Atlas of Cork City

The Editors and Publishers would like to thank our sponsors for their generous support:

Allianz

Ordnance Survey Ireland

University College Cork

Geography Department, University College Cork

Cork 2005

Atlas of Cork City

Edited by

John Crowley, Robert Devoy,
Denis Linehan and Patrick O'Flanagan

Cartography by Michael Murphy

First published in 2005 by
Cork University Press
Youngline Industrial Estate
Pouladuff Road, Togher
Cork, Ireland

© The Editors and Contributors, 2005

All rights reserved. No part of this book may be reprinted or reproduced by any electronic, mechanical or other means, now known or hereafter invented, including photocopying and recording or otherwise, without either the prior written permission of the Publishers, or a licence permitting restricted copying in Ireland issued by the Irish Copyright Licensing Agency Ltd, 25 Denzille Lane, Dublin 2.

British Library Cataloguing in Publication data
A CIP catalogue record for this book is available from the British Library.

ISBN 1 85918 380 8

A CIP record for this publication is available from the Library of Congress.

Printed in Ireland by ColourBooks

Designed and typeset by Redbarn Publishing, Skeagh, Skibbereen, Co. Cork

www.corkuniversitypress.com

Contents

List of Contributors — *viii*
Preface — *x*
Acknowledgements — *xii*

1. The City in the Landscape: The Environmental Heritage — 1

Introduction — 2
1. Cork City and the Evolution of the Lee Valley — 7
2. The Climate of Cork — 17
   A Climate Synopsis — 18
   Weather and Natural Disasters — 21
3. Flooding in the City — 25
   Floods and Climate Change — 31
4. Nature's Immigrants — 32
   Cork's Botanic Gardens — 36
   Wild Plants — 38
   Distillery Field: A Final Refuge — 40
5. The First People — 45
   Ringforts — 52
   Mills — 54
6. Urban Beginnings and the Vikings — 56
7. Medieval Cork — 64
   Lanes and Streets — 74
8. St Finbarr and Early Christian Settlement — 79
9. Christianity, Churches and Burial Places — 85
   St Mary's of the Isle — 93

2. Transformation: A Minor Port Town Becomes a Major Atlantic Port City — 99

Introduction — 100
10. The Anglo-Normans and Beyond — 104
    The Charters of Medieval Cork — 111
11. Sixteenth- and Early Seventeenth-Century Cork — 112
12. The Evolution of Cork's Built Environment, 1600–1700 — 119
13. City, Seasons and Society — 127
    Irish in Eighteenth-Century Cork — 135
    Nano Nagle and Catholic Cork: 1718–1784 — 137
    Shandon — 142

14.	Beef, Butter, Provisions and Prosperity in a Golden Eighteenth Century	149
15.	Cork City's Protestant Culture	160
	The Huguenots of Cork	168
	Quaker Enterprise	171

3. The City in the Nineteenth and Twentieth Centuries — 177

Introduction		178
16.	Industry 1750–1930	183
	Murphy's Brewery	190
17.	Connecting Cork	194
18.	Place, Class and Politics	202
	Musical Bands and Local Identities	209
	Father Theobald Mathew (1790–1856)	213
19.	Cork's 'Golden Age': Great Houses and Art Collecting in the Early Nineteenth Century	215
20.	The Royal Cork Institution	223
	Presbyterians in the City of Cork	229
21.	'The College': University College Cork	231
22.	Famine	239
	Queenstown/Cobh: An Emigrant Port	246
	New Arrivals: Cork's Jewish Community	252
23.	Conflict and War, 1914–1923	256
24.	Cork City in the Twentieth Century	265
25.	The Suburbs	278
26.	Buildings and Architecture	290
	St Fin Barre's Cathedral	300

4. Culture and the City — 305

Introduction		306
27.	The Culture of Food	308
	The English Market	312
28.	Sport	316
	Soccer in Cork City	322
	Hurling and The Glen	325
	Road Bowling	331

29.	Music	336
	Rory Gallagher (1948–1995)	341
	Music and Place: The Lobby, Charlie's and The Phoenix	343
	John Spillane's Cork: A Geography of Song	346
30.	Literature and the City	351
	Frank O'Connor: The Writer and the City	357
	Patrick Galvin's City	359

5. Contemporary Transformations — 365

	Introduction	366
31.	Industry and Employment	369
32.	The Mobile City	377
	Moving Around	384
33.	Underneath the City	386
	Cork Harbour and the Challenge of Change	391
34.	Living in the City	396
35.	Urban Difference	403
	The City at Night	409
36.	Community Development and the Catholic Church	410
	The Marian House Names of Cork	417
37.	Migration	419
38.	Planning and Development	424

Notes	433
Index	450

LIST OF CONTRIBUTORS

Kelly Boyle lectures in the Department of Music, University College Cork (UCC).

Grainne Brick is a graduate of the Department of Geography, UCC.

Barry Brunt lectures in the Department of Geography, UCC.

Cornelius Buttimer lectures in the Department of Modern Irish, UCC.

Plunkett Carter is a local historian who has written extensively on the history of Cork soccer.

Marcus Connaughton is a Senior Producer with RTÉ Radio One and has been based in RTÉ's Cork Studios for the past ten years.

Patrick Cotter is the Director of the Munster Literature Centre. He is also a poet and publisher.

A. S. Cromie was the minister of Trinity Church Cork and Aghada between 1950 and 1955. He is presently Father of the General Assembly of the Presbyterian Church in Ireland.

Maura Cronin lectures in History in Mary Immaculate College (UL), Limerick.

John Crowley lectures in the Department of Geography, UCC.

Valerie Cummins is Manager of the Coastal and Marine Resources Centre, UCC.

Ian d'Alton works with the Housing Finance Agency plc, Dublin. He has published a number of studies on Cork Protestant society in the eighteenth and nineteenth centuries.

Noreen Dalton has lectured in the Department of Geography, UCC.

Robert J. N. Devoy is Professor of Geography at UCC and founding Director of the Coastal and Marine Resource Centre, UCC.

David Dickson is in the Department of Modern History and is the Registrar in Trinity College Dublin (TCD).

Denis Duggan is Chief Project Engineer of the Cork Main Drainage Scheme.

Marita Foster is an academic adviser in the International Education Office, UCC.

Laurence M. Geary lectures in the Department of History, UCC.

Millie Glennon is a researcher in the Department of Geography at the University of Cambridge.

Richard S. Harrison has written on Irish and Quaker commercial themes and has been a frequent contributor to the *Journal of the Cork Historical and Archaeological Society*.

Kieran Hickey lectures in the Department of Geography at the National University of Ireland Galway (NUIG).

Michael Holland is the University Curator for University College Cork. He was previously the Registrar of the Hunt Museum, Limerick.

Kevin Hourihan lectures in the Department of Geography, UCC.

Maurice Hurley is Cork City Archaeologist with Cork City Council.

Gina Johnson is an archaeologist and urban researcher working with Cork City Council.

David Joyce is an Administrative Officer for the Traffic Division, Roads and Transportation Directorate, Cork City Council.

Fintan Lane is a historian and joint editor of *Saothar*, the journal of Irish labour history.

Mary Leland is a freelance journalist and author.

Denis Linehan lectures in the Department of Geography, UCC.

Piaras MacÉinrí lectures in the Department of Geography, UCC.

Kieran McCarthy has lectured and published widely on the history of Cork city.

CONTRIBUTORS

Mark McCarthy lectures in the Department of Heritage Studies, Galway-Mayo Institute of Technology (GMIT).

Kieran McKeown lectures in the Department of Sociology, UCC.

Nicholas Mansergh is a Senior Planner with Cork County Council and has also lectured in the Department of Geography, UCC.

Michael Monk lectures in the Department of Archaeology, UCC.

Adrian Murphy is a doctoral candidate in the Department of Geography, UCC.

John A. Murphy is Emeritus Professor of Irish History at UCC and was an Independent member of Seanad Éireann, 1977–82, 1987–92.

Peter Murray is the Curator of the Crawford Municipal Art Gallery.

Kenneth Nicholls is a retired lecturer at the Department of History, UCC.

A. F. O'Brien is a retired lecturer at the Department of History, UCC.

Tomás Ó Canainn was Dean of Engineering at University College Cork and also lectured there on Irish music.

Donncha Ó Cinnéide lectures in the Department of Environment and Civil Engineering, UCC.

Cathal O'Connell lectures in the Department of Applied Social Studies, UCC.

Raymond O'Connor lectures in the Department of Geography, UCC.

Vicki O'Donnell is a researcher at the Coastal and Marine Resources Centre, UCC.

Diarmuid O'Donovan is the Circulation Manager of the *Evening Echo*. He also contributes a weekly column on sporting matters to the newspaper.

Donal Ó Drisceoil lectures in the Department of History, UCC.

Mary Pius O'Farrell is a Presentation Sister based in Cork and the author of two books on the life of Nano Nagle.

Patrick O'Flanagan is Professor and Head of the Department of Geography, UCC.

Pádraig Ó Riain lectures in the Department of Old and Middle Irish, UCC.

Séamus Ó Tuama lectures in the Department of Government, UCC.

Colin Rynne lectures in the Department of Archaeology, UCC.

Colin Sage lectures in the Department of Geography, UCC.

Regina Sexton is a food historian and food writer.

John Spillane is a singer/songwriter whose roots are very much in Cork city.

Alicia St Leger works as a freelance historical researcher based in Cork.

Denis Walsh is a sports feature writer with the *Sunday Times* (Ireland), having previously worked with the *Sunday Tribune*.

Pádraig Whelan lectures in Plant Science in the Department of Zoology, Ecology and Plant Science, UCC.

Richard Wood has lectured widely on Irish art and architecture.

Preface

Cork's distinctiveness in many respects derives from its physical location. If one were to choose a site on which to build a city, then Cork, in the midst of a marsh and surrounded by steep hills, would not be one's ideal location. Yet from such unlikely beginnings a city has evolved and taken shape. Sometimes serene, sometimes chaotic, Cork has grown to become the principal city in the south of the country.

This *Atlas* sets out to explore the city and its development over time. The result is a book that draws upon the power of maps and the expertise of our contributors to offer new perspectives and insights. Maps are important in learning about Cork. Side by side with reproductions of the cartographic heritage of the city, over two hundred new maps have been commissioned as a means of exploring Cork's transformation. But this *Atlas* moves beyond what might be expected of a conventional atlas. Collected together is a rich collage of aerial photographs, drawings, illustrations from private and public archives, satellite images, paintings and fragments from memory and folklore. A diverse range of authors, including geographers, poets, musicians, historians, journalists, painters, novelists, photographers, cartographers, archaeologists, climatologists, sociologists, planners and engineers, combine here to tell the story of Cork. They reveal a city that, like many other European cities, is modest in size but rich in history, passionate about its culture and concerned about the pace and direction of change.

The five sections of the *Atlas* are not encyclopaedic, but present a broad canvas upon which the city is portrayed. The opening chapters locate the city in its environmental setting and follow its physical development from prehistory to the earliest monastic settlement. Cork is built on water and how it took shape from its river channels and its loose collection of islands and marshlands is central to its story. Using the most recent archaeological findings, the earliest settlements of the city are reconstructed to present a vivid picture of life during the medieval period.

Essays on the eighteenth century investigate the city's progress in the colonial contexts of the Munster Plantation and map out the influence of Huguenots, Quakers and the Protestant ascendancy in shaping the original streetscapes of the modern city. Cork's significant maritime heritage and the prosperity that derived from it are examined, while the growth of the merchant city and the links to the Atlantic world are also charted. The changing nature of Cork in the nineteenth and twentieth centuries is addressed through a series of essays on industry, transport, learned societies, architecture, urban planning, the city's neighbourhoods, laneways and tenements, wars and famine. The cityscape bares the imprint of the various peoples who have lived and settled there. The lives of the great and good are intermingled with the ordinary and so it should be. Not one story then, but a myriad of stories, some better known than others but all contributing to the making and remaking of the city.

Cork's attraction in one sense can be found in its compact nature and the familiarity it breeds. Its island centre – the commercial and cultural hub – can be crossed in a matter of minutes. This familiarity may have its drawbacks, but it also creates at times a fierce loyalty and independence that do not go unnoticed for long amongst those who come to visit. There is no denying Cork people's sense of place in the world. No greater honour can be bestowed than to be acclaimed as 'one of their own'. Countless generations have given the city its unique character and identity. Enquiries into the tastes, pleasures and passions of Cork society are more fully explored through essays that look into the city's traditions and heritage: food, literature, music and sport are all considered in terms of their role in the cultural life of the city.

The present state of Cork is the concern of the final part of the *Atlas*. The questions of jobs and economy, transportation, planning, housing, immigration, religion, social inclusion and housing are all considered and surveyed. Based on original research, these essays present insights into the contemporary changes which have transformed the city, where seemingly in the blink of an eye old buildings are disappearing and a new city is rising up and expanding all around us.

This *Atlas* demonstrates how a survey of social and geographical change can allow us to know more about a city and its place in the world. It is a unique guide to Cork and offers a new visibility to the urban landscape for locals, visitors and travellers alike. An atlas should always allow us to find our place. We hope you find yours here.

Acknowledgements

The preparation of the *Atlas of Cork City* was a large project on any terms and numerous individuals and organisations have made valuable contributions to its production. For generous financial support we gratefully acknowledge the assistance of Allianz Ireland Plc., the Cork City of Culture Committee, the Faculty of Arts, University College Cork, the Office of Public Works and the National University of Ireland. We would also like to thank *Evening Echo* Publications (Cork) for their sponsorship related to the use of photographs from the *Irish Examiner* Library.

As a project that reached deeply into the resources of the city and beyond, the editors and contributors are indebted to a broad range of individuals who gave generously of their time and expertise. Brian Magee, Cork Archives Institute, and Peter Murray and Colleen O'Sullivan of the Crawford Art Gallery gave us constant support and access to valuable materials during the course of the project. Special thanks also must be made to Tomás Tyner, UCC, for his dedication in the production of aerial photography of the city. We would like to thank in particular: President Gerard Wrixon, UCC; Michael O'Sullivan, Vice President, UCC; Ciarán Burke, Cork City Library; Carol O'Connor, Cork School of Music; Caitríona Mulcahy, Heritage Officer, UCC; Michael Holland, University Curator, UCC; Fiona Kearney, Director of the Glucksman Gallery; Raphael Siev, Curator of The Irish Jewish Museum and Heritage Centre; Tony Perrot, Audio Visual Services, UCC; Anne Collins, the Boole Library; Virginia Teehan, Hunt Museum, Limerick; Suzanne O'Sullivan and Brendan Dockery, Department of Geography, UCC; Carol Quinn, Boole Library Archivist, UCC; Patrick Cotter, Director of the Munster Literature Centre; Denis McGarry, Kevin Terry and Ronnie Mc Dowell, Cork City Council; Prof Séamus Ó Catháin and Prof Ríonach Uí Ógáin, Department of Irish Folklore, UCD; Dr William Nolan, UCD; Caroline Meaney, Allianz; Kevin Forde, O'Leary Insurances; Margaret Fitzpatrick and David Kearney, Department of Geography, UCC; Prof Patrick J. Murphy, Department of Electrical and Electronic Engineering, UCC. Special thanks are due to Prof Philip O'Kane and Jim McGrath, the Department of Civil and Environmental Engineering, UCC, for providing digital imagery of the city and harbour; Vicki O'Donnell, Coastal and Marine Resources Centre, for accessing satellite and other imagery; Donal Anderson, Rosanna Devoy and Eamon Smith in the production of reconstruction drawings; Dr Kieran Hickey, NUIG; Dr John Cullinane, Dr Tom Kelly and Dr Ivor MacCarthy, UCC, who gave generously of their time, advice, source literature and graphics in the production of chapter materials; the NRA archaeologists Ken Hanley and Clare McCarthy and also the archaeological companies (ACS and Sheila Lane Associates) and their directors (Donald Murphy, Ed Danagher, Ian Russell, Eamon Cotter, Rory Sherlock, Avril Purcell, Brian Halpin) for access to information from archaeological excavations from the Ballincollig and the Glanmire and Watergrasshill bypasses; Avril Purcell, of Sheila Lane Associates, for permission to refer to the general results of her archaeological excavations at Ballinure on the Mahon peninsula; Judith Monk and Gina Johnson; the European Union, Framework 3, SHELF Project, for research funding on Cork harbour; Dr Colin Rynne, UCC, for advice on and provision of illustrations for chapters. We would like also to thank Maria Minguella, Social Inclusion Unit, Cork City Council, Dr Claire Edwards, Department of Applied Social Studies, UCC, and Helen Bradley and Deirdre Ní Neill, Department of Geography, UCC, for their work on the 2002 census.

We are indebted to Ordnance Survey Ireland for their permission to reproduce maps under Ordnance Survey Ireland Permit No. MP 001705. Unless otherwise indicated, all maps published in the *Atlas of Cork City* remain under the copyright of Ordnance Survey Ireland and the Government of Ireland. For permissions to use graphics, photographs and other copyright material we acknowledge and thank the British Library, Bus Éireann, the Central Statistics Office, the Coastal and Marine Resources Centre, UCC, Cork Airport Authority, Cork City Council, Cork County Council, Cork Harbour Commissioners, the Department of Archaeology (UCC), EG Pettit

ACKNOWLEDGEMENTS

& Company, Gamma Ltd, Meithal Mara (www.mmara.com), Met Éireann and Urban Initiatives Ltd. Special thanks must be made also to Anne Kearney, Library Manager *Irish Examiner* Publications (Cork) Ltd, for her assistance in sourcing photographs. We would also like to especially thank Diarmuid O'Donovan, *Evening Echo* Publications (Cork), and Denis Minihane, Photographer, *Irish Examiner* Publications (Cork) Ltd. For permission to reproduce other photographs and graphics, we are most grateful to Darragh MacSweeney, Provision Photographic Agency; Dr Pat Wallace, Director, National Museum of Ireland; Inpho Photography; Maeve and Ruth Fleischmann; John O'Leary, Freakscene Ltd; Fucino Matera, Eurimage; Carol Hunter; Dr Daphne Pochin-Mould; Ralf Kleemann; Mick Mackey; Maurizo Vallebella; Annilies Verboist; Stella Cherry and the Cork City Museum. In addition, we thank and acknowledge the contributions of Tom Dunne, Today FM; Cork International Choral Festival Archive; Con Houlihan; William Rohan; Ionad na Gaeilge Labhartha; Gael-Taca; Colette O'Flaherty, the National Library of Ireland; Ashmolean Museum, Oxford; Bodlean Library, Oxford; Chris and Amy Ramsden (for the Alec Day Collection); the British Library; the National Gallery of Ireland; the Bodleian Library, Oxford (for MS Rawl.B.485, fol. 118v); the Ashmolean Museum, Oxford; the National Museum of Ireland; the Public Record Office, London; Luke Cassidy, Cobh; Robert Wilson, Wilson Collection Ireland, Cobh; Adrian Brady, Private Collection; *The Irish Times*; Denis McGarry, Cork City Council; and Seán Ó Laoi. Thanks are due also to Jim McKeon, Mark McClelland and *Evening Echo* Publications for permission to use and adapt their map of Frank O'Connor's city.

As editors we would like to acknowledge the work of the contributors, who produced excellent material in a timely fashion and worked with us to shape maps, illustrations and text into a format suitable for the *Atlas*. We also express thanks to the staff of Cork University Press who managed the book with patience, care and professionalism. Finally, but not least, we would like to show personal appreciation to Patsy Devoy, Ríoghnach O'Flanagan, Katharina Swirak and our families and friends for their ongoing interest in the development of the book over the last two years.

John Crowley
Robert Devoy
Denis Linehan
Patrick O'Flanagan

LANDSAT false colour image of Cork city and harbour. The city is shown as a dense area of pink-purple west (left) of the harbour (blue shades). Elsewhere, pink represents mainly bare ploughed ground and smaller settlement areas; green shows vegetated surfaces. (Source: © Fucino Matera, 2001, distributed by Eurimage.)

1
The City in the Landscape

THE CITY IN THE LANDSCAPE
THE ENVIRONMENTAL HERITAGE

INTRODUCTION

Robert Devoy

Cork, a county of contrasts, is characterised in its personality, ballads and legends by its capital city. A fiercely individual city and, for such a relatively small area of *c.* 61 km² with a total metropolitan population of *c.* 345,100, it is full of differences, in topography, landscapes, accents, religion and culture.[1] The city lies on the coast, eccentric to the county and not even at the centre of its long coastline, of *c.* 1,100 km. Despite this location, the city does focus and unify the different areas of the largest county in Ireland. Unlike larger cities (Paris, London or Dublin), Cork avoids the stifling dominance that forces of size, history and inertia tend to engender in capitals. Yet, as John A. Murphy writes about the *essence* of Cork, 'Cork is undeniably the commercial, cultural and services mecca not only of the county but of the province of Munster'.[2] The city has evolved a functionality and lively human relationship with its hinterland that has become woven into its fabric, to be seen no more clearly than in the importance of farming, agricultural trade and products in the life of the city up to the late twentieth century.

This first section of the *Atlas* provides insights into the environmental character of the city and its region. In the physical landscape context, Cork services a diverse region of mountains, boglands, large areas of broad plateau-like lowlands, river valleys and coasts. Four distinct physical landscapes have been recognised: 'the western peninsulas, the southern coasts, the central valleys and the northern hills'.[3]

Land use, reflecting the effects of glaciations, soils and vegetation patterns, defines a broadly fertile east from a rocky and progressively barren west to the county. Cork city is situated close to the divide between these two parts. To the east and north of the county, brown podzols and acid brown earths, with gley soils where lowlands and poor drainage occur, dominate the soil cover. Westwards, the occurrence of uplands and a wetter climate result in the development of poorer peaty podzols and gleys.[4] Whilst earlier people's organisation of the land reflects these environmental differences, later political changes and sixteenth-century colonisation overrode and merged these to create the modern county's social and administrative patterns.[5]

However, too much can be made of these differences in landscape and history. Some physical integrity is given to the county through its topography, rivers, coast and geology (see *Cork City and the Evolution of the Lee Valley*, Chapter 1). A rim of uplands, more than 550 m at the highest point, loosely defines the county boundary with the Sheehy, Derrynasaggart, Mullaghareirk, Ballyhoura and Galty mountains. Within this rim, three main parallel rivers flow from west to east to unite the interior: the Blackwater, Lee and Bandon. Ancient folding over 275 million years ago of the dominant sandstones and

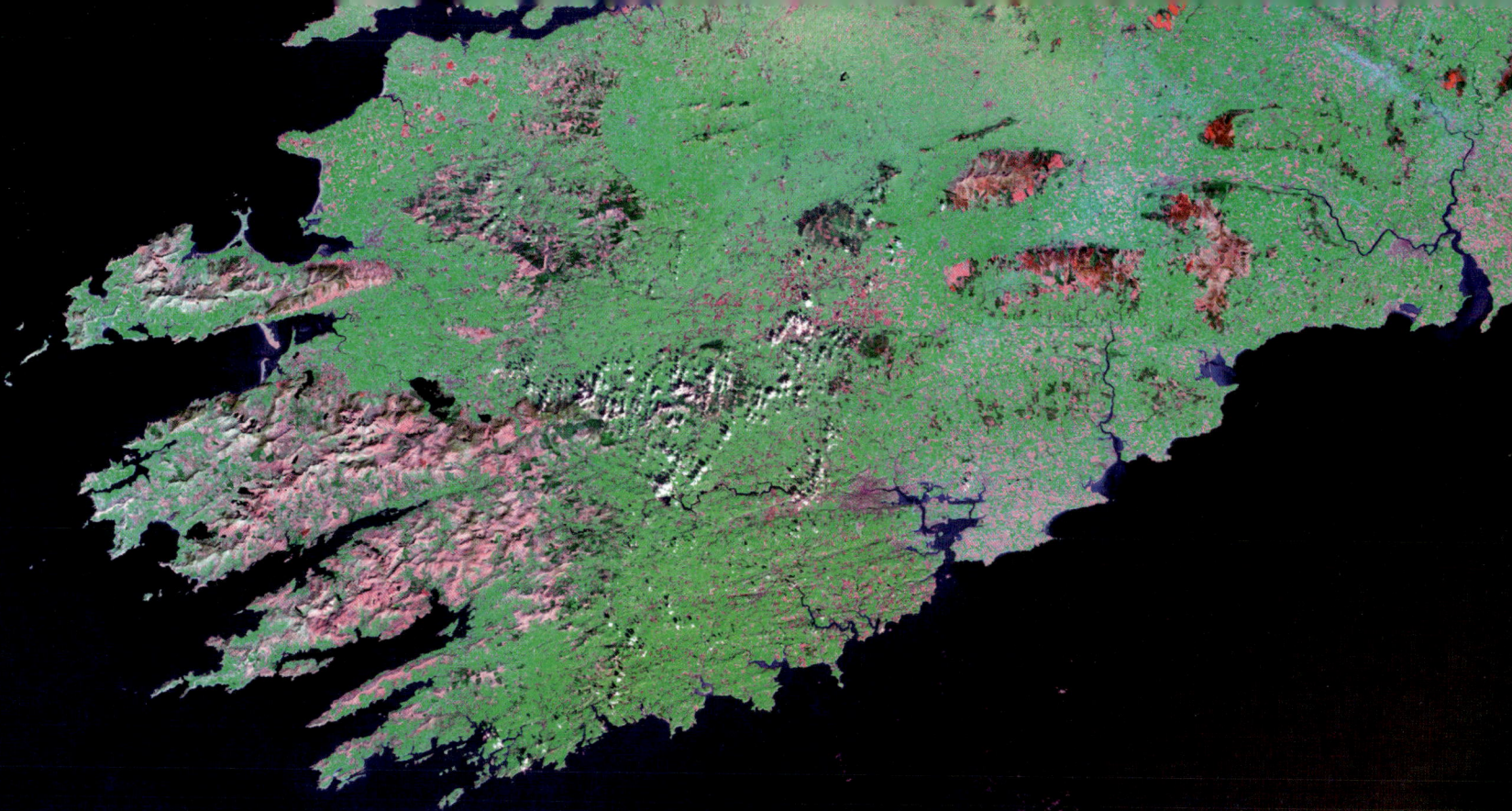

Fig. 1.1 LANDSAT false colour image of County Cork and south-west Ireland, 2000. Bare ground, comprising mainly the uplands, some coasts, agricultural tillage and urban areas, appears as light pink-purple in colour, vegetated areas as green. Cork harbour (blue) and Cork city (pink) are located close to the centre of the south coast. (Landsat TM 5 © Fucino Matera, 2001, distributed by Eurimage.)

limestone rocks, which mirror Cork's emblematic colours of red and white, provides structural guides for these three main rivers. The same rock-folding also creates a central east-to-west spine of lower uplands between 300 and 500 m high: the Boggeragh, Nagles and Knockmealdown mountains. As any traveller approaching Cork city from the north, or particularly by train from Limerick, will know, the effect of these uplands on the topography is to create the impression that, after Mallow, it is all downhill to Cork! At the coast the three main rivers mingle with the many other streams and water courses of the region to form estuaries and frequent coastal indentations of varied shape, size and origin. The Cork coastline, however, is distinctively 'bay–headland' in type. This is largely the result of the geological controls of rock composition and structure, in combination with the effects of long-term coastal erosion by wave action and sea-level changes.[6]

In more recent geological times the Ice Age, spanning the last two to three million years, covered the region almost everywhere with a thick coating of glacigenic sediments, particularly of stony, sandy clays (boulder clay, or till) which often acquire a back-breaking stickiness when waterlogged. The glacial inheritance leaves differences in the landscape resulting from: the effects of mountain terrain on glaciation, the different cycles of ice advance and retreat and spatial patterns of ice melt. These differences, allied with those in the regional climate, form the basis for the marked east-to-west changes in soils and land capability. Climate and weather impacts are also important for the city (see *The Climate of Cork*, Chapter 2; *Flooding in the City*, Chapter 3).

The current vegetation in the region, particularly as linked to agriculture, is influenced by land capability. However, ancient vegetation patterns were more complex.[7] Before their final clearance in the sixteenth to seventeenth centuries, extensive oak woods covered much of the region. These mainly sessile oak woodlands also commonly contained hazel, birch, alder, elm and pine. Ash and hazel flourished in limestone areas, or where steeper slopes and higher light availability allowed. In the river valleys and areas of poorly drained lowland extensive wetland plant communities occurred, composed of lakes, fens and oak-alder-yew swamplands. The most famous of these oak-alder swamps, the Gearagh, lies close to Cork city and survived largely intact until the mid-1950s and the building of reservoirs on the River Lee. In the Gearagh, the glacial rock debris left by the retreating ice over 16,000 years ago resulted in the Lee developing a complex of braided river channels on which the swamplands of fen carr vegetation developed.[8] Such environments were once common throughout Europe prior to their removal by forest clearance, river channelisation and land drainage. By the early twentieth century, the Gearagh had become almost unique. The Cork artist and writer Robert Gibbings famously described the Lee here as flowing past 'a thousand

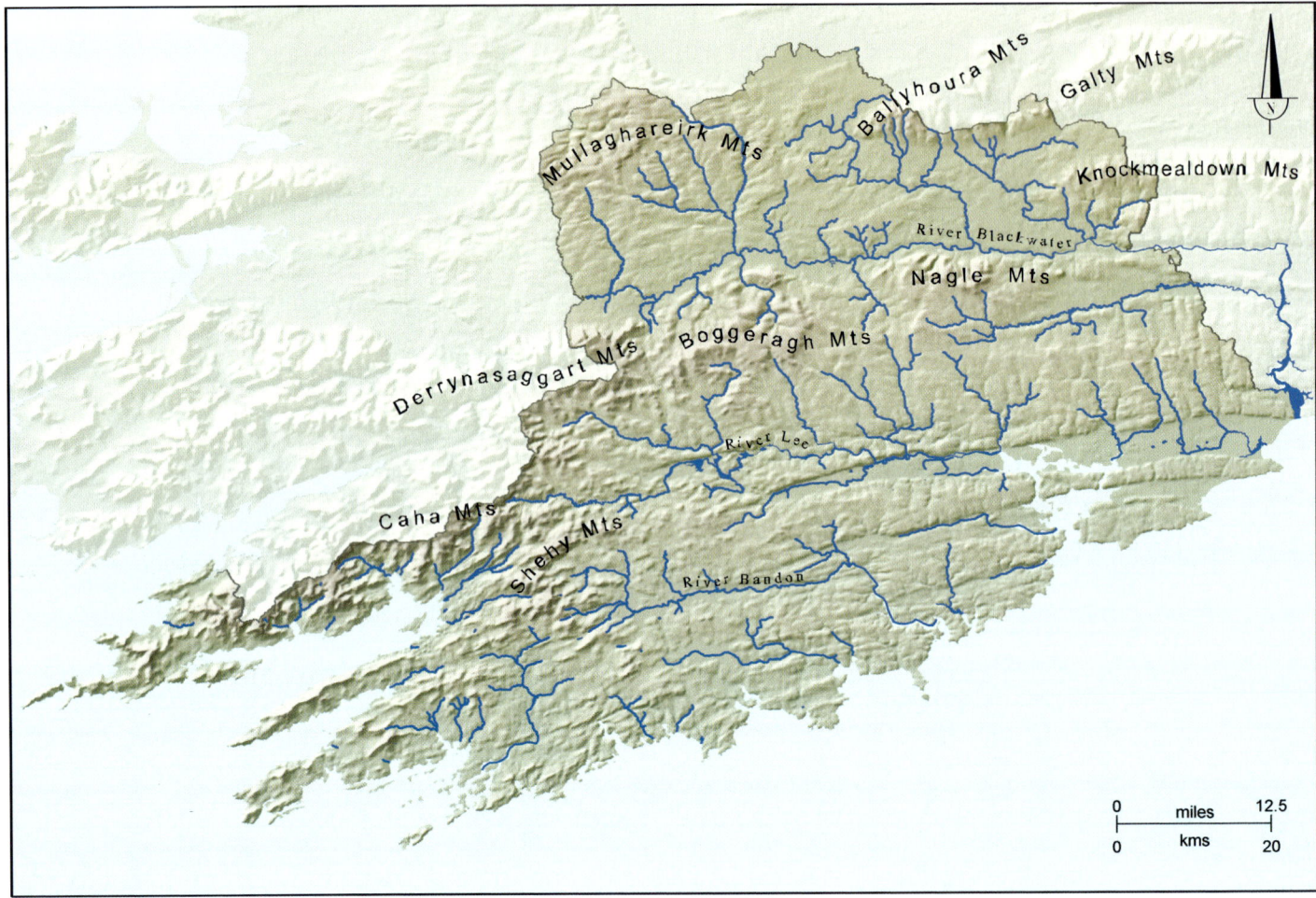

Fig. 1.2 Topography of Munster, showing the main rivers, central uplands and 'mountain' rim of County Cork.

wooded islets, under the overhanging fern-laden, moss-covered oaks; under the alders and hazels; through tangles of rushes, swaying tall weeds; through tortuous channels, trailing long grasses; an almost impenetrable jungle'.[9]

Elsewhere, in the uplands, higher rainfall and, to the west, acid poorer soils modified the vegetation patterns. These conditions allowed pine, hazel and birch to become more prominent in the oak forest. Extensive open pine woodlands dominated upland areas like the Boggeragh mountains between 6,000 and 5,000 years ago. Since about 4,500 years ago, the impact of fires, the first farmers and climate change have led to the disappearance of these pine and mixed oak woods. In the uplands, they were replaced by blanket bog as a result of a cooler, wetter climate and soil leaching. In the lowlands, boglands progressively clogged the east-to-west valleys of the region, prior to drainage of the bogs and their removal from the eighteenth century onward.

Cork city offers a rich archaeological record. There has been settlement in the Cork region from at least the Neolithic and later Bronze Age periods onwards (see *The First People*, Chapter 5). Into this setting came the monastic foundations of St Finbarr and later the Viking and medieval settlements (see *St Finbarr and Early Christian Settlement*, Chapter 8). From these beginnings Cork developed its long tradition of seafaring, stretching back to its Viking origins and early sea-based trade (see *Urban Beginnings and the Vikings*, Chapter 6; *Medieval Cork*, Chapter 7). The process of woodland removal occurred most dramatically from the fourteenth century onward under the impetus of political changes.[10]

Clearances from colonisation and farming, combined with demand for the numerous industrial uses of timber (for charcoal, barrels, shipbuilding, urban construction), had significant consequences for the rivers and estuaries. The sediments released from this deforestation, and later on from bog reclamation, silted up the many small ports along Cork's coastline. This silting continues today at rates of around four to eight millimetres a year, though the role of people-pressure in this process has been exacerbated by the work of coastal erosion and storms.[11] As the shallower and smaller ports were abandoned, a process intensified

THE · CITY · IN · THE · LANDSCAPE

Fig. 1.3 Clogheenmilcon fen, Blarney. A) View eastwards along the remaining wetland and fen areas of the Blarney valley, bounded to the north by the Cork to Mallow road. (Photo: Tomás Tyner.) B) The fen, showing areas of reedswamp, colonising shrubs and associated waterlands. Such environments would have been common in and around Cork city until the mid-nineteenth century. (Photo: John Crowley.)

Fig. 1.4 Cork city's coat of arms. (Cork City Public Museum.)

historically by political and economic factors, so the port of Cork emerged as pre-eminent in the region.

People have made a home in the physical environment of Cork and moulded the natural landscape of water, soil, forest terrain and coast to suit them. This time-honed process has shaped Cork, a city at the boundary between land, river and sea and, as shown by Cork's coat of arms, the county's window on the world.

1. CORK CITY AND THE EVOLUTION OF THE LEE VALLEY

Robert Devoy

The city of Cork is situated close to the coast in the valley of the River Lee. The Lee is *c.* 65 km long and has a drainage area of *c.* 1,200 km². The river begins its journey eastwards to Cork from the area of Gouganebarra, a lake and former ice basin on the border of the counties of Cork and Kerry. The river's flow is direct and fast, with the valley rarely more than 5 km at its widest and often bounded by steep slopes (see *Introduction*, Section 1). Before recent glaciations the river probably followed a southerly route through the present Bride valley, but the deposition of ice debris (moraine) disrupted this former drainage line. At its eastern end the Lee discharges to the sea through the complex estuary zone of Cork harbour. The sandstone ridges of the region control the distinctive double box-like shape of the inner and outer harbours.

The physical setting for the city and its region has been studied from different viewpoints, especially from its geology and geomorphology, which help establish the character of the city and its environment. The name 'Cork' derives from the Irish *corcach* (a marsh) and the Vikings established their first settlement in the estuary on low, flood-prone islands in the estuarine marshes (see *Urban Beginnings and the Vikings*, Chapter 6). The sixteenth-century poet Edmund Spenser referred to the city's setting as 'the spreading Lee, that like an Island fayre, encloseth Corke with his divided flood', which describes well the original nature of the Lee as a braided river. It offered a good location for the Vikings and the need for defence and water-based communications. However, the city's steep-sided valley-bottom location presents a number of problems, of flooding and drainage, the supply of fresh water, air quality and difficulties for road, rail and air communications (see *Flooding in the City*, Chapter 3). This physical setting has also had its benefits. At the head of a deep natural harbour, the

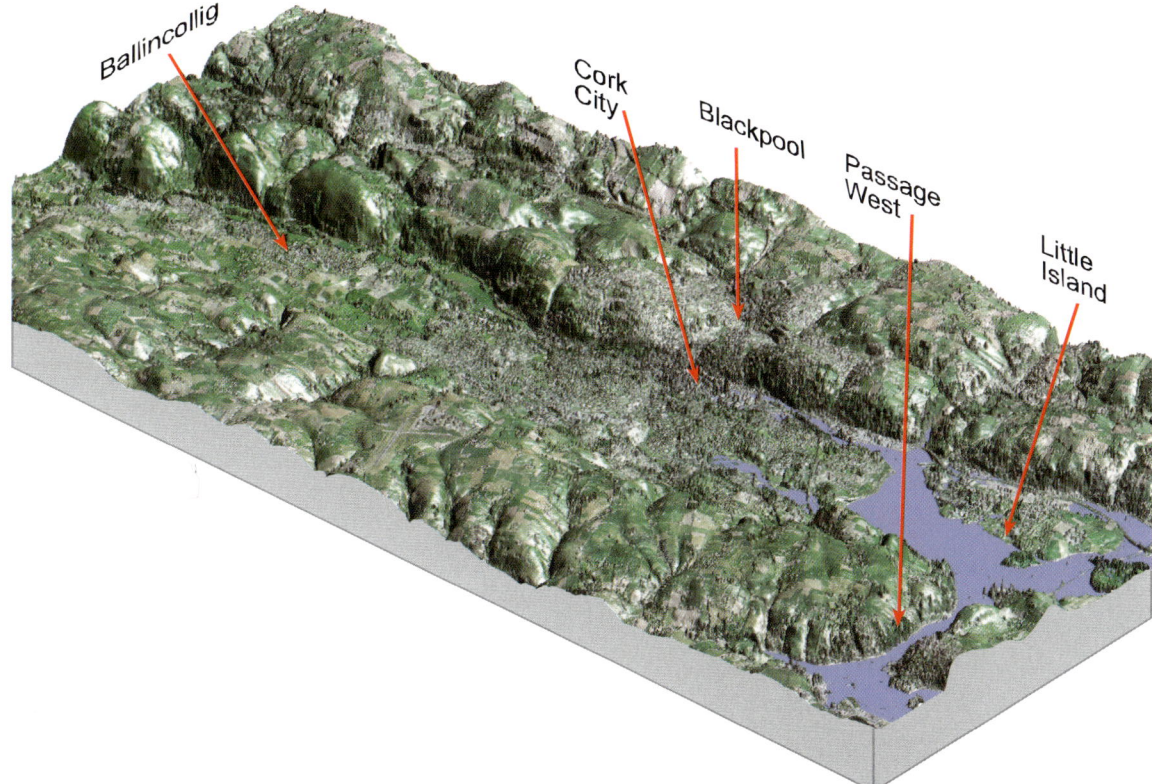

Fig. 1.5 Digital elevation model (3-D view), based upon an aerial photographic image of the Cork city and harbour region, showing the main topographic features. (Terrain graphics by Jim McGrath and Philip O'Kane, Department of Civil and Environmental Engineering, UCC.)

city grew as a port from the early medieval period. It has flourished on the trade of agricultural products drawn through the routeways provided by the Lee and neighbouring rivers (see *Introduction*, Section 1). In turn, the port and its consequent trade encouraged the establishment of a cosmopolitan population and commercial and cultural links with maritime Europe.

The importance of the city's physical environment and climate for its development, character and buildings cannot be denied. In the present age of concrete, steel and glass uniformity, one of the striking images of Cork is the dominant use of two varieties of stone in its buildings, the local white-grey limestone and the purple-red sandstones. Whilst the sequencing of environmental changes have been important in creating this physical character for Cork, key elements may be isolated as most significant: geology, rivers, ice erosion and deposition, and the integrating controls of climate and sea-level changes.

GEOLOGY: ROCKS AND TIME

Cork and its region sit upon an ancient geological boundary between rocks of the Devonian and the Carboniferous periods (Fig. 1.7). This boundary evidences a change from land to deepening ocean conditions over 340 million years ago, when the part of the earth's crust that is now Ireland lay close to the equator. The underlying rocks around Cork are of the Devonian period (345–400 million years) and comprise thick sequences of sandstones and finer-grained silt – mudstones (Old Red Sandstone). These were deposited as sediments in riverine environments on a continental landmass, marginal to upland and mountain areas. The sediments accumulated in a progressively deepening crustal hollow, the Munster basin.[1]

The end of the Devonian crustal movements resulted in a marine invasion of the basin and heralded the onset of the Carboniferous period. Sandstones replaced the former land-based sediments and mudstones of shallow marine deltaic and coastal swamp settings (345 million years ago). Continued subsidence and differential uplift, associated with changes in coastal position and water depth, led to the later deposition of calcareous muds and the formation of shallow marine mudbank limestones. These rocks form the widespread white-grey Carboniferous limestone of County Cork. The continued deepening of this marine environment is also recorded in the development of the Upper Carboniferous sandstones, siltstones and shales in the region.[2]

The current land surface and distribution of these Devonian and Carboniferous rocks reflect the region's subsequent tectonic history. Intense folding and faulting of the rocks began towards the end of the Carboniferous

Fig. 1.6 Use of limestone and red sandstone in Cork's stone buildings, seen in the offices of Deloitte and Touche, Lapp's Quay. The building was originally Furlong's Mill, built in 1852. (Photo: John Crowley.)

period. It continued on, *c*. 290 million years ago, into Permian times as part of the Variscan (Hercynian) mountain-building. This major phase of earth-folding affecting Cork comprised part of a broad belt of linked crustal movements stretching from Russia to North America. The subsequent separation of this massive Eurasian-to-Greenland-to-North-American crustal zone took place through the later phases of ocean spreading and the opening of the North Atlantic, beginning 60 million years ago. For Cork, the result was the creation of the prominent ridge-and-trough fold topography of south-west Ireland.[3] These structures are aligned east to west with the ridges supporting steep surface slopes, commonly of 15–30°. The ridges form the uplands of the region, with a series of separated plateau-like surfaces developed along the axes of the ridges at heights of between 150 and 180 m Ordnance Datum Malin (OD) (see *Introduction*, Section 1). These uplands are composed of the tough Devonian sandstones and related quartzites. The intervening valley troughs are floored by the less resistant Carboniferous rocks.[4] The city and harbour region today is cut by numerous north-to-south

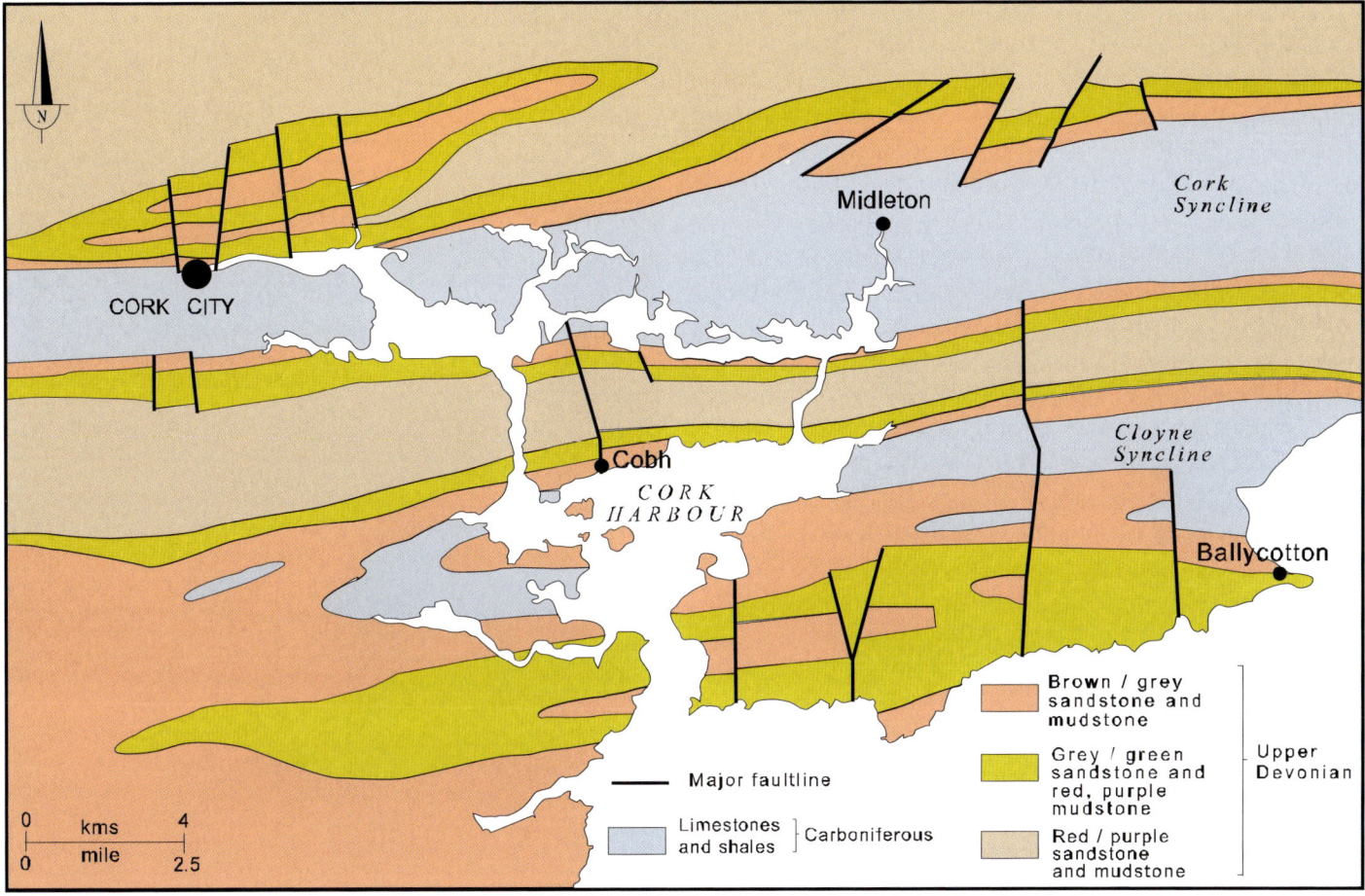

Fig. 1.7 Summary geology of Cork and Cork harbour. (Adapted from Ivor MacCarthy.)

tear faults and by less frequent east-to-west thrust faulting, produced by the Variscan mountain-building.

Geological history in Cork city and county, as recorded from the solid rocks, stops with the Carboniferous period. Any records of subsequent rock deposition have been removed. A thick sequence of marine carbonates (chalk) was deposited here in the Upper Cretaceous period (65–95 million years ago) and once overlay the Carboniferous rocks.[5] This chalk rock cover was removed through long periods of exposure of the region as land from 60 million years ago, culminating in the intense water and ice erosion of the Ice Age (Pleistocene).

RIVERS AND MARINE PLANTATION

The geological setting was a key influence in the subsequent work of rivers, sea and ice in sculpting the present landscape.[6] This has been decisive in the development of the distinctive shapes of the regional drainage pattern and the appearance of flattened tops to the uplands. The Lee effectively alters its flow direction at Cork. It breaks away southward through the rock ridges of the harbour area to reach the sea at Monkstown through the narrow north-to-south aligned rock-cut channel of Passage West (Fig. 1.5). This abrupt discordance with the controlling east-to-west flow direction, mirrored by other rivers in south Munster, has been the cause of much debate as to the origins of the drainage system in south-west Ireland.[7]

Reconstruction of the regional rock-folding shows that at least 250 m of the Carboniferous and Devonian rocks have been eroded in the Cork region. This rock removal resulted from a combination of marine and river action. The low, regular upland surfaces around the city, developed regionally at heights of between c. 180 and 245 m OD, are evidence of land uplift and emergence from times of high sea levels, or so goes the standard explanation.[8] Waves and marine erosion created these relatively uniform flattened tops to the sandstone ridges, subsequently providing a convenient surface for Cork Airport. This ancient wave action created a southward-sloping marine-cut surface over the entire Cork region, on which later emergent rivers developed.[9] As these eroded down through the Carboniferous rocks and met the harder underlying sandstones, so the rivers would have changed direction to follow the east-to-west folds.

Opinions differ as to whether sufficient evidence exists to support the theory of marine erosion and whether such marine surfaces originally sloped southward at all. Some suggest that this process of river superimposition must have developed initially from a southward-sloping former chalk land surface, and it was weathering and erosion that brought about the complete removal of the chalk, not marine processes.[10] However, explanation of the north-to-south diversion of the Lee and of neighbouring rivers remains a problem in evolutionary models proposed for the region. An ingenious solution argues for the existence of structural *sags*, low points along the axes of the sandstone ridges.[11] The positions of these sags determined preferential north-to-south groundwater flows in the limestone that formerly overlay these ridges. These low points would be preserved later as river valleys as this limestone cover disappeared. Geomorphological action is seen as having removed the limestone completely, except in the emerging east-to-west valley folds, such as in those of the Blarney, Lee and Bride river valleys (Section 1, *Introduction*). An alternative view is that the limestone cover was only finally removed during the Ice Age. At times of glacier retreat, meltwater torrents would have maintained the elements of any former north-to-south drainage. The position of the numerous north-to-south rock faults and earth movements

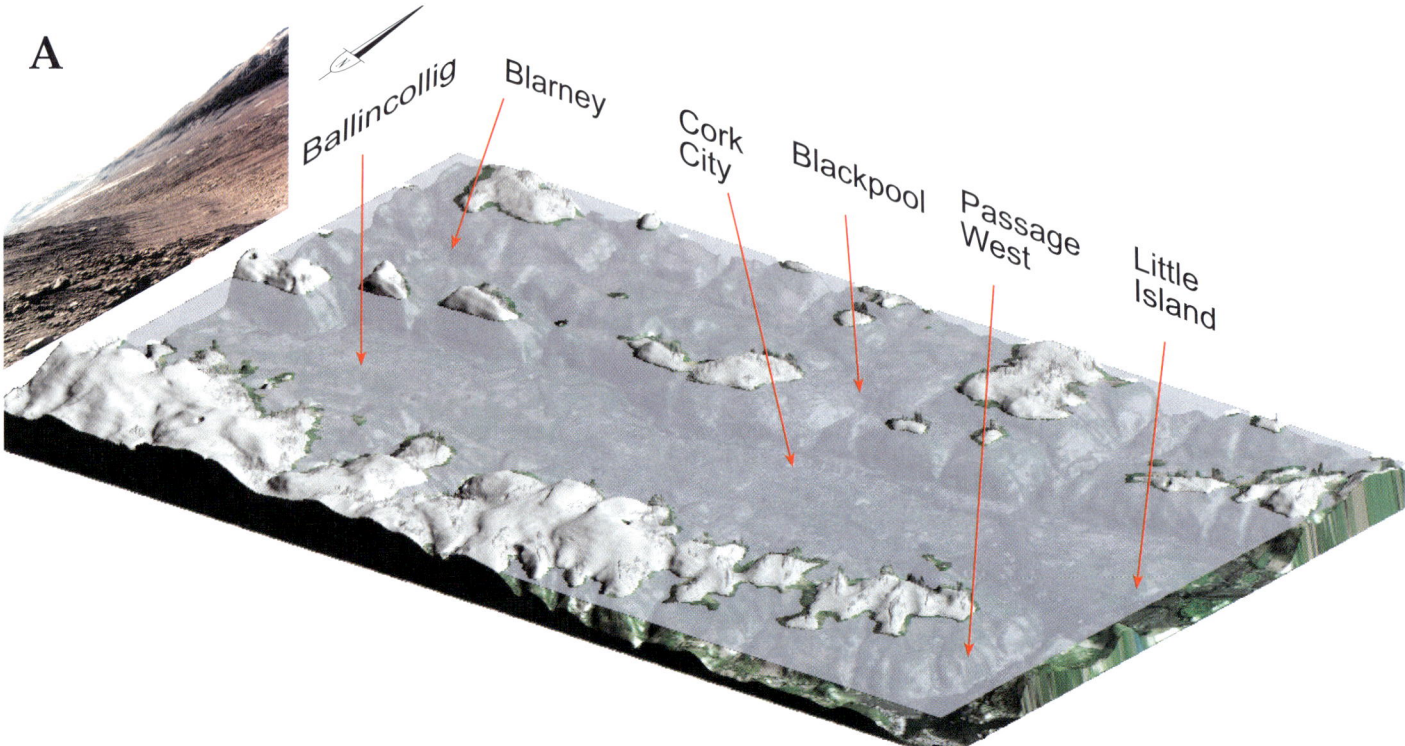

Fig. 1.8 A) Digital elevation terrain model of the Lee valley in the city area showing a reconstruction of ice infill of 100 m thickness in the valley, as at the time of ice retreat westwards from Cork *c*. 18,000 years ago. (Terrain graphics by Jim McGrath and Philip O'Kane, Department of Civil and Environmental Engineering, UCC.) B) Valley view along the Tasman glacier, New Zealand, illustrating the type of glaciated valley environment existing most recently in the Lee valley *c*. 20,000 to 17,000 years ago. (Photo: Richard J. Wood.)

caused by ice-loading (neotectonics) must also have played their part in this complex story.

In the emerging east-to-west valleys, the deep weathering of the limestones (karstification) continued into the Pleistocene period under warm climatic conditions. Although now only a remnant of the formerly extensive limestone terrain, elements of this landscape are still found throughout the city region, for example in the Blackrock to Mahon areas of the city, in Ballincollig and in Blarney. Common features are small-scale solutional holes and fluting in limestone exposures. Occasional bigger swallow holes and cave passages also occur. Deep solution hollows in the limestone and remnant rock pinnacles also lie buried beneath the present cover of glacial sediments, presenting a recurring problem for construction work.[12]

THE WORK OF ICE

Cork was covered by ice, but how often and exactly when is uncertain. Glaciers covered the city most recently c. 20,000 years ago at the end of the Ice Age. Ice flowed from the Kerry mountains eastwards towards the city as valley glaciers, joining with thicker ice from the north and north-west to reach a thickness of up to 250 m in the Lee valley (Fig. 1.8).[13] From here the ice extended eastwards and southwards across the present coastline and onto the exposed bed of the Celtic Sea (Fig. 1.9).

At this time, the relative sea level would have been 100 m lower than at present. Glacier action, together with meltwater release, had cut down the floor of the Lee and neighbouring valleys to meet these low sea-level positions.[14] As revealed by the numerous building excavations and borehole data in the city region, the result has been the creation of the Lee as a rectilinear, U-shaped glacial trough. The base of this rock-cut channel falls towards the sea in irregular steps, from depths of about 11 m below sea level (OD) west of Cork city to 40–60 m below sea level before

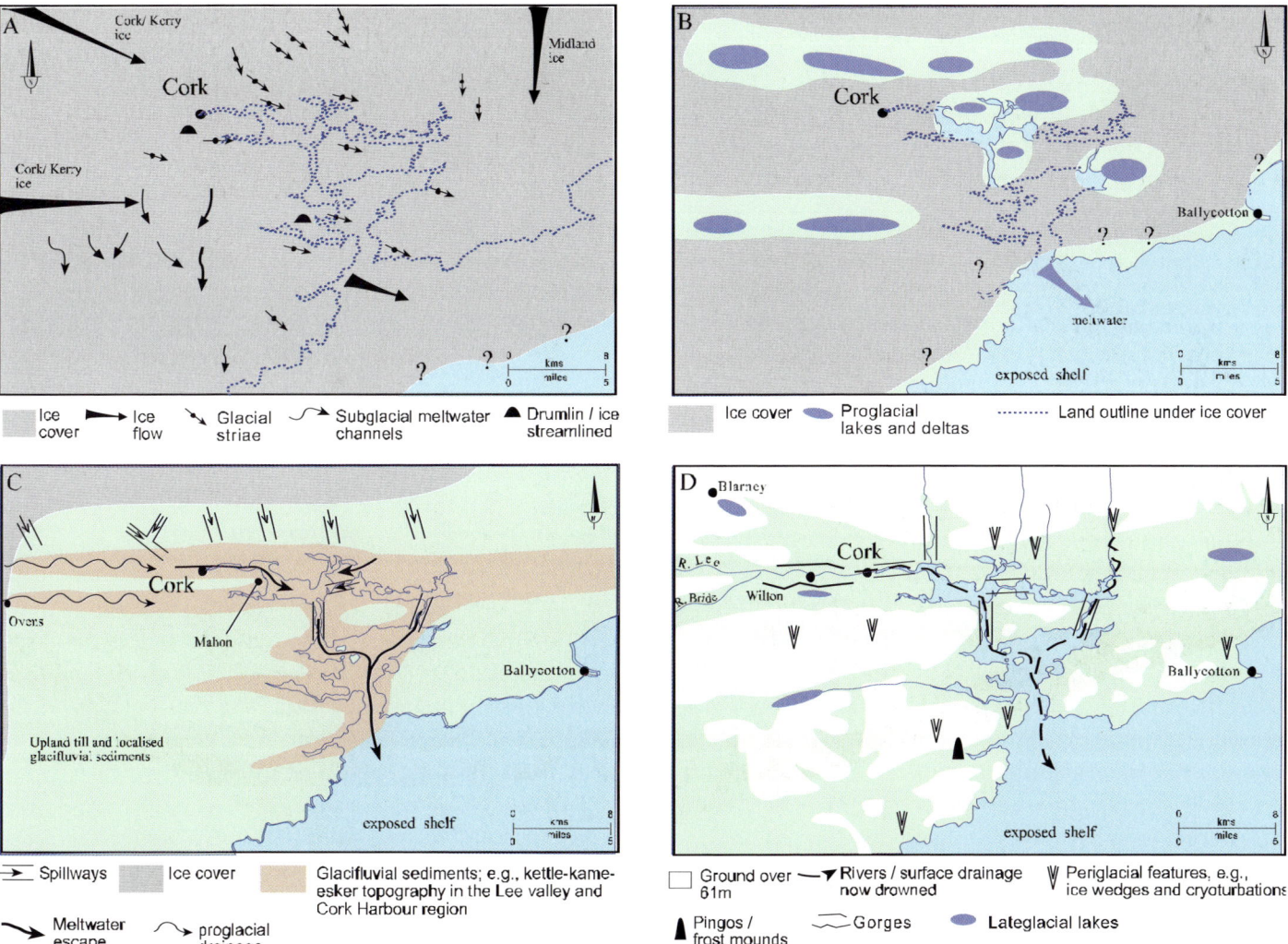

Fig. 1.9 Geomorphological and palaeoenvironmental reconstructions of the Cork and Cork harbour region, OIS 2–4. A) Maximum ice cover 24,000 to 20,000 years ago. B) and C) Deglaciation phases 20,000 to 16,000 years ago. D) Late-glacial phase 13,000 to 10,000 years ago.

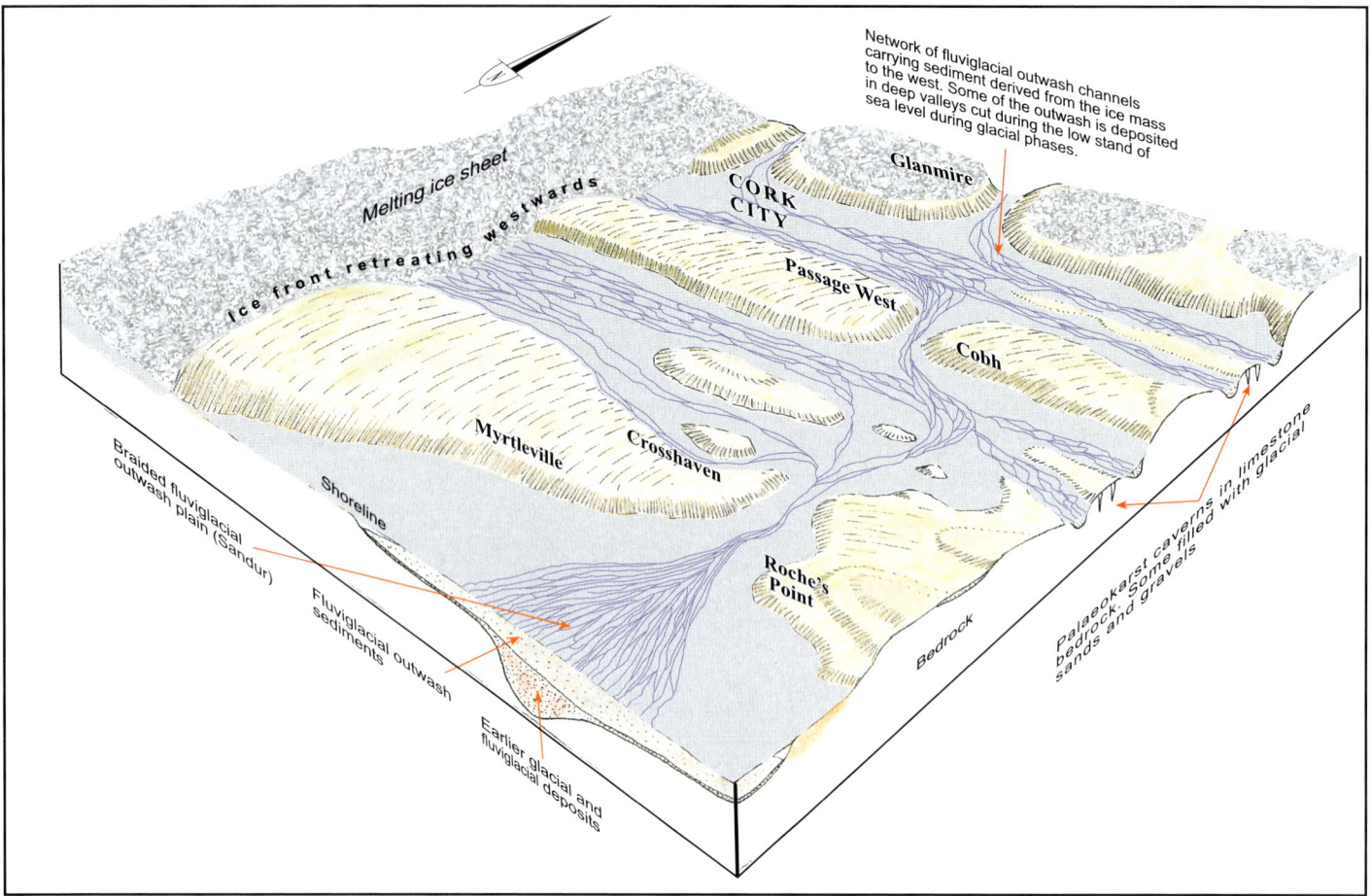

Fig. 1.10 Ice retreat and palaeoenvironmental model of the Cork and Cork harbour region, during phases B and C in Fig. 1.9 (adapted from Ivor MacCarthy). The 3-D reconstruction emphasises the occurrence of the north-to-south former stream valleys cutting the east-to-west sandstone ridges and acting as meltwater channels. It also shows the glacifluvial braided streams and outwash sediments issuing from the ice front. In the area of Roche's Point, geophysical and coring data support the existence of an extensive outwash plain, with interbedded sands and gravels filling the former river channel of the Lee. Marine processes reworked the surfaces of these glacigenic sediments during the Holocene rise of sea level. The sediments have been carried out to the continental shelf and also reworked into present-day beaches.

entering Lough Mahon and to greater than 70 m below sea level at the coast (Fig. 1.10).[15] Even within these three zones, further over-deepened and ice-scoured areas exist, with the valley cut locally to depths of 40 m below sea level, as at Victoria Cross. These deep features are characteristic of all the region's glaciated valleys.

Thick sequences of ice-crushed rock debris (boulder clay or till) line the valley floors and hillsides around the city. On the surrounding hills these sediments are thinner but still show that ice once covered the hill summits. As the ice moved eastwards it sculpted this debris into streamlined, drumlin-like shapes and esker ridges. These features have now been largely built over or quarried, but some can still be recognised, as in the cliffs at Ringaskiddy (Fig. 1.11).[16]

Elsewhere in the harbour, as at Mahon, approximately north-to-south aligned submerged ridges of glacial rock debris, over 5–8 m high, mark stillstands as the ice melted during the final stages of ice retreat 17,000 years ago (Figs. 1.9 and 1.12). The retreat of the ice, northwards to the Boggeragh mountains and westwards along the Lee and Bride valleys back to Gougane Barra and the ice-source regions, released vast volumes of meltwater. Sands and gravels carried by the seasonal meltwaters also cover the city region. Today everywhere has its local sand and gravel quarries. These outwash deposits form the low, hummocky *kettle and kame* terrain of Fota Island and the harbour eastwards.[17] Along the valleys westwards the sand and gravels indicate the former existence of outwash fans, as at Ovens and Killumney. Trapped between the ice and the valley sides, the gravels form thick stepped terraces, or *caims*, from which the glacial term *kame* is derived.

This last phase of glacial cold affecting the city region began over 70,000 years before, though it would have been interrupted periodically by short phases (up to 3,000 years long) of warmer climate. In these warmer times, pine-birch-willow-juniper woodlands and scrub, similar to areas of the southern Baltic today, replaced the prevailing Arctic-cold and tundra-like environment. These conditions returned to

Fig. 1.11 Glacial features in Cork harbour. A) Coastal cliff composed of till (glacial boulder clay) at Ringaskiddy. B) The prominent limestone glacial erratic boulder of Golden Rock on the foreshore in front of the cliffs. (Photos: Robert Devoy.)

the Cork city area about 14,000 years ago.[18] Earlier, lakes had formed at the retreating ice margins, as at Blarney and at the exits to the re-emerging north-to-south stream valleys. In Blarney, and in others of the east-to-west valley-folds, such as the Tramore and Owenboy rivers, these lakes survived after ice retreat, filling with glacially derived clay and silt sediments. The warmer climate and returning vegetation made the lakes magnets for grazing animals, evidenced by the numerous remains of the giant Irish deer (*Megaloceros giganteus*) found at Wilton, south of the city.

At Passage West, Passage East and Glanmire, elements of the former north-to-south rivers have acted as conduits for glacial meltwater and sediment, leaving these channels as deeply incised gorges (Fig. 1.10).[19] In some areas ice melted more rapidly than in others, creating lakes trapped by encircling ice, as in the Shandon and Blackpool areas of the city. When this ice eventually melted back, the released lake waters also cut deep channels into the underlying sediments

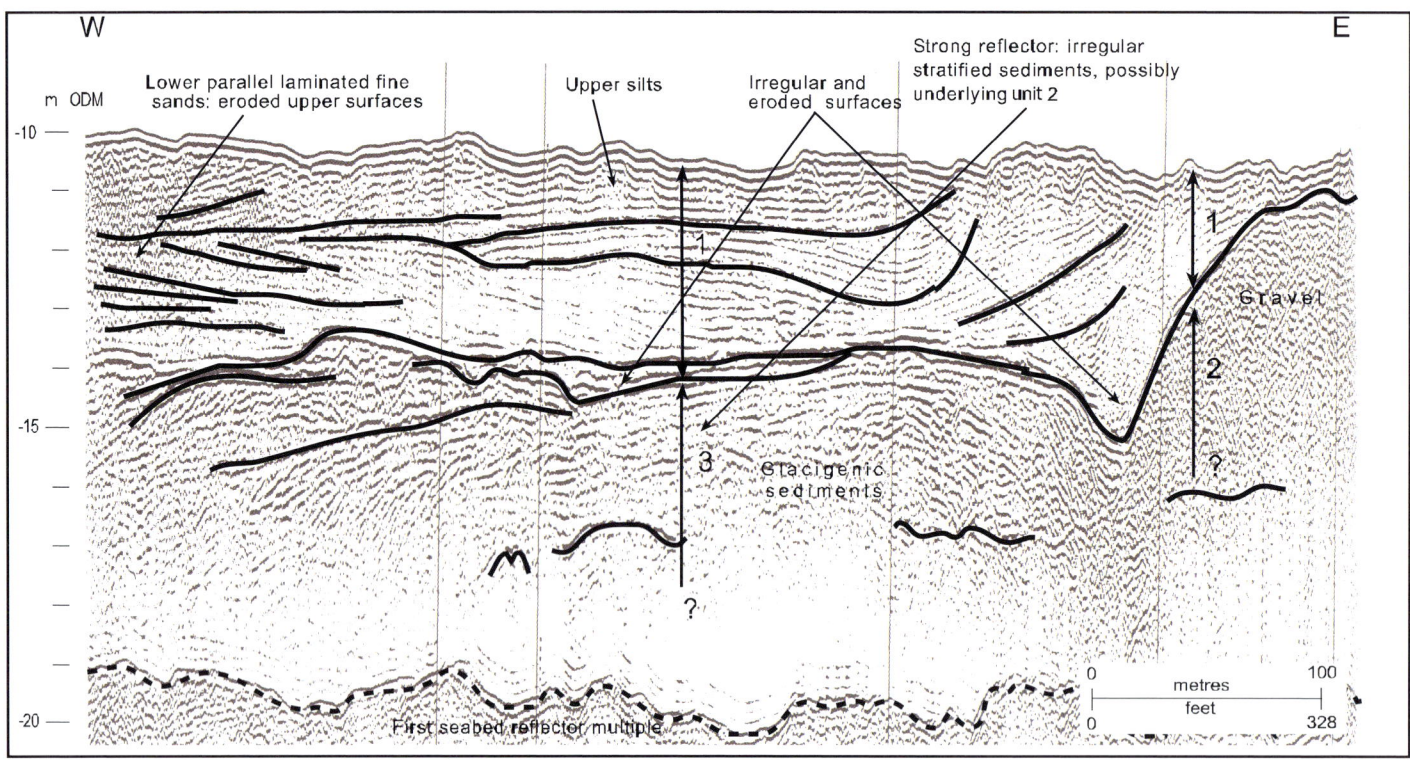

Fig. 1.12 Seismic stratigraphic profile from Lough Mahon, Cork harbour. Unit 1 represents a complex Holocene sequence of cross-bedded and laminated clays, silts and sands, showing internal erosion surfaces. This Unit overlies the channelised surface of what are probably glacigenic materials, containing interbedded sands and gravels (Unit 3). The composition of seismic layers marked by '?' are unknown. Beneath Unit 3 occur the interglacial plant beds and estuarine clay-silts. Eastwards into Lough Mahon, Units 2 and 3 also form prominent moraine ridges (see Fig. 1.14).

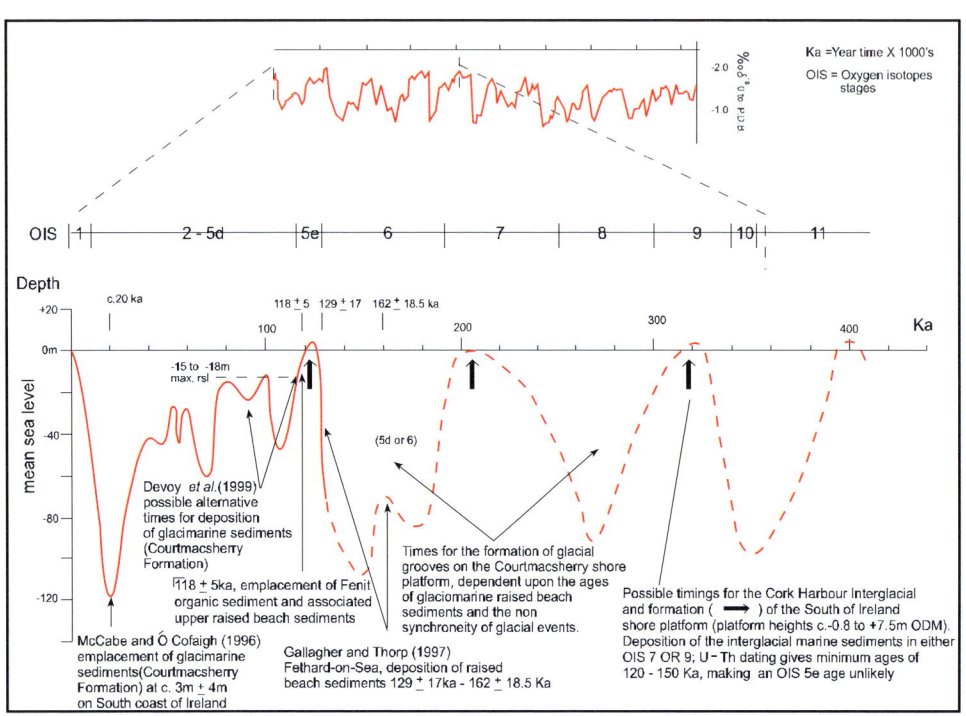

Fig. 1.13 Trends of global ocean volume and of related relative sea-level changes based on oxygen isotope records ($\delta^{18}O$), ancient shorelines, coral terraces and speleothem data. The curve shown at the top, from the Pacific Ocean core V28-238 of $\delta^{18}O$ data, provides a timescale. The central curve, of ocean volume change and annotations, gives the timing and sequence of Quaternary (Late Cenozoic) events for Cork harbour and south-coast regions, Ireland.

and rock. The Glen, in Blackpool, is an example of such a meltwater escape channel.[20] The sands and gravels of the former lake here were used for many years in city building work. The quarries are now worked out and have been filled in with refuse, or reclaimed for housing and recreational areas.

Information about this final stage of the Ice Age is abundant, but evidence for earlier glacial times in the region is more difficult to find. Oxygen isotope analysis of sedimentary records from the oceans shows that the earth experienced multiple phases of glacial cold and low sea levels during the Pleistocene, alternating with interglacial times of warmer climate and high sea levels (Fig. 1.13).[21] It is unclear whether any of these earlier glacial phases can be identified securely in Ireland. Traditional views recognised the

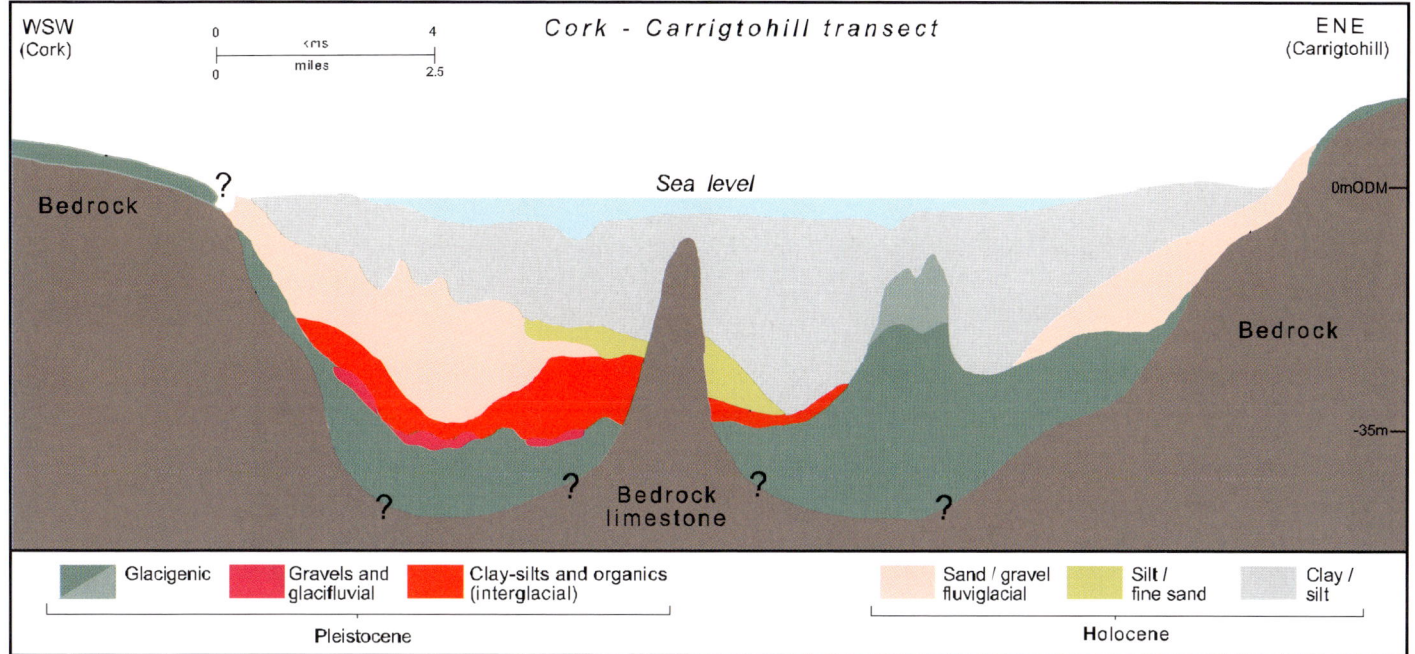

Fig. 1.14 East-to-west model cross-section through the Quaternary (Late Cenozoic) sediments of Cork harbour. The estuarine interglacial sediments (OIS 7/9) are shown diagrammatically, sandwiched between till and gravels of glacigenic origins. The occurrence of the irregular weathered limestone bedrock surface and end moraine ridges is also illustrated.

glacial sediments around Cork city as representing the last two glacial stages: the Midlandian and the Munsterian.[22] There was no good evidence of the intervening times of climate warmth. Neither the last interglacial, oxygen isotope stage (OIS) 5e, nor earlier interglacials had been identified from the region.

Construction work in and around the city has involved drilling many boreholes through the glacial deposits and these have provided new information (Fig. 1.14). Interglacial sediments have been found in Cork harbour that are pre-Munsterian in age and date to OIS 7, or earlier.[23] These sediments seal underlying glacial materials that must be at least 250,000 years old, much earlier than the Pleistocene history envisaged formerly. The sedimentary sequences found in the Lee and inner harbour indicate that the last three stages of ice and glacial cold definitely affected Cork.[24]

Sea-level changes and Cork's harbour

The rise of relative sea level and the creation of Cork harbour, after the last ice melted (the Holocene), happened slowly at first and then accelerated into rapid flooding (Fig. 1.12). The first marine invasion of the sands and gravels left by the ice in the harbour occurred about 8,000 years ago at levels of just over 15m below sea level (OD).[25]

The sea rose rapidly, then proceeded to flood towards the city at rates of up to 7 mm annually, covering the vegetation that had colonised the former glacial surfaces. Rivers, sea and tides combined to leave thick sequences (over 4 m) of sticky blue-grey clays, silts and sands in the harbour as a record of these events. By 1,350 years ago, high tides had reached present mean sea levels in the inner harbour and the modern coast was forming.

This 'final' flooding had not been the first creation of Cork as a harbour. Cork preserves a unique record in Europe of earlier Pleistocene sea levels, evidencing former interglacial marine environments and post-glaciation flooding events. Boreholes taken for the De Valera Bridge revealed sequences of rock-hard green-grey estuarine clay-silts rich in plant debris, including the remains of pine, yew, alder and willow. Water-loving algae (diatoms) in the sediments showed the existence of an almost complete record of a Pleistocene marine invasion cycle (Fig. 1.15).[26]

Analyses show a remarkably similar pattern to the later Holocene events. First, the retreat of ice from Cork (pre OIS 7/9 ice) left a deep basin. This was exposed initially to tundra-like conditions and then to the freshwater stream and marsh development of an earlier River Lee and tributary streams. The sea subsequently flooded in, recorded at levels of 35 m below sea level (OD) at the Custom House. Thousands of years of marine presence then occurred before the return of ice and low sea levels once more.[27] These former estuarine conditions stretched eastwards in behind Fota Island and Carrigtohill and south-westwards along the Tramore valley. Most importantly, the timing and elevations of the estuarine sediments show that they drop down across the harbour westward along a line

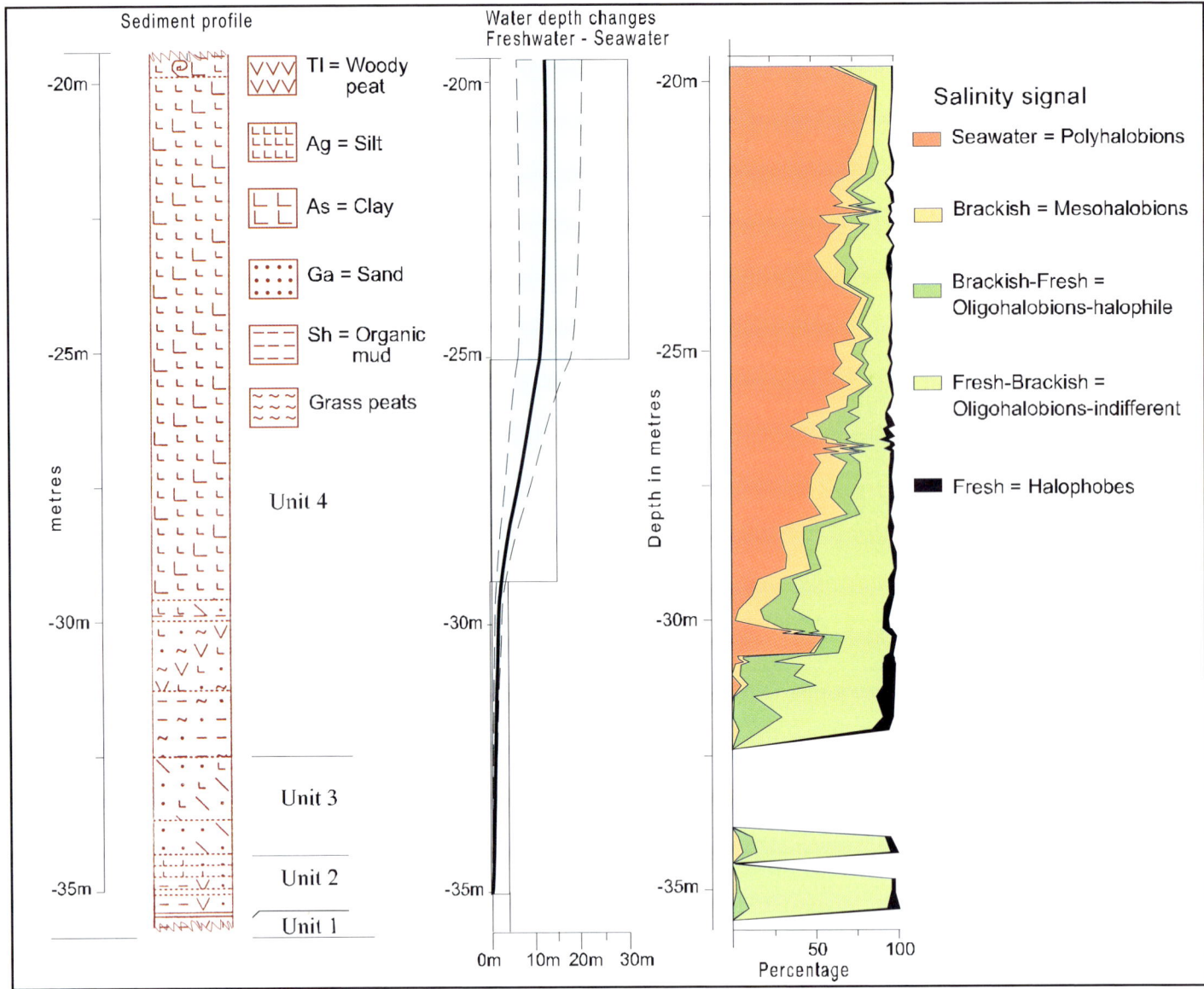

Fig. 1.15 Interglacial diatom salinity groupings and relative sea-level changes from the Custom House (core CB2), Cork harbour (diatom values are as a percentage of Total Diatoms). The seawater (marine) diatom grouping is shown to dominate the harbour area, following the initial freshwater and fresh-brackish water phases. Water depth changes over time are shown by the solid vertical curve; the blue-shaded area shows the possible water depth error margin, based upon palaeoenvironmental reconstructions.

from Carrigtohill to Cork by up to 24 m. The simplest explanation for this is that the underlying rocks have moved, due to the effects of the later ice loading on the rock faults of the region (neotectonics).[28] The marine record shows, ironically, that in recent geological times Cork has been longer without a harbour than with one.

Conclusion: Times of change

Cork was once described as a city 'of elegant limestone buildings reflected in the burrowing waters of the Lee'.[29] Its distinctive valley location has been created by natural processes generally operating over millions of years, though with some times of distinctive rapid change. Today we are again experiencing one of those times of rapid change. Human intervention via the construction initially of weirs and locks, then of dams and finally now of a regional stormwater drainage system provides rigorous controls on the Lee.[30] The impacts of future climate warming may overwhelm these controls. Heavy storm rainfall may well occur with future climate warming and, combined with rising sea levels, may again cause flooding in the city in the twenty-first century.[31] The environment once more will pose a challenge for building and change in Cork, particularly for the docklands, harbour installations and coast.

2. THE CLIMATE OF CORK

Kieran Hickey and Robert Devoy

Fig. 1.16 Mists in the Lee valley, west of County Hall and the city, caused by cold air draining down into the valley and temperature inversion. (Photo: Robert Devoy.)

Fig. 1.17 Snow over Cork. View in 1995 over St Fin Barre's Cathedral to snow lying on the hills to the south of Cork. (Photo: *Irish Examiner*.)

Cork's valley location imposes a series of climate-related characteristics on the city; for example, its problems with flooding (see *Flooding in the City*, Chapter 3), which distinguishes it from the climate of the wider region. The valley topography can, under specific air conditions, create air temperature inversions. This is particularly visible on cold, frosty mornings in the Lee and other valleys around the city, in the magical sight of ethereal layers of mist hovering mid-air.

Before the introduction of smokeless fuel regulations in 1995, those inversions exacerbated the problems of smog and air pollution in the city, and significant respiratory problems resulted.[1] The city climate is also modified by height, from the exposed surrounding uplands to the valley bottoms, heights ranging from close to sea level to over

150 m (see *Cork City and the Evolution of the Lee Valley*, Chapter 1). Distinct changes in temperature, rainfall and wind speeds occur with these differences in elevation and exposure, as also with distance from the coast. When it snows, a much less common event today, a clear snowline is often visible just below the top of the Lee valley.[2] In the city, as with most urban environments of any size, a distinct heat island effect emanates from the buildings, which is noticeable both diurnally and seasonally.[3] Yet the climate of Cork remains similar to that of the southern coastal region of Ireland: an equitable, maritime climate, though for some it is too relentlessly grey and overcast.[4]

A climate synopsis

Kieran Hickey and Robert Devoy

Note. The climate statistics used are based on meteorological observations from Cork Airport, Roche's Point and other primary weather stations supplied by Met Éireann.[5] Data cover the observation periods 1930–1960, 1961–1990 and 2003–2004.

Cork city and region straddles the temperature threshold between areas above and below 10.5°C. The January daily air temperatures range from *c.* 5.5°C inland to *c.* 7°C at the coast, rising to more uniform values of 15.5° to 16°C in July, though the city does stand out as a summer 'heat island' (Fig. 1.18B). A low number of air frost days are recorded, beginning in mid- to late October and ending by mid-April, with *c.* 24 frost days inland (ground frosts *c.* 77 days), falling to *c.* 7 frost days for coastal areas (ground frosts *c.* 45 days).[6]

The Cork city region, in common with south-west Ireland and the southern coastal strip, has a relatively warm climate in comparison with the rest of the island. A distinct inland and elevation gradient with milder coastal areas is notable though, even over the short distances involved (ten to twenty kilometres). The overall climate characteristics reflect strong environmental controls: Cork's southerly location in Ireland (latitude 51° 50′ N), its coastal position and the added influence here of the warming effects of the North

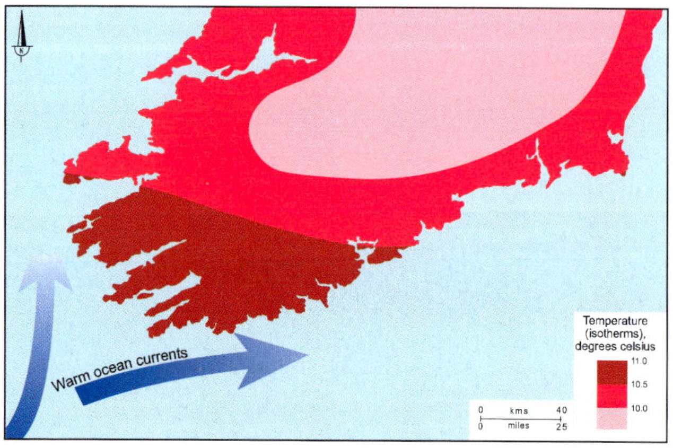

Fig. 1.18A) Mean annual daily air temperature in degrees Celsius (°C) for Cork and the south of Ireland (1951–1980, Met Éireann). Cork lies on the temperature line (isotherm) of 10.5°C. (Air temperature is reduced to mean sea level; this removes the effect of altitude, where the higher one ascends the lower the temperature. Blue arrows indicate the offshore flow directions of the North Atlantic Drift.)

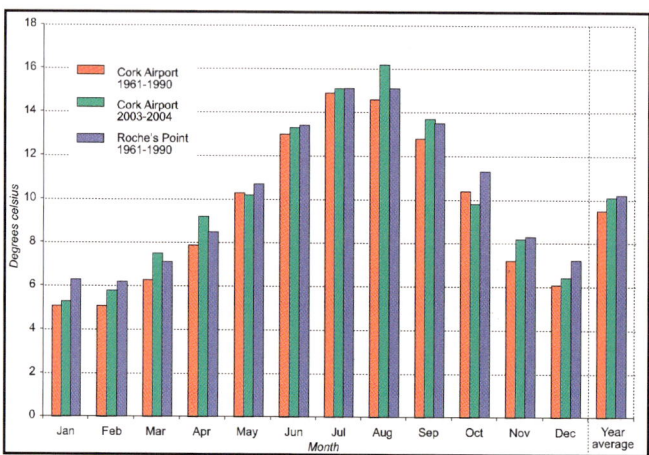

Fig. 1.18B) Mean monthly and annual air temperatures for Cork Airport (1961–1990) and Roche's Point (2003–2004). Data sources are as for Fig. 1.18A.

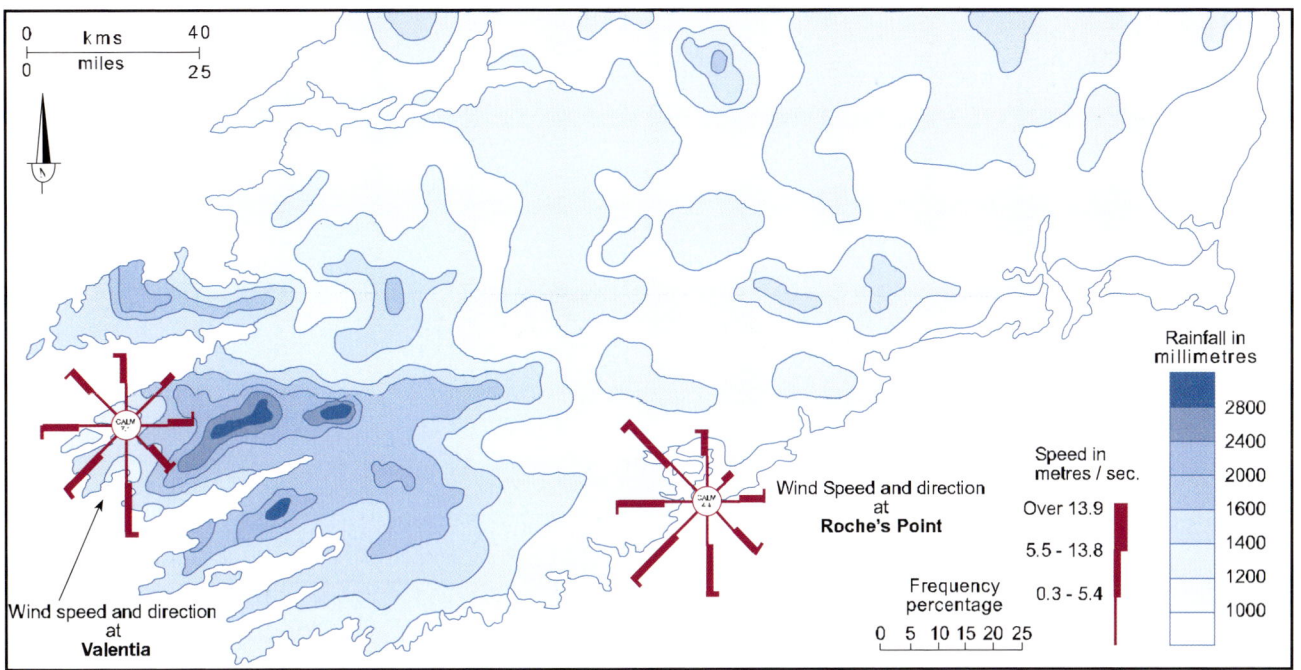

Fig. 1.19A) Mean annual precipitation for Cork and the south of Ireland (1951–1980), mm per year, and mean monthly wind speed and direction for Cork and south-west Ireland (1951–1990), metres per second.

Atlantic Drift, originating as the Gulf Stream.[7] These factors allow sea surface temperatures to remain relatively high all year (9–12°C) and in the marine environment this has permitted the survival of a number of chance arrivals of marine biota from southerly latitudes. Cork falls into the southerly sunshine belt of Ireland, with 1,400 to 1,500 hours of bright sunshine a year, and only 70 days of no sun (fully overcast). However, Cork frequently finds itself on the edge of a high-pressure system centred further east. The result is calm air and overcast skies: high-pressure gloom!

Annual precipitation in the region of *c.* 1,050 mm per year occurs primarily as rainfall (Fig. 1.19A and B). Despite the perception that it rains in Cork all the time, this mean value is *c.* 100 mm below the national average of 1,150 mm. The number of rain days (recorded as > 1 mm per day) for the city is between 150 and 160 days per year.[8] A coastal to inland and altitude gradient may also exist for rainfall. Immediately to the south and east of the city, the precipitation declines to less than 1,000 mm per year. At Roche's Point, on the coast, a value of 935.7 mm per year is recorded. This increases inland to 1,194 mm at Cork Airport (Fig. 1.19C). To the north and west of Cork, values rise to 1,200 mm, rising to over 2,000 mm in western upland areas, showing the importance of south-west to westerly weather systems in combination with elevation in producing the precipitation pattern for Ireland.

These weather systems are also notable in producing strong gales. Approximately 33 gale days are recorded at Roche's Point with maximum wind gusts of over 45 m per second, though strong wind speeds are also recorded at higher elevations inland.[9] Winds affecting Cork are predominantly from the west, with important wind direction components from the north-west through to the south.[10] Easterly winds and storms are

Fig. 1.19B) Roche's Point lighthouse and weather station at the entrance to Cork harbour. (Photo: Tomás Tyner.)

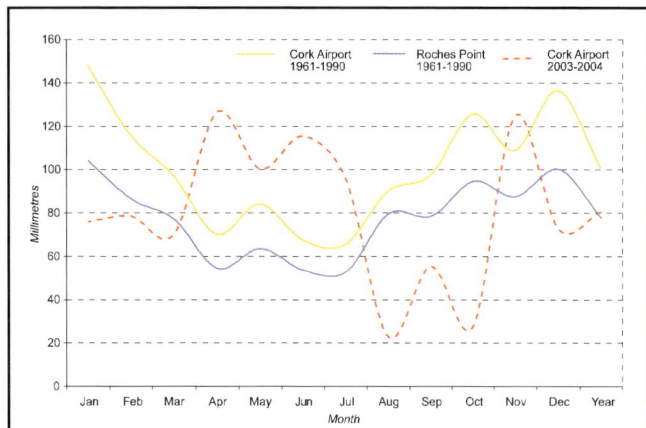

Fig. 1.19C) Mean monthly and annual precipitation for Cork Airport and Roche's Point. Data sources are as for Fig. 1.19A for the years 1961–1990 and 2003–2004.

less common but have a higher significance for coastal erosion and other damage, due to the openness of the landscape to the east. However, long periods of relative calm are common in Cork.

In the twentieth century, Cork seems to have been getting wetter (Fig. 1.20). Future predictions indicate a regional warming with an average annual temperature increase of 1°C by c. 2050.[11] Existing temperature trends show decreasing numbers of 'cold' days and winter warming, along with a marginal increase in 'hot' days and an overall reduction in seasonal extremes.[12] These trends are consistent with predictions. Drier summers are forecast, with a five per cent reduction in precipitation. Wetter winters (ten to fifteen per cent increase) and a reduced storm frequency are predicted, though winter storms of a higher magnitude may occur.[13]

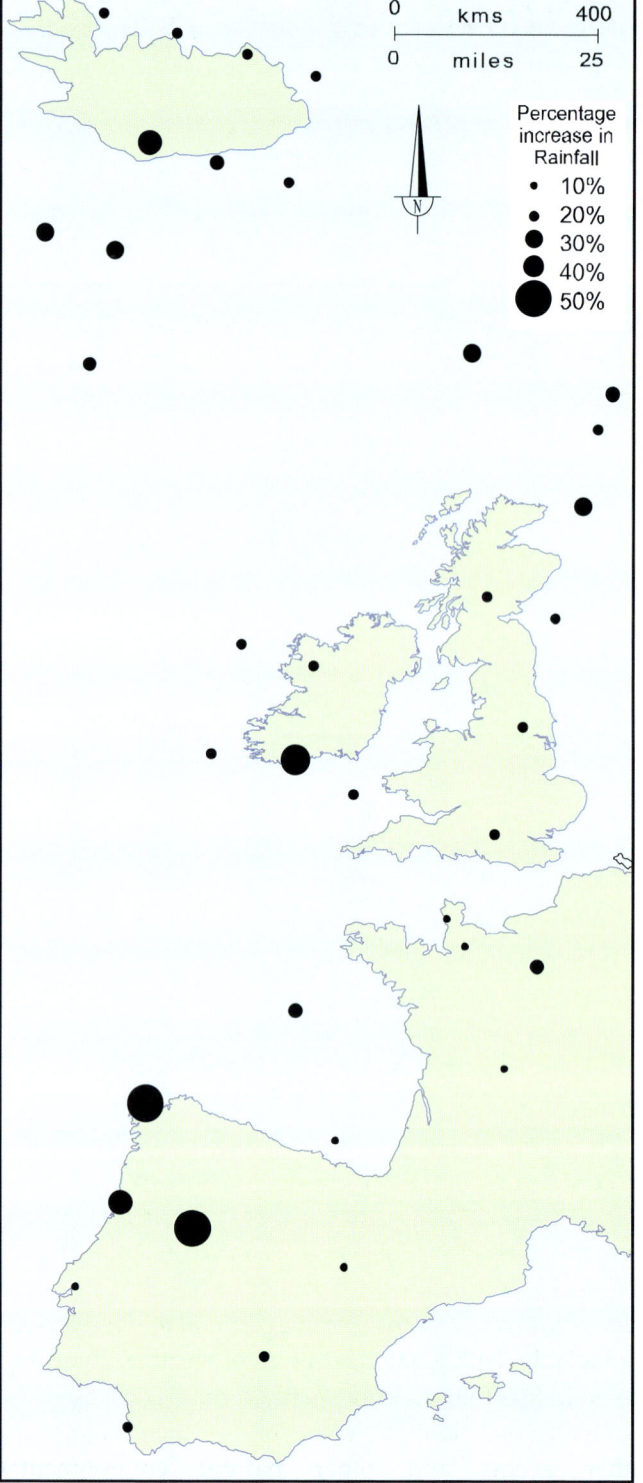

Fig. 1.20 Trends in annual precipitation for Atlantic Europe during the twentieth century, shown as percentage change per century. Black circles show increased precipitation. Cork's distinctly wetter climate is based upon Met Éireann data from the period 1961–1990. Inaccuracies probably exist in these weather station data and the trends should be viewed with caution. (Adapted from Intergovernmental Panel on Climate Change, 2001.)

THE • CITY • IN • THE • LANDSCAPE

Weather and Natural Disasters

Kieran Hickey and Robert Devoy

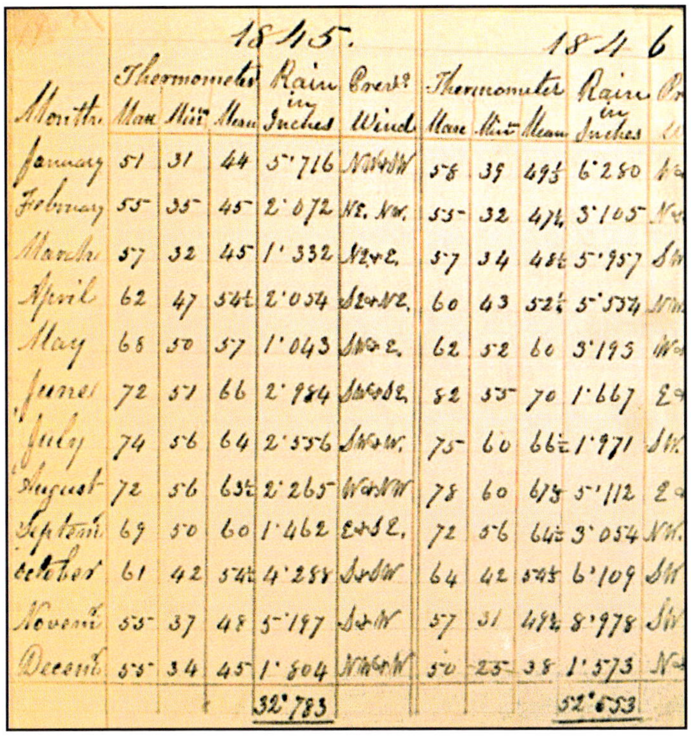

Fig. 1.21 Extract from an 1845 notebook containing weather records for Cork. (Royal Cork Institution Papers, Cork Archives Institute.)

Introduction

A huge variety of weather and other natural phenomena have been recorded in Cork city over the period known as the Little Ice Age. This spanned times of significant climate change from the 1400s until as late as the early 1850s. During this time Ireland was colder and often stormier than at present.[1] Historical records also suggest that the climate was more variable, with greater extremes of weather occurring. Various archival sources of weather conditions exist for Cork. Here, we highlight some of the most significant weather events and other natural environmental phenomena that affected Cork city up to 1850. Events occurring after 1850 are given comprehensive coverage in the *Cork Examiner* (now the *Irish Examiner*) archives.[2] Flood events are discussed in Chapter 3, *Flooding in the City*.

Freeze-ups

The first and notable weather event in the historical records dates from the winter of 1517: 'There was so great a frost, that all the rivers of the country were frozen up for several weeks; particularly the Lee.'[3] This was not a unique occurrence as the Little Ice Age became more severe. In 1683: 'There was a most severe frost, the River Lee was frozen many weeks, and carriages passed over from the ferry slip to the east marsh'.[4]

The most significant of the freeze-ups occurred from 26 December 1739 to 4 January 1740, when the Lee was frozen by one of the sharpest frosts in human memory, called 'the hard frost'. During that time, 'tents were fixed on the River Lee, from the north strand to Blackrock, and several amusements were carried on there, which continued even after the commencement of the thaw'. Accounts from Cork stated that 'all the rivers in and about the city are frozen and that people walk three miles on the ice'.[5] This freeze-up was associated with the terrible conditions of intense cold and exceptional drought that started in December 1739 and continued until the harvest of 1741. It was so cold that liquids froze indoors and ice floes were to be seen at the mouths of rivers.[6] Between 300,000 and 400,000 people died in Ireland as a result of starvation and associated illnesses, a quarter of the population of the country at that time, brought about by these exceptional weather conditions over an eighteen-month period. In Cork, the development of the North Infirmary in 1744 and the poorhouse-cum-foundling hospital in 1747 are attributed to the impact of this event on the city.

Further freeze-ups occurred in early February 1766, 2–17 January 1767 and 14–18 December 1788, when 'the South Channel from Parliament Bridge to the edge of Lapp's Island was frozen, and the navigation of ships greatly impeded'. Similar freezing conditions returned in January 1820, when the cold continued for a period of up to five weeks and caused much hardship amongst the poor, including one poor woman who 'perished in a heap of snow near Gallows-Green'.[7] However, some people still managed to find enjoyment at some of these cold times.

Snow and hail

In addition to these big freezes, major snowfalls also occurred. On 11 January 1768, snow was recorded as six feet high in places. Other heavy snowfalls occurred on 31

January 1776 and 3 May 1779 ('a most remarkable late date for snow and hail'),[8] the end of February 1838[9] and 3 February 1841 (when parts of the city 'were covered to a depth of four to five feet').[10] There were also other notable hailstorms, as on 1 May 1753 and 20 February 1819.[11]

WARM SPELLS

In contrast to the freeze-ups there is much less evidence of exceptionally warm and dry conditions. The first of these is recorded for the summer of 1539, which was 'so dry that the Lee at Cork was almost dried up, and several other rivers also, for want of rain'.[12] The spring and summer of 1740 were exceptionally dry, as was 1761 when, on 20 June, 'prayers for rain were offered up in all the churches, because no rain had fallen for thirteen weeks prior to this day'. In May 1786, it was stated that 'the season being very dry, the poor inhabitants of this city suffered greatly from want of water'.[13]

THUNDER AND LIGHTNING

The worst weather-related disaster to have affected Cork, including flooding, was on 31 May 1622, when a considerable part of the city was burnt. A very severe thunder-and-lightning storm started between 11 and 12 a.m. It began with the city being covered by dark clouds, probably a thunder super-cell. Numerous flashes of lightning quickly followed the clouds. Some of the lightning strikes hit buildings on the east and the highest parts of the city. Within minutes, fires caused by these strikes raged, as many buildings were either wooden or thatched, or both. Within fifteen minutes, fire was also occurring on the west

Fig. 1.22 Snowfall on St Patrick's Street, 1963. Though less common in recent years, the city can still experience snowy conditions. (Photo: *Irish Examiner*.)

Fig. 1.23 Depiction and account of the fire of 1622, which destroyed much of Cork city. (Source: C. Smith, 1893.)

of the city, which led to widespread panic; many people fled the city into the surrounding fields and an unoccupied island on the Lee. Others fled to the stonewalled and slate-roofed churches of the city, where they felt safe. Many people became trapped in their homes and on the streets and were burnt to death. The death toll ran into the hundreds.[14] Clearly, Cork suffered enormous damage and it was many years before the city had recovered to its previous state. In hindsight, the famous 'Battle of the Birds' of 12 and 14 May 1622 was seen as an evil portent of the disaster to come: tens of thousands of starlings in 'two armies' engaged in an aerial battle, causing several thousands to plunge to the earth dead.[15]

As a result of the intense convection cells found in thunderstorms, the potential for large hailstones is high. On 20 June 1726 and 18 June 1748, severe thunder-and-lightning storms occurred. On these occasions the storms were associated with exceptionally large hailstones, measuring 'five inches square, and others had five or six forks projecting from them, of an inch long each, by which several windows were broken, and other considerable damage done in and about Cork'.[16] On 14 July 1783 a thunderstorm near Cork was also stated to have 'included balls of fire which were seen to fall in several fields, tearing the ground as they entered. Several sheep, cows, horses and pigs were killed, and many persons scorched'.[17] This refers to the rare form of lightning known as 'ball lightning', a phenomenon still poorly understood by scientists. Further damaging lightning storms occurred on 22 September 1818, 'which included incessant flashes of very vivid lightning and very heavy rain',[18] and again on 7 September 1849, 'during which over two inches (> 51 mm) of rain fell in just six hours', and on 8 February 1850.[19]

Gales and storms

Cork has long been plagued by gales and storms (Fig. 1.24). One of the worst of these storms occurred in November 1692.[20] Again, on 23 February 1723, 'a violent south-westerly storm, along with other damage to chimneys and roofs, demolished a great part of a wall twenty feet high on the right hand side of the Sunday's Well Road, and with the force of the fall the opposite wall was broken'. This was followed by another violent south-westerly storm on 25 January 1725, which caused 'a large breach to be made in the same road by part of the rock giving way'.

Additional damaging storms occurred on 18 November 1808 and 15–16 December 1814 (in which three people were killed and others severely hurt).[21] The largest and most devastating storm in the historical records, which occurred on the night of 6 January 1839 and is known as 'The Night of the Big Wind', had a surprisingly limited impact on the city. No fatalities were recorded, in comparison with the rest of the country, where at least 300 people lost their lives.[22] However, damage was done to chimneys and roofs throughout the city and some people had lucky escapes from falling chimneystacks and roofs. Another notable gale occurred in March 1848. This was reported as causing the bog, 'which for years had been accumulating in the centre of the lough near Cork City, to commence moving steadily, until it became connected with the Old Kinsale Road, in which position it remains'.[23]

Wet spells

These wet spells are ones for which there is no evidence of flooding in the city. The summer of 1491 is the first of the records found that was described as 'exceedingly wet'. In the eighteenth century prayers for fair weather were

Fig. 1.24 Meteosat-7 satellite image for 16 June 2004 of an Atlantic cyclone. Thick cloud on the storm's southern edge can be seen approaching Ireland. The cyclone's centre is moving eastwards towards northern Scotland. (Source: Eumetsat and Met Éireann, Dublin.)

offered up on 31 July 1763 in all the churches of Cork, 'it being the wettest summer ever remembered'. In October 1782, 'the very inclement weather during the whole harvest' caused 'a great scarcity of bread, which continued to the end of the year, the bread was perhaps the worst that was ever made, owing to the continued rains which had totally ruined the corn'.[24]

OTHER NATURAL PHENOMENA

Other unique events were recorded in Cork city that are worth mentioning. On 7 April 1234, 'there appeared in Cork and several other places the resemblance of four suns'. This was most likely to have been a rare halo phenomenon, caused by the reflection of the sun in ice crystals in the sky. Later, notable blazing stars or comets were seen in August 1506 and December 1680, of which the tail was described as 'extending 40 degrees in length'.[25] If this date was incorrect by a couple of years, then the latter comet was in fact Halley's comet, which was seen in 1682. A spectacular *aurora borealis* (Northern Lights) occurred on 21 January 1750 and was described as 'extending from east to west over the heart of the city, tinged with so deep a scarlet, that at a distance the town seemed to be in flames, during which time, it moved in a compact body from north to south with a very slow motion'.[26]

On 1 November 1755, Cork was 'affected by a violent shock of an earthquake at thirty-six minutes past nine o'clock in the morning, but did no injury'.[27] This was the famous Lisbon earthquake, the epicentre of which occurred several hundred miles due west of Portugal under the Atlantic and devastated that great city and much of the Portuguese coastline, causing more than 30,000 fatalities.[28] The fact that the earthquake was clearly felt in Cork indicates its strength. On 31 March 1761 an earthquake tremor was again felt in Cork.

On 23 November 1772, a strange event happened around two o'clock, 'when the sun was nearly eclipsed by a large cloud from the west, so as to cause nearly a total darkness for about two minutes; some persons in this city imagined they felt the slight shock of an earthquake at the same time'. This was possibly an exceptionally dark thunderstorm super-cell. On 8 November 1786 another celestial event occurred: 'a remarkable meteor was seen this night, much brighter than the moon, and of double in diameter. It was of a white colour inclining to blue, had no tail, and was of a globular form not well defined; it scattered luminous particles as it passed along'.[29]

LOOKING BACK

Records and anecdotes of natural phenomena are fascinating, having something of a voyeuristic attraction, but they are not unique to Cork.[30] Their significance for Cork, or elsewhere, lies in what they show of the lives and times of the people. Weather extremes underline in particular how many of the city's inhabitants lived on a knife-edge of survival. However, it is important to remember that natural events and disasters are more the exception in the human time span. It is only when the analysis of such events shows sequences and patterns that their real environmental significance becomes apparent, as in recording climate change and its impact on people.[31]

3. FLOODING IN THE CITY

Kieran Hickey

CAUSES OF FLOODING

One of the realities of living in Cork is the almost yearly flooding that can wash over the flat central part of the city and many of the coastal suburbs. This flooding is rooted in a variety of causes that include the estuarine location and topography of the city, the history of its development and growth through marshland reclamation and the nature of its urban structure (see *Cork City and the Evolution of the Lee Valley*, Chapter 1).

Cork was originally founded on two of approximately thirteen flat marshy islands in the Lee (see *Urban Beginnings and the Vikings*, Chapter 6; *The Evolution of Cork's Built Environment*, Chapter 12). These islands were chosen for two main reasons: their defensive potential and their accessibility to the sea for port activities. However, the site was, and is, vulnerable to flooding. Even the origin of the name Cork, *Corcaigh Mhór Mumhain*, or the Great Marsh of Munster, signifies its waterland location.[1] Relative to mean

Fig. 1.25A) Flooding in Blackpool on 21 November 2002. Floodwater reached depths of over one metre. (Photo: *Irish Examiner*.) B) Flooding on Patrick's Street in October 2004, caused by a combination of floodwaters from the Lee, a spring high tide and a storm surge in the harbour resulting from an easterly wind. C) Floodwaters over the Lee fields, October storms 2004. (Photo: *Irish Examiner*.)

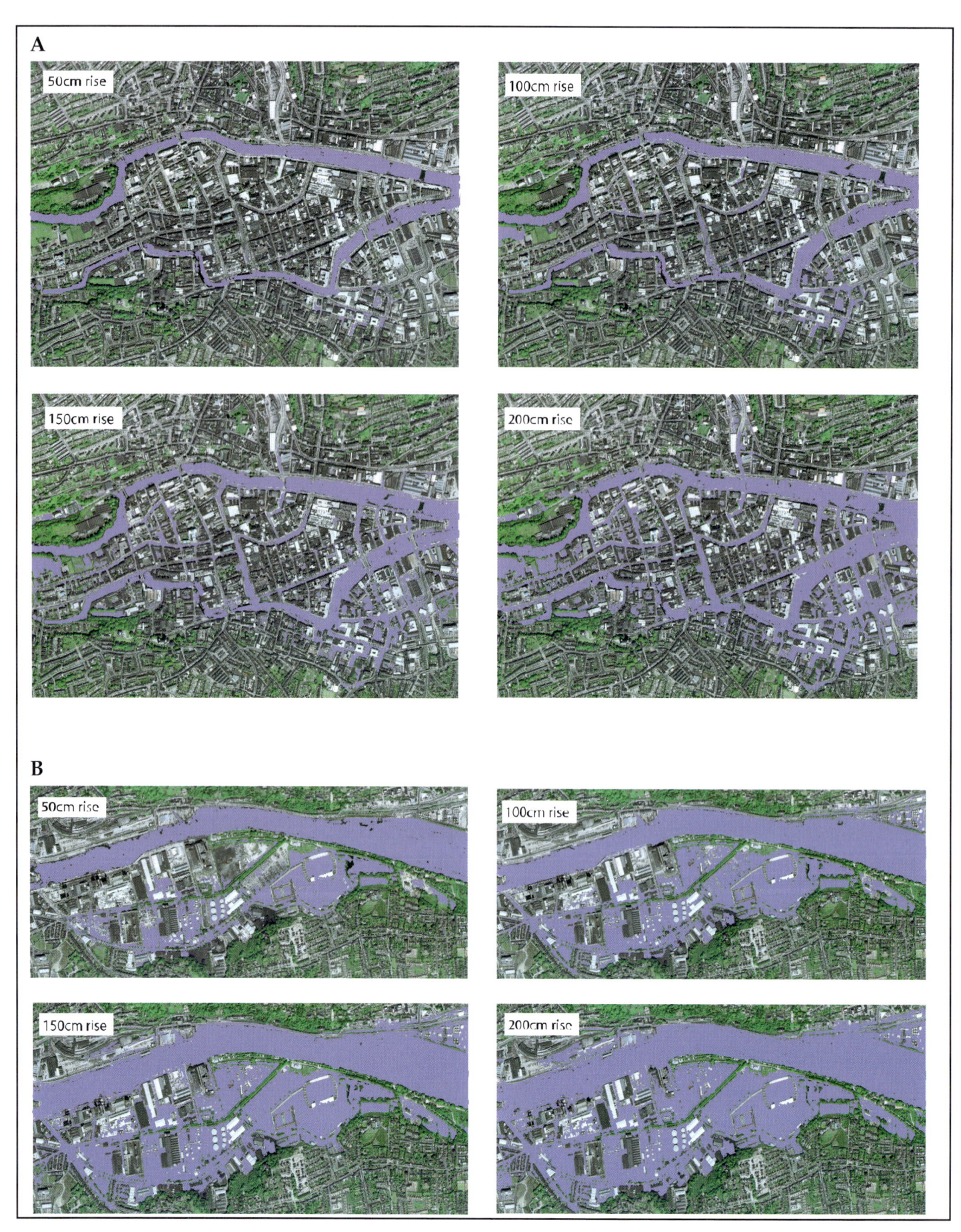

Fig. 1.26 Areas of Cork vulnerable to flooding by the Lee, rising sea levels and high tides or storm surges, shown in increments of 50 cm above current levels of the mean high-water mark of spring tides, c. 4.2 m OD. A) The centre of the city. B) Cork's southern docklands. Areas at risk from flooding are shown in blue and violet. Current best estimates of global mean sea-level rise are between 0.13 and 0.68 m by the 2050s. (Digital elevation model data are from J. McGrath, K. Barry, J.P.J. O'Kane and R.C. Kavanagh, UCC.)

THE · CITY · IN · THE · LANDSCAPE

A

B

A) SMITH'S 1750 MAP
   North-east Marsh – fully reclaimed
   East Marsh (Dunscombe's Marsh) – partly reclaimed
   Pike's Marsh – partly reclaimed
   Hammond's Marsh – partly reclaimed

B) ROCQUE'S 1759 MAP (CHANGES IN COMPARISON TO SMITH'S MAP)
   Green's Marsh – unreclaimed
   Pikes Marsh – fully reclaimed
   Hammond's Marsh – fully reclaimed
   East Marsh (Dunscombe's Marsh) – partly reclaimed
   Reap's Marsh – partly reclaimed
   Dunbar's Marsh – starting to be reclaimed
   South-east Marsh – starting to be reclaimed

C) ROCQUE'S 1773 MAP (CHANGES IN COMPARISON TO HIS EARLIER MAP)
   Devonshire Marsh – fully reclaimed
   Reilly's Marsh – starting to be reclaimed
   Dunbar's Marsh – fully reclaimed

D) MURPHY'S 1784 MAP (CHANGES IN COMPARISON TO ROCQUE'S LATER MAP)
   Reilly's Marsh – fully reclaimed
   South-east Marsh – fully reclaimed
   Green's Marsh – fully reclaimed
   East Marsh (Dunscombe's Marsh) – fully reclaimed
   Reap's Marsh – fully reclaimed

As the city grew, reclamation and colonisation occurred (see *The Evolution of Cork's Built Environment*, Chapter 12) (Fig. 1.27). One after another, each of the thirteen islands was attached to the rest of the city with a bridge, reclaimed and then built on.[4] The initial costs would have been so high that this process was not undertaken lightly. As part of the reclamation the size and shape of the islands were stabilised, but all continued to be vulnerable to flooding. As the process of reclamation progressed into the 1700s, urban development also led to the canalisation of the Lee between the islands. Eventually the lesser channels were either filled in or culverted over. All these islands were eventually converted into one large central city island between the north and south channels of the Lee, although a few smaller open and culverted channels are still in existence (see the case study, *Lanes and Streets*, in Chapter 7).[5]

The steep topography and narrow valley of the Lee also generates flooding (see *Cork City and the Evolution of the Lee Valley*, Chapter 1). The slopes encircling the city focus incoming rainwater onto the valley bottom. Before the spread of buildings out of the city core, there would have been water percolation on the valley slopes into the underlying soil and bedrock. However, as the city grew, it covered both the valley bottom and the valley sides with impermeable surfaces like roads and buildings, leading to a significant increase in run-off, which can cause flooding and a reduction in percolation. This process is still continuing today.

Cork's weather plays a key role in generating floods, caused by prolonged rainfall, or intense downfalls during thunderstorms (see *The Climate of Cork*, Chapter 2). Other floods resulted from the rapid melting of snow and ice in the catchment of the Lee. Flooding can also be caused by tidal surges associated with large storm systems that push a wall of water up the estuary, increasing water heights well above the normal tidal cycle. They are also associated with reduced barometric pressure, which also allows the water to rise a little higher. It is really the combination of the two, high rainfall often associated with big storms and a storm surge occurring at high tides, which causes the most severe floods (Figs. 1.26 and 1.28). This is predominantly around the central city island and on the opposing banks of the south and north channels, but it can also occasionally affect some coastal suburbs. Oliver Plunkett Street, Patrick's Street and the Grand Parade dominate the most frequently named flooded locations within the city (Fig. 1.29).[6]

Major floods

Very large floods have affected the city over the last four centuries. The earliest known description is from the winter

Fig. 1.27 Cork's marshlands. A) The Lee at Cork and its blocking marsh islands; drawing, *c.* 1720. (Source: British Library.) B) Cartographic evidence from a series of eighteenth-century maps for Cork city shows that the process of marsh reclamation was spurred on by the pressure of population and also by mercantile activity requiring new buildings and quays. C) Excavation showing the culvert at Grand Parade, 2005. (Photo: Darragh MacSweeney, Provision Agency.)

sea level, Ordnance Datum Malin (OD), much of the central city island is within the normal spring tidal ranges and is estuarine. Without quay walls and other obstructions, parts of the city would be flooded virtually every spring tide. Oliver Plunkett Street is the lowest street in the city, at only 4 m above sea level, whereas the normal spring tidal range can reach heights of > 4.3 m OD (Fig. 1.26).[2] This also leads to a high water table within the city (the layer of permanent water that varies very slowly over the seasons). As a result there is very little capacity for the ground to absorb incoming water. Chief Justice Willis, writing in 1762, put it succinctly: 'The situation of the town is on a marsh, and during a very high spring tide the whole town is overflowed to the great prejudice of the merchants.'[3]

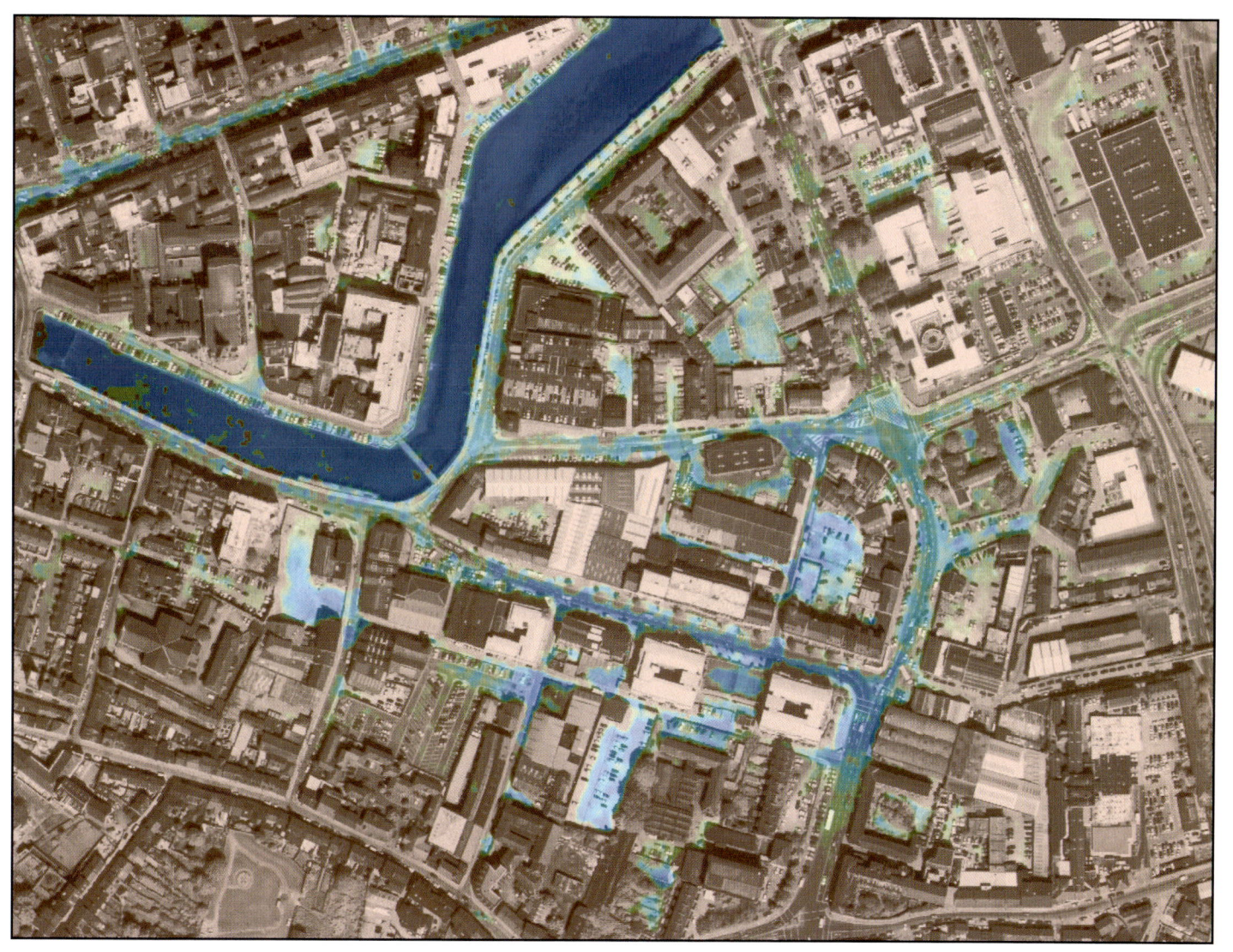

Fig. 1.28 Flood risk map of South Terrace, George's Quay area, using photographic and digital elevation model data. The most vulnerable areas are shown in blue and lie below the level of the present-day high tide; red represents areas that are 1 m or more above this level and areas of intermediate heights appear as green-grey. (Source: J. McGrath, K. Barry, J.P.J. O'Kane and R.C. Kavanagh, UCC.)

of 1633, when there was 'a prodigious flood which, among other damage done, ... carried away the old North and South Gate bridges and the castles on top of them'.[7] The flood that occurred on 17 January 1789 was one of the largest ever to have affected the city. Remarkably, only one person lost their life: ironically, a man called Noah. The main cause of this flood was heavy continuous rain that caused snow cover to melt quickly. The flood is described as 'breaking every boundary and overflowing the entire city between the gates'; water depths were between one to over two metres in many places. The impact of the flood was serious, with a few houses completely washed away and many others badly damaged. One of the bridges (unspecified) was destroyed, others were damaged, and many of the quays were also badly affected. The mayor ordered the markets to be opened on Sunday, 'so that people could get food and other urgent provisions'.[8]

The only other flood that can compete with 1789 is that of 1–2 November 1853. This flood was caused by a combination of heavy rainfall following a prolonged wet spell lasting several weeks, and occurred independently of the tidal action of the estuary. The whole central city island from the Western Road seaward was completely covered in water, including Grand Parade, Patrick's Street and the South Mall. The average height of the floodwaters was close to two metres. However, at the Mardyke the water depth was estimated to have approached three metres. A flood of this magnitude is likely to cause fatalities and this was certainly the case. The old Patrick's Bridge collapsed in the flood, sweeping eleven people to their deaths. The western portion of a pier near Camden Quay also collapsed, causing the loss of between eight and twelve people, and three people were lost when 'Mr Perrott's Foundry was washed away'.[9] The

Rank	Location	Total (out of 277 floods)
1	Oliver Plunkett Street	102
2	Patrick's Street	49
3	Grand Parade	40
4	South Terrace	39
5	Winthrop Street	34
6	Carrigrohane	32
7	Victoria Road	30
8	Rutland Street	27
9	South Mall	27
10	Blackpool	25
11	Cook Street	21
12	Princes Street	20
13	Victoria Cross	20
14	Lavitt's Quay	19
15	Marlborough Street	19

Fig. 1.29 The fifteen most frequently identified flooded locations in Cork city 1841–1988. The actual flooding totals are higher than those shown, as no specific sites are mentioned in some of the flood descriptions.

impact on the heart of the city was enormous, with other quay collapses, damage to virtually all the bridges, numerous buildings impacted upon and a few destroyed.

The flood of 26–27 September 1875 is a classic example of the different causes of flooding in the city. It resulted from a combination of high water levels due to a week of heavy rain, particularly heavy rainfall immediately preceding the event and a high spring tide driven in by a westerly gale. This flood affected the western districts of the city especially, with water depths approaching two metres in places, including on the Mardyke, the Western Road and Washington Street. Flooding also affected the main shopping streets, where water depths were generally less than one metre. The flood also caused considerable damage to Pope's Quay. In the flood record repeated flooding has occurred at high tides over a number of days and, although the individual floods may not have been too damaging, the cumulative effect was significant. In 1945, flooding occurred on one of the high tides on 17, 18 and 19 December, on both high tides on 21 December and again on one high tide on 22 December. This sequence of floods was caused by a combination of high rainfall and above-average tides. The most notable of the floods in the sequence was on the morning of 21 December, when a very exceptional tide height of over five metres OD was recorded. There was extensive flooding on the central city island, with water depths of one metre in places, including on Patrick's Street, Oliver Plunkett Street and South Mall. Many other streets were affected and much damage was done to shops and other premises in these areas.[10]

The most significant flood of recent times to affect the city was that of 21 November 2002. The main cause of the flooding was a night of torrential rain, with 44.5 mm of rain falling in twelve hours from six p.m. on 20 November to six a.m. on 21 November, during which almost 25 mm fell between midnight and one a.m. Unusually, this flood did not really affect the central city island and the usual flood-prone parts of the city. Instead it affected suburban locations, particularly Blackpool, where the River Bride burst its banks, probably due to an obstruction. The streets most badly affected were Great William O'Brien Street and Thomas Davis Street (Fig. 1.25A). The next worst-hit area, again caused by a stream bursting its banks, was the Greenwood Estate in Togher, with 'muddy water' recorded here almost a metre deep. Also affected were roads around Ballincollig and Carrigaline. That plans for flood relief works in Blackpool were scheduled for 2003 was said to be of 'little comfort' to the affected residents.[11] The overall damage was estimated to be in excess of 10 million euro. Insurance companies have reassessed the flood liability of properties in the face of the possible repercussions of climate warming on flooding.

Floods and Climate Change

Kieran Hickey and Robert Devoy

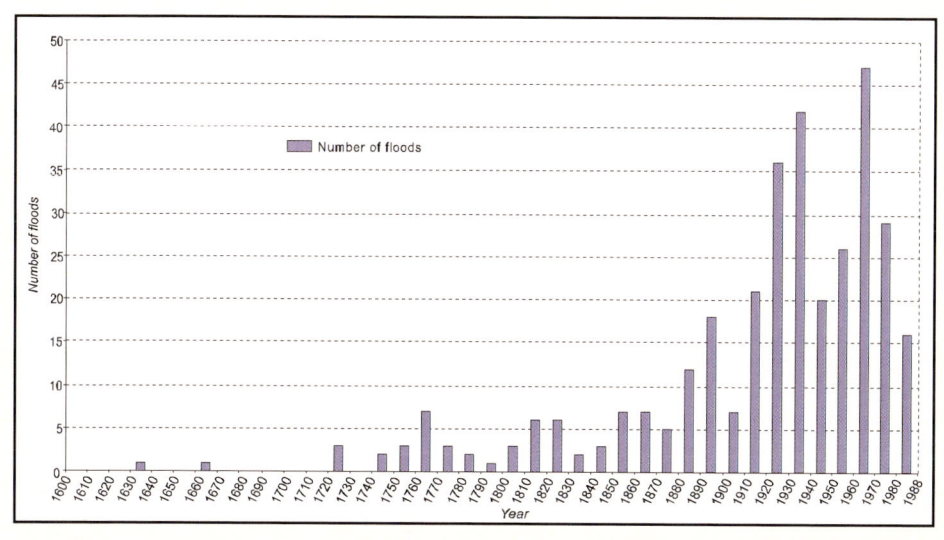

Fig. 1.30 Floods recorded in Cork city between 1600 and 1988 from various archival sources. The chronology depends on the availability of historical information and hence the record shown here is likely to be incomplete. The figures for the 1940s are also inaccurate, as no weather events were reported in the newspapers due to the restrictions of the 'Emergency' (World War Two).

A tentative 'flood chronology' for Cork city has been assembled using two information sources.[12] The first being the many histories of the city and the quantity of published historical research. The second is the newspaper archive, mainly the *Cork Examiner*, which yielded an almost continuous record of floods from 1839 onwards and is more comprehensive than any other source. Only the damaging floods were recorded prior to 1839 and this must be borne in mind when looking at the chronology.

The first decade with more than one flood recorded was the 1720s. Three decades stand out as having more floods recorded than the rest: the 1760s, 1810s and 1820s. These decades are easily comparable in terms of floods recorded for the first four decades of the *Cork Examiner* record from the 1840s to the 1870s. Thereafter, much higher numbers of floods were recorded, but many of these would be small and localised in effect, the size of floods not being recorded previously. There are three decades of higher numbers of floods: the 1920s, 1930s and 1960s. The three most flood-prone years on record were 1928 (ten floods), 1929 (nine floods) and 1935 (ten floods). This pattern is also replicated in other studies across north-west Europe and resulted from an increase in the frequency of bouts of high rainfall.[13] After the 1960s, the number of floods recorded declined up to 1988, as a result of the building of the Inniscarra dam and reservoirs on the Lee in the mid-1950s. Subsequent records show that the city still remains vulnerable to flooding, as indicated by the events of 2002 and 2004.[14]

It is difficult to accurately predict the future prospects for flooding in Cork city, but certain natural processes will make flooding more likely, assuming there is no significant human intervention. The first process is that of rising sea levels. Global climate warming will cause sea levels to rise, through the expansion of the oceans and the addition of ice meltwater.[15] This will have the knock-on effect of increasing surge heights during major storms, making the city more vulnerable when they coincide with high tides (Fig. 1.26). Secondly, global warming will make Ireland wetter in the winter, with storms of a higher magnitude over the next fifty years.[16] Such changes would increase the number of large floods in Cork by raising river water levels and causing heightened storm surges, the ideal combination for causing flooding in the city. The commissioning of the city's new storm-water drainage scheme may make a significant difference, but it has yet to be tested.

4. NATURE'S IMMIGRANTS

Pádraig Whelan

We do not see cities as places that we share with plants, birds and other animals. We may give a passing thought to birds, or to people's gardens and pets, as we go about our business. Rarely, though, do our thoughts dwell on these things for long. Yet plants and animals were there before us. As the city environment has grown, so the flora and fauna have had to adapt in order to survive (Fig. 1.31). Both consciously and by chance, people have brought in new species and the native ones have had to cope. This is the general pattern for plants and animals in any city: the only significant difference is where the city is located. Cork's flora and fauna have distinctive aspects that arise from the city's natural setting and its urban past and present (see Section 1, *Introduction*; *Cork City and the Evolution of the Lee Valley*, Chapter 1; *The Climate of Cork*, Chapter 2). Given the complexity of this story, one way of approaching the range of ecological changes, patterns and processes recorded in the city is to examine some examples.

The Lough

The Lough, south-west of the city centre, is one of Cork's most fascinating amenities (Fig. 1.32). It delights a wide range of the city's citizens of all ages who engage in a large range of activities, from team games to jogging, walking, reading and nature study. As an urban amenity, its lake and surrounding grass area provide respite from the built environment that surrounds it. It teems with wildfowl and, for many of Cork's youngest citizens, this may be their first experience of seeing wildlife at close quarters. It has also proved to be a nursery for many of Cork's amateur and professional biologists. The wildfowl interact closely with humans, especially during feeding, but the large body of

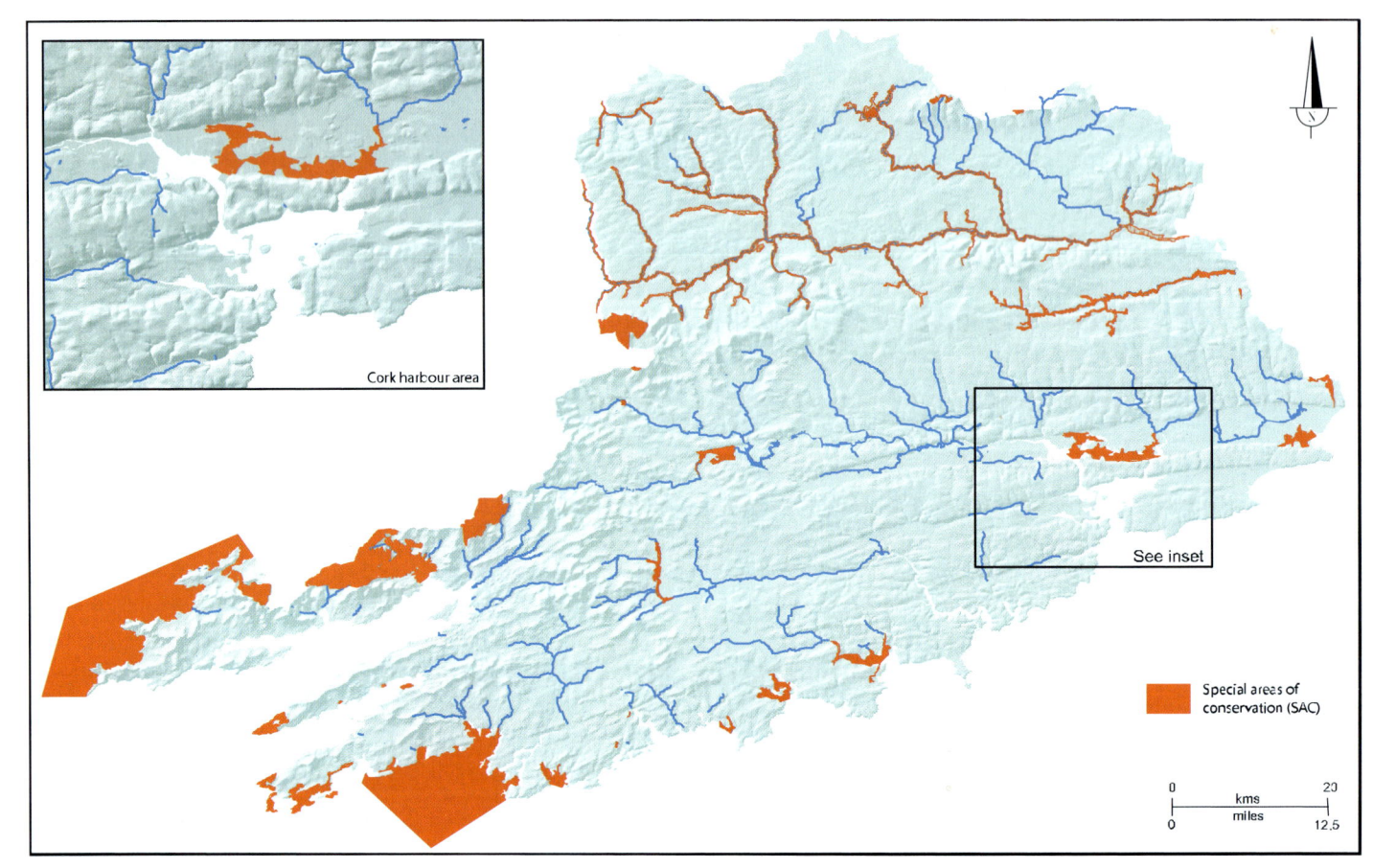

Fig. 1.31 Areas of special conservation, of ecological and natural heritage interest. Few such sites have been designated in urban areas. (Adapted from Dúchas.)

Fig. 1.32 Aerial view of The Lough, 2004, showing the vegetation island in the lake and the surrounding urban setting. (Photo: Tomás Tyner.)

water and the vegetated island provide a safe refuge for them. The Lough was declared a Public Wildfowl Refuge as early as 1881 and is one of Ireland's oldest protected areas.[1]

As a small freshwater limestone lake in a shallow depression, The Lough receives its water from springs and from water percolating from the ridge to the north, on which stands The Lough parish church. No river flows into the lake, but there is an outflow drain in its south-west sector. The Lough is shallow and many people remember it being sufficiently frozen to support the weight of a human. The mean depth of both the north and south basins of the lake is just less than one metre. Overall, depths vary between 0.21 m and 1.6 m with sediment thicknesses of $c.$ 0.1 m to 0.9 m. A high maximum water temperature of 28°C has also been attributed to its shallow nature.[2]

The area of The Lough has varied as its circumference has become more symmetrical and well defined. In 1893, Doran reported the area to be 7.3 ha ($c.$ 18 acres), though an Ordnance Survey map for that same period gives 6.6 ha.[3] The Lough was shown then as larger and more irregular in outline than its current oval shape.[4] In 1984, the size of The Lough was established as 6 ha, with the island occupying 1.5 ha of the total.[5]

VEGETATION

The southern part of The Lough features an island, on which the most visible vegetation consists of fully developed willows. These trees are now tall enough to partly obscure a view of the opposite shore. It was not, however, always so. Photographs from 1870 indicate that the island has been present since at least then, although until the 1930s the vegetation was much lower and contained a different assemblage of species to those seen there today.[6]

By means of a natural process called *succession*, the island is gradually converting to land. The rate of this succession has been accelerated by partial drainage in 1765 and again in the 1920s. The high nutrient levels of the surrounding water, a feature of recent decades, have aided the influence of the drainage. In the 1930s, the island consisted of large amounts of Greater Reedmace (*Typha latifolia*) with some

Fig. 1.34 The Lough. The water margin, July 2004. (Photo: John Crowley.)

Fig. 1.33 Swans and other wildfowl on The Lough. (Photo: John Crowley.)

willow (*Salix* species), vegetation typical of many lake margins.[7] At this stage the island was really just a raft of vegetation with the roots anchored loosely in soft mud. It would have been unsafe to walk upon the emergent island without the real danger of sinking into the water. This gradual process of vegetation succession and lake infilling would have been common in the wetlands around the city before vegetation clearance, draining and other human interventions took effect (Section 1, *Introduction*).

Since the 1930s, the willows on the island have become progressively more dominant. By the 1960s, the Greater Reedmace had been substantially reduced and there were areas that were still free of willows.[8] From the 1970s to the present, willows have come to dominate the island, almost to the exclusion of any other large vegetation. Comparison of photographs shows that the island in The Lough has grown upwards, in terms of vegetation height, but has not increased in area.[9]

To a person looking into the open water areas of The Lough today, they appear to be free of submerged or floating vegetation. This contrasts sharply with The Lough in the 1940s and 1950s, when the abundance of floating and submerged weeds made sailing of model yachts very difficult.[10] At that time, the Water Fern (*Azolla filiculoides*) had been introduced and floated on the surface, while Hornwort (*Ceratophyllum demersum*) and Water Milfoil (*Myriophyllum* species) were growing on the shallow lake bottom.[11] Hornwort and Water Milfoil are characteristic of shallow limestone lakes. A 1954 report indicated that at least 'ninety per cent of The Lough was covered by weeds' and that eels, sticklebacks and rudd were common.[12] By 1956, the weed growth had been drastically reduced and by the mid-1960s these plants were no longer present in The Lough.[13] This collapse in aquatic vegetation in the 1950s and 1960s can be attributed to the introduction of carp (herbivorous fish) in 1954.[14] If aquatic vegetation had been seen as a problem, then the introduction of carp would have been an easy remedy.

Fish

The Lough was once famous in the city for its fishery, so much so that in the eighteenth century all nets and boating on The Lough were banned. Prior to the 1950s the lake was more important as a fishery than as a wildfowl reserve. Freshwater eels (*Anguilla anguilla*) and three-spined sticklebacks (*Gasterosteus aculeatus*) probably occurred naturally in The Lough and, at least up to 1985, the largest freshwater eel ever captured in Ireland had come from The Lough. This hoary veteran, caught in 1974, weighed 3.54 kg (7 lb 13 oz) and was estimated to be 207 years of age.[15]

There have also been several introductions of other fish species to The Lough. Carp (*Cyprinus carpio*) and tench (*Tinca tinca*) were introduced in the 1950s, pike (*Esox lucius*) in 1965 and perch (*Perca fluviatilis*) in 1973. Eighty carp were released into The Lough in 1954. The carp were reported as not breeding and were subsequently restocked, with 500 fry in 1974 and again in 1975.[16] The date of introduction of rudd (*Scardinius erythropthalmus*) is not known. The rudd fishery has been decimated by the introduction of the perch (a competitor) and pike (a predator). The extinction of sticklebacks in The Lough in 1975–1976 may have been linked to the reduction in aquatic vegetation and the 1974 introduction of perch, whose fry would compete with sticklebacks.[17]

Birds

Today wildfowl are the most visible wildlife feature associated with The Lough and the place is now more famous for its wildfowl than its fish. To people visiting The Lough,

Black Headed Gull (*Larus ridibundus*)
Bonaparte's Gull (*Larus philadelphia*)
Common Gull (*Larus canus*)
Glaucous Gull (*Larus hyperboreus*)
Great Black Backed Gull (*Larus marinus*)
Herring Gull (*Larus argentatus*)
Iceland Gull (*Larus glaucoides*)
Kittiwake (*Rissa tridactyla*)
Laughing Gull (*Larus atricilla*)
Lesser Black Backed Gull (*Larus fuscus*)
Mediterranean Black Headed Gull (*Larus melanocephalus*)
Ring Billed Gull (*Larus delawarensis*)
Thayer's Gull (*Larus thayeri*) – a first record for Ireland

Fig. 1.35 Gulls recorded at The Lough.

the swans, geese and ducks are its most striking feature (Fig. 1.33). While the birds come close to humans when they are being hand-fed, the large body of open water and the island act as refuges to which the birds can retreat if they feel threatened. However, the birds cope admirably with children, dogs, joggers and the city environment. The birds occur in large numbers and originate from native wild populations and introduced ornamental waterfowl. Until the early 1960s, the birds were all wild free-flying birds, living either as permanent residents, regular visitors, or as migrants arriving there to breed or to overwinter.[18]

In 1962, nine pairs of ornamental waterfowl, consisting of Canada Geese (*Branta canadensis*), Magellan Geese (*Chloephaga picta ssp. leucoptera*), Chiloé Wigeon (*Anas sibilatrix*), Caroline Duck (*Aix sponsa*) and Mandarin Duck (*Aix galericulata*), were introduced and subsequent introductions also took place.[19] Whilst some of this original group did not become established, the numbers of birds at The Lough are now considerable. The introduced wildfowl increased fivefold between 1962 and 1984. The density of birds (geese, swans and ducks) was estimated as varying between 575 and 880 birds per hectare from July to October 1984. Two-thirds of this population were ducks and of these 66 per cent were 'wild free-flying birds'.[20] Swan numbers varied between 153 and 247 per hectare, depending on the month. The greatest variation in bird numbers was found in the geese, which ranged from 135 birds per hectare in July to 22 birds per hectare in September. Many of these leave The Lough for coastal sites in August and September. While the birds are the most visible feature of The Lough, their high numbers have resulted in the problem of hyper-eutrophication, or over-enrichment, caused by the nutrient input from their excreta.[21]

The Lough's location, close to one of the city's sanitary landfill sites on what is now the South Link Road, has resulted in the attraction of gulls to The Lough area and some interesting gull records have been noted (Fig. 1.35).[22] As management of landfill sites improves, the opportunities for visits by gulls become reduced. The closure of the nearby landfill site will also reduce visits by rare gulls to the area and may have an impact on bird diversity at The Lough.

Cork's Botanic Gardens

Pádraig Whelan

Fig. 1.36A Green Cork. A palimpsest of the city's small, open green spaces. (Photo: Philip O'Kane, Department of Civil and Environmental Engineering, UCC.)

The place of plants in Cork city is distinctive. Viewed from the air it is striking how many open and backyard green spaces fleck the city. If not Cork the garden city, then it is certainly a city of spaces for plants to inhabit (see the case study, *Distillery Field: A Final Refuge*, in Chapter 4). A formal interest in plants in Cork dates from at least the nineteenth century and the work of the Royal Cork Institution (RCI) in setting up the Botanic Gardens (see *The Royal Cork Institution*, Chapter 20).

In 1809, the RCI purchased land for a botanic garden at what is now St Joseph's Cemetery, on Tory Top Road in the Cork suburb of Ballyphehane.[23] Regrettably their history as gardens is a short one. James Drummond (1784–1863) was the curator of the Cork Botanic Gardens from their beginning until their closure in 1829. In May 1826, a series of robberies of plants, including plant grafts 'for which there were no duplicates', and vandalism to the property led the RCI to consider the future of the

Fig. 1.36B View of the arboretum, Fota House, Cork harbour, a continuation of Cork's botanic garden tradition. (Photo: Tomás Tyner.)

Botanic Gardens. The situation worsened when shortage of funds meant that the services of a watchman had to be discontinued.[24] By late 1827, the financial situation was so critical that proposals were put to the RCI to rent the gardens or even 'surrender' the premises. The formation of a new botanic garden was considered. In January 1829, the RCI decided to sell the 'Botanical Garden'.[25] By February the RCI had received twenty pounds for removable articles in the garden and, soon afterwards, the garden was purchased by Fr Theobald Mathew and became St Joseph's graveyard (see boxed section, *Father Theobald Mathew*, in Chapter 18).

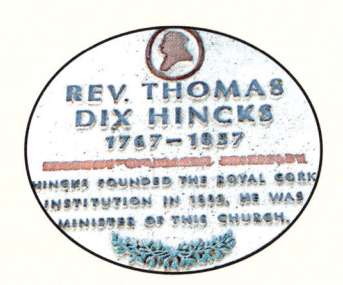

Burials in the garden (the older, walled, area of the graveyard) date from 1830, as seen from several extant headstones. Fr Mathew's own grave lies in the centre of this same walled portion. Next to his grave is the stump of a large tree that was blown down in January 1973.[26] It is reported that this was a cedar tree and probably the last remnant of the Cork Botanic Gardens. The name of nearby Botanic Road preserves the link with Cork's first botanical garden, as do local people's references to burials in the Botanic Gardens.[27]

Fig. 1.37 A) Plaque to the Reverend Thomas Dix Hincks (1767–1857), who ministered in the Unitarian Church in Princes Street in Cork and founded the Royal Cork Institution in 1803. (Photo: Pádraig Whelan.) His son, William Hincks, was the first Professor of Natural History in Queen's College, Cork. B) St Joseph's Cemetery, formerly the Cork Botanic Gardens, showing the remains of a cedar tree from the garden and Fr Mathew's grave. (Photo: Patrick Whelan.)

Wild Plants

Pádraig Whelan

by ants. All these occurrences are, therefore, thought to have arisen by the same spontaneous mutation of the more common purple form.[32]

The rarer, white-flowered form of Ivy-leaved Toadflax is termed an acyanic mutant, because it lacks the purple anthocyanin pigment that gives the commoner purple-flowered form the purple tinge on its flowers and leaves. The leaves of the acyanic mutant are green. While the purple form is widespread throughout the city, the white form is most frequently found on bridges and vertical walls on the north and south channels of the Lee.[33] Both forms grow together on weathered limestone surfaces. The success of this plant on walls is due to the ability of the species to manoeuvre its developing seeds into wall crevices, where they are protected from drought and excessive sunlight in the early stages of growth. The flower stalk pushes the fertilised seed capsule away from sunlight and into cracks in walls near the parent plant. A city such as Cork, which is full of stone walls, offers the plant an ideal environment.

The white form of Ivy-leaved Toadflax, with its green leaves, grows better in shade, while the purple form is more of a sun plant, whose leaves are not damaged under high light conditions.[34] The purple anthocyanin in the purple form of the Ivy-leaved Toadflax, in effect, acts

Fig. 1.38 Ivy-leaved Toadflax. A) Purple form. B) White form. (Photos: Pádraig Whelan.)

A NATURAL MUTANT – IVY-LEAVED TOADFLAX (*CYMBALARIA MURALIS*)

Ivy-leaved Toadflax, with its purple-tinged flowers and leaves, is common throughout Ireland. In Cork city, and in a number of other locations, there also occurs a rarer, white-flowered form of this species that has arisen by natural mutation.[28] Locally, ants spread this introduced plant.[29] However, the widely separated populations of the white-flowered form in such dispersed places as Cork city, Portrush (County Antrim)[30], Sallins (County Kildare) and Killorglin (County Kerry)[31] are too distant for its dispersal

Fig. 1.39 Fuchsia in Cork. (Photo: Pádraig Whelan.)

as a sunscreen, protecting plants from the damaging effects of ultra-violet light. The absence of such a pigment explains, at least in part, why the white-flowered form is restricted in Cork to locations that are shaded from intense sunlight.

Fuchsia (*Fuchsia magellanica*)

Another introduced plant is the Fuchsia, with its distinctive red flowers (Fig. 1.39). Fuchsia grows throughout west and south-west Ireland in hedgerows and near dwellings and is frequently found in the city. Its flowers are a visual feature of Irish summers. Tourists from mainland Europe are amazed by its profusion, given that many people there can only grow the plant in pots. It is so abundant that many consider it native to Ireland and the 'Fuchsia' brand is even used as a logo for what is best in West Cork food produce and accommodation (see *The Culture of Food*, Chapter 27). The specific epithet *magellanica* in its scientific name refers to its South American origins. In Cork, it is used as a hedging plant in older parts of the city and it also occurs on urban walls and waste ground.[35]

Common Cord Grass (*Spartina alterniflora*)

At the head of an estuary and open to the sea, the city's environs also provide opportunities for coastal plants to thrive. The sheltered, shallow muddy shores of Cork harbour have undergone considerable changes in recent decades. These changes relate to the growth of *Spartina alterniflora*, an introduced hybrid plant that has colonised large stretches of the intertidal areas of the harbour, converting them from mudflats to Cord Grass meadows. The original introduction was at the east bank of the estuary of the Glashaboy River.[36] This grass was introduced in November 1925, probably from the south coast of England, by Professor Henry Cummins of Queen's College, Cork.[37]

While the original plants do not seem to have prospered in their initial site, they have successfully colonised large areas of mudflats in the sheltered upper reaches of the harbour. The dense, stiff, upright stems of the plants act as baffles and reduce water flow. The result is the deposition of waterborne sediments and the gradual raising of the surface of the former mudflat, sometimes

Fig. 1.40 *Spartina* meadows, Fota Island area, Cork harbour. (Photo: Pádraig Whelan.)

resulting in the emergence of dry land. Ornithologists have differing views on this introduced hybrid. Some regard it as a bonus because of the seeds and plant material it contributes for consumption by birds and mud-living invertebrates. Others regard it as a threat to intertidal mudflats as a habitat and to the many species of wading birds that probe these muds for their invertebrate food. When the plant dies back, the trapped sediment is also released, causing channels and harbours to silt up.

Distillery Field: A Final Refuge

Noreen Dalton

A GREEN SPACE

Distillery Field is a green, semi-natural area that lies just west of the centre of Cork city. It is located along the banks of the Lee, at the end of North Mall.

This area is of historic interest and is thought to be the last reclaimed marsh in the city.[1] Marsh reclamation began in Cork as early as the thirteenth century. However, the main thrust of reclamation occurred during the seventeenth and

Fig. 1.41 Map and aerial view of Distillery Field. (Photo: Philip O'Kane.)

eighteenth centuries (see *Flooding in the City*, Chapter 3; *Urban Beginnings and the Vikings*, Chapter 6). Distillery Field marsh was not fully reclaimed until 1850. Along the banks of the Lee and the millrace, stone walls can clearly be seen at low tide. These walls were built as part of the reclamation and the area behind them back-filled to raise the land level above that of the river.

Distillery Field must also be considered as a potential amenity in its context within Cork. Apart from sports facilities, there are few recreational green spaces within the city itself. The increasing pressure from development on some of the urban open areas – for example, the Glen recreation area on the city's northside – emphasises the importance of the preservation of such spaces in Cork. The Distillery Field site is a quiet and peaceful place, close to the city's heart, and presents one of the last chances to conserve and develop a green public space for the benefit of the city (Fig. 1.42).

The importance of keeping green spaces has not gone unnoticed. The Distillery Field site was an integral part of an action plan that was unsuccessfully submitted for millennium funding for the regeneration of one of Cork's main recreational areas, the Lee Fields. The Recreation, Amenity and Culture Department of Cork City Council, jointly with University College Cork, are now constructing a pathway at the site. The university has purchased Mardyke Gardens on the other side of the river, which has facilitated the construction of a new pedestrian bridge (Fig. 1.45). This pedestrian link will shorten the commuting time between outlying university departments on the northside of the river and the main campus.[2]

A visible part of the site's amenity value is its greenness: Distillery Field is an important location for flora and fauna within the city. During the foot-and-mouth disease restrictions in Ireland in March–July 2001, many of the locations used for educational and research purposes by biologists from UCC were inaccessible. Consequently, Distillery Field was used as a temporary study site and its value quickly became apparent. Preliminary surveys carried out by undergraduates revealed the area to be rich in plants and wildlife. Thirty bird species were recorded, among them Sparrow Hawks (*Accipiter nissus*), Grey Herons (*Ardea cinerea*) and Pheasants (*Chrysolophus* sp.) and 90 invertebrate taxa were found. Mammals have also been reported on the site, including stoat (*Mustella erminea*), foxes (*Vulpes vulpes*) and otters (*Lutra lutra*).

The site contains a mix of plant communities. There is an area of semi-natural wet Alder (*Alnus glutinosa* (L.) Gaertner) woodland located north of the millrace and the Lee. The area to the south of the millrace contains a mixture of woodland and more open areas that are heavily infested with the alien plant species Japanese Knotweed (*Polygonum cuspidatum* Siebold & Zucc.). The northern part of Distillery Field consists of disturbed open grassy areas that give way to a steep cliff that rises up to Sunday's Well Road. This area is also home to some alien plant species. Although the species

Fig. 1.42 Panorama eastwards of Distillery Field and the Lee.

Fig. 1.43 Infestation of Traveller's Joy, *Clematis vitalba* in woodland, Distillery Field. (Photo: John Crowley.)

are not large in number, they are well established, invasive and abundant. Sycamore (*Acer pseudoplatanus* L.) is found throughout the site, including the wet woodland area near the water. Winter Heliotrope (*Petasites fragrans* (Vill.) C. Presl) occurs mainly in open areas and drier banks. Traveller's Joy (*Clematis vitalba* L.) is by far the most invasive species on the site, engulfing most of the cliff and trees along the northern boundary. In recent times, this plant has started to spread into the woodland along the water.

Mapping

During 2002–2003, a survey of the vegetation in part of Distillery Field was undertaken so that this could be catalogued and understood. Another primary objective was to examine the suitability of Geographical Information Systems (GIS) as a tool for mapping vegetation.[3] This involved the setting up of a 10 m × 10 m surveyed grid over

Fig. 1.44 Butterfly bush, *Buddleia variabalia*, growing in open space around the woodland. (Photo: John Crowley.)

the area, using wooden stakes and tape to mark the location of each grid point.[4] Plants were identified and catalogued around the gridded stakes, based upon a 5 m × 5 m quadrat method. The results were input to a spreadsheet in Microsoft Excel™. This spreadsheet was used to construct a GIS that could manipulate the vegetation results in a 'spatial tabular comparison'.[5]

In this GIS device, each quadrat was given a location, as a simple x, y co-ordinate, based on its location on the base-grid and in relation to the river and site boundaries. Each of the total of 178 plant species found was represented as a separate layer in the GIS. By switching on and off the layers that represented different species, a map of the vegetation associations was generated (Fig. 1.46). Further layers were constructed within the GIS to represent the vegetation associations present in relation to characteristic vegetation associations for Ireland.[6] By indicating the number of diagnostic species present at every quadrat, it was possible to quickly assess the degree to which a quadrat was representative of a particular vegetation association.

The results show the Distillery Field to contain a number of vegetation types. A typical Irish ash wood with a well-developed herbaceous layer best describes the woodland along the millrace and the river (*Corylo-Fraxinetum typicum*). This vegetation association is a member of the Oak–Beech class. On this site, however, alder and ash replace beech and oak, indicating its very wet environment. The remaining vegetation associations fall into three types: woodland margins (*Artemisietalia vulgaris*), bank vegetation (*Convolvuletalia sepium*) and grassland types (*Filipendulo-Iridetum pseudacori*, *Seneciono-Juncetum acutiflori* and *Centaureo-Cynosuretum*). They all reflect varying levels of the disturbed and wet environment that would be expected in this riparian urban site.

Fig. 1.45 Pedestrian bridge (built 2005) to Distillery Field over the Lee, linking UCC campus areas. (Photo: John Crowley.)

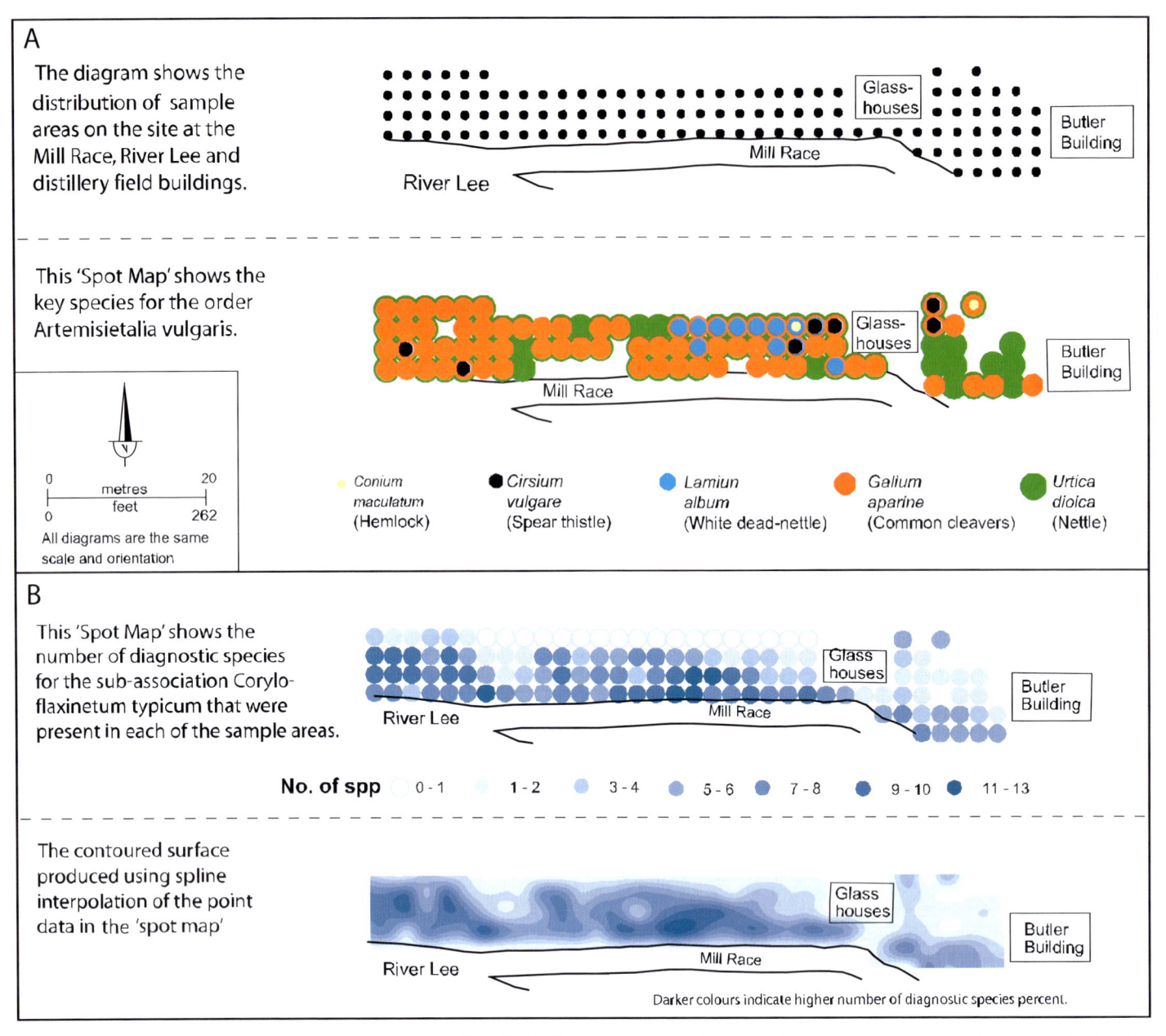

Fig. 1.46A) GIS-generated 'spot' maps for part of the Distillery Field. B) An example of a 'spot map' for a vegetation association commonly found at Distillery Field.

FUTURE PLANS

Distillery Field contains a good example of a species-rich wet alder and ash woodland. It provides a link to the type of vegetation that may once have been found in Cork's marshy estuary. In addition, it is a haven for wildlife in an urban environment. In terms of its survival and conservation, issues that need to be addressed include future development, particularly the location of a pathway, habitat management, the removal of alien plant species, and wetland development and security.

The ecological sustainability of riparian fragments, such as Distillery Field, depends on cultural sustainability.[7] It is not enough to draw up a well-meaning plan; local people must feel the need to follow plans through and see tangible gains, be they recreational or economic in form. The development of a public pathway and recreational areas, possibly with osier beds or other historical and educational links to the area's former uses, would serve to focus attention on this site.

5. THE FIRST PEOPLE

Michael Monk

HUNTERS

In prehistory there was no city of Cork. Settlement was spread across a diversity of landscapes and environments in south-west Ireland. The prehistoric setting of Cork helps in understanding how the later city fits within the human context of immigration and settlement in the region. Cork city's site and its elongated hinterland, to the west along the Lee and to the east and south along its elaborate estuary, provided both opportunities and limitations to prehistoric people who came to dwell there.

The earliest people to settle in and around where the city is now located were Mesolithic hunter-gatherer-fishers (Fig. 1.47). The attraction for them was the rich riverine and marine resources, not least the fish and shellfish that abounded in the shallow water around the harbour. These people hunted wildfowl in the sloblands and the alder carr along the valley (see Section 1, *Introduction*). The lowland wooded areas surrounding the harbour would have supplied wild boar and a diverse range of plant foods.

Although evidence for hunter-gatherer communities has been found elsewhere in Ireland, dating from *c.* 7000 BC, the evidence from the Cork area is intermittent and mostly consists of finds of stone tools. At Gyleen, Ballintra West, east of the harbour on higher ground, a scattering of stone tools including Bann 'flakes' were found. The use of these 'flakes' is uncertain, but they are typical of late hunter-gatherer times (Fig. 1.48).[1] However, settlement commonly was located on the water margins and many sites are now lost to view due to the subsequent rises in sea level. Evidence of such settlement possibly exists in the shell middens in the eastern harbour area, although these mostly appear to be Early Iron Age or later in date.[2] One excavated at Carrigtohill produced thirteenth- and early fourteenth-century pottery; another, at Sunday's Well, produced seventeenth- and eighteenth-century glazed pottery.[3]

THE FIRST FARMERS

Farming became established in Ireland *c.* 4000 BC. Evidence of this was discovered during excavation work on the Ballincollig bypass, west of the city, in 2001–2002 (Fig. 1.49). At Ballinaspig More, early Neolithic pottery was found. This site was occupied throughout prehistory. In Barnagore townland, evidence of a Neolithic house was discovered. It was rectangular in shape, measuring 6.4 m by 5.4 m. Upright timbers, set in trenches, formed the walls and these were supported by earth-fast posts at the corners and internally.[4] Other evidence comes in the form of stray finds of polished stone axes, three from the Mahon peninsula and another from Ballinaspig More. Highly polished and hafted with a wooden handle, these tools were effective in clearing away not only the trees but also undergrowth and roots in preparation for tillage (Fig. 1.50).

By comparison with elsewhere in the country, no evidence remains in the city of the characteristic megalithic monuments, formed with large upright stones, associated with these early farmers. There are only two definable megaliths in the city region and neither of these fit established categories. An earthen mound, similar to the long mounds of southern Britain, probably covered the Castlemary megalith near Cloyne. The megalith at Rostellan, at the eastern edge of the harbour, assumes the appearance of a portal tomb, but its capstone is only supported on three upright stones (Fig. 1.51).[5] This site is covered by water at high tide, indicating later sea-level rises and suggesting that other Neolithic sites may now lie under water.

AGE OF METALS

Copper
The metal age began in Ireland *c.* 2400 BC, when people began to use copper. Important sources of this metal were exploited in south-western Ireland, in west Cork at Mount Gabriel and in Kerry at Ross Island.[6] They produced flat axes like the example discovered at Carrigaline West.[7] These first metal users also made a type of pottery called Beaker, because of its similarity to a modern drinking vessel. There have been no well-attested finds made of this pottery type in the Cork area. Some possible Beaker pottery has been recovered recently, however, from pits at Ballinure on the Mahon peninsula, along with stone tools and a saddle quern. Close by, a hearth surrounded by numerous stakes and a linear feature were found and excavated. The latter could have formed a windbreak for the hearth.[8]

These people became proficient workers in copper and then in bronze, once tin was added to produce the alloy, but they also worked in gold. There have been several finds of Bronze Age gold objects from the greater Cork area, including three gold discs decorated with wheel-and-cross motifs, two from Cloyne and one from Castletreasure, Douglas. These were probably sown on to clothing. Gold lunulae were also found in the nineteenth century near

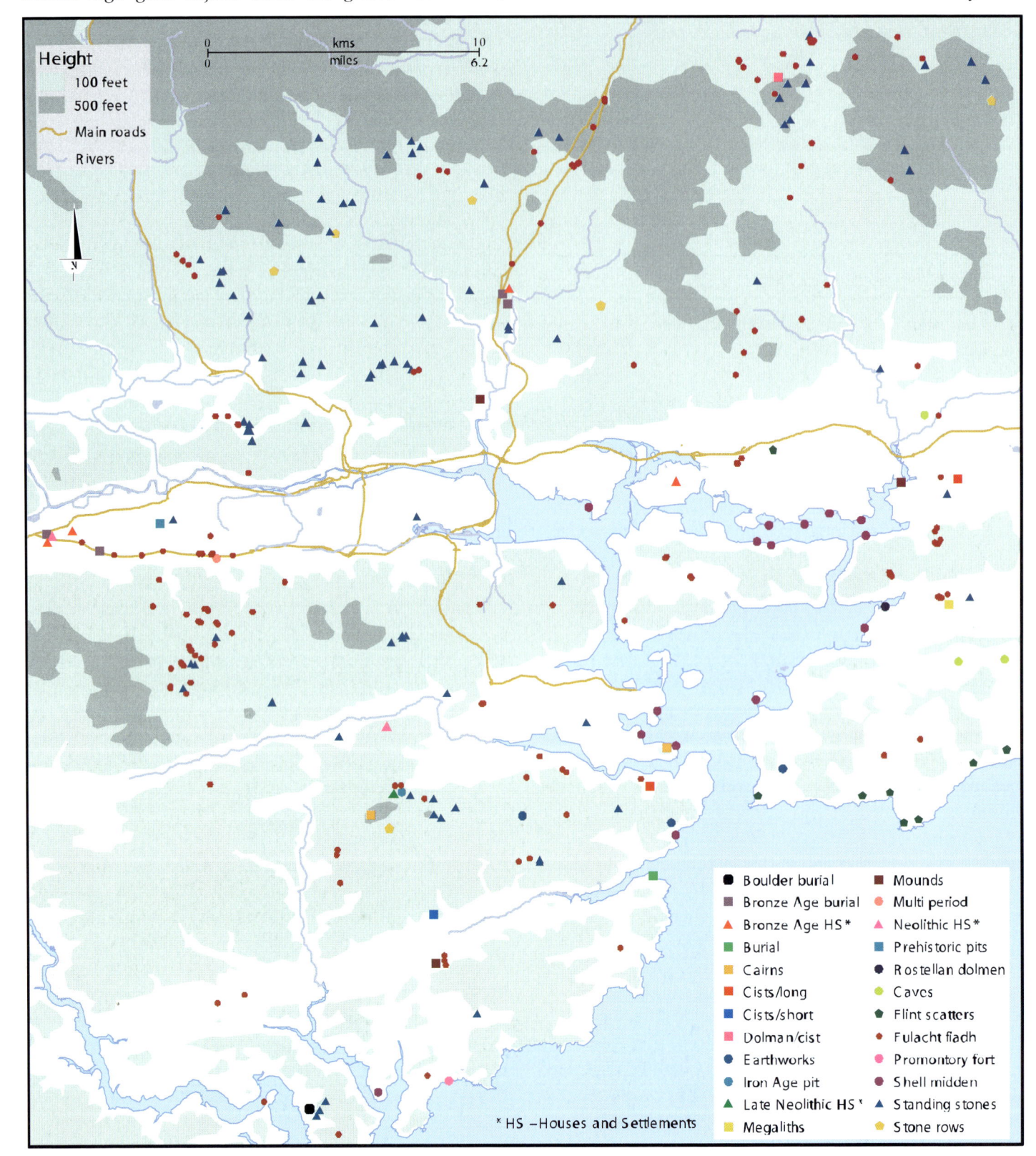

Fig. 1.47 Distribution of prehistoric sites and artefacts in the Cork harbour area. (Adapted from D. Power et al. and County Cork Archaeological Survey.)

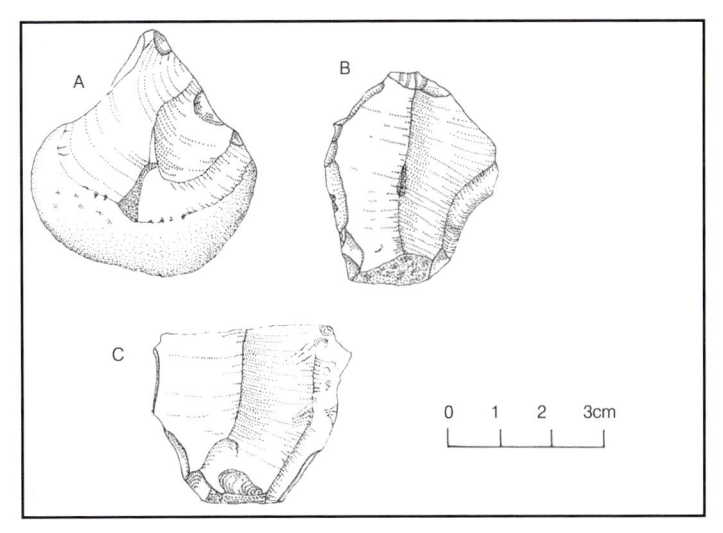

Fig. 1.48 Mesolithic stone tools (lithics) from Gyleen and Inch, in Cork harbour. (Source: Woodman, 1984.)

Midleton (Fig. 1.52). The design on these classic-style lunulae, which boast more gold content than other types, is reminiscent of designs on Beaker pottery and suggests that they date to the end of the Early Bronze Age (c. 2400 to 1600 BC). Other Early Bronze Age objects found within the hinterland of the city include a few amber objects: three amber beads and a unique amber ball.[9]

Bronze

The Middle Bronze Age (c. 1600 to 1100 BC) is partly defined by the change in axe type: from the flat axe of the Early Bronze Age to those with flanged sides to facilitate hafting (such as the one found at Carrigaline) (Fig. 1.53A and B). In the later Bronze Age (c. 1200 to 600 BC), the flanged axe evolved into the palstave, or socketed axe with side loops (as found at Kilbarry and at Ravenswood, near Carrigaline) (Fig. 1.53C). The socket completely contained the crooked haft and the axe was further secured to the handle by the loop. It is possible that these axes could have been used as weapons, but their primary use would have been for working wood. Possession of metal objects (swords, spears, axes) would also have conferred status on their owners. Few Bronze Age weapons have been found within the area of Cork. One socketed spearhead, with loops to attach it to the shaft, was found with the Ravenswood hoard. Three Later Bronze Age swords were also found: one again in the Carrigaline area, the other two nearer the city.[10] All seem to be characteristic of the Late Bronze Age.[11]

Evidence for the Bronze Age in the city and its hinterland is not only restricted to finds of artefacts. A number of sites and monuments have been identified, including burial sites,

Fig. 1.49A) Construction of the Ballincollig bypass (above) unearthed many new archaeological sites indicative of the region's rich archaeological heritage. (Photo: Tomás Tyner.) B) Archaeological excavations at Mitchelsfort during work on the Watergrasshill bypass. (Photo: Avril Purcell, Sheila Lane Associates.)

Fig. 1.50 Neolithic polished stone axe from Castlemary, Carrigtohill, Co. Cork. (Photo: Cork City Museum.)

fulachta fiadh (ancient cooking places) and standing stones and there is also recent evidence for Bronze Age settlements. On Little Island, a large enclosure with associated settlement evidence was excavated in the early 1990s.[12] This structure consisted of several stake and post holes forming an oval plan measuring 8 m by 4.5 m. The size and shape of the structure suggests a Bronze Age date. There were several pits and areas of burnt material and finds were made that included a sharpening stone and flint tools.

Evidence for Bronze Age settlement has also been excavated in advance of the constructing of the Ballincollig bypass.[13] The work has shown, for instance, a late Bronze Age oval structure, or enclosure, at Greenfield 2. This is of similar overall appearance to the one on Little Island. A number of Bronze Age sites have also been found along the Watergrasshill and Glanmire bypass. These include a 6 m diameter circular house in Killydonaghue townland with associated pits that contained broken saddle querns. In two cases these were found in the basal fill of the pits and indicated some kind of ritual deposition. Relatively close to this site evidence of two disturbed cremation burials was found. Both were found in urns and in one case another decorated vessel was found in association with it. Worked flint objects were also found in adjacent pits.[14]

Other Bronze Age urn burials in pits have been investigated at Castlerichard and Oatencake, County Cork.

Fig. 1.51 Rostellan megalithic tomb. (Photo: Department of the Environment, Housing and Local Government, courtesy of the National Archaeological Survey of Ireland and County Cork Archaeological Survey.)

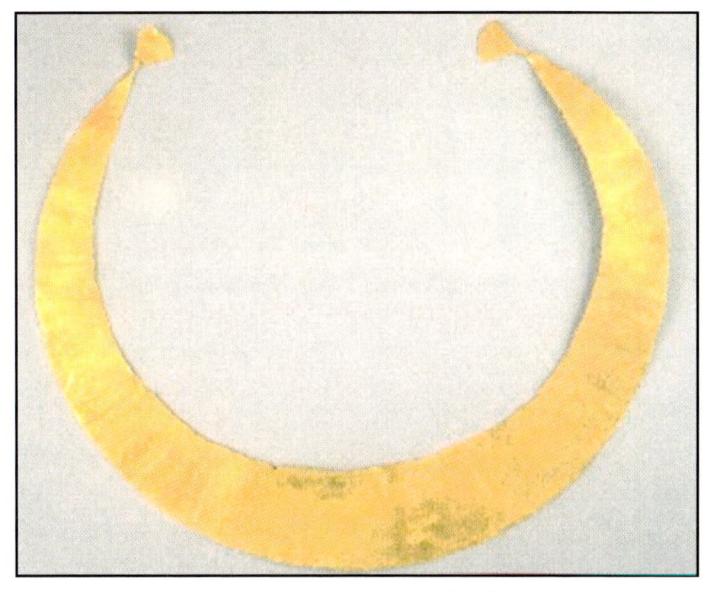

Fig. 1.52 A gold lunula from Midleton. (Photo: Ashmolean Museum, Oxford.)

At Castlerichard a tripartite collared urn had been upturned over the cremated human remains.[15] The grave context of the Oatencake burial had been destroyed. The decorated cordoned urn still contained the remains of a possible adult female.[16] In the same area of Cork, at Clonleigh, an example of a 'boulder burial' of probable Bronze Age date has been noted. In common with the boulder burials more frequently found in west Cork, from which this forms an outlier, the monument consists of a large quartz boulder resting on smaller stones. These burials consist of a larger one to the west and another quartz one to the east, as well as a bed of smaller stones. At one time there was a standing stone close by.[17]

At Currabinny, a hilltop cairn of stones 15 m in diameter and revetted by a stone kerb was excavated in the 1930s. An inner arc of stones was defined within it and in the centre there was a platform of clay and embedded stones where the burial would have been. This was covered with charcoal, among which cattle teeth were found. A ring of loose stones was also identified adjoining the circle on the east side and fragmentary cremated human bone and charcoal was found between the stones with a post hole near the centre.[18] Several earthen tumuli have been identified in the area as well during various investigations, mostly in the nineteenth century. Human remains were discovered in two tumuli at Ballyvorisheen and Clasharinka. The latter example could even have been Iron Age in date.

Apart from burials, evidence of life and settlements of these early people is found in other features in the landscape. Many *fulachta fiadh* have been excavated in the Cork area.[19] These consist of a mound of burnt stones, which surround a localised source of water, into which was set a wooden trough. Close by would be a hearth (Fig. 1.54). The earliest excavations of these ancient cooking sites in the Cork city area were undertaken in the 1950s, on three examples located on marshy ground at Killeens, north-west of the city.[20] All consisted of overgrown mounds of burnt stone of varied size. One of these had two phases of use. In the first phase, the bottom part of a dugout wooden trough was set in a pit and packed with stones. It had a constructed hearth consisting of an arc of stones with a paved floor. Another hearth was found to the north-east of the trough. In the second phase, a further trough was dug to the south-west of the earlier trough. Only the four corner stakes for the trough setting were still in place; the rest had been removed, probably intentionally. Another example had a more classic

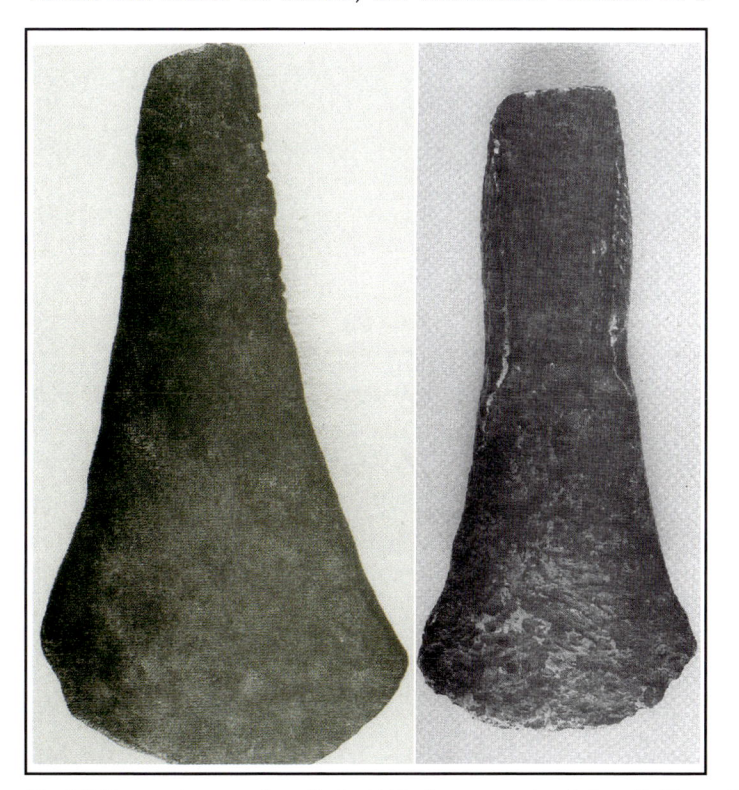

Fig. 1.53 Bronze Age axes from Cork. A) Flat bronze axe-head, from Ballinure (9.1 cm long). B) Flanged bronze axe, from Carrigaline (10.5 cm long). C) Three bronze socketed axes from Ravenswood (the largest of these is 6.5 cm long). (Photos: National Museum of Ireland.)

Fig. 1.54 Reconstruction of a *fulacht fiadh*. (Drawing: Rosanna Devoy.)

horseshoe shape. Within the opening between the two arms of the horseshoe was a pit, containing a rectangular trough with both the sides and base formed of planks. Below the trough a small, gold-plated copper ring was found and the site produced a radiocarbon date that placed its use at the beginning of the later Bronze Age.

Recently, a further 27 *fulachta fiadh* sites have been excavated, seventeen along the Ballincollig bypass and ten along the Glanmire and Watergrasshill bypasses. All of them had been disturbed but all consisted of an irregular spread of burnt stone, earth and charcoal, varying in thickness from a few centimetres to half a metre. In several cases, this material covered hollows or pits of various sizes, but generally up to 2 m by 1 m, that probably represented the emplacements for the trough. Remains of these troughs have been discovered in several of the sites, including two of the eight *fulachta fiadh* in Curraheen townland, near Ballincollig. One of these had most of the timbers that formed it still in place. A re-used dugout canoe was adapted for the purpose at Killalough near Watergrasshill.[21] In several cases near Ballincollig there was evidence of an associated hearth, which included two examples at Curraheen, one at Greenfield, one at Ballinaspig More and the Killalough example near Watergrasshill.

In several of the sites, associated features may suggest ancillary structures at the cooking sites. Post holes exist at Killalough and stake holes at the two Ballinaspig sites; at Ballinaspig More 6 these might indicate a windbreak. At Curraheen 5.7 a linear feature was found that might have represented an overflow channel for the trough. For the most part, however, these sites have not produced *in situ* finds, though there have been a few. At Ballinaspig More 7, a whetstone was found, a plain disc-headed pin at Curraheen 4.1 and, at Meenane (AR24), a piece of struck flint. Some sites have also provided radiocarbon dates indicating a broad date range from the late Neolithic and Early Bronze age: from a clearly two period site at Ballinaspig More 7 to later Bronze Age use at two of the Curraheen sites. The radiocarbon dates show a concentration of use from the later Middle Bronze Age into the Late Bronze Age.[22]

Standing stones are classic archaeological features of the County Cork landscape, and many still exist in the city region.[23] Such stones are usually associated with the Bronze Age. They may have functioned primarily as grave markers or as markers of routeways or boundaries. Only one site near Cork, at Ballynagrumoolia, Ballygarvan, has been excavated.[24] At this location three shallow pits were found filled with organic remains but no artefacts were there to suggest their date.

Iron

The Iron Age began *c.* 600 to 500 BC. A few key pieces of evidence indicate the presence of people in the Cork region at this time. The recent excavations on the multi-period site at Ballinaspig More 5, along the route of the Ballincollig bypass, showed Iron Age settlement in the form of a circular structure.[25] Earlier, an important find of three Bronze 'horns' was made at Victoria Road, Cork, in 1909. The running floral and spiral-type design on these curious artefacts is characteristic of the La Tène style of the later Iron Age. The design is similar to other pieces of Iron Age metalwork, not least the Bann Disc and the unprovenanced Petrie Crown, dated to the first century AD.[26]

The later Iron Age in Ireland was also contemporary with the Roman occupation of Britain. There is evidence, mainly from coastal regions within Ireland, of Roman and Romano-British artefacts that show some level of contact at this time. This was most likely in the form of trading and raiding. A hoard of third- and fourth-century Roman coins was found at Cuskinny close to the entrance of Cork harbour.[27] These could have been the spoils of a successful raid!

CHANGING PATTERNS

The question has to be posed whether the archaeological evidence reflects a representative picture of the presence of prehistoric people in Cork. Artefacts have been found, mainly by chance; for the most part these are *old* finds without a specific provenance. The sites that have been identified consist mainly of ancient cooking places and standing stones. The distribution of these sites suggests clustering in particular areas. For example, a concentration of standing stones exists in the area between the Blarney and Glashaboy rivers but no *fulachta fiadh*.[28] Furthermore, the majority of sites found around Cork are located at a height of between 60 m and 150 m. This might explain the absence of sites in such dissected upland areas as towards Watergrasshill, north-east between the Butlerstown and Owennacurra rivers. Such upland areas may have continued as uncleared woodland until early medieval times. However, a similar dearth of sites also occurs in a relatively lower area between the Owennacurra and Dungourney rivers.

Archaeological surveys also indicate an absence of sites east of the harbour, in the city and, particularly, in the surrounding urban areas (Fig. 1.47). Many of these are valley bottom areas and may have been too wet for use. Yet it is also likely that sites did exist in these locations but have gone unrecorded and been destroyed as the city grew. The lands around Cork city, particularly east of the harbour, include large areas of tilled farmland and many areas immediate to the city were intensively used for market gardening in recent historical times. Such tillage areas are not conducive to the survival of archaeological sites.

The evidence for prehistoric people is clearly influenced by the visibility of their surviving remains.[29] The truth of this observation for Cork is currently coming into sharp focus as more and more sites come to light in advance of large-scale land-use changes in the region. The infrastructural development of roads has been of considerable importance in altering the understanding of such sites. The Ballincollig, Watergrasshill and Glanmire bypasses have produced evidence of timber-house sites and burials from Neolithic and Bronze Age dates. This new evidence provides an invaluable glimpse into the activities of Cork's prehistoric people.

Ringforts

Michael Monk

Ringforts are the most numerous archaeological monuments in this country. Estimates put the total between 40,000 and 60,000 for Ireland. There are over 600 in the east and south Cork Archaeological Inventory, covering the greater Cork area.[1] Excavations show that these circular-shaped earthen banks and ditched enclosures date from the early medieval

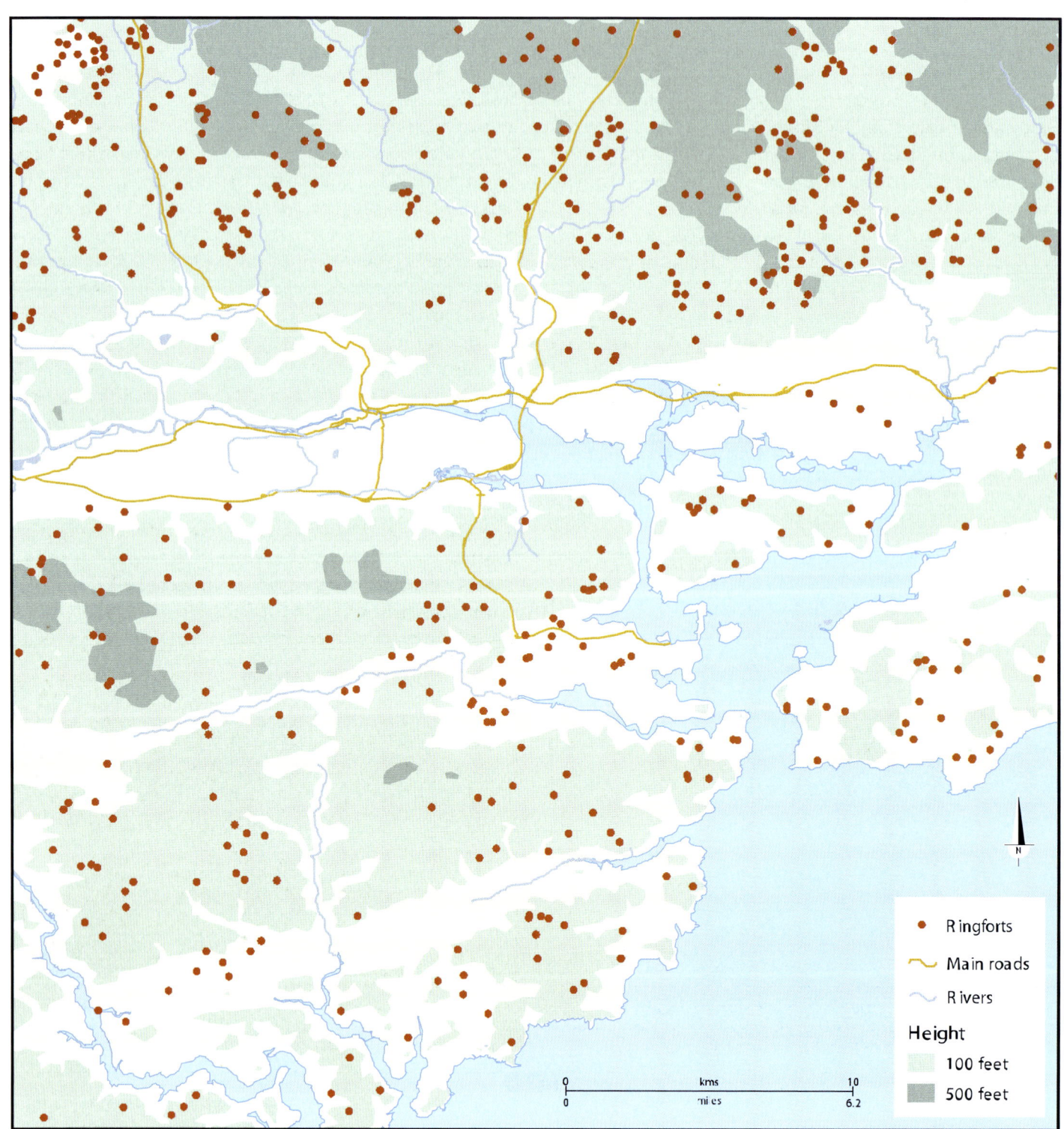

Fig. 1.55 Distribution of ringforts in the greater Cork city region. (Adapted from Dúchas.)

period (c. 550–1000). They represent the defended farmsteads of the middle ranking to stronger farmers of the period.[2] The development of ringforts in such numbers probably illustrates the relatively short-term socio-economic success of a social system based on clientship, requiring co-operative farming. The evidence for agriculture at this time indicates both an upsurge in tillage agriculture and in pastoral farming. This social system encouraged a growth in population, which may also have prompted some instability. This expressed itself in cattle raiding, cattle being of key importance in the clientship system. It is in this context that the ringforts were constructed. Not surprisingly, they are located on the better land or just above it, often on south-facing slopes between elevations of c. 30 to 50 m (Fig. 1.55). Many overlook the larger rivers and are close to the headwater streams feeding these rivers.

Many of the sites known to have existed in the greater Cork area are no longer extant and can only be seen now from the air. Their demise results from the attrition caused by farming, as well as from the spread of urban areas. There have been few excavations of such sites and most of these have been in recent years; for example, at Coolawen, Glanturkin, Killanully and Ballygarvan and at Raheens 1 and 2 near Ringaskiddy, Carrigaline.[3] The two close Raheens ringforts were excavated in 1989 in advance of the construction of the Sandoz chemical factory. The evidence from these sites is characteristic of other ringforts in Ireland. Raheens 1 showed two enclosing ditches, the bank having been removed long ago. Evidence of two circular timber buildings was discovered and their sizes (5 m and 6 m) indicate that they were houses. The few artefacts found included a knife blade and a sharpening stone. The evidence from Raheens 2 was more substantial. The site has a lower than average diameter enclosure of 28 m (sites can range from 20 m to over 90 m in diameter). Some of the encircling bank remained on the east and south sides and reconstruction shows the bank was originally up to 2 m high (Fig. 1.56). A causeway across the ditch and a paved entrance were also discovered in its south-west perimeter. Two posts at the outermost point indicate the presence of a wooden gate.

Within the enclosure evidence for eleven timber buildings was discovered (Fig. 1.57). Although they varied in size, all but one of them was round and their wall construction was similar. The larger buildings range from 4 m to 6 m in diameter and were probably houses, while smaller buildings may have been outhouses or stores. Not all the buildings were contemporary and there was a succession in their use. On most other ringfort sites the occurrence of rectangular houses follows on from that of round buildings, but at Raheens 2 a rectangular house (6.5 m × 4.5 m) with rounded corners was replaced by a circular building.[4] No hearths were found in any of the structures. This suggests that, if they were houses, either the surfaces on which the hearths were set had been eroded away or the hearths were laid above ground level.

Souterrains, common in ringforts, were also found at Raheens 2. These structures were built below ground. They may have served variously as cool stores for dairy products, safes for valuables, or refuges for people during attacks, particularly as people became commodities for the slave trade organised by the Vikings. Three souterrains

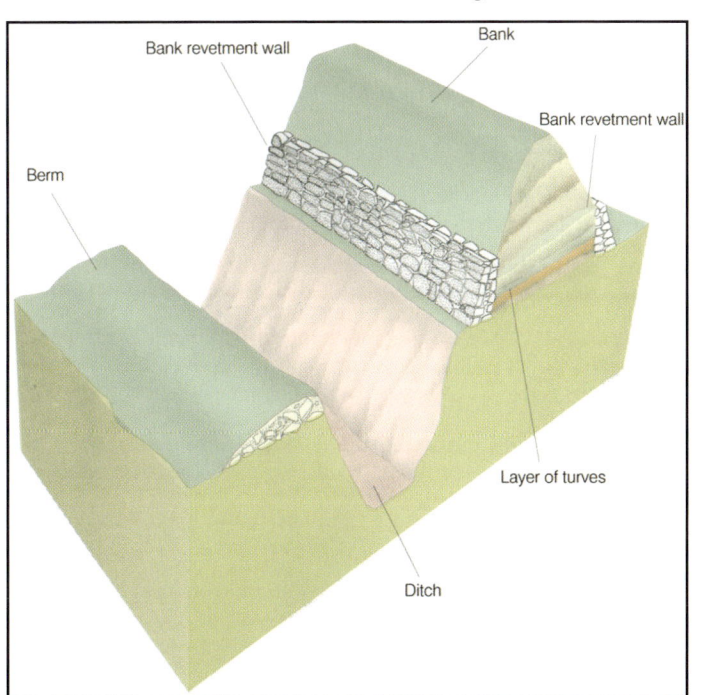

Fig. 1.56 Cross-section through the ditch and bank of a ringfort. At Raheens 2 the ditch outside the bank is 4.3 m wide and 2.1 m deep and the bank could have been up to 2 m high. (Drawing: Colin Rynne.)

Fig. 1.57 Excavation of circular enclosures (houses and outhouses) at Raheens 2 showing slot trenches in which upright posts had been set. (Photo: Anne-Marie Lennon, Department of Archaeology, UCC.)

were discovered on Raheens 2, two inside the ringfort and one outside it. They consisted of single chambers, each with narrow passages leading into them from the outside. The structures had been dug into the ground and the sides revetted with stones. They were probably roofed with wood, except souterrain 2, on the outside of the fort, which was partly corbelled and then closed with three capping stones. In common with souterrains excavated at other ringforts, they represented a late period in the occupation of Raheens 2.[5]

Artefacts excavated at this ringfort include several shale bracelets, two sharpening stones, a stone bead and a perforated stone disc (spindle whorl), all typical of an early medieval date. Both Raheens sites produced a small amount of mostly calcined bone, mainly of cattle and sheep/goats. Part of an articulated dog skeleton was found in souterrain 2 at Raheens 2. As well as animals, this site also yielded shellfish remains (oyster, whelk, periwinkle), fish (cod-like species) and a cetacean vertebra, probably from a small whale.[6]

Mills

Colin Rynne

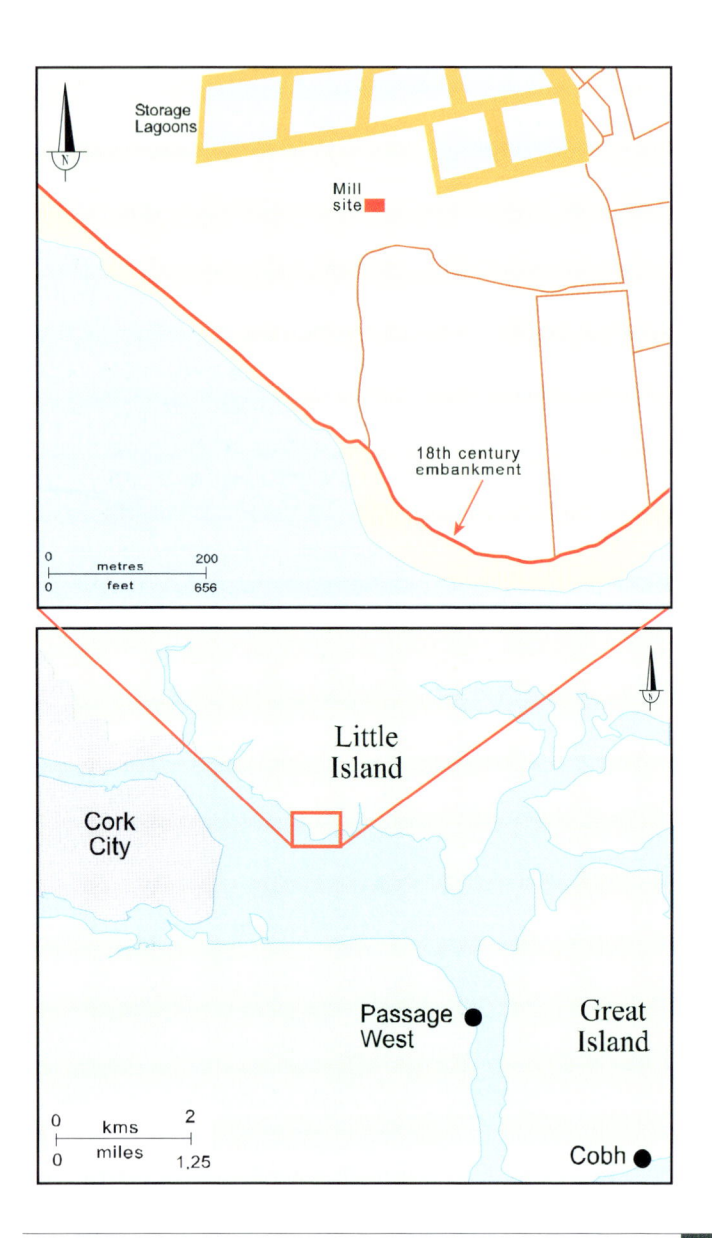

In 1979 clearance work for a series of large storage lagoons on Little Island in Cork harbour revealed the remains of two watermills. These were subsequently dated by dendrochronology to c. AD 630.[1] The mills had been built alongside one another. While one of these was a horizontal-wheeled mill, the other was a vertical-wheeled mill, an unprecedented arrangement for early medieval Irish mills. The horizontal-wheeled mill, which seems to have employed two waterwheels, is the earliest known example of its type in either Europe or Asia. The other mill is the earliest example of its type yet to come to light in Ireland (Fig. 1.59). The most remarkable aspect of the Little Island discovery was the area which the builders had chosen for the mills and the means by which the mills were powered.

Today, Little Island is joined to the mainland along its northern edge. In the seventh century it would have been a true island, with extensive areas of tidal marshes around its shoreline. The area in which the mills were discovered was reclaimed in the late eighteenth century. The mill site is approximately 250 m from the present coast, but, as the estuarine deposits that eventually destroyed the site indicate, this would not have been the case in the early seventh century. The foundations of these mills were covered by up to one and a half metres of estuarine gravel and mud. This suggests not only that the site was eventually destroyed by tidal flooding, but that, in the period when these mills were built, the tidal waters of Lough Mahon extended inland as far as the mill site. Further, the mills' foundations had been built

Fig. 1.58 The mill location at Little Island.

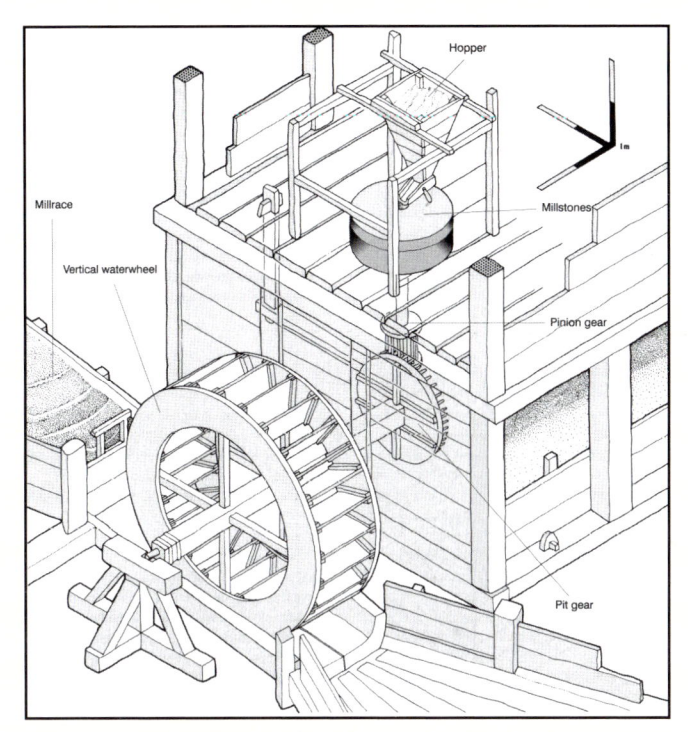

Fig. 1.59 Reconstruction of a seventh-century vertical-wheeled watermill at Little Island, County Cork. This is the earliest example of its type yet to come to light in Ireland.

on riverine mud, indicating that the mills had been constructed on what was then a marsh.

Little Island is one of the most low-lying areas in Cork harbour. The possibility that this small, low-lying island had streams large enough in the early seventh century to power two large watermills cannot be entirely ruled out. But, if a freshwater supply was intended for these mills, why build them in an exposed area subject to tidal flooding? If it had been the intention of the mills' builders to utilise freshwater streams for power, then they would have sited these mills well away from areas covered by the tides. Similar mills with both horizontal and vertical waterwheels are known to have been at work on the coasts of Britain, France, Holland, Portugal and Spain from at least the medieval period onwards. Some of these were in existence up until quite recent times and a small number are still in operation.

The choice of the Little Island site was not accidental. The builders were fully aware of the risks involved in erecting a complex of this size in such a location. Whereas the foundation beams of more conventional early Irish watermills were simply laid on the ground, those at Little Island were firmly pinned to the mud with substantial oaken piles over two metres long. The scale of the carpentry used for the mills has much in common with medieval waterfront revetments. It is perhaps no coincidence that the type of piling used at this site is to be found in structures that were subjected to the scouring action of the tides. So how could the builders of these mills have gained from choosing this location? The answer is probably that these mills were indeed operated by tidal power, exploiting the daily ebb and flow of the tides to fill their millponds. The millponds would have been filled by the rising tide and the mills would have been operated when the tide went out.

Within the last two decades, a large number of early medieval horizontal-wheeled mill sites have come to light in Ireland, but none of these can match the scale of operations at Little Island. This discovery in Cork harbour pushes back the origins of tide mills in Europe by some three centuries; it also provides us with clear-cut evidence of the advanced nature of mill-wrighting in Ireland during the early seventh century. Since the Little Island discovery, a contemporary site dated to *c.* AD 617 has also now been investigated at Nendrum on Strangford Lough, County Down.

6. URBAN BEGINNINGS AND THE VIKINGS

Maurice Hurley

FIRST SETTLEMENT

The social, economic and infrastructural patterns of Ireland owe a significant legacy to the Vikings. The historic power centres of, for example, Cashel, Ferns, Tara and Uisneach faded from their pristine greatness in the face of the growing economic power of the Viking port towns. Within two centuries of the arrival of the Vikings, the controlling influence of their towns had become critical for regional and even national supremacy.[1] The Irish kingdoms, while often allowing the Vikings a surprising level of autonomy, were well aware of the importance of the towns as economic powerhouses and as conduits to the international economy. As a consequence of their increasingly significant roles, the Viking towns became the pawns of warring kingdoms, both Gaelic and Scandinavian, which alternately coaxed or coerced the urban residents into supporting one side or the other. It was these settled Vikings who were to establish Cork as one of their principal towns, through their trading activities. These Vikings intermarried with the Irish and are more appropriately called the Hiberno-Norse.[2]

The location and topography of Cork fundamentally influenced the city's development.[3] The settlement was built in a river valley on estuarine islands with steep hills rising to the north and south (see *Cork City and the Evolution of the Lee Valley*, Chapter 1). The choice of location was based on converging traffic routes, on land and by river and sea. The Lee flows from the west into Cork harbour and several low-lying marshy islands once occurred where the river merged with the tidal water. The islands on which the city developed offered the lowest fording point of the river, thereby connecting the land to the north and south. Recent excavations at Washington Street, Tuckey Street and South Main Street indicate that the topography of the initial Hiberno-Norse settlement may be more complex than was initially thought.[4] What was originally considered to be two

Fig. 1.60 Artist's impression of the Hiberno-Viking settlement at Cork. (Drawing: Eamon Smith, courtesy of Meitheal Mara.)

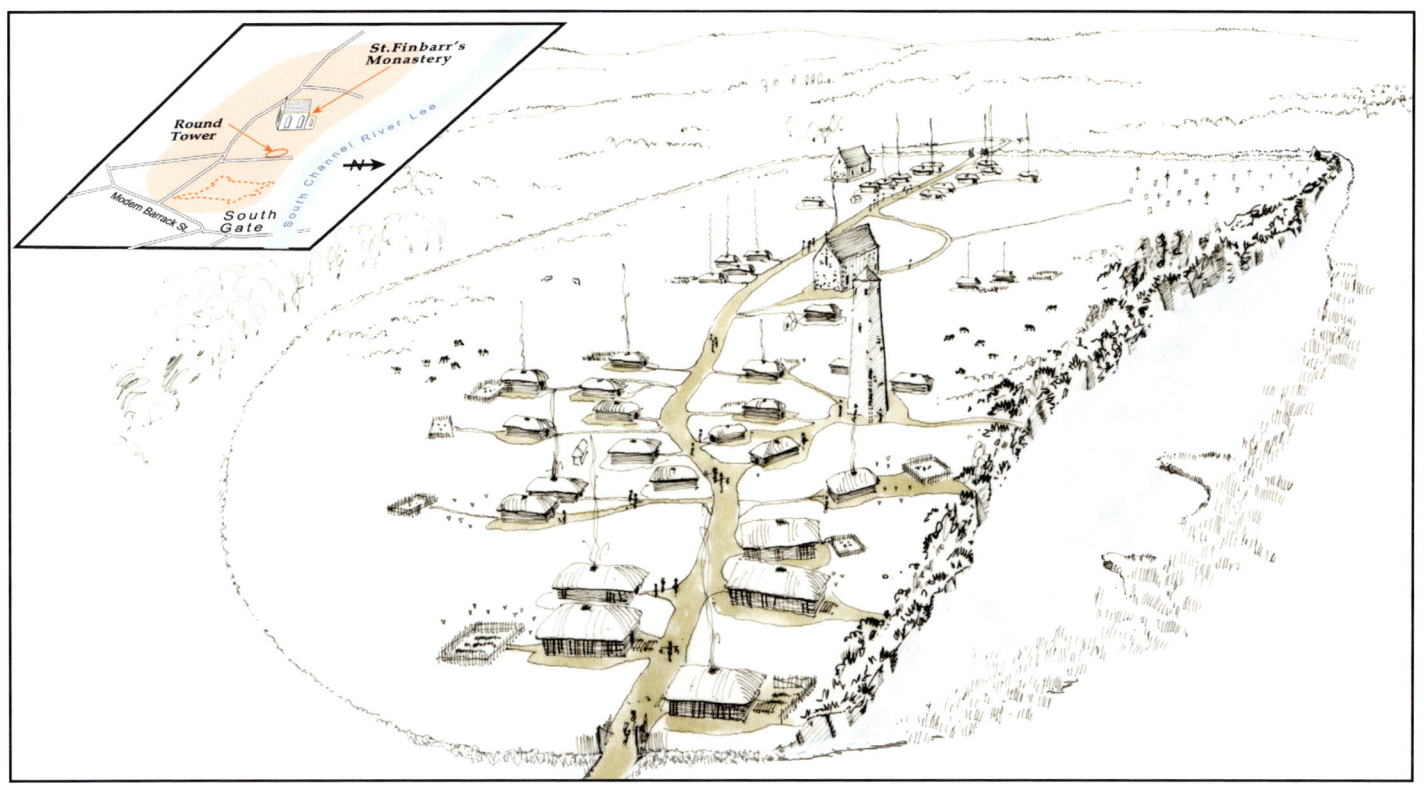

Fig. 1.61 Artist's impression of St Finbarr's monastic enclosure, tenth century. It shows typical contemporary site features, including several churches, a round tower and housing for monks and students. (Drawing: Donal Anderson.)

islands might, in fact, have been a series of artificially raised clay platforms surrounded by the tidal river. Over the years, the areas of solid ground were expanded, the channels infilled and enclosing walls constructed, until Cork took on the well-known form first depicted on sixteenth-century maps and described by Camden in 1568 as being 'of oval shape, surrounded by walls and encompassed and intersected by the river and accessible only by bridges' (see *Medieval Cork*, Chapter 7).

While the foundation of Cork is generally attributed to St Finbarr, who allegedly founded a monastery in the area in the seventh century, the Vikings introduced the ideas of urbanisation in the form we understand today (Section 2).[5] As many as several hundred monks and students lived at St Finbarr's monastery. Also, many people in the surrounding hinterland may have worked to sustain the monastic community. Nevertheless, the monastery cannot be described as truly urban in character. The monastery was located on the shoulder of the south bank of the Lee, an area now occupied by St Fin Barre's Cathedral and its precincts (see *St Finbarr and Early Christian Settlement*, Chapter 8; *Christianity, Churches and Burial Places*, Chapter 9; *Famine*, Chapter 22). The continuity of worship on the site, the discovery of carved stone from many periods and the convergence of historic routes, together with cartographic and historical references from later times, all point to the likely location of the monastery.

The Vikings first made their appearance in Cork in AD 821 and there are historical references to many subsequent plunderings and burnings of the monastery.[6] The Vikings were not welcome visitors, for their raids on Ireland were largely focused on the riches of the monasteries. St Finbarr's, lying close to the riverbank within a sheltered tidal estuary, was an easy target. One of the most beguiling paradoxes of the time concerns the mechanisms by which these foreign raiders began to settle and eventually exert such a profound influence on Irish life. Cork is the most acute example, for the already powerful monastery of St Finbarr was to see the Viking settlement develop at its doorstep. It is evident from documentary sources and archaeological evidence that the monastery and the Scandinavian town co-existed and that a symbiotic relationship developed.

Within 25 years of the first Viking raid in Cork, historical accounts record the existence of a Viking *dún*. The 'foreigners of Cork' are mentioned in references from the mid-ninth century, but nothing more is known until a renewed phase of Viking activity began in the early tenth century. Even then the references to Cork are scant.[7] A reference for the year 1088 describes an attempted raid on Cork by the Norse (Vikings) of Dublin, Wexford and

Waterford. This resulted in a great slaughter of the attackers by the local tribe, the Uí Echach Muman.[8] From this account it can be concluded that by the eleventh century the Viking town was under the control of Gaelic overlords (see *St Finbarr and Early Christian Settlement*, Chapter 8; *The Anglo-Normans and Beyond*, Chapter 10). By the early twelfth century, Cork was central to the emerging kingdom of Desmond. The McCarthy kings of Desmond chose Cork as their administrative capital and established a royal residence there, probably at Shandon. It is difficult to judge what level of autonomy, if any, was retained by the Vikings by this time and how genetically or culturally distinctive they still were. Despite Gaelic dominance, the historical records continue to refer to the population of the town as Ostmen (Northmen). The last Ostman ruler of Cork was Gilbert, son of Turgerius, who commanded the Cork fleet when it sailed out to intercept the Normans. Gilbert was killed in a naval battle at Youghal in 1173 and with him ended the era of Ostmen power in Cork. When the Normans conquered Cork four years later, the Ostmen were expelled from the town and thereafter they faded from the historical record.[9]

Locations

Given the lack of documentary detail, an assessment of the significance of Viking influence on the location, development and growth of Cork must now be sought primarily from archaeological sources. There is no evidence for the exact location of the first Viking settlement at Cork.[10] It is known from other Viking towns identified in Ireland that defence was of paramount importance. Initially, defence was not provided by fortifications but by the natural qualities of the terrain, more particularly by a combination of inaccessible land in close proximity to water. A place to anchor, draw up and secure the boats was also an essential protection against the natural elements and integral to the settlement (Fig. 1.60). In the case of the initial Viking settlements, the best form of defence was seaborne mobility. As expert seafarers, their highly manoeuvrable boats allowed them to flee from situations where sheer numbers could overwhelm them. It is hardly coincidental, therefore, that the most enduring Viking towns (Dublin, Waterford, Wexford, Limerick and Cork) were located at the tidal head in river estuaries. Settlements were established in places where the natural elements of promontories or islands provided security from surprise attack and where, in due course, the settlers could maximise the convergence of land and water routes to capitalise on trade.[11]

The first Viking settlements in Ireland are variously referred to in early records as a *longphort* or *dún* (ships' harbour or fort).[12] The site of the first Viking settlement at Cork is unknown, but by analogy with Dublin and Waterford it is likely to have been within the area that subsequently developed as the medieval town.[13] In Cork, this was on the south island, an area of marshy ground lying between the south and central channels of the Lee (see *Flooding in the City*, Chapter 3) (Fig. 1.62). The later administrative centre of the developed medieval town was 'The Castle', or King's Castle, located at the north-east corner of the south island, in the area to the south of modern Castle Street[14] (see the case study, *Lanes and Streets*, in Chapter 7; *The Anglo-Normans and Beyond*, Chapter 10). Indications from other Irish towns are that their medieval administrative hubs, such as Reginald's Tower in Waterford and Dublin Castle, evolved within the nucleus of the initial settlement areas and the same may be true of Cork.[15]

History records that the *dún Corcaighe* was attacked in AD 846 by Ólchobhar mac Cináeda, the King of Munster.

Fig. 1.62 View over South Main Street, Barrack Street and the South Gate Bridge area of the former south island of Cork, the likely area of the earliest Viking settlement. (Photo: Tomás Tyner.)

Fig. 1.63 Artist's impression of medieval Waterford, showing Reginald's Tower and surrounding buildings. (Source: Crawford Municipal Art Gallery.)

Other contemporary references also record the Viking *caisteal* (castle), which was destroyed in AD 865. Thereafter, the historical references are few until the twelfth century. While archaeological evidence for ninth- to mid-eleventh-century Cork has not been uncovered, there is a growing body of archaeological and other information that indicates the existence of a highly developed late eleventh- and early twelfth-century settlement on the south island.[16] This covered both sides of the present South Main Street, as well as some associated settlement across the river adjacent to Barrack Street. The suburban settlement extended during the twelfth century on this south bank of the Lee, especially to the south-east of South Gate Bridge. A trackway of roundwood dated by dendrochronology to *c.* 1085 was excavated on the east side of Barrack Street and its existence supports this interpretation of the development of the early settlement. The trackway may have led through swampy ground close to the old riverbank towards a ford or bridge at the South Gate. Most recently, excavations at North Main Street, north island, have also provided material that is probably Viking.[17]

The earliest historical reference to a bridge at Cork occurs in 1163, when Muircheartach Ua Maelseachlainn, son of the King of Mide, is recorded as having fallen off the bridge at Cork and drowned in the river.[18] As soon as one ford or bridge existed, then two others would have been equally

Fig. 1.64 Wooden boundary wall (revetment) at Tuckey Street, dated by dendrochronology to *c.* 1120. (Excavation: Mary O'Donnell.)

essential, as three bridges would have been needed to cross the river. In the later medieval town all traffic entering the main street had to pass over either the North or South Gate bridges, while through traffic had to cross both these bridges and a third one joining the south and north islands.[19] The linear main street, bisecting the islands, clearly developed as a connecting route between the bridges, just as the network of roads to the north and south converged on the bridges via accessible terrain. The pattern of bridges and roads, recorded in early historical references and in sixteenth- and seventeenth-century maps, is still intact today as are the North and South Gate bridges.

TAKING SHAPE

Knowledge of the development of the south island is still sketchy, despite recent significant archaeological discoveries. The earliest recorded levels uncovered in the archaeological excavations in the South Main Street area date to the late eleventh and early twelfth centuries.[20] Wooden walls – revetments – were built to contain clay platforms, while the houses were arranged to face towards the main street. The settlement was truly urban in character, with contiguous houses in an architectural style of Scandinavian origin. The houses excavated in Cork are remarkably similar to those found in Dublin, Wexford and Waterford.[21] This indicates that the emerging urban centres, in spite of the recorded wars and power struggles, shared a distinctly homogenous cultural sphere.

Until the second quarter of the twelfth century, almost all construction was of wood. The bridges were certainly of wood and the surface of the main street was carried on wooden rafts.[22] The thatched roofs of the houses were supported on trestles, carried on four earth-fast wooden posts, while the rafters and wall-posts were of lighter *scantling*. Wattle wands were woven between the wall-posts to create single or double wattle walls and the cavities between the wattle rows were packed with bracken and ferns. The walls may have been little more than one metre in height, as the thatched roofs hung low and may have over-sailed the walls, which formed an enclosing element with little or no structural significance. Ash was the preferred timber for structural supports, while alder and hazel were

THE • CITY • IN • THE • LANDSCAPE

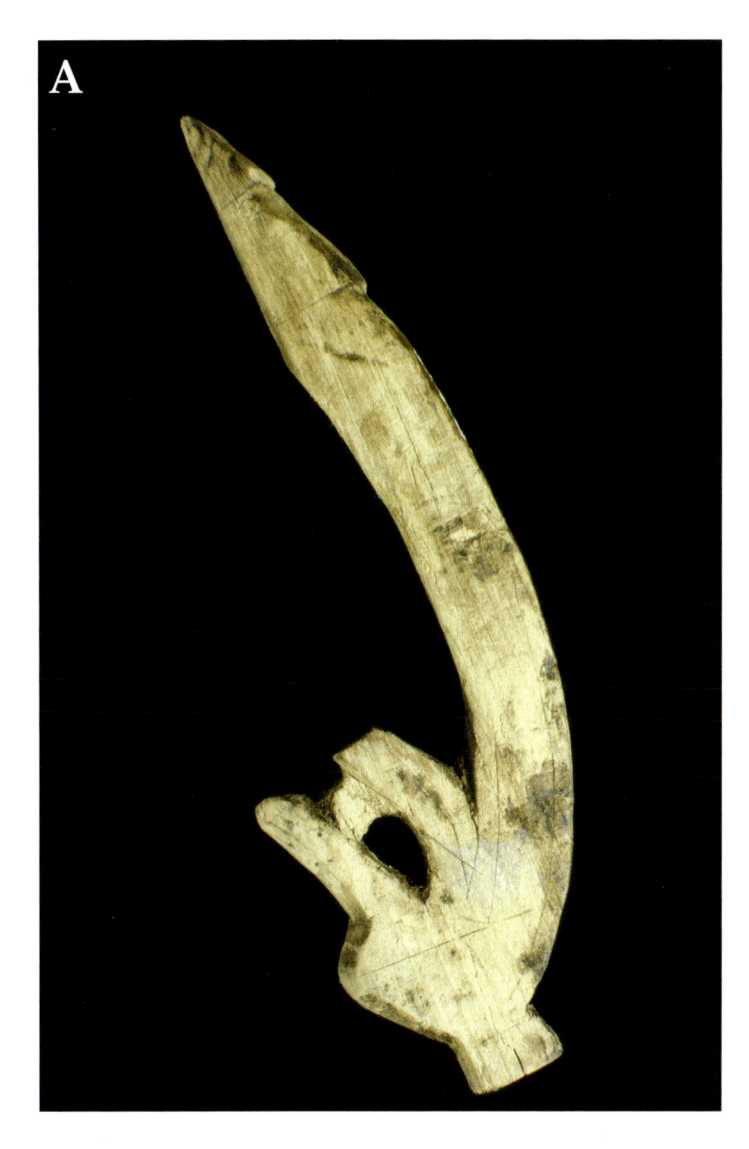

Fig. 1.65 Domestic items found in the excavation of early medieval Cork. A) A child's toy depicting the head of an animal, late eleventh century. It was carved from yew wood and excavated from Holy Trinity (Christ Church). B) Selection of bone and antler gaming pieces, including counters (flat items), an ivory *hnefetafle* piece (bulbous), two chess pawns and four dice. (Photo: Cork Public Museum.) C) Detail of the ivory *hnefetafle* gaming piece.

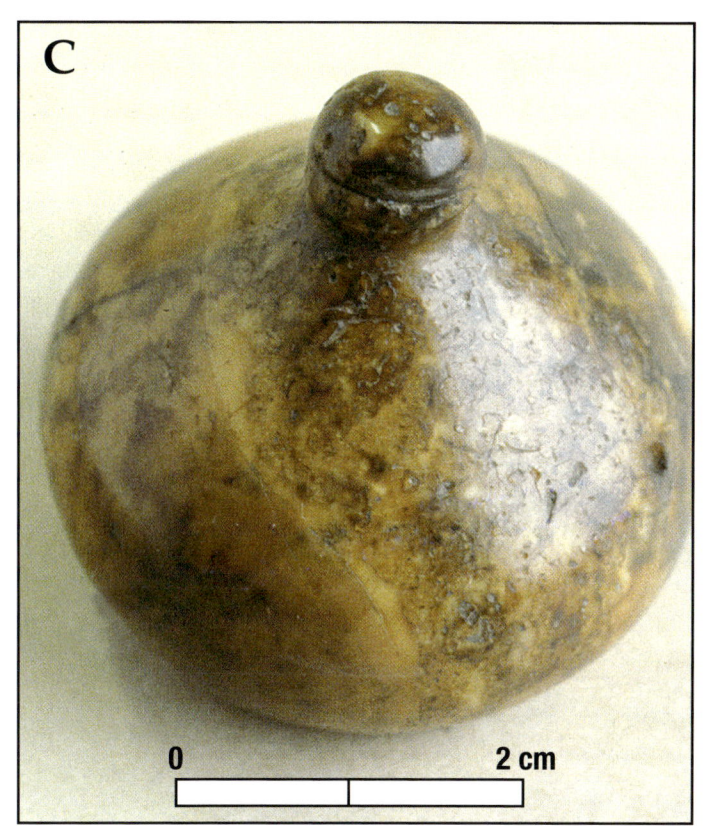

used for the wattle and lighter elements of the buildings. All these materials would have been available close by in the river and estuary environments (see Section 1, *Introduction*; *Cork City and the Evolution of the Lee Valley*, Chapter 1).

The location of the roof supports, in a rectangular plan within the houses, fundamentally influenced the internal layout of space. The house plans had a strong tripartite division with a wide central space. The side aisles had low bench beds in the middle and storage areas at either end. The hearth was in the centre of the house and was thus the focus of all daily household activity. By night, the hearth was *curfewed* by being covered with clay. The houses were single storey and the smoke was emitted through the roof. Doorways were centrally placed on the short walls of the houses; hence the front door faced the street, or a pathway leading to the street, while the back door gave access to the backyard.[23]

The layout of formal burgage plots implies a level of urban municipal organisation. The main house on the property fronted the street, but frequently a subsidiary house stood to the rear, often flanking a path.[24] The second building was generally smaller than the street-fronting house, and its construction usually involved a variation on the main architectural features. These subsidiary houses may have formed additional sleeping accommodation for the residents of the main house and probably represent the initial development of a private chamber for the householder and his wife. This trend later became a feature of the more privileged groups of medieval society. Other features of the plots lying behind the houses were wood-lined wells, animal pens and latrines, in which toilet seats stood above wood-lined cesspits. Domestic refuse and dung were dumped at the rear of the properties in a deliberate effort to raise the ground above tide level.[25]

Hinged wooden doors and possibly wooden window shutters were a feature of these houses, but household furniture was minimal, except for three-legged stools. Most domestic implements and utensils were also wooden. Archaeological finds include: carved vessels for the storage, preparation and consumption of food; spoons for mixing and stirring; distaffs, spindles and looms for spinning and weaving; shovels, rakes and pitch-forks for digging and collecting; combs for the hair and also wool-combing; long bows and arrow shafts for hunting and warfare; gaming boards and counters for play; and wooden toys for the children (Fig. 1.65). The craftsmen had an innate knowledge of the suitability of wood species for the item required and clear preferences for certain woods for particular objects are apparent. Antler and bone were used for items requiring even greater durability; the production of hair combs from antler was a highly skilled craft. Many other small everyday items were carved from antler, while the bones of large birds such as goose or swan were ideal for adaptation as flutes and whistles. Stone was used for sharpening knives and for weights and moulds. Iron was essential for weapons and tools, such as swords, arrow- and spearheads, knives and axes (Fig. 1.66). Silver was highly valued by the Vikings and metalworkers and craftsmen had a special status.[26]

Changing style

The early twelfth century was a period of profound economic and cultural change, culminating in the social and political upheavals occasioned by the Anglo-Norman conquest of the 1170s. The Normans conquered England a century before they arrived in Ireland. During this time the influence of the Anglo-Norman world in Ireland grew progressively stronger. Throughout the twelfth century international trade increased in importance and the Hiberno-Norse towns such as Cork were the focus for mercantile activity.[27] Within Ireland the towns became the centres of power and gateways for the introduction of new trends. Imported English and French pottery is a significant feature of the cultural layers excavated in late eleventh- and twelfth-century port towns, and Cork is no exception. Ceramics from Bristol as well as the south coast of Britain and the Norman homelands of north-western France dominate the cultural assemblage of early twelfth-century Cork (Fig. 1.66).[28]

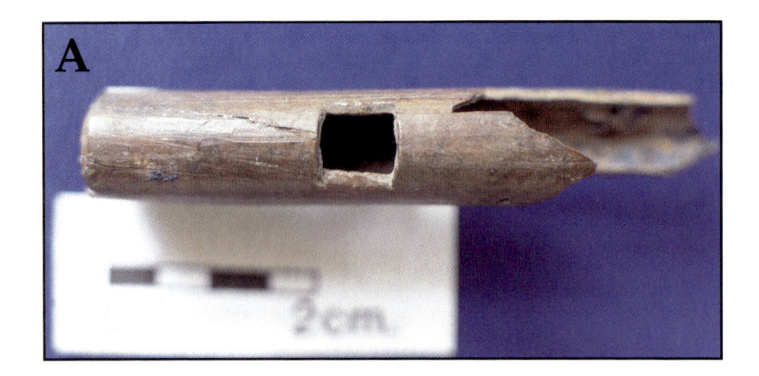

Fig. 1.66 Artefacts from Cork. A) Bone whistle. B) Iron knives, excavated from Hanover Street. The knives are from the later medieval period but are similar in pattern to those used in the early medieval period. C) Jug face, Bristol Redcliffe pottery from Kyrl's Quay, showing stylised face from a jug rim that served as a spout. (Source: Cork Corporation and Cork Public Museum.)

Even greater manifestations of cultural change are apparent in twelfth-century domestic architecture.[29] The long-established tripartite wattle-walled houses gave way to a new form of building, the sill-beam house. This new form of architecture removed the four-post trestle support from within the house and, thereafter, the roof, and possibly even an upper floor, was supported by the outer walls of the house. The houses were built of large, squared earth-fast timber posts, set in opposing pairs in the long walls. The intervening bay was filled by staves set in a grooved beam or sill-beam, hence the term *sill-beam house*. The technique was based on a concept of construction fundamentally different to that used for the post-and-wattle-walled houses. The rapid and widespread adoption of new techniques and concepts of domestic space are indicative of a profoundly changing society. A development in the arrangement of buildings within the plots is also apparent in the twelfth century, with the emergence of large houses, possibly halls, in the backyards of the plots.[30]

The adoption of a new building type had implications not only for the arrangement of domestic space but also for the craftsman and for those who procured the requisite raw materials. Construction of sill-beam houses was of stout, radially split oak posts and beams and no longer of slight ash posts and hazel wands. Coppiced groves, essential for the production of light hazel poles, were no longer necessary. Instead, large, straight-grained oak trees had to be felled in forests and transported over increasingly long distances to urban centres (see Section 1, *Introduction*). The splitting and shaping of planks and staves was very different to the more organic technique of wattle weaving. It is likely that the new building techniques were accompanied by a parallel social development, whereby community co-operation based on a sharing of skills was replaced by increased professionalism and division of labour. Domestic artefacts were also the subject of increased specialisation in the twelfth century. Vessels carved from single blocks of wood were no longer in evidence, as high-quality stave building and lathe turning became increasingly accomplished and common. Even the Old Norse board game, called *hnefetafle*, was replaced by a new form played with discoid counters, and this was eventually replaced by chess, which made its first appearance following the Norman conquest (Fig. 1.65B).[31]

Use of stone and the end of an age

The earliest use of stone for building in Irish cities dates to the second half of the eleventh century and the medium became increasingly common in the early twelfth century. While stone was used in a limited way for domestic architecture, it had become ubiquitous for urban churches and defensive structures by the middle of the twelfth century. Evidence for a stone-built Romanesque church at St Fin Barre's Cathedral is provided by the discovery of several carved voussoirs in the Romanesque style.[32] The decorative influences are said to be derived from Poitou, in France. The carved stones were embedded in the masonry of the eighteenth-century building (see *Famine*, Chapter 22) (Fig. 1.67). The several parish churches constructed in Cork during the twelfth century were also probably built of stone.

Stone-built defensive walls may have enclosed some or all of the south island by 1177, but there is no archaeological evidence for this. It is likely that the south island was fortified before the arrival of the Normans; however, clay banks or wooden revetments may have been used without the addition of masonry. The development of such Norman-style defences presages the closing phases of Viking Cork and its transition to a Norman city.

Fig. 1.67 The Dean's Gate, a Romanesque-style archway from the walls surrounding St Fin Barre's Cathedral. This probably dates from the thirteenth century and it may have come originally from the medieval St Finbarr's church, or possibly from the Dominican priory of St Mary's of the Isle (see boxed section, *St Mary's of the Isle*, in Chapter 9). (Source: Cork Corporation and Cork Public Museum.)

7. MEDIEVAL CORK

Maurice Hurley

A NEW AGE

The term 'medieval' is generally taken to cover a period of several hundred years before and after the first millennium. Such medieval elements as feudalism, chartered towns and religious orders were not a feature of Irish life until after the Norman conquest in the late twelfth century. Medieval, therefore, as applicable to an Irish town, is taken *de facto* as referring to the period 1170 to 1550 (see *The Anglo-Normans and Beyond*, Chapter 10).[1] In some respects, the years between 1537 and 1541 may be regarded as the close of the medieval period, for the general suppression of the monasteries was a defining event in the decline of the medieval system. The medieval world of Cork continued up to the year 1690, when the Williamite army defeated the besieged Jacobite defenders.[2] Seventeenth-century maps of Cork depict a settlement little changed in size, form or character from that of several hundred years earlier. The year 1690 signalled the disappearance of the old order, both socially and culturally, while changes in the economic sphere and physical form of the town which had slowly begun to take place in the previous fifty or so years accelerated rapidly thereafter. In reality, the term 'medieval' could be argued to cover the period 1170 to 1690.[3]

The Anglo-Normans took control of Cork in 1177 and almost immediately began to settle and expand the town (see *The Anglo-Normans and Beyond*, Chapter 10). They initially expelled the Ostmen, the Hiberno-Norse descendants of the Vikings, occupied the south island and shortly after consolidated their gains by the construction of a new town wall. At this stage, the urban area was confined to the south island. Some unenclosed settlement may have existed in the suburb of Dungarvan (on the north island) and in the suburb of Fayth (now Barrack Street), on the south bank of the Lee, the area to which the Ostmen were expelled.[4] Suburban settlement soon developed in the Shandon area, probably associated with the routes from the North Gate via Shandon Street, Blarney Street, the route to Youghal via Dominick Street, as well as areas in the flood plain of the river adjacent to the Franciscan friary, now the North Mall. The suburban settlement of Dungarvan grew throughout the thirteenth century until the area became integral to the economy of the town and was completely enclosed within the town wall in the early fourteenth century.

THE URBAN LAYOUT

The developments between 1177 and 1603 are chronicled by royal charters, while the most vivid record of the development of Cork in the sixteenth and seventeenth century is provided by a series of pictorial maps (see Section 2). There are no surviving early medieval maps or plans of

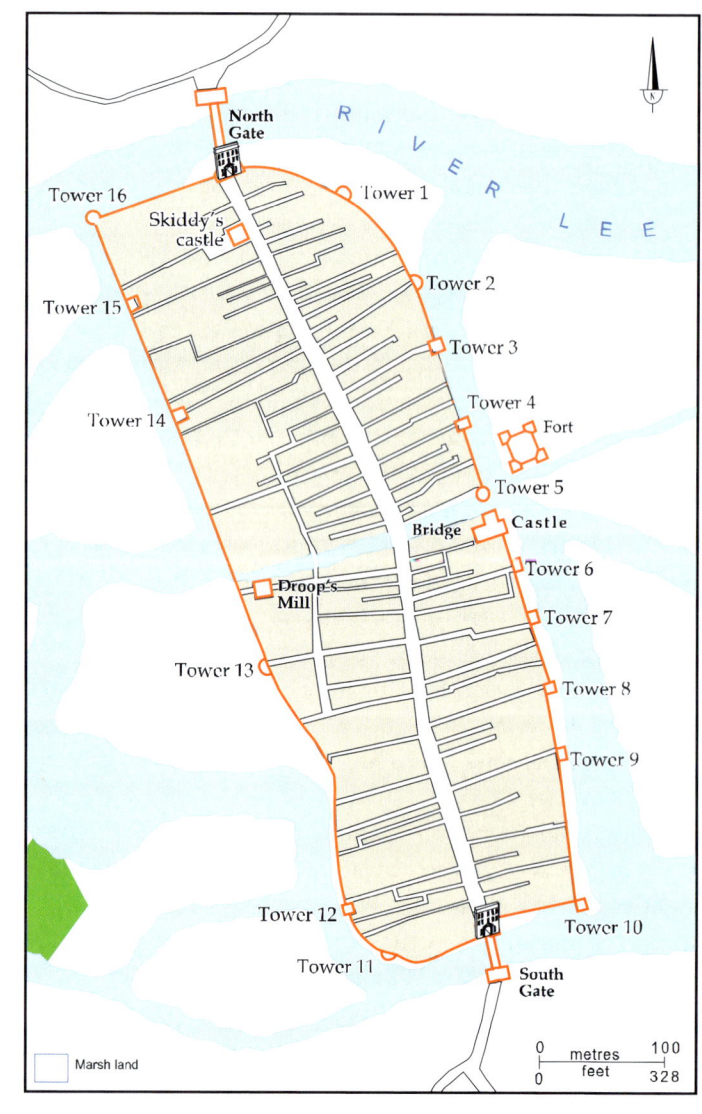

Fig. 1.68 Medieval walled town of Cork, including the main river channels and marsh areas.

Cork and the earliest plans date to the sixteenth century. By that time, the layout of the town and its enclosing walls had been fully established for over three centuries.[5] In examining the maps, one is struck by the significance of the town wall. Medieval towns and cities were most conspicuously defined by their walls (Fig. 1.69). These not only provided defence but also defined the urban borough and its privileges and gave expression to the power and prestige of the inhabitants. The walled town of Cork effectively remained an island development for over half a millennium. The enclosure of the two islands was not the result of a single episode of construction but a protracted effort taking almost 150 years in order to complete the circuit and its sixteen mural towers. The image of a consistent enclosing wall regularly punctuated by mural towers, as depicted in the *Pacata Hibernia* plan of *c.* 1585, masks centuries of expansion, collapse and rebuilding. The unified circuit also belies the vulnerability of a stone wall built in a marsh. The wall would constantly have been affected by factors such as subsidence, tides and riverine floods. In addition, private interests would have maintained personal gateways, thus altering the wall even further. Public authorities frequently maintained the wall with no more than an outward appearance of consistency and strength.

A bridge roughly at the junction of where Liberty Street and North and South Main Streets are today spanned the channel between the north and south islands. Bridges at both ends of the town led to the north and south banks of the river. The area enclosed by the walls was about 640 m long and 220 m wide. The central waterway provided a protected wharf where ships could dock within the safety of the walls. The *Pacata Hibernia* plan depicts ships in full sail within the channel, evidently a case of artistic licence, whilst a quay is shown flanking the north side of the channel. On the plan a watergate was protected by castles at either side of a portcullis. The image of Cork portrayed by the *Pacata Hibernia* plan is echoed by contemporary accounts, such as Edmund Spenser's reference to 'the spreading Lee' (see *Cork City and the Evolution of the Lee Valley*, Chapter 1).

Within the town walls a spinal main street provided the main artery between the bridges. Laneways developed at right angles to the main street and gave access to the rear of the street-fronting properties (Fig. 1.70). The extent to which the laneways were public thoroughfares is unknown. Some may have provided access from the main street to strategic points on the town wall. Others, however, were private or semi-private, providing access only for the property owner, or those with legitimate business at the rear of the plots (see the case study, *Lanes and Streets*, in Chapter 7).[6]

THE TOWN WALLS

Archaeological excavations in Cork have been undertaken since the mid-1970s and a vast amount of evidence has been unearthed detailing many aspects of medieval Cork.[7] Standing remains of its wall survive in only a few places. The wall was largely demolished in the early eighteenth century to make way for the rapidly expanding town. Surprisingly, below ground level Cork possesses what is arguably the most intact circuit of walls of any Irish city (Fig. 1.71).[8] The reason for its preservation lies with Cork's marsh location. The nature of the marshy ground was such that every effort was made by the inhabitants to constantly raise their habitation level above the tidal floodwaters. Between three and four metres of introduced clay and dumped organic material were built up within the town between the twelfth and fourteenth century. As a result, the lower levels of the walls have been sealed and these survive in a

Fig. 1.69 The Hiberno-Viking and later medieval core of Cork. The contemporary roads form a virtual ring around the core, marking the former line of the town's walls. The excavation site of the walls at Kyrl's Quay can be seen at the bottom left corner. (Photo: Tomás Tyner.)

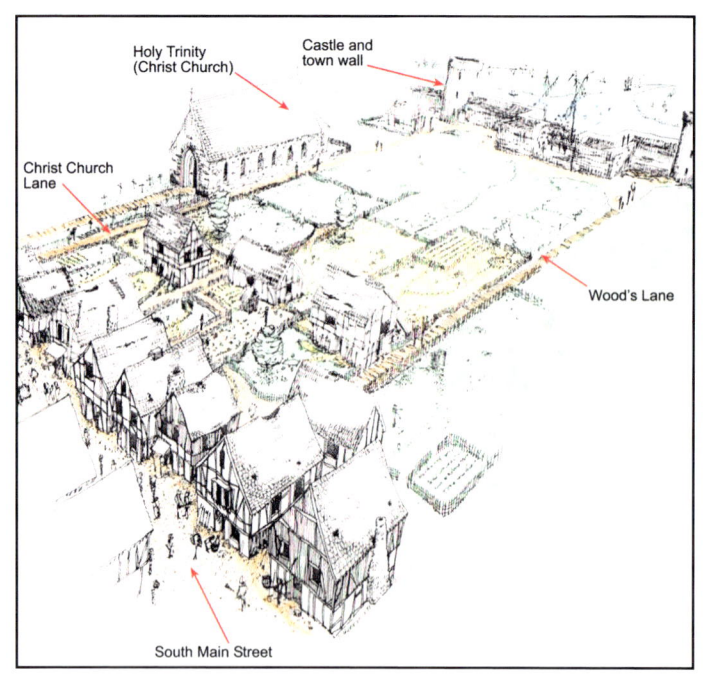

Fig. 1.70 Conjectural view of South Main Street in medieval times. (Drawing: Donal Anderson.)

remarkably intact condition. The walls have been recorded in over twenty archaeological excavations, ranging from a 60-metre length of wall exposed at Kyrl's Quay to small, deep incisions beneath the streets undertaken in the course of the Cork Main Drainage Scheme (Fig. 1.71B).[9]

The Anglo-Norman town wall of late twelfth- and early thirteenth-century date was built on river gravels at the extremities of the island, seemingly without recourse to a wooden raft foundation. The outer face of the wall was widely splayed (battered) (Fig. 1.72). This feature, as well as having a defensive function, served to broaden the base of the wall, thereby spreading the load over a wider area. Even at the time of construction, the lower courses of the wall were submerged in the silt and by the mid-thirteenth century up to 3 m of the wall lay buried in the silt and accumulated refuse. The river channels which formed a ring around Cork supplemented the defences, while the intractable marshes lying to the east and west were a virtual no-man's land until deliberate reclamation and canalisation of the channels commenced in the mid-seventeenth century.

Fig. 1.71A The town walls. View of the wall at the Grand Parade. The medieval wall can be seen underlying a seventeenth-century phase of building. (Excavation and photo: J. Wren.)

THE • CITY • IN • THE • LANDSCAPE

Gate: the Queen's Castle on the north and the King's Castle on the south. The castles are impressionistically depicted on the Cork coat of arms with the motto *Statio Bene Fida Carinis*, presumably referring to the security provided by the enclosed wharf within the walls (see Introduction, Fig. 1.4).[10]

More recently, the well-preserved foundations of the early eighteenth-century gatehouse were found on the north-east side of South Gate Bridge. Following the destruction of the medieval castles at North and South Gates by the floods of the 1630s (see *Flooding in the City*, Chapter 3), the old castles were reconstructed. They were rebuilt in the emerging classical tradition in the early eighteenth century, probably to the design of the Cork architect John Coltsman. Several illustrations of the eighteenth-century bridges and gatehouses were produced by Nathaniel Grogan and copied by Fitzgerald in the early nineteenth century (Fig. 1.74). Both gatehouses were used as prisons (see *Christianity, Churches and Burial Places*, Chapter 9). Within the main street the effect of the gatehouses was grim. A French chronicler, Chevalier de Latocnaye, writing in *c.* 1798 described how 'it would seem as if it were wished to hinder the wind from drying the filth, for the two ends of the street are terminated by prisons, which close the way entirely and prevent the air from circulating'.[11] For these reasons, and due to the impediment to traffic, the gatehouses were demolished in the early nineteenth century.

The island town of Cork remained a defensive bastion of colonial administration throughout the medieval period. Despite numerous attacks from Gaelic rebels and the frequent burning of the suburbs, Cork did not fall. The strategic advantage of an island site was offset to some

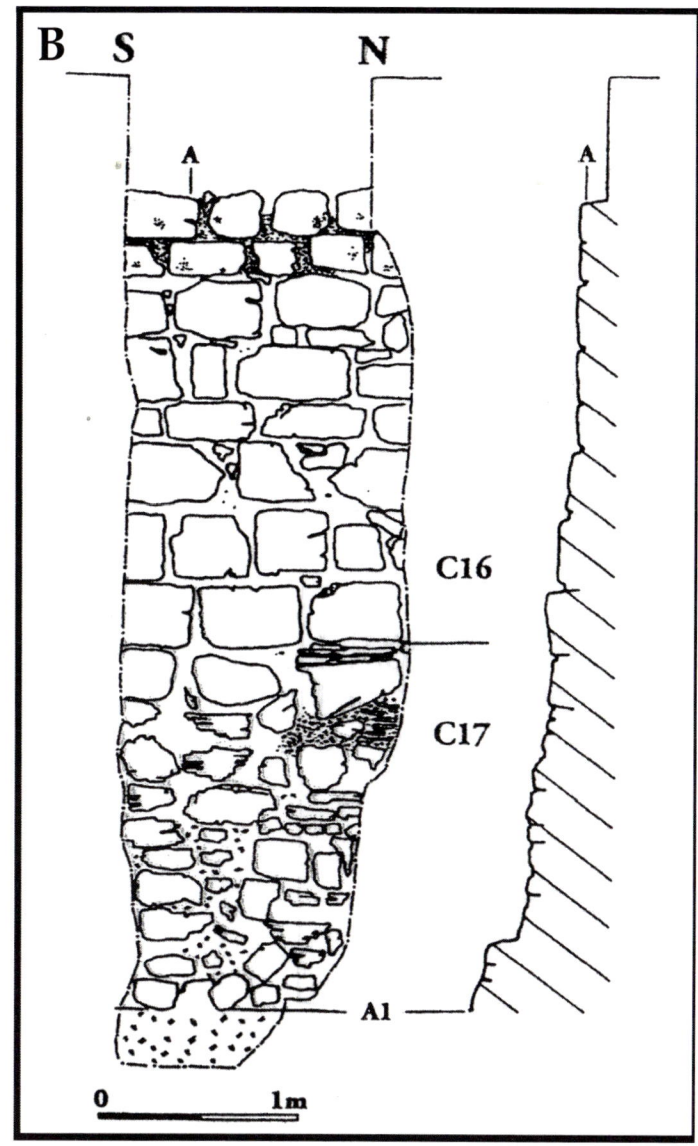

Fig. 1.71B) Excavated section of the wall at Washington Street; the plan drawing shows the remains of the east-facing elevation of the wall. (Source: Maurice Hurley, courtesy of Cork City Council.)

The town, with its towers, battlements and crenellations, must have been a spectacular sight, judging from the circuit that survives below ground. The mixture of vivid white limestone contrasting with dark red sandstone must have created a unique mottled effect reminiscent of many of the old stone warehouse buildings still to be seen in Cork today (see *Cork City and the Evolution of the Lee Valley*, Chapter 1) (Fig. 1.71A). Of the many towers and castles that punctuated the wall, not a single upstanding element survives. The foundations of three towers have been unearthed by archaeological excavation: a D-shaped tower at Kyrl's Quay, fragments of a tower known as Hopewell Castle at Grand Parade and part of the circular foundations of a round castle at Castle Street, which is probably the Queen's Castle (Fig. 1.73). This was one of two castles that flanked the Marine

Fig. 1.72 Reconstructed section of the medieval wall. The foundation consisted of three or four courses of stepped stone blockwork on the outside and a single offset course of stonework on the inside. The inner face was usually vertical. The wall was generally *c.* 2.5 m wide and originally stood at a height of over 6 m, surmounted by battlements and a protected wall walk. (Drawing: Rosanna Devoy.)

Fig. 1.73A) Foundations of the Queen's Castle, under excavation in 1987. (Photo: Cork Main Drainage Scheme, courtesy of Cork City Council.) B) Drawing of the Queen's Castle. (Source: *Pacata Hibernia*, 1585.)

extent by the constant threat of flooding and the erosion of the walls by the tide (see *Flooding in the City*, Chapter 3). One particular collapse was attributed directly to the fact that 'the city is founded on watery soil [and the walls] are daily penetrated by the ebb and flow of the sea'.[12] Today, archaeological excavations in Cork city centre are frequently conducted at depths below sea level, where tidal flooding is a fact of life and tide charts dictate the daily schedule. Historically, the most disastrous flood recorded occurred in 1633. However, layers of silt recorded from archaeological excavations indicate that the flooding was a periodic if largely unrecorded event. Archaeological excavations have also produced ample evidence for the repair and rebuilding of the town wall. The walls at Kyrl's Quay, Grattan Street and the north-west end of Grand Parade were extensively rebuilt in the seventeenth century. The evidence is corroborated by records in the Council Book of Cork. In 1613 the Corporation of Cork raised a tax of £500, which was partly intended to finance 'the erection of the walls of the city, now ruinous and ready to fall except speedily repaired'.[13] The post-medieval rebuilding of the wall was generally of inferior workmanship to its medieval predecessor. A notable exception is a length of wall at Grand Parade, from St Augustine Street to south of Washington

THE • CITY • IN • THE • LANDSCAPE

Fig. 1.74 North Gate Bridge, from a drawing by Nathaniel Grogan (1740–1807).

Street, where it was rebuilt in ashlar blocks not dissimilar to the eighteenth- and nineteenth-century quay walls that we are familiar with today.

The outward appearance of the defences belied numerous weaknesses, which were mostly initiated for reasons of personal advantage. Excavations have revealed no less than three private gateways or posterns. One gateway at Kyrl's Quay gave access to a slip where boats could be drawn up within the safety of the walls.[14] The opening was masked on the outside by a skin-deep blocking of stone. Other gateways at Kyrl's Quay and Grattan Street date to the seventeenth century. This was a period when the town increasingly came to rely on the strength of its outlying fortifications and the defensive function of the town wall was greatly diminished. In particular, the development of artillery meant that Cork was no longer impregnable. Quite the opposite in fact, for the town was vulnerable to naval bombardment from the river and was overlooked by high hills to the north and south.

In 1601, Sir George Carew described Cork as 'one of the weakest places to defend from an enemy that ever I saw'.[15] For this reason, Carew commissioned the construction of an artillery fortification on a ridge above the South Gate (Fig. 1.75). This fortification became known as Elizabeth Fort (see *Christianity, Churches and Burial Places*, Chapter 9; *Sixteenth- and Early Seventeenth-Century Cork*, Chapter 11). The fort, along with an outlying earthwork to the south-west known as Cat Fort, and Shandon Castle to the north of the town, became integral to the defensive plans of the Jacobites in 1690. Despite the perceived impregnability of Elizabeth Fort, the town succumbed to bombardment after a siege lasting only four days. The town wall was damaged in the course of the siege, especially in the south-east quadrant along Grand Parade. In the following years the wall became obsolete and was not maintained.

Although the medieval wall was demolished, its influence has survived in many contemporary property boundaries. The former river channels surrounding the walls were canalised and eventually culverted to form new streets, including Grand Parade, Cornmarket Street and Grattan Street. These streets create a virtual ring on the east, north and north-west sides of the old town (Fig. 1.69). Only on the south and south-west sides does the river still flow against the line of the old wall.

DOMESTIC BUILDINGS

There are no surviving houses in Cork pre-dating 1730, but here and there the fabric of late medieval stone buildings has been incorporated into later structures. Occasionally diagnostic elements such as a carved stone door, window surrounds and fireplaces are identified in the walls of buildings of otherwise eighteenth- or nineteenth-century appearance. Only a small number of pictorial sources exist of medieval Cork's domestic architecture; the first architecturally accurate illustrations date to the eighteenth century. Several documentary sources are also available, but these are limited and relate to descriptions of the houses of a wealthy minority.

Cork experienced rapid growth in the early eighteenth century (see *The Evolution of Cork's Built Environment, 1600–1700*, Chapter 12; *Beef, Butter, Provisions and Prosperity in a Golden Eighteenth Century*, Chapter 14). The records for public buildings indicate an unprecedented building programme.[16] This is most vividly illustrated by the rebuilding of churches, while at least six secular public buildings were built between 1715 and 1730 (see *Christianity, Churches and Burial Places*, Chapter 9). Several new bridges

Fig. 1.75 Walls and fortifications. Elizabeth Fort, the site of Sir George Carew's artillery fortification, overlooking the South Gate area. (Photo: Robert Devoy.)

were also constructed during this period. Despite this widespread replacement of medieval buildings in Irish cities in the early 1700s, the street patterns, layout and plot size frequently remained unaltered from the medieval plan. This is nowhere more evident than in Cork (see the case study, *Lanes and Streets*, in Chapter 7).[17]

In Irish medieval towns the impact by the late twelfth century of the Anglo-Norman conquest was detectable in most aspects of urban life. In the domestic architecture of ports such as Cork, however, the impact was not so novel, as they had been open to external influences long before the arrival of the Anglo-Normans. Furthermore, uniquely Irish and Hiberno-Norse influences also persisted in the domestic architecture of the developing medieval settlements. Importantly, wood continued to be the ubiquitous raw material of medieval construction for domestic buildings, although stone became increasingly common for churches and the houses of the wealthy. From the surviving documents for medieval Cork, for example, we learn that in his will, dated 1306, John de Wynchedon bequeathed to his sons 'two stone houses' near Holy Trinity church, Cork. A document of 1314–1315 refers to 'a stone house' of Nicholas de la Wythye being taken over by the English Crown as a prison. The 'great stone house' of Walter Reych is also referred to in 1442.[18]

Archaeological excavations show that many aspects of domestic urban life, particularly the use of domestic implements of all types, remained little changed. Ceramics, for instance, were always in use but the use of glass increased in the seventeenth century (Figs. 1.77 and 1.78). By the early thirteenth century, advances in carpentry facilitated the development of fully framed timber buildings. Large earth-fast uprights were no longer necessary, for the new buildings stood entirely on the surface, or more frequently were raised on meagre stone footings (see *Urban Beginnings and the Vikings*, Chapter 6). Full framing, whereby tenons fitted into shouldered mortises and joints were secured by dowels, have left remarkably little archaeological evidence. Only fragmentary remains of dwarf walls and occasional stone settings for hearths are indicative of this type of structure.[19] While the evidence can be elusive, the foundations of at least ten stone-footed medieval houses were excavated at North Gate.

Stone-walled houses became common from the fourteenth century onwards. One of the most interesting aspects of the later medieval development of stone-walled houses in Cork is the occurrence of a series of substantial houses at distances of between 20 and 50 m from the street frontage.[20] This possibly reflects the development of rows of houses within the established long and narrow burgage

Fig. 1.76 Fifteenth-century twin light window at rear of a later period building, North Main Street. Elements of medieval architecture have been incorporated into and occasionally survive in such later buildings. (Photo: Cork City Council.)

plots. All of the houses in each burgage plot, extending back from the street, are likely initially to have been in the ownership of one family, but subdivision of the plots must inevitably have occurred as time passed (see the case study, *Lanes and Streets*, in Chapter 7). At North Gate, excavations have shown that the second or even the third house to the rear of the street frontage was generally of more robust stone-walled construction. Access to these houses was invariably by way of paved laneways or alleys that developed within the plots. Late medieval stone houses of Cork are often represented by very substantial foundations resting on broad offset footings. Some of these houses may have been two to three storeys high and conceivably were comparable in size to the smaller urban tower houses.

Fortified houses

Urban tower houses, or fortified town houses, were built in Irish towns from the fifteenth to the mid-seventeenth century. They were usually referred to as castles but were not part of the municipal defensive system of mural castles and towers. They were, however, frequently located at critical defensive locations and would have dominated the late medieval streetscape. The buildings are analogous with the tower houses of rural Ireland (Fig. 1.79). The initial timing for the construction of tower houses is frequently dated to 1429, when a grant of ten pounds was offered by King Henry VI to his 'liege men' in the counties of the English pale to erect fortified buildings.[21] The origin of the form of tall fortified houses may in fact be of an older date. The genesis of the urban form may lie in the unfortified stone dwellings common in the late thirteenth- and fourteenth-century towns. In Ireland, the fortified urban tower houses of the fifteenth century and later can be seen as 'a response to the unstable political climate of the period', as well as a means whereby minor notables demonstrated their prestige and wealth within the community.[22]

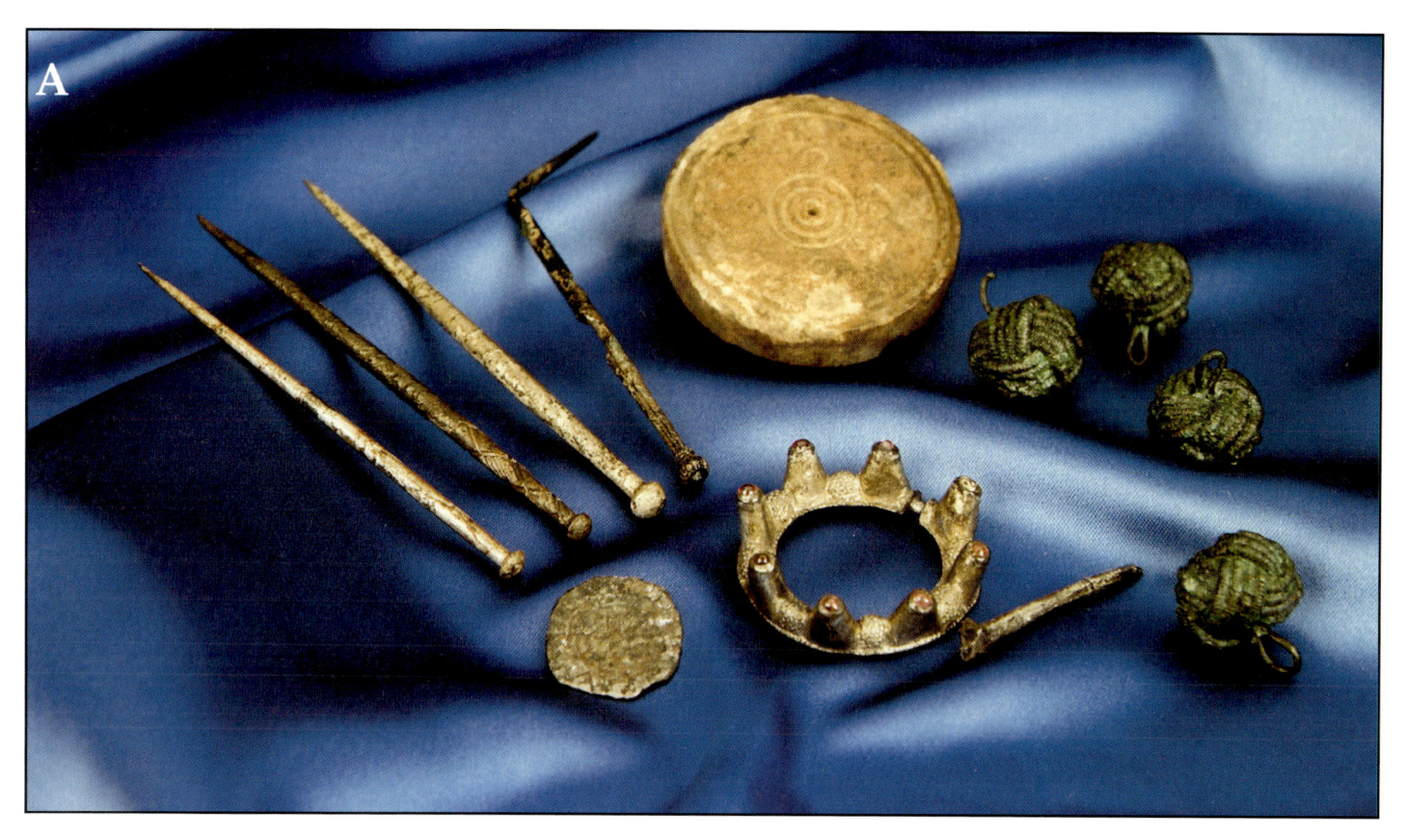

In Cork, one of these tower houses, known as Skiddy's Castle after the family of merchants who built it, was excavated (Fig. 1.80).[23] The castle's crenellated battlements must have been a significant landmark, for it is depicted in

Fig. 1.77 Medieval artefacts discovered in excavations from Cork. A) Thirteenth-century artefacts, showing (left to right) a silver penny, four stick pins and a gaming piece (excavated from the city centre), four buttons (green) and a ring brooch (centre), excavated at Barrack Street. (Photo: Jim McCarthy, courtesy of Cork City Council.) B) Seventeenth-century glass wine bottle, corkscrew and seal, excavated from Kyrl's Quay. (Photo: Cork City Council.) C) Mid-thirteenth-century amber paternoster (prayer beads), excavated from Grand Parade. (Photo: Cork City Council.)

Fig. 1.78 Henry III silver penny excavated from Grand Parade. Head and reverse sides shown. (Photo: Cork City Council.)

ROOFS

The survival of ground plans and floor levels encourages archaeologists to omit mention of the single most important component of houses of every period, the roof. As roofs became heavier it became necessary to build stronger walls. In essence, the tripartite ground plan of the Hiberno-Norse house was dictated by the location of the internal roof supports. The eleventh- and twelfth-century houses were probably roofed entirely with thatch. Tile and slate was first used in the thirteenth century and gradually became more common. Tiles were used in association with other materials such as slate or shingle. The decoration of houses, especially the embellishment of roofs with finials and crested ridge tiles, appears to have been normal practice throughout the medieval period. Following a disastrous fire in 1622, Cork Corporation ordered the removal of thatched roofs within the town walls (see the case study, *Weather and Natural Disasters*, in Chapter 2). In 1663–1664, the Civil Survey records that the majority of Cork's houses were slated.

FIRES AND FIREPLACES

Chimneys would have become necessary as upper floors were added and, consequently, it was no longer feasible to have the hearth in the centre of the house. The earliest recorded evidence of a fireplace on the end wall, in a building excavated at Kyrl's Quay and North Main Street, was dated to the late thirteenth/early fourteenth century. A large stone house of seventeenth-century date excavated at North Gate had a chimney-breast on the sidewall of a large room. A ceramic firedog, imported from north Devon, found on the same site was probably typical of the hearth furniture

all of the sixteenth- and seventeenth-century pictorial maps of Cork (see Section 2). It was a three- to four-storey structure built *c.* 1445 by John Skiddy, bailiff and later mayor of Cork. When excavated, the undercroft (basement) was found largely intact. The walls stood above an elaborate wooden raft foundation; the builders were evidently familiar with the risks involved in building on river mud. Historical sources indicate that other 'castles' stood within the walls of medieval Cork. In these cases the use of the words 'house' and 'castle' appear to be interchangeable. A description of Cork in 1620 states that the buildings in Cork were 'of stone, and built after the Irish forme, which is Castlewise, and with narrow windows, more for strength than for beauty, but they begin to beautify it in better forme'.[24] Some of the castles were known by name, for example Parentiz (Paradise) Castle, or Roche's Castle, which was located at the junction of North Main Street and Castle Street.

Fig. 1.79 Blarney Castle (foreground), one of the few surviving tower houses in the Cork area. (Photo: Tomás Tyner.)

Fig. 1.80 Drawing of Skiddy's Castle. (Source: *Pacata Hibernia*, 1585.)

of wealthy households of this period. Also, internal ovens, generally brick built and of semi-circular shape, are known from eighteenth century houses in Cork city, but some may be of an earlier date. Carved mantelpieces surrounded the fireplaces of the grander buildings; an example from Skiddy's Castle is now incorporated into a twentieth-century façade on North Main Street. The finest carved mantelpiece from Cork, dating to 1585 and said to have come from the College of Holy Trinity, is now housed in the Crawford Municipal Art Gallery.

Doors and windows

Hiberno-Norse houses of the eleventh and twelfth centuries had front and back doors; the front doors gave access to the street and the back to the plot. The doorways were usually represented by a threshold flanked by doorjambs. The jambs were sometimes slender posts, but more frequently they were planks of rectangular or wedge-shaped cross-section. The thresholds were mostly wooden beams laid between the jambs or, more frequently, inside them and held in place by small posts driven into the ground. Bolt brackets were attached to the jambs, or inner faces of doors, by iron rivets. In excavations in the city a door pull, a wooden handgrip attached to the inner or outer face of a door, was found in a late medieval context.[25]

Decorated stone surrounds, frequently using imported stone from Dundry Hill in Somerset, were widely used in Irish churches and castles from the thirteenth century onwards. The use of Dundry stone was especially common in port towns and cities. Moulded stone was rarely used for the detail surrounding the doors of domestic buildings. A stone-walled house of fourteenth-century date excavated at Philip's Lane, Cork, was provided with two opposing doorways. The door surrounds were faced with moulded yellow sandstone blocks. By the late 1400s, with advances in the quality of stone-carving chisels, local hard carboniferous limestone was in regular use for moulded architectural details, such as door and window surrounds and corbels. Chamfered edges, pick-dressed panels and foliar designs such as trefoils and the figure-of-eight design known as the 'Tudor knot' became common motifs on sixteenth-century stonework.

Wooden shutters may have been used at windows in the houses of the eleventh- and twelfth-century Irish towns. There is limited evidence for window glass in the domestic architecture of medieval Ireland. There was no medieval glass industry in Ireland, but glass was imported. As a result, the use of glass was confined to churches and perhaps the houses of the wealthiest. Neither is there evidence from Ireland for the use of horn as a means of admitting daylight to medieval houses, but it is known that horn, having been pressed into broad flat sheets, was utilised for lantern covers. By the 1600s, glass was in more widespread use in domestic architecture in Cork and this is evidenced by finds of window lead and glass grooves in window mullions.

Conclusion

The development of this valley-bottom, stone-fortified medieval town with its waterways and bridges must have given Cork a distinctive appearance: another 'Venice of the north'. To a traveller approaching the town from land or the sea it would have been an impressive and possibly unexpected sight, rising suddenly from a landscape of woodlands and estuary marshes. The loss of its walls in the city's eighteenth-century expansion, heralding the beginnings of urban sprawl, did not diminish Cork's unique form and its medieval roots are still imprinted upon the city today.

Lanes and Streets

Gina Johnson

Medieval Cork was a walled town with three entrances, two of which were connected by a central north–south main street. The late sixteenth- and early seventeenth-century maps give a general impression of the layout of the city, showing dozens of laneways leading to the east and west off this spinal main street (see *The Anglo-Normans and Beyond*, Chapter 10).

Individually these lanes were not exceptional, but they formed a herring-bone pattern that made the layout unique. The massive enveloping wall defined the extent of the medieval town, providing defence and a means of regulating the population and trade within. It also affected the internal layout of the streets and lanes, restricting the extent of the passageways and influencing their positioning.[1]

An east-to-west waterway flowing just south of modern Castle Street and on the north side of Liberty Street served as the central quay of the medieval town. This was guarded at the eastern end by the Marine Gate, also known as Martin's Gate. The waterway is today culverted beneath the buildings on the south side of Castle Street (Fig. 1.82).

The laneways in Cork's medieval core are now built over or have been incorporated into modern buildings, but the original positions of many are still indicated by doorways leading to private corridors, halls or short passages (Fig. 1.83). Others partially survive but no longer function as thoroughfares (Fig. 1.84).

Excavated laneways

The evidence from excavations in the city is currently too fragmented to detail the development of the laneway network from the early medieval period. There is, however, enough information to suggest that the first laneways were simply compacted clay, some covered or defined by wicker, wood or timber. The earliest trackways, from within the area of the walled town, were uncovered during the 1970s excavations at Christ Church, Holy Trinity College. Two thirteenth- or fourteenth-century wattle trackways, a mid-twelfth-century trackway of horizontal wooden planks on a matrix of wood chips and various cobbled pathways were uncovered in what is now Bishop Lucey Park.[2] Some of these medieval paths were in the same position as two post-medieval laneways (Edmond Sarsfield's or Gillman's Lane, and Woods Lane), indicating a notable degree of continuity.[3]

Fig. 1.81 Detail of the centre of Cork, 'A description of the cittie of Corke and the places next adjacent', from the Hardiman Atlas 1602 (Trinity College Dublin, MS 1209/45). The main street was the spinal focus for the two approaches to Cork from the county. At either end of the street, gate towers (later replaced by the city and county gaols) defended the island settlement and bridges connected to the evolving suburbs on the north and south banks of the Lee. From the North Gate Bridge, the road rises steeply uphill along Shandon Street onto what was to become Gerald Griffin Street and from there on to Mallow. Consequently, the upper end of Shandon Street and Gerald Griffin Street were originally known as Mallow Lane; from South Gate Bridge the road also climbs steeply onto Barrack Street and west to the Bandon Road. The northern approach seems to have been a natural craggy route that was gradually modified to ease movement through the steep sandstone ridges that shadowed the walled town.

Fig. 1.82 A nineteenth-century painting of what is now Castle Street, indicating the source of the street name: Roche's Castle is in the foreground, while in the distance a ship enters between the Queen's and King's castles. (Photo: Cork City Council.)

The archaeological evidence indicates that the earliest lanes were informal pathways to backyards and houses behind the main street-fronting properties. Although the orientation was often east to west, this was not consistent amongst the earliest lanes. The introduction of stone houses in the late thirteenth and early fourteenth century seems to have regularised the layout of the lanes (Fig. 1.85).

In many cases, an arrangement evolved whereby a single lane served two adjacent burgages or property lots. Others led from the main street directly to the front door of houses that lay behind the main street-fronting buildings. When the defence of the town was critical, some of the lanes also led to strategically important features along the town wall: to steps leading to the walkway and to the mural towers that studded the wall. These lanes were amongst the most substantial and enduring: Old Post Office Lane, Tuckey's Lane, Christ Church Lane, St Peter's Church Lane, Hoare's Lane (now Adelaide Street) all led to mural towers and all survive today as thoroughfares.

As Cork became more densely populated, many of the east–west lanes became lined with buildings. Portney's Lane and St Peter's Church Lane, off North Main Street, retain this arrangement with residential properties defining one side of both lanes. The earliest plans of the town, particularly the one from *Pacata Hibernia*, depict a similar layout.

THE DEMISE OF THE LANES
The residents of the walled town were privileged in several ways, being afforded the protection of the walls but also having defined trading rights and the status conferred on citizens of an important trading port. The wall, which was heavily damaged during the 1690 siege of Cork, was demolished, built over or incorporated into new buildings during the early years of the eighteenth century, effectively removing the advantage of living within its confines. Throughout that century, the marshes to the east and west of the medieval town were filled in and the focus of Cork shifted to the newly developed areas to the east.

By the mid-eighteenth century the population had outgrown the area of the medieval town and the wealthiest

Fig. 1.83 The gate to Meeting House Lane, also known as Cross Court. The gate's design represents the eighteenth-century layout of North and South Main Streets. The lane led to the Quakers' Meeting House, which stood on the site of the Southern Health Board property on Grattan Street. (Drawing: Ben Reilly. Photo: Cork City Council.)

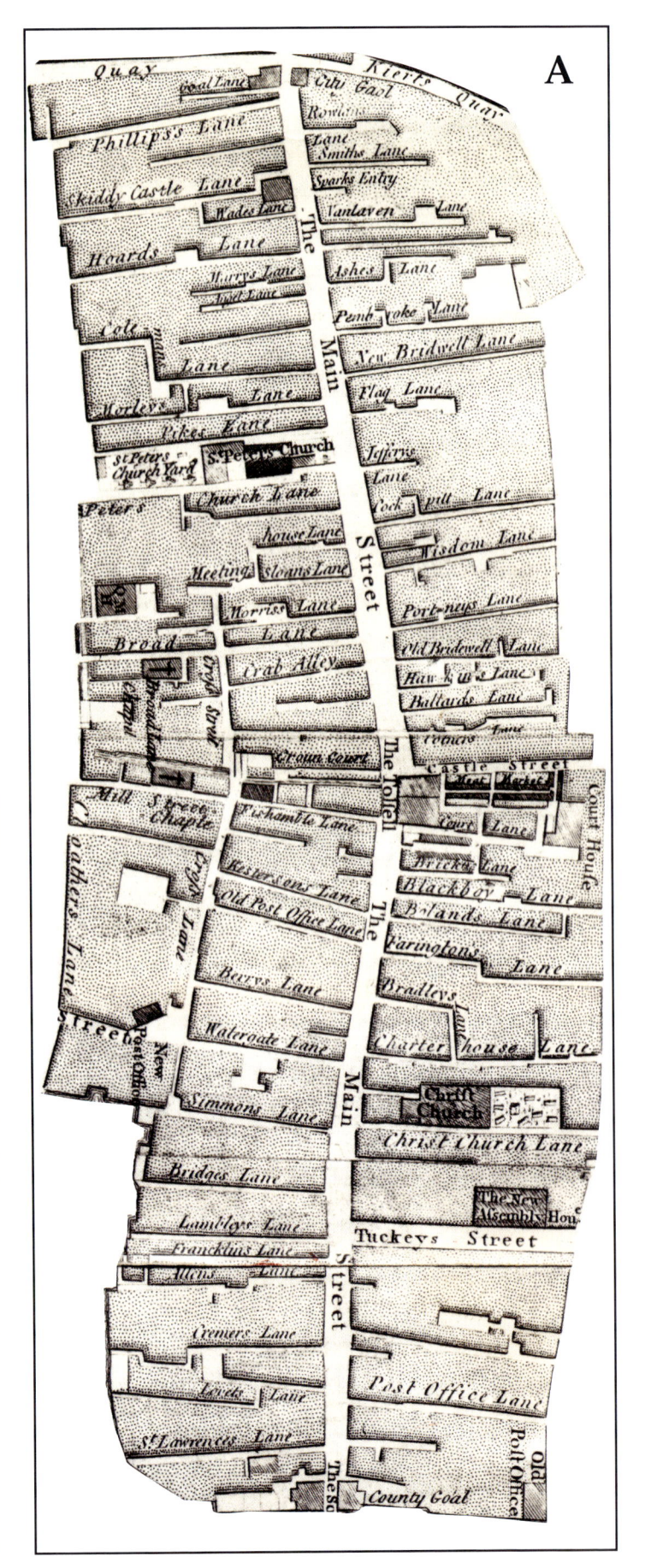

citizens emigrated to the areas that eventually became city suburbs and to the countryside. The laneways that had given access to the elegant merchants' houses and trading properties were transformed to accommodate squalid tenements housing the poorest citizens. By 1841, three-quarters of Cork city's population were classified as living in slum accommodation and a decade later 80 per cent of the city's housing comprised run-down tenements.[4] During the 1800s over 200 people lived in tenements along St Peter's Church Lane and a staggering 423 people lived in 21 tenements along Coleman's Lane. It was not until the formation of the Improved Dwellings Company in the late nineteenth century that significant measures were taken to move people to purpose-built houses in the suburbs. By the mid-twentieth century virtually all the laneways in the area of the medieval town had been cleared of their residents. In the 1940s Broad Lane, off North Main Street, was the last of the major residential lanes to disappear from the streetscape.

Lane names

The first formal naming of streets and lanes in Cork occurred in 1787, although earlier limestone street plaques still survive: Farren's Street 1732, Tuckey's Street 1761, Millerd's Street 1766 and James Street 1767. Before the eighteenth century, lanes were identified mainly by property ownership. The lane was usually named after the dominant property owner on that lane. One of the earliest comprehensive sources of post-medieval lane names is the *Survey and valuation*, a survey of about half of the property in the area of the medieval city *c.* 1641–1664.[5] Of 68 streets and lanes named in the survey, all but nine are named after individuals or families such as the Skiddys, Copingers,

Fig. 1.84 A) Detail of John Rocque's 1759 map, revised in 1773. The area of the walled town is depicted as a densely built-up island, almost entirely surrounded by waterways. The three editions of Rocque's map (1759, 1772, 1773) provide names for the vast majority of the lanes in this area. Of these, the following survive as public thoroughfares (clockwise from North Gate Bridge): Jeffery's Lane (now Kyle's Street), Portney's Lane, Castle Street, Charterhouse Lane (now Tobin Street), Christ Church Lane, Tuckey's Street, Kift's Lane (not named by Rocque), [Old] Post Office Lane, Watergate Lane (now Hanover Street), Kesterson's Lane, Mill Street/Fishamble Lane (now Liberty Street), St Peter's Church Lane, Coleman's Lane and Hoare's Lane (now Adelaide Street). B) Present-day views of 1) North Main Street, 2) Kift's Lane. (Photos: Cork City Council.)

Fig. 1.85 A fourteenth-century laneway excavated at the North Gate is typical of the medieval laneways, with its traditional white limestone and red sandstone and its east-to-west alignment. (Photo: Cork City Council.)

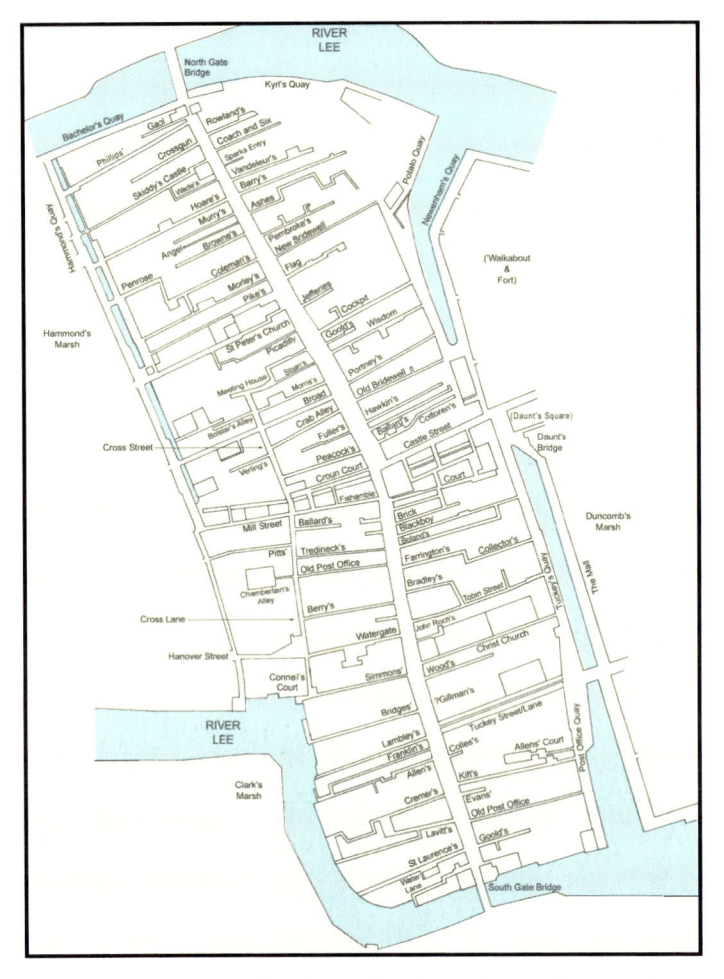

Fig. 1.86 Schematic map of Cork's medieval core showing the approximate location of the laneways. The outline is based on eighteenth-century cartography and the nineteenth-century Ordnance Survey maps.

The Williamite conquest of Cork in 1690 swept aside the old order and instigated an almost total renaming of the lanes (Fig. 1.86). Consequently, John Carty's map of 1726 does not include a single old family lane name but introduces some of the newcomers: the Newmans, Fenns, Dunscombes and Tuckeys, who were amongst the sponsors of his map. By 1759, when John Rocque mapped Cork, at least 41 lanes in the area of the old medieval town were named after individuals, none of whom had traditional roots in Cork (Fig. 1.84A). The only names that were retained from the *Civil Survey* of the 1600s were Christ Church Lane, Court Lane, Cross Street, Mill Street, (Skiddy's) Castle Lane and St Peter's Church Lane. The common denominator was that they were all called after the significant buildings with which they were associated, with the exception of Cross Street, which was simply descriptive.[6] The eighteenth-century surnames did not have the longevity of the medieval lane names and by the mid-nineteenth century, when the Ordnance Survey mapped the city, many had again disappeared. By this time the streetscape had changed drastically in the area of medieval Cork and, with the culverting of the remaining waterways, the construction of Washington Street and the Court House and the expansion of the breweries in the southern quarters, the lanes had begun to disappear. Of the 75 laneways identified on Rocque's maps, only eight survive today as public passageways; an additional six have been modified to serve as relatively broad modern streets, such as Castle Street, Liberty Street and Adelaide Street.

Tirrys and Gallweys. Other documentary sources indicate that this trend had been established during the medieval period.

8. ST FINBARR AND EARLY CHRISTIAN SETTLEMENT

Pádraig Ó Riain

This chapter provides an outline of the ecclesiastical and related processes that led to Cork's establishment as a religious and administrative centre and later, in the medieval period, as an expanding town.[1] A casual visitor to the island on Gougane Lake today will feel transported back to the days of early Irish Christianity by the sight of monastic cells, which are scarcely three hundred years old, grouped around a raised timber cross.

Equally, a reader of the biography written for St Finbarr will doubtless also be convinced of its essential authenticity, despite its obvious concern with episcopal and diocesan issues that first came to the fore in the twelfth century.[2] For more reliable information, however slight, on what was happening in the Cork area in early Christian times, we must turn to other sources. Some of these are archaeological in character. Others consist of ogham inscriptions and names of saints, contained either in place names or in genuinely early hagiographical documents.

Seeds

There was considerable trade between the Cork area and south-west Britain in the fifth and sixth centuries, when Christianity was becoming established in Ireland.[3] The

Fig. 1.87 A) Gougane Barra. (Photo: Michael Murphy.) B) Depiction of St Finbarr on a seventeenth-century silver chalice from St Mary's, Pope's Quay. (Photo: Tomás Tyner/UCC.)

distribution of ogham-inscribed stones, which are mainly found in south Munster and in south-west Britain and which date to the period AD 350 to 550, bears out these contacts. There is an obvious kernel of truth in the claims of such later texts as Cormac's glossary and *History of the Britons*, attributed to Nennius and dated to c. AD 830, that the sons of Liathán and the Déise enjoyed great power in Britain.[4] Liathán forms the origin of the place name Castlelyons (Caisleán Ó Liatháin) and the Déise is the name for the baronies of Decies in County Waterford. Since Christianity had already put down roots in south-west Britain by the fourth century, it is reasonable to assume that the south Munster kindred of the Irish who had settled there would also have learned of the new religion and, in many cases, adopted it. Although the literary concept of pre-Patrician Christianity in Ireland appears to be a late medieval invention, it has a basis in fact in the case of south Munster (Fig. 1.89).[5]

If Christianity was first brought to the Cork area as a consequence of contacts among kindred or trading activity, then its local adoption would not have involved serious disruption to hereditary entitlements of land and office. The smooth transition from paganism can still be glimpsed at several Cork ecclesiastical sites. In Ballyvourney, archaeologists expected to find traces of early Christianity, in keeping with the seventh-century date assigned to the local cross-inscribed stone; instead they discovered extensive remains of iron-working activity.[6]

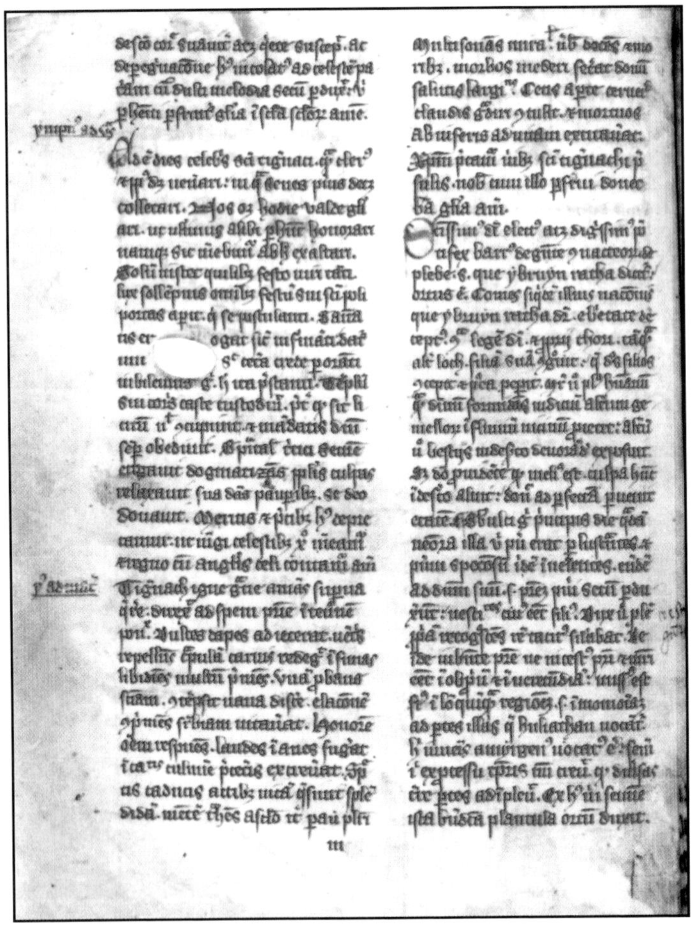

In fact, the archaeological findings are at one with the implications of the name of the local saint. Gobnat takes her name from Gob(ba), a pet form of a name based on goba (*gabha*), meaning smith or ironworker. Kilgobnet is the name of four churches in the wider Cork area, and the corresponding male saint, Gobán, is remembered in the names of several churches, at Bantry (St Goban's), near Bandon (Kilgobbin) and at Ballyclogh in north Cork (Kilgobban). Ironworkers in these areas continued to venerate their ancient pagan divinities, albeit in transmuted Christian form.

The many churches in the Cork area named after pre-Christian divinities points to an early phase in local Christianity that was superficial in character and that left intact the structures or practices relating to land ownership and title to office that had previously obtained. Besides Gobnat and Gobán, we find Lug, the greatest of the Celtic gods, whose name survives at Templemolaga near Mitchelstown and at Timoleague, near Clonakilty, both of which derive from *molaga*, 'my (dear) Lug'.[7]

FINDING CORK'S SAINT

Towards the middle of the sixth century, a form of monasticism centred on the churches of north-east Ulster, most notably Bangor, began to extend its influence throughout Ireland and beyond. Spurred on by a renewed religious enthusiasm and intellectually imbued by increasing extended contact, Irish ecclesiastics found the energy not only to propagate reform and revival at home but also to evangelise outside Ireland. Although initially confined to the Irish in Scotland, the *peregrinatio pro Christo* soon extended to the Picts, Northumbrians and (with the departure of Columbanus from Bangor c. AD 590) to the European mainland. The vigour of the external dimension of this movement can easily be measured by reference to the documents that recorded its progress, in Bobbio, Péronne and elsewhere.[8]

At home, among a people that had traditionally preferred the oral mode, the otherwise undocumented progress of the reform can now best be gauged by reference to place name evidence. Hundreds of churches throughout Ireland are reputed to have been founded by, or named after, Colum Cille, one of the most notable exponents of the

Fig. 1.88 Extract from a c. 1385 copy of a manuscript of 'The Life of Finbarr', originally composed in Cork in the late twelfth century. (Source: Bodleian Library, Oxford.)

movement, the first truly Irish saint. One sign of this saint's popularity is the variations on his name, including Colmán, Caimín, Cuimín, Comán, Cainnech, Mochonna, Mocholla, Mochuille, that are preserved in churches named after him.[9]

By the time Adamnán wrote his Life of Colum Cille, shortly before AD 700, south Munster had clearly embraced this new form of Irish Christianity. Colum Cille is reported to have visited Terryglass in north Tipperary, where his name is still attached to the local church. Adamnán made no mention of Cork. However, he revealed the name of Colum Cille's teacher, Bishop Finbarr, alias Finnian (†AD 579), who can be identified with the patron of the church of Movilla, near Bangor in County Down. This man is probably the same famous scholar whom Columbanus described as having corresponded with Gildas, the celebrated historian of Britain, on a question of monastic discipline. Bishop Finbarr also composed one of the earliest known penitentials, a book containing directions for confessors regarding grades of penance.[10]

Not surprisingly, as the cult of Colum Cille spread throughout Ireland, the role played by his teacher, Finbarr, also received local attention. At Terryglass, the designation of a neighbouring church, Kilbarron (Irish *Cill Bhairrfhionn*), preserves the name of the saint's teacher in one of its many possible variations, which include Finnio (Finnian), Finnén, Finne, Finnu, Munnu, Bairrfhionn, Bairre, and Barra. The *Bairrfhionn* version of the name first put down roots in Cork, as is shown by the entry on the saint's feast in the two oldest surviving Irish martyrologies, composed at Tallaght, near Dublin, about AD 830. In one, the prose Martyrology of Tallaght, the name reads *Bairrind*; in the other, the metrical Martyrology of Óengus, the pet form *Bairre* is preferred. That Cork's patron saint was originally Colum Cille's teacher is shown not only by his name but also by his September feast, his reputation as a teacher and his association with a narrative involving a gospel book.[11]

We have no documentary means of dating the arrival of the cult of Finbarr in Cork. However, it probably became established locally about the time that it was adopted in the Terryglass area, certainly before the end of the seventh century. The earliest recorded abbot of Cork, Suibne († 682 AD), belonged to an ecclesiastical family named Uí Meic Brocc, which, like other families of its kind, appears to have been itinerant in character. Branches of the family are also known from north Cork and the Carrickmacross area in County Monaghan.[12] From texts on saints' lives composed in the latter half of the seventh century, such as the lives of Patrick, Brigit and Colum Cille, we can gather that there was a great deal of clerical itinerancy in the country about this time, with the churches of Armagh, Kildare and Iona contending for ecclesiastical advantage.[13]

Perhaps it was then that the authorities in Cork first heard the story of St Finbarr, as related possibly by a member of the Uí Meic Brocc. Finding much of interest in it, the church authorities in Cork set land aside for the erection of a church in the saint's honour. The usual preparation of the site for the purpose of its consecration involved three days of fasting and prayer, together with a solemn procession along the bounds of the site. There followed the erection of a church, at that stage no doubt of timber (see *Christianity, Churches and Burial Places*, Chapter 9). Once this was consecrated, and a relic of the saint placed at or near the altar, the history of St Finbarr's long association with Cork may be said to have begun. In the writing of saints' lives, the sacredness of the site was often distinguished by additional features, comprising angelic guidance to the chosen place and the prior presence there of an animal (Fig. 1.90).[14]

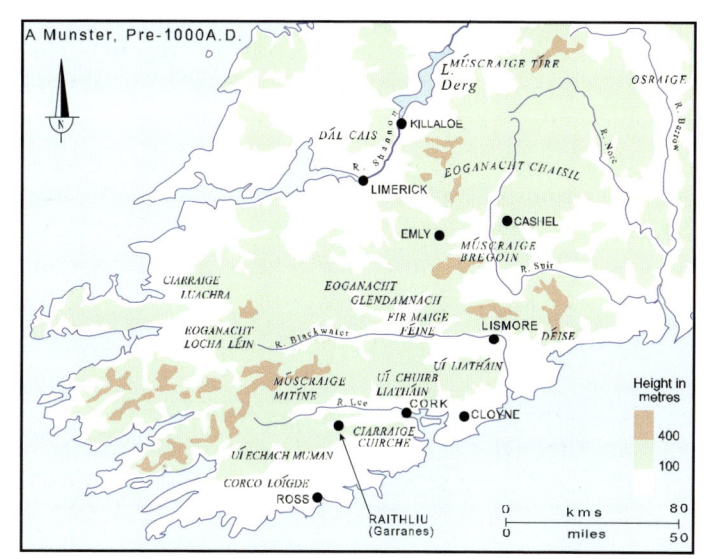

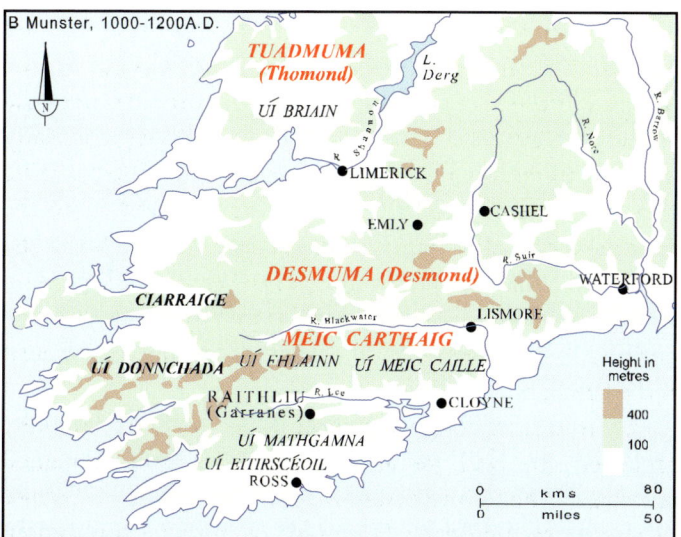

Fig. 1.89 A) Pre-Christian and B) early Christian place-name distributions and territorial divisions.

Fig. 1.90 Raithliu (Garranes), County Cork, the reputed site of St Finbarr's birthplace. (Photo: Daphne Pochin Mould.)

FINBARR BECOMES CORK'S OWN

During the centuries that followed, control of the abbacy of Cork for the most part alternated between the various hereditary ecclesiastical families that were attached to it. These were landed families with considerable stakeholds in the local area. The Uí Meic Brocc, for example, held lands near Spike Island in Cork harbour. Similarly, the Uí Meic Iair (later known as the Uí Shelbaig), who provided several abbots of Cork between 1016 and 1140, held the greater part of what was to become known as the civil parish of St Finbarr's. The continuing importance of this family in the twelfth century led to the naming of an ancestor, Áed mac Comgaill, as the donor of the site on which the church was built.[15]

The hereditary entitlement of such local families to the office of abbot often received short shrift at the hands of powerful political dynasties. These power groups made a habit of intruding members of their own families into the abbacies of the more important churches. As early as the eighth century, Ciarraige abbots were intruded into the abbacy of Cork by the kings of west Munster. This practice was maintained by the Eoganacht kings of Cashel (later the Meic Carthaig) and by the Dál Cais (later the Uí Briain) in the period between the ninth and twelfth centuries. The last known 'intruder', Gilla Pátraic Mac Carthaig, died in 1157.[16]

By the twelfth century, when Cork's importance was confirmed by its selection as a diocesan centre, its outward appearance would no doubt have reflected its status as a church of substance. An entry in the Annals for 1081 recording the burning of Cork shows that it was then surrounded by 'its churches'. An abbey, later named Gill Abbey after the first known diocesan bishop of Cork, was built near the church in 1134. The names of no fewer than eight churches, within or in close proximity to the medieval

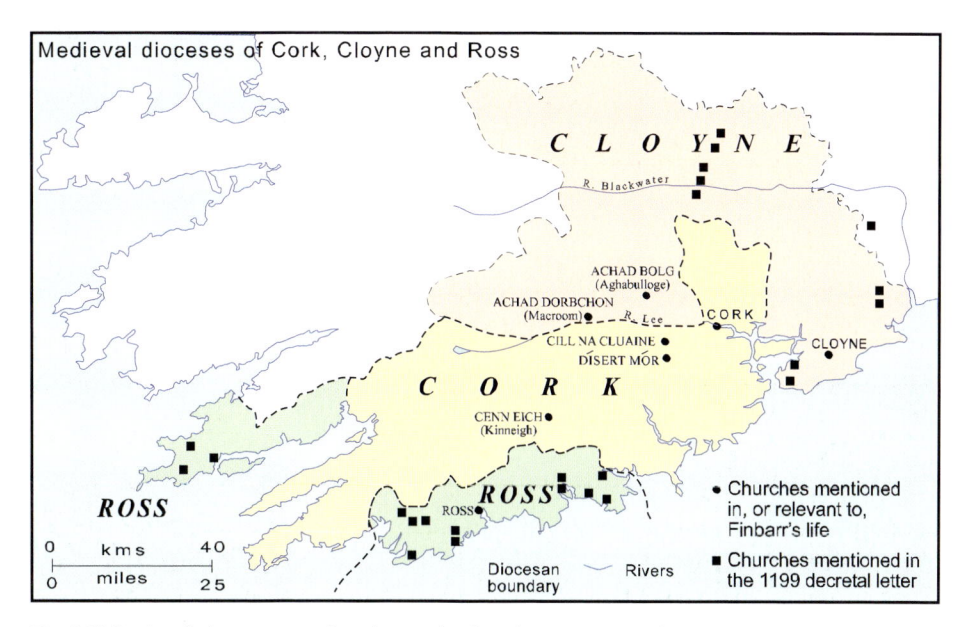

Fig. 1.91 Regional place names, churches and cultural sites associated with St Finbarr in the diocese of Cork, Cloyne and Ross.

town, are contained in the 1199 decretal letter sent by Pope Innocent to the bishop of Cork in confirmation of his privileges and entitlements (see *Christianity, Churches and Burial Places*, Chapter 9) (Fig. 1.91).[17] Like other Munster centres of ecclesiastical importance, Cork would presumably have had its church rebuilt around this time in the new Romanesque style.

Although chosen as an episcopal see at Ráith Bresail in 1111, Cork remained without a diocesan bishop until the Augustinian Gilla Áeda Ua Muigin was elected *c.* 1140. This was a contentious appointment, as is made clear by the only surviving record of the event, the Life of St Malachy of Armagh written by St Bernard of Clairvaux in 1148. Bernard describes how Malachy resolved the differences between the contending parties, doubtless the local hereditary families and perhaps also the Meic Carthaig, by naming 'a poor man whom he knew to be both learned and holy and he happened to be an outsider'. Gilla Áeda, who came from Errew near Lough Conn in County Mayo, enjoyed a long tenure of the see until his death in 1172.[18]

Gilla Áeda's legacy was destined to be enduring, in at least three important respects. First, at the synod of Kells-Mellifont in 1152, he gave his consent to a radical contraction in the boundaries of his diocese, large parts of which were allocated to the sees of Cloyne and Ross. Secondly, in keeping with his own western origins and with the traditional view of the need for a family relationship between a patron saint and his successor, he imposed upon Cork's saint a Connacht origin, which has since become an integral part of Finbarr's hagiography. Thirdly, his name became attached to the Augustinian abbey to which he himself had belonged. Originally named *Ecclesia Sancti Johannis Apostoli*, this later became known as *Mainistir Ghiolla Aodha* or Gill Abbey.[19]

FACT OR FICTION

Gilla Áeda's death in 1172 coincided with the arrival in Cork of the Anglo-Normans, an event that immediately gave rise to the need for documentary evidence of title to land and office. Numerous charters and other such documents bearing their signatures indicate that Gilla Áeda's immediate successors were conscious of the importance of written evidence. Two more substantial documents composed towards the end of the twelfth century also responded to the pressing need for written evidence of title. One of them, the decretal letter, confirms that Pope Innocent III sent 'the possessions, rights and privileges' of the diocese of Cork to its bishop in 1199. In this extremely valuable and detailed document, a draft of which was doubtless first prepared in Cork and subsequently sent to Rome for papal sanction, the various churches under the jurisdiction of the bishop of Cork are named. These included several key churches belonging by right to the dioceses of Ross and Cloyne. The then bishop was clearly concerned with restoring to Cork its earlier hegemony over the ecclesiastical lands of the two neighbouring dioceses.[20]

Precisely the same message is spelt out in the second document, the Life of St Finbarr, composed in Cork in the late twelfth century. This document purports to set out the earliest history of Christian Cork. Its contents are often at variance with the history given here. The basis of disagreement with the author of the saint's 'Life' is given now in brief outline.[21]

Since their authors were mainly concerned with establishing precedents assignable to the time when Christianity was becoming established locally, the lives of saints were a powerful means of promoting traditional ecclesiastical interests. Finbarr's biographer was well aware of the great benefits to be drawn from his text, as is made clear by his continuous depiction of the patrons of Cloyne and Ross, Colmán and Fachtna as subservient to Finbarr (Fig. 1.91). Using a series of fabricated incidents, he created for these two saints a primordial indebtedness to Finbarr, which implicitly was adjudged to have remained valid in perpetuity. Colmán and Fachtna are mentioned explicitly as

Fig. 1.92 Sites associated with Finbarr's 'last days' and death. A) Dísert Mór (Desert More), which St Finbarr is said to have visited shortly before his death. (Photo: Daphne Pochin Mould.) B) Cill na Cluaine (Kilnacloona), County Cork, where St Finbarr is said to have died. (Photo: Cork Archaeological Survey.)

in the list of those who were allegedly Finbarr's pupils in the school which he is said to have founded in Cork. In the Ossory section of the 'Life', the biographer ingeniously capitalised on a belief that the Ross and Kilkenny areas were closely connected and the deference shown by Fachtna to Finbarr is incurred vicariously through relatives of the former saint.

Another pointer to a late twelfth-century date for the 'Life' is its accommodation of the interests of the Meic Carthaig, who had been forced by the arrival of the Anglo-Normans to leave their earlier headquarters at Shandon in the town of Cork and re-group west of what is now Ballincollig. This peripheral area was selected as the place of Finbarr's final illness and death. The church specified as the place of his death, Cill na Cluaine (in the townland of Ballineadig, parish of Aglish), is now marked neither by name, which has become obsolete, nor by physical remains, which are only scarcely visible above the ground (Fig. 1.92). Yet its saints, named Cormac and Baíthín, are said to have been directed to found their church there by no less a figure than Ruadán, ancestral patron of the Meic Carthaig. The purpose of the episode is quite clear: the Meic Carthaig, whose connection with the town and diocese had only begun in the early part of the twelfth century, were accorded the signal honour of presiding over the final moments of Cork's patron saint.

These and other emphases in the 'Life' are concerned with late twelfth-century politics, both ecclesiastical and secular. Yet this patently tendentious document is still frequently cited as a window on the early history of Christian Cork (Fig. 1.88).[22] Through its enthusiastic adoption of the cult of the celebrated northern teacher and writer, St Finbarr, Cork assumed a role in keeping with its own high ecclesiastical status. Namely, the diffusion of the cult of a saint who deserves to be ranked as Ireland's fourth most important early saint, after Patrick, Brigit and Finbarr's pupil, Colum Cille.

9. CHRISTIANITY, CHURCHES AND BURIAL PLACES

Maurice Hurley

The first churches

In order to understand the nature, extent and location of churches and burial places in any long-established city, it is necessary to understand the origin and development of the urban area and its prevailing religious traditions. Cork owes its foundation to Christianity; namely, a sixth-century monastery (see *Urban Beginnings and the Vikings*, Chapter 6; *St Finbarr and Early Christian Settlement*, Chapter 8). The Vikings, who were initially pagan, provided the main impetus towards urbanisation during their Christianised period in the eleventh and twelfth centuries. The continuous occupation of Cork for over fourteen hundred years spans many changes in Christian doctrine, interpretation, ecclesiastical organisation and ritual, as well as associated burial practices and traditions.[1]

The earliest positively identifiable site likely to contain evidence for both settlement and burial is St Finbarr's monastery. It was founded in the sixth century and subsequently expanded into a thriving monastery. This later became a cathedral in the course of the transformation of the Irish Church from a monastic to diocesan system. The significance of St Finbarr and the monastery remains strong in contemporary tradition and he is generally credited with the founding of Cork. The tradition, while rooted in documentary references, is largely based on legend and propaganda (see *St Finbarr and Early Christian Settlement*, Chapter 8). There is little doubt that St Fin Barre's Cathedral occupies the site of an early Christian monastery. A burial

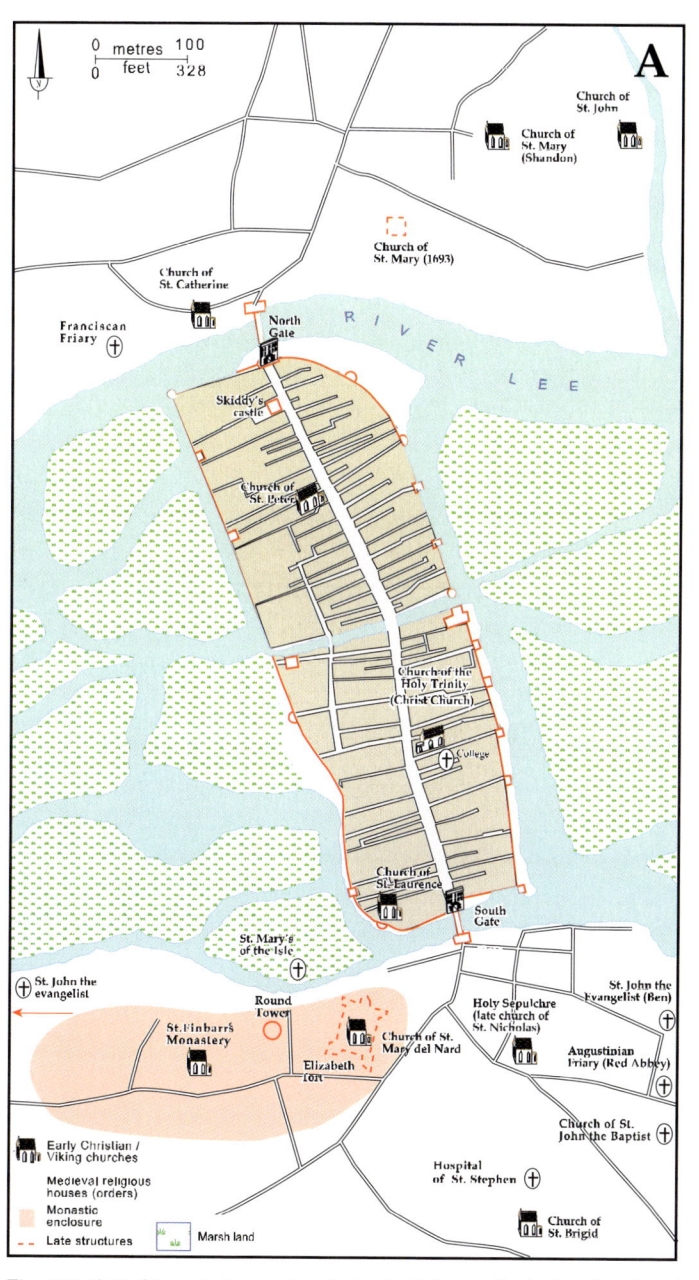

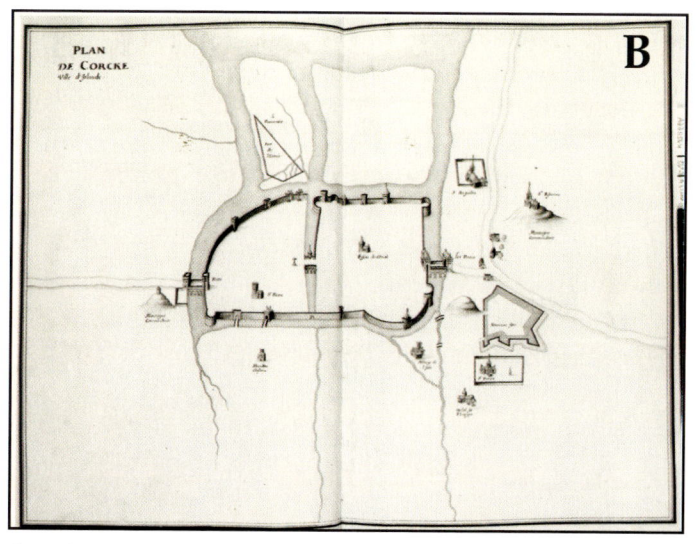

Fig. 1.93 A) Multi-period map of ecclesiastical sites in Cork city, showing the outline of the medieval town and the site of St Finbarr's monastic foundation and of medieval and later religious houses. B) *Plan de Corke, Ville d'Irlande*, of c. 1610–50 (French artist) showing the town walls and key churches. (Source: Private collection.)

Fig. 1.94A) St Peter's church, North Main Street. This was probably the site of an early Christian monastery founded on the marsh islands in the Lee and later of an early church. There are several references to St Peter's throughout the medieval period, when it is recorded as the church of the parish of St Peter. (Photo: Robert Devoy.) B) Drawing of St Peter's church. (Source: *Pacata Hibernia, c.* 1585.)

ground is likely to have existed in association with this monastic site. Archaeological excavations of such sites elsewhere in Ireland have provided evidence for the prevailing burial practices: extended inhumations, showing no grave goods, in either unlined or stone-lined graves, with an east-to-west orientation.

St Finbarr's monastery did not stand alone as a Christian site in Cork. The tradition that St Finbarr first dwelt in a cave is supported by the establishment of a house of the Canons Regular of St Augustine called Gill Abbey in 1137. The monastery was known as *de Antro Barre*, or the Cave of Barra. It is likely that a tradition of the sanctity of this place had persisted for several centuries, culminating in the choice of site for the first authenticated establishment of the new ecclesiastical orders in south Munster.

It has also been suggested that an early Christian monastery stood in the marsh centring on the site of St Peter's church, North Main Street. The name 'Dungarvan', as applied in the medieval records to the north island of Cork, may be derived from *Dún Garbhain*, or Garbhán's Fort, after the saint mentioned in the Irish Life of St Finbarr (see *Medieval Cork*, Chapter 7; *St Finbarr and Early Christian Settlement*, Chapter 8).[2] His name occurs in a list of saints, all of whom were with Finbarr at Loch Irce and gave their churches to him.

It is likely that there was a church and ecclesiastical community on the north island and a burial ground may have occurred in association. The dedication to St Peter may have been applied to an older church site. St Peter's church is listed in the year 1199, but the church and dedication are likely to be of pre-Norman origin, in common with similar churches in Dublin and Waterford. The excavation of a pre-thirteenth-century ditch close to Grattan Street may be tangible evidence for the reputed monastic settlement. St Nessan was also listed as one of the saints who were with Finbarr at his school at Loch Irce. The precise site of St Nessan's church and monastery is uncertain, but it is likely to have been on the north bank of the Lee, re-dedicated to St Catherine in the early thirteenth century. It stood to the west of North Gate Bridge and Shandon Street.

Several other churches, monasteries and burial places probably existed beyond the core of the emerging Hiberno-Norse town of Cork. It is impossible to pinpoint the location of the many churches and monastic sites recorded in historical references, as most of them have been engulfed by modern urban expansion. One such site is at Temple Hill in Ballintemple. A small graveyard enclosed by a stone wall still exists. The name 'Temple Hill' is applied to the adjacent house and local reports of the discovery of human skeletons in the area abound. Other indications of the former existence of a church associated with the burial ground are provided by names like Churchyard Lane, while Boreenmanna Road, meaning 'the little road of the monks', points to the former existence of a monastery. In the course of a survey undertaken in 2003 by Cork City Council several topographical features indicating previously unrecognised elements of a large sub-circular enclosure were identified.[3] Such enclosures normally surrounded and defined the area of early Christian monasteries. The names Temple Hill and Ballintemple have been taken by some to suggest the presence of a Knights Templar house on the site in the late fourteenth century, but it is more likely to reflect an early twelfth-century dedication.

EARLY MEDIEVAL FOUNDATIONS

When the Vikings arrived as raiders in Ireland in the early ninth century, they followed pagan burial practices: generally extended inhumation accompanied by grave goods, such as swords, axes and silver jewellery with the males and domestic and weaving implements with the females. No burials of this era have come to light in Cork. By the eleventh century the settled Scandinavians were embracing Christianity. In the twelfth century, the Hiberno-Norse port towns were a significant force in the introduction of new ideas leading to the reform of the Irish Church. Holy Trinity, Christ Church, was the parish church of the Hiberno-Norse town of Cork. It was located in the heart of the south island (see *Urban Beginnings and the Vikings*, Chapter 6). The dedication and location of the main parish church in a central and dominant part of the town is paralleled in Dublin and Waterford. In the latter towns, the churches dedicated to Holy Trinity, Christ Church, became cathedrals in the early twelfth century. In Cork, however, the dominance of the McCarthy kings of Desmond resulted in the favouring of the traditional Gaelic monastic site of St Finbarr's, to the detriment of the Hiberno-Norse church.

Other contemporary parish churches of the Hiberno-Norse era were St Peter's, on the north island, St Nessan's, St Brigid's, St Michael's, St Mary del Nard and St John's in Civitate (Fig. 1.93). These churches were in existence before 1199, when they are recorded in the decretal letter of Pope Innocent III.[4] All of the churches may, however, have originated as Gaelic monasteries, or were founded in a Hiberno-Norse Christian milieu as parish churches. St Brigid's parish church stood on the south side of the town, reputedly in the area later occupied by Cat Fort; namely, the area between Tower Street and Friar Street. It may have continued in use from the early Christian to the late medieval period. St Mary del Nard was another southside parish church which was later engulfed by a military

Fig. 1.95 A) Holy Trinity (Christ Church), South Main Street. (Photo: John Crowley.) B) The late eighteenth- to nineteenth-century graveyard at Holy Trinity church. (Photo: John Crowley.)

fortification, Elizabeth Fort. 'Nard' is probably a corruption of the Irish words *an tard*, meaning 'the height', hence it was also referred to as Sancte Marie in Monte, or St Mary on the height, and was dedicated to the Holy Rood or Holy Cross. The church survived until the early seventeenth century, for it is depicted in Speed's plan within the newly constructed Elizabeth Fort, where it is identified as 'Holly Rode' (see *Sixteenth- and Early Seventeenth-Century Cork*, Chapter 11) (Fig. 1.93).

St Michael's church is also listed in 1199 as within the same churchyard as St Mary del Nard. The dedication of a church on a height to St Michael corroborates the reference. St John's in Civitate is even more elusive. The word *civitate* implies 'within the walls', as St Peter's is similarly described. St John's may have been located where St Lawrence's later stood, close to South Main Street. There is no trace of a church above ground in this area today, as the likely site lies in the yard of the Beamish and Crawford brewery. The church of the Holy Sepulchre is equated with the later church of St Nicholas. St Nicholas' continued as a place of worship until the 1990s.

Some, if not all, of the churches named as parish churches in the decretal letter of 1199 had associated burial grounds.[5] The size and extent of the burial grounds probably depended on the topography, available land and the demography of the parish. Burial grounds within the walled town are likely to have been smaller than their suburban counterparts, due to the pressure on available land. These burial grounds are generally more densely packed with inhumations, as soil was often introduced to create new burial levels above an existing graveyard; in effect a multi-layered graveyard could be created, as at St Peter's church, Waterford.

Monastic orders

The arrival of the Anglo-Normans in Cork in 1177 brought no significant changes to the established diocesan or parochial situation. The most significant impact on ecclesiastical affairs was the appearance of several new religious orders in the wake of the conquest. In Cork, Anglo-Norman lords patronised at least five new religious houses and four hospitals in the course of the twelfth and thirteenth centuries. The dominant orders were the Benedictines, Franciscans and Dominicans. The foundation date of the Franciscan friary in Cork is uncertain. Conflicting entries range in date from 1214 to 1240, with the foundation being variously credited to Diarmaid MacCartaigh Mór, the Gaelic chieftain, and to various Norman lords, including de Barry, de Burgo and Philip or Gerald de Prendergast, as founders or benefactors. The Franciscan friary was located on the north bank of the Lee, to the west of the North Gate. The site was midway along low-lying ground between the cliff face and the river. Burials associated with the friary are known to occur over a wide area on North Mall.

In addition to the Franciscan and Dominican friaries, Cork possessed at least three other religious houses throughout the medieval period. The Augustinian priory of St John the Evangelist continued to thrive at the Gill Abbey site, while the Augustinian friary at Red Abbey existed from at least the early fourteenth century but was probably founded in the thirteenth; burials from this site have also been uncovered in the course of archaeological excavation (see *The Anglo-Normans and Beyond*, Chapter 10). There are no visible remains of the four medieval hospitals recorded in the documentary sources and there have been no diagnostic archaeological discoveries. Burial places existed in association with the hospitals, especially the leper hospital. The leper house was the beneficiary of a bequest from John de Wynchedon in 1306 and was recorded as being 'beside the bridge near the priory of the Friars Preachers'.[6] This would place its location close to the point where Proby's Quay joins Bishop Street.

Post dissolution

The fortunes of religious houses had varied considerably since the dissolution of the monasteries in 1541. Some of the monasteries were restored to the orders during the reign of Queen Mary but were again suppressed under Queen Elizabeth. Throughout the seventeenth century some of the religious houses continued to exist and both the Franciscan and Dominican friaries were flourishing in 1689. When King James II visited Cork he is recorded as having 'lodged in the House of the Dominican fathers and on Sunday, heard mass in the church of the Franciscans, called North Abbey'.[7] Burial continued at these sites up to the late seventeenth century, since it was a significant function of friary churches.

The religious houses ceased to exist in the period of Protestant supremacy in the eighteenth century, when the old abbeys were demolished and houses and industrial buildings were built over the burial grounds. Within 35 years of the fall of the Catholic Jacobites in 1690, the old medieval parish churches were largely swept away in a wave of rebuilding and modernisation. Between 1693 and 1725, no less than six city-centre churches were rebuilt.[8] Some of the churches had been damaged in the siege. Nevertheless, the replacement of Gothic architecture with classical buildings had more to do with a symbolic significance (see the boxed section, *St Fin Barre's Cathedral*, in Chapter 26). Single volume buildings, with regular lines and light and uncluttered interiors devoid of graven images, personified the taste of the dominant Protestant élite.

THE • CITY • IN • THE • LANDSCAPE

The Franciscans are recorded as living in a thatched cottage in Shandon and they 'worked openly until the Penal period during which they were forced to go into hiding'.[9] They re-established a monastery in Broad Lane before 1759, for Rocque's map names Broad Lane Chapel as a church on the south-western side of the lane (see *Sixteenth- and Early Seventeenth-Century Cork*, Chapter 11) (Fig. 1.98). The Franciscans continued to reside at this site and a new friary was opened in 1813, with a church added in 1829. The modern church and friary were rebuilt on an extension of the same site in the 1950s. The Augustinians resided between Blackboy Lane and Brunswick Street, where a new church was built before 1789.[10] The church was replaced by a much larger building on the same site in the 1930s.

BURIAL PLACES AND GRAVES

The provision of burial places, a core function of the medieval religious houses, was no longer a feature of the eighteenth- and nineteenth-century monasteries. Neither did the newly established orders of brothers and nuns provide burial grounds, although some monasteries

Fig. 1.96 St Anne's, Shandon, completed in 1722, with its simple, classical-style steeple in white limestone. (Photo: John Crowley.)

Several of the small medieval parish churches disappeared from the record. Many of the new classical churches were built over basement or semi-basement crypts. Vaulted crypts survive at St Anne's church, Shandon; Christ Church, South Main Street and St Paul's church, Paul Street. Crypts were not constructed beneath the classical building of St Fin Barre's Cathedral (1725–1735) or St Peter's (1780) (see *Famine*, Chapter 22).

RELIGIOUS ORDERS RE-EMERGE

The nineteenth century witnessed the growth of several Roman Catholic religious orders. Many of the old medieval orders flourished again: the Dominicans at Pope's Quay, the Franciscans at Broad Lane–Liberty Street and the Augustinians at Washington Street. The orders had continued to exist throughout the eighteenth century but generally as small communities with humble quarters and small churches hidden away in the back streets of the city. The Dominicans first re-established a house in Old Friary Place in 1721 and later transferred to Pope's Quay, where the friary and church of St Mary's, Pope's Quay, still flourishes.

Fig. 1.97 St Fin Barre's Cathedral, photographed *c.* 1850s, as seen prior to its reconstruction in the nineteenth century. (Photo: Colin Rynne; Day Collection.)

89

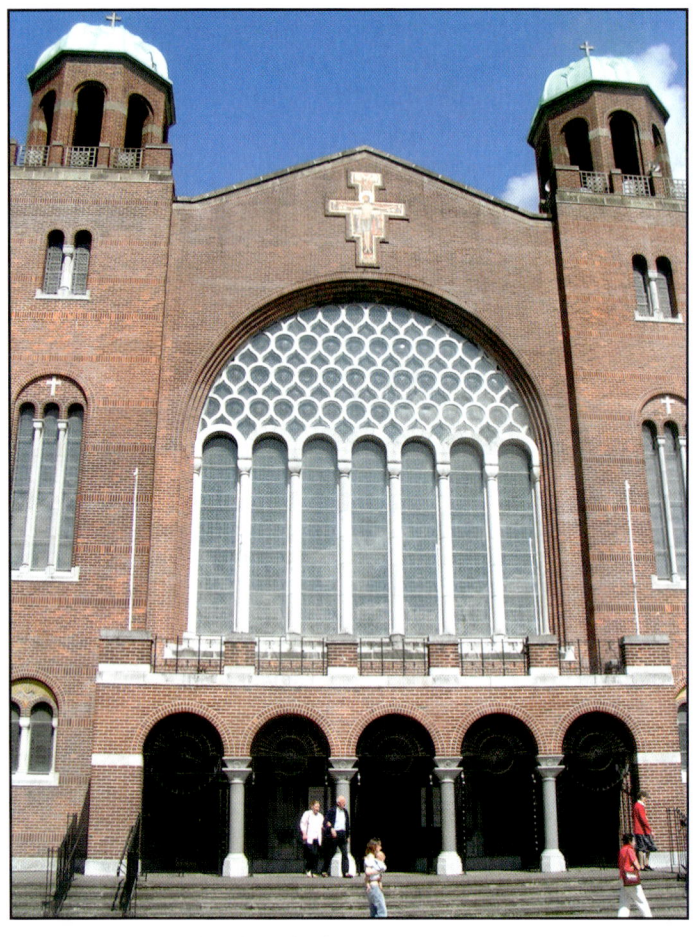

Fig. 1.98 St Francis church, in the former area of the Franciscan monastery and church at Broad Lane. (Photo: John Crowley.)

contained a burial place for their own community; examples of these include: South Presentation on Douglas Street, Ardfoyle Convent in Blackrock and the Christian Brothers at Mount St Joseph's. Some orphanages also provided burial places for infants and children that died in their care; for example, the Good Shepherd Convent in Sunday's Well.

The established Protestant Church, the Church of Ireland, retained the medieval parish burial grounds such as St Anne's, Shandon, St Peter's (Christ Church), St Nicholas' and St Fin Barre's Cathedral as burial grounds for parishioners. Parish churches newly created in the eighteenth century, such as St Paul's, Paul Street, and St Mary's, Shandon, contained crypts and burial grounds adjacent to the churches (Fig. 1.99). The Huguenots had their own parish church, known as the French Church, with an associated burial ground extending from French Church Street to Carey's Lane (see the case study, *The Huguenots of Cork*, in Chapter 15). The church is still standing but is now the locale for a number of shops, while a small portion of the graveyard remains in private ownership within the backyard of commercial premises. Several nineteenth-century buildings overlie most of the former burial ground.

In common with the late nineteenth- and twentieth-century Roman Catholic churches, the churches of most of the Nonconformist Protestant denominations did not provide burial grounds for their parishioners. The period saw responsibility for burial pass from the churches to the municipal authorities. The City Council established cemeteries at: St Michael's, Blackrock; St Joseph's, Tory Top Road in Ballyphehane; and St Finbarr's in Glasheen. All three continue to service the city's population. The former existence of a Jewish burial ground in the Douglas Street area was also a notable addition to the map of Cork burial places.[11]

There are several references to burials in mass graves and pits. Joseph Pike's account of the aftermath of the 1690 siege tells how the defeated Jacobites of Cork, along with soldiers of the Williamite army, were 'buried . . . together in a hole almost every day'.[12] Similarly, it was noted that Lapp's Island was 'a place of melancholy note in penal times, for on it was a great open grave, into which the bodies of men hanged at Gallows Green (now Greenmount) used to be thrown and also those who died of epidemics'.[13] Further, an archaeological study undertaken by Cork City Council has identified several hitherto unrecognised burial sites.[14] It has also pinpointed several areas outside the existing boundaries of churches where burials may lie beneath modern buildings and streets. This study brings to our attention several references to burials outside of known cemeteries where, due to taboo or desperation, bodies were dumped in pits and mass graves.

Burial practices

In medieval times, the burial practice was invariably extended inhumation. Wood-lined graves were popular in the eleventh century, constructed either from planks laid end to end or occasionally from hollowed tree trunks. Charcoal-filled graves were a rare feature of eleventh-century funerary practice, while partial charring of coffins to delay the decomposition of the wood remained a common practice until the thirteenth century. Stone-lined graves predominated from the twelfth to fourteenth centuries, while simple earth-cut graves were a constant feature throughout the medieval period.

Burials within the body of the church were common from the mid-eleventh century onwards. Those who could afford it were buried in special places within the church, such as close to the chancel or within chantry chapels, as it was believed that proximity to the chancel ensured greater consideration in the after-life. Tomb effigies, carved slabs and memorials became increasingly popular in the medieval period. Outside the medieval churches few graves were marked with enduring memorials. Inscribed slabs became increasingly common in the eighteenth century, while the wealthy began to construct elaborate tombs and mausoleums based on classically derived architectural motifs. Such tombs are generally associated with the Protestant ascendancy and fine examples survive at St Anne's, Shandon, and St Fin Barre's Cathedral (Fig. 1.100).

The use of crypts became a feature beneath early eighteenth-century churches. This was influenced by the contemporary fashion for burial within the church building; the crypt avoided disturbing the interior of the church. Burials within the crypts were not interred, but the wooden and metal coffins were stacked in locked chambers within the vaults. Such burials remain in St Anne's, Shandon, and St Paul's. Pre-existing burials within the floors of the medieval churches must have been exhumed and re-buried or dumped along with the demolished buildings.

Except for crypts and mausoleums, the vast majority of post-medieval to modern burials were in earth-cut graves, generally in wooden coffins. Lead caskets are occasionally used by the wealthy, whilst in the 1980s and 1990s there has been an increase in the popularity of cremation and urn burial. Modern funerary practices are in the early phase of transition and, in common with the Late Bronze Age and Early Iron Age, both extended inhumations and urn burials are on occasions placed in the same grave within Cork's municipal cemeteries (see *The First People*, Chapter 5). Outside of the dominant Christian burial traditions, the occurrence of human remains in mass graves and pits without any significant ritual associations was always a factor. In times of war or epidemic, such contingencies were the only resort. Unbaptised infants, unidentified sailors, suicides and executed criminals were generally refused burial in consecrated ground by church authorities. As a result, the burial of executed criminals frequently took place in pits close to the gallows or in other designated places, while the tradition of burying unbaptised infants in specially set apart places was a common practice throughout Ireland from at least the eighteenth century, although the practice ended in the early twentieth century.

TREATMENT OF BODIES

The dismembering of the bodies, especially the decapitation of those convicted of treason, was common in medieval times. Heads and other body parts were frequently displayed in prominent positions on medieval city walls or gates. Heads impaled on spikes, for example, are represented outside the North and South Gates castles in the *Pacata Hibernia* plan of Cork *c.* 1585. Five decapitated heads on spikes are also shown on John Fitzgerald's 1797 drawing of South Gate Bridge). Such skulls were frequently discarded in the mud where they fell or were dumped with

Fig. 1.99 A) Crypt and burial from Cornmarket Street. (Photo: *Irish Examiner*.) B) Excavation of a stone-lined grave, of a twelfth- to fourteenth-century date, in the area of St Mary's of the Isle, Cross's Green. (Photo: Cork Corporation.)

Fig. 1.100 A) Eighteenth- and nineteenth-century grave slabs and more elaborate tombs at St Fin Barre's Cathedral. B) Tomb of the Murphy family and graveyard memorials at St Peter's church, Carrigrohane. (Photos: Robert Devoy.)

refuse. Finds of several perforated skulls from Dublin excavations provide grim evidence of this practice.[15]

Some bodies were deliberately hidden and the remains of victims of unsolved murders lie undetected. The remains of bodies acquired for anatomical research in the past may also be poorly documented. The skeletal remains uncovered at Cove Street in the early 1980s are reputed to have been the result of the burial of body parts used in such research.[16] Perhaps the most unusual and least considered source of human remains is that of poorly recorded archaeological finds. An example of this is the recovery of an Egyptian mummy beneath the floorboards of the Pathology Lecture Theatre at UCC; this discovery was the result of an undocumented acquisition by an academic![17]

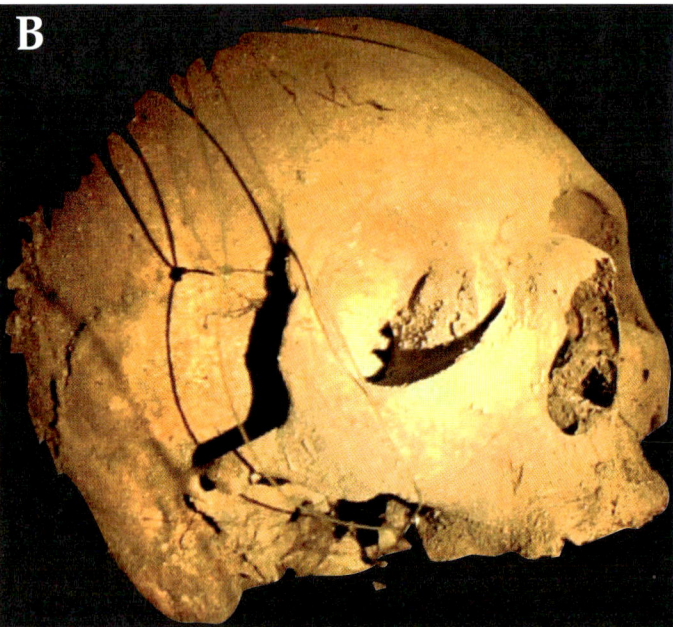

Fig. 1.101 A) Drawing of heads on spikes, North Gate Bridge. (Source: *Pacata Hibernia*, c. 1585.) B) An ancient skull from a burial in Cork. (Photo: *Irish Examiner*.)

St Mary's of the Isle

Maurice Hurley

The Dominican priory of St Mary's of the Isle, Cross's Green (also known as Crosses Green), founded in 1229, was one of an early group of houses established by the order in Ireland.[1] The priory was founded by Lord Philip de Barry on a marshy island to the south-west of the walled city. The site was excavated in 1993.[2] Two hundred graves were excavated, 109 in the area of the church and 91 in the cloister area. The burials included men, women and children, confirming the historical evidence that the Dominican priory at Cork was a favoured burial place for rich and poor alike. The Earl of Desmond's petition to Queen Mary in 1557 stated that the restoration of the church to the Dominicans would 'do much good amongst your grace's poor savage people of these parts that knoweth not decently where to be buried'.[3] The Earl's letter also stated that 'a great part of all the gentlemen and lords here abouts have their monuments', implying that the friaries were favoured by the nobility over parish churches as burial places.

The important part played in the development of Cork by the Dominicans is not widely recognised. Before the excavation of the priory of St Mary's, the main sources for the physical appearance and location of this monastic site were ancient maps. The island on which the priory stood lay to the west of the medieval walled town. This island was shown on several ancient maps. The *Pacata Hibernia* map of *c.* 1585 depicts a church of St Mary's of the Isle with a spire on the south-west side of Cork (see Chapters 10, 11 and 12). A mill building straddling a stream is also shown and the island is linked to the south bank by a bridge. The domestic buildings are not depicted. Similarly, on John Speed's plan of 1610, the church, with a central tower, is shown on a triangular island and there are no associated buildings. In a map of Cork from *c.* 1690 St Mary's is shown in a similar location. The church appears to have a tower and associated buildings to the north and south. A curved wall encloses an area to the north-east of the church and the island is linked to the south bank by two bridges. A mill appears to straddle the stream.

The Dominicans, or Black Friars, first came to Ireland in 1224, initially establishing their priories in Dublin and Drogheda. Within 30 years they had moved into many parts of Ireland in the wake of the Norman colonisation. By 1250 the Dominicans had a dozen friaries in Ireland.[4] The Dominican priory in Cork, known as St Mary of the Isle (also called St Mary's of the Isle, or St Dominick's Priory, or Abbey, and now St Marie's of the Isle) was one of the first houses established by the order. The rapid spread of the Dominicans, as well as the Franciscans, in Britain and Ireland owed as much to the patronage of the new orders by powerful Anglo-Norman lords as to the zeal and religious conviction of the friars. Gaelic chieftains were also connected with many of the early Dominican foundations; for example, at Limerick,

Fig. 1.102 Excavation of a grave from the priory church and cloister area at Cross's Green. (Photo: Cork Corporation.)

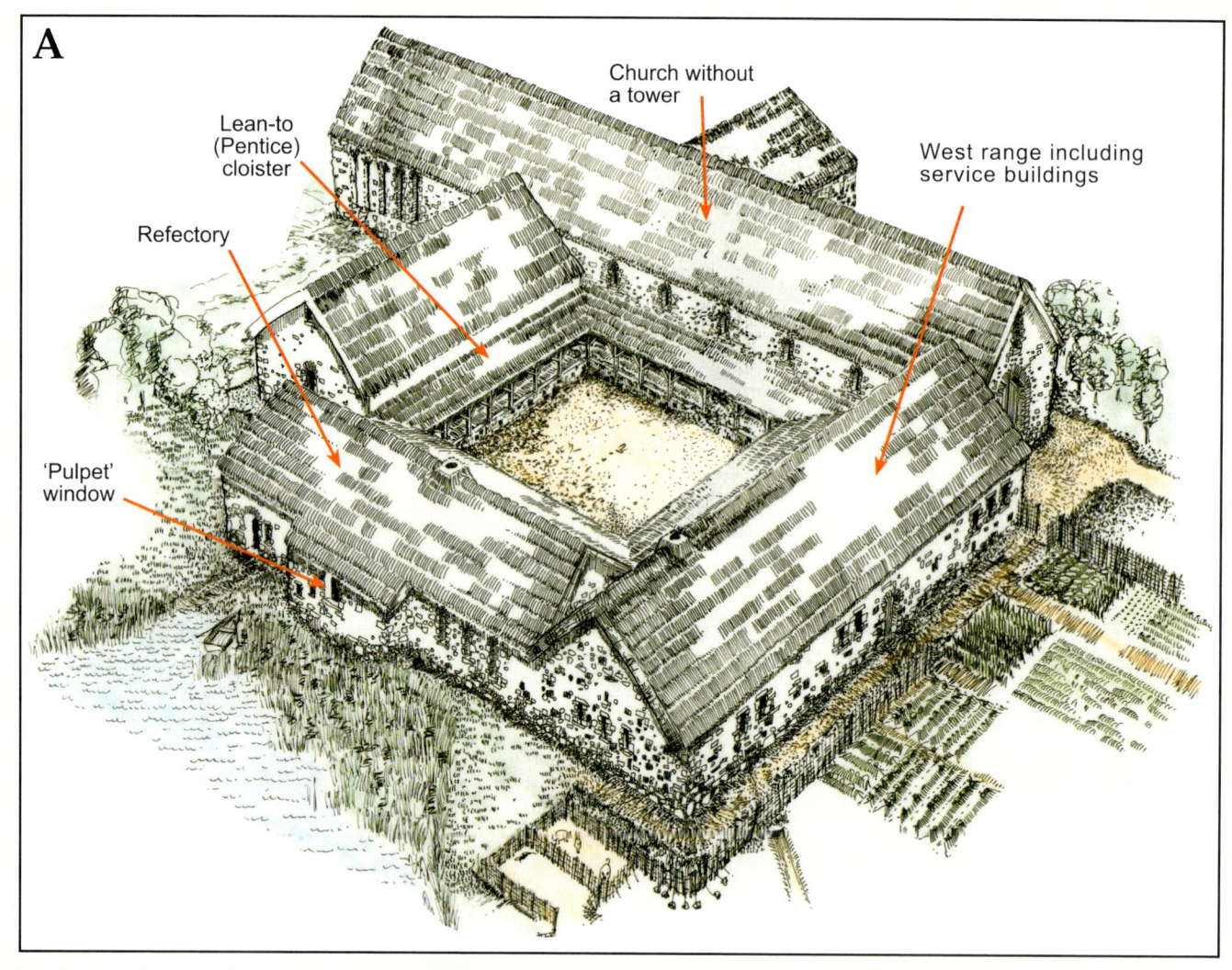

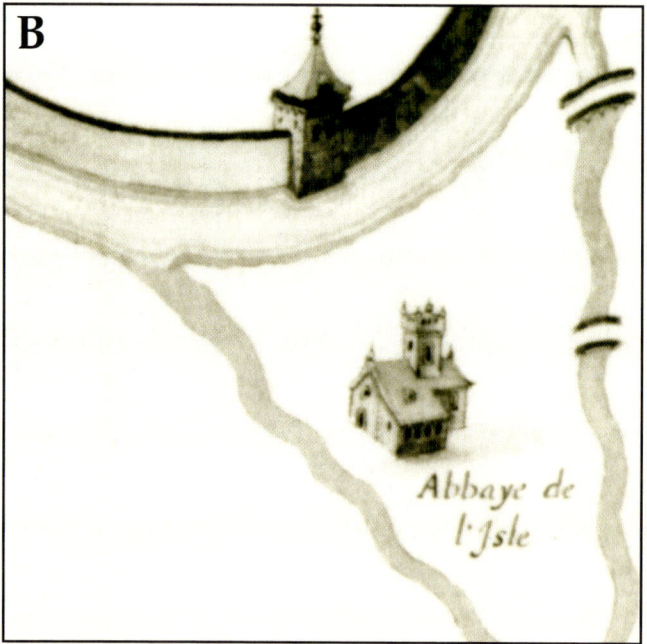

Fig. 1.103 A) An artist's impression of the thirteenth-century Dominican priory of St Mary's of the Isle. (Drawing: Donal Anderson, Cork City Council.) B) Depictions of St Mary's of the Isle from *Plan de Corke* (Abbaye de L'Isle) *c.* 1610–50. (Source: Private collection.)

Athenry and Roscommon. Regardless of racial divide or political interest, the orders were eager to establish themselves in, or as close as possible to, urban centres, though in Ireland rural sites were also used. The establishment of the priories in the thirteenth century closely reflects the growth of towns and cities in the Anglo-Norman colony.

Early Dominican churches were required to be low and without a tower, but the church at St Mary's of the Isle, Cork, was described as magnificent, 'magnifica ecclesia'. Perhaps a greater testimony to its stature was the residence, in 1381, of Edmund Mortimer, who came to Cork as Lord Lieutenant of Ireland and resided at the Dominican priory until his death.[5] Historical records that

Fig. 1.104 A) Excavated areas of St Mary's of the Isle and B) a reconstruction of the ground plan of the buildings.

refer to the physical layout, nature and extent of the priory mostly relate to lists and grants post-dating the Dissolution in 1541. It was reported that 'the church belfry and two chapels can be thrown down . . . All other buildings and houses in the precinct are suitable for the necessary use of the farmer'.[6] In 1557, during the reign of Queen Mary, an attempt was made to restore the priory to the Dominicans. Its post-medieval history is sketchy though. In 1578 the Protestant bishop publicly burnt a statue of St Dominic. The Dominicans were re-established on the site in the reign of James I and remained there until the Williamite capture of Cork in 1690 (see *Sixteenth- and Early Seventeenth-Century Cork*, Chapter 11). In 1689, King James II is recorded as having 'lodged in the house of the Dominican fathers, and on Sunday heard mass in the church of the Franciscans, called the North Abbey'. After 1690 the priory was used as the residence of the mayor of the city and was called the Great House of St Dominic's. In 1721 the Dominicans

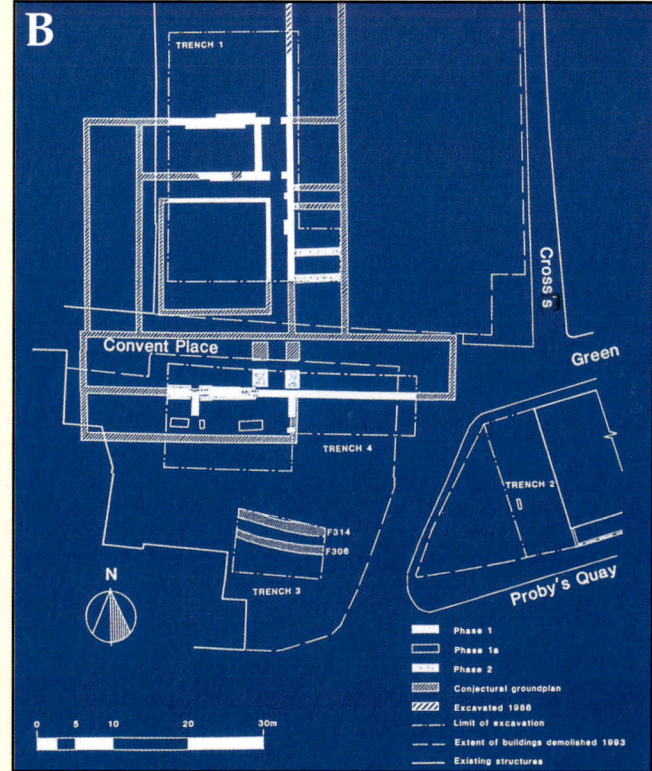

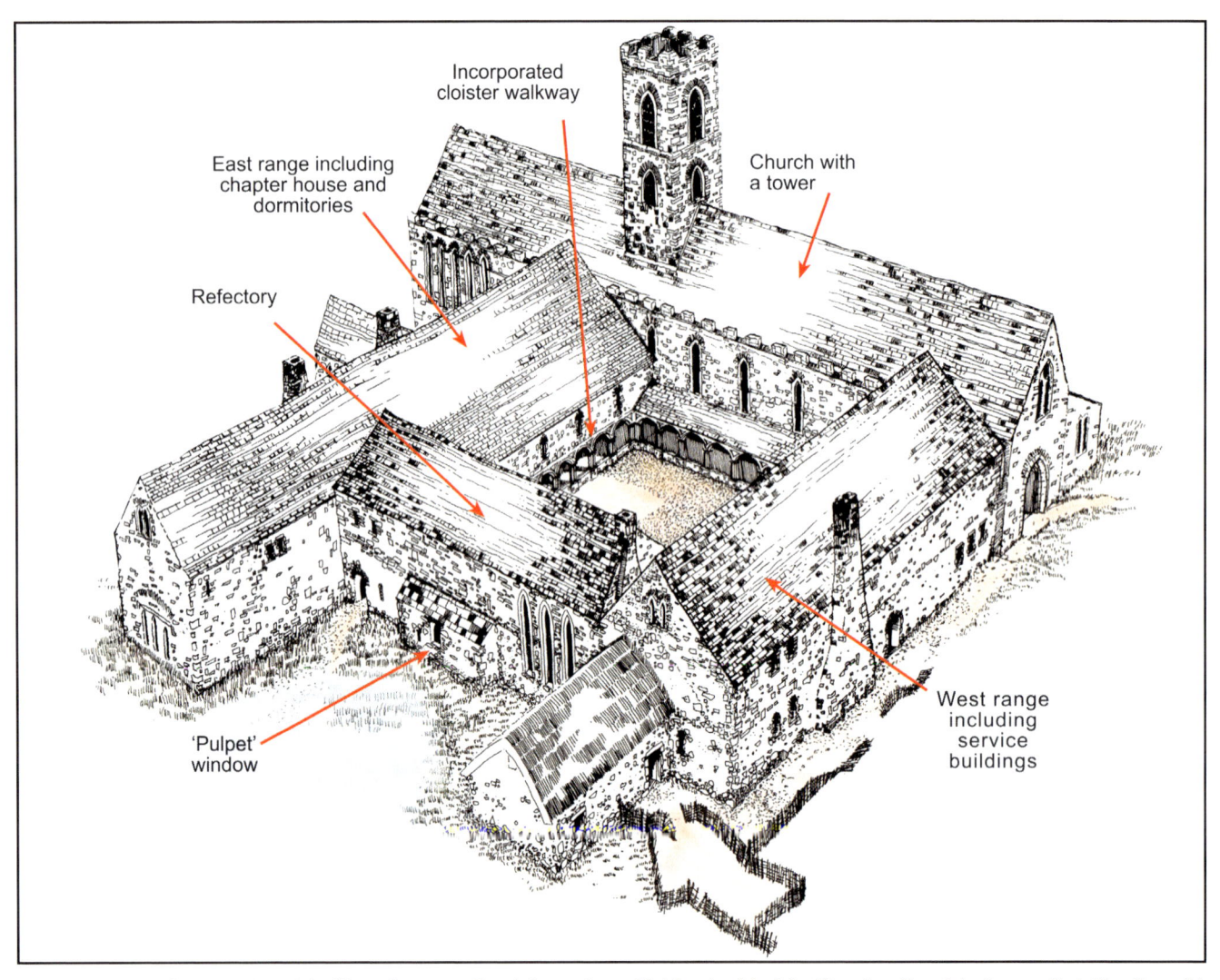

Fig. 1.105 An artist's impression of the fifteenth-century Dominican priory of St Mary's of the Isle. (Drawing: Donal Anderson, Cork City Council.)

established a new community residence in Shandon, and today the order is located at St Mary's, Pope's Quay.[7]

Excavation of the priory site was necessitated by the re-development of the area. At the time of excavation, the site had most recently been occupied by two mills, a few domestic houses and a large complex of sheds and related structures.[8] The excavation of the priory evidenced two major structural phases and in both of these the buildings were of stone. The evidence for the church was fragmentary, due to extensive disturbance by modern foundations. It was not possible to establish a clear ground plan of the thirteenth-century church, although a number of walls were found from this building. The church was modified in the late fourteenth to fifteenth century (Fig. 1.104). The second church was probably a taller building with a tower at the crossing (Fig. 1.105).

The cloister of St Mary's of the Isle was located to the north of the church. The excavation centred on the north side of the cloister and the north range of domestic buildings. The cloister was probably square, measuring approximately 20 m × 20 m, and two phases of building were identified. The first phase was free standing. It was defined by a continuous low sill-wall. This may have been a footing that supported a series of wooden arcade pillars. It was probably a lean-to structure, as the north and east ranges were likely to have been single-storey buildings at this time. The second cloister (Phase 2) overlay the first. This cloister was probably of the integrated type, in that associated domestic buildings may have had an upper storey that projected over the cloister ambulatories. Stone arcading carried on twin shafts linked together probably supported this upper

Fig. 1.106 Excavation of St Mary's of the Isle, Cross's Green (also known as Crosses Green), showing the refectory, with the cloister and ambulatory. The well, seen in the centre, is a later addition. (Photo: Cork City Council.)

storey (Fig. 1.105). A cloister ambulatory of this type would have been open and without window glass.

Though the plans of Dominican priories were not the same everywhere, some common elements occur.[9] Characteristic features of a large room excavated in the north range of St Mary's of the Isle clearly define it as the refectory. A small room found to the east, with two opposing doorways, is of the proportions of a hall, or vestibule. The refectory was usually situated on the opposite side of the cloister from the church. At St Mary's it was a long rectangular room set parallel to the cloister ambulatory. Within the refectory a ribbon of stones formed a border surrounding a central rectangular zone. This is likely to have been the 'foot-pace', a feature usually located along the side walls where benches and tables for the community were placed. A pulpit was set in one wall towards the upper end of the room. This projected from the north wall of the refectory, was reached by a narrow flight of mural steps from within the room and probably contained a reader's window.

'A survey of the city and suburbs of Cork' by John Rocque, 1759.

2
Transformation

TRANSFORMATION
A MINOR PORT TOWN BECOMES
A MAJOR ATLANTIC PORT CITY

INTRODUCTION

Patrick O'Flanagan

In this section we look at the processes responsible for the conversion of a small regional port into a significant maritime commercial centre with a powerful transatlantic presence. For Cork this entailed the settlement passing through a number of phases, evident in the nature, rhythm and scale of its physical expansion, its population

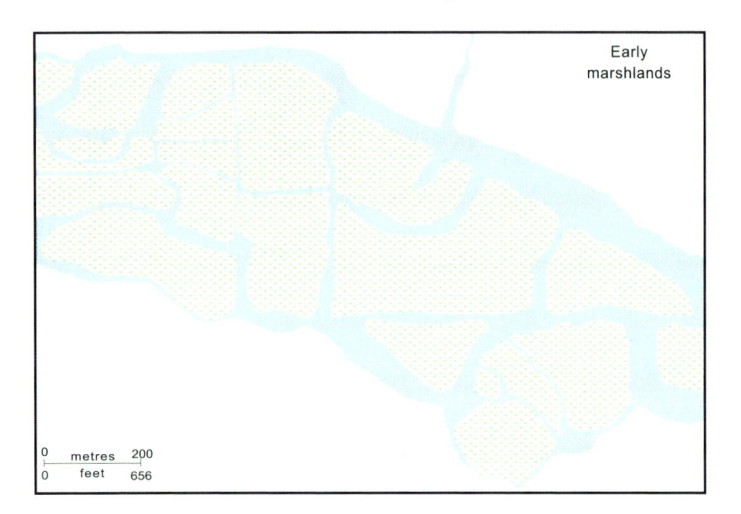

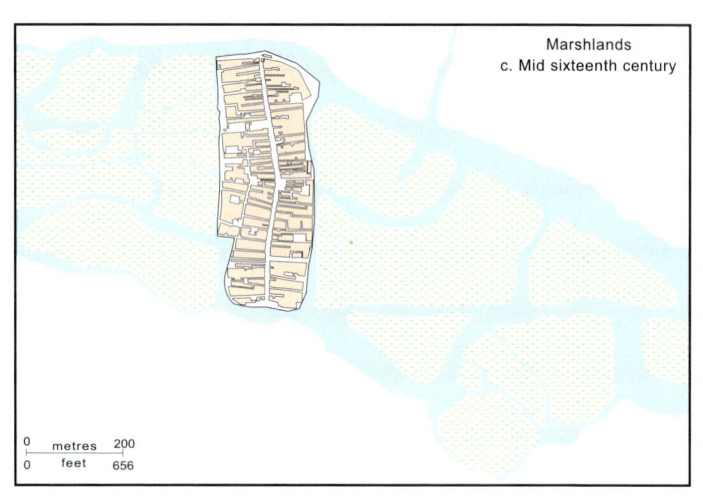

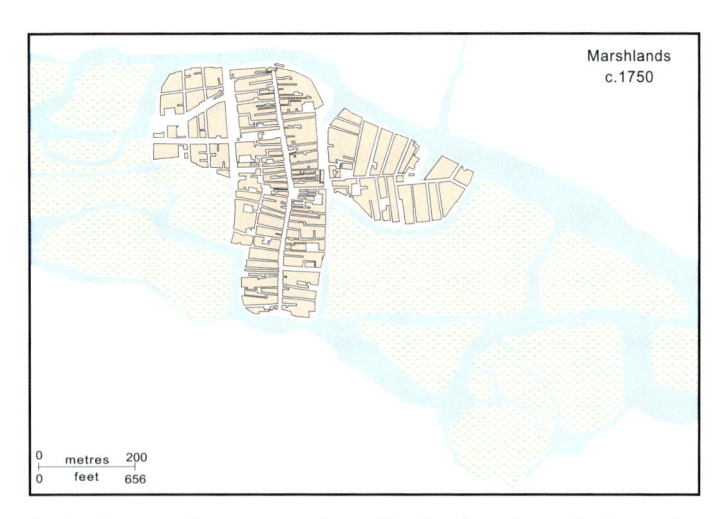

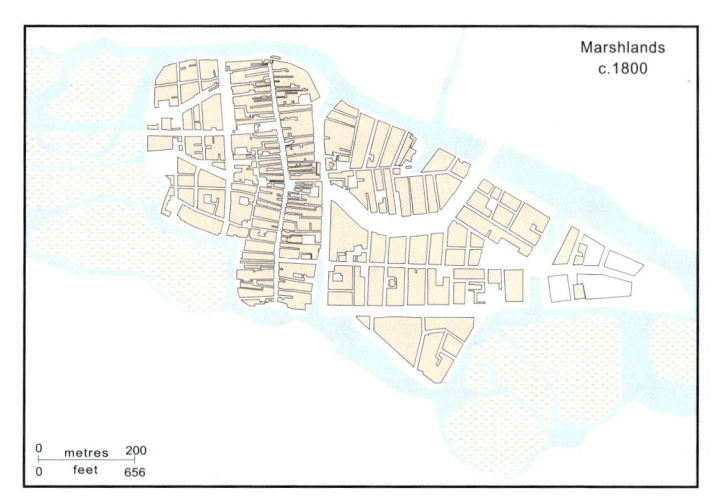

Fig. 2.1 Stages in the sequence of marshland reclamation and urbanisation.

Fig. 2.2 'View of Cork', John Butts, *c.* 1760. This famous and iconic view of Cork allows us to focus in on particular buildings and recognise Dutch and Flemish house styles. It provides a marvellous prospect of the waterfront and indicates dense development around Shandon. (Crawford Municipal Art Gallery.)

growth rates, the amplification of its foreland and hinterland, its emergence as Ireland's premier transatlantic port city and the evolution of its distinctive confessional and ethnic content.

It would be a misconceived endeavour to regard Cork's development as somehow unique. Many other port cities along Europe's Atlantic façade, such as Porto and Vannes, shared its robust growth based on the successful commercialisation of the products of their hinterlands. In an Irish context, however, Cork's success is distinctive. With few early buildings surviving, an understanding of its street plans at different times helps us comprehend how the marshes were embanked and reclaimed, the channels culverted and the islands urbanised (Fig. 2.1).

Up to the sixteenth century, in terms of commercial vitality and population, it was only third or fourth in the league of Munster's major ports, smaller than Waterford, Youghal and perhaps even Kinsale. By 1242, Cork was already acting as a pivotal wine-importing centre. In the late sixteenth century, because of Europe's deepening involvement with the transatlantic world, Ireland's location became increasingly commercially and strategically significant. Mercantile and military competition between several European states prompted England's re-engagement with Ireland. The Munster plantation was England's first major attempt to pacify and exploit what was then regarded as both a suspect population occupying a strategic territory with the bonus of being a well-endowed resource base.

While the town of Cork was not 'planted', it increasingly experienced a series of consequences of English commercial and military involvement. These pressures culminated in sustained ethnic cleansing during the Cromwellian interlude of the 1650s, which was subsequently repeated after the 1690 siege. Floods and fires over the same period also precipitated a number of calamities.

One of the products of outside involvement was the early appearance of a series of intricate maps, paintings and plans of the settlement. By the eighteenth century, some of these were masterpieces in their own right. They allow us to reconstruct the physical expansion of what had now become a city. The rapid rise of the provisions trade underwrote Cork's commercial success. Functional specialisation and

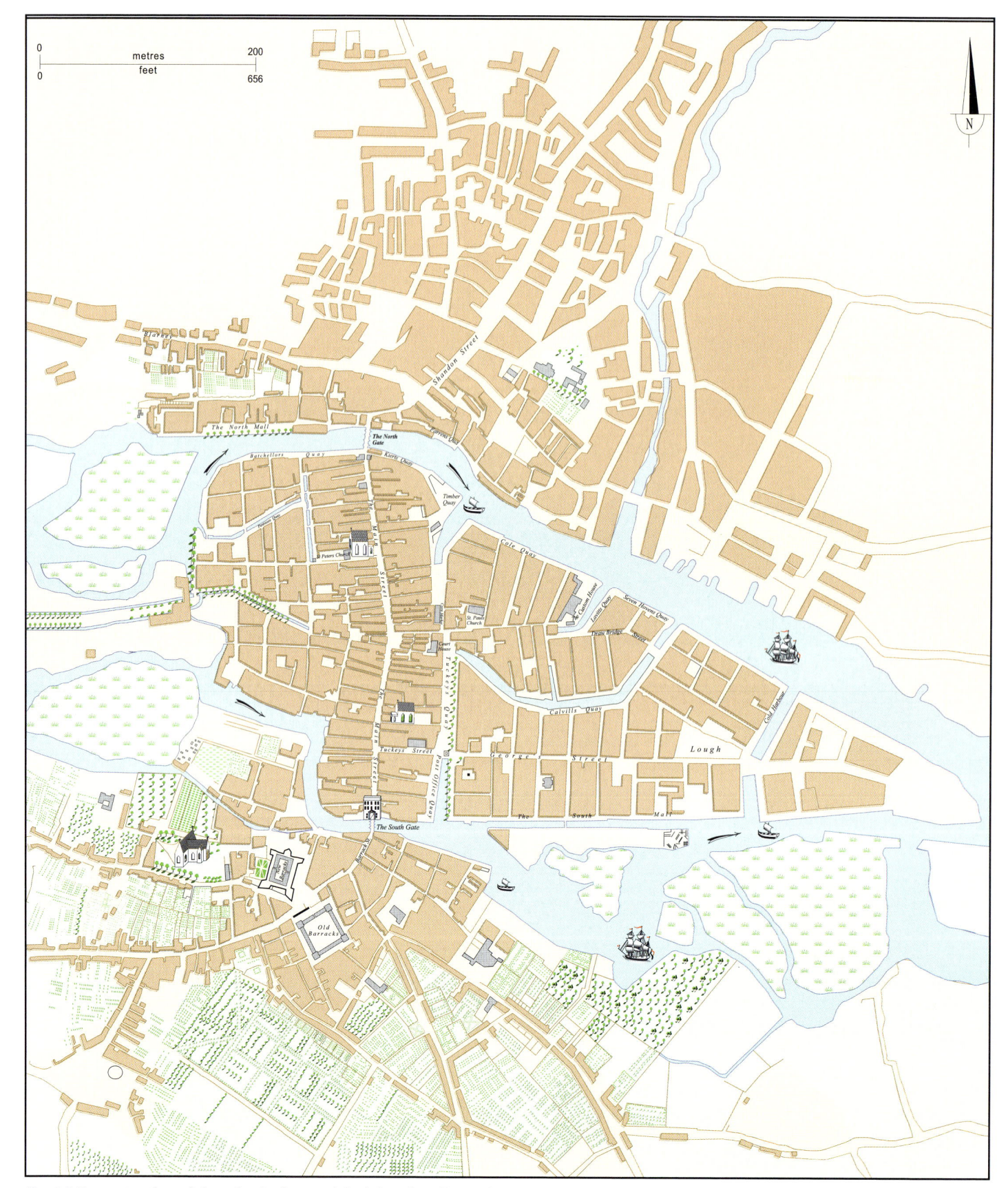

Fig. 2.3 Reconstruction of the urbanised core of Cork based on Rocque's 1759 map. Rocque's two maps, dating to 1759 and 1773, represent critical cartographic landmarks. Rocque's work was anticipated by Carty's fine 1726 depiction, which is the first real 'map' of the city.

Fig. 2.4 This magnificent portrayal of St Patrick's Quay by Gilbert gives a clear impression of wharf activities. (Source: Crawford Municipal Art Gallery.)

occupational diversification during the golden years of the eighteenth century generated many paradoxes. The Anglican community was acutely proud of its achievements; it was equally cognisant of the growing challenges that it faced from a hesitant but burgeoning Catholic underbelly. Roman Catholics were evident in the professions and controlled some key areas of the urban economy, notably the butter sector.

Mercantile achievements were by no means the sole outcome of Anglican endeavour and the crucial contributions of other newcomers, notably the Huguenot and Quaker communities, are underlined. In addition, functional diversification had a finely tuned spatial representation, especially in the Shandon district. For some, Cork was a honey-pot of opportunity and promise. For most, especially the immigrant poor, it was a prison of unfulfillable aspirations. The life-work of one of the city's outstanding eighteenth-century inspirational characters, Nano Nagle, resonates with its own peculiar geography and underlines the gravity of Cork's social problems.

10. THE ANGLO-NORMANS AND BEYOND

Kenneth Nicholls

Before the Anglo-Norman, or Anglo-French, invasion of Ireland, the Ostman city of Cork consisted of the present South Main Street area, with its church dedicated (as in other Ostman towns) to the Holy Trinity (Christ Church), and a small area south of the South Gate Bridge. To the south-west was the ancient ecclesiastical establishment of St Finbarr, with a group of dependent churches, joined from the mid-twelfth century by a community of Augustinian Canons Regular, the abbey of St Finbarr's Cave (Gill Abbey). On the north side of the river the MacCarthy kings of Desmond had established their residence at the 'old fortification' (*sean dún*), which gave its name to the present Shandon. When Henry II granted 'the kingdom of Cork', that is the MacCarthy kingdom of Desmond, to Robert FitzStephen and Milo de Cogan in 1177, he reserved the town and 'the cantred of the Ostmen' (Kerrycurrihy), and between 1185 and 1189 his son John, Lord of Ireland but not yet king, gave the first charter of incorporation to Cork (Fig. 2.5).

He granted them the privileges enjoyed by the city of Bristol, the main English port trading with Ireland, from which many of the new settlers who had arrived in Cork certainly came. A further charter of 1242 granted a new series of municipal and commercial privileges to the town, including exemption for its citizens from the tolls levied in other towns.[1] Before the invasion the MacCarthy kings had erected at Shandon that essential symbol of medieval lordship, a gallows for the execution of malefactors; when Shandon was no longer under direct royal control after 1177, the gallows moved south, eventually ending up on the Green or Faythe (*faithche*) of Cork, which became known as Gallows Green, the present Green Street. The bishop's claim to this area, for which the citizens paid a heavy rent to the king, was firmly rejected, and henceforth Gallows Green and the surrounding area remained an enclave of the town's jurisdiction surrounded by the lands of the bishop's manor. Confusingly, the manor was also called Faythe, as was the small corporate borough established on it. It was later called the manor of St Finbarr's.[2]

Shandon had been included in the extensive grant of territory made by Robert FitzStephen to his nephew Philip de Barry, and the latter had in turn granted it and the surrounding district (Uí Cuirb Liatháin) to Philip de Prendergast, who established at Shandon a corporate borough. The inhabitants of Shandon irritated the citizens of Cork by their infringement of the latter's monopoly on trading privileges, until they were eventually crushed by decrees of the Justiciar's Court in 1289 and 1300 (Fig. 2.6).[3]

Religious houses

Following the Anglo-Norman invasion a large number of new religious establishments sprang up around Cork (see *Christianity, Churches and Burial Places*, Chapter 9). Lands to the south-east of the town had been granted *c.* 1180 to the Benedictine monks of St Nicholas priory, Exeter. Here they

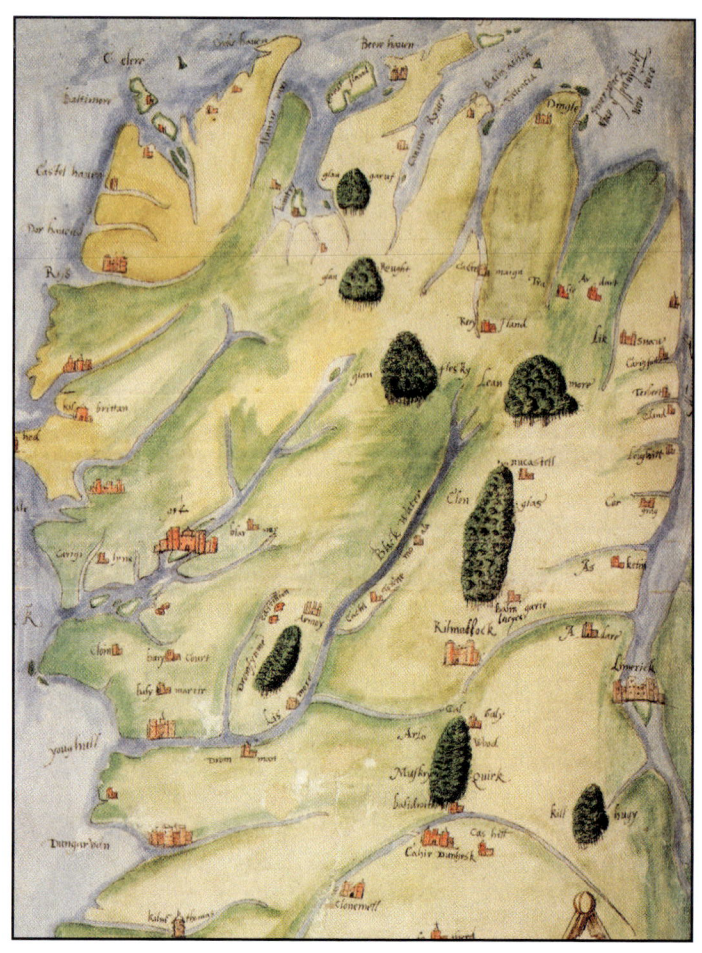

Fig. 2.5 Map of Munster, *c.* 1580. This early map provides a contemporary impression of the lie of the land in Munster on the eve of the great plantation. It depicts Cork as a bulky settlement and indicates the position of the principal rivers and forests. (Source: PRO.)

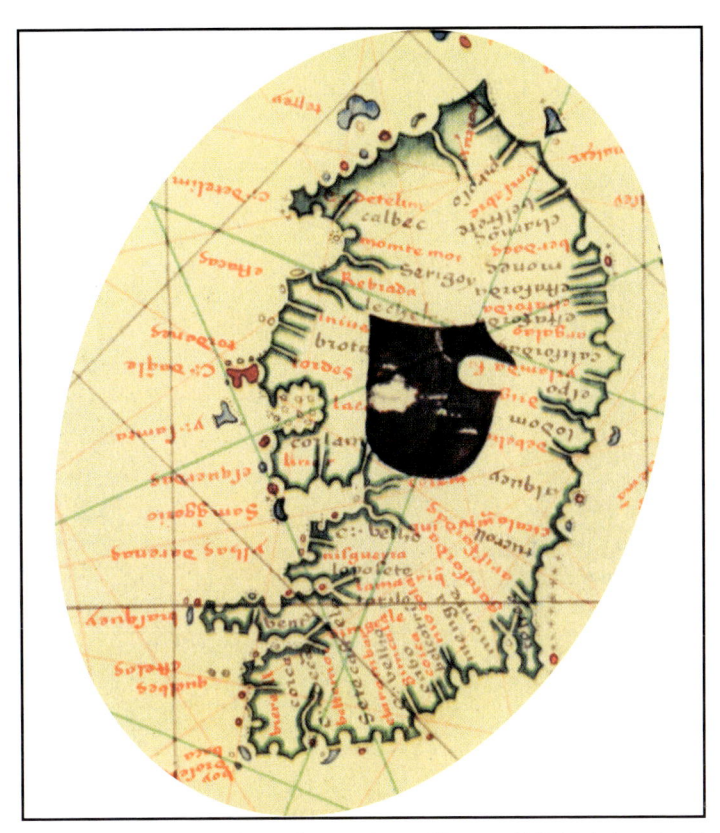

Fig. 2.6 A Portolan of the Irish coast, Lopo Homen, 1519. This is a detail from a larger plan of Atlantic Europe. Portolan charts were produced to aid navigation, colonisation and commerce. They often represent the very first systematic attempt to map landmasses, islands and oceans. (Source: A Cortesão and A. Teixeira da Mota, *Portugaliae monumenta cartographica*, Volume 1, Lisbon, 1960.)

major and many minor urban centres. As usual, they settled in the suburbs.

The Franciscans in Shandon and the Dominicans on a probably unoccupied island to the south-west (St Mary's of the Isle) both seem to have arrived around 1229; the Augustinians, whose house (later called the Red Abbey) was between the two St John's, came later in the century. The mention in 1479 of a lane in Shandon called 'the little bowhyr (*bothair*) of the Sakeris' (apparently the modern Eason's Avenue, formerly Old Chapel Lane) suggests that the short-lived order of the Friars of the Sack may have arrived at Cork, as they did in Dublin, in 1268, before their suppression by the Council of Lyon in 1274. Finally, Cork's two hospitals for the lepers whose facial disfigurement inspired such contemporary horror, St Stephen's in the south suburbs and St Mary Magdalene's in Shandon, were apparently insufficient to cater for the victims of this

established the cell or priory of St John the Evangelist, which between 1191 and 1199 obtained a confirmation of its possessions from John as Lord of Ireland, and which before that had been transferred (perhaps in consequence of some property deal in England) to the priory of Bath. It subsequently came under the control of the latter's dependent priory of St John at Waterford. The priory was charged with maintaining a hospital for the poor and sick, though we are told that this duty was sometimes neglected. It possessed a street of houses, St John Evangelist Street (apparently the present Cove Street), subject to its own manorial jurisdiction and exempt from that of the town – which in 1297 sued the inhabitants for infringing their monopoly rights – but the exact location of this important establishment has not been positively identified.[4]

Further east, the Knights Hospitallers of St John of Jerusalem had already, before 1182, set up a house, with the attached church of St John the Baptist, and also possessed a street of houses (St John Baptist Street, now Douglas Street) subject to their own manorial jurisdiction. In the thirteenth century, that new religious phenomenon, the friars, established themselves at Cork, as they did at all

Fig. 2.7 Red Abbey Tower. The tower is one of Cork's most ancient buildings and prominent landmarks and was formerly part of an Augustinian foundation. (Photo: Maurice Hurley.) Inset shows a detail of Shandon Abbey, *Pacata Hibernia*, c. 1585.

disease, as we hear in 1306 of another small group of lepers settled outside the Dominican friary. By the sixteenth century, leprosy, which had been so prevalent in the thirteenth century, had become virtually extinct in Ireland.

BLACK DEATH

Thirteenth- and fourteenth-century Cork thus represented a sizeable settlement. The town itself had spread to include the island of Dungarvan, the North Main Street area around St Peter's church, which – although within the city walls – continued to be referred to as a 'suburb' as late as 1609.[5] North of the river was the feudal (and rival) borough of Shandon and on the south side was the bishop's borough of Faythe around Barrack Street and St Finbarr's and the autonomous streets of St John the Evangelist and St John the Baptist. But this was to change. The implosion of the English colony in Ireland had begun even before the devastating Bruce invasion of 1316–1318. It was helped by the private wars between the rival 'Anglo-Norman' lineages; that waged by the Barrys and Roches against the Cogans in the 1310s was particularly devastating and was exacerbated by the climatic deterioration which set in after 1316, leading to a switch from tillage to grazing, which ate away at the social and economic foundations of the colony.[6] Into this rapidly deteriorating situation came the disaster of the Black Death, which reached Ireland in July or August 1348 and quickly spread through the crowded urban communities. Ports were probably separately infected by ship-borne disease, and Cork seems to have suffered particularly heavily, while the plague coincided with a serious accidental fire which burned a quarter of the town and with attacks on its neighbourhood by 'Irish' enemies, probably Dermot MacDermot MacCarthy and his allies. In July 1351, the citizens dispatched the first of a series of petitions to the king in London, seeking a respite in the payment of the fee-farm, the rent which they paid to the king, and detailing their calamities and the loss of population through the plague, which had resulted in many empty houses.[7]

SUBURBAN CONTRACTION

In 1374–5 the suburbs north and south were burned by 'Irish enemies and English rebels', the latter led by William Barret; they were again burned in the early 1380s and were finally abandoned soon after 1400. The new charter granted to Cork by Edward IV in 1462 states that the suburbs, north and south, had been destroyed some fifty years before. This is abundantly supported by documentary evidence. Fifteenth- and sixteenth-century deeds (which for Shandon are relatively abundant) indicate that rebuilding did not

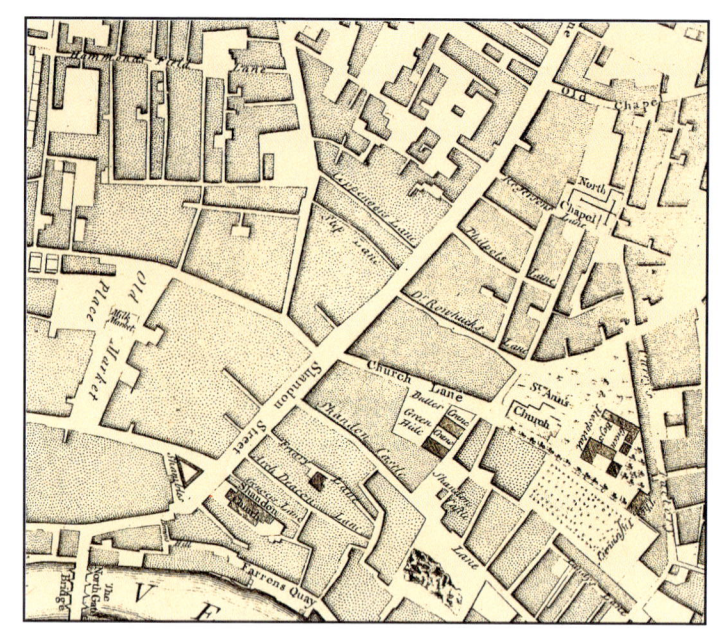

Fig. 2.8 This 1759 detail of Shandon Street by Rocque stresses its ancient and intricate urban fabric.

commence until late in Elizabeth's reign at the earliest. References to property in Shandon from the 1440s down to the 1570s are to gardens and orchards, not houses, although the survey of 1660 shows that by 1641 most of the area around Shandon Street (or Mallow Street as it was then called) and Blarney Street had been built over (Fig. 2.8). There is much less documentary evidence for the southern suburbs, but the surveys made at the suppression of the monasteries in 1541 again refer to gardens and empty house-sites, rather than houses. The dissolution of the religious houses in 1541 did not mean the destruction of their buildings, which remained in existence and were used for secular purposes into the seventeenth century. Again, it was not until the early seventeenth century that the orchards and gardens south of the river, like those of Shandon, began once more to be filled with dwellings.

EARLY CORE

Cork in this period, therefore, had been reduced to the two islands, separated by a narrow channel along the line of Castle Street and Liberty Street and linked by the single long street which survives as North and South Main Streets (Fig. 2.9). Elizabethan writers characterised Cork as 'but one street'. At each end, the North Gate and South Gate, there were wooden drawbridges (Fig. 2.10). On the wall at each gate was cut the standard perch measure, 29 feet in length, which formed the basis of the acre and mile used in the county. The buildings of the town, or at least the principal houses fronting the main street, are described by Luke Gernon in the 1620s as 'of stone and built after the Irish

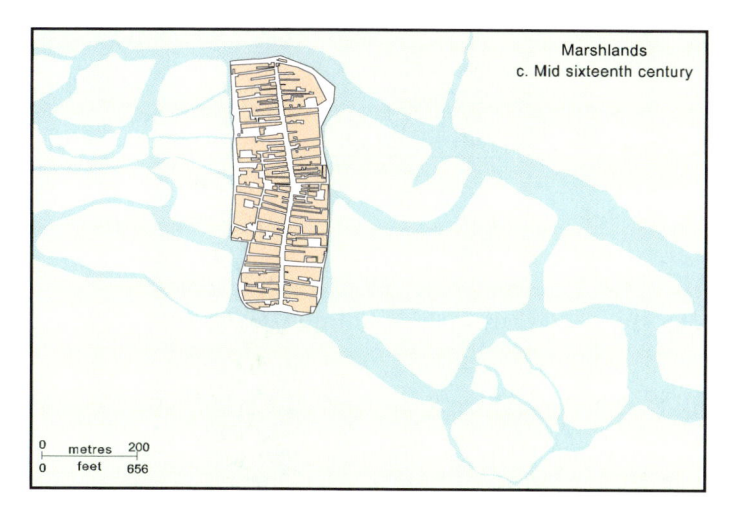

Fig. 2.9 Marshlands and urbanisation. This tentative mid-sixteenth-century depiction emphasises that most of Cork's marsh islands remained unreclaimed and their clogged channels were a hazard for shipping.

Fig. 2.10 Detail of wooden drawbridge, *Pacata Hibernia*, c. 1585.

forme, which is castle-wise and with narrow windows, more for strength than for beauty'. Most of this building in stone probably dated from the prosperous period of the late fifteenth and early sixteenth centuries. It seems likely that the early fifteenth-century town was mainly of timber and clay construction, as indeed were most of the smaller houses and buildings even in the seventeenth century. Most of the houses were thatched and, after the terrible fire of 1622, the Corporation decreed that all thatched roofs must be replaced by slate or shingles without delay.

Conditions within the narrow crowded confines of the town must have been unsanitary and unpleasant, and when plague came its ravages were severe. In April 1582 there were 200 deaths from plague and famine within the town. This was an an almost incredible figure, considering that only eight years before the Limerick Jesuit David Wolfe had estimated Cork's population within the walls at only 800, 'all merchants, fishermen and artisans'. Wolfe's figure seems remarkably low when one considers that in 1641 the old town on the islands had at least 159 'front houses' facing onto the street and perhaps twice that number of 'back houses', situated behind them in the plots which ran back from the street to the town wall (Fig. 2.11).

It is possible, of course, that many of these 'back houses' were of later date than Wolfe's time and represented an infill of the gardens behind the 'front houses' in response to a shortage of accommodation caused by population growth in the later Elizabethan period, before the reoccupation of the suburbs by housing in the more settled conditions after 1603. Another possible explanation is that Wolfe only counted the freemen and permanent inhabitants and their families, ignoring servants and other non-natives. We must, however, accept one or other of these explanations. If Wolfe's estimate of the population is correct, then the town within the walls must have been much less densely built up in 1574 than it had become by 1641; if, on the other hand, the density of housing had remained much the same, then his figure cannot be correct.

The collapse of the Anglo-Irish colony and the retreat of English administration and control during the fourteenth century left the port towns of the southern and western coasts, including Cork, isolated among territories ruled by Gaelic and Gaelicised lords, although in the early portion of the fifteenth century their position would seem to have been one of considerable stress and their relations with their neighbours generally hostile. A *modus vivendi* appears to have been reached by the second half of the century. An upturn in foreign trade led to an improvement in the position of the towns, which by 1500, although small, were prosperous and, by Irish standards, rich.

At the opening of the fifteenth century, Cork still retained links with the Dublin administration, although these were becoming increasingly tenuous. The town sent two representatives to the parliament of 1421, John Mythe (Miagh or Meade, to give the more usual forms of the name) and Geoffrey Galvy (Gallwey), but the county was only represented by the same John Mythe and by Thomas Halle, a Dublin administrator with no Cork connections. This would seem to be the last occasion on which the town and county agreed to contribute to the royal subsidy, for which collectors and assessors were duly appointed. It is uncertain, in the absence of evidence, whether the town of Cork returned members to the Irish parliament at any date

Fig. 2.11 Detail of streetscape and houses from a 1601–1602 plan confirms the view of Elizabethan writers that Cork was just 'one street'; many of the houses on 'the main street' were substantial buildings. (Source: Fig. 2.26 in Chapter 12.)

between 1421 and 1558, when parliamentary representation recommenced for certain.

REVIVAL

The impression from English customs records and other sources for the period is that, in the early fifteenth century, Kinsale may have been a more important and prosperous trading centre than Cork. If this impression is correct, then the cause is perhaps to be found in the geographical situation of Cork, situated at the head of a long harbour where shipping would be vulnerable to piratical attacks in the event of the breakdown of authority in the surrounding areas. In the early years of the fifteenth century the western shore of Cork harbour, Kerrycurrihy, constituted the last surviving portion of the once-great lordship of the Cogan family; under a succession of feeble lords it had collapsed, to the benefit of the ruthlessly expanding MacCarthys and the rising and Gaelicised Barrets. Robert Cogan, lord of Kerrycurrihy, was still listed among the magnates of County Cork in 1421, but in 1439 he sold his lands to James, sixth earl of Desmond. East of the harbour, the barony of Imokilly, whose feudal centre was Inchiquin near Youghal, was finally, after a century of dispute, brought firmly under Desmond control in this same period. It is hard not to believe that the union of the two sides of Cork harbour under the direct control of the great ruling family of Munster, once it had been firmly consolidated, would not have dramatically improved the security situation for shipping coming up to Cork itself and so lead to a revival of its trade at the expense of Kinsale (Fig. 2.12).

The 1441 acquisition by the great merchant family of Tirry of the island of Inysewenagh (later Inisheynagh or Haulbowline) may have been inspired by the desire to secure a post for the defence of shipping at a strategic point in the harbour mouth. The middle of the fifteenth century probably marked the beginning of an upsurge in the city's fortunes, an upsurge in fact shared by all the Irish port towns and arising from a dramatic increase in commercial activity, this time primarily oriented to the Iberian peninsula, not towards England as it had been in the thirteenth and fourteenth centuries.

CHARTERS

The municipal and commercial privileges granted to Cork in 1242 had been widely extended by royal charters in 1318 and 1323. Subsequent charters of that century were merely confirmations of these privileges. With the mid-fifteenth century begins a new series of royal charters conferring additional privileges and immunities on the Irish port towns, in part in response to successive petitions which stressed their largely spurious claims to be bastions of

Fig. 2.12 Thirteenth-century green glazed jug from Saintonge, France, excavated in South Main Street. (Photo: Cork Public Museum.)

'Englishness' and of obedience to royal authority (Fig. 2.13). The grant of fiscal privileges and exemptions, however, may also be seen as a practical recognition by the Crown and the Dublin administration of the impossibility of collecting taxes or customs duties in these isolated places. In 1443, the Irish Council had sought to compel the ports of Cork, Limerick and Galway to pay their fee-farms by asking the English Council to have their ships arrested at Bristol until they discharged the amounts due, but this attempt was dropped and the debts of Limerick and Cork were remitted soon after on the payment of a nominal sum.

Edward IV's charter of 1 December 1462 not only discharged the citizens of Cork from the payment of the hitherto accustomed fee-farm but also granted to them the cocket (the custom duty on wool, sheepskins and hides, the most important Irish export commodities) 'until such time as the citizens might peacefully go one mile beyond the walls'. This clause must have been inserted in response to an outrageous piece of deception put forward by the citizens of Cork to a gullible English monarch and Council. It is true that on account of the insecurity of the surrounding region and the danger of nocturnal raids, for fear of which the gates of the town were kept unopened from sunset to sunrise throughout the sixteenth century, the suburbs had been abandoned. But, to imagine that the citizens of Cork, with their network of trade connections in the adjacent regions, lived permanently beleaguered within their island town strains credulity.

However this may be, Cork's citizens retained possession of the cocket, and even the royal proceedings of 1609 against the fiscal exemptions of the Irish port towns failed to wrest it from them. Further charters of privileges to Cork from successive English monarchs followed in 1482, 1500, 1510 and 1537. In 1543, citizens claimed the right to trade in enemy goods in time of war. In 1576 Queen Elizabeth I conferred on Cork the right to appoint the customs officials, like a searcher or a gauger, whose appointment had hitherto rested (in theory) with the Crown. Also granted was the privilege to trade, except in arms and munitions of war, with enemies and foreigners (except pirates) in time of war, provided that such foreigners and enemies coming to trade should not be molested in the town

Fig. 2.13 Cork's evocative coat of arms reminds us that Cork's prime function was that of a well-defended port. This version is by Maclise and is set on the Custom House. (Source: Crawford Municipal Art Gallery.)

Fig. 2.14 A seal found in Cork.

or port. In addition, her charter granted them the right to receive all fines imposed within the town, even by the royal judges. This latter grant enabled the town to remit to its citizens, if it so wished, fines imposed on them by agencies of the central administration.

Fig. 2.15 Coat of arms of the Terry family, one of Cork's leading merchant families in medieval times. Later, branches of the Terry family were established at Cádiz and Málaga, indicating the importance of Cork merchant trading orbits in the wider Atlantic. (Source: K. Terry, *Terry's of Cork, 600–2000*, 2005.)

A further privilege unique to Cork was its right, dating from Henry III's charter of 1242, to the 'prize' of wines; a duty of one 'tun' of wine from every ship laden with up to twenty tuns and two tuns if it carried more. In all other Irish ports, except Waterford, the prize was an hereditary perquisite of the Butler family of Ormond. In Waterford, the town and the Ormonds shared the prize wines between them. In the early seventeenth century, the wine so taken was auctioned off privately among the members of the Corporation, the proceeds going to the municipal funds. Besides the formal privileges granted by charter, the numerous Elizabethan statutes which prohibited under penalty the export, especially to the Continent, of so many of Ireland's basic raw materials were not enforced against the merchants of the chartered port towns and in fact simply enhanced their monopolistic position. This turning of a blind eye was due to the financial reliance of the Irish administration on the duty on imported wines: if exports were prevented, there would be nothing to pay for the imported wine.[8]

PATRICIATE

A list of 'the ancient natives and inhabitants of the city of Cork', drawn up in 1652 after they had been finally expelled by the New English, contains 253 names: they include 36 Goolds, 28 Roches, 19 Tirrys, 18 Gallweys, 18 Coppingers and 18 Miaghs or Meades (two forms of the same name).[9] The Sarsfields, Morroghs and Mortells each numbered ten. More than half the freemen of the city at the end of the old order, therefore, belonged to six surnames, an illustration of the degree to which control of the town, its trade and administration at this period was exercised by a 'patriciate' of great merchant families. The ownership of the house property within the town would seem to have become similarly concentrated; unfortunately we have few records regarding the ownership of property in fifteenth-century Cork, but its pattern presumably resembled that in contemporary Kinsale, where it was quite widely distributed among the townsfolk, with individual artisans often owning their own dwellings. By 1641, as the Cromwellian surveys show, the ownership of house property in Cork had been monopolised by the urban patriciate referred to above. The rent return from urban property was extremely high when compared with the low value of land in the countryside, at least until the 1620s.

The Charters of Medieval Cork

A.F. O'Brien

A clear distinction must be made between the establishment of an urban, or proto-urban, settlement and the granting of a charter to it.[1] Cork's first charter did not mark the beginning of settlement in the location of the future city of Cork. Rather, it conferred on the existing settlement a legal personality whereby it became a body corporate enjoying a measure of autonomy under the English Crown. The charter, therefore, was a feudal instrument intended to mark off the settlement at Cork from its fully feudalised hinterland.

Urban boroughs would be profitable but could only thrive if they generated a level of economic activity appropriate to their status and situation. In order to attract settlers to a borough in the first place, it was essential to confer on it a measure of autonomy, whereby it would be freed from the more rigid constraints of the feudal socio-economic system which prevailed outside it. The charter was an instrument designed to confer this autonomy and a device designed to unleash economic prosperity.

Henry II's charter of 1177 granted the kingdom of Cork, the whole demesne of Desmond, to Robert FitzStephen and Miles de Cogan, and retained to the English Crown in perpetuity 'the city of Cork' and the lands of the Ostmen adjacent to it. That charter, however, did not confer any distinctive urban rights. In the following half-century the basis of Cork's municipal autonomy was established and the model chosen for Cork – and for the king's other larger Irish towns, Waterford, Limerick and Dublin – was the one granted to the city of Bristol. Accordingly, Cork's first charter of liberties, privileges and immunities was granted by Prince John, as lord of Ireland, possibly in 1185, but probably in 1189. The original charter no longer exists and we are, therefore, dependent on a thirteenth-century undated transcript.

The charter made two provisions. It granted the burgesses of Cork the land on which it was situated to hold off the English Crown in free burgage in perpetuity. The principal characteristics of free burgage were (1) the payment of money rent in lieu of all services and (2) the right of the holder of land in free burgage to sell and devise his property at will. The burgesses held that their burgages were free from other feudal obligations and charges. The charter, moreover, granted to the city of Cork in perpetuity all the franchises and free customs which Bristol had, but these laws and customs were not specified. This matter was clarified in a number of subsequent charters, whereby the autonomy and jurisdiction of the city was significantly extended.

The charter of 1242 provided for a wide range of autonomy, both administrative and judicial, while it sought to promote the internal and external trade of the city. The basic privilege it bestowed, central to the question of autonomy, was the right to hold the town of the English Crown in free burgage on payment of a yearly fee-farm rent. In addition to the concession of the fee-farm, the charter gave the burgesses wide jurisdiction in the administration of law and justice. Notable among the provisions was the stipulation that the burgesses of Cork were to distrain for debt within the town and all pleas concerning debts incurred there were to be heard in accordance with its customs.

A further charter of 20 July 1318 confirmed the charter of 1242 and augmented the privileges enjoyed by the citizens under existing charters. Subsequent charters of 1323 and 1330 reiterated existing liberties and further extended them. Cork's charters were confirmed in 1382, 1400, 1413, 1423, 1464, 1482 and 1500. All of them, with the exception of the charter of 1482, added little to existing privileges and immunities. The particular importance of the charter of 1482 is that it extended the area of Cork's jurisdiction to include much of the harbour region. By the early fourteenth century, Cork's basic urban autonomy, enshrined in a series of charters, was well established.

11. SIXTEENTH- AND EARLY SEVENTEENTH-CENTURY CORK

Kenneth Nicholls

The exclusion of the craftsmen and tradesmen from the local government of the Irish towns in favour of the merchant class was probably a development of the late fifteenth century, though its roots may well have been earlier. In the Scottish towns an exactly similar development took place at the same period, resulting in the permanent depression of the crafts and trades in favour of the merchants. The economic backwardness of both Ireland and Scotland was probably an important factor in bringing about this change in both countries, since it meant that, on the one hand, local crafts and industry were weak and there was perhaps even a lack of demand for their products. On the other hand, comparatively large profits were to be made from the foreign trade of the merchants who exported local products; largely raw materials and the produce of unorganised rural crafts, imported manufactured goods and such staple necessities as iron, salt and wine.

In the case of the Irish towns, supplies of grain and other foodstuffs had also to be continually imported, since it was not until the establishment of peace in the seventeenth century that they could secure sufficient supplies from the depopulated and underdeveloped countryside. There is no doubt of the wealth – by the standards of so poor a country as Ireland, if not by those of England or the other richer parts of contemporary Europe – which the merchant communities of the Irish port towns derived from their trading activities between the late fifteenth and early seventeenth centuries, a wealth to be seen in the silver plate and household goods owned by Cork merchants of the Elizabethan period. From that period on, it was to be massively invested in land purchase in the regions surrounding the ports.

The trading activities of the Irish merchants were not confined, either, to an exclusively Irish trade. In an unpublished study, A.F. O'Brien has confirmed the involvement of merchants from the south Irish ports in

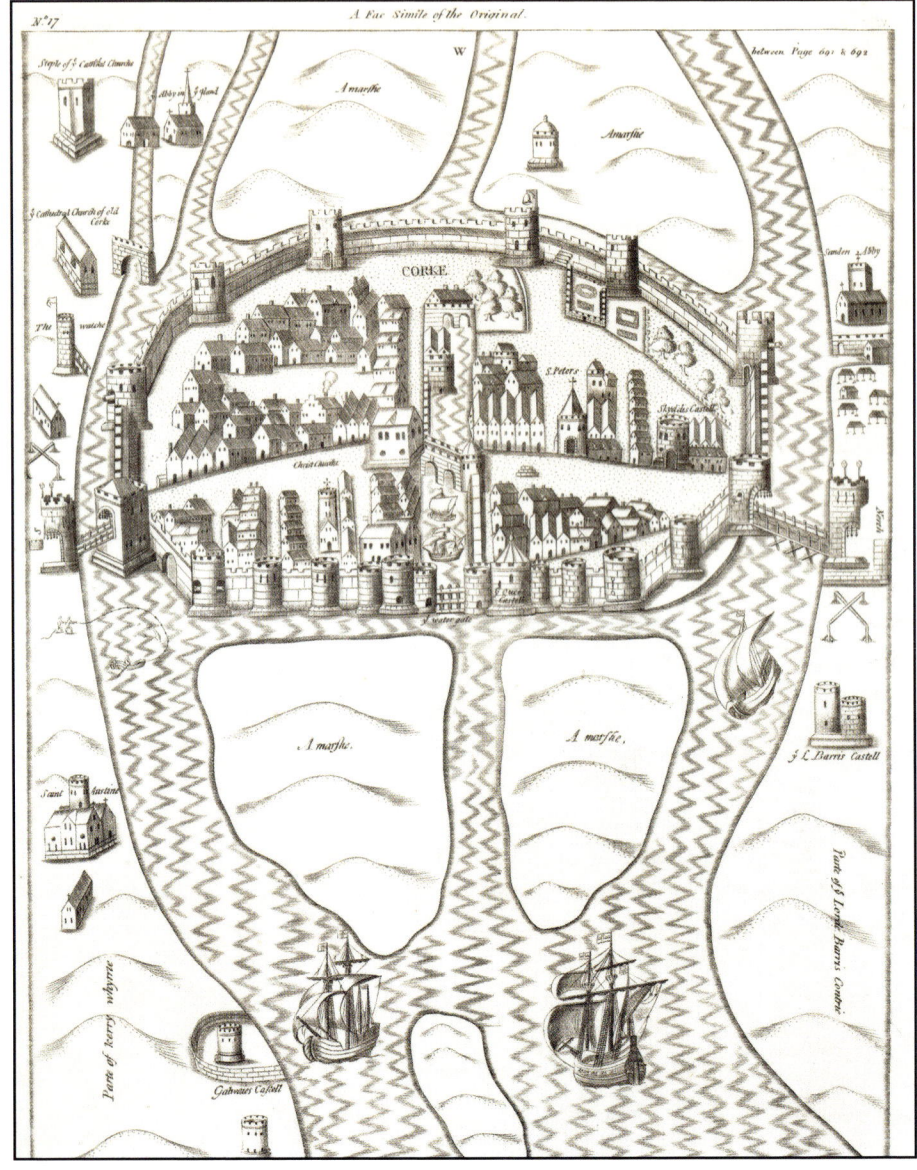

Fig. 2.16 The *Pacata* plan of Cork, dating to the 1580s, is the first known attempt to illustrate Cork's urban fabric. Besides providing a useful impression of the city walls, it is possible to identify some of the settlement's major public buildings. (Source: *Pacata Hibernia*, Dublin, 1810.)

carrying Spanish and Portuguese produce and, after the discovery of the sea route to India in 1497, Indian produce brought to Lisbon and on to England. From England, foodstuffs and manufactured goods would be brought to Ireland, while Irish produce – most importantly hides, but also furs, timber, linen and the heavy Irish mantles and other wool products – went both to England and to Spain, Portugal and the Mediterranean region. Enormous numbers of Irish hides went as far as the leather industries of Tuscany, and Spanish and Bordeaux wine, Basque iron and 'bay salt' from Brittany came into Ireland.

Merchants

The wealth of the merchants and the weakness of the artisans combined to secure the permanent exclusion of the latter from any say in local government. In the earliest surviving Cork Council Book, of 1609 to 1643, there are only two references to the craft and trade guilds. In 1614 the Company of Butchers, who had been forced to move their slaughterhouses outside the walls, petitioned for a reduction in the duties levied on them by the sheriffs. In 1626, the Corporation legislated against the 'rich artificers' who, on being chosen masters of their companies, insisted on giving 'many superfluous entertainments and feasts' so that at the end of their year of office they were forced 'to betake themselves to foreign countries to get relief for themselves, their wives and children'. The Corporation decreed that they should be heavily fined if they gave more than one feast to their company in their year of office. Control of the 'city' government by a narrow group was easy, as the outgoing mayor and the two bailiffs to be replaced – in 1609, when the 'city' became a county of its own – by sheriffs nominated their three successors, out of whom the Common Council chose one to be mayor.

By the seventeenth century, it was the accepted rule that the eldest sons of previous mayors were to be automatically preferred for nomination as mayors or bailiffs. Admission both to the Common Council and to the rank of freeman was by favour and the payment of an entry fine, and although entry to the freedom by outsiders was never actually forbidden it was made very difficult. In 1606, for fear 'that strangers take up the benefit which might redound to the decayed citizens' children', the Corporation ordered that merchants might take apprentices from outside Cork or the sons of artificers within it only on stringent (and expensive) conditions, and this statute was strengthened in 1609 and again in 1631. Only such apprentices as were the sons of freemen who were 'merchants or gentlemen dwelling in the city' were exempt from giving security to observe the rules. The standard merchant apprenticeship was for seven years, the first two or three years being spent as apprentice and the last four as a junior partner trading on a jointly subscribed capital and dividing the profits. Cork was in no way peculiar in falling under the control of a narrow merchant oligarchy and in the rigid exclusion of the crafts and trades. The same development occurred in all the Irish towns; Limerick and Galway were, if anything, controlled by an even narrower patriciate than Cork. In Waterford and Dublin the merchant communities were larger and more open, but the principles were the same.

Of the existing patrician families in sixteenth-century Cork only a handful of names (Skiddy, Lavallin and

Fig. 2.17 Detail of 'Skiddis Castell' from *Pacata Hibernia*, 1585. It was originally built as a residence, but later it was demolished to make way for an almshouse, which was opened in 1711.

Fig. 2.18 Elizabeth Fort is one of Cork's earliest surviving structures. The contemporary building has been continuously modified since it was originally erected in the early 1600s. This detail is from Rocque, 1759. Recently refurbished, it is one of Cork's major heritage sites.

Fig. 2.19 Blackrock Castle was built in the early 1600s, with a twin castle erected on the other side of the channel, as a formidable harbour defence. Later it was used by the Corporation for ceremonial occasions. The original structure was destroyed by fire in 1827, but a new more ornamental building designed by the Pains was completed in 1829. (Crawford Municipal Art Gallery.)

Fig. 2.20 Detail of 'ye Cathedral Church of old Cork' (St Fin Barre's) from *Pacata Hibernia*, c. 1585.

Lombard) appear among the city magistracy before 1400 (see *Medieval Cork*, Chapter 7). Of these, the Skiddys fell behind in the race: although they continued to provide mayors and sheriffs until the seventeenth century, there were only five freemen of the name in 1652. The Lombard family were of rather unusual origin; they were originally a family of Florentine bankers called Donati delle Pape who had established themselves in Ireland in the late thirteenth century. John Donati, the heir of the family, was forced to bring a legal action in 1338 to compel the citizens of Cork to admit him as a freeman, but he eventually (as John Lombard) became mayor in 1361. There were only three Lombard freemen in 1652 and most of their property had passed to other families. The Wynchedons, who later changed their surname to Nugent, a name that was very prominent in fourteenth-century Cork, eventually dropped

Fig. 2.21 Dundanion Castle on the Mahon peninsula is the nearest surviving example to the city of a tower house. It dates to the sixteenth century. (Photo: Caroline Somers.)

Fig. 2.22 Monkstown Castle was built in 1636 by the Archdeacon family and is a good example of a fortified house from the period. Its elaborate features testify to the considerabe wealth of the Archdeacon family (Photo: Cork Archaeological Survey.)

out of the town, surviving only as landowners in the Carrigaline area. A number of the merchant families had been prominent in Kinsale before moving to Cork, among them the Gallweys and the Ronans or Ronaynes, originally O Rónáin, one of several families of unquestioned Gaelic origin. In 1487, Maurice Ronayne was simultaneously a freeman of Cork, of Youghal and of Kinsale, seemingly a not unusual situation. The Coppinger family was similarly prominent in all three posts.

Many of the most prominent families of the patriciate were landowners from the countryside who had moved into Cork to escape the exactions of the Gaelicised lords. Such were the Tirrys and the Sarsfields from Barrymore, the Miaghs or Meades from Kerrycurrihy, the Roches of Dunderrow near Kinsale and the Whytes of Killaminoge near Innishannon. These retained a claim to their rural lands until, with the reimposition of English rule in Elizabethan times, they were able once again to enjoy them unmolested, although they did not then renounce their urban position. The history of the Sarsfields is particularly well known through the fortunate preservation of a brief sixteenth-century account of the family, which illustrates the fate of those family members who failed to make good and the prevalence of emigration to England.[1] The Sarsfields had been lords of Glanmire and Sarsfield's Court from around 1240, and in the mid-fifteenth century two younger brothers moved as merchants to Cork. The line which remained at Glanmire ended with James Sarsfield, who in 1535 sold his property to his cousin (and former guardian) William Sarsfield, a Cork merchant, and emigrated to Bodmin in Cornwall, where he earned his living as a shoemaker and his sons were also tradesmen. Another cousin, David Sarsfield, likewise emigrated to England, in his case to Minehead in Somerset, where he worked as a carpenter and his son was a carpenter after him. But the members of the family who stayed in Cork prospered.

CORK AND THE PLANTATION

The 1590s saw the emergence of a new and well-organised settler community, especially strong in Munster after the Munster plantation of the 1580s. This was accompanied by the triumph of counter-Reformation Catholicism in the towns which rendered them politically suspect to the administration, so that a change in official attitudes to them and their mostly Roman Catholic urban patriciates began to be evident. The commission of enquiry into the state of Munster reported in 1592 that the grants of extensive financial and other privileges, much greater than those of any city in England, which had been made to the towns 'in respect of their assured loyalties in doubtful and troublesome times' were now unsuitable 'in time of peace and civility'. The strains imposed by the Nine Years War of 1594–1603 – the only struggle of the Tudor period to extend to the whole of Ireland and which spread into Munster in 1597, sweeping away the plantation and filling the towns with English fugitives – increased the growing alienation between the towns and the English administration. The port towns, especially Cork, served as the centres of the English war effort and were forced to receive large numbers of soldiers, both as garrisons and soldiers on their way to campaigns. These were compulsorily quartered on the citizens and caused serious disputes, both as regards payment for their maintenance and for criminal jurisdiction over their misdeeds.

The loyalty of the citizens, who were accused of supplying arms to the rebels and of being sympathetic, on religious grounds, to the Spaniards, was questioned. During this period Cork had an active devil's advocate in the person of its Protestant bishop, William Lyon, whose letters to London are full of complaints against the citizenry. In 1600, he accused the Cork merchants of travelling among the rebels and supplying them with gunpowder that they had purchased from France in exchange for hides which they duly traded back to the French.

The position of Cork was forced upon the attention of the English authorities when in the same year the mayor and citizens petitioned for a new charter with fresh privileges. In a supporting letter Alderman Edmond Tirry outlined the losses which the citizens had sustained during the war, in which they had been plundered of their cattle and the rents of their rural lands, and had been restricted to trading within the city itself. No doubt the losses were genuine enough, but there may have been some compensations: a few years later it is said that during the war Cork had taken over the whole hide trade of south Munster, to the exclusion of the lesser ports which had formerly shared in it and which had fallen victim to the war. The number of hides exported from Cork during the war years had risen from a yearly total of 6,000–8,000 to some 20,000.

Some of the concessions petitioned for by Cork in 1600 were insignificant, such as that for the remission of the arrears, since 1576, of the 20 pounds of beeswax a year for which the original fee-farm of the town had been commuted since 1482, or that entitling the city to levy a toll on the herring fishery, ostensibly for the maintenance of Blackrock Castle. But other concessions sought were much more important.

A new charter would make Cork and the area for three miles around it a county of itself, which would mean that the wide administrative and law-enforcing powers of the county sheriff would be vested in two sheriffs elected by the Corporation. More distasteful to the government was the request that the soldiers quartered in the town would in future be subject to the ordinary judicial authority of the town authorities, instead of being under the sole jurisdiction of their officers. Even more objectionable to the government was the request that Cork should have the same jurisdiction in criminal matters as had Waterford; that is, the power to try all criminal cases arising within the town in its own courts. The authorities at once perceived that this would make the trial

192 (folio 3)	CENSUS OF IRELAND, 1659 THE SUBURBS OF CORKE CITTY					
	Suburbs	Number of People	Tituladoes Names	Eng	Irish
Shandon	North Suburbs	733	Jonas Morris and James Peercy Esqrs Nicholas Lee John Harris gents Dr John Messick alien Esq William Delahide Ignatius Goold Thomas Wills Francis Rogers gents and Phillip Mathews Esq Jonas Morris Junir John Craine Symon Everson alien Michaell Stanton Thomas Farren Dauid Barry James Skiddy Richard Goold James Tomlin James Finch Patrick Ronane William Meagh George Caple John Morley & John Skiddy gents Noblett Dunscombe Esq Henry Bennett John Johnson Richd Johnson James Barry John Welsh Thomas Combel John Verkers Thomas Ô Herne Phillip Ronane John Guyn William French John Steuens Martin Boohier and Walter Gallwey gentlemen	223	510
(folio 4). St Johns	South Suburbs	421	Thomas Mills Richard Beare John Sinhouse Lawrance Harrison Dauid Goold Sampson Roberts George Hopson John Bayley Dauid Meskell Richard Meskell Thomas Crooke Christopher Fagan William Field Phillip Hayes William Heydon Francis Goold Edmond Roch and Nicholas Skyddy gentlemen	102	319
St Finbarry	South Suburbs	160	Barthollomew Rice John Meade Zachariah	043	117

Fig. 2.23 Page from the 1659 census, which provides the numbers of people on a street-by-street basis and segregates the population into ethnic groups, either Irish or English. It also lists the élites of society, curiously identified by the Spanish term *tituladoes*. (Source: S. Pender (ed.), *A census of Ireland circa 1659*, IMC, Dublin, 2002.)

and conviction of Cork citizens on charges of treason impossible, as had been shown in Dublin.

The Cork requests produced several extremely hostile memoranda from officials urging that they be rejected. Hugh Cuffe, who was both a soldier and a Munster planter, speaks of 'the cities and towns which have been the roots of all these mischiefs, as in sending their sons into Spain, whereof some have been brought up as seminar priests, who had returned to seduce Her Majesty's subjects from their allegiance'. Others, trained as soldiers, had returned as rebels. 'All the principal rebels have a Christian gossip or fosterer in the towns, and they supply them with munitions ... They are loyal to the Pope and the king of Spain, as well as supplying the rebels, and yet sue the Queen for an increase of their privileges. Since they have grants of the fines imposed within the city, they ignore fines imposed for religious matters.'

When the English forces set out from the 'cities' on any expedition against the rebels, the townsmen would send messengers in advance to warn the latter. Traditional Irish modes of cementing friendships or alliances, 'Christian gossipred' (the sponsoring of children at the font) and fosterage, were prevalent among the townsmen as well. In most cases, this practice did not mean rearing the child but rather a relationship which involved taking a friendly interest in it, with the right to a child's portion of the fosterer's goods on his death.[2]

The fervent Catholicism of the towns, from which – and not from the Gaelic countryside – the early recruits to the continental seminaries were drawn (returning, as Cuffe observed, as trained and devoted apostles of the counter-Reformation), combined with economic grievances such as the government's tampering with the currency in an effort to pay its debts and the embargo on Spanish trade imposed early in 1603 (over-ruling the legal right of such towns as Cork to trade with enemy countries), led, on the news of the death of Elizabeth I (24 March 1603), to the uprising known as the 'Recusant revolt' of the Munster towns. A mistaken belief in the secret Catholicism of the new sovereign, King James VI of Scotland, who now became king of England as well, played a large part in inspiring this essentially religious uprising. This belief was grounded not, as has been alleged by a succession of Irish historians ignorant of Scottish history, in his being the son of Mary, Queen of Scots, from whom he had been separated when he was a few weeks old, but in his sympathetic policy towards the Scottish Catholics, who were the only element among his subjects he could rely upon to give him unconditional support against the Presbyterian clergy, and on the fact that, believing that he might have to fight for the English throne on Elizabeth's death and seeking in that event the support of the Catholic powers, he had employed gullible Catholic secret agents on the Continent to spread the disinformation that he was a Catholic at heart.

The Munster towns, in the event, shut their gates against the English authorities, drove out the few Protestant residents and re-established the Catholic images and rituals in the churches. The revolt was soon crushed, bloodlessly, by the Lord Deputy, Lord Mountjoy, and an attempt to prosecute the Recorder, the former Mayor of Cork, William Meade, for treason failed. Its suppression ushered in a period of governmental repression in the towns, at least where religious matters were concerned. The Mandates, a policy of severe religious repression and of enforcing compulsory attendance at the state church, was commenced in July 1605. As the churches in the countryside were mainly in ruins and there were few Protestant clergy, it was initially put into effect in the towns. In the following year, during a progress of the Lord President of Munster and the judges, more than one hundred citizens and burgesses of Cork were heavily fined for non-attendance at the official service. The Mayor, William Sarsfield, after being fined £100, gave way and attended church, but in the following year it is recorded that many citizens and aldermen of the town had been in prison for a long time for their refusal.

In 1608, however, Cork received a new charter, which established it and the surrounding area as an independent county (later, the Barony of Cork), as had been requested in 1600. The two Cork bailiffs subsequently became sheriffs. A number of minor extensions of the town's judicial authority were granted, but the independence of Cork, like that of the other Irish towns, was severely restricted in the following years by the re-imposition of royal control over the customs. Although Cork kept its possession of the old custom known as 'cocket of hides', the new duties of tonnage and poundage were henceforth collected in the port and the appointment of customs officials was resumed by the Crown.

In 1611, the export trade of Cork was valued by an observer at £20,000 yearly, equalling that of Drogheda (and ranking after Dublin and Waterford). The exports consisted of rugs, friezes, hides, tallow, sheepskins and pipestaves (planks for making barrels). The imports were the usual Irish staples of wine, salt and iron, as well as 'various commodities', probably principally manufactured goods, from the twice-yearly Bristol fairs. A few years earlier, the export of hides, the most important single item in Irish exports, had amounted to 6,000–8,000 yearly, sent to St Malo in Brittany, to Lisbon, Seville and the Canaries. A raw hide in Cork was worth 6 or 7s (shillings), while at its destination it fetched 10s, a tanned hide fetching respectively 10s or 12s and 15s. There is little information on the growth of trade between then and 1641, but, with the rapid growth of the Irish economy, it was substantial. The trade in butter and meat, exported in casks, which played so great a part in the economy of eighteenth-century Cork, may have had its beginnings in this period.

In these same years, too, with the acquisition of the first English colonies on the American mainland and in the tropical West Indies, a direct trade developed between them and the south Munster ports. This was a period of an expanding Irish economy, even if a disproportionate amount of this expansion, and of its benefits, involved the new English settler community. In 1622, there were probably around 12,000 English settlers on the lands of the Munster plantation and there must have been a good many more outside its limits on purchased or rented land. The class who do not seem to have benefited from this general expansion of the economy were the native Irish gentry and landowners, many or most of whom, even the greatest, seem to have been under extreme financial pressure and to have been forced to sell or mortgage their lands wholesale. Much of this sale or mortgaging was to the new English settlers but much was also to the merchant families of the towns, including Cork. All through the southern and western parts of the county, large estates were bought up by the merchants of the Cork patriciate, a proof of their continuing prosperity and the profits of their trading enterprises. Such great mansions as Coppinger's Court, built by Sir Walter Coppinger on his newly acquired lands near Rosscarbery, or Monkstown Castle, built by the family of Archdeacon, also testify to considerable wealth (Fig. 2.22).

The outbreak of the Irish rising in November 1641 left the Catholic patriciate of Cork in a difficult position. Although their sympathies, like those of the other old port towns, must have been with the Catholic cause, Cork (unlike, for example, Waterford or Galway) was heavily garrisoned and was the headquarters of the English and Protestant administration of Munster under the 'excitedly belligerent' and brutal Lord President, Sir William St Leger. Although Cork withstood a siege by the Confederate forces in the first flush of the Confederate success, in March and April 1642, it soon reverted to being solidly within the English and Protestant lines, a testimony to the strength of the settlement in County Cork, and the citizens thus had no chance to throw in their lot with their fellow Irish Catholics. After the truce of July 1644, against which the Munster Protestant forces based in Cork protested, the local Irish commander, Lord Muskerry, plotted with some of the citizens to get possession of the town. The plot was discovered and Fr Francis Mathews or O'Mahony, O.F.M., who seems to have acted as an intermediary, was tortured and executed by the Protestant commander, Murrough O'Brien, Lord Inchiquin.

EXPULSION

On 26 July 1644, the mayor and aldermen were dragged from their beds in the early morning by Inchiquin's soldiers, summoned to his presence and informed that the entire Irish and Catholic population – in the context of the time, the terms were synonymous – were to be expelled from Cork. The expulsion was carried out next day, and the houses of those expelled were looted by the soldiery. Although some of the expelled inhabitants secured readmission to the town during the peace of 1648–1649, this was the end of the old patriciate in Cork (Fig. 2.23). Many former inhabitants established themselves at Macroom, Lord Muskerry's residence; others seem to have scattered throughout west Cork and south Kerry, where some of their descendants were to be found as local merchants in the following period. Henceforth Cork was to be a new English town, and a strongly Protestant one. In the eighteenth century, the descendants of the Cork merchant patriciate, unlike those of their congeners in Galway or Waterford, are of little importance in the exiled Irish merchant communities in France or Spain. The clue to this may lie in those years between 1641 and 1644, when, by their own account, they paid out £30,000 to the royalist cause and, under the control of their enemies, would have had no opportunity to transfer their liquid assets abroad.

TRANSFORMATION

12. THE EVOLUTION OF CORK'S BUILT ENVIRONMENT, 1600–1700

Mark McCarthy

Cork's present streetscape facilitates a captivating entry-point into a scrutiny of Ireland's 'multifaceted past'.[1] In this chapter we investigate the evolution of this urban space during the seventeenth century as it transformed from a late medieval town into a modern and fully-fledged Atlantic port settlement.

As a colonial settlement in an expanding British empire, Cork's development during the early modern period was strongly influenced by the globalisation of commodity and labour markets, culture, government, capital markets and warfare. Cork began losing its late medieval character after 1600, when it started to increase its size and population, and by 1641 it had developed a much stronger economy. It was not long, however, before its progress was dramatically halted by the large-scale reorganisation of property and the social changes that resulted from repeated expulsions of the Catholic and Irish inhabitants. Despite this political trauma, Cork recovered and experienced economic renaissance and urban growth from the early 1660s onwards as a result of its growing status within the expanding Atlantic colonial trade

Fig. 2.24 The town of Cork, *c.* 1601. This early plan of Cork shows that it was a very well defended and compact port settlement. The outline of Elizabeth Fort and other prominent buildings can be easily identified. (Source: TCD, MS. 1209, No. 46, The Towne of Corke in Ireland, *c.* 1601. Size of original 19" × 10". Reproduced by permission of the Board of Trinity College, Dublin.)

in provisions, notably beef and butter. By 1700, Cork bore some of the hallmarks of a buoyant Atlantic port centre. By then, it had assumed a much higher rank in the general European urban hierarchy as a result of the dramatic eight-fold increase in its population between 1600 and 1700.

Urban design and evolution, 1600–1641

In February 1600, Cork was described as one of the 'two principal maritime cities' of the province of Munster. Cartographic evidence permits a detailed reconstruction of the morphology of the port town of Cork in the first decade of the seventeenth century. When compared to the pictorial *Pacata Hibernia* plan of Cork (*c.* 1585), a colour representation of the town in 1601 entitled 'The Towne of Corke in Ireland' displays a number of new features, including Elizabeth Fort in the south suburbs and a 'walkabout' around the newly reclaimed north-east marsh. Cork was then a small island town surrounded by walls. Its main street ran along a north-to-south axis which was typically fronted by three-storey buildings aligned in an east-to-west direction, with their gable ends facing onto the street. The roofs of public buildings in the town are coloured blue on the map, while the residences are distinguished by their red and orange roofs. Narrow laneways set at right angles to the main street ran eastwards and westwards to the town walls.

Cork's street pattern can be categorised as 'chequered', resembling the plot-determined layout of other Irish towns. Good surviving examples of the narrow medieval and early modern laneways in the town of Cork include Christ Church Lane and Old Post Office Lane. Located between the laneways and fronting the main street were the long, narrow, individually owned properties known as burgage plots, which also ran at right angles to the main street to the town walls. Excavations of property boundaries at Kyrl's Quay/North Main Street in Cork found that the lines of property boundaries to the east of North Main Street 'remained virtually unchanged for almost 700 years', with each successive rebuilding superimposed on the previous one, and respecting 'the division of the backyards into linear plots' (see the case study, *Lanes and Streets*, in Chapter 7).

The *c.* 1601 map confirms that ships could dock inside the safety of the walls in the central waterway along a line immediately south of present-day Castle Street (Fig. 2.24). The central waterway was enclosed by a gateway between King's Castle to the south and Queen's Castle to the north. It was not possible for ships to travel upstream to the site of Droop's Mill, as there was a bridge connecting the northern and southern halves of Main Street. A wooden drawbridge joined the walled town to the north-east marsh.

The parish church of Holy Trinity sited in the south-east part of the walled town is depicted in 1601 as a large church with a nave and north and south aisles. St Peter's church in the north-west part of town is also depicted. One of the most impressive tower houses was Skiddy's Castle, built by the Skiddy family in the late fifteenth century.[2] A market cross is depicted in the centre of the street, a few metres to the north-east of a bridge that enabled the citizens to cross the central waterway. Both North and South Gate bridges are illustrated as timber structures. Other recognisable features include the rough outline of nine (green-coloured) marshes, four to the east and five to the west of the town, a fort sited on the north-east marsh, residences in the suburbs, Franciscan, Augustinian and Dominican abbeys and St Fin Barre's Cathedral.

During the seventeenth century, the walls surrounding Cork proved to be an integral element of its defences. Those who lived within their confines could consider themselves to be more privileged than those who lived in the small suburbs outside. Cork's walls in the early seventeenth century were ten feet thick in places and measured 50 feet high. Many other Irish towns had thinner and lower walls, as their corporations simply lacked the financial resources to build strong defences. Limerick's walls were seven feet thick, Kilkenny's were four and a half feet thick and Athlone's three feet thick, while the walls at both Athenry and Youghal were only two feet thick. Cork's walls had a stepped platform near the top for sentries, called a wall walk, while its parapet had crenellations (see *Medieval Cork*, Chapter 7). Eighteen towers are depicted by the 1601 map along the course of the walls, two less than the number depicted on the *Pacata* plan, *c.* 1585.

A second plan of the town of Cork dating to 1602 is entitled 'A description of the Cittie of Cork, with the places adjacent thereto' (Fig. 2.27). It bears a close resemblance to the 1601 plan, with the roofs of residential buildings in the walled town coloured red. The roofs of suburban houses, however, are coloured green on the 1602 plan. John Speed's

Fig. 2.25 The 'Queen's Castell' was one of the best-known buildings in early seventeenth-century Cork. (Source: *Pacata Hibernia*, *c.* 1585.)

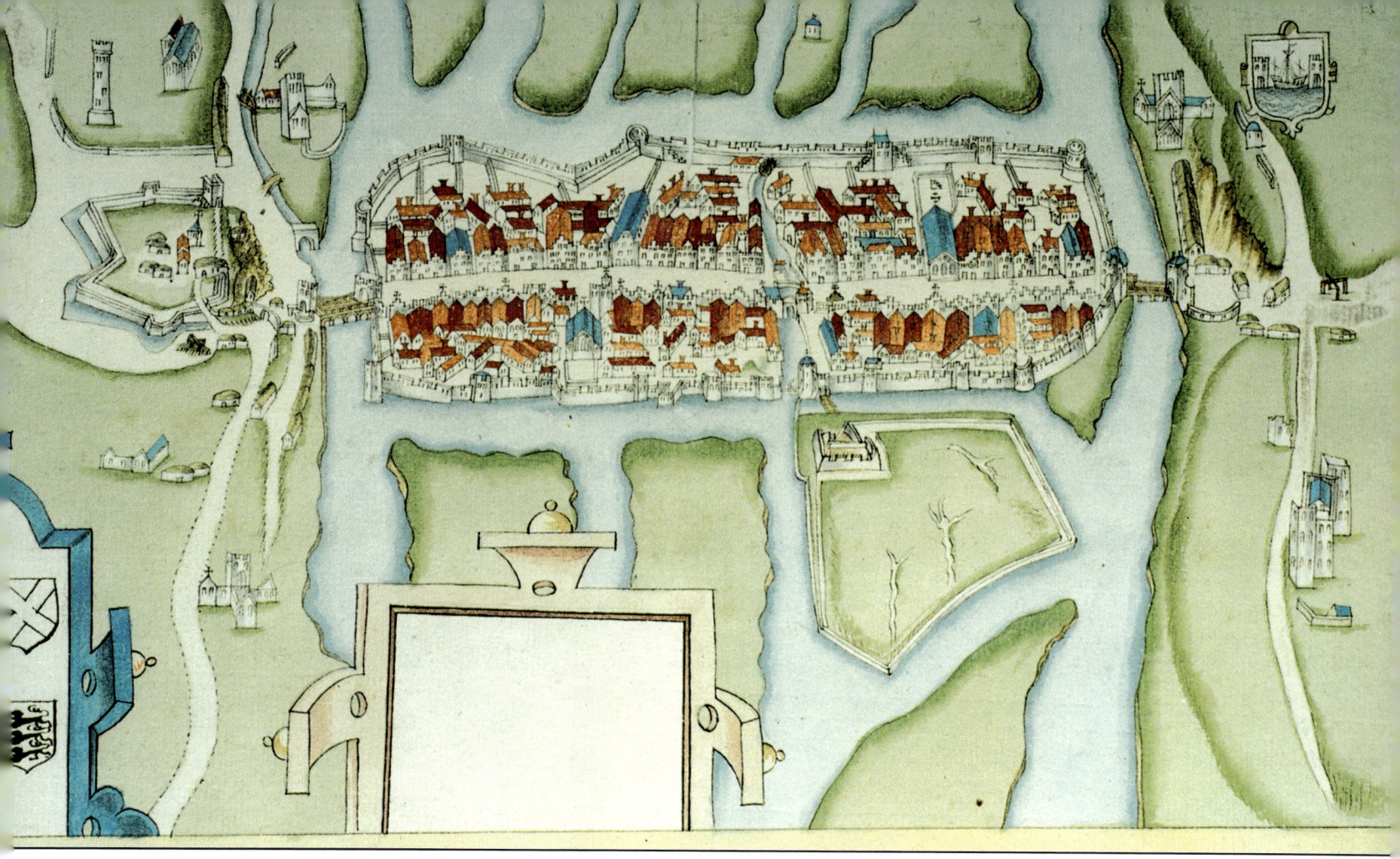

Fig. 2.26 The town of Cork, 1602. The colours employed by the unknown maker of this plan make Cork appear as a vital settlement arrayed along a spinal street. Many of the buildings on this main street were substantial three-, sometimes four-storyed, structures. Space remained for development within the walls, on the western side of the settlement. (Source: TCD, MS. 1209, No. 45, Plan of Cork, 1602, entitled 'A description of the Cittie of Cork, with the places adjacent thereto'. Size of original 22″ × 16″. Reproduced by permission of the Board of Trinity College Dublin.)

1610 map of Cork again confirms the outline plan of the early seventeenth-century town as shown on the 1601 and 1602 plans.[3]

An important element of Cork's modernisation was that the 1608 charter officially extended the geographical limits of municipal jurisdiction from the line of the town walls to three miles outside of them. This area became known as the 'County of the City of Cork'. Another way of measuring the degree to which Cork had grown physically is to compare the multiplication that occurred in the number of streets, lanes and buildings between 1601 and 1641. This can be achieved by scrutinising the 1602 plan and comparing this to information concerning the town's topography in 1641 contained in the *Survey and valuation of the city of Cork, AD 1663–1664*.

There were some 29 laneways in the walled town in 1602 (28 led at right angles from the main street) and a further 15 streets in the suburbs to the north and south of it, making a total of 44. By 1641, the number of streets and lanes in the walled town had doubled to 69, while the equivalent for the suburbs had increased to 24. This meant that streets and lanes in the town and suburbs had more than doubled, from 44 in 1602 to 93 by 1641.

Over the same period, dwelling houses in the walled town and suburbs had nearly tripled. Cork's population had also nearly tripled, from about 2,906 in 1602 to 8,262 in 1641. As the space within the walled town came increasingly under pressure, more of the expanding population resided in the suburbs. During this period, the harbour became more significant as a naval base.[4]

REORGANISING ETHNIC SPACES IN CORK IN THE 1640S AND 1650S

During the 1640s and 1650s, Cork's population decreased slightly, largely as a consequence of Protestant reaction to the 1641 rebellion. Catholic and Irish inhabitants were expelled from Cork in 1644, 1649, 1651 and 1656 and replaced by New English Protestant settlers. Following these expulsions, municipal control of Cork's administration gave way to military rule until 1656. Thereafter, the walled area continued to remain a space of Catholic exclusion.[5] The general effect of the Cromwellian conquest of Ireland was to secure, in both rural and urban areas, the ascendant interests of the Protestant population, which had been gradually expanding since the late sixteenth century.

Fig. 2.27 John Speed's plan of 'Corcke' *c.* 1610. Although an impressionistic plan, its lack of clutter provides a clear guide to its leading structural features. It supplies good definition of defences and shows that gardens and orchards were still evident within the walled area. (Sources: C.A. Webster, *The Diocese of Cork, Preface by the Lord Bishop of Cork, Cloyne and Ross, with Illustrations*, 1920; *Pacata Hibernia*, facsimile ed. 1810.)

A remarkable insight into Cork's population geography soon after the expulsions of the Catholic inhabitants is provided by the so-called 1659 Census, an abstract of the poll-tax returns for 1660. Because the 1659 Census only listed adult males over the age of fifteen, a multiplier of three has to be employed for calculating Cork's population. Based on this exercise, the total population of the walled sector in 1659 stood at 3,605, while the combined total for core and suburbs was 7,547. In terms of ethnic composition, the New English Protestant settlers in the walled area totalled 2,356 residents, outnumbering the Irish and Old English by nearly two to one. Such a tally again confirms the hypothesis that 'the larger the settlement the greater the proportion of New English residents in mid-seventeenth-century County Cork'. Bandon was the only other town in County Cork in 1659 to have a New English population amounting to more than 60 per cent, while those at Youghal and Kinsale amounted to 40 per cent.

In spite of the 1644 expulsions, there were still 1,249 Irish and Old English living in the walled part of Cork in 1659; they formed a minority of 35 per cent of the residents. While the Irish and Old English in the walled settlement were outnumbered by the New English by nearly two to one, this situation was in stark contrast to the conditions which existed immediately before the expulsion in 1644. Then the Old English and Irish outnumbered the New English by at least six to one and only about one-tenth of the freemen admitted in the years between 1610 and 1641 were New English. Nevertheless, the fact that 35 per cent of the population in the walled settlement after the Cromwellian period were Irish and Old English Catholics confirms that expulsion was only partial. The large 1659 residue can be explained by the fact that, as a bureaucratic undertaking, 'the eviction of all Catholics proved impossible', even though the Cromwellians were successful in excluding them from municipal office and trade.

The population was slightly larger in the suburbs than in the walled settlement. The Irish and Old English population was nearly triple that of the New English. Of the 3,942 people who lived in the suburbs, 2,838, or 72 per cent, were Irish and Old English, while 1,104, or 28 per cent, were New English. Taking the total population of the walled area and suburbs together, over half was Irish and Old English. However, the combined Irish and Old English population was only slightly greater than the New English population. Out of a combined total of 7,547, 4,087 (54 per cent) were Irish and Old English, while the New English accounted for 3,460 (46 per cent). The 7,547 people living in the walled sector and suburbs of Cork in 1659 represents a small decrease in the 8,262 residents in 1641. Its 1660 population total was still much greater than the 2,906 residents living there in 1602.

The proprietorial reorganisation of ethnic groups that crystallised in Cork after the expulsions can be understood by examining the *Survey and valuation of the city of Cork, AD 1663–1664*. Fifty per cent of all the property in the city and suburbs of Cork in 1664 listed in the *Survey and valuation* formed part of the war booty owed to the '49 Officers'. This source lists the names of the 1641 property owners (mainly Catholics) and those who owned them in 1664 (mainly Protestants). Out of 92 streets surveyed in the city and suburbs of Cork in 1663–1664, 'innocent' Catholics were restored to their property in a total of 39 streets. Twenty, or more than half, of these were located in the suburbs, while the other nineteen were located in the walled area.

In both the north and south suburbs, virtually every street (20 out of 24) registered one or more 'innocent' Catholics who had had their property restored. In contrast, less than one-third of the 68 streets and lanes in the walled settlement counted even one. While the total number of proprietors in 1641 numbered 200, this figure had risen to around 500 when the port's lands had come into the ownership of the New English in 1664.[6] Gone were the days when the vast majority of urban property was held by fourteen powerful Catholic families, which included the Goolds, Galweys, Tirrys, Roches, Skiddys, Barrys and McCarthys. Once the expulsions occurred, most properties came into the hands of the New English. In the process, property ownership in Cork became more fragmented and new names, such as the Alwins, Fletchers, Harrisons, Hawkins, Newmans, St Legers and Youngs, made their debut on the property scene.

A PERIOD OF RENAISSANCE: THE FORGING OF AN ATLANTIC PORT, C. 1660–1700

Despite the turmoil caused by the expulsions of Catholic and Irish inhabitants between 1644 and 1656, Cork soon recovered and experienced a period of economic renaissance in the closing decades of the seventeenth century. This was a time when it transformed into an Atlantic port thriving on colonial trade to the West Indies and America. As these changes unfolded, the physical extent and population of Cork increased. Population expansion resulted not only from an increased birth rate among established and dispossessed inhabitants, both Anglican and Roman Catholic, but also from an influx of other immigrant Protestant settlers – Huguenots and Quakers, along with some Baptists and Presbyterians. A

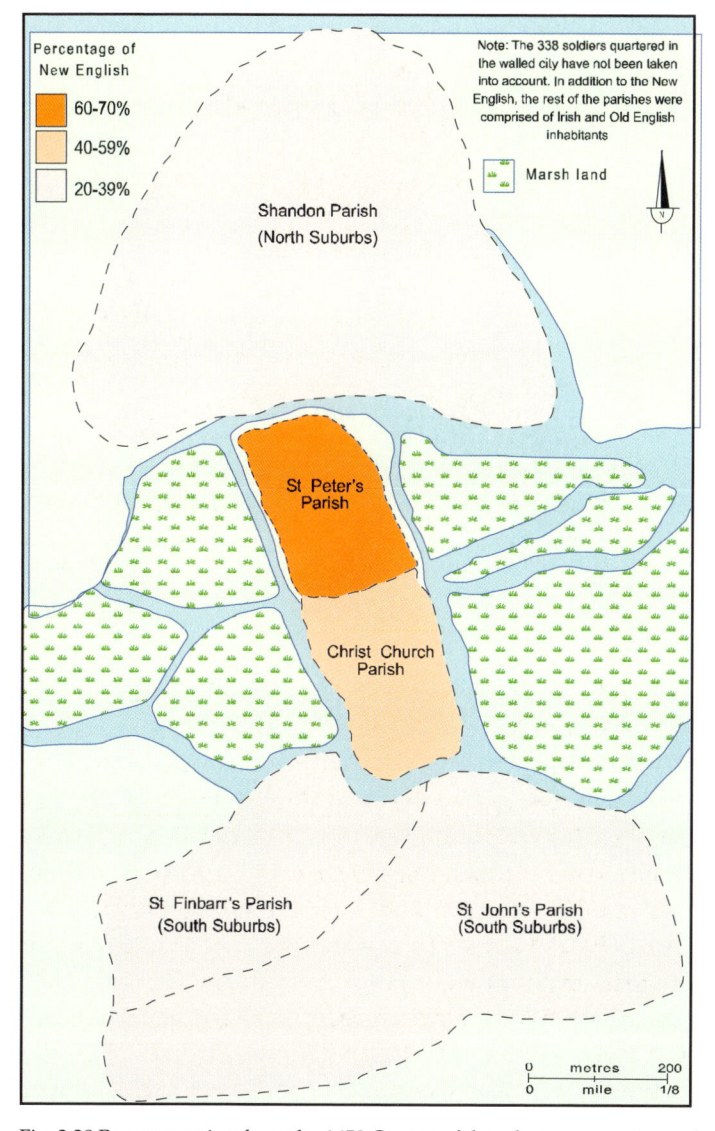

Fig. 2.28 Reconstruction from the 1659 Census of the ethnic composition of parish residents in the walled area and Cork's suburbs. More New English lived inside the walled area than outside it. (Sources: S. Pender (ed.), *A census of Ireland, circa 1659. With supplementary material from the poll money ordinances (1660–1661)*, Irish Manuscripts Commission, Dublin, 1939. Redrawn from McCarthy, 'Turning a world upside down: The metamorphosis of property, settlement and society in the city of Cork during the 1640s and 1650s', *Irish Geography*, 2000.)

	New English	Irish and Old English	Total Number of People
Christ Church parish			
South-east quarter	372	276	648
North-east quarter	582	366	948
South-west quarter	291	219	510
Total population of Christ Church parish	**1,245**	**861**	**2,106**
St Peter's parish			
South-west quarter	318	162	480
North-west quarter	477	204	681
Total population of St Peter's parish	**795**	**366**	**1,161**
Soldiers in Cork city*			
Lord Broghill's Company	80	8	88
Captain Courthop's Company	84	6	90
Captain Wakeham's Company	84	6	90
Captain Tenche's Company	68	2	70
Total number of soldiers	**316**	**22**	**338**
Total population of Cork City	**2,356**	**1,249**	**3,605**
Suburbs of Cork city			
Shandon parish, north suburbs	669	1,530	2,199
St John's parish, south suburbs	306	957	1,263
St Finbarr's parish, south suburbs	129	351	480
Total population of suburbs	**1,104**	**2,838**	**3,942T**
Total population of city and suburbs	**3,460**	**4,087**	**7,547**
Liberties			
South Liberties of Cork	480	3,360	3,840
North Liberties of Cork	249	2,166	2,415
Total population of Liberties	**729**	**5,526**	**6,255**
Total population of city, suburbs and Liberties	**4,189**	**9,613**	**13,802**

* In the case of soldiers, a multiplier of 3 has not been used, as the garrison presumably comprised only adult males.
(Source: As for preceding figure.)

Fig. 2.29 Population of Cork from the 1659 Census.

tantalising glimpse into the high birth rate in Cork at the time is given by the parish registers for Christ Church (Holy Trinity), which was then a parish that recorded almost one-third of its 1659 population in the walled core and suburbs combined. Births recorded in the parish between 1643 and 1666 outnumbered deaths by two and a half; in fact, there were 892 christenings, as opposed to only 357 burials. Between 1660 and 1666, births amounted to 367, more than double the 166 deaths that were recorded.[7]

A contemporary estimate of Cork's population was made by Richard Cox in 1685: 'The suburbs are grown twice as big as the citty, and altogether do containe 20,000 souls.' Cork's population still managed to rise to around 24,275 by 1700. This figure appears reasonable, especially when one considers that a population increase in Cork in the last decade and a half of the seventeenth century would have borne similarities to much of the rest of the county of Cork. It was one of only six Irish counties between 1685 and 1702 to register a rise in hearth tax revenue and presumably thereafter in population, in spite of the

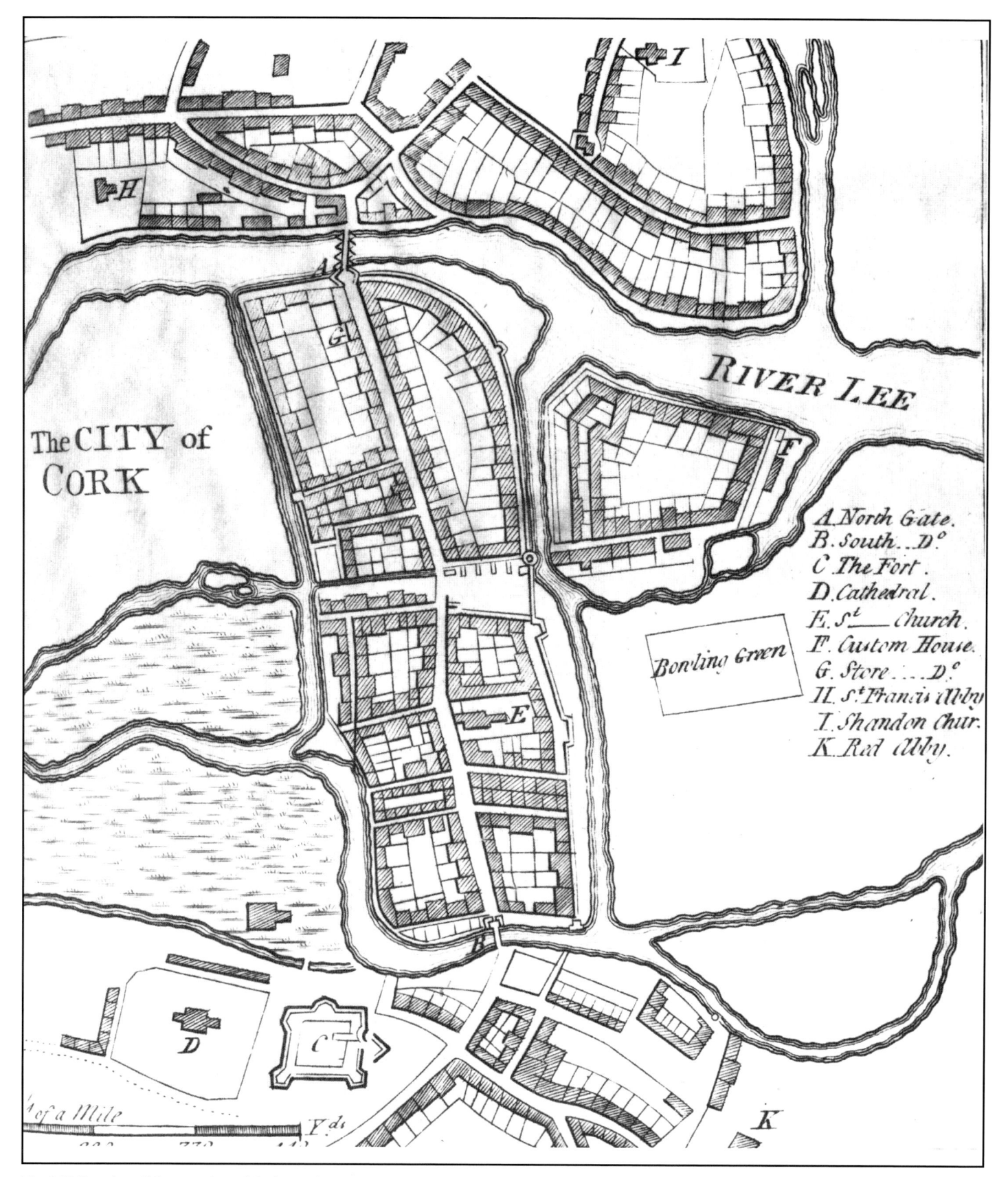

Fig. 2.30 Story's well-known plan of Cork, produced during, or soon after, the 1690 siege. This is an important cartographic landmark, in that it depicts for the first time extensive and ordered suburban expansion on both sides of the Lee. Strangely, the urban core is tantalisingly blank. (Source: G. Story, *A continuation of the impartial history of the wars of Ireland*, 1693.)

disruptions caused by the Williamite wars in the early 1690s.[8] Remarkably, the increase in Cork's population from 7,547 to 24,275 between 1659 and 1700 represents an annual growth rate of 5.3 per cent, a higher figure than that recorded in Dublin and London.

Three maps of Cork survive for the late seventeenth century, and they all depict a town enlarged by a booming economy and rapid demographic growth. The first of these maps is a pen and watercolour map in Thomas Phillips' *Military survey of Ireland* of 1685. A virtually identical 1690 plan of the city was produced in George Story's *A continuation of the impartial history of the wars of Ireland* (Fig. 2.30). Finally, there is a coloured 1690–1695 map of Cork by the French cartographer Goubet.

Compared to the maps of the late medieval town that survive for 1601, 1602 and 1610, Story's plan of Cork in 1690 shows the expansion of the port downstream. The central waterway within the walls is shown partly filled in or arched over at the eastern side of North Main Street. Downstream from the central waterway, the north channel of the River Lee and its associated quays was the new zone for shipping activity.

The north-east marsh is shown embanked with a quay located along its northern edge. This was the area where ships docked and would have been the place where 'people came to work or to find employment, to learn the news or to exchange information, to greet travellers, to send or receive shipments, or simply to observe or enjoy the animation that came from so many activities in such a well-defined space'. Cork by 1698 had 349 ships registered, compared to Waterford's 203 and Dublin's 951, involved 'in the importing of goods and merchandise into the several ports of Ireland'.

Eleven towers mark the circuit of the walls on Story's plan. The street pattern remains linear and the North Gate and South Gate are also depicted, as is 'The King's Storehouse', formerly known as Skiddy's Castle. The Bowling Green on Dunscombe's Marsh had been left to the Corporation by Michael Gallwey. Francis's Abbey, on the north bank of the River Lee, then formed part of the estate of the Earl of Orrery. In addition to the downstream expansion of the port through the reclamation of the Northeast Marsh (which first began to be reclaimed in the early 1600s), there are signs in Story's plan that many other marshes to the east and west of the walled city were being reclaimed. The process of marsh reclamation absorbed several generations of speculative merchant capital and enterprise. The strategic development land of the marshes (including Dunscombe's Marsh, Reap Marsh and Hammond's Marsh) was promoted by the Corporation and sections were let in long leases to its members, and sometimes to non-members like prominent Quakers.[9]

Conclusion

While the 2,906 recorded for Cork's population in 1602 made it a relatively small town, its increase by over eight-fold to 24,275 by 1700 enabled it to assume a much higher rank in the European urban hierarchy. This figure of 24,275 was nearly five times larger than Liverpool's population of 5,000 in 1700 and three times the size of the populations of Leeds and Boston. Cork's exceptionally rapid growth had strong parallels with the equally buoyant economies of other port cities of the British empire, such as Bristol.

Without doubt, Cork by the end of the seventeenth century was one of Europe's more prominent Atlantic port cities. Its commercial vitality was reflected in many dimensions: these included a twenty-fold increase in its annual customs returns between 1610 and the 1680s, the cosmopolitan nature of its society, the establishment of trading connections with British America, the formation of new guilds, the demolition of the town walls, the shift in the core area of shipping activity further downstream, the dramatic expansion of the suburbs on the hilly ground to the north and south of the walled area, improvements in Cork's infrastructure and the construction of market places in order to meet the demands of the early modern capitalist world system.

13. CITY, SEASONS AND SOCIETY

David Dickson

Autumn

The municipal governors of Cork have always had a legitimate sense of their own importance and so it was in the eighteenth century when the town on the marsh first became a city. Despite the total rupture in the 1640s when the old Catholic merchant dynasties were swept aside, the new standard-bearers of Protestant Cork took pride in the antiquity of the Corporation and were jealous of its privileges and ancient rights. Old customs and traditions, many of them common to corporate towns of medieval origin in Ireland and England, continued to be acted out each year. Indeed, with the official calendar shorn of many of the Popish festivals of former times, civic feasts and rituals took on a heightened public importance in the eighteenth century.

In Cork, as in every Irish corporation, the civic year began around Michaelmas, 29 September, when the new mayor, elected by the Council the previous month, took the oaths of office. The start of the municipal year had two distinctive local elements: a public pelting of the mayor with bran and coarse flour when he first showed himself to the citizenry and a mounted parade of civic officers, led by the mayor, that wended its way around the legal boundaries of the city. These apparently ancient rites incorporated a more modern and contested anniversary: that marking the return of Cork to Protestant control in 1690, when the Jacobite garrison had surrendered to Williamite forces under the command of the Duke of Marlborough. Out of the ashes of that siege, the eighteenth-century city had emerged.

September was also the month when the seaways and roadways converging on the city became busier. The maritime approaches to Cork were never short of sailing vessels in motion, but through the autumn and early winter months there was a noticeable increase in the number of ships present in the lower harbour. These ranged from small coasters, fishing smacks, cross-channel colliers and packets to the long-haul merchantmen travelling to Iberian, North American and Caribbean destinations and the naval men-of-war. Most were seeking out the products for which eighteenth-century Cork was famous: salted beef, tallow, hides and butter.

September was the month when the slaughtering season began. Since the 1660s an export trade in salted beef had become one of the main elements of the urban economy. In early years, supplies were purchased at a great three-day fair held on the edge of town that opened on St Matthew's Day, 21 September. But as the trade grew, twice-weekly markets were held north of Blarney Lane and later again they became daily. Thousands of grass-fattened bullocks were driven to Cork for sale and slaughter throughout the autumn. The processing of the meat, the hides, the fatty residues and the cattle horns supported a range of specialist crafts. The numbers of cattle herded from the prime fattening grounds north of the Blackwater and beyond had reached 80,000 per annum by the 1760s, the peak of the trade, by which time up to 900 beasts were being slaughtered each day during the 90-day season.

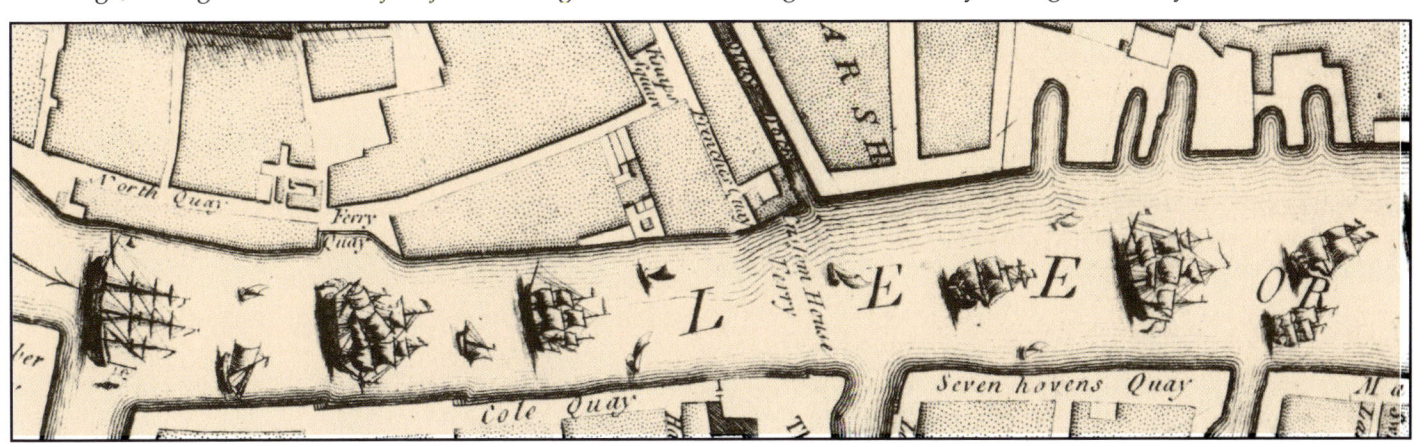

Fig. 2.31 Detail of ships sailing around the inner harbour in Rocque's 1759 plan. The insertion of a virtual flotilla of vessels was an astute decorative device achieved probably by the employment of transfers.

Life in the city hinged on the business of the butchers; the wealthier ones spent much of their summertime on horseback, making forward deals with the big graziers who were bringing large herds of bullocks into prime condition. Cattle were then driven to Cork and usually rested for several days on 'standing ground' at the edge of the city before being brought to slaughter. Abattoirs were concentrated close to the steep streets and running water of the north suburbs, but the detritus and the ensuing stench affected most folk in this closely packed area.

John Rogers, a leading city doctor writing in 1735, was struck by the way the slaughtering season changed the popular diet:

> In no part of the earth, a greater quantity of flesh-meat is consumed, than in this place, by all sorts and conditions of people during the slaughtering season. The vast profusion and plenty, and the low price, tempt the poorer sort to riot in this *luxuriant* diet: these suffer most by it, by the sudden change from a meagre fare.

He saw a correlation between the shift in diet and the seasonal pattern of epidemics and fever in the city. Rogers believed that the almost exclusively meat regime of those who could not afford to balance it with 'bread well fermented' and citrus fruit gravely weakened their constitution.[1] In Rogers' time, the waste products were sold locally by slaughter-houses, but a generation later merchants found external markets for much of this – for bullock heads and hearts, kidneys and 'skirts', 'at which [trade] the poor are very angry'.[2] Autumn and winter remained, however, the time of comparative plenty, as oatmeal carts and potato boats converged on the city. Employment picked up sharply in these months and, with it, casual wages: 'in the slaughtering season, great butchers require a vast number of journeyman and cleave-boys whom they pay very handsomely on the spur of the moment – but when the hurry is over, they leave them to live on offals till the next season'.[3]

The heightened demand for labour in the slaughteryards, the cooperages, the tallow chandleries, the salt-works and in port-related handling and transport triggered wage demands from journeymen, particularly the coopers.[4] It also encouraged seasonal migration into the city, mainly from Cork and Kerry. When Arthur Young first visited the 'amazingly thronged' streets of Cork in September 1776, he was told that in summertime the population of the city was 67,000 souls but that after the beginning of September it was '20,000 increased'. Both figures are on the high side, but Young was almost unique among eighteenth-century visitors to the city in commenting on this population movement.[5]

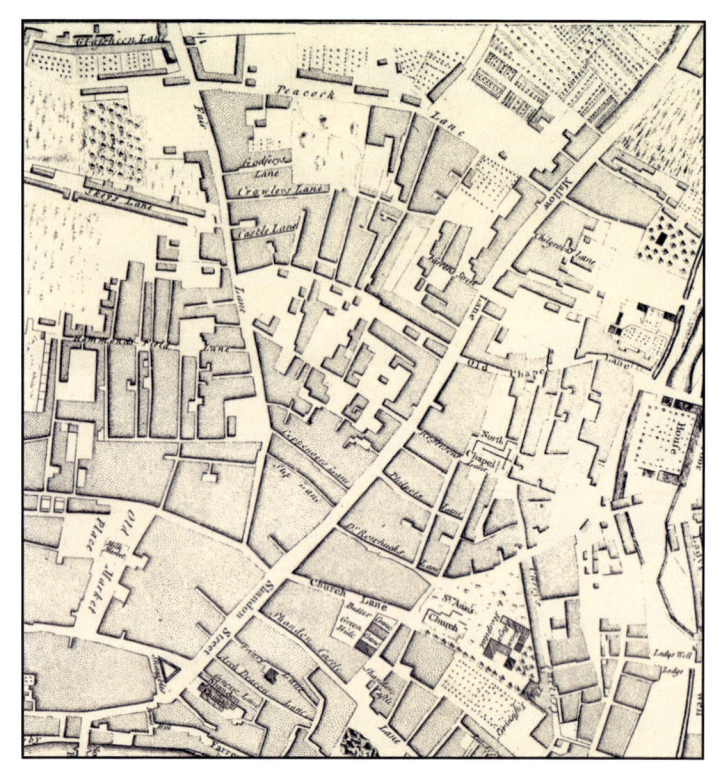

Fig. 2.32 Fair Lane and Mallow Lane from Rocque's 1759 map. Huge volumes of black cattle were moved in to support many abattoirs and tanneries.

Where did these seasonal workers live? Most of them probably boarded with close relatives, for Cork like every pre-industrial city needed a constant flow of country migrants just to hold its numbers. The impressive growth of the city since Williamite times had only been possible with the ample influx of young adults. Many of the unskilled settled on the northside alleys and lanes close to Mallow Lane, Blarney Lane and Fair Lane, in the single-storey thatched houses captured in John Butts' panorama of the city *c.* 1760.

The much-travelled Frenchman, de Motraye, who spent some weeks in Cork in the late 1720s, noted of the Blarney Lane neighbourhood that it was '*habitée par les plus pauvres gens dont les maisons ne valent pas mieux que les hutes de pescheurs* [sic]'. A few years later 'Alexander the Coppersmith' labelled nearby Mallow Lane as the city's 'nursery of villainy'.[6] By the end of the century, as parts of the inner city became more dilapidated, garret and cellar tenants became more numerous in the older multi-storey buildings near the river, and many of these folk no doubt were country 'swallows'.

Winter

Life in the shadow of the provisions trade was harsh and the twelve-hour working day punishing: some business went

Fig. 2.33 Detail from Butts' 'A View of Cork', 1760, showing the Custom House and a busy quayside. (Source: Crawford Municipal Art Gallery.)

Fig. 2.34 The 'Wren Boys', *c.* 1841, by D. Maclise captures the ethos of a very popular pageant.

on through the night at the peak of the season and street lamps, formerly extinguished early in the night, stayed burning through the whole night between September and April from the 1770s. The number of street lamps was gradually extended to over 2,200 by the beginning of the nineteenth century.[7] Work in these stockyards was seen by some as 'debauching' and unsavoury. References in the eighteenth-century press to brothels and to intermittent attempts by the Corporation to stamp them out occurred in mid-winter.[8]

Christmas and St Stephen's Day provided a momentary break in the bruising routine; the Wren Boys, strongest in Munster, were out on the city streets begging for money for feasting. The mayor suppressed the practice in 1845, a year or two after Daniel Maclise's striking depiction. For the respectable classes, wintertime social activity centred on the coffee-houses by day and the assembly-house by night, where from the 1750s concerts and 'drums', gambling and backgammon sessions were held at least once a week.[9]

Mid-winter was a time of danger: torrential rainfall in the catchment area of the Lee in conjunction with high tides have always spelt trouble (see *The Climate of Cork*, Chapter 2; *Flooding in the City*, Chapter 3). Sections of the recently reclaimed land along the eastern quays were poorly reinforced and there were several disastrous floods, most of them in mid-winter, notably in January 1725 and 1726, January 1750, December 1771, December 1773, January 1789 and January 1796. The 1789 flood, coming amid a commercial building boom, cost city merchants £50,000.[10] These exceptional weather events destroyed older houses and traders' stock, damaged the primitive systems of urban water-supply and drainage and on occasion wrecked city bridges, quays and shipping. Some must have despaired at the limitations of the site of the city when nature could wreak such havoc. Prudent builders, like those on the South Mall, kept their cellars at or above street level.

A less frequent hazard was prolonged frost, sufficient to freeze the Lee and halt the mills. The winter of 1683–1684 was one such event, when

Fig. 2.35 The South Mall became progressively urbanised during the eighteenth century and was transformed from being dockland with many warehouses into a more salubrious locale for many offices and residences. The steps leading to first-floor entrances remind us of a time when goods from waterborne traffic had to be brought 'upstairs'. (Photo: John Crowley.)

gentlemen's coaches were driven across the river channels. In the eighteenth century the main channels froze on at least five occasions, the most severe being the great frost of December–January 1739–1740. That winter of unparalleled cold started with recreational feasting on the ice, but a bizarre sequence of weather extremes, first frost then drought, triggered a chain reaction of disasters in town and countryside. The whole of northern Europe was affected, but the social consequences in Ireland were appalling: spring cereals and potatoes were decimated. The impact on Cork and its hinterland was particularly severe; the excess death rate in city and county during 1740 and 1741 was probably higher than that of the Great Famine a century later.[11]

In more temperate years, winter gave strength to the streams and rivers around the city. In an age when the most advanced technology was water-powered mills, winter was the season when this energy was most easily harnessed. In the city itself and at mill settlements outside the city – as along the Glanmire valley, at Douglas and around Blarney with its paper-making and metal-working, cloth-tucking and seed-grinding – wintertime was, therefore, busy. After the harvest, the industrial processes based on cereals – namely grinding, milling, baking, malting, brewing and distilling – tended to be most vigorously pursued.

The other weather hazard, storms, was an ever-present concern in an age of sail. On the whole, the ample lower harbour was regarded by mariners who knew their way around the north Atlantic sea-lanes as a friendly haven in wintertime. Compared to the treacherous shallows of Dublin Bay, Cork Harbour, even in the busiest winters, seemed relatively safe. Larger vessels cast anchor off Passage, and most cargoes were shuttled by lighter to the city quays. The construction of the tracking wall and eastward extensions of the quays allowed vessels of 300 tons draught to sail up to the city by 1800.

Spring

As Lent approached, the bullock-slaughtering season was finished, export merchants were making up their orders from foreign merchants and the ancillary trades such as the tallow chandlers, the tanners and the glue-makers had by now acquired stocks sufficient to keep them busy through the year. The city was becoming somewhat quieter. It is true that the butchers' season was lengthened after the 1760s with the growing importance of the pig trade. Barrelled pork was becoming by then an attractive alternative to salted beef as the price differential narrowed and it found growing favour among continental and naval purchasers. Pigs were a small-farm business and they were generally fattened on potatoes. They were brought to market from New Year onwards when the beef season was over. However, it was not until Napoleonic times that pigs eclipsed the bullock trade.

The eve of Lent was carnival time and the goodbye to meat for most families was not just for the Lenten days of abstinence but until the next slaughtering season. The days before Lent were a time of sport – specifically cock-fights.[12] In addition, there was the custom for which the city later became famous – the Skellig list. This tradition had old roots but its evolution is unclear; the taunting of bachelors and unmarried women in the days leading up to Ash Wednesday was no doubt commonplace. The printing of lists of those to be 'shamed' was an early nineteenth-century local elaboration. By then, Cork's Skellig night was a time of carnival and licence. James Beale's atmospheric painting of South Mall on Skellig night *c.* 1845 suggests an inclusive, gently subversive civic moment in an otherwise much-divided city (Fig. 2.36).[13]

Fig. 2.36 'Skellig Night on the South Mall', c. 1845, by James Beale (1798–1879). (Source: Crawford Art Municipal Gallery.)

The end of Lent meant more to the Catholics than their Protestant neighbours, but as bells were only permitted in the Church of Ireland churches, the proclamation of Easter and of every formal religious holiday always came from Protestant steeples and churches. It is striking though that a pre-Reformation relic, a parade by the company of butchers symbolically tossing the herring as the symbol of Lent, survived as a civic event in the city marking the end of Lent. It was painted by Nathaniel Grogan, presumably in the 1780s or 1790s. Grogan's image of the huddle of unkempt butchers at North Gate was hardly a tribute to the dignity of the big slaughter-house owners. The figures shown here were more likely to have been stall-holders in the 'English Market' who retailed meat to the respectable citizenry.[14]

When the previous year's cereal harvest or potato crop had been deficient, this would begin to affect retail prices in the late winter and early spring; oatmeal prices would edge upwards and the size of a fixed-priced loaf would diminish as farmers and dealers played the market. If the suspicion grew that big merchants were hoarding stocks for export, or excessively delaying the release of grain onto local markets, public irritation erupted. Crowds, led by weavers and butchers, made for the houses and stores of the supposed hoarders and on more than one occasion there was major violence before order was restored. In the February riot in the famine year of 1729, the mayor, Hugh Millerd, was the butt of crowd anger and his house was destroyed. At least three were killed on that occasion before the military garrison restored order.[15]

Prevailing prices usually fell a little after these spontaneous outbursts; more to the point, city merchants were discouraged from becoming involved in the shipping of cereals from Cork to other parts of Ireland, even in comparatively good years. It also meant that the city Corporation was proactive, notably in 1740, in commissioning orders for flour and wheat from European and transatlantic sources ahead of private merchants. There was a gradual elaboration in the kind of emergency food relief provided by voluntary parish and city committees: between spring and autumn in 1797, over 14,000 people were being regularly fed from charity boilers in the city.[16] A hungry spring also meant an influx of rural beggars seeking help and

Fig. 2.37 This evocative painting by Grogan entitled 'Whipping the Herring' captures the vibrant atmosphere of a popular ritual enactment. (Source: Crawford Municipal Art Gallery.)

Fig. 2.38 Millerd Street, named after a family that was deeply involved in eighteenth-century civic life. (Photo: John Crowley.)

cheaper food in the city. Many resented their presence, not least because in the worst of years beggars brought famine fever and other infectious diseases into renewed currency.

In most years there was a moment of festive relief at the end of spring: May Day, celebrated on the first Sunday of the month. No other day in the urban calendar was as important, both as a moment of general conviviality and excess and as an opportunity for territorial contests between northside neighbourhoods, especially in the days leading up to it. Fair Lane and Blarney Lane were the two contesting factions who, between the 1740s and the 1770s, did battle, occasionally with fatal results. Paramilitary gangs engaged

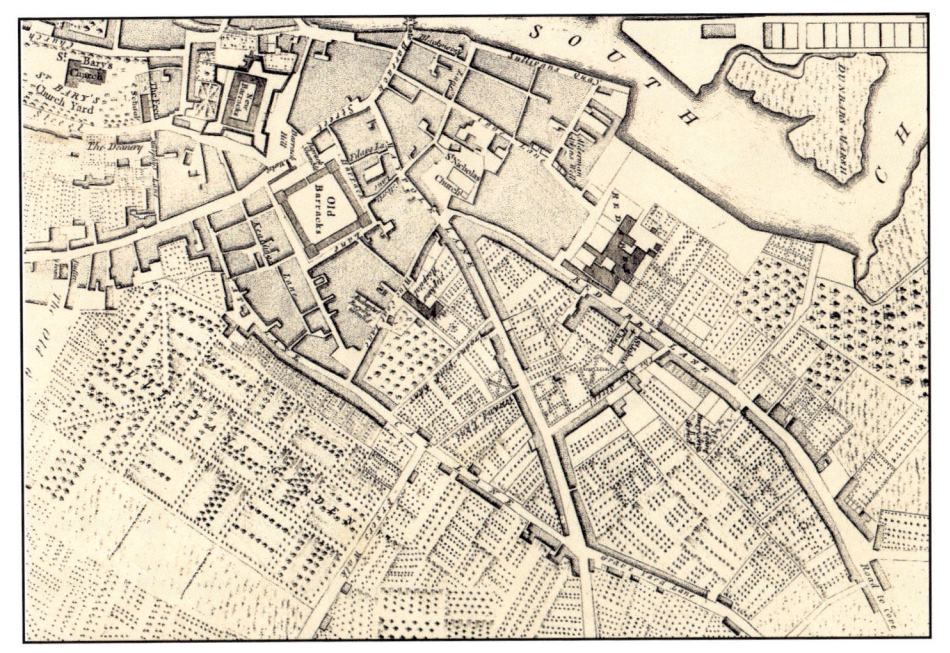

Fig. 2.39 Maypole Lane, now Evergreen Street, shown by Rocque in 1773 as a lane running out from Barrack Street into a maze of well-cared-for gardens and orchards.

in street displays, 'with colours flying, bagpipes playing', during the competition for Maypoles.[17] These faction fights, which sometimes flared up on other Sundays in spring and summer, became less prevalent, or at least less violent, later in the century. Vast numbers streamed out to spend a bacchanalian day in the pastoral surrounds of Glanmire, and May Day continued to be a holiday which happily united the lower-class urban Protestants and Catholics.[18]

Summer

In those exceptional years when rain failed in spring or summer, its absence could be disastrous for both the economy and the health of the poor. And there was the risk of fire in a city with no effective fire prevention: in June 1762, after a period of almost no rain for five months, fire broke out on the southside along Cat Lane (Tower Street) and swept through some 150, presumably thatched, houses; fire ravaged several dozen cabins in the Fair Lane district in June 1775; and the terrible drought of 1800 led to some 50 houses being destroyed in August, again in poverty-stricken Cat Lane (see the case study, *Weather and Natural Disasters*, in Chapter 2).[19]

In normal summers, the landscape outside the city was green, the grass grew strongly and the region's ubiquitous cows lactated. Before May was out, the first pack-horses reached the city laden with freshly salted butter. In the months following, thousands of small farmers, farm servants and carriers made their way to the city butter market, and thence to the stores of parishes across Cork, Kerry and west Waterford. Unlike the bullock trade, the butter business brought vast numbers of countrymen to the city in summertime. Those who travelled with their modest cargoes from west Cork or south Kerry, as was increasingly the case by the later eighteenth century, lingered on for a night or two.

The shops and taverns, both in the central parishes and the suburbs, depended on this country trade and equipped themselves for it. The striking variety of shop signs and symbols in the less fashionable streets of the city helped guide and attract the illiterate consumer. Groceries and salt, timber and metalware, such as spades, helped fill the carts and truckles of the thousands of returning dairymen, who might visit the city no more than two or three times a year.

All classes of retailer sought to have new stock for the summer, whether the produce of the city's workshops or the latest fashions brought in from Dublin and London. The wagon trade from Dublin carrying high-quality goods, such as fine woollens, silks and furnishings, reached a peak during the summer months. Indeed, in the second half of the century there were several attempts by local craftworkers, notably the weavers of Blackpool, to hijack these vehicles on their way into the city. This was either a response to hard times or the fear of outside competition.

The strength of summer business rested not so much on the small farmer's purchases as on those made by the people of higher station, like the gentry who also came to town in

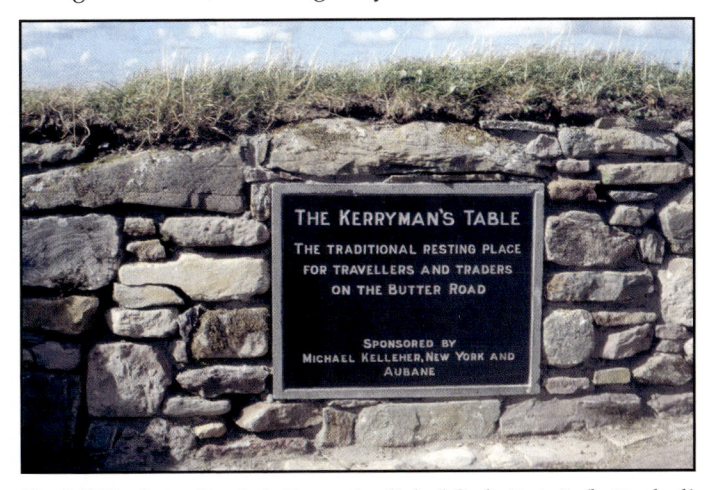

Fig. 2.40 The Butter Road – better roads – linked Cork city to its 'buttershed' in counties Cork, Kerry and Limerick. It is a typical gun-barrel road, in that for most of its course it is dead straight. It pays little attention to topography and curves are only evident when it encounters severe topographical challenges. (Photo: P. O'Flanagan.)

Fig. 2.41 The Exchange, North Main Street, was one of Cork's most renowned public buildings and a prominent skyline feature. This was the locale where bankers, merchants and shippers transacted business. (Source: Cork Archives Institute.)

had sprung up on every eminence over Cork harbour since the beginning of the eighteenth century. Indeed, the abundance of suburban sites commanding views of the harbour or, west of the city, along the Lee valley explain why so few wealthy citizens engaged in conspicuous architectural display in the city itself. The harbour was the great attraction, especially in summertime. The precocious founding of the Cork Water Club in the 1720s revealed how the harbour was already seen as an extension of the city and that its sheltered waters could be a zone of élite recreation and display. Summer on the water was capped by a civic show marking the end of the muncipal year, when the outgoing mayor led a flotilla downstream to Blackrock, accompanied by musicians. This culminated in the ritual throwing of a dart into the harbour waters to mark the limits of the city's jurisdiction.[20] But all fashion percolates through society, and one of the great moments in the social calendar of city folk by the beginning of the nineteenth century was the July fair at Passage, a carnival of excess that rivalled Dublin's Donnybrook fair, but with an added maritime dimension.

summer. There were in fact two points in the year when men of property and business from across south Munster always tried to be in the city: the spring and summer assizes, when the judges on circuit came to Cork to hear criminal cases before the county grand jury. These times were critical points of contact between central government and the Protestant community at large. The first assize was held in early April, the second and generally larger in late August. It was generally also in the summer months that the rare vice-regal visit to the city occurred.

In the wake of the judges followed a retinue of barristers. One of the things that made Assizes Fortnight so important was the opportunity it gave for people of property to meet and settle business, arrange deals, locate debtors and get a sense of the local political breeze. It was not merely a male-dominated occasion. Wives and daughters of wealthy farmers and gentry seized assizes gatherings as an opportunity to socialise and search out partners and future spouses. Much of this social calendar, notably the theatre season, began around the August assizes and ran for a further three to five weeks. It was socially restrictive without being exclusive.

With maritime trade temporally slack, the export merchant and professional city families retreated to the countryside, or rather to the panoply of villa residences that

The end of summer was marked in town and countryside by St Bartholomew's Day, 24 August. A less exuberant occasion than May Day in Cork, it was nevertheless a time when vast crowds congregated around a holy well outside the suburbs. According to one witness, the pilgrimage culminated in 'wrestling and yelling, dancing, noise and merriment'.[21]

By September, the professional players who played the Cork stage every summer were moving on as the slaughtering season got under way. The gentry were gone, as Dublin and its seasonal delights began to beckon, while the merchants were back in full force on The Exchange and a new crop of ill-prepared migrants were preparing to enter the jostling, unhealthy but vibrant city. It was autumn again.

Irish in Eighteenth-Century Cork

Neil Buttimer

Irish speakers reacted to the city in this period in various ways. Some who settled and worked there seem to have achieved a degree of familiarity and perhaps ease with its urban life. This may be seen in the case of the anonymous author of the poem *Fógraim, leathaim is scaipim i measc na tíre* ('Now shall I spread about the voice of fame'). The text is centred on Paul Street, a precinct which developed east of the old town walls during the late 1600s. It speaks of Uilliam Ó Ceallaigh, a tailor who operated in the area. The work praises him for his skill in making, from the finest scarlet, what appears to be a bellows or bag for the composer's *uilleann* pipes. The instrument now plays as powerfully as the bells of St Fin Barre's (*cloig Naoimh Barra*), according to the piece. This reference suggests the poem was completed after 1752, when Cork's Church of Ireland cathedral installed its new carillon. The sounds of the city and the activities of its craftsmen thus resonate naturally in the fabric of this literary creation. Its author had no hesitation in recommending that residents of east, north and west Munster (where Irish was normally in use), who wished their cloth to be cut and made up according to the best London and Parisian fashions, seek out Ó Ceallaigh for their requirements.

The document containing the earliest version of *Fógraim, leathaim* was compiled by the copyist Stephen Cox. He is probably identical with an individual of the same name based in nearby Half Moon Street, and was apparently a sailmaker. Others involved in maritime matters were also Gaelic scribes. One of these was Muiris Camshrónach Ó Conchubhair, a shipwright (*saor loingis*) living in Leitrim Street, to whom codices containing poetry, historical and devotional works are attributed. Members of other professions were present in the city as well. Among these was the manuscript writer, Peadar Ó Féichín, a teacher with an address in Barrack Street, near Elizabeth Fort or Cat Fort. Teaching may also have been the occupation of another penman, Séamus Ó Broin, as indicated by the survival among his writings of a dictionary, together with tracts on orthography and grammar. Of particular interest is the appearance in his papers of a handwritten list, in English, of the mayors of Cork from 1333 to 1776. It draws, perhaps, on a similar register in Charles Smith's *Antient and Present State of the County and City of Cork* (1750) and is interspersed with perceptive comments on the strengths and weaknesses of the city's magistrates. These entries reveal acute observation of civic affairs on the part of the scribe or others in his general circle.

Assimilation of the Gaelic community did not occur to such an extent that Irish became a lasting vernacular in Cork. However, the language undoubtedly left its mark on how English was spoken there. Some facets of its imprint are not easy to quantify, but other influences are more definite. Falling into the first of these two categories may be the speed and pitch associated with aspects of the Cork accent (itself a social hybrid). Use of metaphor to express a fact or a concept is an established practice in Gaelic speech patterns. This second feature may surface in the city's English also. Residents of Cork's northside, who might characterise a journey south of the Lee (a distance of no more than a few hundred metres in length) as tantamount to going on a world tour, would convey through such an image the not inconsiderable differences in topography and society that distinguish both parts of the same urban environment, as well as the degree to which each is unknown to the other. The use of word-play can be simultaneously inventive, challenging and defensive. The more demonstrable trace elements from Irish are lexical. Thus, an English speaker who unselfconsciously describes a cantankerous female neighbour as a *badhb* employs a term attested from the earliest stages of Gaelic literature onwards, where it designates a 'scald-crow', the embodiment of the war goddess. These phonological, stylistic and semantic layers were more than likely set down in Cork English substantially before the 1700s. However, the drawing in of new inhabitants from all of Cork's contiguous Irish-speaking counties and from farther afield which led to the remarkable increase in the city's population throughout the eighteenth century must be credited with a consolidation of such tendencies.

Persons associated with the Gaelic world did not have a uniformly positive impression of Cork at the time, however. The story of Muircheartach Óg Ó Súilleabháin (Morty Oge Sullivan) illustrates the argument. This native of the Beara peninsula was involved in coastal trading, smuggling and the press-ganging of local youths for service in Wild Geese regiments in continental European armies. In March 1754, he and some associates assassinated John Puxley, a tax official who had sought to curtail trade in contraband, even though his family was earlier involved in it. Government forces pursued and shot Morty Oge in May and arrested two of his collaborators. Ó Súilleabháin's body was attached to the back of a boat and drawn into Cork harbour from Bereheaven. His companions were hanged in late August, all three decapitated and their heads placed on spikes in the Cork Gaol at South Gate Bridge (see *Christianity, Churches and Burial Places*, Chapter 9).

The incident was the subject of a number of poems in Irish, one of which attempts to conjure up the sentiments of Ó Súilleabháin's assistant, a Domhnall Ó Conaill, in Cork just before his execution. He speaks of having been bound in chains and dragged by 'the dogs of the street' through the mud (*Madraí na sráide, im cháibleadh ar fuaid ghutaigh*), while his tormentors bayed arrogantly (*a' búirtheach le mustar*). A text attributed to Sullivan's fostermother claimed that Morty Oge's decapitation would give particular satisfaction to what appear to be the city's purse-holders (*lucht sparán i gCorcaigh*). The sense of alienation revealed in this extreme instance is replicated elsewhere. Diarmuid mac Eoghan na Tuinne Mac Carthaigh travelled from north-west of the county to Cork's city's butter-market, where he died. In retrieving his remains and lamenting his loss, his mother mourned his demise among churls and English and the families of merchants (*búir nú Sasanaigh nú clann ceannuithe*). These would have been unlikely to wake and mourn him as his own community might have done, or even to regard his departure as being of any consequence. Other parts of Cork and a range of alternative experiences are therefore at issue in these examples. All combine to underline the complex interaction, in human, cultural and linguistic terms, one would have encountered in the city in its earlier heyday.

Nano Nagle and Catholic Cork: 1718–1784

Mary Pius O'Farrell

Eighteenth-century Cork was a city where education was the preserve of the privileged few. There was little educational provision for the poor, the vast majority of whom were Catholic. The Penal Laws prohibited both Catholic teachers and schools. As a result, the education of Catholics was largely driven underground or abroad. The establishment of charter and charity schools in the city reflected a desire amongst the city's Protestant élite to cater for the educational needs of the poor. A Blue Coat school for boys was founded on the south side of the city c. 1699, while the Green Coat charity school was founded in the Shandon area in 1716. Religious instruction in these schools was principally in the Protestant faith.[1] This presented a major challenge to Catholic interests in the city. The increasing affluence of Georgian Cork could not hide the dire conditions of the Catholic poor. By mid-century, the vacuum was eventually filled by the pioneering educational endeavours of a Cork woman, Nano Nagle, whose work with the poor would leave a lasting impression on the city and its people.

Nano Nagle was born in 1718 in Ballygriffin, Killavullen, about six miles east of Mallow in the county of Cork and in the diocese of Cloyne. The family were descendants of once powerful Anglo-Norman settlers, the Nagles of Cork and the Butler–Mathew family of Kilkenny/Tipperary.

> Although the eighteenth-century Nagles had come down in the world, and were threatened by the Penal Laws, and by their Protestant neighbours, it would be wrong to think of them as hopelessly downtrodden, like say, the poor Catholics of the northwest. Munster was different and Munster Catholics of the Nagle class were resilient.[2]

Her parents were Garret Nagle and Ann Mathew and she was the eldest of seven children. After elementary education in her own home and perhaps in a hedge school, she was obliged to go to Paris for further training.

In Paris, she enjoyed an attractive lifestyle circulating in the social milieu of descendants of her grand-uncle, Sir Richard Nagle. Richard Nagle had fled Ireland in the aftermath of the 'War of the Two Kings' (1689–1691), losing in the process some 5,000 acres of land that extended from Mallow to Waterford. Her uncle was Joseph Nagle, whose nephew, also named Joseph, wrote that a little triangle of land in the city – where Douglas Street and Evergreen Street now meet – was the only land saved from a Bill of Discovery. Here she was to live and die. The portion of land would become central in her attempts to evangelise and educate the poor of the city.

In Paris, she witnessed first-hand the terrible suffering of the poorer classes. This affected her deeply. Called home when her father died c. 1746, she went to Bachelor's Quay in Dublin to live with her mother and her sister Ann. Dublin, like Paris, was a breeding-ground for the destitute. In 1748, her mother died. Shortly afterwards, Ann also passed away and Nano returned to Ballygriffin to stay with her brother David. In Cork city, she again encountered many oppressed people reduced to idleness, ignorance and drunkenness. Uncertain of her future and filled with a sense of her own helplessness, she left Ireland 'for a convent in Paris' but soon returned to Cork.

In the early 1750s, she secretly opened a school in Cove Lane (now Douglas Street) that attracted children from nearby Pender's Alley, Willow Lane, Gould's Lane, Donovan's Lane and Primrose Lane. Located in a cabin, the school consisted of two earthen-floored rooms, a garret and a thatched roof. In such conditions began her life-long involvement with a poverty-stricken people. Several months passed before her brother Joseph was informed of the school's existence. It was her uncle Joseph (Nagle), 'the most disliked by the Protestants of any Catholic in the Kingdom', whom she feared most.[3] However, her uncle did not place any obstacles in her path and supported his niece with generous contributions.

In a relatively short time she was operating seven poor schools across the city. Three were located in Cove Lane in the city's southside, while three others were situated on the northside of the city in the vicinity of Philpott Lane. A further school was located in the 'middle parish' at the junction of the present Grattan Street and Sheares Street. Two of these schools catered exclusively for boys, with a master for each. She continued steadfastly with her mission, constantly walking the streets of Cork, meeting the poor at

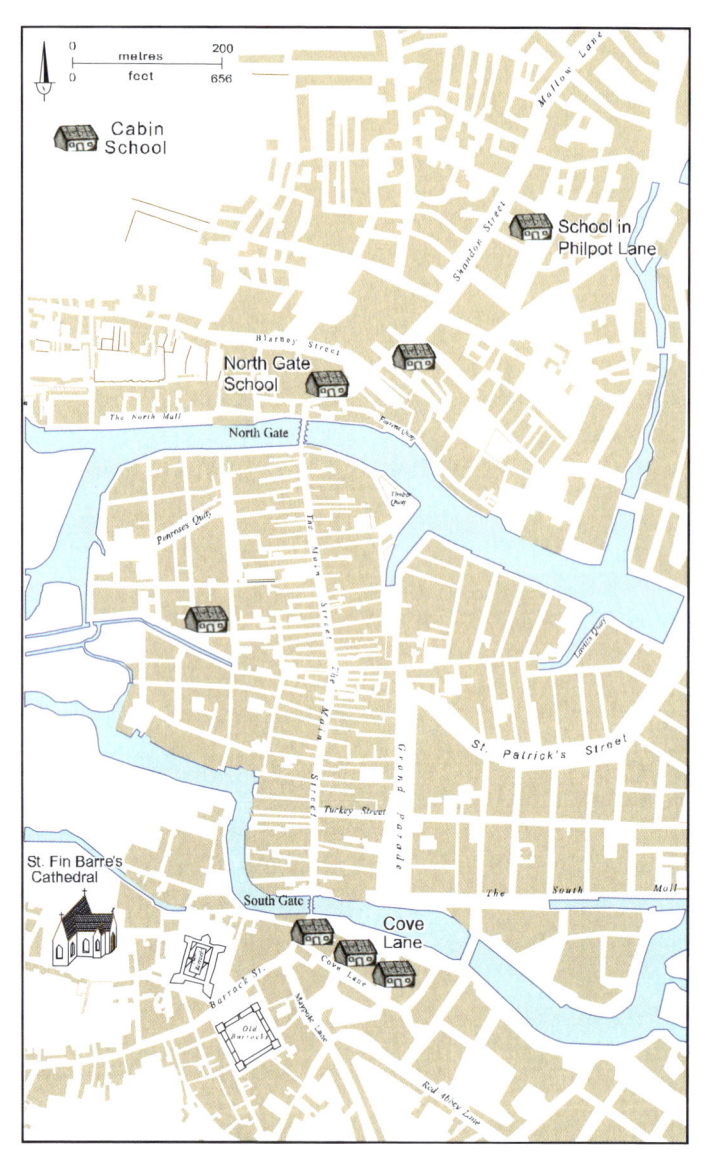

Fig. 2.42 The incidence of cabin schools, each one of which drew on highly localised pupil catchments.

every turn and extolling the virtues of the Gospel. 'How often have we seen her', wrote Bishop Coppinger, 'after a well-spent day, returning through the darkness of the night, dripping with rain, mingling with the bustling crowd, moving thoughtfully along by the faint glimmering of a wretched lantern, withholding from herself in this manner, the necessaries of life, to administer the comfort of it to others'.[4] Eminently practical, she paid teachers to train the children, not only in reading, writing and arithmetic, but also in skills like needlework by which they could earn a living. She herself would teach matters pertaining to the spiritual development of the child. By 1769, she wrote that she was 'taking delight and pleasure' in her schools:

> They learn to read and when they have the Douai Catechism by heart, they learn to write and cipher.
> There are three schools where the girls learn to read and when they have the catechism by heart, they learn to work. They all hear mass every day, say their morning and night prayers, say the Catechism in each school by question and answer together. Every Saturday they all say the beads, the grown girls every evening. They go to confession once a month and to communion when their confessors think proper. The schools are open at eight, at noon the children go to dinner, at five o'clock they leave school.[5]

Her evangelising spirit would take her inexorably beyond the schoolroom and into the heart of the communities she served. Through daily contact with the children, she got to know widows and orphans, the old, the sick and the abandoned. Over a period of 30 years, it is quite possible that she got to know 'every garret in the city'.[6] Finances were scarce and the burden of supporting the schools weighed heavily on her shoulders. Hers was a constant search for new benefactors. In that respect, she was not alone a teacher but a social activist.

The schools she founded represented the bedrock of her mission in the city. Despite financial constraints, she

Fig. 2.43 A portrait of 'Nano Nagle and her Pupils' by James Butler Brennan, 1825–1889. (Source: Crawford Municipal Art Gallery.)

Fig. 2.44 Foundation dates of Presentation houses in Ireland.

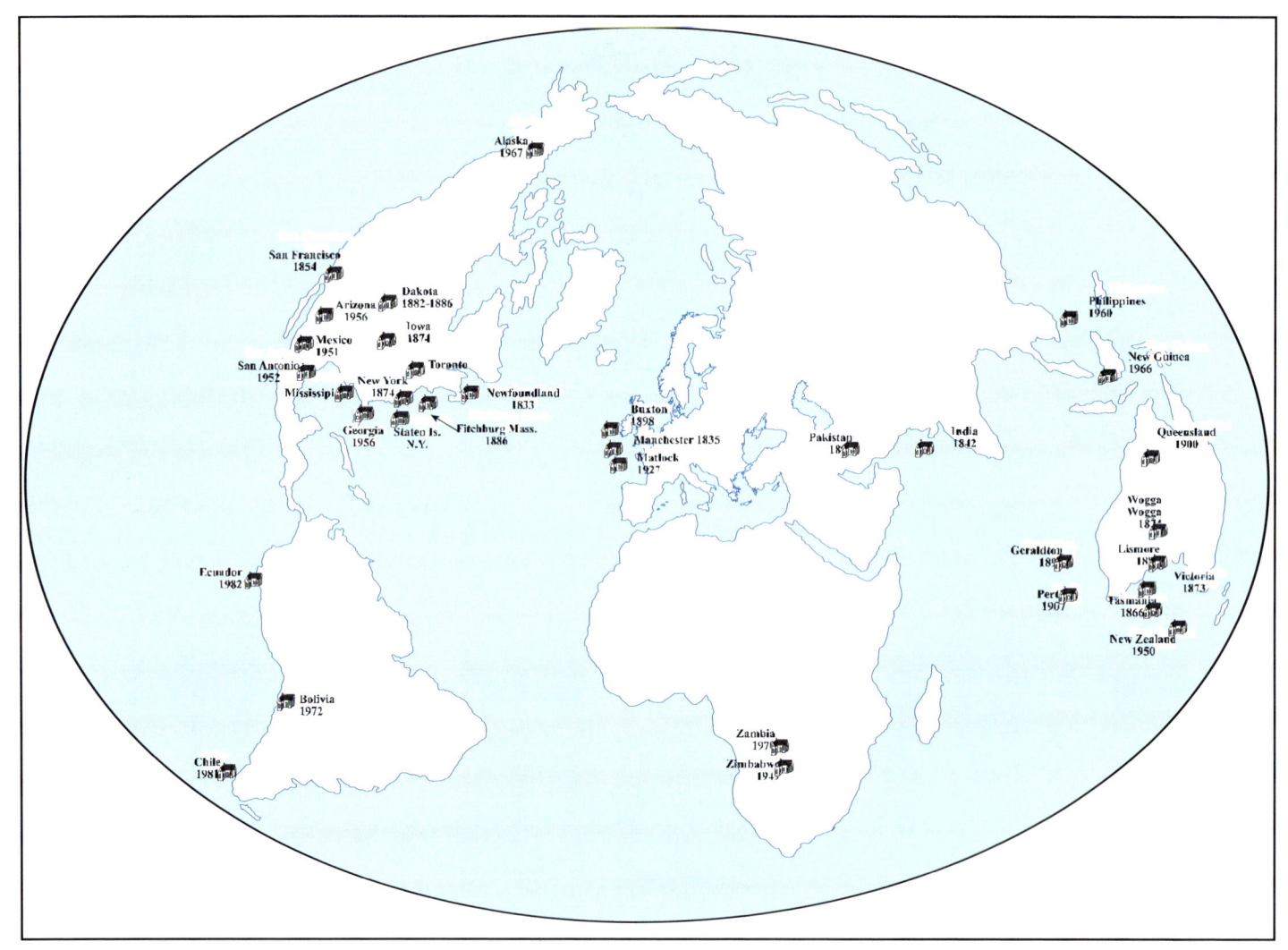

Fig. 2.45 Worldwide foundation dates of Presentation houses.

remained resolute in her commitment to the schools and their future. To secure that future, she funded the training of four Ursuline sisters in Paris. By 1771, five Ursuline sisters had settled in Cork city. Administering a school for the poor, however, could not disguise the fact that the Ursulines primarily served the Catholic gentry in the city.

That they opted for enclosure went against the grain of her vision for the sisters. In response, she founded a new religious congregation on Christmas Eve 1775. Known as the Sisters of the Charitable Instruction of the Sacred Heart of Jesus, it would later be called the Presentation Order. The new congregation represented a radical departure. As Clear explains, 'it was the first of the modern, socially active congregations in Ireland. It was intended as a sisterhood without enclosure and with a multi-dimensional function of work amongst the poor.'[7]

The new congregation was drawn mainly from the teachers and associates in her schools who were close to the people she cared for most. Elizabeth Burke, Mary Fouhy and Angela Collins were talented women and she had them 'perfected in the art of teaching'. It was to her close friend Teresa Mulally that she poured out the perplexities of each day, all the while hoping that Teresa would join her in her new undertaking. The close bond of friendship that existed between them is very much evident in a letter dated 31 January 1783 in which she revealed to Teresa her hopes for the future of the Order.[8]

Finding suitable candidates for both the Ursuline foundation and her own was a constant worry. Her struggle to formulate constitutions – an abiding and troublesome necessity – also caused her much anxiety. The Bishop of Cork, Francis Moylan, would finally complete this task. In 1782, the laws that excluded Catholics from teaching in schools were rescinded, but by then she had but two years to live. The shadow of the Penal Laws had in effect followed her from the cradle to the grave. She died on the 26 April 1784. The *Hibernian Chronicle* of the day recorded her loss to all those in need, noting 'that she had won the esteem of all

Fig. 2.46 The tomb of Nano Nagle at the Presentation convent, Douglas Street. (Photo: John Crowley.)

accounted for 55 per cent of convents in Ireland. Teresa Mulally, who completed her novitiate in the Presentation convent in Cork, would later return to her native Waterford to found a poor school there.

Edmund Rice, the founder of the Christian Bothers, 'saw in the religious life and rule of the Presentation Sisters a pathway to perfection through the Catholic training of childhood'.[11] Rice and his associates would take their first religious vows in the chapel of the Presentation Sisters in Waterford in 1808. The model of education which Nano Nagle had devised in her Cork schools provided a template for Rice and his followers. The work of the Presentation Sisters would also influence Mary Aikenhead (1787–1858), who established the Irish Sisters of Charity in 1815, and Catherine McAuley (1778–1841), who founded the Sisters of Mercy in 1828.

Formal Papal recognition of the Presentation Order was bestowed in 1802. The missionary zeal of the sisters became more apparent as the nineteenth century progressed. The Presentation convent in Galway, founded in 1815, sent its first mission abroad to Newfoundland in 1833. A number of congregations soon followed suit and the Presentation Order firmly established itself in places such as Manchester in 1836, Madras in 1842, California in 1854 and New York in 1874. The flame that had been lit in Cork soon spread across the globe.

Nano Nagle resolved at an early stage that education could provide a solution to the widespread poverty in the city and this became the kernel of her mission amongst the city's poor. The congregation that she founded in 1755 would become a leading element in Catholic education. Aside from her own deep faith, the single thread of her humility and solidarity with the poor stands out amongst all her attributes. Her burial place today is situated within the Presentation convent in Douglas Street. Her life remains an integral part of the story of the city and its people.

ranks of people'.[9] The Protestant journal, *The Volunteer*, predicted that 'her name would resist the all destructive hand of time and that a monument would be raised in her honour'.[10]

In the aftermath of her death, the congregation that she founded went from strength to strength. From its humble beginnings in Cove Lane, it diffused throughout the country at a rapid rate. Congregations were founded in Killarney in 1793, Dublin in 1794, Waterford in 1798 and Kilkenny in 1800. By the mid-nineteenth century, the Presentation Sisters

Shandon

Colin Rynne

The present Shandon church was completed in 1722 as a 'chapel of ease' to the former St Mary's, Shandon, on Mallow Lane (latter-day Shandon Street) and was financed by subscription. John Rocque's map of Cork of 1773 shows St Anne's as 'Upper' Shandon church and St Mary's as 'Lower' Shandon. The original St Mary's church occupied the site of the present St Anne's, but was severely damaged in the siege of Cork in 1690. This latter site actually overlooked that of Shandon Castle, a key artillery station for Marlborough's besieging army in 1690. In 1690, the northern suburbs around Shandon were set alight by the Jacobites and Shandon Castle was abandoned, early on, to Marlborough's army. After the siege it was deemed inadvisable for the successor church to be built at a location that compromised the security of the castle. In consequence, the successor to St Mary's was built on a small eminence overlooking the North Gate Bridge on the former Mallow Lane, where it continued in use until it was demolished in 1879. The site of this latter chapel is currently occupied by the car park of an apartment building complex on Pope's Quay.

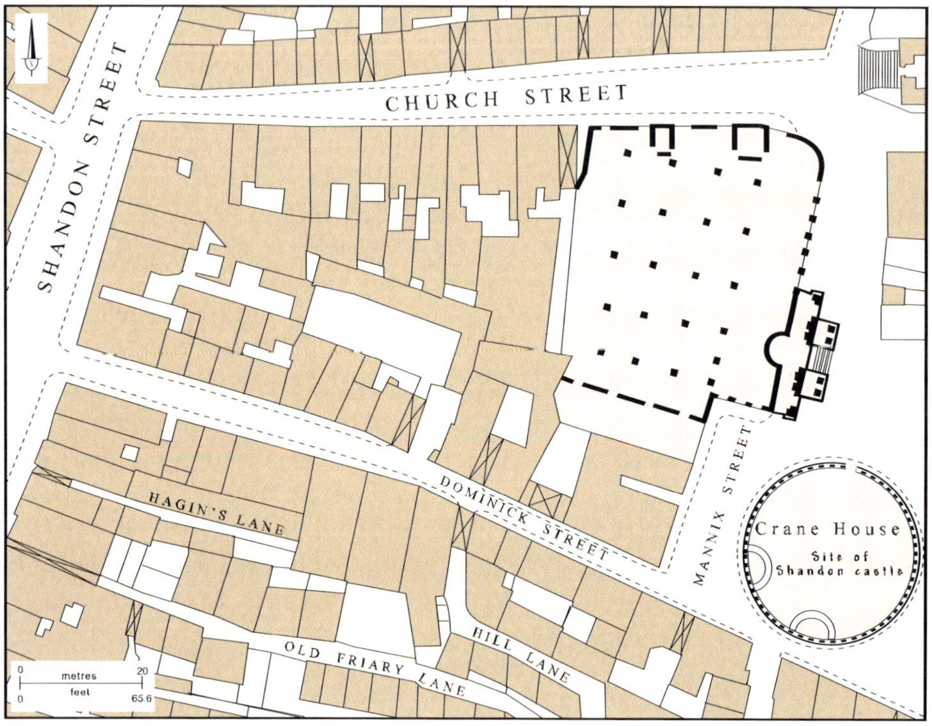

By the beginning of the eighteenth century the Mallow Lane area, the emerging centre of the Cork provisions industry, was also becoming the focal point of the Cork butter trade. By the 1730s, the Shandon area had become the most important butter-trading location in Ireland (Fig. 2.47).

The subsequent development of the Shandon area, and of the church itself, is intricately linked with that of the butter crane (a weighhouse) and the development of a formal butter market within the environs of the crane in 1770. In the early decades of the nineteenth century, a proper butter-market building was established on the site of the original crane house, and in a normal working day the area around the church was thronged with carters, farmers bringing butter to market, butter brokers and butter merchants. Indeed, until the closure of the Cork Butter Market in 1924, Shandon remained one of the busiest areas of the city, but in the aftermath of the closure its importance quickly declined.

The design of the church and its construction has been traditionally ascribed to John Coltsman, a master stonemason who had built the present South Gate Bridge in 1716. The church of Holy Trinity, Christ Church, on South Main Street was completed in the early 1720s and is also tentatively attributed to Coltsman. The use of ashlar limestone in all three structures is the only putative link between each structure.

Upon its completion in 1722, the original church tower comprised three diminishing stages, with a west-facing doorway flanked by fluted limestone pilasters and surmounted by an aedicule. The church has a simple basilican form – a nave and two aisles – but with a squared-off apse at its eastern end and no transepts. Even by the standards of the early eighteenth century, this church was quite plain, but its elevation enabled its original tower to take full advantage of the city skyline and there can be little doubt that its designer fully intended that it

Fig. 2.47 Shandon and its intricate streetscape (Source: Ordnance Survey Ireland, 1869).

would be visible from any point in the city. At the corners of each stage, the original tower also has pineapple sculptures, a common feature of eighteenth-century Cork ecclesiastical architecture. Similar features can be seen on Christ Church and the original entrance gateway (1765) of St Fin Barre's Cathedral. Nevertheless, the limestone used in the church could only have been sourced from quarries to the south of the Lee. The stone used for St Anne's is a massive pale-grey, Carboniferous limestone; the only likely outcrops regularly worked during the early eighteenth century would have been at either Gillabbey or Windmill Road; the Blackrock quarries only came to prominence in the late eighteenth century. The ashlar work incorporated into the church is of the highest quality, as are the window and door dressing employed throughout. From the outset, this church was intended to be a high-status building.

The two-tier extension to the original tower was started in 1750 to accommodate the new bells cast in England for Shandon. The tiers diminish from the base and are surmounted by a faceted copper dome. By the early 1770s, by which time the church had attained parochial status, the gilded weather vane in the shape of a salmon, colloquially known as the goldie fish, was added. The first bells for the tower were cast in 1750 by Abel Rudhall of Gloucester, but these were not installed until 1752. At least four of these bells were recast, one in 1869, the other in 1908. Nevertheless, all of the bells still retain their original inscriptions: *When us you ring we'll sweetly sing; God preserve the Church and King;* and *We were all cast at Gloucester in England by Abel Rudhall, 1750.* On the symbolism of the salmon, however, there can be little doubt. The salmon fisheries of the Lee, from the Duke of Devonshire's weir near the present city waterworks to the west to Blackrock, were internationally famous, and the weather vane salmon is a clear reference to this.

In the early 1840s, Cork Corporation decided to make use of the church tower's elevation and extraordinary visibility

Fig. 2.48 St Anne's, Shandon, must be Cork's best-known building. A crowd has gathered at the Butter Exchange beside the church. (Source: J. Mahoney, *The Tourist's illustrated Handbook of Ireland*, 1854.)

by installing a series of clock faces. The clock was manufactured by James Mangan of Cork and installed in 1847. Only on the hour are the four clock faces in agreement about the time, which gave rise to the local sobriquet for the clock, 'the four-faced liar'. The machinery for the clock is believed to weigh in the region of two tonnes and each of the clock faces is three metres in diameter.

A number of artefacts from the original seventeenth-century St Mary's church have been retained. The most important of these is a font with the inscription: 'Walter Elinton William Ring 1629. Made this Pant [the font] at their charges.' A pewter bowl with wide flanges was inserted into the latter in 1773 and bears the name of the churchwardens of that year. In the vestry room, a memorial originally erected for George Peircy, in 1635, also survives. The graveyard of the church also has seventeenth-century gravestones.

Skiddy's almshouses

The early development of the almshouse site was as an adjunct to the Green Coat school of 1716. In 1715, two charity schools were to be built on a 'waste piece of ground belonging to the incumbent of St Mary Shandon' by the Green Coat charity. Subscriptions were to be raised for the construction of these schools, while 'an excellent quarry was found within 30 feet of the spot of ground designed for the buildings, which sav'd £40 in the stone work'. The incumbent of St Mary's, Shandon, gave £10 towards the opening of the quarry. The foundations of the charity schools, along with the master's house and an apartment for the '18 decayed house-keepers' of St Mary's parish, were laid on 6 March 1715. By December 1720, over £81 had been spent on the building work. However, by 1716 the construction work was threatened by a scarcity of funds, but £60 was eventually found to buy stone and timber. A Cork merchant, Daniel Thresher, funded these endeavours and also paid for a clock on the hospital building in the south wing. After all the original difficulties were resolved, the charity school was opened on 12 August 1716.

In 1716, workmen were already finishing off the interiors of the other buildings. Further donations were both inventive and much-needed. William Pope, for example, donated £6-worth of 'dutch tiles' for floors of the boys' school and the master's apartment, while in September 1716 'John Harrison Esq; concerned in the lead-mines in the county of Tipperary' donated five hundredweight of lead for the buildings. Furthermore, almshouse accommodation was also to be provided for the '18 poor decayed house-keepers', which were equipped with 'several chambers' for their use in January 1716. In the left wing of the building, in which the master's residence was located, a public library was installed, 'furnished with many useful and instructing books'.

In 1717, an act of parliament became vested with grounds for support of the almshouses, for the benefit of the poor then maintained by the Bettridge and Skiddy foundations. Their directors were of the view that their existing buildings were too cramped, and they decided to sell their existing almshouses and use the profit to build a larger one. Representations were made to the trustees of the Green Coat hospital to provide land for this purpose and they agreed to provide a fee-farm lease forever. The foundation for the new almshouse was laid in July 1718 and the complex, which now formed a U-shaped courtyard with the Green Coat school, was completed in 1719.

Skiddy's charity had originally been set up by Stephen Skiddy in his will of 1584, in which he bequeathed an annuity of £24. This sum was to be distributed among twelve of the city's 'poorest honest citizens', who had to be over 40 to qualify to be housed in the almshouse. In Skiddy's will, the mayor of Cork was 'to make provision of some convenient place to continue forever an almshouse for said poor persons to dwell'. This institution was certainly in existence in 1630, by which time it was overcrowded. The almshouses were rebuilt next to the Green Coat school by the Corporation between 1718 and 1719. By 1848, the almshouse provided accommodation to 22 women, half of whom were Roman Catholics.

Bettridge's charity had been established under Captain Roger Bettridge's will of 1683. Under its covenant £33 was to be bequeathed for the children of poor Protestant soldiers and an estate of £30 yearly for the support of seven old soldiers. These funds were available from 1717 onwards. Their residue was allocated for the

Fig. 2.49 Skiddy's almshouse remains one of Cork's least-known heritage structures. Its erection in 1717 marks the beginning of a rash of building that arguably culminated in a Catholic and Protestant church building frenzy, which reached a peak in the early nineteenth century. (Photo: Cork Archaeological Survey.)

Fig. 2.50 An attractive and engaging representation of 'Shandon' by Kate Dobbin, 1868–1955. (Crawford Municipal Art Gallery.)

in 1964 they announced their intention to demolish the almshouses. This was opposed by an ad hoc committee, which eventually became the Cork Preservation Society, and they came up with proposals for the reuse of the buildings. In 1968, a temporary preservation order was made permanent. A restoration scheme was begun in 1975 and the buildings were transformed into flats.

THE BUTTER MARKET

By the early decades of the eighteenth century, the Mallow Lane area of the city had become the focus of the Cork butter trade within the city, probably because of its greater accessibility for travellers from the surrounding countryside and later, perhaps, because of the concentration of both coopers and butter dealers in the area. The importance of this informal trading centre for butter was further enhanced by an act of 1721. Under the provisions of this act all local authorities were to build public weigh-houses, at which all butter offered for sale within their jurisdiction was to be weighed by public weigh-masters. Thereafter, it was illegal to sell butter which had not been weighed and branded at municipal weigh-houses.

In practical terms, after March 1722, any butter passing through the city had to be brought to a weigh-house at Church Street, near St Anne's church at Shandon, or to a second weigh-house in North Main Street. By the 1730s, however, the Shandon weigh-house was already regarded as the main butter-trading area. The expansion of the Cork butter trade necessitated further legislation, which increased the number of weigh-masters in Cork to three in 1739.

The focus of the trade was thus switched to the Shandon weigh-yards, but as yet no formal market structure had been established. Little is known about the fortunes of the second weigh-house, known as the 'south weigh-house', in the North Main Street area, which was presumably intended for butter coming into Cork from the south-west of the county.

apprenticing of sons of the soldiers, or donated to the sons of Protestants at the discretion of the mayor. Cork Corporation henceforth undertook to provide apartments for the seven selected old soldiers.

In 1963, the trustees of the Skiddy and Bettridge charities decided to build a new home on the southside of the city and

ATLAS · OF · CORK · CITY

At the end of the eighteenth century, the prospect that Cork's most profitable trade could be lost haunted many Cork butter merchants. The international complexion of the butter trade was slowly changing and Cork's pre-eminence in it could only be assured by innovation. Voluntary regulation was devised to sustain the trade. A 'Committee of Merchants' was created in March 1769 by some 23 exporters of butter. Although it had no statutory powers during the 115 years of its existence, it sought to regulate the Cork butter trade. In the committee's view, owing to 'the visible decay of our butter trade', combined with 'the severe losses which attended the adventurers in it', immediate action was required.

The formal market structure which was eventually created out of the firm resolve of these merchants was not,

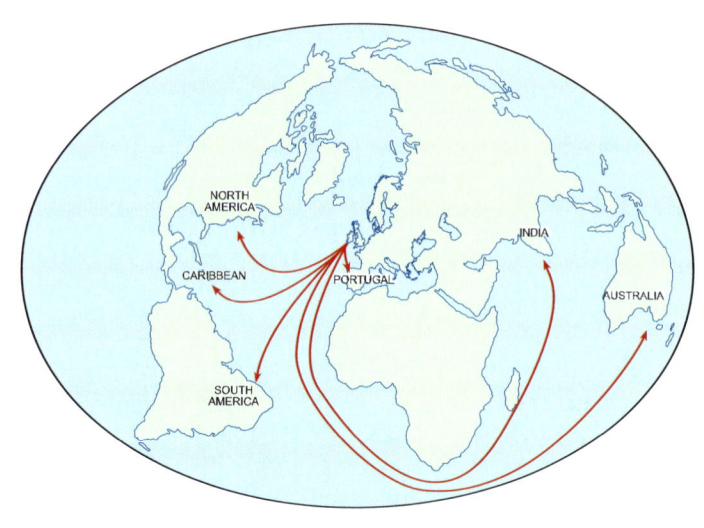

Fig. 2.51 Cork's eighteenth- and nineteenth-century butter foreland had truly global dimensions. Its main components changed over time. Portugal remained one of its chief markets and the long-term presence of a Portuguese commercial consul at Cork was a testament to the value of this trade.

In the early years of the nineteenth century, however, butter carts from the Bandon district went almost directly to the Shandon weigh-house. The south weigh-house, commemorated by Weigh House Lane off North Main Street, was closed in 1849 when the new butter-market building was opened on the site of the main weigh-house at Shandon.

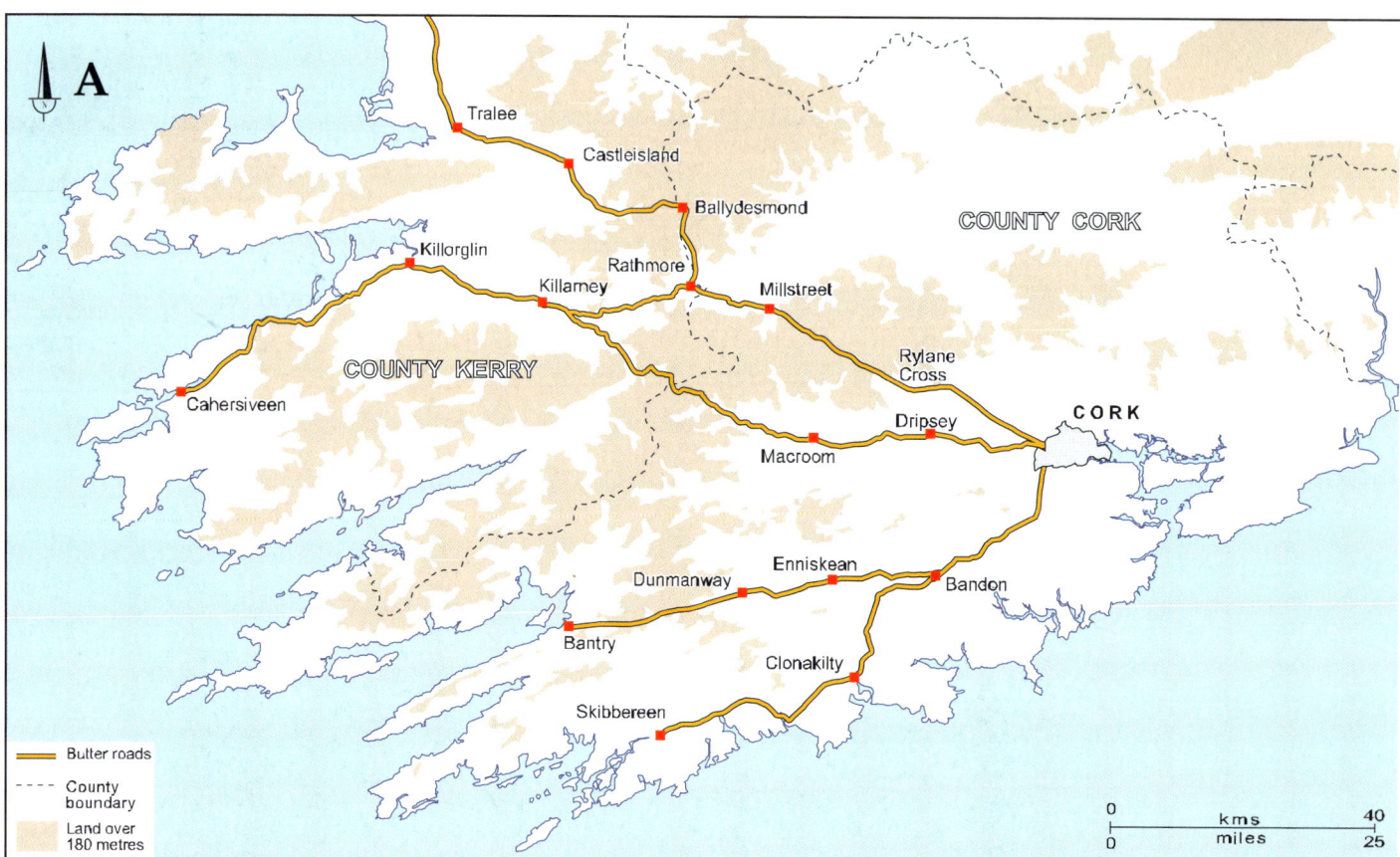

Fig. 2.52A) series of butter roads connected parts of the western marginal fringe and later producer zones to Cork's butter-markets. B) Butter road in north Cork. (Photo: P. O'Flanagan.)

TRANSFORMATION

however, an eleventh-hour development. Indeed, it does not appear to have been forced upon the trade by its own falling standards. The amount of butter exported from Cork in the years leading up to the establishment of the Committee of Merchants had remained at high levels. Moreover, there are no indications that the price of butter had fallen significantly. Butter merchants had to tailor their product for the newly opened English market rather than to remedy a perceived decline in local standards from Cork.

The phenomenal success achieved through the formal market system established by the Committee of Merchants did not simply create new markets for Cork butter in Britain. In an age of widespread corruption and jobbery, in both public and private life, the quality-assurance system associated with it ensured fair dealing for seller and purchaser alike. It was a commercial innovation unique to Cork in an

Fig. 2.53 An 1868 notice to dealers relating to the Butter Exchange activities. (Photo: Cork Archives Institute.)

Fig. 2.54 The hub of the butter business was Cork's Butter Exchange, as depicted here from an 1859 edition of the *Illustrated London News*.

Fig. 2.55 The Firkin Crane building was constructed on the site of the former Shandon Castle.

Irish context and it was regulated on a voluntary basis by the Committee of Merchants and their salaried officers.

As a physical entity, the Cork Butter Market was originally conducted in the weigh-house and around the weigh-yards at Shandon. Despite the scale and importance of its dealings, it was not until the early nineteenth century that a covered area was constructed. The butter and hide cranes were situated near the corner of what is now Butter Market Lane and Church Street. These buildings were separated by a small courtyard and were flanked on the west by a large open area of land. Before 1832, this area was enclosed and covered and a formal market concourse was thus created. By the late 1840s, the size of the trade and the constraints placed on the conduct of the inspection process compelled the Committee of Merchants to extend their existing market facilities.

In 1849, the Committee and the Wide Streets Commissioners began to acquire houses within the vicinity of the weigh-house to enable a new market building to be erected and the surrounding streets to be widened. In 1850, the street immediately in front of the new market portico was narrowed from nine metres to six metres to make it easier for carts to drive into the Exchange. The impressive classical portico designed by the county surveyor John Benson was completed in 1849, and by June of 1850 Benson had completed the new market, at a cost of just over £200, for the Committee of Merchants. In the 1860s, the present Firkin Crane building was constructed on the site of the former Shandon Castle. This large circular building, in which the butter was now weighed and branded, is unique in Ireland; by then the main exchange building was largely concerned with the inspection process.

14. BEEF, BUTTER, PROVISIONS AND PROSPERITY IN A GOLDEN EIGHTEENTH CENTURY

Patrick O'Flanagan

Cork in the eighteenth century was Ireland's premier port city and most of its achievements during that century owed much to the vitality of its port. Other large Irish urban centres of the period also had vibrant ports, but none of them could match Cork's performance. To appreciate these accomplishments in Cork during those golden years it is relevant to place them within an Atlantic European context. Our quest involves an identification of the attributes and sequence of Cork's physical growth and an explanation of its patterning. Rapid population increase, seismic physical enlargement, the changing spatial and structural architecture of its resident society, the startling diversification of its functional base and massive growth in the value and volume of trade passing through the port are telling indices of change. The burgeoning reach of its trade allows us to define its expanding foreland and hinterland, which explains Cork's dramatic expansion (Fig. 2.56).

What was a port city and what were its defining characteristics? Were they different to other large urban centres in eighteenth-century Europe? Port cities were amongst the most common and oldest types of urban settlements in Europe and included ports like Bordeaux, Cádiz, Marseilles, Istanbul and London. Astonishingly, scholarship has little to tell us about them as a ubiquitous generic settlement type. What then were their most representative characteristics? First and foremost, they were centres of exchange and trade and many were entrepots; that is, they assembled, redirected and redistributed merchandise of all kinds. They acted as hubs of maritime and terrestrial communications, while many developed important financial and insurance sectors. They were centres of business, enterprise, speculation and particularly trade. Commerce involved the movement of colonial goods such as bullion, spices, exotic wood and medicines. Many port settlements also sent out agricultural raw materials, semi-processed goods and re-exported manufactured goods to the colonies. The tertiary sector provided most work. Hordes were employed as accountants, administrators and scribes by regulatory and surveillance agencies and merchant 'houses'.

Larger and more complex port cities were characterised by a small, but often wealthy, merchant sector, a significant proportion of whom were of foreign origin.[1] Many residents worked as seafarers of all kinds. Port-related activities also provided large numbers with work and legions of people held posts connected with the unloading, storage and dispatch of merchandise. Craftspeople, especially carpenters, were active in preparing containers. Family enterprises were common; they combined retailing, wholesaling and fabrication under the one roof. Many maritime-related functions, from sailmaking to shipbuilding, also furnished employment. Manufacturing was rare and usually on a small scale. Only exceptionally were goods processed at the ports, as in the cases of sugar refining and tanning. The jury is still out over the question of whether proto-industrialisation was a fact of life at some ports. Port activities also generated other trades, such as the sourcing and preparation of massive amounts of wood and salt for preserving processed foods.

The wealthy merchant sector invested resources in lavish residences. Some port cities are characterised by discrete merchant districts organised into emblematic streets. Others were engaged in philanthropic enterprises resulting in the construction of ornate churches, schools and hospitals, sometimes funded by the proceeds of lucrative slave-trading expeditions. Often merchants diverted their assets into urban and rural properties, which inflated property prices and forced nearly everybody, except the super-rich, to share residences in high-rise situations. These favourable conditions often drew in famous architects and embellishers from all over Europe, as well as legions of domestic servants of all kinds. Living conditions for the infirm, the retired and the unemployed were appalling. Many port cities had a huge underbelly of depravity, a feature rarely accurately recorded.[2]

Power in these settlements was connected with commercial success and mediated by the merchants through municipal institutions. Agencies of the state, especially the army and navy, wielded enormous civic influence, given the strategic significance of ports and their exposed situations. Their concerns were represented by the appearance of imposing fortifications. In Atlantic Europe, the heyday of these settlements between 1500 and 1800 coincided with the great expansion of colonial trade, which was initially focused on the metropoles of Seville–Cádiz and Lisbon and later in the northern ports of Antwerp, Amsterdam and London.

Population of Cork c. 1584–2002				
Year	Population	Year	Population
1584	800 (houses)	1881	80,124
1600	c. 3,000	1891	75,345
1659	c. 14,000	1901	76,122
1680	20,000	1911	76,673
1706	17,600	1926	78,490
1719	27,000	1936	93,322
1725	35,000	1946	89,877
1744	38,000	1951	112,009
1752	41,000	1956	114,428
1760	45,000	1961	115,689
1766	52,000	1966	125,283
1793	54,000	1971	134,430
1796	57,000	1979	138,267
1821	72,000	1981	136,344
1841	80,720	1986	133,271
1851	82,625	1991	127,253
1861	79,594	1996	127,187
1871	78,642	2002	123,062

Sources: Burke, 1967; Campbell, 1778; Day, 1902; Dixon, 1977; MacCarthy, 1997; O'Flanagan, 1993; Nicholls, 2005; Smith, 1750.

The figures before 1841 can only be regarded as an estimate. In the middle of the eighteenth century Dixon indicates that each year the population was temporarily swollen by the influx of 20,000 workers. For the seventeenth century, the population of the Liberties is only a best estimate. For the duration of the twentieth century, the population of Cork's suburbs have been omitted. The total tally for Cork and its suburbs in the 2002 census was 186,239 residents.

Fig. 2.56 Population of Cork, 1584–2002; a summary of the growth of Cork's population. Before the mid-nineteenth century, it includes both core and immediate suburbs and sometimes Cork's Liberties. Thereafter it refers to the county borough and, since 2001, to Cork city.

Figure 2.56 provides an extended overview of Cork's demographic expansion over more than two centuries. It doubled in the first half of the eighteenth century and nearly doubled again during the second half. A peak nineteenth-century figure of 82,000 residents was recorded in 1851. What drove this cataclysmic expansion?

People lived longer than before, food supplies were more secure, birth rates were higher, while rates of inward migration to the city in the 1770s may have been low. Cloth production provided prosperous off-farm employment for many rural residents at this time.[3] However, a swing away from tillage to pastoral activities towards the close of the century may have triggered greater population movement to the city as land clearances of people were reported.[4] Greater distress in the countryside during the early decades of the nineteenth century certainly forced many to leave and industrial failures at larger centres like Bandon, at the same time, created other waves of human detritus. Economies of scale promoted the concentration of manufacturing and production at large centres like Cork.

When then did Cork become a city? Charters had certainly endowed city privileges in the past. Population tallies provided urban credentials, but it was Cork's deepening port function in the early eighteenth century that transformed it from a port town into a major Atlantic port city and ushered in a golden age of achievement.

Structural change

Several renowned cartographers turned their attention to production of large-scale maps of the city during the period under review. John Rocque is certainly the best known and his portrayals of the settlement in 1759 and his update in 1773 represent milestones in cartographic understanding.[5] Before that, valuable maps were made by John Carty in 1726 and one published by Charles Smith in 1750. Additional maps by John Connor in 1774 and William Beaufort in 1801 bring us beyond the century. Detailed analysis of these primary sources helps us reconstruct the nature, incidence, scale and intensity of change in Cork's layout.

Smith's printed map of 1750 and Rocque's map of 1759 confirm that several important extensions to the urban fabric had been added since the 1726 map had been produced. The city was still intimately connected to the sea, mainly in the form of tidal channels that are usually described as quays. Many of these were cut and maintained for drainage, leading to reclamation, embankment, culverting and finally urbanisation.

Between the publication of Story's plan in 1690 and Carty's map in 1726, the area around the present-day site of the Opera House had been reclaimed. Paul Street and Drawbridge became its axis. This and other blocks of reclaimed land appear to have been systematically laid out for subsequent urbanisation. Morrison's Island, formerly Dunbar's Marsh, may also have been partly embanked over this period.

The period between 1726 and 1759 witnessed several vital changes, not least the emergence of George's Street (Oliver Plunkett Street), resulting from the drainage of the area including Dunscombe's Marsh extending to Reap Marsh. Later, this zone emerged as a vital spine of the 'New City', as titled by Connor in his later map. South of the river, in the area between Sullivan's Quay and Cove Lane,

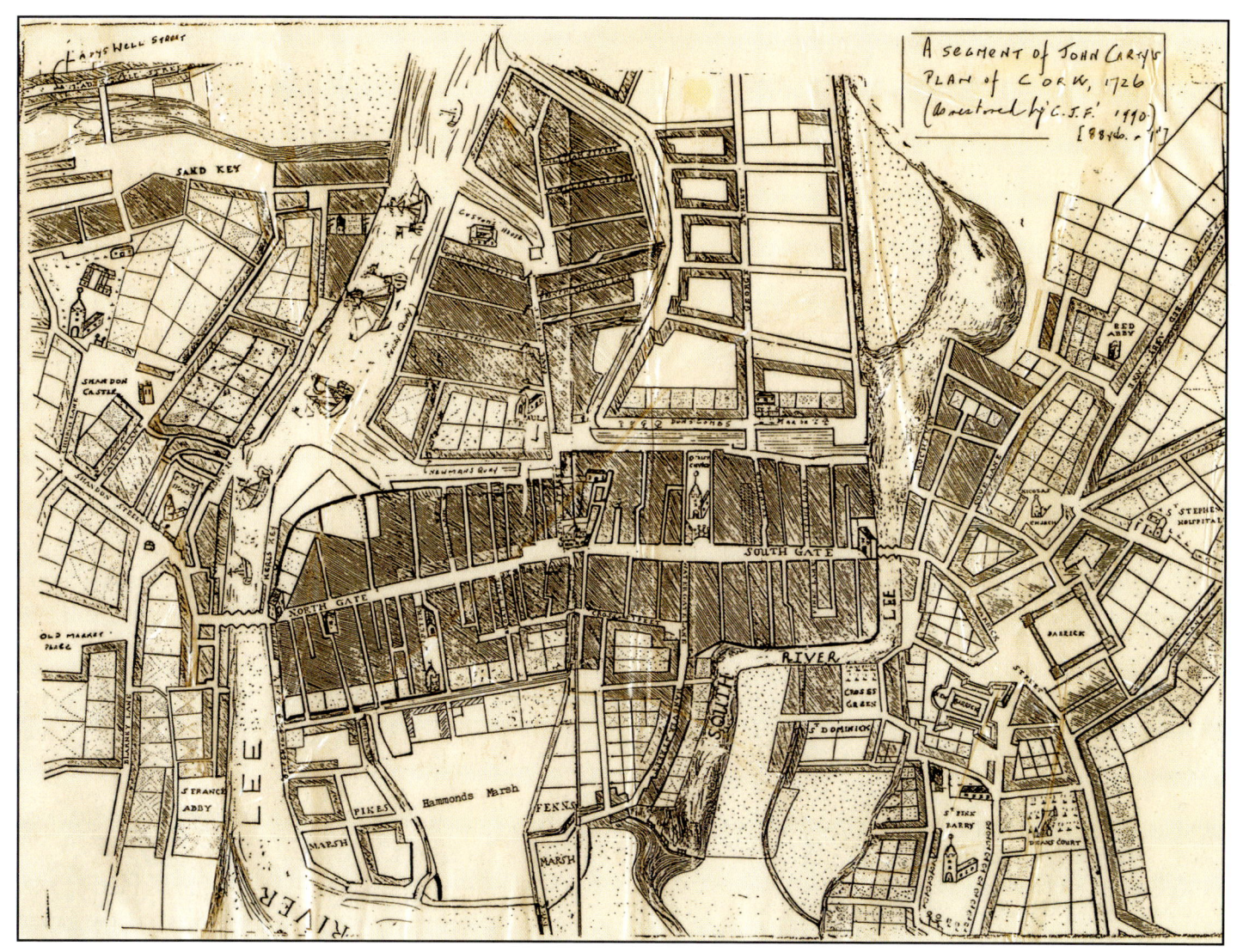

Fig. 2.57 'The new and exact plan of the city and suburbs thereof' was produced by J. Carty of Cork and published in 1726, making it the first real 'map' of Cork. While it is not entirely an accurate representation, it depicts in a credible manner Cork's leading structural features. Dublin had to wait nearly twenty years before Rocque published his now famous map of that city.

significant urbanisation had also taken place. To the west of the core, only desultory progress is evident in the transformation of 'Pike's Marsh', 'Hammond's Marsh', 'Fenn's Marsh' and 'West Marsh', which spanned both sides of the 'South River Lee'.

The main axis of the settlement remained 'The Main Street' and its herring-bone arrangement of lanes, which extended between North and South Gate bridges. Its circumference was still almost entirely surrounded by water and behind these channels were a plethora of quays. To the west there was 'Hammond's Quay' and to the east, where the present Coal Quay is sited, was an unnamed 'Timber Quay' and a 'Potato Quay'. Separating it from what is now Grand Parade was a 'Corn Market' and then a new bridge erected at what is now Daunt Square. The Grand Parade then consisted of two quays, namely 'Tuckey's Quay' and 'Post Office Quay'; opposite was 'The Mall'. On the other side of this bridge lay 'Cavill's Quay', covering most of the area now known as Patrick's Street. Today's South Mall was then a novel planned element of the waterfront, as it was an extension of the south channel.

Between the two main channels, named as 'The River Lee' and 'The South Channel', Rocque's 1759 map suggests the existence of several different types of new urban areas, in terms of the scale of reclamation and the degree and nature of their urbanisation. There were areas which had the appearance of being recently reclaimed and partially urbanised. An example is 'Hammond's Marsh', which is partly coincident with today's Middle Parish or 'Marsh'. The process of reclamation was incomplete in 1773, as a major drainage channel, named as 'Penrose Quay', almost bisected this area. Only one street, Francis Street, was named

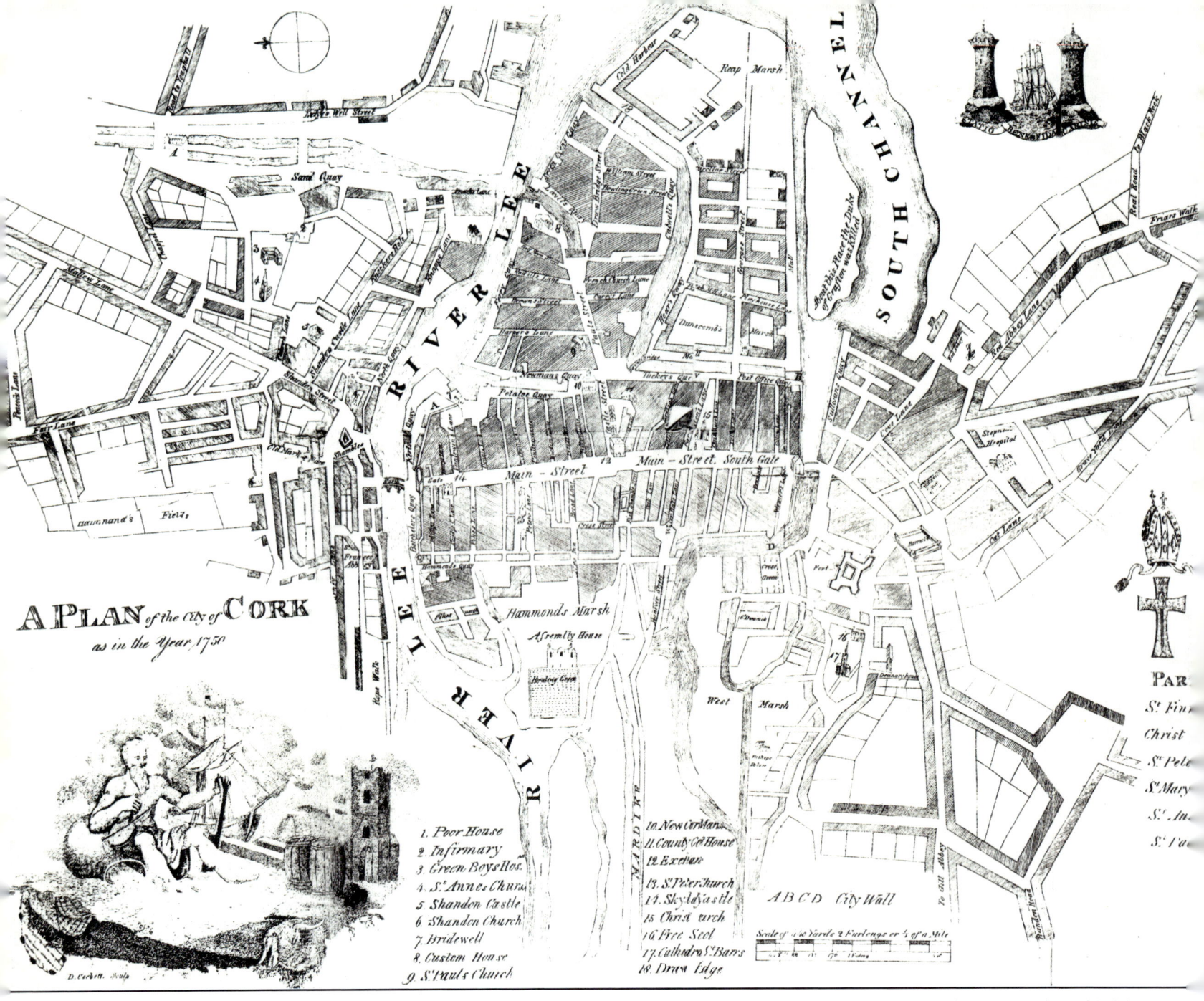

Fig. 2.58 'A plan of the city of Cork as in the year 1750' was one of the most daring illustrations in *The antient and present state of the county and city of Cork*, by C. Smith. Smith's work was one of the earliest and most substantial county histories, which has run into several reprints. His map is a key source for appreciating the evolution of Cork's urban fabric and, together with its descriptions of life in the city and a famous 'view' of the same date, his book constitutes a major sourcebook for understanding the city.

here on the 1759 map, indicating that the area was not completely urbanised.

The third area that stood out was 'George's Street', now Oliver Plunkett Street, and the entire area on both sides of it extending between the South Mall and Merchants Quay, then called Marsham Quay and Cold Harbour. The presence of new buildings in all but the western sector of this area and the remains of some marshy ground there suggest that Georgian Cork was only beginning to take shape.

The northern suburbs centred around Shandon Street were then far larger than their counterparts to the south. Here there were essentially two sectors. Between it and 'Lady's Well Street' were a warren of lanes, most connected with 'Shandun Street'. On the other side of this street, urban development was arrayed around two of the settlement's main northern entry points, 'Blarney Lane' and Fair Lane. The southern suburbs were far less extensive and much development was focused around 'Barrack Street', 'Maypole Lane' and 'Red Abbey Lane'. Most noteworthy here was the spectacular extent of ornate gardens, which at one point extended down to the banks of the south channel. Smith's exciting depiction of the city 'from the north' in 1750 identifies the bulky urban core, the leading civic buildings and extensive suburban development in and around Shandon.

Analysis of two later maps, of 1773 (Rocque) and 1774 (Connor), allows us to monitor the extent and scale of physical

TRANSFORMATION

change over a fourteen-year period since the publication of Rocque's 1759 map. Significant developments are evident. To begin in the west, Hammond's Marsh and 'Pick's Marsh' were now more urbanised and the erection of the 'Mayoralty' confirmed that most of Penrose's Quay had been filled over, as had also happened at 'Finn's Quay' (Fenn's Quay).

Patrick Street still functioned as part of the port and entry to it was by means of a raised drawbridge. Connor refers to it as 'The Long Quay' while Rocque calls part of it 'Cavill's Quay' and marks the other side as 'Travers's Quay'. By 1773, the Grand Parade had been filled in and only a minute vestigial dock remained. South Mall still functioned as a quay and the entire George's Street area was now urbanised, except for a zone at its eastern end referred to by Rocque as a 'Lough'. Likewise, Morrison's Island was fully reclaimed, embanked and divided into a series of unnamed streets and lanes. Connor supplies street names and quay names.

The erection of Parliament Bridge in 1764 opened new opportunities for development on Morrison's Island and the area directly across the river around 'The Red Abbey' and 'Margaret Street'. Urban expansion replaced the gardens in this sector of 'The South Channel'. There is no evidence of significant urban expansion in the suburbs at either end of 'The Main Street' over these few years. Strangely, Connor's map of 1774 shows 'The New Wall' extending out from a marsh beside Morrison's Island which acted as a formidable southern embankment for the Lee. This was a prelude to the drainage of a vast marsh; a year earlier, Rocque's map does not depict this feature.

By 1801, this phase of inner urban expansion and reconstruction was almost complete. The marshes on and around the island core had been filled in and urbanised. Even more dramatically, Connor refers to this reality as the 'New City'. Beaufort's 1801 map emphasises the ordered

Fig. 2.59 Rocque's map, entitled, 'A survey of the city and suburbs of Cork' and published in 1759, was the most accomplished portrait of the city to date. It is both a work of art and a generally accurate map. It is a mine of information relating to all aspects of Cork's morphological development and it serves as a gazetteer of street and lane names.

development in this area, in contrast to older and less regular blocks of the then 'North' and 'South Main Street'. By now, all of 'Hammond's Marsh' was developed and was linked to the 'Mardike Walk' by 'Nile Street'.

Crucially, 'St Patrick's Bridge', built in 1789, provided a new, now fully reclaimed, urban axis, 'St Patrick's Street', with dedicated access to the northern side of the river. The development of a further block at the eastern end of the 'island' was now well under way on 'Lapp's Island'. Further careful development, no doubt encouraged by the presence of Parliament Bridge, is evident across the channel around 'Morrison's Place', and the 'South Parade' was well under way too. Here also, for whatever reason, there was a

Fig. 2.60 'Wisdom Lane'. First confirmed in 1714 documents, it connects North Main Street to Cornmarket Street. It seems to have been named after a well-known local family. (Source: Johnson, 2002. Photo: John Crowley.)

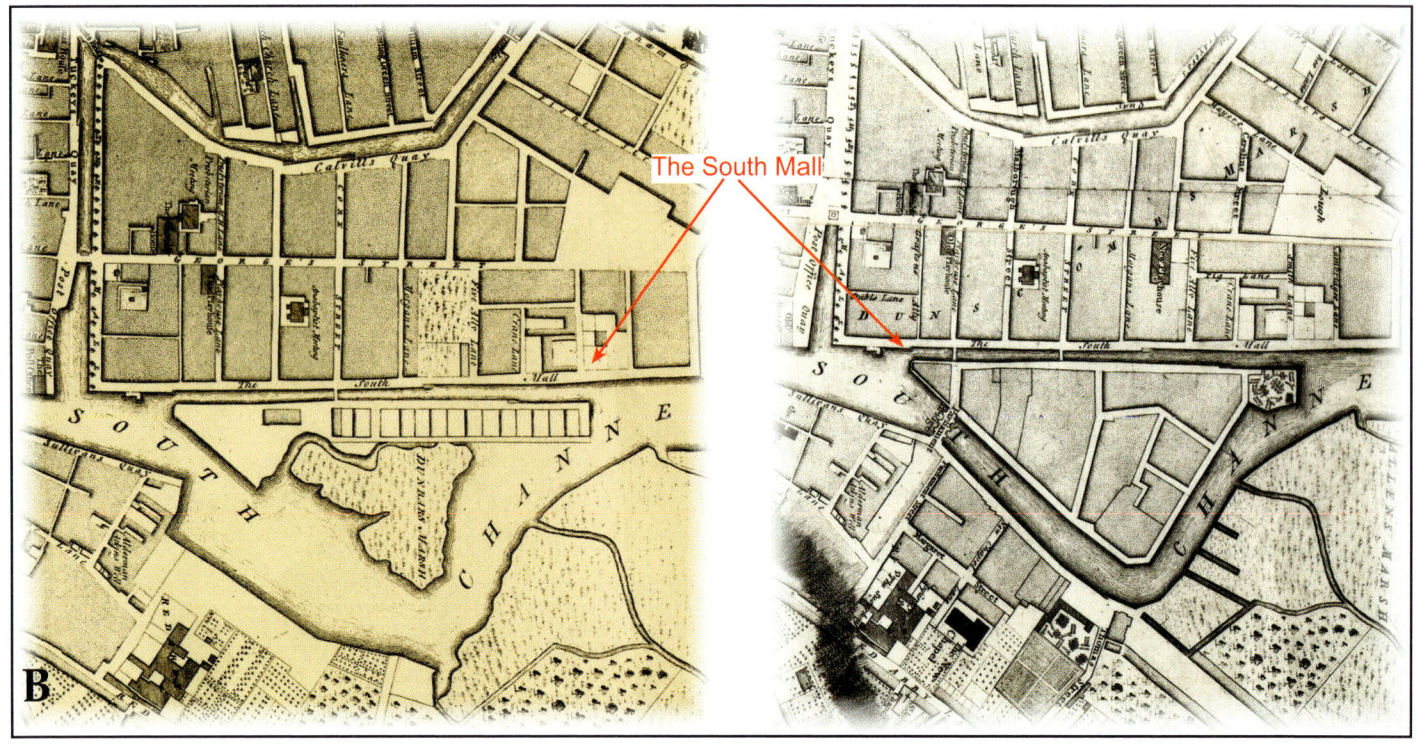

Fig. 2.61 A) Cartouche of quayside activities, indicating the presence of foreign traders, beside a schematic version of Cork's coat of arms. (Source: Rocque, 1759.) B) As a measure of urban fabric change, a similar sector of Cork is depicted on two maps by Rocque dating respectively to 1759 and 1773. It confirms that the pace of reclamation, culverting and urbanisation accelerated over the years in question.

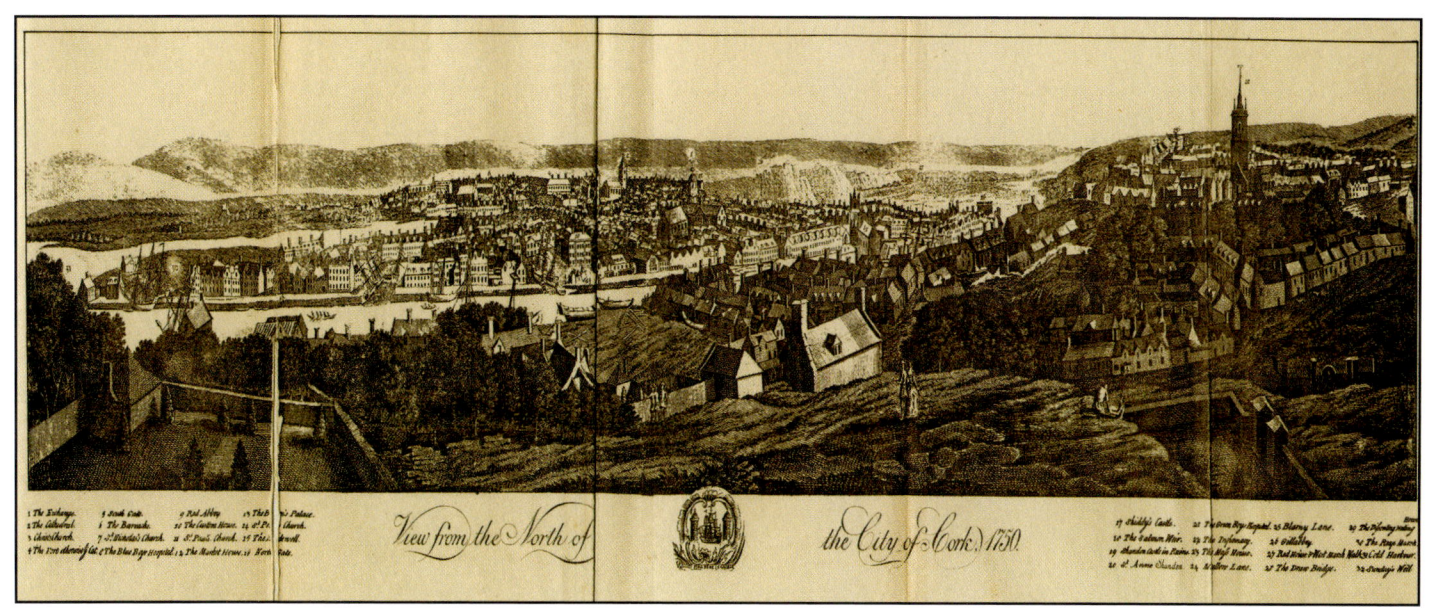

Fig. 2.62 Ten years earlier than Butts' painting, Smith's 1750 'View from the north of the city of Cork' is a magnificent portrayal of a rapidly expanding port city. This stunning 'view' provides an in-depth representation of Cork's urban fabric. Housing styles, quays and notable buildings are recognisable. It confirms that significant urbanisation had occurred in the Shandon area. (Source: Smith, 1750.)

massive reduction in the extent of gardens and nurseries.

On the northern side of the Lee, the nature and scale of expansion is more difficult to determine, as areas mapped by the various cartographers do not coincide. While it is possible to trace the broad sequence of morphological developments, it is not feasible to confirm that there was a commensurate level of improvement to port infrastructures. If anything, the wharfage was drastically reduced as a consequence of bridgebuilding and culverting programmes and by the activities of the Wide Streets Commission after 1812. By 1801, Rocque's 'Green Marsh', named by Connor as 'Devonshire Marsh', was one of the last 'inner' marshes beside Lavitt's Quay to be filled in and partially converted into a dock, as shown in Beaufort's map. Its completion effectively ended this phase of inner reclamation and urbanisation.

The eighteenth century was truly a seismic century for Cork. It witnessed a minor port town change into a regional centre and then become a major European port city. The city itself was transformed by the emergence of a new 'Georgian' settlement, which was quite unlike anything anywhere else in Ireland.

What were the implications of these changes for the confessional structure and functional organisation of the city? Suddenly, a series of new urban spaces had become available for commerce and occupation. Who then was able to take advantage of these new opportunities? The reconstruction of Cork's historical functional characteristics must be based on a reliable categorisation of Cork's occupational structure. The occupational classification scheme outlined in Figure 2.66 was produced by scrutinising several relatively comprehensive contemporary directories for the city.[6]

Many craftspeople also doubled as traders, so distinctions between producers and traders were never too abrupt (Fig. 2.67). In addition, very few streets documented an exclusive dedication to a particular profession, except in the cases of merchants, coopers, shipbuilders and butter merchants. Often streets recorded repeated occupational and confessional associations: for instance, some indicated a preponderance of skilled artisans with small numbers of craftspeople, or there was a combination of high incidences of craftspeople with lower-order shops, as in Barrack Street, Blarney Lane and Bandon Road. Other streets registered a majority of professionals with either higher-order shops or

Fig. 2.63 The Mayoralty house, now the Mercy Hospital, was first built in 1767. When erected, it acted as a potent development stimulus for urbanisation in a zone of newly reclaimed marshes.

Fig. 2.64 Connor's 'A map of the city and suburbs of Cork', published in 1774 by P. Butler, is a sophisticated and dexterous production which clearly distinguishes between the 'old' and the 'new' city. Coincidences between it and Rocque's excellent 1773 map have led some to assert that here is an example of cartographic plagiarism.

craftspeople. Morrison's Island provides an example of this kind of structure, where there were many merchants and a few coopers. Castle Street and Paul Street recorded a high incidence of higher-order shops and skilled artisans. By way of contrast, Mallow Lane recorded significant numbers of lower-order shops and the presence of many craftspeople.

In addition, some of Cork's central streets, such as the 'Main Streets' and Grand Parade or Patrick's Street, recorded 'mixed' functional and occupational characteristics. These were streets where there were five or more different occupational groups, often almost in equal proportions. Regrettably, we do not have sources that fill in the stories of the less skilled.

What then were the distinctions evident in occupational geography between the 'Old' and the 'New' city? Were differences also evident between the northern and the southern suburbs? Broadly, some of the new streets or districts such as the South Mall registered a significant number of professionals, as did Morrison's Island. Patrick's Street recorded a more varied range of occupations, but even here many professionals were evident, among them several attorneys. Exceptionally, there were functional clusters, as at Coach Street, with its several coachmakers.

The occupations of the southern suburbs were forcefully influenced by a military presence on Barrack Street and it was also an area with few sophisticated producers. The situation in the northern suburbs was different. At its extremities, in the Watercourse and Blackpool districts, there were several 'manufactories'. Elongated 'Mallow Lane' counted a very diverse range of occupations, with many craftspeople and a host of lower-order shops, no doubt serving the dense resident population. Exceptionally, at Churchyard Lane, there was a cluster of butter merchants.

Another arresting feature of Cork's late eighteenth-century occupational and residential geography was its acute sectarian foundation, which was to be gradually transformed over the next half century. Suddenly, a significant amount of land became available for residence during the eighteenth century. What were the implications of the occupation of these areas on the functional, occupational and sectarian geography of the port city? What would come to be their leading confessional attributes and how were they represented spatially?

Surname data from Lucas's Directory for 1787 have been validated from other sources and then mapped in Figure 2.68. Clear relationships between religious affiliations and specific occupations were immediately evident and there were strong spatial connections between occupations and residential locations. These distinctions were particularly evident between individual streets and entire districts, such as 'The Old City' and 'The New City', and between the north suburbs and their southern counterparts.

Firstly, there was frequently a dominant and sometimes overwhelming Anglican presence in some occupations, evident at several locations. The same cannot be said for Roman Catholics, except in the case of butter merchants, which was almost exclusively a Catholic profession. Most attorneys, barristers and surgeons were not Roman Catholics. Figure 2.68 dramatically illustrates the extraordinary prevalence of Protestants in street-by-street profiles of work and residence. Several streets notched up a 90 per cent plus majority. Protestants still formed a two-thirds majority in 1787. Protestant supremacy was even more pronounced in most of the streets in 'The New City', where a significant mix of occupations was recorded.[8] Nowhere in the 'New' nor in the 'Old' city did Roman Catholics constitute even a simple majority of producers,

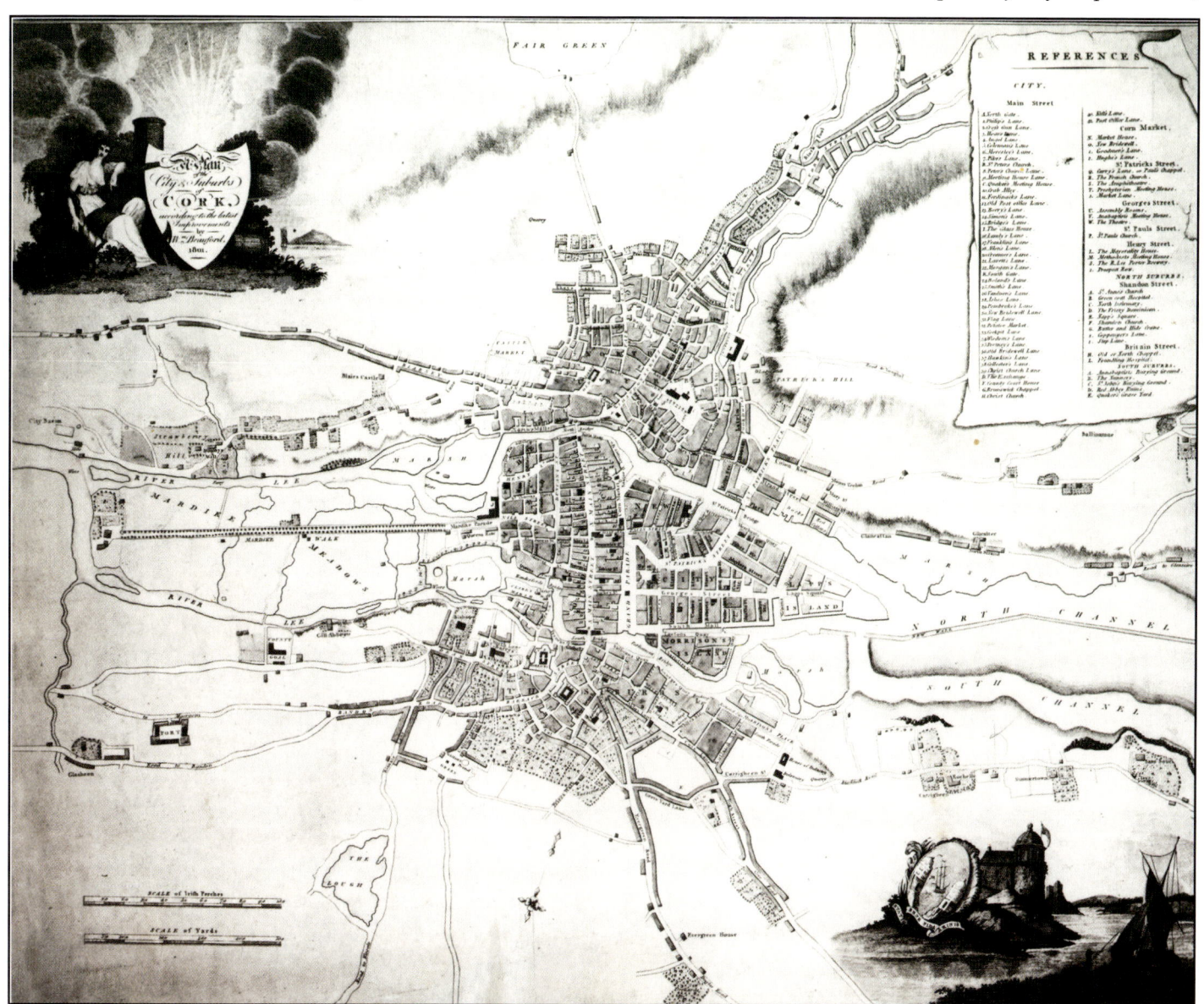

Fig. 2.65 William Beaufort's 1801 'A plan of the city of and suburbs of Cork according to the latest improvements' depicts a mature turn-of-the-century port city at the height of its vitality.

Occupational categories, 1787

Professional	Merchants, clothiers, attorneys, surgeons, barristers and manufacturers
Producers	
	Skilled artisans: Watchmakers, cabinetmakers, instrument makers
	Craftspeople: Tailors, coopers, tanners, carpenters, masons, soap boilers
Shopocracy/dealers/makers/traders	
	Higher-order retail: perfumers, druggists, wine merchants, toymen
	Lower-order retail: Grocers, shopkeepers, linen drapers, victuallers
	Butter merchants

Fig. 2.66 Occupational categories in 1787.

traders or professionals. Even in places like Blackpool and Barrack Street, Protestants formed an overwhelming preponderance of active workers. Mallow Lane was the exception where a significant Roman Catholic majority was evident.

These data refer to the year 1787, when Cork's successful Atlantic commercial career was buttressed by a largely Protestant sector. They reflect a snapshot of the occupational hegemony in 1787, on the eve of massive and sustained Catholic expansion into a range of occupations from which they previously had been barred from entering.

Fig. 2.67 Lucas in his 1787 directory records all artisans, professions and sellers; the unskilled and women were excluded from his reckoning. This representation emphasises the significant variations evident in Cork's 1787 occupational patterning.

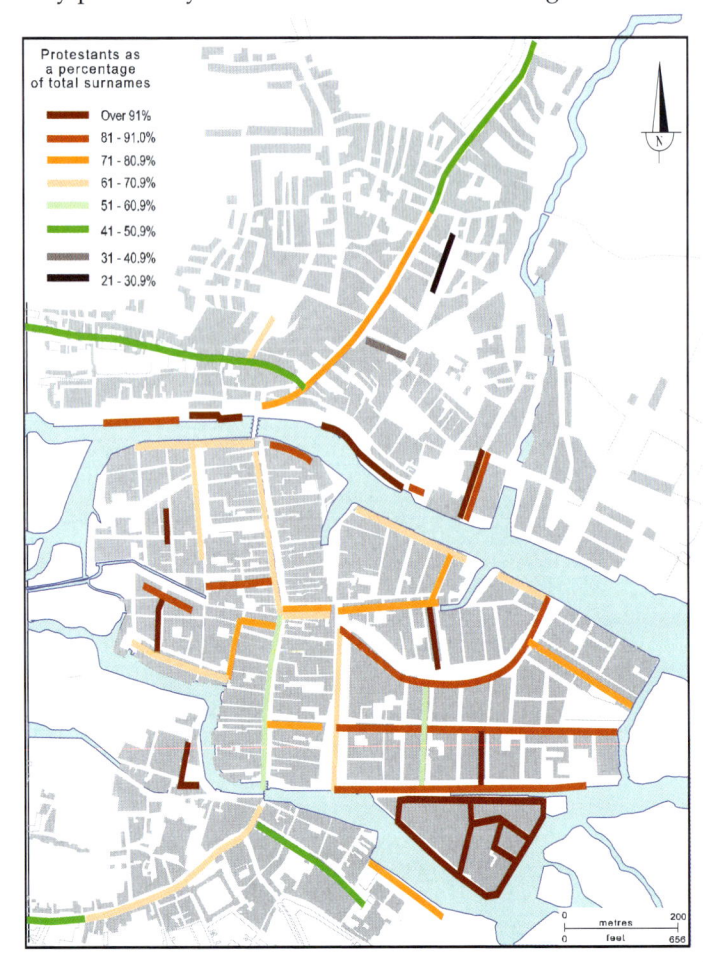

Fig. 2.68 Cork's confessional structure in 1787. Using surnames mentioned by Lucas in 1787 as a crude index of religious affiliation, this illustration of Cork's confessional structure can only be regarded as a best estimate and it should be interpreted with d'Alton's section in this volume, Chapter 15.

Fig. 2.69 South Gate Bridge by John Fitzgerald, 1797. (Source: Crawford Municipal Art Gallery.)

Fig. 2.70 'A lease/bargain and sale of september 3rd 1733, for one year by Eliz Pike, Sunday's Well, North Liberties of the City of Cork, widow to Joshua Beale, City of Cork, Merchant. Property: The little stable and dunghole backward of the Chairehouse and the little yard thereunto adjoining also the underground cellar belonging to Joshua Beale's present Dwelling house situate Meeting House Lane in the City of Cork. Terms and conditions: For one year at rent of one peppercorn at the feast of Easter. With enclosed extract from a will concerning the Beales' dwelling house.' Witnessed by F. Rodgers and James Lee. (Source: Cork Archives Institute Pilot Digitisation Project, 2003.)

15. CORK CITY'S PROTESTANT CULTURE

Ian d'Alton

Despite its increasing economic significance as an 'Atlantic city port', Cork's politics remained local, its concerns selfish. If, in 1690, Cork was described as 'a neat, wealthy and populous city', it did not appeal to all; it was 'an ambitious but ugly metropolis' and in 1736 the earl of Orrery excoriated 'the natural dullness of the place', where 'the butchers are as greasy, the Quakers as formal, and the Presbyterians as holy and full of the Lord as ever'. Alexander the Coppersmith, a year later, described the Christian 'Stiles' in the city as 'Episcopacy, Quakerism, Anabaptism, Huguenotism, Popery and Hypocrisy'.[1]

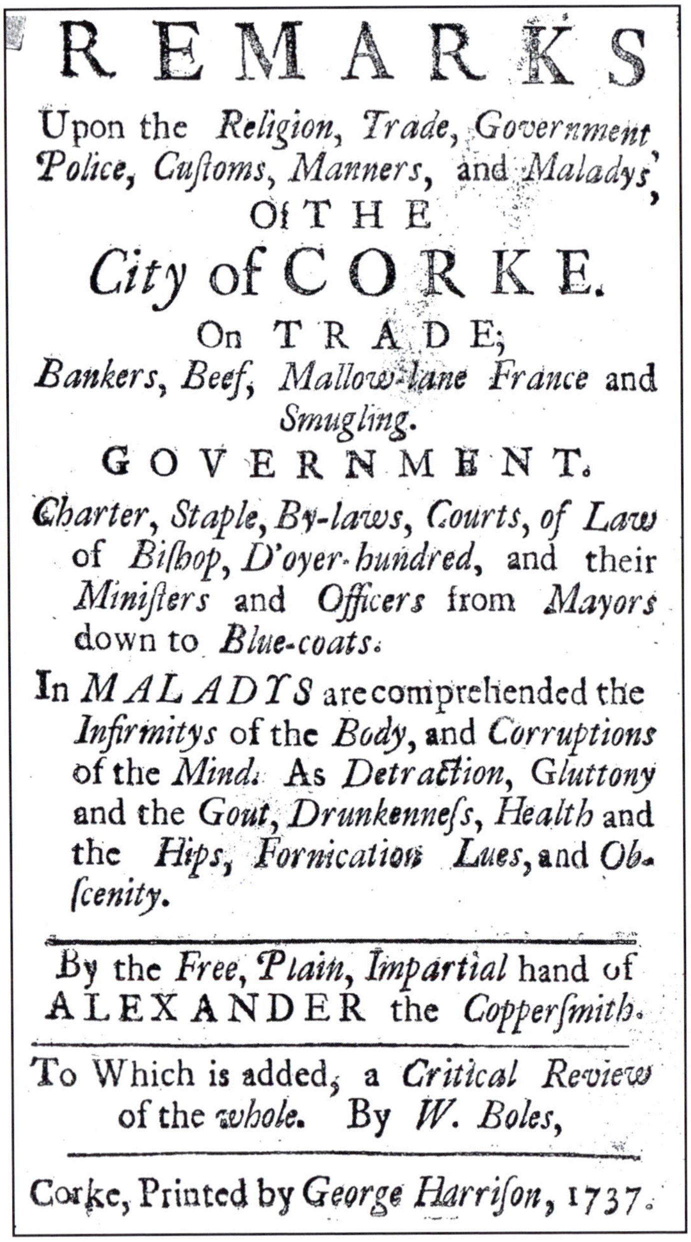
REMARKS

Upon the *Religion*, *Trade*, *Government* *Police*, *Customs*, *Manners*, and *Maladys*,

OF THE

City of CORKE.

On TRADE;

Bankers, *Beef*, *Mallow-lane France* and *Smugling*.

GOVERNMENT.

Charter, *Staple*, *By-laws*, *Courts*, *of Law* of *Bishop*, *D'oyer-hundred*, and their *Ministers* and *Officers* from *Mayors* down to *Blue-coats*.

In *MALADYS* are comprehended the *Infirmitys* of the *Body*, and *Corruptions* of the *Mind*. As *Detraction*, *Gluttony* and the *Gout*, *Drunkenness*, *Health* and the *Hips*, *Fornication Lues*, and *Obscenity*.

By the *Free*, *Plain*, *Impartial* hand of ALEXANDER the *Coppersmith*.

To Which is added, a *Critical Review* of the *whole*. By *W. Boles*,

Corke, Printed by *George Harrison*, 1737.

Fig. 2.71 Alexander the Coppersmith was the author of a critical essay relating to civic, commercial and religious corruption in eighteenth-century Cork.

Decline of Protestant ascendancy

At the beginning of the eighteenth century, Cork Protestants were rapidly leaving a settler past behind them. Their outlook was shaped by the Jacobite and Williamite episodes. What is most significant about them, as they now lived in a recognisably English town, is that their ascendancy, seemingly dominant, was already starting a process of disintegration. Two interrelated developments were responsible: the rapid growth of the city and the rise of a Catholic middle class. The population of the city was estimated at 17,000 in 1706. It had reached 41,000 by mid-century and, despite famines and plagues, stood at over 57,000 by 1796. By 1834, it had climbed possibly to a centurion peak of 85,000.

The 'English' population was dominant in the city-centre parishes (two-to-one in St Peter's) by 1659. Thereafter, Protestants, despite increasing from 13,000 in 1736 to 17,000 by 1834, were proportionately in decline. They accounted for 33 per cent of the city's population in 1736; by 1834, the proportion had halved to 18 per cent. An increase in absolute Protestant numbers, over a century, of some 31 per cent was impressive, but it was dwarfed by the 185 per cent increase in the Catholic population.[2]

At the same time, the growth of Catholic economic power further weakened the city's Protestantness. In the 1700s Cork was a mercantile city. A rich hinterland of pasture encouraged an export trade of cattle and cattle products, together with other products manufactured locally, such as textiles. In particular, provision exports became pre-eminent during the century, especially the export of butter. Protestant pragmatism saw Catholics admitted to the Committee of Merchants in 1769 to ensure that quality standards for provisions were maintained.[3]

In the lower trades, Catholics boasted a two-to-one majority by the 1730s and four-to-one by 1800. In contrast,

Fig. 2.72 Nathaniel Grogan's (1740–1808) etching of 'The North Gate Bridge', c. 1790, captures the atmosphere of one of the city's busiest entry points and reminds us that this bridge acted as a potent inner urban boundary. (Crawford Municipal Art Gallery.)

they only held 20 per cent of the foreign trade in 1758, a proportion that rose to little more than 30 per cent even by the 1820s. Protestant hegemony was in the professions, the law and banking. Nevertheless, from a standing start in 1700, by the beginning of the nineteenth century nearly half the barristers and physicians in Cork were Catholics. A sectarian economic head count should not be construed as a zero-sum game. If Catholics were entering the professions and the trades, it was largely because the city was growing. From the 1770s onwards, the port became most significant for provisioning the king's armies and navy on the way to North America.

Within the Protestant merchant nexus there was an unusually high turnover of families in both Dublin and Cork. Once money had been made, merchants headed for the social uplands, aspiring towards gentry and rentier status. There were also other outlets for Anglican sons, in the armed forces and the Church, which reduced potential recruits to the merchant classes. These openings were denied to Dissenters. With more intense intermarriage patterns, it is perhaps not surprising to find more complex merchant pedigrees within Dissenter and, indeed, Catholic families. While merchant families waxed and waned, movement for Protestants in the lesser trades to the merchant classes was rare.

Several cities

Cork was several 'cities' in this period; relationships within Protestantism and between it and Catholicism was influenced by the 'city' in which one perceived oneself primarily to have lived and moved. The administrative city was the Corporation's area of control, originally walled, but extended as development progressed. The political city was the parliamentary borough, which was quite extensive, including huge rural and semi-rural tracts. The ecclesiastical city was the Anglican parishes of St Fin Barre's, Holy Trinity, St Peter's, St Paul's, St Nicholas's, St Mary's, Shandon, and St Anne's, Shandon, which were part urban, part suburban and

Fig. 2.73 John Fitzgerald's watercolour representation of Elizabeth Fort and old St Fin Barre's is a reminder of this site's enduring position as a centre of worship within the ecclesiastical topography of Cork. (Source: Crawford Municipal Art Gallery.)

part rural. The differences between the old and the new city were also hardening. The social city was defined by the new, fashionable and salubrious suburbs in the north-west and south-east, where merchants began to build their residences.

The greatest concentration of Protestants and Dissenters was found in the centre island parishes of St Peter's, St Paul's and Holy Trinity. Densities here were more than six to ten times those in the other parishes. Holy Trinity and St Peter's were one-third non-Catholic; they particularly stand out from the rest in that regard. Even as late as 1834, there was a close correlation between the proportion of Protestants and the valuation of a parish, with Holy Trinity, St Paul's and St Peter's evincing the greatest wealth. Within Anglicanism, however, the relative position of parishes was a little more complicated. Suburbanisation in the eighteenth century transformed the social and economic mix (Fig. 2.74).

By the 1780s, the professional classes and larger merchants were moving their residences out of the city centre and were to be found proportionately more in the relatively low-valuation parishes of St Anne's, Shandon, and St Nicholas's. Another measure of relative wealth is the cost of church pews. On this basis a two-tier society crystallised: tier one formed Holy Trinity, St Fin Barre's and St Anne's, Shandon; tier two embraced St Paul's, St Peter's, St Nicholas's and St Mary's, Shandon (Fig. 2.75). The centre was no longer holding and the richer Protestants were now migrating to parishes in which they were a more visible minority.[4]

The admixture of Protestant and Catholic, particularly amongst the lower orders, is evidenced by Thomas Newenham's street-by-street census of 1807 for the parishes south of the river and the 138 small schools which children of all denominations attended in 1826. This highlights another feature of Cork Protestantism: it retained a complete class structure through to the late nineteenth century. Cork and Dublin had substantial numbers of artisan Protestants, evidenced by craft guilds in Dublin and charities in Cork

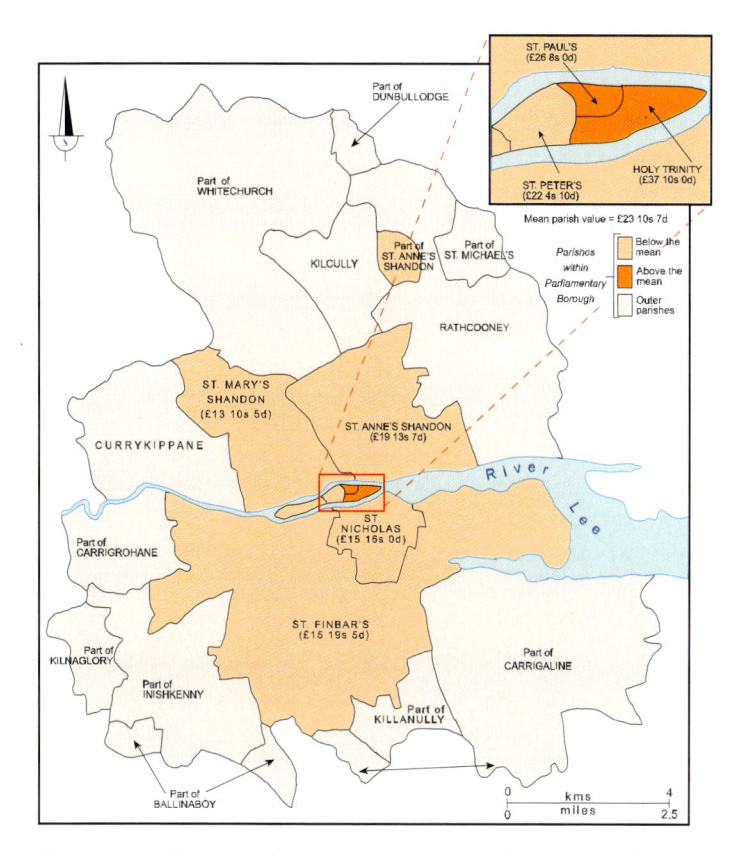

Fig. 2.74 Anglican parish valuations in the early 1830s confirm the concentration of wealth in the 'New Georgian City' on the island.

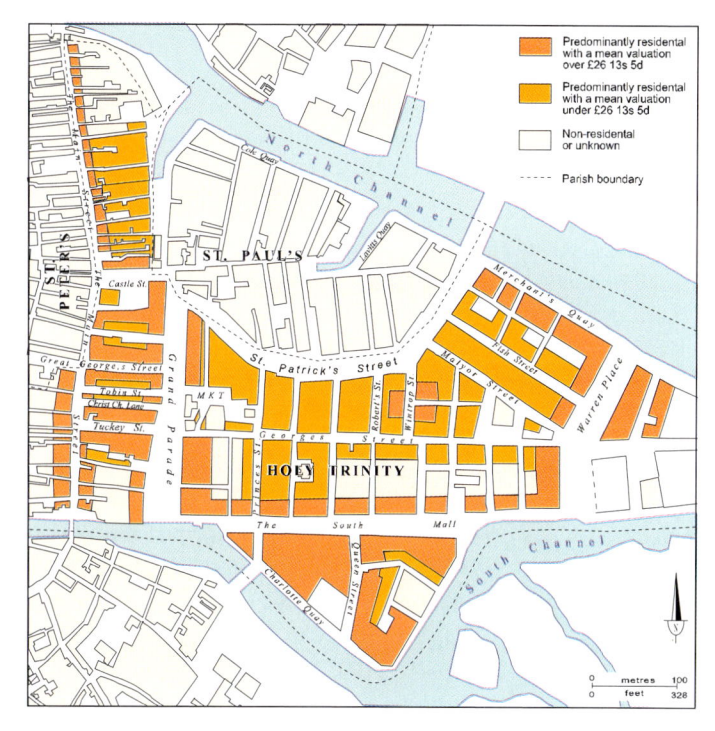

Fig. 2.75 Residential valuations in Trinity parish, 1831, illustrate the gradations of property valuations in the inner 'New City'.

devoted specifically to aid for working-class Protestant apprentices. Proportionately more of these artisans lived in the north city parishes of St Anne's, Shandon, and St Mary's, Shandon. As late as 1845, the Anglican rector of one of these was writing angrily about the plight of his parishioners: 'hundreds of them in the greatest distress'. Father Mathew's famous Temperance Movement was predated by Reverend Nicholas Dunscombe's activities on behalf of his Protestant parishioners.[5]

At the other end of the social hierarchy, the aristocracy and landed gentry were well represented politically, as well as economically, in city life. Peers such as the earls of Shannon, Cork and Orrery and Donoughmore, and merchants and recently elevated gentry such as the Longfields, Smith-Barrys and Newenhams, owned substantial lands within the Liberties and thus had considerable political influence within the constituency.

OTHER PROTESTANTS: DISSENTERS IN THE CITY

What of Dissenters? The congregations of (Ana)baptists, Quakers, Presbyterians and, later, Methodists (1752) were relatively small. Accounting for one-third of all non-Catholics in the 1670s, they had rapidly declined in numbers and proportion by the early eighteenth century. Prominent in city trade, the modesty of their places of worship at this time reflected their small numbers; for instance, there were 200 Quakers in 1700, who desired to remain unobtrusive.

In 1834, Dissenters accounted for only one per cent of the city population, but seven per cent of the total non-Catholic population. One-third was concentrated in one city-centre parish, Holy Trinity. Dissenters had achieved a disproportionate influence in the city's cultural and intellectual life. Their relationship with Anglicans was complex, ranging from religious hostility to an acceptance on both sides that, ultimately, in the face of Popery, they were as one. Cork Corporation was charging Quakers 'toleration money' in the 1690s while at the same time resolving to borrow from them when needed. Again, by 1756, Dissenters were allowed to accept and hold commissions in the local militia, thus endowing them with civil parity with the Anglican establishment.

Wealth stirred feelings of envy and rage; Bishop Wetenhall in 1699 ranted against 'the Quakers' eager pursuit of wealth, and their effectual, wily and secret ways of getting it'. Tensions with Methodists arose during the episcopate of Jemmett Browne (1745–1772) when a mini-pogrom was conducted against them by alderman Millerd, a relation of the bishop. The imposition of tithes and vestry-cess on Dissenters also fuelled anger in the early 1800s and pushed many towards radicalism. Families of Huguenot origin numbered about 300 souls in the mid-century and, with their ministers ordained as Anglicans by the 1740s, they were prominent in civic politics: five mayors bore Huguenot names between 1690 and 1800.[6]

A window on Protestantism: The Corporation

Cork Protestant activities were channelled through the two principal institutions with which it was most closely identified locally: namely, the city Corporation and the Church, particularly in its physical manifestations.

In 1827, *The Freeholder*, a radical newspaper, wrote that: 'If ever Mammon reigned in a country, it is in this. Every thing is measured by money, and the idea of consideration not derived from money, or the means of making it, is unintelligible.'[7] The Corporation may not entirely have justified one hostile description of it as 'a set of low vulgar city jobbers', but this view might not have been too far off the mark. The Corporation benefited enormously from the growing revenues of a prosperous city over the eighteenth century. Income increased from £900 in 1715 to about £1,200 by 1732, reaching £7,000 per annum by 1820. This was used to fund a lavish municipal edifice.[8]

Between one-third and one-half of the funds went on salaries. The mayoralty was the great prize, with total emoluments in the early nineteenth century of about £2,000. The two sheriffs, next in dignity to the mayor, were paid £50 per annum up to 1787 and, thereafter, were given a piece of plate worth about £100 as salary. Each alderman of the ward received £180 per annum from court fines and fees. There were many other offices, including the town clerk, with £600 in the late eighteenth century and a host of minor posts: butter weigh-masters, bridewell keepers, sword-bearers and calculator of the assize of bread.

Under various charters dating from Henry III to Charles I, the sovereign power in electing the Corporation officers had lain with the freemen. In 1721, however, the Corporation approved two bye-laws which, taken together, concentrated power in the hands of a small clique. In effect, the nomination to the mayoralty was confined to those who had served as sheriff. The nomination to sheriff was likewise restricted to nominees of the great officers of the Corporation. This put enormous power in the hands of the sheriffs, who also had substantial patronage.

The institutional bodies which governed the Corporation were the Court of d'Oyer Hundred, which included the entire body of freemen, and the Common Council, which included the great officers and other ex-sheriffs, totalling 24 individuals. The freemen were exclusively Protestant and numbered 2,500. A freeman had to be the eldest son of, or apprenticed for seven years to, a freeman.

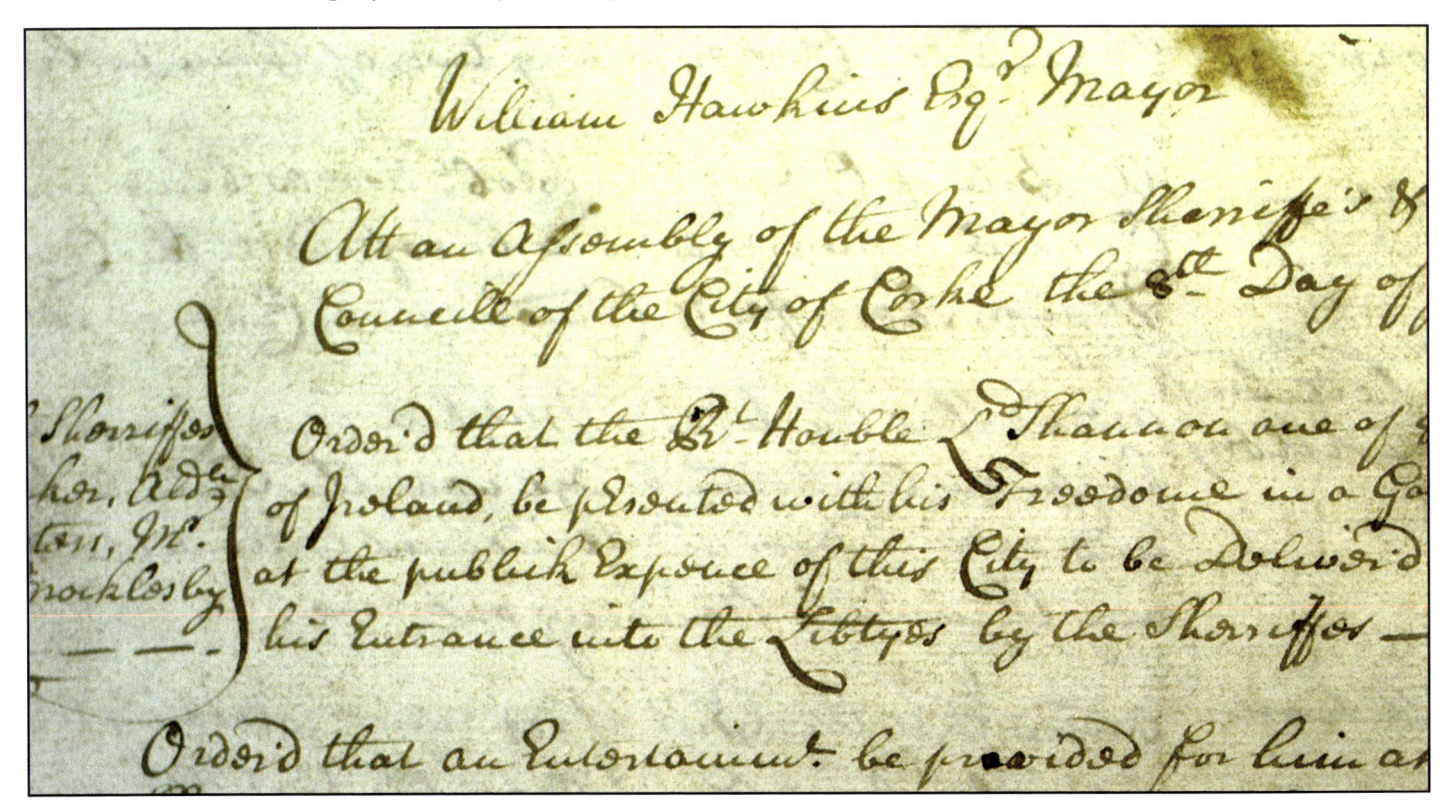

Fig. 2.76 An 8 July 1722 extract from the Council Book of the Corporation minutes (1710–1732) notes: 'At an assembly of the Mayor, Sherriffe's & Common Council of the City of Cork . . . Order'd that the Rt. Honble Ld Shannon one of the Lrds Justices of Ireland be presented with his freedome in a Gold box . . . to be deliver'd him at his entrance into the Libertyes by the Sherriffes . . . Order'd that an Entertainment be provided for him at the Council Chamber and his attendance and such other Gentlemen as is proper to invite with hime . . . Directions to be given for preparing the said Entertainment by Mr Mayor, and two Sherriffes Mr Saml Croker, Mr James Focault . . .'. (Source: Cork Archives Institute.)

The body of freemen was by no means homogenous. Residents in the city accounted for 1,000, county outvoters (mainly the middle gentry of the Liberties) numbered another 1,000 and there were 500 who were resident outside Cork county and who had generally been granted the freedom because of their status or position, such as the Lords Lieutenant (the Duke of Rutland), prominent politicians and judges (such as William Pitt the Elder) and military commanders (such as the Duke of Wellington).[9]

The Common Council abrogated to itself the right of admitting freemen. The freemen chose the Common Council. Thus a closed circle was established similar to, for instance, the governance of Dublin from the late fifteenth century. However, just in case this did not achieve the desired level of control, a further, inner, group had formed, known as the Friendly Club. The club was founded in the 1760s, when a group of Protestant merchant families felt that Lord Shannon, a large landowner within the city, had too much influence over the selection of mayor and resolved to do something about it. 'The effort was successful', noted the Corporation commissioners laconically in 1833, 'but the members of the club, having discovered their power, continued it for other purposes, and its organisation has been ever since maintained so effectually, that the members of it, by acting together in the court of d'oyer hundred, possess all the power in corporate affairs'.[10] The club's strength was that it operated informally. Its ultimate objective was to elect the sheriffs, thus recognising their primacy in the Corporation. The club evolved a system of control that was devastatingly effective, requiring only that its nominees were supported by all members. In this it exhibited all the ruthlessness and discipline of the modern political party.

The club itself was dominated by a tightly bound clique. An examination of mayoral, shrievalty and common speaker lists for the period confirms that a small group of families was at the centre of the Corporation's web. By the late eighteenth century, a recognisably stable group had emerged, principally the families of Newsom, Lane, Allen, Besnard, Perrier, Gibbings, Bagnall, Leycester and others, often originally Huguenots. In many cases these were closely connected through intermarriage as well as business dealings.[11]

Patronage and profit must be set within the prevailing cultural mores of eighteenth-century Ireland; nevertheless, it is tempting to characterise the Corporation as little more than an extensive system of outdoor relief for certain Protestant families in Cork. Even though it may have seen itself as the linchpin of the city's Protestant establishment, pragmatism prevailed; when it suited them, Corporation Protestants were quite willing to admit the right sort of Catholic into the system. By the end of the century, 70 prominent merchants were bestowed with the freeman title.

Anglican churches

In the eighteenth century, staking out territory was the imperative, especially after the unsettled period between 1641 and 1690 in which Protestants were visibly put on the back foot. The seventeenth century had seen Cork city as a 'contested space, with Catholic and Protestant groupings vying for superiority and recognition within the landscape'. In the eighteenth century, Protestants largely prevailed in this space, the most obvious manifestation of this being the building and rebuilding of Anglican churches. The most significant were Christ Church (Holy Trinity), between the Grand Parade and South Main Street and in which the Corporation assembled and worshipped,

Fig. 2.77 Interior of Christ Church (Holy Trinity), once one of the principal Anglican centres of worship in the inner city. The dwindling numbers of parishioners forced its closure and now it houses the Cork Archives Institute, where much of the city's documentary past is preserved.

and St Peter's on North Main Street, the fashionable church for the upper orders.

The Anglican churches were in a poor state of repair at the end of the seventeenth century, largely due to wartime upheavals. In 1693, St Peter's had been rebuilt. It was also planned to reconstruct St Mary's, Shandon, in the northern suburbs, to cater for the growing Protestant population in that area. The insecurities of the seventeenth century had left their mark and made local Protestants cautious; ultimately the church was built closer to the centre of the city.[12]

Some observers see the wave of church-building and renovation in the early eighteenth century as demonstrating the economic and social superiority of Protestant over Catholic rather than furnishing a built environment within which a better spiritual life could flourish.[13] Even as late as 1800 Protestants and Dissenters had thirteen places of worship in Cork city, compared to nine Catholic chapels. The spate of Anglican church renewal in Cork city during the century was impressive and includes the rebuilding of Christ Church in 1720 and St Nicholas's, to serve the southern Liberties, in the same year. A new church of St Anne's, Shandon, was built in 1722, which was followed by another new church, St Paul's, in the city centre in 1723. The reconstruction of the city's cathedral, St Fin Barre's, began in 1735 and it was opened for worship in 1738 for the exclusive use of the upper tier of local Protestants. None of these projects was cheap. For instance, the new Christ Church cost £5,328, despite being poorly constructed. The churches, including the cathedral, were largely built in utilitarian styles and with a keen eye on cost.[14]

Architecturally, they did not particularly enthuse contemporary, or later, observers.[15] The best that the antiquarian Charles Smith could say of Christ Church was that 'The body of this church is capable of containing three thousand people, with good pews and galleries, and is all built of hewn stone.' Cork's eighteenth-century ecclesiastical architecture exhibited little of the dazzle of Dublin, yet the city saw in that period the construction of a number of

Fig. 2.78 A hand-coloured print of St Patrick's Bridge by Nathaniel Grogan (1740–1807) depicts one of the earlier structures to span the Lee at this point. (Crawford Municipal Art Gallery.)

Fig. 2.79 The Custom House was originally built beside a quay. The Crawford Municipal Gallery now occupies its site. (Source: Crawford Municipal Gallery.)

substantial civic buildings, including the Custom House (1724), Corn Market (1740), Mansion House (1767) and stone bridges over the Lee in 1712, 1713 and 1789.

Though the state may have provided funds for church-building, it is evident that the real impetus came from local interests. Building activity in Cork coincided with the energetic and reforming episcopacy of Peter Browne (1709–1735).[16] Again, while resources came from taxes and imposts, a significant part of the funding was raised from local and voluntary contributions. In 1726, the parishioners of the two new churches of St Mary's, Shandon, and St Paul's raised £1,079, which was 30 per cent of the cost of building the churches. This period of vigorous construction ended in 1738, but there were some modifications and embellishments made to the city's churches later in the century, notably the addition of a bell-tower to the cathedral in 1772. The last significant building project took place between 1783 and 1788, with the demolition and reconstruction of one of the city's oldest churches, St Peter's (see *Christianity, Churches and Burial Places*, Chapter 9).

NEW CHALLENGES

For Cork Protestants, the eighteenth century ended as had the seventeenth, with wars, rebellions and insecurity. The city was a vigorous centre of the Volunteer Movement, the Court of d'Oyer Hundred, at one time granting 300 guineas for the raising of a corps. The Cork Boyne Society, formed in 1776 to provide mutual assistance and to protect peace and prosperity, restricted its membership to the upper echelons of city Protestant society: no 'apprentice, menial servant, papist, or any person married to a papist' was to be admitted. Another Volunteer corps, which had its origins in the local militias of the 1720s and 1730s, was the True Blues. It was one of the oldest societies in Ireland, formed in 1745 and reconstituted as a Volunteer corps in 1778. Protestant Cork, however, was perhaps too busy making money out of the American and French wars to involve itself as heavily in the patriot game as Dublin and Belfast.

Protestant culture in eighteenth-century Cork may not have sparkled with intellect, but it was not without its coffee houses, convivial societies such as the Water Club, the Cold Bone Club, the Atlantic Club and the Free Debating Society (founded in 1772), theatres, music gallery and 'French airs'. Its first newspaper was established in 1715, and English broadsheets were plentiful by 1748. Lord Orrery's 'dullness' should not necessarily be taken as the leitmotif for the city's life of the mind during these years. Nevertheless, it is not until the early 1800s that an artistic flowering is seen.

The Huguenots of Cork

Alicia St Leger

'We live here with many satisfactions and lack nothing', Pierre Farie wrote in 1711, describing life in Cork, having fled from persecution in his native France.[1] Farie was just one of about 300 Huguenot refugees who settled in Cork in the late seventeenth and early eighteenth centuries.

Huguenots were French Protestants, followers of the teaching of John Calvin (1509–1564), whose numbers and power grew in the seventeenth century. Their perceived threat to the established religious and political order in France led to periods of intense persecution in the late sixteenth century. By the 1680s, a Roman Catholic revival prompted an increasing number of challenges to the liberties of Huguenots, culminating in the revocation of the Edict of Nantes in 1685.

Huguenot emigration had occurred prior to 1685, but it was the revocation that convinced many that they had no future in France. While Huguenot ministers were forced to leave France, all other Huguenots were forbidden to emigrate. Therefore, those deciding to flee France had to do so surreptitiously, leaving from ports or across land borders bound for countries like Holland, Britain, Germany and Switzerland which welcomed Protestant refugees. Between 200,000 and 250,000 Huguenots fled from France in the late seventeeth century.[2]

Protestant countries valued the contribution that Huguenot refugees could make to society. Many brought with them skills, knowledge and a reputation for hard work, which not only made them self-supporting but also contributed to the expansion of existing industries. In addition, the British authorities regarded them as loyal and trusted members of society. Several parliamentary acts were passed encouraging Huguenot settlement in Britain and Ireland. In 1662, the Lord Lieutenant, the Earl of Ormond, sponsored an act to encourage 'Protestant Strangers' to settle in Ireland by granting them privileges regarding naturalisation and the freedom to trade in towns.

Huguenot troops played an important role in the victory of the Williamite forces and many were rewarded with pensions and land in Ireland, particularly in Portarlington and Youghal. The act encouraging Huguenots to settle in Ireland was restored in 1692 and enhanced by granting them 'the free exercise of their religion'.[3] Huguenots arriving in Ireland settled mainly in urban areas in the east and south and especially in Dublin.

The Huguenots who came to Cork did so after the 1685 revocation, but some were recorded in the city before that time, including members of the Carré (Quarry), Goble and Covert families. Greater numbers arrived in the late seventeenth century, often coming to the city via Holland and Britain. In 1685, the Cork Register of Freemen recorded the names of Peter Rogue, John James Ribet (Riblet) Vigié,

Fig. 2.80 The Huguenot Cross became a symbol of the Huguenots. It represents Christianity and the fleur-de-lis (between the arms of the cross) symbolises France, while the dove represents the Holy Spirit.

increased every day, for Cork is a great business centre, and has a fine port . . . I was well-received at Cork by the French as well as by the English.'[5] A Huguenot church was built in 1712 between Ballard's Lane (now Carey's Lane) and Lumley Street (now French Church Street). An adjoining property was purchased in 1733 and that site was used as a graveyard. The church in Cork was initially Nonconformist but by the 1740s the ministers were ordained in the Church of Ireland and obeyed the rules of that Church. Huguenots attended their own church until 1813, when declining numbers led to its closure. The building was subsequently used by Methodist congregations and in 1845 was replaced by a new Methodist chapel. A portion of the original graveyard still remains on Carey's Lane.

The existence of a Huguenot minister in Cork from the 1690s encouraged other Huguenots to settle in the city. Although some were poor, others brought resources with them and soon established themselves in the economic life of the city. The refugees and their descendants set themselves up as merchants, craftsmen and manufacturers. Members of the Lavitt and Perrier families, for instance, amassed wealth that enabled them to expand into other areas such as property and shipping. The Huguenots and their descendants fitted well into the ruling urban Protestant élite and several served as mayor.

Huguenot gold- and silversmiths were renowned for the high quality of their work and those settling in Ireland in the late seventeenth and eighteenth century benefited from the increased demand for their products for ecclesiastical and domestic purposes. In this period there were several Huguenot craftsmen working in Cork. Most significant were the Goble family, who were prominent in the guild of goldsmiths in the city. Other Huguenot silversmiths included William and John Armour, Adam Billon, Stephen Mackerill, John Rickotts, Thomas Robinette, Anthony Semirot, William Teulon and James Verdaile.[6] Huguenot descendants

Fig. 2.81 Jacques Fontaine (1658–1728) was the first Huguenot minister in Cork. (Source: Putnam, 1853.)

Peter Billon, Samuel Ablin, Mathew Savory, Zacharia Trebuseth and Peter Segen, all recently arrived Huguenot refugees.[4] The Huguenots settled in Cork city with relatively little difficulty. By the early eighteenth century their numbers were sufficient to enable them to build their own church.

The first Huguenot minister in Cork was Jaques Fontaine, a dedicated man of religion who led an adventurous and colourful life. He fled from France to England in 1685 and in 1694 arrived in Cork to minister to the growing Huguenot population. He wrote: 'The church

Fig. 2.82 These silver items were made by Cork Huguenot silversmiths. Left to right: a tankard by Anthony Semirot, early eighteenth century; a chalice by Robert Goble, inscribed 'Parish of the Holy Trinity Cork' and 'This chalice, made in the year 1675, Martine Stokes and William Ballard Church Wardens'; a snuff box by Stephen Mackerill, mid-eighteenth century; a jug by William Teulon, who operated from St Patrick Street between *c.* 1791 and 1844. (Source: Cork Public Museum.)

continued to practise as silversmiths into the nineteenth century. By 1853, this activity had died out because of competition from cheaper mass-produced English silver.

The textile industry was one in which Huguenot skills were well known, particularly in the London silk industry and in linen production in places such as Lisburn and Dublin. A short-lived silk industry in Inishannon from 1765 was run by Huguenots who were encouraged to settle there by the local landlord, Thomas Adderley. However, the silkworms failed to thrive in the damp climate and the venture collapsed. The cotton industry was important in Cork in the late eighteenth century, thanks to imported English technology and protection by the Irish parliament. One of those involved in 1792 was Michael Quarry, who was probably descended from an early Huguenot settler, Augustus Carré.

An existing sailcloth factory in Douglas developed by the firm of Perry and Carleton became associated with the Huguenot families of Perdrian and Besnard by 1783. The venture thrived because of high demand for sailcloth during the French Revolution and the Napoleonic Wars and the Douglas factory benefited from the introduction of improved mechanised production.[7]

Huguenots in Cork remained a close-knit community, intermarrying with and apprenticing their children to other Huguenots. They progressively began to assimilate into Cork society and by the early nineteenth century no longer had a need for a specifically French church. Today there are few Huguenot surnames still evident in the city. Some Huguenot names were lost in marriage, although some were preserved as first names. Not all have disappeared, though. Names such as Fleury, de Foubert and Dukelow are reminders of these seventeenth- and eighteenth-century arrivals in Cork, while oral traditions in many families preserve the proud heritage of the Huguenots of Cork.

Quaker Enterprise

Richard S. Harrison

'Baker and Wright, Harris and Beale, Newsom and Pike, and old Becky Haughton' – this answer in a Cork schoolchildren's game encapsulates the names of the city's Quaker families. Cork streets remind us of the formative influence of Quakers – The Religious Society of Friends – on the city's physical development. Quakers have been in Cork since 1655. The communal and egalitarian assumptions of their Christian belief were a challenge to the political power and earned them immediate persecution. Although many of them had been Cromwellians, they evolved a pacifism that made them useless as soldiers and rendered them politically suspect. Other early Quaker centres were at Charleville, Bandon, Skibbereen, Kinsale and Youghal.

Most Quakers were small tradesmen and shopkeepers but with a developing class of bigger merchants trading with Europe and America. Much of their trade was centred on

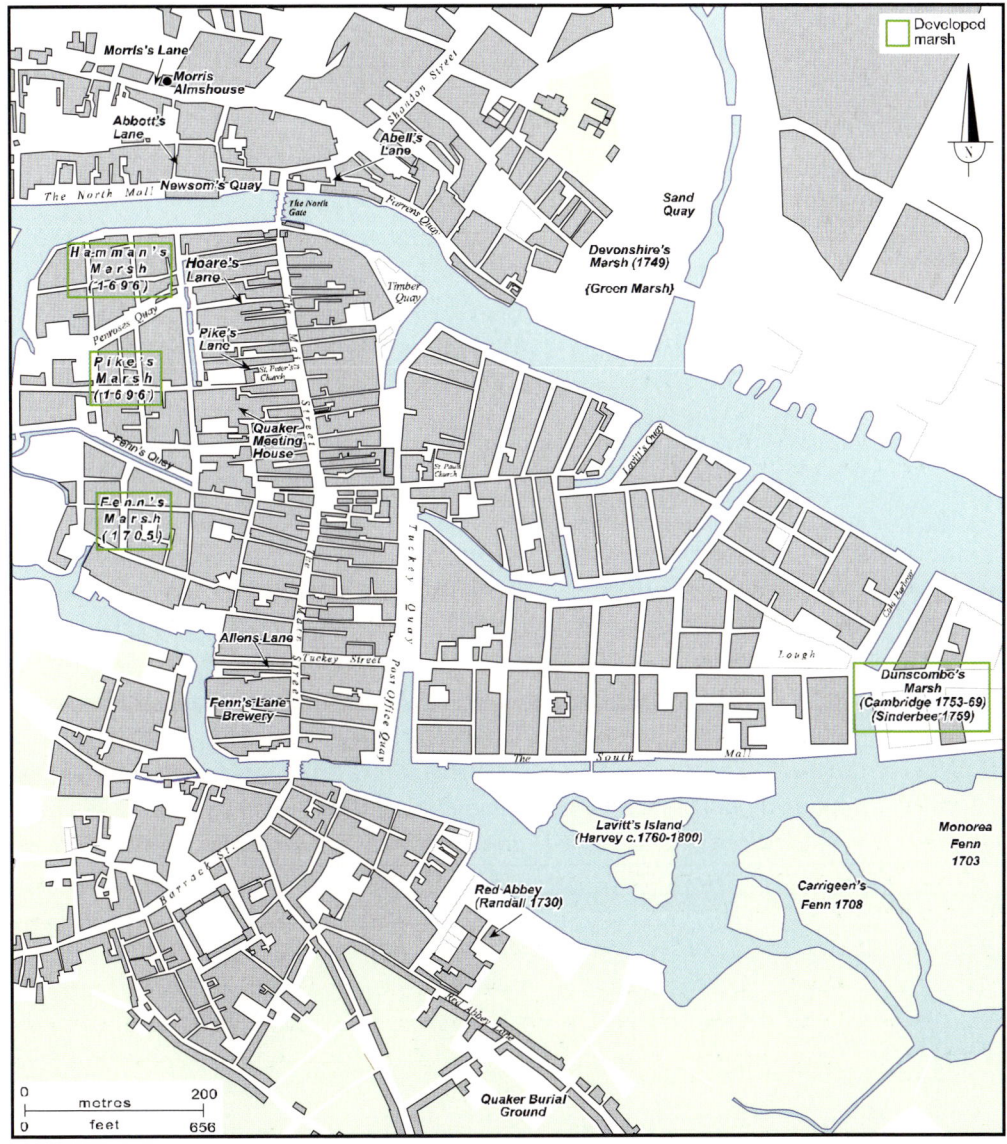

Fig. 2.83 Although numerically a minute minority, Quakers owned many substantial and valuable properties within the city.

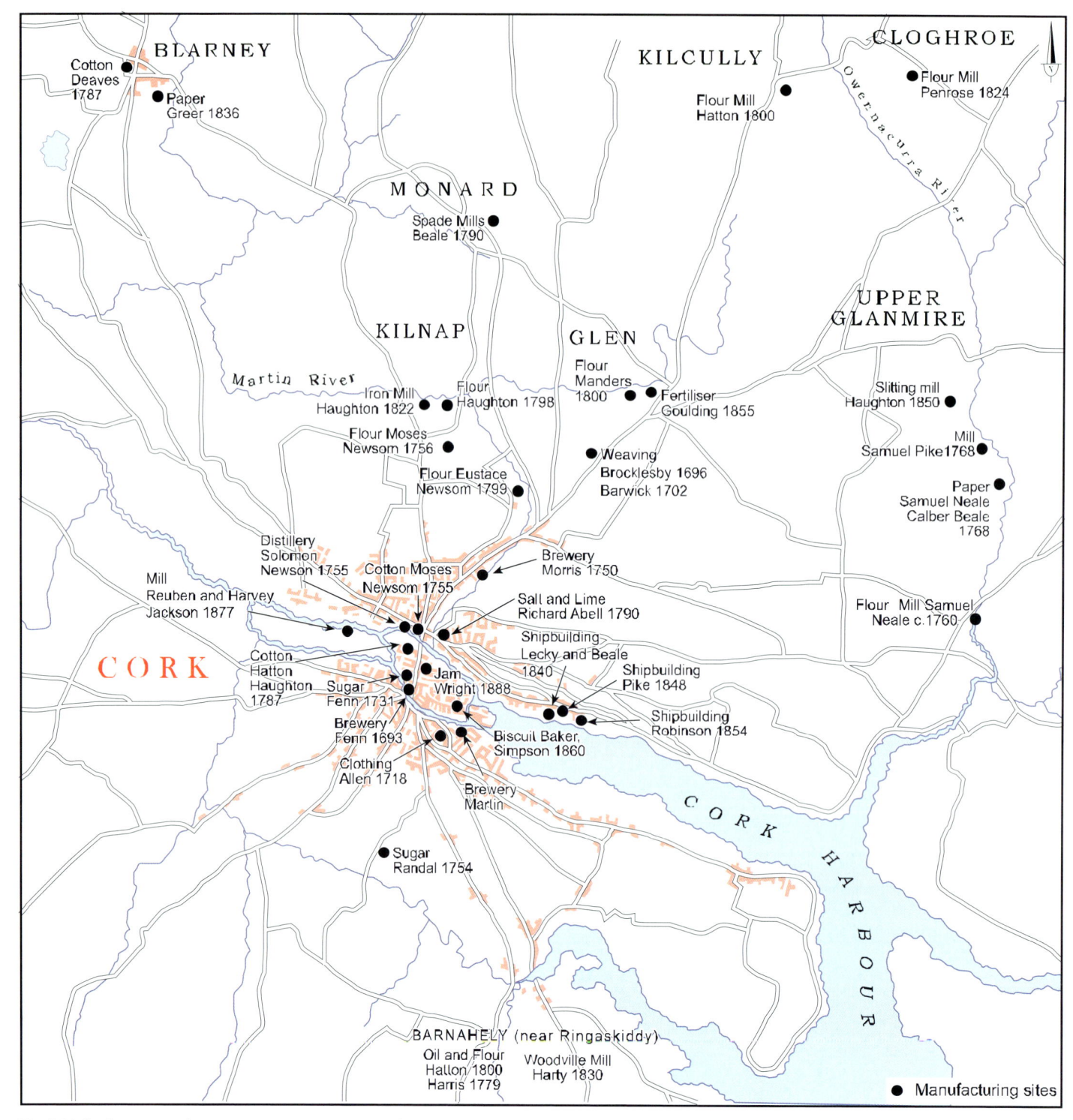

Fig. 2.84 Quakers were also prominent in commerce and initiated many new 'manufactories'.

cloth and textile production. Business was the private concern of each Quaker family, but the community worked together to see that Friends paid their debts and were honest in word and deed. The Society, though not a secret or business society, reminded members of their secular responsibilities. They developed a practice of endogamous marriage that tended towards the maintenance of assets among Quaker families.

The 'War of the Two Kings' (1689–1692) proved decisive to the better acceptance of Quakers in Cork. They shunned military forces of any hue and suffered losses of property yet found a role in giving humanitarian service. Irish Quakers, by fair-dealing and honesty, gained the confidence of their fellow citizens. They consciously avoided monopolies, cartels and political involvement,

TRANSFORMATION

but were accepted as freemen of the city. Although they refused to take the required oaths, they were in some cases accepted on payment of a 'fine' and in other cases even that was waived.

In the wake of the turmoil of the 1690s, Cork's civic finances were in a bad way. The richer Quaker merchants loaned money to the Corporation to discharge its debts. Some individuals were already leasing land from the Corporation and now started to buy cheap development land in the marshes to the west of the city, particularly in the north Liberties: the Pikes purchased Pike's Marsh and John Hamman (or Hammond) acquired Hammond's Marsh. The names of other Quaker families were perpetuated in Fenn's Marsh, The Green Marsh and Sleigh's Marsh (Monrea). These marshes were reclaimed, embanked and urbanised.

CONSOLIDATION

There were 200 Quakers in Cork at the beginning of the eighteenth century. Their gradual numerical decline was made worse by the 'disuniting' that resulted from infringement of the Quaker rules and particularly from the many young people who 'married out'. The 1760s marked an improvement in Irish commerce in which Quakers played a creative part, in spite of disabilities because of the Penal Laws and tithe system. They also, like the wider population, increased in numbers. Not all were wealthy, but all were counselled to choose simplicity in their lifestyles and a movement towards spiritual reform made them more inward-looking. Nevertheless, Cork Quakers, like their fellow citizens, had a necessary interest in land. As a consequence of a limited banking system and the absence of other investment outlets, land formed a safe haven for capital, giving a guaranteed return. Land could be traded for mortgage loans and for marriage settlements and other family and business purposes.

Wealthy Quaker merchants acquired large tracts in development areas east of the city walls and at Dunscombe's Marsh. This investment was usually directly related to getting new warehousing for their own businesses. The Carrolls, importers of Baltic timber, invested in land around Leitrim and in Dring's Marsh east of the Penrose holdings. Reuben Harvey, who exported linen and salt beef to the West Indies and North America, acquired Lavitt's Island and built warehouses and houses there. The Beales owned land around Myrtle Hill, above Beale's Hill. The Penroses, uniquely, embarked on a deliberate land-investment policy designed to earn them an income independently of their timber-importing business. Through marriages with the Denis family, they already owned many plots of city land, but in about 1785 they purchased large areas of desolate land to the north-east, in Glankittane, later known as Penrose's Marsh.

Commercial changes implied changes in the physical appearance and development of Cork. When the bay-yarn export declined, many Friends reinvested surplus capital in activities such as flour-milling and cotton-spinning. Several of these Quaker-owned plants were situated on the northside of the city in Blackpool, along the Watercourse and the Bride. This all implied land purchase or sale and the use of inherited capital made available through family networks and extended partnerships. Already, a few of the richer Quaker merchants had houses in the suburbs: the Penroses at Woodhill, the Carrolls at Hyde Park, the Harveys at Pleasant Field and Chiplee and the Newenhams at Maryborough.

DECLINE

By 1810 Cork Quakers had peaked at 450–500 members and thereafter deaths exceeded births by 40 per cent in each successive decade. The economic position of Quakers was more weighty than their numbers alone would suggest. The partnership of Harvey, Deaves and Harvey, for example, controlled ten per cent of

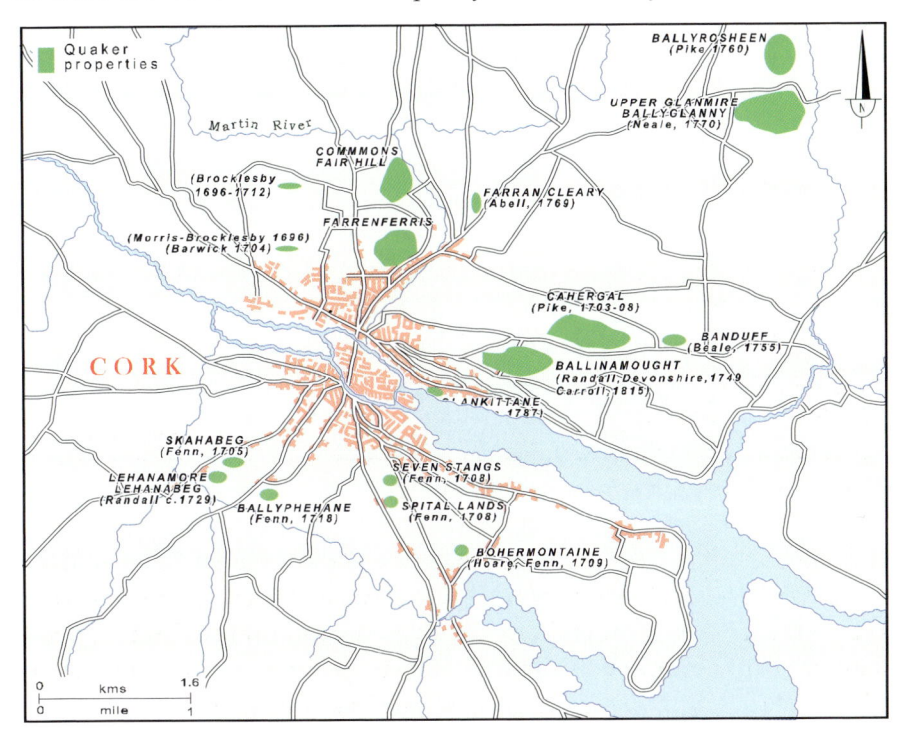

Fig. 2.85 Major Quaker properties outside Cork confirm that some families were amongst the earliest to move outside the congested city.

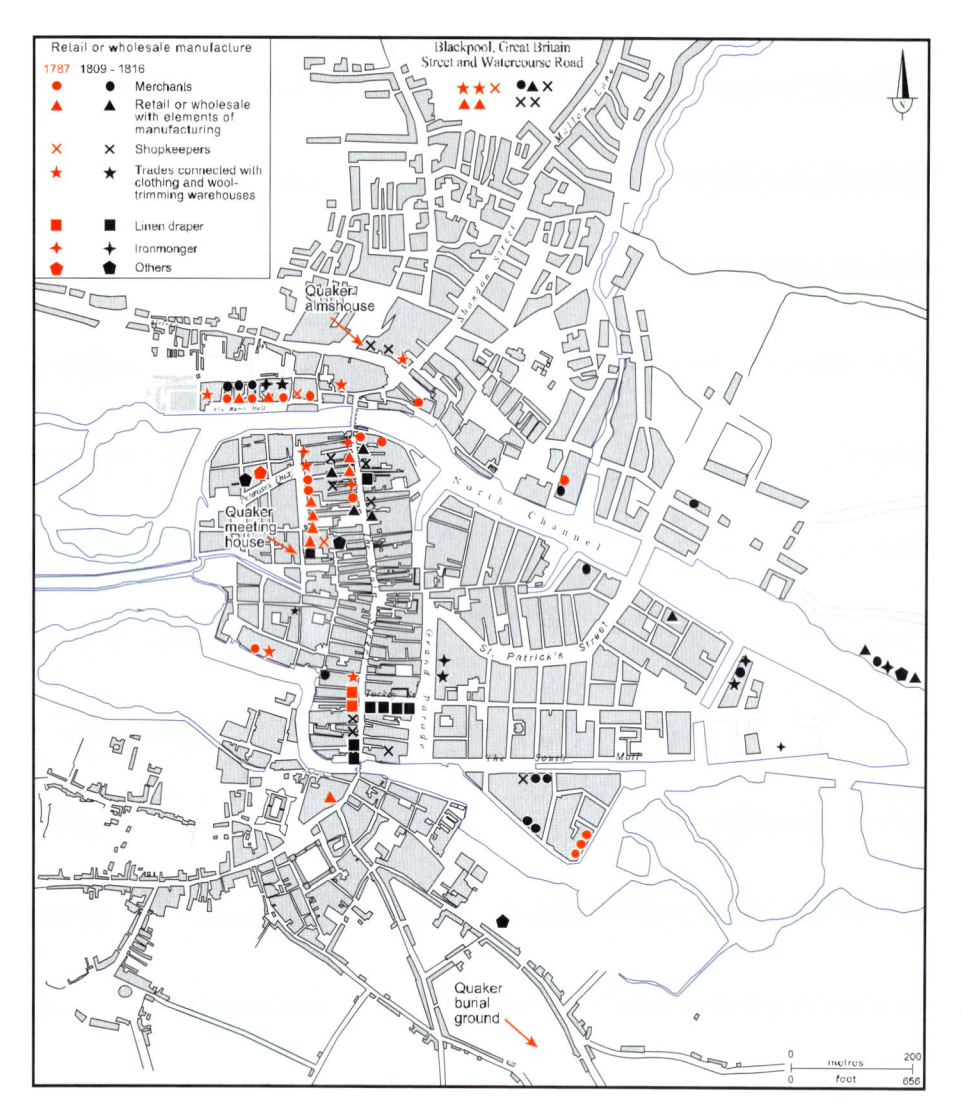

Fig. 2.86 Quakers were also deeply active in business and in the professions.

Cork's import of the barrel-staves so important to Cork's trade. There was an increasing degree of product specialisation among merchants and a growing number of smaller retailers. Any competition was probably qualified by claims of family and familiarity.

Sixty per cent of the Quaker population was elderly or otherwise dependent and a simple form of welfare was available to the incapacitated. Some lived with relatives or above their shops, were clerks or apprentices, or derived an income from pensions and annuities. Quakers preferred to live and socialise in proximity to their meeting-house in Grattan Street.

After the depression of 1816 that hit Cork following the French wars, a reconstruction of commercial and investment strategies occurred. The old Penrose lots at Glankittane had formed a useful block of property, well laid out with streets and warehouses. Many Quakers had moved out of the older city and set up business in Patrick Street or on the Grand Parade. Specialist grocery shops became noticeable. These premises were on long leases and land investment was less attractive as commercial and financial infrastructures improved. By the 1820s many Cork citizens invested in the Quaker-inspired St George's Steam Packet Company, which further focused commercial attention on England. In 1838, this company, under the leadership of James Beale, produced the *Sirius*, the first steam-powered vessel to voyage to America.

By 1838, there were only 280 Quakers in Cork, but a new meeting-house, designed by George T. Beale, was built at Grattan Street. Many Friends with city businesses were now settling in the suburbs at Summerhill North and the Middle Glanmire Road, sometimes renting or buying houses on land owned by relatives. Some Carrolls lived at Clarence Terrace and 'Carrolina' was named after them. The Beale family lived at Adelaide Place. An attraction, besides the fresh air, was to be outside the claims of city taxes. The south-eastern suburbs Blackrock and Monkstown also proved popular and available. Ebenezer Pike lived at Bessborough and the Newsoms at Tellingana.

Cork Quakers are remembered for their non-sectarian administration of relief during the Great Famine from 1845 to 1848. The events marked a watershed in the development of new agricultural, commercial and industrial patterns. Land owned by the Penroses at Glankittane and by the Carrolls at Dring's Marsh proved crucial to the establishment of the Lecky and Beale ship-building concerns and to the Pike and the Robinson shipyards, which employed hundreds of men.

There is no sign that Quakers had any great desire to be landowners. They were chiefly shopowners or were active in the new professional classes mainly living in the suburbs. Numerical decline led to the building of a smaller meeting-house at Summerhill South in 1939 in a corner of their burial ground at Quaker Road. Since the 1980s, the Quaker community has seen steady growth and, in 2003, numbered 130 members.

Fig. 2.87 The *Sirius* sets sail for New York. (Source: Crawford Municipal Gallery.)

'View of Cork City', by Thomas Sautell Roberts (1760–1826), watercolour on paper. (Source: Crawford Municipal Art Gallery.)

3
The City in the Nineteenth and Twentieth Centuries

THE CITY IN THE NINETEENTH AND TWENTIETH CENTURIES

INTRODUCTION

John Crowley

The aftermath of the Napoleonic Wars saw a marked decline in the provisions trade in the city. Nevertheless, the wealth generated by the city's merchant princes underpinned the development of a new civic consciousness. This expressed itself in the establishment of literary, scientific and artistic institutions and societies. Indeed, the early decades of the nineteenth century witnessed an artistic flowering in the city, which has never been subsequently equalled. The nineteenth century saw the founding of the Royal Cork Institution (RCI), as well as a School of Art and Design. The city also acquired its university, Queen's College, built on the foundations laid down by the RCI. The hosting of a national exhibition in mid-century was also indicative of a new confidence and pride. The widening and building of new streets as well as the construction of imposing buildings continued throughout the century. The construction of bridges facilitated the growth of the city beyond its island centre, while new developments in transport allowed for further suburban expansion.

The distinguished architects, Sir Thomas Deane, the Pain brothers James and George Richard (Cork Gaol, 1818; Holy Trinity church, 1832; St Patrick's church, *c.* 1836, and the Court House, 1835) and William Burges (St Fin Barre's Cathedral, 1865), left their stamp on the city. Deane, who designed Queen's College, was one of the principal lights in this new civic crusade. However, while building work continued on Queen's College the city was engulfed by the horror of famine as thousands of people from the surrounding countryside converged on the city seeking refuge from the torment of hunger. The Cork workhouse soon overflowed with the dying and the dead. Mortality levels in the workhouse soared during the famine years (1845–1852), principally as a result of overcrowding and the consequent spread of disease. The city's quaysides would also bear witness to a mass exodus of famine refugees bound for Britain, the United States and Canada. Emigration was a constant feature of life throughout the remaining decades of the nineteenth century, with Queenstown (Cobh) taking over as the principal emigration port in the Munster region. The arrival of a small group of Jewish refugees in the city in the 1880s and 1890s marked a minor reversal of what was an overwhelming pattern of emigration.

The nature of local politics in the nineteenth century altered considerably, reflecting new realities. A Protestant élite had controlled municipal government across the eighteenth century. During the course of the nineteenth century, Catholics would become much more prominent in municipal affairs. The campaign for Catholic Emancipation along with the Repeal movement had firm adherents within the city. The case for Repeal was made eloquently

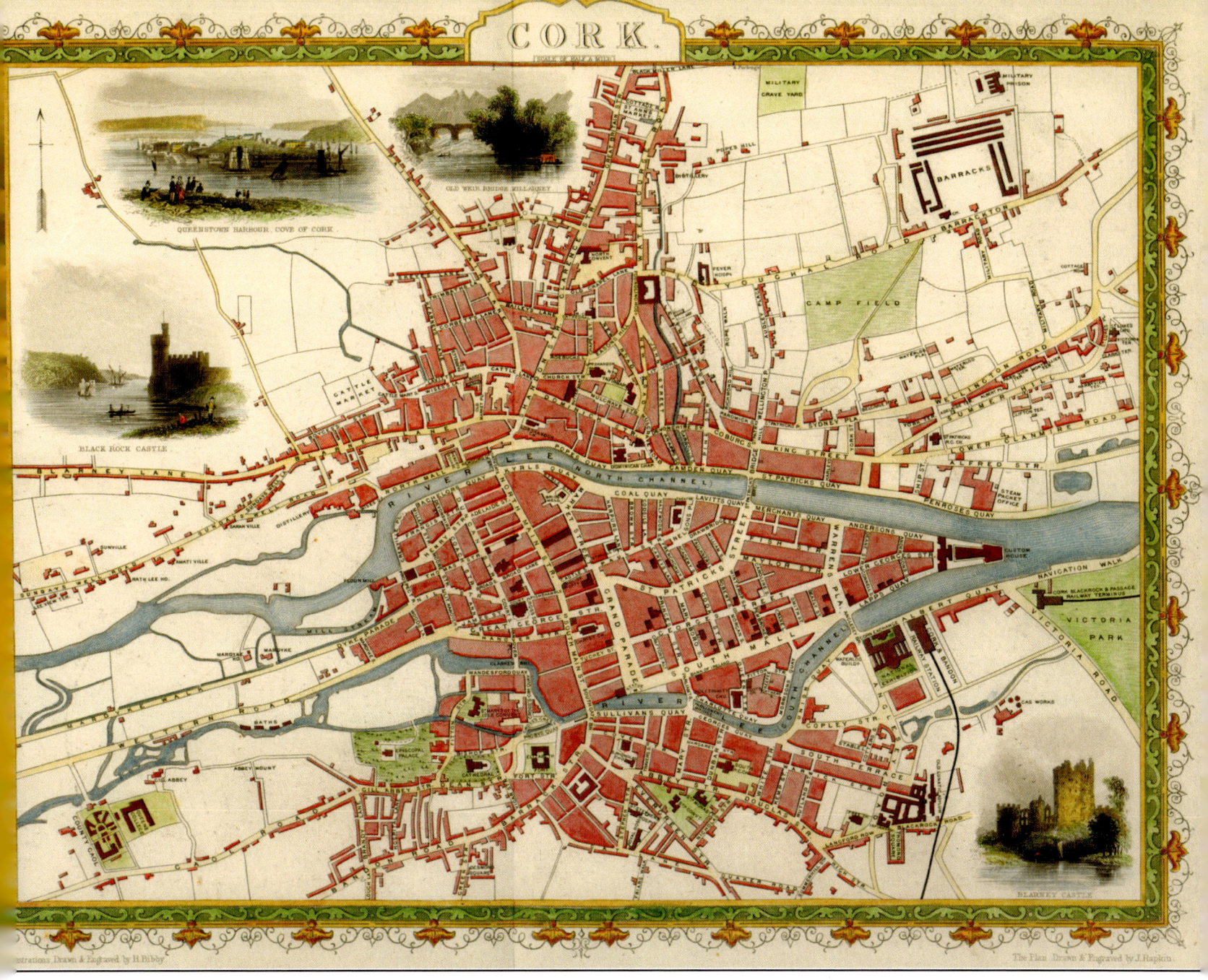

Fig. 3.1 This map shows the extent of Cork city *c.* 1850. The modern streetscape is clearly visible in the city's island centre. Expansion beyond this island centre was greatly facilitated by the construction of new bridges, including St Patrick's Bridge (1791), Parliament Bridge (1806) and Anglesea Bridge (*c.* 1830s). (Source: Private collection.)

by John Francis Maguire, MP for Cork. He established his own newspaper, the *Cork Examiner*, in 1841 as a rival to the Unionist-dominated *Cork Constitution*. Maguire – a future Lord Mayor – also championed Father Mathew's temperance campaign, which sought to counteract the evils of drink in a city famous for its distilleries and breweries. Cork in that sense was a typical Victorian city in its search for civic and moral improvement.

Residential segregation continued in the nineteenth century. The outward movement of the city's mercantile élite to suburban villas in Blackrock, Douglas, Lota and Glanmire in the eighteenth century was a sign of things to come. In the nineteenth century, an emerging middle class increasingly decamped to fashionable suburbs at Sunday's Well, the Western Road, Ballintemple and Blackrock. Tenements and slums invaded the former high-class residential areas in older parts of the city. The provision of suitable housing for the working classes became a priority in the latter decades of the century, with private philanthropic bodies taking the lead. Cork Corporation eventually followed their example. Schemes such as Madden's Buildings and Horgan's Buildings reflected a desire amongst the city's municipal authorities to ameliorate the living conditions of its working-class citizens.

By the end of the nineteenth century, Cork's once vibrant economy had stagnated. The population was in decline and

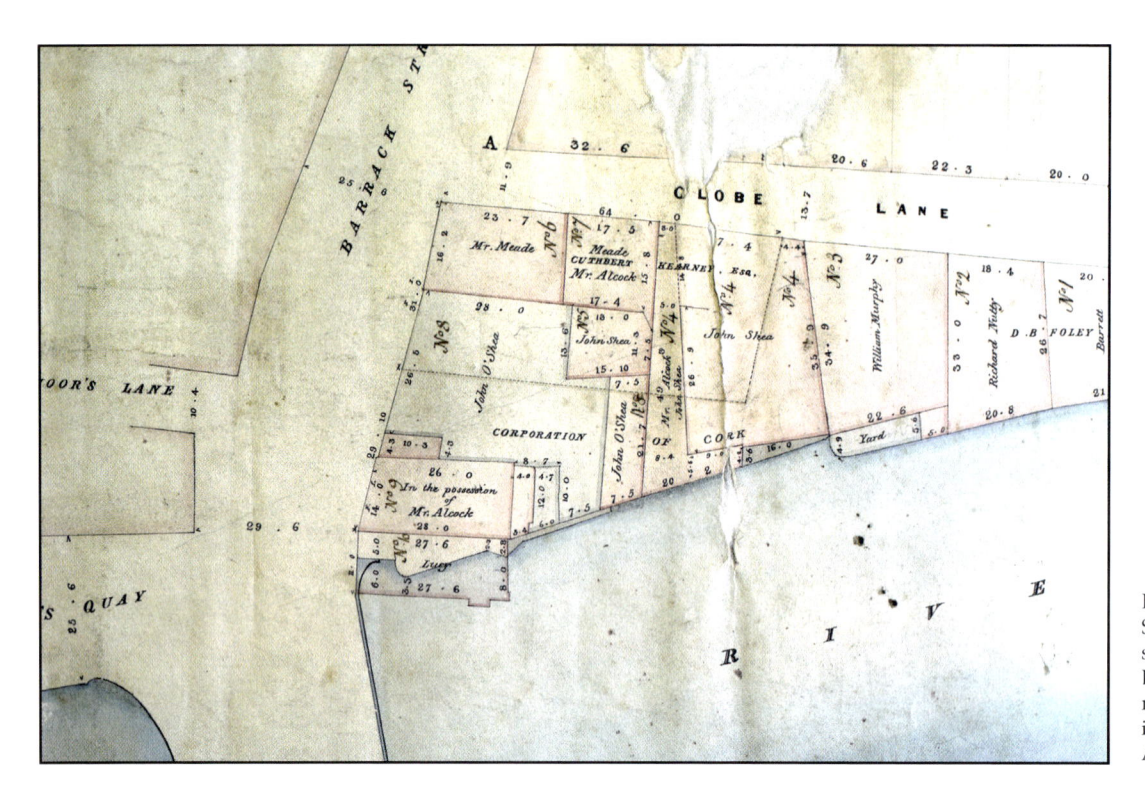

Fig. 3.2 Extract from the Wide Streets Commission Plan, showing properties at the end of Barrack Street which were removed during street improvements. (Source: Cork Archives Institute.)

Fig. 3.3 'Emigrants at Cork', *c.* 1840, artist unknown, oil on canvas. (Reproduced by kind permission of the Department of Irish Folklore, University College Dublin.)

THE · CITY · IN · THE · NINETEENTH · AND · TWENTIETH · CENTURIES

Fig. 3.5 A farm adjoining the city being put up for auction in 1900. New housing would fill these green-field sites. (Source: Cork Archives Institute.)

arrival of the Ford plant (1917) on the site of the former Victoria Park, a racecourse and amenity area situated on the Marina. Goulding's and Dunlop's later joined Ford's at its Centre Park Road location. All would become central to the social and industrial fabric of the twentieth-century city.

The city experienced dramatic change from the 1920s onwards. The scale and tempo of suburban expansion, for example, intensified, reflecting the desire of Cork Corporation to clear overcrowded laneways in central and northside areas. The provision of public housing on green-field sites hastened the demise of slums and tenements. The introduction of town planning played a critical role in these new developments. The publication of the Cork Civic Survey in 1926 and the passing of a Town Planning Act in 1934 marked a watershed in the city's growth. The local economy, however, remained volatile throughout much of the twentieth century. Periods of high unemployment resulted in many Cork people

Fig. 3.4 John Francis Maguire, Mayor of Cork 1862–1864. (Source: Cork Archives Institute.)

its prospects were bleak. The population of the city in 1901 was 76,000, a decline of six per cent from 1841. The turbulent war years – the Great War, the War of Independence and the Civil War – also took their deadly toll. Many who enlisted in the British Army did so principally for economic reasons. However, work conditions improved for some with the

Fig. 3.6 'View of the Ford Factory in Cork', 1953, by Alfred Dobbin (1911–1960), watercolour on paper. (Source: Crawford Municipal Art Gallery.)

'taking the boat' to Britain. Emigrants boarding the *Inisfallen* became an all too familiar sight in the 1950s. Emigration levels in the early 1980s mirrored those of the 1950s. The closure of Dunlop's (1983) and Ford's (1984) in particular dealt a serious blow to the morale of the city.

By the last decade of the twentieth century, the city and region had recovered economically, with both the information technology sector and pharmaceutical industry very much to the fore. The city itself has been the subject of a series of urban plans whose principal objectives have been to make Cork a more attractive place to live and work in and to visit. The redesign of St Patrick's Street acknowledges the need for higher-quality civic spaces. While the impact of the Celtic Tiger is more readily visible in Dublin and Limerick, the potential for development in Cork, especially down river, has been recognised. The spread of the city has been its most dynamic feature in the twentieth century. However, the ongoing revitalisation of the city centre remains key to its future.

16. INDUSTRY 1750–1930

Colin Rynne

At the end of the eighteenth century, the port of Cork, Ireland's leading transatlantic shipping port, was experiencing incipient industrialisation and appeared destined for greater things. Its future success, indeed, seemed assured. As the second city, Cork's burgeoning industrial development had already eclipsed its nearest rivals Waterford, Kinsale and Youghal. Its main textile industries were of national – and in at least one instance international – importance, while the largest porter brewery and distillery in Ireland had also been established there. The quality of Cork butter was assured by one of the most innovative and rigorously enforced systems of quality control then known in Europe, which laid the foundations for the largest butter market in the world. Cork's exports of beef and pig-meat were also nationally significant, whilst the by-products of the slaughter-houses provided the raw material for a plethora of allied trades.

Yet Cork's success as a port was too closely aligned with the provision trade. Foreign markets for Irish provisions had already declined by the turn of the eighteenth century, and the establishment of large industrial units within the city and its immediate environs generated too few spin-offs to provide a firm base for future industrial development. The false optimism of contemporary accounts of Cork's foreign trade is laid bare by the subsequent lack of industrial concentration in the nineteenth century. Brewing and distilling, its principal textile industries, sailcloth manufacture, linen and woollens, along with a number of other important local industries such as shipbuilding, engineering and gunpowder manufacture, experienced mixed fortunes after 1800. So why did Cork, like so many other Irish ports during the eighteenth and nineteenth centuries, fail to industrialise?

The expansion of Cork's trade in the eighteenth century cannot simply be explained by geographical advantages. Human factors, such as the changing patterns of English and Irish overseas trade and the military and economic benefits accruing to England from its continued development, were important. Nevertheless, Cork harbour was endowed with considerable natural advantages, not least of which was being one of the largest natural harbours in the northern hemisphere. The lower harbour could easily accommodate the larger transatlantic convoys or British naval squadrons. From the American War of Independence onwards, British naval facilities became increasingly concentrated in the lower harbour and, between 1777 and 1779, £90,000 was spent on improvements and on naval repair work at Passage West.[1] Britain's American war and the later Napoleonic campaigns were a source of considerable financial gain for Cork merchants. Each of these episodes concentrated the greater bulk of transatlantic trade on the port of Cork, while underlining the strategic importance of the harbour to the Admiralty. The fact that Cork was far enough from Dublin not to be threatened by direct competition from the capital, while close enough to important markets in Britain, was also an important factor.

By the end of the seventeenth century Irish provisions, principally salted beef, butter and pork, had become a significant element in the maintenance of the West Indian plantations.[2] Cork and Dublin had by this time already become the most important Irish ports engaged in this trade. The expansion was a direct result of the preference of British shipowners for victualling their ships at Irish ports and then sailing to the Continent and the American colonies.[3] In the eighteenth century most vessels involved were English owned and registered, and these were assembled in naval centres such as Plymouth to be escorted, under convoy, to their destinations in Europe or in the American colonies.[4] Cork became the seat of the Admiralty's victualling agent in Ireland and its pre-eminence in the Irish provisions trade as a whole led to the accreditation of Spanish and Portuguese consular officials there.[5]

INDUSTRIAL LOCATION

Immediate access to the port of Cork was the main factor in the location of industry within the immediate environs of the city during the eighteenth century. Indeed, while certain large industrial concerns such as brewing and distilling were geared towards a localised market, most of the others (particularly the textile industries) primarily manufactured for export. Industries dependent on mechanisation needed power; for the vast majority of eighteenth-century Cork industries, that meant water power. There were, of course, some notable exceptions, principally urban breweries and distilleries, where water power was not an important concern, as all of the essential plant could be worked by horse-powered machinery. However, their future expansion could only be assured by the adoption of steam-powered prime movers, and Cork's distilleries and breweries became some of the first in Ireland to do so.[6]

By the later 1700s, the tidal marshes upon which the city had been built were in the process of being reclaimed, and the passage of the Lee through the city was increasingly confined to larger channels. The effectiveness of the water flowing through these channels, particularly of those flowing through the city itself, provided no great inducement to the establishment of water-powered mills, as the tidal reaches of the harbour extended to slightly beyond the built-up area of the city itself. In the medieval and post-medieval periods, a small number of grain mills were built on these channels, and it seems quite likely that many of these were tide mills. A water-powered manufactory, however, required a much larger and more dependable source of water of a magnitude beyond that which the tidal channels of the Lee could provide. Thus the water-powered industries which utilised the Lee within the city were few; all were sited to the west to extract water from stretches of the river beyond its tidal reaches. In consequence, large units of mechanised industry were located within the immediate environs of the city adjacent to non-estuarine stretches of the Lee's main tributaries.[7]

From the second half of the eighteenth century onwards, the Bride and Glen rivers (which converged to form the Kiln River in Blackpool), flowing southwards through the northern suburbs of the city, were impounded to power a number of industrial processes. The Blarney, Glasheen and Curraheen rivers to the north-west and west of the city were also harnessed to serve large industrial units. Only when steam power arrived in Cork in the late eighteenth century did the location of mechanised industries within the city itself become a viable option. Immediate access to Welsh coal discharged directly at the city's quaysides, which reduced transportation costs, doubtless provided a further stimulus to establishing steam-powered industries within the city. The increased importation of American wheat in the nineteenth

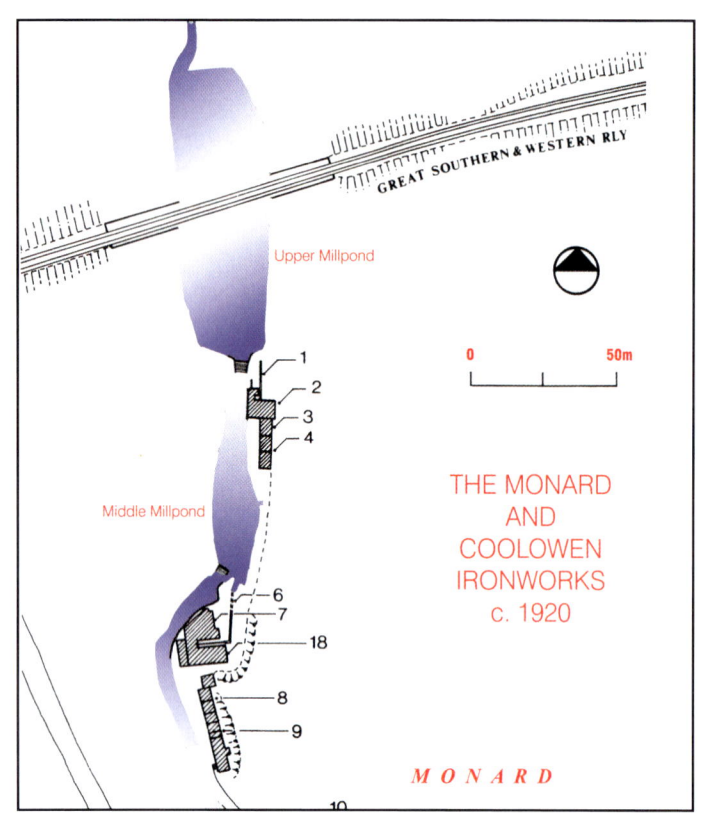

Fig. 3.7 Water power was the backbone of all industrial activity in the eighteenth and early nineteenth century. In the Monard and Coolowen Ironworks (a Quaker industrial settlement, established by the Beale family c. 1780), the Blarney River was used to power a series of spade and shovel mills. The four water-powered mills (2, 7, 13 and 16) were serviced by a community of smiths, who lived in comfortable houses built by the owners (8 and 9).

Fig. 3.8 A cross-section through the Coolowen spade mill in the Monard complex showing a large wooden waterwheel (2), which powered a trip hammer (4) for forging and welding shovels and spades and a grinding stone for sharpening the hammer heads (5). A second, smaller, iron-framed waterwheel powered the forge bellows.

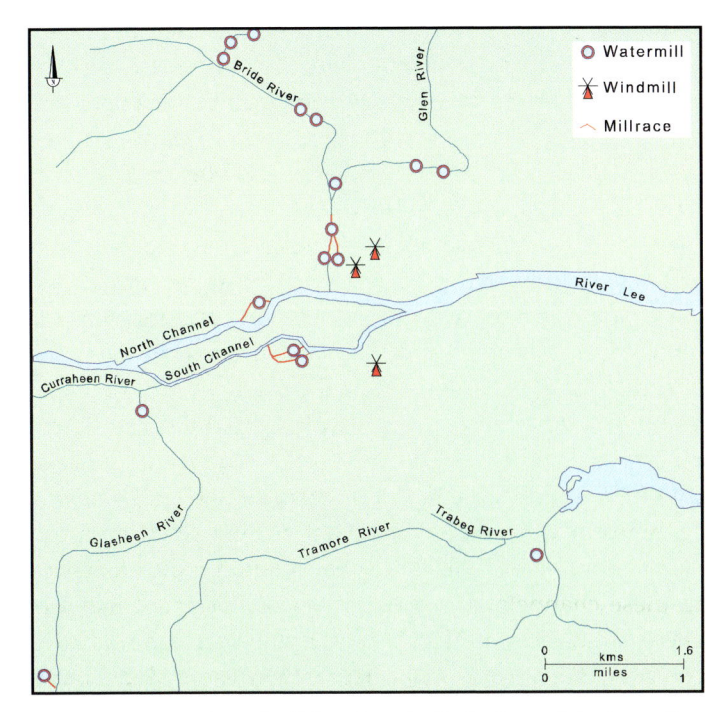

THE CITY IN THE NINETEENTH AND TWENTIETH CENTURIES

Fig. 3.9 Water- and windmill locations in Cork city and its immediate environs between 1750 and 1880. There was a clear concentration of water-powered sites to the north of the Lee, where the fall of water was more conducive for conversion to industrial energy. Windmills were a rarer phenomenon. As in the rest of Ireland, they were a supplemental energy form and those in Cork, as elsewhere, were built to take advantage of favourable trends in the flour-milling industry in the late eighteenth and early nineteenth centuries.

century also stimulated the establishment of steam-powered flour mills on the city quaysides, where both grain for the mills and fuel for their engines could easily be unloaded.[8]

INDUSTRIAL FOUNDATIONS

In the second half of the eighteenth century, the woollen, linen and cotton industries established around Cork were becoming nationally important. Their establishment in the outlying areas of Blarney and Douglas provided the focus of later settlements, which were, in every sense, 'industrial villages'. Cork county was, by this stage, the centre of the Irish woollen trade. The Lane family, who had established a large manufactory at Riverstown in the early nineteenth century and who had created a near monopoly of the manufacture of army clothing, employed approximately 1,000 workers in their Riverstown and Cork city works.[9] The O'Mahony family, later to become synonymous with the Blarney tweed industry, also established themselves in the Blackpool area in the 1790s.[10] One-half to two-thirds of Ireland's supply of combed wool passed through the hands of the city's worsted manufacturers by the early years of the nineteenth century. This in itself was a good index of the success of the industry in Cork. It was one that was to a certain extent equalled by those engaged in linen manufacture.

The establishment of linen manufacture within the city dates to the early decades of the eighteenth century and was associated with the Besnard family at Douglas. With the development of the port and the subsequent growth in the manufacture of ship's chandlery, the establishment of sailcloth manufacture was a natural progression. In 1726, an important linen industry developed near the village of Douglas; by the turn of the nineteenth century, it became the first linen factory in Ireland to operate water-powered spindles and the largest sailcloth factory in Europe.

The manufacture of cotton was reputedly introduced into Cork by French prisoners of war in the early 1750s. The substantial operation begun by Henry and James Sadleir in 1781 drew on the expertise of skilled workers who, along with machines, were directly imported from the Manchester cotton industry. The Sadleir brothers had a large manufactory on the south quays, while outside the city, at Glasheen, a former linen mill became the centre of their finishing and printing operation. By the end of the eighteenth century, the various textile industries established in Cork were already in serious decline.[11] Sailcloth manufacture was continued in Douglas, but throughout the county this industry declined to the extent that the growing of flax had to be effectively re-introduced from scratch in the mid-nineteenth century. Nevertheless, Cork's woollen and linen industries were partially revitalised in the second half of the nineteenth century, by which time existing market conditions favoured their success. For the most part, however, the large-scale industrialisation and consequent prosperity which the late eighteenth-century textile industries had promised was not subsequently fulfilled.

BREWING AND DISTILLING

During the eighteenth century, the brewing and distilling industries established a firm foothold within the city. The output of the largest fifteen breweries in the 1770s was relatively small and of poor quality. Towards the end of the century, however, the units of production tended to be larger. Beamish and Crawford's porter brewery, established in 1792, became the largest in Ireland by the early years of the nineteenth century. Nevertheless, the main Cork breweries in the late eighteenth century were locked into what were primarily localised markets, and were unable to compete on the national market until the establishment of the rail network in the nineteenth century.

The first large distillery in the city was built on the quayside adjacent to the North Mall in 1779, and from 1782 onwards was controlled by the Wise family. By 1796, the total for the city was ten, which accounted for more than four-fifths of the Cork region's still capacity: two of these were the largest in Ireland, each with a capacity of 2,000

Fig. 3.10 Workers at O'Brien's Woollen Mill in Douglas, 1933. (Photo: *Irish Examiner*.)

gallons.[12] Early in the nineteenth century, the proprietor of the Crosses Green Distillery, Thomas Walker, was said to have been 'the greatest distiller in the kingdom'.[13] Indeed, as early as 1808, the Crosses Green Distillery was considered to be the largest in Ireland, and was certainly the first to utilise steam power.

The commercial success of Cork industries associated with the latter half of the eighteenth century could provide no solid foundation for industrialisation. Cork was never to become an industrial city; the aftermath of the Napoleonic Wars, indeed, served only to highlight the extent to which its commercial and industrial fabric had worn very thin. In other industrial sectors, the decline, though gradual, was irreversible and the provisions trade was seriously undermined by the end of government contracts, which, in turn, followed a general depression in British and Irish agriculture.[14]

However, the more important food-processing industries such as brewing and distilling continued to develop apace. When the commercial clauses of the Act of Union began to be implemented after 1824, English textiles were dumped on the Irish market, with truly devastating consequences for the Cork-based textile industries.[15] The failure of Cork's textile industries to adopt new technology also contributed significantly to their decline in the early nineteenth century.[16] All of the main Cork industries that experienced growth in the period 1780–1840 declined in the second half of the nineteenth century. Despite some notable successes, principally in iron foundries and shipbuilding, large-scale industrialisation did not occur within the region. Rapid

Fig. 3.11 Beamish and Crawford's brewery is perhaps the city's most enduring large-scale industrial concern. Its nucleus was a brewery and maltings in Cremer's Square (off the present South Main Street). William Beamish and William Crawford bought the lease in 1791 and began porter production in 1792. Beamish and Crawford's output was of national importance and it was the largest Irish brewery until 1833, when Guinness of Dublin exceeded its output.

technological change in some areas (the woollen textile industry) was equally matched by technological stagnation in others (tanning) and even active technological regression, as in the distilling industry.

The Cork region, like so many others within Ireland during the nineteenth century, failed to develop sustainable industries. A general erosion in the region's economic base caused by a declining home market, a more impoverished population after the Great Famine of the 1840s and geographical isolation from leading English industrial regions militated against the industrialisation of the greater Cork area. The lack of large-scale industry within the region by the end of the nineteenth century was not simply a symptom of general decline. Cork had never been an important industrial city at any stage of its development.[17] In 1841, 40 per cent of the males employed within the city were engaged in manufacturing; in 1901 this figure was 19 per cent. A similar decline is discernible in the employment figures for women – all this in a period when the labour force always outran the amount of gainful employment available to it.[18]

Even by working to its strengths the Cork region was unable, in the long term, to develop industries that could successfully exploit the raw materials produced within its hinterland. In the 1860s and 1870s the Cork Butter Market controlled 30 per cent of the Irish butter trade.[19] However, Cork butter failed to compete with butterine and factory-blended butter imported into England (its main market) from Europe. As in the case of the local distilling industry, the Cork Butter Market failed to respond to market conditions and its strict regulations, once a hallmark of its quality, became a restraint on innovation.[20]

By the early decades of the twentieth century the port of Cork served mainly as a conduit for imported goods. Local industry failed to rise to the challenge of foreign competition and, while industries such as porter brewing and textiles continued to expand, growth in other sectors could not be sustained. Even the establishment of the Ford tractor works

Fig. 3.12 Thomas Addison Barnes established the Hive Ironworks on the western end of Hanover Street in 1800. The foundry may well have been the first to manufacture steam engines in the city. It was the first in Ireland to manufacture marine steam engines. The first wholly Irish-built steamship, the *Waterloo*, built at Andrew and Michael Hennessy's yard at Passage West, was fitted with engines built at the Hive Ironworks under the supervision of James Atkinson. In 1829, T.A. Barnes and Company built the three-storey warehouse shown here on Great George's Street (now Washington Street), a formal structure with elaborate pilasters and moulded parapets facing the street. (Photo: Colin Rynne.)

industries such as brewing, distilling, bacon curing and certain textile industries were, in varying degrees, able to survive until recent times. Murphy's and Beamish and Crawford's breweries continue to make important contributions to the city's economy, whilst the flour-milling industry enjoyed a revival; other industries (shipbuilding, gunpowder manufacture and tanning) have long since disappeared. Many important industries with eighteenth-century roots were severely affected by adverse international economic conditions which prevailed in the aftermath of the Napoleonic Wars. The impact of the commercial clauses of the Act of Union in the later 1820s, the Great Famine of the 1840s, along with the localised effects of Father Mathew's temperance campaign, all took a heavy toll on Cork industries. However, Cork, when compared to Dublin, Waterford and Limerick, was by no means exceptional in failing to work to its strengths.

at the Marina in 1919 was largely a philanthropic gesture by the founder of the Ford empire. 'Cork', wrote Henry Ford in 1926, had 'no real industry'. During the First World War, the city's textile and engineering industries received a temporary boost. In its aftermath and immediately before partition, the city's textile and food-processing industries continued to be the main employers but, as in Dublin, the work force in manufacturing industries had effectively halved in the second half of the nineteenth century. Local initiative in the form of the Cork Industrial Development Association, established in 1902 to promote Cork industry, achieved little to reverse this trend. The entire Irish economy was depressed after the boom years of the Great War, although it was still very closely tied to Britain, its principal export market.[21] Even the presence of the Ford Motor Works at Cork, which was employing 1,600 workers in 1923, was not enough to attract further large-scale foreign investment.[22]

Cork was a commercial rather than an industrial city and this was the characteristic pattern in all of Ireland's ports, with the sole exception of Belfast, in the eighteenth and nineteenth centuries. Nevertheless, the more important city

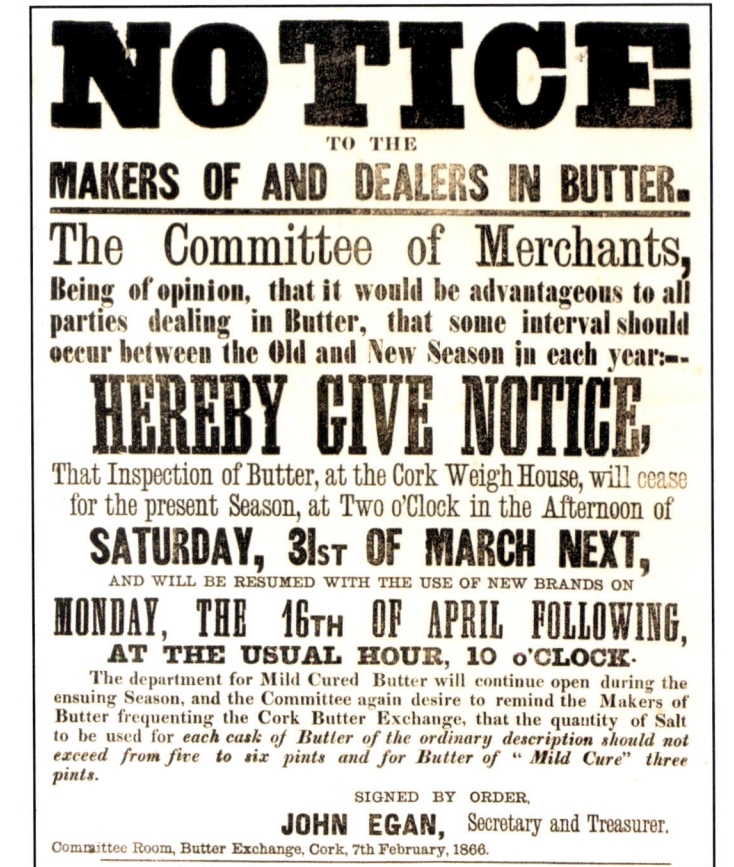

Fig. 3.13 The late nineteenth century would witness a decline in the once thriving butter market. (Source: Cork Archives Institute.)

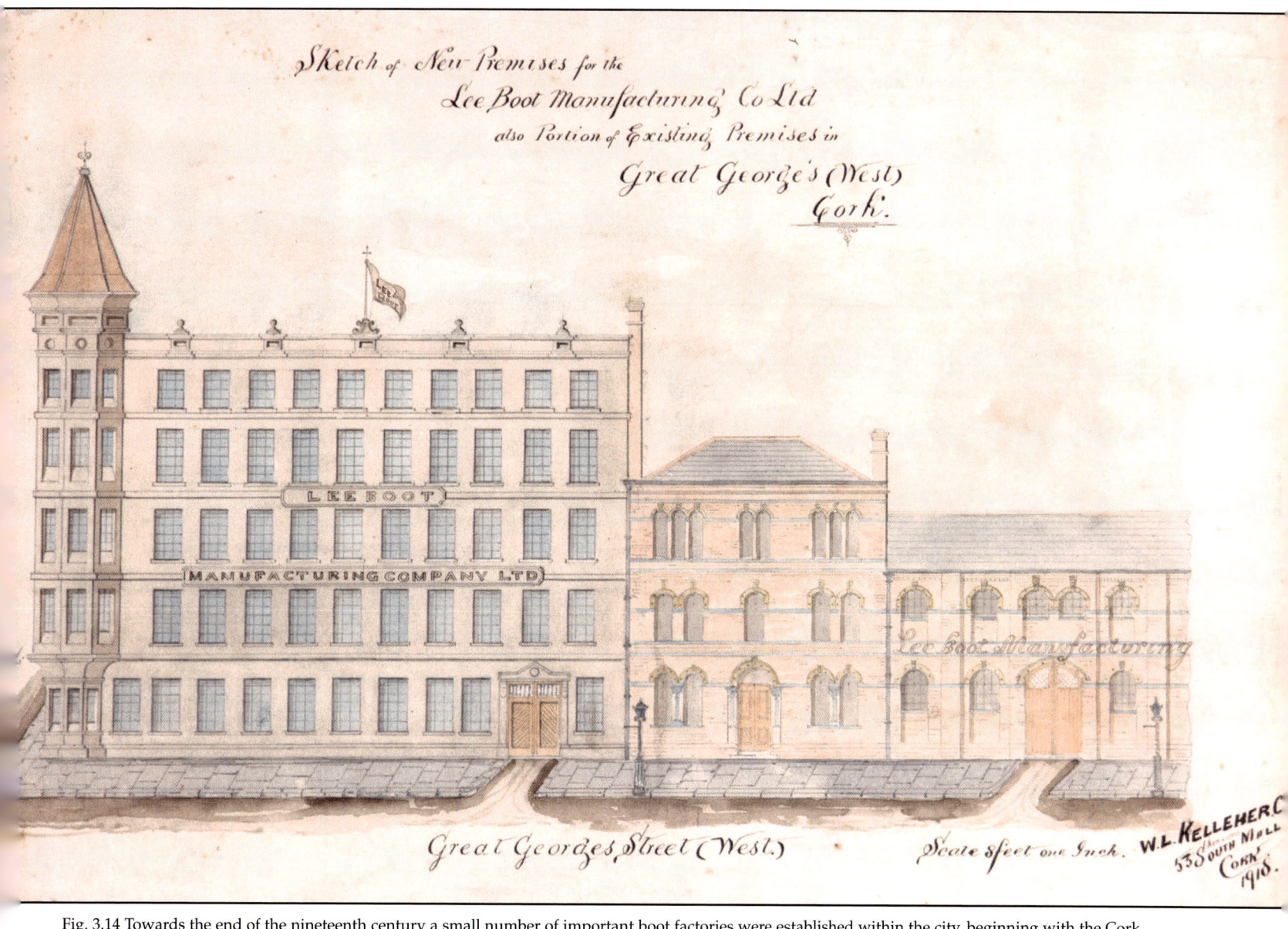

Fig. 3.14 Towards the end of the nineteenth century a small number of important boot factories were established within the city, beginning with the Cork Boot Factory in Blackpool. A high degree of mechanisation clearly distinguished such factories from more traditional craft-based boot- and shoemakers. Dwyer and Company began boot manufacture in Hanover Street and expanded into new premises, the Lee Boot Manufacturing Company at Great George's Street (now Washington Street), in 1885. The almost total disappearance of the Cork tanning industry by the end of the nineteenth century was partly compensated for by the relative success of the Cork footwear industry. The Lee Boot Factory survived until the early 1980s. (Source: Cork Archives Institute.)

Murphy's Brewery

Donal Ó Drisceoil

From the mid-eighteenth century the small-scale Irish brewing industry had been in decline in the face of competition from the large British porter breweries. This decline was reversed towards the end of the century as Irish brewing was gradually reorganised into larger and more efficient units. Commercial breweries displaced the formerly dominant retail operators.[1] The increasingly large-scale and technically efficient Irish porter breweries, led by Guinness of Dublin (1759) and Beamish and Crawford of Cork (1792), rapidly saw off British competition and established brewing as a major Irish industry. Small-scale brewing continued – a dozen small breweries survived until the 1840s in Cork city – but the larger concerns gradually put them out of business. By mid-century, Cork brewing was dominated by the large brewing concerns of Beamish and Crawford and Lane's on South Main Street, and Abbot's (later Arnott's) on Fitton Street (later Sharman Crawford Street). The decreasing popularity of spirits, due to tax increases and temperance campaigns, together with increased spending power in post-Famine rural Ireland and the advent of the railway age, saw the Irish brewing industry enter a period of sustained growth in the second half of the nineteenth century.

Five Cork entrepreneurs saw a business opportunity and added the name of Murphy's to the Irish brewing scene. Five young brothers from one of Cork's 'merchant prince' families established Murphy's Lady's Well Brewery in 1856. It grew rapidly to become an established part of Cork life. A century and a half later, the brewery still stands on its original site on Leitrim Street and, though Murphy's has become an international brand, it remains very much a local favourite.

Fig. 3.15 'View of Cork City', c. 1870, showing Lady's Well Brewery.

THE · CITY · IN · THE · NINETEENTH · AND · TWENTIETH · CENTURIES

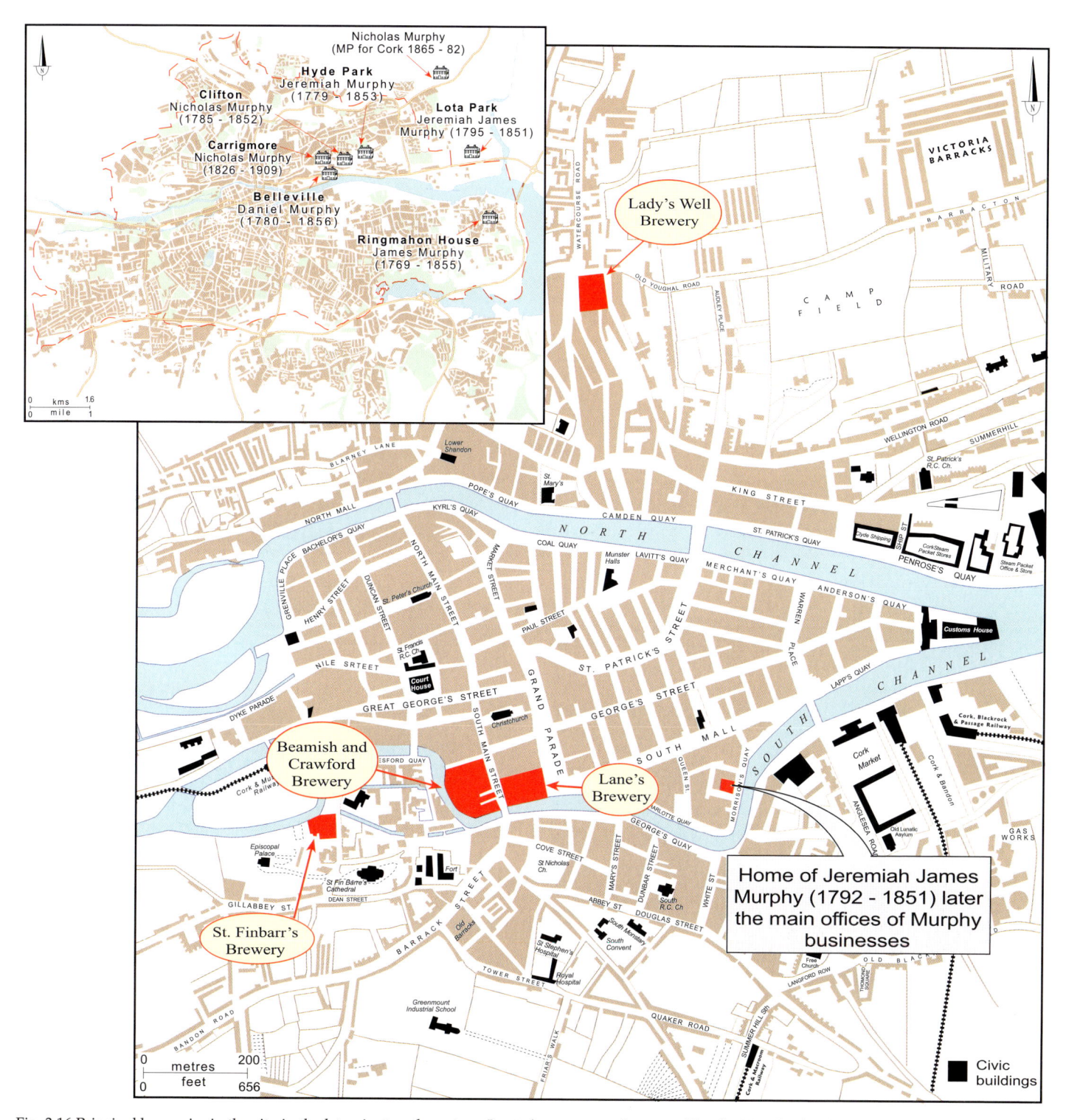

Fig. 3.16 Principal breweries in the city in the late nineteenth century. Inset shows properties owned by the Murphy family in the city and its environs.

MERCHANT PRINCES: THE MURPHY FAMILY

The Murphy family had grown prosperous through a variety of commercial and industrial ventures and their wealth was translated into political, social and cultural power. A flavour of their wealth and status is discernible in the elegant houses in the fashionable outskirts of the city occupied by various members of this clan. Having initially prospered in tanning, the family branched out into shipping and international trading from their base at Morrison's Island. Their ships brought luxury exotic goods such as sugar, rum, spices, coffee and tea into Cork from the Americas and the Far East. In 1825, James Murphy (1769–1855) of Ringmahon House and three of his brothers established the James Murphy and Company distillery in

191

Midleton, which amalgamated with four city firms in 1867 to become the Cork Distilleries Company. Another brother, John, was Catholic bishop of Cork from 1815 to 1847. In 1829, their nephew Jeremiah Stack Murphy became Cork's first Catholic MP. His brother Francis Stack Murphy and cousin Nicholas Murphy were both later elected to parliament also, and their cousin John Nicholas Murphy was Lord Mayor and High Sheriff of the city in the 1850s. The Murphys were major benefactors of the Catholic Church in the city, helping to build St Peter and Paul's and to secure the lease on the old Mayoralty House, which in 1857 became the Mercy Hospital, the first hospital in Cork to be placed in the charge of a religious order.

JAMES J. MURPHY & CO.

James J. Murphy (1825–1897) and his four brothers, William, Jerome, Francis and Nicholas, bought the premises of Cork's Foundling Hospital on Leitrim Street in 1854 and in 1856 James J. Murphy & Co. opened Lady's Well Brewery, named after the holy well situated across the street.[2] They began by brewing Lady's Well Ale and Murphy's Porter, but from 1862 concentrated on porter alone. In 1889, stout, a stronger version of porter, was added. By the 1920s, stout had supplanted porter as the staple Murphy's product. Murphy's quickly established itself as the city's second largest brewery, surpassing Arnott's and Lane's and becoming a serious competitor to Beamish and Crawford's. County trade was supplied through the newly established railway network that radiated out from the city, while city trade was based on 'tied houses', pubs acquired by the brewery and let to tenants who were obliged to sell only Murphy products. This tied house system was common in British brewing, but in Ireland was unique to Cork, and partly explains the survival of the two Cork stouts of Murphy's and Beamish in the face of Guinness's virtual monopolisation in the rest of the country in the twentieth century. One of the company's first acquisitions was No. 1 Union Quay, now The Lobby Bar, purchased in 1858 for £600. By the beginning of the twentieth century, the Murphy tied estate numbered 200 houses.

CORK'S LEADING BREWERY

By the late 1880s, when it became a limited company, Murphy's had become Cork's leading producer, brewing just under half of the city's total porter output. In the early 1890s the brewery was remodelled, upgraded and expanded. The new malt-house built in this period was converted into the main offices of Murphy Brewery Ireland Ltd. in the early 1990s. Exports to Britain and the colonies also began at this time. In 1896 a subsidiary, the West Cork Bottling Company, was established in Bandon and in 1901 the company took over and closed down Arnott's St Finbarre's Brewery in Fitton Street and its ale brewery at Riverstown. Lane's Brewery had been taken over and shut down by Beamish's the previous year, leaving the city with only two breweries. Murphy's success in these years was aided by the growing profile of the Murphy family and its Catholic philanthropy, and by the rescue of the Munster Bank in 1885 led by James J. Murphy, which saved many businesses and individuals in the city from ruin. He was also a patron of the nascent GAA, whose Cork County Board adjourned its meeting as a mark of respect on the day of his death in 1897. The brewery's success can be gauged from the fact that the individual annual incomes of the two senior partners (over £11,000 each) were almost double the total annual wage bill at a time when the brewery employed up to 200 workers.

SLOW DECLINE

Francis Murphy became chairman after the death of his brother, followed by James J.'s three sons in succession – Charles Eustace, Albert St John and Fitzjames. They

Fig. 3.17 James J. Murphy (1825–1897), founding chairman of James J. Murphy and Company.

Fig. 3.18 Lady's Well Brewery in the late nineteenth century.

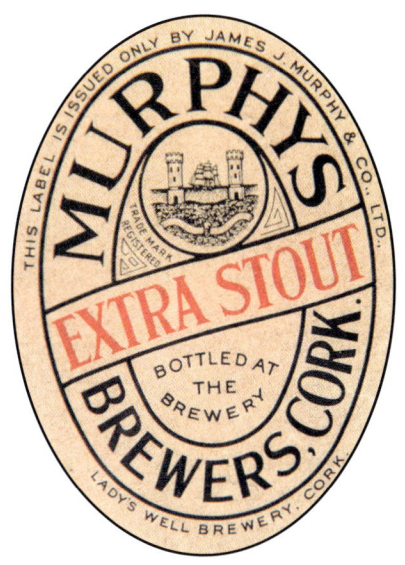

Fig. 3.19 A Murphy's brand label.

presided over a period of slow decline that began with the disruption caused by the First World War. As well as the immediate problems caused by the war, the lowering of the strength of beer, the tax-related price increases and the restrictions on opening hours that were introduced at this time remained a permanent feature. The fact that Cork county, the heart of the Murphy trade, was the most violent region during the War of Independence and Civil War meant continuing disruption. Four Murphy pubs were destroyed in the burning of Cork city in December 1920. A five-week strike by the city's brewery workers in early 1920 seriously curtailed production and gave Guinness a foothold in the city that it never subsequently relinquished.

Stagnation best describes the brewery's fortunes during the early decades of independence. It celebrated its centenary in 1956 against a backdrop of Irish economic and social crisis. In 1958 the last Murphy to head the company, 'The Colonel', John Fitzjames, a grandson of James J., took the helm. He oversaw a rare successful initiative as the company responded to changes in the city in the late 1950s and early 1960s by closing down old pubs in the depopulating city centre and opening new premises in the expanding suburbs – the Outpost in Bishopstown, the Tory Top in Ballyphehane and the Orchard in Ballinlough. Another major shift was the switch from the old wooden barrel to the new metal casks in the early 1960s, which marked the end of the line for the coopers, craftsmen associated with the brewery since its inception. By 1964, all the remaining breweries in the rest of the country had either been closed down or taken over by Guinness, which was beaten in the race to buy Beamish and Crawford by Canadian Breweries in 1962. Murphy's rebuffed a Guinness offer, but was forced to take action to keep pace with its competitors in the rapidly changing industry and diversifying market.

TAKEOVERS AND SURVIVAL

In 1965 Murphy's entered a partnership with British brewing giants Watney Mann, which acquired a majority shareholding in 1967. Its Red Barrel Ale was a failure on the Irish market and in 1971 Murphy's was on the brink of liquidation when the British brewers pulled out. It was rescued by the state, and an interim board kept the company afloat until it was taken over by a group of vintners in 1974. Despite initial successes, including the introduction of new brands – most significantly Heineken in 1975 – the company was in trouble again, and in 1982 it went into receivership. In 1983 it was bought by the Dutch brewing giant Heineken, which created Murphy Brewery Ireland Ltd and began a new era in the history of this Cork institution.

17. CONNECTING CORK

Colin Rynne

As the locus of an important international trading network, in terms of provisions and textiles, both sea and land communications within the greater Cork harbour area were considerably improved during the eighteenth and nineteenth centuries.[1] Of these, the pace of both road and railway development fell well within national trends. Yet curiously enough the physical development of Cork harbour, arguably the region's most important natural asset, did not. For a harbour of its international importance, wet docks were never provided for the city itself, while as late as 1870 large ships could not progress from the upper to the lower harbour except on the spring tides.

ROADS

There were two principal means by which roads were constructed and maintained: by grand jury presentment and by turnpike trusts. From the early seventeenth century onwards, Irish grand juries were empowered to levy direct taxes for the repair and construction of roads, causeways, toghers and bridges which were 'broken or decayed'. In Ireland, the grand jury was the forerunner of the latter-day county council, which succeeded them under the Local Government Act of 1899. In 1710, grand juries were empowered to undertake the construction and repair of roads by presentment. Under the presentment system anyone could make a proposal to the grand jury to build or repair a road. If the grand jury accepted this proposal, it could make a presentment that monies be allocated from the county cess (rates) to pay a contractor to build the road. An act of 1727 specified that all roads built by presentment had to be gravelled to a width of 12 feet and be at least 30 feet wide. In 1739 the grand juries were empowered to 'facilitate the laying out of roads in straight lines from market town to market town' and were now enabled to buy land for this purpose. An act of 1777–8 further enabled the grand juries to grant contracts for the repair of roads, by which time the repair and general maintenance of most of Ireland's roads had become its complete responsibility.

The 1739 act encouraged the construction of long straight roads. The stipulation that these roads should link market towns was an attempt to stop landlords from diverting roads to suit their own ends. Straight roads were also cheaper to build and, until the 1760s, grand juries showed a marked preference for laying out 'geometrical' roads, laid out in straight lines without any reference to the terrain they traversed. However, roads of this type tended to have steep gradients unsuited to wheeled vehicles, and were also impassable on certain stretches during the winter months. Nevertheless, the system was efficient enough to ensure that the quality of Irish roads by the early nineteenth century greatly exceeded those of contemporary Britain. Compared to the roads built by Richard Griffith in parts of Munster in the period 1822–1836, the surfacing of presentment roads often may have left much to be desired. Nevertheless, the general lightness of the wheeled traffic using them was such that they fared tolerably well during the winter months, while many appear to have been able to dry out quickly after wet spells. The main problem with the grand juries of Cork, Limerick and Kerry, however, was that they were ineffectual in dealing with county link roads, particularly in hilly or mountainous areas. Indeed, in certain areas there were no roads other than pack-horse tracks.

Cork Grand Jury's responsibility for the county road network increased steadily throughout the nineteenth century. In 1834 it had some 1,599 miles of road within the East Riding of the county under contract and this increased to 2,300 miles by 1844. In 1854, all 85 miles of road within the county previously under the jurisdiction of the Board of Works became the responsibility of the grand jury, along with all of the county's turnpike roads and piers, and by the 1870s the maintenance and construction of roads and bridges had become Cork Grand Jury's single most important function. In 1817, all Irish grand juries were legally obliged to have any works conducted by presentment certified by engineers, a measure calculated to prevent waste of public funds. This legal obligation eventually led to the creation of county surveyors, who fulfilled this monitoring function on a full-time basis.

TURNPIKE ROADS

The system by which roads were built by turnpike trust, in existence in England since 1663, was not introduced into Ireland until 1729. For the most part, turnpike roads, like presentment roads, were a product of local initiative. A turnpike road was built and maintained by a turnpike trust, usually run by local landowners who could raise the finance necessary to obtain an act of parliament. The Turnpike Act invested powers in named trustees to erect gates and tollhouses (turnpikes) with which to collect tolls. These tolls were collected from most road users, save pedestrians and local farmers who used the road on a daily basis, and were spent on the upkeep of the road. Tollhouses were built near large towns or important crossroads, and a gate was built across the road. On payment of the requisite toll, which varied in accordance with the size of the vehicle and the type of wheel it employed, the tollhouse keeper would open the gate.

The first turnpikes constructed in Munster in the early eighteenth century were generally a reflection of the importance of the port of Cork. The first turnpike linking the city of Cork with Dublin via Kilworth mountain was constructed under a Turnpike Act of 1731. The road 'leading from the town of Newcastle in the County of Limerick to the City of Limerick and from thence to the City of Cork' also became the responsibility of a turnpike trust in the same year. A direct link with County Kerry was enabled under a Turnpike Act of 1747, which was to become the most significant route for the Munster butter trade. The Irish grand jury system of road construction and repair saw to it that there was no shortage of good, toll-free roads in Ireland by the end of the eighteenth century. Road users could use alternative routes, and turnpikes, starved of income, rapidly went into decay. By the 1770s, poorly maintained Irish turnpike roads were a key target for the criticism of English visitors to Ireland.

In the wake of the legislation of 1783 that established an independent Irish post office, mail-coach services were introduced to serve the principal Irish towns, beginning with the Cork–Dublin line in 1789. The tolls paid by mail-coaches using turnpikes were a welcome and often lucrative source of income for the turnpike trusts, and the early decades of the nineteenth century saw an upturn in their fortunes. In consequence, the state of many Irish turnpikes improved substantially in the first half of the nineteenth century, when the condition of many of them began to compare favourably to that of the presentment roads. By 1837, they were accommodating high traffic densities. Nevertheless, the existence of so many good toll-free roads and the advent of the railways brought a terminal decline in the fortunes of Irish turnpike roads, the extent of which had fallen from 1,500 miles in 1820 to 300 in 1856.

The turnpike roads involved with the butter trade, the Cork to Limerick turnpike and the Cork to Tralee turnpike, were administered by conventional turnpike trusts in the early nineteenth century. The Cork to Limerick via Mallow turnpike road, which had 31 trustees, was in good condition by the early 1830s. Over £2,157 was expended on its upkeep in 1830 and, although all of the tolls collected on it were spent on the road, this was said to 'have hardly been adequate to keep the road in repair'. In comparison, the 60 miles of turnpike road between Cork and Tralee, administered by no less than 173 trustees, was built with 'pounded stone' and surfaced with gravel of the 'best description sometimes'.

Fig. 3.20 Cork's road network as depicted in George Taylor and Alexander Skinner's *Maps of the roads of Ireland* of 1778. By then most of Cork's inter- and intra-county roads had been turnpiked. The main road to Dublin ran via Shandon Street, rather than as today via the Lower Road.

Under legislation enacted in 1857, Irish turnpike trusts were dissolved and all turnpike roads in Munster came under the jurisdiction of county grand juries.

Railways

No less than five county-based rail networks and one national rail link had established termini within the city of Cork by the end of the nineteenth century.[2] The national rail link and three of the county lines were built to the Irish standard gauge of five feet three inches, with two county lines built to the Irish narrow gauge of three feet, one of which had actually been converted from standard to narrow gauge early in the twentieth century. Four of the Cork city railway termini were established to the south of the Lee, but

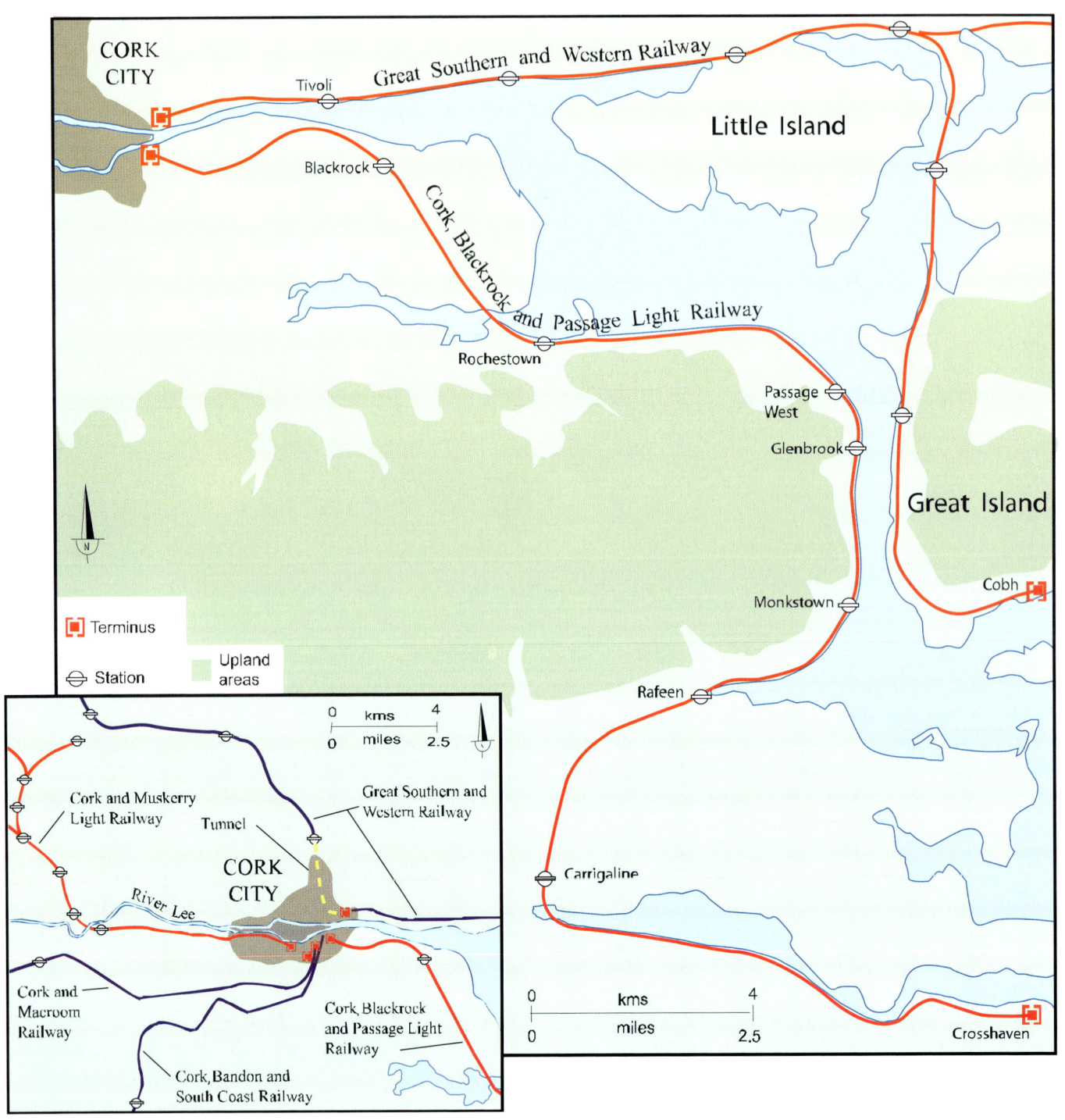

Fig. 3.21 The Cork city railway network in 1890. All of the termini of the county lines were to the south of the Lee. Two of these, the Cork, Bandon and South Coast Railway and the Cork, Blackrock and Passage line, had prized quayside locations. All, with the exception of the line to Cobh and the east Cork line to Youghal, were closed by 1961.

Fig. 3.22 The Chetwynd ('Bandon') viaduct was built as part of the Cork, Bandon and South Coast line. The entire stretch of line between Cork and Bandon was opened to the public on 6 December 1851. (Photo: Denis Minihane, *Irish Examiner*.)

it was not until the early twentieth century that any attempt was made to provide a cross-city link between a county line and the national rail network.

For the most part, Cork railway companies sought quayside locations for their termini. The early companies, such as the Cork and Bandon, Cork, Blackrock and Passage and Great Southern and Western, built stations with direct access to the city quaysides. However, while Penrose's Quay and the Custom House Quay experienced the considerable advantages of feeder lines, the only industrial units within the city to benefit from such a provision were the much later Marina mills and the Ford tractor works. Indeed, long-established institutions such as the Cork cattle and butter markets, on the northside of the city, would surely have benefited considerably from direct access to rail heads.

The city railway network facilitated travel between Cork and many of the county towns that in its own way was a social revolution of sorts. Commuter traffic was now possible between out-ports and villages on the edge of Cork harbour, while tourist rail traffic to Cork county's main seaside resorts, and even popular inland tourist destinations such as Blarney Castle (on the Cork and Muskerry Light Railway), could now be accommodated. The Cork, Blackrock and Passage Railway also operated a loss-bearing fleet of river steamers, which it ran in direct competition to the River Steamer Company, a conflict that affected its early financial development. Beginning with a single river steamer (the *Queenstown*) in 1851, the railway company was operating four steamers by 1854, in the early stages of a battle for passengers which only ended by agreement in 1860. The railway company was granted permission to expand its fleet of harbour steamers in 1881, although the company's profits from the river steamers only bore some fruit when the service was extended to Aghada. The steamers departed from Patrick's Bridge to take in a route which included Passage, Glenbrook, Monkstown, Ringaskiddy, Haulbowline, Queenstown and Aghada, or an alternative route which included Spike Island, Curraghbinny and Aghada.

For the most part, the county network accommodated both passenger and goods traffic and, in at least one instance, quickly usurped the existing overland trade in butter to Cork. With the arrival of the railways in the 1850s, the traditional importance of the horse cart in bringing butter all the way to Cork declined. The first line to serve areas to the west of the county was the Cork, Bandon and South Coast Railway, the earliest section of which opened in 1849. Between 1851 and 1893 the mileage of the west Cork line was extended from 20 to 94. Beginning with the Kinsale branch line (opened in 1863), the west Cork network was extended to Dunmanway in 1866. These developments greatly alleviated the effort involved in getting the butter to Cork. The opening of the West Cork Railway to Dunmanway in 1866, for example, reduced the time taken to transport butter to Cork by around three-quarters. The line was further extended to Skibbereen (the Ilen Valley Railway) in 1877, Bantry in 1881, Clonakilty in 1886, Timoleague and Courtmacsherry in 1890 and Bantry Bay in 1892. The final extension of the line was to Baltimore in 1893. In 1866 a further west Cork line, the Cork and Macroom Direct Railway, was opened to traffic. Thus small butter producers could now simply bring their firkins to a railhead and save both the time and the expense of transporting their butter all the way to Cork. In the 1850s, when the Great Southern and Western Railway was extended to Killarney and west Cork, butter producers were also brought into the net. Farmers in the Knocknagree area of County Cork, for example, brought their butter by cart to Rathmore railway station, on the Cork–Killarney line.

The decline of the Cork rail network began in the late 1920s when transport by both bicycle and motor vehicles, unfettered by timetables and expensive infrastructure such as stations and signalling systems, superceded locomotives and rolling-stock. Lines serving the city and its environs, such as the Cork, Blackrock and Passage Railway (1932) and the Cork and Muskerry Railway (1934), were the first to close. Others, such as the Bandon and west Cork network, survived up to 1961. At present, the only surburban line in the region is the Cork and Cobh links, although there are currently plans to revive the east Cork link with Midleton.

Tramways

In 1870 work began on the Cork city horse tramway, with a total track length of just under two miles at the Irish standard gauge of five feet three inches. It was laid at a cost of £10,000.[3] The new line opened in 1872, operating with six tramcars built by Starbuck and Company of Birkenhead, each drawn by two horses. The horse tram network in Cork did not survive beyond its first three years of operation and proved to be a costly failure. By 1876 the trackway was torn up by Cork Corporation.

The network of electric tramways, which operated within the city and its main suburbs in the period 1898–1931, was an arrangement made between Cork Corporation and the Cork Electric Lighting and Tramway Company. Under this arrangement the company not only operated a network of electric tramways within the city, but also provided electricity from its own independent electricity generating station for public lighting and domestic use. The tramway company (which had close links with the British Thomson-Houston Company), ran three cross-city routes: Blackpool to Douglas, Summerhill to Sunday's Well and Tivoli to Blackrock, a total length of ten miles.

Between 1898 and 1931, the tramway company operated 35 tramcars from its depot adjoining the Albert Road electricity-generating station, all manufactured by the Brush Electrical Company of Loughborough, each equipped with two British Thomson-Houston 27 hp electric motors. The eventual demise of the tramway system in Cork was brought about by three main factors: the rise of motor transport, the nationalisation of the electricity supply in the Irish Free State and the humble but ubiquitous bicycle. The Cork trams were badly hit by the growth of motor omnibus services within the Cork area and, like the local narrow-gauge railways, did not survive beyond the 1930s.

The river and harbour communications

As late as the early 1870s, large ships were forced to tranship part of their cargoes at Passage West. The single most important artery of communication linking the city with its international markets remained underdeveloped for the greater part of the nineteenth century, adding significantly to the cost of importing goods into Cork. Furthermore, vital physical links between the main railway terminals were not brought about until the early twentieth century. The

Fig. 3.23 The Cork city electric tram and the Cork and Muskerry Light Railway train (the 'Muskerry Tram') running side by side on the Western Road early in the twentieth century. (Photo: Day Collection.)

Fig. 3.24 'Sailing Vessels in Cork Harbour', c. 1850, by George Mounsey Wheatley Atkinson (1806–1884), oil on canvas. (Source: Crawford Municipal Art Gallery.)

nineteenth-century development of the port of Belfast, which overcame similar difficulties to those experienced by shipping in contemporary Cork, was critical to its industrial success, despite the fact that it did not have a superb natural harbour like Cork's.

The eighteenth century witnessed the direct involvement of civic authorities in the improvement of Ireland's ports and harbours. During the nineteenth century the development of steam packet ferries in the Irish Sea area also led to the creation of new port facilities, as did direct government intervention (through the Board of Public Works) in western fishing harbours.

Port and harbour improvements c. 1750–1900

Shallow shipping channels and the silting up of harbours presented the biggest problem to port development in the

Fig. 3.25 The bonded warehouses on Custom House Quay were designed by William Hargreaves. Work began in 1814 and was formally completed in 1818. The warehouses have brick-arched interiors as a defence against fire and fireproof spiral staircases on the exterior walls. This type of infrastructure was important in early nineteenth-century Irish ports. (Photo: Colin Rynne.)

eighteenth and early nineteenth centuries, and invariably required both an institutional response and a considerable cash outlay.[4] Before the advent of the steam dredger, little could be achieved by traditional methods. Manual dredging, by private contract, of the shipping channel linking the upper and lower harbours at Cork commenced in 1822 on the shoal near Tivoli, and the 12 hp dredger acquired from Waterford was followed by a second, 20 hp, dredger in 1839. Large amounts of estuarine deposits were removed from shipping channels during dredging operations, but not all of it was dumped at sea. Dredge stuff was also used in harbour reclamation works at Cork in the 1850s, where it was brought ashore behind the navigation wall to form what eventually became the Marina embankment, and later to fill in slobland near the city.

In Cork harbour, two new dredgers were at work in the late 1850s in the creation of a new deepwater channel, and in the deepening of the berths at the city's quaysides. Six 120-ton barges were purchased to remove dredge materials from the harbour in 1865. In the same year Cork Harbour Commissioners became the first in Ireland to explore the use of hopper barges, whose successful use on the River Clyde had aroused their interest. In 1865, they dispatched their mechanical engineer to assess their utility for the dredging operation in the upper harbour. The hopper float, or barge, was equipped with bottom-opening doors. When the vessel had been filled by the dredger, it could be towed out to sea where, by opening the bottom doors, the load could be emptied in a location where it could be washed away by tidal currents.

The main channel of the Lee from Passage West to the city was only three feet deep in many places, and vessels of over 80 tons could only reach the city quays safely on the spring tides. As late as the early 1870s large vessels were obliged to tranship at least part of their cargoes to lighters at Passage West. Another remarkable feature, given the size and relative importance of the port, is that it was never provided with basins or enclosed docks, which would have enabled larger vessels to unload irrespective of the tides. In the 1870s, the problem was partially solved by the provision of deep-water berths, and subsequently by extending the available wharfage downstream.

The first real attempts to improve the upper harbour for shipping were made in the 1760s, when work began on the construction of a 'navigation' or 'tracking' wall. The north and south channels of the Lee currently converge to the east of Custom House Quay, but in the eighteenth century the south channel at this point was separated from the north channel by a large marsh. The 'navigation wall' was intended to regularise the current in the north channel of the river by directing the flow of the south channel into it at a point nearer to the city quays, and to enable ships facing contrary winds to be pulled by horses up to the city quays.

THE CITY'S QUAYSIDES

In 1815 the Scottish engineer, Alexander Nimmo (1783–1832), reported that the city's rubblestone quays were poorly founded, being constructed on the strand at high-water level, and that no ship drawing more than 15 feet of water could safely sail upstream beyond Passage West. Nimmo also questioned the benefits of the navigation wall, a view which later commentators shared. Before 1813, the city's quaysides had been developed in a piecemeal fashion, with individuals enlarging them at their own expense after obtaining liberty to do so from the Corporation. The Corporation assumed responsibility for the repair and enlargement of sections of the city's quaysides, as was the case with Bachelor's Quay in 1767. Indeed, alterations to the city's quays were also carried out by grand jury presentment. Cork quaysides bear the names of the merchants responsible for their development – Penrose's Quay, originally built between 1800 and 1808, Lapp's Quay, named after John Lapp, and Anderson's Quay, named after the Scottish magnate John Anderson. The newly established Harbour Commissioners also considered the maintenance of the city's quay walls to be within its remit and undertook a large-scale programme of quay repairs between 1820 and 1833. Repairs were undertaken on Charlotte Quay, Morrison's Island, Camden Quay, French's Quay, Grenville Quay and Merchant's Quay.

The shoals in the main channel, however, which prevented larger ships from proceeding beyond Horsehead, proved to be a much more serious impediment for the Harbour Commissioners than the repair of quay walls. The only practical solution, and one which the Commissioners wholeheartedly adopted when finance was available, was to dredge the main channel. Although the dredging of the channel began in earnest in 1822, larger vessels could only proceed to the city quaysides in 1874. In 1850 there were 26,359 feet of quay walls at Cork, of which some 5,047 feet were on the north channel and 6,370 feet on the south.

The lack of proper deep-water berths at Cork added substantially to the cost of importing goods into the city. In 1849, 67 ships which were obliged to tranship their cargoes at Passage incurred extra costs which averaged at around two guineas per lighter-load carried from Passage to the city. However, while the Great Southern and Western Railway Company was to obtain government sanction to construct a floating dock on a four-acre site at Penrose's Quay in 1850, the Harbour Commissioners' attempts to acquire parliamentary approval for their proposed improvements to Cork berthage facilities did not bear any fruit until the 1870s.

In the 1870s a number of important steps were taken towards the modernisation of the city quays. Hitherto, many seagoing vessels had been unable to discharge afloat at the city quaysides, but in 1874 timber jetties were built at Victoria Quay, whilst dredging to a depth of 20 feet near these berths enabled vessels of 18 feet draught to be accommodated without resting on the bottom. By 1875, some 1,000 feet of deep-water berthage was available at Victoria Quay. The Cork Harbour Act of 1875 sanctioned the deepening of the berthage at Victoria Quay and a further act of 1877 allowed work to proceed on the north bank of the channel.

In the first half of 1894 the Commissioners contracted out work on the addition of over 1,200 feet of timber wharfage to St Patrick's Quay and Penrose's Quay, which was to have 13 feet of water alongside. These works were completed in 1896. After 1903 the extent of the city's deep-water berthage was extended up the quaysides on the north and south channels, and the Custom House Quay was reconstructed to facilitate dredging to a depth of 22 feet alongside it. In addition, greenheart wharves were erected on the north channel as far as Parnell Place, and up as far as the Cork, Bandon and South Coast Railway on the south channel.

Up to the end of the nineteenth century, the development of the port was stymied by the relatively slow progress in improvements to access to the upper harbour. Larger ships were still forced to tranship their cargoes (at considerable expense) to lighters, which could negotiate the shallow channels separating the upper and lower harbours. This, in turn, led to the creation of outports such as Passage West, which increasingly began to control this trade. Indeed, commercial interests in these outports successfully scuppered attempts to construct wet docks at the city quaysides and thereby continued reliance on transhipping facilities in the lower harbour.

18. PLACE, CLASS AND POLITICS

Maura Cronin

Cork city's population and prosperity grew progressively during the eighteenth century, so that by 1800 it seemed destined to rival Dublin. The nineteenth century, however, saw a reversal of fortune. Traditional industries declined and population stagnated. By 1900 Cork's population of 76,000 was six per cent less than that of 1841.[1] Yet, during the same period the city expanded physically, local and parliamentary government opened up to the city's middle classes, and the living conditions of working people improved. In these developments, place, politics and social class played their part.

CLASS AND RELIGION

Social class in Cork was shaped by denominational alignment. In 1861, 84 per cent of the population were Catholic, 13 per cent were Protestant, and slightly over 2 per cent were categorised as Dissenters and 'others'. Protestants, whose presence in the city's working class had weakened significantly since the eighteenth century, were strongly represented among the medical profession, bankers, magistrates and the army, and within the employer and commercial sector. In 1877, when between 50 and 60 per cent of the city's employers were Catholics, some of the more prominent wholesalers and the proprietors of concerns like the Steam Packet Company and the Cork Docks Company were Protestant. At the lower end of the social scale, Catholics predominated, particularly among the tanners, dockers, carters and general labourers, whereas printers and engineering workers had a sizeable proportion of Protestants in their ranks.[2]

OCCUPATION, WEALTH AND CLASS

While occupation and class were not completely interchangeable, they did overlap in nineteenth-century Cork. As the population structure of the city changed after the Famine, so did its occupational structure in both skill and gender terms. The proportion of males employed in the building trade and retailing sectors remained fairly constant, those in transport increased ten-fold, while those in manufacture were halved by a combination of insufficient capital, mechanisation, foreign competition and the employment of low-paid female and 'boy' labour.[3]

After 1800, the city's labour force constantly overran the available employment; there was always a wide fringe of 'casual labour', male and female, picking up an odd day's work and eking out a precarious existence. Further up the social scale were labourers with near-constant employment, who benefited from the expanding transport sector and by advances in unionisation among the semi-skilled towards the end of the century. Still further up were the skilled artisans, mostly employed in small cooperinng, printing and builders' workshops or as outworkers in the tailoring and shoemaking trades. On a par with the upper ranges of these skilled trades were the up-and-coming retailers – shopkeepers, vintners and pawnbrokers – their livelihoods dovetailing with both the poor below and the more prosperous classes above. Occupying the top rungs of the city's social ladder were merchants, manufacturers, clergy and professionals.

Personal wealth also played its part in defining class. Surviving wills indicate that personal fortunes of between £20,000 and £60,000 were left by the mercantile élite, while a modest master craftsman might leave as little as £100. However, personal fortune alone did not determine class. Some prominent merchants left as little as £800 on their deaths, some master craftsmen's wills totalled £4,000, and many apparently comfortably off employers left no personal fortunes at all.[4]

CLASS MOBILITY

Transition from one class to another was not usual, but was possible, particularly at the upper end of the scale. From the late eighteenth century, particularly after the relaxation of penal legislation, wealthy Catholics advanced through the city's thriving provision and butter trade and put themselves on a par with their Protestant peers by buying land and educating their sons in the law and medicine.[5] Such upward mobility was also possible further down the social scale. The occasional shopkeeper's son could ascend into the merchant class, as did John Daly, mayor and parliamentary representative of Cork in the 1870s and 1880s.[6] Among skilled artisans, similar upward mobility was possible, local trade union records making occasional reference to members' progression to the position of masters, though the reverse occurred when capital failed or when a trade went into decline.[7] At the bottom of the ladder, however, there was usually no way up for the destitute, the only exit being via either the workhouse or the graveyard.

Classes in Cork city were not completely segregated. At public meetings and court sittings, the élite were exposed to the merciless witticisms of the plebeians in the crowd and maintained their popularity only by joining in the repartee and giving as good as they got.[8] Such familiarity between high and low was possible in a small city like Cork where different socio-economic groups lived cheek by jowl. Nevertheless, this familiarity was also largely illusory and was becoming more so as postal address came increasingly to reflect social status.

Residential segregation

The mercantile élite began this trend towards social segregation, moving out to suburban villas dotting the Blackrock and Douglas areas and the picturesque slopes at Sunday's Well, Lota and Glanmire.[9] This outward move was facilitated from the 1760s onwards as bridge-building between the island city and its hinterland commenced; by the early 1900s a dozen structures spanned the river's twin channels.[10]

From the early nineteenth century, Montenotte became the most fashionable villa suburb, housing merchants and manufacturers, while the marginally less exalted resided in the imposing terraces of Sunday's Well, Tivoli, Monkstown and on the Wellington Road and Summerhill North. Professionals still lived in the high-class terraced housing of the city centre, especially along the North and South Malls, until the middle of the nineteenth century, only then succumbing to the suburbs like the now slightly faded Sunday's Well and the up-and-coming Western Road.

This race for the suburbs from 1850 onwards accelerated with the building of railways linking the city centre with Blackrock, Passage, Bandon, Kinsale, Mallow (on the Dublin line) and Blarney. The Great Southern and Western (Cork–Dublin) line had little enough impact on residential patterns in the city, since, as soon as the train departed from the station (completed in 1855) on the Lower Glanmire Road, it entered the tunnel and did not emerge again until it was outside the city proper at the edge of Blackpool. The other three railways encouraged the building of middle-class terraces (slightly less ostentatious than those of the previous half-century) to the south-east, south and south-west of the city. The Cork, Blackrock and Passage Railway, in particular, opened up a sweep of territory from Albert Quay to halfway down the southern side of the harbour, while the Muskerry line facilitated the development of the Western Road around the newly fashionable neighbourhood of the Queen's College.[11] The tramlines (horse-drawn from the 1870s and electric from 1898) also encouraged the building of more terraced residences for upwardly mobile professionals and retailers, especially around Blackrock, Douglas and the Western Road.[12]

Within a half-mile radius of the city centre, a less socially differentiated zone existed where the lower levels of the middle class lived in close proximity to the less prosperous. Comfortable retailers lived over their shops and public houses, dotted along secondary thoroughfares like Shandon Street, Blarney Lane and York Street north of the river, and Barrack Street and Douglas Street to the south. A few yards away, in the lanes surrounding the Butter Market and radiating off Barrack Street and Douglas Street across the river, lived relatively prosperous artisans, while the permanently poor lived in the slum tenements of the decaying city centre, the lanes on the northern and southern slopes, and the cabin suburbs around Glasheen, Douglas and Blackpool – all centres of the dying textile trade.[13]

Fig. 3.26 Maryborough House dates to the mid-eighteenth century and originally belonged to a branch of the Newenham family. It is a good example of the suburban style villa built in this period. (Photo: John Crowley.)

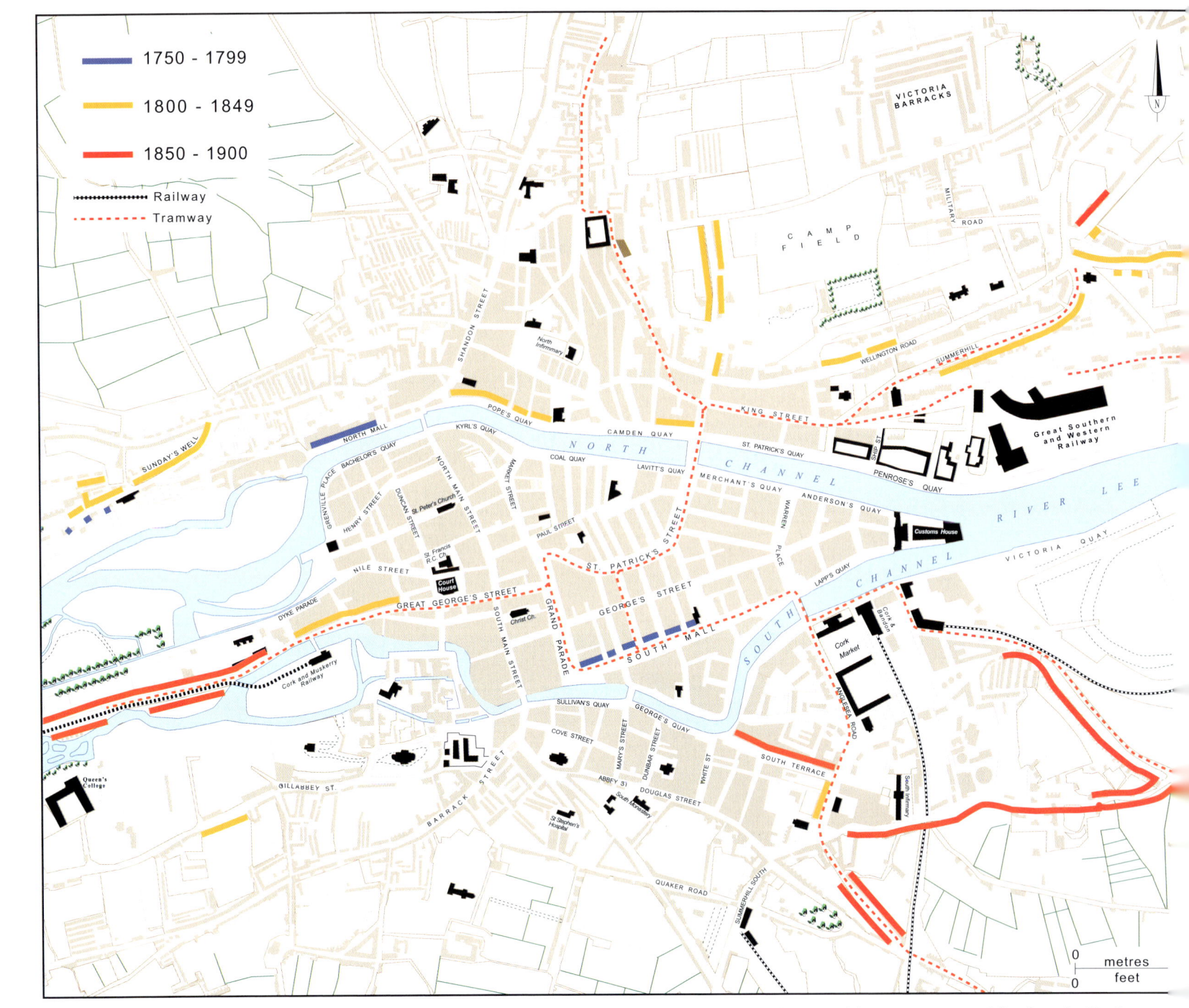

Fig. 3.27 In the early nineteenth century, professionals tended to live in the well-designed terraced housing of the city centre, especially along the North and South Malls. However, during the course of the century the professional classes were increasingly attracted to suburbs such as Sunday's Well and the Western Road. The South Terrace and the Old Blackrock Road also became fashionable in the latter decades of the nineteenth century.

Conditions in these cabins and tenements were at their worst in the pre-Famine period, but misery still prevailed in the latter part of the century, when the Glasheen cabins were described as 'wretched places' falling into decay. At the same time, a house-to-house inspection by Cork Corporation of the city centre and the surrounding slopes revealed houses which were 'much overcrowded, dilapidated, in many instances mere hovels, internally dark, filthy, [and] ill-ventilated ... [while] the larger the house, the greater the evil of overcrowding'.[14] In these conditions, disease spread rapidly. Typhus, for instance, was always present in the city, but it was most prevalent in cold weather when people huddled together for warmth in crowded accommodation. When the houses were closed up to stem the disease, the displaced people simply moved in with other families and accelerated the contagion.[15]

REHOUSING THE WORKING CLASS

The rehousing of these lane and tenement dwellers did not become a public issue until late in the century. Some cosmetic rather than socially ameliorative demolition of slums around Broad Lane (off North Main Street) in the 1850s actually aggravated the problem, since those displaced by the demolition were not rehoused and simply moved into other already over-crowded accommodation nearby. In the late 1870s, Cork Corporation took advantage

Fig. 3.28 The overcrowded laneways that converged on Shandon Street c. 1870. (Source: OSI.)

of the provisions of Crosses' Act to initiate slum clearance and rehousing. Over 100 houses were demolished in areas particularly prone to typhus, smallpox and cholera, south of the river in the environs of Evergreen and Barrack Street, around North Main Street, and in the area between Fair Lane and the Watercourse Road. Some of the land so cleared was leased to the local Improved Dwellings Company, whose combination of philanthropy, profit-making and self-help was reflected in the names of their housing schemes: Prosperity Square and Industry Street (off Evergreen Street) and Prosperous Place (off York Street, now Thomas Davis Street). This company built 418 houses in the last 30 years of the century, just as Cork Corporation itself began to provide housing for the working classes. In 1886, the first of these schemes, Madden's Buildings, was built between the Watercourse Road and Great Britain Street (now Great William O'Brien Street). Other schemes followed in quick succession. On the north side of the river were Ryan's, Sutton's and Barrett's Buildings, all off Blarney Street (1888 to 1906), Roche's Buildings off Pope's Road (1892) and Kelleher's Buildings near Dillon's Cross (1905). In the city centre, Corporation Buildings were built near the Coal Quay (1900), and south of the river Horgan's Buildings were erected behind the Queen's College (1891).

Initially, people were to be transferred within the existing built-up area, utilising land made available through clearance of slum housing, an approach which facilitated housing by the Improved Dwellings Company. The first Corporation housing was located on cleared ground: Madden's Buildings were on the site of the old Blackpool Market, Sutton's and Barrett's were on the former Cattle Market, and Corporation Buildings were on land cleared when the Harpur's Lane Market was demolished. Such land was in short supply, however, and subsequent schemes had to be built on suitable land leased or purchased by the Corporation. Later schemes of working-class housing, red-bricked terraces fronting on to the street and with a small yard to the rear, crept outwards and upwards from the

ATLAS · OF · CORK · CITY

Fig. 3.29 In the nineteenth century it became clear that new housing stock was needed to improve the living conditions of the city's working classes. Slum clearance by the Corporation, however, was not always followed by the provision of new housing. The task of providing suitable housing was initially undertaken by the Improved Dwellings Company, a commercial and philanthropic body intent on improving housing conditions. It was responsible for housing schemes such as Prosperity Square and Industry Place, off Evergreen Street, and Prosperous Place off York Street (now Thomas Davis Street). Cork Corporation eventually followed their example and built schemes such as Madden's Buildings, Barrett's Buildings and Horgan's Buildings.

Fig. 3.30 Horgan's Buildings, built in 1891. (Photo: John Crowley.)

traditional working-class areas, preparing the way for the more extensive suburbanised local-authority housing in the half-century after 1930.

Other factors limited the social impact of these early housing schemes. Firstly, insufficient finance restricted Cork Corporation's capacity to replace demolished houses, so that by 1901 there were actually 700 fewer houses in Cork than there had been in 1891 and acute congestion prevailed in the poorer parts of the city, especially around the northern slopes between Patrick's Hill to the east and Shandon Street to the west. The second factor was the relatively high rent charged for the new houses, far beyond the means of the poorest tenement dwellers in most need of rehousing. Thus, although a small number of labourers' and a greater number of skilled workers' families were housed in these schemes, many other houses were occupied by white-collar workers like clerks, insurance agents and teachers. Consequently, despite the early attempt to rehouse and relocate the city's working classes, the population patterns of the 'flat of the city' and the hillside lanes remained largely unchanged well into the twentieth century.

Politics and class

At first sight, political divisions in nineteenth-century Cork followed denominational lines, with Protestant conservatives upholding the union with Britain and Catholics generally supporting forms of nationalism. In reality, attitudes among the middle classes of both denominations were more complex. Not all Cork Protestants clung doggedly to support for the union, and not all Catholics favoured the restoration of an Irish parliament, while a small minority advocated militant means to achieve an independent republic.[16]

It is impossible to calculate precisely the social and geographical distribution of support for these different political standpoints. The franchise was narrow and the introduction of the secret ballot in 1872 completely cloaked voting patterns. Most middle-class men (professionals, merchants and prosperous retailers) were enfranchised in 1832 or 1850, and many skilled artisans in 1867. Other working men had to wait until 1885, or even as late as 1918, when women over 30 years of age were also enfranchised. The general pattern of the city's political alignments can be traced by reference to the ward boundaries. In elections both to parliament and to Cork Corporation, the greatest conservative support came from the north-east ward, centred on Glanmire and Tivoli, where the most prosperous Protestant merchants resided. The north-west and north central wards, on the other hand, dominated by the Catholic shopkeepers of Shandon Street and Blackpool, traditionally voted nationalist, occasionally separatist; it was in these wards that the highest vote was given to the veteran revolutionary, John Mitchel, when he stood unsuccessfully in the city election of 1872.

For the city's middle classes, the two most significant political developments in the nineteenth century were Catholic Emancipation in 1829, facilitating propertied Catholics' entry to parliament, and the 1840 Municipal Reform Act, increasing their access to local government. This latter measure opened up deep socio-political divisions in the ranks of Cork's middle class. The most serious division was between the major merchants (who controlled

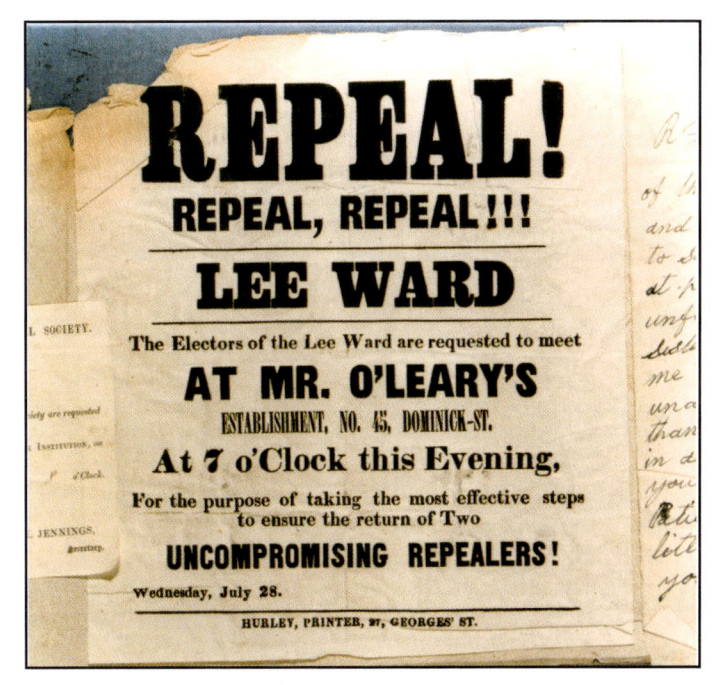

Fig. 3.31 A Repeal poster from the Richard Dowden papers. Dowden was Mayor of Cork in 1845. (Source: Cork Archives Institute.)

40 per cent of Corporation seats for the remainder of the century) and the ambitious retailers who had not progressed as far as they would have liked within municipal government. These vintners, pawnbrokers and shopkeepers from Shandon Street, Blackpool and Barrack Street formed a succession of Burgess Associations over the remainder of the century, acting as watchdogs over Corporation proceedings, voicing the grievances of the ratepayers and exercising considerable influence on local city politics.[17]

Among the city's working classes, political awareness increased over the course of the century as literacy levels rose, newspapers became cheaper and political movements deliberately canvassed popular support. Nationalism (both constitutional and separatist) was the main beneficiary of this development as the local Protestant working class shrank in size, and as Protestant conservative power in Cork and throughout the island receded in the face of continuing government reform. Widespread popular support favoured O'Connell in the pre-Famine decades and Parnell four decades later, while sympathy for Fenianism in the late 1860s and 1870s led to frequent rioting in the environs of North Main Street and Castle Street. This popular commitment to nationalism did not preclude an enthusiasm for monarchy, as evidenced by the reaction to royal and vice-regal visits and celebrations from 1849 onwards, while recruitment to the army in both the Boer and First World Wars was most successful in the poverty-stricken lanes and streets which had produced pro-Fenian rioters thirty years earlier.

Radical politics

Despite the increasingly frequent use of the 'language of class' from mid-century onwards, it is difficult to identify any clear strand of working-class consciousness in nineteenth-century Cork. The city's trade unions, the most organised and cohesive bodies within the working class, were socially conservative, avoiding Chartism in the late 1830s and actively campaigning against the First International in the 1870s and the nascent socialist movement of the late 1890s. Though this attitude may have been influenced by a conservative Catholic Church, it was also shaped by the skilled worker's sharp contempt for the unskilled, and his fear that the gap between the two groups might be narrowed by radical political activity.[18]

On the other hand, internal divisions within the working class could be bridged, by common pastimes and loyalty to place. This was particularly evident in allegiance to sporting bodies and musical bands. From the 1870s onwards, bowling and harrier clubs and, later in the century, hurling clubs faced each other in sporting rivalry.

Except for its declining population, nineteenth-century Cork was a classic Victorian city with a prosperous commercial élite, aspiring retailing sector and impoverished lower class. Inter-group division, shaped by religion, access to wealth and occupation, was bridged by the relative smallness of the city but progressively widened as suburban expansion accompanied city-centre stagnation. By 1900, place had begun to reflect class and politics, but the identification remained incomplete. While the élites monopolised the suburbs, comfortable retailers and master craftsmen lived in the city centre and on the surrounding hill-slopes, and working-class housing schemes achieved only a minor transfer of population. It was well into the twentieth century before the combined development of industrial zoning, town planning, bus services and large-scale public authority housing clearly differentiated between the élite, the middle ranks and the working classes.

Fig. 3.32 Denny Lane's certificate of membership of the Home Rule League. Denny Lane (1818–1895) was a well-respected businessman, nationalist and patron of the arts. A friend of Thomas Davis and the Young Irelanders, at one stage he was imprisoned for his political activities. He continued to support the nationalist cause, as indicated by his membership of the Home Rule League. He was also a founding member of the Cork Historical and Archaeological Society. In addition he penned a number of ballads, the most notable of which remains 'Carrigdhoun', which first appeared in the pages of *The Nation* newspaper in 1845. (Source: Cork Archives Institute.)

Musical Bands and Local Identities

Fintan Lane

Musical bands have existed in Cork city from at least the early 1800s. In 1832 the weavers, the butchers and the Cork Trades Association each had their own band and participated in demonstrations in favour of 'home manufactures' and for the repeal of the Act of Union.[1] However, it was in the late 1830s and 1840s that bands became especially popular in the city. Many were formed by the temperance movement of that time as an alternative activity for those who wished to avoid the public house. These bands were locality based and had numerous followers who would accompany them on excursions through the city. This extended interest was indicated on Easter Monday 1842, when at least 23 city bands, each containing 20 to 30 musicians, participated in a huge temperance procession through the centre of Cork.[2] Many came from poor localities such as Fair Lane, Blarney Street, Blackpool and the Barrack Street area.

The number of bands decreased in the later nineteenth century, but there were still seven brass bands and ten fife-and-drum bands in Cork at the beginning of the 1880s. While some were still referred to as 'temperance bands', most had long-since dissolved this connection.[3] Indeed, it was now not uncommon for young men to drink alcohol as they followed their local band through the streets. Some of the bands, mostly the brass bands, were connected to various trade societies, or to workplaces such as the Butter Exchange. Locality-based bands, on the other hand, were normally fife-and-drum bands, simply because the cost of properly equipping a brass band was significantly higher and beyond the means of a membership drawn from impoverished working-class communities. This was the case with the seven fife-and-drum bands involved in the 'band nuisance' riots of 1879–1882. All seven were located in areas of serious social and economic deprivation: Quarry Lane (in Blackpool) and Fair Lane on the northside; Cat Lane/Tower Street, Abbey Street, Globe Lane (on French's Quay), Green Street and Gillabbey Street on the southside. Other fife-and-drum bands were situated in York Street, Duncan Street and Evergreen Street.[4]

'Following the bands'

These local working-class bands met in the evenings during non-work hours, except on Sundays when they convened earlier in the day. Occasionally they played at nationalist demonstrations or at social events such as weddings. In the main, their activity consisted of promenades through the streets of the city. Supporters, often numbering over 100 people, would regularly follow the bands on these musical excursions, which could last late into the night. In general, the police, the priests and the press viewed the fife-and-drum bands and their supporters as undesirable. The nationalist *Cork Examiner* castigated them as 'the ordinary

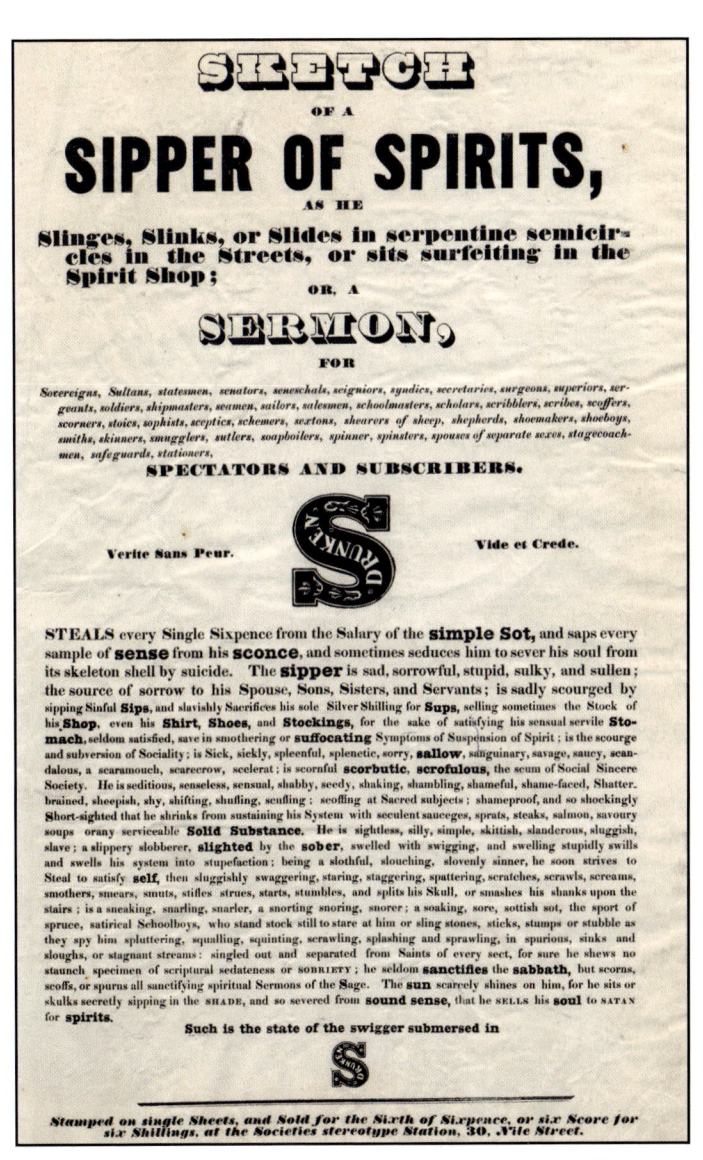

Fig. 3.33 Temperance poster *c.* 1840, from the papers of Richard Dowden, Mayor of Cork in 1845. (Source: Cork Archives Institute.)

crowd of roughs', among whom were 'several "wets" [drunks]', and it reported sneeringly of 'the usual band-following class', while the unionist *Cork Constitution* described the band followers as 'the great unwashed'.[5] The majority of those who followed the bands were young unskilled labourers and factory workers, including many girls and women. Some band members had served in the British Army and played previously in military bands. Ex-soldiers played an important role in maintaining the band culture in Cork. Frank O'Connor's father, Big Mick O'Donovan, played the big drum with both the Munster Fusiliers and the Quarry Lane Band at the beginning of the twentieth century.[6]

Local rivalries: the 'band nuisance'

Rivalries between bands, based on pre-existing local identities, probably existed from the outset. However, in 1879 these deteriorated into serious violence and over the following few years Cork bands and their followers engaged in a sustained bout of rioting and street-fighting, known euphemistically as the 'band nuisance'. Locality rivalries between Fair Lane/Shandon Street and Blackpool erupted in open fighting between supporters of the Fair Lane and Quarry Lane bands; on the southside the Cat Lane Band engaged in a prolonged feud with the Abbey Street and Gillabbey Street bands. The Fair Lane and Cat Lane bands were also mortal enemies, and the factions would, on occasion, cross the city to 'invade' each other's territory. Between 1879 and 1882 two people were killed during these riots and scores were seriously injured.[7]

Labourers were more likely to be involved in street fighting than artisans or clerks who had 'positions' to maintain and it is undoubtedly the case that those who followed the bands emanated from the poorer strata of the working class. These elements included some hardened street-brawlers such as Daniel Creed ('the worst character in Cork', according to the police) of the Quarry Lane faction and Jeremiah 'Cowboy' Crowley, who belonged to the Cat Lane faction.[8] The 'band nuisance' cannot be categorised as an entirely male business. The involvement of women was noticeable from the beginning and a number were jailed for participating in the fighting.

These Cork band riots flourished during a period of exceptional political tension (such as the Land War of 1879–1882) and a national weakening of law and order, probably encouraged the participants. However, the

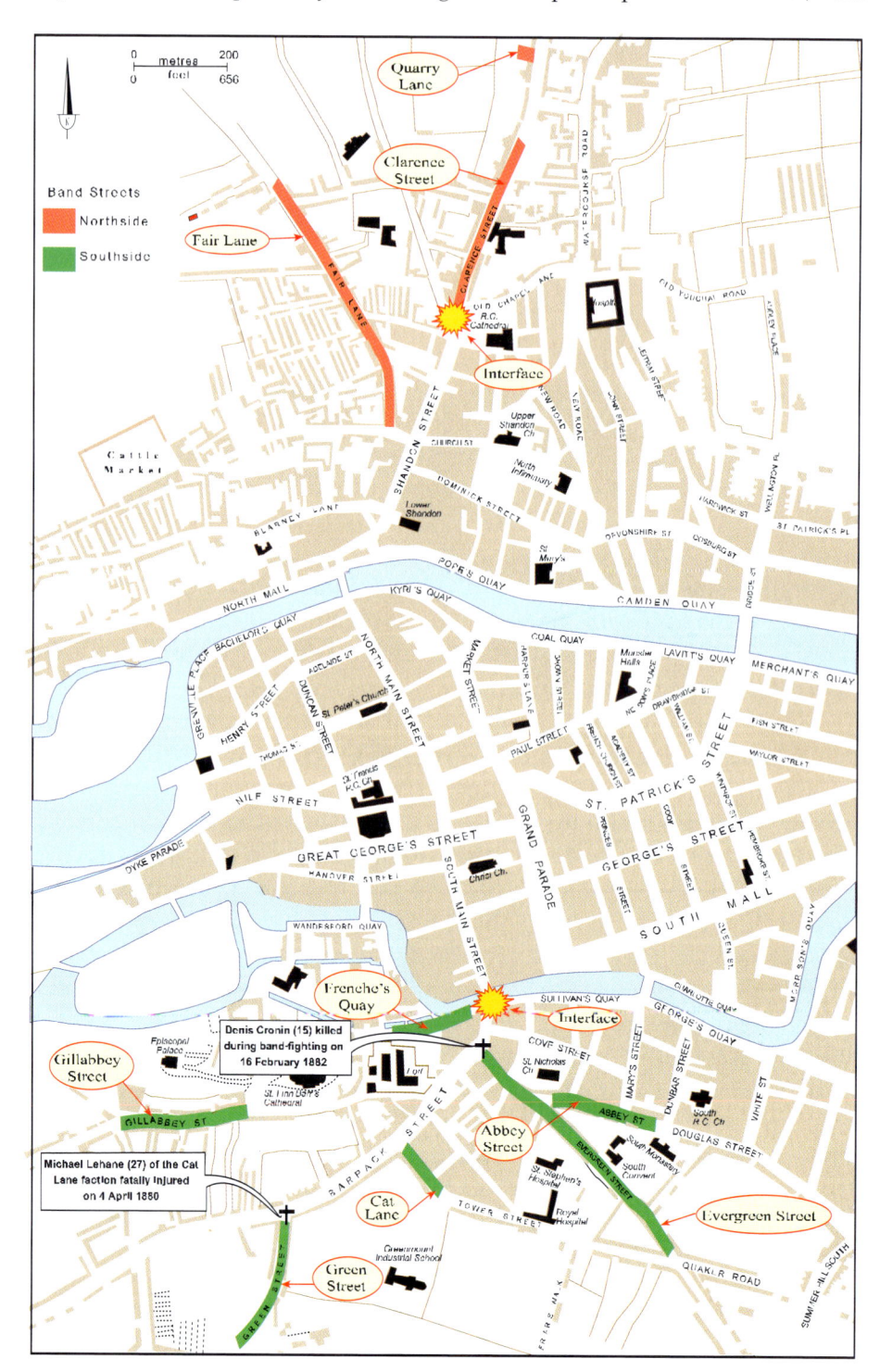

Fig. 3.34 Locations involved in the 'band nuisance' of 1879–1882.

immediate origin of the Fair Lane and Blackpool disturbances had absolutely no political connotations and was rooted in bad feeling over money given to the Fair Lane Band for entertaining guests at a wedding at which Quarry Lane had also played. Supporters of the Quarry Lane Band, including Creed, subsequently attacked the Fair Lane Band as it passed through Blackpool, smashing the big drum and setting off a chain of events that led to a riot on 4 May 1879 outside the North Cathedral involving 2,000 people.[9] The area adjacent to the cathedral became an interface area during subsequent fighting between the factions. Indeed, the acrimony between these bands had distinct communal overtones and people from Fair Lane were assaulted, sometimes quite savagely, as they passed through Blackpool on their way to work in the local flax factory.

The disputes between bands on the southside had similar origins and minor slights could spark off serious confrontations. It is not clear what sparked the conflict between the Cat Lane and Fair Lane bands, but these factions were not slow to interfere in other feuds. The Fair Lane Band struck up an alliance with the Gillabbey Street Band to instigate attacks on the Barrack Street area. Band instruments were used occasionally as bludgeons during these confrontations, though sticks, stones and fists were more commonly deployed. Incursions by the Fair Lane faction typically ended with a stand-off at the interface zone in front of the South Gate Bridge before the northsiders were finally driven out of the area.

The 'band nuisance' was ultimately checked in early 1882 as a result of joint action by the Catholic clergy and the magistrates. The bands were repeatedly condemned from the pulpit and the arrest of 'Cowboy' Crowley and two of his associates in early March deprived the belligerent Cat Lane faction of some key figures. Nevertheless, the intense band rivalry continued after 1882. In fact, the Parnellite split of 1890–1891 provided new justifications for violent conflict between rival bands; not surprisingly, the Quarry Lane and Fair Lane bands found themselves on opposite sides in that dispute. The Quarry Lane Band (known as the 'Antis') was anti-Parnellite; the Fair Lane Band was pro-Parnell.[10] Band-fighting in Gillabbey Street in the early twentieth century was directly related to splits within the Home Rule movement.[11] The political divisions were real and the bands were associated with nationalist movements throughout the nineteenth century and early decades of the twentieth century.[12] The band members and their followers came from politicised communities where nationalism was an intrinsic part of local culture. However, there were other factors at play also and, particularly prior to the growth of the GAA, band-following and band riots served multiple social functions.

For many participants the band riots were a form of recreational violence. Certainly this was true for seasoned street-brawlers such as Creed and Crowley, and the fife-and-drum bands, with their martial music, were especially conducive to this type of activity. Band-following was also a pleasurable recreation in itself and friends would meet up to pass the evening listening to the tunes while strolling the streets. Bandstands were erected in places such as the Marina and the Mardyke in the late nineteenth century and many people congregated there to listen to the various bands.[13] The numerous bandrooms, many little more than tenement rooms, also provided a meeting place for those more intimately associated with the bands. Moreover, for many young men and women, the late-night band-following had attractions other than the pleasure of musical excursions or the excitement of street-fighting: social constraints, in a culture that restricted 'courting', were

Fig. 3.36 Three members of the Cork Volunteer Pipe Band relax following an excursion to Carrigtohill in 1955. (Photo: Private collection.)

Fig. 3.35 The Fair Lane Band ('Parnell Guards Band') on parade in the early 1900s. (Photo: *Irish Examiner*.)

Fig. 3.37 The Barrack Street Band at Musgrave Park in 1999. (Photo: *Irish Examiner*.)

undermined and the long late-night promenades provided useful opportunities for meeting the opposite sex in an unsupervised setting. In 1880, Fr James Fleming of the South Parish declared that 'any girl' who followed the bands 'must be lost to all sense of shame and female delicacy'.[14] Two years later a resident magistrate claimed that 'the most indecorous conduct is occasionally pursued sometimes leading up to the destruction of females'.[15]

Decline

The band culture survived well into the twentieth century, but the continued development of the GAA and other forms of entertainment led to its demise in the latter half of that century. Fighting between bands dissipated early in the 1900s as the locality-based bands gradually disappeared. Pipe bands emerged in the city during the Gaelic revival and among the best known was the Cork Volunteer Pipe Band, formed in 1914, which was active until quite recently. Today, the city has no more than a handful of marching bands, though these include two brass bands that have survived from the nineteenth century: the Barrack Street Band, formed in 1838, and the Butter Exchange Band, formed in 1878, neither of which were involved in the band riots of 1879–1882.[16] The Barrack Street Band was established as a 'temperance band' and it remained 'respectable' throughout its history and was consistently popular in the city. Likewise the Butter Exchange Band was workplace-based originally, although it has survived the closure of the Exchange and is now firmly community based.

Father Theobald Mathew (1790–1856)

John Crowley

The statue of Father Theobald Mathew, which is situated on Cork's main thoroughfare, St Patrick's Street, celebrates the life of the well-known Apostle of Temperance. Colloquially known as 'the Statue', it is a familiar landmark in the city. It was in the vicinity of Sullivan's Quay in Blackmoor Lane that the Tipperary-born priest began his ministry in Cork in 1814. The Capuchin Order to which he belonged was of Italian provenance and followed the Franciscan way of life. In 1824 Mathew started a school for girls in a converted store near the Capuchin chapel in Blackmoor Lane. The achievement of Catholic Emancipation would allow for the building of a more substantial church at Charlotte Quay (now Father Mathew Quay). The foundation stone of Holy Trinity Church was laid on 10 October 1832.

A Quaker, William Martin, would later elicit Fr Mathew's support for a newly established temperance campaign. From its local development in Cork it spread extensively throughout the provinces of Ireland and beyond. By January 1839 it was estimated that over 200,000 people had enrolled.[1] Much was invested in the

Fig. 3.38 Fr Mathew monument on St Patrick's Street. (Photo: John Crowley.)

Fig. 3.39 Detail from the 1869 Ordnance Survey map showing the location of the old Capuchin chapel in Blackmoor Lane. (Source: Ordnance Survey Ireland.)

person of Fr Mathew, to whom the campaign owed a great deal of its success. A number of temperance bands in the city were established during this period, including the Barrack Street Band, which was founded by Fr Mathew in 1838.

During the Famine years Mathew leased a section of the Botanic Gardens in Ballyphehane, which was set aside for the free burial of Catholics. His own burial place is located on this site (now St Joseph's Cemetery). The statue in Patrick's Street was unveiled on the 10 October 1864 by the then Lord Mayor, John Francis Maguire.

Fig. 3.40 Holy Trinity church, designed by George Pain. (Photo: John Crowley.)

19. CORK'S 'GOLDEN AGE': GREAT HOUSES AND ART COLLECTING IN THE EARLY NINETEENTH CENTURY

Peter Murray

International conflicts in the late eighteenth century brought hardship to both sides of the Atlantic. However, those same years also brought prosperity to the farmers and merchants of Cork, who supplied the armies of Britain with horses, butter, beef and gunpowder. Travelling through Cork in 1790, the French diarist Charles Étienne Coquebert de Montbret commented on an appetite for calamity among the merchants of Cove: 'This small town . . . rather poor in times of peace, flourishes in wartime with the result that the inhabitants are always longing for the conflicts so bewailed by others. When we were there England and Spain appeared to be on the brink of war, but as belief that war was about to be declared grew less, faces obviously grew longer.'[1] As a result of these dividends of war, life in the south of Ireland from 1790 to 1820 was comfortable for the wealthy and tolerable for many. With peers and members of parliament largely based in London after the Act of Union in 1800, the merchants of Cork became princes by default and built many of the county's finest houses during this period. In his *Directory of Cork*, published in 1810, William West describes the palatial new villas and mansions that dotted the wooded banks and shores of the harbour, among them Tivoli, Woodhill, Lota Beg, Lota Park and Dunkettle. Designed by skilled architects Abraham Hargrave, James Morrison and James and George Richard Pain, houses such as Coolmore, Dundanion and Convamore were designed

Fig. 3.41 'View of Coolmore, County Cork', eighteenth-century Irish school, artist unknown. (Source: Richard Wood.)

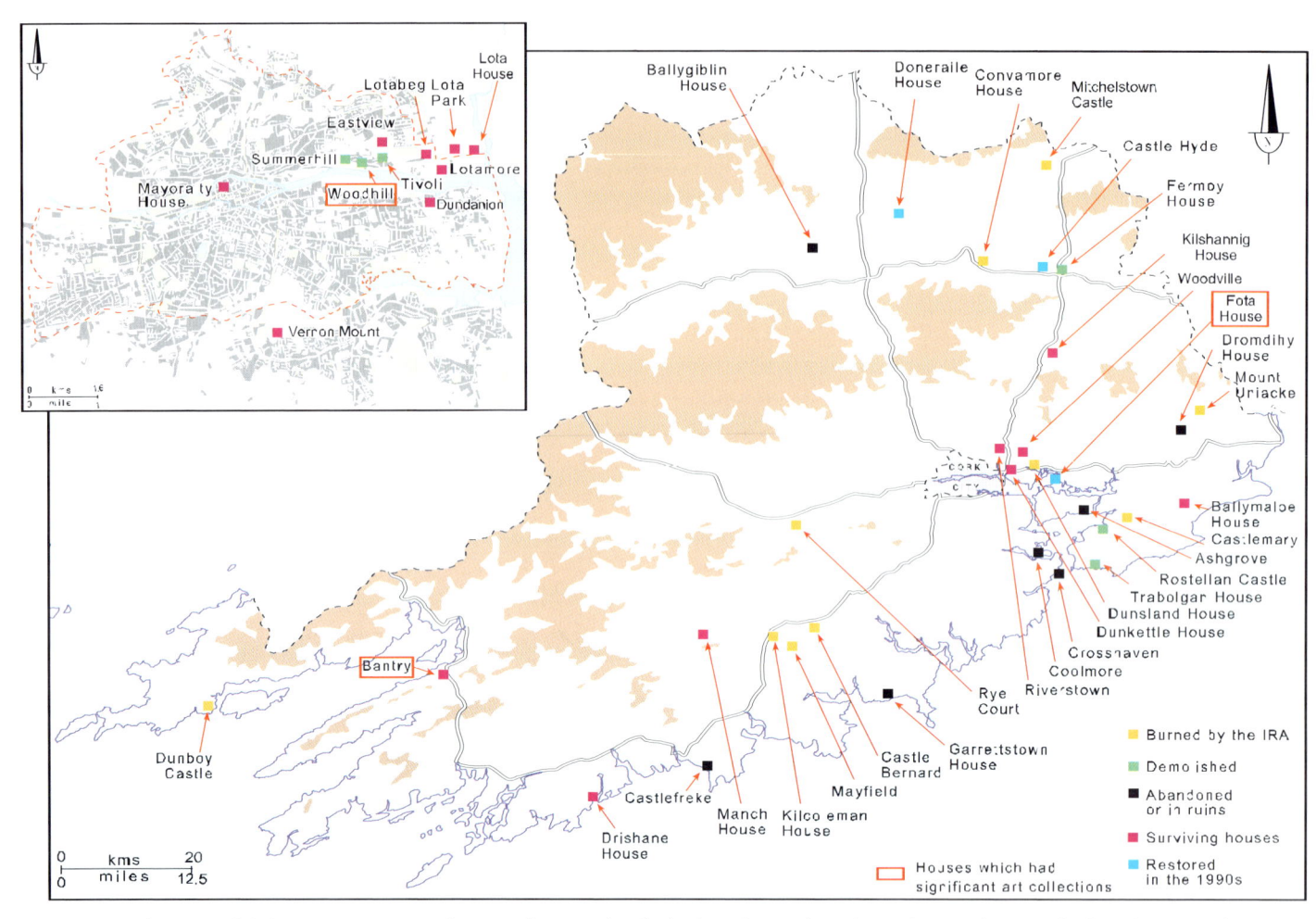

Fig. 3.42 Great houses. While by no means comprehensive, this map details the fate of a number of great houses that were built in the city and county in the eighteenth and nineteenth centuries. During the Irish War of Independence and the Civil War in the 1920s, many houses were burned by the IRA, ostensibly to prevent them being used as military barracks. Those that survived were slowly abandoned by their owners in the 1940s and 1950s as the cost of maintaining them grew onerous. Their contents, including libraries, furniture and works of art, were dispersed – either gradually or by public auction. The economic resurgence of the 1990s has seen a few, such as Fota House, Castle Hyde and Crosshaven, restored. However, many of the most important houses in Cork remain unoccupied and face an uncertain future, the society that created them having faded into history. (Source: Margaret Fitzpatrick.)

and built to a standard that reinforced the claims of their newly rich owners to be seen as people of culture and taste. Fifty miles west of the city, a similar degree of sophistication was demonstrated at Drishane in Castletownshend, a house built by merchant Tom Somerville, and Manch House in Ballineen, built for the Conner family in 1826 and designed by the Pain brothers. Accomplished and restrained essays in neo-classicism, these two houses are representative of a type common in Cork during this period, in which the opulence of the eighteenth century was tempered to the needs of merchants and farmers who, perhaps mindful of the French Revolution, were less eager than their forebears to engage in ostentatious displays of wealth.

The symbolic values expressed in these new great houses of Cork and their art collections were not overly complicated. For the most part, in terms of their design they followed the Palladian type established in eighteenth-century Ireland by Ducart. However, by the turn of the nineteenth century, this was a Palladianism pared down to essentials. Although classical in general form and detail, Castle Hyde, Coolmore and Dunkettle were plain structures, built on a large scale to accommodate social activities amongst inhabitants and guests. Not all were neo-classical; Richard Morrison was equally adept in designing houses, such as Castlefreke in west Cork, in a medieval revival style. Embellished with paintings and sculptures and surrounded by tennis courts and croquet lawns, these great houses served as centres for entertainment on a lavish scale in the nineteenth century. They also provided employment for considerable numbers of domestic staff. Their art collections were available for viewing by connoisseurs and visitors with letters of introduction, but not by the general public.

The city's art collections

In contrast with the county, the relatively few art collectors living in the city of Cork tended to be amateur antiquarians

Fig. 3.43 Fota House was designed by Richard Morrison and his son William for the Smith-Barry family. (Photo: Tomás Tyner.)

Fig. 3.44 Dunkettle (Dunkathel) House was designed in the Palladian style by Abraham Hargrave for the Morris family *c.* 1785. (Photo: Tomás Tyner.)

Fig. 3.45 'View of Castle Hyde' (detail) by Nathaniel Grogan (1740–1807), watercolour on paper. (Private collection: Knight of Glin.)

such as John Fitzgerald and Richard Sainthill. Sainthill's house on Emmet Place is one of the few early eighteenth-century houses surviving in Cork city. A collector of coins, he was an early patron of the artist Daniel Maclise. Sainthill and others were involved in more formal attempts to improve the city's art collections. The Cork Institution, founded in 1803 by Nonconformist minister Thomas Dix Hincks, was housed around 1827 in the former Custom House (the older section of the present Crawford Municipal Art Gallery), during which time it took over the art collection of the Cork Society for Promoting the Fine Arts. The Institution's collections were diverse and included religious and ritual artworks from Polynesia, Canada, China, Tibet and Egypt. Participation in the business of empire building, as army officers, or as medical staff or traders, was commonplace among Cork's professional classes. The objects they brought back from their travels were treated as 'curiosities' and, in keeping with a eurocentric viewpoint, were displayed as secular artefacts, alongside natural history specimens, rather than as works of art with their own specific religious significance.

At the heart of the Institution's growing art collection in the former Custom House was a collection of over 100 replicas of classical and neo-classical sculptures in the Vatican Museum. Presented by the Prince Regent to his friend Viscount Ennismore (Lord Listowel), President of the Cork Society of Arts, the arrival of the 'Canova Casts' in Cork in 1818 prompted the establishment of a School of Art in a former theatre in Patrick Street. Although this school, directed by an artist named Chalmers, was initially welcomed by the merchant princes of the city, the writer of a short biography of Samuel Forde relates how the 'Mecaenases and Medici of the hour' fled to 'their villas and their counting-houses' when they realised that the expense of supporting an academy of fine arts might fall on their shoulders.[2] Forde, who assisted Chalmers in theatre scene painting, produced home-made mezzotint portraits and also taught architectural drawing at the Mechanics Institute. Among the commissions he undertook was the decoration of a ceiling at Tivoli, a Palladian house on the outskirts of Cork city, which was the home of James Morgan. In addition to the main house, Tivoli was noted for its garden temples, one a reproduction of the Temple of Vesta, the other built in the neo-Gothic style. The house, with its garden and temples, is depicted in an important painting by Nathaniel Grogan, 'Landscape at Tivoli, Cork' (National Gallery of Ireland). In his journal, Forde describes the ceiling decoration he painted at Tivoli: 'In the four angles were shepherds, vine-gatherers, reapers, mariners; at one end an old man reading – at the other, a man in an attitude of reflection, and finished by three figures in adoration.'[3] Also at Tivoli were neo-classical sculptures by another student of the art school, James Hogan. Lent by Morgan to the 1821 exhibition of the Society of Arts, these included a statue of Antinous and a statue of Venus Canova. Tivoli, along with its painted ceiling and much of its art collection, was destroyed by fire around 1820, when Morgan's children were playing with fireworks.[4]

THE CORK SOCIETY FOR PROMOTING THE FINE ARTS

The roll-call of members of the Cork Society for Promoting the Fine Arts gives a great insight into who was collecting art in Cork in the early 1800s. In 1816, the presidents were the Earl of Shannon and Viscount Ennismore. The Earl of Shannon's house, at Castlemartyr in east Cork, had been for centuries noted for its furniture and extensive art collection, while Lord Listowel's house, Convamore, on the river Blackwater, was one of the first great houses in Ireland designed by James Pain, who, along with his brother George Richard Pain, settled in Cork in 1815. The old house at Convamore was transformed into a large but quite plain house, its greatest asset being that it overlooked a beautiful stretch of the river Blackwater, near Fermoy. Its owner, himself once plain Mr William Hare (1751–1837), was MP for Cork in 1796 and purchased Convamore four years later from the Callaghan family. After voting for the Act of Union, he was rewarded in 1801 with the title Baron of Ennismore.

William's father, Richard Hare, having made a fortune as a merchant in Cork in the eighteenth century, had also purchased large estates in north Kerry. The collection at Convamore included Nathaniel Grogan's 'The Itinerant Preacher' and 'The Wake'.[5] The Cork Society of Arts had no less than eighteen vice-presidents, including the Duke of Devonshire, the Earl of Kenmare, Sir Nicholas C. Colthurst, Colonel Longfield, Daniel Callaghan, members of the Crawford, Roche, Penrose and Beamish families and Robert O'Callaghan-Newenham. The real work of the Society of Arts was carried out by a committee that included the architect Sir Thomas Deane.

Given the membership of the Cork Society of Arts and the conservative nature of Cork society, it was inevitable that disagreements would arise as to what might or might not be shown in the Society's annual art exhibitions. The most notable example of censorship was the removal, on the grounds of indecency, by the Society's exhibition committee of James Barry's 'Venus Rising from the Sea'. This large painting (now in the National Gallery of Ireland) had been loaned for the exhibition by Cooper Penrose (1736–1815), who lived on the outskirts of Cork city. The Penrose family had first come to Ireland from Yorkshire around 1660. William Penrose built up a thriving timber business in Waterford and his grandson Cooper Penrose moved to Cork, married Elizabeth Dennis and set up a glass factory and other enterprises. Cooper Penrose commissioned the Yorkshire architect Abraham Hargrave to design a large new house overlooking the Lee, just west of Tivoli. The original gate lodge to the house, an octagonal Gothic structure, still survives. The main house, neo-classical in style, was begun around 1775 and completed five years later. It was described in later years by Daniel Maclise as containing 'a very remarkable picture gallery, one of the chief in the south of Ireland'. Along with seashells and other natural history exhibits, Woodhill contained a number of paintings by James Barry, including the controversial 'Venus Rising from the Sea', a large portrait 'The Prince of Wales in the Guise of St George' (now in the Crawford Art Gallery), 'Lear and Cordelia' and 'Jupiter and Juno upon Mount Ida'.[6]

Described by William West as 'the Irish Vatican', probably on account of its collection of Greek and Roman sculpture casts, Penrose's gallery also contained Angelica Kaufmann's 'The Return of Telemachus' and a painting, 'The Sacrifice of Gideon', ascribed by Maclise to Boucher.[7] Crofton Croker records that Penrose also owned works by Nathaniel Grogan.[8] As well as being a patron of James Barry and John Butts, Cooper Penrose had his own portrait painted in France by Jacques Louis David (this portrait is now in the San Diego Museum, California).[9] The Quaker, Lewis Dillwyn, who visited Cork with his friend Joseph Woods in 1809, gave a brief but vivid description of Woodhill and the Penrose family:

> About four Cooper Penrose called on us and insisted on our accompanying Mr Woods to dine with him at his Villa, which is beautifully situated on the north bank of the city about one and half miles from the city. He has a fine collection of pictures for which he has been building a gallery as also five other rooms for statuary, and they are all very tastily lighted by cupolas from the ceiling. We returned to our Inn about eleven o'clock well pleased with the hospitality and polite attention of Mr Penrose & his son.[10]

Fig. 3.46 'Fishermen at Old Blackrock Castle' by Nathaniel Grogan (1740–1807), oil on canvas. (Private collection: On long-term loan to the Crawford Municipal Art Gallery.)

After the death of Cooper Penrose, his son James, who had settled near Whitegate, reluctantly moved with his family into Woodhill in 1819. He lived there for a decade before economic circumstances forced him to move to Germany for a number of years. For the next century, Woodhill was rented and became progressively more run down until it was finally demolished in the 1980s, to be replaced by a modern house.

Sir Thomas Deane (1792–1871)

Another committee member of the Society of Arts was the architect and property developer Thomas Deane. The Society's first exhibitions, in 1815 and 1816, were held at 'Deane's Buildings' on the South Mall, not far from the home of the Cork Institution. Tuckey's *Cork Remembrancer* records that the Institution's building on the South Mall was completed in September 1811. Thomas Deane's own house, Dundanion, near Blackrock, was also constructed around this time. Although Deane supervised the construction, it was actually designed by the Morrisons.[11] The satirical eye of 'Father Prout' was brought to bear on Thomas Deane, who acquired a set of statues from Blarney House, mentioned in Richard Milliken's *Groves of Blarney*:

> Who bought the castle, furniture and pictures, O!
> And took off in a cart
> ('Twas enough to break one's heart),
> All the statues made of lead and the pictures, O![12]

According to the Reverend J. Quarry, writing in 1899, Deane had called his new house Herculaneum, 'because at the foot of the lawn just over the water, stood a statue of Hercules which formed one of the series from old Blarney Castle into which Milliken introduced bold Neptune, Plutarch and Nicodemus'. Quarry goes on to state that he himself had for a long time owned two of the statues from Blarney, which stood in a courtyard 'before a house in a cross street near the Custom House in which resided a brother of Sir Thomas, commonly known as 'Sandy Ball'.[13] Thomas Deane married three times; the son of his second marriage, to Eliza O'Callaghan-Newenham, was the architect Thomas Newenham-Deane. Eliza's father, Robert, had been a founder in 1816 of the Cork Society for Promoting the Fine Arts.

Another member of the Society of Arts was William Crawford, who lived at Lakelands (now demolished), which stood at Mahon, about a mile south-west of Dunkettle. The site of the house is marked by two surviving monkey-puzzle trees, which flank the new dual carriageway. Described by William West as the former home of Benjamin Bousfield Esq., by 1810, when West published his directory, Lakelands had become the home of Crawford, who had made his fortune in banking and brewing. Bousfield's library, or part of it, remained at Lakelands after his departure and formed part of the Crawford library, which was eventually donated to Queen's College Cork. Although closely associated with the Cork Society of Arts, little is known of the paintings or sculptures assembled by the Crawford family at Lakelands.

By 1818, the committee of the Cork Society for Promoting the Fine Arts had grown considerably. The third exhibition was characterised by the inclusion of works by old masters, calculated to 'add to the refinement of public taste'. Among the lenders were James Penrose, Dr Woodroffe, James Roche, William Carleton and the Earl of Bessborough, who had a number of valuable paintings at his house near Carrick-on-Suir. The inclusion of works by old masters totally changed the character of the Cork Society of Arts exhibition, for now Thomas Crofton Croker, with his five flower and landscape pen sketches, found himself surrounded by paintings ascribed to Rembrandt, Ruysdael, Berghem and Hobbema. M. Crosbie attempted to rise to the occasion by exhibiting his 'Woman Taken in Adultery', copied from the picture by Rubens. E.W. Penrose also rose to the occasion by exhibiting his own painting of a moonlit landscape, in addition to lending works by Hobbema, Jervis and Guido. Another whole-hearted supporter was E. Parks, who lent several works, including 'Mars and Venus' by Sebastian Ricci, while also contributing his own portrait of the late much-lamented Princess Charlotte ('not finished').

Most of the old master works loaned from private collections were ambitiously, and probably erroneously, attributed to Rembrandt, Canaletto and other Dutch and Italian artists, with James Penrose also lending paintings ascribed to Murillo. Amongst the Irish 'old masters', Butts, Grogan and Barry were again featured as examples of excellence. Works by one of the Sadler family of artists were also included. Even by the standards of the day, the Cork Society of Arts exhibitions must have been dull affairs at this juncture, with views of Dutch seaports, eruptions of Vesuvius, landscapes with cattle, sheep, ruins or figures, enlivened perhaps by the occasional drunken cobbler, or a sea view with a brisk gale. There were few enough works by contemporary Cork artists. A portrait bust by John Hogan, done sometime before 1821, depicts George Newenham, a prominent Cork banker and art patron, who died that same year. Newenham's house at Summerhill in Montenotte was frequented by Daniel Maclise, who described it in his autobiography written many years later 'as . . . a residence entirely congenial to his dawning tastes. For Mr N. had a gallery of pictures very well selected and, besides being the resort of all who could at all pretend to taste, there was in the house, carried on by the daughter and the father, the actual exercise of the arts of Painting and Modelling. Colours, canvas and the easel, the model stand and clay were familiar objects.'[14]

Amongst the early paintings executed by Maclise at Newenham's house were portraits of 'his old lady patroness', Miss Spratt, and another old lady, Miss Parks.[15] George's sister Mary was also an artist, showing work at the 1815 Society of Arts exhibition. Like his neighbour Cooper Penrose, George Newenham regularly loaned paintings to the exhibitions of the Cork Society of Arts, including a painting by John Butts, 'The Finding of Moses'. This painting was later described in Bolster's Quarterly Magazine as 'not unworthy of Francis Mola; it is rich and mellow, both in effect and colour'.[16] In 1818, Newenham loaned two works by Grogan, 'Terpsichore' and 'Innocence', to the Society's exhibition, and the following year this shift in emphasis away from living artists was continued. Of the 132 works listed in the catalogue, over four-fifths were old masters from private collections; less than a fifth came from local artists' studios – and a good half of these were either by 'a young lady' or one of the Misses Newenham. In 1822, the indefatigable Miss N. Newenham showed no less than eleven works. George Newenham was also interested in science and constructed a telescope for astronomical observations. Late in life he developed a taste for sculpture and caught his death from a cold in 1821 while clay-modelling, shortly after his bank was wound up.[17]

With the Cork merchants vying with one another to amass the most important art collection, it comes as something of a relief to find a Mrs Jones (about whom little is known) lending no less than eight Grogans in 1818, including an interior view of Buttevant Abbey, which had also been shown in 1815, 'South Gate Bridge and Jail', 'The Triumph of Bacchus', various landscapes and humorous figures as well as 'Philip Baptising the Eunuch'. The 1820 Society of Arts exhibition differed little from those of the two previous years, with a preponderance of works ascribed to Canaletto, Cuyp, Teniers, Veronese, Guercino, Poussin and other old masters. Over one-third of the 155 works shown were from the private collection of James Roche ('J.R.' of The

Fig. 3.47 Lotamore House. (Photo: Tomás Tyner.)

Gentleman's Magazine), who lived at Lota Park, a late Georgian house overlooking the Lee at Glanmire. All 58 paintings lent by Roche, mostly Italian and Dutch old masters, but including several works by Nathaniel Grogan which had previously been seen in the 1815 and 1816 exhibitions, were sold by auction after the exhibition closed.

Several houses along the Lee towards Glanmire bear the name Lota. The oldest is Lota itself, a house designed around 1765 by Davis Ducart. Then there are Lota Beg, Lotamore, Lota Park and Lota Lodge, all dating from around 1800. Lota Beg, a fine Palladian house on the outskirts of Cork, was designed *c.* 1800 by architect Abraham Hargrave Senior for Sir Richard Kellett. Lota Beg is a large, square late-Georgian house with an impressive cantilevered staircase, typical of Hargrave's architectural designs. The ionic triumphal arch that still stands at the entrance to the demesne was designed by George Richard Pain and erected some 25 years later. In 1810, William West described Lota Beg as having 'an excellent library, selected with a chaste and classical taste'.[18] According to a contemporary newspaper account transcribed by Windele, Sir Richard Kellett at Lota Beg owned Nathaniel Grogan's painting 'The Country Fair'.[19] Although painted for Kellett, this work, also known as 'The Breaking up of the Fair', was later owned by Mr Denny, who lived on Duncan Street.[20] It was described in *Bolster's Quarterly Magazine* some years after as a scene of 'frolic, farce and riot'.

The 1822 exhibition included works by, or attributed to, Vandyke, Zucarelli and Vandervelde that were loaned to the Society of Arts by Robert Hedges Eyre (curiously, not listed as a subscriber), who also loaned a painting of William III at the Battle of the Boyne by Wyck. Hedges Eyre lived at Macroom Castle, originally a fifteenth-century castle of the MacCarthys, which he was rebuilding around this period. To some degree the Society's seventh annual show marked a return to the form of the first exhibitions. The representation of local artists improved, with John O'Keeffe (*c.* 1797–1838) exhibiting seventeen works, predominantly depictions of biblical scenes, nearly all of which had been loaned to the exhibition by the Right Reverend Dr Murphy.

By the 1830s, Cork's brief 'golden age' was on the wane. Daniel Maclise had emigrated to London, John Hogan was in Rome and the Society of Arts was no more. Samuel Lewis's 1837 *Topographical Dictionary* gives a summary of the more important Cork houses and their owners at this time. Woodhill, the former home of Cooper Penrose, was rented to a Thomas Arbuthenott, while Tivoli, the home of James Morgan, had been badly damaged by fire and much of its art collection destroyed. Ennismore (or Eastview), a house built by Joseph Leycester, founder of the Cork Steam Ship Company, for his son William was also occupied by tenants. Sadly for 'Old Joe', William preferred travelling on the Continent with his wife Babs to taking over the management of the family firm. The paintings at Ennismore, among them 'The Singing Boy' by Adam de Coster and marine views by Van de Velde and Guardi, were eventually sold.[21]

The art collection of the Royal Cork Institution grew slowly but most accounts of the Custom House during the mid-nineteenth century emphasise its run-down condition, and the damage this caused to the sculpture collection. It was not until the later nineteenth century that William Crawford's munificence to the city resulted in the remodelling and extending of the old Custom House to make the Crawford Municipal Art Gallery. A small number of paintings and sculptures were transferred, by donation or purchase, from private collections in Cork to the Crawford during these years; many more were sold or otherwise dispersed.

20. THE ROYAL CORK INSTITUTION

Kieran McCarthy

The eighteenth and early nineteenth centuries represented a period of great intellectual ferment in Europe. The questioning of traditional beliefs and practices became commonplace. New ideas in science and technology were transforming society. In Britain these ideas rapidly took root in urban centres. The establishment of cultural and scientific institutions became widespread and played a critical role in the awakening of intellectual and scientific curiosity. Such institutions also aspired to advance the moral values of their members. The improvement of society became a general concern amongst the middle classes. Terms such as 'progress' and 'improvement' entered their vocabulary for the first time. In the nineteenth century the Royal Cork Institution (RCI) would become central to the intellectual and cultural life of the city. As well as cultivating an appreciation of science and the arts, it also aimed at increasing intellectual awareness across a broad range of disciplines.

Origins

The beginnings of the RCI can be traced to the growth and influence of a number of British institutions that were active in the eighteenth century. The most important of these included the Royal Society of London and the Lunar Society of Birmingham. The latter was established in 1766. Many of its members were 'working' natural philosophers. These were practical men who owned mills, ironworks, potteries and dyeworks. Amongst the Society's most distinguished members were James Watt, renowned for developments in steam power; Matthew Boulton, famous for his work in iron foundries; Josiah Wedgwood, whose pottery was highly prized; and Joseph Priestley, who is regarded as the father of modern chemistry and a founding member of the Unitarian Society. Priestley was a writer with liberal views on religious and political freedom. He also advocated the need for a new concept of practical education: 'While serving as a Presbyterian minister, he opened his own school to develop his ideas on education and especially how science could improve the quality of human life.'[1]

Many members of the Lunar Society were religious Dissenters who openly challenged the privileged position of the established Church of England. They challenged in particular its monopoly in civic life and higher education. Many Dissenters, for example, were excluded from public schools and universities on religious grounds. As a consequence, they established academies for the higher education of their offspring, offering a curriculum of practical subjects and modern languages. Priestley taught at two of these academies, one at Warrington and the other at Hackney. The existence of the Lunar Society along with other similar institutions in cities across Britain would greatly influence the founding of the RCI. Priestley's ideas on education, for example, would later find expression in Cork in the person of the Reverend Thomas Dix Hincks (1767–1857).

Reverend Thomas Dix Hincks

Hincks came to Cork in 1790 to take up his ministry at the Presbyterian church on Princes Street. His arrival coincided

Fig. 3.48 'Rev Thomas Dix Hincks' (1767–1857), artist unknown.

with the city's golden age in terms of economic prosperity and cultural development. He was the son of a custom's official and was initially educated at Chester. He spent a short time at Trinity College Dublin before making known his intention to enter the Church of Ireland ministry. He eventually decided to study under Joseph Priestley at Hackney. Hincks brought to Cork the ideas and vision of Priestley and his associates. The improvement of society was a key objective, which could be achieved through better education, better hospitals, better sanitation and good civic design in the laying out of streets and squares. Like Priestley, he also sought religious freedom for those not subscribing to the established Church.[2] Shortly after his arrival in the city, Hincks opened a school at his house on Patrick's Hill, where he taught not only classics but also a broad range of subjects including mathematics and elementary science.

By 1802, Hincks wished to put his academy on a more formal footing. He eagerly sought funds from local businessmen to support his annual course of private and public lectures. Many responded generously to his requests. In the following year, 1803, the Cork Institution was established. Leading members included the notables William Crawford, William Beamish and Cooper Penrose. Hincks's course of lectures covered languages, literature, logic, elementary mathematics, natural history and experimental sciences. Hincks noted that 'the course took in the whole range of school education; it commenced in some instances with the elements of the English language, spelling, reading and writing, but the greater number of students were learning the Greek and Latin languages. I also instructed them in mathematics, geography, history and in as many branches of useful knowledge as circumstances

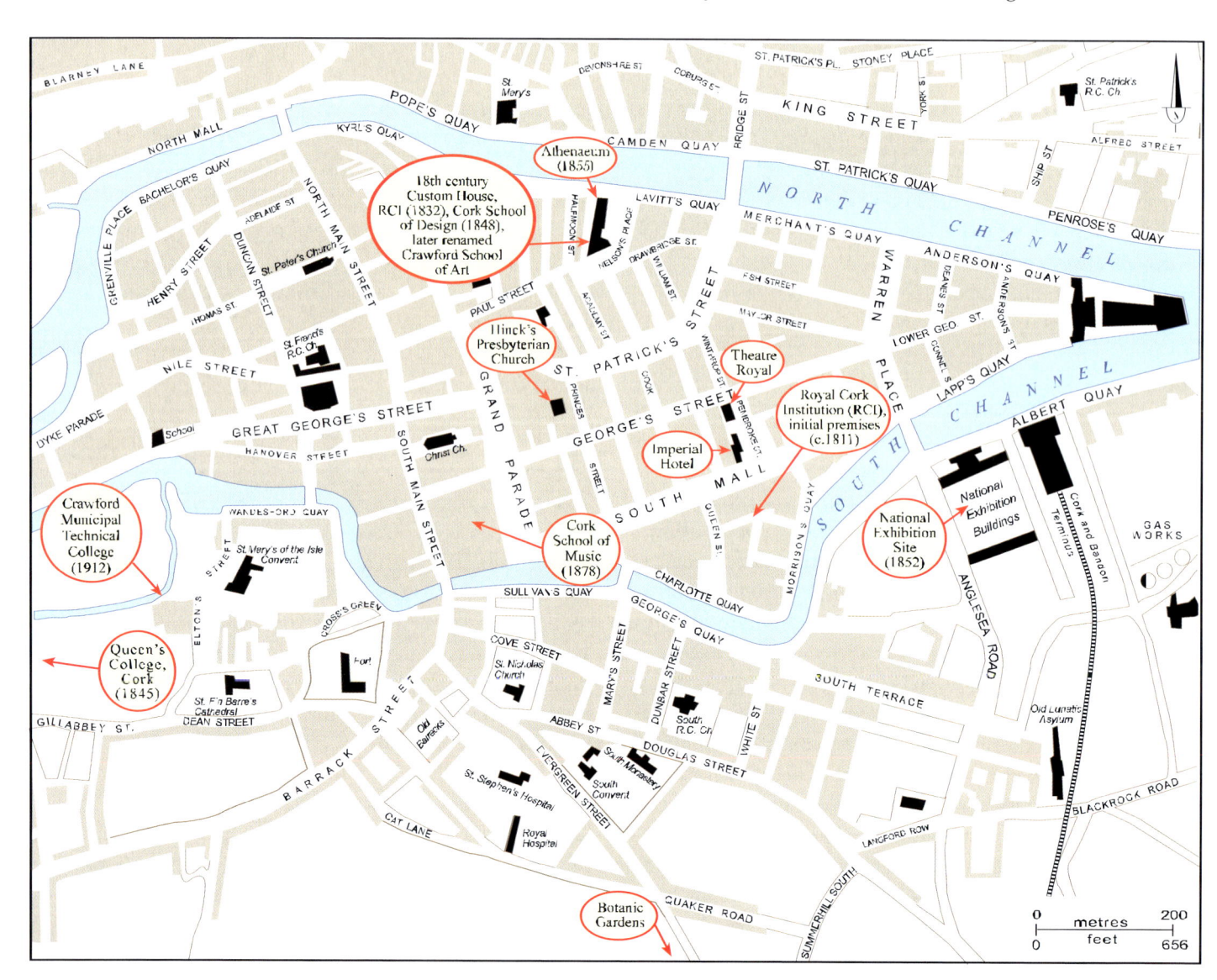

Fig. 3.49 By the mid-nineteenth century there had been a significant increase in cultural and educational institutions in Cork.

would permit.'[3] The numbers enrolled in Hincks's initial classes varied between twelve and twenty persons. He charged four guineas per person for those attending, which was a higher fee than schools in general at the time. The commercial middle classes were well represented amongst the initial intake.

A suitable premises was obtained to hold his lectures and this was located in Jameson's Row on the South Mall, opposite the Imperial Hotel, until its move in 1832 to what is now the Crawford Municipal Art Gallery. In 1806, Hincks introduced specialised courses in chemistry, natural history, natural philosophy (science) and agriculture. He later secured an annual government grant of £2,000. The latter was formalised on 20 March 1807, when a Royal Charter of Incorporation was granted. Public investment in education at any level was only in its infancy. Soon Cork was to become a centre like Dublin, London and Edinburgh, where scientific ideas could be exchanged, where a library of scientific books and journals could be consulted and where a laboratory existed for experimental work.

Fig. 3.50 The former Custom House, which was presented to the Royal Cork Institution in the 1830s. (Photo: Kieran McCarthy.)

Evolution

After the granting of the charter, professors were appointed and lectures given in natural philosophy, chemistry, natural history and agriculture. A library was opened and this was to be supported by the Institution's own funds. In addition, the proprietors of the RCI began the search for a suitable location for a botanic garden. Land in Ballyphehane was eventually purchased. James Drummond, an eminent Scottish botanist, was appointed the first curator of the Cork Botanical Gardens.[4]

The Institution went from strength to strength in the early decades of its existence. However, financial problems worsened due in no small part to the Institution's activities and its wider role in Cork society. The Institution appealed to the government to have its financial position inspected by a Commission of Inquiry.[5] By mid-winter 1826 the Commission was able to return a verdict. The pedagogic content of the lecture courses was not criticised, but a key recommendation was that the Botanic Gardens be disposed of in order to lessen expenditure. Because of its general appearance, its remote location and difficult access, the inspectorate expressed grave doubts about the future of the gardens. In addition, on the 31 December 1826, Henry Goulbourn of the Commission of Inquiry sent a letter to the Institution detailing the fact that the parliamentary grant was being reduced to £1,500 and that agricultural activities had to be seriously curtailed.

By 1830, the entire parliamentary grant was withdrawn. To compensate for this, Cork's former Custom House on Emmet Place was given to the Institution. This departure provided greater space for scientific activities. The most popular included demonstrations in chemistry, electricity, botany and mineralogy. The Cork middle classes willingly embraced the opportunity for such scientific study. In 1843, the RCI was closely involved in organising a meeting of The British Association for the Advancement of Science. Over a thousand people assembled in the city in August of that year to attend the various lectures, soirées, excursions and grand balls. Lectures were held in the former Custom House, while the Imperial Hotel was the main venue for the various social activities.

The RCI and the emergence of Queen's College Cork

During the 1830s, members and patrons of the RCI campaigned vigorously for the establishment of a Munster college.[6] In 1845, the Colleges of Ireland Act was passed, which provided public funding to establish one or more colleges in Ireland. It was decided initially to establish Queen's colleges (after Queen Victoria) in Belfast and Cork, whilst a later decision was taken to establish a college in

Galway. The establishment of Queen's College Cork was to be a critical factor in the demise of the Royal Cork Institution. Key lecturers in the Institution moved quickly to lecture in the new Queen's College.[7] By 1850, due to inadequate funds and lack of public support, the influence of the RCI began to fade.

Besides scientific matters, the Institution would also leave its mark on the artistic life of the city. From the outset the RCI developed a keen interest in art. It already possessed a collection of casts of Vatican sculptures, made under the supervision of the curator of the Vatican Museum, Antonio Canova. These casts were influential in the artistic training of two of Ireland's foremost nineteenth-century artists: painter Daniel Maclise (1800–1858) and sculptor John Hogan (1806–1870).[8] On 3 April 1848, a discussion took place with regard to proposals for the establishment of a government School of Design in the old Custom House. Sir Thomas Deane, a manager, proposed that the school obtain the upper floor of the building, at a rent of £80 per annum. The proposal was accepted. The Cork School of Design was one of a number of similar schools established throughout England, Scotland, Wales and Ireland. In 1883, the wealthy Cork merchant William Crawford was persuaded to donate the necessary finance to complete a renovation and

Fig. 3.51 Canova cast in the Crawford Municipal Art Gallery. (Photo: Kieran McCarthy.)

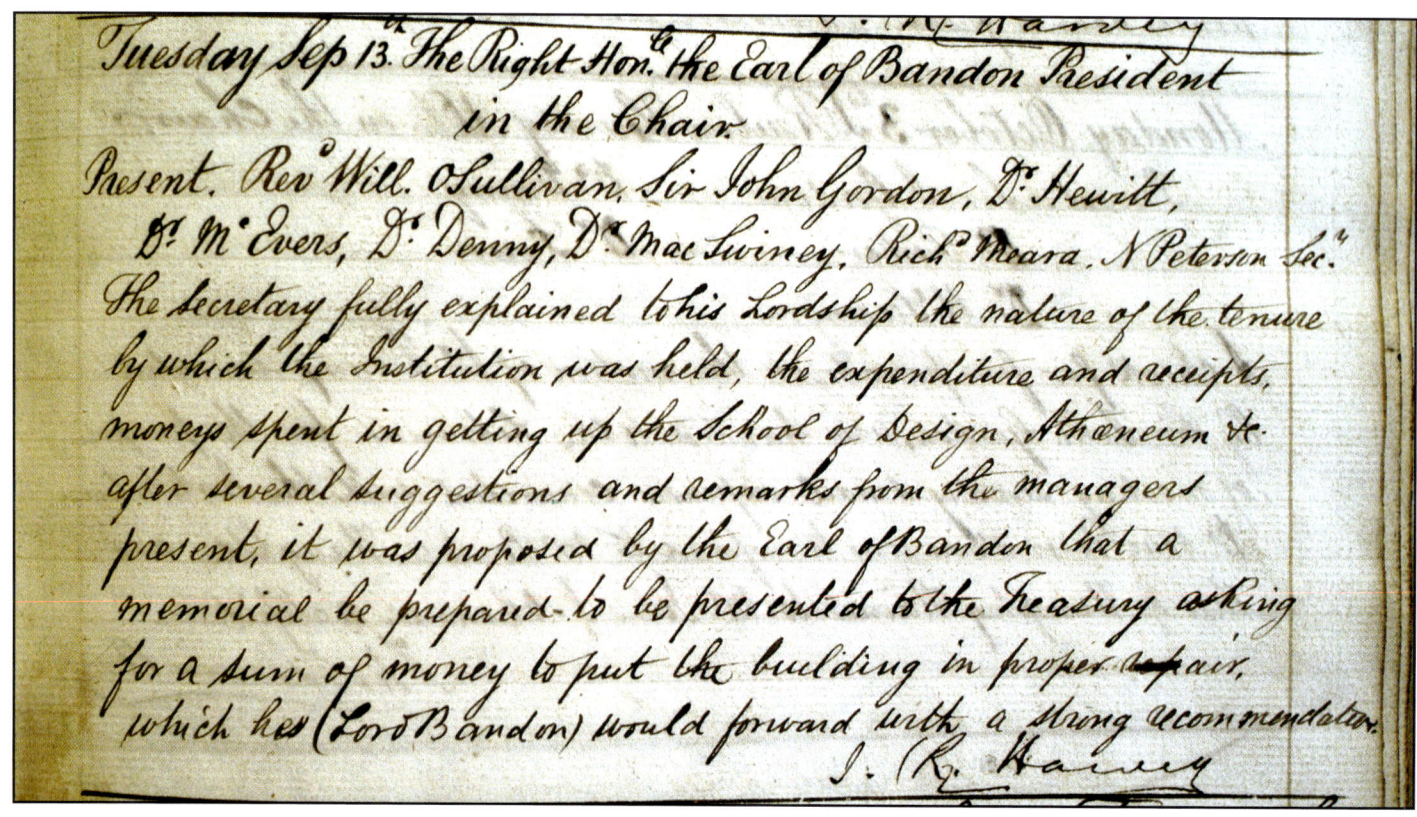

Fig. 3.52 Minute Book of the Royal Cork Institution, 13 September 1864. The extract refers to the financial position of the Institution – specifically its expenditure on the School of Design and the Athenaeum – which was a constant source of worry for the managers in the Institution's final years. (Source: Cork Archives Institute.)

Fig. 3.53 The extension to the former Custom House, funded principally by William Crawford. (Photo: Kieran McCarthy.)

the use of the 'Great Hall' as a venue for promoting culture, the fine arts and practical sciences. John Benson's iron-and-glass exhibition building was to be transferred from its site overlooking the south channel of the Lee to waste ground overlooking the north channel, the present-day site of the Cork Opera House.[9] Beautiful ornamental pillars modelled on those of the temple of Jupitor Stator in Rome were installed in the interior and the exterior roof was covered with new slates. The Cork Athenaeum's unofficial opening took place on 29 January 1855. Over 2,000 people attended a benefit concert for the Cork Blind Asylum. The Athenaeum was used principally as a concert venue. It would later be renamed the Cork Opera House.

By the time the scientific and cultural activities of the RCI, and indeed its offspring the Cork Cuverian Society for the Cultivation of Sciences (1835–1878), had come to an end, it had bequeathed to the city a rich legacy: 'Its record had been an impressive one, pioneering adult education in the city and paving the way to the later Queen's College.'[10] The ideas of the RCI on the 'diffusion of useful knowledge' would also live on in the early twentieth century in the form of the Crawford Municipal Technical College, founded in 1912, which eventually evolved into the Cork Regional Technical College in 1974, now known as the Cork Institute of Technology.

extension of the school. The renovated building and extension were designed by Arthur Hill of the architects' firm Hill and Company and were built at a cost of £20,000. It was renamed the Crawford School of Art.

THE ATHENAEUM

The RCI also played a significant part in the construction of an Athenaeum. This was to be a large extra space for displaying the artistic endeavours of students at the Cork School of Design. The architect John Benson was commissioned to design an exhibition hall for the highly successful National Exhibition, which took place in the city in 1852. In the months after the exhibition, the President of the RCI, Thomas Tobin, formed a committee for converting

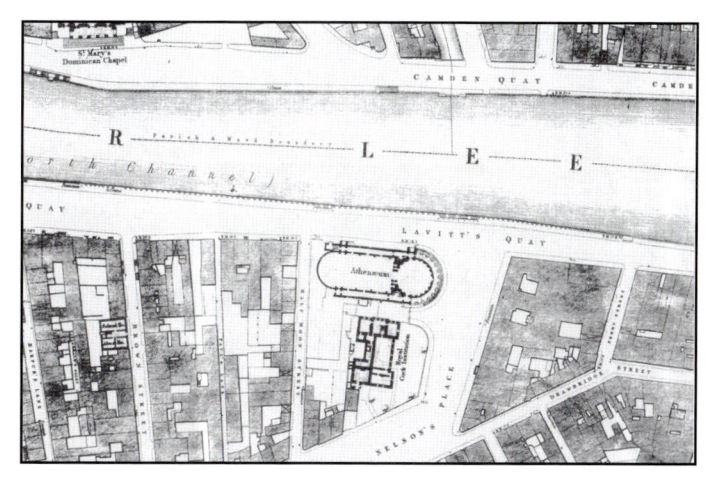

Fig. 3.54 Detail from the Ordnance Survey map showing the location of the Athenaeum (later Cork Opera House) at Lavitt's Quay.

Fig. 3.55 'View of Cork Opera House', *c.* 1857, by Samuel McDonnell, watercolour on paper. Copy after Robert Lowe Stopford (1813–1898). (Source: Crawford Municipal Art Gallery.)

Presbyterians in the City of Cork

A.S. Cromie

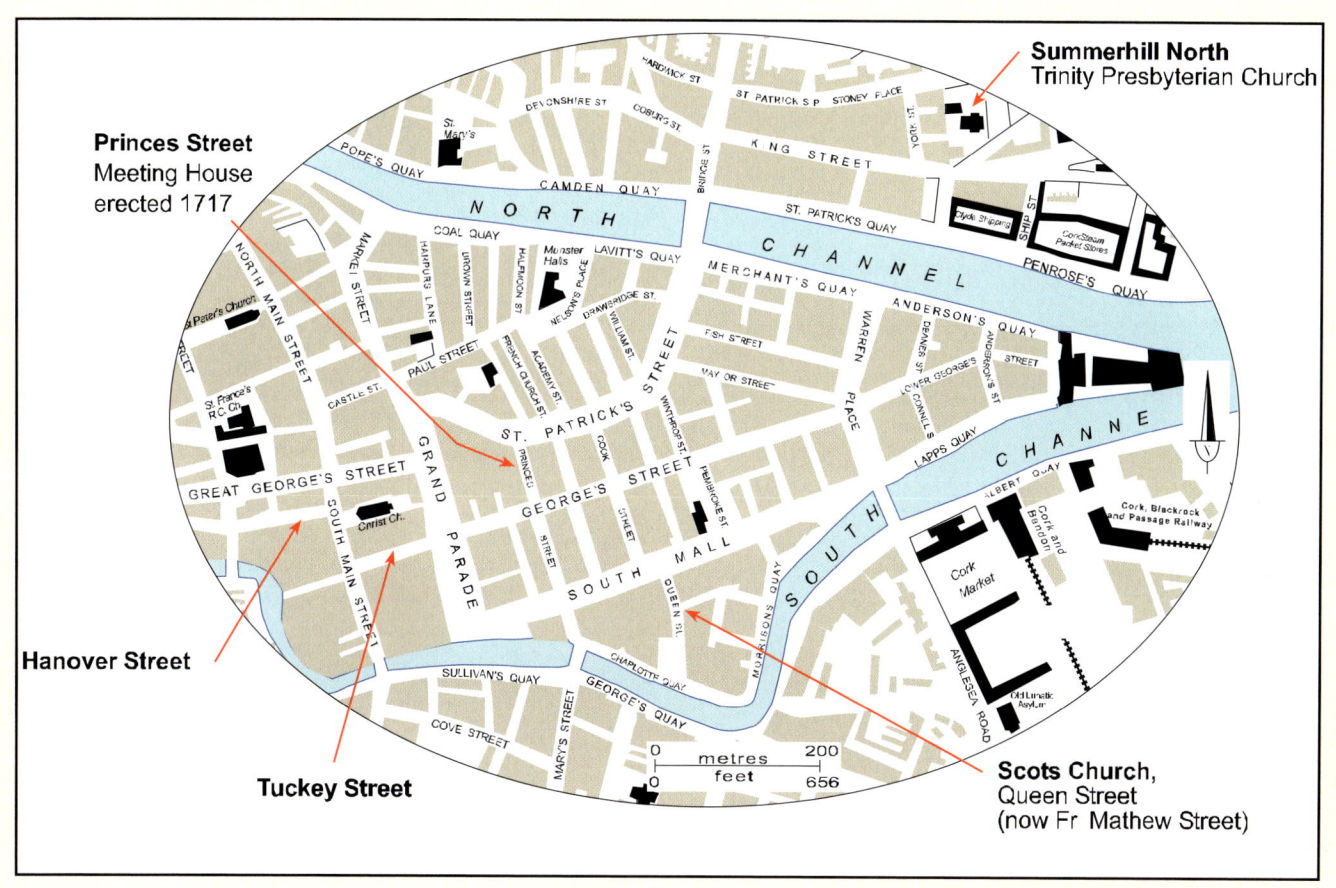

Fig. 3.56 Location of significant sites associated with the Presbyterian Church in the city.

Thomas Dix Hincks and his son Edward are remembered by two plaques on the pillars of the gateway leading to the First Presbyterian Church on Princes Street. Thomas was minister of the church from 1792 until 1814. The son became an eminent scholar and deciphered ancient Syrian writing. The Princes Street Meeting-House was built in 1717. Prior to that date there was a meeting-house in Watergate Lane, the present Hanover Street. The congregation was founded by Englishmen and was heterodox or non-confessional. It was during Dr Thomas Dix Hincks's ministry that a pipe organ was installed in January 1802, the first pipe organ in any dissenting church in Ireland. The famous painter Daniel Maclise, who later befriended Charles Dickens, was a choirboy in the congregation and he left his mark by carving his initials on the back of an oak pew.

The congregation was linked to the Presbytery of Munster, which united in 1809 with the Presbytery of Dublin to form the Southern Association of United Presbyteries, later the Synod of Munster. About 1838, doctrinal differences in the Princes Street congregation caused a schism and the Trinitarian members withdrew, most of them joining the then recently established Scots Church. The Princes Street congregation came to be regarded as Unitarian. In 1816 it claimed an average attendance of 300, but over the years numbers declined until only one member was left. Recently a service of worship has been restored.

Fig. 3.57 Holy Trinity Presbyterian church at Summerhill. (Photo: John Crowley.)

The Scots Church, established in 1831, was formed in connection with the Synod of Ulster. Services were held in the Baptist Chapel, then in Tuckey Street and finally in new premises erected in 1839 in Queen Street (now Father Mathew Street). The words 'Scots Church' were carved into the stonework above the doorway. This name referred not to the nationality of the worshippers but to the fact that the doctrines proclaimed were in accordance with the doctrines of the established Church of Scotland. In 1860, the congregation of Scots Church erected on Summerhill, off King Street (now MacCurtain Street), the Trinity Presbyterian church, with a seating capacity of 700. It is a remarkable example of the decorated style of Gothic and has a tower and spire 140 feet high. It stands on a very commanding height and is the only example of Kentish-rag stonework in the city. It is sometimes referred to as the church with the crooked spire. The building was dedicated for worship on 28 July 1861. However, a section of the congregation formed a separate congregation by reopening the former Scots Church under the name of 'Queen Street'. In 1904, a pipe organ was installed in the back gallery over the entrance hall of the church in Summerhill. The seats there were arranged to accommodate the choir. A three-tiered seating arrangement, for both conductor and choir, is positioned below the manual, which has a central dip to allow for visibility of both the preacher and the conductor of the choir. The music from the unseen choir prompted a visiting worshipper to remark as he left the church: 'Today we heard the angels sing.'

As a result of the First World War, the War of Independence and the Civil War, the membership of both congregations was greatly reduced and the two congregations united in 1928. The former Scots meeting-house was sold and the united congregations now worship together in the Trinity Presbyterian church on Summerhill. Many of Cork's most prominent businessmen, including lord mayors and aldermen, have been faithful members. Today the size and nature of the building creates problems as regards its upkeep; its size makes it very difficult to preserve the atmosphere of togetherness in worship for a greatly reduced congregation. Relocating is not a viable option. However, in the early years of the twenty-first century we are seeing a trend whereby people from the area around the church, including language-school students, asylum-seekers and others whose job has brought them to Cork city, are attending Trinity. This is very encouraging and suggests that the church should stay on that site, although the question of the suitability of the building remains.

21. 'THE COLLEGE': UNIVERSITY COLLEGE CORK

John A. Murphy

'A university city since 1845', proudly proclaim the signs on the main approach roads into Cork. Though we might quibble with the date (the enabling legislation was enacted in 1845; the building was completed and opened in 1849) Queen's College, or University College Cork, in popular parlance simply 'the College', was the only third-level institution in the city until recent decades and it gave Cork a distinctive academic and cultural personality. It became the focus of development of the inner western suburbs and today it stimulates industrial research in the region as well as being a major generator of jobs and spending power in the urban economy.[1]

Origins

Why and how did it all begin? The general demand for social reform that characterised the United Kingdom in the early nineteenth century was expressed in the sphere of education in a movement to make universities accessible to the new professional and commercial middle classes. This development was seen as conducive to political and social stability. This was particularly to be desired in Ireland, where an ambitious Roman Catholic middle class sought its place in the educational sun, which certainly did not shine for them in Trinity College Dublin, where any welcome for non-Anglicans was grudging and limited. Providing public

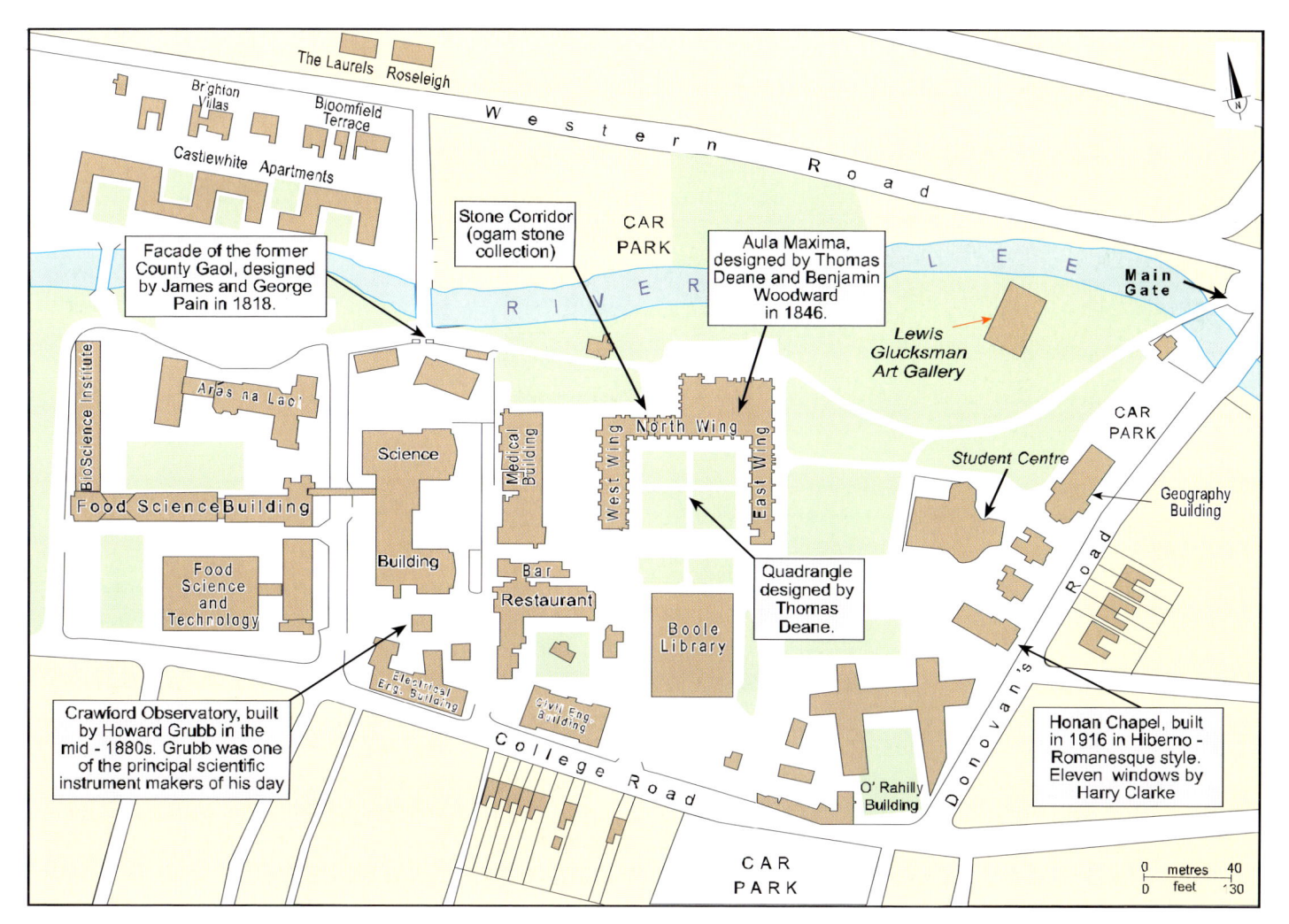

Fig. 3.58 Significant sites in University College Cork.

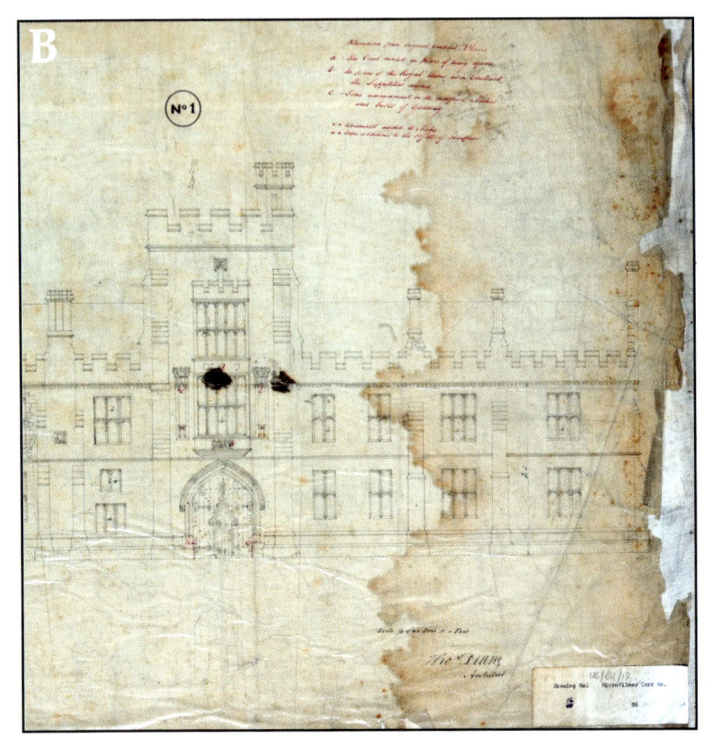

Fig. 3.59 A) The quadrangle designed by Sir Thomas Deane. (Photo: Tomás Tyner.) B) Deane's original drawings for the quadrangle. (By kind permission of the University Heritage Office, UCC.)

money for a lay Catholic university was unacceptable to the Protestant establishment, so setting up the Queen's Colleges, which were secular in structure and ambience while relegating religion to the private and voluntary sphere, was a compromise.

Independently of national considerations, there was a strong public demand in the 1830s and 1840s for a higher-education institute in Munster. A campaign was led by the prominent MPs, Thomas Wyse and William Smith O'Brien, as well as by a representative committee of Catholic and Protestant bankers and businessmen including James Roche, Richard Dowden and the influential Beamish family. There were rival lobbies in Limerick and Cork for the location of such a Munster college, but the larger and more prosperous city won out. Cork had a lively interest in the arts and sciences and two high-level learned societies – the Royal Cork Institution and the Cuverian Society. Moreover, and this was a strong argument by Cork proponents, there was already a well-established tradition of medical training in the city.

The Queen's Colleges of Belfast, Cork and Galway were established by act of parliament in 1845, under the government of Sir Robert Peel. They were to be nonresidential and non-denominational. There would be 'no religious tests' for staff or students, though students would be permitted, indeed encouraged, to attend instruction and worship in the religion of their choice. Students would also pay 'reasonable fees' to the professors 'for attendance at their lectures'. The Crown (in effect, the chief secretary in Dublin Castle) would appoint, and dismiss, the president and professors. This would not only check any tendency 'to tinge general instructions with peculiar religious tenets', but it would also put a premium on the loyalty of academics to the Crown – that is, to the Union.

Location

The 'Gillabbey site' as the chosen location of Queen's College Cork (QCC) met with general satisfaction, the chief architect Sir Thomas Deane describing it as 'excellent and commanding and most beautiful for a public building'. Mr Denis Hayes of Blackpool Nurseries tried to secure the site for the northside but to no avail. The building began early in 1847 and was completed within two years. The manpower involved was considerable and workers from the County Cork countryside thus found some relief from the devastating consequences of the Great Famine. During her brief visit to Cork in 1849 the young Queen Victoria witnessed her statue being hoisted to the apex of the easternmost gable as her procession passed below on the Western Road.

The splendid neo-Gothic structure on its spectacular clifftop site aroused enthusiastic admiration among contemporary observers. The high-quality limestone quadrangle, unfinished, like Schubert's Eighth Symphony, remains to this day a place of soft brightness and tranquillity and, in sunshine, of basking warmth. Presumably it was the stunning view of the battlemented site from the Western Road that provoked Macaulay's reference to 'a gothic college worthy to stand in the High Street of Oxford'. In an 1874 memorial to the lord lieutenant, the president and professors were concerned that the 'chief public view of the College' be not 'injured' by the building of houses along the Western Road, in the area that is known today as Perrot's Inch. There were drawbacks. The people in the immediate vicinity were 'of a very low class' with insalubrious habits, according to the professors, who also repeatedly expressed their distaste for having to live cheek by jowl with the denizens of the adjoining County Gaol. Social undesirables congregated in the roadway common to the College and the gaol, particularly on the occasion of public executions, which staff and students found very distressing. In the 1850s, the college authorities expressed their desire for 'a new approach' on the eastern side, which would shorten, both physically and psychologically, the distance from town. All the disadvantages of class and location were overcome, or at least diminished, in time. Eventually, the physical presence of the College influenced the development of a socially desirable residential area.

Governance and early problems

The appointment of Robert Kane as the first president was an auspicious beginning. Kane was a chemist of international renown and the author of *The Industrial Resources of Ireland* (1844), which became a favourite text for economic nationalists, from the Young Irelanders, to Sinn Féin, to Fianna Fáil. He was the exemplar of the concept of higher education as 'useful knowledge', then very much in the ascendant. His immediate task was to put flesh on the bare bones of the College, which was officially inaugurated on 7 November 1849. Kane promised that the new institution would 'educate young men for the active age and world in which we live'. He also appealed to deeply cherished local tradition when he asserted that 'Fin Barra, the patron saint of Cork, left to his followers the charge of founding a seat of learning in this place: here, after nearly a thousand years, we open now the portals of this edifice and accept the task of training the youth of Munster.'

Fig. 3.60 Portrait of Robert Kane, first president of Queen's College Cork. (By permission of the College Archivist.)

After the celebrations, academic work commenced for the 112 students across the faculties of arts (including science, agriculture and engineering), law and medicine. Kane had numerous problems to face, the main one being the religious issue. Despite his own Catholic persuasion and his repeated claims that the College provided safeguards for the religious faith of students, the Catholic bishops denounced the 'neutral' Queen's Colleges as unacceptable and 'godless'. Though lay involvement and attendance was never explicitly prohibited, nevertheless sustained disapproval by the Catholic Church largely explains the disappointing lack of progress by Queen's College Cork for the remainder of the nineteenth century. With the Crown firmly in command and with no community representatives in administration, the College was seen as alien, autocratic and élitist by an increasingly nationalist-minded citizenry. When a mysterious fire destroyed the west wing in 1862, the town had precious little pity for the badly singed gown. The investigator appointed by the Dublin Castle authorities reported that 'amongst the lower order of people here, there is no feeling of regret felt at the occurrence, some say it is a pity any of the building escaped'.

Kane's 28-year presidency was often stormy. He seems to have had a temperamental difficulty in dealing with the academic staff – including George Boole, the distinguished first professor of mathematics whose algebra was to form the basis of computer science. But then rows between presidents and professors, or between professors themselves, are an inescapable part of university life, it would seem. *Odium academicum* has raged across the college spectrum from that day to this.

Developments under Sullivan

Under the vigorous direction of Kane's successor, President William K. Sullivan (1873–1890), a native of Dripsey, County Cork, Queen's College expanded in area, student numbers and amenities. The student body reached 300 in 1879–1880, of whom 60 per cent were Catholic, despite their church's disapproval. Land was acquired to secure 'free space about the College' to develop a botanic garden and plant houses and (in 1879) to make a new entrance from the Western Road, some yards to the west of the present main gateway, which was constructed in 1929. The College grounds took on the dimensions they were to maintain up to the mid-twentieth century. Berkeley Hall (later the Honan hostel, in turn demolished in 1995 to make way for the multi-purpose O'Rahilly Building) was opened in 1884–1885 as residential accommodation for male Church of Ireland students: it was located in the south-east corner, bounded by College Road and Donovan's Road.

A most notable development in the mid-1880s was the building of a fine observatory, complete with major astronomical instruments. The project (today under active restoration and refurbishment) reflected the intense

Fig. 3.61 George Boole (1815–1864) was born in Lincoln, England. The son of a shoemaker, he would make his mark in the world of mathematics. Boole had already acquired a reputation for original mathematical ideas and research when in 1849 he was appointed the first professor of mathematics in the then newly established Queen's College Cork. He was responsible for significant developments in algebra. In December 1864, he died from pneumonia at the tragically early age of 49, having walked four miles from Ballintemple to his lectures in a rainstorm. A large stained-glass window in the Aula Maxima is dedicated to his memory. The library at UCC bears his name.

contemporary interest in astronomy and meteorology. It attracted funding from people like the Duke of Devonshire, but it was named after another generous donor, W.H. Crawford, a wealthy brewer who admired Sullivan's qualities and achievements. Among his donations was the provision of money for plant houses and books for the library, which enhanced the latter's function as a reference resource for the south of Ireland. Crawford was one of the very few substantial benefactors in the history of the College, despite countless appeals over the decades by presidents for public donations.

WOMEN: STAFF AND STUDENTS

The excessively male world of the College was breached in the 1885–1886 session with the admission of the first female students, but their number remained tiny until the transformation of QCC into UCC in 1908–1909. President Sullivan commented on these pioneering young women: 'The presence of ladies in the classrooms and in the library greatly contributed to the preservation of order, and I expect their example will stimulate the men to more attentive and regular work.' The College continued to be ruled by a male establishment and, right down to the 1950s and 1960s, 'ladies' had to observe extra regulations made especially for them: they were not to smoke in public, for example, and most famously 'not to lie about on the grass'.

In those early days, medicine was a particularly resistant male preserve and women medical graduates struggled in getting access to, and achieving equality of treatment in, posts as house doctors. In the early twentieth century, women began to get positions on the academic staff of the College and a major milestone was reached with the appointment of Mary Ryan, from a well-known Cork family, to the professorship of Romance Languages (1910–1938), the first woman in the United Kingdom of Britain and Ireland to hold a chair. It remained – and remains – a man's world at the top in UCC. Women account for little more than ten per cent of professorial appointments.

Meanwhile, female students have significantly increased in numbers and confidence, particularly since the 1960s. The general trend has been towards full integration in the student body, with a common students' club, for example. There were 76 women out of 430 students in 1913–1914, 296 (out of 906) in 1934–1935 and 1,165 (3,181) in 1969–1970. By the late 1980s, a century after the first admission, women outnumbered men.

DECLINE AND RESURGENCE: QCC TO UCC

The last decade of the nineteenth century and the first years of the twentieth saw the College touch rock-bottom in terms of two successive disastrous presidencies, under-financing, poor morale, dubious student material and declining numbers. The Catholic authorities were still hostile to the Queen's Colleges and were pushing to denominationalise the university system. The Cork College's future seemed fated to be that of a glorified medicine school. The university framework was the Royal University of Ireland (1882–1909), an examining and degree-conferring body that did not require lecture attendance at the Queen's Colleges. This had a detrimental effect on entrance standards and student numbers at Queen's College Cork. To the nationalist and Catholic population of Cork and Munster, the College was still an alien and irrelevant institution. A radical change for the better took place with the appointment of Sir Bertram Windle, one of the outstanding presidents (1904–1919) in the history of the College. He revitalised College life, promoted student welfare and established strong links with the city. Under his presidency, the physics and chemistry building (the present civil engineering department) was opened in 1911, the athletic grounds on the Mardyke were acquired in the same year and the Donovan's land area (site of the future dairy science institute, now the Geography Building) was added. With Windle's encouragement, the Honan bequest resulted in the establishment of the Honan hostel, the Honan Biological Institute and the building in 1916 of the Hiberno-Romanesque gem, the Honan Chapel.

It was in Windle's time and, in no small measure, due to his hard work that the College experienced the most important turning-point in its fortunes. Under the Irish Universities Act of 1908, within the federal framework of the National University of Ireland, Queen's College became University College Cork (UCC). It had now entered the second phase of its history, with a new name, a new charter and a greatly extended range of departments – archaeology, economics, education, music and so on. This was a revolutionary expansion of academic disciplines confidently inviting a corresponding growth in student numbers – 404 in 1910–1911, up from 171 in 1900–1901. The transformed UCC now flourished, local graduation ceremonies being a symbol of new vigour and colour. Ecclesiastical disapproval was lifted. Catholic parents could now send their children to the College (if they could afford it!) with a clear conscience. From a religious standpoint, it was no longer an alien institution; indeed, it was to be increasingly Catholicised over the next five decades.

TOWN AND GOWN

During the Queen's College days, the institution remained a place apart from the community and the 1908 changes did not make UCC a people's college overnight. Though Windle had done his best to fulfil his promise of identifying himself 'with the city', he made an observation in 1913 that would hold true today for some Cork citizens: 'I am often surprised to find how many people in the city of Cork, educated people, too, who have never been inside the walls of the University College and have no idea of what kind of place it is.'

Working-class and trade-union sentiment still tended to be apathetic, if not hostile, to UCC, and their representatives were sensitive to perceived snubs from college quarters. There had been popular enthusiasm in the early 1900s for university change: 20 to 30 years on, there was corresponding disenchantment that the changed institution was not flinging open its gates for the benefit of 'the poor man's son'. The *Cork Examiner*, in its editorials and correspondence columns, reflected the position of the interested general public – supportive but critical.

For all that, the citizens were proud that Cork was a university town and they appreciated the consequent advantages to the urban and regional economy. From the 1920s onwards, there was a gradual strengthening of the links between town and gown and the College made a considerable effort to improve the relationship. In the words of a prominent local businessman in 1928: 'College came down town and fraternised with the business associations, with the workers' associations, with the other educational schemes – in fact the College became a citizen.'

Fig. 3.62 A stained-glass window by Harry Clarke in the Honan Chapel. (Photo: Andrew Bradley, by permission of the Honan Trust.)

Fig. 3.63 The largest collection of ogam stones (28 in total) on open display in Ireland is located in the 'Stone Corridor' at UCC. (Photo: John Crowley.) There are over 330 ogam stones in Ireland, with a major concentration in counties Cork, Kerry and Waterford. The College acquired many of the stones in its collection in the latter decades of the nineteenth century and the early part of the twentieth century. The inscriptions on these stones, which date from the fourth to the seventh centuries, represent the oldest form of script in Ireland. (Source: D. McManus, *Ogam stones at University College Cork*, Cork, 2004.)

the college farm. Over the decades, also, links between the College's medical school and local hospitals were strengthened. It was to be the late twentieth century, however, before the College felt the need to establish a public relations unit to explain itself to the wider community.

CONTINUITY AND CHANGE FROM THE 1960S

The 1950s were a period of financial conservatism and debt containment. UCC did well in staving off disaster for the dental school and in securing continuing recognition by British and American registration bodies for the medical school. In the 1960s, students were protected by their solid conservatism from the shock of student revolution worldwide. (This lack of radicalism was due to the middle-class complexion of the student body and its strongly local base: a pleasant inner-suburb campus favoured stability, tradition and the continuity of conservative values.) Student power was expressed reasonably and responsibly, but there was no return to the deferential and hierarchical modes of a former age. For the students of the 1960s, activism took the form of a constructive 'teach in' rather than quadrangle or street rioting. And, soon enough, in the 1980s students turned inwards and became absorbed in the mundane concerns of responding to higher examination standards, problems of finance and overcrowding and the beckoning demands of the market economy outside. Gradually, the introduction of student grants, together with the raising of entrance standards, achieved an increased measure of educational opportunity.

Part of the process of popularising and 'nativising' UCC was the arranging of open days so that citizens could 'see for themselves the full scope of the work of the university'. Other additions included the provision of extension lectures and the development of close links with the Cork Municipal School of Commerce and the Municipal Technical Institute in the 1930s and 1940s. One very popular College area that had visitors from all over Munster from its inception in the late 1920s was the dairy science institute. Groups were frequently shown around the creamery and

In more recent years the College has responded successfully to challenges posed to its erstwhile monopoly of third-level education in the city and the province – from a thriving Cork Institute of Technology and a vibrant new university in Limerick. In 2003, the College was named Irish University of the Year by the *Sunday Times*, a signal recognition of the institution's excellence in research and

Fig. 3.64 An aerial view of University College Cork. (Photo: Tomás Tyner.)

teaching, the cultural richness of the student mix and UCC's contribution to national life. The Lewis Glucksman Gallery in the lower grounds is the latest example of the College's commitment to the visual arts. The launch of a new School of Pharmacy in 2003 was another exciting departure, as has been the development of the new Schools of Research Excellence.

The eternal student

Meanwhile, the ultimate continuity in the college experience is provided by the students themselves. The bulk of them are drawn as always from the city, the county and south Munster but now are increasingly leavened by a welcome intake from many countries, particularly from the EU and the USA. Underneath all the changes since 1849 the eternal student persists, creating the charming illusion of changelessness and immortality and sharing a priceless elixir with the academics. In that homely phrase, the students are the life of the place: *semper sint in flore*.

22. FAMINE

Larry Geary and Marita Foster

Between 1845 and 1852 general starvation and opportunistic diseases were responsible for more than one million deaths in Ireland, and at least another one million emigrated. During the previous century, the Irish population had more than trebled, from 2.5 million people in 1750 to more than 8.5 million in 1845.[1] This rapid population increase, which was most marked among the poor – the landless labourers, cottiers and small farmers – put enormous pressure on the country's resources and reduced the majority of the people to a dangerous dependency on a single food source: the potato.

In the autumn of 1845 potatoes in Ireland were attacked by a new phenomenon, *phytophthora infestans*, or blight, a fungal disease that originated in the north-east of the United States in 1843 and spread to western Europe. By the time the blight was first detected in Ireland in September 1845, the early potatoes had been harvested and it was the second or late crop that was affected. In total about one-third of the second crop was lost, but in County Cork the loss was only slightly more than 20 per cent.[2] In the following year, blight appeared early and destroyed almost the entire crop. This marked the commencement of the Great Famine in Cork city and county, no less than in the country generally.

IMPACT OF THE FAMINE ON CORK CITY

The speed with which potato blight spread and the devastation it caused were vividly captured in a letter written by Fr Theobald Mathew to Charles Trevelyan on 7 August 1846:

> On the 27th of last month I passed from Cork to Dublin, and this doomed plant bloomed in all the luxuriance of an abundant harvest. Returning on the 3rd instant, I beheld with sorrow one wide waste of putrefying vegetation. In many places the wretched people were seated on the fences of their decaying gardens, wringing their hands and wailing bitterly [at] the destruction that had left them foodless.[3]

The winter and spring that followed witnessed the utmost distress in Cork and throughout the country. This was a period of extreme and debilitating food shortages, spiralling food prices, food stealing and food riots, and a grossly inadequate public works programme. The resident population of Cork city was augmented by starving people from the county and further afield who swarmed into the city in search of relief, 'walking masses of filth, vermin and sickness'.[4] These rural refugees scattered famine-related diseases in every direction and swamped the city's limited charitable and relief mechanisms. Dr John Popham, one of the physicians attached to the North Infirmary, recorded:

> The pressure from without upon the city began to be felt in October [1846], and in November and December the influx of paupers from all parts of this vast county was so overwhelming that, to prevent them from dying in the streets, the doors of the workhouse were thrown open, and in one week 500 persons were admitted, without any provision, either of space or clothing, to meet so fearful an emergency. All these were suffering from famine, and most of them from malignant dysentery or fever.[5]

Dr Callanan, one of the workhouse physicians, captured the situation in Cork during the fateful winter and spring of 1846–1847 in imagery that was such a haunting feature of contemporary writing on the Great Famine:

> From the commencement of 1847, however, Fate opened her book in good earnest here, and the full tide of death flowed on everywhere around us. During the first six months of that dark period one-third of the daily population of our streets consisted of shadows and spectres, the impersonations of disease and famine, crowding in from the rural districts, and stalking along to the general doom – the grave – which appeared to await them at the distance of a few steps, or a few short hours.[6]

RELIEF EFFORTS DURING THE FAMINE

The Cork Relief Committee was established in March 1846, following a public meeting in the city. From 28 March, the committee sold Indian meal for one penny per pound at three city outlets: York Street in Blackpool, Little Market Street and Barrack Street. According to one observer, 'the crowds of poor persons who gathered around them were so

Fig. 3.65 A soup depot located in Barrack Street: 'It is impossible to overrate the valuable services rendered by the gentlemen who attend here, and undertake the arduous duty of administering the daily rations of food to the famishing and clamorous crowds who beset the gates. The average number supplied every day at this establishment for the past week has been 1,300, and many hundreds more apply, whom it is impossible at present to accommodate.' (Source: *Illustrated London News*, 13 March 1847.)

turbulently inclined as to require the immediate interference of the police'.[7] By October 1846, ten Relief Committee depots were operating and an average of 25,000 people were receiving relief every day.[8] The Relief Committee launched a public works scheme, which by May 1846 included the construction of a road from the Lough to Pouladuff Road, a new road from St Joseph's Cemetery to Friar's Walk and improvements to the Fever Hospital Road and to the old barracks.[9] The Relief Committee also provided loans to the Wide Street Commissioners and the Harbour Board for various public works, including the extension of Penrose's Quay by about 700 feet and the reconstruction of the navigation wall. By November 1846, more than 400 labourers were employed on the Great Southern and Western Railway works on the northside of the city.

As the situation in the city deteriorated, private charities played an increasingly important role in the provision of relief. A conference of the Society of St Vincent de Paul was established in Cork in March 1846 and the society distributed Indian meal, bread, coal and, in some cases, money to the needy. The Quakers opened a soup kitchen in Cork in November 1846 and by the following January they were supplying 1,500 gallons of soup on a daily basis. The *Illustrated London News* reported that:

> The present calls are for from 150 to 180 gallons daily, requiring 120 pounds of good beef, 27 pounds of rice,

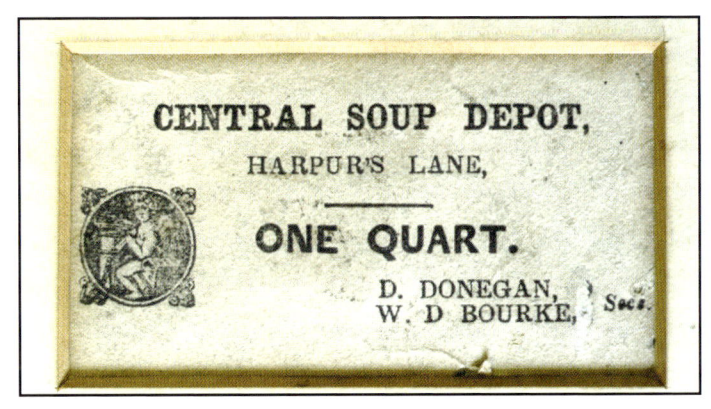

Fig. 3.66 Ticket for soup depot in Harpur's Lane. (Source: Cork Archives Institute.)

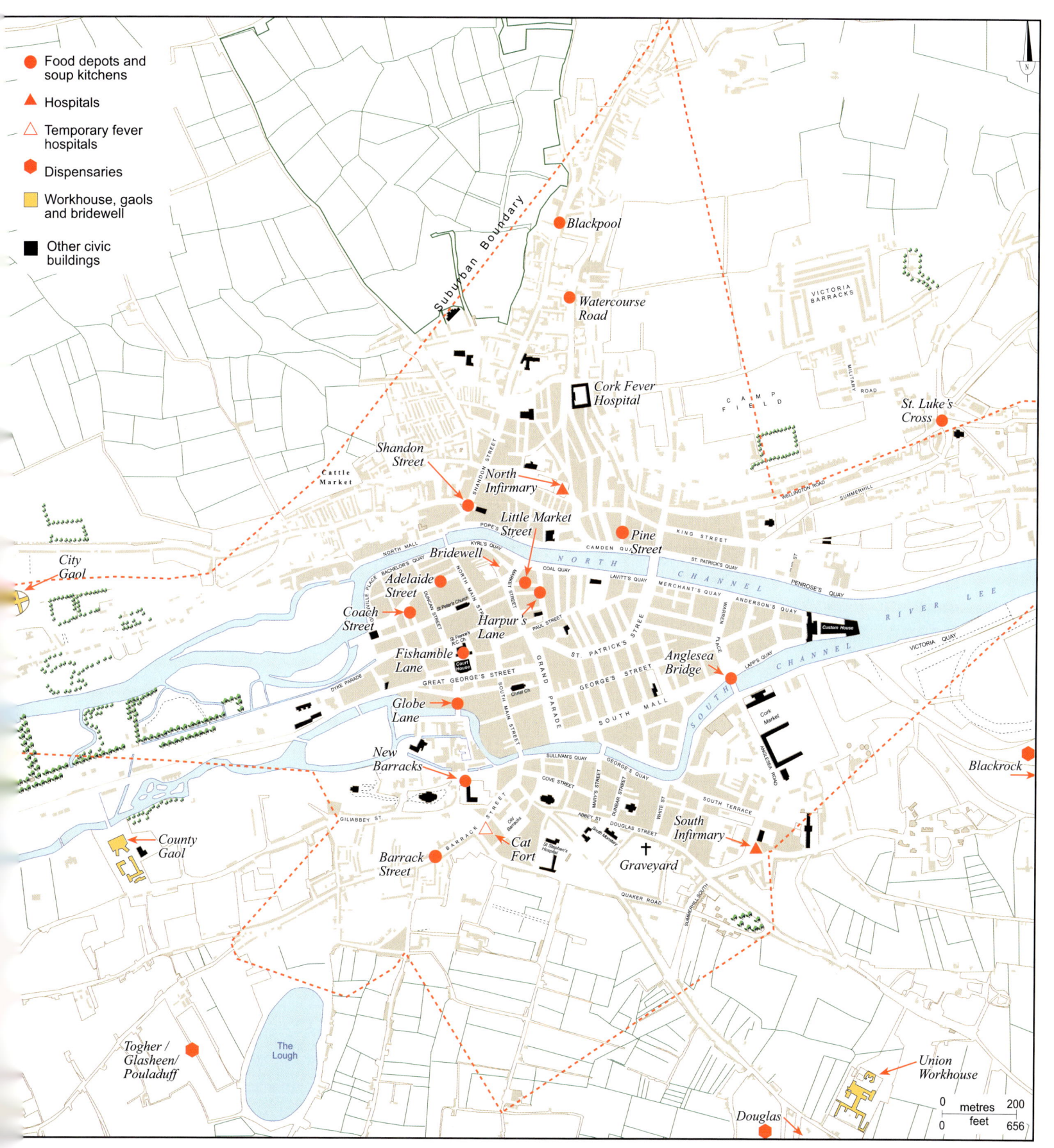

THE · CITY · IN · THE · NINETEENTH · AND · TWENTIETH · CENTURIES

Fig. 3.67 Location of medical and relief facilities and burial grounds in the city during the Famine.

27 pounds of oatmeal, 27 pounds of split peas, and 14 ounces of spices, with a quantity of vegetables. Tickets, at one penny each, are unsparingly distributed, on presenting one of which, each poor person receives one quart of soup, with half a small loaf of bread; and both are of good quality.[10]

The Cork Relief Committee encouraged local parish committees to establish soup kitchens in various parts of the city. By December 1846, there were five such outlets: at Adelaide Street, Barrack Street, Blackpool, Harpur's Lane and Shandon Street. By the following February additional depots at Pine Street had been established by Baptists with the assistance of Fr Mathew and his associates, and at Coach Street, operated by Congregationalists. On 12 April 1847, the *Jamestown* arrived in Cork harbour with relief supplies valued at over $35,000 for distribution within the city and county. The ship's captain recorded in graphic terms the horrific conditions he witnessed in the city:

> I went with Father Mathew only a few steps out of one of the principal streets of Cork into a lane; the Valley of the Shadow of Death was it? Alas! No it was the valley of death and pestilence itself. I saw enough in five minutes to horrify me; hovels crowded with the sick and the dying; without floors, without furniture, and with patches of dirty straw covered with still dirtier shreds and patches of humanity; some called for water to Father Mathew, and others for a dying blessing. From this very small sample of the prevailing destitution, we proceeded to a public soup kitchen under a shed guarded by police officers. Here a long boiler containing rice, meal etc. was at work, while hundreds of spectres stood without, begging for some of the soup which I can readily conceive would be refused by well-bred pigs in America. Every corner of the streets is filled with pale, careworn creatures, the weak leading and supporting the weaker; women assail you at every turn with famished babes imploring alms.[11]

THE INSTITUTIONAL RESPONSE

The starving and the sick besieged the Cork Union Workhouse and the city's hospitals, food depots and soup kitchens. Numbers in institutions mounted rapidly and overcrowding soon became both a logistical and public-health problem. By the end of January 1847 there were 5,309 individuals in the workhouse, almost twice its intended capacity, and 1,480 of them were sick, mostly from fever or dysentery. There had been 91 deaths in the workhouse in the last week of January, a figure that increased to 164 for the second week in February and continued to rise inexorably in the following weeks.[12] The huge increase in typhus and relapsing fever in the city in the opening months of 1847 obliged the Cork Fever Hospital to refuse any further admissions from the workhouse and in February the North Infirmary was converted from a general hospital into one catering solely for individuals suffering from fever and other contagious diseases.

The high mortality in the workhouse prompted the Central Board of Health in Dublin to order an inquiry into its causes. Dr Stephens, the board's medical inspector, concluded that the debilitated or dying condition of the poor on admission and gross overcrowding were responsible for the unacceptably high number of deaths. The Poor Law Commission in Dublin, on the advice of the Central Board of Health, informed the Cork Board of Guardians that it was essential to reduce workhouse numbers and to suspend further admissions temporarily. The Central Board of Health and the Poor Law Commission in Dublin were gravely concerned about institutional overcrowding, fearing that it would lead to outbreaks of disease which would then spread to the general community. These fears were all too often realised during the Famine. Invariably, fever and other contagious diseases began among the poor and spread to the higher social classes,

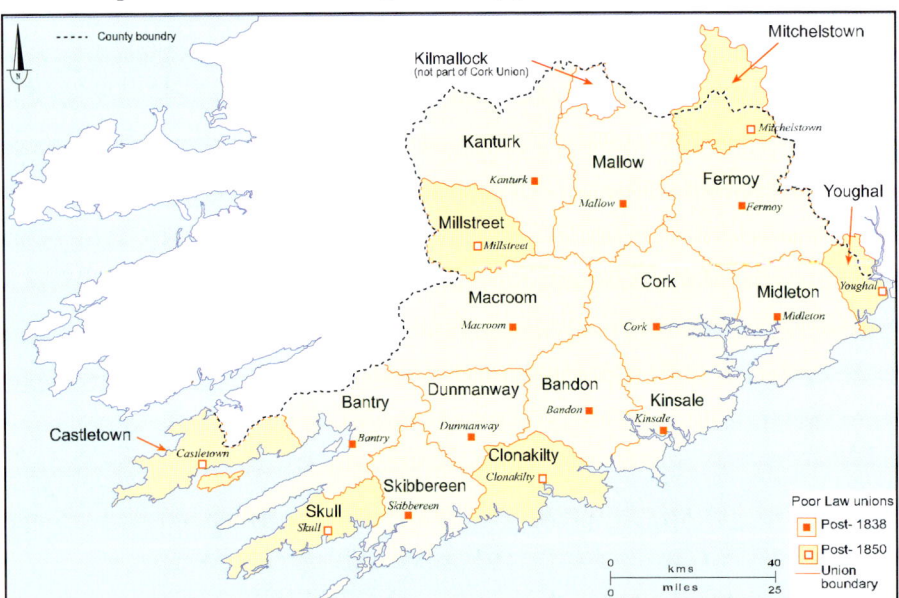

Fig. 3.68 Eleven Poor Law unions were established in County Cork under the 1838 Poor Law Act. Six additional unions were created in 1850.

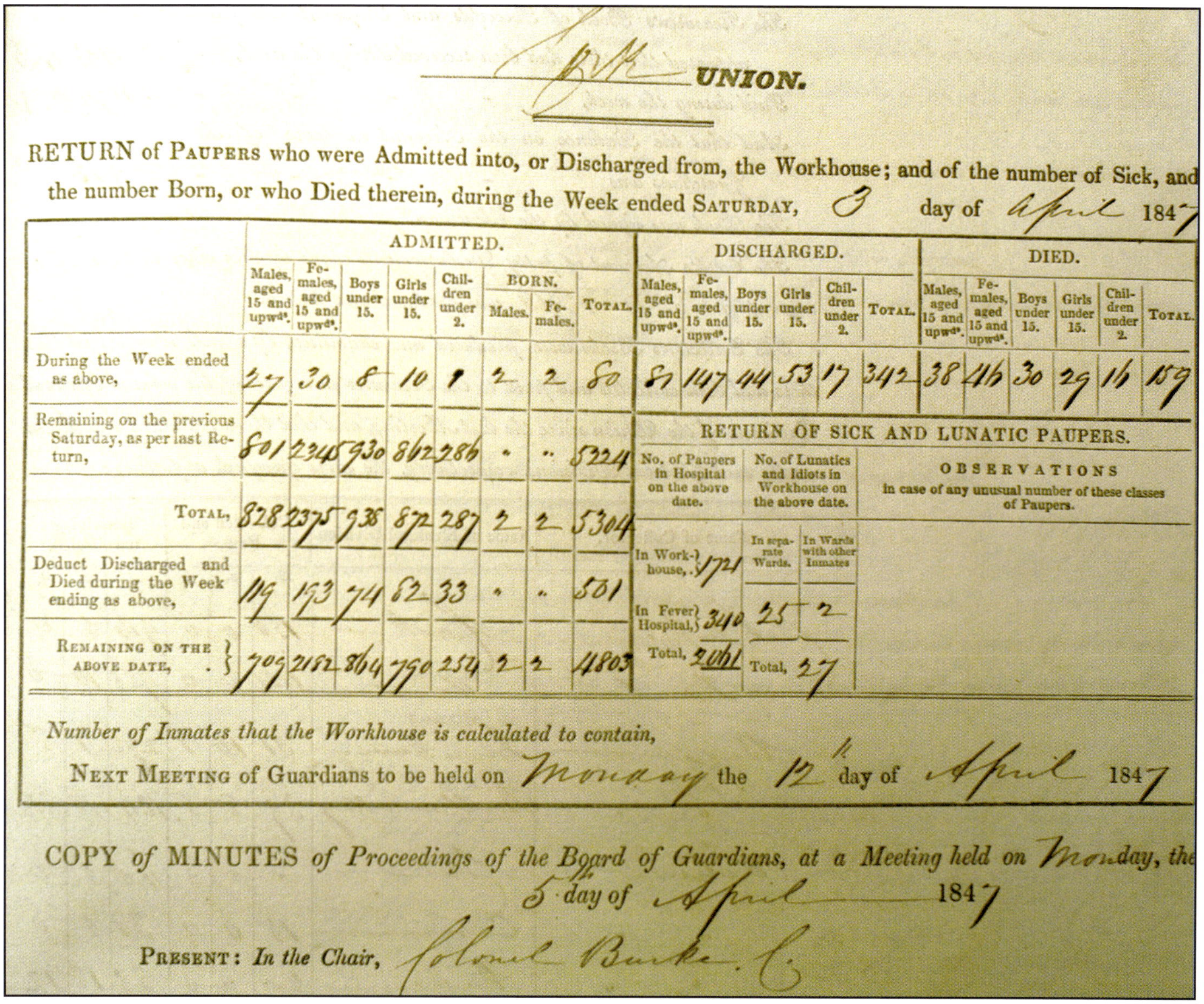

UNION.

RETURN of PAUPERS who were Admitted into, or Discharged from, the Workhouse; and of the number of Sick, and the number Born, or who Died therein, during the Week ended SATURDAY, 3 day of April 1847

	ADMITTED.								DISCHARGED.						DIED.					
	Males, aged 15 and upwds.	Females, aged 15 and upwds.	Boys under 15.	Girls under 15.	Children under 2.	BORN. Males.	BORN. Females.	TOTAL.	Males, aged 15 and upwds.	Females, aged 15 and upwds.	Boys under 15.	Girls under 15.	Children under 2.	TOTAL.	Males, aged 15 and upwds.	Females, aged 15 and upwds.	Boys under 15.	Girls under 15.	Children under 2.	TOTAL.
During the Week ended as above,	27	30	8	10	1	2	2	80	81	147	44	53	17	342	38	46	30	29	16	159

	Males, aged 15 and upwds.	Females, aged 15 and upwds.	Boys under 15.	Girls under 15.	Children under 2.	BORN. Males.	BORN. Females.	TOTAL.
Remaining on the previous Saturday, as per last Return,	801	2345	930	862	286	"	"	5224
TOTAL,	828	2375	938	872	287	2	2	5304
Deduct Discharged and Died during the Week ending as above,	119	193	74	82	33	"	"	501
REMAINING ON THE ABOVE DATE,	709	2182	864	790	254	2	2	4803

RETURN OF SICK AND LUNATIC PAUPERS.

No. of Paupers in Hospital on the above date.		No. of Lunatics and Idiots in Workhouse on the above date.		OBSERVATIONS in case of any unusual number of these classes of Paupers.
		In separate Wards.	In Wards with other Inmates	
In Workhouse,	1721			
In Fever Hospital,	340	25	2	
Total,	2061	Total,	27	

Number of Inmates that the Workhouse is calculated to contain,

NEXT MEETING of Guardians to be held on Monday the 12th day of April 1847

COPY of MINUTES *of Proceedings of the Board of Guardians, at a Meeting held on* Monday, the 5 *day of* April 1847

PRESENT: *In the Chair,* Colonel Burke. C.

Fig. 3.69 An extract from the Minute Book of the Cork Poor Law Union showing the number of inmates in the workhouse on 3 April 1847. (Source: Cork Archives Institute.)

among whom disease generally proved more lethal, possibly because of a lack of acquired immunity. The Poor Law Commission concluded that, if the present numbers were maintained in the workhouse, the institution would become a source of disease and contagion for the city and environs. On 29 March 1847, after the deaths of 757 inmates during the course of the month, the guardians closed the workhouse against further admissions until 'the physicians report the house in a wholesome and healthy state'.[13]

To relieve the pressure on the workhouse and the city's hospitals, auxiliary workhouses and temporary fever facilities were established. A fever hospital for the southside of the city was opened at Cat Fort (the former Orphan Asylum) on 19 April 1847 and another, containing 330 beds, in Barrack Street. Fever sheds were also erected at the latter location and at the Cork Fever Hospital. By the end of May 1847 there were 228 patients in the Fever Hospital, 120 in the North Infirmary, 118 in Cat Fort, 172 in the Barrack Street hospital and 32 in the sheds. By early July, the patients in the various fever facilities had increased to 845. Numbers in the different institutions continued to swell for the remainder of 1847 and during the following years, reflecting the worsening famine crisis. For instance, there were 7,015 individuals in the workhouse and its auxiliaries in June 1849, after which the number decreased steadily. In the same year, 4,149 patients were admitted to the temporary fever hospital in Barrack Street, 777 of whom died.[14]

The expansion of workhouse and hospital accommodation to meet the continuing crisis was an enormous and increasingly resented burden on the

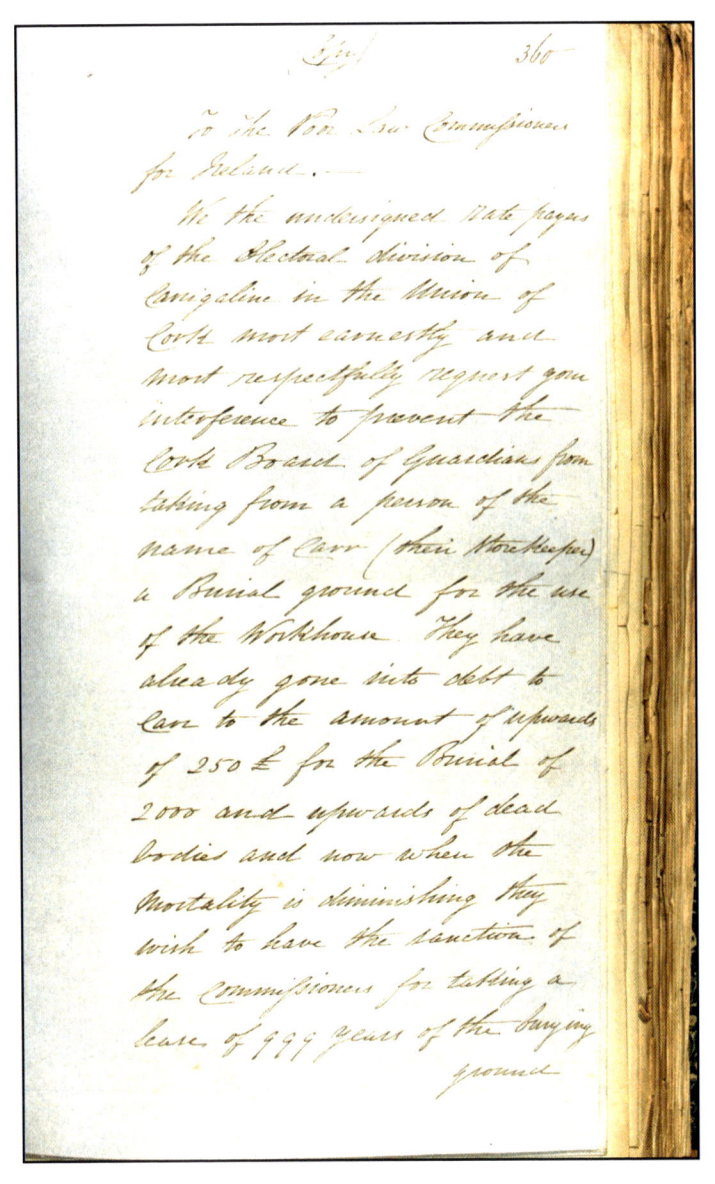

Fig. 3.70 An extract from the Minute Book of the Cork Poor Law Union relating to the acquisition of burial grounds on the Carrigaline Road (Carr's Hill). (Source: Cork Archives Institute.)

men, to be placed at the principal entrances to this city, to prevent the further influx of country paupers'.[15] The mayor's acquiescence to both requests prompted Fr Mathew to complain to the government of the authorities' 'heartless and cruel' response to the Famine, claiming that it was distinctly contrary to the express word of God. According to Fr Mathew, strangers who were caught begging for food were confined without sustenance in an open market overnight, after which they were handed over to the constables, taken five or six miles from the city and given a modest quantity of bread to sustain them. Fr Mathew, in a reference to the large amount of aid that was flowing into the country from overseas, observed: 'We are all strangers to the benevolent of all countries and thankfully receive what we refuse to the famine-stricken natives of our own country.'[16]

The high mortality that occurred in Cork put enormous pressure on the city's cemeteries and the proper disposal of the dead created both an ethical and an additional public-health problem. In the workhouse alone, 5,142 individuals died between 1846 and 1848, 3,329 of them in 1847, which Dr Callanan described as an 'appalling return'.[17] At the beginning of June 1847 St Joseph's Cemetery was closed to further interments and the Cork Relief Committee began to send corpses from the city's northside to Curraghkippane Cemetery and arranged for the opening of a new graveyard at Carr's Hill on the road between Douglas and Carrigaline. Here, the volume and manner of interment gave rise to public disquiet and complaints.[18] In late October 1847, the mayor, aldermen and burgesses of Cork complained to the lord lieutenant about the shortage of burial space in the city, observing that attempts to establish temporary burial grounds had provoked breaches of the peace because of fears that they would lead to the spread of disease.[19]

ratepayers' pockets. In particular, migrants from the country, individuals who were not native to the Cork Poor Law Union, met with hostility, fear and rejection. The agency of fever and other diseases was not discovered until later in the nineteenth century, but there was an empirical awareness that such diseases were contagious, and mendicants and vagrants were blamed for the spread of disease. A meeting of church wardens, officers of health and magistrates in the city on 23 April 1847 sought 'to diminish the very great number of strolling beggars who infest Cork'. The meeting called on the mayor to reactivate legislation passed in 1819 that allowed for the expulsion of infected persons and paupers from the city in order to prevent contagion. In addition, the meeting requested the civic authorities 'to organise a staff of able bodied and if possible well disciplined

DEMOGRAPHIC TOLL

In the late 1840s and early 1850s, the Irish people were confronted with a catastrophe of unprecedented dimensions and with morbidity and mortality on a scale never before recorded. The poorest and most vulnerable were stripped of entitlement and choice. For the more advantaged, there was the option of flight and some two million emigrated from Ireland in the decade 1845–1855. Cork was an important emigrant port in the pre-Famine period, drawing prospective emigrants from all of the Munster counties and beyond. However, the scale of emigration changed with the onset of the Famine. Hundreds arrived in the city every week from mid-1846 onwards. On 15 April 1847 the *Cork Examiner* reported:

The quays are crowded every day with the peasantry from all quarters of the country, who are emigrating to America, both direct from this port and 'cross channel' to Liverpool, as the agents here cannot produce enough of ships to convey the people from this unhappy country. Two vessels – the *Fagabelac* and *Coolock* – were despatched this week, the former with 208, the latter with 110 passengers. There are two other ships on the berth – the *Wandsworth* for Quebec, and the *Victory* for New York; both are intended to sail on Tuesday next. There are nearly 1200 passengers booked in these vessels.[20]

Conditions in the port for intending passengers were generally appalling. John Besnard, who had twenty years' experience of the emigrant trade, estimated that travellers spent nine days in the city before embarking, adding that they lodged 'in the lowest and filthiest houses in the city' because they were the cheapest.[21] Duross, the constable in charge of passenger regulation in the port from 1849, described how runners:

> would fall in with the emigrant as soon as he comes to town; and the runner brings him to the emigration broker; and the emigration broker generally gives from 1s to 2s for each passenger brought to him. The runner then brings him to the grocer, where he gets from 1s 8d. to 3s in the pound, according to whatever purchases the emigrant makes; then to the fish store, then to the bacon store, and the bakery.[22]

Besnard was critical of these runners, observing that they were 'just as unprincipled, but not so numerous, as the sharks who prey upon the whole of the emigrants at Liverpool'.[23]

Fr Mathew, a severe critic of the emigrant trade, argued that many of the individuals departing from Cork were totally unprepared for the sea journey, particularly in relation to the amount of provisions they carried with them for the voyage:

> Very painful instances came before me during the prevalence of fever in Cork, with respect to the amount of sea stores, which these people had. Many of the emigrants, especially from Kerry, remained in Cork till their funds were exhausted; some got sick and died: their boxes with sea stores were left in my care till their friends sent for them; it was afflicting to see the small provision they had made for the voyage, perhaps a little oatmeal, a pig's head, or half a pig's head, and a little tea and sugar.[24]

Those who were familiar with the emigrant trade in Cork agreed that shopkeepers in the city charged an exorbitant price for provisions, which were generally of poor quality. Duross, assessing the difficulties facing passengers departing from Cork, concluded: 'there is a general impression that the emigrants are defrauded from the date they start from their homes until they are at sea'.[25] The volume of direct emigration from Cork during the years 1845–1851 is estimated at 72,000,[26] and was much larger than from any other Irish port, while Cork emigration via Liverpool averaged at least 25,000 a year in mid-century.[27]

Nationally, the numbers who died during the Famine years were on a par with those who emigrated. Between 1841 and 1851 the population of County Cork declined from 854,118 to 649,903, or by almost 24 per cent, although the city's population increased from 80,720 to 85,745 as a result of the influx of rural migrants.[28] The demographic impact was the most dramatic and enduring of the Famine's seismic shocks, but there were others, political, social and economic, that were to rumble for the remainder of the nineteenth century and into the next.

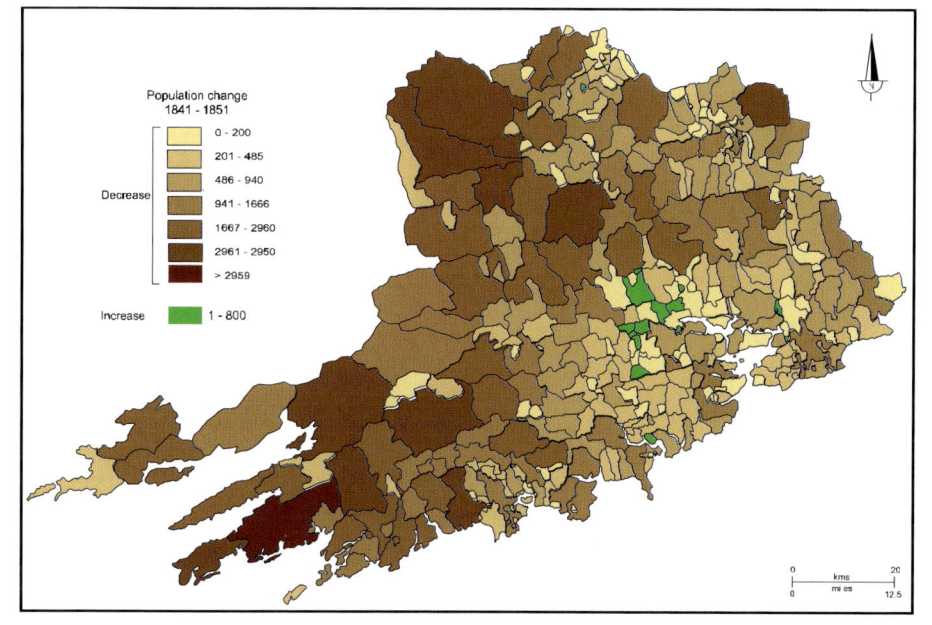

Fig. 3.71 Population decline, County Cork, 1841–1851. (Source: 1841 and 1851 census.)

Queenstown/Cobh: An Emigrant Port

Marita Foster

In 1859, the Inman Line, one of the major steamship companies carrying emigrants on the North Atlantic route, began a regular call at Queenstown, with ships calling on the day following departure from Liverpool.[1] This marked the beginning of the town's association with the transatlantic steamship companies involved in the emigrant trade, an association that continued until 1968 when the Cunard Line closed its Cobh office.[2] During the intervening years, the majority of passengers departing from the town were emigrants destined for the United States of America. The passenger trade was hugely important for the town, as services developed to cater for travellers who passed through the port. Indeed much of the town's prosperity in the second half of the nineteenth century and during a considerable part of the twentieth century was due to the emigrant/passenger trade.

1859–1899

The Inman Line was followed by the Cunard Line later in 1859 when the company's ship, *Canada*, sailing from Liverpool for Boston, began a fortnightly call at Queenstown, outwards and homewards. By 1875 steamships of the Inman, Cunard, National, White Star, Guion, American and Allan lines were calling at the town. All offered passage to the United States, normally on a weekly basis, while the Allan Line operated a twice-weekly sailing to Canada. The number of shipping companies in Queenstown fluctuated throughout the remainder of the nineteenth century, but there were always at least half a dozen companies competing for emigrant traffic. The demand for passage was significant, particularly from April to September, when hundreds of emigrants departed from Queenstown on a weekly basis. In periods of heavy emigration, such as 1863–1866 and 1880–1883, the extent of the exodus was the subject of newspaper comment. In April 1866 the *Cork Examiner* reported:

> The emigration season opened this year much earlier than usual, and, up to the present, it has surpassed in the number of emigrants, any of the last few seasons ... The number that actually departed from Queenstown for America is estimated at 12,000 to 14,000 souls, or nearly a thousand per week ... The numbers have varied according to circumstances. Thus, while in one week not more than six hundred departed, during last week, when there were no less than seven steamers leaving, fully two thousand souls embarked at this port – the vast majority of these being the young, strong, and healthy children of toil.[3]

In May 1883 the newspaper again referred to the scale of emigration:

> The exodus of our people via Queenstown continues at an extremely high rate. Not less than nine or ten steamers per week now call at this port for passengers, and despite the fact that the greater number of them are vessels of very large size and great capacity for emigrants, the accommodation falls somewhat short of the demand. Since yesterday week eight steamers have called, and though nearly every one took very full complements, still some were left behind.[4]

STEAMSHIP COMPANIES AND THEIR AGENTS

The steamship companies were represented by agents throughout the country, as was noted by the *Cork Examiner*:

> No town of importance is without its shipping agent or passenger broker, whose office is now as much an institution of the place as the post office or the grocer's shop. Once the fortunate possessor of the few pounds required to pay his fare and provide the scanty outfit necessary, the intending emigrant repairs to the agent and books for the first steamer in which a berth can be had.[5]

In Queenstown the steamship companies' agents were responsible for the embarkation of passengers and baggage and the provisioning of ships. The offices of the agents were located in the centre of the town – of the six emigration agents listed in *Guy's Directory* in 1886, four were located in Scott's Square, one on Lynch's Quay and one on West Beach.[6] The emigration agents were important residents of the town, involved in a lucrative trade. These agents had numerous other interests. They were representatives of marine insurance companies, of shipping companies; some were consuls for various countries, others owned lodging

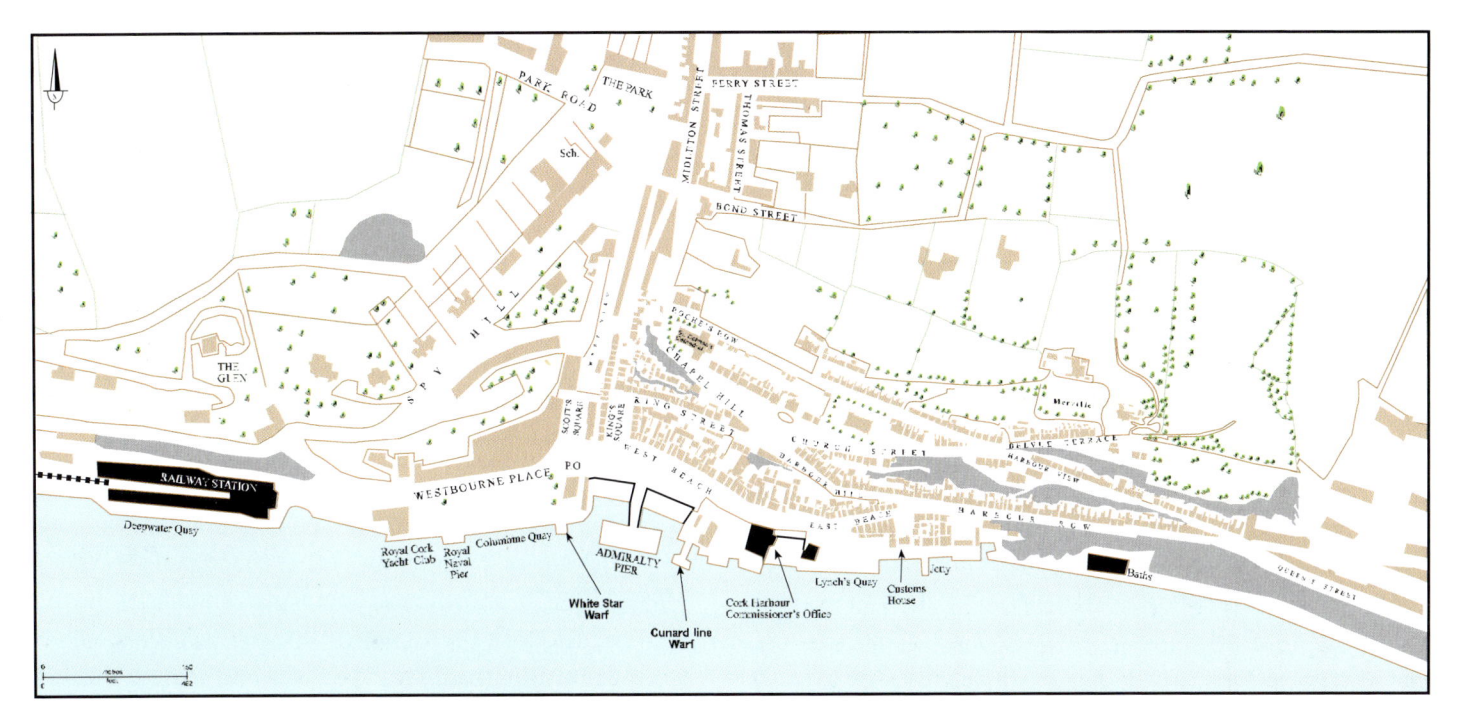

Fig. 3.72 Map of Queenstown.

houses, while still others were justices of the peace. They also played a pivotal role in the development of Queenstown in the second half of the nineteenth century.

James Scott and Co. was the principal emigration/shipping agency in Queenstown and the Scott family initiated many improvements in the town. Philip Scott was involved in the construction of Bellevue and King's Terraces, the Upper and Lower Parks, Westbourne and Scott's Square. The Seymours, another prominent family engaged in the shipping and emigrant trades, were responsible for the construction of fine terraces (St Maur's, Athenian and Wilmount) located at the eastern end of the town. The jetties and quays whence emigrants embarked were built on behalf of the shipping companies, most notably the Inman Quay, a project undertaken by William Inman, one of the founders of the shipping line which bore his name.[7]

The offices of the emigration agents were located close to the railway station. The first passenger train on the Cork–Queenstown railway line ran on 10 March 1862 and the railway played a vital role in emigration. Emigrants travelled to the town from all over the country, particularly from the south and west, and many made the journey by rail. In 1866, a report noted:

> By train and steamer they hurry on to Queenstown, dropping in almost incessantly, yet in largest numbers on the day immediately preceding the departure of a steamer. At the stations and landing places they are met by a crowd of nondescripts, mostly old men and ragged boys, who, for what to some would appear an exorbitant remuneration, become the *chaperons* [sic] of the emigrants, pilot them to the offices of the agents for the particular steamers by which they are to proceed, and cart their luggage to the stores in which it is to be temporarily deposited. Having presented their tickets at the agent's office and seen their luggage safely stowed away, they have now to while away the anxious interval till the arrival of the steamer, as best they can.[8]

'RUNNERS' AND LODGING HOUSES
Emigrant runners (touts) were also employed by lodging-house keepers to 'escort' emigrants to their respective premises:

> The proprietors of the houses into which emigrants are taken to lodge, have in their employ persons, male and female, who visit the railway station to attend on emigrants on arrival and guide them to their establishments. The persons thus employed at Queenstown seem to have come to a common understanding among themselves whereby contentions over the persons of arriving emigrants are avoided on the arrival of a train.[9]

Runners, found in every emigrant port, had a poor reputation and were frequently accused of defrauding emigrants. A system of licensing and registering emigrant runners was established under the Passenger Act of 1855.

The Merchant Shipping Act of 1894 permitted the forfeiture of a runner's licence on the grounds of misconduct.[10]

Lodging houses were located along the front of the town in Westbourne Place, Scott's Square, King's Square, Lynch's Quay, Harbour Row, King's Bench and Queen Street, within walking distance of the railway station, the offices of the emigration agents and the jetties and quays. Referring to accommodation available in the town in the 1860s, the *Cork Examiner* commented:

> When night comes, shelter is found in the numerous lodging houses, which have become one of the principal sources of income to the humbler townspeople. For a few pence, sleeping accommodation is provided, generally of a sufficiently comfortable and cleanly character, but sometimes, too, of a very meagre and unsatisfactory kind. For a long time after these thousands of strangers first began to crowd into the town, the places in which they were lodged were a gross scandal to a civilized community. Regardless of health, and often of decency, and only anxious to grasp at the opportunity presented of making money, the owners of these premises literally crammed their small, ill ventilated rooms with persons of both sexes, young and old, married and single. Now the system is much improved, thanks to the operation of the provision of the Common Lodging House Act, administered by the local Board of Town Commissioners.[11]

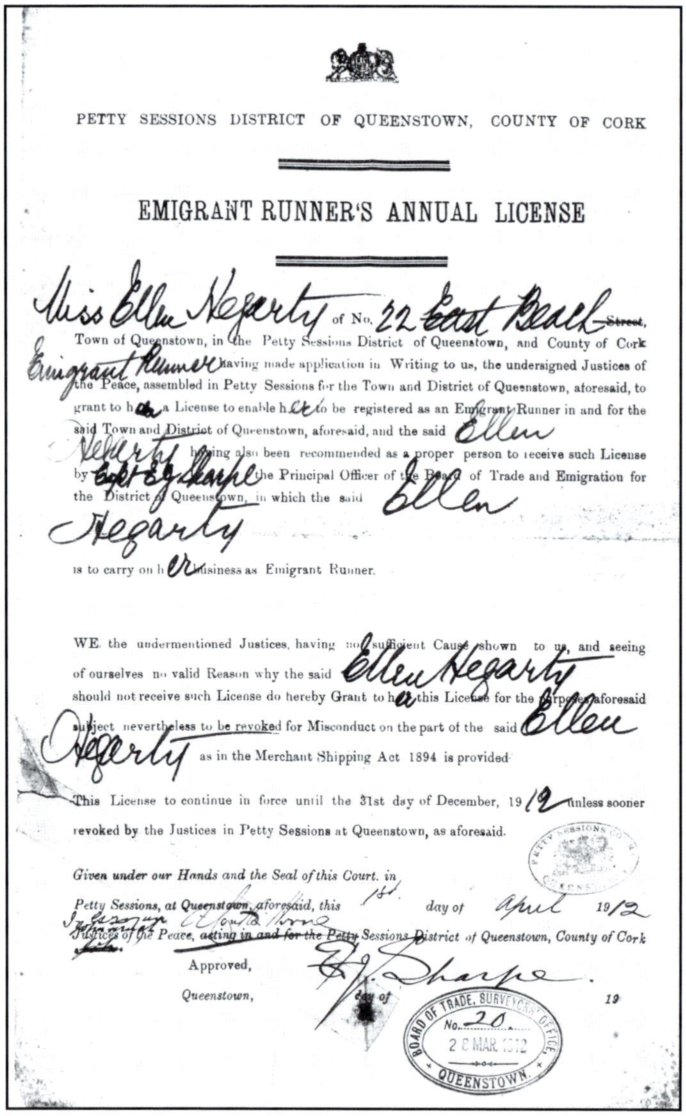

PETTY SESSIONS DISTRICT OF QUEENSTOWN, COUNTY OF CORK

EMIGRANT RUNNER'S ANNUAL LICENSE

Miss Ellen Hegarty of No. 22 East Beach Street, Town of Queenstown, in the Petty Sessions District of Queenstown, and County of Cork Emigrant Runner having made application in Writing to us, the undersigned Justices of the Peace, assembled in Petty Sessions for the Town and District of Queenstown, aforesaid, to grant to her a License to enable her to be registered as an Emigrant Runner in and for the said Town and District of Queenstown, aforesaid, and the said Ellen Hegarty having also been recommended as a proper person to receive such License by Capt E J Sharpe the Principal Officer of the Board of Trade and Emigration for the District of Queenstown, in which the said Ellen Hegarty is to carry on her business as Emigrant Runner.

WE the undermentioned Justices, having no sufficient Cause shown to us, and seeing of ourselves no valid Reason why the said Ellen Hegarty should not receive such License do hereby Grant to her this License for the purpose aforesaid subject nevertheless to be revoked for Misconduct on the part of the said Ellen Hegarty as in the Merchant Shipping Act 1894 is provided.

This License to continue in force until the 31st day of December, 1912 unless sooner revoked by the Justices in Petty Sessions at Queenstown, as aforesaid.

Given under our Hands and the Seal of this Court, in Petty Sessions, at Queenstown, aforesaid, this 1st *day of* April 1912

Justices of the Peace, acting in and for the Petty Sessions District of Queenstown, County of Cork

Approved, E J Sharpe

Queenstown, day of 19

BOARD OF TRADE, SURVEYOR'S OFFICE No. 20 2 MAR 1912 QUEENSTOWN

Fig. 3.73 An Emigrant Runner's Annual Licence (1912), granted to Ms Ellen Hegarty of 22 East Beach Street.

A Board of Trade report on the *State of lodging houses in Queenstown* published in 1882 claimed that 'there is no system of licensing the lodging-houses, no organised system of inspecting or registering them, no system of taking returns of the numbers they are fit to accommodate, nor of the numbers actually on the premises at any one time'.[12] The report was critical of many of the lodging houses in the town (it listed 36 lodging houses catering for emigrants):

> Four or five men are sometimes put into one bed, while others lie about the floor, and that 26 people have been known to lie in a room of about 17 feet by 10 feet, but emigrants do not in the busy season occupy during the whole night even these closely-packed places . . . While some of the emigrants snatch an hour or two of rest, others are afforded facilities elsewhere for singing and dancing, so that the same bed or floor place may be occupied by different persons during the 24 hours.[13]

These observations were supported by Dr Brodie, the Board Inspector:

> When the beds in the lodging-houses are full, an itinerant musician is introduced to attract the attention of the 'sleepers', who are encouraged to rise and join the dance in which those who have been unable to obtain sleeping accommodation are engaged. And when this ruse has succeeded in getting those in bed to vacate their places, the beds are then occupied by those who first commenced the dancing, so that the same bed or floor place may be occupied by different persons during the night. It is therefore not difficult to comprehend the fearful state of overcrowding that must necessarily exist, and consequent poisonous state of the air.[14]

As a result of the ensuing bad publicity, the Town Commissioners reluctantly agreed to adopt bye-laws

Fig. 3.74 West Beach, Queenstown/Cobh, early 1880s. In the foreground is Charlotte Grace O'Brien's Emigrants' Home, 7 West Beach. (Photo: Lawrence Collection, reproduced courtesy of the National Library of Ireland.)

implementing the lodging-house clauses of the Public Health Act of 1878. In 1883, the *Cork Examiner* referred to the impact of the bye-laws:

> The lodging houses of Queenstown are, on the whole, considerably improved. The agitation that was very properly set up a few years ago, has, I believe, to a great extent removed overcrowding and every lodging house must be licensed and the number of lodgers for each room be stated in a card hung on the walls.[15]

In an attempt to provide comfortable accommodation at a reasonable rate to emigrants passing though Queenstown during the early 1880s, Charlotte Grace O'Brien (daughter of William Smith O'Brien) opened the Emigrants' Home, situated at 7 West Beach. The boarding house could accommodate 105 emigrants and the charge was two shillings a night for a 'good supper, bed, breakfast and thorough protection'.[16] The establishment of the Emigrants' Home was part of O'Brien's crusade to improve conditions for Irish emigrants, particularly female emigrants. In 1881, following a tour of the White Star Line's ship *Germanic* in Queenstown, she criticised conditions for steerage passengers in the *Pall Mall Gazette*. The subsequent inquiry found her allegations were without foundation, but nevertheless recommended improvements to sanitary facilities and to the arrangements regarding the supervision of single women while on board ship.

Such controversies did not deter prospective emigrants. Thousands continued to leave Ireland on an annual basis. Between 1876 and 1899, over 670,000 emigrants departed through the port, with the vast majority destined for the United States.

1900–1968

Queenstown's position as the premier port of departure for emigrants was maintained throughout the early decades of the twentieth century, although the outbreak of the First World War meant an end to the passenger trade for the duration of the hostilities. Immigration restrictions imposed by the US in the 1920s resulted in a decline in numbers emigrating from Ireland to that country. Despite the restrictions, the liners continued to call at Cobh. Tourists

Fig. 3.75 The tender *Blarney* approaching the Deep Water Quay, Cobh, 1954. (Photo: reproduced by permission of Luke Cassidy, Cobh.)

now made up a significant proportion of the passengers being carried on the North Atlantic route; passengers embarking and disembarking at the port were often former emigrants who had returned home on holiday, many for the first time since their original departure from Ireland. However, the global recession of the 1930s impacted on the emigrant and tourist trade and on the shipping companies. In 1934, the Cunard and White Star lines merged to form the Cunard–White Star Line. This merger resulted in the closure of Cunard's office in Cobh and the transfer of business and staff to the White Star Line's office beside the post office.

In 1939, six companies were still carrying passengers, mail and cargo to and from the port – Anchor Line, Cunard–White Star Line, French Line, Hamburg–America Line, North German Lloyd Line and United States Lines. The Second World War brought an end to the transatlantic emigrant and tourist trade. Referring to the expected impact of the war on the town, the *Cork Examiner* commented:

> The shipping industry will be hard hit here by the outbreak of hostilities and that at a time when our harbour is again coming in to its own as the premier port of call for trans-Atlantic liners. Soon after the outbreak of the Great War, liners ceased to call here, either to embark or disembark passengers and hostilities had ended some considerable time before resuming their calls here and disemployment was rife amongst the shipping community in consequence, and history is likely to repeat itself in the present instance. Hotels and boarding houses will suffer through lack of ocean going travellers and while this was compensated for during the Great War by the influx of British naval and army officers' wives and families coming over here to stay with their husbands, there is no compensatory factor in the present case.[17]

1946 saw the resumption of the transatlantic liner calls at Cobh, with almost 2,300 passengers embarking from the port during that year. During the 1950s and early 1960s thousands of emigrants, mainly from the west and midlands, departed for the United States.[18] The decline of the linen industry in Northern Ireland resulted in the emigration through Cobh of large numbers of textile workers and their families to Canada. Tourist traffic became increasingly significant. However, from 1956 onwards the number of people embarking at Cobh was in decline, falling from 11,783 in that year to 5,156 in 1964. Competition from the airlines was primarily responsible for the decline: one by one the shipping companies withdrew from the town, starting with the closure of the United States Lines' office in 1964:

> The US Lines' Cobh office at Westbourne Place, closed its doors for the last time last evening, following the company's decision to sell the *America* and to abandon the Irish trans-Atlantic passenger service. No ceremony marked the breaking of the thirty five years' connection with the port, the staff quietly slipping away at their scheduled hour, as they would on a normal working day.[19]

Cunard, which began its regular call to Cobh in 1859, was the last company to withdraw from the town, closing its office in 1968. Thus ended Cobh's long association with the emigrant trade.

Fig. 3.76 Intending passengers outside the United States Lines' Office, 12 Westbourne Place, Cobh, *c.* 1950. (Photo: The Wilson Collection, Ireland, reproduced by permission of Robert Wilson, Cobh.)

Fig. 3.77 Aerial view of Cobh. (Photo: Tomás Tyner.)

New Arrivals: Cork's Jewish Community

John Crowley

Cork's Jewish community peaked at the turn of the last century. This community had its origins principally in Lithuanian Jewry. The Jews who arrived in the city in the latter decades of the nineteenth century were fleeing persecution in their own country. Those who settled in Cork came 'almost exclusively from the districts of Vilna and Kovno' – the majority from a small village called Akmijan.[1] On arrival in Cork they gravitated to a part of the city near Albert Road that would later become colloquially known as 'Jewtown'. It is said that the early refugees committed the error of mistaking Cork for New York. However apocryphal the story, the disappointment it induced amongst the new arrivals did not necessitate them boarding a second ship to find their true destination. Cork city was in the grip of an economic slump. The emigrant ship which had proved to be an escape from the harsh conditions of life for many Cork people now delivered a group of Lithuanian Jews who would eventually form a community in the heart of an already overcrowded city.

Unlike Limerick, where the Jewish community found itself in conflict with the local population, the Cork Jews, after some early altercations, soon acquired a way of living with their new neighbours. The pogrom in Limerick, which had been sparked off by the rabid sermon of a local Redemptorist priest, was widely condemned, but it ultimately compromised Limerick's Jewish community. Cork society in the latter half of the nineteenth century was strongly polarised, where the wealthy lifestyle of the few

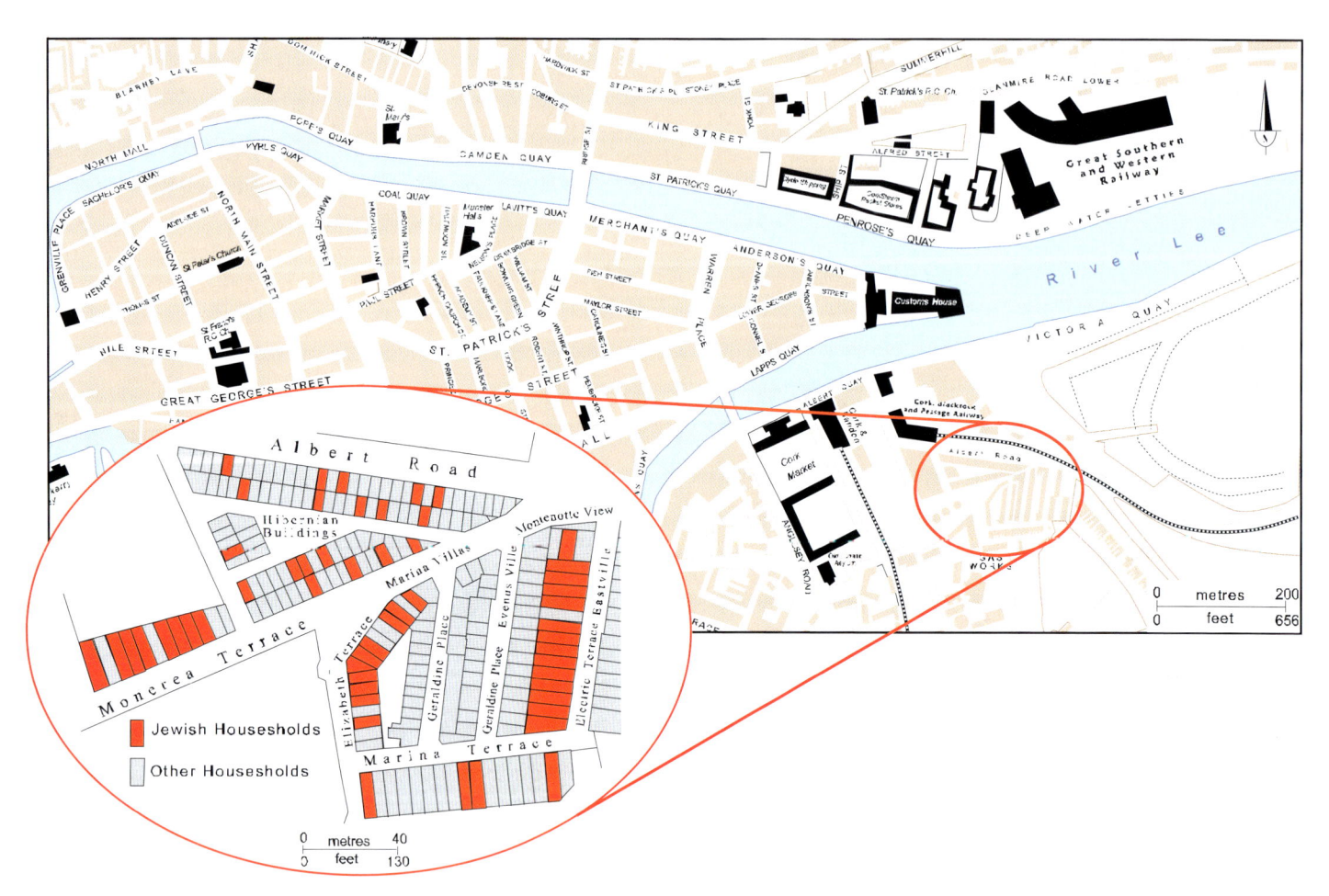

Fig. 3.78 Hibernian Buildings and environs ('Jewtown') in 1901.

contrasted with the poverty of many. The intrusion of an alien people was bound to be seen as unwelcome competition in a city where the poorer classes eked out a precarious existence. The failing Irish economy would almost inevitably elevate the Jewish people to the mantle of competitors, a fact recognised in a letter to *The Times* in 1888 by the then Lord Mayor of Cork, John O'Brien:

> They like so many of my race are strangers in a strange land and the little wonder is that the rich and influential leaders in England, the most powerful body for its members in the world should be unable to divert their co-religionists from trying their fortune in an impoverished land where the natives are compelled to hasten from at the rate of a hundred thousand per annum and in which the struggle for existence among those who remain is so keen and so bitter.[2]

Even in the face of such misgivings, the Jewish community in Cork would quickly establish itself and increase in number.

THE COMMUNITY IN THE EARLY TWENTIETH CENTURY

The census manuscripts for 1901 and 1911 afford us an opportunity to explore the largely hidden world of these refugees, in that they furnish us with a snapshot view of the community on census night. The census material for the Clein family of 38 Hibernian Buildings reveals how quickly the new arrivals adapted to their surroundings after the initial dislocation. Ester Clein, the head of household, could neither read nor write. However, the first three children, Ben (22), Joseph (20) and James (13), were all registered as literate and engaged full-time in the peddling trade. Lena Clein, aged 14, listed dressmaking as her occupation. The three youngest children were attending school in the synagogue on the South Terrace under the supervision of Rev Joseph Myers. Attempts by the community to enlist financial support from the more prosperous Jewish communities in Britain to build a Jewish school in the city failed, with the result that Jewish children mingled with their Irish counterparts in local Catholic and Protestant schools. The community was gradually becoming more affluent. The Steinberg family of 82 Hibernian Buildings could afford the luxury of a general servant.

Peddling was the source of much-needed income in the community and also provided a means of integration with the locals. Each Jewish family engaged in the selling of their wares along selected routes in the city and county. Corkonians were glad of the service proffered by the peddler. The churlish taunts of 'Jewman' with its peculiar Irish flavour took root in the years that followed. The often malign image of the Jewish peddler stemmed in part from the determination of the emigrant to provide for his family in an environment that offered little succour. Such a lifestyle presupposed a certain discipline that did not go unnoticed amongst their Cork neighbours. While the circumstances of their arrival in Cork may have been fortuitous, the success of the community in the peddling trade owed little to chance. Nobody could really place a barrier to the march of the Jewish peddler. As Joseph Levi claimed, 'I was never molested but was treated by both Fenian and policeman with the same respect'.[3]

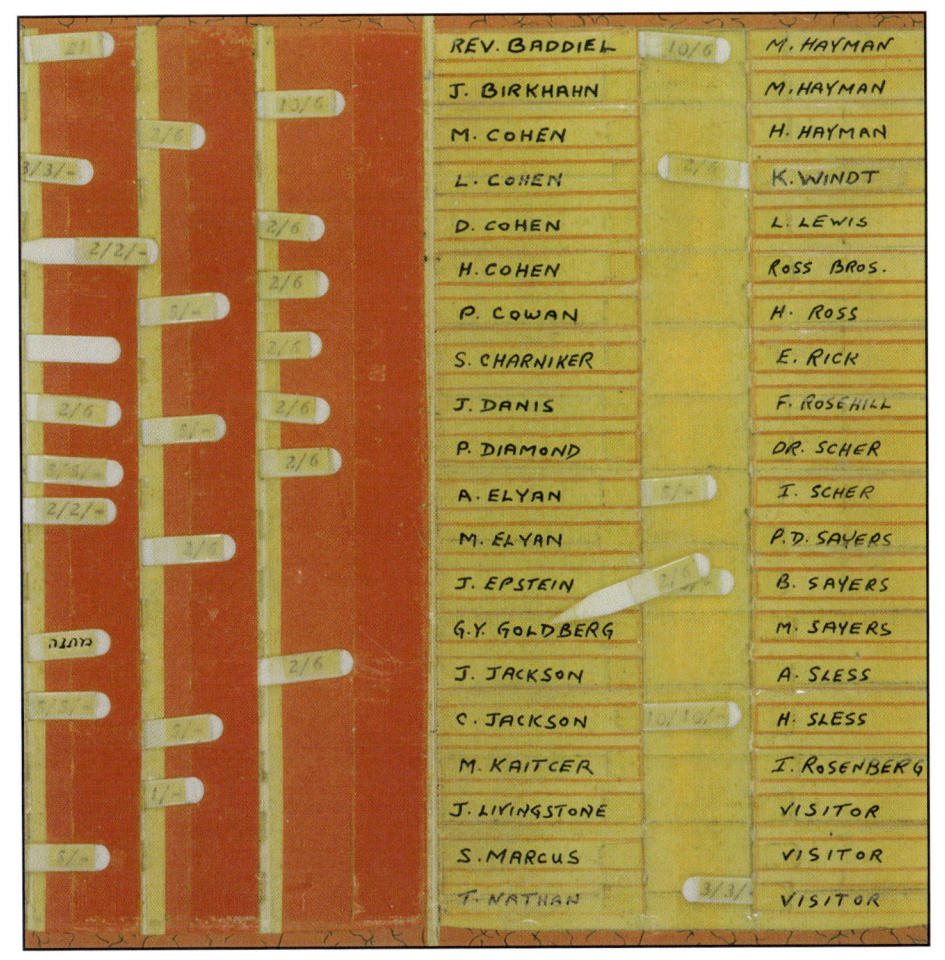

Fig. 3.79 Donation table, Cork Synagogue, *c.* 1960. The Jewish religion did not allow any financial transactions to take place on the Sabbath Day. Hence donations took the form of a pledge. The table is revealing insofar as it lists many familiar Jewish family names. (Source: The Irish Jewish Museum.)

Fig. 3.80 Gerald Goldberg receiving his chain of office in 1977 from outgoing Lord Mayor Seán French. (Photo: *Irish Examiner*.)

community declined. Eleven families remained in 'Jewtown', down from a peak of 55 in 1901. The lack of employment opportunities for young Jews as well as problems finding marriage partners contributed to the decline. Some families joined the larger Dublin community, while others emigrated to Britain and the United States. News of a mining boom in South Africa also prompted a number to seek their fortunes there. Given the demographic structure of the community in 1901 and its youthful disposition, such a migration flow was certainly no surprise. Of those families who remained in Cork, a community of sorts would emerge centred on the Mardyke, Western Road, College Road and Connaught Avenue.

Jewtown in every sense resembled a Lithuanian village. Those who had been neighbours in Akmijan contrived to be so again as family followed family. Thus many of the customs and traditions of village life remained intact. The custom of the marriage match was an integral part of Jewish village life. Many of the Jewish families who arrived in Cork knew each other well, some would say too well. The match and subsequent marriage contract was made between families who had known each other for many years. Each family literally breathed down the necks of their fellow Jews. A significant rift would develop in the early years that had its roots in village rivalries in Lithuania. The community split into two congregations. Such was the divided nature of the community that religious services were held in two separate houses, Number 2 and Number 10 respectively, on the South Terrace. Meyer Elyan (1844–1928), who came to Cork from Zhogger in 1881, served the congregation at Number 10. The two factions would eventually come together in the late 1920s, with the children of the feuding families soon intermarrying.

INTEGRATION AND EMIGRATION

As families grew wealthier, the prospect of leaving Jewtown became more real. The more affluent moved to other parts of the city, while some would leave the country altogether. The dual process of integration and sustained emigration precipitated in many ways the disintegration of Cork's Jewish community. *Guy's Directory* in 1939 reveals how rapidly the

Fig. 3.81 Synagogue on the South Terrace. (Photo: John Crowley.)

Fig. 3.82 Aerial view of Hibernian Buildings and environs. (Photo: Tomás Tyner.)

Here such families as the Jacksons, Epsteins, Sandlers, Marcus, Hertzogs and Sayers maintained a community that was based on a certain degree of territorial proximity, but even this was to wane when the impetus for emigration became more sustained in the years 1946–1961.

The climb up the social ladder was facilitated in no small way by the strong desire of parents to educate their young. A new professional class supplanted an older generation of peddlers, drapers, tailors and shopkeepers. Cork Jews such as David Birkhan, Ivor Scher and Gerald Goldberg attended the school run by the Presentation Brothers on the Mardyke. Goldberg would later coin the term 'Catholic-Jew'. This description captured for him the subtle nuances of his own educational upbringing.[4] A distinguished lawyer by profession, he would become the backbone of the Jewish community in Cork.[5] In 1977, Gerald Goldberg made his own mark on the history of the city by becoming its first Jewish Lord Mayor.

The community today has declined to a handful, but reminders of the city's Jewish heritage are still visible in the streetscape. The synagogue on the South Terrace remains a significant cultural landmark, while a public park near Hibernian Buildings bears the name 'Shalom' in honour of the Jewish community that once resided there.

23. CONFLICT AND WAR, 1914–1923

Donal Ó Drisceoil

'Rebel' Cork of 1919–1922 would have been hard to imagine in August 1914, as the city was engulfed by a wave of popular enthusiasm for the British war effort. 'It was red, white and blue everywhere', remembers Liam Ruiséal.[1] Soldiers marched past cheering crowds and people flocked to recruitment rallies as the Catholic and Protestant churches, the city's newspapers, political parties and all its public bodies united in support of Britain's war. Cork's employers declared that any employee joining the British Army would have their job held until their return. Although little dissent was visible, it did exist, and the cabal who offered it would emerge after the war as the dominant political force in the city and the vanguard of the military campaign against British rule.

This small but resilient group of 'Irish-Ireland' cultural nationalists and Irish Republican Brotherhood (IRB) activists, which included the likes of Tomás MacCurtain, Sean O'Hegarty and Terence MacSwiney, organised the founding meeting of the Cork branch of the Irish Volunteers in December 1913.[2] In the early months of 1914 several

Fig. 3.83 The British Army recruiting in Cork during the early years of the First World War. (Photo: *Irish Examiner*.)

dozen unarmed Cork Volunteers regularly drilled in the Cornmarket on Anglesea Street, peripheral to the mainstream of Cork politics (which was still dominated by the rival nationalist parties, the Redmondite Irish Parliamentary Party [IPP] and William O'Brien's All-For-Ireland League) and the consciousness of most Corkonians. When John Redmond declared his support for the Volunteers, it was transformed into a mass movement of over 100,000 nationwide. In Cork city and county, over 6,000 enlisted; 700 joined in the city in one week alone. This united nationalist movement was short-lived, however. Following the outbreak of war in August 1914, the organisation split, with the vast majority supporting the British war effort for the sake of Home Rule. The minority, about 300 in the county and 60 in the city, who resisted were mainly the original advanced nationalist Volunteers, who continued to drill and organise, while many of their former comrades joined the British Army. In September, Terence MacSwiney launched the Cork republican weekly *Fianna Fáil*, which, until its suppression in December, attempted in vain to convince Corkonians to resist the rallying call of 'England and Empire'.[3]

'LOYAL' CORK

Cork's position as one of the most important harbours in the British empire, its high concentration of troops and its role as a staging post meant that the city was immediately drawn into the war declared by Britain. Within 48 hours the first detachments of army reservists were boarding trains at Glanmire railway station, bound for the battlefields. British soldiers immediately began to commandeer horses from city businesses for military use, and buildings were leased or taken over. St Peter's (indoor) Market on Cornmarket Street, for example, was closed down and converted into an ammunition factory. Victoria Barracks (now Collins Barracks) on the city's northside was the headquarters of the British Army garrison. The barracks also became the administrative centre of the army recruitment drive and a

SALONIKA

Chorus:
So right away, so right away
So right away, Salonika
Right away, my soldier boy

My husband's in Salonika
And I wonder if he's dead
I wonder if he knows he has
A kid with a foxy head

Chorus

Now when the war is over
What will the slackers do
They'll be all around the soldiers
For the loan of a bob or two

Chorus

But when the war is over
What will the soldiers do
They'll be walking around with a
 leg-and-a-half
And the slackers will have two

Chorus

And they tax their pound o' butter
They tax their halfpenny bun
But still with all their taxes
They can't beat the bloody Hun

Chorus

And they tax th' old Coliseum
They tax St Mary's Hall
Why don't they tax the bobbies
Wi' their backs ag'in' the wall

Chorus

But when the war is over
What will the slackers do
For every kid in Americay
In Cork there will be two

Chorus

For they takes us out to Blarney
They lays us on the grass
They puts us in the family way
And leaves us on our arse

Chorus

There's lino in the parlour
And in the kitchen too
A glass-backed chiffonier
That we got from Dicky Glue

Chorus

And before that I got married
Sure I used to wear a shawl
But now the war is over
'Tis hanging in Jones' pawn

Chorus

And never marry a soldier
A sailor or a Marine
But keep your eye on the Sinn Féin
 boy
With his yellow, white and green

Chorus

Fig. 3.84 'Salonika'. The Greek port city of Salonika was a base for the British Army in the Balkans campaign from October 1915, including Corkmen serving in the 10th (Irish) Division. Slackers were men who refused to join up. The last two verses were probably added later, reflecting the changed circumstances at the war's end.

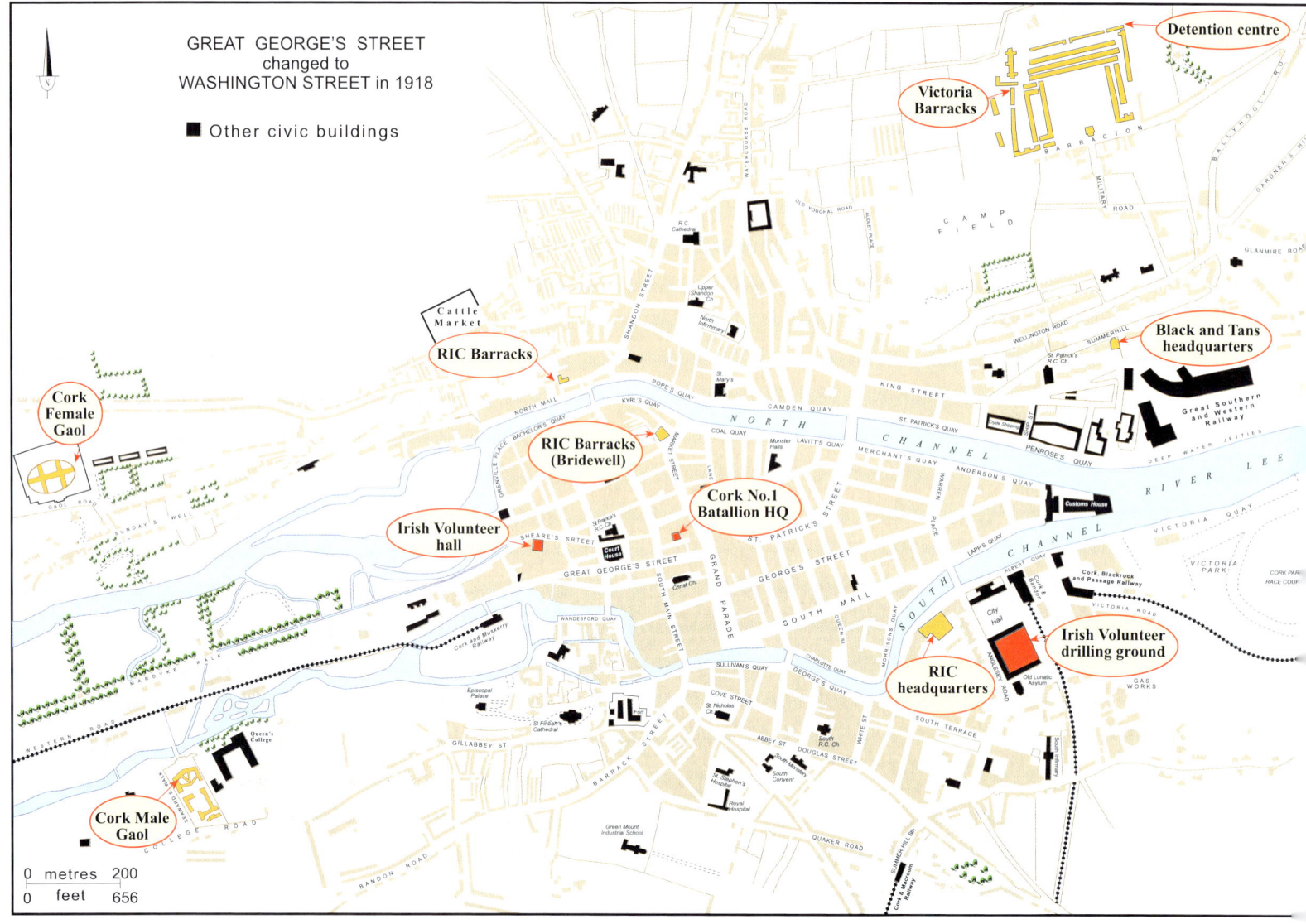

Fig. 3.85 Key locations in Cork city associated with republican and British forces, 1913–1921.

temporary base for the tens of thousands of soldiers from across Ireland who passed through Cork en route to war. Accommodation for these troops was provided in a special camp established adjacent to Assumption Road, north of the barracks, known locally as 'Tintown' because of the corrugated huts that housed the soldiers. North of 'Tintown' a system of trenches was created for training, giving soldiers a very mild foretaste of what awaited them in the killing fields of Europe.

Between 1914 and 1918, 12,000 men from County Cork joined the British Army (a sixth of whom perished), over half from the city and its environs. One in every seven families in the city had a member fighting in the war. Their reasons for joining varied: unionists were motivated by a duty to king and country; nationalists were convinced by their political leaders that the granting of Home Rule, suspended at the outbreak of war, depended on their participation; economic factors, especially the dependants' Separation Allowance, encouraged the majority of recruits, men from the impoverished working-class districts, to join. A taste of the popular impact of the war on working-class Cork is contained in the ballad 'Salonika', written from the perspective of a 'separa', a woman in receipt of the allowance.

As the war dragged on, enthusiasm waned and recruitment numbers levelled off, though events such as the sinking of the *Lusitania* off the Cork coast in May 1915 revived interest. The torpedoing of this liner, with the loss of 1,198 civilian lives, brought the realities of the war to Cork's doorstep. Bodies were brought ashore and laid out in Cobh before burial in mass graves. The injured were brought to the military hospital in Victoria Barracks, where survivors were put up in the Imperial Hotel on the South Mall and provided with clothes and tickets for their onward journeys. Items recovered from the *Lusitania*, as well as images and memories of the disaster, were used extensively by the authorities in their attempts to maintain a steady flow of recruits. From mid-1915, 144 recruits per month were enlisting in the Cork region, in comparison to a monthly average of 620 in the first months of the war.

The 1916 Rising and its aftermath

Advanced nationalist propaganda fed into and encouraged anti-war and anti-British sentiment. The Irish Volunteers in Cork continued to drill and organise under the leadership of MacCurtain and MacSwiney. By the end of 1915, there were 46 companies across the county, comprising up to 1,500 men, 150 in the city. Their headquarters were in the new Volunteer Hall on Sheare's Street (later, St Francis Hall). In the plans for the Easter Rising of 1916, the Cork Brigade was to join units from Kerry and Limerick along the Cork–Kerry border to receive their quota of weapons, which were to have been landed in Kerry on Easter Sunday. The weapons never arrived, because of the capture of the *Aud* arms ship, and the brigade was stood down amidst confusion and contradictory orders from Dublin. The result was that Cork did not participate in the Rising. The Volunteer leadership occupied the hall on Sheare's Street, while the British Army took up strategic positions around the city and warned the Volunteers that any action by them would result in the shelling of the hall and other targets. Following negotiations with the Lord Mayor and Catholic bishop, the Volunteers surrendered their weapons to the Lord Mayor, from whom they were later seized by the British Army. The Volunteer Hall was shut down by the authorities in 1917.

The leadership of the Cork Volunteers joined thousands of other republicans in British prisons after the Rising. Following their release in late 1916 and early 1917 they led an invigorated advanced nationalist movement, in the shape of the Volunteers and Sinn Féin, which was now a force in Cork politics, as in Irish politics generally, for the first time. The growth in participation and support was fed by the shift in public opinion in the aftermath of the Rising and the severe British response, together with growing disenchantment with the war and declining confidence in Redmond's influence and British intentions with regard to Home Rule. The German offensive of March 1918 led the British to advocate the extension of conscription to Ireland in April. This provoked a massive response as all nationalist political parties, the Catholic Church, public bodies and the trade union movement united in opposition. On 23 April over 30,000 workers joined a Cork Trades and Labour Council demonstration against conscription, part of a nationwide general strike. The leading role taken by Sinn Féin in the successful opposition to conscription laid the basis for its success in the general election of December 1918.

Towards 'rebel' Cork

The conscription crisis shattered the remaining vestiges of belief in British intentions with regard to Home Rule, and the hopes of many nationalists were now transferred to US President Woodrow Wilson and his promise to facilitate the right to self-determination for all nations. In September 1918, Cork Corporation changed the name of Great George's Street to Washington Street 'as a compliment to America'. (America and Wilson would fail to deliver recognition of Irish self-determination in the post-war settlement, and the *Cork Examiner* expressed the popular shift in opinion towards Wilson with its heading 'Making the World Safe for Hypocrisy'.)[4] The war ended in November 1918. The immediate response in Cork was muted, and the changed attitude in the city since 1914 was reflected in the following month's general election, when Sinn Féin, standing on a

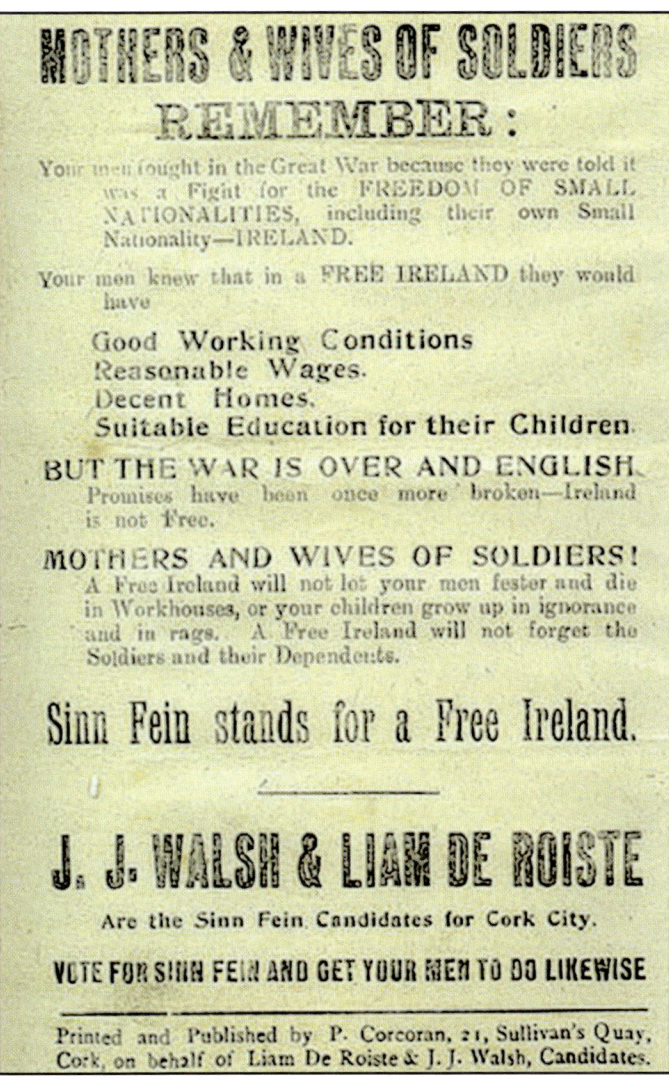

Fig. 3.86 Sinn Féin election poster. (Source: Cork Archives Institute.)

separatist platform, was victorious. In the seven Cork county constituencies, Sinn Féin candidates, including Michael Collins in Cork South and Terence MacSwiney in Mid Cork, were returned unopposed. In the city, the Sinn Féin candidates J.J. Walsh and Liam de Róiste won 20,654 votes, against 7,321 for the Home Rule candidates and 2,386 for the Unionists – in other words, over two-thirds of the votes cast. The Volunteers, now numbering 8,000 in the county, became increasingly visible, assertive and militaristic in the face of what they saw as the British refusal to recognise the democratic will of the Irish people, as expressed in the Sinn Féin victory.

Bans on drilling, the wearing of uniform and the carrying of weapons were openly defied and the police force, the Royal Irish Constabulary (RIC), together with the courts and the prisons were put under increasing pressure. Isolated armed attacks on police patrols and barracks in the county became more commonplace in 1919, as the IRA (as the Volunteers became known from August 1919, when they pledged themselves to the defence of the Republic) set out to procure arms and render British authority untenable. The first police fatality in Cork occurred in Kilbrittain in December 1919, by which time the rule of law in the county had effectively broken down.

War of Independence

The IRA in the county was organised into three brigades: 'Number 2' (under Liam Lynch) and 'Number 3' (under Tom Hales) covered the north and west of the county respectively, while 'Number 1' extended from Youghal in the east to the Kerry border in the west, under the command of Tomás MacCurtain. The city was a part of the 'Number 1' Brigade area and was subdivided between the First Battalion (city centre and northside) and the Second (south of the southern channel of the Lee). The Brigade's secret headquarters were located in the city, in the home of the Wallace sisters on St Augustine's Street. Victoria Barracks was the centre of the British military presence in the city, augmented by garrisons in Ballincollig, Buttevant, Fermoy, Bandon, Cobh and Kinsale. Police headquarters were in Union Quay. Other city-centre stations were in Tuckey Street, King Street (now MacCurtain Street), the Bridewell and Barrack Street. IRA volunteers in the city were mainly upper working class/lower middle class, male, Catholic and under thirty. Most became involved through family, neighbourhood or peer connections. Volunteers recruited co-workers, schoolmates, brothers, GAA clubmates and so on. As the situation became more militarised, a hard core of guerrilla fighters, later formed into flying columns, took the lead, leaving the majority in a support role.

Fig. 3.87 Obituary card of Terence MacSwiney. (Source: Cork Archives Institute.)

In January 1920, Sinn Féin triumphed in the municipal elections. The commanding officer of the IRA's 'Number 1' Brigade, Tomás MacCurtain, was elected Lord Mayor and the tricolour was raised above Cork City Hall. The conflict intensified in that month as IRA headquarters authorised open attacks on Crown forces, which resulted in a wave of assaults on police barracks in Cork city and county over the following months, resulting in the closing down of most of them in the county and city suburbs. By the summer of 1920, Togher, Commons Road, Blackrock, King Street, Victoria Cross and St Luke's barracks had all been destroyed by the IRA. The RIC in the city was effectively under siege and generally confined to barracks. Morale was low, resources inadequate, frustration and absenteeism rife.

Following the shooting of policemen in March 1920, the RIC began to retaliate, aided and abetted by their newly arrived reinforcements, the notorious 'Black and Tans', who established their Cork base in a house in Empress Place on Summerhill, halfway between the army and police headquarters. In the early hours of 20 March, a police death

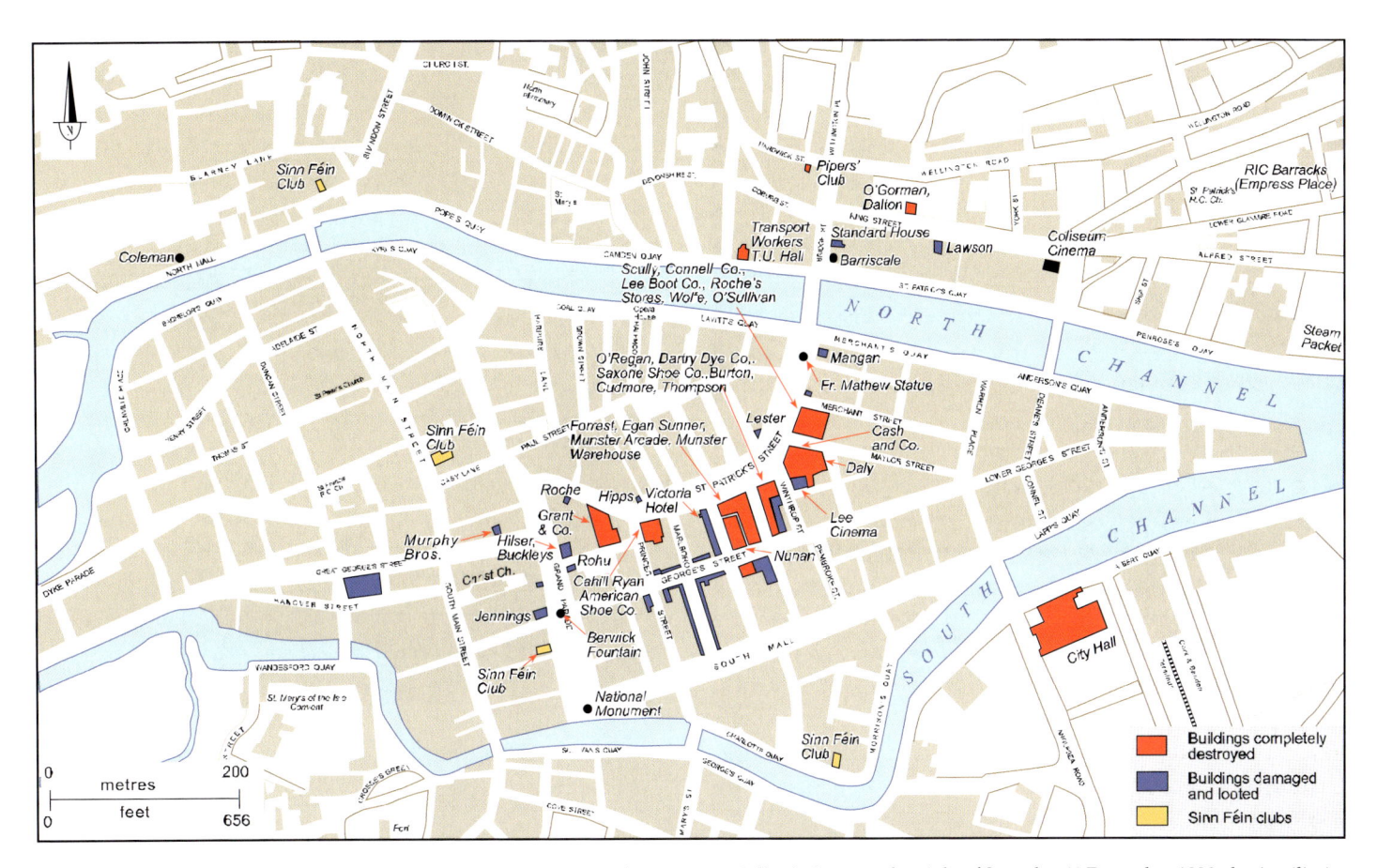

THE • CITY • IN • THE • NINETEENTH • AND • TWENTIETH • CENTURIES

Fig. 3.88 The burning of Cork city. Following an IRA attack on an Auxiliary party at Dillon's Cross on the night of Saturday 11 December 1920, the Auxiliaries and Black and Tans went on a rampage of looting and burning in the city. It is likely that the ambush provided the opportunity to carry out what was probably a pre-planned operation. After the burning of houses in Dillon's Cross, they proceeded to set fire to the city's main department stores on Patrick's Street, including the Munster Arcade, Roche's Stores and Grant's. In the early hours of Sunday morning, City Hall and the historic Carnegie Free Library nearby were also torched. Despite the best efforts of the fire brigade, which was subjected to harassment and shooting from British forces, all of these buildings were completely destroyed. Many other premises were damaged. (Source: *Who burnt Cork city? A tale of arson, loot and murder*, Dublin, 1921.)

squad with blackened faces broke into Tomás MacCurtain's home on Thomas Davis Street in Blackpool and shot him dead on his thirty-sixth birthday. The city came to a standstill for MacCurtain's funeral on 22 March, and on 31 March his replacement as 'Number 1' Brigade commander, Terence MacSwiney, was elected Lord Mayor. A cycle of terror and counter-terror, reprisals and tit-for-tat attacks, characterised life in the city throughout the spring and summer of 1920. Following the killing of a high-ranking RIC officer in the County Club on the South Mall in July 1920, the army imposed a curfew between 10 pm and 3 am covering a three-mile radius from the city centre.

In August the army swooped on a secret IRA officers' meeting in the City Hall and arrested many leading figures in the Cork IRA, including Terence MacSwiney, who was sent to Brixton Gaol in London, where he commenced a 74-day hunger strike which received worldwide attention and sympathy for the republican cause. He died on 25 October and his body was returned to Cork, where he lay in state in the City Hall for two days before a huge funeral on 31

Fig. 3.89 The destruction visited on St Patrick's Street. (Photo: *Irish Examiner*.)

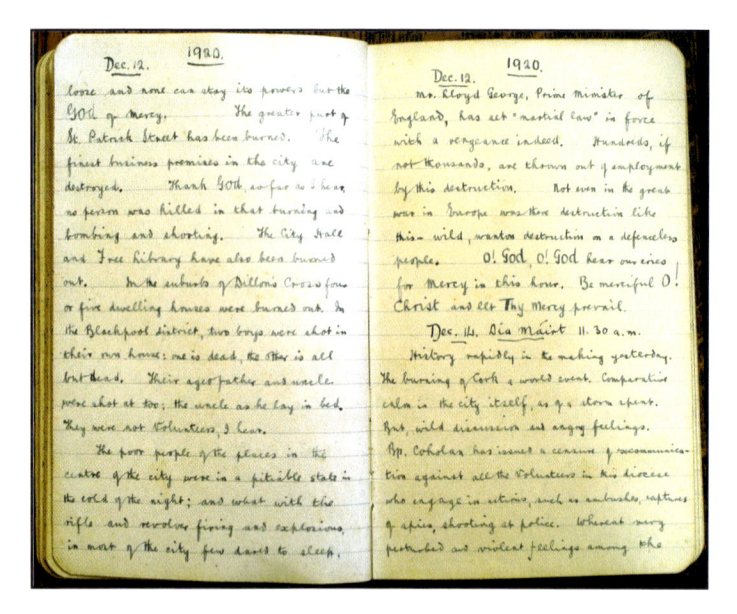

Fig. 3.90 Liam de Róiste's diary entry for the 12 December 1920 describing the burning of Cork city. De Róiste was one of the two Sinn Féin MP/TDs elected in December 1918. He took the Treaty side in the Sinn Féin split and was returned as a pro-Treaty Sinn Féin TD for Cork city in 1922. (Source: Liam de Róiste papers, Cork Archives Institute.)

October. MacSwiney was replaced as brigade commandant by Sean O'Hegarty, the IRB's leading man in Cork and a ruthless militarist. IRA strategy was increasingly centred on active-service units, or flying columns, and in the city most of the fighting was carried out by a full-time active service unit of sixteen to twenty men that had been formed in September from the two city battalions.

In October, the newly formed Auxiliary Division of the RIC (the Auxies), a mobile force made up of ex-commissioned officers of the British Army, arrived at Victoria Barracks. They immediately made their presence felt on the streets of Cork, harassing and intimidating civilians, raiding houses and gaining a reputation for drunkenness, violence, thievery and racism. Tom Barry led his flying column in an ambush of an Auxiliary party at Kilmichael on 28 November in one of the most famous battles of the period, which resulted in the death of seventeen Auxiliaries and three IRA men. On 10 December martial law was declared in Cork, Limerick and Tipperary. The following night the IRA ambushed an Auxiliary patrol close to the Victoria Barracks

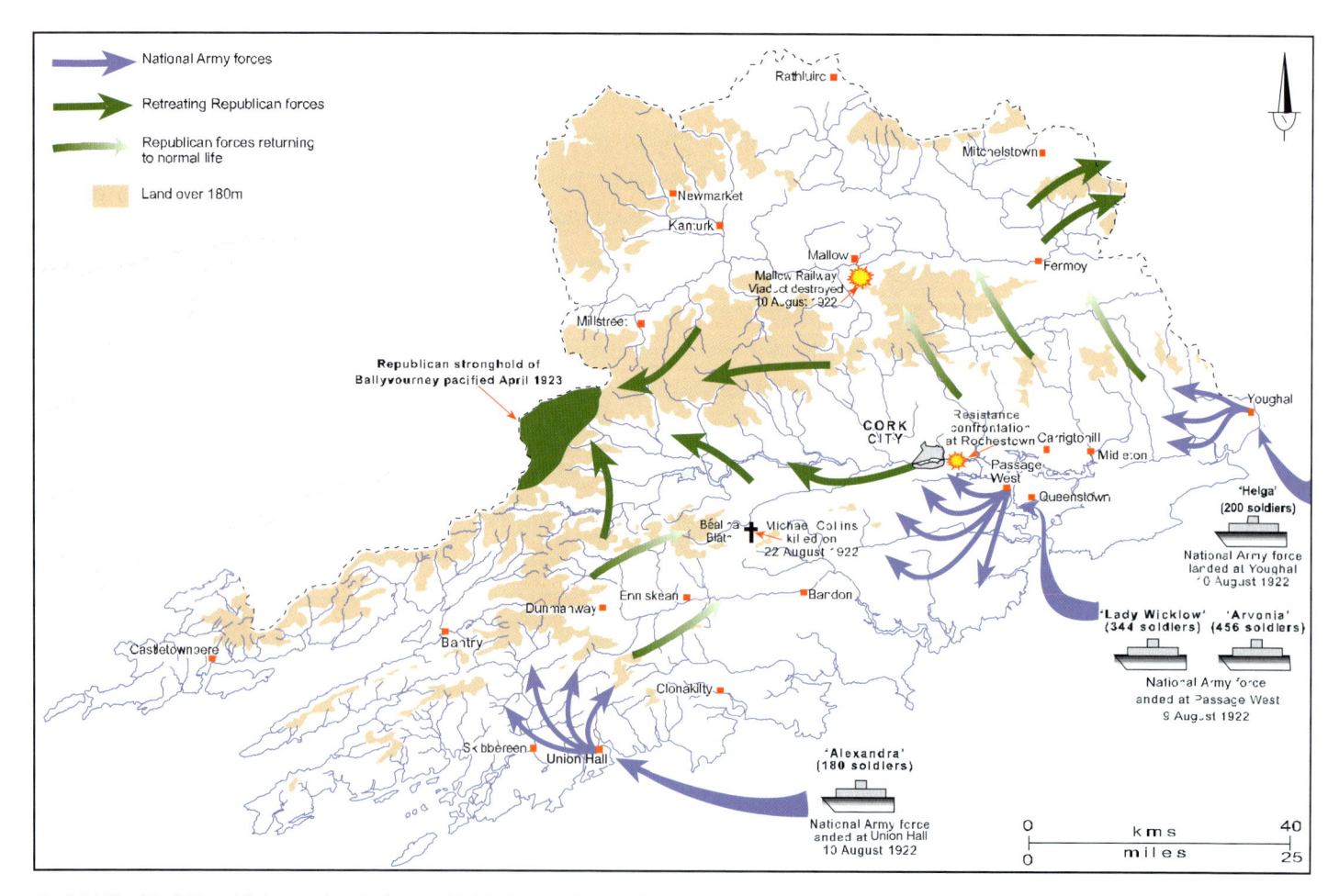

Fig. 3.91 The 'Cork Republic' was taken in August 1922 by National Army forces, who landed by boat at Youghal, Passage West and Union Hall. Republicans retreated or went underground in the face of the advance. The only immediate resistance was a clash at Rochestown. Republicans subsequently launched a guerrilla campaign, which claimed Michael Collins as an early and prominent victim.

Fig. 3.92 Michael Collins at St Francis church, Broad Lane, 1922. (Photo: *Irish Examiner*.)

at Dillon's Cross, killing one and wounding a further twelve. The Auxiliaries and Black and Tans exacted a terrible revenge, burning large areas of the city centre, as well as the City Hall and Carnegie Free Library.

On 28 February 1921, six IRA men were executed in the military detention barracks in the city. In retaliation, the IRA killed six British soldiers in different parts of the city. A separate Cork city command had been established that month, and in April the three Cork brigades, together with six from Kerry, Limerick and Waterford, were formed into the First Southern Division. The IRA's Cork city bomb factories supplied most of the mines and grenades for the Division. Grenades were cast in a central factory on the Ballinlough Road, and the bombs were secretly completed by Volunteers working in the Technical School and in the laboratories in UCC.

Cork's citizens lived in an atmosphere of fear, suspicion and betrayal, with nightly killings, disappearances and arson attacks. The IRA remained strong and the British forces were supplemented (Major Bernard Montgomery, who later found fame as British Commander in Africa during the Second World War, was sent to Cork as a brigade major in early 1921), but the conflict had reached a stalemate, and on 11 July 1921 a truce was agreed. Both sides remained armed and wary, ready to resume hostilities. However, the truce held and, following the signing of the Treaty in December 1921, army and police detachments gradually withdrew and handed over the barracks to the

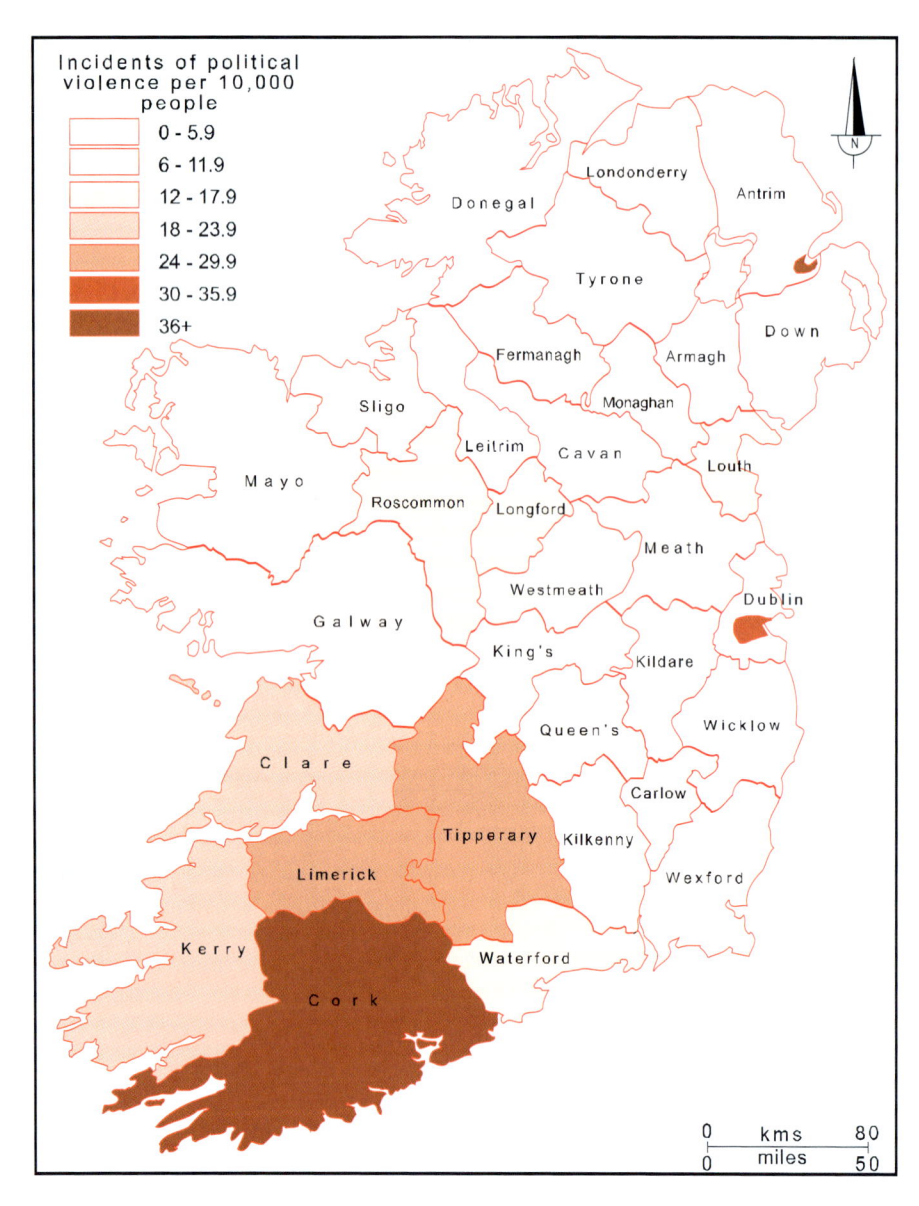

Fig. 3.93 Incidents of political violence per 10,000 people in Ireland between 1917 and 1923. Cork was the most violent county during the revolutionary years. (Source: Peter Hart, *The IRA at war 1916–1923*, Oxford, 2003.)

IRA. A number of British Army units remained in Victoria and Ballincollig barracks until May 1922, but the city and county were effectively in the control of the Cork IRA, which overwhelmingly rejected the Treaty, giving rise to the so-called 'Cork Republic'. The IRA collected taxes, censored the press and even issued its own postage stamps. Sporadic violence continued, directed against British soldiers, former RIC men and informers rather than against pro-Treatyites.

Civil War

The Civil War began with the 28 June shelling of the IRA Four Courts garrison in Dublin. Many of the Cork IRA, including Sean O'Hegarty, remained neutral rather than taking the Free State side. The anti-Treaty republicans, who kept the IRA name and were dubbed Irregulars by the new provisional government, failed to take the initiative despite their initial numerical advantage, particularly in the south, and adopted a primarily defensive strategy. The provisional government adopted an aggressive war plan and built up its army and armaments. Following the capture of Limerick and Waterford in late July, Cork was the last major stronghold of the 'Munster Republic'. Government forces landed at three points on the Cork coast on 8 August: 200 at Youghal, 180 at Union Hall, and the main force of 800 men, armoured cars and artillery guns at Passage West. IRA resistance at Rochestown, which left nine National Army soldiers and seven republicans dead, delayed their advance, but they took the city on 11 August. The IRA units retreated west, while the other towns in the county fell one by one with even less resistance over the following days. IRA men who had not abandoned the fight went underground to begin the guerrilla phase of the Civil War. An early victim was Michael Collins, chairman of the provisional government and commander-in-chief of the National Army, who was killed in an ambush at Béal na mBláth in west Cork on 22 August. His body arrived in Cork after midnight and was laid out at Shanakiel Hospital. The next day it was brought by sea to Dublin for burial.

Cork city experienced only sporadic violence in this period, as most of the city's activists had either been arrested or had fled. In addition, the National Army had far more control, local knowledge and support than the British forces had enjoyed, and most of the city's population were war weary and eager for a return to some sort of normality. In the county, republican units were confined mainly to the mountainous regions in the far west. The civil war ended in May 1923. A decade of militarism had come to an end and Cork city and county, the most violent region in the country in the period 1917–1923 and the 'storm centre' of the revolution, began to experience the novelty of peace.[5]

24. CORK CITY IN THE TWENTIETH CENTURY

Kevin Hourihan

Cork city began the twentieth century as a cramped and stagnant port whose best days had long passed, and ended it as the second city of the Republic, a bustling business and industrial centre surrounded by suburbs and a ring of commuting towns. This transformation was not a steady, continuous process; the first 60 years saw only slow development, while the last few decades have been a period of unprecedented change.

In 1901, Cork's population was 76,000, confined to an area of just 4.2 square miles. Despite the health and housing reforms of the previous twenty years, conditions in the city were still very poor, and the economy was stagnant. Notwithstanding the nineteenth-century conditions, one characteristic feature of the twentieth century was evident at this time: population loss at the centre of the city. This was to continue uninterrupted for the next 90 years.[1]

Although commerce dominated the city centre, there was still a substantial residential population, with one-tenth of the city total living there. By 1991, this would fall to half a per cent of the city's population. The traditional industries, especially butter processing, were gone, but a new era of heavy industry in Cork began with the arrival of the Ford Motor Company in 1917 and its factory in the City Park. These former sloblands to the east of the city centre and the nearby docks became a major industrial centre, with Dunlop's Tyres, Rank's Flour Mills and Goulding's Fertilisers all locating there. These would remain central to Cork's economy for the next 60 years.

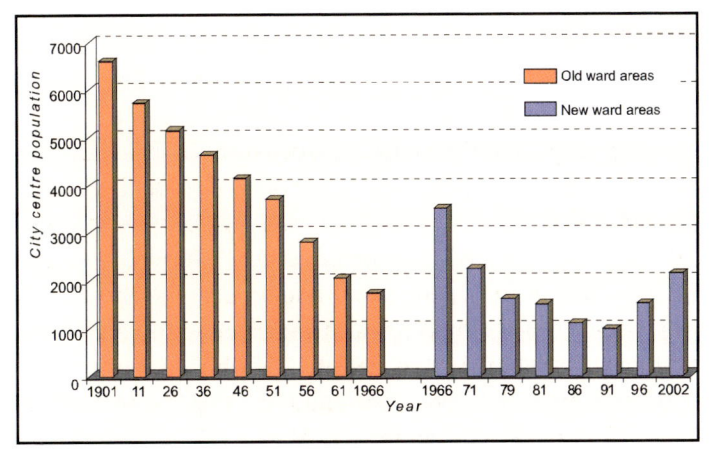

Fig. 3.94 From the beginning of the twentieth century, the population of the city centre was in decline. It fell from over 6,600 in 1901 to 1,700 in 1966. The ward boundaries were changed in 1970, hence it is not possible to continue the sequence exactly. The new wards are larger than the previous ones, with over twice the population (3,500 people) in 1966. They continued to decline to less than 1,000 in 1991. Since then, urban renewal has encouraged a population increase to over 2,100.

CORK IN THE NEW FREE STATE

The 1920s brought several developments. The first was the burning of large parts of St Patrick's Street and Oliver Plunkett Street by British forces in December 1920. Compensation paid for the construction of several of the city's landmark buildings, including the first department stores (now operated by Roche's and Brown Thomas) and the new City Hall. In 1923, the Cork Progressive Association was founded to demand an inquiry into alleged mismanagement of the city by Cork Corporation. A public inquiry confirmed the allegations and the Corporation was dissolved in 1924. In 1929, a modern council-manager system replaced the discredited Corporation and, with only a change of name (to Cork City Council), this is the local authority that still manages the city today.

In the early twentieth century, many cities in Britain and Ireland undertook civic surveys as a first step towards urban planning. Dublin's was published in 1925 and Cork's appeared the following year.[2] The *Cork Civic Survey* remains an impressive document, with many maps and data on conditions in the city in the 1920s. It identified three large areas of slums and argued that one-fifth of the entire population needed rehousing. Within a few years, the Corporation began its huge housing estates on the south and north outskirts of the city, initiating a programme which continued for the next 50 years. The Census of Population of 1936 identified a suburban population for the first time and backdated it to 1926. Some of these suburbs were incorporated into the city through boundary extensions in 1955 and 1965, but the process of suburban expansion has continued to the present day.

The *Civic Survey* also documented the shortage of public open space in Cork, with only 0.54 acres per 1,000 population compared to Dublin's 5.7 acres, partly because of giving the City Park to Ford's. This problem would not be addressed for the next 50 years. Another modern concern raised by the *Survey* was boundaries and

Fig. 3.95 A view of Cork city centre from the east showing the island formed by the two channels of the Lee. It was in turn the site of the Norse settlement, of the Anglo-Norman walled town and of the commercial and residential developments of the eighteenth century. It remains the shopping, commercial and entertainment centre of the region. In the foreground are the old docks and industrial sites, which will be redeveloped in the near future. (Photo: Tomás Tyner.)

extensions, an issue still unresolved today. Although it is in many respects a very modern report (and still relevant in many ways), it also contains some appealing anachronisms, like a map showing cattle movements through the city (see *The Culture of Food*, Chapter 27).

In 1934, Cork Corporation became responsible for planning both the city and its hinterland under the new Town and Regional Planning Act, although little was done until Manning Robertson was commissioned to produce a plan in 1941.[3] Robertson proposed a green belt surrounding the city and limiting it to a population of a quarter-million on seventeen square miles, with generous areas of public open space throughout. His detailed proposals for new roads and bridges, a central bus station and ring roads on the outskirts are close to what have emerged over the past 30 years since the Land Use and Transportation Study (LUTS), but unfortunately in the 1940s the Corporation had neither the will nor the finance to implement the Robertson scheme. Instead, the focus was on continued housing development on the outskirts of the city with little reference to the overall plan.

The 1950s brought no improvements to Cork city. It was a decade of economic and demographic stagnation for the entire country, although the population of the city and suburbs increased by ten per cent. The Corporation continued, indeed accelerated, its policy of slum clearance in the city centre, rehousing people in large estates on greenfield sites. The result was rapid population loss in the centre, 45 per cent over the decade.

THE 1960s: THE DECENTRALISED CITY

Since the beginning of the century, Cork had been expanding outwards with new housing developments, but the 1960s brought a new dynamism to this process. The national population increased for the first time in a century, with the cities experiencing the greatest growth. Cork's population

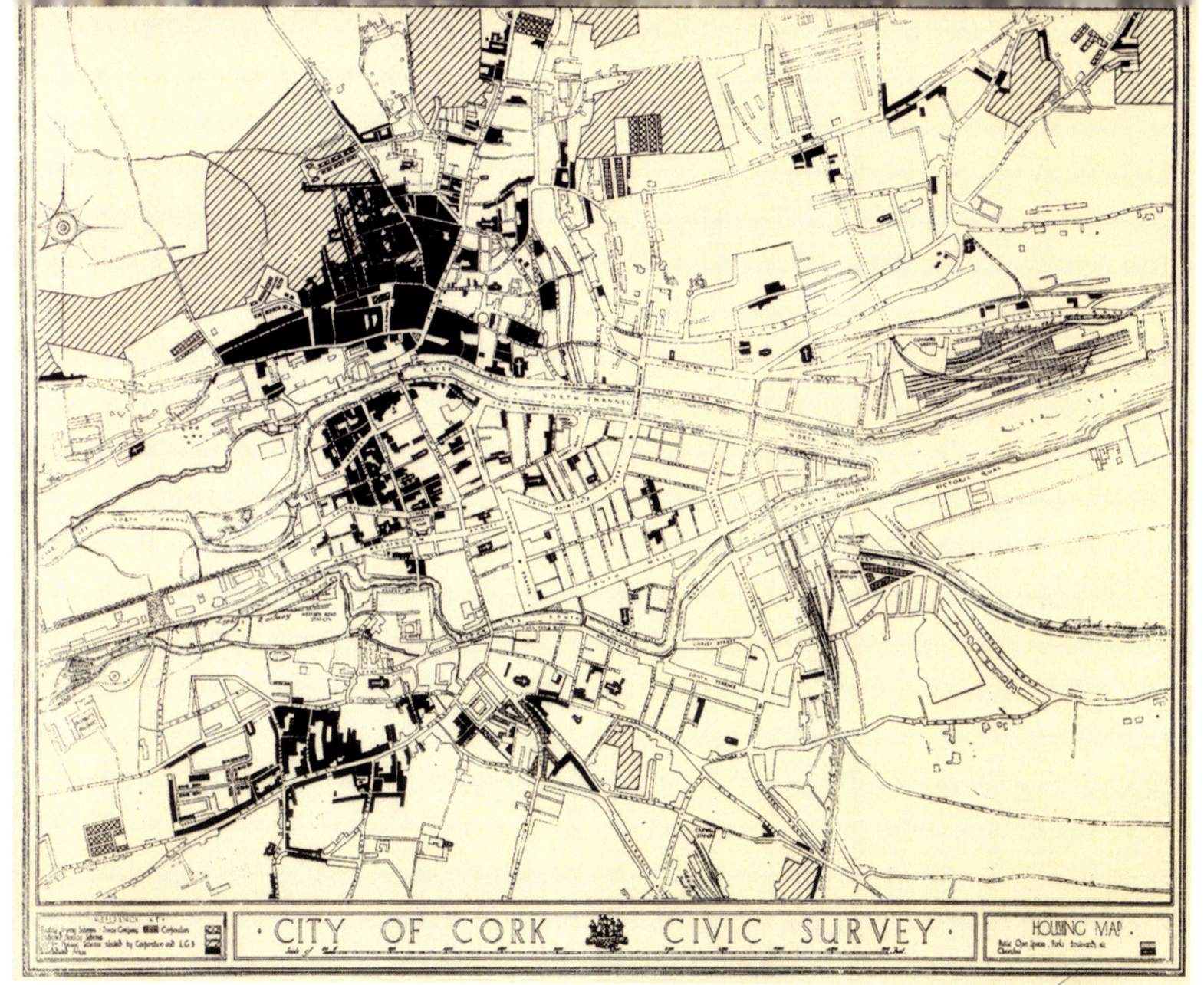

Fig. 3.96 The maps in the *Cork Civic Survey* are a valuable record of the city in the 1920s. While slum clearance had taken place before then, it was limited in extent. Large tracts of housing on the western side were very dilapidated and unfit for inhabitation.

Fig. 3.97 Large families in small, mean houses on a narrow lane indicate the reality of the slum areas outlined in Fig. 3.96.

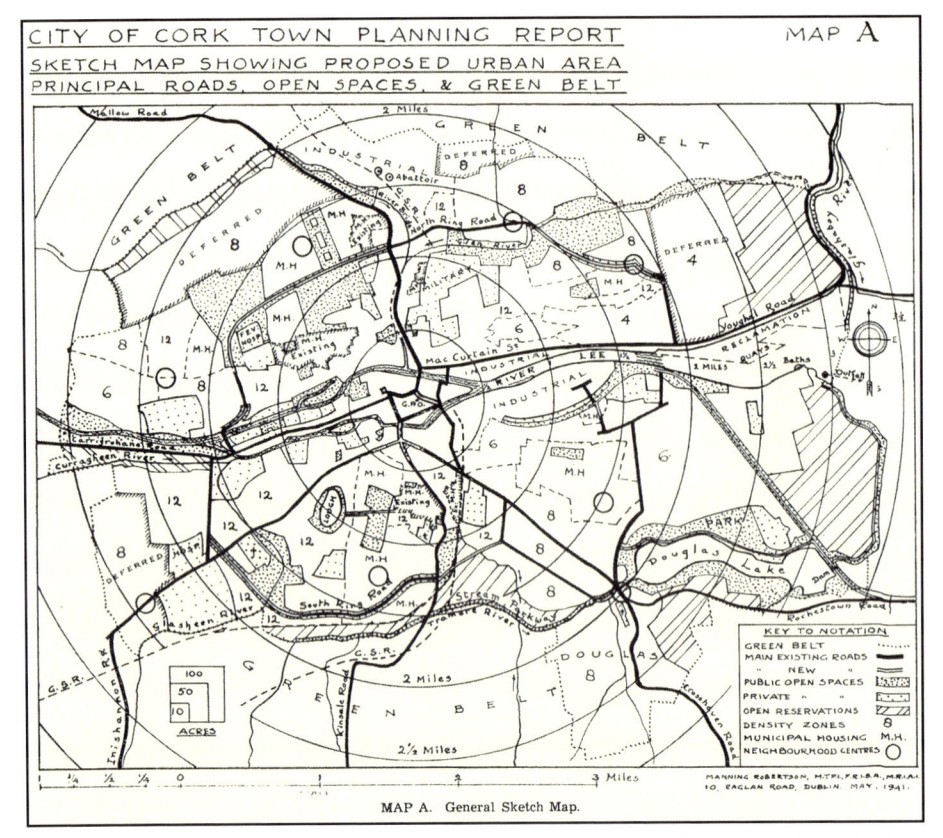

Fig. 3.98 Manning Robertson's 1941 plan for Cork city was very advanced for its time. It emphasised greenery, open space and good-quality housing, and could have provided a very worthwhile model for post-war development.

grew by 20 per cent between 1961 and 1971. The economic growth and increased prosperity that lay behind this was clearly welcome, but it also brought many changes and presented new problems.

Suburban housing development accelerated, with speculative, private estates outnumbering Corporation houses for the first time. Car ownership became more widespread and started to replace public transport. The first suburban shopping centre opened in Togher in 1970. Larger centres followed in Douglas in 1971 and in Wilton in 1979, both on the southside, while Ballyvolane, Mayfield and Hollyhill opened on the northside in 1979 and 1980. Since then, the only large new developments have been Douglas Court in 1990, Bishopstown Court in 1994, Blackpool in 2000 and Mahon Point in 2005, but most of the earlier centres have been expanded and modernised. Retail warehouses, dealing especially in DIY and homecare, are mainly located in the southern suburbs. The suburban centres would inevitably take an increasing share of Cork's retail sales. They are more accessible to motorists and have large areas of free parking. Increasingly, they are attracting non-retail services like banks, credit unions and restaurants, providing for all of their customers' needs. They overtook the city centre in about 1990, but the recent renewal and repopulation of the inner city has probably changed the balance again. Overall, though, there is little fear in Ireland that suburban malls might take on the dominant role they have in the USA, where many older downtowns have been wiped out by the malls and the issue of 'public' space which is privately owned and controlled has created many difficulties.[4]

The 1960s also began the decentralisation of the manufacturing industry and the 1970s brought the closure of many factories after accession to the EEC. New industrial estates and parks were developed on the outskirts of the city, both by the Industrial Development Association (IDA) and private enterprise. The advantages over traditional locations were the classic push-and-pull factors; the cramped, inaccessible, obsolete premises could not compete with purpose-built developments and better accessibility. By the 1980s, the only large manufacturing plants left in the inner city were the two breweries, both of which had invested heavily in modernising their operations and

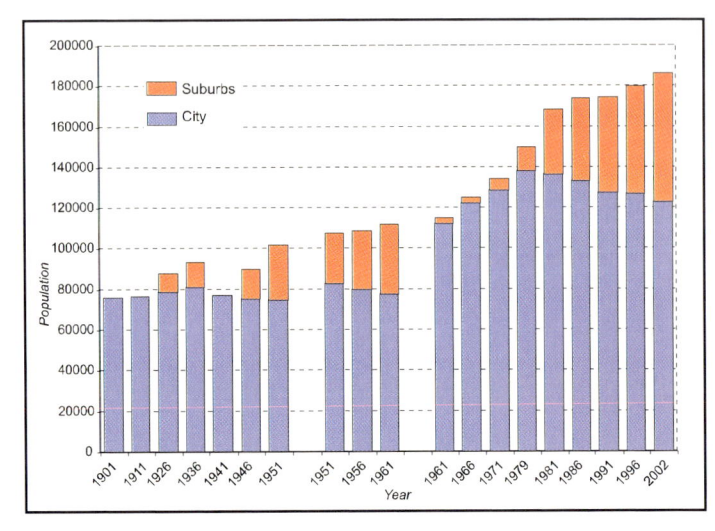

Fig. 3.99 Examining population change in cities and suburbs can often be complicated by boundary changes and extensions. The city's boundary was expanded twice in the twentieth century, in 1955 and 1965, to incorporate adjacent suburbs. The Central Statistics Office always backdates the next census to show the population that previously lived in the newly defined area, in this case for the censuses of 1951 and 1961. The city's population changed slowly over the first 60 years and did not exceed 100,000 until the extension of 1965. It peaked at over 138,000 in 1979 and subsequently declined to 123,000 in 2002. In contrast, the contiguous suburbs have grown continuously, from 9,200 in 1926, when they were first defined for census purposes, to over 63,000 in 2002.

THE • CITY • IN • THE • NINETEENTH • AND • TWENTIETH • CENTURIES

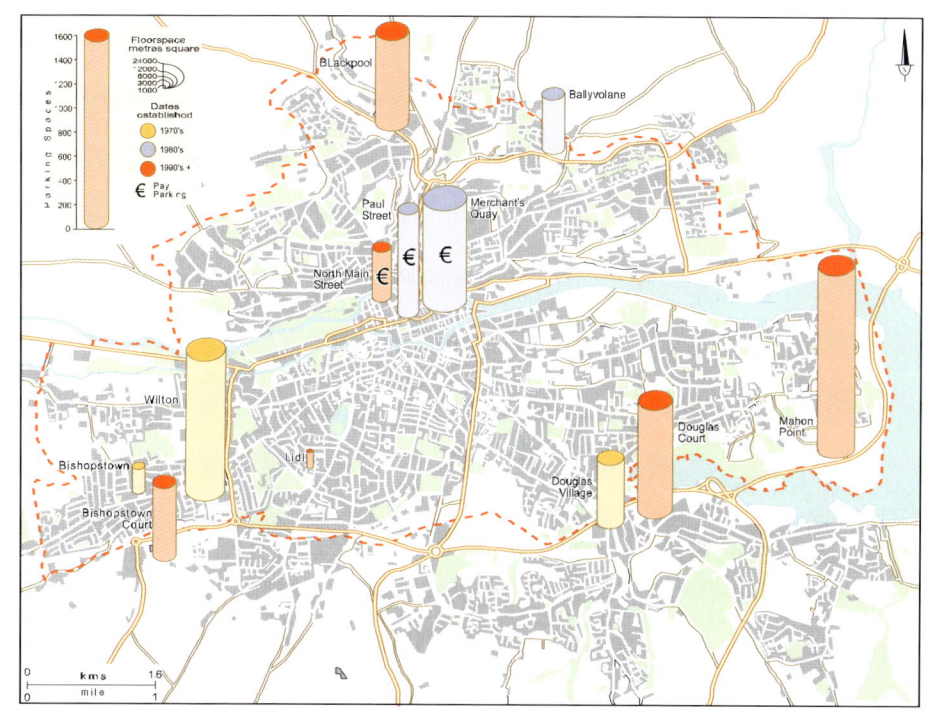

Fig. 3.100 Over the past 35 years, suburban shopping centres have begun to dominate retailing in Cork. The malls in the city centre provide about 2,100 parking spaces, but at a cost, while the suburban centres have almost three times as many spaces for free. Combined with easier accessibility and longer opening hours (in some cases, 24-hour opening), the suburbs have considerable advantages. The future of the city centre increasingly depends on comparison, rather than convenience, shopping.

also had traditional ties to their sites. The Ford and Dunlop factories closed, and were followed later by Verolme and Irish Steel in Cork harbour.

The old docklands also became obsolete. The passenger ferry, *Inisfallen*, had been the emigrant ship to Britain in the 1950s used by scores (probably hundreds) of thousands of exiles. In the 1970s, the ferry terminal was first relocated to Tivoli and later to Ringaskiddy, and the docks near the city centre lost most of their traffic.

In terms of planning, decentralisation was encouraged. The development plan accepted by Cork County Council in 1972 was ostensibly an attempt to control suburban sprawl on the outskirts of the city.[5] It concentrated development into three 'satellite towns': Carrigaline, Ballincollig and Glanmire–Riverstown. In practice, however, it only displaced the housing estates to these centres, leaving people with even longer commuting trips to the city. In addition, the green belt, an essential component of the plan, was not properly controlled. Scores of one-off houses (urban-generated rural houses) were built on it, often in the form of ribbon development. The use of green belts and new towns derives from the Greater London Plan of 1944, then the largest city in the world. Cork city, with its 1971 population of 135,000, hardly required this kind of dispersal. More imaginative and comprehensive planning could have better addressed Cork's problems.

Although by modern standards the number of private cars in Cork in the 1960s was quite low, the city still experienced serious congestion and the Corporation commissioned a major plan to deal with the issue. The resulting BKS report, published in 1968, was an extraordinary document, even in an era when cities all over the world were trying to facilitate private motorists.[6] It proposed a raised limited-access distributor road (100 feet wide) circling the city centre, with most of the central streets adapted for traffic and large areas given over to surface parking. Altogether, some 2,000 homes would be demolished for these developments. The report admitted that these ideas were 'of a scale . . . completely new to Cork'. The Corporation accepted the proposals, despite widespread public concern. Disquiet was reinforced by an environmental study of the city by Peter Dovell, published in 1971.[7] This examined the townscape quality of Cork and illustrated through a series of sketches the terrible impact that the distributor road would have on visual amenity in the city. Nevertheless, the BKS proposals hung over the city like a sword of Damocles for the next decade. Planning blight began to appear in many of the streets designated as traffic arteries and there were several instances of buildings collapsing without any warning.

LUTS AND ITS AFTERMATH

The disquiet over the BKS proposals and increasing concern over the impact of private car ownership forced local authorities to commission a new strategic plan for the Cork region in 1976. This was the Land Use and Transportation Study (LUTS), which was accepted in 1978, revised in 1992, and remained the guiding framework for development until the year 2001, when the Cork Area Strategic plan (CASP) replaced it.[8]

In many respects, LUTS was ground-breaking. It was the first regional plan for a city in the Republic, incorporating a commuting area that was objectively defined, and it had the backing of not only the city and county authorities, but all the other bodies involved in development, like Córas Iompar Éireann (CIE), the Electricity Supply Board (ESB) and the Cork Harbour Commissioners. It also explicitly recognised the symbiotic relationship between land use and transport.

Fig. 3.101 Douglas, a former industrial village, was separate from the city until the 1960s, when the suburbs (top) reached it. Since then, two large shopping centres, a cineplex and other facilities, all geared towards private transport and the South Link Ring Road, have been developed. Over the past decade, the most intensive suburban development around Cork has been to the south of Douglas. (Photo: Tomás Tyner.)

The population and employment projections in LUTS were conventional, with increases predicted for the suburbs and outlying towns. The transport elements, on the other hand, were a major reversal of the private motorist orientation of BKS. LUTS made only limited proposals for new or expanded roads and these involved little disruption, as they used the abandoned railway lines for the most part. Three new bridges over the river and the downstream tunnel were designed to relieve congestion in the city centre, and these have all subsequently been built.

The most radical proposal was termed Area Traffic Control, which was to allow private motorists into the centre only as and when space was available for them in the area. This was a modification of a scheme known as 'zones and collars' which had been tried in Nottingham in England.[9] It had proved successful in reducing congestion, but was associated by the public with aggressive, anti-car ideologues and became politically unacceptable. After only two years, it was scrapped abruptly in 1976. The planners and politicians in Cork seemed to learn from this experience, hoping to introduce the measures gradually and quietly, without the kind of fanfare that proved disastrous in Nottingham. In practice, though, it was repeatedly deferred and eventually abandoned. Controlling private cars has again become imperative in the third millennium, with London's road pricing scheme becoming major news in 2003, and calls for something similar for Dublin. The LUTS plan of 1978 could have given Cork an advantage if fully implemented.

In another area also LUTS was a failure. It argued for concentrating new housing and population increase within the existing city and towns, but this was not implemented. Instead, one-off houses and small estates proliferated in the countryside and by 1986 the census showed the largest suburban expansion yet recorded.

1986–2005: Renewing the city centre

The past twenty years have brought dramatic changes to Cork. The urban renewal incentives for redevelopment near the centre began in 1986, but Cork Corporation had previously taken its own initiatives. It funded small-scale housing development through a revolving fund, and designated housing protection areas in vulnerable neighbourhoods near the city centre to prevent commerce from encroaching on them. In 1985 it

Fig. 3.102. Carrigaline, one of the satellite towns of the 1972 development plan, had a population of 11,191 in 2002, but has become a low-density suburban sprawl. (Photo: Tomás Tyner.)

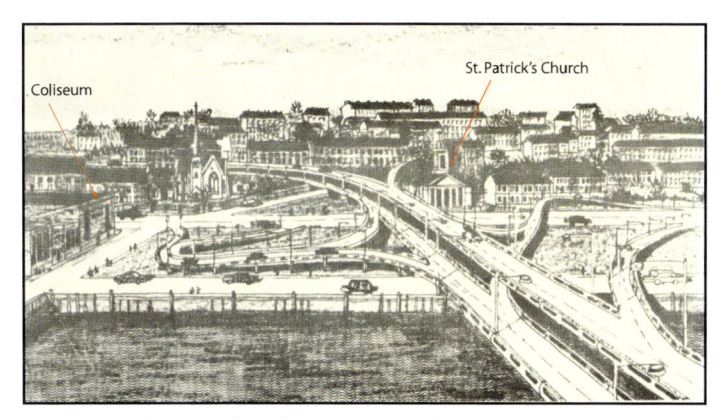

THE · CITY · IN · THE · NINETEENTH · AND · TWENTIETH · CENTURIES

Fig. 3.103 The visual and environmental impact of the BKS inner distributor road is well illustrated in this diagram by Peter Dovell. The entire area between the Coliseum corner and Kent Station would have been the site for a huge, spaghetti-junction-like interchange.

developed Bishop Lucey Park in the medieval city as part of the eight hundredth anniversary of the granting of the city's first charter. Although small, this park has become a very popular amenity, given Cork's historic lack of public open space.

At national level, the first urban renewal scheme was really designed for Dublin rather than Cork, where dereliction was much less widespread. Initially, 81 acres were designated, mainly to the south and west of the business district, with another 18 acres in Blackpool. In 1990 another 31 acres were added, to the north and east of the commercial core.

At national level, the first phase of urban renewal has been criticised on several grounds, including favouring office and commercial developments over residences and encouraging new construction rather than rehabilitating older buildings.[10] These criticisms certainly apply in Cork, but not as badly as elsewhere, and there were many important benefits. Over 800 residences (both flats and houses) were built close to the city centre, increasing the population in an area which had been in continuous decline. The new buildings are reasonably attractive and there are few of the fortress-like apartment blocks that are so widespread in Dublin. Some buildings successfully capitalise on their riverside sites, with balconies

3.104 The city centre, east of the medieval town, was developed through reclaiming the marshes, mainly during the eighteenth century. The new development dense, with no squares or parks left for public use. The line of St Patrick's Street (centre) followed one of the river channels and was not completed until the nineteenth century. The LUTS plan would have controlled the number of cars entering this area, reducing congestion. (Photo: Tomás Tyner.)

Fig. 3.105 In the early twentieth century, St Patrick's Street was a major junction for the electric trams which were then the mainstay of public transport. The trams and horse-drawn carts were replaced by buses and private cars, but St Patrick's Street remained a major thoroughfare through which most traffic was funnelled until the new bridges and ring roads of the 1980s.

overhanging the water, unlike their predecessors that turned their backs to the river.

Urban renewal was a mixed blessing. Over 80 per cent of the new dwellings are flats and many are too small for families. Gardens, play areas and amenities for children are non-existent. Noise disturbance is a problem for residents because of poor sound insulation. Most of the inhabitants are young single adults, including a large number of students and a group of asylum-seekers. Very few intend staying there in the long term. Most newcomers have no contact with people living in the old established communities nearby, and there is little interaction even among people in the same block.[11]

Renewal also began outside the designated areas. Obsolete buildings like the Savoy and Pavilion cinemas and the Queen's Old Castle department store were converted into modern shopping centres and purpose-built malls were erected at Paul Street, Merchant's Quay and North Main Street. These developments were vital in stopping what looked like an irreversible displacement of shopping to suburban locations. Although the city centre is no longer the dominant shopping destination, it can at least now compete with the suburban shopping centres.

A revised urban renewal scheme was introduced in 1994 designating three smaller areas totalling 35 acres. In contrast to the earlier programme, refurbishment of older buildings was favoured over new construction. In addition, seven streets were to receive assistance under a new scheme to encourage 'living over the shop' (LOTS). This especially seemed desirable because a large number of the upper floors in the city centre were completely vacant. Many families who own businesses in the city and traditionally lived over their premises moved to homes in the suburbs, and most of the older flats were closed in the 1980s when fire regulations were enforced after the Stardust disaster in Dublin. By the end of these new schemes in 1998, another 120 homes were available in the city centre.

The Historic Centre Action Plan (HCAP) was another major initiative of the 1990s.[12] This was partly funded by the European Commission under the Conservation of European Cities programme and was focused on the area of the old medieval walled town and its surrounds. Cork was the first Irish city to plan for its historic core, predating Dublin's Historic Area Rejuvenation Project (HARP) initiative by several years. Most of the HCAP proposals were sensitive and thoughtful and avoided any kind of 'Disneyland' makeover for the city centre.

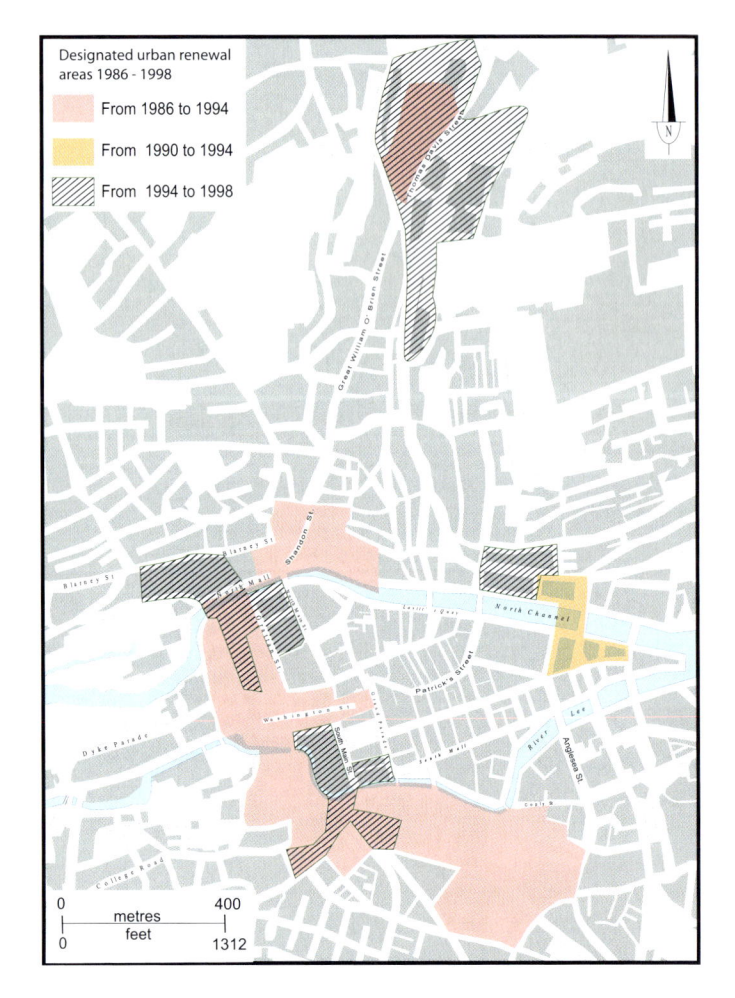

Fig. 3.106 From 1986 to 1998, large areas near the city centre were designated for urban-renewal incentives. Although they vary widely in quality and appearance, new developments have reversed the population decline of the previous 90 years and given the area a more vibrant, lively atmosphere.

THE · CITY · IN · THE · NINETEENTH · AND · TWENTIETH · CENTURIES

Fig. 3.107 The Shandon area was the centre of the butter trade in the eighteenth century. The site of St Anne's church is very much the symbol of Cork city. In the 1980s this traditional housing area was the scene of one of Cork Corporation's earliest local regeneration plans, and benefited from urban renewal after 1986. It is currently coming under increasing pressure from commercial developments (foreground). (Photo: Tomás Tyner.)

The restoration of Fenn's Quay (possibly the oldest terrace in Ireland) and St Peter's church were significant in their own right, but they also acted as training schools in conservation skills. Small items, like the plaques commemorating the lanes of the medieval city, are tasteful and instructive. It is difficult to assess the economic content of HCAP, and the 'dynamic traffic management' seems to have had little impact on congestion, but overall the plan has been beneficial. It coincided with, and incorporated, the 1994 renewal scheme and incentives for living over shops. It was also explicitly aimed at pump-priming the private sector for city-centre renewal, by demonstrating the economic viability of older buildings. One result is the so-called 'Huguenot Quarter' of French Church Street and

Fig. 3.108 Like Shandon on the northside, the South Parish and Barrack Street on the southside is also changing. The transition from the inner city to the suburbs of the early twentieth century is evident in the foreground. (Photo: Tomás Tyner.)

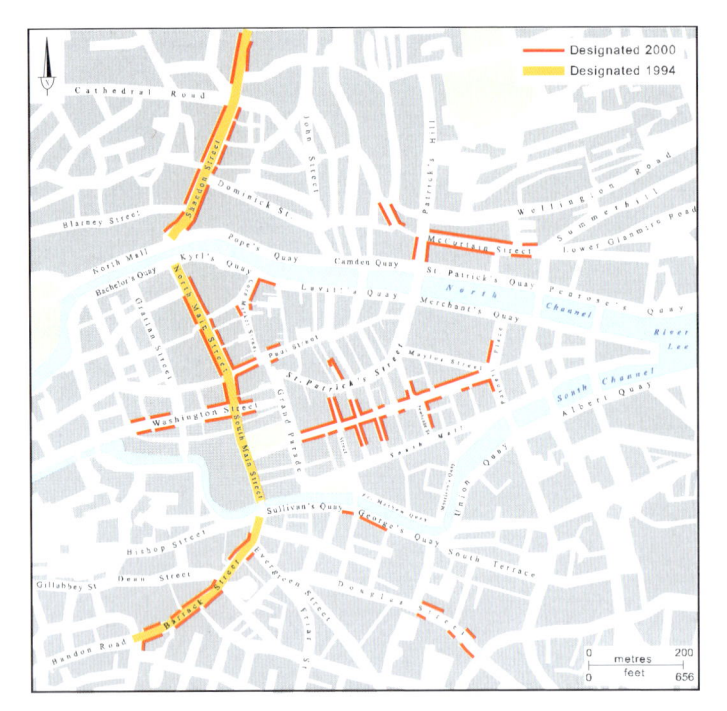

Carey's Lane, where eighteenth-century warehouses have been adapted for shops and restaurants, with considerable success. Generating pride in the city centre is an intangible but lasting legacy of the Historic Centre Action Plan.

The third millennium has not seen the end of urban renewal. In 2001, another series of streets (totalling three kilometres of frontage) was designated for living over the shop for a three-year period. An integrated area plan was produced for the Blackpool/Shandon area. This has encouraged considerable economic and infrastructural development, but has left many of the residents of the area dissatisfied. They blame severe flooding in early 2003 on building over marshy fields that previously absorbed heavy rainfall, and are concerned at the new road that slices through the area.

Fig. 3.109 Living over the shop (LOTS) incentives began in 1994, in conjunction with the Historic Centre Action Plan and the second phase of urban renewal. Although they can be difficult to see at street level, many upper storeys have been refurbished or converted for living purposes and are a very positive contribution to the repopulation of the city centre.

Fig. 3.110 The conservation of Fenn's Quay was one of the showpiece elements of the Historic Centre Action Plan. Possibly the oldest terrace of buildings in Ireland, its name dates from the late medieval period, when it lay just outside the town walls on one of the many waterways that threaded through the area. (Photos: Denis McGarry, Cork City Council.)

THE · CITY · IN · THE · NINETEENTH · AND · TWENTIETH · CENTURIES

Fig. 3.111 The new lampposts on St Patrick's Street were specially designed by Beth Gali as a reminder of Cork's maritime heritage. The new layout of the street is certainly visually attractive, but will need careful management for anti-social behaviour. (Photo: John Crowley.)

The redesign of St Patrick's Street was originally envisaged as a project for the millennium, but was delayed by funding problems and the main drainage works, which caused considerable disruption in the city's streets. Beth Gali, a Catalan architect with an international reputation in this field, was given the commission. The result is a striking innovation for an Irish city, and the street is transformed from a traffic artery to a pedestrian-friendly layout, almost plaza-like in places. As Cork's main shopping thoroughfare, St Patrick's Street has always been busy. Over five hours on Saturdays in March and September, the numbers (aged sixteen years and over) passing Roche's Stores and A-Wear have generally exceeded 30,000, and in September 2002 were almost 45,000 (according to pedestrian counts conducted by the Centre for Retail Studies in UCD). It will be interesting to see whether the redesign of the street will lead to increased numbers. In general, Cork people seem pleased with the work.[13] Some dislike the lamp-posts, but Gali's explanation that they were inspired by ships' masts in the harbour seems

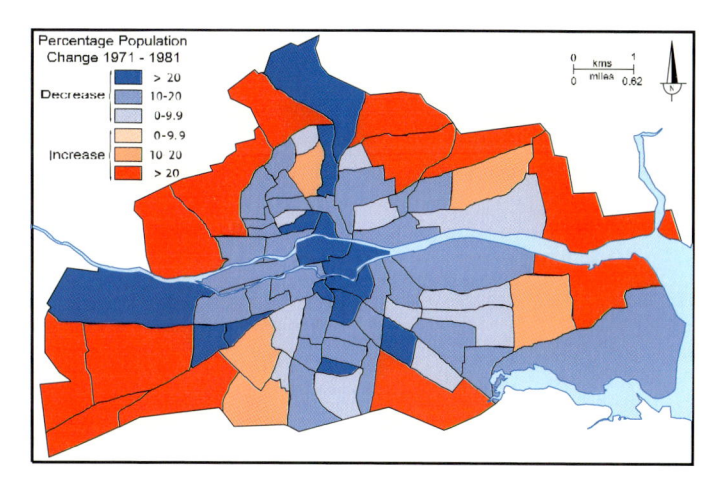

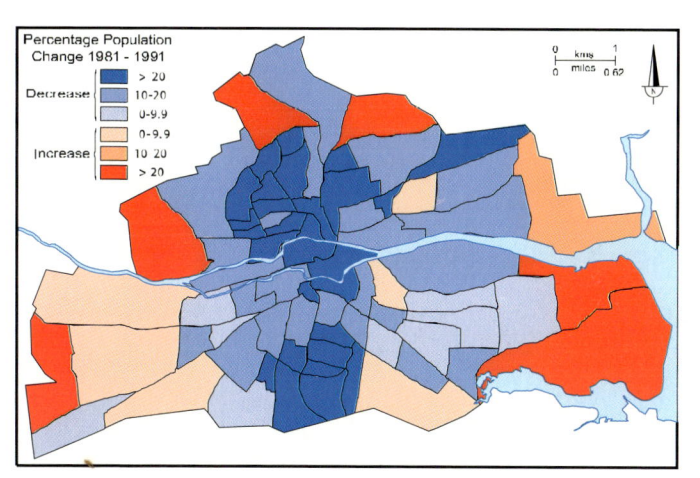

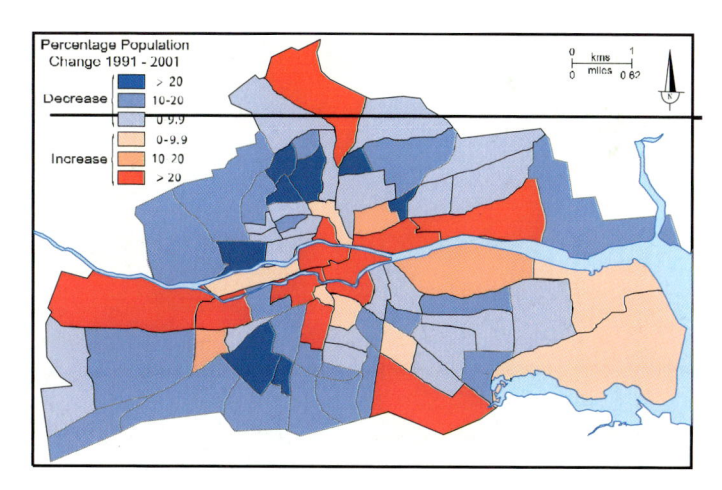

Fig. 3.112 Since 1970, Cork city has been subdivided into 74 wards for electoral and census purposes. The three maps show the patterns of population change for each decade since then. In the 1970s, only eighteen wards had a population increase, all of them on the outskirts of the city. In the 1980s, only twelve were increasing, with ten of these near the city boundary. In both decades, the inner city had heavy population losses. In contrast, between 1991 and 2002 the population grew in 22 wards with the largest increases in and around the city centre. By then, the wards near the city boundary were in decline, although suburban areas outside the city were growing very rapidly.

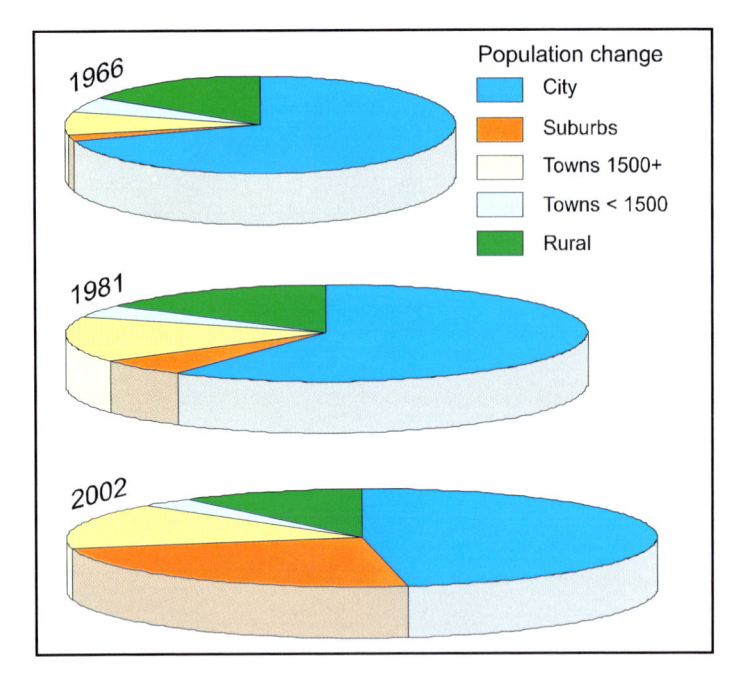

Fig. 3.113 Since the LUTS plan of 1978, the planning area which was defined in the plan has been very useful for identifying population change. In 1966, the total population was almost 175,000; by 1981 it was over 228,000 and almost 259,000 in 2002. The relative shares in the city, suburbs and the nearby towns have been changing in a clear and continuous manner.

reasonable. Many of the new details, like the paving, seats and bicycle racks, are of a high standard.

It is difficult to predict the future for St Patrick's Street. Irish cities have no tradition of using public space like Mediterranean cultures do, although the experience of Copenhagen has shown that Danish people will use spaces that have good amenities and design.[14] In the best scenario, residents of Cork will respond in the same way, and 'doing Pana' will be an enjoyable experience. The city centre dominates the social life of Cork, with its concentration of pubs, clubs, restaurants, cinemas and theatres. Like Dublin, Cork has had its share of drunken hooliganism and violence in recent times. St Patrick's Street has no residents who might take responsibility for reporting incidents to the police, and many, especially females, are already afraid of the area after dark. Unless it is carefully managed and policed, St Patrick's Street could deteriorate into an expensive no-go zone at night.

There were other worthwhile innovations in the 1990s. Emmet Place was redesigned as a pedestrian plaza, providing a forecourt to the Opera House and Crawford Gallery, and, along with Bishop Lucey Park, helping to

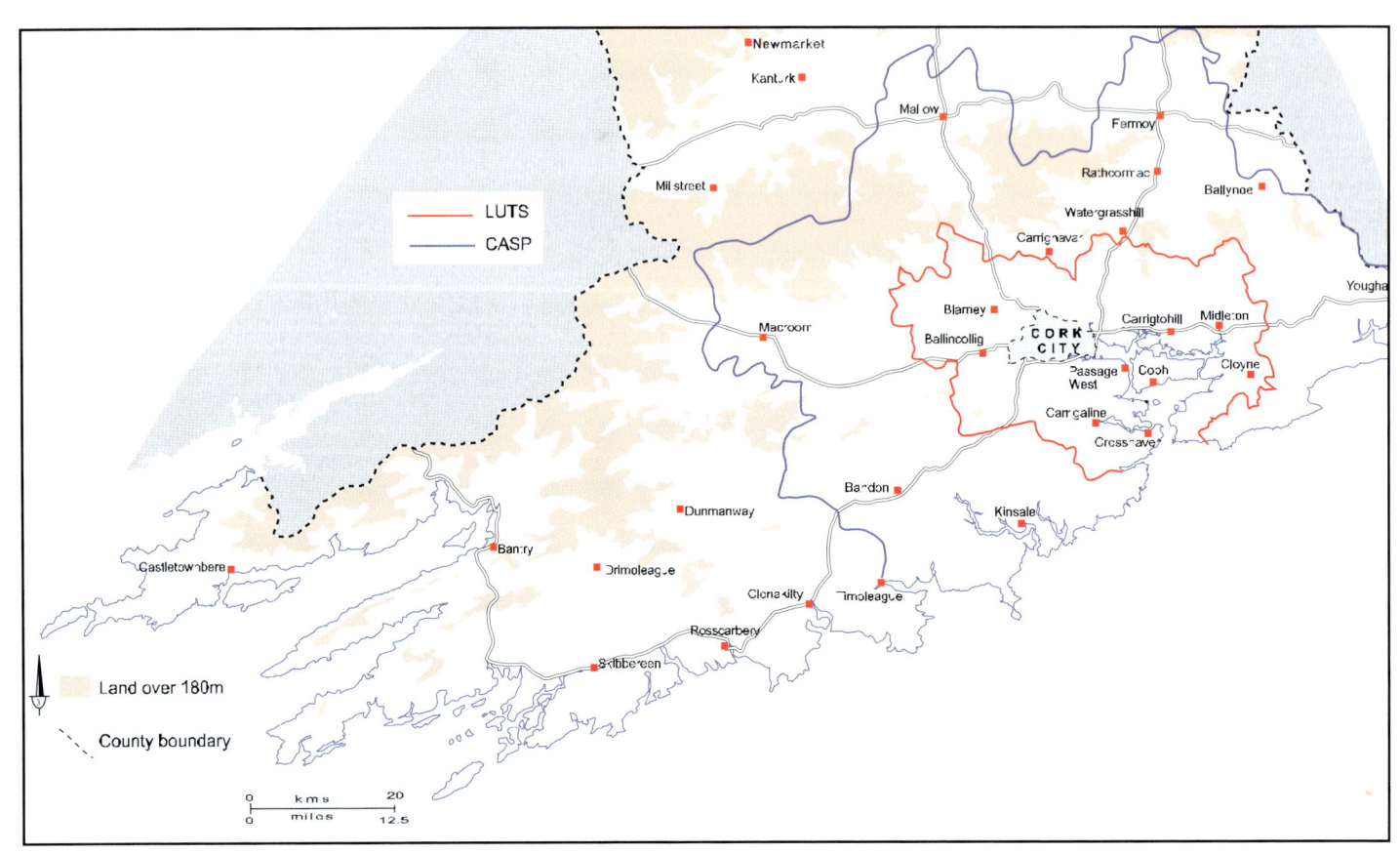

Fig. 3.114 The increasing dominance of the Cork Metropolitan Region, as it was called in the Cork Area Strategic Plan (CASP), is shown in the new boundary identified in 2001. This contrasts with the LUTS area of 23 years earlier. Old market and industrial towns like Macroom and Mallow are now identified as 'ring towns' rather than the kind of independent centres they were previously. This type of urban dominance is a worldwide phenomenon, but is often seen as a threat by people in more remote areas, where they see themselves as marginalised and forgotten. In Ireland, this is well illustrated by the editorials in local newspapers, like, for example, the Skibbereen-based *Southern Star*.

reduce the historic shortage of public open space in Cork. St Fin Barre's bridge over the south channel of the Lee was opened in 1999, linking with the first new street (as opposed to roads) to be built in the city for many years.

Together, these policies for the city centre have reversed the pattern of population change that characterised the twentieth century. This had involved population growth in new suburbs on the outskirts of the built-up area, with decreases in the old inner city and particularly in the centre. In contrast, since 1991 the centre's population has almost doubled and many of the outlying wards have started losing population as they pass through the family life cycle and little space is available for new residential development. The work of the city council and planners was recognised by the Royal Town Planning Institute in the year 2000, when it awarded Cork a Silver Jubilee Cup, the first such distinction for an Irish city. In the near future, the city hopes to build on this success with the redevelopment of the docklands.

Cork in the twenty-first century: an urban region

Although the inner city has been revived over the past twenty years, the outward push of new development still dominates. Of the contiguous built-up area, the suburbs outside the city boundary are growing fastest, by 45 per cent in the 1980s and by 34 per cent in the period 1991–2002. Over one-third of the total population lived in these suburbs in 2002, compared to just 4.3 per cent in 1971 and 9.0 per cent in 1981.

Even these figures understate the blurring of boundaries between the city and countryside. The LUTS plan of 1978 defined an area of 828 km^2 as Cork's daily urban system. This included three towns with legal status – Cobh, Midleton and Passage West – the satellite towns of 1972, and several villages, as well as rural areas. In 1981, the population of the LUTS area was 222,000, of which some two-thirds (67.5 per cent) lived in the city and suburbs. By 2002, the total increased by 16.7 per cent to almost 259,000, with the city and suburbs accounting for almost 72 per cent of the LUTS total.

The Cork Area Strategic Plan (CASP), which was commissioned by the city and county councils in 2000 and accepted by them in 2001, formalised the LUTS area by identifying it as the Cork Metropolitan Region. It argued that it constitutes a single market in terms of jobs and property, and in access to social, cultural and educational facilities. Beyond this, CASP defines a city region extending to about 25 miles from the city (or 45 minutes' journey time) and including a series of 'ring towns' – Kinsale, Bandon, Macroom, Mallow, Fermoy and Youghal. In effect, this is the LUTS area for the early twenty-first century, and, in turn, this will be replaced by a wider area when CASP II is produced in 2020, unless the trends of the past 40 years are suddenly reversed. Already there are reports of daily commuting to Cork from distances of 50 miles or more.

Already, it is clear that new and improved roads are encouraging more dispersed housing developments on a larger scale. Recently, new estates have been built in or near small villages like Ovens, Killumney, Aherla and Cloghduv, to take only the road on the south side of the Bride valley west of Cork. These will be much more accessible by the Ballincollig bypass, and their example will attract even more dispersal from the city proper.

This change in the nature of cities, from the dense concentrations of the early twentieth century into dispersed entities labelled 'urban fields' or 'daily urban systems', is a worldwide phenomenon.[15] In Ireland, it is more advanced in Dublin than in Cork. At its worst, in the United States, it has resulted in many depopulated, almost abandoned, city centres, and the emergence in the countryside of 'edge cities'.[16] The past twenty years suggest that Cork will avoid this kind of doomsday scenario. Change is inevitable, but, if managed properly, a reasonable balance can be maintained between the city and its surrounding region.

25. THE SUBURBS

Kevin Hourihan

We are often inclined to regard suburbs as typically modern, but this is inaccurate. A suburb is an area of housing on the outskirts of the city proper, showing some of the characteristics of both the city and the countryside. The history of suburbs is almost as old as that of cities. It seems, for example, that the ancient city of Ur, in modern-day Iraq, had suburban housing; classical Rome had a prestigious suburb at Tivoli; and even the compact cities of the medieval period had suburban developments outside their walls. In Cork, Sunday's Well and Montenotte developed as high-status suburbs in the late eighteenth and early nineteenth centuries.

The twentieth century has brought the development of mass suburbs, however, and these differ significantly from their predecessors in their size and extent. In most cities nowadays the bulk of the population lives in suburbs, rather than in the older city areas, and these often spread for miles outside the cities. Mass suburbs have developed in response to population growth and rising living standards, but the greatest single influence has been improvements in transportation. The introduction of the electric tram, the motor bus and the electrified commuter railway were important stimuli for development, but the increased ownership and use of private cars since the 1940s has been the most important factor in the spread and design of suburbs.

The image of modern suburbs in both academic writing and the popular media is not favourable.[1] Social life in the suburbs is often viewed as being superficial and transitory, with problems ranging from excessive conformity to a lack of community spirit. The physical design of many suburbs has also been condemned. The lower-density suburban housing lacks the townscape qualities of cities, while the open spaces and greenery compare badly with the countryside.

Five sequential phases of suburban development in Cork during the twentieth century can be identified. These are not simply chronological periods, but rather reflections of different social and economic circumstances and the changing responses of public-housing authorities and private developers. The role of international models and influences is also evident in these phases.

THE INTER-WAR SUBURBS

The need for suburban development in the 1920s and 1930s did not derive from population growth, but rather from terrible housing and health conditions. The *Cork Civic Survey* of 1926 estimated that one-ninth of the city's population (2,900 families) lived in slum-like tenements, most of which were incapable of repair, and 2,400 other houses were unfit for habitation. In total, 16,000 people, one-fifth of the city's population, would need rehousing in 'probably new sites'. An associated problem identified in the survey was the severe lack of open space in the city.

The solution to both problems lay in suburban development on greenfield sites. The Corporation had been active in building new houses since 1886. Between then and 1892, four schemes of bye-law style buildings were constructed, totalling 346 homes.[2] In a second phase in 1905–1906, another 169 houses were provided in three schemes.[3] Although all of these were on greenfield sites, they were terraced buildings of very high density and lacking any gardens or open space, so they did not have the rural element which characterises the modern suburbs.

The three schemes that the Corporation built in 1922–1923 are the first examples in Cork of the modern mass suburb. Even their names, MacCurtain's, MacSwiney's and French's 'Villas', express their aspirations. The inspiration for these developments came from British cities, where there were concerted efforts to combine the best of town and country living in schemes like garden cities and garden suburbs.[4] The best local authorities in Britain had responded with cottage estates, like those in London, and immediately after the end of the First World War there were attempts to establish general standards for suburban housing.[5] In 1918, the Local Government Board recommended a density of twelve houses per acre and the Tudor Walters Report of 1919 suggested design criteria which have had a lasting influence. These included two-storey, single-family houses, separated from facing houses by a general width of 70 feet to allow sunshine to reach all rooms in winter, and with standardised components like doors and windows.

Cork Corporation's villas are two-storey houses with gardens to the front and rear. MacCurtain's (76 houses) and MacSwiney's (40 houses) are mainly laid out in short

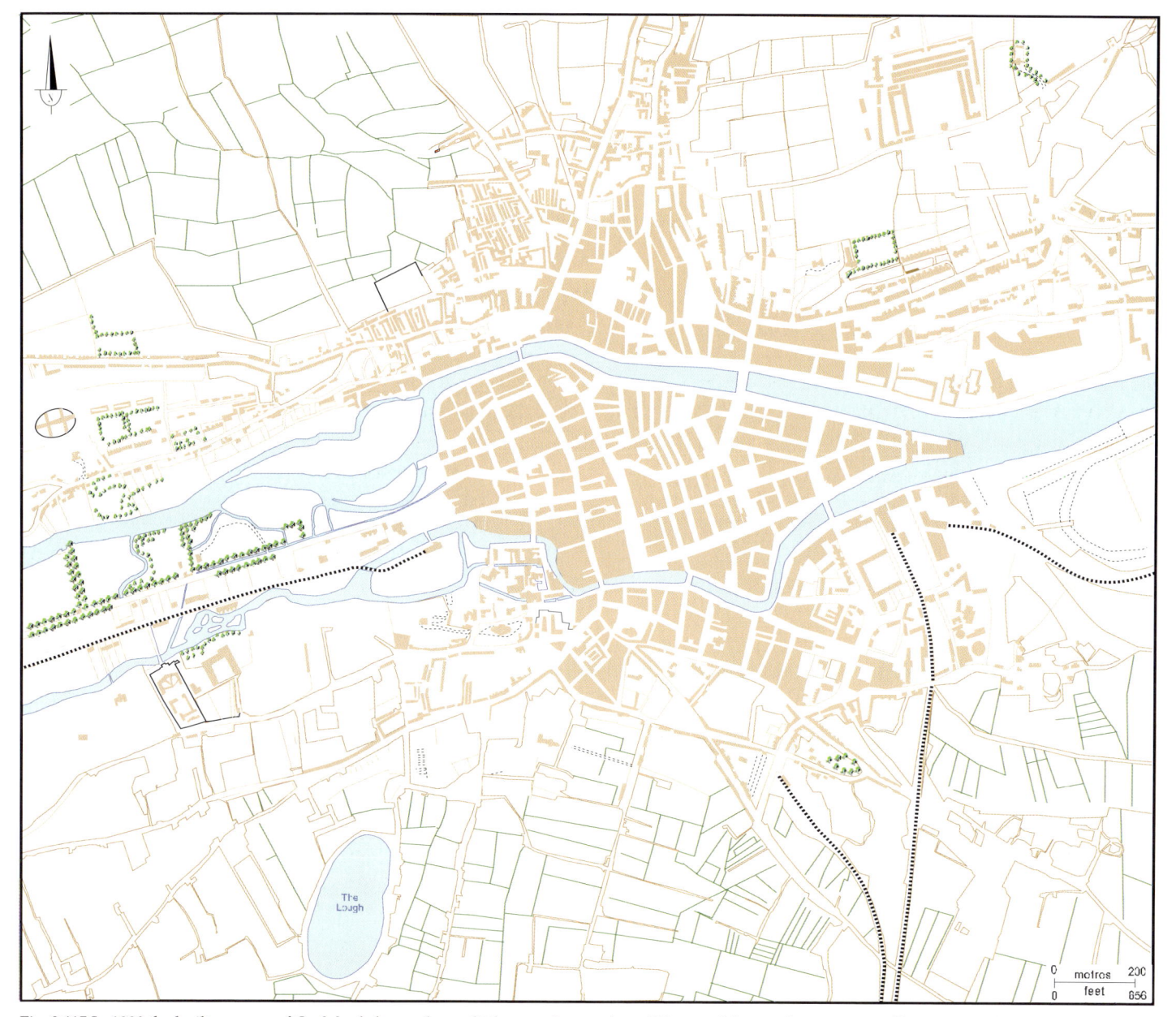

Fig. 3.115 In 1900 the built-up area of Cork had changed very little over the previous 150 years. Most settlement was still concentrated in the medieval core and the eighteenth-century extensions, with later developments to the north and south. Features like The Lough, Queen's College and Victoria Barracks were separated from the city by green fields and open space.

terraces of four (with a few terraces of up to eight buildings). French's Villas, with 30 semi-detached houses laid out in a cul-de-sac, was the most adventurous of the three schemes. The semi-detached house was partly a reaction to the way in which terraced housing had become associated with the working classes and tenements, but it also provided access to back gardens for deliveries of coal, and so on. The semi-detached building became the middle-class standard during the nineteenth century, and its use in French's Villas in 1923 was an enlightened step by Cork Corporation.

Private house building was very slow during the 1920s, averaging less than 20 houses per annum.[6] The Soldiers and Sailors Land Trust built 29 houses at Evergreen and another 60 in a cul-de-sac behind French's Villas on Fair Hill. The Fair Hill Villas scheme (now Kerryhall Road) was made up of short terraces of four to six dwellings and, although the buildings have been modified (originally of brick, they are now mainly pebble-dashed) and the cul-de-sac is open to the green space on Valley Drive, the villas were a progressive development for the 1920s.

Soon after the publication of the *Civic Survey* of 1926, the Corporation began a concerted effort to provide new houses in the city. In 1928, the Capwell development provided 148 homes, laid out in short terraces of four like MacCurtain's Villas. These homes were mainly four-roomed, at a relatively high density of sixteen per acre. They were mainly laid out

Fig. 3.116 Madden's Buildings in Blackpool were the first to be built by Cork Corporation after the Cross Act. Dating from 1886, they comprise 76 houses on two streets, on a site only slightly larger than one acre. Cork was then subject to periodic outbreaks of diseases like cholera and typhoid, which were thought to be caused by miasmas, or putrefying atmospheres. Madden's Buildings were designed with small yards to the rear to allow through ventilation for health purposes. The photograph shows some of the recent modifications to the houses, like the dormers on the roofs to increase the living space. (Photo: Kevin Hourihan.)

Fig. 3.118 French's Villas, built by Cork Corporation in 1923, was one of the best of the early public-housing schemes.

Most of the Corporation's efforts in the years 1934–1941 were concentrated in the north-west of the city. Slum clearance in the Ballymacthomas area had provided space for redevelopment, and the higher, sloping ground was seen along one road over 550 yards long, so they lack the spatial qualities of French's Villas. The same basic design has been repeated dozens of times since 1928, both by the Corporation and by private developers. Another 152 houses were built nearby at Turner's Cross in 1930 at the higher density of nineteen per acre and, in 1932, 168 more houses, all five-roomed in this case, were added. Altogether, the Corporation had provided 468 houses in these three developments in four years, but this was well short of their annual target of 350 houses if the slum problem were to be resolved.

Fig. 3.117 Privately built semi-detached houses on Wilton Road show the 'villa' aspirations of middle-class homes, with classical motifs on their façades. (Photo: John Crowley.)

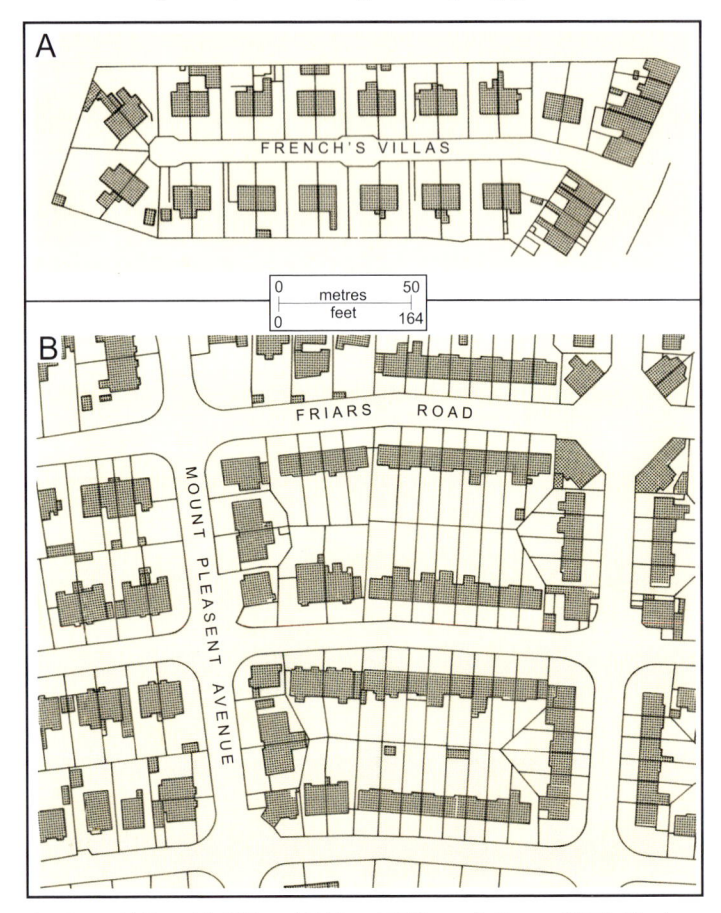

Fig. 3.119 A) French's Villas of 1923 and B) Turner's Cross of 1930. The later scheme shows many of the features which are characteristic of public housing around this time: terraces, often up to eight or ten buildings, laid out on straight lines, roads with many intersections, and very few communal amenities or public open spaces.

as being healthier than the low-lying centre of the city. Another factor was the greater freedom of location afforded by the new public bus system which replaced the trams in 1931. Henceforth, transport could follow new suburban developments, rather than determining it. This new freedom was enhanced by the Town and Regional Planning Act of 1934, which allowed the Corporation to designate a contiguous planning area around the city if necessary, thereby reducing potential conflict between itself and Cork County Council. This useful measure would remain in force until the Planning Act of 1963.

Intensive building began in Gurranabraher in 1934, with over 500 houses built by 1936. These houses were laid out in terraces of up to ten with short gardens to the front and longer ones to the rear. The overall layout is dense and unimaginative, but the terraces follow the contours of the slope and do have a southerly aspect. The same cannot be said of the 1936 development at Spangle Hill, where 170 houses were laid out in north–south terraces on an east-facing slope, in what was then an isolated location. Aside from the gardens, these developments were as unimaginative as Madden's Buildings of 1886.

There were some innovations in the Corporation schemes of the 1930s. Bathrooms were introduced in 1936. The first six-roomed houses were occupied at Assumption Road in 1938 and a variety of house types were built at Farranferris in 1939. There was a marked improvement in the health conditions of the population. Deaths from typhoid and tuberculosis in particular had been greatly reduced since the beginning of the century. The building of almost 1,900 new houses by the Corporation between 1934 and 1941 was a major achievement and, when the priority was providing large numbers of houses as efficiently as possible, social, environmental and design considerations were generally of less importance.

THE POST-WAR SUBURBS: 1946–1965

The Corporation built no new houses in the period 1942–1945, and when building resumed in 1946 it was guided by the same philosophy of suburban development. This was reinforced by the development plan prepared for the Corporation by Manning Robertson in 1941.[7] He endorsed the use of two-storey houses with gardens, with generous provision of parks and open space. The suspension of slum clearance in the war years caused housing conditions to deteriorate and there were serious outbreaks of tuberculosis, diphtheria and poliomyelitis. The late 1940s were fairly depressed and the Corporation built only 212 new houses in the period 1946–1949. By 1950, the city's medical officer estimated that over 4,100 families still needed rehousing. These problems were exacerbated by the population increase of the 1950s and 1960s: between 1946 and 1966 the city's population grew by 18,000 persons. This demand would be met by the Corporation and, increasingly, by private suburban development.

In 1948, the first city architect was appointed and the Corporation formed its Direct Labour Unit for house building. Over 3,000 new municipal dwellings were built in the 1950s. At first, the heaviest concentration was on the southside, with 525 houses at Ballyphehane in the period 1950–1955, and 260 houses to the west at Killeenreendowney.

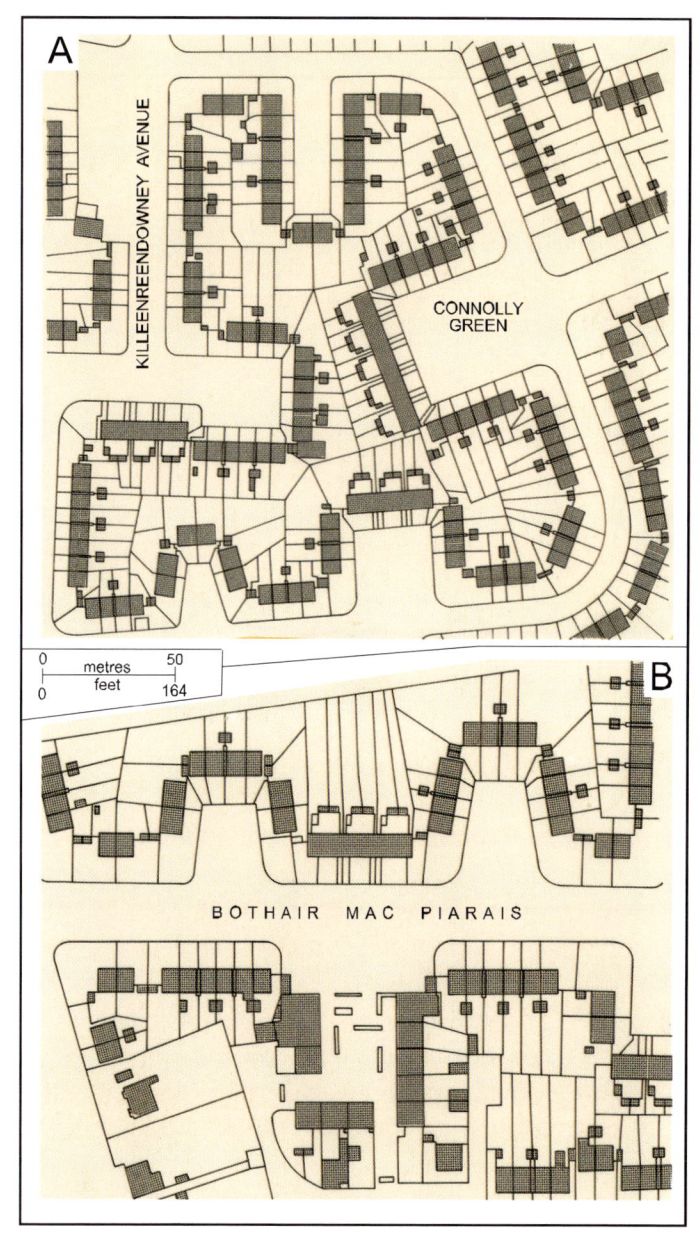

Fig. 3.120 Almost 800 homes were built by the Corporation in Ballyphehane and Killeenreendowney in the 1950s and they were the most attractive and innovative suburbs in the city, probably until the 1980s. They reduce through traffic, provide generous green areas and open space, and contain a variety of house types. These qualities were totally absent in middle-class estates of this time.

Fig. 3.121 Ballyphehane, with its housing squares and greenery, was a major advance in Corporation housing. (Photo: John Crowley.)

The latter scheme in particular was of a high standard, with a variety of house types (from one to three storeys in height) laid out in short terraces along a continuous loop road that was designed to discourage through traffic. The terraces themselves were staggered to break up the continuous façades that had characterised earlier developments, and there is an imaginative distribution of small green spaces and squares. There was not much landscaping and planting was confined to some shrubs and avenue lines of cherry trees. A few forest trees would have provided better vertical contrasts to the horizontal layouts, but, in their absence, the cherry trees ensure that for at least a couple of weeks each year the area is a blaze of colour.

The northside estates at Fairfield and Churchfield were not as attractive. There were some small squares and culs-de-sac, but most of the terraces are laid out in continuous lines along straight roads. Landscaping was negligible and there was an unwelcome appearance of SLOAP (Space Left Over After Planning).[8] Cork Corporation have required two hectares of open space per 1,000 population in new developments to ensure adequate public green areas in the suburbs. Much of the open space along Valley Drive in particular is steeply sloping, and would possibly be unacceptable to the Corporation by present criteria and of little value for recreational or amenity purposes.

In the 1960s, the Corporation's emphasis moved from the periphery to cleared sites in the inner city, where their developments were, of necessity, smaller. Most of these developments were three-storey terraces without gardens, like Fort Street and St Finbarr's Road, and in Blackpool four-storey blocks of flats were developed at Green Lane.

The post-war suburbs also saw speculatively developed estates and those of the 1940s included Wilton Road, Belvedere in Douglas, Beaumont Drive in Ballintemple, and St Christopher's, St Anne's and St Joseph's Drives in Montenotte. These earlier developments were often not contiguous with the existing built-up area, but rather tended to spread along the arterial roads. This ribbon development had been widespread in British cities before the war, where it had caused transport and environmental problems. Post-war planning controls restricted it in Britain, but it would continue in Ireland through the 1950s and 1960s and it continues even today in many towns and cities.

The semi-detached house became the standard form in speculative estates, clearly distinguishing it from the terraced municipal housing. In these earlier estates, garages were generally not provided. Car-ownership was relatively low, and motorists could park their cars in the space beside their houses. Since then, many have built garages, often linking with those next door and so removing one of the main advantages of the design, access to back gardens. Visually, the garages exacerbate the jagged, uneven appearance of these estates.

Private estate development became more rapid during the 1950s and 1960s. Almost all continued the basic characteristics of middle-class suburbia: large numbers of semi-detached houses, with garages added more frequently, laid out in straight lines along a rectangular road system and with open space in the form of one large patch. Landscaping or planting was minimal. The middle-class suburbs were increasingly dependent on transport by private cars, so road widths and design were based on this. There was no provision for separating pedestrian, or cyclist, and vehicular movement. In short, none of the planning innovations of the twentieth century was evident in Cork's suburbs.[9]

HOUSING PRESSURES AND SUBURBAN SPRAWL: 1965–1980

Cork's population increased by 2,000 per annum between 1961 and 1979. Combined with increasing affluence, this generated great demand for new housing and resulted in the building of over 700 new houses annually on average through the 1960s and 1970s. In 1965, more houses were built by private developers than by the Corporation and, increasingly, speculative estates provided a greater share of the new houses in Cork.

Economics was the overriding influence on the middle-class estates of the 1960s and 1970s. The main influence on house builders was the buyers' capacity to finance their purchase, followed by site and building costs.[10] Design considerations were far less important. It was a time of high inflation, particularly of house prices, and the result was suburban estates that were built as cheaply as possible. Roads were long and straight, as this saved on road length

Fig. 3.122 From 1930 to 1980, most development on the north-west side of Cork was Corporation housing (left), built in response to severe housing needs but lacking most other amenities. (Photo: Tomás Tyner.)

Fig. 3.123 Many of the middle-class estates that were developed in the post-war period were laid out on busy traffic roads. Today they are exposed to heavy noise, pollution and congestion. (Photo: John Crowley.)

per house and the cost of utilities. Economies were also achieved through building large estates, sometimes of hundreds of houses, and of standardising the styles as much as possible. Typically, the estates of that era have only a couple of house types in them: three and four-bedroomed semi-detacheds. The cost of marketing just a couple of house types was less than if a variety of designs had been used.

Despite this, the housing market was competitive and in the 1970s an increasing number of cost-saving measures were introduced. The space between buildings became progressively smaller, so that even detached houses were separated by only a few feet in some cases and garden sizes became diminutive in order to save on site costs. The quality of materials also disimproved, with items like cavity blocks, and untreated window frames that rotted after only a few years. Some builders even returned to the use of terraced houses, despite its continued association with municipal estates. Middle-class aspirations were maintained through 'neo-Georgian' motifs in some cases (although few of these terraces have the proportions and harmony of eighteenth-

Fig. 3.124 The 'town houses' of the 1970s and 1980s made many attempts to distinguish themselves from Corporation terraces. (Photo: Kevin Hourihan.)

century Georgian housing), and in others by incorporating garages, usually by an extension to the front. These developments were invariably marketed as 'town houses' rather than 'terraces', and were invariably also described as 'luxury' or 'de luxe'. This marketing is still evident today.

Another legacy of this period is a clear distinction between the names of speculative and Corporation estates. The latter were usually called after distinguished persons in the War of Independence or public life, but private developers preferred increasingly 'posh' and foreign-sounding names, to add social status to their estates. Terms like 'mews', 'close' and 'court' were used inappropriately. Often the developments fell far short of the images conjured up by the names. Another undesirable trend of this time was the activity of 'trading-up'. The rapid inflation of house prices encouraged people to sell their current houses after only a short period and buy a more expensive house in a more desirable location. The rapid turnover of residents in many estates militated against community development and trading-up added to the status distinctions of different parts of the city. Suburban houses were no longer just homes; increasingly, they became consumer products that reflected a more materialistic and ostentatious culture.

The residents of the private suburbs depended heavily on private motor cars for transport, and the road networks were designed for cars rather than the safety or convenience of pedestrians, much less their visual attractiveness. They were, however, inefficient, with many junctions which cause congestion on arterial roads. The main roads, often poorly designed, were frequently blocked with traffic and many motorists resorted to using 'rat runs' through housing estates. This brought serious disruption and danger for residents. Attempts to control it through ramps and rumble strips have had little effect and it remains visible throughout the suburbs today. Public transport was not a realistic alternative to private cars, as buses, or any other mode of mass transit, need a certain population density to be viable. Few bus lines run through the private estates, and people are often unwilling to walk any distance to the main roads.

The demand for more public housing also increased during the 1960s. The Corporation responded by giving a contract to the National Building Agency (NBA) for over 1,800 dwellings in three estates, Mayfield, The Glen and Togher. Almost 70 per cent were houses, mainly three-bedroomed, with the remainder being flats. Their construction was a new development for public housing in that they were system-built of pre-fabricated units. If the speculative estates of the period generally comprised solid housing in poor layouts, the reverse was true of the NBA developments. The houses were centrally heated and had no chimneys. There were problems of ventilation and consequently of condensation and damp. With their dull grey colour, the buildings looked unattractive. Yet, their layout was superior to anything in the private sector at that time. The best of the three estates was that at Togher, where the 318 dwellings form terraces of six in short culs-de-sac leading off a loop road. A central spine of green space runs through the development and there is a good system of pedestrian paths separated from vehicular traffic. The same elements are used in the other two developments, but their larger size (864 dwellings in Mayfield, 630 in the Glen) and less focused layout are not as attractive as Togher. The remedial work that the Corporation carried out on the NBA houses has greatly improved them.

The other large Corporation development of the 1970s was at Knocknaheeny. This comprised 715 houses in terraces of four and six. These were built by direct labour and structurally were far better than the NBA developments. Some of the details, like pedestrian paths, are quite good, and the western part of the estate that was built later has more culs-de-sac and squares. There was an attempt at social mixing by providing land nearby for private developments, albeit separated by Harbour View Road. Overall, though, the size of the estate, its isolated, exposed location on the summit of the ridge, and the unemployment

Fig. 3.125 What's in a name? These two are separated by two miles and forty years. One is unmistakably Irish, the other probably more appropriate for Hampshire or Beverly Hills. (Photo: Kevin Hourihan.)

and social problems that arose soon after its construction have caused difficulties at Knocknaheeny.

The two major plans of the late 1960s and early 1970s both reinforced the trend of large-scale suburbanisation. The BKS report of 1968 wanted to sacrifice much of the city centre to the needs of private motorists, most of them commuting from suburbs. Combined with this was the satellite town policy adopted by the County Council. This may have limited suburban developments near the city boundary, but it encouraged them further out in the designated towns.

Towards better suburban design

By the 1970s, dissatisfaction with suburban design was increasing in many countries. In Britain, Essex County Council was the first local authority to issue a design-guide manual for new developments in 1973, but it was quickly followed by many others.[11] These made many useful recommendations about housing, density, spacing, landscaping, roads and traffic. Although Cork County Council produced a design guide for rural houses in 2004, there is still no equivalent for suburban developments around the city. In Sweden, also, new standards were being set, and Dutch planners developed the idea of the 'woonerf'. This involves adapting roads to control traffic rather than facilitating it, by narrowing the surface, planting small gardens in a staggered fashion on it and providing spaces for children along the road. Even now, these principles could profitably be applied to many of our suburban roads. Oscar Newman's study of 'defensible space' in New York also generated interest.[12] This design involves locating dwellings so that other homes can be casually overlooked, and organising space so that residents develop a sense of proprietorship and responsibility for it. These principles were completely lacking in Cork's suburbs, where housing was located to increase privacy, and space was clearly demarcated into just two types: private and public. Most residents had no identification with the public spaces and the result was litter, graffiti and green spaces with very little maintenance. Newman's ideas also seem particularly relevant at present, with neighbourhood watch schemes occurring in many areas.

The mid-1970s brought a number of critiques of Irish suburbs by professional bodies. The 1975 publication *Dublin: A city in crisis*, included three chapters devoted to the suburbs and in 1976 An Foras Forbartha published *Streets for living*.[13] Semi-detached housing was critically examined by James Murphy in 1977.[14] As well as criticism of current suburbs, all of these papers made positive suggestions for future designs and, fortunately, these have become increasingly evident in the developments of the past 25 years.

As with previous suburbs, the Corporation led the way. Mahon was the only remaining large area to be developed within the county borough, and the Corporation made great efforts to avoid the problems of past estates. A design team was set up, which was actually based in Mahon to monitor progress and to be available to developers and residents. Corporation housing included a range of sizes and styles, mixed together and laid out in an imaginative fashion around courts and culs-de-sac, incorporating many of the recommendations from An Foras Forbartha and others. An attempt was made to have a mix of municipal and private housing, but this has not materialised, partly because of the recession of the early 1980s, but also through the reluctance of speculative builders to become involved.

The Curraheen estate in Bishopstown was built for the Corporation by the NBA in the late 1970s, but using direct labour rather than the prefabricated units of the earlier schemes. It is an excellent design and visually far more attractive than the nearby estates that were speculatively developed. It also has playing fields and open space adjacent to it and a primary school was built very soon after the estate was occupied. The long delay in providing local services like schools had been very difficult for many earlier suburbs. The Corporation maintained these high

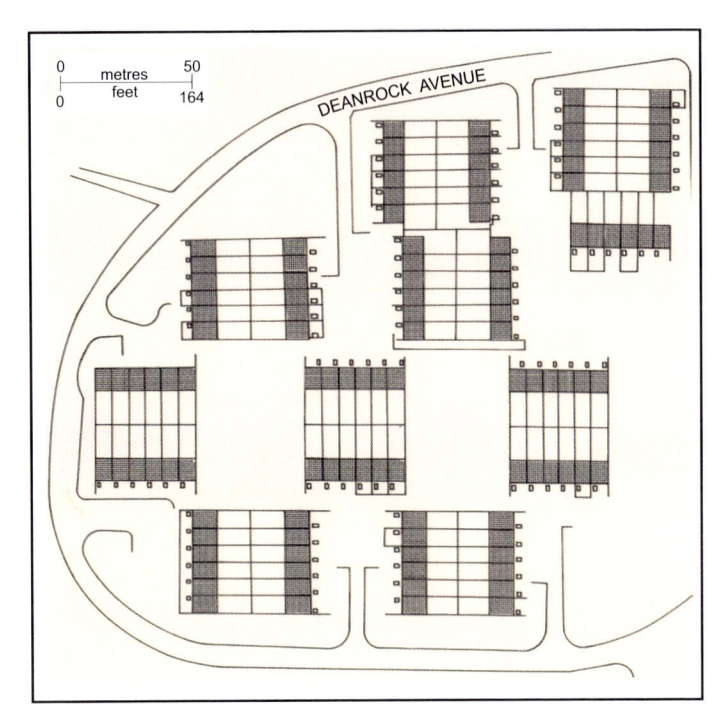

Fig. 3.126 The Deanrock estate in Togher, built by the National Building Authority (NBA) in the 1970s, had a far superior layout than any of the speculative estates of that time. Unfortunately, the buildings themselves were prefabricated, with flat roofs, and were very unattractive. They also had serious problems of condensation.

in Grange and Donnybrook. These guidelines have created a more attractive environment through the use of culs-de-sac and squares, better landscaping and open space, and more sensitive use of the natural site. These estates still use semi-detached houses, but in the Oakdale–Briars Court development in Shanakiel neo-Georgian terraces are used in an effective fashion to create a suburban version of the city squares of the eighteenth century. At present, layout and landscaping have become important considerations in standards in their other suburban developments, like Leesdale on the Model Farm Road, but during the 1980s most attention was focused on the inner city. The Corporation attempted to revive this declining area through infill developments on small sites (like Cobh Street and Broguemakers Hill), designating housing protection areas, restoring old homes through a revolving fund and encouraging redevelopment under the Urban Renewal Bill of 1986. This emphasis, together with financial constraints, meant that few suburban houses were built by Cork Corporation during the 1980s.

Private suburban development also slowed considerably during this period. The emigration of many young people who would otherwise have bought houses and the recession and unemployment greatly reduced the demand for new houses. On the positive side, the quality of development improved significantly. This was encouraged by new planning criteria introduced by Corporation planners in 1985. Prior to this, new housing developments had to meet quantitative standards of density, open space and services. The 1985 development plan also included qualitative criteria designed to improve the visual appearance of new estates. The result has been some innovative developments on the outskirts of the city: like Barnavara and The Downs in Mayfield, Parklands off the Commons Road, Palmbury in Togher and the newer estates

Fig. 3.127 After refurbishment, the Deanrock homes were greatly improved (A), although some of the flats remain in their original condition (B). (Photo: Kevin Hourihan.)

THE • CITY • IN • THE • NINETEENTH • AND • TWENTIETH • CENTURIES

Fig. 3.128 The Curraheen estate (right foreground) was one of the earliest attempts by the Corporation to break from the conventions of the previous 50 years. It is ringed by privately built speculative estates of the 1970s, where the layouts are monotonous and unappealing. These were heavily used by commuters as 'rat runs' for years before the completion of the Ballincollig bypass (background). (Photo: Tomás Tyner.)

marketing new suburban developments, as is evident in most advertisements.

THE URBANISATION OF THE SUBURBS

Despite the improved appearance and aesthetics of Cork's suburbs over the past twenty years, other factors are changing the quality of suburban life in many respects, not for the better. By the 1970s, American suburbs were becoming increasingly city-like.[15] As the inner cities declined, their economic functions – manufacturing, retailing, services and offices – were all decentralising to the suburbs. This has also occurred in Cork, although it has been balanced by the renewal of the city centre over the past twenty years. Nowadays, there are several large employment centres located in Cork's suburbs. Wilton/Bishopstown is a good example, with the University Hospital, Cork Institute of Technology, shopping centres, factories, services, recreation and leisure amenities, and local authority and private offices. In many respects, it is self-contained, virtually independent of the city centre.

In other respects also, the suburbs are changing. In the past, Cork's suburbs were almost exclusively single-family homes, which were owner-occupied or rented from the Corporation. This has changed since the introduction of Section 23 tax relief in 1981 for investment in property for renting. This will finally run out in 2006, but it has encouraged the construction of large numbers of apartment blocks throughout the suburbs. Planning policies for higher residential densities have also favoured these developments. They are not popular with the residents of nearby housing estates, who often view them as excessively large and out of character with their own homes. In the south-west of the city, feelings ran so high that one candidate for the city council election in 2004 campaigned expressly against 'high-rise' developments. He was not elected but did receive over 600 first-preference votes. Technically, the apartment blocks are not 'high-rise'; most do not exceed three or four storeys in height. Probably their most negative impact will be through increased traffic on suburban roads that are already severely congested. Section 50 tax relief was first introduced in 1999 to encourage purpose-built student accommodation. It will also expire in 2006, and is having a similar impact to Section 23. A good example is the huge 'Edenhall @ The Village' complex on the Model Farm Road. Advertisements describe it as a 'futuristic campus style environment with five star accommodation'. By any standards, it is a long way from the suburbs of the early twentieth century.

Fig. 3.129 A new private estate in Lehenaghmore on the southern outskirts of the city. The houses are arrayed on loops, adapted to the terrain and with open space running through the development. In the foreground are parts of an industrial estate and older, once-off houses. (Photo: Tomás Tyner.)

Another American innovation that has surfaced in Cork is the so-called 'gated community'. In Irish cities, housing has always been divided by social class and, because of the scale of development during the twentieth century by both city councils and private builders, entire areas of our cities are now identified only as working class or middle class. Attempts at social mixing have been weak and unsustained. The policy of requiring private developers to provide 20 per cent of land for social housing was abandoned after just a few years. Social mixing may be generally unsuccessful, anyway, as research in America suggests.[16] However, gated developments go far beyond living among one's own social class. Most are managed by private homeowners' associations, to which the residents pay dues. If they are incorporated, the residents' property tax payments can be deducted from federal and state income taxes. In effect, many gated communities have privatised traditional public rights and responsibilities. They have been labelled 'privatopias', heralding a future 'Fortress America'.[17] Although it is unlikely that gated developments in Ireland can resort to these extremes, they have emerged in small numbers, motivated by the same ethos of privilege and exclusion. They may be rationalised on the basis of fear of crime and mistrust of outsiders but are not a desirable social feature.

Other characteristics which many people associate with cities have also become widespread in Cork's suburbs. Traffic congestion can now be as severe in many suburban areas as in the city centre. Changing travel patterns in the city are reflected in the new orbital bus routes. Car-ownership is continuously increasing, as are rat runs and disruption of residential areas. Joy-riding no longer receives the publicity it formerly did but it does continue. Behaviour which many people associate with vagrancy in the city centre, like alcohol and drug parties in public places, are now more common among teenagers in the suburbs. Design innovations of the 1960s and 1970s, like pedestrian paths and open spaces, are now being used for crime and vandalism.

There have always been inherent contradictions in the suburban ideal. Lewis Mumford encapsulated some of these in his description of suburbs as 'a collective attempt to live a private life'.[18] On the one hand, people are living in close proximity to their neighbours, while attempting at the same time to maximise their own privacy. In the same way, suburbs lie next door to other suburbs and the older city, while attempting to stay apart. Neither attempt can be entirely successful. It may be that the idealised suburban family and its home was always unrealistic, but the social and economic changes in the recent past make even the image of the ideal difficult to maintain nowadays.

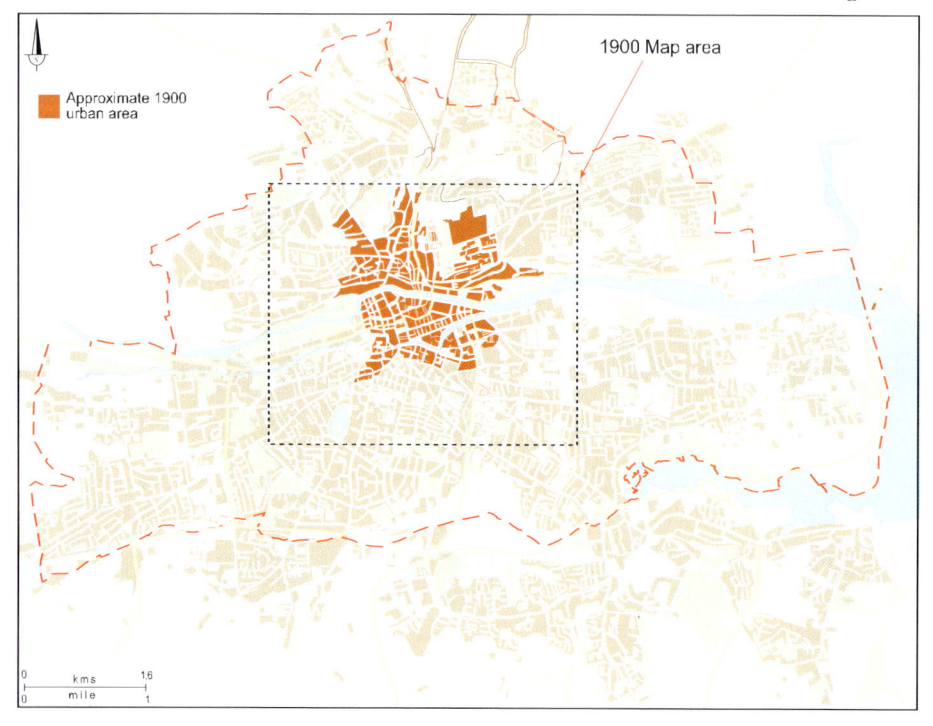

Fig. 3.130 By the year 2000, Cork city had expanded dramatically since 1900, with the suburbs continuing to spread outwards. Very little undeveloped land remains within the city boundary, and the largest recent developments have been on the slopes to the south. More recently, many substantial estates have been built several miles outside the city, with the residents commuting every day.

Conclusions

Buying a house is the most expensive purchase of a lifetime. The housing environment is a crucial aspect of family life, community development and the socialisation of children. However, providing an attractive and efficient environment has not been a major consideration for much of the past century. Rather, economic and traffic concerns have been the major influences. Nevertheless, the aesthetic quality of our housing is important and people would be better off living in attractive designs rather than in monotonous estates. The best visual designs are also superior for traffic safety, crime reduction and, probably, social interaction.

Over 88 per cent of the homes in Cork city and suburbs in 2002 had been built since 1919, most of them in the suburbs of their times. One-third were built after 1980, when suburban designs improved, so over 31,000 homes date from the period 1919–1979. Most of these are structurally sound and could be improved though the redesign of roads and open spaces, with landscaping and tree planting. The balance between town and countryside inherent in a suburb is always delicate. As long ago as 1876, one critic of the new developments in London stated: 'A modern suburb is a place which is neither one thing nor the other, which has neither the advantage of the town nor the open freedom of the country, but manages to combine in a nice equality of proportion the disadvantages of both.'[19]

Whatever about 1876, this certainly has a ring of prophecy about many twentieth-century developments. Community architecture, as propounded by Rod Hackney and his associates in Britain, has been concerned with the problems of multi-family blocks.[20] The deficiencies of single-family suburban housing are not as serious, and imaginative improvements could be achieved at far less expense. In the USA also, the source of so many contemporary suburban developments, a movement called the New Urbanism, has started a serious debate about American suburban design.[21] In Ireland, we have followed the British and American lead in our housing areas; it will not be incongruous if we also have to copy their solutions.

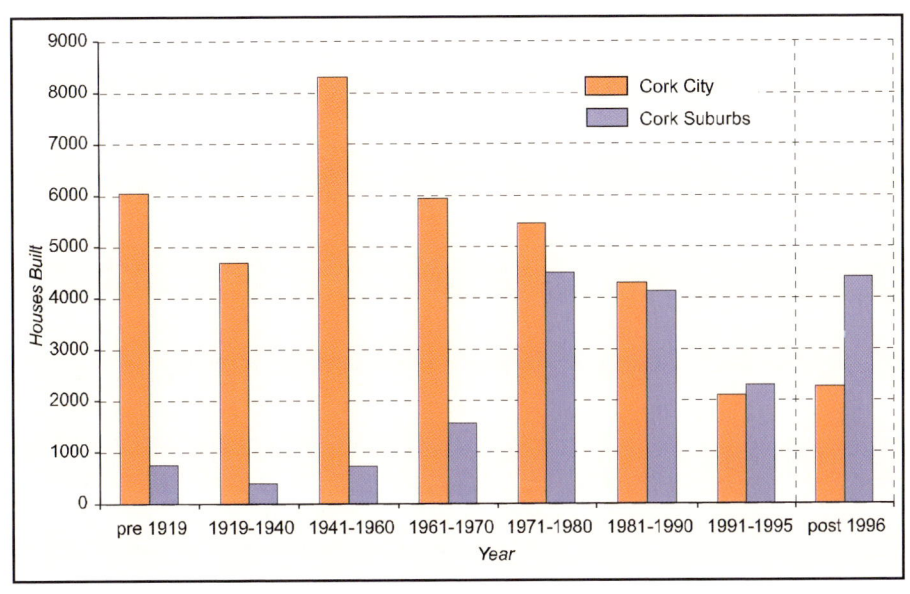

Fig. 3.131 Much of the current suburban development has a 'scatter-shot' appearance, with large estates springing up in the middle of green areas. These depend heavily on private transport for work, school, shopping, etc. (Photo: Tomás Tyner.)

Fig. 3.132 Until 1970, most new houses in Cork were built within the city. Between 1970 and 1990, almost as many were built in the suburbs as within the city. Since 1991, suburban development has dominated and this trend looks certain to continue.

26. BUILDINGS AND ARCHITECTURE

Richard F. Wood

The city's troubled past, its fertile hinterland, its spectacular harbour, together with its provincial status, religious rivalry and an ambivalent relationship with the British Empire, were elements that contributed to the development, as well as sometimes to the destruction, of buildings in Cork.

The effects of wars and poverty during medieval times has meant that few buildings now remain from that period: the tower of the Red Abbey, the recently discovered town wall on the Grand Parade, the star-shaped Elizabeth Fort watching the old part of the city from its rocky crag off Barrack Street and the Dean's Gate in the precincts of St Fin Barre's Cathedral, which served as the west door of the cathedral until 1865 when the present one was built. William Burges, the Cathedral's architect, did this gate the honour of copying its scalloped design for the porch of the estate church of Newby Hall at Skelton in Yorkshire, his next commission.

Medievalism persisted longer in Ireland than elsewhere in Europe because of the unsettled state of the country, and as late as 1650 we see a defended house being built at

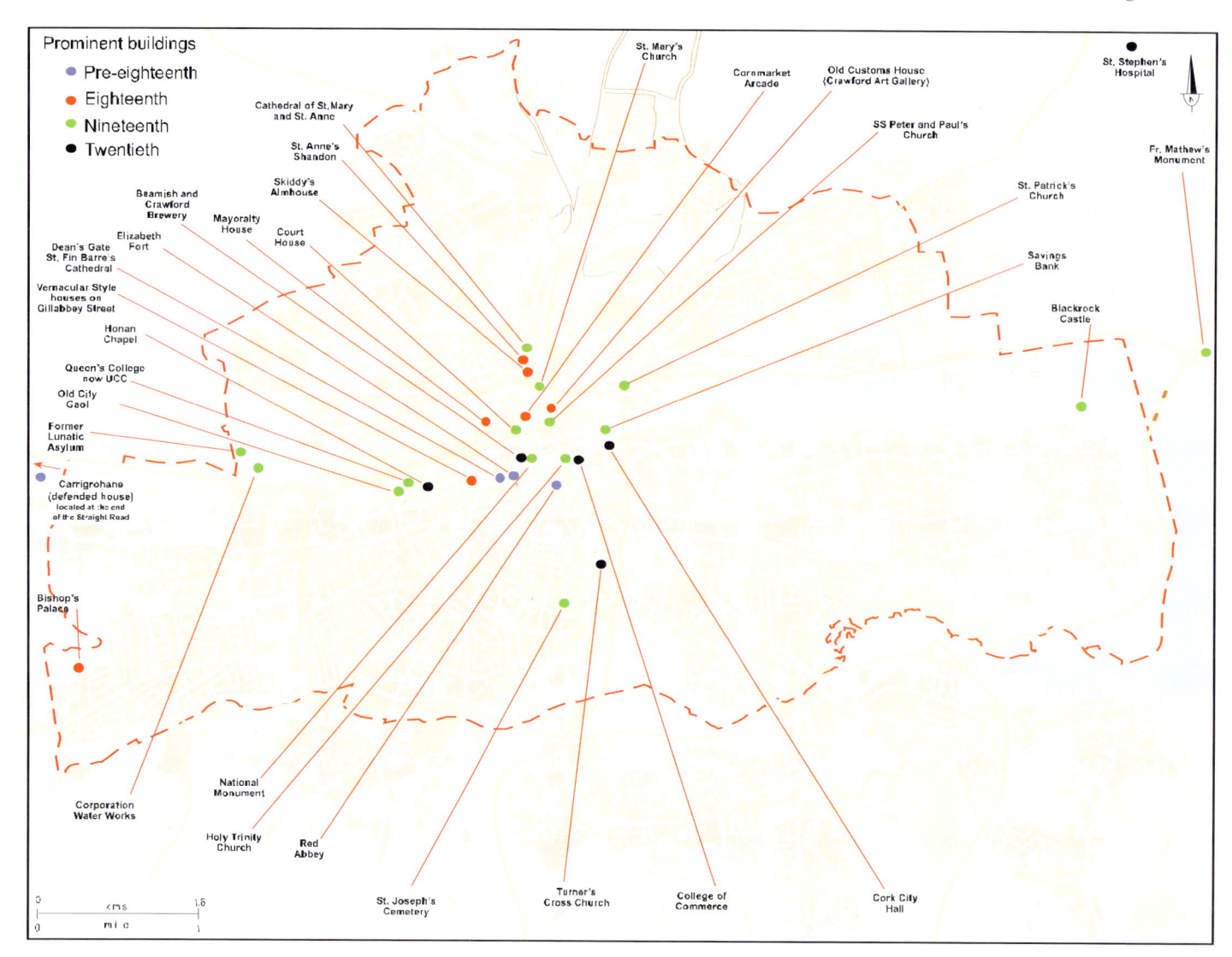

Fig. 3.133 Location of significant buildings in Cork.

THE · CITY · IN · THE · NINETEENTH · AND · TWENTIETH · CENTURIES

Fig. 3.134 Carrigrohane Castle, a fortified house which was built *c*. 1650.

Fig. 3.135 The Bishop's Palace (*c*. 1720s), whose sole concession to grandeur is its impressive stone doorcase clearly marking the entrance. (Photo: Richard Wood.)

Carrigrohane, where a cautious move was made away from the old castle to something more comfortable. With its small Gothic door, mullioned windows, bartizans and battlements, it is a perfect example of a transitional building.

Anglican dominance

The Battle of the Boyne in 1690 brought with it greater stability as well as Anglican hegemony, reflected vividly in the early-eighteenth century Bishop's Palace at Bishopstown (1721–1726). The palace was built by Bishop Peter Browne as a country retreat for himself and his successors and now belongs to the western suburbs. It is defenceless and though relatively humble it is distinguished both by the good manners of its simplicity and the imposing nature of its doorcase. This simple style, hiding panelled rooms, corner fireplaces and carved staircases, can also be found at Carrigrohane House and at the terrace on Kyrl's Quay. In more ambitious buildings of this date there is even a hint of the Renaissance. The arcaded courtyard of Skiddy's Almshouse (1718–1719) is Cork's first building to have such a flavour. Beside it stands St Anne's, Shandon (1722), possibly by Coltsman, which is famous for its bells. St Anne's is a typical classical temple-like church, redolent of the age of reason.[1]

The Corn Market arcade, again probably by Coltsman, on the Coal Quay is a most satisfying essay in early classicism. From the same period is the Old Custom House in Emmet Place, now part of the Crawford Municipal Gallery, though medievalism lurks still in its mullioned windows and corner towers. Nearby is a delightful pedimented house with the strong features of this period, including quoin stones, a stone doorcase and the added sophistication of a varied window disposition to emphasise the central bay.

Increased self-confidence and wealth is shown in the Mayoralty House (1765–1773) on Henry Street, off Grenville

Fig. 3.136 Baroque plasterwork by Patrick Osbourne on the staircase ceiling in the Mayoralty House (1765–1773), now part of the Mercy Hospital. (Photo: Richard Wood.)

Fig. 3.137 Small houses on Gillabbey Street, most probably eighteenth-century. (Photo: Richard Wood.)

Place, and now part of the Mercy Hospital. Designed by Davis Ducart, it happily retains its imperial staircase, which rises to the second floor forming the processional route to the principal reception room. Baroque plasterwork by Patrick Osbourne of Waterford enlivens the ceilings of the building. By way of contrast, the tiny houses on Gillabbey Street built in a vernacular style may well also date from this period. Some are no more than one door and one window wide and back on to the extensive grounds of the Church of Ireland's Bishop's Palace of 1786. This building was almost certainly designed by Thomas Ivory and is among the finest surviving buildings from the late eighteenth century, only surpassed by the Ursuline convent at Blackrock, finished in 1780.

CATHOLIC EMANCIPATION (1829) AND CHURCH BUILDING

Catholic Emancipation in 1829 was the catalyst for the construction of Cork's finest Catholic churches. The Catholic cathedral of St Mary and St Anne, however, had been built in 1802. In 1828 George Pain gave it a Gothic interior, which is now much remodelled on account of expanding congregations and liturgical restlessness. Its finest feature is the tower, by Sir John Benson, which was built in the 1860s.

Fig. 3.138 St Mary's church at Pope's Quay. (Photo: Denis McGarry.)

THE · CITY · IN · THE · NINETEENTH · AND · TWENTIETH · CENTURIES

Fig. 3.139 Stone carvings in the portico of St Mary's church. (Photo: Richard Wood.)

The Dominican church of St Mary's on Pope's Quay is the most perfect and splendid expression of neoclassicism in the city. The church, happily, remains intact, down to its light fittings. Built by Kearns Deane between 1832 and 1839, the crisp carving of its exterior is matched by the bold plasterwork and carved Corinthian capitals of its interior. It contains a fourteenth-century Flemish carved ivory sculpture of Our Lady of Grace. Other fine Catholic churches of this period include St Patrick's on the Lower Road by George Pain (1836), with a splendid campanile surmounted by a drum with carved figures bearing a cross. Regrettably its interior was destroyed by a fire in the 1890s. There is also Holy Trinity on Father Mathew Quay, again by George Pain (1825), though completed after his death in slightly modified form. Further fine architectural carving in a variety of styles can be seen at St Joseph's Cemetery on Tory Top Road, where Cork's citizens' achievements are recorded with a splendour that fully echoes the best of the city's stonework and buildings.

The crisp classicism and light-hearted Gothic styles used by church architects during the first half of the nineteenth century gave way to something altogether more serious during the 1850s. One such example is the church of Saints Peter and Paul (1859) on Carey's Lane, just off St Patrick's Street. Edward Welby Pugin was partnered by George Ashlin for this commission and they created a sumptuous church, rich in decoration, that triumphs over its awkward site and transports its worshippers into a world of colour, carving and angels. For members of the Church of Ireland, with their inadequate Georgian cathedral attached to the squat medieval tower, this must have been the last straw.

The response was William Burges's new cathedral built on the site of its predecessor.

Great George's Street (built *c.* 1830), now Washington Street, provides an entry to the city of increasing excitement and interest. Its regular redbrick buildings gain in height, as its beautifully designed shopfronts become grander and more complex, some with superb carving. Alas, its fine qualities have been ignored and it has suffered from neglect. However, the street's red brick provides the perfect setting for a key public building, Cork's Court House, by George and James Pain. Its gleaming white limestone and commanding Corinthian portico and low dome are set off by a surprisingly benign representation of Justice. The Savings Bank on Lapp's Quay (1839) is by the Deane brothers,

Fig. 3.140 The plaster ceiling and Corinthian columns on the inside perfectly complement St Mary's exterior. (Photo: Richard Wood.)

Thomas and Kearns. It is a fine essay in crisp neoclassicism and retains its interior intact. Nearby, on Fr Mathew Street, stands a much-altered church, now a nightclub, built in stone with vaguely Grecian elements. It is by Robert Howard, whose brother Henry emigrated to Louisiana and became the finest architect of that state in the mid-nineteenth century.

Further down the river, at Blackrock, stands Blackrock Castle, by the Pain brothers, an inventive though diminutive essay in medieval romanticism. It rises on the foundations of an earlier structure which guarded the channel, as it flows close to this rocky promontory. The Pains fully realised the picturesque nature of the site and answered it by decorating the landscape with a vision of a 'many-towered Camelot'. Some decades ago the castle was converted to a restaurant and in the process the Pain interior was ripped out.

In 1843, a tower was built, to the design of George Pain, on a hill a little downstream from Blackrock and on the opposite side. It commemorates the fact that Father Mathew, the 'Apostle of Temperance', was well received on a visit to London. His statue, in composite stone, stands outside. Decay, on this occasion, was responsible for the loss of

Fig. 3.142 The tradition of stone cutting and stone carving in the city was vividly portrayed by Seamus Murphy in his autobiography *Stone Mad* (1950). The photo shows Murphy at work in his Blackpool studio in 1947. (Photo: *Irish Examiner*.)

the splendid fan-vaulted ceiling of the principal room, and of other features. However, the exterior of this tower and those of Blackrock Castle across the river, whether by design or not, create an intriguing effect: the city's coat of arms is evoked each time a ship passes between them on the river. Such fancy was not beyond the wit of nineteenth-century romantics.

Back on the other side of Cork, another Deane building is to be found, that of Queen's College, now University College Cork (UCC), dating from 1845. Magdalen College, Oxford, as well as Pugin's 'Ancient Residence of the Poor', were major influences on the design. Details for the chimneypieces and wall carvings were borrowed, again

Fig. 3.141 The former premises of monumental sculptors Denis McCarthy and Sons at White Street. (Photo: Ralf Kleeman.)

Fig. 3.143 The Pain brothers enhanced the landscape of Lough Mahon on the estuary of the Lee by adding the bold verticals of the towers of Blackrock Castle. (Photo: Richard Wood.)

incongruously, from the Waking Bier at Holy Cross Abbey and from the French Prison at Kinsale. In size, scale and detail the Deane and Woodward building is impressive, romantic and satisfying. It takes full advantage of its dramatic site, with its principal elements rising from the cliff on which it is perched looking northwards over a channel of the Lee. In contrast the arms of the quad stretch southwards as if opening themselves to the warmth of the sun. Nearby stands the entrance gate to the old gaol designed by the Pains (1818), who made it as forbidding as the classical style would allow. It guards a stone bridge of 1833 designed by the engineer Brunel, though whether it is by the famous father or by the equally famous son nobody seems to know.

Vernacular buildings of the late eighteenth and early nineteenth centuries are best – though hardly typically – represented by Cork's characteristic bow-fronted houses. Few, alas, remain. The three or four that do, 'like Hardwick Hall, more glass than wall', demonstrate daring engineering, fine craftsmanship and a desire for elegance. In the example illustrated, which still stands on George's Quay, even the mullions that divide the windows are made of glass, their decoration being a variant on the fanlight. It is believed that this form of craftsmanship derives from Cork's maritime tradition, as such windows are to be found mainly in the county's port towns, Kinsale in particular.

A little west of UCC, at the beginning of the Lee Road, is a group of buildings that are rich in polychromatic stone and brickwork. Their function is not obvious, though a tall and crisply elegant chimney suggests something industrial. They contained the city's waterworks and were built in 1858 by Sir John Benson, who was also responsible for St Patrick's Bridge as it now stands. Sadly, Benson's magnificent design for Cork's railway station, an elongated version of the Old Parliament House at College Green, Dublin, was not realised, though the railway tunnel is his, as presumably are the fine limestone classical ruins still standing in the railway yard. The red-and-white-banded building at the waterworks that seems to lie on the river is somewhat later and was designed by Barry McMullen.

A little further out on the Lee Road stands Our Lady's Hospital (the former Lunatic Asylum), on a commanding site. Designed by William Atkins and started in 1846, its prominence, enhanced by gables, towers and spires originally topped with metal flags, seems to suggest a pride in this method of housing the mentally ill. They, however, must have finally abandoned all hope when they saw its grim Gothic features. Originally built as three separate blocks, they had to be joined together in 1861 due to demand for accommodation. It is now being developed as an apartment complex.

More cheerfully, in the centre of Cork is the English Market, started in 1840 and finished in 1860 to the design of Sir John Benson. The building stretches from the Grand Parade to Princes Street, each with a ceremonial entrance façade. The Byzantine one on Princes Street, with polychromatic brickwork and limestone pillars, unfortunately painted blue, is the finest.

Little more than the portico survives of Cork's other great building, which owed its existence to the city's fertile hinterland, and that is the Butter Market at Shandon. It gives fitting, if rather pompous, architectural expression to the importance of Cork's butter trade, the Exchange here having operated since 1730. The building was completed in 1849 and all evidence points to Sir John Benson as its architect. It now functions as a craft centre and museum. It stands at the end of the Kerry Pike road, which runs straight through the lush dairying lands between the city and Millstreet. Along this road can still be seen vernacular farmhouses set in their courtyard of farm buildings, and dating back perhaps two hundred years.

Fig. 3.145 Cork Corporation Waterworks at the Lee Road. (Source: Colin Rynne.)

During the 1880s the old Custom House was extended by Arthur Hill and his father Henry, of the Hill family of architects, to create the Crawford Municipal Art Gallery. The junction between the old and new building is marked by a tower, the qualities of the existing building being fully recognised and respected. The Hill extension is strong and

Fig. 3.144 A pub on George's Quay, built *c.* 1800. It is one of the few surviving vernacular, bow-fronted buildings once so characteristic of the city.

Fig. 3.146 The courtyard of a farm on the Kerry Pike road (or Butter Road). (Photo: Richard Wood.)

Fig. 3.147 The church of Christ the King at Turner's Cross. (Photo: John Crowley.)

handsome, though its florid interior provides much competition for the works of art.

The national monument at the south end of the Grand Parade represents the end of a self-confident and vigorous century of building in Cork. Designed by Coakley, it was built to celebrate the centenary of the 1798 Rebellion and is a worthy structure in muscular Gothic.

Twentieth-century buildings

The twentieth century began with much promise on Bishop Street where, just below Burges's monumental cathedral, the brewing company Beamish and Crawford erected (in 1900–1902) stabling for their dray-horses and offices for their clerks. Like the cathedral opposite, the architect was English.

The delightful building, by the firm of Houston and Houston, rejects both classical and Gothic. It looked forward with confidence to the possibilities of the new century. Happily, the building has survived a change of function. Architects and their patrons, however, looked backwards as much as forwards, and the Honan Chapel at UCC, built in 1915, is in the Hiberno-Romanesque style of the early medieval period. Designed by James McMullen, it is a jewel-like showcase of the Irish arts-and-crafts movement. Sadly, most of the movable items have been moved, but splendid stained glass by Sarah Purser and spectacular glass by Harry Clarke are amongst the features still worth enjoying.

The Catholic church at Turner's Cross (1927–1931) was a pioneering work and of European importance. In a brilliant move, the Roman Catholic Bishop of Cork, Dr Cohalan, commissioned Barry Byrne of Chicago to design it. Byrne rejected worn-out styles and relied on common materials, daring engineering and a focus on purpose to create here a thoroughly modern building that is functional and also deeply spiritual. The striking sculpture of the entrance front is by John Storrs of America.

The Cork School of Commerce and Domestic Economy (1934–1935) on Morrison's Island is by Henry Haughton Hill, the third generation of the family to practise architecture. The building is a worthy 'essay' in the stripped classical style, with elements of art deco. The overall attention to both spatial effect and detail is impressive. The recent addition of an attic floor has managed to improve the building further. Nearby, on Albert

Fig. 3.148 A pavilion in the grounds of St Stephen's Hospital. (Photo: Richard Wood.)

Fig. 3.149 The millennium extension at the Crawford Municipal Art Gallery. (Photo: Richard Wood.)

Fig. 3.150 The Lewis Glucksman gallery at UCC. (Photo: Denis Minihane, *Irish Examiner*.)

Quay, is Cork's City Hall (1935), which was designed by Jones and Kelly. Definitely looking backwards, it owes something – though not much – to Gandon's sublime Custom House in Dublin.

The tuberculosis epidemic of the 1940s and 1950s produced St Stephen's Hospital at Sarsfield's Court, Glanmire (1950–1955). It was designed by Norman White of New Zealand, who led the Department of Health's architectural team. Its bulk is rendered almost graceful by the judicious use of glass and metal. However, one of its satellite pavilions would have been the envy of any Côte d'Azur millionaire. Its simple elegance testifies to extraordinary sophistication of concept and design. The lawn outside is terraced to reflect the shape of the pavilion.

Cork's Opera House (1965) was designed by Michael Scott for an island site in the south channel of the river on the Western Road, where the soon-to-be-replaced Jury's Hotel now sprawls. There, the famous blank wall of the Opera House would have been broken up by the wooded landscape. At the last moment the building was relocated, the authorities being overcome with nostalgia for the original site in Emmet Place. Here it continues to obscure the northern façade of the Old Custom House. For the new millennium its entrance façade, its best feature, was enlivened by Murray O'Laoire and Associates.

Also for the new millennium, an awkward V-shaped yard at the Crawford Gallery was filled in by Erik van Eegeraat and Partners of Rotterdam. Here the logic of gravity is turned on its head, with a brick wall on the first floor resting on a ground-floor continuous window. The wall itself bulges, further defying gravity. Inside, its soft white surface undulates, with light entering at various points in baroque fashion. These galleries, like their earlier neighbours, provide much competition for the works of art.

Currently, in spite of the country's unprecedented wealth, architectural aspirations are swept aside, by and large, in the rush for riches. The outstanding exception to this generalisation is the Lewis Glucksman Gallery in University College Cork, completed in 2004. Its architects, O'Donnell Tuomey, have been respectful of its beautiful site and have created a building of elegance and style.

St Fin Barre's Cathedral

Michael Holland

The cathedral dedicated to St Finbarr, its three spires visible from much of the city of Cork, was commissioned in 1861, begun in 1865, consecrated in 1870 and was almost complete by 1879. It stands on the site of a succession of cathedrals. An eighteenth-century cathedral, begun in 1735, was demolished to make way for the present structure. That previous cathedral was itself built on the site of a medieval cathedral, and retained a medieval tower. A fine doorway from that medieval tower survives in the present cathedral grounds and a set of eighteenth-century bells survive in the present North Tower.

The medieval cathedral, and its successors, were each built on part of the site of the seventh-century Early Christian monastery traditionally associated with St Finbarr, patron saint of Cork, after whom the cathedral is named. The large D-shaped enclosure of this early foundation, overlooking the

Fig. 3.151 St Fin Barre's Cathedral, with the Bishop's Palace in the background. (Photo: Tomás Tyner.)

Fig. 3.152 Detail from the central portal on the West Front depicting the five wise virgins (Matthew 25:1–13). (Photo: John Crowley.)

Burges was one of the leaders of the nineteenth-century Gothic revival and St Fin Barre's was his first important ecclesiastical design to be built. It is inspired by French cathedral architecture, but is not slavishly copied from it. While the source of specific details can be identified, they are combined into a composition that is consistent and dramatic and bears witness to the great artistic vision of Burges. He was a contemporary and friend of the leading lights of the arts-and-crafts movement, and of the Pre-Raphaelites. His work includes Cardiff Castle and Castel Coch in Wales, Knightshayes Court in Devon, Tower House in London, Skelton and Studley Royal churches in Yorkshire, the jewel-like second chapel in Mountstuart on the Isle of Bute in Scotland and, closer to home, Templebreedy church in Crosshaven, County Cork. These too are marked by his distinctive vision, lush use of colour and attention to detail.

His design for Cork was for a building in the Gothic style, small in relative size but giving the impression of being much larger. He assembled a team of artists and craftsmen skilled in stone, wood, metal, mosaic and stained glass. Chief amongst his team was Thomas Nicholls of London, artist and sculptor. Nearly 1,300 pieces of sculpture were drawn by Burges and plaster maquettes of them were prepared by Nicholls. Some were carved by Nicholls but the majority by an R. McLeod and his team of local stonemasons. Today these stand as eloquent testimony to the skill of 'the dust', the community of workers in stone in Cork immortalised by Seamus Murphy in his book *Stone Mad*.

south channel of the Lee, extended west from the cathedral to the grounds of University College Cork.

The present St Fin Barre's Cathedral may be nineteenth-century in terms of its construction, but is firmly thirteenth-century in the date of its inspiration. It is the design of William Burges (1827–1881), a short-sighted, eccentric, humorous, English bachelor architect-designer who immersed himself in the life, art and architecture of the Middle Ages, particularly the 1200s. He designed and oversaw the construction of cathedrals and castles, fairytale interiors, fabrics and furniture and from his imagination sprang into form intricate cups, carvings and bejewelled objects of all kinds.

With the workers in stone were others: the artists Fred Weekes and H.W. Lonsdale, and glass-manufacturers Saunders & Co. of London, led by William Worrall (stained glass); Jones & Willis, Hart & Co. and Hatfield, all of London (metalwork); Barkentin & Krall (silver inlay); W.R. Harrison of Cork (stonework); Walden & Co. of London (furniture and woodwork); Burke & Co. of Paris (mosaic); and Hill & Co. (the organ). The result is a riot of colour, high craftsmanship and intricate detail within a co-ordinated and layered iconographic scheme. On the exterior, the scheme is a reflection of that of the great medieval cathedrals and declares the purpose of the building. Telling the Bible story, it offers salutary lessons about preparedness for the next life and deals with the themes of Judgement and Resurrection. Fantastic creatures and symbolic gargoyles depicting Virtue conquering Vice are grouped with depictions of professions and occupations, angels, demons, the natural world, saints and biblical scenes.

Inside, the scheme moves through the Old Testament and the New Testament, showing the Creation and the Apocalypse, the firmament of stars, Christ resurrected, Christ enthroned in glory and the workings of the Holy Spirit. Burges also mixes beautiful and uplifting imagery with the stark and almost brutal, forcing us through this shock effect to consider the course of our lives. The decorative designs and motifs, in a variety of media, provide a rich background to the figurative work on the interior.

Overall, the cathedral speaks to us of how we should make an act of Christian faith, and of how Christ's life and death are the fulfilment of the Gospels. The variety, richness, quality, organisation and occasional quirky humour of the iconographic and decorative scheme of the cathedral are remarkable; their order and symbolism raise the building to the level of the sublime.

The artistic expression of these scenes and themes was controversial amongst some in the congregation of the time. In contrast to the plainness and simplicity of the eighteenth-century cathedral, the imagery and decoration of the new building in 1861 seemed to some to be too rich, unsuitable for use in the Church of Ireland, and the cost too high. The background to the choice of Burges and his scheme lies in the thinking of the Oxford movement, which emphasised the need for ceremony and a sense of mystery. They regarded Gothic architecture as the most appropriate style and that of the Age of Enlightenment to have had almost pagan overtones. In the face of opposition, Burges was backed by the Bishop, John Gregg, himself a remarkable character, who was as able in dealing with the internal politics of the project as he was in fundraising for it. Overcoming the opposition, the cathedral is itself a statement of great confidence, being built at a time of political tension and of great uncertainty for the Church of Ireland, which was then in the process of losing its privileged position as the established state Church.

Burges closely supervised the design and construction of all aspects of the project, from the largest to the smallest, giving the finished building a remarkable consistency of artistic content, style and high quality. It is an architectural gem, and a national treasure. The structure, fixtures and

Fig. 3.153 The St Patrick's day service at St Fin Barre's Cathedral, 2001. (Photo: Denis Minihane, *Irish Examiner*.)

fittings are only part of the picture; there also survives a remarkable archival and artefactual record of the design process, in the form of a mass of documentation (including contract drawings and design cartoons), architects' and builders' models, as well as an extensive collection of plaster maquettes from which the cathedral carvings were executed in stone.

This is an irreplaceable record of the creation of a major public building and the work of a master architect. Dedicated to God, inspired by the Middle Ages and executed as the grand design of a most unusual man, St Fin Barre's Cathedral is a remarkable chapter in the story of Cork. It is a heritage of faith, of art and of the lives of those who created it. It deserves to be better known and better appreciated, not least by the people of Cork.

Fig. 3.154 St Fin Barre's Cathedral and Frenche's Quay with Elizabeth Fort in the background. (Photo: Caroline Somers.)

B flat and E flat tubas reflecting Emmet Place along with the afternoon sunshine as the band of the First Southern Brigade gives a recital during the fiftieth Cork International Choral Festival. (Photo: Denis Minihane, *Irish Examiner*.)

4
Culture and the City

CULTURE AND THE CITY

INTRODUCTION

John Crowley

This section explores the cultural city. It is broad in its approach, for culture is a difficult concept to define. Culture can be found in libraries, museums and galleries but it can also be found in the city streets. The language of food and drink, sport and song, is deeply embedded in the world of the everyday. The city abounds in pubs, restaurants, sporting clubs and musical venues. These are places where experiences are shared. More significantly, they are places in which people find fulfilment. Culture, in this important respect, is what makes life worth living.

The city's distinctive contribution to the heritage of food is rooted in the provisions trade that flourished in the eighteenth and early nineteenth centuries. The city was one vast slaughterhouse, as trade in grain, butter, beef and bacon expanded. Culinary traditions associated with this period include spiced beef, tripe and drisheen (still sold in the English Market). Cork cuisine has continually been shaped by both internal and external influences. The changing face of Cork over the last decade is reflected in the increasing number of restaurants in the city. The more affluent the city has become, the greater the choice in terms of quality food and eateries. The city region has also embraced culinary artists such as Myrtle Allen, Darina Allen, Denis Cotter and Seamus O'Connell. Such names are an integral part of a growing culture of food in the city.

Fig. 4.1 Chefs preparing local fish dishes in the English Market. (Photo: Annelies Verbiest.)

CULTURE • AND • THE • CITY

Fig. 4.2 Sonia O'Sullivan running in the Cork City Sports at the Mardyke. (Photo: Inpho Photography.) 'Hers is the classic arc of the gifted athlete, world standard since she was first introduced to spikes... one of the great sights in Irish sport is still Sonia bursting a gut down the home straight'. (Tom Humphries, *Irish Times*.)

If Cork people are passionate about anything, it is sport. Corkonians have always revered their sporting heroes. Sport is central to many people's lives. It is an expression of culture and culture is very much rooted in place.[1] Sport creates its own emotional attachments, rivalries and jealousies. It unites as much as it divides. Different localities in the city have been defined by their sporting loyalties and achievements. Whether it is Blackpool, Fair Hill, Mayfield, Togher or Turner's Cross, the talk of sport is never far away.

The city in particular has had a long love affair with hurling and the sport continues to produce its share of artists. Jack Lynch, Christy Ring, Ray Cummins and Jimmy Barry Murphy have always been held in high esteem. The genius of Cork's most famous hurler, Christy Ring, lay not only in his consummate stick work but also in his ability to see openings that baffled his opponents. Ring had strength and determination, but perception was key to his greatness. Cork people rarely cede ground when quizzed about the greatest hurler of them all. There is only room for Ring on that particular pedestal.

The true artist constantly expands our horizons. Iconic figures in the world of literature and music have pushed the limits of their art and provided us with new ways of seeing, understanding and imagining. Discovery is an integral part of the writer's art. Cork writers have helped us to see the city in new and varied lights. One cannot ignore the accomplishments of Frank O'Connor, Sean O'Faolain and Patrick Galvin. O'Connor and O'Faolain in particular remain towering figures in the city's literary landscape. Both have praised but also cast a cold eye on the city.

Fig. 4.3 Coach Jimmy Barry Murphy celebrate's Cork's victory over Waterford in the Munster Senior Hurling Championship semi-final at Thurles in 1999. (Photo: Denis Minihane, *Irish Examiner*.)

Fig. 4.4 Seán Óg Ó hAlpín pursued by Kilkenny's Henry Shefflin during the 2004 All-Ireland Hurling Final. (Photo: Brian Lougheed, *Irish Examiner*.)

The city's musical scene is vibrant. It can boast impressive credentials when it comes to the quality and quantity of its musicians and musical venues. The city is home to musical festivals, including its choral festival and its internationally renowned jazz festival. In terms of a musical heritage, the city has had its important figures. While Seán Ó Riada's heart lay elsewhere, nevertheless his links to University College Cork were strong. The achievement of guitar legend Rory Gallagher has been memorialised in the city centre. The city has also been celebrated in song. Contemporaries such as Jimmy Crowley and John Spillane continue this rich tradition.

27. THE CULTURE OF FOOD

Colin Sage and Regina Sexton

The food habits of a city reflect its personality; they recall its past, detail its present and influence its future. The existing food culture of Cork city reflects a peculiar blend of localised historical and contemporary developments. The fusion of past and present food patterns gives Cork a complex, distinctive and dynamic food character. As a result, divergent food systems and structures run side by side. While the mainstream food industry continues to grow, traditional specialities linger and an expanding network of small-scale food producers and market retailers provide a greater choice of innovative, high-quality food products. Cork is also home to some of the country's leading chefs and opinion formers. The city hosts an extensive mix of product and producers, of celebrity chef and chip shop, of farmhouse cheesemaker and multinational dairy co-op, of supermarket chain and farmers' markets, of buttered eggs and burgers, of tripe and tagliatelle, of drisheen and dim sum.

TRADITIONAL SPECIALITIES

Notable food products lend a characteristic local and regional individuality to Cork food: drisheen (a type of blood pudding made with the blood serum of sheep and cows' blood), tripe (a variety of pig offal) and, to a lesser extent, buttered eggs, spiced beef and salted ling or cod. The origin, availability and popularity of the beef and pork by-products can be traced to commercial developments in the city between the seventeenth and nineteenth centuries. In this period, Cork's exportation of salted beef, butter and bacon was estimated to have been 'greater than those of any town in the King's dominions'.[1] By 1741, Cork was annually exporting 10,300 barrels of bacon to England, America and the Continent and by 1776 over 100,000 barrels of salted beef were annually delivered to ports in England, Europe and as far away as the West Indies and Newfoundland.[2] Thus, by the mid-eighteenth century, the victualling trade had eclipsed all others in the city. Consequently the city earned itself the titles 'the slaughterhouse of Ireland' and 'the ox-slaying city of Cork'.[3]

A rapidly expanding victualling trade effected a marked increase in meat consumption, particularly among the wealthy members of the community, while the poor were left with the coarser, less desirable cuts. The vast quantities of quick-spoiling blood and entrails to hand during the slaughtering season gave rise to the easily and swiftly made by-product, drisheen. Traditionally three varieties of drisheen were manufactured in Cork city: sheep drisheen, beef drisheen and tansy drisheen. The first was a pudding of sheep's blood boiled in sheep's casings. The second was a mixture of beef and sheep's blood boiled in beef casings, while the tansy drisheen was prepared with either blood type and flavoured with a little tansy. Beef drisheen is the only variety available today. This foodstuff has been under threat since the 1930s when the city Corporation embarked on a policy of house clearance, particularly on the northside of the city, in Ballymacthomas, Cattle Market Street and Wolfe Tone Street. This demolished quarter was not only a concentrated housing area, but it was also the heart of the city's drisheen industry.

With the destruction of the slaughterhouses, the allied enterprise of drisheen-making failed to re-establish itself in the city. Today, the best-known drisheen factory is run by the O'Reilly family, a father and son team with a small number of additional staff. Typically the process of beef drisheen-making began with the blood of ten cattle (20 gallons). Although the pudding is called a beef drisheen, it is always necessary, for reasons of palatability, to mix in a quantity of sheep's blood. The proportions of cattle and sheep blood vary according to the season of production. During the summer and autumn months, the drisheens are predominantly of sheep blood, as the heavier and richer cattle blood would render an extremely tough and unacceptably dark final product. During the winter and spring months, the proportions are reversed.

After blending, the hot bloods are left to rest and within a few minutes the mixture begins to coagulate and solidify. After a number of hours it is scored with a knife and is again left to settle overnight. By morning, the mixture has separated into blood serum and coagulated residue. The serum is now ready to be drawn off and poured into prepared beef intestines. Approximately two and a half gallons of usable serum are yielded from the original mixture of 20 gallons. The waste blood residue makes excellent manure and was widely sought by orchard owners

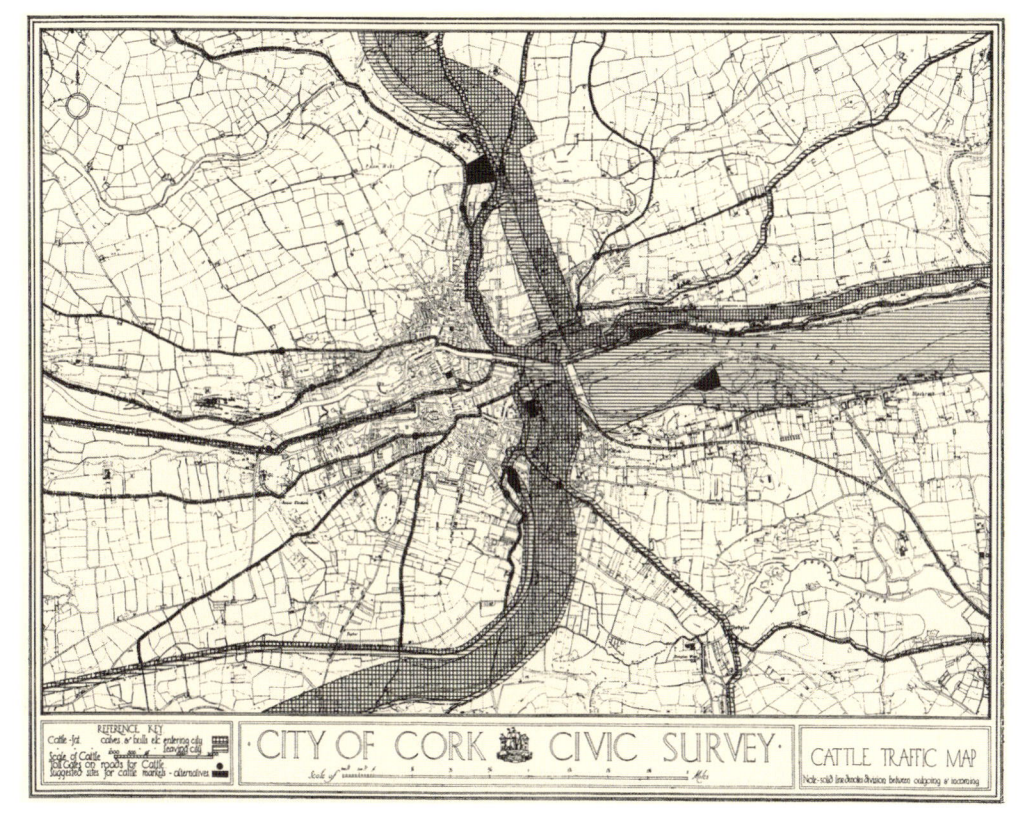

Fig. 4.5 A map taken from the *Cork Civic Survey* of 1926 illustrates the relative volumes of cattle entering and leaving the city, principally by railway. The city has played a significant role in the cattle trade, being an important exporter of salted beef and, later, live animals.

and market gardeners up to the 1950s. Large quantities were also collected by farmers and used as pig feed.

While sheep and tansy drisheens were also produced, the O'Reilly family has now abandoned the manufacture of these varieties. Preparing sheep drisheens is extremely labour-intensive, as the high fat content surrounding the intestines requires copious cleaning and scraping. Once cleaned, the thin-walled casings frequently tore at the filling or boiling stage. By the 1940s the O'Reillys decided that their preparation was not worth the time and labour involved. Tansy drisheen suffered a similar fate. This was available only on special request at specific stalls and was made to order. Gradually, the orders dwindled and tansy drisheen manufacture was no more. Today, the O'Reillys manufacture 1,000 pounds of beef drisheen per week and it is extremely popular among the city's older populace. Drisheen sales are slow during the summer, but the increased sales in the cold winter months compensates for the seasonal decline.

Drisheen heated with milk is a traditional and popular Cork dish on its own, but more commonly it is complemented by the equally traditional tripe. Today, any tripe offered for sale is invariably beef tripe. The most abundantly available comes from the first stomach (rumen) and is locally termed 'plain', 'blanket' or 'vein'. More popular, however, is honeycomb tripe, which comes from the second stomach (reticulum). It is named because of its characteristic honeycombed texture and it is the decided favourite with Cork housewives, who consider it more tender and flavoursome. The tripe is washed with soda and bleached with lime to give it its white colour. In the past, however, this process was less vigorous and the tripe, although darker in colour, was deemed more tender. Two further varieties of beef tripe, locally called 'book' and 'reed', have become but distant memories. Book tripe comes from the third stomach (omasum) in cattle and consists of a complex arrangement of leaf-like layers, thus the term 'book'. The thin nature of this tripe was its characteristic feature. The cleaning of this tripe was laborious, as it required careful washing between each of the leaves.

The process became too cumbersome and time-consuming and has been discontinued by the triperies. A fourth beef tripe, known as 'reed' or 'the black,' from the fourth stomach chamber (abomasums), is no longer carried by tripe sellers, because of its dark greyish/black colour. Despite being considered the most flavoursome of all tripes, it was stigmatised by its colour and was not charged for by the sellers: they would simply 'throw in a bit of black' for their favourite customers.

Despite vociferous assurances to the contrary by many Corkonians, tripe is a bland dish. It relies almost exclusively on its accompanying sauce for its flavour. The tripe is cut into small one-inch squares and is given at least one full hour of boiling. The smell from this process is strong and lingering and very familiar to many Corkonians. When ready for eating, the tripe is reheated in a mixture of milk and onions. At this reheating stage, drisheen is added.

Throughout the nineteenth century, commercial and economic developments combined to bring about a change in the range of foodstuffs available in the city. First, Cork's cured beef export trade declined steadily throughout the nineteenth century. The ending of the Napoleonic Wars in

1815 lost Cork its British Navy provisions contract, while in the 1820s and 1830s the Newfoundland and West Indian markets were lost to the better competition.[4] The introduction of the steamship in the cross-channel livestock trade in 1825 facilitated an increase in the exportation of live cattle to Britain.[5] Yet, while one industry declined, another rose to fill the gap. The expansion of the factory bacon-curing industry in the second half of the nineteenth century supplied both the home and foreign market. Exportation of cured meats accelerated after 1876, due to the combined efforts of the Cork and Munster bacon curers to improve the quality of bacon. By the end of the nineteenth century, three main bacon-curing factories, Lunham's, Denny's and Murphy's Evergreen, supplied the city markets with a wide variety of pig off-cuts that provided cheap and sustaining fare for the urban poor. Pigs' heads, crubeens (feet), bodice (ribs), tails, shoulder and breastbones, knuckles and skirts (diaphragms) and kidneys continue to linger in the diet, although their consumption and popularity are in notable decline.

Eating in and dining out

Until the second half of the twentieth century, the diet of the city, cooking methods and food purchasing patterns followed typical urban trends. Grocers' shops and dry stores, fresh meat shops, dairy co-op stores, huckster shops and bakeries supplied the staples, while market gardeners working in the north and south suburbs provided fruit and vegetables to the Potato Market, the stalls on Cornmarket Street and the old English Market. From 1700 to 1950, market gardening was strongly associated with the townland of Killeenreendowney (the suburbs of Ballyphehane, Friars' Walk, Pouladuff and Togher). Smallholdings up to six acres in size were cultivated with potatoes, cabbages, broccoli, peas and turnips, while apples, pears, cherries, plums and soft fruits, especially gooseberries and strawberries, provided a surprising variety of fresh produce.

Specialist outlets, for example Woodford Bourne on St Patrick's Street, offered coffee, spices and what in their day were viewed as exotic and high-value commodities like canned sweet and savoury goods, potted and preserved meats and fish products. However, one of the main players in food retailing was the English Market. As a central and convenient asset to the city, it also enabled the consumer to maintain a close and tactile relationship with fresh food. In addition it provided fresh food on a daily basis, thus encouraging shoppers to buy in limited supplies suitable to a single or alternated day's needs, a feature of practical significance in the period before refrigerated storage facilities were common or widespread.

In the home kitchen the staples were simply prepared and, if food patterns varied in accordance with social class, this is possibly best reflected in greater access to better cuts of meat, the consumption of a wide variety of fruits and vegetables, the use of spices, and up-to-date kitchen equipment amongst those of means. A comprehensive picture of typical middle-class Cork food and cooking is detailed in the Cork manuscript receipt (recipe) book of Mary Conor.[6] She began compiling her collection of close to 200 recipes in 1829, although many are clearly of a later date. Sweet puddings feature highly, as do recipes for pickling (oysters, salmon and tongue) and preserving (apples, raspberries, strawberries, lemons, carrots, white onions, ginger and walnuts). Some recipes may be viewed as very 'modern' for their time. There are, for example, recipes for home-made mayonnaise, raspberry vinegar and 'East Indian curry powder'. Colonel Pollock supplied this last recipe and it is tempting to conclude that he was a member of the British Army serving in India who brought the recipe back home to Cork in the nineteenth century. The nature of the Cork diet, at least in some quarters as revealed in Mary Conor's recipe books, was aligned to British styles and trends – borrowings from contemporary British published cookery books are apparent – while distinctive Irish tastes are evident in such recipes as colcannon and soda cake. It was a diet that was neither static nor bland but rather dynamic, varied and abreast of current fashion.

For those of more modest means, a repetitive range of food was marshalled into a weekly regime of set meals which centred upon baked and fried meats, stews of fresh and cured meats, steamed or fried white fish and steamed smoked coley and haddock. Choice cuts of meat and poultry were saved for the Sunday roast, while potatoes, and green

Fig. 4.6 Herding pigs on Brian Boru Street in the 1930s. (Photo: *Irish Examiner*.)

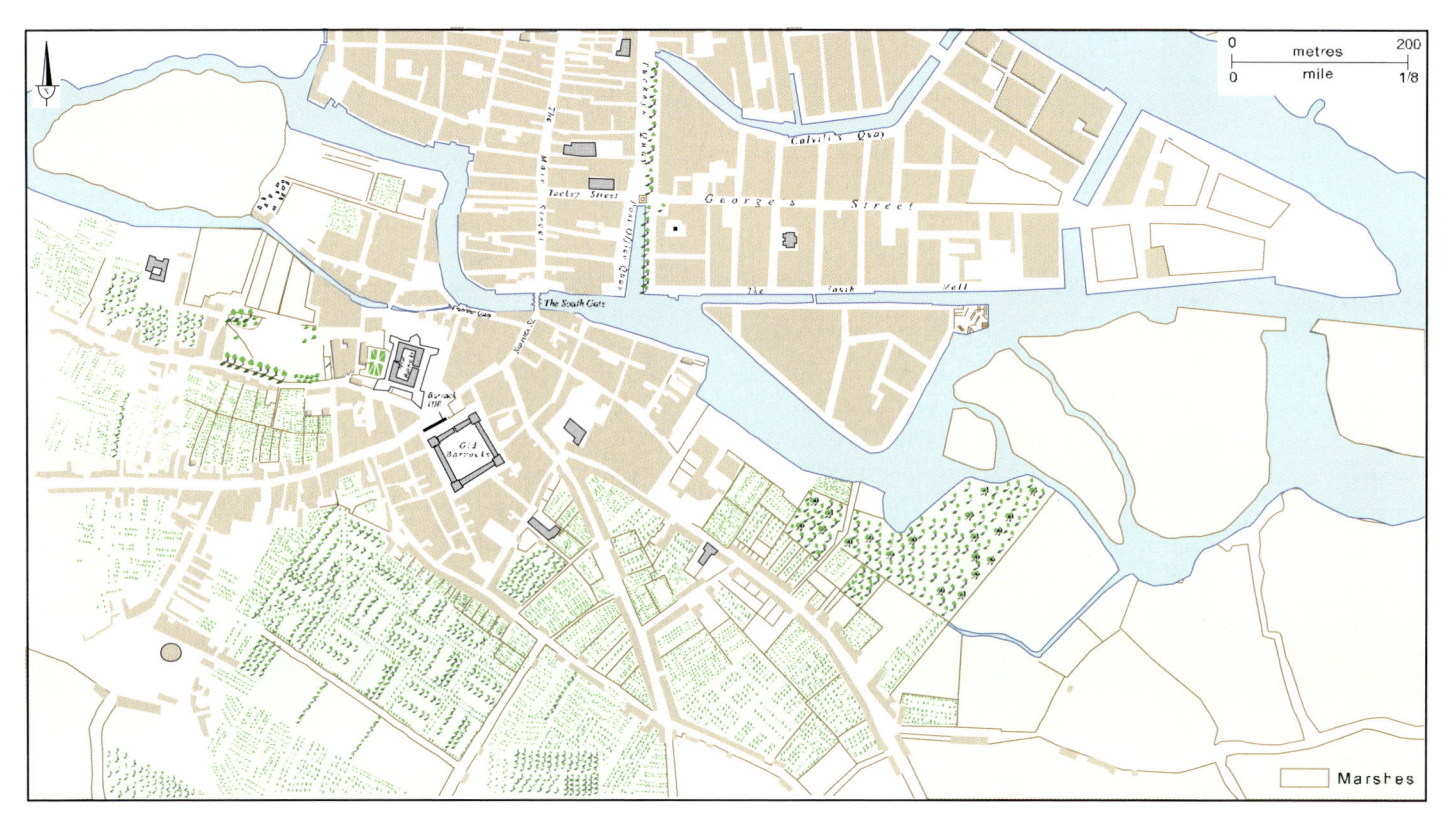

Fig. 4.7 This map is based on the original Rocque map of 1759 and shows the extent of market gardens across the townland of Killeenreendowney and beyond. A wide variety of vegetables and fruit were produced for provisioning Cork city.

and root vegetables were the routine accompaniments. Shop-bought sundries – white yeast bread, cakes, canned fruits, jam, rice, semolina and tapioca – bulked out the diet. Until well into the twentieth century, the dietary pattern of many followed that described by Maisie Flynn in her reminiscences of life in Cork between the 1920s and 1940s.

> The child was the main thing in those days, especially with the women. My grandmother would give us everything she could. She gave us good food and she gave us plenty of warmth. What more could you ask? We ate better than many around us. Potatoes and cabbage and corned beef, and bacon and pig's tails and pig's head and pig's feet, and offal and tripe and carrots, onions and custard and jelly. My grandmother had a set routine. Sunday it would be corned beef and cabbage. Monday was leftovers because it was wash-day. Tuesday, tripe and drisheen. Wednesday, steak and chops and onions. Thursday, ribs and cabbage. Friday, battenburg fish [battleboard-salted cod or ling]. We got the best food going, even a boiled egg for our breakfast. And we loved the crubeens. We'd boil them for hours, 'Do them to baby rags'. We'd waste nothing. Even the core of an apple. If you were eating an apple now, I'd say, 'First on your ox.' That meant the core was mine. We just hadn't the food to waste.[7]

The diet followed not only a weekly regime but it also acknowledged religious duty, with fish on Wednesdays and Fridays. Similarly, the practice of dining out, which until quite recently was a rare treat for many Cork people, was considered most usual for celebratory occasions, in particular rites of passage. A handful of good restaurants like the Oyster Tavern on Market Lane off St Patrick's Street and the Tivoli, together with hotels like the Imperial, the Metropole and the Victoria, offered substantial food with a strong emphasis on meat. For more casual dining, establishments like the Savoy Grill, in the Savoy picture house on St Patrick's Street, were frequently patronised and where the mixed grill enjoyed considerable popularity, while the city's numerous fish-and-chip shops and cake-and-milk shops served cheap and tasty take-away and snack food. In addition, a number of early-opening 'eating-houses' catered for country people who delivered their produce to the city's shops and markets. Here the food was simple in a home-cooked style and rarely extended beyond sustaining fries with mugs of tea and bread and butter.

However, at the other end of the scale, the epitome of fine dining in the city was the Arbutus Lodge Hotel. Run by

The English Market

Colin Sage

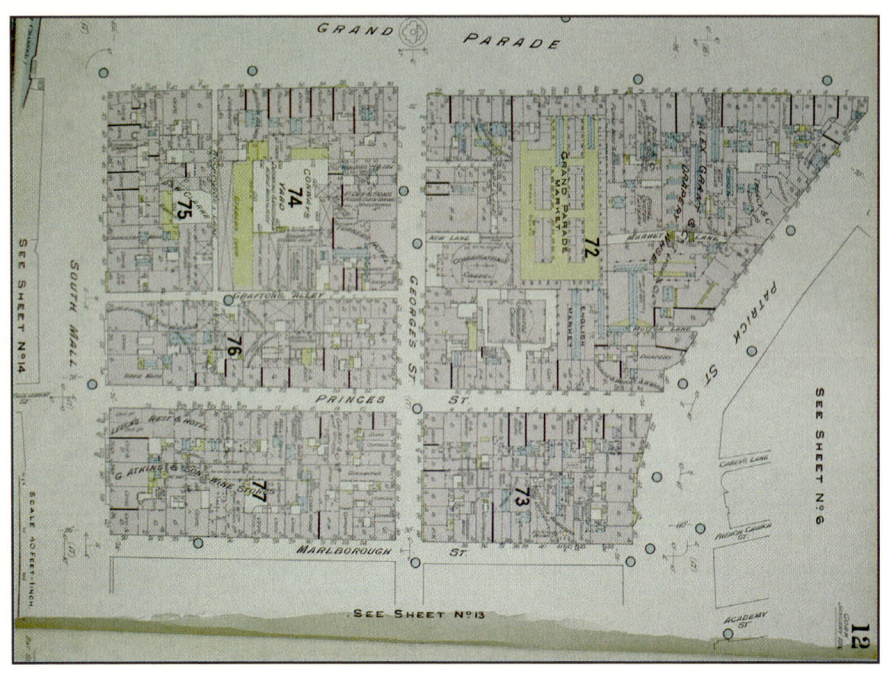

Fig. 4.8 The English Market and adjoining buildings, from Goad's Insurance map 1897. (Source: Cork Archives Institute.)

Markets are vital places that provide the backbone of the local food economy. Invariably occupying a strategic central location, markets draw together local people in the buying and selling of food. For the traveller, markets are privileged spaces that offer a window on 'real life', an opportunity to observe people engaged in an everyday activity and a microscopic lens on the local food culture. In an age when the giant retail chains appear to be sweeping all before them, local markets here in Ireland are undergoing a renaissance. Local markets deal principally in fresh products with shorter life spans, much of it sourced within the region. People who return to markets appreciate the human interaction, the character and taste of the food and the sense of trust that comes from shopping personally.

The English Market first opened on 1 August 1788 and has long occupied a central place in the heart of the city. Then known as the 'Root Market', with its entrance on Princes Street, the narrow access afforded by its original entrance encouraged the Corporation in the 1860s to seek tenders for its redevelopment. The commission was awarded to the architect Sir John Benson, a native of County Sligo and designer of many important Cork landmarks, such as the Butter Market, the waterworks and the old Opera House. The refurbished Princes Street market was opened in 1868 and within fifteen years was further extended with the opening of the Grand Parade market. For a full one hundred years the English Market, as it had become known, supplied the people of Cork with fresh meat, poultry, fish, fruit and vegetables. On 20 June 1980 fire badly damaged the Princes Street part of the market. However, an appreciation for Benson's Italianate design, with its cast-iron pillars and ornate brackets, brickwork and lofty vaulted glass roof, encouraged the Corporation to restore the damaged building as faithfully as possible to the original, although the fountain was moved from its original location.

Fig. 4.9. A plentiful supply of geese for sale in the English Market, December 1947. Note the rim of the fountain in the bottom left-hand corner of the picture. (Photo: *Irish Examiner*.)

CULTURE • AND • THE • CITY

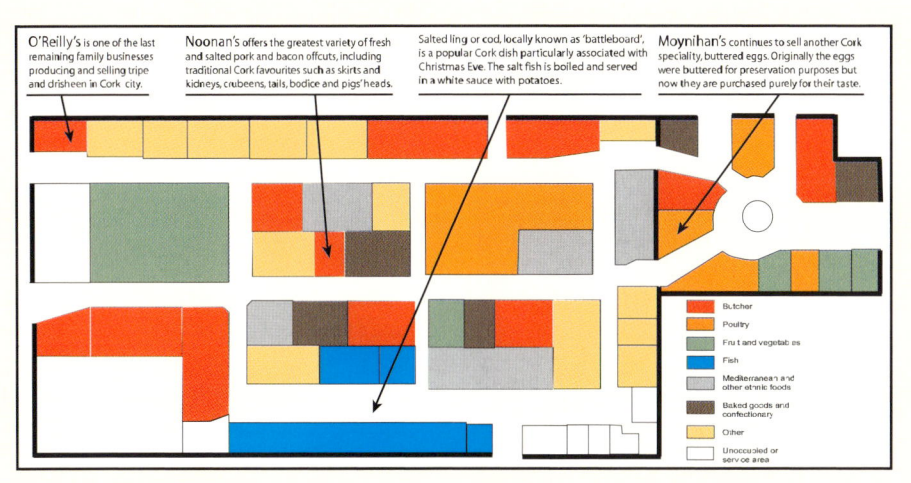

Fig. 4.10 The current layout of stalls in the English Market.

Today the English Market features a greater diversity of food products than ever before. Indeed, it has been described as 'the mother of all Irish markets ... a cornucopia of delicious ancient and modern foods'. So, while such Cork specialities as tripe and drisheen are available from O'Reilly's and offal and pigs' feet from Noonan's, the market also offers a wide range of contemporary European products such as cheese, olives, pasta, champagne and Belgian chocolates. Alongside these new products is a display of fish that would not look out of place in a Mediterranean market, quality meat, fruit and vegetables (organic and conventionally produced) and baked goods. Upstairs in the Farmgate Café one can taste many of these products freshly prepared. The English Market provides the visitor with a privileged glimpse of Cork people engaged in the serious business of buying and selling food.

Fig. 4.11 The English Market, from the Princes Street entrance. (Photo: John Crowley.)

Fig. 4.12 Market gardens at Assumption Road, July 1941. (Photo: *Irish Examiner*.)

brothers, Declan and Michael Ryan, the restaurant won local and national acclaim and, between 1974 and 1984, was the only Irish restaurant to continuously hold a Michelin star. After a training period in France, Declan directed the kitchen towards French-style cooking and the restaurant's signature dishes included *côté de boeuf sauce beaujolais moelle* and *cassolette* of fresh prawns. Despite the strong French resonances, the Ryan brothers also acknowledged the city's specialties and for a time it was the one restaurant in Cork to serve tripe and drisheen. French-style food, attentive table service, starched linen and silver, such were the perceptions and expectations of formal dining until well into the 1980s. It was around this time, too, that an alternative dining destination and experience emerged with the establishment of the Kinsale Good Food Circle and its spin-off event, the Gourmet Festival, held in early October. Yet, in this period, reputable food and travel guides to Ireland continued to pinpoint three of Cork's classic restaurants as the country's best: the Arbutus Lodge Hotel, Ballylickey House in west Cork and, of course, Ballymaloe House in east Cork.

It is impossible to imagine writing a chapter about the food culture in Cork without mentioning Ballymaloe House, and especially its proprietor, Myrtle Allen. Ballymaloe today enjoys a worldwide reputation for the quality of its food and hospitality, yet it retains an enduring appeal to a more local clientele, who appreciate its magic on those special family occasions. Ballymaloe has maintained its integrity as an establishment because of the inspiring leadership displayed by Myrtle Allen over the years and her promotion of high-quality food of local origin cooked in a style reflecting Irish culinary tradition. In addition to opening and running a highly successful restaurant and hotel at home, Myrtle Allen has proven an outstanding ambassador of Irish food abroad. She has organised food promotional events in Europe and the US, run a highly regarded restaurant in Paris and has made a major contribution to the European Community of Cooks (Euro-toques). She has provided a source of moral authority for those concerned with good food, combining unswerving practical support for small local producers with a constant vigilance in defending them against bureaucratic efforts to impose uniformity through excessive regulation.

Myrtle Allen's leadership has played a vital role in strengthening the distinctive character of Cork food, not least as many of the important chefs in the city have passed through the Ballymaloe House kitchen and the Ballymaloe Cookery School run by Myrtle's daughter-in-law, Darina Allen. One such Ballymaloe-trained chef is Canice Sharkey, who, together with Michael Ryan, runs the highly sucessful Isaac's restaurant on MacCurtain Street. The opening of Isaac's in 1992 may be seen as a turning-point in the city's restaurant culture. Modelled on the style and ambience of a French bistro, it brought a relaxed air of dining to the city while at the same time introducing good and varied food at a reasonable price. These elements made restaurant dining more accessible to a wider clientele and the choice of ingredients and style of cookery, tinged with pan-Pacific influences, diversified Cork's relationship with food. Denis Cotter of Café Paradiso is another chef who has been directed in his craft by both home-based culinary movements and foreign trends. With expertise gained in Lettercollum House in west Cork and in New Zealand, Cotter has emerged as one of the country's best vegetarian chefs and his restaurant can be isolated as a centre of innovation.

Today the city supports a broad range of restaurants and food outlets, from fast-food chains to contemporary Irish, Mediterranean and ethnic (most recently taking in Eastern European and African food), that satisfy both the vagaries of palate and the constraints of budget.

Change

The mid-twentieth century may be seen as a benchmark for change in the food ethos of Cork. The expansion of the city into the northern and southern suburbs brought an end to the tradition of market gardening in these areas, while the Corporation's programme of slum clearance in quarters associated with drisheen-making brought a rapid decline in the industry. Furthermore, lifestyle changes created a more flexible and open attitude to food. Foreign travel, especially package holidays, and television revealed the wonder of different cuisines and hitherto little-known ingredients. In 1963, for example, the engaging cook, Monica Sheridan, sprang onto Irish television in her series *Monica's Kitchen*, delivering, in the midst of the more routine, instructions for cooking spaghetti, pizza, risotto and *escargots à la bourguignonne* and quick lessons in the cheeses of Italy, France and Switzerland.[8] An inquisitive younger population, especially university and college students living away from home, were open to culinary change. Indeed, there is no shortage of anecdotal evidence to reveal that it was in the flats and bedsits of Cork that spaghetti, sweet peppers, garlic and tinned tomatoes were tasted for the first time. The movement for change and ever-increasing variety was satisfied by the arrival of the supermarket, which in time was instrumental in diversifying the ingredients base of the city. The desire for variety and the attraction to the illusion of gleaming aisles of plenty was also detrimental to the small producer and retailer.

Of particular note is the considerable change in the structure of food retailing over the past twenty years, with an increasing concentration of market share in the large multiple retailers and a halving in the number of independent grocery shops. This change in food retailing has been accompanied by the 'speeding up' of working lives that has made convenience seem such a desirable feature, along with lower prices. Supermarkets have consequently become an indispensable ally of modern life, offering foods manufactured for easy preparation and 'ready-to-eat' convenience.

Cork city has witnessed a significant decentralisation in food retailing, with an extraordinary growth of suburban shopping centres in Wilton, Douglas, Bishopstown, Blackpool and Mahon Point. While there remain important food retailing names in Paul Street, St Patrick's Street and North Main Street, the overwhelming bulk of food purchased by Cork residents is in the suburbs. This has significant repercussions for the economic well-being of the city centre as food retailers move into non-food goods and ever-larger suburban retailing units provide for all our needs. This has implications for traffic congestion in the suburbs, as people drive from an ever-wider hinterland attracted by the mall experience. It has reverberations for our diet and nutrition, as supermarkets stock durable commodities able to withstand the rigours of long-distance transportation, central warehousing and long shelf life, but perform poorly in providing fresh produce of local origin.

The pace of structural change in the retail sector in Ireland in recent years has been accelerated by increased international penetration through mergers and acquisitions. Many will see this internationalisation as inevitable, a desirable process that offers a future of lower prices and greater choice. Others are less sanguine about the megaretailers and are working hard to create a healthier, tastier and more sustainable future in which farmers, food producers, small retailers and consumers can all benefit. The growing market trend towards sourcing, supporting and advancing endogenous Irish produce has been directed by national and international developments. At home, the favourable performance of the existing producers and the dissemination of their produce is a dynamic development that has encouraged the emergence of a vibrant food culture whose needs are subject to refinement and evolutionary change. Furthermore, the availability of quality-crafted produce has offered an alternative market for those who have been disillusioned by large-scale commercial food production. The growth of a small-scale artisan food sector within the Cork region has thus created a milieu where questions of ethics, aesthetics, positive health benefits and sensory appeal can be measured against the mainstream.

On a broader level, the globalisation of food trade and production has redirected consumers towards local and regional produce, as many people now demand access to information regarding the origin and production techniques. The disdain for cheap, inferior food amongst certain socio-economic groups is manifest in the upsurge in the number, popularity and commercial success of the country and farmers' markets within the county (Midleton, Skibbereen, Clonakilty and other places besides). Meanwhile, the Irish branch of the Slow Food Movement, which began its life in Cork, continues to spread across the country, reflecting a groundswell of support for the ethos of small-scale food production.

The concentration in Cork, therefore, of quality small food producers, well-known and articulate chefs and others concerned with maintaining our authentic culinary culture has cumulatively given rise to an influential 'Cork food voice'. Cork has an evident commitment to supporting high-quality food produced from sustainable practices; this nurtures our proud culinary traditions and will ensure Cork's claim to be the food capital of Ireland.

28. SPORT

Denis Walsh

On the morning of the 1999 All-Ireland football final between Cork and Meath, Professor John A. Murphy raised his Cork colours on the flagpole of the Sunday Independent. Murphy's father won an All-Ireland football medal with Cork in 1911, but the piece addressed the greater issues of sporting identity and what we might loosely call 'Corkness'. Murphy began with an apocryphal anecdote, rooted in the most telling truth: 'Sean MacReamoinn, a Corkman, alas only by desire', he wrote, 'tells the story of the Leeside father seeing off the son and heir to his first job in Dublin. "Now, boy, whenever you're in company, don't be too inquisitive. Never ask people where they're from. If they're from Cork, they'll tell you anyway. If they're not you don't want to embarrass them."'

There are kinder, softer ways to describe the native Cork condition, but it can't be entirely fudged in euphemisms. Outsiders fail to miss the arrogance of Cork people and Cork people can't deny it. For Cork people, humility is available as a lifestyle choice or as an acquired social grace; however, it is not the state into which they are born. It is an aspect of mind and sport provides for its most robust expression. Cork people have achieved great things in literature and the arts, in music and scholarship, but those other pursuits lack the edge of competition and tribalism, shared victory and noisy bragging. Critically, they lack the arena which sport has offered Cork people, not just to win but to win in public. For those who never read a word of Frank O'Connor it would be much harder to claim ignorance of Christy Ring, Roy Keane or Jimmy Barry Murphy, because their status was effortlessly conveyed by sport's unique facility to spread and invade. Sport became the empire which Cork people built beyond their city walls.

Hurling's unique place

The city's relationship with sport is layered and full of cross-references. It used to be said that it was the only city in the world where children played hurling in the streets. That was never strictly true, but it reflected the city's passion for a game whose constituency was overwhelmingly rural. It could not be said now that hurling is any more popular than soccer in Cork city, and, in terms of playing numbers, GAA clubs in the city are finding it easier to recruit young Gaelic footballers than hurlers. None of this undermines hurling's unique place in the cultural life of the city. Blackrock, St Finbarr's and Glen Rovers share 82 of the 116 senior championships listed on the roll of honour. When Cork people referred, with typical hubris, to their county championship as 'The Little All-Ireland', these were the clubs that had given it such status in the local imagination. When an All-Ireland club championship did come into being in the 1970s, these giants of hurling in the city shared seven of the first eight titles between them. Modesty would have been out of place all along. The most fevered and enduring sporting rivalries in the city have existed between GAA clubs, essentially because they appealed to an audience far beyond the protagonists, because there was a critical element of continuity from generation to generation and because, at one time at least, they were sprinkled with stardust.

Fig. 4.13 Jimmy Barry Murphy in conversation with Christy Ring during training at Pairc Uí Chaoimh in 1978. (*Irish Examiner*.)

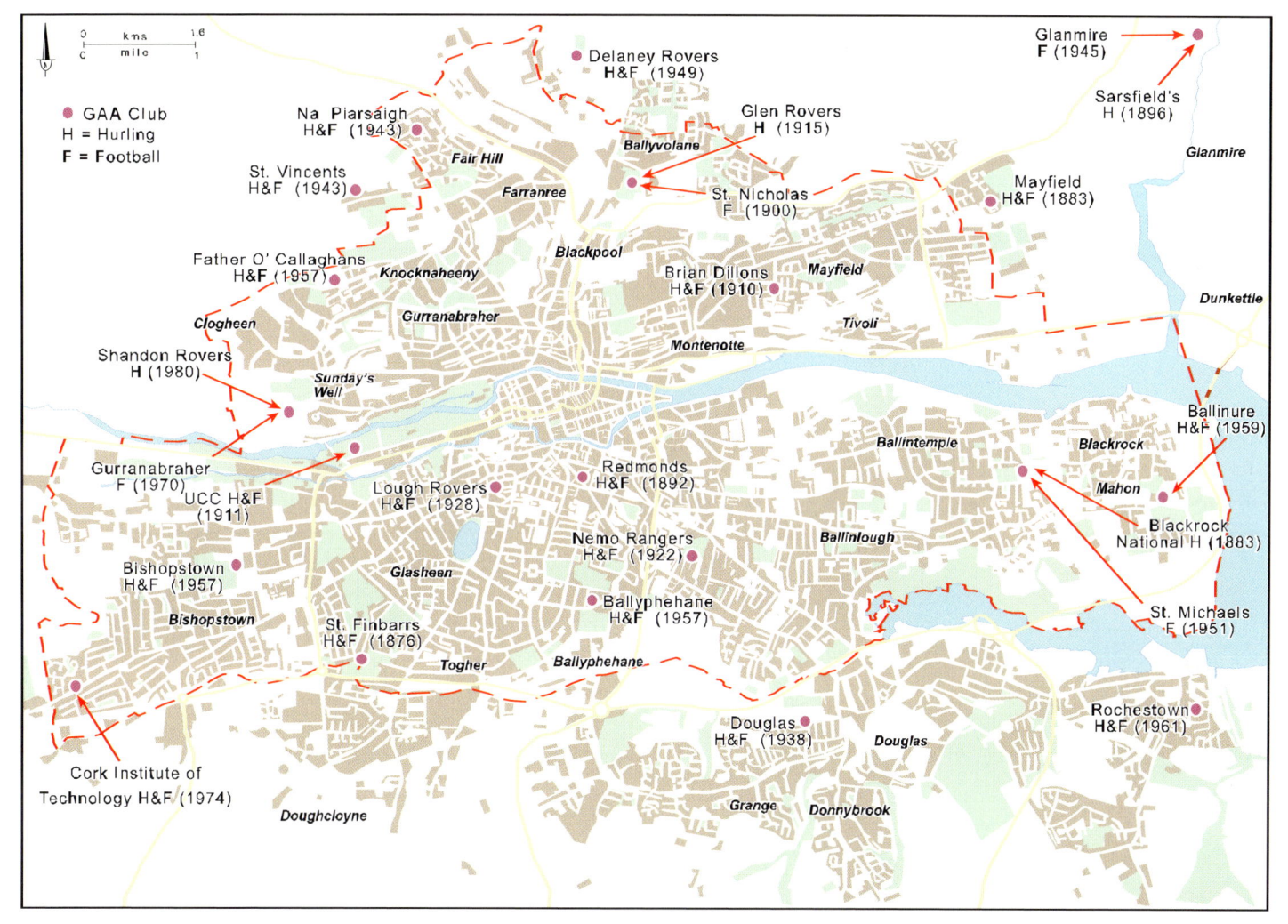

Fig. 4.14 GAA clubs in the city and their founding years. The club in each parish was key to the success of the GAA, both in the county and the city. Clubs forged identities principally based on parish loyalties. Clubs like the 'Barrs' (Togher) and the Glen (Blackpool) became part of the social and cultural fabric of the city. As Cork expanded in the 1940s and 1950s, new clubs were formed which also had their roots in their respective localities. The strength of the GAA in the city remains its attachment to place and locality.

Rugby

Those factors did not exist to the same extent in the other major sports. Cork has been home to the same five senior rugby clubs for the last fifty years or more, but spectator support for club rugby in the city was always only a fraction of that enjoyed by the GAA. Different dynamics were at work. Rugby clubs had no real connection to the areas where they happened to have their clubhouses and play their matches, and the communities in those areas did not, by and large, hang their sporting identity on the local rugby club. Sunday's Well and Dolphin, for example, are both based in Musgrave Park in the Ballyphehane area of the city, which remains a soccer stronghold largely resistant even to the GAA's loving advances. Cork rugby clubs draw their players from the two rugby-playing schools, Christian Brothers College (CBC) and Presentation Brothers College (PBC), and from the professional classes, though not exclusively the professional classes and not with the same level of élitism as existed in Dublin rugby.

The upshot, however, was that the rugby community was never defined by place. The ties that bound had a different quality and, in modern times, were more easily undone. The establishment of the All Ireland League in the early 1990s initiated a trend of talented players, leaving the smaller Cork clubs to join Cork Constitution, the most powerful and successful club in the city. This situation was not unique to Cork; it was mirrored in Limerick and Dublin too. Neither, in a sense, was it unique to rugby, because the biggest GAA clubs in the city always accepted talented outsiders and were inclined to approach good prospects from smaller clubs; but none of the GAA clubs ever enjoyed Cork Constitution's status as the singularly most desirable destination for any talented and ambitious young player. When Sunday's Well ceased to pay their senior players at

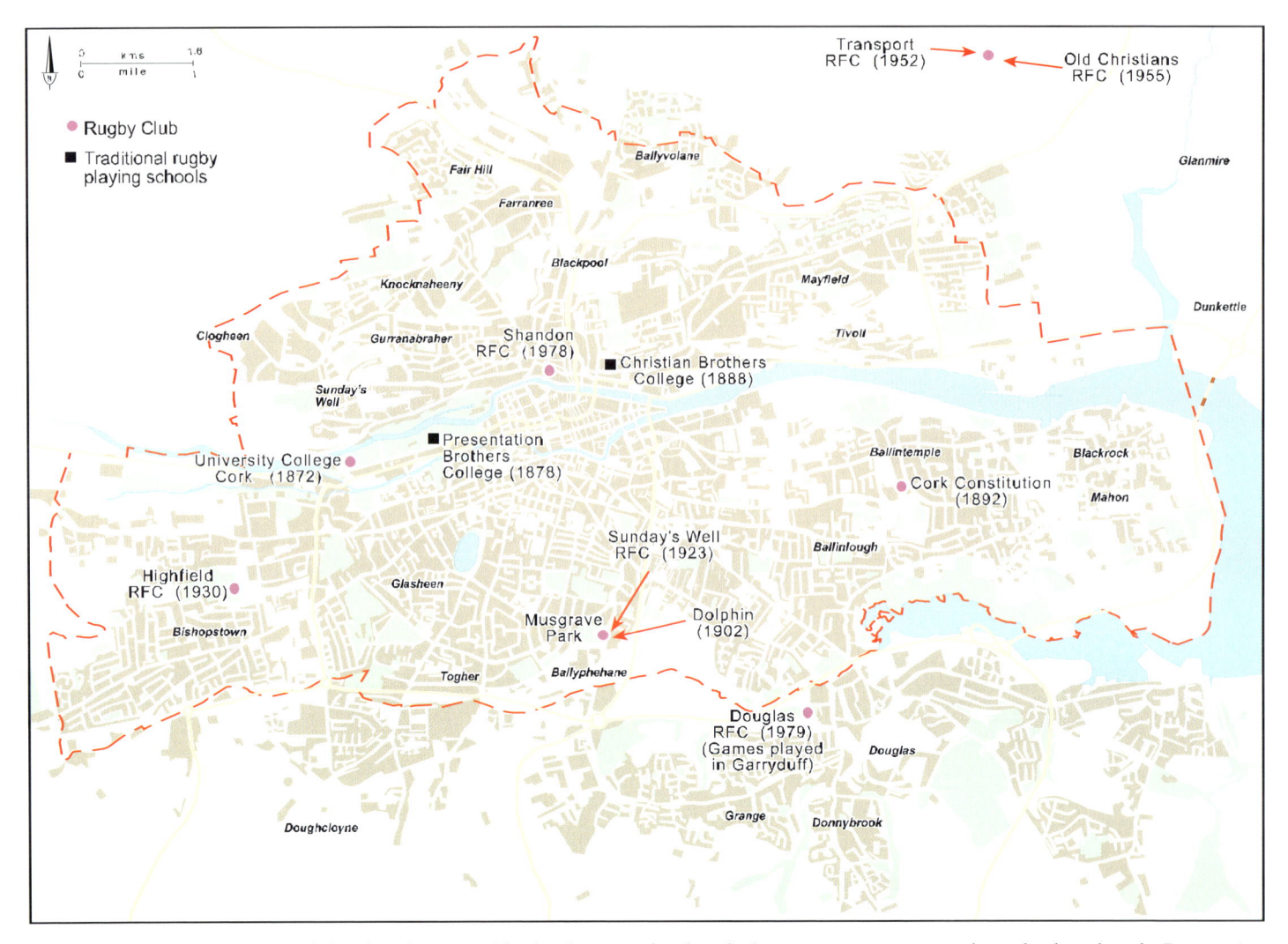

Fig. 4.15 Rugby clubs in the city and their founding years. The development of rugby relied to a great extent on secondary schools such as the Presentation Brothers College (PBC) on the Mardyke and the Christian Brothers College (CBC) on Wellington Road. University College Cork also played a pivotal role in nurturing talented young players. Students who attended these schools and colleges received not only an academic but also a rugby education that allowed them to graduate later to established clubs such as Cork Constitution, Sunday's Well, Dolphin and Highfield.

Fig. 4.16 CBC scrum half Tom Martin gets the ball away against PBC in their Barry Cup clash in 2004. (*Irish Examiner.*)

the end of the 2002–2003 season, thirteen of the first team defected. This had a lot to do with the influence of professionalism, but it also demonstrated rugby's comparative rootlessness. It made it easier for players to swap one shirt for another.

At different times over the last 80 years Cork soccer boasted two teams simultaneously in the League of Ireland, and those derbies were naturally big games that commanded big attendances. Cork clubs in the League of Ireland had a history of folding and these rivalries were relatively short-term affairs. In short, soccer or rugby had nothing to compare with the longevity, intensity or richness of the Glen–Barr's rivalry. From the 1930s onwards, even in years when they did not meet in the championship, the annual Eucharistic match between the clubs was a significant event in the local GAA calendar. By the 1940s it was attracting thousands to the Mardyke and continued to do so consistently until the late 1960s. It was a cherished set piece in the sporting life of the

Fig. 4.17 Cork Constitution's Ronan O'Gara watches the ball go between the Welsh posts for the match-winning drop goal scored in injury time in the 2003 Six Nations Championship at the Millennium Stadium, Cardiff. (Photo: Denis Minihane, *Irish Examiner*.)

city. Ostensibly, it was only a tournament game, but it was played in the temper of a championship match, with outbreaks of fisticuffs to authenticate the seriousness. People will tell you now that for those fixtures two ambulances used to be parked down the lane between the hurling field and Fitzgerald's Park so that casualties could quickly be attended to. If, in fact, such a provision did not exist, the gist of the story is that it should have. When these clubs met in the 1977 senior hurling county final, a crowd of 33,000 thronged to Pairc Uí Chaoimh. It was an extraordinary crowd for a club match and remains a record for the championship. If a county championship match anywhere in the country ever exceeded that figure, we have yet to hear of it.

Cork heroes

These clubs produced not just Cork players but Cork heroes. Just a year earlier, in 1976, an iconic figure from both clubs conspired to swing an All-Ireland hurling title for Cork. Jimmy Barry Murphy from the Barr's was playing his first senior hurling final and Christy Ring, holder of eight All-Ireland medals, was a Cork selector. Mick Jacob, the stylish Wexford centre-back, had broken Cork's heart all afternoon but he was starting to tire late in the second half and Barry Murphy was moved from the wing to the centre to use his pace and take him on. The legend has it that Ring conceived and executed the move independently of the other selectors, but in any event he invested himself completely in the strategy. For one of Barry Murphy's solo runs, Ring can be seen in the television footage keeping pace as best he could down the sideline. Barry Murphy flashed over three points in ten minutes, one of which brought Cork level, another of which put them ahead, and at the final whistle Ring ran directly to Barry Murphy and wrapped him up in a hug. Only Cork people would have instantly understood the resonance of such an image and the cultural history on which it drew. A Barr's man and a Glen man embracing in the middle of Croke Park flew in the face of one of the city's most enduring partitions.

Glen Rovers are dealt with in greater detail elsewhere but they demand passing reference here. The club has won just one Senior Championship since the 1970s, having won 24 between 1934 and 1976; however, they retain an identity, which is arguably the most vivid and powerful in the Cork sporting universe. Even before the club fell on lean times, the Glen's past had an irresistible means of forcing humility on the present. This, after all, was the club of Ring and Jack Lynch, 'Fox' Collins and the Buckley brothers, Vincie Twomey and Jim Young. The first Glen Rovers team to win a county championship went on to win eight in a row. The standards were merciless. Winning was the banner they followed, more than excellence, and not just winning but the imperative to lay your body and every atom of your being on the line for the jersey. The Barr's and Blackrock both enjoyed reputations founded on classy hurling, but an element of machismo was central to the Glen's identity and the club was comfortable with that.

There was an aura about the Glen, which they recognised and manipulated. Conor Hayes, the former Galway captain, played with the club for a year in the early 1980s and was struck by the ingrained arrogance: 'The old Glen saying', he remembers, 'was hang the jersey on the gate of the field going in.' The implication was that opponents would be cowed and beaten before a ball was pucked. The Barr's and Blackrock had that cockiness too which, up until twenty years ago, country clubs around the county would have both envied and resented. And Cork teams drew on it. The cockiness of the city hurlers filled the red jersey.

During their decline, the Glen's experience has echoed in other clubs around the city struggling to cope with demographic and cultural shifts. The dynamics of community life in Blackpool, where Glen Rovers was founded, resembled a village more closely than a suburb, the terraces and lanes a hothouse of clannishness, so that the bond to the Glen had a rural zeal to it. But the fabric of that life has long since been eroded.

In the 1950s families started to leave Blackpool for new and better housing – most of it south of the river – and it was not until the 1970s that significant amounts of new housing was built in the Glen's orbit. Some Glen fathers sent their sons across the city to play for the club of their youth, but more of them allowed their sons to play with their friends in whichever club was nearest.

Nemo Rangers have taken over from the Glen as the great brand name of city GAA, even though all of their glorious history is modern and all of their truly great players are still with us and active in the club. With seven All-Ireland club football titles they are the most successful club in the history of the competition, in either football or hurling. Yet they would bring no more than 500 supporters to their All-Ireland finals and the parish of Turner's Cross, where the club sits almost as an enclave, would scarcely miss those who had gone to the match. The little village club has been the primary unit of the GAA throughout the association's history and Nemo Rangers, like the old Glen, has all the qualities of a village in the city, a minor miracle of self-sufficiency and regeneration.

Turner's Cross: The city's soccer heartland

In Turner's Cross, Nemo are surrounded by the city's soccer heartland. Cork's most celebrated soccer players hailed from here: Peter Desmond and Tommy Moroney, who played for Ireland in the famous win over England at Goodison Park in 1949; Owen Madden, another international whose cross-channel career was cut short by the Second World War; Frank O'Farrell, once manager of Manchester United. Spread the net wider around the city and the trawl will bring in Noel Cantwell, Charlie Hurley, Roy Keane and Denis Irwin, not just great Cork soccer players but some of the greatest ever to play for Ireland.

Soccer has always enjoyed a strong if unstable presence in Cork. The city has been home to nine different League of Ireland/National League clubs, eight of which folded for one financial reason or another. Cork City entered their twentieth year in 2004, which took them past Cork Hibernians as the longest surviving League of Ireland/National League club in the city's history. Turner's Cross is Cork City's home now, but they also played for a while in Flower Lodge and in specially developed grounds

Fig. 4.18 Crowds watching a soccer match from outside the railings on the Mardyke, 1936. (Photo: *Irish Examiner*.)

Fig. 4.19 Waterford's Ned Power taking flight, with sliothar in hand, as Cork's Christy Ring thunders into the square during the 1963 Munster hurling final in Thurles. (Photo: *Irish Examiner*.) 'And of all the great hurlers whose names filled the newspapers and surfaced in everyday talk, one name stood out: Christy Ring. Over the border in the next county from Cork I heard his name spoken with admiration and, sometimes, with resentment, for he had been at the helm of too many defeats which other teams had endured. In so far as I had any mental picture of Cork, Ring was its shape and its achievement' (Waterford-born writer, the late Seán Dunne (ed.), *The Cork anthology*, Cork, 1993).

in Curraheen. Over the years the old greyhound stadium, the Showgrounds and the Mardyke have hosted Cork's other clubs and until the early 1970s it was a booming, if volatile, scene. Between 1941 and 1947, the original Cork United won an amazing five Leagues and two cups; their average home crowd in the Mardyke was 9,000. Yet they went out of existence in 1948. There was an all-ticket sell-out crowd of 28,000 in Flower Lodge for the final game of the 1971–1972 season between 'Hibs' and Waterford, which was effectively a title decider. Hibs lost that day but won the FAI Cup the following weekend, retained it the following season and went out of existence three years later.

The experience of League of Ireland clubs reflected the rhythm of soccer in the city. According to Plunkett Carter, author of three books on the history of Cork soccer, there have been between 600 and 700 clubs in the city of all types and sizes over the last 80 years. Many flickered in and out of existence in the space of a few years. Most clubs would have started off with roots in one part of the city but, unlike the GAA, there was no restrictive parish rule and soccer clubs in the city tended to have loose ties with local communities. Glasheen and Tower Rovers were the first giants of schoolboy soccer in the city in the 1950s and, although they were both southside clubs, they happily accepted and even courted good players from the northside. Leeds, the outstanding Cork schoolboys team of the 1990s, had players on their books from Kerry. Cork teams in the League of Ireland were hardly ever entirely made up of natives, which was often the case for the Barr's, Blackrock and the Glen too. For an insular place, Cork people were happy to allow outsiders to contribute to their excellence on the playing fields of Ireland – as long as they realised how lucky they were to have the opportunity.

KEANE AND RING

Roy Keane is the Christy Ring of Cork soccer and they rank as the two most successful sportspeople the city has ever produced (although Ring was born and reared in the village of Cloyne twenty miles east of the city and was already established on the Cork senior team when he joined Glen Rovers in 1941). Unlike Ring, Keane could never claim to be the all-time greatest in his chosen sport, but Keane was up against a much bigger field. If Ring had lived to see Keane he would have recognised a lot of himself in the Manchester United captain: the extraordinary will to win, the aggression, the power and the drive. Keane's relationship with the Cork public, though, is not straightforward, no more than Ring's was. In a Cork jersey Ring was adored, but in club matches for the Glen his combativeness drew hostility from supporters of the Glen's opponents. As Keane documents in his autobiography, he became entangled in various spats and scrapes around the city as a young and already successful professional with Nottingham Forest. Cork people defend their own against the outside world, but a successful Cork person might go deaf waiting to hear a compliment and Cork's sports stars are not exempt from this.

Fig. 4.20 Roy Keane in action at Lansdowne Road in a friendly international against Russia. (Photo: *Irish Examiner*.)

Because of his personality, his understandable desire for privacy and the demands of the English soccer season, there is a certain distance between Keane and Cork now. If such a generalisation can be made, it might be said that he is respected by the Cork public but not held in the same doting affection as Jimmy Barry Murphy or, in another generation, Jack Lynch. The former Taoiseach remains the only man to have won six All-Irelands in a row, five hurling and one football, and his standing in the city was enormous. Professor Dermot Keogh of UCC's History Department was once told by 'a distinguished scion of Fianna Fáil' that campaigning with Lynch was like 'walking into a town with Cuchulainn'.

The thing about sport in the city, though, was that it was never short of stars and matinée idols. In his wonderful memoir of growing up in Cork during the 1920s and 1930s, *Six o'clock all over Cork*, Tom McElligott recalls childhood certainties: 'We knew and of course boasted that Cork had the best golfer in Jimmy Bruen, the best tennis player in Harry Cronin, the best cricketer in N.C. Mahony, the best yachtsman in Harry Donegan, the best swimmer in Bill Noonan and the best rugby player in Jack Russell. And if some of these excelled in what some Christian Brothers were known to describe as *Cluichí na hImpireachta*, so be it. Each of them was *one of our own*.'

For Cork people, sport merely confirmed a superiority God had given them.

Soccer in Cork City

Plunkett Carter

Prior to the foundation of the original Munster Football Association in 1901, soccer was being played in Cork: several clubs preceded the birth of the association. Munster Senior League competitions began in 1901 and were dominated by military teams comprised mainly of British servicemen. Three city-based civilian teams, Cork City, Cork Celtic and Millfield, competed in the senior division. After the completion of the first decade of the new league, Cork Celtic were the only civilian team still competing at senior level, while famous names like Barrackton, Freebooters and Clifton were among those competing for the Tyler Cup in the junior grade. Matches were played in Turner's Cross, Victoria Cross, Douglas, Blackrock, Dublin Pike and in the 'garrison' towns of Cobh, Passage and Kinsale.

The growth in soccer was unprecedented in the early 1900s and to cater for the influx four divisions had to be organised. Many of the teams which came into existence during the first decade of organised football, survived the vacuum created by the First World War and the Troubles to re-enter when soccer was again organised in 1922. Four Cork-based teams were amongst those to enter when competitions resumed in 1922. A year later the demand for soccer intensified and junior and minor (under-age) competitions began. In 1924 Fordsons (the majority of its players worked in the Ford factory in the Marina) became the first Cork team to enter Free State Senior League competitions. Between 1930, when Fordsons disbanded, and 1984, when Cork City was founded, eight other city-based teams had spells as members; all were forced to resign due to financial difficulties or irregularities.

There was a huge increase in entries to junior and minor soccer during the 1930s, a decade during which the senior grade failed to attract entrants. A perilous situation was eventually averted when some high-ranking junior clubs agreed to upgrade. In the early 1940s, there was a stream of withdrawals and the Munster Football Association (MFA) in emergency action suspended the existing leagues and created Regional Leagues Divisions One and Two, which enabled competitions to continue. After the war football returned to normality and the winds of change blew stronger than ever. New teams failed to gain entry into the Munster Leagues and a new organisation, the Cork City and County Athletic Union Football League (Cork AUL), answered the urgent call to promote soccer. It commenced its competitions in 1947 with twelve teams and by 2004 was catering for 158 teams. A year later the Cork Schoolboys League was founded and is now providing organised soccer for over

Fig. 4.21 Soccer clubs and their founding years.

50 clubs, with teams from under ten to the under sixteen age groups. Roy Keane (Rockmount) and Denis Irwin (Everton) learned their football in the Schoolboys League.

Soccer in the workplace was also popular and inter-house competitions attracted great interest after their inception in the 1930s, when its games were played during the normal season. In the 1950s the playing season was changed to the summer months. This change contributed to the formation of the Cork Shipping League (Business League), which commenced operations in 1953 and provided football throughout the regular season for hundreds of soccer enthusiasts. The main difference between the Shipping and Inter-House Leagues was that those players playing in the latter could also assist teams in other leagues, while those registered in the Shipping (Business) League would require a transfer to do so.

The Munster Senior League provides fixtures for 76 teams, while the AUL caters for 158. A new club must have the use of a regulation-sized ground and changing facilities before it is accepted. Of the 23 teams competing in the MSL Senior Divisions, fourteen originated in the city and suburbs. Teams competing in the lower grades are mainly reserve squads of higher-grade teams. Fifty-two city teams are affiliated to the AUL.

One cannot deny the popular appeal of soccer in the city. The number of teams in the various leagues provides evidence of high participation rates. Teams are clustered around Shandon Street, Blarney Street and Gurranabraher in the northside of the city and Turner's Cross, Ballyphehane and Togher on the southside. These remain the strongholds of soccer in the city. Club grounds and facilities are often located a significant distance away from these original catchments (which were primarily working-class areas). Soccer clubs over the years have been built more around teams than the communities in which they are based. This trend has changed in recent decades with the procurement by many clubs of better and more permanent facilities. This has allowed them in turn to become more fully integrated into their respective communities.

Fig. 4.22 Spectators young and old watching Cork *v* St James' Gate at the Mardyke in 1931 from their vantage point at Shanakiel. (Photo: Private collection.)

Fig. 4.23 Cork City's Colin O'Brien gets away from Aurelieh Capoue during their Intertoto Cup clash against FC Nantes in 2004. (Photo: *Irish Examiner.*)

Hurling and The Glen

Diarmuid O'Donovan

Oh old Blackpool, I dread ye,
God knows you're never 'bate',
For a fighter or poet, or cry in the throat
Of a hound at a five-bar gate.
And all your pigeons fly farther,
Long and true like your bowl playing men,
But most of all I love ye,
For the spirit of the Glen.[1]

'Blackpool', Val Dorgan

Glen Rovers hurling club was founded in 1915. The idea to start the club emerged from men who worked in Goulding's fertiliser factory, then situated in Goulding's Glen. Their plans received a major boost when several of their friends and workmates fell into dispute with another northside club, Brian Dillon's, founded in 1910.[2] These rebels joined forces with the Blackpool lads and Glen Rovers was born. The colours of the club jersey, green, white and gold, reflected the political ideals of the founders. A black band was later added which commemorated the executed 1916 leaders. From modest beginnings the club would quickly prosper, becoming a potent cultural symbol for the tightly knit working-class communities of Blackpool and its environs. The GAA in Cork city would largely be defined by such loyalties and attachments to place.

Blackpool had a reputation for sporting achievement even before the arrival of the Glen. Its intricate network of lanes, streets and alleyways produced a fiercely competitive people, whether it was in bowling, boxing or pigeon racing. The nineteenth-century antiquarian John Windele noted such qualities when describing Blackpool and its inhabitants.[3] It was no coincidence then that hurling would thrive in such an environment. Hurling more than any other sport captured the pulse of a people and a place. The character of Blackpool people shaped Glen Rovers hurling club and the never-say-die spirit which was instilled in its teams.

Prior to the foundation of the club the balance of hurling power in the city lay south of the Lee. The main rivalries were between St Finbarr's, Redmond's and Blackrock. Between 1888, when the first county title was contested, and 1919, these three clubs won 21 of the 31 championships that were completed. Until the emergence of Glen Rovers, no club on the northside had challenged this dominance.

A number of factors helped the Glen establish itself as a club. In 1920 it merged with another juvenile club, Thomas Davis. Paddy O'Connell, who was already playing hurling with the Glen, was the principal organiser of the Thomas Davis Club. The merger introduced an under-age structure to Glen Rovers and O'Connell was the driving force behind this. He later became instrumental in turning talented young players such as Jack Lynch and Din Joe Buckley into some of the greatest hurlers in the history of Cork hurling. In addition to O'Connell's influence, the Glen would also draw strength from the expulsion of St Nicholas football club (based in Blackpool) from the GAA in 1918. Many of their players joined Glen Rovers, including Tom O'Reilly, who played a pivotal role in the rise of the Glen.[4]

Glen Rovers quickly established itself on the playing fields. It won its first county title in minor hurling in 1922, followed by the 1924 junior and the 1925 intermediate championship.[5] During these years, a defining moment was its victory over St Anne's (a rival club founded in 1919 and based in the North Cathedral and Shandon area) in the 1924 City Junior League final. The Glen won, after a highly publicised and much talked about four-game saga. Like Glen Rovers, St Anne's was a young and progressive club and aspired to play in the senior championship. It was always

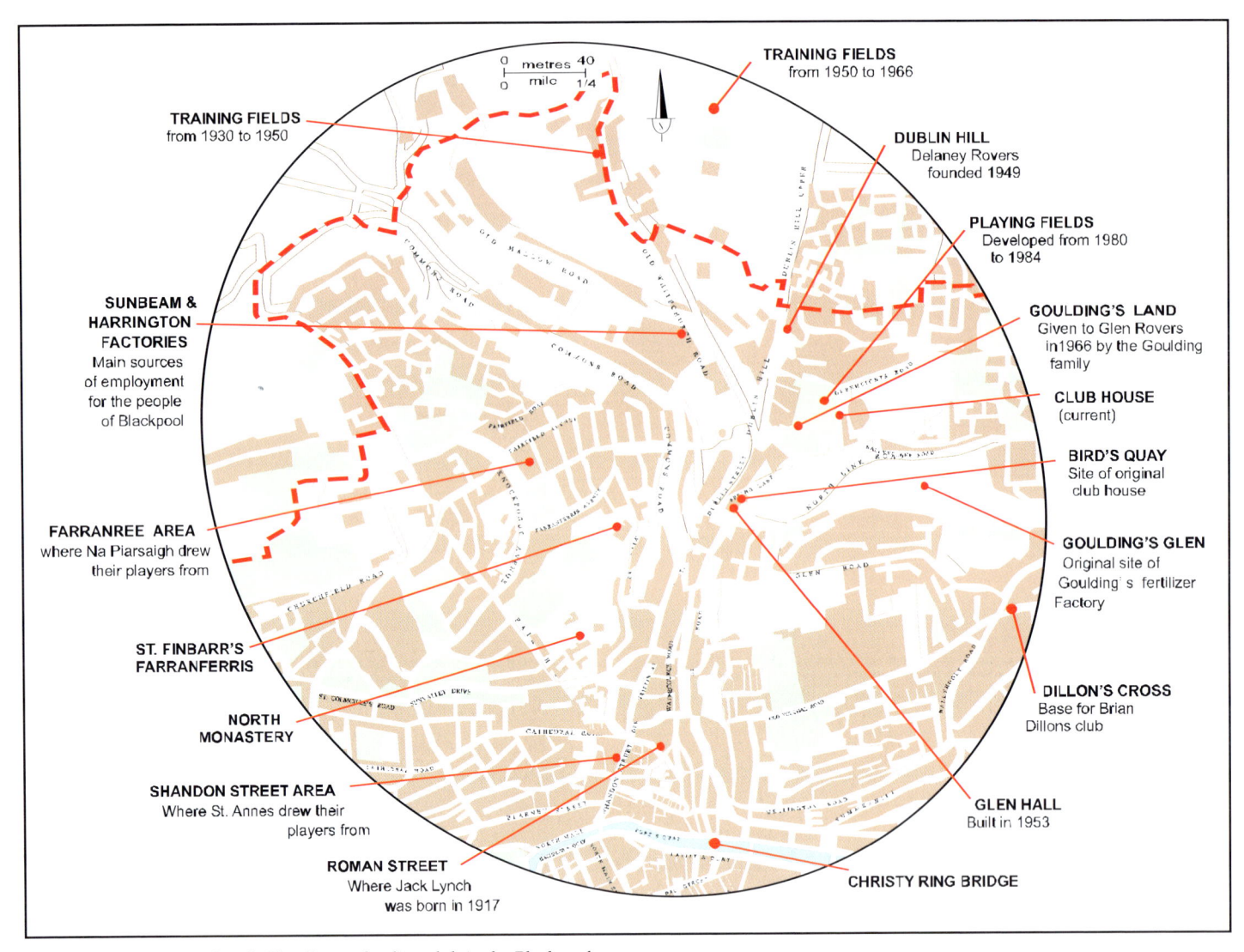

Fig. 4.24 Sites associated with Glen Rovers hurling club in the Blackpool area.

likely that only one club would succeed. The league final ultimately proved to be the defining moment in the history of both clubs. After the 1924 defeat, St Anne's were always trailing in the wake of Glen Rovers. The club faded out of competition in the early 1940s largely due to emigration. The Glen entered the senior championship for the first time in 1926 but made little impact in the early years.

Despite the initial lack of success at senior level, Glen Rovers was progressively getting stronger. Paddy O'Connell had put in place a highly efficient under-age recruiting and development structure.[6] His passion for the game was instilled in every young hurler who came in contact with him.[7] He was also instrumental in cultivating a brand of hurling that was fast, direct and intense. In addition, he forged strong links between the Christian Brothers in the North Monastery Secondary School and Glen Rovers. He also recruited hurlers from the neighbouring St Finbarr's Seminary, Farranferris.[8] Such schools played a critical role in nurturing local talent and acted as feeders for clubs like the Glen. Developing such links and structures was a novel idea at the time and would underpin much of the club's future success.

THE FIRST COUNTY TITLE AND EIGHT-IN-A-ROW

1934 was the Golden Jubilee of the foundation of the GAA. It was also the year that Glen Rovers toppled the old St Finbarr's/Blackrock aristocracy of Cork hurling. The Glen won their first championship title by defeating St Finbarr's; more significantly, the Cork title had crossed over the Lee to the northside of the city for the very first time. Wild celebrations followed the win. Blackpool people, well renowned for their individuality, their temperament and 'devil may care' outlook to life, now at last had reason to celebrate what they always believed, that they were the best in Cork. To prove their point, the Glen retained the title for the next seven years. Their eight-in-a-row sequence in such a highly competitive championship is unique in the history of the GAA. In 1941, Christy Ring joined Glen Rovers from Cloyne and won his first county title. His name has been synonymous with the Glen ever since. When the club finally relinquished the title in 1942, it had completely regenerated itself in terms of playing personnel. This was due in no small part to the club's strong minor committee, the North Mon's successes in the Harty Cup and the recruitment of players from nearby Farranferris. One player, Sonny Buckley, played in all eight winning teams.[9]

A second generation

By the early 1940s, a keen rivalry developed between Glen Rovers and St Finbarr's. This rivalry replaced the old Barrs and Blackrock enmity of the pre-1934 era. St Finbarr's, a very strong team, won county titles in 1942 and 1943 and were threatening to build a dynasty as strong as the Glen's 1930s side. This was the context of the 1944 county final between the two clubs. It became the focal point of both clubs' ambitions. St Finbarr's were favourites, on the basis that the Glen had nine players playing in their first county final. They were also without Jack Lynch (who had moved to Dublin) and Jim Young (who was tied to UCC). Glen Rovers rose to the challenge and easily won the game. It marked the beginning of a second golden era that would last until 1956. Between 1944 and 1956 the Glen contested eleven county finals and won seven.

Throughout this period the Glen's insatiable appetite for success showed no signs of abating. The club's members began to benefit from their association with Glen Rovers. The confidence that success brought, albeit in one aspect of their lives, began to spread into their lives in general. Jack Lynch was an example of this. On the playing field, he was one of the finest hurlers in Ireland. Off the field, he completed his education, joined the Civil Service, studied law and eventually was elected to represent the people of Blackpool in Dáil Éireann.[10] To the people of Blackpool, Jack Lynch was one of their own and Lynch never pretended to be anything else. He set standards that infused his community with expectation rather than aspiration.

Fig. 4.25 The Glen team, with some of the officers and supporters, after they had defeated Ballincollig in the senior hurling county final, October 1941. It was the Glen's eighth consecutive senior title. The photograph features Christy Ring, who won the first of his fourteen senior county medals that day, along with many of the most successful hurlers in the club's history. These include Jack Lynch, Jim Young, Paddy O'Donovan and Din Joe Buckley, all of whom went on to win four All-Ireland Senior Hurling medals in a row with Cork between 1941 and 1944. The only major player of the eight-in-a-row era that is missing from the photograph is Paddy 'Fox' Collins. 'Fox', as he was known, was the first real superstar of the Glen Rovers hurling club. He retired from playing after the Glen defeated Sarsfields in the 1940 county final. Front row: Dan Moylan, Willie Hickey, Joe Looney, Dan Coughlan, Jim McCarthy (children not included). Middle row: Teddy Healy, Mick O'Keeffe, Paddy O'Donovan, Din Joe Buckley, Paddy Hogan, Connie 'Sonny' Buckley (captain), Christy Ring, Dave Creedon, Jim Young. Back row: Tom McCarthy, Charlie Tobin, Paddy 'Chancer' Barry, Christy McSweeney, Jack Lynch, Willie Mackey, Rev Fr Barrett (President), Frank Casey, Denis McDonnell, Jerry Looney, Fred Richmond, Jack Buckley, Ned Porter, Mick O'Brien, Jack O'Connor. (Source of names: *The spirit of the Glen*, Cork, 1975. Photo: *Irish Examiner*.)

Fig. 4.26 Jack Lynch (1917–1999). (Artist: William Rohan.)

As a result of this confidence and their fame, club players were employed even in times of high unemployment in the city. However, this brought its own problems. Steady employment resulted in steady incomes. This meant that people began to aspire to owning their own houses. Despite all the new housing developments across the northside, there was no provision for private housing. It resulted in a trickle of migration across the city to new private housing developments in Bishopstown, Blackrock and Douglas. Here were the first signs of the dilution of the 'all for one, one for all' ethos of Glen Rovers.

In 1949 the club decided to build new clubrooms. From the beginning the club had been based in a small premises in Bird's Quay. The members now wanted a clubhouse more in keeping with the Glen's status as one of the finest clubs in the country. A new clubhouse was built in Thomas Davis Street, and the building became known as 'the Glen Hall'. It cost £10,000, a large sum in the economically depressed Ireland of the early 1950s. The Glen was the first club to complete a project of this magnitude.

The Glen's second golden era reached its peak in 1954. That year the club won the senior and intermediate county hurling titles. It was the Glen's fifteenth senior title in 21

Fig. 4.27 Crowds paying their last respects to former Taoiseach Jack Lynch as the funeral cortège crossed St Patrick's Bridge, 1999. (Photo: Denis Minihane, *Irish Examiner*.)

CULTURE • AND • THE • CITY

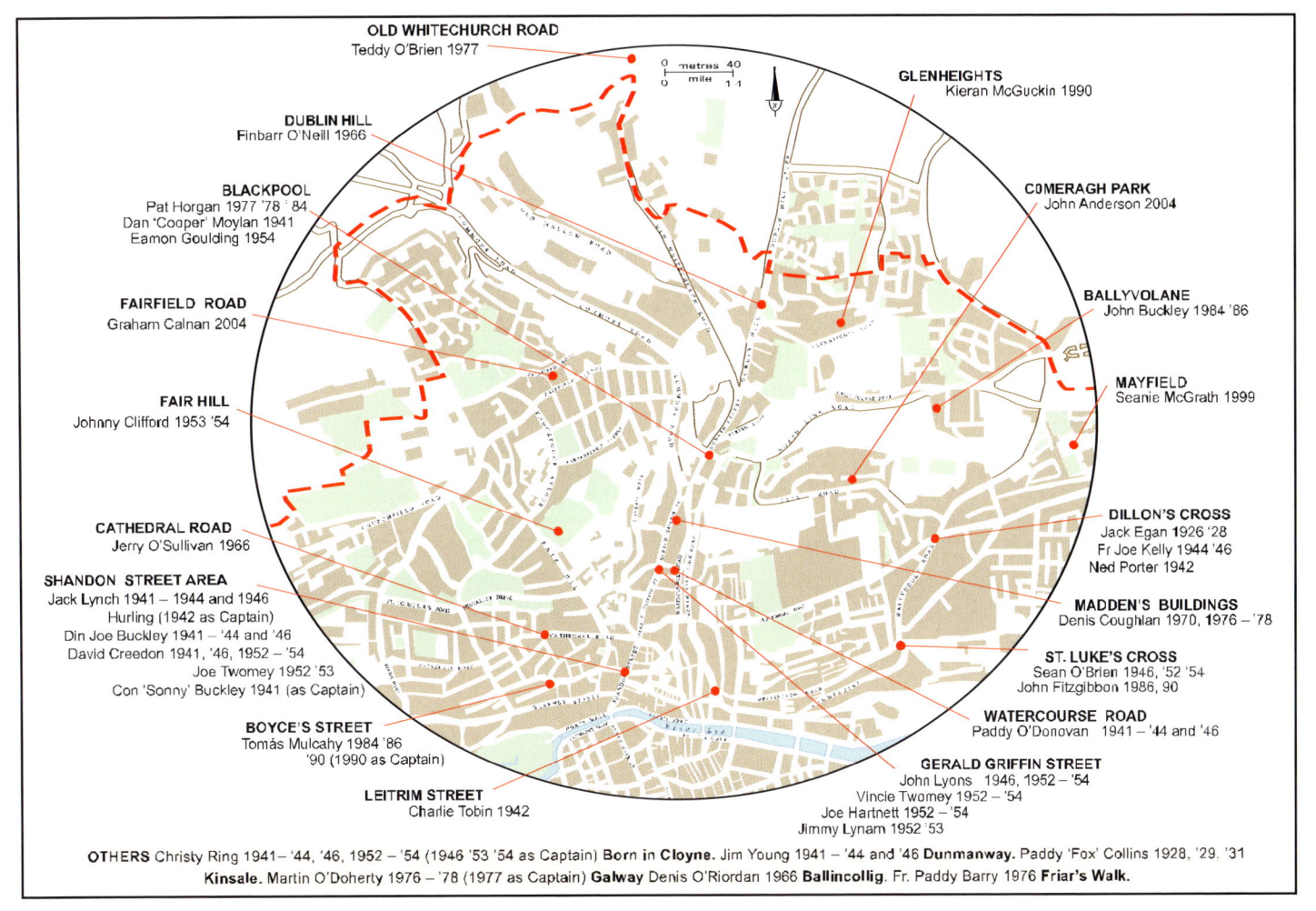

Fig. 4.28 The birthplaces of Glen Rovers players who have won senior All-Ireland titles with Cork.

seasons. Also in 1954, Christy Ring captained the Cork senior hurling team to All-Ireland success against Wexford, winning a record eight All-Ireland medals. Six other Glen players lined out with Ring that day – Dave Creedon, John Lyons, Vincie Twomey, Joe Hartnett, John Clifford and Eamonn Goulding. These All-Ireland winners lived within a stone's throw of each other. To round the year off, thirteen of the players that won senior county medals with the Glen helped St Nicholas to win the county senior football title.

BUILDING A THIRD ERA

After defeats in the 1955 and 1956 county finals to St Finbarr's and Blackrock respectively, many veteran players retired. The Glen's next appearance in a county final was in 1958, when they won a sixteenth championship title. This 'new' team was built around emerging minors like Bill Carroll and Jackie Daly. The victory was sweet because the Glen was forced to line out without Christy Ring. It also heralded a third golden era, which would see the club contest eight finals between 1958 and 1972 and win them all. The club retained the title in 1959 and 1960. Jerry O'Sullivan,

Finbarr O'Neill and Patsy Harte were among several young players that broke into the team in those years. But ominously, other clubs were beginning to challenge the Glen's dominance of the minor grade. Blackrock won five and northside rivals Na Piarsaigh (founded in 1943) won four of the ten minor county championships contested in the 1960s. The Glen only won one. An important well for developing senior talent was beginning to dry up.

The changing social geography of Cork's northside also impacted on the club. The expanding city had spawned new housing estates, which in turn saw the formation of new clubs. Whereas the Glen had been the dominant force on the northside of the city, they now faced competition from newly established clubs intent on creating their own sporting identities. Clubs such as Delaney Rovers (1949), Na Piarsaigh and St Vincent's (1943) now competed with the Glen for up-and-coming players. The impact on the club would be keenly felt in later years. The 1960s was also a decade of change in the administrative side of the club. Many of the founding members were reaching the autumn of their lives. Theo Lynch, who had been secretary for fifteen years, stepped down from his post in 1960. Paddy O'Connell died in 1962, while Tom O'Reilly was still chairman of both Glen Rovers and St Nicholas when he died in 1966. Despite these changes the club continued to expand. A new field and dressing room were acquired in Spring Lane in 1966 and a members' bar opened in 1970. Consequently, the administrative workload grew out of all proportion. The day-to-day management of the club was taking up valuable time which had previously been devoted to the organisation of hurling alone.

THE GLEN AND UCC

The Glen's near monopoly of the Cork senior hurling championship continued into the 1960s. However, new arrivals were emerging on the scene. Principal among these was University College Cork. 'The College' put together a formidable side in the early 1960s, and managed to reach six county finals between 1960 and 1970. The rivalry between UCC and the Glen became intense and the games caught the imagination of the Cork hurling public. Over 20,000 people attended the 1960 final, which the Glen won, while 17,000 people watched the drawn 1962 final. The quality of that game was so good that 25,000 people paid to see the replay, which the Glen also won. The College would eventually win hurling titles in 1963 and 1970. In the 1968 county championship quarter-final the exchanges between the sides were heated. At one stage the game was stopped as a consequence of a brawl. Following a subsequent County Board inquiry, a Glen Rovers player was severely disciplined. The decision infuriated the club to such an extent that the senior team was withdrawn from the championship. The Glen players and members who were involved with Cork withdrew from these panels also. The club gained some compensation when they had a comprehensive victory over UCC in the 1969 final.

ALL-IRELAND CLUB CHAMPIONS

By the time the Glen qualified for the next final in 1972, seven of the team that beat UCC in the 1969 final had retired. However, it was business as usual and the club defeated Youghal in the final. The All-Ireland club championship had been established in 1972. The victory over Youghal gave the Glen its opportunity to become All-Ireland champions. The club defeated St Rynagh's of Offaly in a final that was delayed until 1973. Some weeks before the final the club lost its first county final since 1956 when Blackrock defeated them. Following another county final defeat in 1975, the Glen bounced back in 1976 to beat Blackrock in the final. They then went on to win a second All-Ireland club title when they defeated Camross of Laois in the final, which was played in Thurles in 1977. The club appeared to be as strong as ever.

Fig. 4.29 The Glen's Donal Cronin breaking free from Na Piarsaigh's Gerard Shaw during a Cork Senior Hurling League game in 2004. (Photo: *Irish Examiner*.)

The first significant sign of a decline in fortunes came in the county finals of 1977 and 1978. The Glen lost to St Finbarr's and Blackrock respectively. The club had contested four finals in four years and lost an unprecedented three. In reaction, the members changed the officers. The new officers undertook a major development of the club's playing facilities at Spring Lane. Once again the management of the club was distracted from playing hurling. In an ironic twist, as the club continued to develop its playing and members' facilities the teams became less and less successful. In 1989, Glen Rovers won their first senior county title in thirteen years.[11]

In 1990, the club moved from its base in the heart of Blackpool to a new club premises in Ballyvolane. A changing population largely dictated this shift. The once venerable suburb of Blackpool had declined steadily through the 1970s and 1980s. The club had always moved with the times in providing the best of facilities for its players and the new complex in Ballyvolane merely reflected a desire to cater for the modern player. While the Glen's star has dimmed a little in recent times, the club continues to produce quality players. It also has a tradition and history that encourages its younger members to aspire to be the best. The real challenge that faces the club in the early years of the twenty-first century is to manage their resources, both human and material, in such a manner as to ensure optimum results on the playing fields. If this can be achieved, then the Glen will surely regain its position as one of the greatest clubs in Ireland.

Road Bowling

Seamus Ó Tuama

Come boys and have a day with our bowling club so gay,
The loft of the bowl it will make your heart thrill,
When you hear the Shea boy say, 'Timmy Delaney has won today'.
Here's to them all says the boys of Fair Hill.[1]

From the 'The boys of Fair Hill'

If you really want to see Cork city you need to journey up to Fair Hill. From Fair Hill you will see the city spreading out below you like an intricate patchwork quilt, with the Lee bidding farewell to the city as it heads to the ocean. That view encapsulates all of life in Cork, its layers of urban growth, its relationship with the sea, the surrounding hills watching over it and the faint traces of the great marsh. Fair Hill's other advantage is the richness of its association with traditional sports, especially with that most 'Cork' of sports, bowl playing – or, as it is more frequently called today, road bowling.

Fair Hill and its bowling tradition
Some years ago I asked Denis Scully, one of the greats of bowl playing, how he got involved in the sport. With neither pretension nor false modesty he simply said: 'Up here you are a bowler or you are nothing.' If that is the criterion for recognition in Fair Hill, then he most certainly is something. He is one among a gallery of great bowling names and families that have helped make Fair Hill the capital. It may not have begun with Timmy Delaney, but he is certainly the most famous name in the Fair Hill pantheon. He was the first Cork bowler to play against an Ulster bowler, when he made the long journey to Armagh in the 1920s to play Peter 'Hammerman' Donnelly. Delaney won that day, making Fair Hill the undisputed capital of bowling until the emergence of Mick Barry, who had the audacity to be born on the southside of the river.

Delaney's road-shower, the equivalent of a caddy in golf, was Jack O'Shea. He is the 'Shea boy' who announces Timmy Delaney's victory in the traditional anthem of Cork City, 'The boys of Fair Hill'. Jack O'Shea was the most famous of all road-showers and his advice was sought for many years after Timmy Delaney had retired from bowling. Denis Scully inherited the Delaney mantle in the 1970s. He became a hero, emerging as a raw unknown youth who took on all-comers, eventually winning All-Ireland and international honours, but most importantly he challenged the hegemony of the greatest bowler of all-time, Mick Barry of Waterfall.

For northsiders, and those from Fair Hill in particular, this was about restoring the balance of power. While Mick

Fig. 4.30 Timmy Delaney of Fair Hill bowling on Dublin Hill, May 1933. (Photo: *Irish Examiner*.)

Fig. 4.31 Fair Hill's Kieran Gould steers his shot though the crowd during the Irish Road Bowling 2004 All-Ireland senior championship final at Ballincurrig. In defeating Michael Toal from Armagh, Gould recorded his first senior title. (Photo: *Irish Examiner*.)

Barry was the undisputed king of bowling, Fair Hill still saw itself as the home of bowling. It is not a claim without justification. Apart from Timmy Delaney and Denis Scully, it could also lay claim to players like Davey Long, Jack Coveney, John Barry (Nash's Boreen), Jack O'Shea, John Murray, Christy McSweeney, Batna Barrett (who also played full-forward for Glen Rovers), Stephen Barrett, Finbarr Casey, James and Michael Buckley, the Gould brothers, James O'Sullivan and Peter Nagle, to name a few champion bowlers of different generations.

In Delaney's time, the Fair Hill bowlers made plans for a full day of bowling on Sunday mornings after the children's mass at the North Cathedral. While purportedly for children, the bowlers used the mass as a meeting-point, as it was at the right time and was usually over quickly. By eleven a.m. the bowlers would assemble at Connie Doyle's (the famous Harrier trainer). A series of scores were played in succession: the first from Connie Doyle's to Johnny Collins' boreen, the next to McSweeney's white wall and from there to the 'gate in the path', the next one to 'the gate over the bridge', then to 'the slate house' on the Kill Road and the last one to Killeens. They then bowled all the way back to Fair Hill. That famous bowling road went out of use after a house was built near the Blackstone Bridge. Many of the other traditional roads familiar to previous generations of Fair Hill bowlers are no longer available. Presently Fair Hill bowlers use what they call the 'Bog Road' or simply 'the Boggy', the Old Blarney Road. Bowlers congregate near the Blackstone Bridge and bowl in the direction of Blarney.

RIVAL BOWLING CAMPS

In the Delaney era, the old bowling roads were like arteries winding their way up to the Fair Field, bringing with them rival bowling camps. The Commons Road contingent, with players like Davey Mulcahy, Davey Long and Connie Collins, bowled from the Sunbeam gate up the factory boreen to Fair Hill. The Blarney Street contingent bowled up Johnny Collins' boreen. They all met at the Fair Field, where the serious business commenced, usually as a challenge between representatives of the different groups.

Sometimes players like Dan O'Neill or Buzzer O'Sullivan would come from Clogheen for a challenge. In a big score involving the likes of Timmy Delaney, the bowlers peeled off at O'Sullivan's pub at the Fair Field and bowled towards the Blackstone Bridge, up the Kill Road, through Killeens, where the houses were lofted, and on down to Scott's Shovel Mills in Monard. Other times the battle was taken to Dublin Hill. Here the big scores started at the Railway Bridge at the foot of Dublin Hill – they later started from the Long Lane – and were played up to the Booth House pub. Blackpool's

Fig. 4.32 Four famous bowling roads from the first half of the twentieth century: Waterfall and Pouladuff on the southside and Fair Hill and Dublin Hill on the northside. Bowling has been synonymous with Cork for hundreds of years. At one time bowling scores commenced close to the city centre, but as the city expanded and roads became busier bowling was pushed to the suburbs.

Jack Murphy was and still is the record holder over the longer course.

There was strong rivalry too with the southside. Here big challenges were mostly played over the famous Waterfall Road or the Pouladuff Road. Scully emerged as Fair Hill's own challenger to Mick Barry in 1968. Their first two meetings were double-hand scores. In the first, Scully teamed up with Derry Kenny of Clogheen to play against Barry and Johnny Creedon at Conna in east Cork on 5 July 1968. Scully was on the winning side that day, but Barry and Creedon reversed the result at Skibbereen on 24 August. They met for the first time in a single-hand score (one-against-one) at Ballymacoda in March 1969. Scully took victory on a technicality, as Barry was injured and unable to finish. Barry won when they met at Waterloo in July 1969, but Scully finally had his say in a final at Ballinadee in May 1973. For Fair Hill it was like the end of a long siege. But Barry was far from finished, as Scully found out subsequently when he tied their four score series with victory at Ring near Clonakilty. Mick Barry strode over the bowling world like a colossus. He was born and spent his formative years in a small cottage on the Waterfall bowling road, one of the premier bowling venues in the country and a bowling hotbed. His home was beside McGrath's farm, adjacent to what is now called the Oxygen Factory. It is not surprising that he was drawn into bowling. His career commenced when he was no more than ten. His first scores were on the Model Farm Road. He played a schoolmate, Paddy Kelly, several times, winning all his scores. They played from Cait's Lane near the Munster Institute to the water pump beyond the Minister's cross. They had return scores at Waterfall from the Mill Lane to the Two-Pot Bridge. He later defeated Joe Kelly, an older brother of Paddy's, and the legend of Mick Barry was already emerging.

Barry could claim to be the most outstanding sportsman produced by Cork in the twentieth century. To measure the impact he had on bowling, one must realise that Ból-Chumann na hÉireann, the national governing body, was not founded till 1954, when he was already 35. He won the last of his eleven senior championship titles when he was 58. From 1962 until 1975, he was Munster senior champion in all but three years. He twice completed All-Ireland four-in-a-rows – 1964 to 1967 and 1969 to 1972.

Most players would have rested happily on that amazing record, but not Mick Barry. He returned to centre-stage in 1991 and won the Munster vintage (over-60s) championship, and again in a magnificent performance in 1994. Mick Barry captured the imagination of the public like no bowler before or since. His fame even transcended sport. He won every possible competition and broke road records, lofted bends, bridges, trees and houses that others would not even

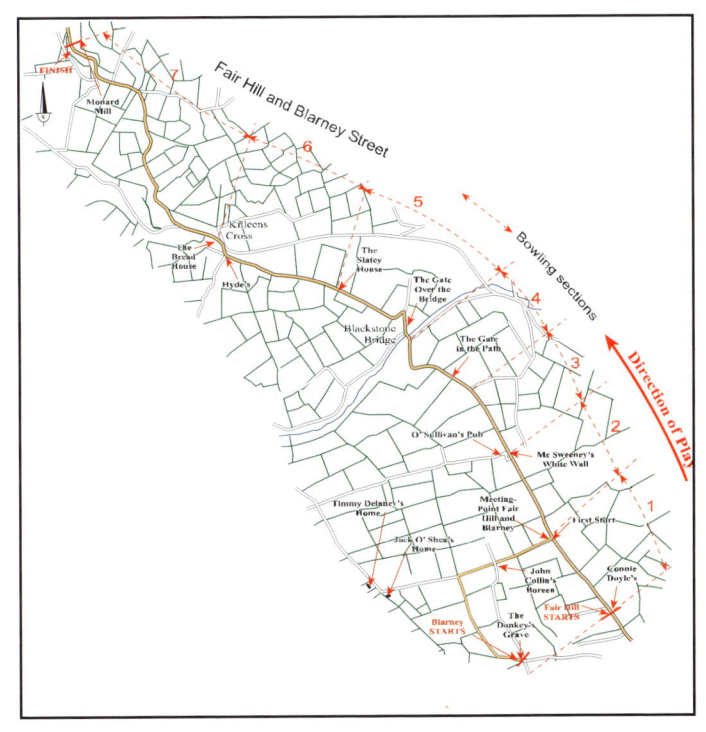

Fig. 4.33 The Fair Hill bowling road as it would have been played in the heyday of Timmy Delaney. This course is no longer used; the 'Boys of Fair Hill' now bowl on the old Blarney Road (Bog Road).

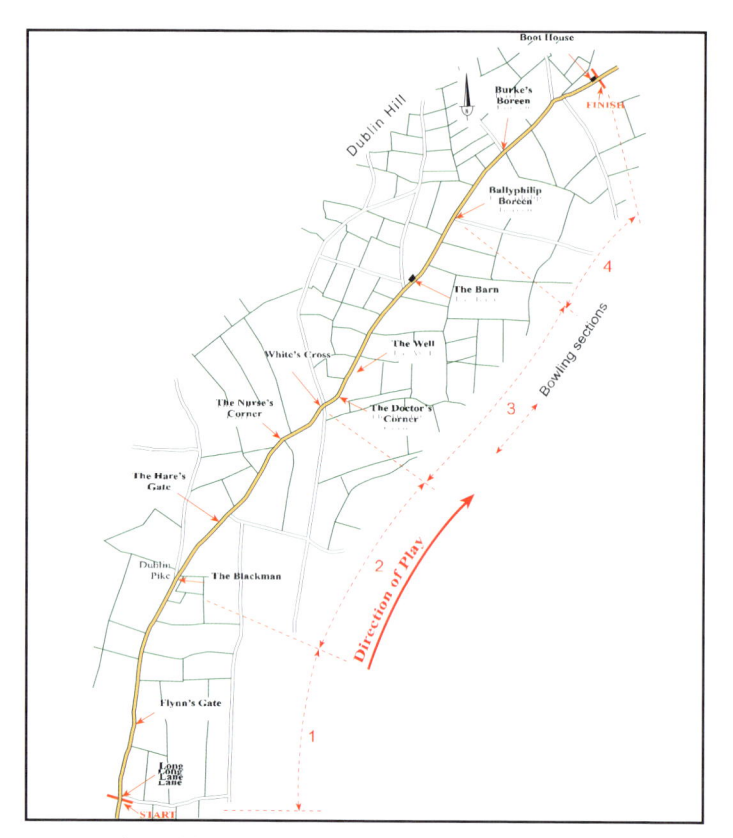

Fig. 4.34 The Dublin Hill bowling road, which was the principal bowling venue in Ireland until urban development and increased traffic volumes reduced its suitability for major events.

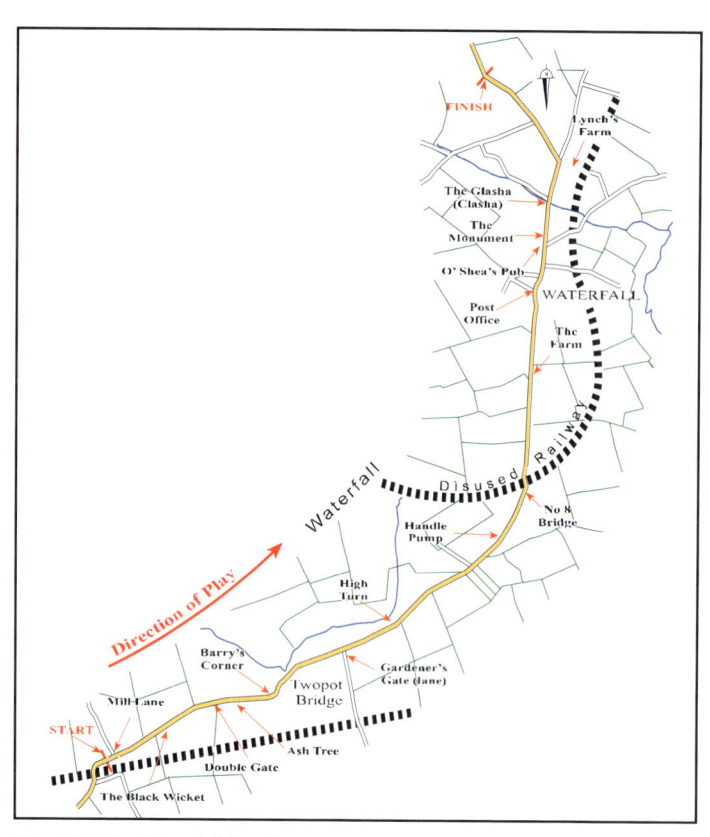

Fig. 4.35 The Waterfall bowling road as played in the 1910 *Cork Examiner* report. Increased urbanisation means that most scores now start at O'Shea's pub and proceed away from the city.

Cork Examiner, 1910
REPORT OF BOWLING MATCH ON THE WATERFALL ROAD

On Sunday the match which was left unfinished on the previous Sunday between those two adepts of the this fine old Irish pastime – Jerry Casey of Killeens and Jerry Riordan of Friars Walk – was played on the same road and £10 was added to the wager. The game lay between Mill Lane and Field's boreen. The greatest interest was manifested by an extremely large concourse of followers of the game. The weather was in striking contrast to the previous Sunday, the roads being heavy and showers fell throughout parts of the game. However it is very hard to damp the ardour of the bowl-player and his sporting qualities . . . It was estimated that between two and three thousand witnessed the game, and the best of order and decorum prevailed. Of the players it must be said they are a very good match, and possess the best sporting spirit. Casey started the game with a fine bowl, which gave him a few feet lead, which he maintained to the 'Two-Pot', where his backers were on 'fore' bowl. When starting from here Riordan got a magnificent shot, and brought his opponent 'hind' and playing splendidly kept increasing his lead to 'No 8' where he had half a bowl to his credit. This he maintained, both players playing strong, considering the slippery condition of the road to Waterfall.

It was the opinion of Riordan's backers that he should have a bowl of odds at 'O'Keefe's'. An incident took place, which partly had the effect of nullifying his chance. An old apple-cart was left to block the thoroughfare, after the road being cleared, and his bowl got blocked by it. Leaving Waterfall both played very cautiously, but there was no material change to the Clasha, where Riordan still had nearly a bowl to his credit. Then Casey did some very fine work. Putting his bowls from him in grand style he brought down the odds considerably on his antagonist, which left them on a level at the second Clasha about four throws from the finish. Excitement now ran pretty high, the supporters of both players evincing new spirit at each performance. It was a real fight now, up what is known as 'Scoura Hill' and tested the stamina of the players. Casey started with a fair bowl. Riordan got a bad break, his bowl was swept off the road, leaving Casey a good advantage which he retained to the finish. (By kind permission of Richard Henchion, *The land of the finest drop*, Cork, 2003.)

Fig. 4.36 An account of a score of bowls at Waterfall, one of the historic senior bowling venues in the western suburbs.

Fig. 4.37 Mick Barry, the most famous name in bowling, at the age of 76, bowling in the 1995 Munster vintage (over-60) championship final at Macroom.

player(s) who reaches the finish line in the least number of throws is the winner. It is a sport that demands high levels of skill to deal with the challenges of the course. Top players can loft over obstacles (launch the bowl in the air) and can spin the bowl left or right to negotiate the camber and curve of the road. A bowling match is called a score, which derives from an earlier tradition of playing twenty shots instead of using a finish line.)

dare. On St Patrick's Day 1955 he lofted a sixteen-ounce bowl over the Chetwynd Viaduct, then fully decked, a feat never equalled.

Barry's prowess and fame united the city bowlers north and south. He put down a mark on the Pouladuff Road that has never been equalled. Starting from O'Sullivan's pub, since demolished, he made the 'barking dogs' in five shots. He was at the top of the hill in seven and was just short of 'the spout' in eight. From there he made the finish at 'the patch' in three more – eleven shots of absolute accuracy and incredible speed.

The passion for bowling remains unflinching in Cork city. It is a sport that exudes authenticity in a world of global superstars. Here is a sport where the contestants have to mingle with the spectators and deal with the topographical challenge posed by standard public roads. Some of the most famous roads are being lost and all the 'point' names that go with them. Mick Barry's birthplace is in ruins, while road improvements and housing plans never take account of one of the most precious cultural assets of the city – its traditional bowling roads.

(*Note*. Road bowling is a traditional Irish sport played on public roads. The rules are relatively simple and similar to golf. The object is to throw a 28-ounce cast-iron bowl over a designated course marked by a start and finish line. The

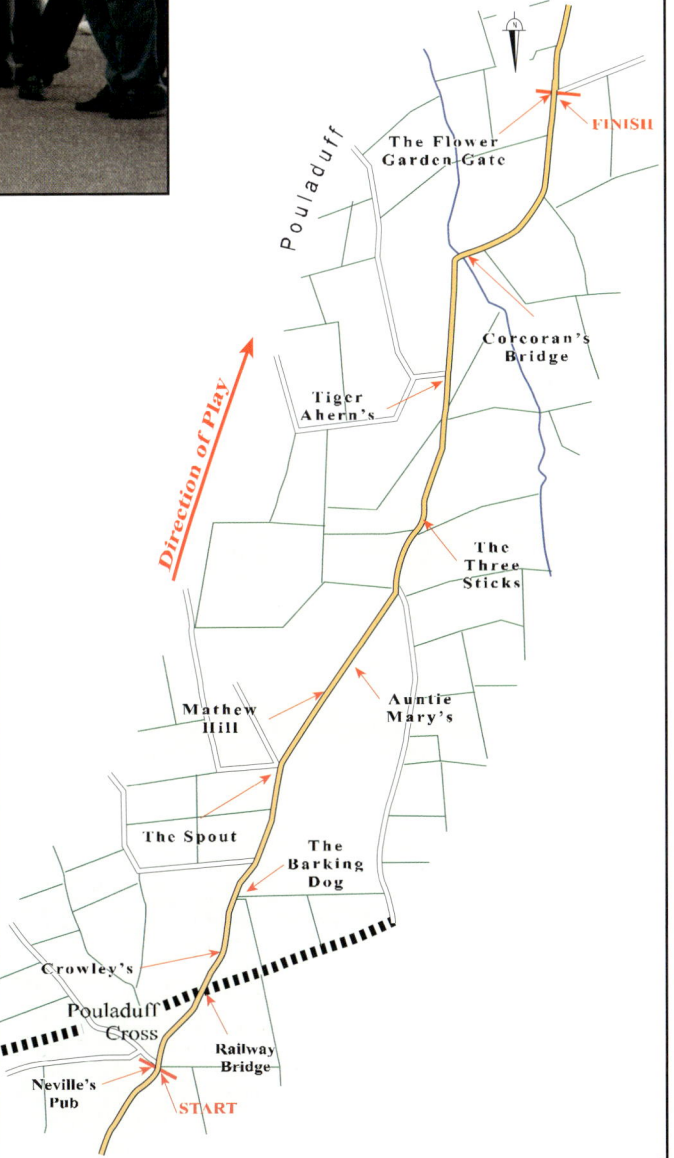

Fig. 4.38 The Pouladuff bowling road was one of the most important venues in the southside of Cork city. Recent housing developments have made most of the original route unplayable.

29. MUSIC

Tomás Ó Canainn

Music means many things and music in Cork means even more than the thousand things it means elsewhere! Classical, traditional, rock, pop, jazz, bluegrass, country, choral – they are all alive and well and vibrating in Cork. Music here is of the past and the present – a kaleidoscopic continuum that points to an even more musical future. Why should a Derryman like myself, a mere blow-in, albeit a blow-in of more than forty years' standing, suggest the possibility that Cork might be Ireland's most musical city? Well, in my forty enjoyable years here, I have been making various musics, listening to many more and reporting on the city's concerts for some twenty years for the *Cork Examiner*, taking over from the late Geraldine Neeson, who had spent a lifetime as a reviewer and piano teacher and who was, incidentally, bridesmaid at the wedding of Cork's famous Lord Mayor, Terence MacSwiney. I have written a number of books on traditional music and have taught music in Cork's two major musical institutions, the university and the Cork School of Music. But more of that shortly.

Let me ask what music means in Cork. It means, or meant, Rory Gallagher and Aloys Fleischmann, Matt Cranitch and Adrian Petcu, the Frank and Walters Band, Jimmy McCarthy, the Cork Symphony Orchestra and John Spillane, the Guinness Jazz Festival and the Cork International Choral Festival, Majella Cullagh, Dog on Stilts, Finbarr Wright, Ruby Horse, Na Filí, the Sultans of Ping. It is not limited in time or space! In this city of so many bands and choirs of all types, what about the RTÉ Vanbrugh String Quartet and Jimmy Crowley, Seán Ó Sé and Angel Climent, Jan Cap, John Gibson, Johnny McCarthy, Cara O'Sullivan, Mary Hegarty, Ger Wolfe, the Four-Star Trio, Any Old Time, Boa Morte and Two-Step Polka, Con Fada, Matt Teehan, the Neffs, the Butter Exchange Band, and Barrack Street Band? Where does one stop? Mick Daly, Niall Vallely, Christy

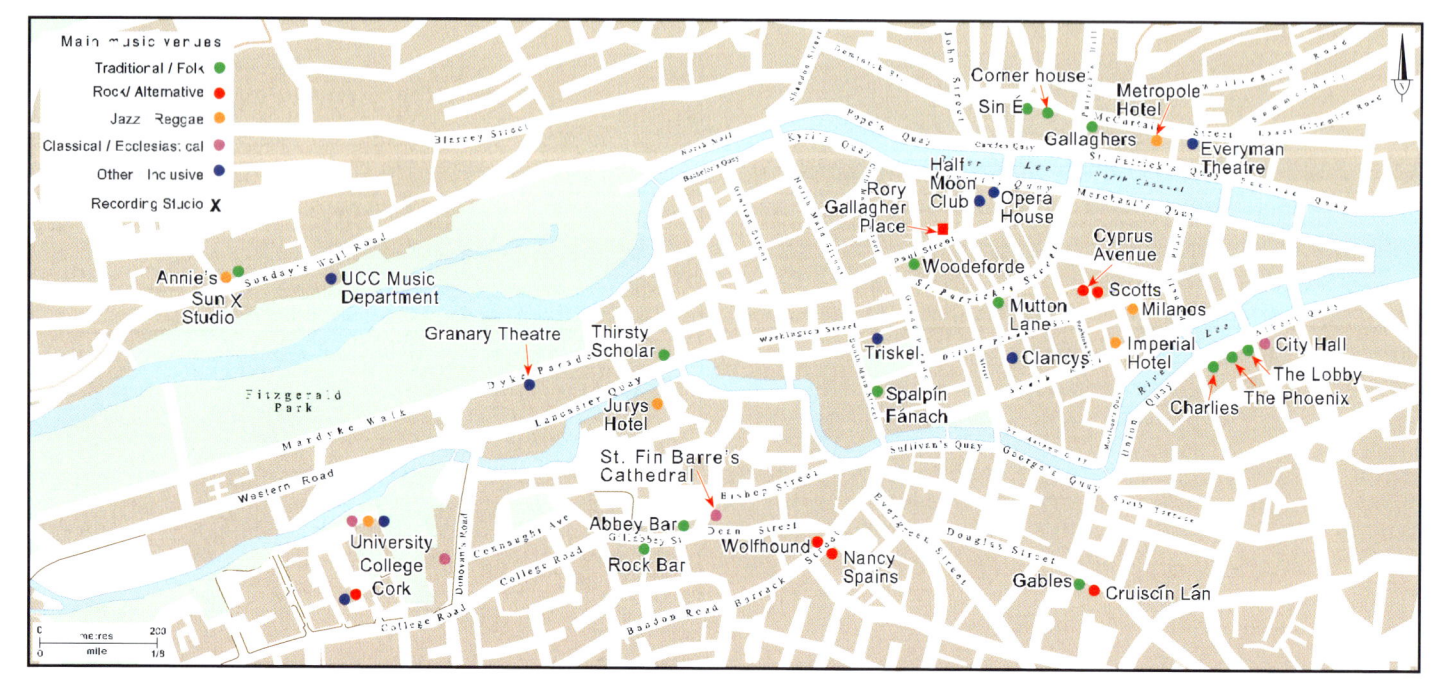

Fig. 4.39 Traditional music is strong in Cork city, both in terms of the quality and the quantity of musicians and venues. The city has many 'open' traditional sessions, which in some venues are accompanied by folk music and ballad-singing. The continuing success of the annual Cork Folk Festival and the UCC Tradfest reflect the strength of this tradition. Venues listed under rock/alternative play host to some of Cork's fine up-and-coming singers and songwriters, many coming from Coláiste Stiofáin Naofa as well as those who have emerged from the popular Battle of the Band's competitions. Jazz in its older forms is performed in many venues, but an increasing number of young musicians include fusions with other styles, particularly reggae. Cork also plays host to a world-famous jazz festival each October. Classical and ecclesiastical music is most often located in churches or larger theatres such as the Opera House and the City Hall. The Cork Choral Festival celebrated its fiftieth year in existence in 2004. The city also hosts the Vanbrugh String Quartet. (David Kearney, UCC.)

Leahy, Séamus Creagh, Dave Hennessy, Mel Mercier, Madrigal 75 and the Lee Valley String Band, the Lynch Mob and the Sixties Band, Pa Johnson's and the Cork Opera House, Paul O'Donnell, Dave Owens and UCC Jazz, the CSM Jazz Big Band, John O'Connor, Red Hat and Calico, Mandy Murphy, Nomos, Evelyn Grant.

I begin to feel that I should be interrupting this long litany with an occasional 'Pray for us' or, perhaps more appropriately, a few interjections of 'Have mercy on us'! I could make the litany much longer, but I'll mention just a few more relevant names . . . Stoker's Lodge, the Stargazers and the Crawford Trio, Len McCarthy, Ken Foley, Ossian Publications, Joe Mac and Teddy Moynihan, Catherine Leonard, Tadhg Crowley, Alf Kennedy, Don Baker and Louis Stewart live in Scotts, the Office and O'Flaherty's, Concorda, Eleanor Malone, Karan Casey and Aidán Coffey.

Forget the litany! Where do you want to go for your music? Well, it depends on what you want. How about the Granary Theatre, the Briar Rose, the Corner House, Acton's Hotel in Kinsale to hear Billy Crosbie, the Lobby Bar, An Spailpín Fánach, the Blue Haven, the Metropole, Morrison's Island, Rochestown Park, Triskel Arts Centre, the Imperial, Sin É, the Long Valley, O'Connell's of Glanmire, Mutton Lane Inn, Gables, Charlie's and many, many more. And then, of course, if you want to go to Ballincollig, Midleton, Carrigaline, northside, southside . . . I trust the above gives some indication of the scope of music in the city.

Grand Opera and the Opera House

My earliest memories are of a city that was given to reminiscing about its former love-affair with grand opera and its knowledgeable *aficionados*, who, it seems, were not shy about letting visiting artistes know their opinions. There was the story, often retold in various guises, of the Italian tenor who got encore after encore and at last thanked his audience profusely, protesting that he could not sing the aria again. A voice from the upper gallery or 'the gods' shouted: 'Yes you will, until you get it right!'

But that was before 1955, when the old Opera House burned down and the Cork habit of weekly trips to the theatre came to an end. Let me say that they saw much more than opera on those visits. The late Seán Beecher described the Opera House fare as 'ballet to boxing and grand opera to Gilbert and Sullivan'. It was culture for the ordinary citizen and the visit of companies like the Carl Rosa Opera caused a real stir, with citizens meeting the stars at the railway station and taking over the job of the horses in pulling visitors' carriages to their lodgings on Lavitt's Quay, beside the Opera House. Sean O'Faolain remembered some of them staying at his home in Half Moon Street.

Cork has quite a few orchestras today, including the Cork Symphony Orchestra, the Cork Youth Orchestra, the County Orchestra and the orchestras of the university and the Cork School of Music. A pioneering figure in the early days was the late Mícheál Ó Ceallacháin. He was the first conductor of the Cork Youth Orchestra, and his children were all top-class musicians and played various orchestral instruments. Generations of Cork teenagers had, and still get, their first orchestral experience in the Cork Youth Orchestra.

Public music-making in the city can easily be traced back to the nineteenth century, when there are references to the Cork Musical Society, a choral unit formed and conducted by Dr Marks, as well as the Band of the Cork Orchestral Union, which had some forty players. The latter gave regular performances in the Assembly Rooms, conducted by W. Ringrose Atkins. At the Cork Exhibition of 1883, the Cork Musical Society gave a very successful performance of Mendelssohn's *Elijah*. For the next thirty years or so, amateur opera in Cork was in its heyday, with performances of Gilbert and Sullivan in the Theatre Royal.

Fig. 4.40 Aloys Fleischmann (1910–1992). (By kind permission of the Fleischmann family.).

However, for the Cork International Exhibition of 1902, an orchestra of foreign players under Signor Grossi was recruited and the conductor and his wife, a pianist, were persuaded to remain in Cork to teach, which they did for some thirty years. Grossi re-formed the Band of the Cork Orchestral Union and they joined forces with the choir of St Fin Barre's Cathedral to form the Musical Art Society in 1908. After one successful concert they disbanded, failing to reach agreement on whether the name of the choral conductor or the orchestral conductor should appear first on its programmes.

George Brady conducted the orchestra of the Cork Philharmonic Society from 1926 to 1937, when it was wound up. The now familiar Cork Symphony Orchestra started life in 1934 as the University Orchestra, conducted by Professor Fleischmann and led by W.E. Brady. It was renamed in 1938, when the Cork Orchestral Society was founded to arrange its concerts.

The Cork School of Music (1878) was the very first such establishment in these islands, preceding even the Guildhall School of Music in London. I was a piano student of the late Bridget Doolin there in the 1960s. She was a very fine pianist and a top-class teacher. I remember telling a colleague of mine that Bridget was so inspirational that she could turn anyone into a pianist – all one needed was a pair of hands and a bum to sit on. Unknown to me, my colleague, who was also a friend of Bridget's, told her what I had said. I was surprised to hear, years later, that she had been quite amused by my offbeat praise.

I had a short-lived connection with the Cork Symphony Orchestra in the 1960s. It came about through the Lanes, who were a very musical family in Cork. I became a cello student with Denise Lane, who later encouraged me to join the Cork Symphony Orchestra for a couple of performances of Handel's *Messiah*, conducted by the late John Murphy. I managed the Handel alright and Denise encouraged me to attend the next orchestral practice, under Professor Fleischmann. I turned up at Lee Maltings on the Monday evening to discover, to my horror, that I was the only cellist. To make matters worse, they were starting the first rehearsal of a Schumann symphony. I spent a very embarrassing evening trying to locate high notes in areas of the fingerboard of the cello that I had never before frequented. I unilaterally terminated my career as a cellist there and then, but remained good friends with the amiable, energetic professor and continued my studies for the BMus degree in the Music Department at UCC. For me, he was always Cork's Mr Music. So much of what is now taken for granted in the local musical scene would not be there if he had not devoted many years to making music an important element in the life of the city.

Seán Ó Riada

I was fortunate, at this time, to make the acquaintance of a great Cork musician, Seán Ó Riada, with whom I shared tunes and studied Irish music. Seán had attended Farranferris College, where he studied piano and organ with Aloys Fleischmann's father and learned fiddle from Willie Brady. While still a student at the college he played at a concert in the Coliseum, performing a classical repertoire and then, when he did not get the attention he felt he deserved, breaking into Irish dance music, to considerable applause. He later did a BMus degree at UCC and, while a student there, played with local dance bands, including Billy Browne's Band, the Kampbell Kombo and various jazz groups.

After graduation he joined RTÉ as Assistant Director of Music, later becoming Musical Director at the Abbey Theatre, and composed much music, including a number of works showing a Greek influence as well as excellent film music, including, of course, *Mise Éire*. All this was accomplished before he returned to take up a position in UCC in 1963 and live with his Irish-speaking family in Cúil

Fig. 4.41 Portrait of Seán Ó Riada (1931–1971) by the artist Mícheál Ó Nualláin. (Source: University College Cork Art Collection.)

Aodha. It was in this period that he composed his liturgical music and was involved with many radio and television programmes. The last concert of his famous group, Ceoltóirí Cualann, took place in the City Hall, Cork, in the last year of Seán's life, as part of the Carolan celebrations.

Seán Ó Riada added considerably to the status of the university, as he was already a famous figure when he arrived as a new lecturer in the Music Department in 1963. His legacy to the city's musical scene was immense.

Irish traditional music is now a very important and lively part of the Cork musical scene, with music every night of the week in many pubs, including our own regular Tuesday night in O'Connell's of Glanmire. It certainly was not so when I first came to the city in 1961. For some six years before then, I had been deeply involved in making traditional music, both solo as an accordionist and as a founder member of the Liverpool céilí band, playing almost every night of the week.

Traditional music

I was shocked to find that traditional music in Cork at that time was confined to a relatively few players, who would have weekly gatherings in the spartan surrounds of the Group Theatre in South Main Street or the CYMS hall in Castle Street. A slightly separate sect would meet in Dún Laoi on the North Mall, presided over by piper Mícheál Ó Riabhaigh, with whom I later started to learn pipes, leading to a gradual desertion of my accordionist status.

The Francis O'Neill branch of Comhaltas Ceoltóirí Éireann used to meet on Thursday evenings to play a few tunes. I remember, among others, Dick Nangle, Ned Maher, Matt Teahan, Mick Milne, Charlie O'Sullivan, Gary Cronin, Mícheál Ó Lochlainn and a young singer, Lena Mullins. We formed bands for Comhaltas competitions and gradually improved. I also attended the Saturday night sessions in Dún Laoi and visited Mícheál Ó Riabhaigh often in his home, where he introduced me to the piping art on a set of Crowley pipes I had purchased second-hand from my dentist. The chanter was one made for me by Alf Kennedy. His father, Moss, always kept me well supplied with good reeds.

Uilleann pipes are not, of course, the only kind of pipes to be found in Cork. There is a long tradition of marching pipe bands – what many people term 'war-pipes'. The better-known names include St Finbarr's, St Mary's on the Hill, Gurranabraher, the Ballyphehane Band and the Volunteer's Pipe Band. If you want to step it out beyond the city bounds, you may sample fine bands in Carrigaline and Cobh.

I joined up with Matt Cranitch and Réamonn Ó Sé and in 1969 we won the trio competition at the All-Ireland Fleadh Cheoil in Cashel, where I was surprised to get first place in the solo piping competition. Later that year we took the name 'Na Filí', recommended by Séamus Caomhánach, and made our first LP for Mercier. Tom Barry soon replaced Réamonn in our line-up and for the next ten years we toured Europe and America, making numerous

Fig. 4.42 The opening gala concert at the Cork International Choral Festival, 1996. Requiem by Giuseppe Verdi; soloists: Cara O'Sullivan, Marie Walshe, Ronan Tynan; bass: Dean Robinson; RTÉ Concert Orchestra and the Festival Chorus composed of four local choirs (Carrigaline Singers, Cantairí Mhuscraí, Cór Cois Abhann and Cór Naomh Muire); conductor: Richard Cooke. (Photo: Choral Festival Archive.)

Fig. 4.43 The Norwegian, Beady Bell, performing at the Cork City Jazz Festival. (*Irish Examiner*.)

Fig. 4.44 Clodagh O'Driscoll of Gaelscoil Douglas playing the violin during the Cork School of Music's annual Suzuki Concert at City Hall, Cork. (Photo: Denis Minihane, *Irish Examiner*.)

television appearances and another half-dozen LPs. It was an unforgettable time.

The Cork International Choral Festival was still fairly new when we arrived, having begun in 1953. I have attended the famous festival for forty years now and have heard the wonderful singing of foreign choirs and witnessed the standard of Irish choirs going up and up. There were many big moments – one of the best for me being Geoffrey Spratt's first win with the UCC Choir in the international competition. Professor Fleischmann's seminar on contemporary choral music was an important part of the annual festival. We always enjoyed his analysis of the new music composed for the occasion. Even the composers were sometimes surprised to be told about the musical thinking behind their new works! Such excitement was there on the final night, with the prize-giving and many sad partings with new friends.

Jazz and the city

Jazz has had an important place in Cork for a very long time, many years before the establishment of the Jazz Festival. Dave Owens, one of the old-timers, told me many stories of the old days in the Gregg Hall and subsequent gigs in various hotels, including the Metropole and the Imperial, and fine sessions in the Long Valley or the Blue Haven in Kinsale, where jazzmen could drop in regularly for a *blow*. Paul O'Donnell, who is now both performer and teacher in the field, told me about their modern weekly sessions in Annie's Bar in Sunday's Well.

The Guinness Cork Jazz Festival, for more than 25 years the biggest event on the Irish music calendar, features almost a thousand musicians and attracts tens of thousands of visitors to Cork. Jazz columnist Pearse Harvey is credited with having suggested the establishment of such a festival to Ray Fitzgerald and Jim Mountjoy of the Metropole hotel in 1978. Jazz greats like Oscar Peterson, Ella Fitzgerald, Gerry Mulligan, George Shearing, Buddy Rich, Cleo Laine, Dave Brubeck, Dizzie Gillespie, Teddy Wilson and BB King have guested at the Cork festival in the intervening years.

The term 'jazz' covers many different kinds of music at the festival, including big band, rock, blues, Dixie, swing and, in some corners, even country music. The Guinness Jazz Trail, where various musicians play in dozens of city pubs, gives patrons a chance to go from one hostelry to another, listening to a variety of jazz that one could not possibly hear anywhere else. Apart from this, major concerts are held in the Everyman Palace Theatre, the Cork Opera House and the Guinness Festival Club at the Metropole hotel, featuring international musicians on six stages.

It is clear that music plays an important role in the cultural life of Cork. The richness and diversity is evident in the musical venues which are scattered around the city. Different influences both external and internal continue to shape the flow of music. From the Lobby Bar to the Opera House to the City Hall, music continues to enrich and enliven. It was Henry James who once wrote that 'art makes life, makes interest, makes importance'. Music in all its various forms has done just that and the city has been a better place for it.

Rory Gallagher (1948–1995)

Marcus Connaughton

Fig. 4.45 'Gallagher was arguably the finest white blues guitar player in the world. Eric Clapton may have had more finesse, but Rory had soul and feeling dripping from his fingers. I remember watching him from the side of a stage in Cork in the mid-1980s, one man, his fender guitar, a Vox AC30 amplier and a breathtaking performance' (Tom Dunne, *Today FM*).

Rory Gallagher, born in Ballyshannon in 1948, was raised in Cork. He considered himself a Corkman and regularly remarked that he was 'home to sharpen up the accent, bhoy'. A cursory listen to 'Home Town' will explain all, with its mention of Ford's and Dunlop's. He was this country's first major rock star and emerged from an Ireland that produced many fine showbands and beat groups in the late 1950s and early 1960s. The Ireland that young Rory grew up in was a country where there was no exposure to popular music except through listening to AFN, Radio Caroline, the BBC and Radio Luxembourg. He got his first guitar at the age of nine and had a determination and an investigative spirit that defies belief, given the limited availability of the music that he so passionately followed and played at that time.

His interest was stirred by the skiffle of Lonnie Donegan and through that he discovered the work of Huddie Leadbetter ('Leadbelly') and Woody Guthrie, the great American poet and troubadour. His early heroes also included Larry Williams, Chuck Berry, Eddie Cochran, Jimmy Reed and the buddha of the blues, 'Muddy Waters' – McKinley Morganfield. The young Cork teenager discovered photographs of some of his idols in *Melody Maker* and the magazine *Banjo, Mandolin and Guitar*. It was from the latter that he extracted the chords and tunings for the repertoire of Big Bill Broonzy, Josh White and Leadbelly. He was later to make his version of 'Out on the Western Plain' by Leadbelly an anthem for acoustic blues fans worldwide.

Rory served his apprenticeship alongside Paul Conway and Tom McCarthy with the Palladium Showband, who played at the rear of Cork City Hall for the Civil Defence. Then it was on to the Fontana, with Rory on lead guitar. This band had its roots in west Cork. At this time Rory stood out, with his shoulder-length hair and his dexterity on the guitar. He travelled to featured John Wilson on drums and Ritchie McCracken on bass. They secured a regular gig at Belfast's now legendary Maritime Club. Gallagher had discovered his sound and revelled in it.

The classic line-ups of the Rory Gallagher band featured as a constant Gerry McAvoy on bass guitar with Wilgar Campbell occupying the drum chair. Other members included Rod De'Ath, Ted McKenna, Brendan O'Neill, Mark Feltham on harmonica and Belfast's radiator of the eighty-eights, Lou Martin.

Rory Gallagher defined modern blues without realising it through his demeanour and his gentleness of spirit, which is reflected in his considerable recorded output. He toured Europe and America relentlessly during the 1970s. If one was to pick a classic year for this musician, then 1972 would be hard to beat: he was chosen by *Melody Maker* as their musician of the year; 'Live in Europe' achieved platinum sales; he recorded the London Sessions with Muddy Waters, his hero, travelling back from the De Montfort Hall in Leicester in his souped-up Ford Continental in which Muddy was to sit alongside Rory. He adorned the cover of *Melody Maker* in the 1970s with the caption 'Rory Rocks Belfast', when few rock musicians wanted to include the city on their touring schedules. Many of us practised air guitar with tennis racquets or hurleys in front of the wardrobe mirror and put those moves to use when Rory paid our respective hometowns a visit over the Christmas holiday period.

As a style icon, Rory cut a dash with his check shirts, converse sneakers and black jeans. In later years he was to sport that classic black leather jacket. If you visit Cronin's or Leader's shops in Cork today, he is still remembered with great fondness. As we say in Cork, we were haunted: we were a lucky generation who saw live music in our teens and could spot a decent rhythm section, never mind one of the world's finest guitarists.

Fig. 4.46 Public sculpture dedicated to the memory of Rory Gallagher, singer and international guitar legend. (Photo: John Crowley.)

Hamburg with Johnny Campbell and Oliver Tobin in 1965 before achieving major success with his group, Taste. The first edition of Taste featured Norman Damery and Eric Kitteringham. Rory then found digs in Belfast, where the second edition of Taste took shape. This

Music and Place: The Lobby, Charlie's and the Phoenix

Kelly Boyle

Charlie's Bar, 2 Union Quay, Cork, on a Monday night. Ensconced in the window behind the door, Hank Wedel and Ray Barron perform their weekly session for a full house. Guitar, mandolin and voice are miked up to fill the room and their sounds spill on to the street outside. Music flows in the form of American folk rock, tunes and ballads. Energy moves between listeners and performers. A perceptible warmth and familiarity bridges any implied distance between them. Participation is encouraged: a guest sings a Bob Dylan song accompanied by Hank and Ray's bed of sound; a local singer-songwriter fills the gap while they take their break, during which time they are enveloped by the crowd, occupied by chat. This event will happen again next week and the week after, as it did last week and the week before. In the meantime, Charlie's will host more evening and afternoon sessions and gigs, welcoming other music-makers and their listeners.

Fig. 4.47 Hank Wedel and Ray Barron performing in Charlie's. (Photo: Kelly Boyle.)

The Phoenix, 3 Union Quay, Cork, on a Tuesday night. On the other side of the wall to Hank and Ray's session, Jimmy Crowley and Tony Canniffe host the regular gathering of the Cork Folk Club. Songs are shared among this small group of singers and listeners, and the invitation to sing extended. Local places are called to mind in lyrics and melody; so, too, are distant places, brought closer by the singing. Stories are recounted and remembered. All are woven into the fabric of local sound and song through the course of the evening. The intimacy signifies a bond and a commitment to this place, this time, this act. Some people have travelled from out of town to be here, a few from as far as Dunmanway, and make the journey weekly. Others come from closer by, all converging on this place with a common interest. On other nights, in this bar and in the room upstairs, different groups of musicians fill the space anew with different sounds, styles and listeners. But for now this is the domain of singers, accompanied only by each other or an acoustic guitar.

The Lobby Bar, 1 Union Quay, Cork, on a Wednesday night. In the upstairs room, a traditional music group, Gráda, play up a storm to a packed audience. The sounds leak down through the ceiling into the quiet bar-room below. Vibrations from the singer-songwriter open-mike night in Charlie's next door carry through the walls. This is one of the few nights of the week when the Lobby's downstairs room borrows its music from elsewhere. From Thursday to Monday the sessions here, Ricky Lynch's and

Fig. 4.48 The three venues on Union Quay, the heart of Cork's live-music scene. (Photo: Kelly Boyle.)

Eoin Conway's, hold their own. Overhead the ceiling continues to pulse from the gigs in the room above. Tickets to Seamus Begley and Jim Murray's up-coming weekend performances sell steadily over the bar. From inside the dimly lit room the eye is drawn to the floodlit limestone buildings outside, to City Hall on the other side of Anglesea Street and one of the Allied Irish banks across the river on the South Mall. Black-and-white pictures on the wall inside show these quayside buildings – the Lobby and its neighbours – in former times. There are ships on the river outside their doors, but they give no indication of any music within.

The section of Union Quay in Cork that is home to three live-music venues, the Lobby Bar, Charlie's and the Phoenix, is a remarkable part of the city's musical landscape. Side-by-side along the south channel of the Lee, these pubs resound nightly with music and song. Viewed from the South Mall on the opposite side of the river, they cover but a short distance: the Lobby itself forms the corner that the quay makes with Anglesea Street; to its immediate right is Charlie's, which is flanked by the Phoenix on its other side.

The imposing structure of the City Hall, Cork's municipal centre, lies to the left of the Lobby, separated from it by Anglesea Street, while further upriver, on Union Quay, one of the city's prominent musical institutions, the Cork School of Music, has its home. Yet, the unassuming physical scale of these venues belies the wealth of musical activity that takes place within.

LOCAL MUSIC-MAKING

An enthusiasm and support for local music-making pervades Cork's character and, just as the city's waterways have defined its identity, history and geography, so too does the music that takes place along this quayside shape its social and musical landscape. The sessions, open-mike nights and concerts in venues dotted around the city, in which local musicians, singers and songwriters take part, constitute a musical contour unique to Cork. While the range of musical styles and genres offered at the Lobby, Charlie's and the Phoenix varies, the venues are strongly characterised by a common commitment to nurturing this local scene, supporting traditional and folk styles in particular. Thus, the concentration of musical activity on this stretch of riverbank makes each of the venues a focal point on the map for local performers and audiences alike.

The vibrancy of the activity evolves from collective input: from proprietors, musicians and supportive audiences. The energy brought by changing schedules, acts that pass through the pubs occasionally, synthesises with the consistency of regular sessions – Jimmy Crowley's in the Phoenix every Tuesday, Hank and Ray's on Monday nights in Charlie's, the mix of acoustic and traditional sessions by Ricky and Ruben, Eoin Conway or the Céilí Allstars from Thursday to Monday downstairs in the Lobby. The coming together of performers and listeners at the same time and place every week eventually creates a special kind of bond, one of familiarity and participation. Musicians become known, ingrained into the scene and into the musical worlds of their audience.

As modes of performance, sessions invite and facilitate participation. Open-mike nights, in particular, provide individuals with a forum for musical expression. In the routine sharing of space for musical experience, communities are formed and local voices sounded. And within this special setting, no two nights are the same. Performance is dynamic. In the context of repetition, even after decades of supporting the same traditions, anything can happen on the night.

Characterised by such a culture of familiarity and participation, the musical worlds in these live-music venues may not be as immediately audible as Cork's higher-profile musical terrain. The city's quieter, everyday scenes can often be eclipsed by bigger events – its festivals of jazz and choral music, symphony orchestra recitals and performances which take place in such landmark venues as the Opera House and City Hall. At close range, however, the local music-making that takes place here is vibrant and the venues are part of the fabric of Cork's musical identity.

Singer-songwriters

A prominent player in this local music world is the singer-songwriter and the scene has yielded many whose songs articulate a special awareness of place and a resonance with the locality. It is fitting, therefore, to find the places that support the scene captured in song. John Spillane expresses a connection to the venues on the quay. 'Magic Nights in the Lobby Bar' gives voice to the beauty and significance of memorable musical moments. It pays tribute to the people who take part and to the sense of community that is formed by them, celebrating the venue as a space in which people can gather for shared musical experience. In his 'Let the River Flow', the Lee is watched from the quay outside Charlie's, evoking in a different way the scene in this same part of town.

By inscribing local places, landmarks and people into song, the singer-songwriter's music takes on a local inflection, a characteristic cadence. These songs create their own musical map of Cork. In performance, the songs become spells, invoking the power of local knowledge, conjuring up the everyday. The experience of those places is then transformed through hearing them being sung. Physical maps become mental maps, inner soundscapes of the city. Thus, through music and song Cork's places, communities and local identities can be transcended, transposed, elided and superimposed on other landscapes – real and imagined, collective and individual – even as they are being reaffirmed. Such musical moments as Hank and Ray's, as Jimmy Crowley's, as John Spillane's, offer an invitation to the experience of elsewhere, a suggestion of connections formed with other places.

In similar but distinct ways, each pub gives the local music of the city shape and form. The music in turn transforms and shapes these social spaces, identifying them as hosts to special musical events. The local musical identities expressed on this quay vary daily and more so with the passage of time; waves of activity rise and fall with movements of people and changes in taste. Difficult as it is to convey the historical and musical depth of the place, its particular contours formed over years of activity, this snapshot of three venues on the bank of the Lee and of the echoes of the music that resounds there, suggests how one corner of Cork's dynamic musical world might look, feel and sound at one point in time. For now, the sounds reflect consistency, in the accommodation of live music and in the support for local voices. The sustained commitment from performers and listeners forms an impetus, which, like the river, flows through the city and shapes its musical landscape in quiet yet powerful currents.

Note. Since this piece was written, The Lobby bar has closed and faces an uncertain future.

John Spillane's Cork: A Geography of Song

John Spillane

I was born in the Bon Secours Hospital on the College Road and taken home to our house on Laburnum Lawn. Laburnum is a type of tree but I did not know that at the time. There were no laburnum trees on Laburnum Lawn but there was one up around the corner in Laburnum Park, in someone's front garden. We were told to stay well away from it, because it was a poisonous tree and you could die if you tasted its fruit. It was all semi-detached houses on our lawn. I am still wondering why the place was named after the laburnum tree and once I wrote a song about it:

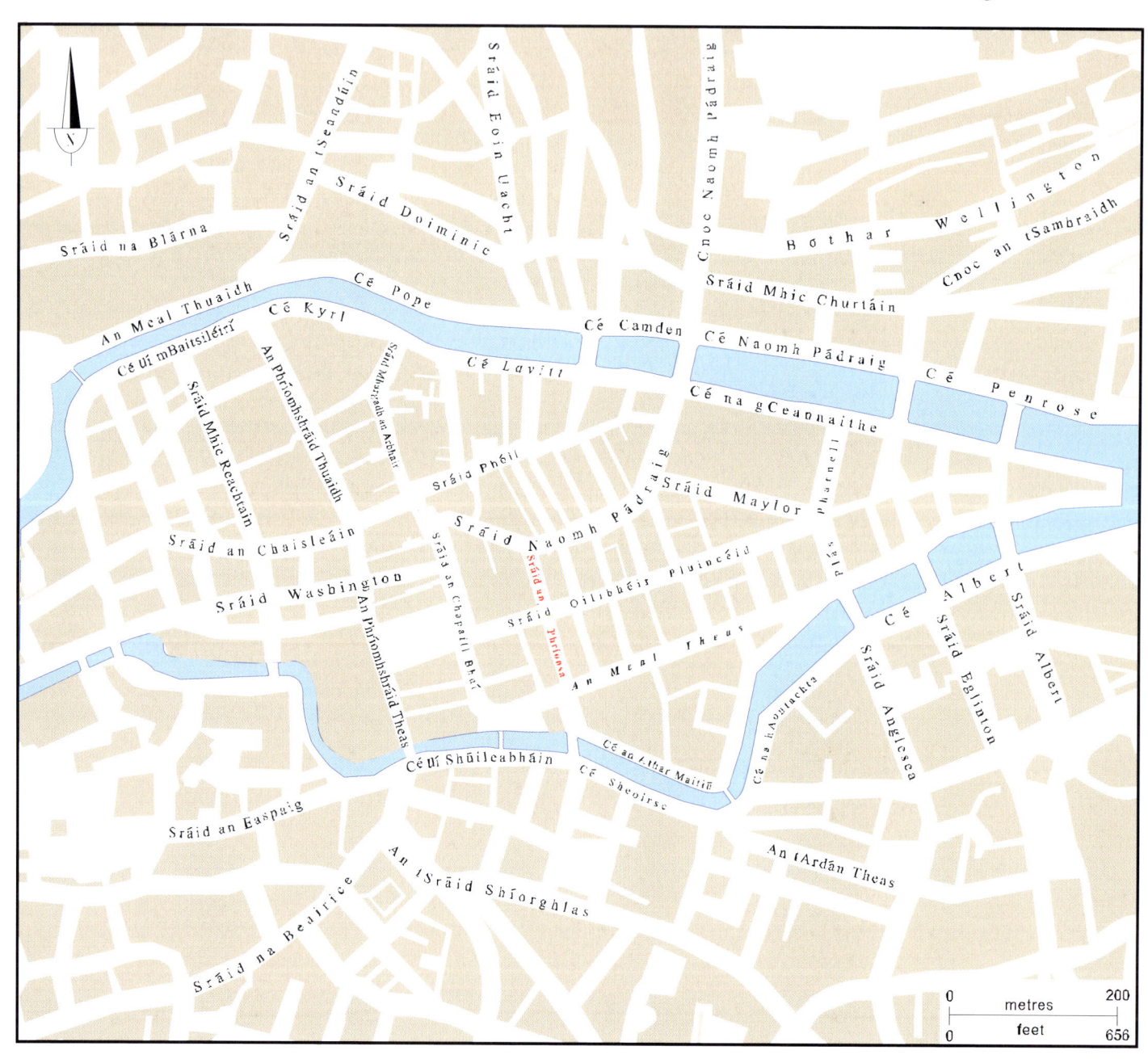

Fig. 4.49 Sráid an Phrionsa (Princes Street), which is located in the heart of Cork city. (Source: Gael-Taca.)

Laburnum Lawn

I live in woods without a tree
Rows of houses follow me
Houses dancing two by two
Like people at a wedding do

We feed the flowers and kill the weeds
In our woods without the trees
Houses dancing on and on
Willow Grove, Laburnum Lawn

There was a well that overflowed
And left us under water
I saw the woods fill up with sea
I heard you laughing after me

I loved a girl in Cedar Park
She disappeared into the Dark
Break the spell if you are able
Your dinner's on the table
And if God smiles on me and mine
I'll be a millionaire in time

There was a well that overflowed
And left us underwater
I saw the woods fill up with sea
I heard you laughing after me

Fig. 4.50 Princes Street.

The houses were built in the 1950s on the edge of Cork city, in a place called Wilton, on a slope on the southside of the Lee valley. At the end of our back garden 'The Country' began. At the bottom of the garden there was what we called the 'Ditch'. This was a country word and it was a big old ditch covered in trees, weeds, elm, whitethorn, elder, and an ancient tree with shiny leaves no one could identify, until one year when we were all grown up it produced one twisted knobbly fruit, just one: it was a pear.

When you crossed the ditch you entered a wonderland; it was like 'The King of Elfland's Daughter' by Lord Dunsany: you had left behind the real world and entered the surreal. First there was 'The Orchard', then 'The Meadow', and finally the strangest place of all, 'The Quarry'. The Quarry filled with a lake every winter and dried out every summer. You were no longer in Cork when you were in The Quarry.

Princes Street was the first street in Cork that was pedestrianised, and for this reason it was a good place to go busking. I was never very good at busking in Cork because I was too self-conscious about people I knew passing by, neighbours or schoolfriends. However, I did busk there for a while in the early 1980s and because I was learning the Irish language at the time – that is, learning how to speak it, not learning it like you do when you are at school – I noticed that the Irish for the street was Sráid an Phrionsa. This just means the Street of the Prince, but because you came at it through another language it was the first time you wondered about, or even noticed the 'Prince' in the street's name. This got me thinking about other Cork placenames, and one day I was up on Strawberry Hill when I noticed that the Irish version was Cnoc na nDrise – the Hill of the Briars. How well they translated the briars, or blackberries, to strawberries! This got me going, and then I wrote this song:

Princes Street

I spent Monday on Strawberry Hill
Till I fell and I landed on your windowsill
I hung there by a golden-fine thread
I had woven from a hair of your head

I spent Tuesday just walking through town
Till I saw a gold angel come tumbling down
And waltzing with seagulls up in an elm tree
Where the wind runs her fingers above the dark Lee

Chorus:
And O will you meet me on Saturday night
We'll dance in the shadows between the streetlights
Between these two rivers I know where we'll meet
On Princes Street

Fig. 4.51 The golden angel that looks out over the city from its vantage point at St Fin Barre's Cathedral. (Photo: John Crowley.)

Fig. 4.52 The golden fish on top of Shandon steeple. (Photo: John Crowley.)

I spent Wednesday doing nothing at all
Till late in the evening the wind came to call
And stood at my window and danced a handstand
The sun on her shoulder and birds in her hands

The next morning I woke from a dream
Of where the fish lie on their beds of deep green
I watched Thursday morning put on its new coat
Of cloud at the elbow, blue sky at the throat

Chorus

I spent Friday just counting the time
Till up in a tower I heard some bells chime
I saw a great goldfish take wing like a swan
And told me that Saturday wouldn't be long

Chorus Twice and Home

The gold angel in the second verse is the golden statue of the Angel of the Resurrection on the roof of St Fin Barre's Cathedral. The story as I have heard it is that the angel fell twice when it was being put up there. It was then fixed so solidly to the roof that it was said that the next time it would fall would be on the Last Day. The goldfish in verse five is the golden fish on the top of Shandon steeple, *an bradán feasa* (the salmon of knowledge). It is said to have a bullet hole in it from the time of 'The Troubles'. The elm trees on the Mardyke were all killed by the Dutch elm disease, except for one small one at the end. Lime trees grow there now.

When I was asked to write a song for Cork European Capital of Culture 2005, I climbed up above the town to Farranree to think about it and I wrote this song:

Farranree

Someday when I'm free I'm going up to Farranree
Up to the King's Country
Someday when I'm free
I'm gonna look down on this town
City of Angels, City of Rivers, City of Bells
City of Women, City of Boys, City of Sorrows, City of Joys
City of Sunsets in a Valley of Gold
City of Secrets that never will be told
That never will be told

Ah running wild and free through the valley of the Lee
The river sang for me from Guagán Barra to the Sea
But still I could not see, Blinded by Angels
Blinded by visions, Blinded by Love
In a City of Sorrows, City of Joys
City of Women, City of Boys
City of Girls, City of Men

City of Heartbreaks that will never come again
That will never come again

Someday when I'm free I'm going up to Farranree
Up to the King's Country
To see what I can see
I'm gonna wander down this town
City of Dreamers, City of Poets, City of Songs
Someday when I'm free I'm going up to Farranree
Someday when I'm free

The name 'Farranree' comes from *Fearann an Rí*, which means the Land of the King. It is high on the hill above Cork.

April can be a very long grey month in Cork. 'Will the summer ever come? Have we not done our time, like?' The ornamental cherry-blossom trees make a spectacular appearance around the third week of April with their bright pink regalia. Originally from Japan, there are many places in Cork where there are large numbers of them, including Passage West, where I now live, and, most spectacular of all, Pearse Road near The Lough.

The Dance of the Cherry Trees

Let me tell ya 'bout the cherry trees
Every April in our town
They put on the most outrageous clothes
And they sing and they dance around
Hardly anybody sings or dances
Hardly anybody dances or sings
In this town that I call my own
You have to hand it to the cherry trees
And they seem to be saying
To me anyway

You know we've travelled all around the sun
You know it's taken us one whole year
Well done everyone
WELL DONE

Cherry blossom in the air
Cherry blossom on the street
Cherry blossom in your hair
And a blossom at your feet

You know we've travelled all around the sun
You know it's taken us one whole year
Well done everyone
WELL DONE

On behalf of me and the cherry trees
WELL DONE

You know me, sometimes I think I'm getting old
Not as young as I used to be
So it means even more to me
To see the dance of the cherry trees
And they seem to be saying
Is it only to me?

You know we've travelled all around the sun
You know it's taken us one whole year
WELL DONE EVERYONE
WELL DONE
ON BEHALF OF ME AND THE CHERRY TREES
WELL DONE!!!!!!

Fig. 4.53 Cherry blossom on Pearse Road. (Photo: John Crowley.)

The Lobby Bar, 1 Union Quay, is the home of good music in Cork. I have had many magic nights there. When I set about writing 'Magic Nights in the Lobby Bar', I picked three moments that stood out in my memory as being especially magical, based around three musicians, Brendan Ring, a piper now living in Brittany, and two songwriters, Ricky Lynch and Ger Wolfe, both from Cork city. Everything in the song either happened in the Lobby or in one of Ricky and Ger's songs, which I quote here using a device I call 'the song within the song'. It was one of the most magical moments in my musical life when Christy Moore sang this song back to me last summer in De Barra's, Clonakilty.

Magic Nights in the Lobby Bar

They were magic nights in the Lobby Bar
With Brendan Ring playing 'Madame Bonaparte's'
And every note that the piper would play
Would send me away, send me away
Away through the window, away through the rain
Away 'cross the city, away in the air
To a field by a river where the trees are so green
The deepest of green that you've ever seen
Where once you have been you can go back again
You can go any time, go any time
'Cos it's only in your mind

They were magic nights in the Lobby Bar
With Ricky Lynch and his golden guitar
Singin' 'Autumn in Mayfield and the barley was ripe
The harvest moon hung low in the sky
We were children and our mothers were young
And fathers were tall and kind'
And every word that Ricky would play
Would send me away, send me away
Away through the window, away through the rain
Away 'cross the city, away in the air
To a field by a river where the trees are so green
The deepest of green that you've ever seen
Where once you have been you can go back again
You can go any time, go any time
'Cos it's only in your mind

They were magic nights in the Lobby Bar
When Ger Wolfe would sing like a lark
Singing 'I am the blood of Erin
Spilt in an empty cave
I am the flower of Ireland
Out on the drifting wave
I am the lark of Mayfield
Tumbling down the hill
I am the child of summer

Fig. 4.54 Singer-songwriter John Spillane. (Photo: *Irish Examiner*.)

I can remember you still'
And every word that Ger would say
Would send me away, send me away
Away through the window, away through the rain
On a carriage of music away in the air
To a field by a river where the trees are so green
The deepest of green that you've ever seen
Where once you have been you can go back again
You can go anytime, go anytime
'Cos it's only in your mind

'It was autumn in Mayfield and the barley was ripe
The harvest moon hung low in the sky
We were children and our mothers were young
And fathers were tall and kind'

(All songs copyright John Spillane, except 'Magic Nights in the Lobby Bar', copyright John Spillane, Ricky Lynch and Ger Wolfe.)

30. LITERATURE AND THE CITY

Mary Leland

There have been novels and short stories set in Cork and it has had its literary presences. Sean O'Faolain was once described by his daughter Julia (herself a writer of distinction) as one who 'mythologised' the city. The city did not care much for his depiction: the self-portrait has never been an applauded civic art. And yet, from Giraldus Cambrensis in 1183 to Patrick Galvin in the Douglas Street of the 1960s Cork has had its explorers, corporeal and spiritual. In fact Galvin as a poet unites these two elements with unique, and characteristic, insight. Can the coalition of the experienced city and the imagined city be mapped? Or is literature itself the only chart of their conjunction? And there is the question: to what degree, or with what accuracy, can an atlas reveal what might be called a civilisation but in this smaller context is better known as a culture?

The literary history of Cork is relatively recent. It was a place visited – it does little for the cultural status of St Patrick's Bridge to know that Charlotte Brontë drove across it during her wedding visit to Ireland – or a place in which to grow up before being sent to school in Dublin or in England, or before leaving for college and a career in London. Its visitors were often luminous and its home-grown practitioners, however far abroad they set their literary sights, were at the last loyal. Amongst both there was no compelling awareness that this colonial city was, of itself, distinguished.

For centuries of Cork's life there was always a world elsewhere and one offering greater prospects of recognition and reward. But a merchant class remained at home. Cork is no Middlemarch, but there was a time, particularly in the early nineteenth century, when its more prominent figures, once described as 'opulent citizens', might have reflected the Bulstrodes (and indeed even the Casubons) of that novel. Cork deserved its George Eliot, but it never got one.

For generations, little that was homegrown found a wider audience. This fact makes Frank O'Connor and Sean O'Faolain stand out like giant landmarks, their American and European successes opening possibilities to the writers who have come after them in their native city. The cluster of contemporary poets around the campus of University College Cork is a flexible grouping, its publications stretching far beyond a national audience. It includes Seán Ó Tuama, John Montague, Greg Delanty, Theo Dorgan, Thomas McCarthy, Eileán Ní Cuilleanáin, Roz Cowman, Paul Durcan, Nuala Ní Dhomhnaill, Robert Welch, Bernard O'Donoghue and Michael Davitt.

Writing in Irish and English, these men and women and the generation which by now is following them have a greater scope than the writers of the early years of the last century. These were years when there were national contestations over what it meant to be an Irish writer, or an Irish-born writer writing in English, or an Irish-born writer but not a nationalist one, or a writer born an Irish Catholic but writing for foreign publishers and journals. These complexities were not unique to Cork, although it was here that they found a specially bitter expression in the triumvirate of Sean O'Faolain, Frank O'Connor and their early mentor Daniel Corkery. In the first few decades of life in the newly independent Ireland was added the censorship of a puritan government that preferred to exile rather than embrace its artists.

LITERARY ASSOCIATIONS

Cork is a small city and the literary markings on the map clutter and jostle in a tangled swirl of intersecting lives. If Cork were to be mapped ward-by-ward, its most cluttered literary neighbourhood would be the triangle of streets and terraces formed south-east from the hill of Shandon, south to St Luke's Cross and east again to Montenotte. However, this process would reveal literary ley-lines rather than cohesive linkages. There are few signs of Edmund Spenser at Christ Church in the city centre, where he is reputed to have married Elizabeth Boyle in 1594, but the air of Shandon is still coloured by the shadow of his friend Colin Clout, in the military persona of Sir Walter Raleigh, a 28-year-old invincible in the 1580s. A few yards beyond the rebuilt outlines of Shandon Castle is St Anne's church. In the churchyard lies the tomb of the self-laicised priest Fr Prout, otherwise known as Francis Sylvester Mahony (1804–1866), son of a Cork woollen-milling family. Through Mahony we are in the literary company of Browning, Thackeray, Dickens, Coleridge, Southey and Carlyle, of Mrs Oliphant and Elizabeth Barrett Browning, of London's *Fraser's Magazine* and its editor William Maginn of Cork and its illustrator Daniel Maclise.

ATLAS • OF • CORK • CITY

Wellington Road
The sculptor Seamus Murphy (1907-75) lived here.

Harrington Square
Juvenile landscape of Frank O' Connor

Gardiner's Hill
Daniel Corkery, teacher, writer, musician and painter was born in a thatched cabin at the foot of the hill; inspired both O'Connor and O'Faolain in their early forays into literature.

St Anne's Church: burial place of Francis Sylvester Mahony (1804-1866); known to the literary world as Fr. Prout, wrote the lyrics of one of Cork's most famous songs 'The Bells of Shandon'.

St. Patrick's Church, Lower Glanmire Road. Fr. Prout's requiem mass was said in this church; also the setting for Frank O'Connor's short story 'First Confession'.

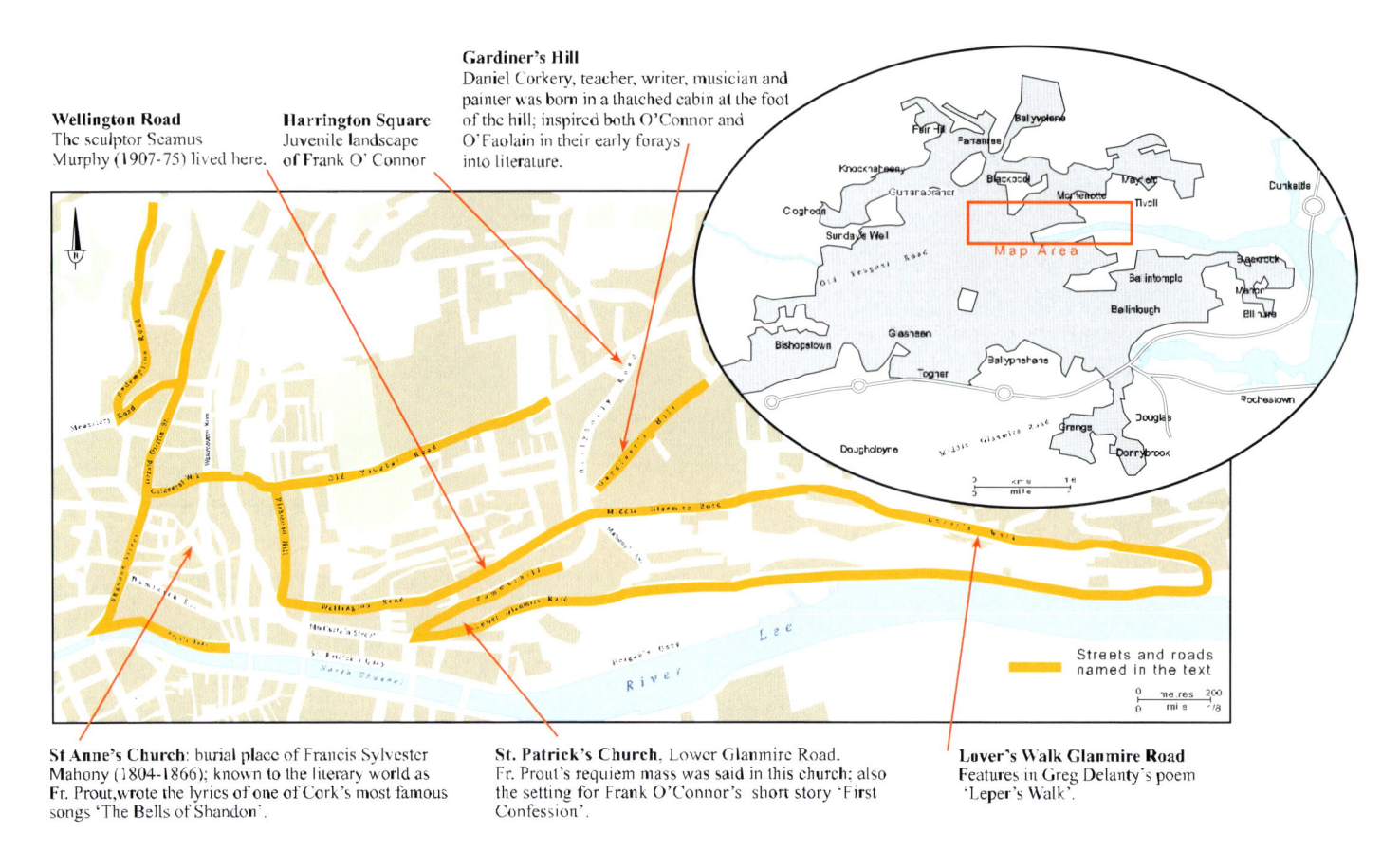

Lover's Walk Glanmire Road
Features in Greg Delanty's poem 'Leper's Walk'.

Fig. 4.55 Literary cluster on the northside of the city.

Irascible, ardent and impetuous, Mahony fled Cork when his pastoral seeds fell on stony clerical ground. In London he became a journalist, inventing a satirical alter ego as Fr Prout of Watergrasshill, the supposed offspring of Dean Swift and Stella. Already dead, his memoirs were later collected as *The reliques of Fr Prout* (1859), edited by the fictitious Oliver Yorke. He remained, although very privately, a priest, what his biographer called 'a half-pay soldier of the church – minus the half-pay'. When he died in Paris in 1866, his obituary in the *Pall Mall Gazette* was written by Robert Browning. Earlier, having known him well in Florence, Elizabeth Barrett Browning wrote of his kindness and warm-heartedness and of his being 'a most accomplished scholar . . . vibrating all over with learned associations and vivid combinations of fancy and experience – having seen all the ends of the earth and the men thereof'.[1] In Paris, he eventually succumbed to diabetes, but not before being recorded by Margaret Oliphant as having 'almost an ascetic face although his life had been not exactly of that description I fear'. When she visited his apartment amid all 'the obliterations of old age', he was encouraged to sing 'his great song, The Bells of Shandon, which he did, standing up against the mantelpiece with his pale head, like carved ivory'.[2]

Fig. 4.56 'Francis Sylvester O'Mahony (1804–1866)', alias Fr Prout. (Source: Private collection.)

If Francis Sylvester Mahony is remembered in Cork at all, it is as the writer of those lyrics, set to music by Morgan D'Arcy of Dublin. Although his clamorous career might suggest otherwise, he did live faithfully his hidden life and, like George Eliot's contributors to the growing good of the world, he rests in an unvisited tomb. How then to draw the mystical thread between that neglected slab and the long flight of steps leading from Summerhill down to St Patrick's church on the Lower Glanmire Road? In one sense the connection is obvious. For the Cork priest only became Fr Prout because his passionate proposal to build a chapel of ease for the North Cathedral was rejected by his bishop. Yet the chapel was built as St Patrick's. It was in this church that his requiem mass was said by a bishop whose appointment he had opposed vehemently in favour of his earlier colleague, Fr Theobald Mathew, the temperance evangelist.

How then can we connect these ironies of events into a link with the boy who would become Frank O'Connor? O'Connor spent most of his young life in the square between Summerhill and the military barracks and, as a writer, set one of his most famous stories in and around St Patrick's church. His short story 'First Confession' takes place in the yard, on the steps, by the railings and in the confessional and sacristy of this church, which grew out of a controversy inflaming Cork a hundred and more years before.

Through O'Connor we can connect with the teacher, playwright, musician and painter Daniel Corkery, who lived at Gardiner's Hill nearby. He taught O'Connor and became his inspiration and later his enemy. He encouraged Sean O'Faolain and became both his rival and critic. Corkery also wrote a novel of Cork, some memorable short stories and two of the most hotly debated volumes of cultural theory and literary criticism of the twentieth century in Ireland: *The Hidden Ireland* (1924) and *Synge and Anglo-Irish Literature* (1931).

This is the juvenile landscape of O'Connor and O'Faolain and their work reflects it. The geography of Cork has these three men meeting and talking and walking through this actual triangle of streets and hills – which were walked around also by Francis Sylvester Mahony. In addition, these streets have seen the visits of Anthony Burgess and John Heath Stubbs and Derek Mahon because of the poets who lived here most recently – the late Seán Dunne, John Montague (who moved from Grattan Hill to west Cork) and Thomas McCarthy at Montenotte.

There is easy access to Shandon from Summerhill and St Luke's Cross via Wellington Road. Here lived another friend of Daniel Corkery's, the late stone-carver and sculptor Seamus Murphy (1907–1975), whose book *Stone Mad* (1950) is ostensibly a memoir of the 'fraternity of masons' he had

Fig. 4.57 St Patrick's church, Lower Glanmire Road, which provided the setting for Frank O'Connor's short story 'First Confession'. (Photo: John Crowley.)

worked with as a youth. Despite what the filmmaker Louis Marcus says was 'the frightened conservatism' which descended on Ireland for decades of the recent past, Murphy retained his faith in a synthesis of craft and art, 'of expression and feeling, towards which this uncertain age is still only groping'.[3] Murphy was also a marvellous raconteur, with an immense appetite for life and a gift for hospitality that he shared with his wife Maighread. They drew writers and artists from Ireland and abroad to their home here, its high-windowed drawing room visited by Leon Uris and Angelica Huston, among many others.

The district is dominated by the now deconsecrated St Luke's church. The narrow lane behind it winds down to the Lower Glanmire Road and the docks; up this lane for centuries came the mariners who made Cork their port of call and who gave thanks at the earlier versions of this church for their safe landfall. Cork's maritime history includes a terror of foreign, seaborne contagions. Many fevers and skin diseases were hastily diagnosed as leprosy and a little beyond the church another road led to the

Fig. 4.58 View of Wellington Road and Summerhill approaching St Luke's. (Photo: Tomás Tyner.)

laneway designated for the quarantined lepers, or, in Irish, *lobhair*, eventually anglicised as lover and thus giving Cork its misleading Lovers' Walk. Greg Delanty remembers it in his poem 'Leper's Walk' as a romantic place, its villas spreading lilac and laburnum over their high stone walls, the generations of affluence making its climb to Montenotte one of the prettiest roads in the city. And yet, for Delanty, it is a city infected by 'the typical small town mycobacterium laprae / the paralysis that no soul dare attempt anything / different, diagnosed as rising above one's station'.[4]

Altitude alters the perspective. From the heights of Lovers' Walk the poet Thomas McCarthy can look down onto the quays and riverside, onto the docks that will soon be gentrified into docklands and into the distinctive vocabulary of plimsoll lines and chandleries and distant registrations. His local terrain expands to the Pacific, the South China Seas, the Indian Ocean, the Baltic, to the lands beyond this immediate shore. So, from this tangle of connections in this one small segment of a small city, the whole world is within reach.

There are other clusters of literary associations in Cork. They reach back as well as forward, internally diffuse as well as alert to external influences. Once a village, now a suburb, Glanmire can offer the pedagogic verses of 'Parliament na mBan', composed in 1697 as the advice to a gathering of the most beautiful women in Ireland and collected here in a textbook of behaviour for James Cotter written by his tutor Fr Dónall Ó Colmáin. Unfortunately, the spirited James ignored this advice and in the end was hanged on a charge of raping a Quaker girl. He is almost lost to history but the verses live on.[5] The legend of Sarah Curran, enshrined for her romance with the patriot Robert Emmet, executed in 1803, who was befriended while living here by Katherine Wilmot. With her sister Martha, Kate Wilmot spent some adventurous years in Russia before returning to the family home at Glanmire and, in 1824, dying in Paris.[6] Martha Wilmot married William Bradford, later chaplain to the British Embassy in Vienna. Before that appointment

Fig. 4.59 Bust of Michael Collins, by Seamus Murphy, in Fitzgerald's Park. (Photo: John Crowley.)

(which was to provide Martha with much of her later material), Bradford had been chaplain of a brigade with Wellington's army in the Peninsular Wars, and it was he who said the hurried prayers over the grave of Sir John Moore at Coruna in 1810. The Rev Charles Wolfe, author of the famous poem marking that burial, lies in a cemetery fifteen miles away in Cobh.

So from this web of interwoven lives, linked only through a place, little can be extracted except the marvel of coincidence – such a coincidence, for example, as is revealed in the presence in modern Glanmire of a small community dedicated to living through the Irish language and, among its members, the poet and musician Tomás Ó Canainn.[7]

WRITING THE CITY: REMEMBERED LANDSCAPES

A city changes, its scribes are constantly rewriting its story. In fiction, transformations are allowed, yet nothing is more moving, surely, than the accuracy of a remembered landscape, a recall that unites both writer and reader. Sean O'Faolain grew up near the northern channel of the Lee. Half Moon Street was named after an American vessel which tied up close to his door. If he followed the river, O'Faolain would still recognise the city, otherwise so changed, which he wrote about in a letter telling of a dream:

> Last night I was in Cork . . . I lay on the steps of the square in Patrick Street . . . and Pigott's front was just two immense doors from roof to pavement in black and gold lacquer, and Egan's the jeweller's had a hallway of great size surrounded by walls covered by life-size brass repousse goddesses and gods and warriors designed by Harry Clarke . . . Suddenly Jack Hendrick and Kitty O'Leary appeared. Jack wore a lieutenant's uniform, Irish army . . . and then lo, and how exquisitely beautiful it was, he flung himself down beside me, threw down the army cap, and Kitty curled up too . . . and my God how he laughed and how Kitty laughed and we were all young again and full of joy.[8]

Pigott's was the music store, packed with pianos and sheet music, and is gone now. Egan's is no longer aglow with

Fig. 4.60 Sean O'Faolain. (Photo: John V. Kelleher correspondence, Boole Library Archives, University College Cork.)

monstrances, vestments and gems; a fashion clothing company has taken over there. O'Faolain's dream of Cork ends in tears of recognition – 'I knew it was only a dream I was dreaming'. It was a young man's dream, it was a Cork both real and imagined, which O'Faolain would leave but in which Jack Hendrick and his wife Kitty O'Leary lived out their own history, a slice of which is caught forever in the memories, fictional and biographical, of O'Connor and O'Faolain. Both writers shook the dust of the streets of Cork from their feet, but the streets were innocent. However they might affect the story, however they might have been transformed by literature, they had done no wrong. They were simply there.

Frank O'Connor: The Writer and the City

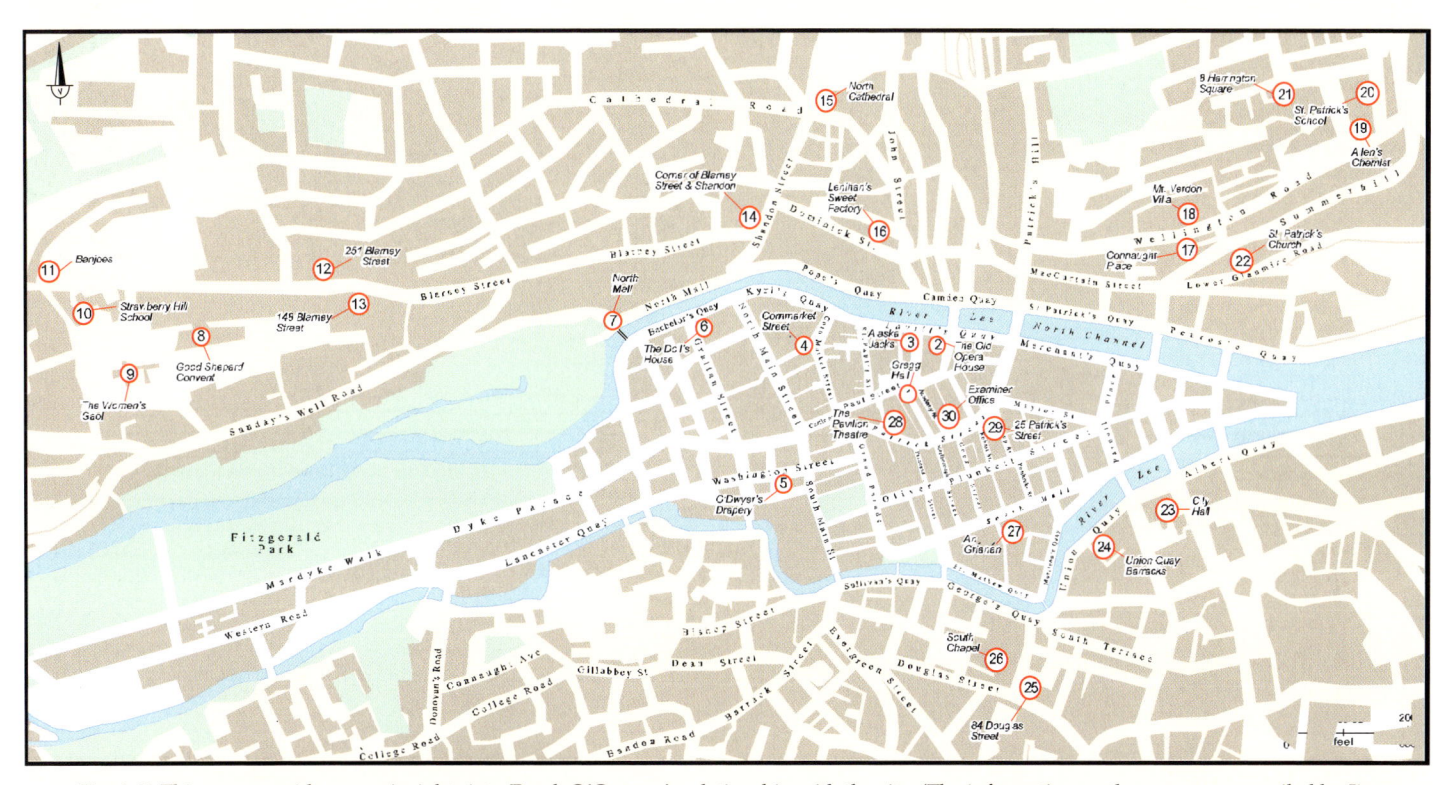

Fig. 4.61 This map provides some insights into Frank O'Connor's relationship with the city. (The information on the map was compiled by Jim McKeon and Mark McClelland, courtesy of the *Evening Echo*.)

1. **Gregg Hall, Academy Street:** Now Meadows and Byrne, this was the venue where Frank O'Connor's Drama League performed. Their first play was *The round table* by Lennox Robinson. It played for two nights in February 1928.

2. **The Old Opera House:** Terence MacSwiney, who became an idol of O'Connor's, wrote a play that had a run of one week here. It is now the site of the current Opera House.

3. **Alaska Jack's:** On the corner of Lavitt's Quay and Half Moon Street, above a pub called Alaska Jack's, O'Connor's best friend, Sean O'Faolain, was born in 1900. O'Faolain was offered the freedom of the city but refused it.

4. **Cornmarket Street:** O'Connor's mother frequently went shopping here, always taking young Frank with her.

5. **O'Dwyer's Drapery:** O'Connor had his first job in O'Dwyer's as a general assistant in 1917. He lasted two weeks. A large building opposite the Court House, it is now occupied by a number of solicitors' firms.

6. **The Doll's House:** On the corner of Grattan Street and Bachelor's Quay, this was a tenement that looked like a doll's house. Knocked down in 1966, it was the setting for O'Connor's novel, *The saint and Mary Kate*.

7. **North Mall:** The setting for the short story 'The Mad Lomasneys'

8. **The Good Shepherd Convent:** This had been an orphanage. O'Connor's mother lived here from the age of seven (in 1872) until she was fourteen.

9. **The Women's Gaol:** Adjoining the convent, this was where O'Connor was kept for the first month of his eleven-month internment after being captured during the Civil War. Although he never actually fought, he did work extensively for the republican cause. In later years he became disillusioned with the futility of Irishmen killing Irishmen. His first book, *Guests of the nation*, published in 1931, was a collection of anti-war stories. In the late 1920s the building was taken over as the headquarters of Radio Éireann and was often used as a rehearsal venue for O'Connor's Cork Drama League.

10. **Strawberry Hill School:** Cork's first national school, this was also O'Connor's first school. It was made from stone left over when the Women's Gaol was built.

11. **Banjoes:** Not its real name, 'Banjoes' was the local name given to this pub (now O'Kennedy's) where O'Connor set his short story 'The drunkard'.

12. **251 Blarney Street:** O'Connor lived here between 1903 and 1910. Although the house is no longer in existence, there is a plaque on the ground outside number 248 commemorating the writer.

13. **148 Blarney Street:** Across the road from number 251 is where O'Connor's mother was born in 1865.

14. **Corner of Blarney Street and Shandon Street:** Now a chemist, this was the shop which featured in the short story, 'Old fellows'.

15. **North Cathedral:** The funerals of Terence MacSwiney and Tomás MacCurtain were held in the North Cathedral in 1920. MacSwiney's death in particular had a great effect on the impressionable young O'Connor.

16. **Lenihan's Sweet Factory:** It was above this that Father O'Flynn, better known as Flynnie, set up the Loft in 1924, where the Cork Shakespearean Company performed. O'Connor and Flynnie did not enjoy a good relationship and at one time, over a period of one week, traded four letters of insults in the *Cork Examiner.*

17. **22 Connaught Place:** On 1 February 1923, Free State soldiers captured O'Connor here. After spending a month in the former Women's Gaol, he was transferred to Gormanstown internment camp. He was freed in Christmas week.

18. **Mount Verdon Villa:** Opposite 22 Connaught Place, this was where Sean and Geraldine Neeson lived. Both appeared in all O'Connor's plays. Sean became the head of Radio Éireann, while Geraldine was a journalist with the *Cork Examiner* and a bridesmaid at Terence MacSwiney's wedding.

19. **Allen's Chemist:** Now Shandon video shop, O'Connor worked here as a messenger boy in 1917 but only lasted a week because he could not ride a bicycle. During that year he had numerous jobs, none of which lasted.

20. **St Patrick's School:** O'Connor went to school here and hated it, but he was influenced by one of his teachers, Daniel Corkery, a well-known writer and nationalist.

21. **8 Harrington Square:** O'Connor lived here between 1910 and 1924 and a plaque on the wall confirms this. The surrounding area and the colourful characters that inhabited it had a huge influence on his later writing.

22. **St Patrick's Church:** This is the church where O'Connor made his first confession. The short story 'First confession' came out of this experience.

23. **City Hall:** This was the last building to be gutted in the burning of Cork, which took place on the 11 December 1920. The adjoining building was the Carnegie Library, where O'Connor spent much of his time between 1910 and 1920. He reputedly read every book in the children's section. It was reduced to a shell and it is believed a tearful O'Connor visited the scene a day after the burning.

24. **Union Quay Barracks:** This is where the British Army took incendiary devices and petrol intended for the attack on City Hall.

25. **84 Douglas Street:** O'Connor was born here as Michael John O'Donovan in 1903 to Minnie and Mick O'Donovan. His midwife was Ellen O'Connell and, as she could not read or write, his birth certificate was signed with a cross. The 'O'Connor' came when Frank adopted his mother's maiden name. 'Frank' came from his confirmation name, Francis Xavier. The writer changed his name to Frank O'Connor on 14 March 1925. The building is now home to the Munster Literature Centre.

26. **South Chapel:** Father Mark Leonard christened Frank here on 20 September 1903. His parents also married here on 8 October 1901. It is Cork's oldest Catholic church.

27. **An Grianán:** The Cork Gaelic League regularly met here in the years before 1916 to speak Irish. A member of the League, this is the place where Frank first met Terence MacSwiney and Tomás MacCurtain, who were to have a big influence on his life. The building is long gone. Its location was on the corner of Finton Street East and Father Mathew Street nearest the South Mall.

28. **25 Patrick Street:** Now Golden Discs, the Cork County Library opened here in 1925 and, at the age of 22, Frank became Cork's first county librarian. His wages were £5 a week, which was a considerable amount at the time. It was while working here that he changed his name to Frank O'Connor. Because his writing at times proved controversial, he did not want to be identified as the author. Changing his name was a means of protecting his job, as one of his colleagues had previously been fired for writing a contentious article.

Fig. 4.62 Frank O'Connor with his first wife Evelyn. (Photo: Munster Literature Centre.)

Frank O'Connor, pseudonym of Michael O'Donovan, was a celebrated short-story writer. He was born in Douglas Street but spent most of his childhood in Harrington Square on Cork's northside – a childhood vividly evoked in his autobiography, *An only childhood* (1961). While O'Connor may have fallen in and out of love with the city at different times during his life, he always remained loyal. As he once wrote: 'Nothing could cure me of the notion that Cork needed me and that I needed Cork. Nothing but death can I fear ever cure me of it.'

Patrick Galvin's City

Patrick Cotter

In the South Side of the city
The City of two rivers
I was born
In the house with the cross on the wall
And on that day
In the fine church of the Holy Trinity
The women wore black shawls
And sat on wine-baskets under the gallery
That day my Father played feck on Albert Quay[1]

'South Side', Patrick Galvin

Not all the towns and cities of the world have their streets portrayed, lovingly or otherwise, in poem or story. Joyce's eulogy to Dublin in *Ulysses* must be the supreme expression of a writer's attachment to a city, but there are other examples, such as Biely's *Petersberg*, *Berlin Alexanderplatz* by Doeblin, *Winesburg's Ohio* by Sherwood Anderson, not to mention Joyce's own *Dubliners*. *Dinnseanchas*, the Gaelic tradition of celebrating a place by naming it in song and poem, has been successfully transferred to the Hiberno-English tradition. Cork has had many gifted literary

Fig. 4.63 Patrick Galvin, writer and poet, on Sullivan's Quay in the South Parish, where he spent his childhood days. (Photo: *Irish Examiner*.)

ATLAS • OF • CORK • CITY

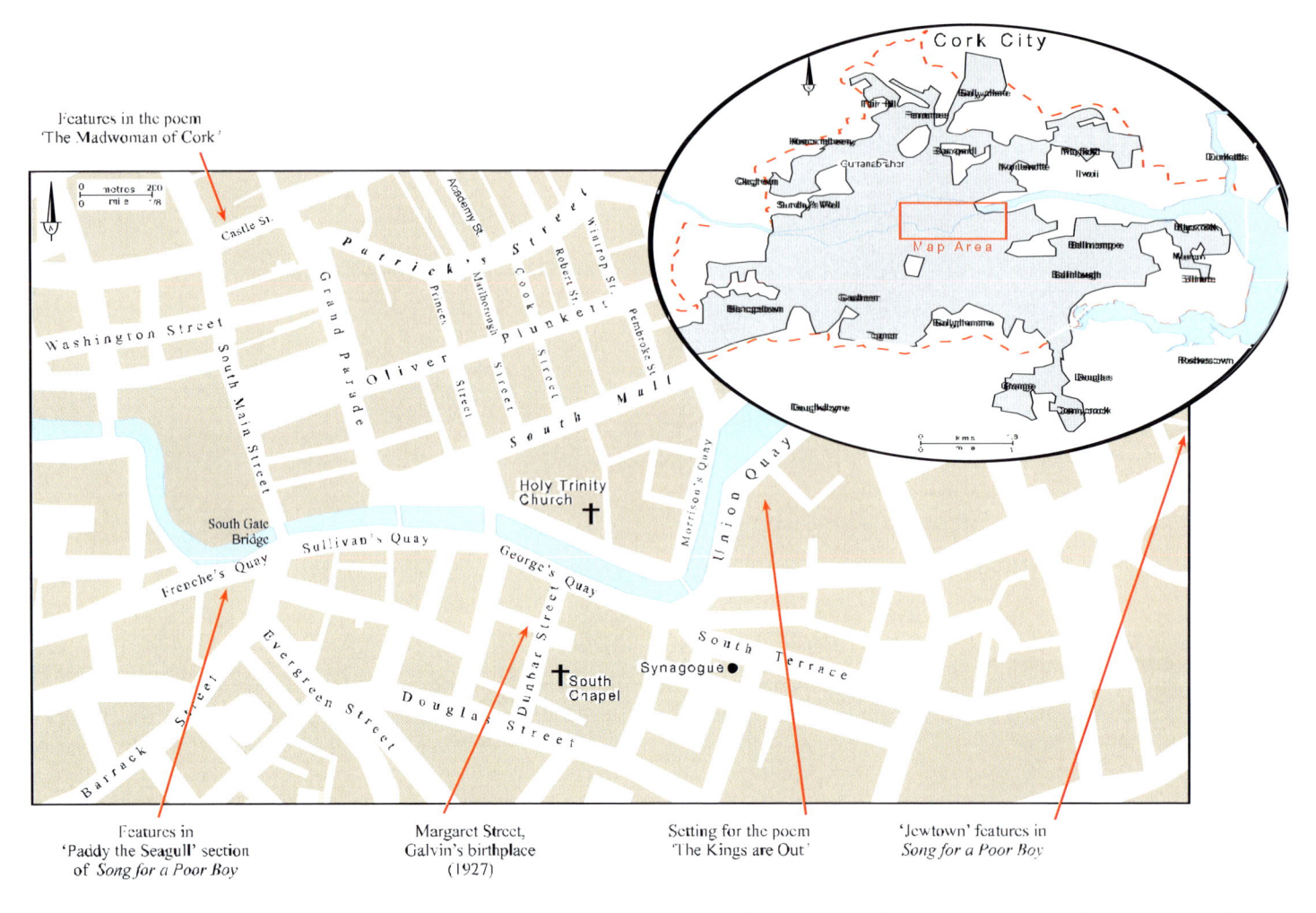

Fig. 4.64 Very often we find ourselves following in the footsteps of the writer, drawn to his or her world by the known and familiar. In the case of Patrick Galvin and the South Parish, the footprints are everywhere: along Douglas Street and Dunbar Street, crossing over by the neo-Gothic Holy Trinity church or close to the parapet of the South Gate Bridge. The specific naming of place allows the reader the opportunity to connect with and share a common ground with the writer. Galvin's work is inhabited with placenames that understandably link his writing to his place of birth. At other times it is the particular tone a writer adopts which permits the reader a foothold in the world which he or she evokes. In many of his Cork poems, Galvin allows the topography of the South Parish and the wider city to emerge as it relates to his own individual situation. The lanes, streets and river, in the end, are very much part of Galvin's own story. (John Crowley.)

celebrants, among whom Sean O'Faolain and Frank O'Connor are perhaps the best known.

Growing up in the 1970s studying Sean O'Faolain and Frank O'Connor on the Intermediate Certificate short story course, it seemed to me the most natural thing in the world that Cork would be a place worthy of great literature. Only upon further maturity and wider travel did the singular absurdity of that fact dawn on me. The world is populated by thousands of towns equal to Cork in size and many that are much bigger, some of which have grander, prettier architecture, others which found themselves located at historical crossroads way more significant than those Cork has found itself at, many of them without a poet or great writer to their name, or at least one who would choose to sing about his or her hometown.

GALVIN'S BACKGROUND

In the context of all the songless cities in the world, Patrick Galvin's being is a miracle. Born into a poor family with none of the educative resources of John Whelan's family, who could afford to send him to the Presentation Brothers and UCC (to emerge as Sean O'Faolain), he became a mitcher and a caffler and petrified inmate of Ireland's own peculiar form of Gulag: the religious-dominated borstal. Galvin himself claims that he owes his literary salvation to an eccentric old Jewish friend, Mannie Goldman (who used books for furniture), and a dissident, secular Spanish Civil War veteran and teacher who was his saviour in that brutal borstal, introducing him to the wonders of poetry.[2] In crediting those men with his literary salvation, Galvin underplays the resilience and resourcefulness of his own genius. Galvin often loved to say that a poet is one who tells

Fig. 4.65 Aerial view of the South Parish. (Photo: Tomás Tyner.)

lies, only with style. Those men make the origin of Galvin's genius plausible on the page and, as every writer knows, plausibility is paramount.

Unforgiving streets

Galvin's Cork is surreal and absurd, populated by loving, lovely people eking out an existence against a backdrop of cruel and unforgiving streets. If the streets appear loved by Galvin, it is only because they are populated by the people for whom he has love and compassion and the love has rubbed off. People like 'The Madwoman of Cork', who is devoid of any sense of being loved herself, her loveless state reducing her world to one where goblins appear at her feet in Castle Street and headless horses convey the dead to their graveyards. Children pelt her with stones and dead priests appear to her in Dunbar Street. She has seen terrible things, such as a woman buried in ice and a child with one eye, and, just as it is not clear to her, it is not clear to us either if those sightings are of the same order as seeing 'death in the branches of a tree, birth in the feathers of a bird'. Another character of this kind is Paddy Tom Kilroy, in Galvin's memoir *Song for a poor boy*. Paddy is convinced he is a seagull, and in Galvin's writing he becomes part of a tragicomedy played out between the Court House in Washington Street and the interior labyrinth of the South Parish. Paddy the Seagull is a source of cheap, harmless amusement for many, harmless until he harms himself by going for a walk on the river, only to be found later floating dead by Blackrock Castle.

In poem after poem, Galvin's Cork is not a happy place. 'The kings are out' is a cry of warning, where the Kings roam The Mall and Union Quay and every street along the Lee dispensing murder, rape and sudden death. In that poem, Cork is a city of green and bitter hate lurking under a darkening moon, shot through with rivers of frost. Lips are murdered, tongues are buried and eyes are gouged. In 'Sullivan's Quay', people walk with lowered eyes, crying out for bread and a saviour for their souls as their blood flows down the tenement walls. In 'South Side', the narrator of the poem tells us that 'no one heeded the music in my voice'; he talks of his mind and sense leaving him and having to wear shoes made of frost and an old coat made of fire. His first love came from Evergreen and died outside the Union (workhouse) doors. Through all these litanies of woe, never is heard the whingeing cry of the victim, only the terrible defiance of the survivor.

A city does not have to be a happy place to be praised in literature. It simply needs to be acknowledged as a place where significant lives are lived. While there is much defeat in the Cork poems of Patrick Galvin, there is also some triumph and courage. The triumph of his father, who has come through it all to rest at a point where he can stop by the parapet of the South Gate Bridge and talk to swans, to speak without fear of his days in India with the Munster Fusiliers. In the same poem Galvin recalls his mother remembering Pearse and Connolly and celebrates how he was born of these two people. Against the backdrop of other poems, we realise the scope of that complex personal triumph.

Fig. 4.66 George's Quay and Frenche's Quay are but a stone's throw from where Patrick Galvin grew up. Beatrice, a fishmonger, features in Galvin's childhood memoir, *Song for a poor boy*. Fishermen have always been synonymous with the quaysides on the southside of the city. A strong fishing tradition existed in Frenche's Quay from the mid-nineteenth to the middle decades of the twentieth century. Families such as the Fahys, Flynns and O'Callaghans strove to make a living from the river. This tradition had its roots in west Cork. The first commercial fishery was established in Frenche's Quay in the 1850s. The fishermen from here were known as the men from the 'Three Steeples', as Frenche's Quay lay in the shadow of St Fin Barre's Cathedral. A keen rivalry existed between themselves and the men from the 'fishing village' of Blackrock. The death of one of the last inshore fishermen, Paddy O'Flynn, took place in 2004. (Photo: *Irish Examiner*.)

fig. 4.68 'When I was seven years of age/And bread was all my reason/I cried through every street in Cork/and Winter was my season', from 'South Side' / Patrick Galvin. Aerial view of Cork's medieval core so familiar to Galvin in his childhood years (Photo: Tomás Tyner).

An aerial view of the Lee, with the Tivoli container port on the north bank and the green suburb of Blackrock on the south. (Source: Philip O'Kane, Department of Civil and Environmental Engineering, UCC.)

5
Contemporary Transformations

CONTEMPORARY TRANSFORMATIONS

INTRODUCTION

Denis Linehan

In 1984, the last of the workers left the Dunlop factory in Cork after the machinery there was finally dismantled, packed in cases and exported to China. Many recognised that moment as a watershed for the city. The closure of Dunlop's, Ford's, the Verholme Dockyards and numerous other industries in the region was a negative outcome of globalisation. Cork was shaken by global forces that undermined its local economy and increased unemployment and emigration. Twenty years later, Ireland is ranked amongst the fastest-growing economies in the world and Cork has become a prosperous urban area with a diverse economy – ranging from ICT and pharmaceuticals to agriculture and tourism. The range of transformations in economy, society and environment have many faces: some require historical consideration, some are commercial and economic, others are cultural and social – many are territorial and geographical. The chapters grouped here explore the nature of these changes, they benchmark some of the directions the city has taken from the recent past and consider the kind of city Cork will be in the future.

At a global level, social and economic change is reflected well in transitions in economy and society. During the early 1980s, there were shops on St Patrick's Street that were boarded up due to lack of custom. The economy in Cork faced a hard restructuring process following the decline of the textile and traditional manufacturing sector. Supported by funding from the European Union, Cork people in their thousands trained for new occupations and, in time, new global industries related to information technology, electronics, pharmaceuticals and internationally traded services were attracted to locate in the region. Cork now boasts the third highest concentration of pharmaceutical companies in the world. This new economic diversity is mirrored in the changing composition of the city's population. From a point twenty years ago when lack of employment and opportunity meant that emigration sapped personal and community life, Cork is now an increasingly multinational and cosmopolitan city, with a

Fig. 5.1 A night-time view of the North Gate Bridge and lower Shandon Street. (Photo: Ralf Kleemann.)

CONTEMPORARY • TRANSFORMATIONS

Fig. 5.2 New housing, such as these recently developed estates near Douglas, continues to expand the city outwards. (Photo: Tomás Tyner.)

growing proportion of the population originating from other European Member States and also from Africa. These new groups add to the rich tapestry of workplace and street-life and challenge the parochialism of the so-called 'Second City'. Likewise, with exposure to a broader canvas of opinion, values and aspirations and the increased tempo of Irish life, neighbourhood life and community development has changed. Where once the Catholic Church was at the centre of the life of the city's neighbourhoods, recent social transformation has displaced its role and shifted the process of parish formation. Cork has gone global. New opportunities and fresh challenges are written both into the fabric of the city and the mentalities of its inhabitants.

There is a sense of the increased Europeanness of Cork, and not only in terms of our embrace of café culture! The city's vibrant cultural life and an increasingly outward-looking sensibility gave it the confidence to become the European City of Culture for 2005. The impact of the EU is also illustrated in the city's urban infrastructure. The drainage system, revamped forms of environmental management and, perhaps most strategically of all, the development of roads, the port and the airport all

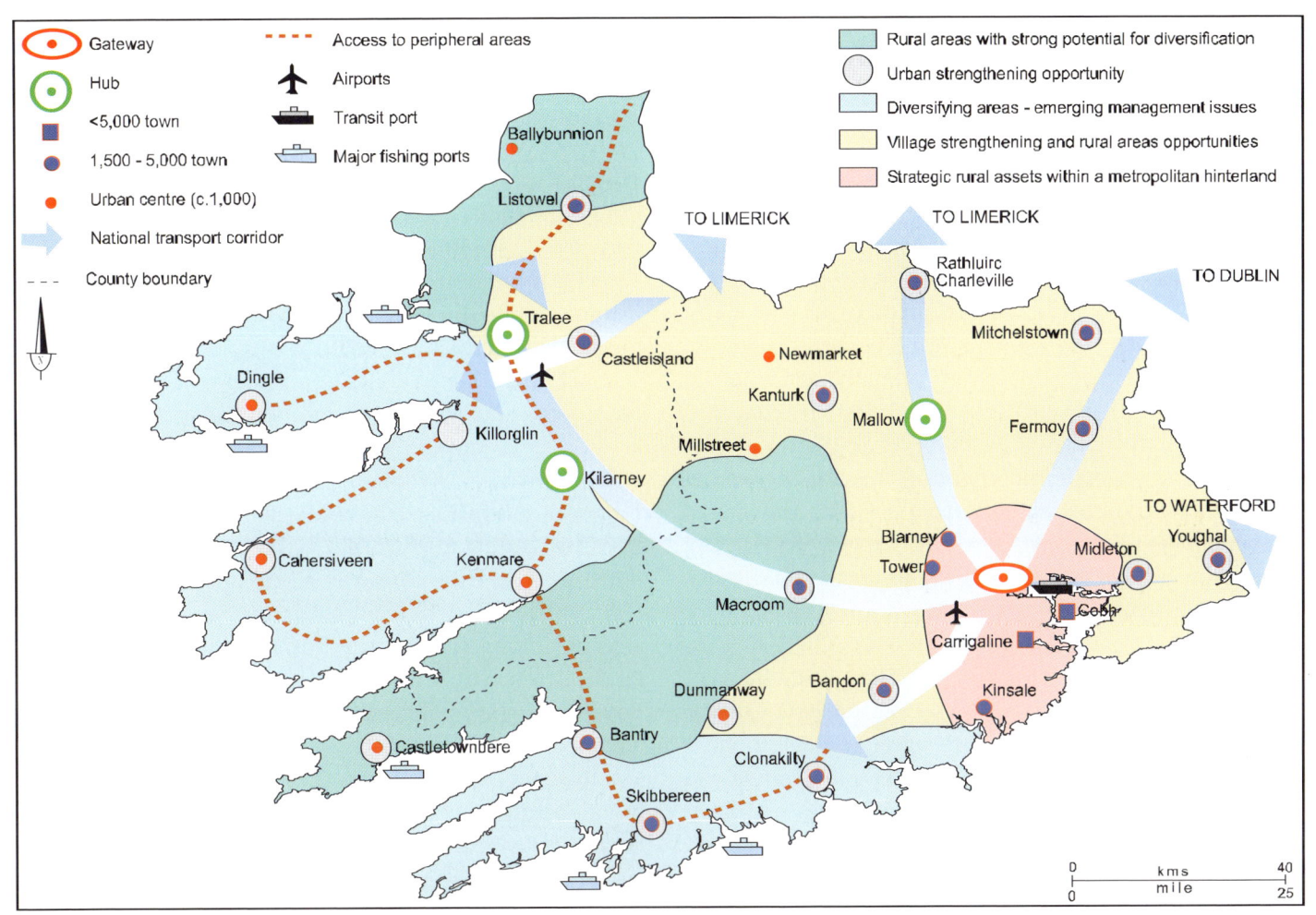

Fig. 5.3 In the National Development Plan, Cork is designated as a 'National Gateway city'. Cork is to be developed as 'a dynamic and progressive European City, attractive to investment in people and ready to act as an effective counter-point to Dublin'. Cork is positioned as the principal city in the south-west region. (Source: National Development Plan.)

Fig. 5.4 Seen here from the rooftop of Brown Thomas, the civic launch of Beth Gali's marvellous reinvention of 'Pana' marked the beginning of a new phase of development for St Patrick's Street. (Photo: Denis Minihane, *Irish Examiner*.)

demonstrate the way in which further European integration has benefited the city region.

Equally, looked at from both national and local perspectives, Cork has also responded to planning changes. At national level Cork has been designated a 'Gateway' city under the National Development Plan 2000–2006. 'Gateway' status guarantees that Cork can expect national support in upgrading its rail, air and telecommunication links. The Cork Area Strategic Plan (CASP) redefines the towns and areas in the immediate hinterland of the city as a single integrated zone known as 'Metropolitan Cork'. The idea of 'Metropolitan Cork' has not yet caught on in the imagination of the city, but the new designation illustrates well the growth of the city and the extension of its influence outwards. The population of this area grew in the 1990s, with an increase from 325,000 inhabitants to the current figure of 345,000 occurring between 1996 and 2002. Current projections suggest that the population of 'Metropolitan Cork' will be 425,000 by 2021. However, illustrating the shifting growth poles of the urban area, Cork city itself experienced a steady loss of population between 1986 and 2002. In part, these new patterns reflect people seeking less expensive housing in the city's fast-growing suburbs, satellite towns and rural hinterlands, but ageing populations, notably in the southside, also play a role in reshaping the population structure of the city.

The impact of national and urban planning, together with increased globalisation, is also evident in new developments in the city itself. If the value of public and private investments is bundled together, an estimated three billion euro has been invested in the fabric and infrastructure of the city since 2000. With flagship urban regeneration projects like the St Patrick's Street development completed in the city centre and novel riverside and dockland developments in place, Cork increasingly shows signs of its new affluence. However, as the city develops, the question of social inclusion continues to be a problem. The 2002 census reveals that poverty in the city has broadly reduced, but that the gap between rich and poor has widened. These issues are most acutely felt in housing and access to health and education services. More specifically, for members of the Travelling Community and for the disabled the city has some way to go in ensuring equality.

Cork, like other Irish cities, is changing rapidly. The map of Cork has many different layers and the interlocking scales at which its destiny is intertwined make the notion of Cork as Ireland's 'second city' increasingly insignificant. The wider European and global context is the playing field on which the city must attract investment to prosper. Cork's experience illustrates that cities require resilience, difference, creativity and a strong sense of social justice to survive. Cork needs its entrepreneurs and its leaders, but, in regenerating the urban fabric, care needs to be taken to defend the public realm, improve access to public and green space and create a city for all. Surveying social and spatial change is an important part of supporting that process and lies at the heart of knowing more about ourselves, our city and our place in the world beyond 'The Banks'.

31. INDUSTRY AND EMPLOYMENT

Barry Brunt

Cork is the most important industrial centre outside of Dublin in the Republic of Ireland. This is due to the many attractions of the city region for industry, including its large labour force, the market potential of the city and its relatively rich agricultural hinterland in south Munster. The country's second-largest city also possesses a good infrastructure to support industrial development, such as centres of third-level education and a well-developed transport network, including proximity to a growing international airport and Cork harbour. In addition, government policies designed to stimulate industrial and regional growth within Ireland have assisted in the emergence of Cork as a counter pole to the dominance of the Dublin region. The influences of these location factors and the types of industry that have developed within the Cork city region have changed significantly since the foundation of the Irish state in 1921. These changes occurred within four distinctive time periods: 1921–1961; 1960–1980; the 1980s; and 1990 to the present.

1926–1961: POLITICAL INDEPENDENCE, PROTECTIONISM AND INDUSTRIAL DEVELOPMENT

Prior to gaining political independence from Britain, Ireland's colonial economy focused on exporting agricultural goods and people to meet the demands of that country's urban-industrial system. The limited manufacturing activities in Ireland were located at the large port cities. These centres provided a market, while their port functions allowed for some industrial development linked to the import/export of goods and raw materials, notably food processing, drink and textiles.[1] In 1926, some 7,000 people in Cork city were involved in industrial activities.

In an effort to increase industrial production and employment, the government, under Eamon de Valera introduced a policy of protectionism in the 1930s. Through a system of high tariffs, the cost of imported goods was raised, thereby creating an opportunity for domestic producers to meet the demands of the Irish market. This approach proved to be successful and, by 1951, manufacturing employment in Cork city approached 12,000. Most of these jobs were in traditional industrial sectors, such as food, drink and tobacco, and textiles, clothing and footwear. These were mainly located near the city centre and in the Blackpool area.

Before the Second World War, two large industries were attracted to Cork and became strongly linked to the city's economic fortunes for the next half century. These were the Ford vehicle assembly plant (1917) and the Dunlop chemical plant (1935). Their success depended on the ease of importing component parts and raw materials. As a result, both were located adjacent to each other at the Marina along the city's inner quays. This created a significant new zone of industrial land use in Cork. Although most manufacturing was concentrated within Cork, several traditional industries were also located in small towns, such as Blarney and Midleton in the city's hinterland. In addition, significant new industries had emerged around Cork's outer harbour, including Irish Steel, on Haulbowline Island (1947), Whitegate Oil Refinery (1957) and Verholme Dockyards (1959), and these provided an early indication of the attractions of this area for large-scale, port-related industrial development.

Despite some new developments, Cork's industrial base was composed of relatively high-cost/low-productivity factories. These could not compete in the export trade and, once the domestic market was satisfied, opportunities for further growth were limited. This became apparent in the 1950s and resulted in a decrease, to 10,000, in manufacturing jobs in Cork city by 1961. The optimism of the early phase of protectionism had evaporated. A new approach was needed to stimulate a more growth-oriented industrial sector. This was to occur in the 1960s.

THE 1960S AND 1970S: A NEW APPROACH

By the start of the 1960s, Ireland's industrial development policy had rejected protectionism. It now focused on free trade and the attraction of foreign multinational companies to locate branch plants within the country. These competitive units would produce goods primarily for export and would help create both new jobs and wealth for Ireland. Generous financial incentives, low land and labour costs and the decision to apply for European Union membership (achieved in 1973), thereby giving access to a prosperous international market, were all vital factors in this new

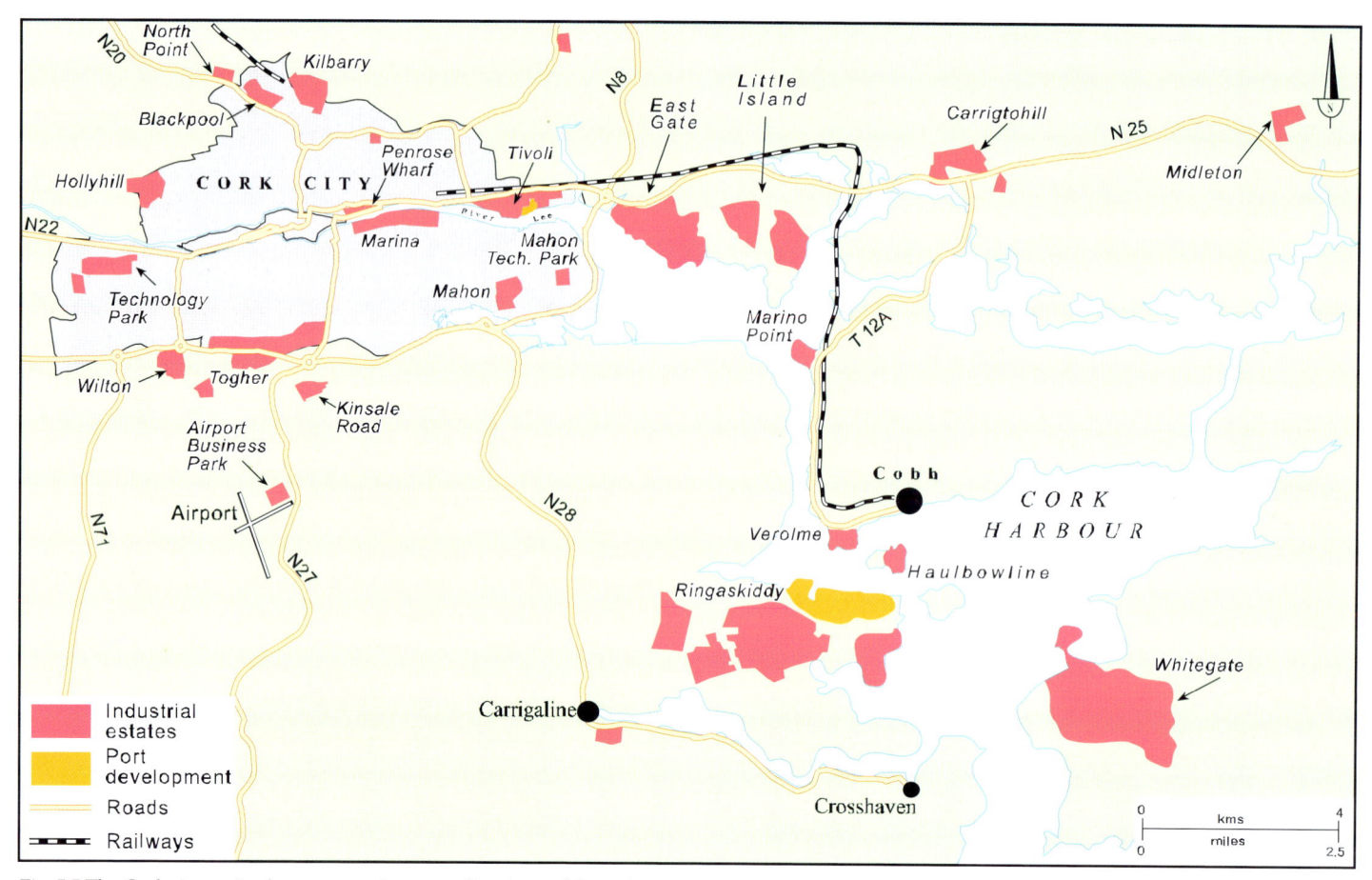

Fig. 5.5 The Cork city region has an extensive area of land zoned for industrial development. Initially restricted largely to the inner-city quays (Marina) and the Blackpool area, since the 1970s industrial estates have been established at a variety of locations throughout the region. This has been crucial for the dispersal of industrial development. Of particular importance are the 'necklace' of industrial estates located around the edge of the city linked to large-scale suburban growth. These city-focused developments have been complemented by extensive tracts of land zoned for industry in the outer harbour and located primarily around the deepwater port of Ringaskiddy. Finally, the large industrial estates on Little Island, together with those that straddle the new N25, have produced an important east–west axis of manufacturing activities.

process of industrialisation.[2] Cork benefited directly from this policy shift. Its industrial traditions, large labour pool, developed urban services and port facilities attracted a new wave of industrial investment into the city region. Such positive developments were further endorsed by an important report which identified Cork, with Limerick–Shannon, as one of two national growth centres to counteract the primacy of Dublin.[3]

During the 1960s, manufacturing employment in Cork city increased by one-third to over 13,000. Impressive gains were made in both the chemical and engineering sectors, while traditional industries also increased their workforce. The city's hinterland shared in these positive trends, as some new industrial developments/branch plants preferred to locate, at lower cost, to green-field sites in rural areas or small towns. Of particular note, however, was Pfizer's decision to locate a large chemical plant at Ringaskiddy in 1969. This development highlighted the beginning of a new phase in the industrial transformation of the Greater Cork Area, and its emergence as 'the chemical capital of Ireland'. The positive trends of the 1960s created a growing optimism within Cork regarding its longer-term prospects for industrial development. This was also encouraged by publication of the Cork Harbour Plan and the Cork Land Use Transportation Study (LUTS).[4] These provided an integrated approach to land use and infrastructural development which would improve the competitive position of the city region in both Ireland and the European Union.[5] Implementation of the LUTS proposals was projected to create an additional 12,000 industrial jobs by 1991.

An important element of the plan was to zone large areas of land in strategic locations for industrial development. This found expression both outside and within the built-up area of Cork city.[6] To accommodate the increasing demand for new industrial sites in rural areas adjacent to the city, large areas of land were zoned for industry at two key locations, Little Island and Ringaskiddy. Three industrial estates were opened at Little Island in the late 1970s to act as a new growth zone along the northern edge of Cork harbour. The physical restriction of the Passage Gorge for bulk shipping, however, prevented the development of large, port-related industries at this location. Proximity to the city's services and labour supplies, together with access to good road and rail links, were the main attractions of Little Island. Priority was given to the promotion of a diversified range of industries which were not dependent on port facilities. By 1980, 1,000 jobs had been created on Little Island, the majority in small and medium-sized engineering and pharmaceutical companies.

Larger-scale industries requiring extensive land area and access to deepwater facilities were zoned for Ringaskiddy. The need to complete construction of a new deepwater port, however, meant that industrial take-off in this zone had to be viewed in the medium term. In spite of this, the outer harbour had already emerged as an area of significant investment in major port-related industries linked to the production of steel, chemicals, ships and oil refining. Irish Steel, Verholme Dockyards and the new Irish Fertiliser Industries at Marina Point (1979) provided 2,300 jobs in 1980. These were vital for the employment prospects of Cobh and its adjacent communities.

Within Cork city, new industrial developments were more limited and manufacturing employment fell by 1,300 in the 1970s. In LUTS, however, a series of new industrial estates were established in expanding suburban areas such as Hollyhill, Togher and Mahon. By adopting a policy of 'taking work to the workers', it was hoped to reduce the journey to work from these large suburban housing estates to the many jobs that remained concentrated in and around the city centre.

The northside industrial estates were of particular significance, given their location near large areas of public housing where unemployment rates were high and rising. The decision of the Apple Corporation to locate a major computer-manufacturing plant at Hollyhill (1978), which provided 700 jobs, was seen as particularly beneficial. It

Fig. 5.6 The Apple plant in Knocknaheeny. (Photo: Tomás Tyner.) Following the successful industrial developments of the 1960s and 1970s, unemployment in Cork was reduced to low levels. Economic recessions in the 1980s, however, resulted in many job losses as factories closed and/or reduced their workforce. By the early 1990s, unemployment had increased four-fold and one in five of the city's labour force was unemployed, making Cork one of Ireland's unemployment 'black spots'. The rise of the Celtic Tiger initially stabilised unemployment levels, but, following 1995, high rates of new jobs creation and fewer job losses caused a significant fall in unemployment. However, unemployment remains well above levels in the 1970s.

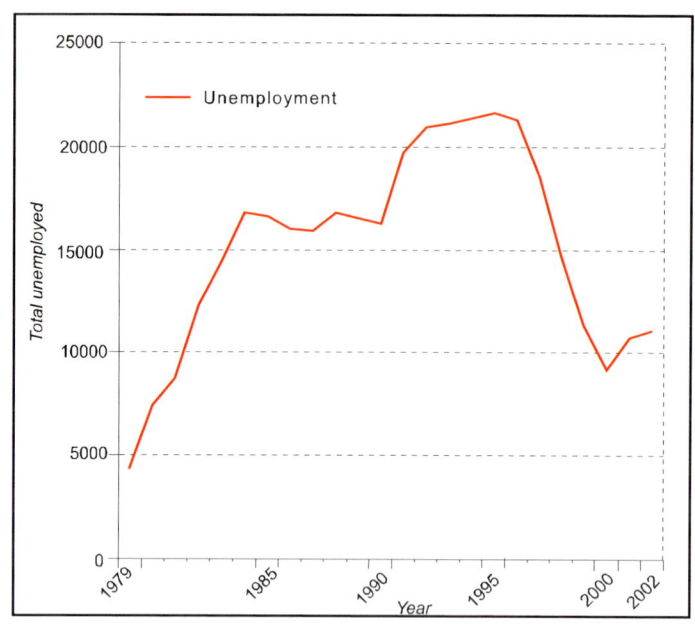

Fig. 5.7 Total employment within Cork city has shown significant changes since 1976. Despite decline in the 1980s, the strong retail and office functions of the city centre ensure that this zone continues to provide most employment. By 2020, it is estimated that 37 per cent of the city's total employment will be focused in the central area. General growth has also occurred throughout suburban Cork and development has been pronounced in the south-western suburbs, due to the attractions of Bishopstown Technology Park and proximity to third-level education institutions. Problems of congestion and scarcity of available sites for expansion will, however, result in a shift of large-scale development to the south-eastern suburbs. In the Mahon area, extensive new retail, office and manufacturing developments are progressing. In contrast, the northern suburbs of the city showed comparatively weak development and, although prospects are improving, they are considered to be less positive than for other zones of the city.

was hoped that this modern growth industry would encourage further investment in the less prosperous northside communities. On a wider level, Apple was the first of a growing number of electronics companies to locate within the city. This complemented the chemical sector, which showed a preference for green-field sites around Cork harbour.

In spite of the optimistic planning proposals and some new industrial investment, a number of problems confronted the regional economy by the late 1970s. Membership of the EU increased competition, especially for the city's labour-intensive traditional industries. The employment base was over-dependent on a small number of large industries, most of which were not competitive and were involved in declining sectors (clothing, steel and shipbuilding). Manufacturing employment declined in the city in the 1970s. Although these losses were offset by gains in Cork's rural hinterland as new factories sought lower-cost locations, the city region seemed to have lost its earlier growth momentum.

THE 1980s: ECONOMIC RECESSION

The 1980s was a decade of economic recession for Cork, with manufacturing employment falling by almost 20 per cent (3,500). The first half of the 1980s was particularly difficult, with closures (2,750) and contractions (2,670) removing 5,400 jobs. In contrast, new openings and expansions provided only 1,270 new jobs. Although conditions improved in the late 1980s, Cork was identified as one of Ireland's unemployment 'black spots', with over one in five of its workforce unemployed. The main problem for the city region was the collapse of its traditional manufacturing base. In the recession, these relatively high-cost/low-productivity industries failed to remain competitive and were forced to close or downsize. In 1983–1984, Ford, Dunlop and Verholme Dockyards all closed, with the loss of over 2,500 jobs. The city also lost over 1,000 jobs in its labour-intensive textile mills. These losses had a devastating impact on local communities which depended on these factories for secure, well-paid employment.

During the 1980s, electronics or, more generally, the information and communication technology (ICT) sector was the only industrial sector to show a growth in employment (see table below). This was linked to an active policy to attract this international growth sector into the city region, resulting in the establishment of the National Microelectronics Research Centre (NMRC), linked to UCC, and the opening of the city's first High Technology Business Park in the Bishopstown suburban area.

In addition to increasing employment opportunities, this new growth sector had three other important influences in Cork. Firstly, since most of the new investment was foreign controlled (especially from the USA), by 1990 one in two manufacturing jobs in Cork was in companies head-quartered outside of Ireland. Secondly, the large reserves of

TABLE: EMPLOYMENT IN ICT INDUSTRIES IN CORK CITY AND COUNTY 1980–2002

	1980	1990	2002
Foreign-owned	733	3,953	10,872
Irish-owned	383	734	1,892
Total	1,116	4,687	12,762

CONTEMPORARY • TRANSFORMATIONS

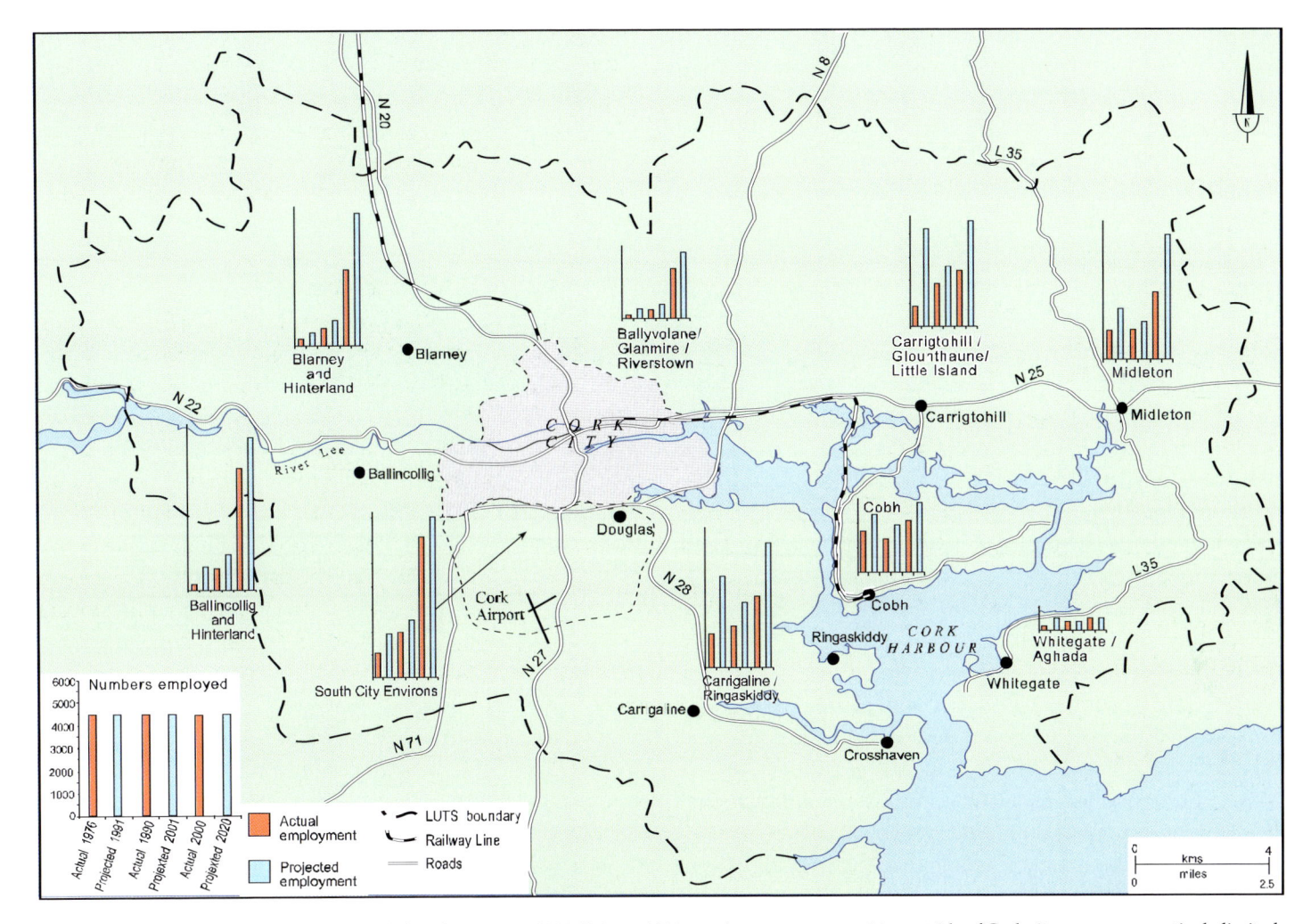

Fig. 5.8 Employment trends in the hinterland of Cork city, 1976–2020. Prior to 1990, employment opportunities outside of Cork city were comparatively limited. Development was focused mainly on two large, planned industrial zones at Little Island and Ringaskiddy. Although growth was significantly less than anticipated since 1990, employment growth has been more impressive and widespread as new investments have opted to locate in attractive rural environments and small towns offering good access to Cork city. This has resulted in two well-defined zones of employment growth: firstly, the area of development to the west and south of the city, including the expanding communities of Blarney and Ballincollig and on to Cork Airport via the South Link Road; secondly, the N25 has been a key factor in promoting an east–west axis of growth for the eastern edge of the city via Little Island and Carrigtohill to Midleton.

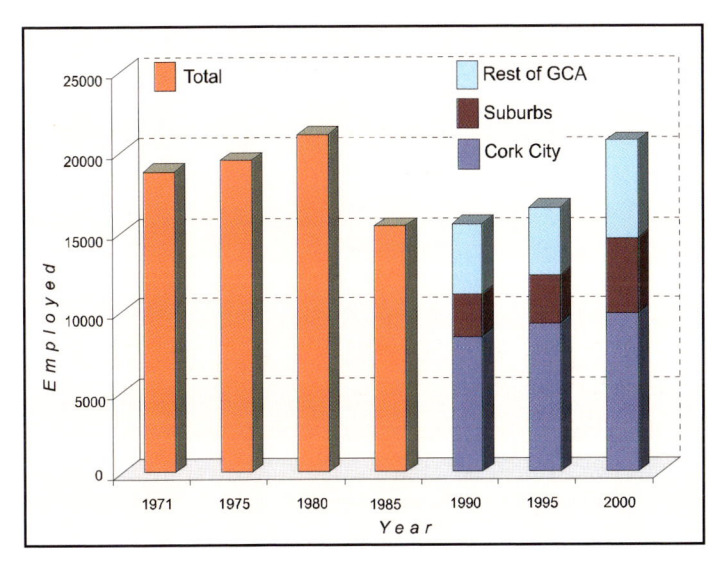

relatively cheap and flexible female labour in Cork proved especially attractive for the electronics sector.[7] By 1991, one in two female manufacturing jobs was in this sector. This helped offset the 86 per cent decline in female jobs in textile and clothing that had occurred from 1971 to 1991. So, while total male manufacturing employment declined n the 1980s, women enjoyed greater job prospects. By 1991, they accounted for nearly one-third of the city's industrial workforce. Lastly, the preferred location for the vast majority of electronics industries was the 'necklace' of industrial estates in suburban Cork.

Fig. 5.9 By 1980 manufacturing employment in Cork exceeded 20,000. Economic recession in the early 1980s, however, saw this figure fall by some 25 per cent. Since the low point of 1985, jobs in manufacturing have increased, especially after 1995. This upward trend has been due primarily to the successful attraction of new industrial investment to the suburbs, especially the smaller towns and rural environment in the hinterland of the city. Less than one-half of manufacturing employment remains in the region.

Although showing trends for total employment rather than only for manufacturing, Figures 5.8 and 5.9 highlight actual and projected changes in patterns of economic development within the Cork region since 1976. The city centre was the location for most employment, due mainly to its retail and office functions. Total employment declined by 1990, however, falling short of earlier projections as recession and high unemployment affected its market functions. In contrast to the city centre, employment increased within *suburban* Cork. Growth was especially impressive in the south-western suburbs, focused on Bishopstown and Wilton. Proximity to UCC, CIT, the new regional hospital and the Technology Park, together with an extensive range of private housing estates, combined to make the area attractive for new investment and especially the electronics industry.

Employment trends in the south-eastern suburbs were more disappointing, with 1990 totals falling below those of 1976. This was due almost entirely to the loss of some 2,000 jobs following the closure of Ford and Dunlop, which were located in this area. During the late 1980s, however, development prospects improved. This was linked to the conversion of the former Ford and Dunlop factories into the new Marina Commercial Park, which offered space for small business operations. In addition, developments at the Mahon Industrial Estate, anchored by a large multinational electronics plant, provided 1,000 jobs by 1990.

The residential environment and underdeveloped social and physical infrastructures combined to make most northside suburban areas less attractive for modern growth industries. This was a major problem, given the high unemployment levels found in the city's large public-housing estates which are located predominantly north of the Lee. In spite of this, total employment increased in northside suburban areas. Vital to this trend were the two IDA industrial estates at Hollyhill and Kilbarry, which had attracted some 1,300 jobs by 1990. It was clear, however, that

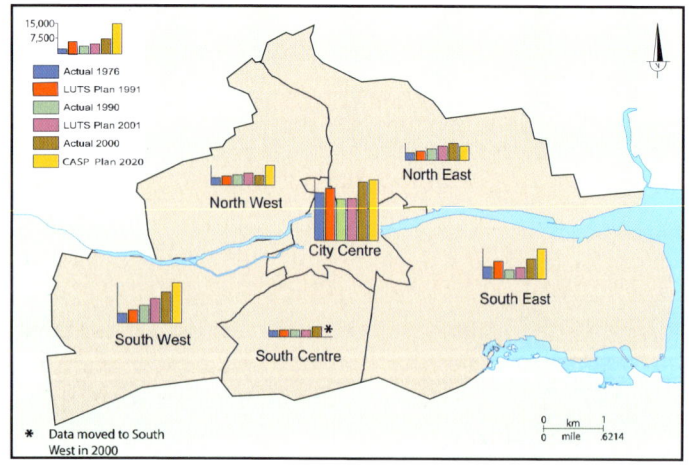

Fig. 5.10 Projected and actual employment growth in Cork city 1978–2020.

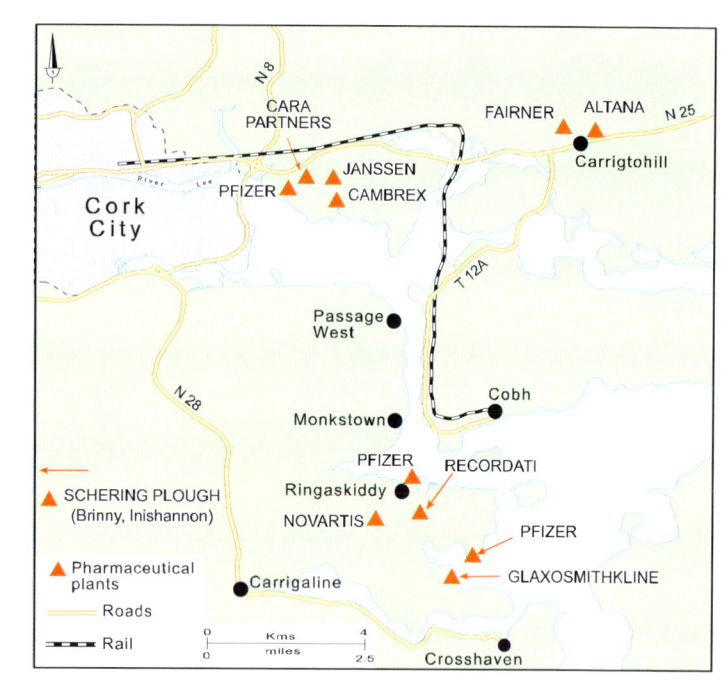

Fig. 5.11 Cork is a key location for some of the world's major pharmachemical industries. More than 25 pharmachemical companies operate in the region and provide direct employment for over 5,000 people. A further 10,000 jobs are in companies that provide this sector with goods and services. The most important concentration of the pharmachemical sector occurs in Cork harbour, especially around the Ringaskiddy deepwater port. Here, nine companies provide some 3,500 jobs. Altogether, Cork provides more than half of Ireland's pharmachemical production and exports. As a result, the city deserves its title of 'Pharmachem City', or the 'chemical capital of Ireland'.

if northside communities wished to compete successfully with those to the south then major investment was required to make such locations more attractive for growth industries.

The hinterland of Cork city recorded some significant gains in total employment. The satellite town of Ballincollig and the rural area south of the city's administrative boundary benefited from overspill from the growing southern suburbs. At both Little Island and Ringaskiddy, employment growth fell well below initial expectations. This was a direct consequence of the downturn in new industrial investment and delays in completing vital infrastructure at Ringaskiddy. In spite of this, both locations provided 2,500 jobs by 1990 and confirmed a shift in manufacturing locations from Cork city to more rural but accessible sites.

CORK AND THE CELTIC TIGER ECONOMY

The 1990s witnessed a major turnaround for the Cork economy. Central to this was the rapid growth of the 'Celtic Tiger' economy. The trickle-down effects from this national development brought major benefits to Cork as the country's second-largest city. An early expression of optimism for Cork occurred in a review of LUTS in 1992.[8]

This suggested a growth in total employment of 15,000 between 1990 and 2001. Actual trends (+26,000) exceeded this forecast. The upturn in Cork's development, however, was relatively slow to take off and occurred mainly from the mid-1990s. This is highlighted in the halving of unemployment figures and the net gain of 4,000 industrial jobs between 1995 and 2000.

In addition to benefiting from the Celtic Tiger, two 'local' factors contributed to the growth of the Cork region. The first was the changing sectoral composition of Cork's industrial economy. The recession of the 1980s greatly reduced the region's dependency on declining sectors and uncompetitive industries. New investment attracted to Cork in the 1990s was not offset by large numbers of job losses. By the start of the new millennium, therefore, Cork's industrial base was dominated by modern, international growth sectors which held good job prospects for the labour market. These include electronics industries such as Apple, Motorola, EMC and Bournes, which regard Cork as a viable alternative to Dublin, thereby generating many industrial jobs. Pharmachem and Healthcare provided over 5,000 jobs by 2003, with new investments, such as Schering Plough, Novartis and Pfizer, consolidating Cork's status as the 'chemical capital of Ireland'. In addition, international services such as RCI generated some 2,500 jobs and are attracted to the city by its improved communication systems and relatively low-cost, but educated, especially female, workforce. Moreover, by 1990 most of the infrastructure, and especially roads, planned under LUTS, was in place. This, together with further large-scale investments (aided by EU Structural Funds) since 1990, has given the city region the efficient infrastructure that is vital for a competitive industrial economy.

Of particular importance have been the Southern Ring Road and the Jack Lynch Tunnel – which provide more direct access to the N8 road to Dublin – an improved N25 link to Midleton and Waterford, and the Blackpool bypass, which provides improved access to the N20 to Limerick. New or enlarged industrial estates have been developed along these new routes, and especially along the Southern Ring Road. The deepwater port at Ringaskiddy was completed, with improved road access to the city. The modernisation of Cork Airport and the development of the business park there is directly linked to this investment strategy. Finally, in 2004, the Cork City Broadband Network was completed, which provides broadband access at reasonable cost to IT-based companies and other companies which require high-speed digital communications. This is vital in encouraging further high-tech investment in the city region.

THE CHANGING GEOGRAPHY OF INDUSTRIAL DEVELOPMENT SINCE 1990

Developments in the 1990s consolidated earlier changes in industrial location but also introduced some new patterns. Five areas of development can be noted, the city centre, the southern suburbs, the northside suburbs, Little Island and the eastern corridor, and Ringaskiddy and Cork's outer harbour.

The City Centre

This remains the largest centre of total employment, reversing its earlier trend of job losses. Urban renewal schemes and further development of the city's retail and office functions created many new jobs. In addition, a growing number of international services companies were attracted to locate in refurbished buildings such as Penrose Wharf. This confirmed the more positive image of the city centre.

The Southern Suburbs

The southern suburbs showed a strong growth in employment. In the south-east, new land for industrial development in Mahon, together with the improved access provided by the Southern Ring Road and the Jack Lynch Tunnel, doubled employment between 1990 and 2003. Employment in the south-west suburbs also grew rapidly. However, the strong attractions of this area for new investment, such as Boston Scientific, has depleted land reserves for further industrial development. One major consequence of congestion in the south-west suburbs has been the continued overspill of investment into adjacent areas. An arc of industrial development emerged between Blarney and Ballincollig along the South Link Road and the airport. By 2003, 30,000 jobs were situated in this arc. This pattern reflects the decentralisation of employment from the city to attractive adjacent areas, and especially those made accessible by improved transport infrastructure.

Northside Suburbs

While some growth in employment was recorded, the northside suburbs continued to experience difficulty in attracting new industries. Despite efforts to promote the Hollyhill and Kilbarry industrial estates, both remain underdeveloped. The conversion of former textile mills into the Sunbeam and Watercourse industrial estates only provided space for a limited range of small industries which generated relatively low-value employment. These activities at the Sunbeam estate were disturbed by a devastating fire in 2003. The Northern Ring Road, however, has improved access to this area and offers new possibilities for the future.

An enterprise centre at Ballyvolane, for example, supports a range of small industries, whilst the Northpoint Business Park attracts mainly retail, wholesale and warehousing functions, and mirrors development occurring around the Southern Ring Road.

Little Island and an Eastern Corridor

Little Island continues to be a major centre of employment, based on the diverse range of growth industries located on its industrial estates. This role has been emphasised by improvements to the N25 which have enhanced its accessibility to Cork and Waterford and to Dublin, via a new link to the N8. This is illustrated by the opening in 2002 of the large East Gate Business Park on Little Island. The upgraded N25 has attracted new investment to Carrigtohill and Midleton. An eastern corridor of development has emerged from Tivoli/Glanmire to Midleton, centred on Little Island and linked by the N25. This is vital for the eastern harbour area and complements the arc of development that is occurring to the south and west of the city.

Ringaskiddy and Cork's Outer Harbour

Despite the closure of Irish Steel in 2003, Cork's outer harbour remains a zone of large-scale, port-related industries focused on the well-serviced industrial land adjacent to the Ringaskiddy deepwater port. Large pharachemical plants, such as Pfizer, Glaxo Smith Kline and Novartis, dominate the landscape and employment structure in this area. The presence of these chemical operations has generated concerns within the local population over environmental pollution. These issues were heightened in 2004 over the decision to build a toxic incinerator plant at Ringaskiddy.

THE FUTURE FOR CORK'S INDUSTRIAL ECONOMY

The outlook for Cork's economic future is optimistic. As emphasised in the Cork Area Strategic Plan (CASP), which covers the years 2001–2020, the city centre is forecast to grow strongly, reflecting ongoing urban renewal and its attraction for labour-intensive services such as in the retail, commercial, legal and financial areas.[9] Employment growth in suburban Cork will also grow, especially in the south-east. Here, continued investment in Mahon and the new Docklands Development Scheme, designed to transform the city's inner quays and the Marina area, will double this area's workforce. This relatively run-down area will be transformed into a waterfront zone encompassing six million square metres of modern office, retail, cultural, leisure and residential units. It will provide a new focus for Cork city and emphasise its image as a modern European city. Growth in the south-west suburbs will be marginal and the central concern here will be to protect the environment from congestion. Further investment will be redirected into the strong arc of development linking Blarney, Ballincollig and the airport. By 2020, this zone could employ over 36,000 people in well-designed industrial estates and expanded urban centres; for example, Ballincollig's planned new urban development on the site of the former military barracks. The northern suburbs will struggle to attract significant new employment. Development in this area is likely to be deflected to the eastern corridor along the N25. Midelton is projected to grow and will be linked by a new commuter railway to Cork. This will enhance the prospects of growth along this transport axis.

Cork's status as the 'chemical capital of Ireland' is likely to be retained, given the established strengths of this sector in Ringaskiddy. While some additional growth in pharma-chemicals can be anticipated, most of the projected gains in employment in this area are likely to come from light industry and office-related functions. To ensure that this occurs, it will be vital to protect the environment of the outer harbour. Overall, the CASP estimates that total employment in the Cork region will increase by one-third to reach some 160,000 in 2020. This increase will be in services, especially as most manufacturing activities will replace workers with automated machines/robotics, in order to increase productivity and remain competitive. In spite of this, Cork will remain a key industrial location and should retain its status as the most important economic centre in Ireland outside of Dublin.

32. THE MOBILE CITY

Donncha Ó Cinnéide

SEA AND AIR CONNECTIONS

Transport change is one of the most important factors in urban growth. The transport system ties together people's lives and affects where we live, work and socialise. It influences our quality of life, limiting what we can do each day and having a significant impact on the environment. Accessibility, traffic management and mobility are key issues for the regeneration of the city. Transport has shaped Cork's land use since the founding of the city on a series of islands in the Lee and the subsequent filling in of the adjacent waterways to make new streets and quays. The tramways and railways of the late nineteenth century and early twentieth century encouraged the growth of the suburbs of Sunday's Well, Douglas and Blackrock as well as the western suburbs and the outlying settlements of Blarney and Monkstown. The car now permits commuters to the city to drive from most parts of County Cork. The city's commuting area now extends well beyond Bandon to the south-west, beyond Macroom to the west, almost as far as Charleville to the north and to Youghal on the east. Well-developed connections via sea and air contribute to Cork's regional and national importance. The port of Cork and its harbour have always been central to the development of the trading capabilities of the city region and today the goods exported and imported from here circulate in the global economy.

Over the years, as land use and shipping technology have transformed, the port has steadily migrated downstream. Located initially inside the original medieval walls, it extended to the city quays as these were progressively developed and from there to the Tivoli docks and the Ringaskiddy deepwater terminal. As a consequence, the harbour zone today can be considered as a number of complementary parts: the city quays, the Tivoli docks and industrial estate, the deepwater terminal downstream at Ringaskiddy, the dockyard at Rushbrook, the commercial harbour towns such as Cobh and Passage and the sailing areas such as Crosshaven. The city quays, once piled high with coal and timber, are now less busy but they are still used by grain ships feeding the tall quayside grain silos, by fishing trawlers and by the occasional visiting naval ship. The port's activities are now located at the rail-connected Tivoli docks, which is the main container terminal, and at the Ringaskiddy deepwater terminal, which accommodates the deepest-drafted vessels capable of being handled at any Irish port. Continued growth in port traffic and changes in shipping require expansion and the Port of Cork Company, a state-owned company, has major plans for development in the lower harbour. However, raising the necessary finance is a problem in the absence of EU funding, which contributed half of the total port investment between 1989 and 2002.

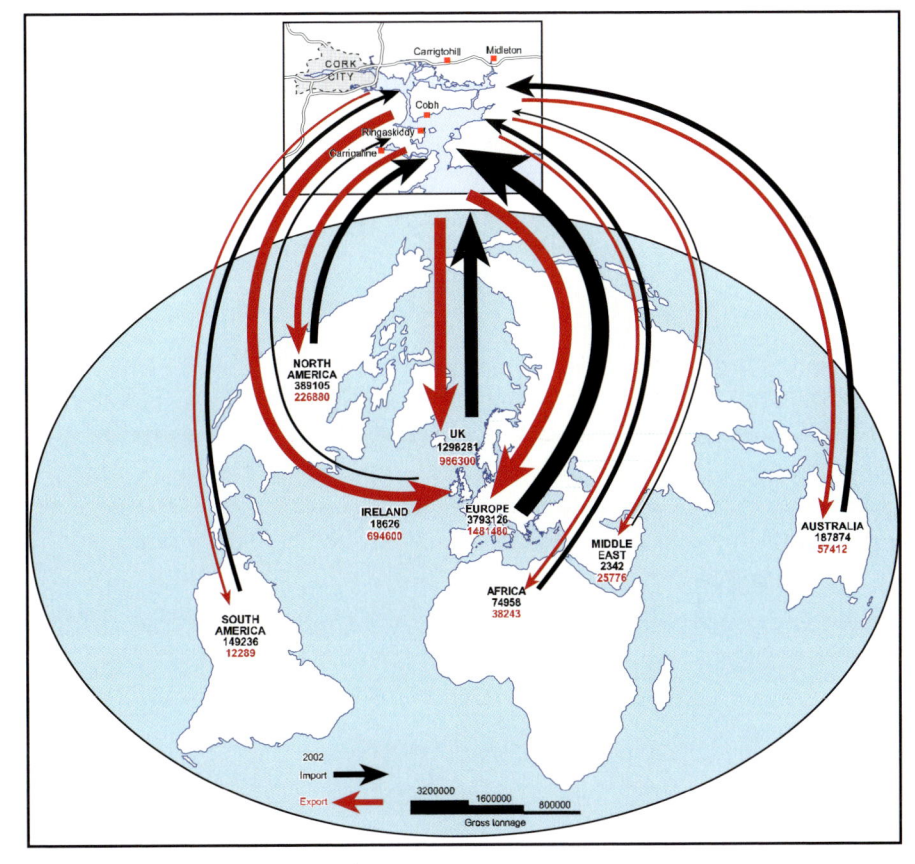

Fig. 5.12 Reflecting the globalisation of the region's economy, imports to and exports from Cork harbour are worldwide.

ATLAS · OF · CORK · CITY

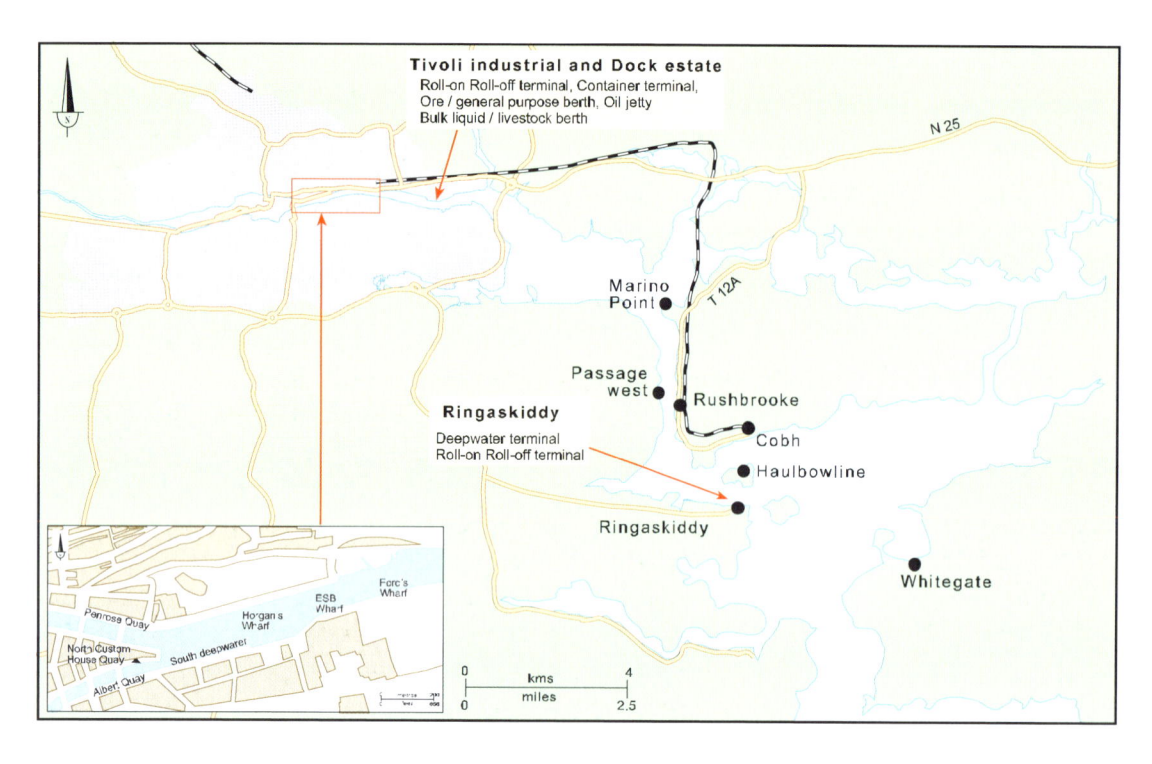

Fig. 5.13 The port of Cork extends from the city centre to Ringaskiddy and incorporates a number of towns and villages. The port benefits from one of the world's great natural sheltered harbours, capable of efficiently and safely handling the largest ships afloat.

Fig. 5.14 The Tivoli industrial and dock estate. (Photo: Tomás Tyner.)

Fig. 5.15 The new airport terminal building at Cork Airport. Supported by the European Investment Bank at a cost of €140 million, the development of a new terminal building makes a major improvement to the quality and capacity of the airport. Overall, the significance of EU membership in facilitating the development of both the airport and the port cannot be underestimated, a situation repeated throughout the region in terms of upgrades to the transport infrastructure. Cork Airport makes a significant contribution to the local economy. By 2010, up to five million passengers will use the airport on an annual basis. (Cork Airport Ltd.)

Cork port currently provides regular freight sailings to continental ports and passenger and freight ferry services to Swansea in south Wales. Weekly direct freight and tourist ferry services are also provided to Brittany in France during the summer. The ferries to south Wales and Brittany operate from Ringaskiddy. Cobh was the main departure point for emigrants to the United States during the nineteenth century and for many years it was the last stopping point in Europe for transatlantic liners. Now, it is regularly visited by luxury cruise ships, which berth at the Cobh Cruise Terminal. In 2004, 37 ships with over 35,000 passengers came ashore here. Apart from Dublin, the modern port of Cork is the only Irish port that provides all five shipping modes of Lift-on/Lift-off, Roll-on/Roll-off, Liquid Bulk, Dry Bulk and Break Bulk. These facilities meet the logistic needs of the diverse range of industries in the region and are used by many of the nearby pharmaceutical and chemical plants. Ringaskiddy is also Ireland's first port-based Freeport, offering important advantages for business. Overall, the port makes a critically important contribution to the local economy and to the economy of the south and south-west of Ireland.

If Cork port supports the manufacturing base of the region, Cork Airport has a significant impact in developing business and tourism, whilst greatly enhancing the accessibility of Cork and quality of life. The airport was officially opened in 1961. Since its early days of fog delays due to its high location, on a ridge 5 km south of the city, it has grown rapidly. It now has excellent navigational facilities, a main runway 2,130 m in length and a shorter cross runway of 1,310 m. Daily services are provided to an increasing number of continental and UK destinations, an average total of 48 scheduled and charter destinations per week, although only London and Dublin have frequent direct services each day. Tardiness in developing a direct connection to the United States has proved to be a competitive disadvantage in attracting direct foreign investment. Cork Airport is now an independent airport operated by a government-appointed board of directors. The airport attracts passengers from the province of Munster and beyond. In recent years there has been a substantial growth in passengers, both for work and leisure purposes; all of Cork now seems to know the Mediterranean and the Canary Islands! Passenger throughput in 2003 was 2.3 million, an increase of 17 per cent on 2002 and an overall increase of more than 60 per cent since 1995. The UK accounted for 1.2 million passengers and, of those, 67 per cent flew to London. The strongest growth area is in the UK regional airport network and several cargo airlines are also based at the airport.

Like many other parts of Cork's transportation infrastructure, the airport has been upgraded. Mirroring similar operations at Hamburg, Nice and Helsinki, there is now a large business park located on a 45-acre site close to the airport terminal. Approved in 1999 by the EU as an enterprise zone, the project received valuable state aid and was built at a cost of €101 million through a partnership between Aer Rianta–Cork Airport, ICC bank and the developer Omnistone Ltd. With an emphasis on high-tech software and electronic-based industries, the Cork Airport Business Park is a flagship for Cork's 'knowledge economy'.

PLANNING THE ROAD INFRASTRUCTURE AND CAR CULTURE

As a mercantile city, Cork always required good road connections with its hinterland. Over the years these roads went through various cycles of improvement and decay. Up to the first half of the twentieth century, the main emphasis was on strengthening the road surfaces and improving narrow sections and sharp bends. Now, even the most minor roads in the Cork area have hard bituminous surfaces. The main roads from Cork to the principal cities in Ireland have been upgraded in recent years and a motorway linking Cork to Dublin is being constructed. Three hundred and fifty million euro has been invested in the road network, a considerable percentage funded through EU structural funding. Traffic congestion has been a feature of life in Cork city for many decades. During the 1960s, delays regularly occurred in the city centre. Although not as bad as then, congestion is still severe and it now occurs throughout the city and suburbs during peak periods and is extending to off-peak times. The large growth in car ownership since the

Car Ownership per Household

	1971	1986	1991	2002
No car	17,354	17,601	17,208	14,606
One car	11,823	15,624	16,277	17,459
Two cars	1,273	3,252	4,035	8,402
Three cars+	121	467	580	2,180
Proportion of households owning a car	43%	52%	55%	66%

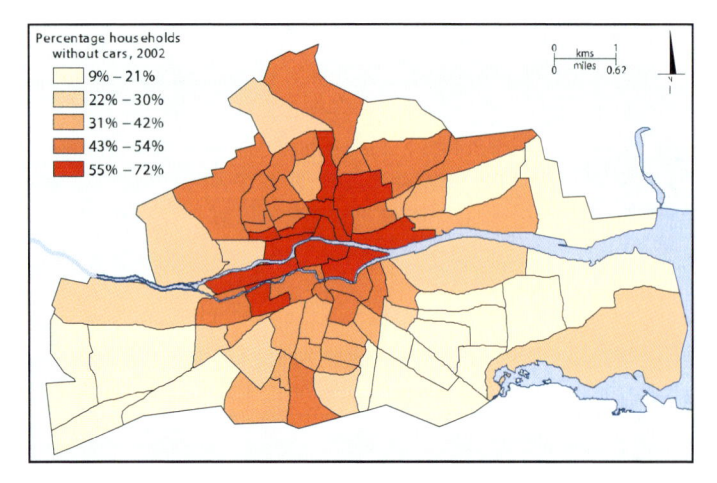

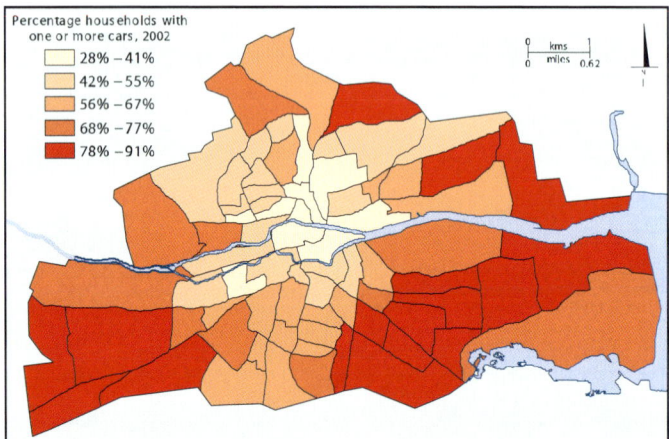

Fig. 5.16 Car ownership has grown substantially since the 1970s and accelerated during the Celtic Tiger period. Improved prosperity, together with social and spatial changes, such as increased participation of women in the labour force and more dispersed settlement in the metropolitan area, has contributed significantly to this expansion.

1960s and the consequential changes in the location of activities have resulted in all the roads near the city carrying heavy volumes of traffic.

The genesis of the current road system lies in the development strategy recommended by the 1978 Land Use and Transportation Study (LUTS). The LUTS transportation strategy included improved public transport services, traffic management measures and new roads. Although road schemes accounted for over 80 per cent of the proposed capital investment, substantial public transport investment was also proposed. Notably, plans for the city centre strategy depended on a substantial transfer from car to bus, particularly by commuters. The LUTS studies meant that Cork was successful in attracting EU and national government road construction funds when they became available in the 1980s and 1990s. The LUTS development strategy was re-evaluated in 1991.

The economic recession of the 1980s meant that the population of the Greater Cork Area and the number employed therein did not increase as predicted; nevertheless, the volume of traffic on the city roads was greater than estimated. This was partly due to the movement of population to the suburbs but was also because bus patronage had severely declined since 1978 due to rising car ownership. The major new roads constructed during this period, including the Southern Ring Road and the Jack Lynch Tunnel under the Lee, opened in 1999. Many roads were constructed as dual carriageways rather than the planned single carriageways. Critically, however, the recommended LUTS funding for public transport did not materialise and the proposed bus priority and car restraint measures were not developed. Consequently, the recommended integrated transportation strategy was not implemented and the seeds for future congestion were planted.

Public transport

The double-track main-line Dublin to Cork rail service reached the city in 1854 on completion of the Cork Tunnel. It is the longest tunnel in Ireland, running to 1,225 metres underneath the steep ridge on the northside of the city. In the second half of the nineteenth century, the regional rail services from Cork city were extended to the county towns of Bandon, Kinsale and Bantry, to Macroom, Cobh, Midleton and Youghal and to the villages west of the city (the Cork & Muskerry Light Railway). There was also a nascent metropolitan network to the lower harbour towns of Passage, Monkstown and Crosshaven via the Marina and the Douglas Viaduct. The line of this railway is now a popular walking and cycle route, with many fine stone bridges.

Apart from the double-track Cork-to-Cobh service which is now being developed as a commuter line, the local lines were short-lived and never economically successful. Scheduled rail services between Cork and Midleton ceased in the early 1970s. Kent Station, the Cork rail terminus, is an impressive Victorian building located immediately after trains emerge from the Cork Rail Tunnel. The main

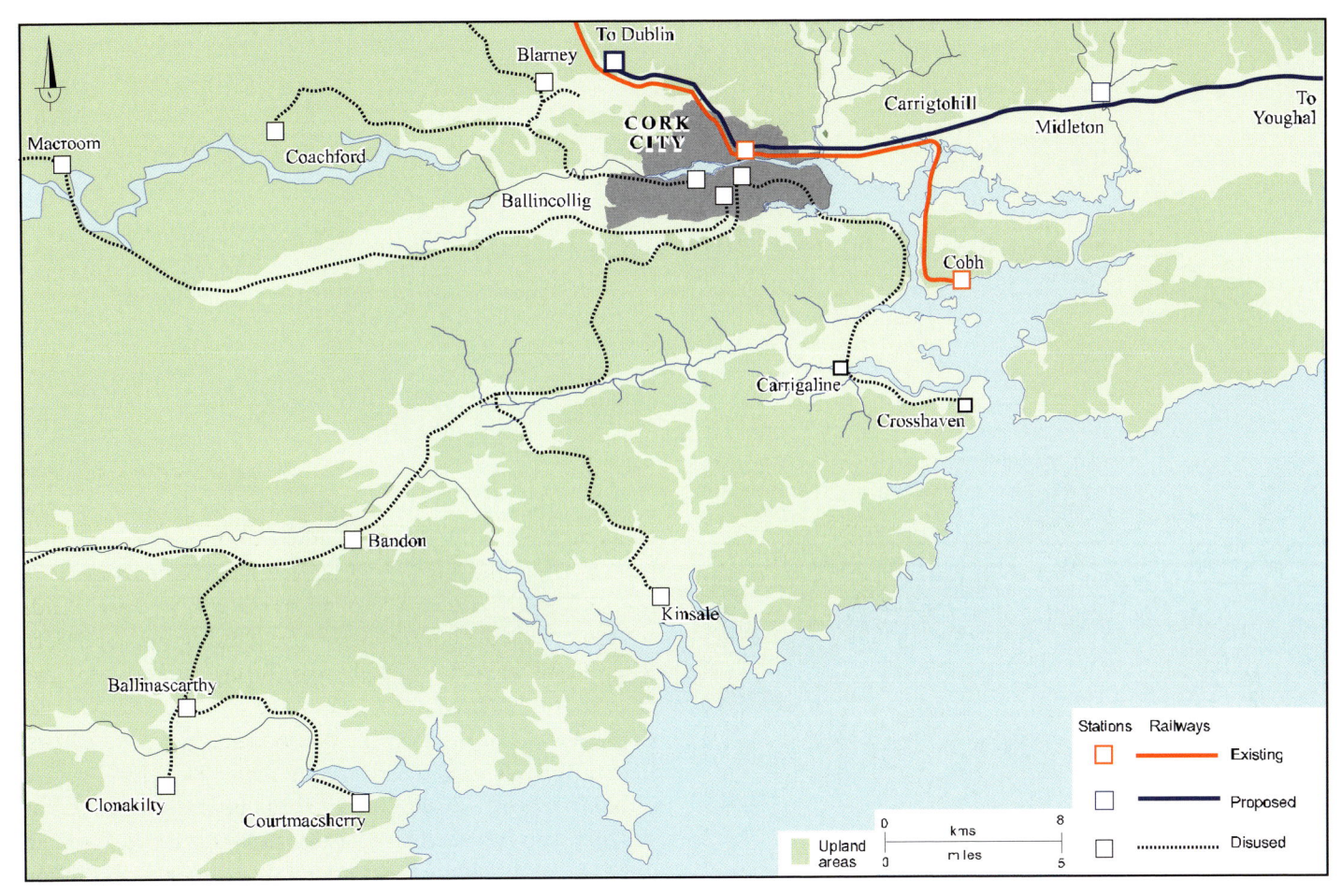

Fig. 5.17 Old, existing and proposed new railway network in the Cork area.

platforms are curved because the track had to be bent sharply through ninety degrees to connect with the Cork–Cobh line. Today, frequent rail services are provided to Dublin (nine per day) and an hourly commuter service to Cobh, but connections to other Irish cities are poor. It is necessary to change at Limerick Junction for Limerick, at Kildare for Waterford and at Portarlington for Galway. The quality of the rail service varies and delays occur regularly, but the main-line service to Dublin is being improved.

The unprecedented economic growth in the 'Celtic Tiger' years has put new stresses on mobility in and around the city. The planning response has been a renewed interest in public transport. In 2002, the development strategy for the Cork area, the Cork Area Strategic Plan (CASP), proposed that one-third of transport expenditure should be on public transport, with the remaining two-thirds on roads and traffic management. Because of the rapid growth in car use, low-density development and the scattered location of new housing and employment, if no action was taken peak-hour traffic speeds would drop from 25 mph to 5 mph in the suburbs and from 15 mph to 5 mph in the city centre. A suite of new proposals included: a commuter rail system linking Mallow to Midleton, Cobh and Youghal; new quality bus corridors to connect Ballincollig, Carrigaline and the airport to the city and Kent Station; priorities for buses in the city; increased bus and train frequencies; denser residential development and the location of development at rail stations; and park-and-ride services at stations and on the edge of the city. New roads included a ring road partly in a tunnel around the north-west of the city and new bridges over the Lee to serve the proposed docklands development.

Following these recommendations, approval has now been granted for a €90 million suburban commuter rail service for Cork city and county. A new and frequent commuter service will be introduced between Cork city and Midleton, a distance of 20 km, at an estimated cost of €56 million. It will involve the relaying of 10 km of new track and the construction of three new stations, at Dunkettle, Carrigtohill and Midleton. All of the stations will have extensive park-and-ride facilities. A train service will run every 15 minutes at peak times and the journey time will be 25 minutes. In addition, the commuter service on the 35-km stretch from Mallow to Cork city on the main Dublin-to-Cork Intercity line will be enhanced. New stations will also

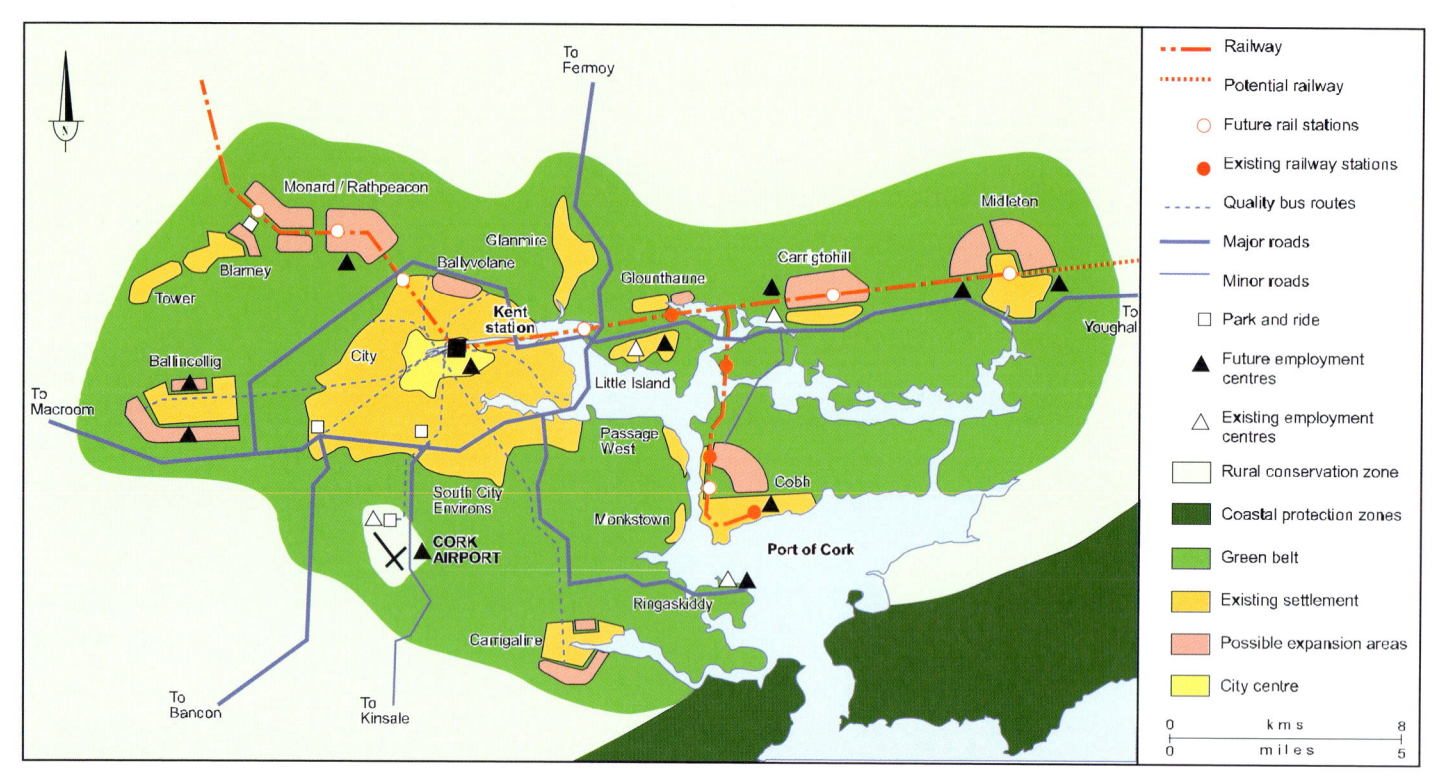

Fig. 5.18 The Cork Area Strategic Plan transportation policy.

be constructed at Blarney, where significant new residential development is planned, and at Kilbarry, on the outskirts of the city, at an estimated cost of €10 million. Passenger trips on the entire Cork suburban rail network, including the existing and expanding Cobh service, will be close to four million per annum, or 16,000 per working day, in the first year of operation.

In terms of bus infrastructure, Bus Éireann, the national bus company, operates a profitable express service from Cork offering frequent connections to the principal towns and cities in Ireland. However, these buses are not easily accessible for the disabled. The express services compete successfully with the rail services to Galway, Limerick, Tralee, Waterford and Rosslare. In the city and its metropolitan area, apart from taxi services, public transport is entirely by bus. The city bus services currently receive a state subsidy covering 20 per cent of their annual costs. Bus Éireann operates services between the city centre and the suburbs and two orbital routes connecting the suburbs on the north- and southsides. Regular services to the adjacent towns and villages in County Cork are also provided. Until recent years, most of the city buses were double-deck and operated by a driver and a conductor. Today, almost all are single-deck low-floor buses, operated solely by the driver, giving easier access for the disabled. During the 1980s the use of the bus services declined significantly with the growth of car ownership and traffic congestion. Whilst the number of people using the bus to get to work has dropped steadily over the last fifteen years, bus patronage appears to have stabilised. Most users are students, women, children and the elderly. Those with an available car seldom use the bus. As a result of traffic congestion, the Cork city bus services are unreliable. During peak periods long delays are common and off-peak services can also be poor. Cork City Council proposes to encourage people to use buses more often by providing priority Green Routes, which will improve the frequency, reliability and speed of services. These will eventually be implemented on routes from Bishopstown, Carrigrohane Road, Farranree, Blackpool, Mayfield, Knocknaheeny, Gurranabraher, the Douglas routes, Kinsale road, the airport and Mahon.

Keeping the city mobile

Traffic, second only to housing, captures the national imagination. Irish people drive longer distances on a daily basis than any other population group, including Americans. In many parts of the world, transport policies struggle to deliver improvements in efficiency, health and safety, but it is usually communities that have to deal with the consequences of these problems. Cork's transport system is under strain, with heavy traffic volumes on all roads leading into the city and congestion affecting even suburban areas. Whilst significantly better than conditions in the Dublin metropolitan region, as more people live

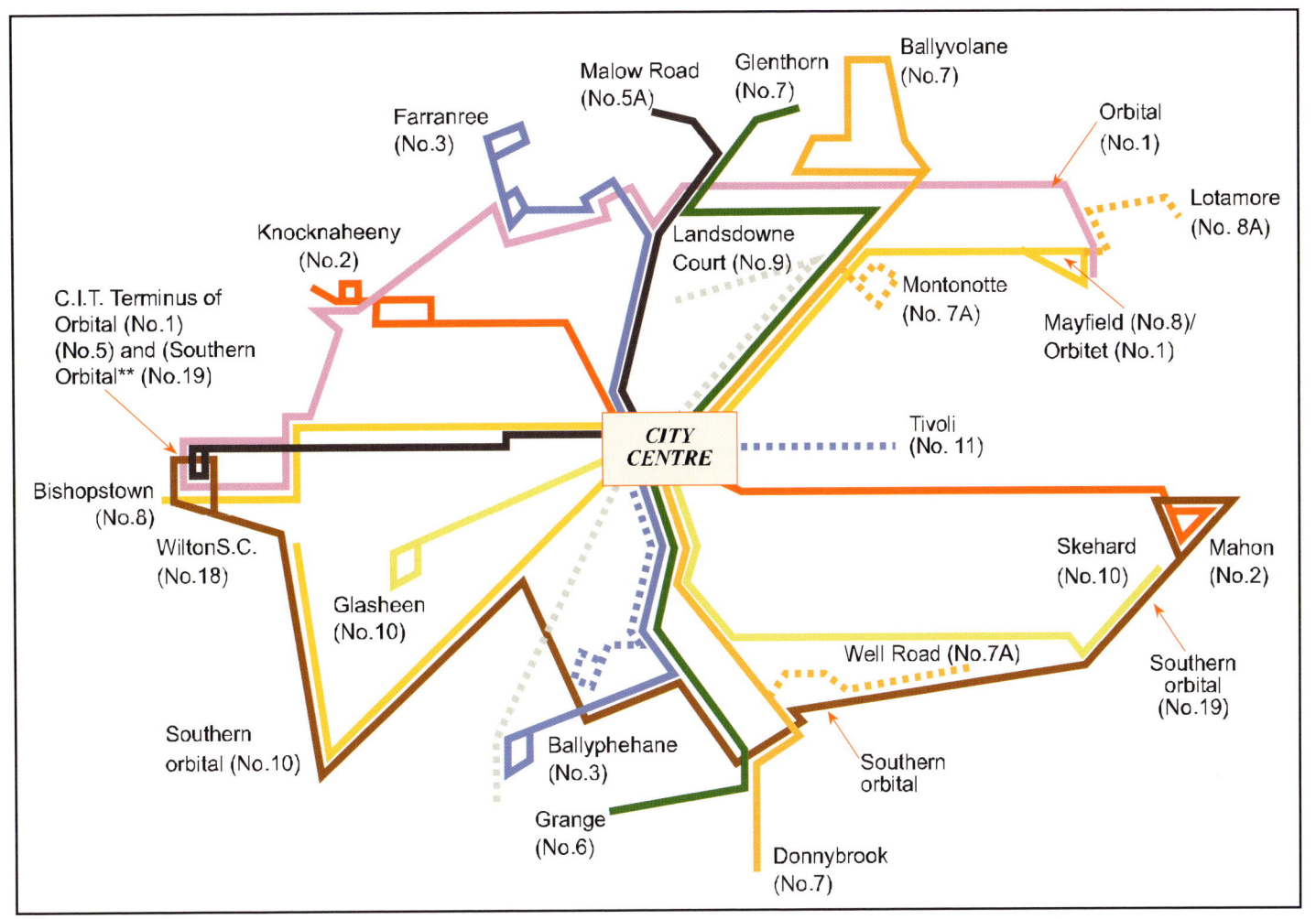

Fig. 5.19 Whilst the bus network is well developed, renewed efforts are needed to ensure it can meet the needs of a growing city and help address increased traffic congestion. To achieve this aim, green commuter routes giving priority to buses have been provided on some of the main city bus routes. Increased bus frequencies and more park-and-ride facilities may encourage car users to avail of more environmentally friendly public transport options. (Source: Bus Éireann.)

outside the city, the traffic problem grows. Commuters and shoppers hope for easy access to the city with free or cheap parking whilst the city authorities try to achieve sustainable growth. This results in stress for drivers sitting in slow-moving traffic or seeking parking whilst avoiding parking wardens, car clampers or tow-away trucks. Either from choice, or because of a lack of alternatives, many Cork parents deliver their children to school by car, adding 20 per cent to the morning peak traffic. To make Cork a more attractive city, realistic options for public transport need to be put in place. The question is how, without harming the economic development of the city and the region and undermining the freedom of individuals, to facilitate movement around the city.

Previous Cork transportation plans depended on the then current solution to the traffic problem, on available finance and on implementation. None were fully developed and the recommended investment in public transport was minimised. The current CASP strategy, by maximising the use of available assets, can potentially reduce car travel and urban sprawl. It locates new developments in areas with good public transport and restricts development elsewhere. The successful implementation of the CASP strategy should reduce congestion but will depend on our willingness to forgo using the car for work and school trips. Twenty-seven per cent of car trips in the city centre must shift to public transport. However, the implementation will be very challenging, as CASP goes against the grain of current development trends and must compete with widespread commitment to the car. Ensuring that Cork stays mobile requires vision, persistence, political participation, funding and a willingness to innovate, characteristics seen in successful European cites which have effective transportation systems, attractive city centres and an excellent quality of life.

Moving Around

Grainne Brick

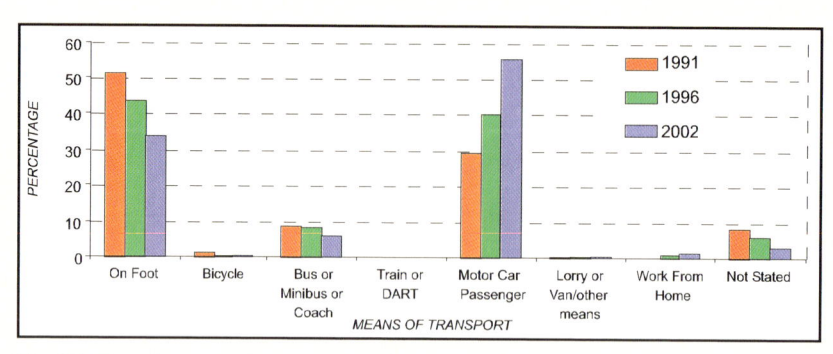

Fig. 5.20 Travel to school by children aged 5 to 12 years.

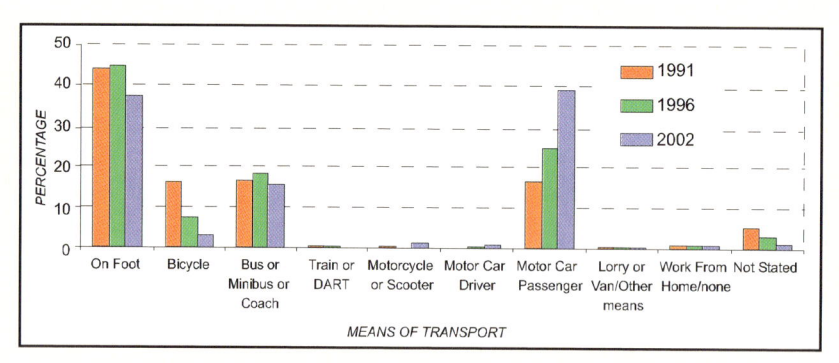

Fig. 5.21 Travel to school or college by children aged 13 to 18 years.

Recent commentaries concerning risks posed to children on their journeys to school, shifts in attitude concerning the paid employment of parents and changing attitudes of policy-makers towards children and the family have all played their part in altering the mobility patterns of people living in and around Cork. School-going journeys are dominated by the huge growth in travel by car. Between 1991 and 2002, all other categories of transport declined in usage by schoolchildren. In 1991, 51 per cent of children travelled to school on foot and only 29 per cent travelled as a passenger in a car. By 2002, these figures had reversed, with 55 per cent travelling by car and 34 per cent on foot. Boys are more likely to travel on foot or by bicycle than girls. In 1991, 10 per cent of children travelled one mile to their school, but by 2002 this figure had dropped to 2 per cent. Between 1991 and 2002 the number of children travelling two miles to school rose from 11 per cent to 18 per cent, the number of children travelling three to four miles to school has risen from 6 per cent to 12 per cent and the number of children travelling five to nine miles has risen from two per cent to five per cent (Fig. 5.20). In total, the journeys of school-going children have been transformed both in terms of distance and means. Reflecting the dispersed urban development of the city, children now travel further from home to attend school and, as a consequence, are less and less likely to travel independently.

The travelling patterns of older school or college students, aged between thirteen and eighteen, have also changed in the past decade. However, this is different to the above group, since they are more independently mobile (Fig. 5.21). Though the decline in walking has not been as sharp as with primary schoolchildren, there has been a drop from 44 per cent to 37 per cent between

1991 and 2002. Changes in this area are dominated by the considerable rise of students travelling as passengers in cars: from 16 per cent in 1991 to 39 per cent in 2002. A small increase is also recorded in the number of students travelling to school or college as a car driver. The distance this group travels to get to school or college has also changed (Fig. 5.22). These students show a predominant reliance on travelling on foot to school or college, more so than any other group examined by the census, with virtually the same proportion travelling on foot between 1991 and 2002. Most notable within this group is the decline in travel by bicycle – a sharp decline, from 24 per cent to 5 per cent between 1991 and 2002. There has been a significant rise in the use of the car – either as a driver or as a passenger. The distance travelled to school or college also shows major change – the proportion of students travelling five to nine miles has increased from 12 per cent in 1991 to 20 per cent in 2002 and travel for all other lesser distances has declined.

In terms of how people get to work, there have been two major areas of change (Fig. 5.23). The percentage of people travelling on foot has decreased from 26 per cent in 1991 to 14 per cent in 2002 and the proportion driving a car has increased sharply, from 37 per cent in 1991 to 59 per cent in 2002. The proportion of those travelling as a passenger in a car has remained the same (11 per cent). Critically important in terms of developing a public transportation policy for Cork, the amount of people travelling to work by bus almost halved between 1991 and 2002, to only 6 per cent. With regard to distance travelled to work, the proportion of working persons travelling under three miles to work has decreased, whilst the number of those travelling three to four miles has remained static. Reflecting the growth in commuting, the greatest increase is in the group travelling five to nine miles, which has increased from 11 per cent in 1986 to 22 per cent in 2002. The increasing dominance of the car for all these groups is stacking up problems for the sustainability of the city in the long term.

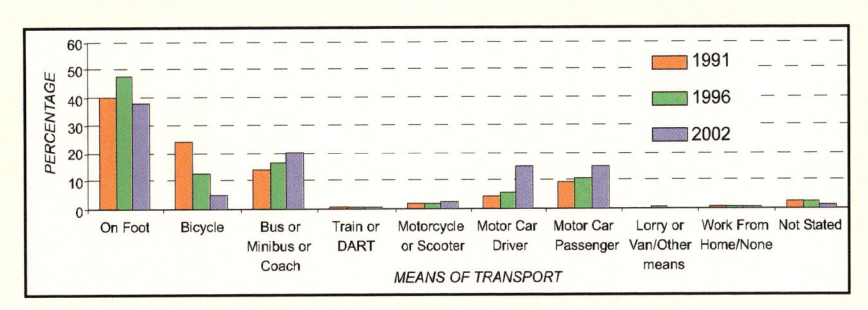

Fig. 5.22 Travel to school or college by students aged 19 years and over.

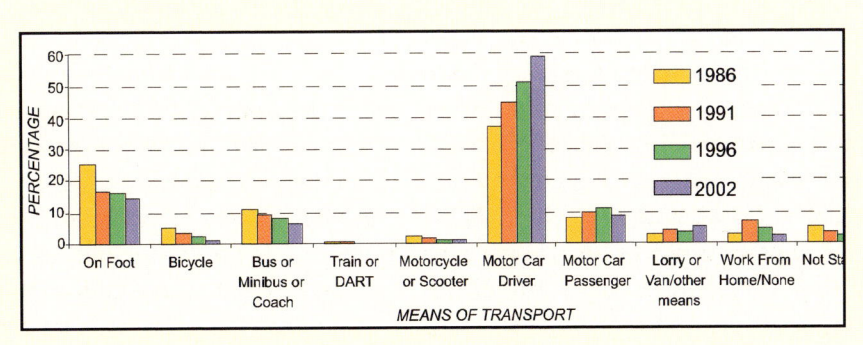

Fig. 5.23 Travel to work by people aged 15 years and over.

33. UNDERNEATH THE CITY

Denis Duggan

The Cork waterways are one of the city's defining features. The Lee separates into two channels to form the central island of the city. Much of the city centre developed in the eighteenth and nineteenth centuries, when stone arch culverts were constructed over the numerous minor meandering rivers and streams. Like Venice or Utrecht, the urban morphology of the city centre owes much to the waterways below it. The curved sweep of St Patrick's Street and its network of lanes are the legacy of the engineering works that reclaimed the city from the marshy environment of the Lee. Cork's wastewater and sewage has always been discharged untreated into these culverts and carried from these into the north and south channels of the river.

As the city developed, this disagreeable situation could not be allowed to continue. Modern standards demand that a city should have a clean, sealed and separate foul-sewer system. Between 1999 and 2004, the Cork Main Drainage scheme sought to eliminate all polluted discharges into the Lee by collecting and conveying them to a new treatment plant located at Little Island.

Managing pollution

River pollution has long been a concern to the city authorities. In 1869, Sir John Benson produced the first major engineering report on the main drainage of the city, followed by a further study by C.P. Walker in 1883. Both reports proposed that sewers should be laid along the quays to collect the waste from the various outfalls entering the river and then discharged at a point downstream of the Custom House. In 1883, the cost of the scheme was estimated at £75,000. However, whilst the condition of the water quality deteriorated over the next century, no work was undertaken due to lack of funding. In 1965, E.G. Pettit, the Cork firm of consulting engineers, devised a series of plans to address pollution in the river. Investment subsequently became available to the city to slowly improve the drainage system. Twenty million pound was spent on the drainage system up to 1999, when sewers to intercept the numerous outfalls discharging to the river were laid along the northern and southern sides of the river channels.

This work moved the point of discharge of the sewage downstream of the city centre at Horgan's Quay and Kennedy Quay. Despite this investment, each day thirteen million gallons of completely untreated raw sewage and polluted water still flowed into the Lee and Lough Mahon. These circumstances were a risk to public health and undermined the use of the river as a resource. Indeed, poor water quality meant over time that the city turned its back to the Lee and the use of riverside space, particularly for recreation and walking, was underdeveloped.

In the early 1990s, stimulated by the EU Wastewater Directive and the government's Environmental Action Plan, Cork City Council was obliged to collect and treat all sewage discharges. Like other large-scale infrastructural projects in other Irish cities, a rigorous and lengthy planning process ensured the participation of the various stakeholders in the city, county and harbour area. In 1992, Cork City Council commissioned E.G. Pettit to design the plans for the Main Drainage Scheme. A planning permission application for the treatment plant was made in 1994. This was followed by a hearing before An Bord Pleanála in 1995, a public health enquiry in 1996 and a final green light from the Ministry of the Environment in 1997. A multifaceted set of agreements and consultations was necessary: these included securing planning permission for various other new structures; agreements for hundreds of way leaves on private properties in the city; arrangements for foreshore licences; and consultation with Dúchas and the Department of Arts, Culture and Gaeltacht in relation to the archaeological supervision of the excavations. The Main Drainage Scheme was a highly integrated project and a good illustration of co-operation between the numerous stakeholders that influence the development of the city. Finally, in April 1999, the Council embarked on one of the largest engineering and environmental projects ever undertaken in Ireland.

The Cork Main Drainage Scheme

The cost was €270 million, of which 80 per cent was from the EU Cohesion Fund, the balance granted from the National Development Plan. At its peak, the scheme employed between 250 and 450 staff and one million euro was spent each week on wages and materials. This money primarily went back into the local economy and the scheme

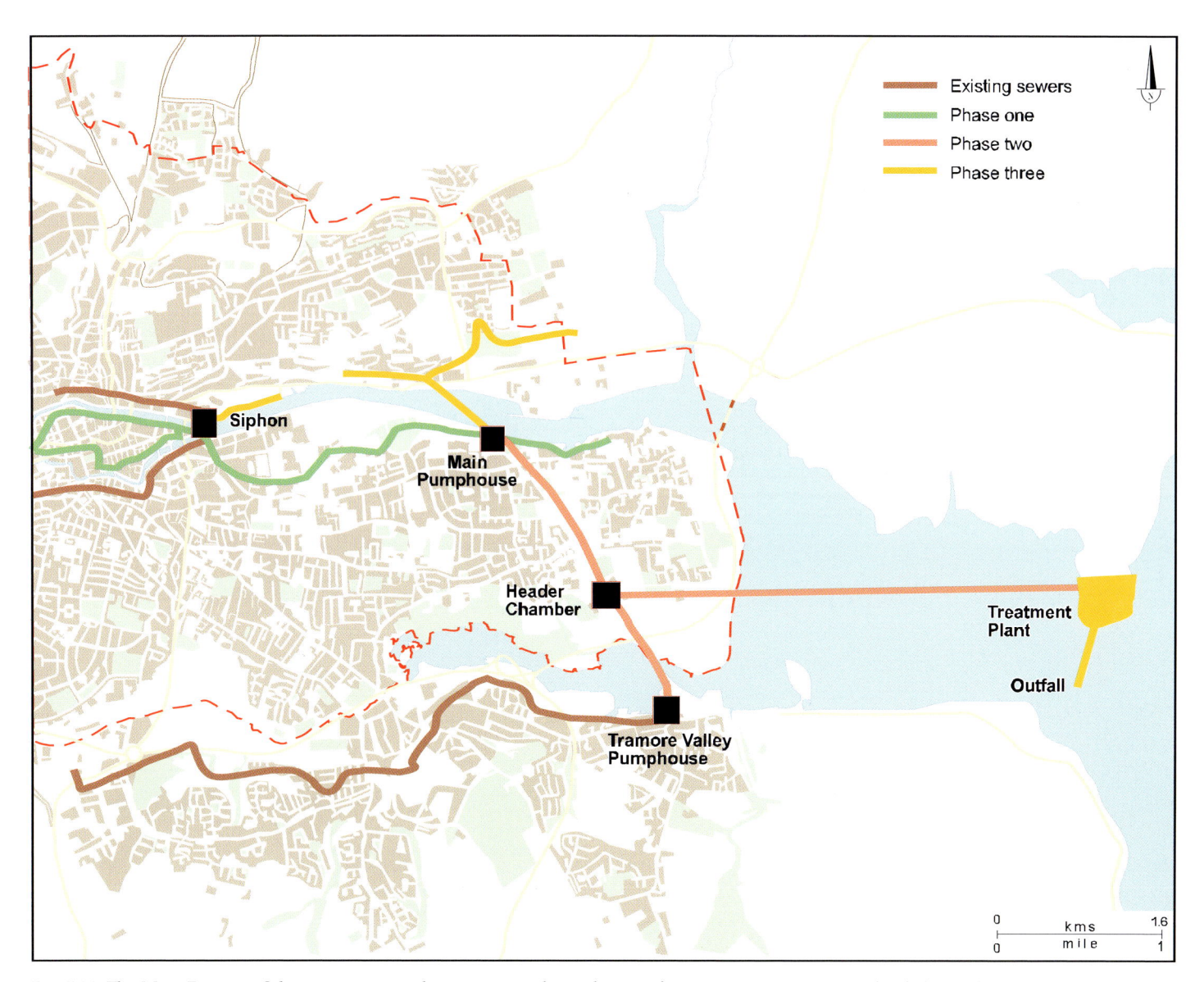

Fig. 5.24. The Main Drainage Scheme was a complex project involving dozens of separate contracts. It was divided into three sections: first, the re-engineering of the foul-water system in the city centre, sealing the outflows into the river channels; second, the construction of the new sewers and distribution system that would pump the sewage for treatment; third, the building of a new sewage treatment plant.

undoubtedly benefited the city of Cork, both in the short and long term.

In the city centre, foul sewers, complete with sewer connections to all properties, were laid in the city central island's streets, comprising over 17 km of drainage pipes. Water mains and ducting for the various utility companies were also laid as part of the works and opportunities have been taken to upgrade both broadband communication and electricity distribution in the city. Beneath the streets, the Cork Metropolitan Area Fibre Network provides the city with state-of-the-art communications for industry, business, hospitals and educational centres.

Local drainage schemes have been constructed in Boreenmanna, Blackpool, Victoria Cross and Blackrock. Within the historic city centre inside the old city wall, special care was taken to facilitate full archaeological excavations. The most significant find was the remains of a wooden house on South Main Street dated at AD 1104, in a style similar to Viking houses of the same period discovered in Dublin. This was the first such structure discovered in Cork from Viking times and resulted in a fresh understanding of the city's origins.

The Main Drainage Scheme's success depended on the construction of the 'siphon' (a structure that allows the transfer of wastewater under the river bed) and the main trunk sewer, both involving complex civil engineering techniques. The siphon now connects the original outfall at Horgan's Quay on the northside and the sewers on the city-island to the newly constructed drainage system on the southside. The main trunk sewer was completed after

Fig. 5.25 Pedestrians walking past works on St Patrick's Street. Building the new system in a busy area was a complex task, and the disruption for business, traffic and daily life had to be carefully managed. The people of Cork – including one of the city's most famous newspaper vendors, Micheal O Reagan – were bemused and sometimes frustrated by these disruptions, but often dealt with the inconvenience with good humour. (Photo: Annelies Verbiest.)

ten months of tunnelling along a 2.65-km route, from the Atlantic Pond, via Monahan Road to Kennedy Quay. A sophisticated tunnel-boring machine was adapted and enlarged to a 3.5-m diameter specifically for the Cork Main Drainage Scheme. The tunnel was wide enough to run a light rail system from the Atlantic Pond up to Kennedy Quay. Each day it transported the work crews to the cutting edge of the tunnel machine and removed spoil from the excavations. Two crews worked 24-hour shifts, five days a week, eight metres below ground level. During this time, a number of main roads remained open to traffic, and motorists and the general public were unaware that just eight metres below them the huge machine, a railway system and 20 personnel were hard at work.

With these systems in place, sewage now flows by gravity from the present main outfall points through a large trunk sewer to a site east of the Atlantic Pond. However, east of the Atlantic Pond, the main trunk sewer is at such a depth that gravity flow is not possible. At this site a large pumping station was constructed which pumps sewage to a substantial tank in Mahon, from where it is again conveyed using gravity to the treatment plant site at Carrigrenan. Using gravity as much as possible to convey the sewage gives considerable savings. The annual pumping cost of the scheme is one million euro.

Dredging was necessary to allow the laying of twin 1.2-m pipes across Lough Mahon to the treatment plant site at Little Island. The large pipes were 450 m long and were manufactured in Norway and then towed behind tugs to Verholme Dockyard, where they were prepared for deployment on the seabed of the harbour. The pipe lengths ensured that a minimum number of joints had to be made and allowed the port of Cork to function without interruption. Other existing drainage schemes had to be connected to the new system. Rising mains have been constructed along the old Passage railway line from both the

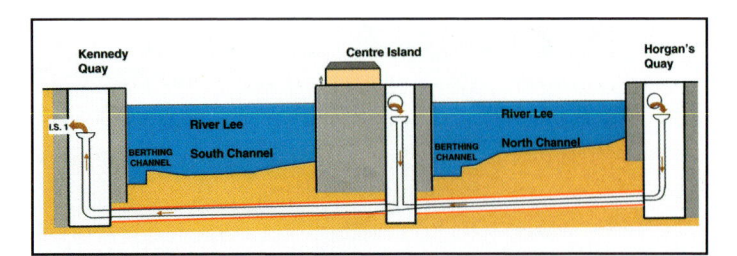

Fig. 5.26 To ensure the effective conveyance of the city's sewage to the new treatment plant via the Atlantic Pond Pumping Station, a siphon was constructed underneath the Lee. This structure connected Interceptor Sewer No. 4 on the North Bank to Interceptor Sewer No.1 on the south bank. The centre island drainage is linked to the siphon via a deep shaft at the tip of Custom House Quay.

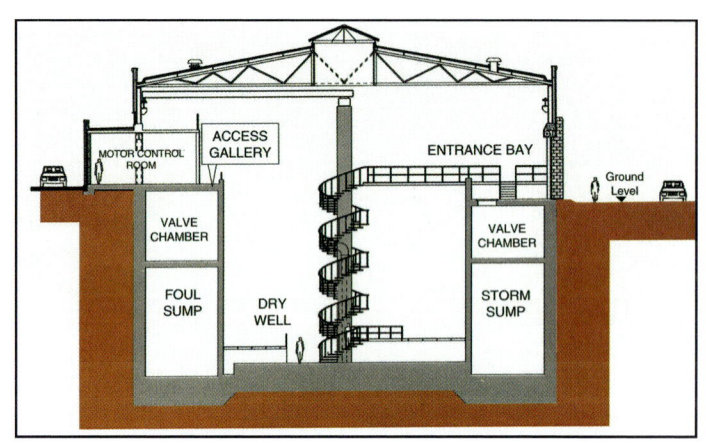

Fig. 5.27 The Atlantic Pond Pumping Station is a circular structure that extends eighteen metres below ground. Designed by consulting engineers E.G. Pettit, the flows in the pumping station are divided into two separate routes, which facilitate effective maintenance whilst ensuring a maximum rate of flow of 2.45 m^3 per second.

Fig. 5.28 The treatment plant at Carrigrenan, Little Island, will be extensively landscaped, planted with seventeen hectares of public parkland and developed into a coastal amenity. (Photo: Tomás Tyner.)

Fig. 5.29 At the heart of the city, the waters of the Lee are central to the city's identity. (Photo: Ralf Kleemann.) 'Some days after school, Connors and I went for a walk down the Marina. We climbed on the quay wall and begged pesetas, drachmas and French francs from the crews of foreign ships. We could see the world from there. The ghosts of corn and timber sails. The flags of nations we would long to visit. The gulls circling over Sweden and Finland, Russia and Scandinavia, and beyond to Egypt where the pyramids stood as a monument to vanity and the death of kings. We played hide and seek between the jetties. Dived naked from the slipway steps. Swam in the dull grey waters of the Lee. And then lay on the grass beside Dunlop's and Ford's to dry out under the rays of the afternoon sun' (Patrick Galvin, *Song for a poor boy*, Dublin, 2002, p. 44).

Atlantic Pond and the Rochestown Road pumping stations. The County Council's main pumping station at Ronayne's Court (Rochestown) was modified to pump across the Tramore River to link with the city's drainage system. A central collection chamber was constructed at Mahon to collect flows from these and other smaller pumping stations. Additional sewers were laid on Little Island to collect discharges from outfall points there and bring them to the treatment plant.

A modern, clean, technologically advanced treatment plant has been constructed at Carrigrenan (Little Island) with an outfall pipeline to Marina Point. The treatment plant was constructed through a contractual arrangement known as 'design, build and operate' and will be managed by Ondeo Degrémont for a 20-year period. Using some of the most advanced wastewater technology, the plant now treats, to a very high quality, domestic and industrial wastewater from the city, the Tramore Valley, Little Island, Glounthaune and Glanmire. Special odour control measures will be undertaken: the main sedimentation tanks are covered whilst other plant processes (screening, grit and grease removal and a sludge treatment area) are enclosed in buildings. Sludge is reduced to an odour-free, pasteurised, dry granular material. It is bagged at the plant and is very

Fig. 5.30A The Lee Swim was an annual event in the city for most of the last century. Because of the poor quality of the water in the river, it was abandoned in the early 1990s. The event is now being revived as a result of the improved water quality. (Photo: *Irish Examiner*.)

turning basin area at Horgan's Quay. An urban beach in the Blackrock–Mahon area is now also a possibility. In time there will be an increase in the numbers and species of wildlife in the estuary. The completed Main Drainage Scheme will be a positive factor in encouraging industrial and commercial growth in Cork city. In facilitating urban shoreline restoration, it returns Cork to the water, to the river and to nature.

suitable as a fertiliser and soil conditioner and is currently distributed under strict conditions laid down by the Environmental Protection Agency. The plant caters for 400,000 people, with industrial flows constituting 50 per cent of the total volume treated.

THE RESTORATION OF THE RIVER

The engineering of the river channels and the construction of drainage schemes have shaped the city's development. From public health, environmental, visual and aesthetic perspectives, the Cork Main Drainage Scheme has been amongst the most significant projects ever undertaken by Cork City Council. The effects on the environment are noticeably positive. Water quality in the city's river channels, Lough Mahon and the estuary generally, all of which were grossly polluted in the past, have now reached EU bathing standards, as water being discharged into Cork harbour is clean enough for swimming. The improved water quality will lead to increased usage of the river and the estuary for recreational activities. The river's new future is vital to the city's post-industrial regeneration.

The restoration of the river will also help in transforming Cork's docklands into a new urban quarter adjoining the city, bringing the area into the heart of the city's commercial, leisure and residential life. The development of four kilometres of riverside walks is proposed and new boardwalk areas are already in place at Lapp's and Horgan's Quay. The development of a marina near the R.H. Hall building is under consideration, as well as new moorings for small craft in the

Fig. 5.30B Brian O'Keeffe and Dave Heffernan of Lee Rowing Club on the river, Christmas morning 2003. (Photo: Denis Minihane, *Irish Examiner*.)

CONTEMPORARY • TRANSFORMATIONS

Cork Harbour and the Challenge of Change

Valerie Cummins and Vicki O'Donnell

THE MARINE GEOGRAPHY OF CORK HARBOUR

Cork harbour continues to shape the lives of the people of Cork city and of the surrounding towns and villages, such as Blackrock, Cobh, Monkstown, Passage West, Whitegate and Aghada. The topography of the landscape is gently undulating, with a diverse coastal environment consisting of built infrastructure, shallow cliffs, inter-tidal mudflats, reed-beds, shingle and rocky foreshores exposed by the tide. The bathymetry of the harbour reflects the morphology of the coastline, with gentle slopes dropping to a water depth of 28 m near the mouth of the harbour. A sheltered environment and deepwater channels make the harbour an ideal location for shipping and boating activities. Its physical geography provides the port of Cork with a strategic location, situated in close proximity to the main shipping lanes to northern Europe. More recently, the harbour has become a primary destination for cruise liners, which berth in the heritage town of Cobh, with its poignant history linking it with the Great Famine and the ill-fated *Titanic*. From an industrial perspective, Cork harbour offers employment in the chemical and pharmaceutical industries that are concentrated mainly in the Little Island and Ringaskiddy areas. The harbour also contains Ireland's only oil refinery, situated at Whitegate. The presence of gas

Fig. 5.31 An aerial view of Cork harbour showing the eastern edge of the city centre, top left, Haulbowline and Spike Islands in the centre and Roche's Point at the mouth of the harbour. (Source: Ordnance Survey Ireland.)

Fig. 5.32 The colourful townscape of Cobh, last port of call to the *Titanic* and home to tourism, fishing and sailing. (Photo: Tomás Tyner.)

fields, almost 50 km off the Old Head of Kinsale, has resulted in the location of many exploration companies in the harbour over the last 30 years, including Conocco Philips, Shell and Marathon. More recently, the port of Cork has been servicing the new Seven Heads gas field located in the Celtic Sea. Gas from the Seven Heads, to be brought ashore at Inch Terminal near the entrance to Cork harbour, will supply ten per cent of Ireland's current gas demand.

While the harbour is marked by concentrations of urban populations and widespread chemical and pharmaceutical industries, much of the coast remains unspoilt and is characterised by rural agricultural land use or protected habitats, which remain less influenced by human activities. A tour around the harbour reveals a whole suite of interesting man-made and natural features, influenced by history and the harbour's link to the sea. Landmarks include Camden Fort (renamed Fort Meagher in 1938) on the west side of the harbour entrance, flanked by Carlisle Fort (renamed Fort Davis in 1838) on the east side. These forts, along with installations on Haulbowline Island, Spike Island, Rocky Island and Fort Templebreedy present an insight into the British military presence that shaped the harbour until the British Royal Navy finally withdrew in 1938. Haulbowline Island is now the home of the Irish Naval Service.

For natural history enthusiasts, the entire harbour is of major international importance for waders (20,000) and wildfowl (5,000). Winter migrants are supported by its extensive mudflat areas around Lough Mahon, the Douglas estuary and the north channel, Lough Beg, Saleen, Rostellan and Whitegate. The harbour hosts the largest number of wintering birds in any area on the east and south-east coasts of Ireland. It is designated for this reason as both a special protection area for birds and a Ramsar site of international importance. Other designations protect the important habitats of salt marsh, reed-bed and intertidal mudflat. The designation 'natural heritage area' has been proposed for Douglas estuary, Great Island channel, Lough Beg, Rostellan Lough/Aghada Shore/Poulnabibe inlet, Whitegate Bay and Cuskinny Marsh. The Great Island channel has been mooted as a candidate for a special area of conservation. The Lee is also designated as a salmon river under the EU Freshwater Fish Directive. This implies an obligation to maintain specific water quality standards and to control pollution in this area. Protected fauna include the otter (*Lutra lutra*), the grey seal (*Halichoerus grypus*) and the common seal (*Phoca vitulina*). Cetaceans

Fig. 5.33 A naval service guard of honour at Haulbowline Naval Base, Cobh. (Photo: Mick Mackey.)

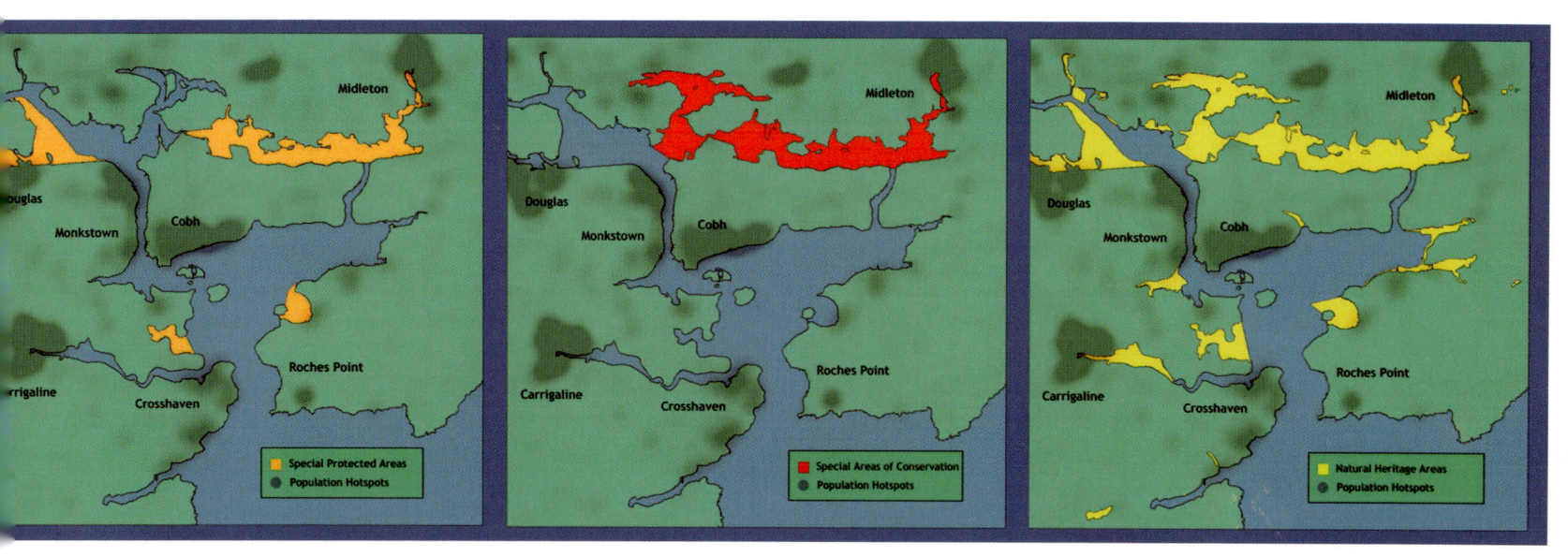

Fig. 5.34 Designated habitats, wildlife protection areas and special areas of conservation in Cork harbour. The darker areas show population hotspots in relation to the areas that are protected.

such as common dolphins (*Delphinus delphina*) and bottlenose dolphins (*Tursiops truncatus*) are occasionally sighted in the harbour. In the summer of 2001, the arrival of a pod of three orca whales (*Orcinus orca*) in Cork harbour attracted considerable attention from local spectators and the national media.

Fishing resources include angling for salmon, trout, coarse fish, sea fish and oyster and there are commercial salmon and eel fisheries. The harbour waters supply important spawning and nursery areas for sea fish species. Draft netting operations are located in areas traditionally known for their salmon movement, the main salmon- and trout-bearing rivers being the Owenacurra, the Glashboy, the Lee and the Owenabue. The coastal scenery around much of Great Island, including Fota, provides scope for many other recreational activities centred in the lower harbour, such as sailing, walking and golfing. The general trend towards increased expenditure on leisure activities within Europe can be seen in the significant growth in the number of recreational boats, with increases in the number of moorings at popular havens such as Crosshaven, Monkstown and Aghada. Cork Week, which is held in Crosshaven every second summer, is one of the most significant sailing regattas in European waters and has a reputation as a world-class sailing event.

Human influences

Pressures which influence the condition of Cork harbour stem largely from human activities such as coastal development, including waste disposal, agriculture, increasing recreational use, transport and over-exploitation of natural resources such as fisheries. Utilising satellite imagery, loss of natural habitat over time can be evaluated to determine the level of degradation of resources from these influences. Two-thirds of the shoreline is dominated by man-made structures such as sea walls and rock reinforcements, many in a state of disrepair and inadequate for current coastal defence needs. One of the most visible indicators of environmental quality within the harbour is water quality, which is threatened by nutrient-loading of phosphorous and nitrogen from agricultural run-off, sewage and industrial discharges. Excessive nutrient-loading from the Lee is an ongoing problem, especially in spring and summer, leading to algal blooms, which can have detrimental effects on the condition of fish stocks. The water quality of the upper harbour region has improved following the completion of the Cork Main Drainage Scheme. Nevertheless, threats to water quality remain and careful regulation is needed to control effluents from local industries. The potential for conflict between the different plans for the harbour is epitomised by the building of a hazardous waste incinerator at Ringaskiddy. Many residents feel that the location of such a facility conflicts with plans to embrace the redevelopment and restoration of the lower harbour as an outstanding natural amenity. Implementation of this vision has commenced with the location of the new National Maritime College at Ringaskiddy, which emphasises the importance of the lower harbour as a hub of maritime expertise and activity. Further planning challenges exist with the recent closure of ISPAT (formerly Irish Steel) at Ringaskiddy and Irish Fertiliser Industry at Marino Point. The remediation and future treatment of these brown-field sites has the potential to influence the future character of the lower-harbour area.

Fig. 5.35 Crosshaven, home of the Royal Cork Yacht Club, founded in 1720, the oldest sailing club in the world. (Source: Ordnance Survey Ireland.)

THE CHALLENGE OF CHANGE

The coastal ecosystem of the harbour is highly productive, containing a rich abundance of natural resources. The harbour also supports a diverse array of related industries, including pharmaceuticals, tourism and shipping, which provide enormous economic productivity. However, urbanisation, agricultural and industrial developments have reduced the biological diversity and cultural distinctness of the coastal landscape. Development pressures, particularly from housing and industry, have resulted in the loss of natural habitats along the shoreline and a deterioration in the quality of the coastal environment. Intensive use of

TABLE: SEASONAL VISITORS TO CORK HARBOUR SPECIAL PROTECTION AREAS (SPAS) AND RAMSAR SITES.

SEASON	BIRD SPECIES
All year	Mute Swan, Mallard, Oystercatcher, Curlew, Kingfisher
Winter	Slavonian Grebe, Black-necked Grebe, Little Egret, Berwick's Swan, Whooper Swan, Canada Goose (feral), Wigeon, Gadwall, Teal, Pintail, Shoveler, Pochard, Tufted Duck, Scaup, Goldeneye, Red-breasted Merganser, Golden Plover, Lapwing, Black-tailed Godwit, Bar-tailed Godwit, Mediterranean Gull, possible Glaucous Gull.
Spring	Whimbrel, terns.
Summer	Breeding Ringed Plover, Common Tern.
Autumn	Passage waders, including possible Little Stint, Curlew, Sandpiper, Ruff, Spotted Redshank, Green Sandpiper, Wood Sandpiper, Common Sandpiper. Migrating terns.

CONTEMPORARY • TRANSFORMATIONS

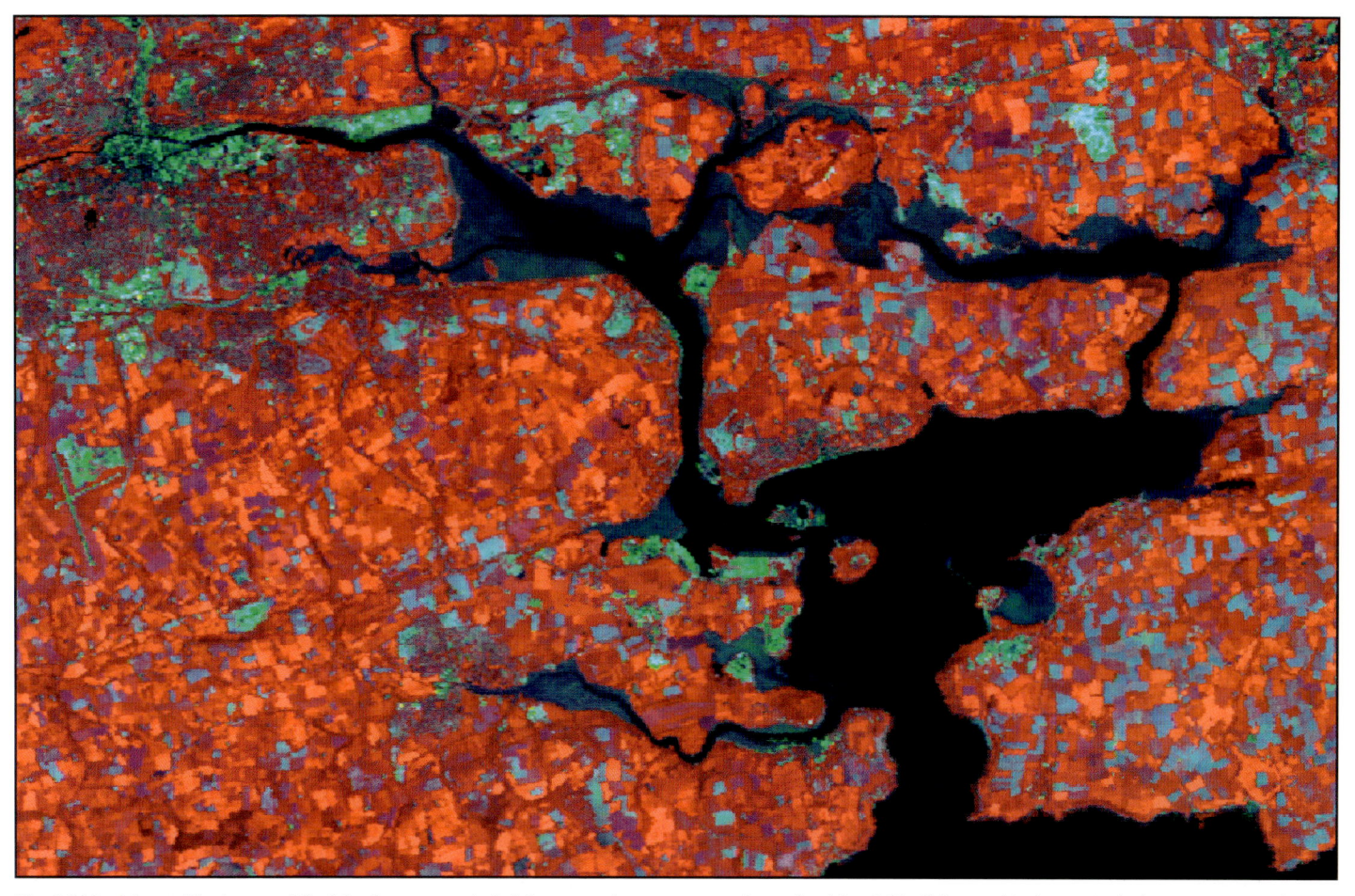

Fig. 5.36 In this satellite image of Cork harbour, areas in bright green show concentrations of residential building and industry, including quarries and Cork Airport. Areas in red represent vegetation, predominantly farming areas. (Photo: Fucino Matera, Eurimage.)

coastal resources by different user groups and the need to reconcile the demands of economic development with environmental protection have caused conflict among the stakeholders living and working around the harbour. The dynamic nature of both human and natural influences on the harbour will ensure that its social, economic and physical fabric will be subject to change. As a result, Corkonians of the twenty-first century will face ongoing challenges to ensure the sustainable development of this marvellous harbour on the doorstep of the city.

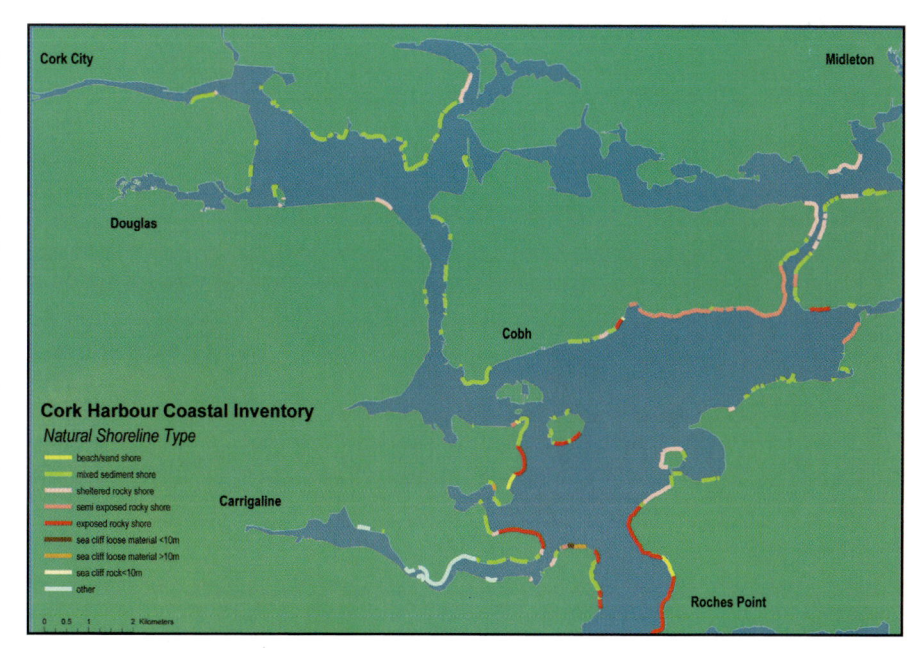

Fig. 5.37 The natural shoreline is predominantly composed of mixed sediment or rocky sections. The western areas of the harbour are more developed than the east and the shoreline here is predominantly made up of sea walls and rock reinforcements.

34. LIVING IN THE CITY

Kieran Keohane and Cathal O'Connell

Anyone viewing Cork today would be impressed by the vibrancy with which the city is being renewed. The skyline is crowded with towering cranes. Streets are in a perpetual state of renovation. The city's built environment is being demolished, refurbished and renewed. Former industrial areas are being revamped as residential and commercial developments, older inner-city houses are being replaced by high-rise apartments and the green hills for which Cork has long been famous are engulfed by the affluent suburban tides of an expanding city. All cities are in a state of perpetual change and transformation and Cork is no different.

CITIZENS, CITY AND THE HOME

The rich diversity of housing styles in Cork, from the substantial villas of Montenotte to the elegant Victorian terraces of Sunday's Well, from model artisan cottages to modern suburban estates, have their foundations in broad historical developments. The revolutions of the late eighteenth century established the ideals of liberal democracy and the democratic republic. The modern liberal democratic republic was premised on the principle of equality of all citizens through political and civil rights. The subsequent development of the nation state through the nineteenth and twentieth centuries entailed the extension of these ideals. On the one hand, the idea of citizenship was expanded from the original 'man of property' to include all men and women, rich and poor. The ideal of equality was elaborated in terms of entitlement to public services in the form of social security, education, health care and housing. These elements came to be defined as the rights of individual citizens and the reciprocal duties of society mediated through the state. Such rights of citizenship reach their apex in the welfare state of the mid-twentieth century.[1]

For the two centuries since the French Revolution, housing has been an integral part of the European city and the liberal idea of European citizenship. Private life in the home complemented the public life of the citizen. The mutually reinforcing relationship between public and private, the home and the *polis*, generated the values that have been integral to modern European civilisation. In the nineteenth century, citizenship was enjoyed by a relatively small number of private-property owners, while the great mass of the population was excluded from the benefits, rights and social status it bestowed. A broadening and deepening of democratic values has been premised on the importance of the house and home in cultivating citizenship.[2] A decent house conferred an identity on the citizen. The householder as a sovereign individual, tied to a particular location, enjoyed dignity through rights that he shared with all other citizens, regardless of wealth or status.

From the late nineteenth century and for most of the twentieth century, European society has seen housing, and thereby full citizenship, become increasingly available on a mass basis, both through private ownership and public housing.[3] However, at the turn of the twenty-first century, the private developer and market emerged as key providers of housing needs, to the detriment of social housing and the appearance of a residual population in that sector. In Cork, this trajectory of progress, exemplified through housing provision, is becoming inverted. In this inversion the patterns of the nineteenth century re-emerge. Once the gated enclave of private houses represented the restricted range of citizenship as rights and privileges enjoyed by middle-class owners of private property. Now the contemporary gated enclave symbolises the exclusivity of citizenship enjoyed by a majority. Meanwhile, a substantial minority have become socially excluded. This trend has profound implications for our vision of the city and our ideas of citizenship and democracy.

PROSPERITY AND PHILANTHROPY

Cork was a boomtown in the late eighteenth and early nineteenth centuries. Great prosperity was generated through the provisions trade, which generated a wealthy powerful local élite, the so-called 'merchant princes'. They gradually moved from their town houses, which were also business premises, in the city centre to the fashionable new suburbs of Montenotte and Sunday's Well. Meanwhile, the city centre was occupied by the labouring classes and the poor, who inhabited the tenemented former town houses as well as overcrowded makeshift dwellings in unplanned housing districts such as the infamous back lanes of Blackpool, Barrack Street and The Marsh. A crisis arose in the mid-nineteenth century when economic decline following the Act of Union coincided with the arrival of thousands of destitute paupers fleeing famine conditions in rural areas. This new population congregated in the already poor, unsanitary and overcrowded quarters of the labouring classes. Cork's pauper population trebled in the decade of the Great Famine.[4] This change placed immense pressure on the existing infrastructure of relief and public health.

These problems of poverty, squalor and associated crime and delinquency, persisted after the immediate crisis of the Famine had passed; unable to emigrate or return to rural districts, the dispossessed population became embedded in the city. This new urban pauperism confronted the city with a challenge which was met by the development of new systems of governance, legislation and social scientific responses to poverty. This new mode of intervention was typified by the model-housing schemes for the working classes, of which Cork boasts several fine examples.

Model dwellings represented the coming together of a diversity of interests whose common goal was the improvement of the city by improving the life of its citizens. Business sought a more productive and contented workforce; merchants were interested in consolidating a more stable and affluent consumer base; public health and municipal authorities desired to eliminate disease and crime through hygiene and public-order initiatives, while philanthropic bodies cultivated the virtues of sobriety, industry and thrift. For the ordinary masses, the model-housing schemes acted as aspirational horizons of respectability and upward social mobility. A classic example of this development is represented by the model schemes around Barrack Street and South Gate Bridge, an area long synonymous with deprivation and urban squalor that had become an unplanned shanty town in the decades following the Famine.

The names of these schemes express the secular and religious values underpinning the improvement: Prosperity Square, Industry Street, Evergreen Road and St Kevin's Road. They constituted the prototypes of public-housing schemes which subsequently developed during the twentieth century. These model schemes became islands of civility in the wider context of urban squalor. They were specifically intended to be occupied by a model population, 'who were to be of good character for sobriety, honesty and cleanliness, who worked for their bread for as long as they were able and could obtain work'.[5]

Prosperity Square, originally a gated enclosure constructed behind a high perimeter wall with a controlled entrance, was organised on the principle of self-management by the tenants themselves. The gated enclave marked an 'exclusive development', physically and symbolically differentiated from its surroundings. This

Fig. 5.38 Prosperity Square. (Photo: Denis Linehan.)

mirrored a feature of middle-class and upper-class life in the better-off districts and suburbs of the city, which were also gated. This reflected the segregation of the city according to distinct social classes: the mercantile and industrial élite in suburban villas, the middle and professional classes in residential enclaves and elegant terraces, the respectable working class in model houses and the impoverished masses in tenements and slums.

THE UTOPIAN IDEAL

By the turn of the century, the institutions of both the municipal authorities at a local level and the nation state were beginning to merge. Philanthropic and local efforts to alleviate poverty had a limited range and catered for a very restricted population, in many cases not extending beyond the workers of particular enterprises. A large-scale intervention was needed and could only be achieved through the aegis of the state. This marked a departure from the nineteenth-century economic ideal of *laissez-faire* to a planned interventionist mode of governance based on taxation, redistribution and management of market forces. The utopian ideal of the welfare state held that the modern democratic republic should constitute a collective home for all of its citizens. This process was part of a broader development in modern European societies reflecting the consensus of capital and labour mediated by the state. The welfare state was based on collective responsibility for meeting fundamental needs. Health, education, social security and, crucially in the present context, housing would be met through income redistribution and programmes of public provision subsidised by tax revenues.[6]

How was this general development manifested in the specific landscape of Cork city? The most striking feature was the clearance of the slums and the relocation of the inner-city population to new estates built on green-field sites outside the city from the early 1930s: Turner's Cross, Ballyphehane, Gurranabraher, Churchfield, Fair Hill, Knocknaheeney, Togher, Mayfield and Mahon. These new estates represented the culmination of the ideals of social democracy and nation-building enshrined in the welfare state, and spanned a period from the 1930s to the mid-1970s, when there was broad political consensus and public support for collective responsibility for achieving a just society. Public policy explicitly endorsed and subsidised the ideal of private ownership for the middle classes through a variety of direct and indirect measures, including first-time buyers' grants, mortgage interest relief, the abolition of local authority rates on domestic dwellings and low property taxes. The consequence was that, as public-sector house-building grew, it was surpassed by heavily subsidised private development. In Cork, neighbourhoods in Bishopstown, Model Farm Road, Douglas and Rochestown belong to this era.

In some ways, the utopian ideals of nineteenth-century model housing were incorporated into the welfare state's aspiration of social improvement. The old slums were demolished and whole communities reconstituted in mass housing estates, which were modern and rational in design and layout. However, three important differences distinguish the welfare era from the nineteenth-century age of improvement. Originally, the model houses were accessible only to a select clientele who fulfilled the strict criteria of moral propriety. In contrast, the primary criterion of mass housing was need, verifiable by the official means test. Secondly, whereas the model houses were intended to be self-managed by the residents themselves, the new public

Fig. 5.39 An aerial view of the city from the 1940s. (Photo: Aerofilm.)

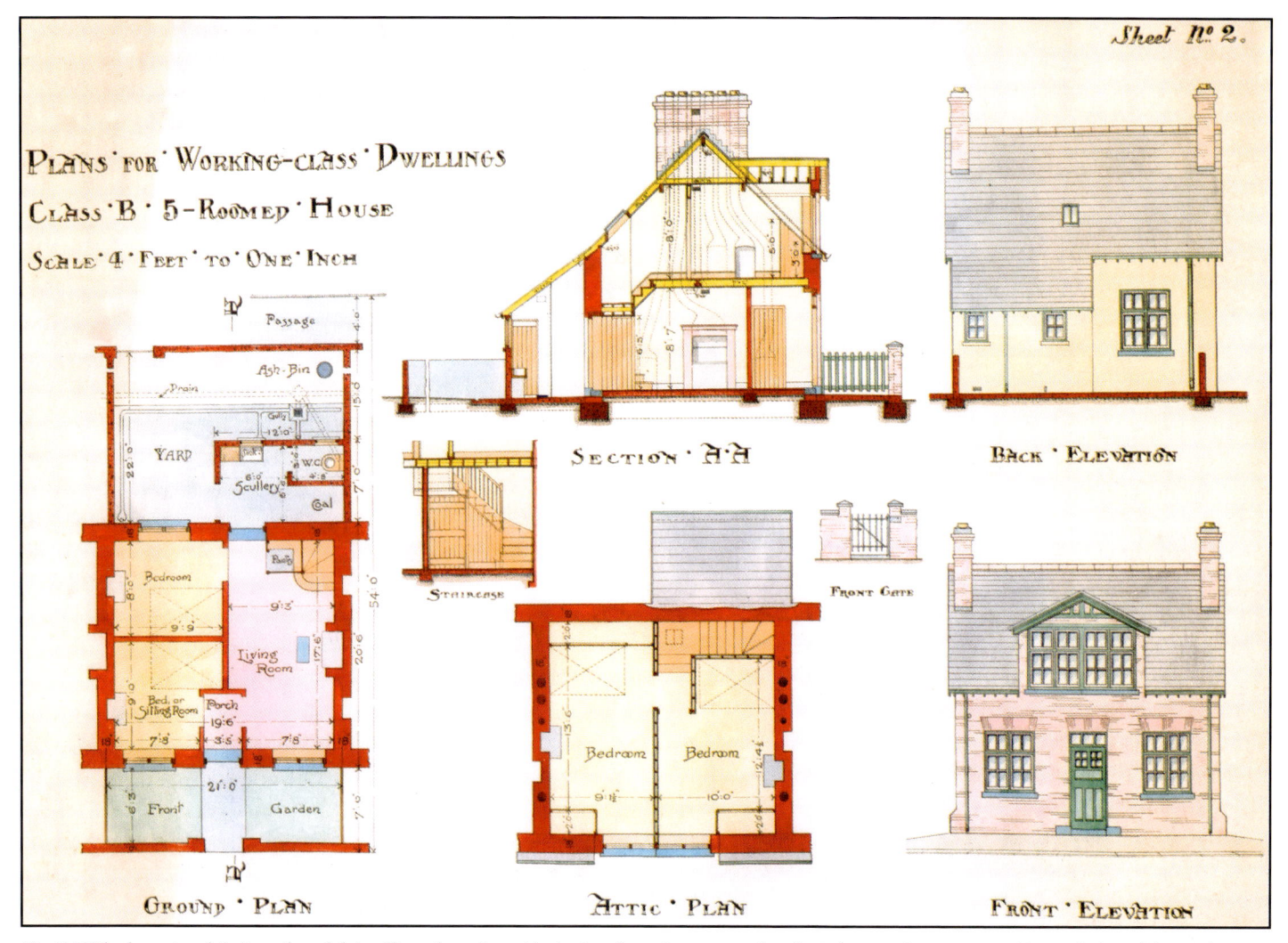

Fig. 5.40 The layout and design of model dwellings from the mid-nineteenth century onwards reflected a growing concern with regulation of domestic space and household behaviour through separation of living and sleeping areas and segregation of the sexes. Underpinning such practices were expectations of respectability through emphasis upon traits such as sobriety, thrift and the work ethic.

housing was centrally managed by a corporation bureaucracy. Third, the model-housing schemes were required to be profitable, where working tenants paid an economic rent. The mass-housing schemes of the welfare state were subsidised from general tax revenues as part of a broader strategy of income redistribution.

Crisis and transition

The welfare state programmes, especially capital-intensive provisions such as housing, required sustained expenditure of public revenue funded by taxation or borrowing. The transformed political and economic landscape was characterised by global economic recession, the end of the old industries and the emergence of political philosophies that rejected the commitment to a social contract based on tax-funded public provision. In Cork, this watershed was marked by the closure of Ford, Dunlop, the Verholme Shipyard and other mainstays of the local economy. Such events had catastrophic consequences for the working-class neighbourhoods of the city. The historical division of the city along a north–south axis was exacerbated by this economic restructuring. Stark social divisions have been reproduced since the nineteenth century, wherein middle-class residential developments and their associated amenities – schools, hospitals, and recreational facilities – have been located predominantly on the southside. The northside has experienced deepening neglect and disadvantage. Under-investment has had chronic implications for disadvantaged communities, whereas resourcing for middle-class neighbourhoods has not been similarly affected.

Gated enclaves and the anti-social society

This pattern of contraction and disinvestment has contributed to new forms of differentiation and the corresponding forms

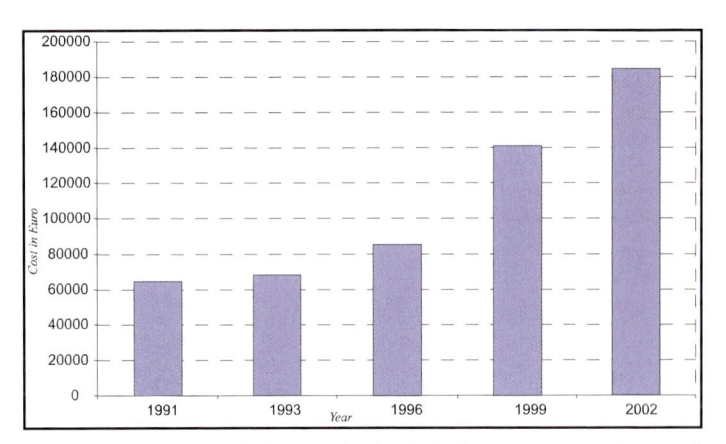

Fig. 5.41 In common with the rest of Ireland, Cork city experienced a period of sustained house price inflation throughout the 1990s. Price rises were moderate in the first part of the decade, but the rate of increase intensified from 1996. In that year, the average price of a house in the city was in the region of €80,000. Three years later, the average price had risen to over €140,000, an increase of 75 per cent. Price increases have persisted in the early years of the new millennium, with a growth of 15 per cent, from €184,369 to €211,980, between 2002 and 2003 being recorded.

AVERAGE NEW HOUSE PRICE IN CORK CITY

Contemporary housing represents an inversion of the relations of social exclusion, as well as the emergence of a new geography that erodes community. This is represented in Cork by the proliferation of privately developed apartment complexes, often underpinned by generous urban-renewal incentives, substantially outpacing social-housing provision. These apartment developments typically fall into two categories: first, a relatively small number of high-end developments aimed at young urban professionals; and second, the dominant, intensively developed, form of standard apartments owned and rented by private investors. The tenants of this latter form constitute a diverse population. Some are transient, such as students and young workers. For others, these apartments of housing that have emerged since the 1990s.[7] Essentially, this has entailed an inversion of the pattern of spatial organisation represented by the gated enclave of the nineteenth century. In the nineteenth century, the gated enclave was an island of civilised society set against a socially excluded mass of poverty and pauperism. The gated enclave was the exception: now it has become the rule. At the beginning of the twenty-first century, the poor are a residual minority experiencing chronic and multiple exclusion, whereas the majority aspire to private home ownership and the security represented by a house in an 'exclusive development'. The twenty-first-century equivalent of the gate takes many forms, both material and symbolic. The security key pad replaces the Victorian superintendent. The moral criteria of private home ownership, thrift, sobriety and diligence, continue to be the implicit mortgage-lending criteria and characterise the life practices of borrowers. However, the ultimate arbiter of social exclusiveness is still the price: within the reach of many, but an impossible ideal for others.

The new pre-eminence of price as the determinant of access to home ownership represents the eclipse of the ideal of the welfare state as a 'collective home' and the exposure of citizens to the vicissitudes of the market. The inversion represented by the gated enclave is a reflection of this more general inversion of political ideals. Now the state withdraws from its redistributive responsibility and increasingly assumes a managerial function directed at the residual population, while the private individual becomes responsible for his or her own welfare.

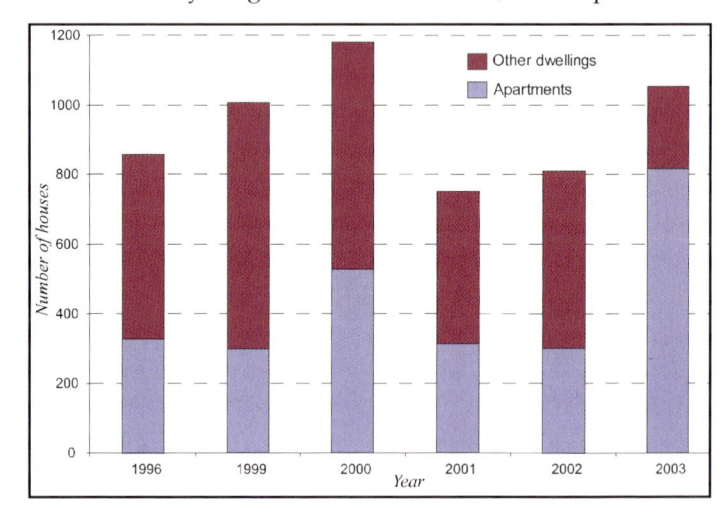

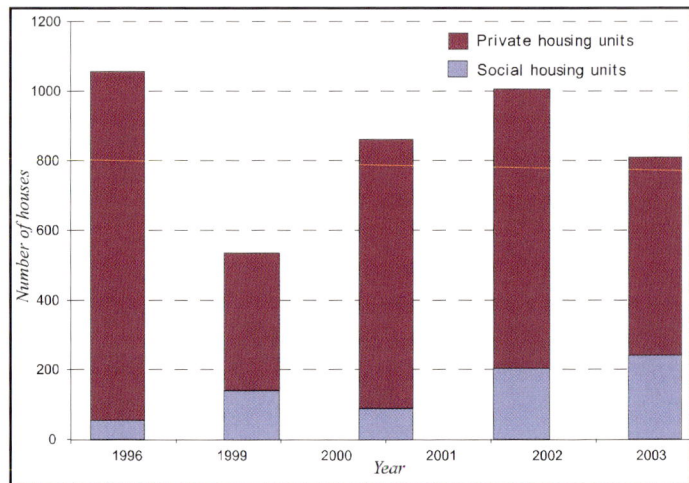

Figs. 5.42 and 5.43 There has been a major shift in the type of dwelling constructed in Cork city within the past five to six years. This reflects the effects of the changing nature of household formation trends, consumption and lifestyle patterns, and state-subsidised urban-renewal incentives on offer to developers. In 1996, of the total number of units constructed, 327, or 38 per cent, were apartments. By 2003, apartments accounted for over 77 per cent of the total residential output in the city. This trend is likely to persist, with schemes such as the Cork docklands coming on-stream at the upper end of the market and growing demand from households in receipt of supplementary welfare rent allowance at the lower end.

fulfil a de facto social-housing function, as they are home to welfare clients, single parents, immigrants, the unemployed and the working poor. Housing priorities and the social objectives that they represent are now inverted. Whereas previously the tenant occupied a subsidised home, now the private investor and landlord enjoy the social subsidy: namely, the initial urban-renewal incentive, tax write-offs and rent allowance paid by the state thereafter. The post-war welfare state in Ireland represented social democratic ideals, whereby responsibility for citizens' wellbeing embraced life 'from the cradle to the grave' through collective systems of wealth redistribution by the tax system. The terrain has radically shifted and, rather than regarding the ideal of home as shelter, some homes have become an anti-social tax shelter for the private investor.

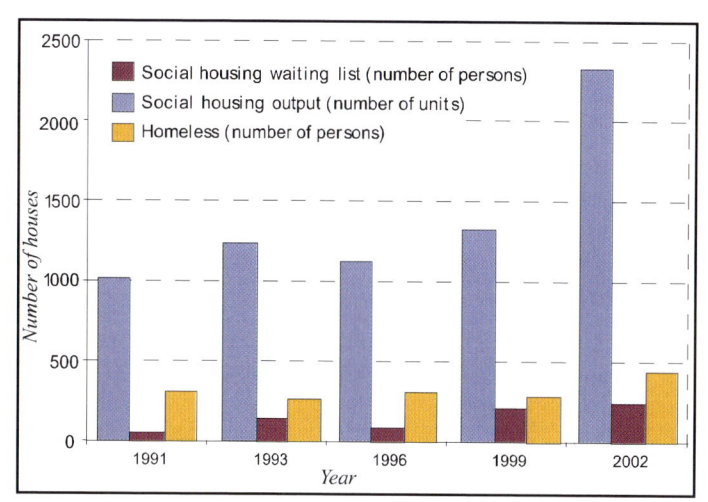

Fig. 5.46 The assessments of housing need undertaken for Cork since the beginning of the 1990s show a clear growth in demand for social housing. Whilst the construction of social housing has risen from 56 to 242 dwellings per annum over the decade, this has not kept pace with growing demand. The waiting list reached 2,282 households by the year 2002. Though Cork City Council provided a total of 1,598 dwellings between 1991 and 2002, it disposed of nearly half of these under the terms of the Tenant Purchase Scheme. As a proportion of overall new construction, social housing has been strongly overshadowed by private provision, which, in common with the rest of Ireland, has been experiencing a boom period over the past seven years. Meanwhile the problem of homelessness persists in the city and has risen from 250–300 persons during the 1990s to an estimated 439 by 2002.

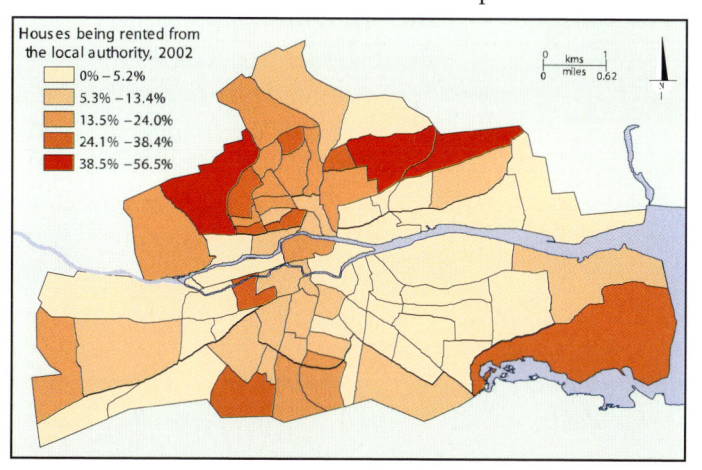

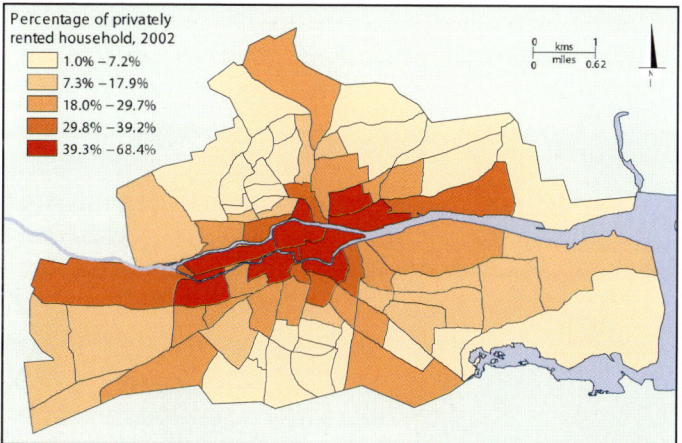

Figs. 5.44 and 5.45 In 2002 there were 5,950 permanent private households being rented from Cork City Council, which constituted 14 per cent of all households in the city. In addition, a further 18 per cent (7,830) of households were privately rented. Fig. 5.44 illustrates a clear concentration of dwellings rented from the local authority in three wards in the city: The Glen A, Mayfield and Knocknaheeny, where between 38 and 56 per cent of households were rented from the local authority. Mahon A and Togher A represent the areas with the greatest proportion of households rented from the local authority in the south of the city. The wards with the highest proportion of privately rented households are found in the city centre, moving out in a strip to the west and east. Between 39 and 68 per cent of households in these areas are privately rented. The outer areas of the city have some of the lowest proportions of privately rented accommodation.

However, the fundamental ideal underpinning our relationship with house and home is the universal human need for security. Shelter, privacy, comfort and domesticity are the elementary components of dwelling. The constellation of dwelling, security and citizenship are enshrined in the Constitution in terms of the right to privacy, which synthesises the relationship between the public person and the private householder. The inextricable links between these elements and their ensuing guarantees stand in stark contrast to the problem of homelessness and the extreme vulnerability intrinsic to that condition. Homelessness is the most extreme form of social exclusion and is tantamount to non-citizenship.

Affluence, unequally distributed, deepens the polarisation between the securely housed and others: the homeless, people in substandard accommodation, those on the social-housing waiting lists, tenants in an inflating rental market and people struggling to get their first foot on the property ladder. Ironically, the construction boom in Cork has been matched by unprecedented levels of housing failure. The predicament of the homeless, of renters and of others is not their failure. Rather, it is the logical outcome of public-policy choices that have systematically favoured wealth accumulation over the ideal of an inclusive society. In the neo-liberal economy, social relations are being recast in terms of consumer relations, and the gated enclave represents the emergence of an anti-social society.

Gated communities

The contemporary emphasis on the market and its attendant anxieties, amplified by the uncertainties of globalisation, have distorted our relations to house, home and sense of place.[8] The heightened anxiety of 'getting a foot on the property ladder' is symptomatic of an accentuated sense of insecurity.[9] The fundamental shift in the context of globalisation is that the forces impacting on the local are far removed from the reach of citizens, both rich and poor. Now, life chances are shaped by events on Wall Street and the World Bank and we are subject to insecurities generated by fluctuations in the global economy that can transform local fortunes overnight. However, as with wealth and property, risks are unevenly distributed. For some, private home ownership can give an exaggerated sense of security; historical experience shows that risks of such magnitude may be better absorbed socially but require political commitment and an adequate revenue base. The welfare state was predicated upon such an adequate revenue base managed by a sovereign nation state.[10] The conditions of globalisation wherein transnational corporations dictate national taxation policy, mean that that base is eroded.

The project of the private home began in the context of the insecurities associated with the emergence of modern society. The industrial revolution, urbanisation and the dissolution of traditional bonds of the extended family, the village and community life exposed modern people to conditions of dislocation. This experience was most acutely felt in the city and manifested as crime and anxiety about moral dissolution. Against this background, the nineteenth-century gated enclave emerged as a haven of security, privacy, comfort and domesticity. The social housing project of the welfare state in the twentieth century can be understood as a generalisation of this practice, and an extension of this model to mass society. In Ireland, as elsewhere, this entailed standard suburban developments. Despite the well-publicised problems of segments of the social-housing stock, families in solid, settled neighbourhoods, from Bishopstown to Ballyphehane, Blackrock to Knocknaheeney, share a common ideal in an uncertain world. People everywhere orient their home around the ideals of security and domesticity. Everyone tries to transform their house into the unique personal space that will be their home. Pride, self-respect and a sense of belonging to a common project are expressed through the everyday but life-affirming work of homemaking. The project of homemaking is universal, regardless of tenure, taste or disposable income. Herein lies the residual trace of our utopian aspiration for the security of family, home and neighbourhood. Cork's designation as European Capital of Culture offers an opportunity for city and citizens to rediscover the common utopian ideals, expressed through our habitat, that have sustained and given meaning to our civilisation.

Figs. 5.47 and 5.48 The gated community, or gated enclave, once a feature of upper-middle-class housing in the nineteenth century (above), has re-emerged in the late twentieth and early twenty-first centuries in Cork and other cities as a commonplace response to the perceived dangers of urban living. Many gated enclaves are now accompanied by a battery of security technologies, such as CCTV, electronic key pads and biometric devices to limit access to residents or authorised individuals.

CONTEMPORARY • TRANSFORMATIONS

35. URBAN DIFFERENCE

Denis Linehan

In celebrating Cork's achievements in sport, culture and economy, it is important not to neglect the social and economic differences that exist within the city and, in particular, the specific concentrations of wealth and poverty. Sales of million-euro homes and new cars may have recently peaked to an all-time high, but, of the 316 primary schools included nationally in the Department of Education's disadvantaged areas scheme, 31 are based in Cork city. Nine of the city's post-primary schools have been designated 'disadvantaged' and eleven of the state's 88 worst unemployment black spots are within the city boundaries. Side by side with economic growth and urban regeneration, a range of inequalities persist in the urban and social fabric of Cork. Over the last two decades, over a third of the population have lived in neighbourhoods experiencing high levels of deprivation.

There is a geography to this inequality that reflects distinctive aspects of development in Cork and also common features of urban Ireland. First, there is a concentration of social disadvantage in areas suffering from physical decline and disinvestment. Second, there are strong links between low educational achievement and low pay and unemployment. Third, these areas tend to have particular social characteristics, such as a high concentration of older people living alone and a higher proportion of one-parent families. In Cork, communities in the northern and south-eastern parts of the city are most at risk from the collective effects of these features. In these areas, most people live in social housing, there are higher levels of unemployment, a higher than average number of one-parent families, higher rates of disability and lower levels of educational achievement.

Urban deprivation

Cork has long been a city of haves and have-nots. Great wealth has lived cheek by jowl with shocking poverty, poor education, lack of amenities and unemployment. During the nineteenth-century, money and power ensured a divergence

Fig. 5.49 The northside is that part of Cork County Borough located north of the Lee. Spread over six square miles, the neighbourhoods include Blackpool, Ballyvolane, Churchfield, Fair Hill Gurranabraher, Hollyhill, Knocknaheeny, Mayfield, Montenotte, Shanakiel, Shandon and the Glen. Whilst 60 per cent of properties currently rented by the local authority are in the north-east and north-west of the city, the northside is not a homogenous area. A short journey from Knocknaheeny to Shanakiel, or from Mayfield to Montonotte, crosses over numerous boundaries of wealth and social class. (Photo: Tomás Tyner.)

in the quality of urban neighbourhoods. For every fine new house built in Sunday's Well or Blackrock, the tenements multiplied in the lanes of the inner city. The scale of early housing interventions by Cork Corporation did little to alter this pattern. In 1919, just before he was elected Lord Mayor of Cork, Tomás MacCurtain complained about the absence of a library and the long distance working people living in the Blackpool area, then one of the most densely populated districts in the city, had to walk to get to the city baths. The construction of new public-housing estates in the mid-twentieth century made a major improvement to the health and quality of life of Corporation tenants. Whilst some new dwellers in Churchfield, used to the vibrant streetlife of The Marsh, initially moved their living-rooms into first-floor bedrooms so they could keep an eye on the street, the gradual nature of the development and the geographical intimacy of the city ensured that the relocation did not undermine the community too much. It is not wholly correct to say that the new neighbourhoods developed at this time still represent the 'real' Cork, but communities in the social-housing areas both north and south of the river have ensured the continuation of valued traditions and rituals in the city that creeping globalisation has undermined.[1]

The social and geographical pattern established by 1970 maintains an important role in shaping the urban experience of Corkonians. These social patterns were consolidated in a wave of investment from the early 1970s, when the city's main public institutions located south of the Lee: the Cork Institute of Technology, the IDA Technology Park, the headquarters of FÁS, the ESB, Cork Gas Company, Cork University Hospital, and University College Cork.[2] These developments enhanced these localities and generated over 10,000 new jobs south of the river. In this period, the northside saw far fewer benefits from comparable public-sector investment. Cork Corporation had little funds available for investment in housing stock and maintenance of the local environment. There was a deficit in amenities and services, parkland and recreational facilities, which affected young people the most. In many areas teenagers lived in crowded houses, often lacking in space and privacy, in neighbourhoods with a dearth of recreational facilities. A gradual concentration of a population experiencing multiple forms of disadvantage in public housing became a feature of the city. It was apparent to community leaders that whole neighbourhoods had been planned without developing focal points for industry, employment and social services.

The legacy of such concentration of public housing without adequate services and sources of employment soon generated acute problems. At the beginning of the 1980s, the consequences of rising unemployment, widespread indus- trial closures and a shrinking national economy was reflected in a dramatic increase in inequality in the city. The live registrar of unemployment for the Greater Cork Area increased a massive 243 per cent in the four years up to January 1984. By March 1984, there were 15,583 unemployed people in the city.[3] The economic downturn affected the whole city, but the failures of the national and regional economy were most intensively felt in the working-class neighbourhoods. The employment opportunities for manual workers were devastated. In Gurranabraher, for instance, the census of 1986 reported that 40 per cent of the labour force was unemployed, and that was not even the highest area. In 1987, the average income of local-authority tenants was 38 per cent below the average income for urban areas. Chronic unemployment, poverty and emigration damaged community life. Real deprivation, in terms of diet, clothing, housing quality, environment and education, gripped many parts of the city. A study of Mayfield at that time described the widespread air of depression and despondency in the Roseville estate, where unemployment ran between 60 and

Fig. 5.50 Passing time and sharing news on the busy thoroughfare of Shandon Street. (Photo: Carol Hunter.)

70 per cent, three times the city average. The absence of industry or commercial development nearby denied the people local employment opportunities. 'Anything less than strict management of money produces poverty and deprivation in the family, while children's schoolbooks and clothes become a nightmare expense.'[4] Under such conditions the health of the population inevitably declined. Poor health among the families of the unemployed resulted in earlier mortality, more frequent hospitalisation and higher rates of drug dependency. Infants born into the lower socio-economic areas of Cork experienced higher relative risks of mortality in comparison with those born in the higher socio-economic areas elsewhere in the city.[5]

Employment and education

Unemployment had declined very significantly by 2002. In 1986 unemployment in the city was at 23 per cent. In 2002, it had almost halved to 12 per cent. The most significant decline happened after 1996, during the growth of the 'Celtic Tiger', when unemployment fell by 8 per cent. However, the decline has not been equal across the city. Higher levels of unemployment are still largely concentrated in the northside and in smaller geographical pockets in the southside neighbourhoods of Togher and Mahon. Whilst there has been a 15 per cent decrease in Fair Hill and Gurranabraher and a 22 per cent decrease in Knocknaheeny, the decline in unemployment in Mayfield was only 9 per cent, and in the Glen A it was only 7 per cent. The shadow of the crisis of the 1980s and early 1990s lingers on in terms of long-term unemployment, disability and poor rates of educational achievement. Unemployment also persists because of the strong relationship between higher rates of unemployment and the prevalence of manual skills among the labour force in these areas. The highest concentration of manual workers in the city is in the northwest wards. Many of these workers are male, which explains in some ways the higher citywide unemployment rate amongst men (14 per cent) over women (10 per cent) citywide. A closer look at the age and skill profiles of the populations here also illustrates that older men and women are at a disadvantage in finding employment. Between 1996 and 2002, unemployment amongst people aged from 45 to 65 rose from 26 to 30 per cent. This represents the highest increase amongst all the different population groups in the

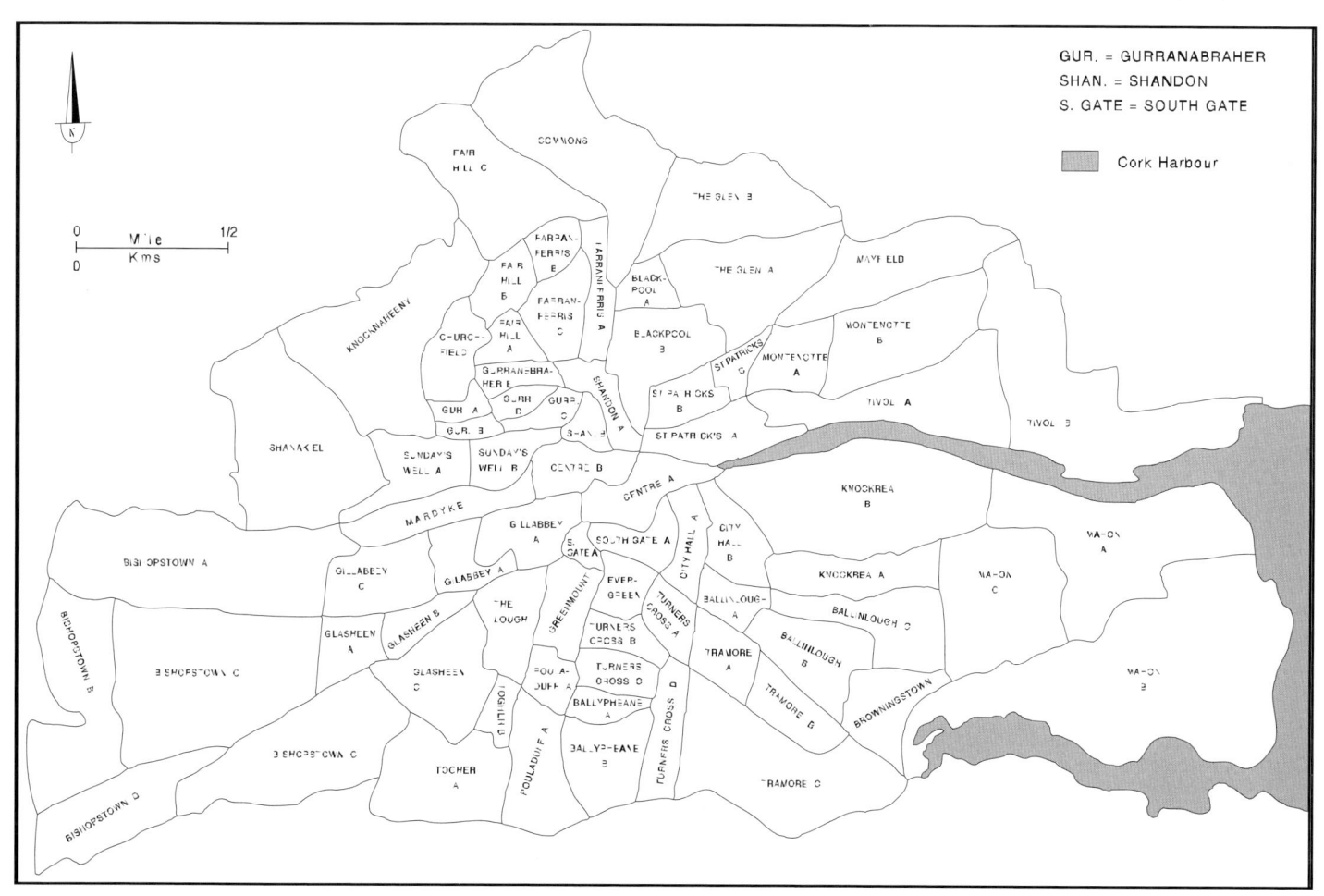

Fig. 5.51 The wards of Cork form the basis of the statistical enumeration of demographic, social and economic trends in the city.

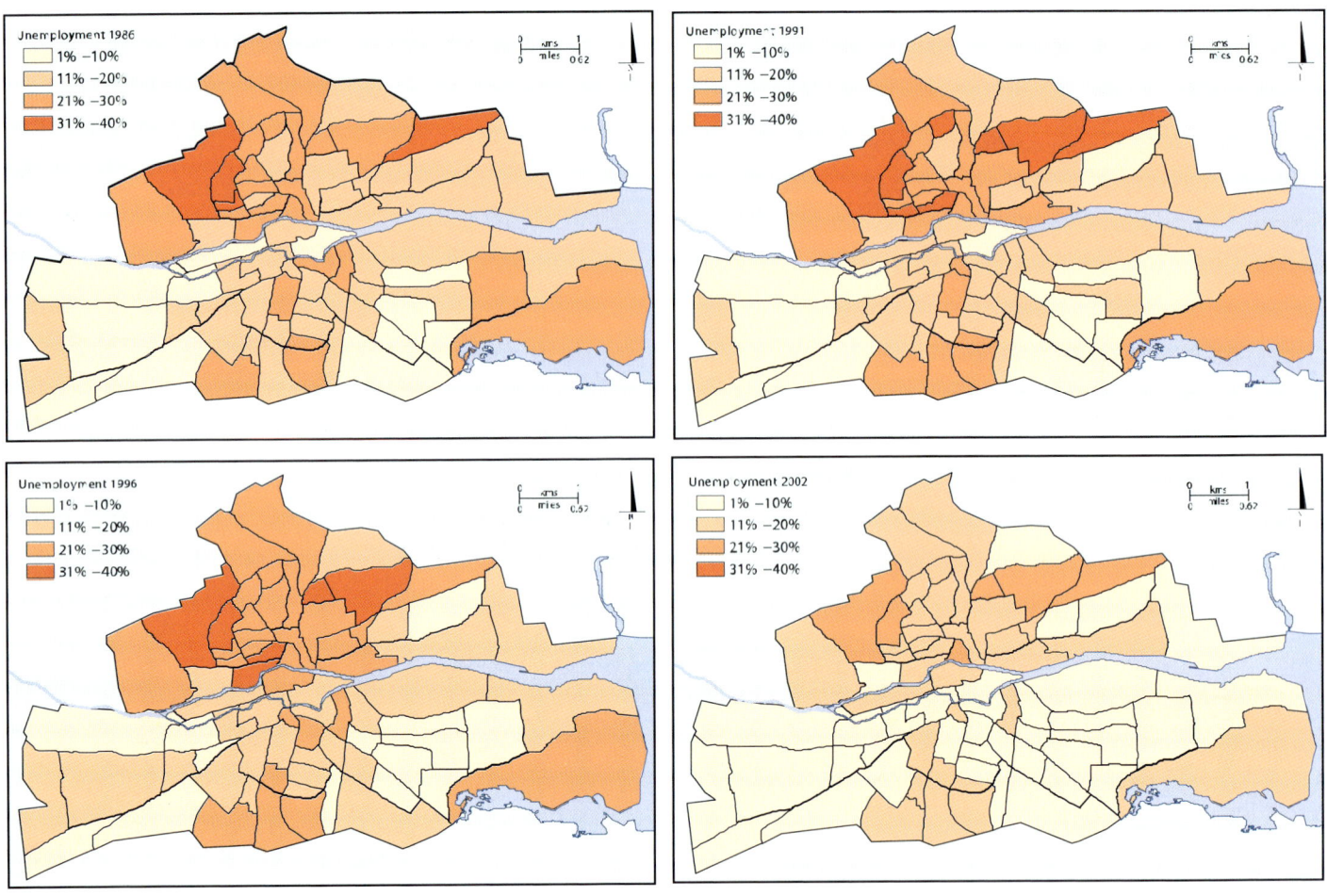

Fig. 5.52 Unemployment fell sharply between 1986 and 2002 but still remains concentrated in a number of neighbourhoods in the city.

city. Long-term unemployment for this age group seems to have solidified and there is a widespread feeling that they have been left behind by the new economy.

It is clear also that certain areas of Cork have higher proportions of people who cannot work due to disability. In the north-west of the city, over 25 per cent of those who are not in the labour force (as opposed to 13 per cent for the city as a whole) are unable to work due to a permanent illness or disability. On the southside, Togher A and Tramore A show similar patterns. Similarly, taking up employment for lone parents can be very difficult. The highest concentration of one-parent households in the city are to be found in Knocknaheeny, Mayfield and Mahon B. Improved provision of child-care by employers and the state could have a dramatic impact on their employability. With 12 per cent of all households in the city now made up of one-parent families, long waiting lists for limited spaces in crèches are commonplace. Problems for lone parents – particularly young women – have been compounded by recent cutbacks that have reduced funding for those attending early school leaving and second chance education programmes.

Whilst the general levels of educational attainment in Cork have shown modest increases since the early 1990s, there are wide differences in the city. In northern wards with

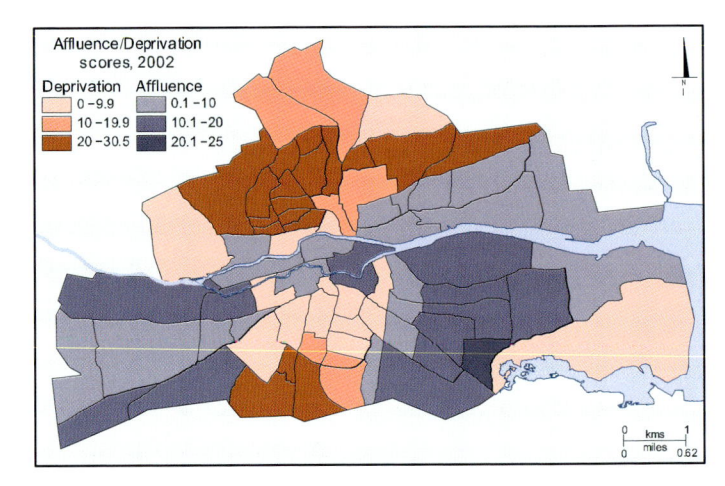

Fig. 5.53 The level of deprivation in Cork city is above the national average. Relative affluence is concentrated in the wards in the east and west of the city. Clusters of disadvantage are in areas from Knocknaheeny and Fair Hill in the north-west through to Mayfield in the north-east. Other deprived areas include Ballyphehane and Pouladuff in south central and Mahon B in the south-east. (Source: Gamma Ltd.)

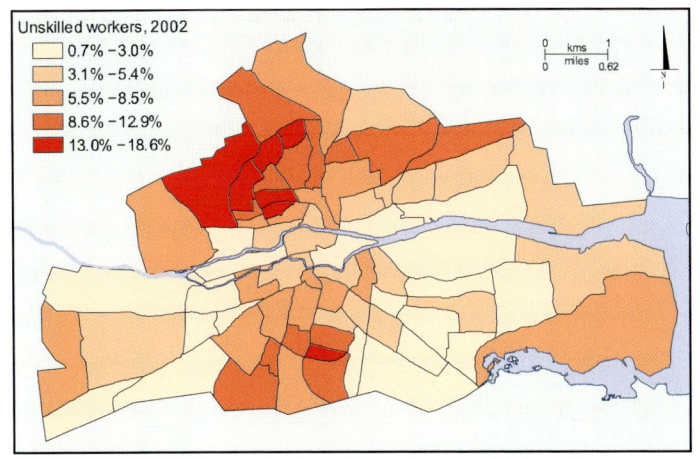

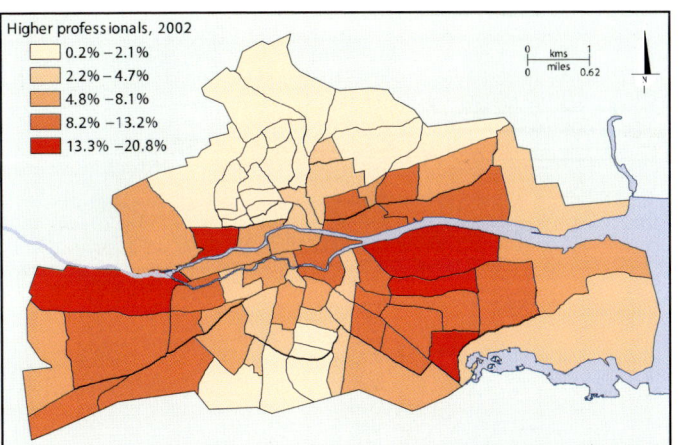

Figs. 5.54 and 5.55 The distribution of skills amongst the population plays a critical role in shaping the prosperity of communities throughout the city.

inequalities abound: in the neighbourhood of Bishopstown the percentage of people who left school at sixteen years of age is 25 per cent, in Mahon, 30 per cent, in Gurranabraher, almost 50 per cent.

Many of these problems have been of concern to policy-makers and community groups in the city. One of the outcomes of high levels of unemployment in Cork during the 1980s and early 1990s was the development of community organisations. There are now over 600 community groups in the city. Many are led by women. The development of Tory Top Park in Ballyphehane, completed in the summer of 1987, which regenerated 8.5 acres of parkland remains testimony to the activities of local communities to address the problems of unemployment. Raising money through dart competitions, pram races and singing contests illustrates well the rich social capital that has kept the fabric of these communities together.

high rates of unemployment – for example, Knocknaheeny, Mayfield and Glen A – most young people leave school at fifteen or sixteen years of age. There are some areas on the southside of the city, such as Mahon B and Togher, which show similar patterns, but the northern wards are more consistently educationally disadvantaged. In 1996, the Northside Education Initiative argued that people living on the northside were most in need of education. But unemployment, poverty, lack of educational tradition within the families and areas in which they live and discrimination through the operation of the educational system worked against them.[6] In 2002, reflecting the national increase in third-level education citywide, there has also been a five per cent increase in those for whom a degree or higher is their highest level of education. But there are stark inequalities across the city. The statistics tell a grim story. In 2002, in only eight of the city's 74 wards do we find concentrations of people with third-level qualifications. There are many neighbourhoods in the city where less than one per cent of the population who have finished their education are graduates. In 17 wards, over 50 per cent of the population ceased formal education aged fifteen or under. Geographical

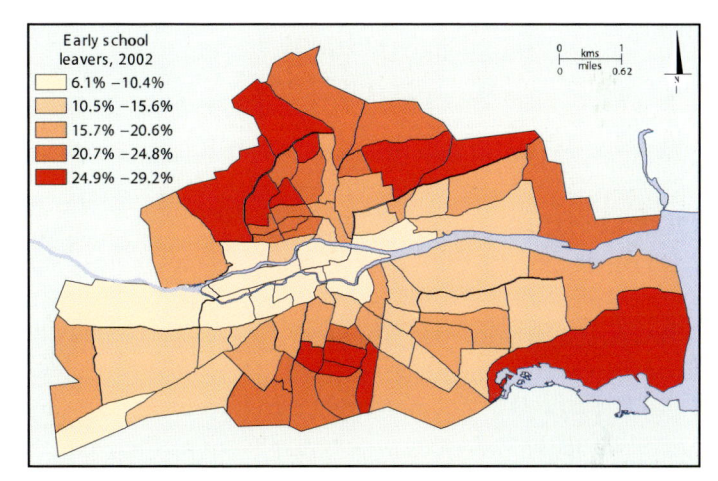

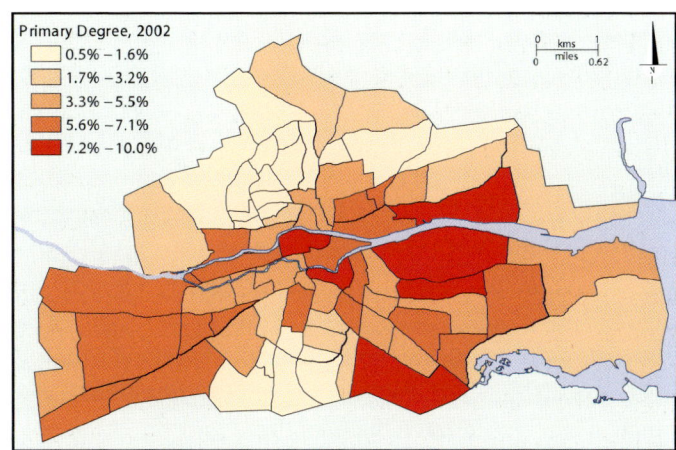

Figs. 5.56 and 5.57 With the exception of a couple of clusters in the south of the city, the northern wards – in particular Knocknaheeny, Churchfield, Fair Hill A and C to the west and the Glen A and Mayfield to the east – have the highest proportion of residents who left school without completing their Leaving Certificate. To the south of the city, Mahon B and Turner's Cross/Ballyphelane A show similar rates. The wards with the highest clusters of people with a primary university degree are to be found in Knockrea and Tivoli, as well as Tramore C. Sunday's Well B and South Gate also have above-average rates.

Community associations now play a diverse role in the provision of services for their local populations.

National and EU programmes are also important. Cork City Partnership, established in 1995, worked in tandem with URBAN I (1994–1999), an EU programme that sought to regenerate urban neighbourhoods and support training, entrepreneurship and employment. Key outcomes included the extension and upgrading of Farranree Community Centre, the construction of an enterprise centre in Ballyvolane and a community resource centre in the Glen. The Cork City Development Board also supports communities to meet local needs and assists socially excluded groups such as Travellers, early school leavers, disadvantaged women, the disabled, refugees, asylum seekers, drug-users and ex-prisoners.[7] Both organisations play a role in managing the National Anti-Poverty Strategy in Cork, particularly through innovative educational provision and implementing the RAPID (Revitalising Areas by Planning, Investment and Development) programme. Mirroring the core areas of social deprivation in the city, the four RAPID areas are: Knocknaheeney/Churchfield; Fair Hill/Gurranabraher/Farranree; Blackpool/the Glen, Mayfield; Togher and Mahon.

CURRENT TRENDS

Despite recent economic growth and new employment, the pattern of urban inequality has remained largely unchanged over the last two decades. The gentrification of a number of inner-city wards has reduced levels of deprivation, but some neighbourhoods – notably Togher and Farranferris – are worse off in 2002 than they were in 1996. The challenge of balancing growth and employment with reducing inequality and building sustainable communities has not gone away, in spite of the city's apparent prosperity. In some ways there is a need to assess the degree to which every development improves the social cohesion of Cork. Whilst the Cork Area Strategic Plan (CASP) seeks to open up a new growth corridor in the north, the employment opportunities available in the first developments in the Blackpool valley are largely in the lower-paid service sector. Despite this investment, Blackpool A lost almost 30 per cent of its population in the period 1996–2002, the largest percentage decline of all the wards in the city. One wonders what Tomás MacCurtain would have made of this!

Meanwhile, the Lee tunnel and the development of the South Link Road have attracted developers to create numerous private industrial estates on the southern side of the city. This has arguably unbalanced the distribution of work in Cork, as, in the absence of good public transport, these developments have increased the relative peripherality of some areas of the northside. Unfortunately, rather than homogenising the city, there is a risk that development of new roads may polarise it, particularly as inaccessibility to transportation can shape people's social and economic future. However, the decision by Cork City Council to regenerate social housing areas in Mayfield, the Glen and Knocknaheeny, and to reinvest capital made from the sale of public lands in Mahon in urban regeneration in the city core, may provide an environment that will attract inward investment into some of the more deprived areas in the city. Whatever the future holds, the history and geography of the inequalities of Cork will continue to mark its population for some time yet.

Fig. 5.58 In 2002, there were 860 members of the Irish Traveller community in the city, many living either on the side of the road or on the edge of the city in isolated halting sites. Whilst the City Council is committed to improving the situation, the experience has been problematic, particularly as the nomadic lifestyle of this group has been increasingly outlawed by the state. 'Travellers who live on the roadside experience risk to their safety, suffer aggression and racist abuse, achieve fewer educational qualifications, die younger, and suffer from a number of illnesses caused by exposure to the elements and unsanitary conditions. Moreover, the existence of roadside sites reinforces negative Traveller stereotypes which fuel anti-Traveller prejudice' (Traveller Visibility Group, *Submission to Cork County Council regarding the Traveller Accommodation Programme 2005–2008*). (Photo: Maurizo Vallebella.)

The City at Night

Adrian Murphy

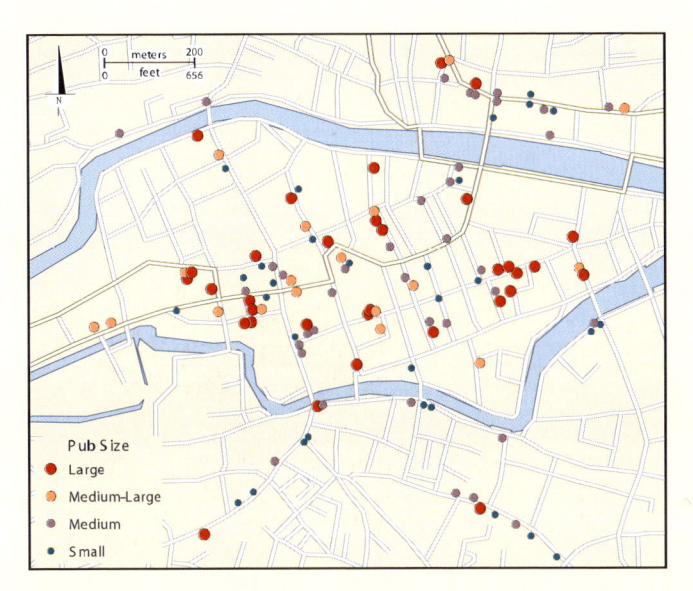

Fig. 5.59 Venues in Cork city centre have numerous forms of ownership. Individually owned bars tend to occupy marginally more remote locations, such as around Washington Street. The most common forms of ownership are partnerships and limited companies.

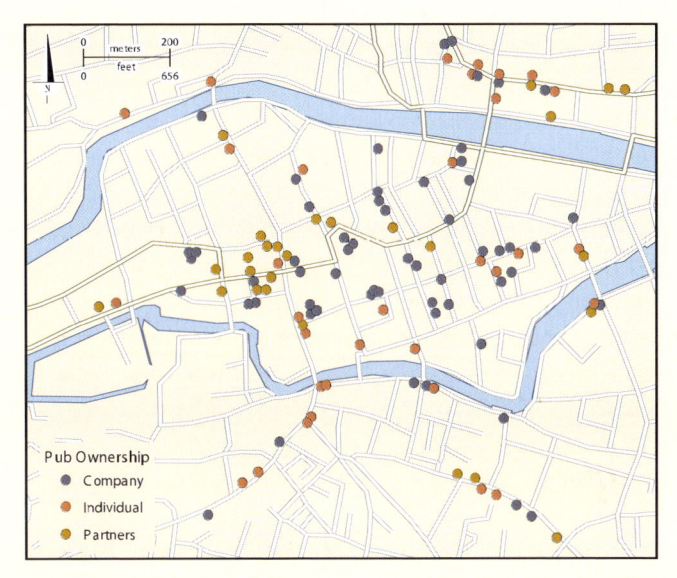

Fig. 5.60 Due to changes in licensing legislation, the 'super-pub' now features in the city centre. Larger venues tend to be clustered together – especially around Washington Street and the eastern end of Oliver Plunkett Street. Smaller venues are less common in the city centre.

In the past two decades, the night-time economy of Cork city has undergone many changes. These have come in the context of increased modernisation and affluence and greater international influences. There have been shifts in the geographies of venues such as bars and nightclubs. As the figures shown here illustrate, the size of venues has changed, as have the ownership structures. Twenty years ago, bars and nightclubs were seen as the social focus for a local community. Today they form the leisure economy of a large urban population – city centre and suburban – and their ties to the locality are diminishing.

Nowadays companies and partnerships own many of the venues (Fig. 5.59). In the city centre, the tradition of family-run pubs has declined. In these new venues it is usual to find a management structure that includes duty managers, bar managers and owners, many with backgrounds in marketing and business studies. Greater attention is being paid to the management and marketing of these venues, and they are generally targeted at discrete markets such as students, young professionals or 'thirty-somethings'. The same partnerships and companies also own many of the venues: Reardens, Havana Browns, Preachers and Scotts, the Raven, the Classic, Cleavers, the Bailey, among others, have common ownership.

While the number of venues in the city centre has not noticeably changed over the last twenty years, they have increased in size (Fig. 5.60). Licensing legislation allows a licence to be transferred to another unconnected premises and so many licences have moved onto larger premises. The interiors of these venues have changed considerably, and a range of 'style-bars' have now developed in the city. The use of design as a marketing tool illustrates the changing tastes of the consumers in Cork and how the spaces of the night-time economy are bound up with the interplay of space, economy and identity. In 1996, the Bodega opened on Cornmarket Street (the building was previously a warehouse), as did the Goat Broke Loose on Grand Parade. Both have been described as Cork's first 'super-pubs'. In 1999, the Bailey re-opened on Courthouse Street in a building which had previously housed two separate venues – these were converted into one larger venue. In 2002, An Bróg was enlarged by extending two adjacent venues. The Old Oak, on Oliver Plunkett Street, continues to expand as buildings surrounding it are purchased. These pressures on space encourage a lively, often boisterous, scene that spills over into the streets, but which, sensibly regulated, greatly adds to the atmosphere of the city centre at night.

36. COMMUNITY DEVELOPMENT AND THE CATHOLIC CHURCH

Raymond O'Connor and David Joyce

Community can take a variety of shapes and forms, but the Catholic Church has provided one of its most visible manifestations in the city. The Church's influence on Cork society may have diminished in recent times, but its historical impact on community life in Cork has been significant. Its network of churches and parishes has created, and continues to create, a sense of place, belonging and identity for a significant number of people in the city.

Church and the City

With the granting of Catholic emancipation in 1829, the church's new-found confidence was expressed most visibly in the urban landscape of Cork through the construction of churches. The city of steeples emerged in this period with the building of the neo-Gothic Holy Trinity church (1832) and St Patrick's (1836), both designed by the architects James and George Pain. The 'devotional revolution' in the later nineteenth century provided a further stimulus in the

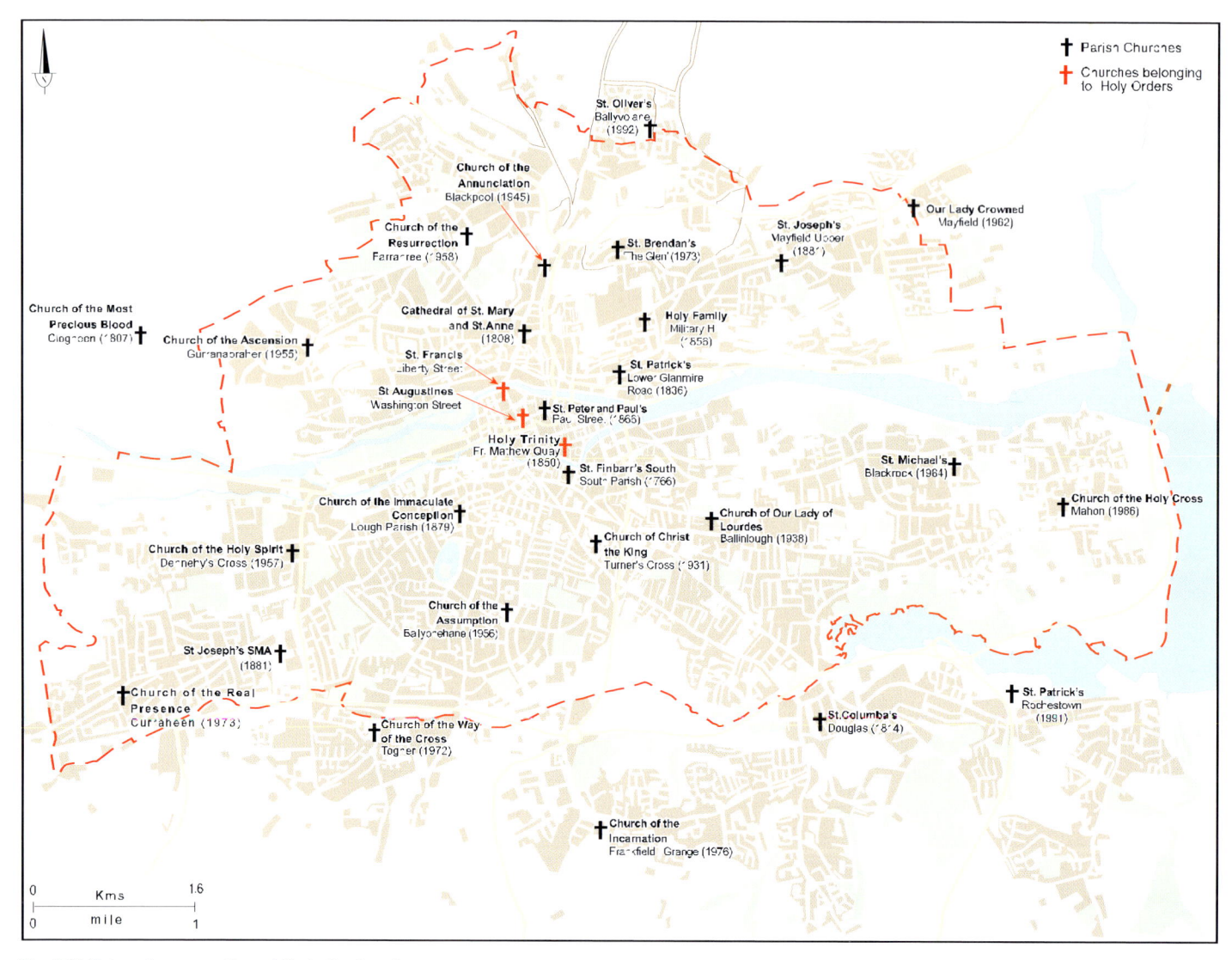

Fig. 5.61 Dates of consecration of Catholic churches.

organisation of the church's rituals and practices. Regular devotions became a staple of many people's lives. With the emergence of the newly independent state in the 1920s, the church's influence on society became even more pronounced.[1] During this time the parochial structure took on an increased significance, as the parish, as a territory, a place and an imagined community, became an essential part of the bond linking Church and people at local level.

As the city's suburbs grew from the 1930s on, the Catholic Church developed new places of worship and schools to cater for the religious and educational requirements of the population. The schools provided a daily focal point for children and parents alike, whilst the churches, commanding central locations within these newly developing suburbs, drew large congregations to their Sunday masses. The importance of these churches as social spaces cannot be underestimated, as they became the focal point for all significant events in their parishioners' lives: baptisms, communions, confirmations, weddings and funerals. Through its parish network, the Church played a pivotal role in structuring community life in the city and provided the social glue in the newly built, sprawling and largely anonymous residential developments.

A key objective of the Catholic Church in Cork was to instil a sense of belonging, to create an attachment to place, to bring the concept of *meitheal*, a traditional form of co-operation between neighbours, from a rural context and breathe life into it in a new urban setting. This process was usually initiated by organising fundraising campaigns so that a church and a school could be built to service the needs of the people. These fundraising initiatives required a high degree of organisation and lasted for many years. It gave

Fig. 5.62 The Church of the Ascension, Gurranabraher, which was consecrated in 1955. (Photo: Tomás Tyner.)

Fig. 5.63 and 5.64 Traditionally the feast of Corpus Christi (usually celebrated on the first Sunday in June) saw the men of each parish north and south of the Lee march in a great act of public devotion. Since 1926, the eucharistic procession has drawn the people of Cork into the streets. The main procession is comprised of civic dignitaries who walk in unison with the bishop, clergy and people of the city. Identification with a parish is integral to the procession. Each parish has its own meeting-point. Traditionally it was the men and boys who walked in the procession and the women and girls who lined the pavements or made their way to St Patrick's Street and Grand Parade in search of the most comfortable vantage point. In the 1990s, the organisers of the event broke with tradition and invited women and girls to walk in the procession for the first time. Falling attendance reflects not only pressures within the Catholic Church but also wider societal change. Despite its decline in latter years, the eucharistic procession remains a living tradition in the city.

those living in the newly established residential areas a common purpose and ultimately a sense of achievement and ownership when the schools and churches were built.

The annual eucharistic procession from the suburban parishes into the city centre was also a ritual expression of parishioners' attachment to their church and parish. Initiated in 1926 by Bishop Cohalan, this annual procession became a major event in the city's calendar and, despite falling participation, remains a unique event in urban Ireland. In the newly formed state, Church occasions inevitably became civic occasions. Nowhere was this more evident than in the eucharistic procession, where civic dignitaries joined with the clergy and the people in a citywide celebration of faith. Parishioners, until relatively recently men and boys only, processed in prayer from their own churches to the city centre for open-air benediction in Daunt's Square and then returned via the North Cathedral to their own parishes. An invented tradition in many respects, the procession symbolised the power and prestige of the Catholic Church in Cork society and, through the annual ritual of walking through the city, embedded a Catholic identity into the streetscapes and mentalities of Cork.[2]

As the suburbs expanded, the Catholic parish network altered considerably. Parishes became smaller in size. This reflected the increased density of housing as green-field sites were transformed into residential areas by Cork City Council. The twin forces shaping the newly independent state – nationalism and Catholicism – were very evident in the naming of the new streets and roads. In the 1930s, the street names reflected the importance of the Catholic Church – Congress Road, Father Mathew Road, Derrynane Road, Sliabh Mish and O'Connell Avenue were all in the parish of Turner's Cross. In the 1960s, the 1916 Rising was commemorated in the street names of Ballyphehane parish – Connolly Park, McDonagh Road, Pearse Road, Kent Road and Plunkett Road.

CONTEMPORARY · TRANSFORMATIONS

Reflecting the growth of the city, the Catholic Church expanded its parish network on a number of occasions. Before 1958 there were seven parishes in Cork: Cathedral, Saint Patrick's, Saint Finbarr's South, Saint Finbarr's West, Blackrock, Douglas and the Middle Parish. Changes initiated by Bishop Cornelius Lucey in the late 1970s, and accelerated by Bishop Michael Murphy in the early 1980s, ensured this expanded to 23 parishes by 1983. Responding to changes in the residential geography of the city, the Cathedral parish experienced the greatest degree of subdivision. By 1983, seven parishes existed where only one had previously. The parish of Upper Mayfield (Our Lady Crowned) was created by Bishop Lucey in 1979, while the parishes of Blackpool (the Glen) and St Joseph's (Mayfield) were created by Bishop Murphy in 1981. In the early 1980s, the Catholic parish network was highly responsive to the changing geographies of residential activity in the city and the need of local communities to identify with their own distinctive parish.

As the parish network expanded, older parishes were subdivided and new churches were built. The high number of vocations to the priesthood ensured that there was no difficulty in allocating priests to the expanding network. It was normal practice for every parish to be staffed by three priests: a parish priest and two curates. So high was the number of vocations that in 1965 the diocese of Cork and Ross initiated an overseas mission in Trujillo, Peru, where priests who were not required at home either volunteered or were directed to serve. In March 2004, all priests serving on this mission were recalled to Cork and Ross, though some sisters remain there. From 1976, the number of vocations began an inexorable downward trend. Only the visit of Pope John Paul II to Ireland in 1979 briefly impacted on this trend. In 2003, only one priest from the diocese was ordained.

In recent years, plans had been formulated to expand the network further and develop a new parish in Rochestown. A church (St Patrick's) was built in 1991 and plans to establish a new primary school were in place. However, a decline in vocations to the priesthood has meant that the Church has had to revise these plans. Rochestown continues to function as an annex of the Douglas parish. As vocations

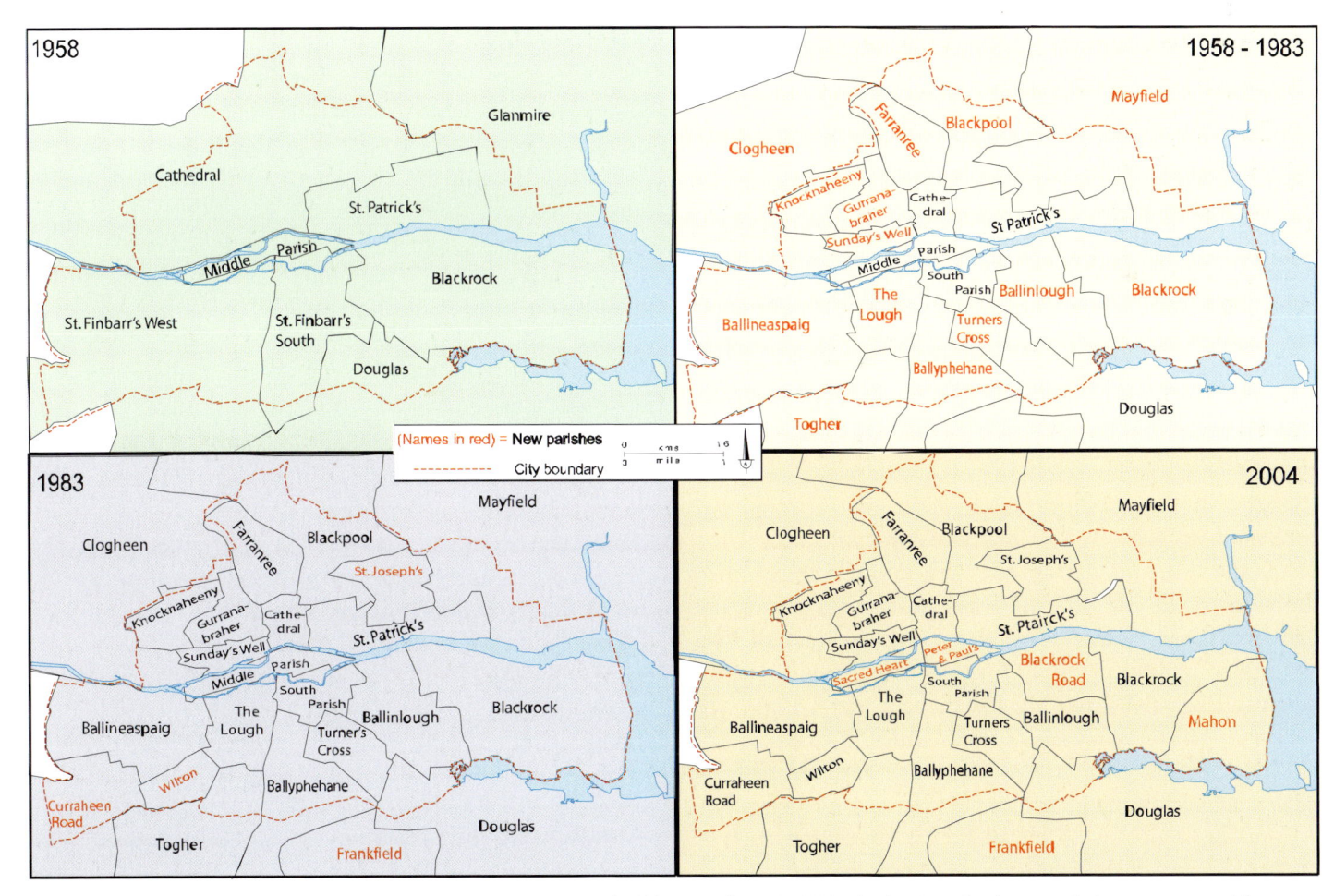

Fig. 5.65 The Catholic Church has altered its parish boundaries considerably since the early 1980s. As the city suburbs expanded, many new parishes were created. Facing into the twenty-first century, the lack of clergy to serve the expanded parish network has meant that the disocese of Cork may soon be obliged to create arrangements whereby priests are based in one parish but work in two or three. It is envisaged that this process may create larger parishes that will be very similar to the network that existed prior to the the Church's expansion in the 1980s and 1990s.

Fig. 5.66 'Hands of Hope'. Crowds gather at the gates of the North Cathedral awaiting the arrival of the relics of St Therese of Lisieux in Cork in 2001. (Photo: Denis Minihane, *Irish Examiner*.)

decline and the average age of priests has risen, the parish network may be less responsive to changes in community life in the future. Faith, however, has deep roots.

During the 1990s, a significant decline in attendance at Sunday mass was witnessed as the ties that bound the people to the Catholic Church came under pressure. Yet, people still wish to avail of the major sacraments offered by the Church for baptisms, communions, confirmations, marriages and funerals. In the early years of the twenty-first century, the parish network has begun to lose its significance. Due to the lack of vocations, the network of parishes in Cork city could not expand to reflect ongoing changes in population distribution and residential expansion. In 2004, Bishop John Buckley published a *Draft pastoral strategy* to assess how the Church might best function in an era of insufficient vocations, where the Church may be reduced to one priest in each parish. The recommendations of this strategy are currently being discussed at parish level.[3] The likelihood is that the laity will play a far greater role in day-to-day church business.

The Catholic Church may also have to rationalise its parish network. Amalgamating parishes does not appear to be a preferred option. So successful has the Church been in creating a sense of attachment to parishes that people do not want to see them dismantled. The preferred choice is an alignment of parishes, where each retains its identity and integrity. These groupings of parishes will co-operate with each other in a loose but formal alliance. Parishioners have expressed a strong desire that any alignments should take place along the lines of the older parish networks. This may result in a *de facto* parish network similar to the one that existed prior to 1958.

CREDIT UNIONS

While the Catholic parish network has rationalised, the Credit Union movement remains highly relevant to changing population and residential patterns. Bishop Cornelius Lucey introduced Credit Unions to Cork in 1960 in the parish of Ballyphehane.[4] Credit Unions would further strengthen the Catholic parish as a meaningful territorial unit in the lives of Irish citizens. He thought that they would complement the work of the Catholic Church and the GAA in fostering a sense of belonging by introducing an economic dimension to community life at parish level. The basic premise on which Credit Unions were based was that money from the community should be circulated within the community. Surplus money from within the community was to be invested in the Credit Union and made available, in the form of loans, to other members who needed short-term low-interest loans.

The money belonged to the community but was managed by volunteers in the Credit Union. Loans to members enhanced the quality of their lives and were usually invested locally. Money was allocated for mundane but important things, such as clothes for job interviews, communion and confirmation expenses, business loans, house improvements, renovations and extensions, cars, education fees and holidays. Any profits were returned to the members in the form of annual dividends or were invested in the community. All Credit Unions sponsor some community-based activities and are particularly important in contributing to the running costs of other voluntary bodies and, specifically, in supporting the activities of caring groups, church-based groups and schools, and educational, recreational and sporting programmes in the community.

Throughout the 1960s Credit Unions were formed in all areas of Cork city. Receiving strong support from the Catholic Church, they operated on a voluntary basis from school classrooms, parish halls and church basements until they were in a position to rent or purchase premises of their own. Once they purchased suitable premises, the opening hours were expanded and permanent staff were employed to provide the highly sought-after services that Credit Unions offered.[5] Credit Unions catered for the small, short-term loans market – a niche market that the banks had, until then, deemed not to be sufficiently lucrative and so had chosen not to develop.

Contrary to Bishop Lucey's expectations, the Credit Union movement chose at a very early stage to develop its own territorial network. It decided not to formally link the newly formed movement's territorial structures to the parish network. The Credit Unions' territorial divisions were called Common Bonds.[6] Only people residing or working within the Common Bond were permitted to become members of the Credit Union. This restriction on membership separated Credit Unions from other financial institutions. Between 1960 and 2004 the ever-changing Common Bond network reflected both the changing residential geography of the city and the increasing levels of mobility enjoyed by suburban residents. The areas covered by Common Bond are generally larger than Catholic parishes and extend well beyond the officially designated city boundary (St Joseph's Credit Union, Mayfield, for example, caters for the residents of Little Island). Some Common Bonds close to the city centre are surrounded on all sides by the Common Bonds of other Credit Unions and are unable to expand. The Middle Parish (established 1968) was one such Credit Union. Unable to expand its Common Bond and suffering because of a decline in the population of the inner city, it was subsumed by Cathedral Credit Union in 1988.

The Credit Union movement was a significant innovation in the city and individual Credit Unions remain an important focal point for their members at a local level. Cork currently has fifteen city-based community Credit Unions. In 2001 over

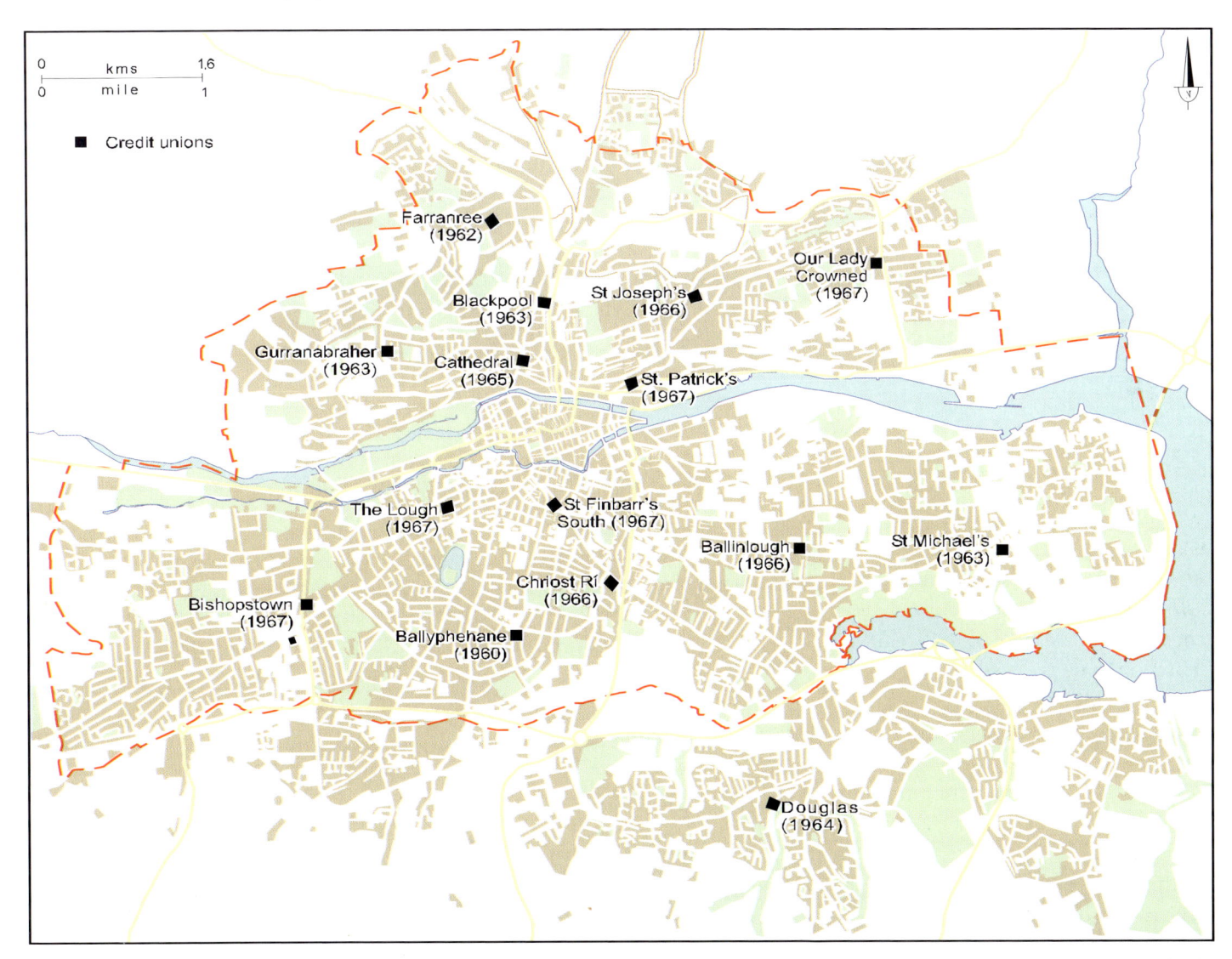

Fig. 5.67 The early 1960s witnessed the rapid expansion of the Credit Union movement in Cork city. Originating in Ballyphehane, the demand for the services offered by the movement was such that very soon every community had its own Credit Union.

126,000 city dwellers were members of a Credit Union and they had purchased shares worth 368 million euro. During the 1990s, many Credit Unions relocated into new purpose-built facilities. By the 1990s, Credit Unions were sufficiently confident to purchase highly sought-after central locations within their communities. The buildings they now occupy are imposing local landmarks with a distinctive architecture; this is a far remove from the church basements and parish halls from which they operated for one or two hours a week in the early 1960s.

Community associations

A more traditional form of community spirit still thriving in Cork is embodied in the community associations. These associations provide services aimed primarily at those members of the community whose needs are not adequately met by the state's welfare system. Community associations are hybrid organisations and their structures are becoming increasingly complex. Many community associations were originally formed either by the Church or by organisations that had strong links to it. However, the links to the Catholic Church have weakened as the importance of the state and its agencies has increased. Community associations act as an intermediary between the state, the Church and the community. To cope with increased demands and bureaucracy, many have developed permanent administrative and management structures. Increasingly, they need to be staffed by highly skilled administrative professionals, but they also require volunteers working in the community delivering services to people. They function to draw down funding and resources for members of their communities who, as individuals, have difficulty in accessing services and they also ensure that the service is delivered locally. They cater for the isolated and the marginalised and try to integrate them into the community. Community associations offer a variety of services including meals on wheels, day-care facilities for the elderly and literacy programmes. They also offer their facilities to other community-based voluntary bodies, such as the Legion of Mary, whose members visit the homes of the ill and the housebound, and the Saint Vincent de Paul societies.

The split between Church and state and the two sets of bureaucracies that community associations have to engage with is evidenced by the fact that both the Catholic Church and Cork City Council keep a register of the community associations operating in the greater Cork area. In Cork city, there are eleven community associations affiliated with the diocese of Cork and Ross. Six are on the southside: mainly, Ballyphehane, Bishopstown, Douglas, The Lough, South Parish and Togher. The remainder are located on the northside: Blackpool, Gurranabraher, Mayfield, Upper Mayfield, St Joseph's Mayfield and Knocknaheeney. Seventeen community associations are currently registered with Cork City Council. Only eight community associations (Ballyphehane, Bishopstown Lough, South Parish, Togher, Blackpool, Gurranabraher and St Joseph's Mayfield) are registered with both the diocesan office of Cork and Ross and with Cork City Council. The nine community associations registered with Cork City Council only are Ballinlough, Blackrock, Farranree, Mayfield East, Middle Parish, Turner's Cross, Mahon, Blarney Street and surrounding areas and Shandon Street. Registering with the different bodies (or both) highlights the differing priorities of these associations. Being community-based, they are aware of the needs and priorities of their own areas and can orientate their structures and activities to meeting these needs.

Since the late 1990s, the existence of some voluntary community groups has been under threat due to the steady decline in the numbers of people prepared to work on a voluntary basis in their communities. Pressure on people's time has increased greatly. People are spending more time both getting to and from work and delivering and collecting children from school and crèches. To compound these pressures, in many cases both parents in a family unit are increasingly forced to work in order to be able to afford the costs associated with house ownership and child-care in the twenty-first century. House buyers today are being compelled by spiralling house prices to travel considerable distances from the city. For many people, having to commute long distances has eroded the time they have at their disposal to engage in voluntary activities in their new communities. Other factors dissuading people from volunteering their time centre on insurance issues and the highly litigious environment that has emerged over the last decade.

Yet the Catholic Church remains a catalyst for voluntary community-based activity. Despite the obstacles described above, voluntary community-based organisations continue to serve their communities as new strategies are implemented to take cognisance of the changing environment in which they operate. The Catholic Church and the concept of community are in transition in Cork city. The future will be shaped by the outcomes of discussions between the Church and local communities on the ideas contained in the *Draft pastoral strategy* (2004).

The Marian House Names of Cork

Millie Glennon

The naming of a house is one of the few naming practices over which ordinary folk have influence. We do not choose our own names at birth, nor do many of us have an involvement in the naming of our streets or towns. House naming is a popular practice all over the world, and this is also the case in Cork, where one-sixth of houses are named. Naming a house creates a sense of identity, as well as a way of differentiating one person's home from another. Names appear on old houses, new houses, mansions, cottages, bungalows and terraces. They are ubiquitous.

In 1941, there was one named house for every 42 inhabitants in Cork. By 2000 there was a named house for every 18 inhabitants. The practice of house naming has grown dramatically in popularity. Religious names have always been significant, but they are of greater relative significance now than sixty years ago, and those associated with the veneration of Mary are strikingly important. In 1941, 1 in every 50 house names was Marian in character; in 2000, they represented 1 of every 15 houses. The 432 Marian house names in Cork city refer to Mary in a variety of ways. Most are explicitly religious in nature. The most popular house name associated with Mary is Genezzano, a place of pilgrimage in honour of the mother of Jesus. Another place of pilgrimage frequently used is Fatima, but there are surprisingly few uses of Lourdes, the most popular pilgrimage destination. Mary has a number of titles, including Star of the Sea and Good Counsel, and these frequently appear on houses in their Latin forms of Stella Maris and Bon Consilio. In Irish, religious use of the name Mary is given in the form 'Múire' rather than the secular form 'Máire'. One hundred houses in Cork bear the Irish name Múire, or Mhúire.

Although such named houses are found across the city, there are four main concentrations. North of the river, named houses are found in Commons ward and Montenotte. South of the river there are two groupings of wards. First, a wedge proceeds west from St Fin Barre's Cathedral bounded by the Lee to the north and Glasheen Road and Bishopstown Road to the south. The second coherent block of house names is bounded by the Lee to the north and the city limits to the south. Its western boundary is formed by a line proceeding south from the City Hall, while on the east it stretches as far as a line proceeding south from the Atlantic Pond. In broad terms, house names are denser in middle-class districts, particularly the suburbs.

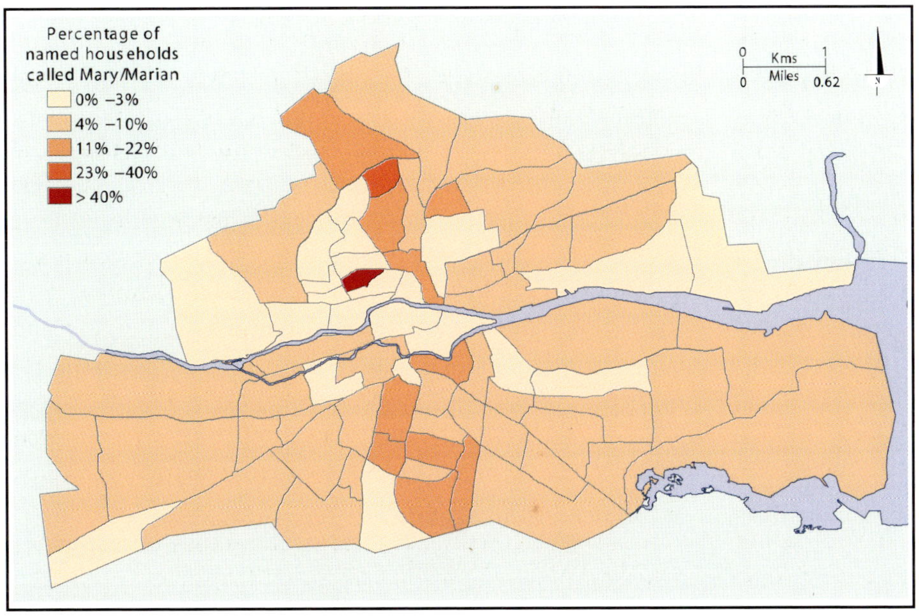

Figure 5.68 indicates the areas where, if people choose to name their house, they have done so by honouring Mary. Blank areas have no Marian names and the next category (up to six per cent) shows those parts of the city with a below-average tendency to use Mary when naming houses. The pattern of above-average use of Marian names is striking. North of the river a wedge of names runs up through Shandon into Farranferris and out to Fair Hill. South of the river another wedge stretches from Turner's Cross and out to Ballyphehane. Neither of these are wards in which house naming is otherwise common and both are districts that are less middle class than those where naming is more

Fig. 5.68 The tradition of naming one's house after Mary has a rich but geographically varied following in the city, as is illustrated here in the percentage of all named houses named after the Virgin Mary.

Fig. 5.69 Whilst practically absent from newer urban developments in recent years, Marian devotion can still be seen in the many grottoes dotted around the city's older neighbourhoods. (Photo: Denis Linehan.)

general. In areas where there are few named houses, a higher proportion are Marian in character. Reverence for Mary may have induced people to name their houses who would otherwise not have bothered.

Why this devotion to Mary and why does it appear to be more intense now than in the 1940s? The upsurge in Marian names occurred in the 1950s under the influence of Bishop Lucey of Cork. Pope Pius XII proclaimed 1954 as the international year of Marian devotion, the Marian Year, timed to celebrate the centenary of the definition of Mary's Immaculate Conception. In 1954, Bishop Lucey of Cork dedicated each issue of *The Fold* magazine to a different aspect of Mary's life and made the recitation of the family rosary the special devotion of the Marian Year in his diocese. The local newspapers of 1954 are replete with references to the building of grottoes and shrines and the organisation of pilgrimages all around the country, all in relation to the Marian Year. In Cork, Bishop Lucey embarked upon a massive church-building programme in 1953, promising to give the county of Cork a rosary of new Catholic churches (three were built within the city). Those who did not have the means for such a grand gesture as building a grotto or shrine to Mary named their houses after her, showing that they could express their devotion to her in a public but personal manner.

37. MIGRATION

Piarias Mac Éinrí

Irish people are accustomed to think of their identities as being rooted in place and time. As a people we have valued the static over the nomadic and stress the importance of continuity. Cities everywhere, by contrast, are composed of populations many of whom originally came from somewhere else. Migration is, therefore, a major part of the history and geography of the urban environment. Cork derived its changing identity from a succession of natives and strangers, from its origins as a monastic settlement to its development as a tenth-century Scandinavian town and the subsequent arrival of the Anglo-Normans. Later, at a time when seaways were still more important than land routes, Cork was very much part of a thriving Atlantic Europe.

The city's merchant families maintained strong links with continental Europe and the wider world. Emigrants left from the city quays long before the Famine and long before Queenstown (now Cobh) became the major port of departure for the New World. North America, though, was not the only destination. In the 1678 census of Montserrat, 'the most Irish isle in the West Indies', the majority of the white population was Irish and most of these were from Cork.[1] Some had been deported during the Cromwellian wars. William Penn, whose family name is now remembered in the US state of Pennsylvania, first proclaimed his Quaker beliefs in Cork city in 1667. London, south Wales and the English Midlands acquired their share of Cork migrants. The British military and colonial services attracted Cork people of all backgrounds, from the impoverished residents of urban tenements to the graduates of Queen's College Cork, now UCC. The British Army was a major source of employment. One of America's most famous labour activists, Mary Harris, or 'Mother Jones', was born in Cork in the 1830s.

One of the first Ford motor works outside the USA was established by Henry Ford at Marina in Cork city, a fact not unconnected with Ford's own Cork ancestry in Ballinascarthy. The subsequent establishment of Ford at Dagenham in Britain led in turn to an exodus of Cork migrants to the new works. A contemporary commentary states:

> Take the 'Dagenham Yanks', for example. Men with winklepickers and blue suits and more money than sense home for the holidays from Ford's giant Essex complex, regaling the clientele in hostelries from Shandon to Barrack Street in Cockney tones as polished as their brown shoes, the jingle louder the first week home than the second. By which time nature would out and the accent had re-tuned itself to the mellifluous local sing-song, 'Jeez boy, that's a great pint of Murphy's, all the same ahh!'[2]

The survival in Cork speech of such phrases as 'Dagenham Yank' is testimony to the cultural effects of these forms of displacement on the local population. Migration was always a complex and multidirectional phenomenon. Michael Collins, who worked in London's Post Office, was one of a generation of lower-middle-class migrant Irish who returned to the home country having decided that their future lay in a nationalist independent Ireland. But many others chose not to come back. With independence, the link with Britain and the British Empire was greatly diminished, but emigration continued, as did the British Army tradition, especially from the poorer parts of the city.

> I was in my early teens when World War Two began. My father had served in the Royal Leinster Fusiliers in World War One and had been wounded in action in that conflict. So at about fifteen years having left the Primary School I persuaded my parents that England was my future and in company with my older sister joined my father in wartime Wiltshire.
>
> On Saint Patrick's Day I wear my shamrock with pride but come November 11th, I am equally proud to wear my 'poppy' and remember those who made the supreme sacrifice for the well being of both countries.[3]

After independence, the Cork tradition of out-migration was sometimes to Dublin rather than London. Indeed, until the recent past, stories about Cork and the Dublin Civil Service were legion. It was said that a Corkman coming to Dublin threw a stone in the Liffey and, if it floated, he went home. In the Civil Service, the GPO was popularly supposed to be 'stone outside and Cork inside'.

Cobh's role as the capital of Ireland's westward emigration only finally petered out when the days of mass passenger shipping ended in the 1950s and air transport took over. Tragically, few records of this westward migration survive in Ireland, as some of the shipping company records were apparently burned on the Cobh quays in the 1960s. Meantime, the quiet haemorrhage of Irish emigrants to the neighbouring island continued unabated, by air, train, bus and ferry. I recall travelling in the 1980s in a packed and hideously smoke-filled Slattery's bus from Cork to London and the long overnight journey by road and ferry, punctuated by endless country-and-western music.

The early years of Ireland's membership of the European Union were painful ones for Cork. After an initial period of tariff protection, the city's antiquated industrial economy was hit harder than many other parts of the country. Heavy and traditional industries proved unable to weather the open seas of international competition. The late 1980s were a time of rapidly increasing emigration, as the shrinking Irish economy proved unable to absorb the baby boomers of the 1960s emerging from Ireland's new publicly funded second-level schools and third-level institutions. The city really only began to recover in the 1990s and even then the 'Celtic Tiger' did not benefit all to a comparable extent.

Those migrants scattered to many destinations, including the newly rejuvenated communities of Irish America, where many Irish found themselves as 'undocumented aliens',

Fig. 5.70 'The good old steam train bore me to Cork in its own time; in that fair city I spent a few hours in Aherne's pub on Penrose's Quay. I could see the *Inisfallen* by looking out the window; there was no fear that she would sail without me. She didn't – and away we sailed down past Blackrock Castle and past Roche's Point and out into the Atlantic. It was late September and, as dusk fell, I could see the lights coming on along the coast that I knew and loved so well. I had bought *The Great Gatsby* that afternoon and had the great fortune to start reading it on my maiden voyage. The sea was calm; I stayed on deck, in the steerage of course – and witnessed a little sight that I could never forget. It was after midnight and I couldn't but feel for a little pale-faced girl who stood at the rails on the land side. I was certain that she too was going to England for the first time; she looked even lonelier than Ruth when she stood in tears amidst the alien corn. I hadn't the courage to approach her and console her by revealing that I too was emigrating for the first time. All, however, was not lost: a young seaman came up from below (he could hardly come up from anywhere else . . .) and handed her a mug of steaming tea – it strengthened my faith in human nature. The transformation in the wee lass was marvellous: her expression had been woebegone – now it said: 'woe, be gone'. And so we sailed on, past The Tuskar and into St George's Channel.' (Source: Con Houlihan; Photo: *Irish Examiner*.)

similar to the 'economic migrants' who would arrive in Ireland from other countries a few short years later. The Irish Immigration Reform Movement (IIRM) was founded in 1987 in New York through the efforts of several prominent members of that city's Cork Association, such as Patrick Hurley, who received one of UCC's first BAs in European Studies in 1985, and Sean Minihane. The IIRM was to play a key role in the regularisation of the many Irish 'illegals' who flocked to the US.[4]

Immigration

In contrast to the story of emigration, we know less about Cork's immigration history, apart from the Huguenots and the city's Jewish community. The more pervasive and long-lasting immigration of English and Welsh settlers, not all of whom were planters and soldiers, has received less attention. Post-independence Ireland found it difficult to deal with this legacy. As Elizabeth Bowen famously queried in *Bowen's Court*, referring to her planter family's background in Cork, 'isn't 300 years long enough?'[5] The War of Independence and the myth of 'rebel Cork' undoubtedly represent a major strand of Cork's history but they have obscured other realities, such as Cork's role as a provisioner for the Empire in the nineteenth century or the warm welcome given to Queen Victoria when she visited the city in 1900.

For most of the twentieth century Cork was not a significant region for immigration, but economic life improved considerably in the city during the 1990s, as it did in the rest of Ireland. Employment grew steadily: whereas only just over one million people were in employment in the Irish economy in 1988, that figure had increased by over half a million, a rise of 42 per cent, just twelve years later.[6] From the mid-1990s onwards, a new phenomenon could be observed as immigrants from other countries began to settle in Dublin, Cork and other parts of Ireland in increasing numbers. Soon migrants were to be found in many sectors of local industry and impacted on local life. A new multi-ethnic geography emerged, with the arrival of people of many different cultures, the establishment of new businesses to cater for the African and eastern European communities and the growth of Islamic, Orthodox and various Christian faiths in the city and surrounding suburbs. The new multicultural Cork is particularly evident in the city's English Market, where the tastes of an increasingly diverse population are catered for in Ireland's best food market. The social and cultural changes that occurred during the 1990s should be understood as having equal importance in the long term as the transition which took place in the Irish economy.

The new arrivals can be divided into a number of categories. The first, return migrants, were not strictly a new group at all. Half of the Irish who emigrated in the 1980s returned in the following decade. Typically, people who had left in their early twenties returned when economic opportunities presented themselves in Ireland, particularly when they reached that stage of their lives when they wanted to raise a family. It is unlikely that such a strong wave of return migrants will recur, as emigration itself fell dramatically in the 1990s and there will therefore be no pool from which substantial numbers of return migrants can be drawn in the future. Although it would be easy to dismiss these returning Irish migrants as being irrelevant to social and cultural change in Ireland, this would be a mistake. For one thing, the country they left was not the one they returned to, and they themselves were not the same people as they were on departure; they brought back with them experiences, attitudes and skills learned from living in other societies. Moreover, whereas migrants left all parts of Ireland in the 1980s, on return they were more likely to settle in an urban area.

The second category of immigrants, and the one which will prove to be of greatest significance in the long term, is labour migrants: 3,445 work permits were issued for labour migrants in Cork city and county in 2003, compared to 2,882

Fig. 5.71 The growth of small businesses and shops catering for the new migrants into Cork has brought life back to many neglected areas of the city. (Photo: Darragh MacSweeney Provision Agency.)

the year before. This figure represents seven per cent of the work permits issued for the country as a whole. This may seem modest, but a further substantial number of labour migrants are from other EU Member States and thus do not appear in these statistics, while a number are accompanied by family members. With the accession of ten new Member States to the EU in 2004, a further, if modest, increase in labour immigrants seems likely. The 2002 census provides pointers to the number of foreign immigrants living in the city and the immediate surrounding area. From a total population of 177,000 for Cork city and suburbs, a modest 5,681 (four per cent) were born in foreign countries other than Britain. If Britain is included, the figure rises to 13,500 (eight per cent), closer to the national average. For the Greater Dublin Area, by contrast, the figure for foreign-born persons is close to eleven per cent.

One recent study focused on identifying Cork labour immigrants and examining how well immigrants in Cork are settling in the Cork region.[7] In general, immigrant workers were satisfied with life in Ireland. People liked the friendliness of the Irish people and the relaxed pace of life, economic conditions and employment opportunities. Dissatisfaction related to inter-racial tension and cultural diversity. The main cause of dissatisfaction with work was low pay and not being able to use their skills. However, despite positive feelings about Ireland, immigrants see themselves as outsiders. Eastern Europeans, more than people from other regions, intend to remain in Ireland. Many of them would like to take out citizenship and have encouraged others to come to Ireland.

The third and more well-known category is made up of asylum seekers, refugees and those given 'leave to remain'. Even though the numbers of asylum seekers never amounted to more than a modest percentage of labour migrants and their families, they have received excessive negative attention and have been the victims of popular prejudice, occasionally

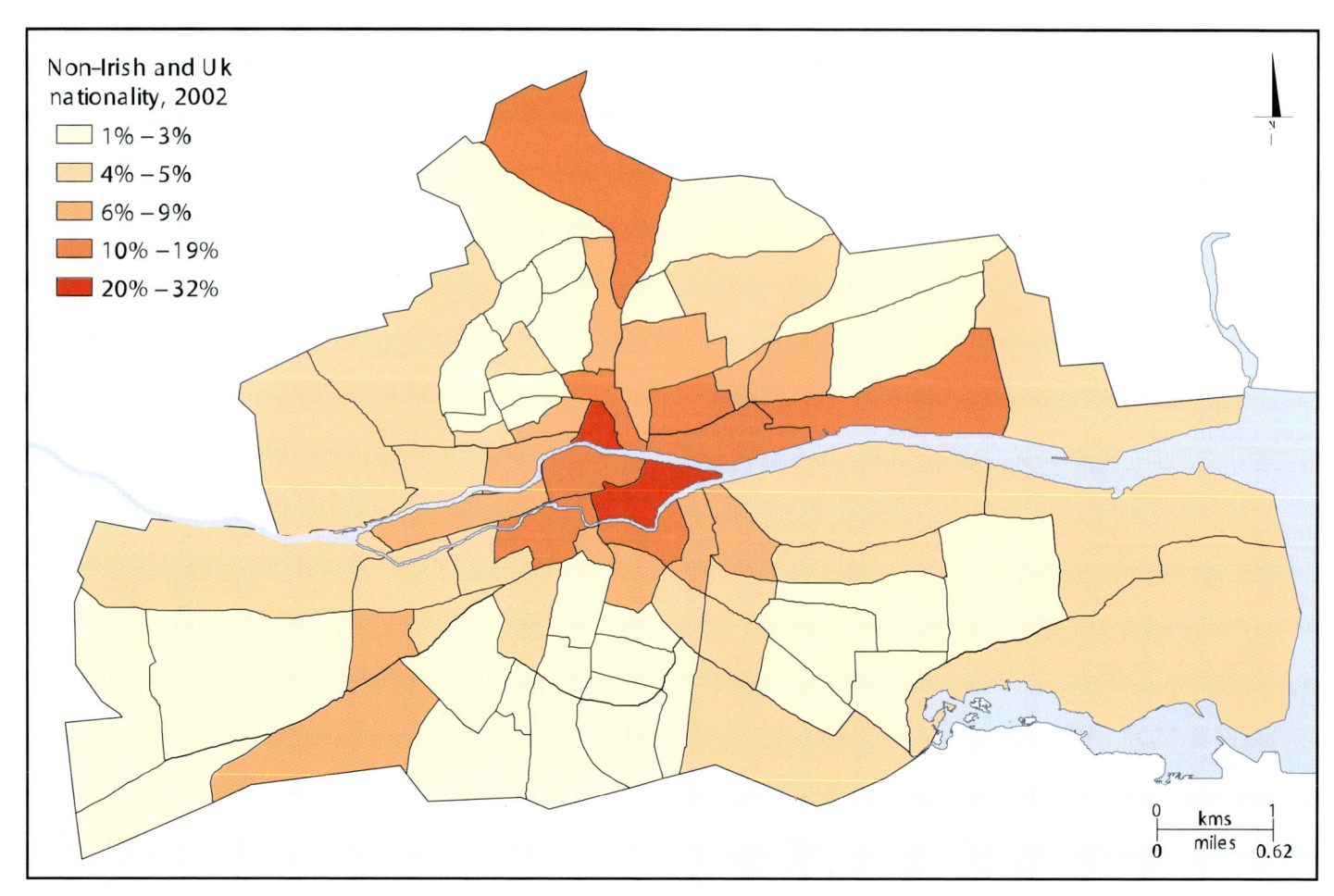

Fig. 5.72 According to the 2002 census, there are 5,681 people in Cork city of a nationality other than Irish or from the UK. As is common in all cities experiencing immigration, a degree of spatial concentration in areas offering less expensive private rented accommodation may be noted. This explains why Shandon B and Centre A have the largest proportions of people of non-Irish/UK nationality (31.5 per cent and 29.5 per cent of their total populations respectively). The adjacent wards of Shandon A, St Patrick's A/B, Tivoli A and, to the north, Commons also have above-average proportions, ranging from 9 to 19 per cent. In contrast, many of the areas to the south of the city have below-average proportions (ranging from 0.85 to 2.5 per cent). Immigration on a significant (albeit still modest) scale to Cork from outside Ireland is still a very new phenomenon. There is little doubt that, with the passing years, new migrants will become more widely dispersed within the city and wider suburbs.

Fig. 5.73 Diwali is amongst the most cherished festivals in Indian culture. Also known as the 'Festival of Light', the celebration brings all members of the community together and the lighting of lamps represents a way of paying tribute to God for health, prosperity, knowledge and peace. The festival was celebrated in 2004 by the Indian community in Cork on the Sacred Heart Missionary site in Wilton. (Photo: Annelies Verbiest.)

biased and inaccurate media coverage and opportunistic political attacks. Asylum seekers first came in numbers to Cork as a direct result of the crisis in housing which occurred in Dublin in 1999 and the consequent decision of the government to disperse asylum seekers across Ireland. There are now asylum-seeking and refugee communities in most local communities. Despite initial forebodings, many have been well received and a plethora of local support groups has sprung up. Two such groups operate in Cork city, the Irish Immigrant Support Centre (NASC) and Cois Tine, a mainly religious group providing pastoral support, while there are informal groups outside the city in Glounthaune, Cobh and Youghal. These groups are strongly supported by the various Christian denominations as well as local Muslims and people of other faiths.

The number of asylum seekers and refugees in the city and surrounding suburbs in early 2002 was approximately 2,500. Sixty-four different nationalities were represented, of which the top ten (in descending order) were Nigeria, Romania, Russia, Democratic Republic of the Congo, Sierra Leone, Algeria, Ukraine, Cameroon, Moldova and Lithuania.[9] The majority are now living in private rented accommodation and many are likely to become permanent members of Cork society.

These developments notwithstanding, can it be said that Cork is now a multi-ethnic city? Certainly, islands of difference exist within the broader geography of the city, but there is as yet relatively little integration of new migrants in the broader community. The geographical distribution of asylum seekers is largely confined to particular city wards and certain areas have managed to avoid receiving any at all. It can hardly be mere coincidence that the two planned reception centres which have not opened are in Rochestown and Orchard Road, while the greatest numbers of asylum seekers are to be found just north of the Lee in Shandon and Blackpool, or isolated in a remote centre on the Airport Road. A politics of integration is clearly needed. Equally, such a politics needs to embrace all of the socially marginalised in the city, whether Irish or foreign, otherwise resentment and conflict are inevitable.

Yet, there are grounds for optimism. Cork City Council, under the slogan 'Cork: one city; many communities', has actively promoted good relations. The initial 'shock of the different' has largely worn off and migrant children are increasingly integrated within local schools and communities. Shops, pubs, clubs and public places have a mixed clientele. Long-term integration and an accompanying respect for diversity will require not just lip-service but debate, participation and change, for the host society and new migrants alike, over a long period of time. The possibilities of integration are reflected well in two quotations from a recent project in Cork city, *New Young Europeans,* which brought together a group of native and newcomer young people:

'I don't want to move again. I want to stay in Cork. It's safe and it's quiet here. I have very sad and difficult memories from my time in Somalia. Some things are just too difficult to talk about. I want to think that I never saw any of those things. It's too much.'

'I think people coming into Ireland with their own cultures is fantastic. What do we want, that the rest of the world shares cultures and different backgrounds and Ireland says "we're alright by ourselves, thank you"? Everyone brings their own thing and shares it and each country just becomes a more interesting and tolerant place.'[10]

38. PLANNING AND DEVELOPMENT

Nicholas Mansergh

A set of closely interrelated plans adopted between 2001 and 2004 will guide the development of the city into the next decade. Jointly commissioned by Cork City Council and Cork County Council, the Cork Area Strategic Plan 2001–2020 (CASP) provides an overall framework for the development of the city and its area of influence. Within this strategic framework more detailed policies were developed in the 2004 City Development Plan, the relevant parts of the 2003 County Development Plan and the Cork Docklands Development Strategy (2001–2025). The City and County Councils also co-operated on joint strategies through the Joint Housing Strategy (2001) and Cork Strategic Retail Study (2003). The successful implementation of these plans depends on sustained economic growth, and on what proportion of national growth occurs in the Cork area. The National Spatial Strategy 2002–2020, which refers approvingly to CASP, outlines policies to prevent undue concentration of growth in the Greater Dublin Area, and designates Cork as the largest of a range of 'Gateways' intended to promote a more balanced pattern of development in the state.

Planning in Cork evolved in three phases. The first generation of plans in the late 1960s and early 1970s

	Generation		
Type of Planning	*First (1963–1977)*	*Second (1978–1998)*	*Third (1999+)*
Strategic Land Use		Cork Land Use Transportation Study (LUTS; 1978) and LUTS Review (1992)	Cork Area Strategic Plan (CASP; 2001–2020)
Transport	BKS Traffic Plan (1968)		
Infrastructure	City Main Drainage Scheme (1965), City & Harbour Water Scheme (1970)		
Local Economy/ Cork Harbour	Cork Harbour Development Plan (1972)		
Cork County (satellite/ring towns)	Satellite Towns Policy (County Development Plans, 1967–1996)		Special Local Plans (2004) for rail-based NE growth corridor
City Centre		City Development Plans (1979–1998), Historic Centre Action Plan (1994)	Docklands Development Strategy (2001–2025)
National Context	Buchanan Report (1968), IDA Regional Plans (1972)	National Development Plans (1989–1993, 1994–1999)	National Spatial Strategy (2001–2020)

Fig. 5.74 Three phases of planning for Cork city and hinterland, 1963–2025.

CONTEMPORARY • TRANSFORMATIONS

produced a series of strategies for environmental, economic and urban development. The difficulty with these first-generation plans was that they were not necessarily compatible with each other. In 1978, the objectives of these earlier plans were integrated into the comprehensive Cork Land Use Transportation Study (LUTS), which formed the centrepiece for a second generation of development plans in Cork city and county. In 1992, the LUTS Review revised the original LUTS policies for the period to 2001, addressed the weaknesses in the local economy and sought a more balanced implementation of the original LUTS objectives. As the third-generation plan, CASP is the successor to LUTS and is the focus of the group of plans adopted since 2001.

THE CORK AREA STRATEGIC PLAN (CASP)

CASP was a product of the boom of the late 1990s. After economic stagnation in the 1980s and modest growth in the early 1990s, the Irish economy suddenly took off in 1995. The boom was initially focused on Dublin and was based on economic sectors with a preference for large urban locations. The opportunities for Cork were obvious, but CASP recognised a growing perception that the city had not capitalised on its advantages:

> The Cork City-Region must strengthen its ability to respond to change, and demonstrate an eagerness for innovation and diversity . . . [It] has outstanding assets – its people, environment, port and harbour, world class industries and education. It has no shortage of developable land on both green-field and brown-field sites. Yet there is an impression that the full potential of these advantages has not been realised and that Cork is 'punching below its weight'.[1]

CASP aimed to remedy this lack of competitiveness through regeneration of inner-city areas. In Cork's

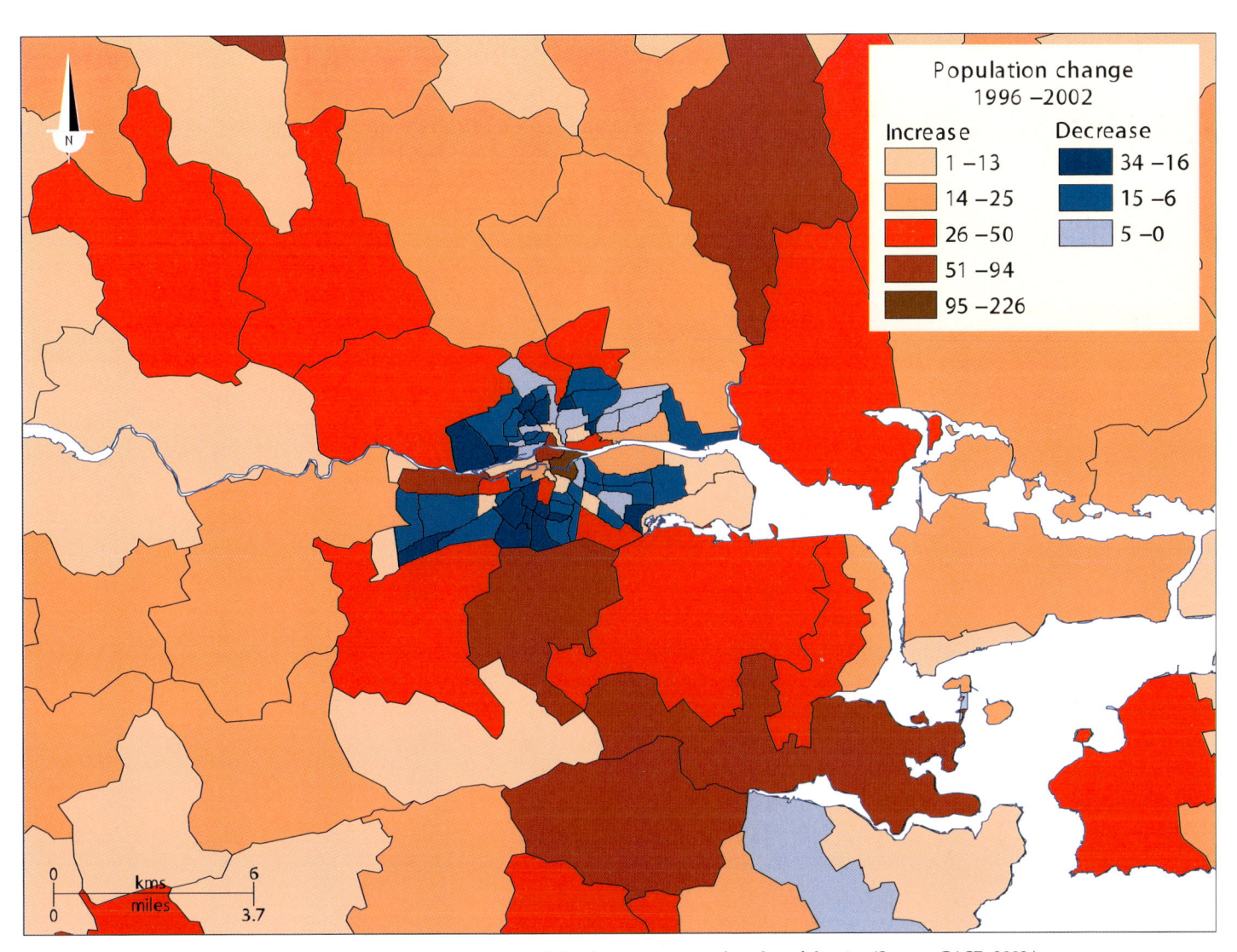

Fig. 5.75 Like many other cities in Europe, recent population growth has been greatest at the edge of the city. (Source: CASP, 2002.)

docklands, it sought to provide new IT-compatible business floor space capable of reversing the tendency for these businesses to locate in suburban business parks on the city's ring road. A bold redesign of St Patrick's Street would complement redevelopment for major expansion of shopping and leisure uses. Redevelopment for high-quality new residential schemes was also actively encouraged, and conservation projects on the lines of the successful URBAN project carried out in the North Main Street area in the mid-1990s can conserve the city's heritage. These various measures would combine to produce a much larger, livelier and more diverse central area, which would act as a more dynamic focus for the region.

The CASP study area was larger than the LUTS one. It added the ring towns 30–50 kilometres out from the city centre (Mallow, Fermoy, Bandon, Youghal, Macroom and Kinsale) to the LUTS study area, and included plans for their expansion. Reflecting the greater inter-connectivity of the settlements in the original LUTS study area, CASP renamed this zone as the 'Cork Metropolitan Area'. At the same time, CASP emphasised the need for critical mass. This strategy concentrates growth in a compact geographical area, to create a pool of high-quality services, major employers, research and educational facilities, and skilled labour close to each other. These clusters of activities will be connected by good transport facilities, including a high-frequency public transport service. In this respect, CASP seeks to combine the economic benefits of concentrating and integrating growth in key settlements with the social and environmental advantages associated with the relatively decentralised strategy adopted by LUTS. LUTS had already guided substantial growth to satellite towns and harbour industrial areas outside the city and, in some cases, at a considerable distance (Ringaskiddy, Carrigaline).

At the core of the CASP strategy is the proposal for a development corridor running from Blarney, through the northern edge of Cork city, and east to Carrigtohill and Midleton. The towns along this corridor are on existing rail lines which run through Kent Station near the centre of the city (the ten-kilometre spur to Midleton is disused but intact). These lines already have suburban services to Cobh and Mallow, the rails are still in place and there is considerable developable green-field land directly adjoining them. Concentrating substantial development along these lines would make it economic to run trains at fifteen-minute intervals, and a service of that quality is in turn needed to change negative attitudes towards the use of public transport.

CASP encourages a major shift towards public transport because Cork risks being strangled by traffic if new housing and employment is not directed into places where it can be served by a first-class public transport system. Cork can achieve the critical mass of mutually accessible employment, services and housing which CASP regards as being needed to promote greater economic dynamism. Obviously, there is much more to CASP than this core project. CASP envisages the suburban rail service connecting with a network of quality bus services running along 'green routes', and movement north of the city facilitated through construction of a northern outer ring road. Even within the Cork Metropolitan Area, substantial growth is envisaged in areas south and west of the city, mainly Carrigaline, Ringaskiddy and Ballincollig. Outside the Metropolitan Area, there are also proposals to expand the ring towns, though emphasis is on those which are connected to the rail system, such as Mallow, or which might eventually be reconnected to it, such as Youghal.

However, the success of CASP is dependent on the rail corridor project. The proposal is not entirely new, as both LUTS studies had also sought to increase the development occurring on the rail corridor, to upgrade rail services on it and to reopen the Midleton branch. However, whilst the LUTS Review did help avert closure of the Cobh line, which was a distinct possibility in 1990, overall investment in public transport, notably bus services, was minimal. The national policy context is more favourable now than it was at the time of the LUTS. There is wider acceptance of the need to invest in public transport. The CASP rail system gained the backing of the 2003 Strategic Rail Review and the Minister for Transport announced funding for the system in 2004.

Plans for the north-east corridor

Development of the north-east corridor and the suburban rail project are interdependent. A growing population in that corridor will support more frequent trains, and more frequent trains will attract more residents and jobs. A sense of momentum has already developed. On lands near Rushbrooke Station, on the Cobh line, residential developments totalling around a thousand houses have recently been completed. Two thousand homes are being built or have planning permission in the area between the main street of Carrigtohill and the Midleton line. In Blackpool, major shopping and associated commercial developments have been built close to the proposed Kilbarry Station. Special local area plans for Midleton, Carrigtohill and the Blarney/Kilbarry area have been prepared by the County Council, in response to the government announcement on the rail project and in order to ensure rapid development in the areas served by it.

Fig. 5.76 Using infrared imagery, different land-use patterns become more apparent. The darker areas represent built-up land while the light pink areas are largely areas undergoing new construction or development. Water, such as at The Lough, is represented as black. Bright pink areas adjacent to farmland on the outskirts of the city are ploughed fields. Of interest is the denser built-up urban environment on the northside, in comparison to the 'leafy suburbs' south of the Lee. The image also effectively illustrates new residential and commercial development in the areas around the South Link Road. (Source: Philip O'Kane, Department of Civil and Environmental Engineering, UCC.)

A sense of momentum is needed, because the project implies a substantial shift in the way local property and transport markets work. Traditionally, much of the northside of Cork city and most of the towns and villages in the corridor have been in secondary property markets. In the 1980s, for instance, development more or less stopped in such areas and retreated to prime property markets in the south and west suburbs and towns (notwithstanding LUTS policies to the contrary). In the 1990s, as the economy recovered, more balanced development resumed, along the lines envisaged by the 1992 LUTS Review. Once a strong development dynamic in the north-east corridor is in place, this vulnerability to recessions should ease. Continued, reasonably rapid, progress with the rail project is needed to give developers, businesses and potential residents the confidence that the overall policy is working.

There is an important social dimension to this. Cork is quite an unequal city. Northern and eastern parts of the city are still affected by the cumulative effects of this inequality, experienced over the last half-century. These areas have a

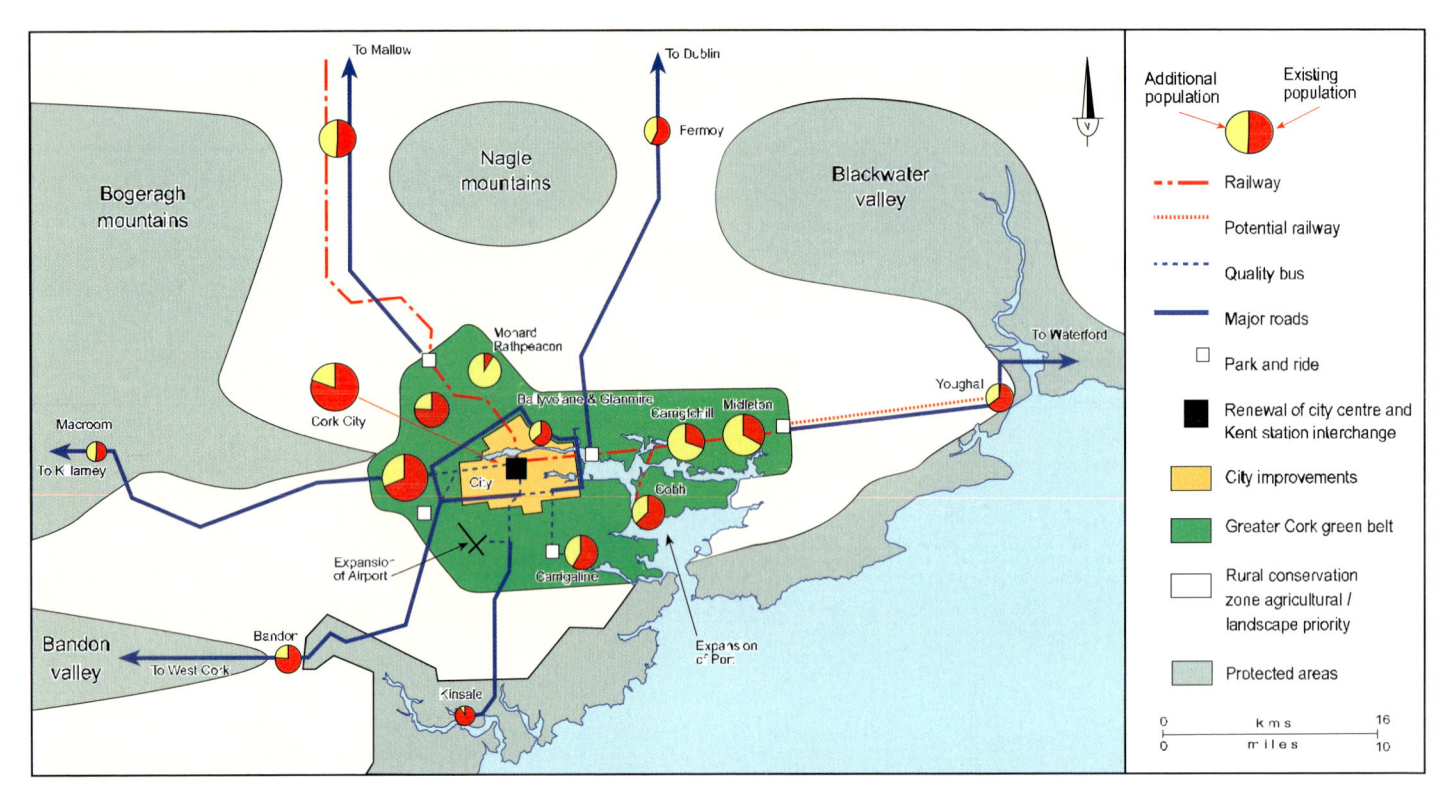

Fig. 5.77 The Cork Area Strategic Plan (CASP) intends to guide development in the city region for the next decade. This plan outlines the strategies and investment needed to promote Cork as a major national strategic growth centre. The priorities of the plan include the revitalisation of Cork city, the improvement of the ring towns, the implementation of rural strategy and the development of new and existing infrastructure. The plan proposes that Cork will become 'a leading European city region – globally competitive, socially inclusive and culturally enriched'. (Source: CASP, 2002.)

higher proportion of social housing, higher unemployment and have received less immediate benefit from the major regional institutions developed from the 1970s onwards (such as third-level education institutions and hospitals), which are concentrated in the south-west of the city. The processes by which growth occurs in some areas and not in others are dynamic ones and, if one wishes to change them, an alternative dynamic is needed. CASP responds to the advantages of the north-east corridor by encouraging greater capacity to accommodate new development and provide it with good transport facilities, in a bid to create such an alternative dynamic.

Docklands

The focus of the proposed rail system is Kent Station, in the docklands area, on the edge of the existing city centre. Kent Station is well placed to serve the large-scale redevelopment proposed for the docklands, which covers 166 hectares, an area similar in size to the existing central area of the city. The Docklands Development Strategy outlines a suggested urban pattern of redevelopment, involving mixed uses and a relatively fine-grain street pattern and plot size, and with new foot and road bridges connecting the north and south quays. This area is still in use, to a greater extent than is normal in dockland redevelopment projects, and ships continue to use the south quays in particular. However, there is also significant vacancy and underuse, and much of the existing use is extensive and industrial in character. There were only 2,000 jobs in the area in 2001 (compared to 29,000 in the central area proper). Assuming relocation of the remaining port activities down harbour, the area has the capacity to accommodate 580,000 square metres of employment uses, and around 6,000 residential units, as well as parks and a marina.

The Docklands Strategy attempts to increase the proportion of CASP area employment and population accommodated in the centre. In this respect, it is more ambitious than previous plans. In 1968 the BKS Traffic Plan assumed that the less prevalent centralised land-use pattern would continue, but also illustrated the difficulty of coping with projected traffic volumes under that assumption. By the time of the 1978 LUTS study, decentralised trends were well established and LUTS aimed at managing these trends in a more coherent and environmentally sensitive manner, rather than stopping or reversing them. Better management of the property market was needed, as vacant land in the central area had doubled between 1963 and 1978 (from 4.5 to 9.5 hectares) and one-sixth of central area property was vacant. The city development plan in 1979 sought to reverse the trend in vacant property through promoting renewal, controlling decentralisation of office and shopping development and slowing the rate at which lower-value but extensive existing uses (such as housing and industry) were lost.

These policies worked. Vacant land in the centre fell to 6.5 hectares by 1987, and to 3.5 by 1997. However, vacancy can be reduced by two distinct methods: by absolute increases in employment and/or population; and by varying the mix of intensive and extensive land uses. Successive city development plans from 1979 onwards aimed for both, but in practice the balance between them changed. In the 1980s, renewal occurred but took the form of higher-quality accommodation with more space per resident or per job (including public open space such as Bishop Lucey Park), and this factor reduced vacancy. In the 1990s, tax relief in the designated areas encouraged substantial apartment construction, and the city-centre population in 2002 was 36 per cent above its 1991 level. The 1990s boom caused a sudden jump in city-centre employment (which had been stable at 20,000 since the early 1970s) to 29,000 in 2002, even though there was very limited new development in the centre at that time.

These changes in market conditions created a realistic context for an explicitly recentralised approach, which had not existed previously. The question was: how recentralised? The Docklands Strategy involves higher average densities than those prevailing in the central area at present, as well as the eastwards expansion of the centre. This strategy is more evident in relation to the employment component of the Docklands Strategy than the residential one. If one assumes one job per 20 square metres, the 580,000 square metres of employment floor space envisaged in the docklands could accommodate 29,000 extra jobs, or a 50–60 per cent share of total job growth projected for the CASP area to 2020. This is a highly re-centralised position, as the city centre currently has 20 per cent of existing CASP area jobs. Prospects for achieving this plan could improve if there were a 'lead sector' to help. Comparable developments in Dublin have been 'led' by an economic sector: the Custom House Docks had financial services; Temple Bar had culture and tourism. In Cork, it might be possible to locate a major institution in the docklands, on the scale of CIT, Cork University Hospital or FÁS when they were established at Bishopstown in the 1970s. However, such institutions are not created very often and their impact is possibly not sufficient.

In contrast, the 6,000 residential units envisaged in the docklands contribute 10 per cent of projected extra housing

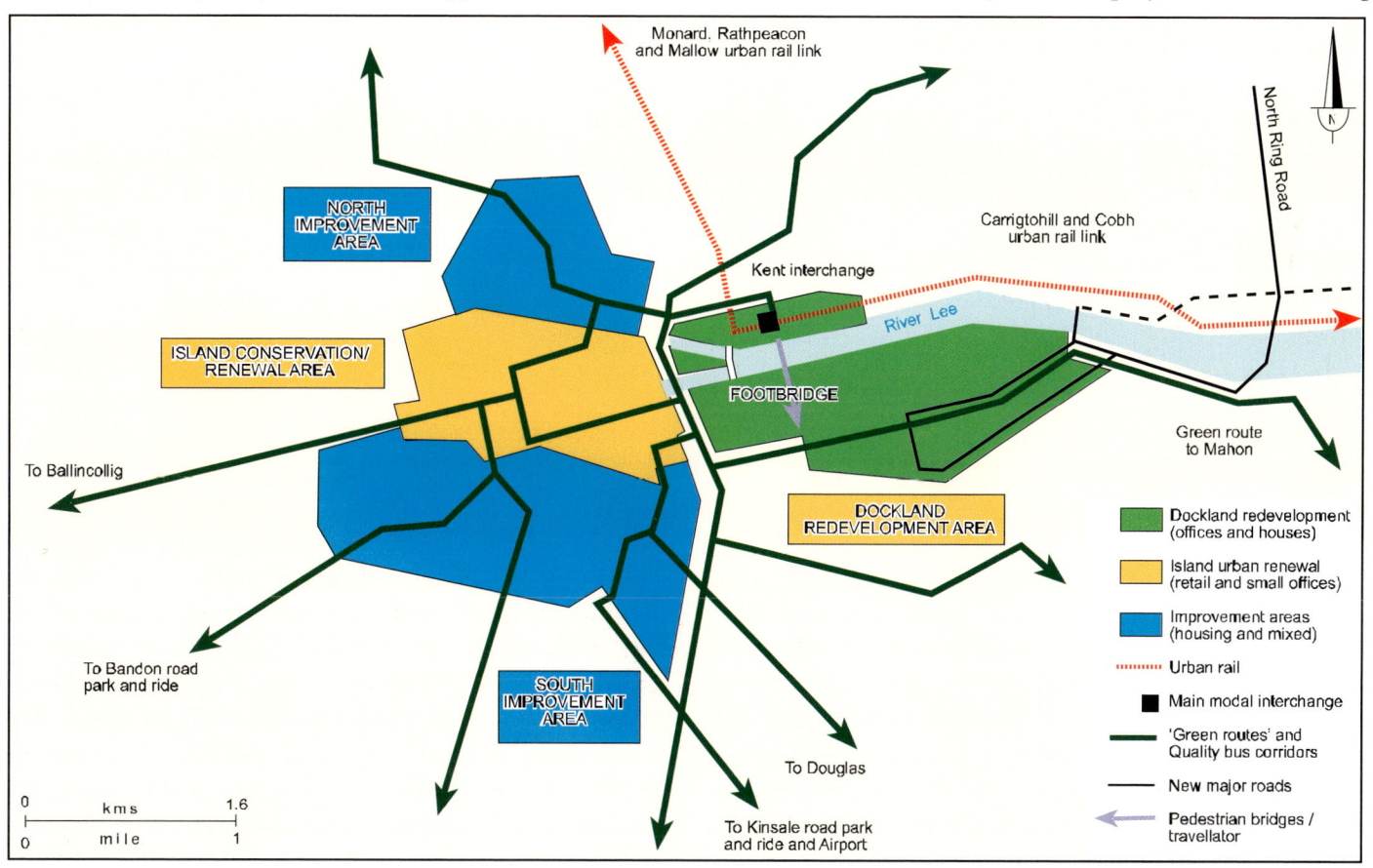

Fig. 5.78 The planning strategy for Cork's inner city will boost population growth, improve the urban fabric, enhance public spaces and support commercial development. Four key areas will be the focus of improvement: the docklands, the central island and both the northern and southern suburban areas. (Source: CASP.)

Fig. 5.79 One of the new developments proposed in the Cork docklands. Launched in 2001, the Docklands Development Strategy initiative simultaneously proposed to regenerate 'brown-field' areas on the site of the eighteenth- and nineteenth-century port while providing new opportunities for urban living and the diversification of the city's economy. Encouraging mixed uses and ensuring public access to the waterfront will be important to the social sustainability of these developments and the city in general. (Murray O'Laoire Architects.)

units in the CASP area over the next 20 years. As 20 per cent of current housing output in Cork city and county are apartments and a further 10 per cent are terraced houses, this is not an unrealistic share of the market. The problem will be to achieve sufficient diversity. Most new apartments in Cork have been sold to investors as private rental units. Many such developments were built in the existing city centre during the 1990s, where they now constitute 5 per cent of city-centre property. In the docklands, they will constitute up to 50 per cent, as relatively little existing development seems likely to be retained. It would be possible to pursue explicitly a diverse mix of tenures and dwelling types, to avoid dominance by the private rented sector. Units with views of the water should be attractive to owner-occupiers, and it should also be possible to promote niche residential markets (such as owner-occupied town houses and apartments, and housing associations) elsewhere in the area.

By encouraging development in this way, it may be difficult to match the supply of centrally located land with demand of adequate quality and diversity. This is not an immediate problem. On the supply side, dockland sites will not all come on-stream in the near future. In the South Docks in particular, relocation of existing uses is not straightforward and cannot be done quickly. On the demand side, new commercial development, which for various reasons (such as demand for technology space which could be provided quickly, in volume, and on an off-the-peg basis; tax designation of Cork Airport Business Park; major changes in accessibility produced by completion of the ring road) had swung drastically towards suburban and edge-of-city locations in the late 1990s, has since swung back towards the city centre. The retail core is benefiting from the redesign of St Patrick's Street and will profit from redevelopment proposals which should attract additional department stores.

The docklands area is held in quite large blocks by a relatively small number of owners. This could be helpful, as it may facilitate incremental development, on a block-by-block basis, and it should minimise the time-consuming assembly of multiple small properties. Notwithstanding the preference of the Docklands Strategy for a fine-grain, urban pattern of development, the potential to offer large businesses substantial sites would make the area more competitive with suburban employment locations.

THE ECONOMIC CONTEXT AND THE NATIONAL SPATIAL STRATEGY

Irish growth rates depend mainly on international economic conditions, but the pattern of growth, both in the state as a whole and in Cork, will also be affected by how far balanced regional development in the 2002 National Spatial Strategy (NSS) is actually realised. Like the earlier (unimplemented) 1968 Buchanan Report, the NSS assumes that mobile investment and growth are most effectively promoted by the economies of scale available in large urban areas with deep

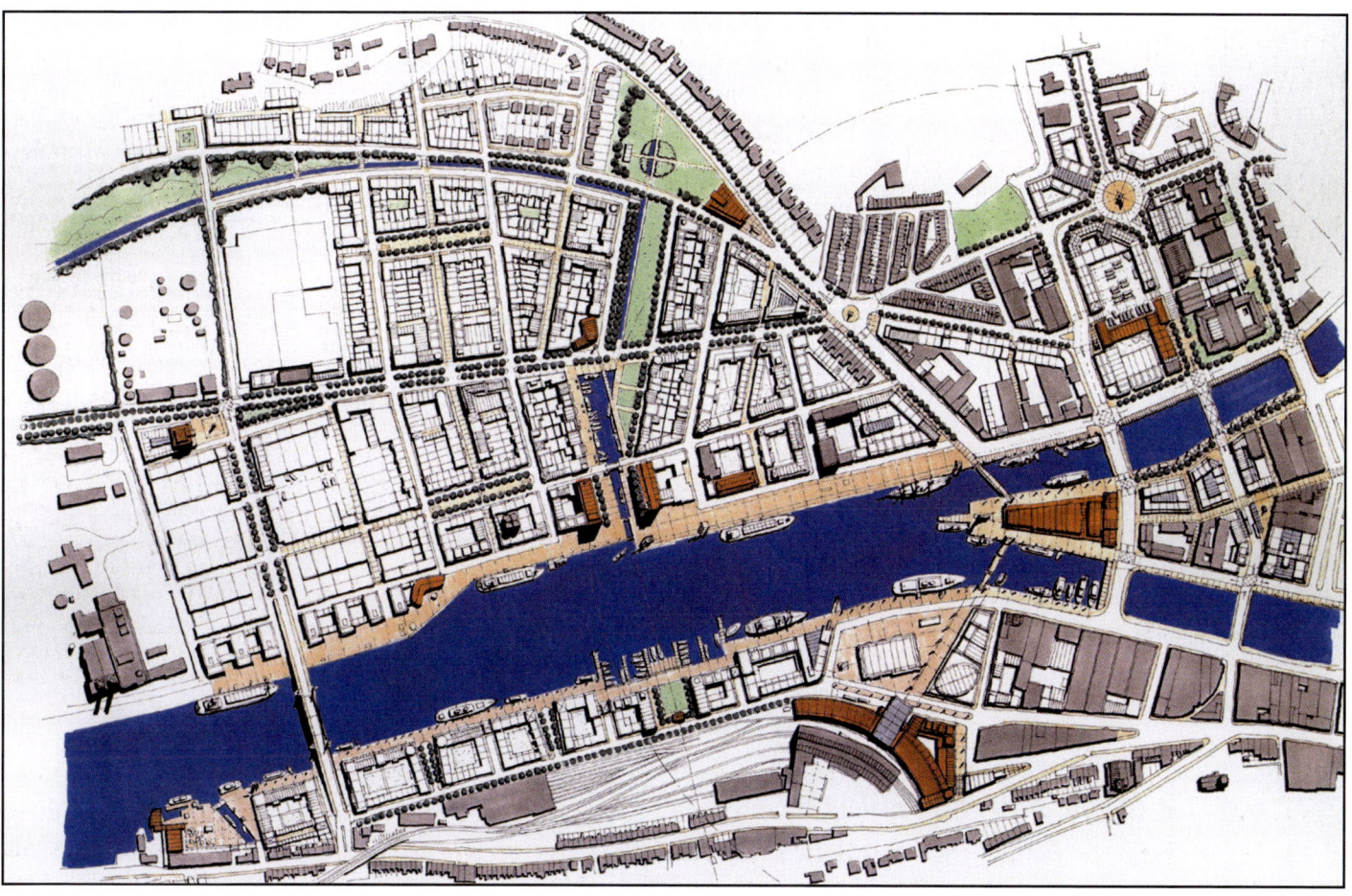

Fig. 5.80 Whilst ensuring that the existing qualities of the area are maintained, the Dockland Master Plan envisages radical transformation. Central to this vision is a diversity of public and commercial uses that will promote the development of a vibrant and sustainable urban quarter. In addition to a number of new bridges, proposals include the establishment of a linear park by Monahan Road, the extension of Marina Park and the creation of a new square at the junction of Centre Park Square and Water Street. (Dockland Development Strategy, 2001.)

labour markets and a wide range of skills and services. If such economies are truly decisive, Dublin will remain the area best placed to achieve them. The NSS view that the 'Gateway' centres should enhance their own competitive advantages implies that they will have to have sources of competitive advantage which are not strictly or linearly related to size.

One possible source is regional economic specialisation. The NSS refers to the need to strengthen regional 'clusters', and to support them through relevant educational, research, training and infrastructure facilities. Cork's most obvious specialisation is in chemicals/pharmaceuticals, of which it is the principal centre in Ireland. Specialisation in this sector is the fruit of a policy of developing industrial estates and infrastructure adjoining Cork harbour from the early 1970s. However, that example illustrates the time and costs involved in building up a critical mass in a particular sector, as well as the eventual benefits. Cork has also developed significant specialisation in other sectors, including electronics/IT and the food industry, both of which are supported by third-level educational institutions and research facilities. Continued support for these areas will be central to the development of the city.

A shorter-term strategy available to the Gateways is to maintain lower levels of congestion and property costs than in Dublin, and to provide a higher quality of life. This is the natural competitive advantage that a smaller city normally has over a larger one. How effective it is depends partly on the quality of planning in each, and partly on whether government funding policies are dominated by the so-called 'worst first' principle. This involves investing in high-cost infrastructure to serve areas already experiencing acute deficiencies and congestion, although such investment will stimulate further growth in those areas, requiring yet more investment and leading to a situation in which capital cities end up with a disproportionate share of modern infrastructure. Governments have little option but to follow such policies much of the time. The crucial question is whether they reserve adequate funding to create capacity for development proactively, at lower cost and ahead of demand, in regional centres. If they do, the prospects for sustained diversion of a proportion of future growth to regional centres are improved.

Economic growth does not happen evenly. It proceeds in surges and pauses. A regional centre is particularly attractive to inward investment during surges, when the primary centre is most likely to be experiencing high congestion costs. If the regional centres have only limited spare capacity, they will quickly be affected by congestion costs as well, and the country as a whole may become less attractive for investment. Cork's future ability to contribute to national economic growth is likely to depend on targeted advance provision of the types of infrastructure which come under most pressure during booms. Transport and accessible, serviced development land are where the pinch was most evident in the late 1990s. The north-east rail corridor is both the principal strategic growth area identified by CASP and also a secondary area, in property market terms, which will benefit disproportionately under boom conditions. What happens in that area is thus likely to be a key factor in determining Cork's capacity to contribute to overall national growth.

NOTES

I. The City in the Landscape

Introduction

1. Cork County Council, *Cork area strategic plan (CASP) 2001–2020* (CASP Office, County Hall, Cork, 2001; http://www.corkcorp.ie/corkstrategicplan).
2. J.A. Murphy, 'Cork: Anatomy and essence', in P. O'Flanagan and C.G. Buttimer (eds), *Cork history and society: Interdisciplinary essays on the history of an Irish county* (Dublin, 1993), pp. 1–14.
3. J.B. Whittow, *Geology and scenery in Ireland* (Harmondsworth, 1974).
4. M.J. Gardiner and T. Radford, *Ireland: General soil map* (2nd ed.) (Teagasc, Dublin, 1980; http://www.teagasc.ie/research/reports/environment/4104/eopr-4104.htm).
5. O'Flanagan and Buttimer (eds), *Cork history and society*.
6. A.M. Sinnott and R.J.N. Devoy, 'The geomorphology of Ireland's coastline: Patterns, processes and future prospects', *Hommes et Terres du Nord, Revue de l'Institut de Geographie de Lille*, 1992–3 (1992), pp. 145–53.
7. F.G. Mitchell, *The Irish landscape* (Glasgow, 1976).
8. Cork County Council, *Cork County Council N22 Ballyvourney–Macroom–Ballincollig road project route selection report* (Cork County Hall, Cork, 2003; http:// www.Phmcc.com/n22_web/n22).
9. M. Andrews, *The life and work of Robert Gibbings* (London, 2003).
10. A.F. O'Brien, 'Politics, economy and society: The development of Cork and the Irish south-coast region', in O'Flanagan and Buttimer (eds), *Cork history and society*, pp. 83–156.
11. R.J.N. Devoy, S.L. Nichol and A.M. Sinnott, 'Holocene sea-level and sedimentary changes on the south coast of Ireland', *Journal of Coastal Research*, SI39 (2004).

1. Cork City and the Evolution of the Lee Valley

1. I.A.J. MacCarthy, *Geological map of the Cork district: Geological surveying and map compilation* (University College Cork, 1988); I.A.J. MacCarthy, 'Guide to the geology of the Cork city and harbour region' (Report Series, 01/02, Department of Geology, NUIC, 2002); I.A.J. MacCarthy, 'Geology of the Devonian–Carboniferous south Munster basin, Ireland' (Department of Geology, UCC).
2. MacCarthy, *Geological map of the Cork district*; MacCarthy, 'Guide to the geology of the Cork city and harbour region'; MacCarthy, 'Geology of the Devonian–Carboniferous south Munster basin, Ireland'.
3. J.B. Whittow, *Geology and scenery in Ireland* (Harmondsworth, 1974); G.L.H. Davies and N. Stephens, *The geomorphology of the British Isles: Ireland* (London, 1978).
4. MacCarthy, *Geological map of the Cork district*; MacCarthy, 'Guide to the geology of the Cork city and harbour region'; MacCarthy, 'Geology of the Devonian–Carboniferous south Munster basin, Ireland'.
5. Whittow, *Geology and scenery in Ireland*; Davies and Stephens, *The geomorphology of the British Isles: Ireland*.
6. Whittow, *Geology and scenery in Ireland*; Davies and Stephens, *The geomorphology of the British Isles: Ireland*.
7. A.A. Miller, 'The origin of the south Ireland peneplane', *Irish Geography*, 3 (1955), pp. 79–86; G.L.H. Davies and J.B. Whittow, 'A reconsideration of the drainage pattern of counties Cork and Waterford', *Irish Geography*, 8 (1975), pp. 24–41.
8. Whittow, *Geology and scenery in Ireland*; Davies and Stephens, *The geomorphology of the British Isles: Ireland*; Miller, 'The origin of the south Ireland peneplane'; Davies and Whittow, 'A reconsideration of the drainage pattern of counties Cork and Waterford'.
9. Miller, 'The origin of the south Ireland peneplane'; Davies and Whittow, 'A reconsideration of the drainage pattern of counties Cork and Waterford'.
10. Whittow, *Geology and scenery in Ireland*; Davies and Stephens, *The geomorphology of the British Isles: Ireland*.
11. Miller, 'The origin of the south Ireland peneplane'; Davies and Whittow, 'A reconsideration of the drainage pattern of counties Cork and Waterford'.
12. R.J.N. Devoy, A.M. Sinnott, Y. O'Connell, L. Dowling and J.D. Scourse, 'Quaternary stratigraphic reconstructions and the marine Gortian interglacial sediments from Cork harbour, Ireland' (Occasional Publication 01/99, Department of Geography, NUIC, 1999); R.J.N. Devoy, A.M. Sinnott, K-L. Knudsen, P. Kristensen and J.D. Peacock, 'Interglacial relative sea-level and Quaternary palaeoenvironmental changes from Cork harbour, Ireland' (Occasional Publication 02/99, Department of Geography, UCC, 1999; http://cmrc.ucc.ie).
13. Devoy, Sinnott, O'Connell, Dowling and Scourse, 'Quaternary stratigraphic reconstructions and the marine Gortian interglacial sediments from Cork harbour, Ireland'; Devoy, Sinnott, Knudsen, Kristensen and Peacock, 'Interglacial relative sea-level and Quaternary palaeoenvironmental changes from Cork harbour, Ireland'.
14. Devoy, Sinnott, O'Connell, Dowling and Scourse, 'Quaternary stratigraphic reconstructions and the marine Gortian interglacial sediments from Cork harbour, Ireland'; Devoy, Sinnott, Knudsen, Kristensen and Peacock, 'Interglacial relative sea-level and Quaternary palaeoenvironmental changes from Cork harbour, Ireland'.
15. A. Farrington, 'The Lee basin, part one: Glaciation', *Proceedings of the Royal Irish Academy*, 60B (1959), pp. 135–66; T.A. Reilly and A.G. Sleeman, *Geological setting for the proposed Mahon–Ringaskiddy pipeline* (Report to Bord Gáis Éireann, Geological Survey of Ireland, Dublin, 1979).
16. MacCarthy, *Geological map of the Cork district*; MacCarthy, 'Guide to the geology of the Cork city and harbour region'; MacCarthy, 'Geology of the Devonian–Carboniferous south Munster basin, Ireland'.
17. J.B. Whittow, *Geology and scenery in Ireland* (Harmondsworth, 1974); Davies and Stephens, *The geomorphology of the British Isles: Ireland*; Devoy, Sinnott, O'Connell, Dowling and Scourse, 'Quaternary stratigraphic reconstructions and the marine Gortian interglacial sediments from Cork harbour, Ireland'; Devoy, Sinnott, Knudsen, Kristensen and Peacock, 'Interglacial relative sea-level and Quaternary palaeoenvironmental changes from Cork harbour, Ireland'.
18. R.J.N. Devoy and A.M. Sinnott, 'Late glacial environments in County Cork: Patterns and processes of change', in P. Coxon

(ed.), *Glacial events* (Irish Quaternary Association [IQUA] Annual Symposium, Dublin, 1993), pp. 15–18.

19 Devoy, Sinnott, O'Connell, Dowling and Scourse, 'Quaternary stratigraphic reconstructions and the marine Gortian interglacial sediments from Cork harbour, Ireland'; Devoy, Sinnott, Knudsen, Kristensen and Peacock, 'Interglacial relative sea-level and Quaternary palaeoenvironmental changes from Cork harbour, Ireland'; Farrington, 'The Lee basin, part one: Glaciation'; Reilly and Sleeman, *Geological setting for the proposed Mahon–Ringaskiddy pipeline*.

20 MacCarthy, *Geological map of the Cork district*; MacCarthy, 'Guide to the geology of the Cork city and harbour region'; MacCarthy, 'Geology of the Devonian–Carboniferous south Munster basin, Ireland'.

21 J.J. Lowe and M.J.C. Walker, *Reconstructing Quaternary environments* (London, 1997); T.H. van Andel and P.C. Tzedakis, 'Palaeolithic landscapes of Europe and environs, 150,000–25,000 years ago: An overview', *Quaternary Science Reviews*, 15 (1996), pp. 481–500; C. Gallagher and M. Thorp, 'The age of the Pleistocene raised beach near Fethard, County Wexford, using infrared stimulated luminescence (IRSL)', *Irish Geography*, 30 (1997), pp. 68–89.

22 F.M. Synge, 'Quaternary glaciation and changes of sea level in the south of Ireland', *Geologie en Mijnbouw*, 60 (1981), pp. 305–15; W.P. Warren, 'Stratigraphy', in K.J. Edwards and W.P. Warren (eds), *The Quaternary history of Ireland* (London, 1985), pp. 39–65.

23 Devoy, Sinnott, O'Connell, Dowling and Scourse, 'Quaternary stratigraphic reconstructions and the marine Gortian interglacial sediments from Cork harbour, Ireland'; Devoy, Sinnott, Knudsen, Kristensen and Peacock, 'Interglacial relative sea-level and Quaternary palaeoenvironmental changes from Cork harbour, Ireland'.

24 J.D. Scourse, J.R.M. Allen, W.E.N. Austin, R.J.N. Devoy, P. Coxon and H.P. Sejrup, 'New evidence on the age and significance of the Gortian Temperate Stage: A preliminary report on the Cork harbour site', *Proceedings of the Royal Irish Academy*, 92B (1992), pp. 21–43; L.A. Dowling, H.P. Sejrup, P. Coxon and H. Heijnis, 'Palynology, aminostratigraphy and U-series dating of marine Gortian interglacial sediments in Cork harbour, southern Ireland', *Quaternary Science Reviews*, 17 (1998).

25 R.W.G. Carter, R.J.N. Devoy and J. Shaw, 'Holocene sea levels in Ireland', *Journal of Quaternary Science*, 4 (1989), pp. 7–24.

26 Devoy and Sinnott, 'Late glacial environments in County Cork: Patterns and processes of change'.

27 Devoy, Sinnott, O'Connell, Dowling and Scourse, 'Quaternary stratigraphic reconstructions and the marine Gortian interglacial sediments from Cork harbour, Ireland'; Devoy, Sinnott, Knudsen, Kristensen and Peacock, 'Interglacial relative sea-level and Quaternary palaeoenvironmental changes from Cork harbour, Ireland'.

28 Devoy, Sinnott, O'Connell, Dowling and Scourse, 'Quaternary stratigraphic reconstructions and the marine Gortian interglacial sediments from Cork harbour, Ireland'; Devoy, Sinnott, Knudsen, Kristensen and Peacock, 'Interglacial relative sea-level and Quaternary palaeoenvironmental changes from Cork harbour, Ireland'.

29 Whittow, *Geology and scenery in Ireland*; Davies and Stephens, *The geomorphology of the British Isles: Ireland*.

30 MacCarthy, *Geological map of the Cork district*; MacCarthy, 'Guide to the geology of the Cork city and harbour region'; MacCarthy, 'Geology of the Devonian–Carboniferous south Munster basin, Ireland'.

31 I. Lozano, R.J.N. Devoy, W. May and U. Andersen, 'Storminess and vulnerability along the Atlantic coastlines of Europe: Analysis of storm records and of a greenhouse gases induced climate scenario', *Marine Geology*, 210 (2004), pp. 205–25; N.J. Shackleton and N.D. Opdyke, 'Oxygen isotope and palaeomagnetic stratigraphy of equatorial Pacific core V28–238: Oxygen isotope temperatures and ice volume on a 10^5 and 10^6 year scale', *Quaternary Research*, 3 (1973), pp. 39–55; D.G. Martinson, N.G. Pisias, J.D. Hays, J. Imbrie, T.C. Moore and N.J. Shackleton, 'Age dating and the orbital theory of the ice ages: Development of a high resolution 0–300,000 year chronostratigraphy', *Quaternary Research*, 27 (1987), pp. 1–29.

2. **THE CLIMATE OF CORK**

A CLIMATE SYNOPSIS

1 E. Barry, *Air pollution in Cork city: 2002 report* (Cork Corporation, 2002). Websites at: http://www.corkcorp.ie http://www.environ.ie/DOEI/DOEIPol.nsf http://www.irishstatutebook.ie/ZZS1403Y1994.html

2 Met Éireann, *Weather reports* (Glasnevin, Dublin, 2004; http://www.met.ie); P.K. Rohan, *The climate of Ireland* (Dublin, 1986); D. Fitzgerald and F. Forrestal, *Monthly and annual averages of rainfall for Ireland* (Met Éireann, Dublin, 1986).

3 Met Éireann, *Weather reports*; Rohan, *The climate of Ireland*; Fitzgerald and Forrestal, *Monthly and annual averages of rainfall for Ireland*.

4 R.J.N. Devoy, 'The Gulf Stream', in B. Lalor (ed.), *Encyclopaedia of Ireland* (Dublin, 2003), p. 464; G. Mills, 'Climate' (Dublin, 2003), pp. 210–11.

5 Barry, *Air pollution in Cork city: 2002 report*; Met Éireann, *Weather reports*; Rohan, *The climate of Ireland*; Fitzgerald and Forrestal, *Monthly and annual averages of rainfall for Ireland*; A. Donnelly, L. McElwain, J. Sweeney and M. Jones, *Climate change and Ireland: Assessing the implications* (Wexford, 2002).

6 Met Éireann, *Weather reports*; Rohan, *The climate of Ireland*; Fitzgerald and Forrestal, *Monthly and annual averages of rainfall for Ireland*; Donnelly, McElwain, Sweeney and Jones, *Climate change and Ireland: Assessing the implications*.

7 Devoy, 'The Gulf Stream', p. 464; Mills, 'Climate', pp. 210–11.

8 Met Éireann, *Weather reports*; Rohan, *The climate of Ireland*; Fitzgerald and Forrestal, *Monthly and annual averages of rainfall for Ireland*.

9 Met Éireann, *Weather reports*; Rohan, *The climate of Ireland*; Fitzgerald and Forrestal, *Monthly and annual averages of rainfall for Ireland*.

10 J.P. Haughton (ed.), *Atlas of Ireland* (Dublin, 1979).

11 Donnelly, McElwain, Sweeney and Jones, *Climate change and Ireland: Assessing the implications*.

12 Ibid.

13 Devoy, 'The Gulf Stream', p. 464; Mills, 'Climate', pp. 210–11; I. Lozano, R.J.N. Devoy, W. May and U. Andersen, 'Storminess and vulnerability along the Atlantic coastlines of Europe', *Marine Geology*, 210 (2004), pp. 205–25; IPCC, *Climate change 2001: Impacts, adaptation and vulnerability* (Cambridge University Press, 2001).

WEATHER AND NATURAL DISASTERS

1 H.H. Lamb, *Climate history and the modern world* (second ed., London, 1995); A. Dawson, L. Elliott, S. Noone, K. Hickey, T. Holt, P. Wadhams and I. Foster, 'Historical storminess and

climate "seesaws" in the North Atlantic region', *Marine Geology*, 210 (2004), pp. 247–59.
2. *Cork Examiner* (www.examiner.ie).
3. F.H. Tuckey, *The county and city of Cork remembrancer* (Osborne Savage and Son, Cork, 1837); G.C. Doran, 'The Lough of Cork', *JCHAS*, ii (1893), p. 197.
4. C. Smith, *The antient and present state of the county and city of Cork* (Guy & Co., Cork, 1893), 2 vols.
5. *Dublin Gazette*, 1740.
6. D. Dickson, *Arctic Ireland: The extraordinary story of the great frost and forgotten famine of 1740–1741* (Belfast, 1997).
7. Tuckey, *The county and city of Cork remembrancer*; Doran, 'The Lough of Cork', p. 197.
8. Smith, *The antient and present state of the county and city of Cork*.
9. *Cork Constitution*, 1838.
10. *Dublin Evening Mail*, 1841.
11. Tuckey, *The county and city of Cork remembrancer*; Doran, 'The Lough of Cork', p. 197.
12. Smith, *The antient and present state of the county and city of Cork*.
13. Tuckey, *The county and city of Cork remembrancer*; Doran, 'The Lough of Cork', p. 197.
14. Smith, *The antient and present state of the county and city of Cork*.
15. Ibid.
16. Tuckey, *The county and city of Cork remembrancer*; Doran, 'The Lough of Cork', p. 197.
17. Ibid.
18. Ibid.
19. *Saunders' Newsletter*, 1850.
20. Lamb, *Climate history and the modern world*; Dawson, Elliott, Noone, Hickey, Holt, Wadhams and Foster, 'Historical storminess and climate "seesaws" in the North Atlantic region', pp. 247–59; Tuckey, *The county and city of Cork remembrancer*; Doran, 'The Lough of Cork', p. 197.
21. Tuckey, *The county and city of Cork remembrancer*; Doran, 'The Lough of Cork', p. 197.
22. K.R. Hickey, 'The night of the big wind: The impact of the storm on Loughrea', in J. Forde, C. Cassidy, P. Manzor and D. Ryan (eds), *The district of Loughrea, volume 1: History 1791–1918* (Loughrea History Project, 2003), pp. 130–42; P. Carr, *The night of the big wind: The story of the legendary big wind of 1839, Ireland's greatest natural disaster* (White Row Press, Belfast, 1993).
23. *Cork Examiner*, 1848.
24. Tuckey, *The county and city of Cork remembrancer*; Doran, 'The Lough of Cork', p. 197.
25. Smith, *The antient and present state of the county and city of Cork*.
26. Ibid.
27. Tuckey, *The county and city of Cork remembrancer*; Doran, 'The Lough of Cork', p. 197.
28. D. Alexander, *Natural disasters* (University College London Press, London, 1993).
29. Tuckey, *The county and city of Cork remembrancer*; Doran, 'The Lough of Cork', p. 197.
30. Lamb, *Climate history and the modern world*; Dawson, Elliott, Noone, Hickey, Holt, Wadhams and Foster, 'Historical storminess and climate "seesaws" in the North Atlantic region', pp. 247–59; Tuckey, *The county and city of Cork remembrancer*; Doran, 'The Lough of Cork', p. 197.
31. Devoy, 'The Gulf Stream', p. 464; Mills, 'Climate'; Lozano, Devoy, May and Andersen, *Storminess and vulnerability along the Atlantic coastlines of Europe*; IPCC, *Climate change 2001: Impacts, adaptation and vulnerability*.

3. FLOODING IN THE CITY

FLOODS AND CLIMATE CHANGE

1. M. Healy and K.R. Hickey, 'Land reclamation on the Shannon estuary', *Journal of Coastal Research*, 36 (2002), pp. 365–73.
2. J. McGrath, K. Barry, J.P.J. O'Kane and R.C. Kavanagh, *High resolution DEM and sea-level rise in the centre of Cork: Blue City Project* (Occasional Publication 2002/01, Department of Civil and Environmental Engineering, UCC, 2002).
3. C. Smith, *The ancient and present state of the county and city of Cork: Containing a natural, civil, ecclesiastical, historical and topographical description thereof* (2 vols.) (Guy & Co., Cork, 1893), vol. 1, p. 419.
4. C. Rynne, *The archaeology of Cork city and harbour* (Cork, 1993); G. Johnson, *The laneways of medieval Cork* (Cork, 2002).
5. Rynne, *The archaeology of Cork city and harbour*; Johnson, *The laneways of medieval Cork*.
6. K.R. Hickey, 'The historical climatology of flooding in Cork city from 1841–1988' (MA thesis, University College Cork, 1990).
7. F.H. Tuckey, *The county and city of Cork remembrancer* (Cork, 1837).
8. Ibid.
9. *Cork Examiner*, 2 and 4 November 1853.
10. *Cork Examiner*, 1945.
11. *Irish Examiner*, 22 November 2002.
12. J.G. Tyrrell and K.R. Hickey, 'A flood chronology for Cork city and its climatological background', *Irish Geography*, 24 (1991), pp. 81–90.
13. Hickey, 'The historical climatology of flooding in Cork city from 1841–1988'; H.H. Lamb, *Climate history and the modern world* (second ed., London, 1995).
14. *Irish Examiner*, 22 November 2002.
15. D. Smith, S.B. Raper, S. Zerbini and A. Sánchez-Arcilla, *Sea-level changes and coastal processes: Implications for Europe* (Brussels, 2000); L.D.D. Harvey, *Global warming: The hard science* (Prentice-Hall, Harlow, 2000); IPCC, *Climate change 2001* (Cambridge, 2001).
16. A. Donnelly, L. McElwain, J. Sweeney and M. Jones, *Climate change and Ireland: Assessing the implications* (Environmental Protection Agency, Wexford, 2002); R.J.N. Devoy, 'Coastal vulnerability and the implications of sea-level rise for Ireland', *Journal of Coastal Research* (in press; http://cmrc.ucc.ie).

4. NATURE'S IMMIGRANTS

CORK'S BOTANIC GARDENS

1. T.C. Kelly, *The status of The Lough: A report compiled on behalf of Cork Corporation* (Department of Zoology, University College Cork, 1985).
2. Ibid.
3. Ibid.
4. C.G. Doran, 'The Lough of Cork, Parts I, II and III', *JCHAS*, ii (1893), pp. 193–244.
5. Kelly, *The status of The Lough: A report compiled on behalf of Cork Corporation*.
6. Doran, 'The Lough of Cork, Parts I, II and III', pp. 193–244; T. Power et al., 'The botanist's guide to the county of Cork', in *Contributions towards fauna and flora of the county of Cork* (London and Cork, 1845).
7. Kelly, *The status of The Lough: A report compiled on behalf of Cork Corporation*; T. O'Mahony, 'A short history of the successional vegetation of Cork's Lough, Appendix II (a)', in Kelly, *The status of The Lough*.

8 O'Mahony, 'A short history of the successional vegetation of Cork's Lough, Appendix II (a)'.
9 Kelly, *The status of The Lough: A report compiled on behalf of Cork Corporation*.
10 Ibid.
11 O'Mahony, 'A short history of the successional vegetation of Cork's Lough, Appendix II (a)'.
12 Kelly, *The status of The Lough: A report compiled on behalf of Cork Corporation*.
13 Ibid.
14 O'Mahony, 'A short history of the successional vegetation of Cork's Lough, Appendix II (a)'.
15 Kelly, *The status of The Lough: A report compiled on behalf of Cork Corporation*.
16 Ibid.
17 Ibid.
18 Ibid; D. Corkery, *The threshold of quiet* (Phoenix, Dublin, 1917).
19 Kelly, *The status of The Lough: A report compiled on behalf of Cork Corporation*.
20 Ibid.
21 Ibid.
22 T. Kelly, Personal communication, June 2004.
23 J.P. Cullinane, *Cork Botanic Gardens* (Department of Plant Science, University College Cork, undated); M. O'Neill, 'The Herbarium of University College Cork', *University College Cork Record* (1969), pp. 45–8.
24 Ibid.
25 Ibid.
26 M. O'Sullivan, Personal communication, May 2004.
27 Cullinane, *Cork Botanic Gardens*; M. O'Neill, 'The Herbarium of University College Cork', pp. 45–8.
28 M. McEvoy, 'Investigations into the mechanism and consequences of anthocyanin deficiency in *Cymbalaria muralis*' (MSc thesis, University College Cork, 2000).
29 S.C.P. Reynolds, 'A catalogue of alien plants in Ireland' (Occasional Paper 14, National Botanic Gardens, Glasnevin, 2002), pp. 1–414; S. Segal, 'Some phytogeographical and taxonomic aspects of mural vegetation', in *Notes on wall vegetation* (Dr W. Junk, The Hague, 1972), pp. 282–3.
30 S.A. Stewart and T.H. Corry, *Flora of the north-east of Ireland* (Institute of Irish Studies, Queen's University, Belfast, 1992).
31 Reynolds, 'A catalogue of alien plants in Ireland' (Occasional Paper 14, National Botanic Gardens, Glasnevin, 2002), pp. 1–414.
32 McEvoy, 'Investigations into the mechanism and consequences of anthocyanin deficiency in *Cymbalaria muralis*'.
33 Ibid.
34 Ibid.
35 Reynolds, 'A catalogue of alien plants in Ireland' (Occasional Paper 14, National Botanic Gardens, Glasnevin, 2002), pp. 1–414.
36 M. O'Neill, Personal communication, 1978.
37 J.P. Cullinane, 150 years: A history of the Chair of Botany and Zoology (University College Cork, 1995).

Distillery Field: A final refuge
1 M.J. Gough, *A history of the physical development of Cork city* (MA thesis, UCC, Cork, 1973).
2 Cork Corporation, *An action plan for the regeneration of the Lee Fields and Mardyke area* (Cork Corporation, 1998); *Irish Examiner*, 3 February 2003.
3 T.R. Smith, S. Memon, J.L. Starr and J.E. Estes, 'Requirements and principles for the implementation and construction of large-scale geographic information systems', *International Journal of Geographical Information Systems*, 1 (1987), pp. 13–31; P.A. Longley, M.F. Goodchild, D.J. Maguire and D.W. Rhind, *Geographic information systems and science* (John Wiley & Sons, New York, 2001).
4 D. Müeller-Dombois and H. Ellenberg, *Aims and methods of vegetation ecology* (John Wiley & Sons, New York); M. Kent and P. Coker, *Vegetation description and analysis: A practical approach* (Wiley & Sons, Chichester and New York, 1992); N. Dalton, *The vegetation and environment of Distillery Field, Cork, Ireland: A comparative GIS approach* (MSc thesis, UCC, Cork, 2003).
5 Dalton, *The vegetation and environment of Distillery Field, Cork, Ireland: A comparative GIS approach*.
6 J. White and G. Doyle, 'The vegetation of Ireland: A catalogue raisonné', *Journal of Life Sciences, Royal Dublin Society*, 3 (1982), pp. 289–368.
7 H. Décamps, 'How riparian landscape finds form and comes alive', *Landscape and Urban Planning*, 57 (2001), pp. 169–75.

5. The First People
1 P.C. Woodman, 'The early prehistory of Munster', *JCHAS*, lxxxix (1984), pp. 1–11; P.C. Woodman, 'The exploitation of Ireland's coastal resources: A marginal resource through time?', in M.R. González Morales and G.A. Clark (eds), *The mesolithic of the Atlantic façade* (Arizona State University Anthropological Research Paper 55, 2004), pp. 42–61; G. Johnson, 'Guileen (Gyleen), Ballintra West', in C. Cotter (ed.), *Excavations 1986* (Wordwell, Dublin, 1987), p. 14.
2 Woodman, 'The early prehistory of Munster', pp. 1–11; Woodman, 'The exploitation of Ireland's coastal resources: A marginal resource through time?', pp. 42–61; Johnson, 'Guileen (Gyleen), Ballintra West', p. 14.
3 M.J. O'Kelly, 'Some prehistoric monuments of Imokilly', *JCHAS*, l (1945), pp. 10–23; M.J. O'Kelly, 'A shell midden at Carrigtwohill, Co. Cork', *JCHAS*, lx (1955), pp. 95–6.
4 T. Condit, 'Neolithic house in Cork', *Archaeology Ireland*, 16 (2002), p. 6.
5 C. Rynne, *The archaeology of Cork city and harbour from the earliest times to industrialization* (Collins, Cork, 1993); D. Power et al., *Archaeological inventory of County Cork, Volume 2: East and South Cork* (The Stationery Office & Wordwell: Dublin, 1994).
6 W. O'Brien, *Mount Gabriel: Bronze Age copper mining in Ireland*, Bronze Age studies 3 (Galway, 1994); W. O'Brien, 'Ross Island and the origins of Irish–British metallurgy', in J. Waddell and E. Shee Twohig (eds), *Ireland in the Bronze Age* (Dublin, 1995), pp. 38–48.
7 Rynne, *The archaeology of Cork city and harbour from the earliest times to industrialization*; Power et al., *Archaeological inventory of County Cork, Volume 2: East and South Cork*.
8 A. Purcell, Personal communication.
9 Rynne, *The archaeology of Cork city and harbour from the earliest times to industrialization*; Power et al., *Archaeological inventory of County Cork, Volume 2: East and South Cork*.
10 Ibid.
11 G. Eogan, *A catalogue of Irish bronze swords* (Dublin, 1965).
12 P. O'Connell and A.E. Rutter, 'Fota Island, Carrigtwohill', in I. Bennett (ed.), *Excavations 1992* (Wordwell, Dublin, 1993), p. 7; E. Rutter and P. O'Connell, 'Fota, Co. Cork', in Cork Public Museum, *Digging up Cork: Archaeological excavations in Cork 1992* (Cork Corporation, 1993), pp. 11–13.
13 D. Murphy, 'Ballinaspig, Greenfield, Greenfield 2, Maglin,

Carrigrohane', in I. Bennett (ed.), *Excavations 2001* (Wordwell, Dublin, 2003), pp. 26, 34, 42–3, 47.
14. R. Sherlock, 'Killydonoghue, Meenane', in I. Bennett (ed.), *Excavations 2001* (Wordwell, Dublin, 2003), pp. 45–6, 49.
15. Rynne, *The archaeology of Cork city and harbour from the earliest times to industrialization*; Power et al., *Archaeological inventory of County Cork, Volume 2: East and South Cork*.
16. M. J. O'Kelly, 'Recent southern archaeological finds', *JCHAS*, lxi (1946), pp. 61–8; M.J. O'Kelly, 'A cinerary urn from Oatencake, Midleton, Co. Cork', *JCHAS*, lii (1947), pp. 126–7.
17. Rynne, *The archaeology of Cork city and harbour from the earliest times to industrialization*; Power et al., *Archaeological inventory of County Cork, Volume 2: East and South Cork*.
18. Ibid; S.P. O'Riordain, 'Excavation of cairn in the townland of Currabinny Co. Cork', *JCHAS*, xxxviii (1933), pp. 80–4.
19. Rynne, *The archaeology of Cork city and harbour from the earliest times to industrialization*; Power et al., *Archaeological inventory of County Cork, Volume 2: East and South Cork*.
20. M.J. O'Kelly, 'Excavations and experiments in ancient Irish cooking places', *JCHAS*, lxxxiv (1954), pp. 105–55.
21. E. Cotter, 'Killalough', in I. Bennett (ed.), *Excavations 2000* (Wordwell, Dublin, 2002); B. Halpin, 'Meenane', in I. Bennett (ed.), *Excavations 2001* (Wordwell, Dublin, 2003), p. 48; A. Purcell, 'Mitchelsfort', in I. Bennett (ed*.), Excavations 2001* (Wordwell, Dublin, 2003), pp. 49–50.
22. Murphy, 'Ballinaspig, Greenfield, Greenfield 2, Maglin, Carrigrohane', pp. 26, 34, 42–3, 47; O'Riordain, 'Excavation of cairn in the townland of Currabinny Co. Cork', pp. 80–4; Cotter, 'Killalough'; Halpin, 'Meenane', p. 48; Purcell, 'Mitchelsfort', pp. 49–50.
23. Rynne, *The archaeology of Cork city and harbour from the earliest times to industrialization*; Power et al., *Archaeological inventory of County Cork, Volume 2: East and South Cork*.
24. J. Tierney, 'Ballynagrumoolia', in I. Bennett (ed.), *Excavations 1993* (Wordwell, Dublin, 1994), pp. 6–7.
25. Murphy, 'Ballinaspig, Greenfield, Greenfield 2, Maglin, Carrigrohane', pp. 26, 34, 42–3, 47.
26. Rynne, *The archaeology of Cork city and harbour from the earliest times to industrialization*; Power et al., *Archaeological inventory of County Cork, Volume 2: East and South Cork*; M.J. O'Kelly, 'The Cork horns, the Petrie crown and the Bann disc', *JCHAS*, lxvii (1961), pp. 1–12.
27. Rynne, *The archaeology of Cork city and harbour from the earliest times to industrialization*; Power et al., *Archaeological inventory of County Cork, Volume 2: East and South Cork*.
28. Ibid.
29. P.C. Woodman, *Seeing is believing: Problems of archaeological visibility*, Inaugural Lecture series 2 (Cork, 1985).

RINGFORTS

1. D. Power et al., Sites and Monuments records, County Cork (Office of Public Works, Dublin, 1988).
2. M. Stout, *The Irish ringfort* (Four Courts, Dublin, 1997).
3. D.C. Twohig, 'Excavation at Coolowen, Co. Cork', *JCHAS*, lxxx (1975), pp. 74–83; B.D. O'Flaherty, 'Ringfort at Glanturkin, Gyleen, Co. Cork', *JCHAS*, lxxxvii (1982), pp. 128–31; C. Mount, 'Excavations at Killanully, Co. Cork', *PRIA*, 95C (1995), pp. 3–57; A.M. Lennon, 'Excavation of a ringfort, Raheens 1 near Carrigaline, Co. Cork', *JCHAS*, xcviii (1993), pp. 75–89; A.M. Lennon, 'Summary report on excavation of ringfort, Raheens No. 2, near Carrigaline, Co. Cork', *JCHAS*, xcix (1994), pp. 47–65.

4. C.J. Lynn, 'Houses in rural Ireland AD 500–1000', *UJA*, 57 (1994), pp. 81–94.
5. Twohig, 'Excavation at Coolowen, Co. Cork', pp. 74–83; O'Flaherty, 'Ringfort at Glanturkin, Gyleen, Co. Cork', pp. 128–31; Mount, 'Excavations at Killanully, Co. Cork', pp. 3–57; Lennon, 'Excavation of a ringfort, Raheens 1 near Carrigaline, Co. Cork', pp. 75–89; Lennon, 'Summary report on excavation of ringfort, Raheens No. 2, near Carrigaline, Co. Cork', pp. 47–65.
6. Ibid; M. McCarthy, 'Appendix 2: Animal bone report', in A.M. Lennon, 'Summary report on excavation of ringfort, Raheens No. 2, near Carrigaline, Co. Cork', *JCHAS*, xcix (1994), pp. 62–5.

MILLS

1. C. Rynne, *The archaeology of Cork city and harbour* (Cork, 1993).

6. URBAN BEGINNINGS AND THE VIKINGS

1. M.F. Hurley and O.M.B. Scully, *Late Viking age and medieval Waterford: Excavations 1986–1992* (Waterford, 1997; M.A. Monk and J. Sheehan (eds), *Early medieval Munster* (Cork, 1998); E.P. Kelly, 'Vikings on the Barrow', *Archaeology Ireland*, 33 (1995), pp. 30–2; E.P. Kelly and J. Maas, 'The Vikings and the Kingdom of Laois', in P.G. Lane and W. Nolan (eds), *Laois history and society* (Geography Publications, Dublin, 1995); P.F. Wallace, *The Viking age buildings of Dublin* (Royal Irish Academy, Dublin, 1992).
2. Ibid; H.A. Jefferies, 'The history and topography of Viking Cork', *JCHAS*, xc (1985), pp. 14–25; H.A. Jefferies, *Cork: Historical perspectives* (Four Courts Press, Dublin), pp. 33–47; J. Bradley and A. Halpin, 'The topographical development of Scandinavian and Anglo-Norman Cork', in P. O'Flanagan and C. Buttimer (eds), *Cork history and society* (Dublin, 1993), pp. 15–44.
3. Ibid.
4. Ibid; R.M. Cleary and M.F. Hurley, *Excavations in Cork city 1984–2000* (Cork, 2003).
5. Hurley and Scully, *Late Viking age and medieval Waterford: Excavations 1986–1992*; Monk and Sheehan (eds), *Early medieval Munster*; Kelly, 'Vikings on the Barrow', pp. 30–2; Kelly and Maas, 'The Vikings and the Kingdom of Laois'; Wallace, *The Viking age buildings of Dublin*; C. Rynne, *The archaeology of Cork city and harbour* (Cork, 1993); P. Ó Riain, *The making of a saint: Finbarr of Cork 600–1200* (Dublin, 1997).
6. Hurley and Scully, *Late Viking age and medieval Waterford: Excavations 1986–1992*; Monk and Sheehan (eds), *Early medieval Munster*; Kelly, 'Vikings on the Barrow', pp. 30–2; Kelly and Maas, 'The Vikings and the Kingdom of Laois'; Wallace, *The Viking age buildings of Dublin*.
7. Ibid; Jefferies, 'The history and topography of Viking Cork', pp. 14–25; Jefferies, *Cork: Historical perspectives*, pp. 33–47; Bradley and Halpin, 'The topographical development of Scandinavian and Anglo-Norman Cork', pp. 15–44; A.B. Scott and F.X. Martin (eds), *Expugnatio Hibernica: The conquest of Ireland by Geraldus Cambrensis* (Royal Irish Academy, Dublin, 1978).
8. J. O'Donovan (ed.), *Annals of the Four Masters* (Dublin, 1848–51); D. Murphy (ed.), *Annals of Ireland from earliest times to 1408* (trans. C. Mageoghan) (London, 1896; reprinted 1993).
9. Hurley and Scully, *Late Viking age and medieval Waterford: Excavations 1986–1992*; Monk and Sheehan (eds), *Early medieval Munster*; Kelly, 'Vikings on the Barrow', pp. 30–2; Kelly and

Maas, 'The Vikings and the Kingdom of Laois'; Wallace, *The Viking age buildings of Dublin*.

10 Jefferies, 'The history and topography of Viking Cork', pp. 14–25; Jefferies, *Cork: Historical perspectives*, pp. 33–47; Bradley and Halpin, 'The topographical development of Scandinavian and Anglo-Norman Cork', pp. 15–44; Cleary and Hurley, *Excavations in Cork city 1984–2000*; Rynne, *The archaeology of Cork city and harbour*; Ó Riain, *The making of a saint: Finbarr of Cork 600–1200*.

11 Hurley and Scully, *Late Viking age and medieval Waterford: Excavations 1986–1992*; Monk and Sheehan (eds), *Early medieval Munster*; Kelly, 'Vikings on the Barrow', pp. 30–2; Kelly and Maas, 'The Vikings and the Kingdom of Laois'; Wallace, *The Viking age buildings of Dublin*; Jefferies, 'The history and topography of Viking Cork', pp. 14–25; Jefferies, *Cork: Historical perspectives*, pp. 33–47; Bradley and Halpin, 'The topographical development of Scandinavian and Anglo-Norman Cork', pp. 15–44.

12 Hurley and Scully, *Late Viking age and medieval Waterford: Excavations 1986–1992*; Monk and Sheehan (eds), *Early medieval Munster*; Kelly, 'Vikings on the Barrow', pp. 30–2; Kelly and Maas, 'The Vikings and the Kingdom of Laois'; Wallace, *The Viking age buildings of Dublin*; E.P. Kelly and E. O'Donovan, 'A Viking *longphort* near Athlunkard, Co. Clare', *Archaeology Ireland*, 46 (1998), pp. 13–16.

13 Jefferies, 'The history and topography of Viking Cork', pp. 14–25; Jefferies, *Cork: Historical perspectives*, pp. 33–47; Bradley and Halpin, 'The topographical development of Scandinavian and Anglo-Norman Cork', pp. 15–44; Cleary and Hurley, *Excavations in Cork city 1984–2000*; M.F. Hurley, 'Below sea-level in the city of Cork', in H.B. Clarke (ed.), *Irish cities* (Cork, 1995), pp. 41–54; M.F. Hurley, 'Excavations in Cork city: Kyrl's Quay/North Main Street and at Grand Parade (Part 1)', *JCHAS*, c (1995), pp. 47–90; M.F. Hurley, 'Excavations in Cork city: Kyrl's Quay/North Main Street (Part 2)', *JCHAS*, ci (1996), pp. 26–63; M.F. Hurley, *Excavations at the North Gate Cork, 1994* (Cork, 1997); R.M. Cleary, M.F. Hurley and E. Shee Twohig (eds), *Skiddy's Castle and Christ Church Cork: Excavations 1974–77 by D.C. Twohig* (Cork Corporation, Cork, 1997).

14 G. Johnson, *The laneways of medieval Cork* (Cork, 2002).

15 Hurley and Scully, *Late Viking age and medieval Waterford: Excavations 1986–1992*; Monk and Sheehan (eds), *Early medieval Munster*; Kelly, 'Vikings on the Barrow', pp. 30–2; Kelly and Maas, 'The Vikings and the Kingdom of Laois'; Wallace, *The Viking age buildings of Dublin*; M.F. Hurley, 'Domestic architecture in medieval Cork and Waterford (11th–17th century)', in M. Gläser (ed.), *Lübecker Kolloquium zur Stadlarchäologie im Hanseraum III: Der Hausleau* (Lübeck, 2001).

16 Cleary and Hurley, *Excavations in Cork city 1984–2000*; Hurley, 'Below sea-level in the city of Cork', pp. 41–54; Hurley, 'Excavations in Cork city: Kyrl's Quay/North Main Street and at Grand Parade (Part 1)', pp. 47–90; Hurley, 'Excavations in Cork city: Kyrl's Quay/North Main Street (Part 2)', pp. 26–63; Hurley, *Excavations at the North Gate Cork, 1994*; Cleary, Hurley and Shee Twohig (eds), *Skiddy's Castle and Christ Church Cork: Excavations 1974–77 by D.C. Twohig*.

17 *Irish Examiner*, November 2004.

18 O'Donovan (ed.), *Annals of the Four Masters*; Murphy (ed.), *Annals of Ireland from earliest times to 1408*.

19 Johnson, *The laneways of medieval Cork*.

20 Cleary and Hurley, *Excavations in Cork city 1984–2000*; Hurley, 'Below sea-level in the city of Cork', pp. 41–54; Hurley, 'Excavations in Cork city: Kyrl's Quay/North Main Street and at Grand Parade (Part 1)', pp. 47–90; Hurley, 'Excavations in Cork city: Kyrl's Quay/North Main Street (Part 2)', pp. 26–63; Hurley, *Excavations at the North Gate Cork, 1994*; Cleary, Hurley and Shee Twohig (eds), *Skiddy's Castle and Christ Church Cork: Excavations 1974–77 by D.C. Twohig*.

21 Hurley and Scully, *Late Viking age and medieval Waterford: Excavations 1986–1992*; Monk and Sheehan (eds), *Early medieval Munster*; Kelly, 'Vikings on the Barrow', pp. 30–2; Kelly and Maas, 'The Vikings and the Kingdom of Laois'; Wallace, *The Viking age buildings of Dublin*; P.F. Wallace, 'The archaeological identity of the Hiberno-Norse town', *Journal of the Royal Society of Antiquaries of Ireland*, 122 (1992), pp. 35–66; P.F. Wallace, *The Viking age buildings of Dublin* (Dublin, 1992); P.F. Wallace, 'Garrda and airbeada: The plot thickens in Viking Dublin', in A.P. Smyth (ed.), *Seanchas: Studies in early and medieval Irish archaeology, history and literature in honour of Francis J. Byrne* (Dublin, 2000).

22 Hurley and Scully, *Late Viking age and medieval Waterford: Excavations 1986–1992*; Monk and Sheehan (eds), *Early medieval Munster*; Kelly, 'Vikings on the Barrow', pp. 30–2; Kelly and Maas, 'The Vikings and the Kingdom of Laois'; Wallace, *The Viking age buildings of Dublin*; Cleary and Hurley, *Excavations in Cork city 1984–2000*; Hurley, 'Below sea-level in the city of Cork', pp. 41–54; Hurley, 'Excavations in Cork city: Kyrl's Quay/North Main Street and at Grand Parade (Part 1)', pp. 47–90; Hurley, 'Excavations in Cork city: Kyrl's Quay/North Main Street (Part 2)', pp. 26–63; Hurley, *Excavations at the North Gate Cork, 1994*; Cleary, Hurley and Shee Twohig (eds), *Skiddy's Castle and Christ Church Cork: Excavations 1974–77 by D.C. Twohig*.

23 Ibid; Hurley and Scully, *Late Viking Age and medieval Waterford: Excavations 1986–1992*; Hurley, 'Domestic architecture in medieval Cork and Waterford (11th–17th century)'; Wallace, 'The archaeological identity of the Hiberno-Norse town', pp. 35–66; Wallace, *The Viking age buildings of Dublin*; Wallace, 'Garrda and airbeada: The plot thickens in Viking Dublin'.

24 Johnson, *The laneways of medieval Cork*.

25 Hurley, 'Below sea-level in the city of Cork', pp. 41–54; Hurley, 'Excavations in Cork city: Kyrl's Quay/North Main Street and at Grand Parade (Part 1)', pp. 47–90; Hurley, 'Excavations in Cork city: Kyrl's Quay/North Main Street (Part 2)', pp. 26–63; Hurley, *Excavations at the North Gate Cork, 1994*; Cleary, Hurley and Shee Twohig (eds), *Skiddy's Castle and Christ Church Cork: Excavations 1974–77 by D.C. Twohig*.

26 Ibid.

27 Hurley and Scully, *Late Viking Age and medieval Waterford: Excavations 1986–1992*; Hurley, 'Domestic architecture in medieval Cork and Waterford (11th–17th century)'; Wallace, 'The archaeological identity of the Hiberno-Norse town', pp. 35–66; Wallace, *The Viking age buildings of Dublin*.

28 Hurley, 'Below sea-level in the city of Cork', pp. 41–54; Hurley, 'Excavations in Cork city: Kyrl's Quay/North Main Street and at Grand Parade (Part 1)', pp. 47–90; Hurley, 'Excavations in Cork city: Kyrl's Quay/North Main Street (Part 2)', pp. 26–63; Hurley, *Excavations at the North Gate Cork, 1994*; Cleary, Hurley and Shee Twohig (eds), *Skiddy's Castle and Christ Church Cork: Excavations 1974–77 by D.C. Twohig*; Hurley and Scully, *Late Viking age and medieval Waterford: Excavations 1986–1992*; Hurley, 'Domestic architecture in medieval Cork and Waterford (11th–17th century)'.

29 Hurley, 'Below sea-level in the city of Cork', pp. 41–54; Hurley,

'Excavations in Cork city: Kyrl's Quay/North Main Street and at Grand Parade (Part 1)', pp. 47–90; Hurley, 'Excavations in Cork city: Kyrl's Quay/North Main Street (Part 2)', pp. 26–63; Hurley, *Excavations at the North Gate Cork, 1994*; Cleary, Hurley and Shee Twohig (eds), *Skiddy's Castle and Christ Church Cork: Excavations 1974–77 by D.C. Twohig*; Wallace, 'The archaeological identity of the Hiberno-Norse town', pp. 35–66; Wallace, *The Viking age buildings of Dublin*; Wallace, 'Garrda and airbeada: The plot thickens in Viking Dublin'.

30 Hurley, 'Below sea-level in the city of Cork', pp. 41–54; Hurley, 'Excavations in Cork city: Kyrl's Quay/North Main Street and at Grand Parade (Part 1)', pp. 47–90; Hurley, 'Excavations in Cork city: Kyrl's Quay/North Main Street (Part 2)', pp. 26–63; Hurley, *Excavations at the North Gate Cork, 1994*; Cleary, Hurley and Shee Twohig (eds), *Skiddy's Castle and Christ Church Cork: Excavations 1974–77 by D.C. Twohig*; Johnson, *The laneways of medieval Cork*; Hurley and Scully, *Late Viking Age and medieval Waterford: Excavations 1986–1992*; Hurley, 'Domestic architecture in medieval Cork and Waterford (11th–17th century)'.

31 Cleary and Hurley, *Excavations in Cork city 1984–2000*; Hurley, 'Below sea-level in the city of Cork', pp. 41–54; Hurley, 'Excavations in Cork city: Kyrl's Quay/North Main Street and at Grand Parade (Part 1)', pp. 47–90; Hurley, 'Excavations in Cork city: Kyrl's Quay/North Main Street (Part 2)', pp. 26–63; Hurley, *Excavations at the North Gate Cork, 1994*; Cleary, Hurley and Shee Twohig (eds), *Skiddy's Castle and Christ Church Cork: Excavations 1974–77 by D.C. Twohig*.

32 J. Bradley and H.A. King, 'Romanesque voussoirs at St Fin Barre's Cathedral, Cork', *JRSAI*, 115 (1985), pp. 146–51.

7. MEDIEVAL CORK

1 A.F. O'Brien, 'Politics, economy and society: The development of Cork and the Irish south-coast region c. 1170 to c. 1583', in P. O'Flanagan and C. Buttimer (eds), *Cork history and society* (Dublin, 1993); J. Bradley and A. Halpin, 'The topographical development of Scandinavian and Anglo-Norman Cork', pp. 15–44; W. O'Sullivan, *The economic history of Cork city from the earliest times to the Act of Union* (Dublin and Cork, 1937); H.A. Jefferies, *Cork: Historical perspectives* (Dublin, 2004).

2 D. Ó Murchadha, 'The siege of Cork in 1690', *JCHAS*, xcv (1990), pp. 1–19.

3 O'Brien, 'Politics, economy and society'; Bradley and Halpin, 'The topographical development of Scandinavian and Anglo-Norman Cork', pp. 15–44; O'Sullivan, *The economic history of Cork city*; Jefferies, *Cork: Historical perspectives*; C. Rynne, *The archaeology of Cork city and harbour* (Cork, 1993); A. Thomas, *The walled towns of Ireland* (Dublin, 1992), 2 vols.

4 O'Brien, 'Politics, economy and society'; Bradley and Halpin, 'The topographical development of Scandinavian and Anglo-Norman Cork', pp. 15–44; O'Sullivan, *The economic history of Cork city*; Jefferies, *Cork: Historical perspectives*; Rynne, *The archaeology of Cork city and harbour*; Thomas, *The walled towns of Ireland*; A. Candon, 'The Cork suburb of Dungarvan', *JCHAS*, xc (1985), pp. 91–103.

5 Rynne, *The archaeology of Cork city and harbour*; Thomas, *The walled towns of Ireland*; M. Hurley and D. Power, 'The medieval town wall of Cork', *JCHAS*, lxxxvi (1981), pp. 1–20; R.M. Cleary, 'Medieval town wall off Lambley's Lane, Cork City', *JCHAS*, xciii (1988), pp. 104–8.

6 G. Johnson, *The laneways of medieval Cork* (Cork, 2002).

7 Hurley and Power, 'The medieval town wall of Cork', pp. 1–20; Cleary, 'Medieval town wall off Lambley's Lane, Cork city', pp. 104–8; R.M. Cleary and M.F. Hurley, *Excavations in Cork city 1984–2000* (Cork, 2003); R.M. Cleary, M.F. Hurley and E. Shee Twohig (eds), *Skiddy's Castle and Christ Church, Cork: Excavation 1974–1977* (Cork, 1997); M.F. Hurley, 'Below sea-level in the city of Cork', in H.B. Clarke (ed.), *Irish cities* (Cork, 1995), pp. 41–54; M.F. Hurley, 'Excavations in Cork City: Kyrl's Quay/North Main Street and at Grand Parade (Part 1)', *JCHAS*, c (1995), pp. 47–90; M.F. Hurley, 'Excavations in Cork city: Kyrl's Quay/North Main Street (Part 2)', *JCHAS*, ci (1996), pp. 26–63; M.F. Hurley, *Excavations at the North Gate Cork, 1994* (Cork, 1997).

8 Rynne, *The archaeology of Cork city and harbour*; A. Thomas, *The walled towns of Ireland*; Hurley and Power, 'The medieval town wall of Cork', pp. 1–20; Cleary, 'Medieval town wall off Lambley's Lane, Cork city', pp. 104–8.

9 Cleary and Hurley, *Excavations in Cork city 1984–2000*; Cleary, Hurley and Shee Twohig (eds), *Skiddy's Castle and Christ Church, Cork: Excavation 1974–1977*; Hurley, 'Below sea-level in the city of Cork', pp. 41–54; Hurley, 'Excavations in Cork City: Kyrl's Quay/North Main Street and at Grand Parade (Part 1)', pp. 47–90; Hurley, 'Excavations in Cork city: Kyrl's Quay/North Main Street (Part 2)', pp. 26–63; Hurley, *Excavations at the North Gate Cork, 1994*.

10 Johnson, *The laneways of medieval Cork*; Cleary and Hurley, *Excavations in Cork city 1984–2000*; Cleary, Hurley and Shee Twohig (eds), *Skiddy's Castle and Christ Church, Cork: Excavation 1974–1977*; Hurley, 'Below sea-level in the city of Cork', pp. 41–54; Hurley, 'Excavations in Cork city: Kyrl's Quay/North Main Street and at Grand Parade (Part 1)', pp. 47–90; Hurley, 'Excavations in Cork city: Kyrl's Quay/North Main Street (Part 2)', pp. 26–63; Hurley, *Excavations at the North Gate Cork, 1994*.

11 S. Dunne (ed.), *The Cork anthology* (Cork, 1993).

12 Cleary and Hurley, *Excavations in Cork city 1984–2000*; Cleary, Hurley and Shee Twohig (eds), *Skiddy's Castle and Christ Church, Cork: Excavation 1974–1977*; Hurley, 'Below sea-level in the city of Cork', pp. 41–54; Hurley, 'Excavations in Cork city: Kyrl's Quay/North Main Street and at Grand Parade (Part 1)', pp. 47–90; Hurley, 'Excavations in Cork city: Kyrl's Quay/North Main Street (Part 2)', pp. 26–63; Hurley, *Excavations at the North Gate Cork, 1994*.

13 R. Caulfield, *The council book of the Corporation of the city of Cork from 1609–1643 and from 1690–1800* (Guildford, 1876).

14 Cleary and Hurley, *Excavations in Cork city 1984–2000*; Cleary, Hurley and Shee Twohig (eds), *Skiddy's Castle and Christ Church, Cork: Excavation 1974–1977*; Hurley, 'Below sea-level in the city of Cork', pp. 41–54; Hurley, 'Excavations in Cork city: Kyrl's Quay/North Main Street and at Grand Parade (Part 1)', pp. 47–90; Hurley, 'Excavations in Cork city: Kyrl's Quay/North Main Street (Part 2)', pp. 26–63; Hurley, *Excavations at the North Gate Cork, 1994*.

15 E.G. Atkinson, *Calendar of state papers of Ireland* (London, 1905).

16 M. Craig, *The architecture of Ireland from earliest times to 1840* (Dublin, 1982).

17 Rynne, *The archaeology of Cork city and harbour*; A. Thomas, *The walled towns of Ireland*; Johnson, *The laneways of medieval Cork*.

18 H.G. Leask, *Irish castles and curtelated houses* (Dundalk, 1977).

19 Cleary and Hurley, *Excavations in Cork city 1984–2000*; Cleary, Hurley and Shee Twohig (eds), *Skiddy's Castle and Christ Church, Cork: Excavation 1974–1977*; Hurley, 'Below sea-level in the city of Cork', pp. 41–54; Hurley, 'Excavations in Cork city: Kyrl's Quay/North Main Street and at Grand Parade (Part 1)',

pp. 47–90; Hurley, 'Excavations in Cork city: Kyrl's Quay/North Main Street (Part 2)', pp. 26–63; Hurley, *Excavations at the North Gate Cork, 1994.*
20 Ibid; Johnson, *The laneways of medieval Cork.*
21 Leask, *Irish castles and curtelated houses.*
22 D. Murtagh, 'The Bridge Castle, Thomastown, Co. Kildare', in G. McNicholl and P.F. Wallace (eds), *Keimelia* (Galway, 1988).
23 Cleary and Hurley, *Excavations in Cork city 1984–2000*; Cleary, Hurley and Shee Twohig (eds), *Skiddy's Castle and Christ Church, Cork: Excavation 1974–1977*; Hurley, 'Below sea-level in the city of Cork', pp. 41–54; Hurley, 'Excavations in Cork city: Kyrl's Quay/North Main Street and at Grand Parade (Part 1)', pp. 47–90; Hurley, 'Excavations in Cork city: Kyrl's Quay/North Main Street (Part 2)', pp. 26–63; Hurley, *Excavations at the North Gate Cork, 1994.*
24 J. Buckley, 'The siege of Cork, 1642', *JCHAS*, xxii (1916), pp. 7–20.
25 Cleary and Hurley, *Excavations in Cork city 1984–2000*; Cleary, Hurley and Shee Twohig (eds), *Skiddy's Castle and Christ Church, Cork: Excavation 1974–1977*; Hurley, 'Below sea-level in the city of Cork', pp. 41–54; Hurley, 'Excavations in Cork city: Kyrl's Quay/North Main Street and at Grand Parade (Part 1)', pp. 47–90; Hurley, 'Excavations in Cork city: Kyrl's Quay/North Main Street (Part 2)', pp. 26–63; Hurley, *Excavations at the North Gate Cork, 1994.*

LANES AND STREETS
1 G. Johnson, *The laneways of medieval Cork* (Cork, 2002).
2 R.M. Cleary, 'Christ Church site excavation', in R.M. Cleary, M.F. Hurley and E. Shee Twohig (eds), *Skiddy's Castle and Christ Church, Cork: Excavations 1974–77 by D.C. Twohig* (Cork, 1997); M.F. Hurley, *Excavations at the North Gate, Cork, 1994* (Cork, 1997).
3 Johnson, *The laneways of medieval Cork.*
4 A. Fahy, 'Place and class in Cork', in P. O'Flanagan and C.G. Buttimer (eds), *Cork history and society* (Dublin, 1993).
5 R.C. Simington, *The civil survey AD 1654–1656: County Waterford, Vol. VI, with appendices . . . also valuations*, circa 1663–4, *for Waterford and Cork cities* (The Stationery Office, Dublin, 1942).
6 Ibid.

8. ST FINBARR AND EARLY CHRISTIAN SETTLEMENT
1 For the most recent edition of Finbarr's Life and for a detailed commentary on its background, see P. Ó Riain (ed.), *Beatha Bharra: Saint Finbarr of Cork. The complete life* (Dublin, 1994); P. Ó Riain, *The making of a saint: Finbarr of Cork 600–1200* (London, 1997); P. Ó Riain, '"To be named is to exist": The instructive case of Achadh Bolg (Aghabulloge)', in P. O'Flanagan and C.G. Buttimer (eds), *Cork history and society* (Dublin, 1993).
2 Ibid.
3 N. Edwards, *The archaeology of Early Medieval Ireland* (London, 1990), pp. 68, 71; L. de Paor, *Saint Patrick's world: The Christian culture of Ireland's apostolic age* (Dublin, 1993), p. 41.
4 For a recent review of the epigraphical and literary evidence, see T.M. Charles-Edwards, *Early Christian Ireland* (Cambridge, 2000), pp. 163–72.
5 R. Sharpe, 'Quatuor sanctissimi episcopi: Irish saints before St Patrick', in D. Ó Corráin, L. Breatnach and K. McCone (eds), *Sages, saints and storytellers: Celtic studies in honour of Professor James Carney* (Maynooth, 1989), pp. 376–99; D. Ó Riain-Raedel, 'The question of the "Pre-Patrician" saints of Munster', in M.A. Monk and J. Sheehan (eds), *Early Medieval Munster: Archaeology, history and society* (Cork, 1998), pp. 33–52.
6 M.J. O'Kelly, 'St Gobnet's House, Ballyvourney, Co. Cork', *JCHAS*, lvii (1952), pp. 18–40; F. Henry, 'The decorated stones at Ballyvourney, Co. Cork', pp. 41–2.
7 P. Ó Riain, 'Traces of Lug in early Irish hagiographical tradition', *Zeitschrift für Celtische Philologie*, 36 (1977), pp. 138–56.
8 K. Hughes, *The Church in early Irish society* (London, 1966), pp. 57–78. Lives documenting the progress of the Irish *peregrinatio* were composed for both Columbanus of Bobbio and Fursa of Péronne shortly after their respective deaths in 615 and 650; see J.F. Kenney, *The sources for the early history of Ireland (ecclesiastical)* (Cornell, 1929; reproduced Dublin, 1979).
9 P. Ó Riain, 'Cainnech *alias* Colum Cille, patron of Ossory', in P. de Brún, S. Ó Coileáin and P. Ó Riain (eds), *Folia Gadelica: Essays presented by former students to R.A. Breatnach* (Cork, 1983), pp. 20–35; P. Russell, 'Patterns of hypocorism in early Irish hagiography', in J. Carey, M. Herbert and P. Ó Riain (eds), *Studies in Irish hagiography: Saints and scholars* (Dublin, 2001), pp. 237–49.
10 A.O. Anderson and M.O. Anderson, *Adomnán's life of Columba* (revised ed., Oxford, 1991), pp. 196, 324, 470; G.S.M. Walker (ed.), *Sancti Columbani opera* (Dublin, 1957); L. Bieler, *The Irish penitentials* (Dublin, 1963), pp. 74–95.
11 R.I. Best and H.J. Lawlor (eds), *The martyrology of Tallaght* (London, 1931), p. 74; W. Stokes (ed.), *Féilire Oengusso Céli Dé: The martyrology of Oengus the Culdee* (London, 1905; reproduced Dublin, 1984), p. 196.
12 P. Ó Riain, *The making of a saint*, pp. 32–5.
13 Charles-Edwards, *Early Christian Ireland*, pp. 241–64.
14 P. Ó Riain, *Beatha Bharra*, pp. 142–4.
15 Ibid, p. 142.
16 P. Ó Riain, *The making of a saint*, pp. 51–2.
17 For the text of the decretal letter, see M.P. Sheehy (ed.), *Pontificia Hibernica: Medieval papal chancery documents concerning Ireland 640–1261*, Vol. 1 (Dublin, 1962–5), 2 vols, pp. 105–9. For a discussion of its place names, see D. Ó Murchadha, 'The Cork decretal letter of 1199', *JCHAS*, cv (2001), pp. 79–100.
18 H.J. Lawlor, *St Bernard of Clairvaux's life of St Malachy of Armagh* (London, 1920), pp. 92–4. For Gilla Áeda, see also P. Ó Riain, *The making of a saint*, pp. 58–61.
19 D. Ó Murchadha, 'Gill Abbey and the "ental of Cong"', *JCHAS*, xc (1985), pp. 31–45.
20 M.P. Sheehy, *Pontificia Hibernica*, Vol, 1, pp. 105–9.
21 For a full discussion of the contents of the Life, see P. Ó Riain, *The making of a saint*.
22 Riain (ed.), *Beatha Bharra*; Riain, *The making of a saint: Finbarr of Cork 600–1200*; Ó Riain, '"To be named is to exist"'; Charles-Edwards, *Early Christian Ireland*, pp. 163–72.

9. CHRISTIANITY, CHURCHES AND BURIAL PLACES
1 J. Bradley and A. Halpin, 'The topographical development of Scandinavian and Anglo-Norman Cork', in P. O'Flanagan and C. Buttimer (eds), *Cork history and society* (Dublin, 1993); A. Candon, 'The Cork suburb of Dungarvan', *JCHAS*, xc (1985), pp. 91–103; A. Thomas, *The walled towns of Ireland* (Dublin, 1992), 2 vols.
2 Ibid; Bradley and Halpin, 'The topographical development of Scandinavian and Anglo-Norman Cork'; Candon, 'The Cork suburb of Dungarvan', pp. 91–103.
3 H. Kelleher, Unpublished excavation report (Cork City

Council, 2003); J. Bradley, A. Halpin and H.A. King, 'Urban archaeological survey: Part XIV CD, Cork city' (unpublished; Office of Public Works, 1985).
4. D. Ó Murchadha, 'The Cork decretal letter of 1199 AD', *JCHAS*, cvi (2001), pp. 79–100; H. Kelleher and F. McCarthy, *Survey of Cork city burial places* (Cork, 2003).
5. Ibid; Ó Murchadha, 'The Cork decretal letter of 1199 AD', pp. 79–100.
6. D. O'Sullivan, 'The testament of John de Wynchedon of Cork, anno 1306', *JCHAS*, lxi (1956), pp. 75–88.
7. A. Coleman, *The Irish Dominicans of the seventeenth century* (translated reprint, with appendix by Father J. O'Heyne, Dundalk, 1902).
8. M. Craig, *The architecture of Ireland from the earliest times to 1880* (Dublin, 1982).
9. P. Conlon, *Franciscan Ireland* (Mullingar, 1988).
10. D. Ó Murchadha, 'The siege of Cork in 1690', *JCHAS*, xcv (1990), pp. 1–19.
11. Kelleher, Unpublished excavation report; Bradley, Halpin and King, 'Urban archaeological survey: Part XIV CD, Cork city'.
12. Ó Murchadha, 'The siege of Cork in 1690', pp. 1–19.
13. J. Fitzgerald, 'The made grounds of Cork city', *JCHAS*, ii (1896), pp. 485–90.
14. Ó Murchadha, 'The Cork decretal letter of 1199 AD', pp. 79–100; Kelleher and McCarthy, *Survey of Cork city burial places*.
15. B. Ó Donnabháin, 'The human remains', in L. Simpson, *Excavations at Essex Street West, Dublin* (Temple Bar Properties, Dublin), pp. 117–20; B. Ó Donnabháin and U. Cosgrave, 'The human remains', in L. Simpson, *Excavations at Isolde's Tower, Dublin* (Temple Bar Properties, Dublin), pp. 97–103.
16. H. Moloney Davis, 'An Egyptian mummy and coffin at University College Cork', *JCHAS*, xcv (1990), pp. 145–52.
17. Ibid.

ST MARY'S OF THE ISLE

1. D. O'Sullivan, 'The monastic establishments of medieval Cork', *JCHAS*, xlviii (1943), pp. 9–18; J.P. Greene, *Medieval monasteries* (Leicester, 1992); G. Coppack, *Abbeys and priories* (London, 1993).
2. M.F. Hurley and C.M. Sheehan, *Excavations at the Dominican Priory of St Mary's of the Isle, Cork* (Cork, 1995); J. Bradley, A. Halpin and H.A. King, *Urban archaeological survey XIV (I) of Cork city* (unpublished; Office of Public Works, Dublin, 1985); J. Bradley and A. Halpin, 'The topographical development of Scandinavian and Anglo-Norman Cork', in P. O'Flanagan and C. Buttimer (eds), *Cork history and society* (Dublin, 1993), pp. 15–44.
3. T.S. Flynn, *The Irish Dominicans 1536–1641* (Dublin, 1993); A. Coleman, *The Irish Dominicans of the seventeenth century* (Dundalk, 1902); A.G. Little, 'The mendicant orders', *Cambridge medieval history*, Vol. 6 (1968), pp. 727–62.
4. O'Sullivan, 'The monastic establishments of medieval Cork', pp. 9–18; Greene, *Medieval monasteries*; Coppack, *Abbeys and priories*.
5. H.S. Sweetman, *Calendar of documents relating to Ireland, 1171–1307* (London, 1875–86), 5 vols.
6. R. Caulfield, *The council books of the Corporation of the city of Cork from 1609–1643 and from 1690–1800* (Guildford, 1876); H.G. Leask, *Irish churches and monastic buildings*, Vol. 2 (Dundalk, 1958) and Vol. 3 (1960).
7. O'Sullivan, 'The monastic establishments of medieval Cork', pp. 9–18; Greene, *Medieval monasteries*; Coppack, *Abbeys and priories*; Flynn, *The Irish Dominicans 1536–1641*; Coleman, *The Irish Dominicans of the seventeenth century*; Little, 'The mendicant orders', pp. 727–62; Caulfield, *The council books of the Corporation of the city of Cork from 1609–1643 and from 1690–1800*; Leask, *Irish churches and monastic buildings*, Vols 2 and 3.
8. Hurley and Sheehan, *Excavations at the Dominican Priory of St Mary's of the Isle, Cork*; Bradley, Halpin and King, *Urban archaeological survey XIV (I) of Cork city*; Bradley and Halpin, 'The topographical development of Scandinavian and Anglo-Norman Cork', pp. 15–44.
9. Caulfield, *The council books of the Corporation of the city of Cork from 1609–1643 and from 1690–1800*; Leask, *Irish churches and monastic buildings*, Vols 2 and 3; K.A. Rodwell, *Church archaeology* (London, 1989); R. Stalley, 'Gaelic friars and Gothic design', in P. Crossley and E. Fernie (eds), *Medieval architecture and its intellectual context* (London, 1990), pp. 191–202; A. Hogan, *Kilmallock Dominican Priory* (Kilmallock, 1991).

II. Transformation: A Minor Port Town Becomes a Major Atlantic Port City

10. THE ANGLO-NORMANS AND BEYOND

1. For the municipal and commercial history of medieval Cork, see A.F. O'Brien, 'The development of the privileges, liberties and immunities of medieval Cork and the growth of an urban autonomy, c. 1189 to 1500', *JCHAS*, xc, 249 (1985), pp. 46–64; A.F. O'Brien, 'The Royal Boroughs, the Seaport Towns and Royal Revenue in medieval Ireland', *JRSAI*, 118 (1988), pp. 13–26; A.F. O'Brien, 'Politics, economy and society: The development of Cork and the Irish south-coast region, c. 1170 to 1583', in P. O'Flanagan and C.G. Buttimer (eds), *Cork history and society* (Dublin, 1993), pp. 83–154.
2. K.W. Nicholls (ed.), 'Inquisitions of 1224 from the Miscellanea of the Exchequer', *Anal. Hib.*, 27 (1972), pp. 11–12; W. Maziere Brady, *Clerical and parochial records of Cork, Cloyne and Ross*, I (Dublin, 1863), pp. 264–5; Bradley and Halpin (in *Cork history and society*, p. 36), who do not cite either of these references, seem to have been unaware of the dual significance of the name Faythe, which, by the eighteenth century, when the bishop's manor had become known as St Finbarr's or St Barry's, was causing confusion.
3. *Cal. Justiciary Rolls, Ire., xxiii–xxxi Edward I*, pp. 313, 334–5.
4. There is no adequate account of St John the Evangelist, which has been consistently confused with St John the Baptist, nor has the fact that it was originally a cell of Exeter been noted. The deed of 1323 (N.L.I. Ms D. 25,886) calendared by R. Caulfield in the *Gentleman's Magazine*, March 1865, pp. 317–18, which Bradley and Halpin (*Cork history and society*, p. 34) cite as evidence that St John the Evangelist stood at the east of the Augustinian Friary (Red Abbey), does not support this conclusion. In fact, as late as 1726 there appear to have been no streets or buildings eastwards of the Red Abbey.
5. Anthony Candon, 'The Cork suburb of Dungarvan', *JCHAS*, xc, 249 (1985), pp. 91–103.
6. For the political situation in the Cork region at this period, see K. Nicholls, 'The development of lordship in County Cork, 1300–1600', in O'Flanagan and Buttimer, *Cork history and society*, pp. 157–211.
7. M. Kelly, *The Black Death in Ireland* (Stroud, 2001), pp. 97–8, 99, 104–5.

8 V. Treadwell, 'The Irish customs administration in the sixteenth century', *Irish Historical Studies,* 20, 80, pp. 384–417; V. Treadwell, 'The establishment of the farm of the Irish customs, 1603–13', *Economic History Review,* 93 (1978), pp. 580–62.
9 Printed in F.H. Tuckey, *The county and city of Cork remembrancer* (Cork, 1837; reproduced 1980), pp. 282–5.

THE CHARTERS OF MEDIEVAL CORK
1 For a more detailed, technical discussion of these charters, their evolution and development and further ancillary grants to later medieval Cork, see A.F. O'Brien, 'The development of the privileges, liberties and immunities of medieval Cork and the growth of an urban autonomy *c.* 1189 to 1500', *JCHAS,* xc (1985), pp. 46–64; 'The royal boroughs, the seaport towns and royal revenue in medieval Ireland', *JRSAI,* 118 (1988), pp. 13–26; Irish exchequer records of payments of the fee farm of the city of Cork in the later Middle Ages', *Analecta Hibernica,* 37 (1998), pp. 141–89. For a general, including an economic, background, see A.F. O'Brien, 'Politics, economy and society: The development of Cork and the Irish south-coast region *c.* 1170 to *c.* 1583', in P. O'Flanagan and C.G. Buttimer (eds), *Cork history and society: Interdisciplinary essays on the history of an Irish county* (Dublin, 1993), pp. 83–154, and *The import of the Anglo-Normans on Munster, the Barryscourt lectures,* II (The Barryscourt Trust and Grandon Editions, Kinsale, 1997).

11. SIXTEENTH- AND EARLY SEVENTEENTH-CENTURY CORK
1 *Gentleman's Magazine,* April 1862, p. 442n.
2 For fosterage and gossipred, see F. Fitzsimons, 'Fosterage and gossipred in late medieval Ireland', in P.J. Duffy, D. Edwards and E. FitzPatrick (eds), *Gaelic Ireland* (Dublin, 2001), pp. 138–49.

12. THE EVOLUTION OF CORK'S BUILT ENVIRONMENT, 1600–1700
1 M. McCarthy, 'Writing Ireland's historical geographies', *Journal of Historical Geography,* 28 (October, 2002), p. 547.
2 J. Bradley and A. Halpin, 'The topographical development of Scandinavian and Anglo-Norman Cork', in P. O'Flanagan and C.G. Buttimer (eds), *Cork history and society* (Dublin, 1993), p. 32.
3 John Speed's map of the town of Cork, *c.* 1610, in C.A. Webster, *The diocese of Cork* (Cork, 1920), facing p. 116.
4 D. Dickson, C. Ó Gráda and S. Daultrey, 'Hearth tax, household size and Irish population change, 1672–1821', *Proceedings of the Royal Irish Academy,* 82 (1982), p. 160.
5 M. McCarthy, 'Cross-sectional reconstructions of historic urban landscapes: An examination of the nature and comprehensiveness of a mid-seventeenth-century survey and valuation', *Journal of the Irish Society for Archives,* 6.
6 M. McCarthy, 'Geographical change in an early modern town: Urban growth, economy and cultural politics in Cork, 1600–41', *JCHAS,* cvi (2001), pp. 53–78.
7 M. McCarthy, 'Turning a world upside down: The metamorphosis of property, settlement and society in the city of Cork during the 1640s and 1650s', *Irish Geography,* 33 (2000), pp. 37–55.
8 S. Hood (ed.), *Register of the parish of Holy Trinity (Christ Church), Cork, 1643–1669* (Dublin, 1998), p. 127.
9 D. Dickson, 'Large-scale developers and the growth of eighteenth-century Irish cities', in P. Butel and L.M. Cullen (eds), *Cities and merchants: French and Irish perspectives on urban development, 1500–1900* (Trinity College, Dublin, 1986), p. 117.

13. CITY, SEASONS AND SOCIETY
1 J. Rogers, *An essay on epidemic diseases . . .* (Dublin, 1734), pp. 47–8. His contemporary, Morgan O'Connell, agreed with him: Morgan O'Connell, *Morborum, acutorum et chronicorum quorundam, observationes medicales experimentales* (Dublin, 1746), pp. xix, xxiii.
2 J. Kelly (ed.), *The letters of Lord Chief Baron Willes to the Earl of Warwick . . .* (Aberystwyth, 1990), p. 49.
3 *Cork Gazette,* 12 March 1796. Cf. *Cork Evening Post,* 2 January 1794.
4 *Dublin Gazette,* 26 August 1732; *Hibernian Chronicle,* 31 October 1776, 2 October 1777, 8 September 1783.
5 A. Young, *A tour in Ireland . . . made in the years 1776, 1777, and 1778 . . .,* II (Dublin, 1780), pp. 65, 66; W. Mason, *A statistical account, or parochial survey of Ireland,* II (Dublin, 1814–19), 3 vols, p. 115.
6 A. de la Motraye, *Voyages en anglois et en françois d'A. de la Motraye en diverses provinces et places de la Prusse ducale et royale, de la Russie, de la Pologne etc. . . .* (The Hague, 1732); F.H. Tuckey, *The county and city of Cork remembrancer . . .* (Cork, 1837), p. lxxxix; A. Crookshank and the Knight of Glin, *Ireland's painters 1600–1940* (New Haven and London, 2002), pp. 131–2.
7 C. O'Mahony, *In the shadows: Life in Cork 1750–1850* (Cork, 1972), 34–5.
8 Mason, *Parochial survey,* II, p. 375; O'Mahony, *In the shadows,* p. 48. For the hours of work, see *Hibernian Chronicle,* 4 September 1780.
9 Tuckey, *Cork remembrancer,* pp. c–ci; K. Danaher, *The year in Ireland: Irish calendar customs* (Cork, 1972), pp. 249–50; S. Ní Chinnéide, 'A new view of Cork city in 1790', *JCHAS,* lxxviii (1973), p. 4. Coquebert de Monbret recounted how in 1790 the mayor entertained some 200 poor citizens to a Christmas banquet and gave them a gift each (suggesting the normality of exchanging Christmas gifts by then): Ní Chinnéide, 'New view', p. 6.
10 *An express from the city and county of Corke . . .* (Dublin, 1724–5); *London Packet,* 4–6 February 1789, quoted in *JCHAS,* xxv (1919), p. 104; Tuckey, *Cork remembrancer,* pp. 132, 160, 166, 200–1; O'Mahony, *In the shadows,* p. 34. For great autumnal floods in September 1745 and October 1767, see Tuckey, *Cork remembrancer,* pp. 131, 149.
11 D. Dickson, *Arctic Ireland . . .* (Belfast, 1997), pp. 25–7.
12 Tuckey, *Cork remembrancer,* p. 155; O'Mahony, *In the shadows,* p. 22.
13 Danaher, *The year in Ireland,* pp. 49–50; P. Murray, *Illustrated summary catalogue of the Crawford Municipal Art Gallery* (Cork, 1991), p. 40.
14 Danaher, *The year in Ireland,* pp. 72–3. For the novelty of Catholic church bells ringing across the city in 1814, see M. Lenox-Conyngham (ed.), *Diaries of Ireland: An anthology 1590–1987* (Dublin, 1998), p. 147.
15 *An express from Corke, with an account of a bloody battle . . .* (Dublin, 1727–8); *Cork Chronicle,* 21 October, 16 December 1765; Tuckey, *Cork remembrancer,* p. 176; R. Caulfield, *The council book of the Corporation of the city of Cork* (Guildford, 1876), p. 600. On the still strong dependence of the city poor on bread (as opposed to potatoes) as late as the 1790s, see T.A. Lunham (ed.), 'John Fitzgerald's diary, 1793', *JCHAS,* xxv (1919), p. 104; *Cork Evening Post,* 1 December 1794.
16 Caulfield, *Cork,* pp. 594–8; O'Mahony, *In the shadows,* pp. 40–1, 43. Cf. *Hibernian Chronicle,* 26 February 1784.
17 *Cork Journal,* 21 April 1755, 30 April 1764; Tuckey, *Cork*

remembrancer, pp. 141, 144, 151, 162, 184. Danaher, *Year in Ireland*, pp. 86, 90, 126. On the southside of the city, the street beside St Nicholas Church was known as Maypole Lane.
18 J. Alexander, *An amusing summer companion to Glanmire, near Cork . . .* (Cork, 1814), pp. 138–9; J. Hall, *A tour through Ireland . . .* (London, 1817), p. 185. On the mock-military character of May Day parades in Munster, see T.C. Croker, *Fairy legends and traditions of the south of Ireland* (London, 1825), pp. 306–7.
19 Tuckey, *Cork remembrancer*, pp. 139, 171, 193, 215. Another huge fire occurred in the suburbs in September 1766 when 73 'straw-roofed hovels' along the Old Bandon Road were destroyed: *Cork Chronicle*, 23 March 1767; Tuckey, *Cork remembrancer*, p. 145.
20 Danaher, *Year in Ireland*, p. 177. This may have been held in late September in some years: Tuckey, *Cork remembrancer*, p. 146.
21 *A tour of two English gentlemen . . .* (London, 1748), quoted in *JCHAS*, ix (1903), p. 70.

Nano Nagle and Catholic Cork: 1718–1784

1 For educational establishments in Cork city, see J.P. O'Donovan, *Unofficial schools in Cork and Ross* (unpublished MA thesis, no. 672, University College Cork; S. Ó Coindealbhain, 'Schools and schooling in Cork city, 1700–1831', *JCHAS* (1943), pp. 44–58; P. McCann, 'Cork City's eighteenth century Charity Schools', *JCHAS* (1979), pp. 102–11.
2 C.C. O'Brien, *The great melody* (Minerva, London, 1992), p. 18. The subject of O'Brien's book is Edmund Burke, a cousin of Nano Nagle, who discreetly supported her educational and charitable work.
3 M.P. O'Farrell, *Nano Nagle: Women of the Gospel* (Cork, 1996), pp. 67–74.
4 W. Coppinger (1753–1831), *The life of Miss Nano Nagle* (Cork, 1794). This was a funeral sermon preached by Coppinger in Cork on the tenth anniversary of Nano Nagle's death.
5 Nano Nagle's letter to Ms Fitzsimons, the first Irish Ursuline sister, dated 17 July 1769; see O'Farrell, *Nano Nagle*.
6 See Coppinger's funeral sermon, op. cit. T.J. Walsh, *Nano Nagle and the Presentation Sisters* (Dublin, 1959), pp. 384–95.
7 C. Clear, cited in S.J. Connolly (ed.), *The Oxford companion to Irish history* (Oxford University Press, Oxford, 1988), p. 377. Also, C. Clear, *Nuns in nineteenth century Ireland* (Gill & Macmillan, Dublin, 1987).
8 Letter from Nano Nagle to Teresa Mulally dated 31 January 1783 (O'Farrell, op. cit.).
9 *The Hibernian*, 26 April 1784.
10 *The Volunteer*, 29 April 1784.
11 J. Prunty, *Lady of charity and sister of faith: Margaret Aylward 1810–1889* (Betaprint, Dublin, 1999), p. 15.

14. Beef, Butter, Provisions and Prosperity in a Golden Eighteenth Century

1 P. O'Flanagan and J. Walton, 'The Irish community in eighteenth-century Cádiz', in H. Clark et al., *Surveying Ireland's past* (Dublin, 2004).
2 A. Bilbao, *Los irlandeses de Bizkaia: 'Los chiguiris' siglio XVIII* (Bilbao, 2004).
3 P. O'Flanagan, 'The "Cork region": Cork and county Cork, c. 1600–1900', in B. Brunt and K. Hourihan (eds), *Perspectives on Cork* (Dublin, 1988), pp. 1–18.
4 H.C. Brookfield, 'A microcosm of pre-famine Ireland: The Mallow district', *JCHAS*, lvii (1952), pp. 7–10.
5 E. Carberry, 'The development of Cork city', *JCHAS* (1943), pp. 48, 67–81.
6 W.A. Armstrong, 'The use of information about occupation', in E.A. Wrigley (ed.), *Nineteenth century society: Essays in the use of quantitative methods for the study of social data* (Cambridge, 1972); P. O'Flanagan and N. Buttimer (eds), *Cork history and society* (1993), pp. 454–61.
7 R. Lucas, 'The Cork directory for 1787', reprinted in *JCHAS* (1967), pp. 135–57.
8 W. Beaufort, 'Plan of the city and suburbs of Cork' (1801, Cork).
9 G. Johnson, *The laneways of medieval Cork* (Cork, 2002).

15. Cork City's Protestant Culture

1 Alexander the Coppersmith, *Remarks on the religion, trade, government, police, customs, manners, maladies of the city of Cork* (Cork, 1737), p. 2.
2 An abstract of 'The number of Protestant and popish families in the several provinces and counties of Ireland taken from the return made by the hearthmoney collectors . . . in the years 1732 and 1733' (Dublin, 1736; reprinted 1786), p. 5. These returns carry a health warning: see S. Connolly, *Religion, law and power: The making of Protestant Ireland 1660–1760* (Oxford, 1992), pp. 144–5; D. Dickson, 'Second city syndrome reflections on three Irish cases: Reflections on three Irish cases', in S. Connolly (ed.), *Kingdoms united* (Dublin, 1999); C. Gibson, *The history of the county and city of Cork*, II (Cork, 1861–64), p. 201. The proportion of Protestant to Catholic families in the city is the highest outside Dublin city and the Ulster counties: 'First report of commissioners of public instruction, Ireland', with appendix (H.C. 1835 (45) (46) xxxiii.1.829, 124c, 136c, 138c, 140c).
3 *Cork Constitution*, 24 October 1833, evidence of Joseph Hayes given to the commissioners appointed to enquire into the municipal corporations in Ireland: Dickson, 'Second city syndrome', p. 105.
4 T. Barnard, *A new anatomy of Ireland: The Irish Protestants* (Yale, 2003), p. 19; 'First report of commissioners of public instruction' (appendix 124c, 136c, 138c, 140c); J. Keane, 'Four tales of a city: The transformation in the social, economic and political geography of Cork city 1780–1846' (unpublished MA thesis, UCC, 1990), p. 121; P. Jupp and S. Royle, 'The social geography of Cork city elections, 1801–30', *IHS*, xxix (1994), pp. 31–2. Sadly, Jupp and Royle do not develop this interesting issue.
5 T. Newenham, *A view of the natural, political and commercial circumstances of Ireland* (London, 1809), appendix xviii; 'Second report of commissioners of Irish education enquiry', appendix 22, parochial abstracts, pp. 1000–23 (H.C. 1826–7 (12) xii.1); J. Hill, *From patriots to Unionists: Dublin civic politics and Irish Protestant patriotism 1600–1640* (Oxford, 1997), pp. 24–32, 39–41; Barnard, *A new anatomy of Ireland*, p. 15; W. Neligan to Peel, 28 January 1845 (B.L. Add. MS. 40558), p. 307; minutes of St Peter's vestry, Cork city (N.L.I. MS. 764); *Cork Constitution*, 7 November 1844, article on Dunscombe's TA society; Keane, 'Four tales', p. 82.
6 Dickson, 'Second city syndrome', pp. 103, 104; M. Costello, 'A symbolic geography of church construction in Cork city from the early seventeenth to the mid nineteenth century' (unpublished MA thesis, UCC, 1994), pp. 136–45; D. Dickson, 'Huguenots in the urban economy of eighteenth century Dublin and Cork', in C. Caldicott, H. Gough and J-P. Pittion (eds), *The Huguenots and Ireland: Anatomy of an emigration* (Dublin, 1987), p. 322; A. St Leger, *Silver, sails and silk: Huguenots in Cork 1685–1850* (Cork, 1990), pp. 9–13, 26–9.

7 *The Freeholder*, 15 July 1827.
8 R. Day and W. Coppinger (eds), *The ancient and present state of the county and city of Cork by Charles Smith, MD*, I (Cork, 1893–94), p. 433; I. d'Alton, *Protestant society and politics in Cork 1812–1844* (Cork, 1980), pp. 92–3, 97.
9 Gibson, *History of Cork*, II, p. 189; R. Caulfield, 'The Council book of the Corporation of Cork from 1609 to 1643, and from 1690 to 1800 (Guildford, 1876), pp. 431, 433, 729.
10 See d'Alton, *Protestant society*, pp. 93–6, and Keane, 'Four tales', pp. 93–9, for a fuller treatment of the Friendly Club. See also K. Milne, 'The Irish municipal corporations in the eighteenth century' (unpublished PhD thesis, TCD, 1962).
11 T. Evans, 'Notes of the Besnard family, *JCHAS*, xxxix (1934) p. 95.
12 C. Webster, *The diocese of Cork* (Cork, 1920), p. 149.
13 E. Bolster, *A history of the diocese of Cork from the penal era to the famine* (Cork, 1989); Costello, 'A symbolic geography', p. 99.
14 Caulfield, *Annals of St Fin Barre's Cathedral, Cork* . . . (Cork, 1871), p. 67; Costello, 'A symbolic geography', pp. 99 et seq., 103–7.
15 For a description of these churches, see J. O'Shea, 'The churches of the Church of Ireland in Cork city', *JCHAS*, xlviii (1943), pp. 30–5. Gibson, *History of Cork*, II, p. 313, describes Christ Church as 'now plain externally, as a barn, with the exception of a cut stone front'.
16 A. Acheson, *A history of the Church of Ireland 1691–1996* (Dublin, 1997), pp. 36–7; A. Winnett, *Peter Browne, provost, bishop and metaphysician* (London, 1974), pp. 54, 60, 62–3, 190.

The Huguenots of Cork

1 J-P. Labrousse, 'Letters from an Irish refugee: The Farie brothers in Cork and Limerick, 1711–25', *Proceedings of the Huguenot Society of Great Britain and Ireland*, XXVIII (2003), p. 58.
2 T. Murdoch (ed.), *The quiet conquest: The Huguenots 1685 to 1985* (London, Museum of London, 1985), p. 51.
3 R. Gwynn, 'Government policy towards Huguenot immigration and settlement in England and Ireland', in C.E.J. Caldicott, H. Gough and J-P. Pittion (eds), *The Huguenots and Ireland: Anatomy of a migration* (Dun Laoghaire, Glendale Press, 1987), p. 221.
4 G.L. Lee, *The Huguenot settlements in Ireland* (London, Longmans, Green & Co., 1936), pp. 28–30, 89.
5 D.W. Ressinger (ed.), *Memoirs of the Reverend Jaques Fontaine 1658–1728* (London, The Huguenot Society, 1992), p. 148.
6 A. St Leger, *Silver, sails and silk: Huguenots in Cork 1685–1850* (Cork Civic Trust, 1991), pp. 17–23.
7 C. Rynne, *The industrial archaeology of Cork city and its environs* (Dublin, Dúchas The Heritage Service, 1999), pp. 106–7, 114.

III. The City in the Nineteenth and Twentieth Centuries

16. Industry 1750–1930

1 D. Dickson, *The economic history of the Cork region in the eighteenth century* (Unpublished PhD, Trinity College Dublin, 1977), p. 527.
2 P.G.E. Clemens, 'The rise of Liverpool 1665–1750', *EHR*, 29 (1976), pp. 211–25; R.C. Nash, 'Irish Atlantic trade in the seventeenth and eighteenth centuries', *William and Mary Quarterly*, 42 (1985), 229–356.

3 J. Mannion, 'The maritime trade of Waterford in the eighteenth century', in W.J. Smyth and K. Whelan (eds), *Common ground: Essays on the historical geography of Ireland presented to T. Jones Hughes* (Cork, 1988), pp. 208–33.
4 L.M. Cullen, *Anglo-Irish trade 1660–1800* (Manchester, 1968), pp. 21–2; W. O'Sullivan, *The economic history of Cork city from the earliest times to the Act of Union* (Cork, 1937), p. 148.
5 Cullen, *Anglo-Irish Trade*, pp. 21–2.
6 C. Rynne, *The industrial archaeology of Cork city and its environs* (Dublin, 1999), p. 13.
7 Ibid, p. 13.
8 Ibid, pp. 13–14.
9 Dickson, *Economic history*, p. 571.
10 Dickson, *Economic history*, p. 571; C. O'Mahony, 'Bygone industries of Blarney and Dripsey', *JCHAS*, lxxxiv (1984), pp. 77–87.
11 A. Bielenberg, *Cork's industrial revolution 1780–1880: Development or decline?* (Cork, 1991), p. 20.
12 O'Sullivan, *Economic history of Cork city*, p. 247; Dickson, *Economic history*, p. 610.
13 E. Wakefield, *An account of Ireland, statistical and political* (London, 1812), p. 732; O'Sullivan, *Economic history of Cork city*, p. 247.
14 J.B. O'Brien, 'Population, politics and society in Cork, 1780–1900', in O'Flanagan and Buttimer (eds), *Cork* (Dublin, 1993), pp. 699–720.
15 M. Murphy, 'The working classes of nineteenth-century Cork', *JCHAS*, lxxxix (1980), pp. 26–51; O'Brien, 'Population politics and society', pp. 704–5; M. Cronin, 'Work and workers in Cork city and county 1800–1900', in O'Flanagan and Buttimer (eds), *Cork*, pp. 721–58.
16 Bielenberg, *Cork's industrial revolution*, pp. 118–19.
17 M. Murphy, 'The economic and social structure of nineteenth-century Cork', in D. Harkness and M. O'Dowd (eds), *The town in Ireland* (Belfast, 1981), pp. 125–54.
18 Murphy, 'Working classes', p. 28.
19 J. Donnelly, 'Cork market: Its role in the nineteenth-century Irish butter trade', *Studia Hibernica*, 11 (1971), pp. 130–63.
20 J. Donnelly, *The land and people of nineteenth-century Cork: The rural economy and the land question* (London, 1975); C. Rynne, *At the sign of the cow: The Cork Butter Market, 1770–1924* (Cork, 1998), 93ff.
21 M.E. Daly, *Industrial development and Irish identity 1922–1939* (Dublin, 1992), pp. 3–13.
22 D. Jacobson, 'The political economy of industrial location: The Ford Motor Company at Cork 1912–26', *IESH*, iv (1977), pp. 36–55.

Murphy's Brewery

1 A. Bielenberg, *Cork's industrial revolution 1780–1880: Development or decline?* (Cork, 1991).
2 D. Ó Drisceoil and D. Ó Drisceoil, *The Murphy's story: The history of Lady's Well Brewery, Cork* (Cork, 1997).

17. Connecting Cork

1 C. Rynne, *The archaeology of Cork city and harbour from the earliest times to industrialisation* (Cork, 1993); C. Rynne, *The industrial archaeology of Cork city and its environs* (Dublin, 1993).
2 C. Creedon, *The Cork and Macroom Direct Railway* (Cork, 1960); C. Creedon, *Cork city railway stations 1849–1985: An illustrated history* (Cork, 1985); C. Creedon, *The Cork, Bandon and South Coast Railway, Vol. 1, 1849–1899* (Cork, 1986); C. Creedon, *The*

Cork, Bandon and South Coast Railway, Vol. 2, 1900–1950 (Cork, 1989); C. Creedon, *The Cork, Blackrock and Passage Railway, 1850–1932* (Cork, 1992). See also S.C. Jenkins, *The Cork and Muskerry Light Railway* (Oxford, 1992) and *The Cork, Blackrock and Passage Railway* (Oxford, 1993).
3   W. McGrath, *Tram tracks through Cork* (Cork, 1981).
4   W. Barry, 'History of the port of Cork steam navigation 1815–1915', *JCHAS*, xxiii (1917), pp. 1–16, 79–93, 125–42, 185–99; D.B. McNeill, *Irish passenger steamship services* (Newton Abbot, 1969 and 1971), 2 vols, and C. O'Mahony, *The maritime gateway to Cork: A history of the outports of Passage West and Monkstown, 1754–1942* (Cork, 1986).

18. PLACE, CLASS AND POLITICS
1   *Census of Ireland, 1821–1901*.
2   M. Cronin, *Country, class or craft? The politicisation of the skilled artisan in nineteenth-century Cork* (Cork, 1994), p. 6.
3   M. Murphy, 'The working classes of nineteenth-century Cork', *JCHAS*, lxxxv (1980), p. 33.
4   Cronin, *Country, class or craft*, p. 4.
5   A. Fahy, 'Residence, workplace and patterns of change: Cork 1787–1863', in P. Butel and L.M. Cullen (eds), *Cities and merchants: French and Irish perspectives on urban development 1500–1900* (Dublin, 1986), p. 41.
6   M. Murphy, 'Cork commercial society 1850–1899: Politics and problems', in P. Butel and L.M. Cullen (eds), *Cities and merchants*, p. 239.
7   M. Murphy, 'The economic and social structure of nineteenth-century Cork', in D.W. Harkness and M. O'Dowd (eds), *The town in Ireland* (Belfast, 1981), p. 134.
8   Cronin, *Country, class or craft?*, p. 140.
9   A. Fahy, 'Place and class in Cork', in O'Flanagan and Buttimer (eds), *Cork*, p. 797.
10 A. O'Callaghan, *Of timber, iron and stone: A journey through time on the bridges of Cork* (Cork, 1991).
11 Fahy, 'Residence, workplace and patterns of change', pp. 802–7.
12 W. McGrath, *Tram tracks through Cork* (Cork, 1981).
13 *Cork Mercantile Chronicle*, 11 January 1832.
14 Murphy, 'Working classes of nineteenth-century Cork', 29.
15 C. O'Mahony, *In the shadows: Life in Cork 1750–1930* (Cork, 1997), pp. 66, 241–2.
16 I. d'Alton, 'Keeping faith: An evocation of the Cork Protestant character 1820–1920', in O'Flanagan and Buttimer (eds), *Cork*, pp. 759–92.
17 Murphy, 'Cork commercial society 1850–1899', pp. 238–9.
18 Cronin, *Country, class or craft?*, pp. 171–95.

MUSICAL BANDS AND LOCAL IDENTITIES
1   F. Lane, *In search of Thomas Sheahan: Radical politics in Cork 1824–36* (Dublin, 2001), pp. 47–8.
2   R.T. Cooke, *Cork's Barrack Street Band* (Cork, 1992), pp. 25–8.
3   *The Irishman*, 14 July 1883.
4   F. Lane, 'Music and violence in working-class Cork: The "band nuisance", 1879–82', *Saothar: Journal of Irish labour history*, 24 (1999), p. 18.
5   *Cork Examiner*, 5 May 1879; *Cork Constitution*, 23 June 1879.
6   J. McKeon, *Frank O'Connor: A life* (Edinburgh, 1998), p. 14.
7   Lane, 'Music and violence'.
8   Ibid, pp. 20, 28.
9   Ibid, pp. 20–2.
10 M. Cronin, *Country, class or craft?* (Cork, 1994), pp. 153, 167; H. Lorton, 'The bands of Cork', *Evening Echo*, 10 April 1975.
11 E. de Barra, *Bless 'em all: The lanes of Cork* (Cork, 1997), pp. 75–7.
12 Cronin, *Country, class or craft?*, pp. 152–3.
13 T. Cooke, 'The old bandstands of Cork', *Middle Parish Chronicle*, 1 (1988), pp. 36–8.
14 *Cork Examiner*, 13 December 1880.
15 *Cork Examiner*, 8 March 1882.
16 R.T. Cooke, *Cork's Barrack Street Band*; C. Bermingham, *The Cork Butter Exchange Band: A living tradition* (Cork, 1996).

FATHER THEOBALD MATHEW (1790–1856)
1   E. Stack, 'Victorian Cork', in H.A. Jeffries (ed.), *Cork: Historical perspectives* (Dublin, 2004), p. 177.

19. CORK'S 'GOLDEN AGE': GREAT HOUSES AND ART COLLECTING IN THE EARLY NINETEENTH CENTURY
1   S. Ní Chinnéide, 'A Frenchman's impressions of County Cork in 1790', *JCHAS*, lxxviii (1973), p. 120.
2   Anon: 'Memoir of Samuel Forde – A Cork artist', *Dublin University Magazine*, xxv (1845), p. 343.
3   Ibid, p. 351.
4   M. Bence-Jones, *A guide to Irish country houses* (Constable and Robinson, 1996), p. 273.
5   *Bolster's Quarterly Magazine*, ii, 5 (1828), p. 56. These paintings survived the burning of Convamore in 1921 and are in a private collection in the United States.
6   T. Crofton Croker, *Recollections of Cork* (unpublished MS 520, Trinity College Library, Dublin, 1833).
7   Daniel Maclise, MS Autobiography (Royal Academy of Arts, London, 1846), pp. 28–9.
8   Croker, *Recollections*, pp. 136, 137.
9   For a full account of Cooper Penrose, see Hugh Read, 'The Penroses of Woodhill', *JCHAS*, lxxxv (1980), pp. 79–98.
10 G.J. Lyne, 'Lewis Dillwyn's visit to Waterford, Cork and Tipperary in 1809', *JCHAS*, xci, 250 (1986), p. 91. Lyne refers to the diary kept by Joseph Woods, an architect, who accompanied Dillwyn on his visit to Cork. This diary is preserved in Cambridge University Library.
11 J.C., 'Sir Thomas Deane, PRHA', *JCHAS*, xxi (1915), pp. 180–6.
12 Ibid, p. 182
13 Letter from J. Quarry DD, Donoghmore Rectory, dated 16 March 1899, quoted by T.F. McNamara, *Portrait of Cork* (Cork, 1981), p. 57
14 Daniel Maclise, MS Autobiography (Royal Academy of Arts, London, MS. no. 5630, 22A (1), 1846). Quoted by J. Turpin, 'Daniel Maclise and Cork society', *JCHAS*, lxxxv (1980), p. 68.
15 Ibid, p. 68.
16 *Bolster's Quarterly Magazine*, ii, 5 (1828), p. 56. Crofton Croker mentions that paintings by Nathaniel Grogan were among the works of art at Summerhill (Croker, *Recollections*, pp. 136–7).
17 J.C., 'Sir Thomas Deane PRHA', *JCHAS*, xxi (1915), p. 184.
18 William West, *Directory of Cork*, 1810.
19 J.C., 'Notes and queries', *JCHAS*, xix (1913), p. 49.
20 Croker, *Recollections*, pp. 136, 137.
21 Information from Christina Leycester, great granddaughter of William Wrixon Leycester. The collection was sold on the death of Christina's grandmother.

20. THE ROYAL CORK INSTITUTION
1   B. Maye, 'Priestley remarkable as scientist and political thinker', *Irish Times*, 2 February 2004.
2   Several of Hincks's early papers, written in Cork, concerning religious and educational matters are available in the Boole Library, University College Cork.

3 *A syllabus of a course of lectures, delivered in the year 1803, by Thomas Dix Hincks, lecturer in the Cork Institution for the diffusion of knowledge* (James Haly, 1803). See also, S.F. Pettit, 'The Royal Cork Institution: A reflection of the cultural life of a city', *JCHAS*, lxxxi (1976), pp. 70–90.
4 Minutes for the Royal Cork Institution 1807–1825, Boole Library, University College Cork.
5 Extensive summaries of the proceedings of the Commissioners of Education relating to the Royal Cork Institution can be examined in *The Southern Reporter*, week beginning 17 July 1827.
6 J.A. Murphy, *The College: A history of Queen's/University College Cork, 1845–1995* (Cork, 1995), p. 8.
7 Murphy, *The College*, p. 8.
8 Several of Hogan's mid-nineteenth-century sculptures are on display in the Crawford Municipal Art Gallery; examples include 'The Dead Christ', 'The Drunken Faun', 'Minerva' and 'Thomas Davis'.
9 The Athenaeum was converted, under the guidance of Corkman James Scanlan, into the Cork Opera House in 1877.
10 T. Eagleton, 'Cork and the carnivalesque', in *Crazy Jane and the Bishop* (Cork, 1998), p. 161.

21. 'THE COLLEGE': UNIVERSITY COLLEGE CORK
1 J.A. Murphy, *The college* (Cork, 1995). Also J.A. Murphy, 'The college and the gaol', *The Graduate* (2002).

22. FAMINE
1 L. Kennedy and L.A. Clarkson, 'Birth, death and exile: Irish population history, 1700–1921', in B.J. Graham and L.J. Proudfoot (eds), *A historical geography of Ireland* (London, 1993), pp. 158–64.
2 J.S. Donnelly, *The land and the people of nineteenth-century Cork: The rural economy and the land question* (London and Boston, 1975), p. 73.
3 J.S. Donnelly, *The great Irish potato famine* (Sutton, 2001), p. 57.
4 *Cork Constitution*, 24 April 1847, quoted in Donnelly, *The land and people*, pp. 86–7.
5 *Dublin Quarterly Journal of Medical Science*, 8 (1849), p. 279.
6 Ibid., p. 270.
7 *Illustrated London News*, 4 April 1846.
8 C. O'Mahony, *In the shadows: Life in Cork 1750–1939* (Cork, 1997), p. 151.
9 Ibid.
10 *Illustrated London News*, 16 January 1847.
11 J. Coleman, 'Voyage of the *Jamestown*', *JCHAS*, x (1904), p. 27.
12 O'Mahony, *In the shadows*, p. 157. See also Chief Secretary's Office Registered Papers (CSORP) 1847 H 1704, 6048, National Archives of Ireland (hereafter NAI).
13 CSORP 1847 H 1704, 6048, NAI; O'Mahony, *In the shadows*, p. 158.
14 O'Mahony, *In the shadows*, pp. 159–60, 169.
15 CSORP 1847 H 5408, NAI. See also O'Mahony, *In the shadows*, pp. 164–6; Donnelly, *The land and people*, p. 87.
16 Fr Theobald Mathew to the Under-Secretary, Dublin Castle, 4 June 1847, CSORP 1847 H 6843, NAI.
17 *Dublin Quarterly Journal of Medical Science*, 8 (1849), p. 270; O'Mahony, *In the shadows*, p. 170.
18 Ibid.
19 CSORP 1847 H 10907, NAI.
20 *Cork Examiner*, 15 April 1847.
21 *Report from the select committee on the Passengers Act; with the proceedings of the committee, minutes of evidence, appendix and index*, British Parliamentary Papers (BPP) 1851 (632) xix.1, p. 707.
22 *Second report from the select committee on emigrant ships; together with the proceedings of the committee, minutes of evidence, appendix, and index*, BBP 1854 (349) xiii.187, p. 80.
23 *Report from the select committee on the Passengers' Act*, BPP 1851 (632) xix.1, p. 708.
24 *Select committee of House of Lords on colonization from Ireland. Report, minutes of evidence, appendix, maps, index*, BPP 1847 (737) vi.1, p. 249.
25 *Second report from the select committee on emigrant ships*, BPP 1854, p. 80.
26 Ibid., p. 162.
27 O. MacDonagh, *A pattern of government growth 1800–60: The Passenger Acts and their enforcement* (London, 1961), p. 41.
28 Donnelly, *The land and people*, p. 120.

QUEENSTOWN/COBH: AN EMIGRANT PORT
1 The town's original name was Cove. In 1849, to mark the visit of Queen Victoria, the town was renamed Queenstown. Following independence, the town adopted the Irish version of its original name – Cobh.
2 Emigrants were a common sight in the town prior to 1859, particularly during the Famine years, but from 1859 onwards emigration through Queenstown was on a much bigger scale than in previous years and the range of services far more extensive than had previously been the case.
3 *Cork Examiner*, 20 April 1866.
4 *Cork Examiner*, 4 May 1883.
5 *Cork Examiner*, 20 April 1866.
6 *Francis Guy's directory and guide, Province of Munster 1886:* N. & J. Cummins, West Beach – National Steam Navigation Company Ltd; American Line for Philadelphia; Henderson Brothers, Scott's Square – Anchor Line; D. McIvor & Company, Scott's Square – British and North American Royal Mail Steam Packet Company; Thomas O'Reilly, Scott's Square – Thomas and Mersey Australian Line; James Scott & Company, Scott's Square – Guion U.S. Mail Company; White Star U.S. Mail Company; Allan Royal Mail Steam Ship Company; C. & W.D. Seymour, Lynch's Quay – Inman Steam Ship Company.
7 Following the construction of public baths by the Sea Baths and Recreation Company in the late 1890s, the quay became known locally as the Baths Quay. During the inter-war years, the building also housed the emigrants' examination station, where prospective emigrants were subjected to a rigorous medical examination, including delousing.
8 *Cork Examiner*, 20 April 1866.
9 *Reports on state of lodging-houses in Queenstown*, British Parliamentary Papers (BPP) 1882 (237) lxiv.563, p. 1.
10 Even as late as 1925, the *Cork Examiner* reported that 'the present system of certain boarding house representatives harassing passengers at Cork Station and other points en route to Cove is strongly deprecated by the steamship companies'.
11 *Cork Examiner*, 20 April 1866
12 *Reports on state of lodging-houses in Queenstown*, BPP 1882 (237) LXIV.563, p. 1.
13 Ibid, p. 2.
14 Ibid, p. 4.
15 *Cork Examiner*, 1883.
16 D. Moloney, *American lay groups and the transatlantic social reform in the progressive era* (London and Chapel Hill, 2002), p. 95.

17 *Cork Examiner*, 2 September 1939.
18 While Great Britain was the destination for the majority of Irish emigrants during the 1950s, 50,000 emigrated to the United States between 1951 and 1960.
19 *Cork Examiner*, 14 November 1964.

NEW ARRIVALS: CORK'S JEWISH COMMUNITY
1 D. Keogh, *Jews in twentieth-century Ireland: Refugees, anti-Semitism and the Holocaust* (Cork, 1998), p. 15.
2 L. Hyman, *The Jews of Ireland from earliest times to the year 1910* (Shannon, 1972), p. 221.
3 *Cork Examiner*, 2 August 1933, p. 9.
4 David Marcus also attended Presentation Brothers College. In his novel, *A land not theirs* (London, 1986, p. 152), he explores the experiences of a young Jewish boy growing up in a city that was predominantly Catholic: 'The one Jew among hundreds of Catholics and his Jewishness instead of making him vulnerable had in fact been his armour. It was as if he didn't exist outside of Jewtown, as if the Jacob attending Presentation College was some *doppelgänger* sent to suffer the pinpricks of its alien world while the real Jacob remained cocooned in his *Yiddisheh veldi.*'
5 'It was thanks to the then Principal of the Presentation Brothers, Brother Edward Connolly, that Gerald Goldberg got a start in the legal firm of Barry Galvin, who told the Brother frankly that without his intervention he would have found it difficult to accept a Jewish apprentice. Goldberg qualified as a solicitor in 1934 after studying in University College Cork' (*Irish Times*, 10 January 2004).

23. CONFLICT AND WAR, 1914–1923
1 L. Ruiséal, *Liam Ruiséal remembers* (Cork, 1978), p. 16.
2 The Irish Volunteers were founded as a nationalist response to the establishment of the Ulster Volunteer Force in 1913, which was pledged to resist Home Rule for Ireland by force of arms. While MacCurtain and O'Hegarty had been in the conspiratorial IRB since 1906, MacSwiney did not join until the eve of the 1916 Rising. MacCurtain and MacSwiney left after the Rising, believing in the need for open rather than secret organisations.
3 F. Costello, *Enduring the most: The life and death of Terence MacSwiney* (Dublin, 1995), p. 51.
4 This is a reference to Wilson's promise on entering the war that America's aim was to make the world 'safe for democracy'. *Cork Examiner*, 13 June 1919.
5 P. Hart, *The IRA and its enemies: Violence and community in Cork 1916–1923* (Oxford, 1998), p. 106.

24. CORK CITY IN THE TWENTIETH CENTURY
1 All population data are from the relevant Census of Population volumes.
2 Cork Town Planning Association, *Cork: A civic survey* (Liverpool, 1926).
3 M. Robertson, *County of Cork and neighbourhood town planning report* (Cork, 1941).
4 To put this decline in city-centre retailing in perspective, it should be noted that by 1982 only three city centres in the United States (New York, New Orleans and San Francisco) had more than five per cent of their metropolitan area sales. By now, this decline is even more acute in the USA. See R.M. Fogelson, *Downtown: Its rise and fall, 1880–1950* (New Haven, 2001).
5 Cork County Council, *County development plan* (Cork, 1972).
6 BKS Consultative Technical Services, *Cork traffic study: Report and recommendations* (Cork, 1968).
7 P. Dovell, *Cork: An environmental study of Cork* (Cork, 1971).
8 Skidmore, Owings and Merrill, Martin and Voorhees Associates, E.G. Pettit and Company, Roger Tym and Associates, *Cork land use/transportation plan* (Cork, 1978); Skidmore, Owings and Merrill, The MVA Consultancy and the LUTS Review Team, *Review of Cork land use/transportation plan* (Cork, 1992); Cork City Council, Cork County Council and W.S. Atkins, *Cork area strategic plan* (Cork, 2002).
9 T. Bendixson, *Instead of cars* (Harmondsworth, 1977).
10 KPMG in association with Murray O'Laoire Associates and Northern Ireland Economic Research Centre, *Study on the urban renewal schemes* (Dublin, 1996).
11 M. Nagle, 'Residential renewal in Cork's inner city, 1986–1996' (MA thesis, University College Cork, 1998).
12 Cork Corporation and Urban Initiatives, *Cork: Historic centre action plan* (Cork, 1994); J. O'Donnell, 'The Cork historic centre action plan', in B. Brunt and K. Hourihan (eds), *Perspectives on Cork* (Cork, 1998), pp. 121–37.
13 T. O'Brien, 'The social use of public space: St Patrick's Street, Cork' (BA thesis, University College Cork, 2004).
14 J. Gehl and L. Gemzoe, *Public spaces, public life* (Copenhagen, 1996).
15 For a discussion of American developments, see R. Fishman, 'Urbanity and suburbanity: Rethinking the 'burbs', *American Quarterly*, 46 (1994), pp. 35–9.
16 J. Garreau, *Edge city: Life on the new frontier* (New York, 1991).

25. THE SUBURBS
1 F.W. Sharpe and L. Wallock, 'Bold new city or built-up 'burb': Redefining contemporary suburbia', *American Quarterly*, 46 (1994), pp. 1–30. For a critical examination of British suburban development, see A.M. Edwards, *The design of suburbia* (London, 1981).
2 The first development was Madden's Buildings in Blackpool in 1886. Ryan's, Horgan's and Roche's Buildings were added between 1888 and 1892.
3 These were Sutton's, Barrett's and Kelleher's Buildings.
4 G.E. Cherry, *Cities and plans* (London, 1988).
5 Edwards, *Design of suburbia*, pp. 94–6.
6 M. Gough, 'Socio-economic conditions and the genesis of planning in Cork', in M.J. Bannon (ed.), *The emergence of Irish planning 1880–1920* (Dublin, 1985), pp. 307–32.
7 M. Robertson, *County of Cork and neighbourhood town planning report* (Cork, 1941).
8 L.B. Ginsburg, 'Summing-up', *Architectural Review*, 154 (1973), p. 264.
9 Cherry, *Cities and plans* (London, 1988).
10 J.D. Murphy, *The semi-detached house: Its place in suburban housing* (Dublin, 1977).
11 Edwards, *Design of suburbia*, pp. 249–55.
12 O. Newman, *Defensible space* (New York, 1972).
13 Dublin Urban Study, *Dublin: A city in crisis* (Dublin, 1975); E. Brangan (ed.), *Streets for living* (Dublin, 1976).
14 Murphy, *Semi-detached house*.
15 L.H. Masotti and J.K. Hadden (eds), *The urbanization of the suburbs* (Beverly Hills, 1973).
16 H.J. Gans, *People and plans* (Harmondsworth, 1972).
17 A. Stark, 'America, the gated?', *Wilson Quarterly*, 22 (1998), pp. 58–79.
18 L. Mumford, *The culture of cities* (New York, 1938), p. 215.

19　Edwards, *Design of suburbia*, p. 223.
20　R. Hackney, *The good, the bad and the ugly* (London, 1990).
21　C. Ellis, 'The new urbanism: Critiques and rebuttals', *Journal of Urban Design*, 7 (2002), pp. 261–91.

26. BUILDINGS AND ARCHITECTURE
1　J. Williams, *Architecture in Ireland 1837–1921* (Dublin, 1994); F. O'Dwyer, *The Architecture of Dean and Woodward* (Cork, 1997); S. Rothery, *Ireland and the new architecture* (Dublin, 1991); M. Craig and the Knight of Glin, *Ireland observed* (Cork); C. Lincoln, *Steps and steeples: Cork at the turn of the century* (Dublin); J.P. McCarthy, *Bishopstown House* (Cork, 1975); the architectural archive database of Irish architects.

IV.　Culture and the City

INTRODUCTION
1　Those involved in sport are in a sense always answering to their own place. Tom Humphries referred to this condition when writing about Roy Keane: 'The refusal of Keane to evolve and to change from the kid from Mayfield seems to run to the core of his being. It is what makes him so hungry and hard. He is answering to his home place all of the time.' Tom Humphries, *Laptop dancing and the nanny goat mambo: A sportswriter's year* (Dublin, 2003), p. 204.

27. THE CULTURE OF FOOD
1　W. O'Sullivan, *The economic history of Cork city from the earliest times to the Act of Union* (Cork, 1937).
2　Ibid, p. 165.
3　Ibid, p. 148.
4　J.S. Donnelly, *The land and people of nineteenth-century Cork* (London, 1987), p. 46.
5　Ibid, p. 148.
6　Receipt book, UCC/U59/1–155, University College Cork.
7　M. Verdon, *Echo boys, the Marsh and the lanes: Old Cork remembered* (Dublin, 1993), p. 48.
8　M. Sheridan, *Monica's kitchen* (Dublin, 1963), pp. 137–43, 147–8, 195–8.

28. SPORT

HURLING AND THE GLEN
1　'Blackpool' can be found in Val Dorgan's book, *Christy Ring* (Dublin, 1980), p. 246.
2　Liam Ó Tuama (ed.), *The spirit of the Glen* (Cork, 1973). Brian Dillon's hurling club was founded in 1910. It is based in the Dillon's Cross area, located at the opposite end of Goulding's Glen from Blackpool. See also *A history of Brian Dillon's* (Cork, 1983).
3　Cited in an article by Denis Long, 'Blackpool, its people', in *Blackpool 800* (Cork, 1985). See also *Windele's Cork: Historical and descriptive notices of the city of Cork from its foundation to the middle of the 19th century*. Revised, abridged and annotated by James Coleman (Cork, 1973).
4　In the 1920s, St Nicholas (St Nick's) became a 'sister club' of Glen Rovers. The clubs enjoy dual membership and to this day many Glen hurlers play football with St Nick's.
5　Prior to 1920, the minor grade was a grade open to players of all ages. Between 1920 and 1925 the competition was confined to boys under the age of seventeen. From 1926 onwards, it was confined to boys under the age of eighteen.
6　O'Connell and Seamus Long (a county Board Officer) are credited with instigating the inter-county minor championships in 1928.
7　At the time very little attention was paid to developing under-age sport in the city. There were 'street leagues' organised in the North and South parishes that were keenly contested. Despite this, strong senior clubs such as St Finbarr's, Redmond's and Blackrock did not put any great effort into developing a juvenile section.
8　It was through O'Connell's efforts that Jim Young (Dunmanway) and Dan Coughlan (Ballydehob), both students at Farranferris, came to play with the club.
9　Other important events occurred in the late 1930s and early 1940s that ensured that Glen Rovers remained the foremost club in the county. In 1936 Tom O'Reilly became chairman of the club. He was a forceful and respected character and a strong chairman. He and Paddy O'Connell formed a powerful axis around which the everyday life of the club revolved. In addition, Gerald Griffin's, a juvenile team based in the North Monastery Technical School, disbanded. This brought players such as John Lyons, Jimmy Lynam and Donie O'Donovan to the club, all of whom became major figures in Glen Rovers over the next 40 years.
10　Jack Lynch was Taoiseach of Ireland between 1966 and 1973 and between 1977 and 1979.
11　Many of the team had won under-21 county medals in 1984 and three of them, Tomás Mulcahy (who was also captain), Kieran McGuckian and John Fitzgibbon, played with Cork when they won the 1990 All-Ireland title.

ROAD BOWLING
1　The original version of 'The boys of Fair Hill' was composed by Seán O'Callaghan.

30. LITERATURE AND THE CITY
1　L. Huxley (ed.), *Letters of Elizabeth Barrett Browning to her sister 1846–1859* (1929).
2　E. Jay (ed.), *The autobiography of Margaret Oliphant* (2002).
3　The *Seamus Murphy exhibition catalogue* (Cork, 1982).
4　G. Delanty, *Leper's Walk* (Cork, 1999).
5　B. Ó Cuiv (ed.), *Parliament na mBan* (Dublin, 1952).
6　E. Mavor (ed.), *The grand tours of Katherine Wilmot* (1992); Marchioness of Londonderry and H.M. Hyde (eds), *The Russian Journals of Martha and Catherine Wilmot* (1934).
7　Ó Canainn has published *Home to Derry* (Belfast, 1986); *Melos* (Cork, 1987); *A lifetime of notes* (Cork, 1997); *Seán Ó Riada* (Cork, 2003).
8　Letter of 1953 to the late J.V. Kelleher, quoted by M. Harmon in *Sean O'Faolain: A life* (Dublin, 1994).

PATRICK GALVIN'S CITY
1　Patrick Galvin, *The madwoman of Cork* (Cork, 1991), p. 7.
2　Patrick Galvin, *Song for a poor boy: A Cork childhood* (Dublin, 1990); *Song for a raggy boy: A Cork boyhood* (Dublin, 1991).

V.　Contemporary Transformations

31. INDUSTRY AND EMPLOYMENT
1　A. Bielenberg, *Cork's industrial revolution: Development or decline* (Cork, 1991).
2　B. Brunt, 'The new industrialisation of Ireland', in: R.W.G. Carter and A.J. Parker (eds), *Ireland: A contemporary geographic perspective* (London, 1988).

3 C. Buchanan and Partners, *Regional studies in Ireland* (Dublin, 1968).
4 Cork Harbour Commissioners, *Cork harbour development plan* (Cork, 1972); Skidmore, Owings and Merrill, Martin and Voorhees Associates, E.G. Pettit and Company, Roger Tym and Associates, *Cork land use/transportation plan* (Cork, 1978).
5 K. Hourihan, 'The Cork land use and transportation study', *Irish Geography*, 12 (1979), pp. 99–104; B. Brunt, 'Industrial and harbour development in Cork', *Irish Geography*, 17 (1980), pp. 101–8.
6 B. Brunt, 'Industrialisation in the Greater Cork Area', in B. Brunt and K. Hourihan (eds), *Perspectives on Cork* (Cork, 1998).
7 A. Barry and B. Brunt (2002), 'Female employment in the multinational electronics industry in Ireland's south-west planning region', *Irish Geography*, 35, pp. 28–39.
8 Skidmore, Owings and Merrill, MVA Consultancy, LUTS Review Team, *Review of Cork land use transportation plan* (Cork, 1992).
9 W.S. Atkins et al., *Cork area strategic plan 2001–2020* (Cork, 2001).

34. Living in the City
1 C. Lefort, *Democracy and political theory* (Cambridge, 1998).
2 N. Elias, *The civilising process: The history of manners* (Oxford, 1978).
3 M. Harloe, *The people's home: Social rented housing in Europe and America* (Oxford, 1995).
4 S. Daly, *Cork: A city in crisis* (Cork, 1978).
5 Cork Artisans Dwelling Company, Minute book (1865).
6 A. De Swaan, *In care of the state: Healthcare, education and welfare in Europe and the USA in the modern era* (Cambridge, 1988).
7 N. Ellin (ed.), *Architecture of fear* (New York, 1997); M. Davis, *City of quartz: Excavating the future in Los Angeles* (London, 1992).
8 Z. Baumann, *Modernity and ambivalence* (Cambridge, 1997).
9 U. Beck, *What is globalization?* (Cambridge, 2000).
10 R. Mishra, *Globalization and the welfare state* (Cheltenham, 1999).

35. Urban Difference
1 Northside Folklore Project, *Life journeys* (Cork, 2000).
2 Cork Corporation, *The northside study* (Cork, 1990).
3 Cork Corporation, *Cork economic monitor* (October 1985).
4 D. Linehan, *Community involvement, Mayfield* (Dublin, 1984).
5 C.A. Ryan et al., 'Trend analysis and socio-economic differentials in infant mortality in the Southern Health Board, Ireland (1988–1997)', *Irish Medical Journal*, 93 (2000), pp. 204–6.
6 C. Forde, *Making education work on Cork's northside* (Cork, 1996).
7 Cork City Development Board, *Imagine our future: Integrated strategy for economic, social and cultural development* (Cork, 2003).

36. Community Development and the Catholic Church
1 L. Fuller, *Irish Catholicism since 1950: The undoing of a culture*, (Dublin, 2004); R.V. Comerford, *Inventing the nation: Ireland* (London, 2004).
2 S. Beecher, *Day by day: A miscellany of Cork history* (Cork, 1992).
3 Cork Catholic Diocese, *The draft pastoral strategy* (Cork, 2004).
4 O. McCarthy, *History and development of Ballyphehane Credit Union 1960–1994* (Cork, 1994).
5 R. O'Connor, O. McCarthy and M. Ward, *Innovation and change in Irish Credit Unions* (Cork, 2002).
6 A.T. Culloty, *Nora Herlihy: Irish Credit Union pioneer* (Dublin, 1990).

37. Migration
1 B. McGinn, 'The black Irish', *Irish Roots Magazine*, 1 (1994) (http://www.irishrootsmagazine.com/about/TheBlackIrish.htm).
2 RTÉ, *Are you still below?* (Dublin, 2003).
3 J. Hegarty, 'A contribution from a Cork boy: Moving here' (http://www.movinghere.org.uk/stories/stories.asp?PageNo=21).
4 R. O'Hanlon, *The new Irish Americans* (New York, 1998).
5 M. Germaine-Dillon, 'The Huguenots', in *Irish family history*, Vol. XIII (1997).
6 E. Bowen, *Bowen's Court* (London, 1994).
7 P. Mac Éinrí and P. Walley, *Labour migration into Ireland* (Dublin, 2003).
8 A. Stavrou and J. O'Riordan, *Labour migrants in Cork City: A survey* (Cork, 2003).
9 A. Collins, *The needs of asylum seekers in Cork* (Cork, 2002).
10 British Council, *New young Europeans* (Cork, 2004).

38. Planning and Development
1 W.S. Atkins et al., *Cork area strategic plan 2001–2020* (Cork, 2001).

INDEX

(Page numbers in italics refer to illustrations and captions)

abattoirs, 113, 127–8, *128*, 308
Ablin, Samuel, 169
Adamnán, 81
Adderley, Thomas, 170
Adelaide Street, 75, 78, 242
Áed mac Comgaill, 82
Aer Rianta, 379
Aghada, 393
agriculture, 45, 53 *see also* market gardens
Aherla, 277
Aikenhead, Mary, 141
air pollution, 17
Airport, 9, 367, 375
  history and development, 379, *379*
Alaska Jacks, 357
alder, 41, 43
aldermen, 164
Alexander the Coppersmith, 128, 160, *160*
algal blooms, 393
Allan Line, 246
Allen, Darina, 306, 314
Allen, Myrtle, 306, 314
Allen family, 165
Allen's chemist, 358
almshouses, *144*, 144–5, 291
Alwin family, 123
amber, 47, *71*
American War of Independence, 183
Anderson's Quay, 201
Anglesea Bridge, *179*
Anglesea Street, 257, 344
Anglicans, 103, 157, 161, 162, 163, *163*, 291–2
  churches, 165–7
Anglo-Normans, 62–3, 64, 70, 83
Antient and Present State of the County and City of Cork, 135, *152*
antler and bone artefacts, 62
apartment blocks, 287
Apple Corporation, *371*, 371–2, 375
Arbuthenott, Thomas, 222
Arbutus Lodge Hotel, 311–14

archaeological artefacts, 45–55, *61*, 62, *62*, *71*, 387
  site distribution, *46*
Archdeacon family, *115*, 118
architecture, 178, 290–9
  church, 142–4, 166, 178, *214*, 230, 297, *297*
    St Anne's, 142–4, 291, *348*
    St Fin Barre's, 300–2, *348*
  great houses, 215–16, *217*, 219–21, 222
  twentieth-century, 297–9
  University College, *232*, 233, 294–5, 297, 299, *299*
  see also house-building
Ardfoyle Convent, 90
Area Traffic Control, 270
Armour, William and John, 169
Arnott's brewery, 190, *192*
art, 178, 216–22
  collections, 216–22
  gallery *see* Crawford Municipal Art Gallery
  Vatican sculptures, 226, *226*
Art and Design, School of, 178, 218, *226*, 226–7
ash, 43
Ashlin, George, 293
assizes, 134
Assumption Road, 281, *314*
asylum-seekers, 272, 408, 422–3
Athenaeum, *226*, 227, *227*, *228*
athletics, *307*
Atkins, William, 295
Atkinson, George Mounsey Wheatley, *199*
Atkinson, James, *188*
Atlantic Club, 167
Atlantic Pond, 388, *388*, 389
Aud (ship), 259
Augustinians, 88, 89, 104, 105, *105*
aurora borealis, 24
Auxiliaries, *261*, 262–3
axes, prehistoric, 45, 47, *48*, *49*

Bachelor's Quay, 201, 357
Bagnall family, 165
Bailey, the, 409
bailiffs, 113, 117
baking, 130
Ballinaspig More, 45, 50, 51
Ballincollig, 84, 269, 277, *287*, *373*, 374, 376, 426
  archaeological finds, *47*, 48, 50, 51
  geology, 11
Ballinlough Road, 263
Ballintemple, 87, 179, 282
Ballinure, 45, *49*
Ballygarvan, 53
Ballymacthomas, 281, 308
Ballymaloe, 314
Ballynagrumoolia, 51
Ballyphehane, *281*, 282, 398, *406*, 407, *407*, 412, 414
Ballyvolane, 268, 376, 408
Ballyvorisheen, 49
Ballyvourney, 80
Band of the Cork Orchestral Union, 337, 338
Bandon Road, 155
Bandon River, 2
bands, 209–12, *336*, 339
  'band nuisance', 210–12
'Banjoes' (pub), 357
banking, 202
Bann flakes, 45
Baptists, 160, 163, 242
barges, 200
Barnagore, 45
Barnavara, 286
Barnes, Thomas Addison, *188*
Barrack Street, *58*, 59, 64, *180*, 211
  businesses, 155, 156, 158
  Great Famine, 239, *240*, 242, 243
  lanes, 152, 205
  urban development, 203, *273*, 397
Barrack Street Band, 212, *212*, 214
barrel-staves, 174
Barret, William, 106

INDEX

Barret family, 108
Barrett's Buildings, 205, 206
Barron, Ray, 343, *343*
Barry, James, 219, 221
Barry, Mick, 331–2, 333–5, *335*
Barry, Lord Philip de, 93, 104
Barry, Tom, 262
Barry family, 106, 123
Barry Murphy, Jimmy, 307, *307*, 316, *316*, 319, 322
bars *see* pubs
baths, public, 404
Beaker pottery, 45
Béal na mBláth, 264
Beale, George T., 174
Beale, James, 130, *131*
Beale, Joshua, *159*
Beale family, 173, 174
Beamish, William, *187*, 224
Beamish and Crawford's, 185, *187*, 188, 190, 192, 193, 268–9, 297
Beamish family, 219, 232
Beaufort, William, 150, 153, 155, *157*
Beecher, Seán, 337
beef
 markets, 127
 slaughtering, 113, 127–8, *128*, 130, 308
 trade, 118, 127, 130, 183, *309*, 309–10
  live exports, 310
  traditional specialities, 308–9
Beg, Lough, 392
beggars, 132, 244
Bell, Beady, *340*
Benedictines, 88, 104–5
Benson, Sir John, 148, 227, 292, 295, 296, 312, 386
Bernard of Clairvaux, St, 83
Besnard, John, 245
Besnard family, 165, 170, 185
Bessborough, Earl of, 221
Bettridge's charity, 144–5
Billon, Adam, 169
Billon, Peter, 169
birds, 32–3, *34*, 35–6, 41, 392
 'Battle of the Birds' (1622), 23
 species in harbour, *394*
Birkhan, David, 255
birth rates, 123–4, 150
Bishop Lucey Park, 74, 271, 276, 429
Bishop's Palace, 291, *291*, 292
Bishopstown, 285, 287, *287*, 291, 315, 374, 398, 407, 429
Bishopstown Business Park, 372, *372*
Bishopstown Court, 268
BKS Traffic Plan, 269, *271*, 285, 428

Black and Tans, 260, *261*, 263
Black Death, 106
Blackmoor Lane, 213, *213*
Blackpool, 211, 242, 387, 396
 'Blackpool' song, 325
 business and industry, 156, 158, 184, 185, *189*, 268, *370*
 convent, 292
 flooding, *25*, 30
 geology, 13, 14
 sport and, 319–20, 325, *326*, 330
 urbanisation, 268, 271, 274, *280*, 282, 315, 408, 426
Blackrock, 179, 203, 364–5, 377, 387
 geology, 11
 quarry, 143
Blackrock Castle, *114*, 116, 220, 294, 295
Blarney, 10, 11, 13, 130, 185, 369, *373*, 377, 382, 426
Blarney (tender), 250
Blarney Castle, *72*
Blarney House, 220
Blarney Lane, 127, 128, 132, 152, 155, 203
Blarney River, 10, 184, *184*
Blarney Road, *181*, 332, *333*
Blarney Street, 357
Blue Coat school, 137
board games, *61*, 63
Bodega, 409
Bog Road ('The Boggy'), 332, *333*
Boggeragh mountains, 3, 4, 12
boglands, 4
Boole, George, 234, *234*
Boreenmanna, 387
Boreenmanna Road, 87
Boston Scientific, 375
Botanic Gardens, 36–7, 214, 225
Bournes, 375
Bousfield, Benjamin, 221
Bowen, Elizabeth, 421
bowling, road, 331–5
Bowling Green, 126
Boyle, Elizabeth, 351
Boyle, Kelly, 343–5
Bradford, William, 355
Brady, George, 338
Brady, W.E., 338
Brady, Willie, 338
Brennan, James Butler, *138*
brewing, 130, 183–4, 185, *187*, 188, 268–9, 297
 history of Murphy's, 190–3
Brian Boru Street, *310*
Brick, Grainne, 384–5

Bride, River, 10, 12, 184
bridges, 59–60, 65, 69–70, 120, 151, 153, 154, *161*, *166*, 167, 178, *179*, 203, 270, 277
British Army recruitment, *256*, 256–9, 419
Broad Lane, 77, 204, *263*
Broad Lane Chapel, 89
broadband, 375
Brodie, Dr, 248
An Bróg, 409
Broguemakers Hill, 286
Brontë, Charlotte, 351
Bronze Age, 46, 47–51
brothels, 129
Brown Thomas, 265
Browne, Jemmett, 163
Browne, Bishop Peter, 167, 291
Browning, Robert and Elizabeth Barrett, 352
Bruen, Jimmy, 322
Brunel, Isambard, 295
Brunt, Barry, 369–76
Buckley, Din Joe, 325, *327*
Buckley, Bishop John, 414
Buckley, Sonny, 327
burgage plots, 111, 120
Burges, William, 178, 290, 293, 297, 301–2
Burgess Associations, 208
burial practices, 86, 87, 90–2
 criminals, 91–2, 136
burial sites, 37, *37*, 89–92, 93, 174
 early Christian, 85–6, 87, *87*, 88
 Famine, *241*, 244, *244*
 prehistoric, 45, *46*, 47, *48*, 48–9
Burke, Elizabeth, 140
burning of Cork (1920), 193, *261*, 262, 265, 358
Bus Éireann, 382, *383*
bus services, 198, 281, 284, 288
 recent developments, 381, 382, *383*, 426
butter
 market, 133, 142, *143*, 145–6, *147*, 148, 187, 296
 roads, *133*, *146*, 195, 198, 296, *296*
 trade, 118, 133, 142, 145–8, 157, 183
 decline, 187, *188*
 exports, 127, *146*, 160, 308
 weigh-houses, 145, 148
Butter Exchange Band, 212
butterfly bush (*Buddleia variabalia*), 42
Buttimer, Neil, 135–6
Butts, John, *101*, 129, 219, 221
Byrne, Barry, 297

451

INDEX

café culture, 367
Café Paradiso, 314
Callanan, Dr, 239, 244
Camden Fort, 392
Camden Quay, 29, 201
Canniffe, Tony, 343
canoe, prehistoric, 50
Canova, Antonio, 226
Cantwell, Noel, 320
Caomhánach, Séamus, 340
Capuchin Order, 213, *213*
car ownership, 268, 278, 282, 379–80
   congestion, 269–70, *271*, *283*, 284, 288, 315, 379, 381, 382–3, 426, 428
   parking, 383
   statistics, *380*
   travel to work/school, 384–5
Carboniferous period, 8–9
Carew, Sir George, 69, *69*
Carey's Lane, 169 274
Carleton, William, 221
Carlisle Fort, 392
Carnegie Free Library, *261*, 263, 358
carnivals, 127, 130–1, *131*, *132*, 132–3, 134, *423*
carp, 35
Carré family, 168, 170
Carrigaline, 269, *270*, 426
   archaeological finds, 45, 47, *49*
Carrigrenan, *388*, 388–90
Carrigrohane Castle, 291, *291*
Carrigtohill, 15–16, 45, 426
Carroll family, 173, 174
Carr's Hill graveyard, 244, *244*
Carter, Plunkett, 322–4
cartography, 150, *151*, *152*, *153*, 156
Carty, John, 78, 150, *151*
Casey, Jerry, 334
CASP (Cork Area Strategic Plan), 269, 276, 277, 368, 376, 381, *382*, 383, 408, 424
   aims and strategy, 425–31
Castlefreke, 216
Castle Hyde, 216, *216*, *218*
Castlemartyr, 219
Castlemary, 45, *48*
Castlerichard, 48–9
Castle Street, 74, 78, 120, 156, 361
castles and forts, 58–9, 67, *68*, 69, *75*, *120*, 392
   fortified houses, 70–2, *73*, *113*, *114*, *115*, *120*, 291, 294
Cat Fort, 69, 87, 243
Cat Lane, 133
Cat Lane Band, 209, 210, 211

Catholicism, 115, 121–3, 160–2, 410–18
   Catholic Church, 367, 410–18
     key objective, 411
   Catholic Emancipation, 178, 207, 213, 292, 410
   Catholics expelled, 118
   community associations, 416
   consecration of churches, 410
   devotions, 410–11
   eucharistic processions, 412, *412*
   growth of middle class, 160, 231
   Marian house names, 417–18
   occupations, 157–8, 161, 202
   parishes, 411, 412, 413, *413*, 414
   politics and, 207–8
   vocations, 413–14
   see also churches
cattle *see* beef
Cattle Market Street, 308
Cave of Barra, 86, 104
Cavill's Quay, 151, 153
'Celtic Tiger', 371, 374–6, 405, 420, 421, 425, 429, 432
cemeteries, 37, *37*, 90, 244 *see also* burial sites
census
   1659, *116*, 122, *124*
   1807, 162
   1901, 253
   1911, 253
   1936, 265
   1951, *268*
   1961, *268*
   1986, 404
   2002, 368, 422, *422*
Ceoltóirí Cualann, 339
cereals, 131
chalk, 9, 10
Chalmers (artist), 218
chandleries, 128, 130
Charlie's Bar, 343, *343*, *344*, 345
Charlotte Quay, 201, 213
charters, 64, 104, 105, 106, 108–10, 111, 117, 121, 225
   petition (1600), 116–17
chemical industry, 182, 366, 370, 371, 374, 376, 391, 392, 432
chess, *61*, 63
Chetwynd viaduct, *197*
child-care services, 406
cholera, 205, *280*
choral music, *307*, *336*, 339, 340
Christ Church, 87, *87*, 89, 104, 120, 142, 143, 162, *165*, 165–6, 351
Christ Church Lane, 75, 78, 120

Christ the King church, 297, *297*
Christian Brothers, 141
   College, 317, *318*
Christianity, early and medieval, 79–97, 104–6
Church of the Ascension, *411*
churches, 63, 69, 81–3, 85–90, 93–7, 135, 162, 165–7, *214*, 292–3, 297, *297*, 353, 410, 413
   consecration of Catholic churches, *410*
   Holy Trinity Presbyterian church, 229–30
   medieval sites, 85
   St Anne's, architecture and building, 142–4, 291, *348*
   St Fin Barre's, architecture and building, 300–2, *348*
   synagogue, 253, *253*, *254*
Churchfield, 282, 398, 404, *407*, 408
Churchyard Lane, 87, 156
Cill na Cluaine, 84, *84*
citizenship, 396
   housing and, 396, 401
City Council, 265, 424
City Development Plan, 424, *424*, 428–9
City Hall
   burnt (1920), *261*, 263, 358
   rebuilt, 265, 299,
city status, 127, 150
civic rituals, 127, 134, 412
Civic Survey (1926), 265–6, *267*, 278, 279
Civil War, 181, 193, *216*, 357, 358
   course of, 264
Clarke, Harry, *236*, 297, 356
Clasharinka, 49
class *see* social class
Clear, C., 140
Clein family, 253
clientship, 53
climate, 17–24, 129–30, 133
   climate change, 16, 19–20, 30, 31
   synopsis, 18–20
   see also flooding
Cloghduv, 277
Clogheenmilcon fen, *5*
Clonleigh, 49
Clout, Colin, 351
Coach Street, 156
coachmakers, 156
Coakley (architect), 297
Coal Quay, 151, 291
coat of arms, *6*, 67, *109*, *154*
Cobh (Queenstown), 178, 215, 277, 371, 377, 391, 392

INDEX

emigration from, 246–51, 379, 419–20
   lodging houses, 247–9
Cobh Cruise Terminal, 379
Cobh Street, 286
cocket, 109, 117
cock-fights, 130
Cogan, Milo (Miles) de, 104, 111
Cogan, Robert, 108
Cogan family, 106, 108
Cohalan, Bishop, 297, 412
coins, *71*, *72*
Cois Tine, 423
Coláiste Stiofáin Naofa, *336*
Cold Bone Club, 167
Cold Harbour, 152
Coleman's Lane, 76
Colleges of Ireland Act 1845, 225, 232–3
Collins, Angela, 140
Collins, Michael, 260, *262*, *263*, *264*, *355*, 419
Collins, Paddy 'Fox', *327*
Collins Barracks, 257
Colmán, St, 83–4
Coltsman, John, 67, 142, 291
Colum Cille, St, 80–1
comets, 24
Comhaltas Ceoltóirí Éireann, 339
Committee of Merchants, 146–8, *147*, 160, *188*
Common Bond network, 415
Common Council, 113, 164–5
community
   Catholic Church and, 410–18
   housing and, 396–402, 403–8, 428–9
community groups, 407–8, 416
Company of Butchers, 113
Confederate War, 118, 121
Connaught Place, 358
Connaughton, Marcus, 341–2
Connor, John, 150, 152–3, 155, *156*
Conor, Mary, 310
conservation, 41, 44, 145
   Cork Harbour environmental issues, 393–5
   special conservation areas, *32*, *392*, *393*, *394*
   see also urban renewal schemes
Convamore House, 215, 219
convents, 90, 139–41, 292, 357
Conway, Paul, 341
Coolawen, 53
Coolmore House, *215*, 215–16
Coolowen Ironworks, *184*
coopers, 128, 156, 193
copper, 45–6

Coppinger, Bishop, 138
Coppinger, Sir Walter, 118
Coppinger family, 110, 115
Coppinger's Court, 118
Cord Grass (*Spartina alterniflora*), 39, *39*
Cork, name origination, 7, 25
Cork Airport, 9, 367, 375
   history and development, 379, *379*
Cork Airport Business Park, 379, 431
Cork Area Strategic Plan (CASP), 269, *276*, 277, 368, 376, 381, *382*, 383, 408, 424
   aims and strategy, 425–31
Cork Boyne Society, 167
Cork City (soccer team), 320–1
Cork City Development Board, 408
Cork City Partnership, 408
Cork Constitution (newspaper), 179, 210
Cork Constitution (rugby club), 317, *318*
Cork Council Book, 113
Cork County Library, 358
Cork Cuverian Society for the Cultivation of Sciences, 227, 232
Cork Distilleries Company, 192
Cork Docklands Development Strategy, 424, 428–31, *430*
Cork Docks Company, 202
Cork Drama League, 357
Cork Electric Lighting and Tramway Company, 198
Cork Examiner, 179, 209–10, 236, 259, 336
   emigration reportage, 244–5, 246, 248, 249, 250
Cork Fever Hospital, 242, 243
Cork Folk Club, 343
Cork Folk Festival, *336*
Cork Gaol, 178, 233
   Women's Gaol, 357
Cork Gas Company, 404
Cork Harbour, 7, 130, 183, 194, 198–201, 377–9, *391*, 391–5, *395*
   creation of, 15–16
   development, 199–201, 240, 370, 376, 377–9, 391–5, *424*, 432
   docks, 269, *364–5*, 366, 368, 370, 376, 377–9, *378*
      Development Strategy, 376, *400*, 424, 428–31, *430*
   dredging, 200, 201
   environmental issues, 393–5
   geology, *9*, 11–16, *391*, *395*
   industry, 369, 370–1, 391–2, 432
   naval base, 121, 183, 392, *392*
   recreation, 134, 322, 393, *394*
   see also shipping

Cork Harbour Commissioners, 200, 201, 240, 269
Cork Harbour Plan, 370
Cork Hibernians, 320
Cork Historical and Archaeological Society, *208*
Cork Industrial Development Association, 188
Cork Institute of Technology, 227, 237, 287, 404
Cork International Choral Festival, *307*, *336*, *339*, 340
Cork Main Drainage Scheme, 386–90, 393
Cork Metropolitan Area Fibre Network, 387
Cork Municipal School of Commerce, 237
Cork Musical Society, 337
Cork Opera House
   old, 227, *227*, *228*, 337, 357
   rebuilt, 299
Cork Orchestral Society, 338
Cork Philharmonic Society, 338
Cork Preservation Society, 145
Cork Progressive Association, 265
Cork Relief Committee, 239–42
Cork Remembrancer, 220
Cork School of Commerce and Domestic Economy, 297
Cork School of Music, 337, 338, *340*
Cork Society for Promoting the Fine Arts, 218, 219–21
Cork Strategic Retail Study, 424
Cork Symphony Orchestra, 337, 338
Cork United, 321
Cork University Hospital, 287, 404
Cork Volunteer Band, *211*, 212, 339
Cork Youth Orchestra, 337
Corkery, Daniel, 351, 353, 358
Corn Market, 151, 167, 257, 291
Cornmarket Street, 69, 257, 310, 357
Corporation, 127, 131, 161, 179, 201, 265
   housing policy, 204–7, 208, 278–89, 404
   institutions and funds, 164–5
   see also planning
Corporation Buildings, 205
corruption, *160*
cosmopolitanism, 366–7, 421, 427
Coster, Adam de, 222
Cotter, Denis, 306, 314
Cotter, James, 355
Cotter, Patrick, 359–63
cotton industry, 185

INDEX

County Council, 194, 424
County Development Plan, 424
County of Cork, 2–6, *276*
'County of the City of Cork', 121
Court House, 178, 293, 362
Court Lane, 78
Court of d'Oyer Hundred, 164–5, 167
Cove Lane, 137
Cove Street, 92, 105
Covert family, 168
Cowman, Roz, 351
Cox, Richard, 124
Cox, Stephen, 135
craftsmen, exclusion of (15th century), 112, 113
Cranitch, Matt, 339–40
Crawford, William, *187*, 221, 222, 224, 226–7, 235
Crawford family, 219
Crawford Municipal Art Gallery, *167*, 218, 222, 225, *225*, *227*, 276, 291
architecture, 296, *298*, 299
Crawford Municipal Technical College, 227, 237, 263
Crawford School of Art, 227
Credit Unions, 414–16, *415*
Creed, Daniel, 210, 211
cricket, 322
crime *see* disorder
Croker, Samuel, *164*
Croker, Thomas Crofton, 221
Cromie, A.S., 229–30
Cronin, Donal, *330*
Cronin, Harry, 322
Cronin, Maura, 202–8
Crosbie, M., 221
Cross Court, *76*
Cross Street, 78
Crosse's Green, 93
Crosse's Green Distillery, 186
Crosshaven, 377, 393, *394*
Crosshaven House, *216*
Crowley, Jeremiah 'Cowboy', 210, 211
Crowley, Jimmy, 307, 336, 343, 345
Crowley, John, 178–82, 213–14, 252–5, 306–7
crypts, 89, 91, *91*
Cuffe, Hugh, 117
Cummins, Henry, 39
Cummins, Ray, 307
Cummins, Valerie, 391–5
Cunard Line, 246
Currabinny, 49
Curraghkippane Cemetery, 244
Curraheen, 50, 285, *287*

Curran, Sarah, 355
Cuskinny, 51, 392
custom duties, 108–10, 126
cocket, 109, 117
fee-farms, 108–9, 116
'prize' wines, 110
Custom House, 167, *167*, 218, 222, 225, *225*, 227, 291, 296–7
Custom House Quay, 197, *200*, 388

Dagenham, 419
Dál Cais, 82
d'Alton, Ian, 160–7
Dalton, Noreen, 40–4
Daly, John, 202
dance bands, 338
'Dance of the Cherry Trees', 349
Daunt Square, 151
David, Jacques Louis, 219
Davitt, Michael, 351
Deane, Kearns and Thomas, 293, 294
Deane, Sir Thomas, 178, 219, 220–1, 226, *232*, 233
Deanrock estate, *286*
Dean's Gate, *63*, 290
deer, 13
Déise, 80
Delaney, Timmy, 331, *331*, 332
Delanty, Greg, 351, 355
democracy, 396
de Róiste, Liam, 260, *262*
Desert More, *84*
Desmond, Peter, 320
Desmonds, 58, 87, 93, 104, 108
Devonshire Marsh, 155
Devoy, Robert, 2–24
Dickson, David, 127–34
diet and food patterns, 128, 308, 310–11, 315
Dillon's Cross, *261*, 263
Dillwyn, Lewis, 219
disability, 406, 408
disorder
'band nuisance', 210–12
contemporary
city centre, 276
suburbs, 288
faction fights, 132–3
food riot (1729), 131
Dissenters, 163–4, 223
Distillery Field, 40–4
distilling, 130, 183–4, 185–6, 187, 188, 192
Diwali festival, *423*
Dobbin, Alfred, *182*

Dobbin, Kate, *145*
Docklands Development Strategy, 376, *400*, 424, 428–31, *430*
Doll's House, The, 357
dolphins, 393
domestic buildings *see* house-building
domestic implements, 62, *62*, 63, 70
Dominicans, 88, 89, 93–7
Donegan, Harry, 322
Donnybrook, 286
Doolin, Bridget, 338
Dorgan, Theo, 351
Dorgan, Val, 325
Douglas, 130, 170, 185, *186*, 268
estuary, 392
urbanisation, 179, 203, *270*, 282, 315, *367*, 377, 398
Douglas Street, 137, 203, 358, *360*
Dovell, Peter, 269, *271*
Dowden, Richard, *207*, *209*, 232
Downs, The, 286
Doyle, Connie, 332
drainage, 9–11, *12*, 16, 28, 31, 33
wastewater, 386–90, 393
see also marshes, reclamation
drawbridges, 106, *107*, 120, 153
dredgers, 200, 201
Dring's Marsh, 174
Drishane, 216
drisheen, 308–9, 311, 313, 315
Droop's Mill, 120
drought, 133
drug users, 405, 408
Drummond, James, 36, 225
Dublin Hill, *331*, *333*, 334
Ducart, Davis, 222, 292
duck, 35, *394*
Duggan, Denis, 386–90
dún, 57, 58
Dunbar Street, *360*, 361
Dundanion Castle, *115*
Dundanion House, 215–16, 220
Dungarvan, 64, 86
Dunkettle House, 215, 216, *217*
Dunlop's Tyres, 181, 265, 269, 366, 369, 374, 399
Dunne, Seán, 353
Dunscombe, Rev Nicholas, 163
Dunscomb's Marsh, 126, 150, 173
Durcan, Paul, 351
Duross, Constable, 245
Dwyer and Company, *189*

earthquake (1755), 24
East Gate Business Park, 376

INDEX

Easter Rising (1916), 259, 412
eclipse of the sun, 24
economy, 369–76
   1900s, 265, 369
   1960s–1970s, 268, 369–72, 404
   1980s, 366, *371*, 372–4, 404–5, 420
   1990s–2000s, *371*, 374–6, *377*, 405, 420, 421, 425, 429, 432
   see also trade
Edenhall @ The Village, 287–8
Edmond Sarsfield's Lane, 74
education *see* schools
education and employment, 405–8
Edward IV, King, 106, 108
eels, 35, 393
Eegeraat, Erik van, 299
Egan's (jewellers), 356
electoral wards, 405
Elizabeth I, Queen, 109
Elizabeth Fort, 69, *69*, 88, *113*, *119*, 120, *162*, 290
Elyan, Meyer, 254
EMC, 375
Emigrants' Home, 249
emigration, 178, *180*, 246–50, 404, 419–21, *420*
   companies, agents and 'runners', 246–50
   Great Famine, 244–5
   lodging houses, 247–9
   return migrants, 419, 421
   1900s, 182, 249–50, 269, 419–21, *420*
Emmet Place, 276–7, 291, 299, *307*
employment, 369–76, 421, 429
   British Army, 256–9, 419
   categories (1787), 157
   children, 202
   class and, 202
   education and, 405–8
   industry and, 369–76
   north–south divide, 404, 408, 428
   religion, 157–8, 161, 202
   unemployment, 366–7, *371*, 372, 403, 404–8, 428
   women, 202, 373, *380*
Empress Place, 260
engineering, 183, 371
English Market, 131, 296, *306*, 310, *312*, 313, 421
   history of, 312–13
Ennismore, 222
Ennismore, Viscount, 218, 219
equality, 368, 403–8
   housing and, 396–402, 403–4
   north–south, 399, 404, 408, 427–8

socially excluded groups, 408
ESB, 404
eucharistic processions, 412, *412*
European Union, 268, 272, 366, 369, 372, 375, 377, 379, 386, 408, 420
Evergreen, 279, 362
Evergreen Road, 397
Evergreen Street, *133*
Exchange, 134, *134*
exports, 113, 116, 117–18, 127, *146*, 160, 183, 308, 310, *377*

Fachtna, St, 83–4
faction fights, 132–3
Fairfield, 282
Fair Hill, 279, 331–2, *333*, 398, 405, *406*, *407*, 408
Fair Lane, 128, *128*, 132, 152
Fair Lane Band, 210–11, *211*
fairs, 127, 130–1, *131*, 132, 132–3, 134
families, one-parent, 406
famine, 107, 131, 397
Famine, Great (1840s), 174, 178, 187, 188, 233, 239–45
   burial grounds, *241*, 244
   effect of, 239–45, 397
   emigration and, 244–5
   relief and response to, 239–44
Farie, Pierre, 168
farm auction, *181*
farmers' markets, 315
Farranferris, 281, 408
Farranree, 408
'Farranree' (song), 348–9
Farranree Community Centre, 408
Farren's Street, 77
FÁS, 404
Father Mathew Quay, 213, 293
Father Mathew Street, 230, 294
fauna, 13, 32–3, *34*, 35–6, 41, 392–3
fee-farms, 108–9, 116
Fenians, 208
Fenn's Marsh, 151, 173
Fenn's Quay, 153, 273, *274*
ferry terminal, 269, 379
festivals and carnivals, 127, 130–1, *131*, 132, 132–3, 134, *423*
   music, *307*, *336*, *339*, 340
Fianna Fáil (paper), 257
Finbarr, Saint, 57, 79, 81–4, 86, 87
   chalice depiction, *79*
   'Life of Finbarr', *80*, 83–4
fires
   1622, 22, *23*, 72, 107
   1762, 133

1920 (burning of Cork), 193, *261*, *262*, 265, 358
1980, 312
Firkin Crane, 148, *148*
First World War, 181, 188, 193, 208
   conscription, 259
   Cork reaction to, 256–9
   recruitment, *256*, 256–9
   'Salonika' (ballad), *257*, 258
fish and fishing, *220*, 362, 377, 392, 393
   herring, 116
   The Lough, 35
   salmon, 143, 392, 393
Fitzgerald, John, 91, *159*, *162*, 218
Fitzgerald, Ray, 340
Fitzgerald's Park, *355*
FitzStephen, Robert, 104, 111
Fleischmann, Aloys, *337*, 338, 340
Fleming, Fr James, 212
Fletcher family, 123
flooding, 25–31, 68, 129, 274
   areas vulnerable, *26*, *28*, *29*, *30*
   causes of, 25–8
   climate change and, 16, 30, 31
   major floods, 28–30, 129
flora *see* vegetation
Flower Lodge, 320, 321
Flynn, Maisie, 311
Focault, James, *164*
Fógraim, leathaim (poem), 135
Fold, The, 418
folk and traditional music, *336*, 339–40, 343–50
   venues, *336*, 343–5
Fontaine, Jacques, 169, *169*
food, 306, 308–15
   diet and food patterns, 128, 308, 310–11, 315
   food relief, 131–2
   restaurants, 311–14
   riot (1729), 131
   traditional specialities, 308–10, 311
   see also famine
An Foras Forbartha, 285
Ford, Henry, 188, 419
Ford Motor Company, 181, 182, *182*, 187–8, 197, 265, 269, 366, 369, 374, 399
   migration to Dagenham works, 419
Forde, Samuel, 218–19
Fort Davis, 392
Fort Meagher, 392
Fort Street, 282
Fort Templebreedy, 392
fortified houses, 70–2, *73*, *113*, *114*, *115*, *120*, 291, 294

INDEX

forts *see* castles and forts
Foster, Marita, 239–50
fosterage, 117
Fota House, *216, 217*
Fota Island, 12, 15, *39*, 393
Fouhy, Mary, 140
Franciscans, 88, 89, 105
Francis's Abbey, 126
Fraser's Magazine, 351
Free Debating Society, 167
Freeholder, The, 164
freemen, 113, 114, *164*, 164–5
freeze-ups and frosts, 21, 129–30
French, Seán, 254
French Church, 90
French Church Street, 273–4
Frenche's Quay, 201, *362*
French's Villas, 278–9, 280, *280*
friaries, 88, 89, 105
Friendly Club, 165
Fuchsia, *38*, 39
fulachta fiadh (cooking places), *46*, 48, 49–50, *50*
Furlong's Mill, *8*
furniture, 62

GAA, 192, 211, 212, 316–18, 320, 325, 326
   clubs and parishes, *317*
Gaelic language, 135–6, 358
Gaelic League, 358
Gali, Beth, 275, *275, 368*
Gallagher, Rory, 307, 341–2
Gallows Green, 90, 104
Gallwey (Galvy), Geoffrey, 107
Gallwey, Michael, 126
Gallwey family, 110, 115, 123
Galvin, Patrick, 307, 351, *359*, 359–63, *389*
games and gambling, *61, 62, 63, 71*, 129
Garbhán's Fort, 86
Garranes, *82*
gas fields, 391–2
gated enclaves, 288, 396, 397, 400, 402, *402*
gatehouses, 67, 69, *69*
'Gateway' city, *367, 368*, 424, 432
Gearagh, 3–4
Geary, Larry, 239–45
geese, 35, *394*
Geographical Information Systems (GIS), 42–4
geology, 2–4, 7–16, 391, *395*
George's Quay, *29*, 295, *296, 362*
George's Street, 150, 152
Gerald Griffin Street, *74*
Gernon, Luke, 106–7

Gibbings, Robert, 3–4
Gibbings family, 165
Gilbert (Ostman), 58
Gill Abbey, 82, 83, 86, 104
Gillabbey, 143
Gillabbey Street, 292, *292*
Gillabbey Street Band, 211
Gilla Áeda Ua Muigin, 83
Gilla Pátraic Mac Carthaig, 82
Gillman's Lane, 74
glaciers, *10*, 10–15
Glashaboy River, 39, 393
Glasheen, 185
Glankittane, 174
Glanmire, 130, 133, 179, 203, 269, 355
   archaeological finds, 48, 50, 51
   geology, 13
Glanturkin, 53
Glasheen, 203, 204
glass, 70, 73
Glaxo Smith Kline, 376
Glen, The, 284, *401*, 405, 407, *407*, 408, 413
Glen Hall, 328
Glen River, 184
Glen Rovers, 319–20, 325–30
Glennon, Millie, 417–18
globalisation, 366, 368, *377*, 402, 404
glue-making, 130
Goat Broke Loose, 409
Gobán, St, 80
Goble family, 168, 169, *170*
gold, 46–7, *49*
   goldsmiths, 169
Goldberg, Gerald, *254*, 255
Goldman, Mannie, 360
golfing, 393
Good Shepherd Convent, 90, 357
Goold family, 110, 123
Goubet (cartographer), 126
Gougane Barra, 7, 12, 79, *79*
Goulbourn, Henry, 225
Gould, Kieran, *332*
Goulding's Fertilisers, 181, 265, 325
Gráda, 343
Grand Juries, 194, 196, 201
Grand Parade, 69, 151, 153, 156, 297
   flooding, 28, *28, 30*
   town walls, *66*, 68–9
Grange, 286
Grattan Street, 69
Great George's Street, *188, 189*, 259, 293
great houses, 215–16, *217*, 219–21, 222, *291*, 291–2
Great Island, 393

Greater Reedmace, 33, 34
green belt, 266, 269, 278, 398
Green Coat school, 137, 144
Green Lane, 282
Green Marsh, 155, 173
Greenfield, 48, 50
Greenmount/Green Street, 90, 104
Gregg, Bishop John, 302
Gregg Hall, 357
Grenville Quay, 201
An Grianán, 358
Griffith, Richard, 194
Grogan, Nathaniel, 67, *69*, 131, *132, 161, 166, 218*, 219, *220*, 221, 222
Grossi, Signor, 338
grottoes, 418
gulls, 35, 36
gunpowder manufacture, 183
Gurranabraher, 281, 398, 404, 405, 407, 408, *411*
Gyleen, 45

Hackney, Rod, 289
hailstorms, 22, 23
Hales, Tom, 260
Half Moon Street, 356, 357
Hall, R.H. (building), 390
Halle, Thomas, 107
Halley's comet, 24
halo phenomenon, 24
Hammond, John, 173
Hammond's Marsh, 126, 151, 153, 154, 173
Hammond's Quay, 151
harbour *see* Cork Harbour
Hardwick Hall, 295
Hare, Richard, 219
Hare, William, 219
Hargrave, Abraham, 215, *217*, 219, 222
Hargreaves, William, *200*
Harpur's Lane, 205, *240*, 242
harrier clubs, 208
Harrington Square, 358
Harris, Mary, 419
Harrison, John, 144
Harrison, Richard S., 171–5
Harrison family, 123
Harvey, Deaves and Harvey, 173–4
Harvey, Pearse, 340
Harvey, Reuben, 173
Haulbowline, 108, 369, *391, 392, 392*
Hawkins family, 123
Hayes, Conor, 319
Healthcare, 375
Healy, James N., 338

INDEX

Hedges Eyre, Robert, 222
Heffernan, Dave, *390*
Hegarty, Ellen, *248*
Hendrick, Jack, 356
Hennessy, Andrew and Michael, *188*
Henry II, King, 104, 111
Henry III, King, 110
herring, 116
Hibernian Buildings, *252*, 253, 255, *255*
Hickey, Kieran, 17–31
hides
   exports, 113, 116, 117–18, 127
   tanneries, *128*, 130, *189*
Hill family (architects), 296, 297
Hincks, Edward, 229
Hincks, Rev Thomas Dix, *37*, 218, *223*, 229
   life and work, 223–5
Hincks, William, *37*
Historic Centre Action Plan (HCAP), 272–4, *274*
Hive Ironworks, *188*
Hoare's Lane, 75
Hogan, James, 219
Hogan, John, 221, 222, 226
Holland, Michael, 300–2
Holly Rode, 88
Hollyhill, 268, 371, 374, 375
Holy Trinity, Christ Church, 87, *87*, 89, 104, 120, 142, 143, 162, *165*, 165–6
Holy Trinity church, 178, *214*, 293, 410
Holy Trinity Presbyterian church, 229–30, *230*
Home Rule League, *208*, 211
homelessness, 401, *401*
Honan Chapel, 235, *236*, 297
Hopewell Castle, 67
Horgan's Buildings, 179, 205, *206*, *207*
Horgan's Quay, 386, 387, 390
Hornwort, 35
hospitals, *155*, 192, 295–6, *297*, 299, 404
   in Great Famine, 239, 242, 243
   medieval, 88, 105–6
Hourihan, Kevin, 265–89
house-building
   apartment blocks, 287
   bathrooms, 281
   docklands proposal, *430*, 430–1
   doors, 61, 73
   Dutch/Flemish style, *101*
   early settlements, 45, 53
   fires and fireplaces, 61, 72–3
   flood protection, 129, *130*
   fortified houses, 70–2, 73, 113, *114*, *115*, *120*, 291, 294
   gated enclaves, 288, 396, 397, 400, 402, *402*
   great houses, 215–16, *217*, 219–21, 222, *291*, 291–2
   Hiberno-Norse, 60–2, 70
   map of significant buildings, *290*
   medieval, 69–73, 106–7, 290–1
   model dwellings, 397, 398–9, *399*
   naming of houses (Marian), 417–18
   roofs, 61, 72, 107
   semi-detached, 278–9, *280*, 282, 285
   sill-beam houses, 63
   slums, 76, 128, 179, 181, 203–5, *267*, 278, 404
      clearance, 205, 265, 266, 280–1, 398
   stone, 8, *8*, 63, 70, 73, 106–7
   stonework, 73
   suburban, 265, 278–89 *see also* suburbs
   timber, 60–1, 63, 70, 387
   town houses, 284, *284*
   town planning, 265–77, 278–89
   urban renewal schemes, 270–7, 282
   valuations (1830s), *163*
   villas, 134, 179, 203, 215, 278
      council-built, 278–9, 280, *280*
   windows, 70, *70*, 73
   see also housing and society
household items, 62, *62*, 63, 70
house-names, 417–18
housing and society, 396–402, 403–7, 428–9
   class and segregation, 202–7, 288
   gated enclaves, 288, 396, 397, 400, 402, *402*
   homelessness, 401, *401*
   house prices, *400*, 400–1
   north–south division, 399, 404, 428
   social housing, 401, *401*, 403, 404, 428
   see also slums
Houston and Houston, 297
Howard, Robert, 294
Huguenot Quarter, 273–4
Huguenots, 103, 123, 163–4, 168–70
   church, 90, 169
   enterprise and settlement, 168–70
   Huguenot Cross, *168*
Hurley, Charlie, 320
Hurley, Maurice, 56–73, 85–97
Hurley, Patrick, 421
hurling, 208, *304–5*, 307, *307*, 316, 319–20, *321*
   Glen Rovers, 319–20, 325–30

Ice Age, 3, 9, 10–15

IDA (Industrial Development Association), 268, 374, 404
immigration, 421–3
   asylum-seekers and refugees, 272, 408, 422–3
   Huguenots, 168–9
   Jews, 178, 252–5
   return migrants, 419, 421
Imperial Hotel, 225, 258, 311, 340
imports, 101, 112, 113, 117, 184–5, 187, *377*
Improved Dwellings Company, 76, 205, *206*
Inchiquin, Murrough O'Brien, Lord, 118
incinerator, 376, 393
Independence, War of, 181, 193, *216*, 421
   burning of Cork, 193, *261*, *262*, 265, 358
   course of, 260–4
Industrial Development Association (IDA), 268, 374, 404
industry, 181, 182, *182*, 183–9, 265, 268–9, 366, 391–2
   Celtic Tiger, *371*, 374–6, 432
   employment and, 369–76
   north–south divide, 404, 408, 428
   protectionism, 369
   recession (1980s), 372–4, 404–5
Industry Street, 205, 397
inequality, 368, 403–8
   housing and, 396–402, 403–4
   north–south, 399, 404, 408, 427–8
   socially excluded groups, 408
information and communications technology, 366, 372, *372*, 375, 426, 432
Inisfallen, 269, *420*
Inman Line, 246, 247
Inman Quay, 247
Inniscarra dam, 31
investment, north–south divide, 404, 408, 428
Irish Fertiliser Industry, 371, 393
Irish Immigrant Support Centre, 423
Irish Immigration Reform Movement, 421
Irish language, 135–6, 358
Irish Republican Army (IRA), *216*, 260–4
Irish Republican Brotherhood (IRB), 256, 262
Irish Steel, 269, 369, 371, 376, 393
Irish Volunteers, 256–7, 259–60, 263
Iron Age, 45, 51
ironworks, *184*, 186, *188*
Irwin, Denis, 320, 323

INDEX

Isaac's restaurant, 314
Ivory, Thomas, 292
Ivy-leaved Toadflax, 38, *38*

Jack Lynch Tunnel, 375, 380, 408
James I, King, 117
James II, King, 88, 95
James, Henry, 340
James Scott and Co., 247
James Street, 77
Jameson's Row, 225
Japanese Knotweed, 41
jazz music, 307, *336*, 340
jewellery, *71*, 356
Jewish community, 178, 252–5
　synagogue, 253, *253*, *254*
John, Prince, Lord of Ireland, 104, 105, 111
John Paul II, Pope, 413
Johnson, Gina, 74–8
Joint Housing Strategy, 424
'Jones, Mother', 419
Jones, Mrs, 221
Jones and Kelly, 299
Joyce, David, 410–16
Jury's Hotel, 299

Kane, Robert, *233*, 233–4
Kaufmann, Angelica, 219
Keane, Roy, 316, 320, *321*, 321–2, 323
Kelleher's Buildings, 205
Kellett, Sir Richard, 222
Kennedy Quay, 386, 388
Kent Station, 295, 380–1, 428
Keogh, Dermot, 322
Keohane, Kieran, 396–402
Kerrycurrihy, 108
Kerryhall Road, 279
Kerry Pike road, 296, *296*
Kilbarry, 47, 374, 375, 382, 426
Kilgobnet, St, 80
Killalough, 50
Killanully, 53
Killeenreendowney, *281*, 282, 310, *311*
Killeens, 49, 332
Killydonaghue, 48
Kilmichael, battle of, 262
Kiln River, 184
Kilnacloona, 84, *84*
Kilumney, 12, 277
King's Castle, 58–9, 67, *75*
Kinsale, 108, 110, 392
Knights Hospitallers, 105
knives, *62*
Knocknaheeny, 284–5, *371*, 398, *401*

employment and education, 405, 406, *406*, 407, *407*, 408
Kyrl's Quay, 291
　town walls, *65*, 66, 67, 68, 69

labourers, 202
'Laburnum Lawn' (song), 347
Lakelands, 221
Land Use and Transportation Study *see* LUTS
landscape, 2–6, 7–16, 391, *395*
Lane, Denise, 338
Lane, Denny, *208*
Lane, Fintan, 209–12
Lane family, 165, 185, 338
lanes, 65, 74–8, 120, 121, 267, *396*, 404
　naming of, 77–8
Lane's brewery, 190, *192*
Lapp's Island, 90, 154
Lapp's Quay, 201, 293, 390
Latocnaye, Chevalier de, 67
Lavallin family, 113
Lavitt family, 169
Lavitt's Island, 173
Lavitt's Quay, 155, 337, 357
lease, example of, *159*
Lee, River, 2, 386, *389*, 392, 393
　canalisation, 28
　drainage, 9–11, *12*, 16, 28, 31, 386
　evolution and geology of, 7–16, 28
　Gearagh swamplands, 3–4
　reservoirs and dam, 3, 31
　swimming, *390*
　water power, 184
　see also flooding
Lee Boot Manufacturing Company, *189*
Lee Fields, 41
Lee Rowing Club, *390*
Leesdale, 286
legal profession, 157, 161, 202
Lehenaghmore, *288*
Leland, Mary, 351–6
Lenihan's Sweet Factory, 358
Lent, 131
Leonard, Fr Mark, 358
'Leper's Walk', 355
leprosy, 88, 105–6, 353–5
Levi, Joseph, 253
Lewis, Samuel, 222
Lewis Glucksman Gallery, 299, *299*
Leycester family, 165, 222
Liathán, 80
Liberty Street, 78
libraries, 144, 225, *261*, 263, 358
lightning storms, 22–3

Limerick, Jewish pogrom, 252
limestone, 8, 10–11, *13*, 67, 142, 143, 233
Linehane, Denis, 366–8, 403–8
linen industry, 185
Listowel, Lord, 218, 219
literature, 307, 351–63
Little Ice Age, 21
Little Island, 48
　industry, *370*, 370–1, *373*, 374, 376
　sewage treatment, 386, *388*, 388–90
　watermills, 54–5
Little Market Street, 239
Lobby Bar, 192, 343–4, *344*, 345, 350
　'Magic Nights in the Lobby Bar', 350
lodging houses, 247–9
Lombard, John (Donati), 114
Lombard family, 114
Long Quay, 153
Longfield family, 163
Lota, 179, 203, 222
Lota Beg, 215, 222
Lota Lodge, 222
Lotamore House, 222, *222*
Lota Park, 215, 222
LOTS (living over the shop), 272, 274, *274*
Lough, The, 32–6, *33*, *34*, 279, 427
Lovers' Walk, 355
Lucas's Directory (1787), 157, *158*
Lucey, Bishop Cornelius, 413, 414, 415, 418
Lug, 80
Lunar Society, 223
Lunatic Asylum, 295
lunulae, gold, 46–7, *49*
Lusitania, 258–9
LUTS (Land Use and Transportation Study), 266, 269–70, *270*, 276, 277, 370, 371, 374–5, 380, 425, 426, 427
Lynch, Jack, 307, 322, 325, 327, *327*, 328
Lynch, Liam, 260
Lynch, Ricky, 350
Lynch, Theo, 329–30
Lyon, Bishop William, 116

McAuley, Catherine, 141
Mac Carthaigh, Diarmuid mac Eoghan na Tuinne, 136
MacCarthaigh Mór, Diarmaid, 88
McCarthy, Denis, *294*
MacCarthy, Dermot MacDermot, 106
McCarthy, Kieran, 223–8
McCarthy, Mark, 119–26
McCarthy, Thomas (poet), 351, 353, 355
McCarthy, Tom (musician), 341

INDEX

McCarthy family, 123
McCarthy kingdom, 58, 82, 83, 84, 87, 88, 104, 108
MacCurtain, Tomás, 256, 259, 260, 261, 357, 358, 404
MacCurtain's Villas, 278–9
McDonnell, Samuel, *228*
Mac Éinrí, Piarias, 419–23
McElligott, Tom, 322
Mackerill, Stephen, 169, *170*
McLeod, R., 301
Maclise, Daniel, 129, *129*, 218, 219, 221, 222, 226, 229, 351
McMullen, Barry, 295
McMullen, James, 297
MacReamoinn, Sean, 316
MacSwiney, Terence, 256, 257, 259, 260, *260*, 261–2, 336, 357, 358
MacSwiney's Villas, 278–9
Madden, Owen, 320
Madden's Buildings, 179, 205, *206*, 280
Maginn, William, 351
Maguire, John Francis, 179, *181*, 214
Mahon, 285, 371, 388, 389, 398, *401*
  employment and education, 405, 406, *406*, 407, 408
Mahon Industrial Estate, 374
Mahon Lough, 12, *14*, 295, 388, 390, 392
Mahon Point, 268, 315
Mahony, Francis Sylvester (Fr Prout), 220, 351–3, *352*
Mahony, N.C., 322
Malachy, St, 83
Mall, The, 151
Mallow Lane, 128, *128*, 142, 145, 156, 158
malting, 130
Manch House, 216
Mandates, The, 117
Mangan, James, 143
Mansergh, Nicholas, 424–32
Mansion House, 167, 192
mansions, 215–16, *217*, 219–21, 222, 215–16, *217*, 219–21, 222, *291*, 291–2
map-making, 150, *151*, *152*, *153*, *156*
Marcus, Louis, 353
Mardyke, 254–5, 348
  sports ground, 318, *320*, 321, *324*
Mardyke Gardens, 41
Marian house names, 417–18
Marina, 369, *370*, 376, *389*, 390
Marina Commercial Park, 374
Marina Park, *431*
Marina Point, 371, 389
Marine (Martin's) Gate, 74

market gardens, 310, *311*, *314*, 315
Marks, Dr, 337
Marsh, The, 396, 404
Marsham Quay, 152
marshes, 3–4, *5*, 126, 392
  reclamation, 28, 40–1, *100*, *107*, 126, 150–1, 153, *154*, 173, 184
Martin, Tom, *318*
Martin, William, 213
Maryborough House, *203*
Mathew, Fr Theobald, 37, 163, 179, 188, 239, 242, 244, 245, 353
  grave, *37*, 214
  life and work, 213–14
  statues, 213, *213*, 294
Mathews, Fr Francis, 118
May Day, 132–3
Mayfield, 268, 284, 286, 398, *401*, 413
  employment and education, 404, 405, 406, *406*, 407, *407*, 408
mayoralty, 113, 127, 135, 164, *164*, *254*, 255
Mayoralty House, *155*, *291*, 291–2
Maypole Lane, *133*, 152
Meade, John, 107
Meade, William, 117
Meade family, 110, 115
medical profession, 157, 161, 202
Meeting House Lane, *76*
megaliths, 45, *46*
Meic Carthaig, 82, 83, 84
meitheal, 411
merchants, 110, 112–15, 160–1, 215, 396
  apprenticeships, 113
  Committee of Merchants, 146–8, *147*, 160, *188*
  expulsion (1640s), 118, 121, 127
Merchants Quay, 152, 201, 272
Mercy Hospital, *155*, 192, *291*, 292
Mesolithic Age, 45
metal age, 45–51
meteors, 24
Methodists, 163, 169
Metropole Hotel, 311, 340
'Metropolitan Cork', 368, 426
Miagh, John, 107
Miagh family, 110, 115
middle classes, 160, 179, 202–3, 231, 282
Midleton, 277, 369, 376, 382, 426
migration, 419–23
  asylum-seekers and refugees, 272, 408, 422–3
  immigration, 421–3
    Huguenots, 168–9
    Jews, 178, 252–5

  return migrants, 419, 421
  labour migrants, 421–2
  seasonal (1700s), 128, *150*
  see also emigration
Mill Street, 78
Millerd, Hugh, 131
Millerd family, *132*, 163
Millerd Street, 77, *132*
Milliken, Richard, 220
mills, 130, 184–5, *185*
  ironworks, *184*
  tidal, 54–5, 184
Minihane, Sean, 421
Mitchel, John, 207
Mitchelsfort, *47*
model dwellings, 397, 398–9, *399*
Model Farm Road, 286, 287, 398
Monahan Road, *431*
Monard Ironworks, *184*
monasteries, 80–1, 85–7, 88, 89–90, 93–7, 104–6
  St Finbarr's, 57, *57*, *85*, 85–6, 87, 104, 300
Monk, Michael, 45–54
Monkstown, 9, 203, 377, 393
Monkstown Castle, *115*, 118
Montague, John, 351, 353
Montbret, Charles Étienne Coquebert de, 215
Montenotte, 203, 278, 282, 355, 396, 417
Montgomery, Major Bernard, 263
Morgan, James, 218–19, 222
Moroney, Tommy, 320
Morrison, James, 215
Morrison, Richard and William, 216, *217*, 220
Morrison's Island, 150, 153, 156, 191, 201
Morrogh family, 110
Mortell family, 110
Mortimer, Edmund, 94
Motorola, 375
Motraye, de, 128
Mount St Joseph, 90
Mount Verdon Villa, 358
Mountjoy, Jim, 340
Mountjoy, Lord, 117
Moylan, Bishop Francis, 140
mudstone, 8
Muircheartach Ua Maelseachlainn, 59
Mulally, Teresa, 140, 141
multiculturalism, 366–7, 421, 427
Mumford Lewis, 288
Municipal Reform Act 1840, 207
Munster Bank, 192

INDEX

Murphy, Adrian, 409
Murphy, Jack, 333
Murphy, James (brewer), 191–2
Murphy, James (housing policy critic), 285
Murphy, James J., 192, *192*
Murphy, John, 338
Murphy, John A., 2, 231–8, 316
Murphy, Bishop Michael, 413
Murphy, Rt Rev Dr, 222
Murphy, Seamus, *294*, 301, 353, *355*
Murphy family, 191–2
Murphy's brewery, 188, 190–3, 268–9
  history of, 190–3
Murray, Peter, 215–22
Murray O'Laoire Associates, 299
music, 307, 336–50
  artefacts, 62, *62*
  musical bands and 'nuisance', 209–12, *336*, 339
  Pigott's store, 356
  venues, *336*, 337, 339, 340, 343–5
Musical Art Society, 338
Muskerry, Lord, 118
Myers, Rev Joseph, 253
Mythe, John, 107

Nagle, Joseph, 137
Nagle, Nano, 103, 137–41, *138*
Nagle, Sir Richard, 137
name origination (Cork), 7, 25
Napoleonic Wars, 178, 183, 186, 188, 309–10
National Anti-Poverty Strategy, 408
National Building Agency, 284, 285, *286*
National Development Plan, *367*, 368, 386
National Maritime College, 393
National Microelectronics Research Centre, 372
National Spatial Strategy, 424, 431–2
nationalism, 208, 256–7, *259*, 259–60, 412
naval base, 121, 183, 392, *392*
Neeson, Geraldine, 336, 358
neighbourhood watch, 285
Nemo Rangers, 320
Neolithic Age, 45
Nessan, St, 87
New English, 121–3, *124*
Newenham, George, 221
Newenham, Mary, 221
Newenham, Thomas, 162
Newenham family, 163, 173, *203*
Newman, Oscar, 285
Newman family, 123

Newsom family, 165, 174
newspapers, 167, 179
Ní Cuilleanáin, Eileán, 351
Ní Dhomhnaill, Nuala, 351
Nicholls, Kenneth, 104–10, 112–18
Nicholls, Thomas, 301
'Night of the Big Wind' (1839), 23
nightclubs, 409
nightlife, 409 *see also* pubs
Nile Street, 154
Nimmo, Alexander, 201
Nine Years War, 116
Noonan, Bill, 322
Normans, 62–3, 64, 70, 83
North Gate, 64, 70, *77*
North Gate Bridge, *69*, 120, *161*, *366*
North Infirmary, 21, 239, 242, 243
North Main Street, 106, 151, 154, 156, 205, 272, 315, 426
North Mall, 64, 203, 357
Northern Lights, 24
Northpoint Business Park, 376
Northside Education Initiative, 407
Novartis, 375, 376
Nugent family, 114–15
nuns, 140–1

Oakdale–Briars Court estate, 286
Oatencake, 48–9
oatmeal, 131
O'Brien, A.F., 111, 112
O'Brien, Charlotte Grace, 249
O'Brien, Colin, *324*
O'Brien, John, 253
O'Brien, William Smith, 232
Ó Broin, Séamus, 135
Ó Canainn, Tomás, 336–40, 355
occupations *see* employment
Ó Ceallacháin, Mícheál, 337
Ó Ceallaigh, Uilliam, 135
Ó Cinnéide, Donncha, 377–83
Ó Colmáin, Fr Dónall, 355
Ó Conaill, Domhnall, 136
Ó Conchubhair, Muiris Camshrónach, 135
O'Connell, Cathal, 396–402
O'Connell, Paddy, 325, 326, *327*, 330
O'Connell, Seamus, 306
O'Connor, Evelyn, *358*
O'Connor, Frank, 210, 307, 351, 353, 356, 357–8, *358*, 360
  place connections, 357–8
O'Connor, Raymond, 410–16
O'Donnell, Paul, 340
O'Donnell, Vicki, 391–5

O'Donnell Tuomey, 299
O'Donoghue, Bernard, 351
O'Donovan, Diarmuid, 325–30
O'Donovan, Mick, 210, 358
Ó Drisceoil, Donal, 190–3, 256–64
O'Driscoll, Clodagh, *340*
O'Dwyer's Drapery, 357
O'Faolain, Sean, 307, 337, 351, 356, *356*, 357, 360
O'Farrell, Frank, 320
O'Farrell, Mary Pius, 137–41
Ó Féichín, Peadar, 135
O'Flanagan, Patrick, 100–3, 149–59
O'Flynn, Father, 358
O'Flynn, Paddy, *362*
O'Gara, Ronan, *319*
ogham inscriptions, 79, 80, *237*
Ó hAlpín, Seán Óg, *304*
O'Hegarty, Sean, 256, 262, 264
Oíchobhar mac Cináeda, 58
oil refinery, 369, 391
O'Keeffe, Brian, *390*
O'Keeffe, John, 222
O'Kennedy's pub, 357
Old Blarney Road, 332, *333*
Old Oak, 409
Old Post Office Lane, 75, 120
O'Leary, Kitty, 356
Oliver Plunkett Street, 150, 152, 265, 409, *409*
  flooding, 28, 30, *30*
O'Mahony, Fr Francis, 118
O'Mahony family, 185
Ó Nualláin, Mícheál, *338*
open spaces and parks, 74, 265–7, *268*, 271, 277, *279*, 282, 404, 407, 429
opera, 337–8
Opera House
  old, 227, *227*, *228*, 337, 357
  rebuilt, 299
orchestras, 337–8
O'Reagan, Michael, *388*
O'Reilly, Tom, 325, 330
O'Reilly family, 308, 309, 313
Ó Riabhaigh, Mícheál, 339
Ó Riada, Seán, 307, *338*, 338–9
Ó Riain, Pádraig, 79–84
Ormond, earl of, 168
orphanages, 90
Orrery, earl of, 160, 163
Osbourne, Patrick, *291*, 292
Ó Sé, Réamonn, 339–40
O'Shea, Jack, 331, 332
Ostmen, 58, 64, 104
Ó Súilleabháin, Muircheartach Óg, 136

INDEX

O'Sullivan, Sonia, *307*
otters, 392
Ó Tuama, Seamus, 331–5
Ó Tuama, Seán, 351
Our Lady's Hospital, 295–6
Ovens, 12, 277
Owenacurra river, 393
Owenboy (Owenabue) river, 13, 393
Owens, Dave, 340
Oyster Tavern, 311
oysters, 393

Pacata Hibernia, 65, *113*, 120
Pain, James and George, 178, *214*, 215, 216, 219, 222, 292, 293, 294, 295, *295*, 410
Pairc Uí Chaoimh, 319
Palladium Showband, 341
Parentiz (Paradise) Castle, 72
parents, lone, 406
parishes, 411, 412, 413, *413*, 414
park-and-ride services, 382, *383*
parking, 383
Parks, E., 221
parks and open spaces, 74, 265–7, *268*, 271, 277, *279*, 282, 404, 407, 429
parliament, members of, 107–8, 215
Parliament Bridge, 153, 154, *179*
'Parliament na mBan', 355
Passage, July fair, 134
Passage East, 13
Passage West, 9, 13, 183, *188*, 201, 264, 277, 377
patriciate, 110, 112–15, 118
Paul Street, 135, 150, 156, 272, 315
Pavilion Cinema, 272
Pearse Road, *349*
peddling, 253
Penal Laws, 137, 140, 173
Penn, William, 419
Penrose, Cooper, 219–20, 224
Penrose, E.W., 221
Penrose, James, 221
Penrose family, 173, 174, 219–20
Penrose's Quay, 151–2, 153, 197, 201, 240, *420*
Perdrian family, 170
Perrier family, 165, 169
Perrot's Inch, 233
Perry and Carleton, 170
Petrie Crown, 51
Pettit, E.G., 386, *388*
Pfizer, 370, 375, 376
pharmaceutical industry, 182, 366, 370, 371, *374*, 376, 391, 392, 432

Pharmachem, 375
philanthropy, 397
Philip's Lane, 73
Phillips, Thomas, 126
Philpott Lane, 137
Phoenix, 343, *344*
Pigott's music store, 356
pigs
  bacon, 188, 308, 310
  cuisine, 310, 311
  herding, *310*
  trade, 130, 183, 188, 308, 310
Pike, Eliz, *159*
Pike, Joseph, 90
Pike family, 173, 174
Pike shipyard, 174
Pike's Marsh, 151, 153, 173
Pine Street, 242
Pius XII, Pope, 418
plague, 106, 107
planning, 181, 265–77, 424–32
  CASP strategy, 425–31 *see also* CASP
  Docklands Development Strategy, 376, *400*, 424, 428–31, *430*
  National Development Plan, *367*, 368, 386
  National Spatial Strategy, 424, 431–2
  phases, *424*
  suburbs, 265–70, 277, 278–89
  urban renewal schemes, 270–7, 282, 287, 375, *400*
  URBAN project, 408, 426
  zoning and industry, *370*, 370–1
plantation, 101, 115–16, 118, 121
plants, 32, 33–5, 38–44 *see also* vegetation
Pleistocene period, 11
poetry, Gaelic, 135, 136
politics, 257
  and class, 207–8
  nationalism, 208, 256–7, *259*, 259–60, 412
  radicalism, 208
Pollock, Colonel, 310
pollution
  air, 17
  Cork Harbour, 393–5
  water, 386, 390, *390*, 392, 393
Poor Law Commission, *242*, 242–4, *243*
Pope, William, 144
Pope's Quay, 30, *292*
Popham, Dr John, 239
population, 150, *150*
  1574, 107
  1600s, 120, 121–6

  1659 census, *116*, 122, *124*
  birth rate, 123–4
  1700s–1800s, 160, 202, 239, 397
    county areas, *245*
  1900s, 181, 265, *265*, 266–8, *268*, *275*, *276*, 277, 282, 368, *425*
  2000s, 2, 368, 422, *425*
  electoral wards, *265*, *268*, *275*, *276*, *405*
  ethnic/religious groups, *116*, 121–3, *124*, 160
  seasonal migration (1700s), 128, *150*
  yearly statistics (1584–2002), *150*
port city, 149–50, 377–9
  emergence of Cork, 100–3, 108, 120, 123, 126, 149–50, 155
Port of Cork Company, 377
Portolan charts, *105*
Portney's Lane, 75
Post Office Quay, 151
Potato Market, 310
pottery, 45, 62, *62*, 108
Pouladuff, *406*
Pouladuff Road, 333, *333*, *335*
poverty, 403–8
  housing and, 396–402, 403–4, 428 *see also* slums
  socially excluded groups, 368, 408
  see also Famine, Great; social class; workhouse
Power, Ned, *321*
Prendergast, Philip de, 104
Presbyterians, 163, 223, 229–30
Presentation Order, *139*, *140*, 140–1, 255
  College, 317, *318*
Priestley, Joseph, 223, 224
Princes Street, 312, *346*, 347, *347*
'Princes Street' (song), 347–8
priories, 88, 89, 93–7, 104–6
Priory of St John the Evangelist, 88, 105
prisons, 67, 178, 233, 357
promontory forts, *46*
Prosperity Square, 205, *206*, 397, *397*
Prosperous Place, 205, *206*
protectionism, 369
Protestants, 118, 121–3, 160–7, 223
  compulsory church attendance, 117
  decline of Ascendancy, 160–1, 178
  Dissenters, 163–4, 223
  occupations, 157–8, 161, 202
  politics and, 207–8
  see also Huguenots; Presbyterians; Quakers
'Prout, Fr' (Francis Sylvester Mahony), 220, 351–3, *352*

INDEX

pubs, 133, 192, 193, *296*, 357, 409
   music, 343–5
   'super-pubs', 409
   venues and ownership, 409
Pugin, Edward Welby, 293, 294
Purser, Sarah, 297
Puxley, John, 136

Quakers, 103, 123, 126, 163, 171–5, 240
   enterprise, 171–5
   Meeting House, *76*, 174
   names, 171, 173
quarries, 12, 14, 143, 144
Quarry, Rev J., 220
Quarry, Michael, 170
Quarry family, 168, 170
Quarry Lane Band, 209, 210
quays, 65, 74, 103, 126, 130, 150, 151, 153, *154*, 155, 197, 362, *362*
   modernisation, 201, 376, 377
Queen's Castle, 67, *68*, *75*, 120
Queen's College *see* University College Cork
Queen's Old Castle Department Store, 272
Queenstown *see* Cobh

radicalism, 208
Raheens, ringforts, *53*, 53–4
railways, 185, 196–8, 203, 240, 247
   commuter services, 381–2, 426
   history of, 196–8
   recent development, 380–2, *381*
   recent proposals, 426, 428
   station, 295, 380–1, 428
rainfall, 19, 23–4, 133
Raithliu, *82*
Raleigh, Sir Walter, 351
Rank's Flour Mills, 265
RAPID (Revitalising Areas by Planning, Investment and Development) programme, 408
Ravenswood, 47, *49*
RCI, 375
Reap Marsh, 126, 150
reclamation, 28, 40–1, *100*, *107*, 126, 150–1, 153, *154*, 173, 184
recreation *see* social activities
Recusant revolt (1603), 117
Red Abbey, 88, *105*, 153, 290
Red Abbey Lane, 152
Redmond, John, 257
refugees, 272, 408, 422–3
religious orders, 88, 89, 93–7, 104–6, 140–1

Repeal movement, 178–9, *207*, 209
reservoirs and dam, 3, 31
restaurants, 311–14
retailers *see* shops
revetments, 60, *60*, 63
Reych, Walter, 70
Rice, Edmund, 141
Rickotts, John, 169
Ring, Brendan, 350
Ring, Christy, 307, 316, *316*, 319, 321, *321*, 327, *327*, 329
Ringaskiddy, *378*, 426
   ferry terminal, 269, 379
   geology, 12, *13*
   industry, 371, *373*, 374, 375, 376, 377–9, 393
   ringfort, 53
ringforts, 52–4
Ringrose Atkins, W., 337
Riordan, Jerry, 334
rituals, civic, 127, 134, 412
rivers, 2, 9–11, 13, 184, 393
   pollution, 386, 390, *390*, 393
   see also Lee, River
Riverstown, 185, 269
road bowling, 331–5
roads, 194–6, *195*, *373*, 376, 379–80, 381
   butter roads, 133, *146*, 296, *296*
   planning, 270, 277, 283, 284
   ring roads, 375–6, 379, 380, 381, 408
   turnpikes, 194–6
Roberts, Thomas Sautell, *176–7*
Robertson, Manning, 266, *268*, 281
Robinette, Thomas, 169
Robinson shipyard, 174
Roche, James, 221–2, 232
Roche family, 106, 110, 115, 123, 219
Roche's Buildings, 205
Roche's Castle, 72, *75*
Roche's Point, *12*, *19*, 391
Roche's Stores, *261*, 265, 275
Rochestown, 389, 398, 413
Rocky Island, 392
Rocque, John, *77*, *78*, *102*, *106*, 127, *128*, *133*, 142, 150, *151*, 152, *153*, *154*, 155, *156*, *311*
Rogers, John, 128
Rogue, Peter, 168
Romans, 51
Ronayne, Maurice, 115
Ronayne family, 115
Ronayne's Court, 389
Roseville estate, 404
Rostellan, 45, 392
rowing, *390*

Royal Cork Institution (RCI), 36–7, 178, 218
   history of, 223–7
   minute book, *226*
   Queen's College and, 225–6, 232
Royal Cork Yacht Club, *394*
Rudhall, Abel, 143
rugby, 317–19, 322
Ruiséal, Liam, 256
Rushbrook, 377, 426
Russell, Jack, 322
Ryan, Mary, 235
Ryan, Michael and Declan, 314
Ryan's Buildings, 205
Rynne, Colin, 54–5, 142–8, 183–9, 194–201

Sadleir, Henry and James, 185
Sage, Colin, 308–15
sailcloth industry, 170, 183, 185
sailing, 322, 393, *394*
St Anne's church, Shandon, 89, *89*, 90, 91, 142–4, *143*, 166, 273, 351
   architecture and building, 142–4, 291, *348*
St Augustine's Street, 260
St Brigid's church, 87
St Fin Barre's bridge, 277
St Fin Barre's Cathedral, 85, 89, *89*, 90, 91, *92*, *114*, 143, *162*, 166, 178, *300*
   architecture and building, 300–2
   angel, 348, *348*
   Dean's Gate, *63*, 290
St Finbarre's church, 63, *63*, 81
St Finbarr's monastery, 57, *57*, *85*, 85–6, 87, 104, 300
St Finbarr's Road, 282
St Finbarr's Seminary, 326
St Francis church, 89, *90*, *263*
St Francis Hall, 259
St George's Steam Packet Company, 174, 202
St John Baptist Street, 105, 106
St John Evangelist Street, 105, 106
St John the Baptist church, 105
St John's church, 87, 88
St Joseph's Cemetery, 37, *37*, 90, 214, 244, 293
St Kevin's Road, 397
St Leger, Alicia, 168–70
St Leger, Sir William, 118
St Leger family, 123
St Luke's church, 353, *354*
St Mary and St Anne cathedral, 292
St Mary del Nard, 87–8

INDEX

St Mary's church (Pope's Quay), 89, *292*, 293, *293*
St Mary's of the Isle, *63*, *91*, 93–7, 105
St Mary's, Shandon, 90, 142, 143, 166, 167
St Michael's church, 87, 88
St Nessan's church, 87
St Nicholas' church, 88, 90, 166
St Patrick's Bridge, 29, 154, *166*, *179*, 295, 351
St Patrick's church, 178, 293, 353, *353*, 358, 410
St Patrick's church (Rochestown), 413
St Patrick's Quay, *103*, 201
St Patrick's school, 358
St Patrick's Street, 151, 153, 154, 156, 182, 315, 358, 366, 386, *388*
   burning of (1920), *261*, 265
   flooding, *25*, 28, 29, 30, *30*
   redevelopment, *271*, *272*, 275–6, 368, *368*
   future plans, 426, 431
St Paul's church, 89, 90, 91, 166, 167
St Peter and Paul church, 293
St Peter's Church, 86, *86*, 87, 89, 90, *92*, 120, 165–6, 167, 273
St Peter's Church Lane, 75, 76, 78
St Peter's Market, 257
St Stephen's Hospital, *297*, 299
Sainthill, Richard, 218
Saleen, 392
salmon, 143, 392, 393
'Salonika' (ballad), *257*, 258
salt-works, 128, 149
sandstone, 8
Sarsfield, William, 117
Sarsfield family, 110, 115
Savings Bank, 293–4
Savory, Mathew, 169
Savoy Cinema, 272
Savoy Grill, 311
Scher, Ivor, 255
Schering Plough, 375
schools, 137–41, 144, 162, 224–5, 253, 255, 286, 357, 358, 411
   'disadvantaged', 403
   employment and education, 405–8
   school journeys, 384–5
   sport and, 317, *318*, 326
'Scots Church', 230
Scott, Michael, 299
Scott family, 247
Scoura Hill, 334
Scully, Denis, 331, 332, 333
sea levels, 11, *14*, 15–16, 31

seals, 392
Second World War, 250
Segen, Peter, 169
Semirot, Anthony, 169
settlements, early, 45–60
   choice of location, 56, 58
Seven Heads, 392
sewage, 386–90, 393
Sexton, Regina, 308–15
Seymour family, 247
Shandon, 13, 64, *101*, 104, 105, 106, *106*, 142–8, *145*, *273*, 274, 351, 353, *422*
Shandon bells, 143, 291
Shandon Castle, 69, 142, 148, 351
Shandon Street, 106, *106*, 152, 203, 242, 357, *366*, *404*
Shannon, Lord, 163, *164*, 165, 219
Sharkey, Canice, 314
Sheare's Street, 259
Sheridan, Monica, 315
sheriffs, 116, 117, 164, *164*
shipbuilding, 174, 183, 186, *188*
shipping, 126, 127, *127*, 130, 183, 198–201
   steamships, 174, *175*, *188*, 197, 199, 202
   transatlantic companies, 246–7, 250
shoe-making, *189*, 369
shops, 133, *158*, 174, 202, 310, 356, 357, 358, 366
   department stores, 265, 272
   shopping centres, 268, *269*, 272, 275, 287, 315, 426
   supermarkets, 315
Showgrounds, 321
shrines, 418
siege (1690), 69, 90, 127, 142
silk industry, 170
silver, 62
silversmiths, 169–70, *170*
Sinn Féin, 259, 259–60, *262*
Sirius, 174, *175*
Sisters of Charity, 141
Sisters of Mercy, 141
Skellig Night, 130, *131*
Skiddy, John, 72
Skiddy, Stephen, 144
Skiddy family, 113–14, 123
Skiddy's almshouses, *144*, 144–5, 291
Skiddy's Castle, 71, 73, *73*, *113*, 120, 126
Skinner, Alexander, *195*
slaughterhouses, 113, 127–8, *128*, 308
Slow Food Movement, 315
slums, 76, 128, 179, 181, 203–5, *267*, 278, 404

   clearance, 205, 265, 266, 280–1, 398
   see also lanes
smallholdings, 310, *311*, *314*, 315
smallpox, 205
Smith, Charles, 135, 150, *152*, 166
Smith-Barry family, 163, *217*
smog, 17
snowfall, 21–2
soccer, 318, 320–4
social activities, 129, 130–1, 132–3, 134
   games and gambling, *61*, 62, 63, *71*, 129
   following the bands, 209–12
   nightlife, 409
   see also music; sport
social class, 202–8
   middle classes, 160, 179, 202–3, 231
   mobility, 202–3
   occupation and wealth, 202
   politics and, 207–8
   residential segregation, 203–7, 288
   working classes, 202, 203–7
Society of St Vincent de Paul, 240
Soldiers and Sailors Land Trust, 279
souterrains, 53–4
South Chapel, 358
South Gate, 69, *69*, 407
South Gate Bridge, *58*, 59, 60, 67, 120, 142, *159*, *360*, 397
south island, 58, *58*, 59, 60, 64
South Link Ring Road, *270*
South Main Street, *58*, 59, 60, *66*, 106, 151, 154, 156, 387
South Mall, 129, *130*, 151, 153, 156, 203
South Parish, *273*, *360*, *361*, 362
South Presentation, 90
'South Side' (poem), 359, *363*
South Terrace, 253, *254*, 255
Southern Star, 276
Spangle Hill, 281
Speed, John, 93, 120–1, *122*
Spenser, Edmund, 7, 65, 351
Spike Island, 82, *391*, 392
Spillane, John, 307, 345, 346–50, *350*
sport, 208, 307, 316–35, *390*, 393, *394*
   blood-sports, 130
Spratt, Geoffrey, 340
standing stones, *46*, 48, 49, 50–1
starlings, 23
steam power, 184–5, 186
steamships, 174, *175*, *188*, 197, 199, 202
   transatlantic companies, 246–7, 250
Steinberg family, 253
Stephens, Dr, 242
sticklebacks, 35

463

INDEX

stone
　masons and sculptors, *294*, 301, 353, *355*
　used in building, 8, *8*, 63, 142, 143, 233
storms, 19, 22–3, *24*, 130
Storrs, John, 297
Story, George, *125*, 126, 150
Strawberry Hill, 347
Strawberry Hill School, 357
streets, 120–1, 150–8, *180*
　animal movements through, 266, 310
　lamps, 129
　naming of, *154*, 278, *285*, 412
　naming of lanes, 77–8
　occupational association, 155–8
　urban renewal schemes, 270–7, 282, 287, 375, *400*
　see also lanes
Streets for living, 285
suburbs
　burned (1374–5), 106
　1600s, 124–6
　1700s, 134, 162
　1800s, 179, 377
　1900s, 181, 203, 265–70, 277, 278–89, 377, 404
　　inter-war, 278–81
　　post-war, 281–2
　　sprawl, 282–5, *367*
　　innovations, 285–8
　planning, 265–70, 277, 278–89
Suibne (abbot), 81
Sullivan, Morty Oge, 136
Sullivan, William K., 234, 235
Sullivan's Quay, 362
Summerhill, 353, *354*
Sunbeam Industrial Estate, 375
Sunday's Well, 179, 203, 278, 377, 396, *407*
Survey and valuation of the city of Cork, AD, 1663–1664, 121, 123
Sutton's Buildings, 205
swans, 35
swimming, 322, *390*
sycamore, 42
synagogue, 253, *253*, 254

tallow, 127, 128, 130
tanneries, *128*, 130, *189* see also hides
Taste, 342
Taylor, George, *195*
Temperance Movement, 163, 179, 188
　poster, *209*
　temperance bands, 209, 212, 214
Temple Hill, 87

Tenant Purchase Scheme, *401*
tennis, 322
Terry (Tirry) family, 108, 110, *110*, 115, 123
Terryglass, 81
Teulon, William, 169, *170*
textile industry, 160, 170, 172, 173, 183, 185, *186*, 187, 186–7, 188, 366, 369
Thresher, Daniel, 144
thunder storms, 22–3
'Tintown', 258
Tirry, Edmond, 116
Tirry (Terry) family, 108, 110, *110*, 115, 123
Titanic, 391, *392*
Tivoli, 200, 203, 269, 278, *407*, *422*
　docks, *364–5*, 377–9, *378*
Tivoli House, 215, 218–19, 222
Tivoli restaurant, 311
Tobin, Thomas, 227
Togher, 30, 268, 284, 286, *286*, 371, 398, *401*
　employment and education, 405, 406, 407, 408
topography, 2–6, 7–16, 391, *395*
Tory Top Park, 407
tourism, 250, 379, 391, *392*
tower houses, 70–2, *72*, *73*
towers, 67, 120
town houses, 284, *284*
town planning *see* planning
Town Planning Act 1934, 181, 266, 281
toys, *61*, 62
trade, 101–3, 113, 117–18, *377*
　bacon, 188, 308, 310
　beef, 118, 127, 130, 183, *309*, 309–10
　　live exports, 310
　butter, 118, 133, 142, 145–8, 157, 183
　　decline, 187, *188*
　　exports, 127, *146*, 160, 308
　decline of trade, 178, 183, 187, *188*, 265, 309–10
　exports, 113, 117, 127, 160, 183, 310, 377
　　butter, 127, *146*, 160, 308
　　hides, 113, 116, 117–18, 127
　grain, 112, 184–5
　hides, 113, 116, 117–18, 127
　imports, 101, 112, 113, 117, 184–5, 187, 377
　pigs, 130, 183, 188, 308, 310
　tallow, 127
　textiles, 160
　West Indies, 118, 123, 183, 308
　wheat, 184–5

wine, 101
trade guilds, 113
trade unions, 208
tradesmen, exclusion of (15th century), 112, 113
traditional and folk music, *336*, 339–40, 343–50
　venues, *336*, 343–5
traffic congestion, 269–70, *271*, *283*, 284, 288, 315, 379, 381, 382–3, 426, 428
　travel to work/school, 384–5
Tramore, 406, *407*
Tramore river, 13, 15
trams, 198, *198*, 203, *272*, 278
transport, 377–85, *424*, 426 see also railways; roads; trams
Traveller's Joy (*Clematis vitalba*), 42, *42*
Traveller Community, 368, 408, *408*
Trebuseth, Zacharia, 169
Trevelyan, Charles, 239
tripe, 309, 311, 313
True Blues, 167
tuberculosis, 281, 299
Tuckey Street, *60*, 77, 230
Tuckey's Lane, 75
Tuckey's Quay, 151
Tudor Walters Report (1919), 278
Turner's Cross, 280, *280*, 297, 320, 398, *407*, 412
turnpike roads, 194–6
tweed industry, 185
typhoid, *280*, 281
typhus, 204, 205, 242–3

UCC Tradfest, *336*
Uí Briain, 82
Uí Echach Muman, 58
Uí Meic Brocc, 81, 82
Uí Meic Iair, 82
Uí Shelbaig, 82
unemployment, 366–7, *371*, *372*, 403, 404–8, 428
　education and, 405–8
　see also employment
Union Quay, 343–4, *344*, 362
Union Quay Barracks, 358
United States Lines, 250, *250*
University College Cork, 225–6, 231–8, *239*, 263, *279*, 339, 404
　architecture, *232*, 233, 294–5, 297, 299, *299*
　Distillery Field and, 41
　history of, 231–8
　Honan Chapel, 235, *236*, 297
　Lewis Glucksman Gallery, 299, *299*

INDEX

urban renewal schemes, 270–7, 282, 287, 375, *400*
   URBAN project, 408, 426
urbanisation
   1600s, *102, 106, 112*, 119–26
   1700s, 150–6, *155*
   1800s, 179, 203–7
   see also planning; suburbs
Ursuline Sisters, 140

Valley Drive, 282
Vanburgh String Quartet, *336*
vegetable growing, 310, *311, 314*, 315
vegetation, 3–4, 12, 32, 33–5, 38–44
   Botanic Gardens, 36–7
   Distillery Field, 41–4
   The Lough, 33–5
   mapping, 42–4
   wild plants, 38–9
Verdaile, James, 169
Verholme Dockyards, 269, 366, 369, 371, 399
Victoria, Queen, 233, 421
Victoria Barracks, 257, 258, 260, 262, 264, *279*
Victoria Cross, 12, 387
Victoria Hotel, 311
Victoria Park, 181
Victoria Quay, 201
Vigié, John James Ribet, 168
Vikings, 56–60, 85, 87, 387
villas, 134, 179, 203, 215, 278
   council-built, 278–9, *280, 280*
Volunteer movement, 167
Volunteer Pipe Band, *211*, 212, 339
Volunteers, Irish, 256–7, 259–60, 263
voting, 207

Walker, C.P., 386
Walker, Thomas, 186
Wallace sisters, 260
walls of Cork, 65–9, 74, 75, 120
Walsh, Denis, 316–22
Walsh, J.J., 260
War of Independence, 181, 193, *216*, 421
   burning of Cork, 193, *261, 262*, 265, 358
   course of, 260–4
'War of the Two Kings', 172
warehouses, *200* 274
Washington Street, 78, *188, 189*, 259, 293, 362, *409*
waste incinerator, 376, 393
wastewater, 386–90, 393
Water Club, 134, 167
Water Fern, 35
Water Milfoil, 35
water pollution, 386, 390, *390*, 392, 393
water power, 183–5, *184*
watermills, 54–5, 130, *184*, 184–5, *185*
Watercourse, 156, 375
Waterfall Road, 333, *333*, 334, *334*
Waterford, Reginald's Tower, *59*
Watergate Lane, 229
Watergrasshill, archaeological finds, *47*, 48, 50, 51
waterworks, 295, *296*
weather *see* climate
Wedel, Hank, 343, *343*
Weigh House Lane, 146
Welch, Robert, 351
welfare state, 397–9, *400*, 402
Wellington Road, *354*
West, William, 215, 219, 221, 222
West Cork Bottling Company, 192
West Indies
   emigration to, 419
   trade, 118, 123, 183, 308
West Marsh, 151
Westbourne Place, 248, 250, *250*
Western Road, 179, 203, 204, 233, 254–5
Wetenhall, Bishop, 163
whales, 393
wheat, 184–5
Whelan, Pádraig, 32–9
whistles and flutes, 62, *62*
White, Norman, 299
White Star Line, 246, 249, 250
White Street, 294
Whitegate, 392
Whitegate Oil Refinery, 369, 391
Whyte family, 115
Wide Streets Commissioners, 148, 155, *180*, 240

wildfowl, 32–3, *34*, 35, 392
wildlife, 13, 32–3, *34*, 35–6, 41, 392–3
Williamite War, 69, 78, 90, 95, 101, 127, 142, 168
Willis, Chief Justice, 28
willow, 34
Wilmot, Katherine and Martha, 355
Wilson, Woodrow, 259
Wilton, 268, 287, 315, 347, 374, *423*
Wilton Road, *280*, 282
Windele, John, 325
Windle, Sir Bertram, 235–6
Windmill Road, 143
windmills, *185*
wine imports, 101
Winter Heliotrope, 42
Wisdom Lane, *154*
Wise family, 185
Wolfe, Rev Charles, 355
Wolfe, David, 107
Wolfe, Ger, 350
Wolfe Tone Street, 308
Women's Gaol, 357
Wood, Richard F., 290–9
Woodford Bourne, 310
Woodhill House, 215, 219–20, 222
woodlands, 3–4, 12, 33–4, 43
Woodrooffe, Dr, 221
Woods, Joseph, 219
Woods Lane, 74
woollen industry, 185, *186*, 187
workhouse, 178, 239, 242–4, 362
Wren Boys, 129, *129*
Wynchedon, John de, 70, 88
Wynchedon family, 114–15
Wyse, Thomas, 232
Wythye, Nicholas de la, 70

yachting, 322, 393, *394*
York Street, 203, 239
Young, Arthur, 128
Young family, 123

zoning, *370*, 370–1